FOUNDATIONS OF INTERNATIONAL MACROECONOMICS

FOUNDATIONS OF INTERNATIONAL MACROECONOMICS

Maurice Obstfeld

Kenneth Rogoff

The MIT Press
Cambridge, Massachusetts
London, England

This book was set in Times Roman by Windfall Software using ZzTeX and was printed and bound in the United States of America.

Library of Congress Cataloging-in-Publication Data

Obstfeld, Maurice.
  Foundations of international macroeconomics / Maurice Obstfeld,
  Kenneth Rogoff.
      p.   cm.
  Includes bibliographical references and index.
  ISBN 0-262-15047-6
  1. International economic relations.   I. Rogoff, Kenneth,
  II. title.
  HF1259.027   1996
397—dc20   96-27824
                                                  CIP

To Leslie Ann, Eli, Clara, and Zachary
M.O.

To Natasha
K.R.

Contents

Preface

The goal of this book is to develop a broad coherent framework for thinking about all of the fundamental problems in international macroeconomics. We are unaware of any previous attempt to accomplish this goal using modern analytical methods.

This project arose from our concern over the widespread view that open-economy macroeconomics (also known as international finance) has become an extremely scattered field, defined more by the people who consider themselves working in it than by any set of unifying ideas. The problem was brought home forcefully in an informal survey conducted by Professor Alan Deardorff of the University of Michigan. In 1990, Deardorff gathered graduate international finance reading lists from eight top economics departments, hoping to find a consensus on which readings should be deemed most essential. To his surprise, he found strikingly little agreement, with only one article appearing on more than half the reading lists. Such idiosyncrasies will come as no surprise to those who have studied international macroeconomics in graduate school. Whereas most students find the major issues compelling, a constant complaint is that the material lacks a unified theme and that radical gear shifts are needed to move from one topic to the next.

Some senior economists at leading departments view the state of the field with such dismay that they teach mostly from articles written in the 1960s and 1970s (or at least articles that should have been written then), disdaining the modern literature for its alleged lack of policy relevance. Unfortunately, that approach is not productive for graduate students who need a vision of the field's present and its future. While the classic literature from twenty and thirty years ago can be admired for articulating and attempting to formalize a number of central policy issues, its limitations are many. The classic approach lacks the microfoundations needed for internal consistency, it fails to deal with dynamics in any coherent way, and its vision of capital market integration may generously be described as narrow. Perhaps most importantly, the older literature simply doesn't deal sensibly with many questions that are central to today's policy world, such as current accounts, government budget deficits, speculative attacks, and the implications of the expanding global markets for securities and derivatives.

Our goal in this book is to show that one can address virtually all the core issues in international finance within a systematic modern approach that pays attention to the nuances of microfoundations without squeezing all life out of this fascinating topic. We knew at the outset that our project was an ambitious one, and we plunged ahead despite having no idea how we would cross some of the vast chasms in the field. We realized that many areas would have to be substantially reformulated, and frankly hoped that some of the gaps would be fortuitously filled in by other researchers over the life of the project. This did happen, but only in small doses. One important missing link we tackled involved bridging the gap between modern flexible-price maximizing models of the current account and the older sticky-price

Keynesian models that still dominate policy debate. The approach we took is the subject of Chapter 10. The reader will have to judge for himself or herself how successful we have been in our goal of offering a unified framework. Whereas we do not pretend that any one model can encompass all issues, you should find that most models and themes we develop appear several times in the book, sometimes in seemingly widely disparate contexts.

The authors of any manuscript this length must stand ready to be accused of self-indulgence. We trust the reader will agree that part of the length is explained by our deliberate attempt to make the chapters easy to follow. We fill in many intermediate steps to guide students through the central models, hoping to save them the frustrations we ourselves often feel when trying to follow the mathematics of elegant but tersely expressed articles. We also devote a considerable amount of attention to providing empirical motivation for the main concepts and themes we introduce. Our notion of empirical evidence is a broad one. If there exists a careful econometric study that casts light on a question we ask, we try to discuss it. But if the best evidence is a suggestive diagram or a relatively unsophisticated regression, we still offer it to illustrate our concepts if not to test them.

How did we ultimately decide on the specific topics to be covered? Two criteria strongly influenced our choices. We biased our selection toward topics that we felt we could integrate with our central microfoundations approach and toward topics for which there seemed to exist an interesting empirical literature. With little exception, nothing appears in the book that is not based on explicit microfoundations. But we have not been so dogmatic as to exclude the most influential ad hoc aggregative models completely. You will find Solow's growth model in Chapter 7, Cagan's model of hyperinflation in Chapter 8, and Dornbusch's classic extension of the Mundell-Fleming open-economy *IS-LM* model in Chapter 9. In each case, however, we go on to show how similar ideas could be expressed in models with microfoundations. Though we try to be up to date, we have also tried not to be slaves to fashion. Target zone exchange rate models are great fun and have generated a tidal wave of papers; we provide an introduction in Chapter 8. But we think the relatively small number of pages we devote to the topic is the right proportion for this book, and we make no apologies for not including an entire chapter on the subject. Other topics such as European Monetary Union (on which both of us have written) are of great current interest, but the relevant academic literature consists largely of narratives and applications of seasoned theory. We examine optimal currency areas in Chapter 9, but not nearly as extensively as others might have chosen to do. We genuinely regret not having more space left over to deal with questions of political economy. We do cover these to some extent in our discussion of international debt and exchange rate policy. But again much of the literature uses rather stylized descriptive models that did not easily fit into our general approach, and so we leave that important subject for later work. In addition to the book's core material in Chapters 1 through 10, we have also included a number of Supplements (five in all) covering the mathematical methods applied in the main exposition, ranging from difference equations to dynamic programming. We were especially concerned to provide useful primers for material that is "folk wisdom" in the field but for which one often cannot find an easily accessible reference.

Some inwardly oriented macroeconomists may look at our coverage and feel that we have somehow usurped standard topics from macro such as growth or inflation. Our simple answer to them is that we do not consider "closed-economy" macroeconomics to be an independent field. We do not see how anyone can. The United States now trades extensively, and even Albania has opened up to the outside world. There are no closed economies, and there are no virtually closed economies. There are only open national economies and the global economy. Macroeconomics is not the only field our analysis crosses. We freely draw on finance and international trade theory throughout. However, we do not necessarily expect our readers to be conversant with all of these topics, and we generally develop any necessary concepts from the ground up.

Finally, the question may arise as to how we intend that this book be used. Is it a treatise? Is it for the core of a graduate international finance course? Or is it aimed at first-year graduate macroeconomics? The answer, we admit, is all three. The book contains a great deal of new research, most notably in Chapter 4, where we present a dynamic version of the classic Dornbusch-Fischer Samuelson continuum model, and in Chapter 10, where we develop a sticky-price dynamic model that finally updates the Mundell-Fleming-Dornbusch model. We also develop a number of useful diagrams and analytical devices, including microfoundations for the classic Metzler saving-investment diagram in Chapter 1, and a "GDP-GNP" diagram for analyzing nontradable goods production under capital mobility in Chapter 4. In Chapter 5, we demonstrate the remarkable analogy between modern finance models incorporating nonexpected utility preferences and standard open-economy intertemporal models that allow for multiple consumption goods. Chapter 6 on international debt contains a number of new results, for example, on the relationship between investment and foreign debt levels. In Chapter 8, we show how to develop a simple tractable general equilibrium model for nominal asset pricing that is more plausible empirically than the alternatives in the existing literature.

Second-year graduate international finance students are certainly an important constituency. We appreciate that this book cannot easily be covered in a semester, but one can conveniently choose parts of it as the basis for a course and use readings to cover other recent research developments. Second-year students may be able to skim fairly quickly past some parts of Chapters 1 through 3, provided this material was adequately covered in their first-year macroeconomics course. As for a first-year macro course, our coverage is fairly comprehensive, although naturally the choice of topics is biased toward open-economy issues. We have endeavored to make most of the chapters relatively self-contained and, except perhaps for Chapters 4 and 10, most material in the other chapters should be accessible to first-year graduate students. Sections making the greatest technical demands are marked with asterisks (*), and the book is written so that these can be skipped without breaking the flow of the development. We hope that both first- and second-year students will appreciate our efforts at working through the models algorithmically, providing many intermediate steps along the way.

Apologies: Although our book includes extensive citations, space limitations simply make it impossible to provide the intellectual history behind every idea. There are numerous excellent surveys (many of which we reference) that are more suitable for this purpose. We also regret (and accept full responsibility for) the hopefully small number of erroneous attributions, equation typos, and other mistakes that may have crept into the manuscript.

We owe thanks to a large number of individuals:

• Rudiger Dornbusch, from whom we both took our first course in open-economy macroeconomics, and who was a major influence on our decisions to pursue research in the field.

• Our graduate students, for helping us think through the material, for assembling data, and for catching numerous mistakes. In particular we thank Geun Mee Ahn, Brian Doyle, Cristian Echeverria, Fabio Ghironi, Harald Hau, Min Hwang, Matthew Jones, Greg Linden, Sydney Ludvigson, Ilian Mihov, Lorrie Mitchell, Giovanni Olivei, Giovanni Peri, Don Redl, Peter Simon, Cedric Tille, Susanne Trimbath, Clara Wang, Keong Woo, and Ning Zhang.

• Reviewers and others who offered helpful comments, including Henning Bohn, Jeremy Bulow, Richard Clarida, Mick Devereux, Charles Engel, Mark Gertler, Michael Huggett, Peter Kenen, Michael W. Klein, Karen Lewis, Enrique Mendoza, Gian-Maria Milesi Ferretti, Jaime Marquez, Paolo Pesenti, Assaf Razin, Gregor Smith, Federico Sturzenegger, Linda Tesar, and Aaron Tornell. In this regard we are especially grateful to Kiminori Matsuyama, who provided valuable criticisms of early drafts of Chapters 1 through 3 and 9, and to Reuven Glick, who read through the entire manuscript.

• Our colleagues, including Ben Bernanke and Michael Woodford, who test drove some of the chapters in first-year graduate macro at Princeton, and Luisa Lambertini, who used several draft chapters for graduate international finance at UCLA. (The authors themselves have, of course, used the manuscript to teach international finance at Berkeley and Princeton.)

• Our assistants, including Barbara Aurelien, Sherri Ellington, Kazumi Uda, and Annie Wai-Kuen Shun, for help in countless dimensions ranging from processing mountains of photocopying to organizing the bibliography to compiling the author index.

• Terry Vaughn, economics editor at MIT Press, for his advice and encouragement.

• The production team of Peggy Gordon (editor) and Paul Anagnostopoulos (compositor) for their high level of skill and for patiently working with us through our extensive fine tuning of the manuscript. We also thank TeX expert Jacqui Scarlott for expertly processing and correcting our original Scientific Word files.

• Finally, and most importantly, our spouses, Leslie Ann and Natasha, for providing essential moral support and cheerfully tolerating the endless hours of work needed to bring this project to fruition.

M.O.

K.R.

World Wide Web addresses (as of August 1996)

For us: http://www.wws.princeton.edu/ObstfeldRogoffBook.html

This book at MIT Press:

http://www-mitpress.mit.edu/mitp/recent-books/econ/obsfh.html

MIT Press Web Site: http://www-mitpress.mit.edu/

Introduction

International macroeconomics is alive with great practical questions. What are the long-term implications of sustained United States current account deficits and Japanese current account surpluses? How do government budget deficits affect interest rates, trade balances, and exchange rates? Is increasing global capital market integration affecting the nature and international propagation of business cycles, and how is it changing the susceptibility of economies to sudden shifts in investor sentiment? What if Europe really goes ahead and adopts a single currency? Is there any tendency for the per capita incomes of developing countries to converge over time to industrial-country levels? How important is monetary policy, and what are the channels through which it affects the economy? These are issues that interest policymakers, business people, and researchers alike. It is no wonder that international macroeconomic issues command the attention of the world's financial press.

This book offers a framework and a general approach for thinking about international macroeconomics. We believe the framework is valuable from both the theoretical and practical perspectives. Central to it is the role of international asset markets in allowing countries to trade consumption goods over time by borrowing from and lending to each other. This *intertemporal approach* certainly illuminates the economics of current account imbalances. But it also discloses the intimate relationship between dynamic possibilities and international trade within periods—trade of distinct commodities, of consumption indexed to uncertain contingencies, and so on. We do not pretend to have definitive answers to all the questions listed at the start of this introduction, but you should find the approach developed here useful for thinking about all of them.

First, a brief road map of the topics and questions covered in the various chapters (for more detail, see the table of contents). Chapters 1 through 7 of the book are all concerned with the "real" side of international macroeconomics. The models in Chapters 8 through 10 for the most part build closely on those of the preceding seven, but they bring money into the picture.

The first three chapters all assume one good on each date and view trade purely from an intertemporal perspective. Chapter 1 covers the many basic insights that can be developed in a simple two-period model with a single asset. Chapter 2 looks at implications of deterministic and stochastic economies with infinitely-lived representative consumers. Richer demographic assumptions are introduced in Chapter 3, which explores various overlapping-generations models. Throughout the book we focus often—though far from exclusively—on the case of a small country that takes the world interest rate (and possibly other external prices) as given by world markets. As the body of international trade theory amply demonstrates, this can be a powerful and illuminating simplifying assumption. We nonetheless systematically study global equilibrium models as well, both to show how world prices are determined and to understand more completely the routes by which various economic shocks are transmitted across national borders.

Chapters 4 through 6 extend and apply the basic approach to myriad new questions that cannot be addressed in a one-good, riskless-lending framework. In the fourth chapter, we introduce the possibility of several consumption goods on a given date, including nontraded goods (one of which could be leisure) and multiple tradable goods (so that the static terms of trade play a role). As we see, the theory illuminates some important facets of the long-term evolution of economic structure. We conclude Chapter 4 by studying the terms of trade within an intertemporal Ricardian model in which nontradability is determined endogenously by international transport costs.

Chapter 5 looks at the economic role of trade in risky assets, showing how models with uncertainty can be understood in terms of the fundamental principles covered in the previous four chapters. The chapter illustrates how international financial markets may dramatically affect the dynamics of the current account and the international transmission of business cycles. It also covers the essentials of international portfolio diversification and the empirical puzzles surrounding observed diversification patterns. One vital application of the models of this section is to international asset pricing, which we explore in depth.

International debt problems are frequently at the center of policy concerns. Chapter 6 shows how they can arise when there is sovereign risk. The chapter also looks at other realistic departures from the idealized complete markets world of Chapter 5, notably models where asymmetric information is the central distortion. The results of this chapter throw light both on the degree to which the international capital market can perform its potential role and on the nature of the instruments that will be traded.

A revival of economic growth theory has been one of the major developments in macroeconomics over the past decade. Chapter 7 surveys this literature. As is appropriate for a book focusing on international macroeconomics, however, we place a relatively heavy stress on open-economy issues and intercountry comparisons. Thus we highlight the role of cross-border capital mobility in economic convergence, the interplay between capital flows and market imperfections, and the growth effects of international diversification under uncertainty.

In an earlier era, the function of money in trade and capital movements was considered the defining characteristic of international finance as a field (as opposed to now, when nonmonetary aspects of international exchange are viewed as at least as important for understanding macro issues). Chapter 8 introduces monetary models, and it does so in the simplest possible setting, one with fully flexible nominal prices. The chapter (which can be read before the first seven) highlights such classic or soon-to-be-classic subjects as seignorage, endogenous price-level instability, speculative exchange rate crises, target zones for exchange rates, and the pricing of risky nominal assets.

Chapter 9 introduces sticky-price monetary models, with an emphasis on empirical stylized facts and the workhorse Keynesian models. The conceptual framework that grew out of Keynes' *General Theory* (1936) furnished the dominant paradigm for more than a half century. The Keynesian mode of analysis started with the pioneering work of Metzler (1942a,b) and Machlup (1943), included Meade's (1951) brilliant and prescient synthesis, and culminated in the systematic incorporation of capital mobility by Fleming (1962) and Mundell (1963, 1964) and of forward-looking expectations by Dornbusch (1976).[1] Chapter 9's coverage of Dornbusch's celebrated overshooting model of exchange rates builds intuition and illustrates some first implications of sticky prices. The chapter concludes with one of the most fruitful applications of the simple Keynesian framework, the strategic analysis of credibility in monetary policy.

Chapter 10 is our attempt to provide a dynamic sticky-price model that preserves the empirical wisdom embodied in the older Keynesian tradition without sacrificing the theoretical insights of modern dynamic macroeconomics. This chapter is difficult if taken in isolation, but once you have learned the building blocks developed in earlier chapters, the analysis should prove quite straightforward and, dare we hope, intuitive. One big payoff from marrying Keynesian price-setting assumptions to an intertemporal framework is an apparatus for the formal welfare analysis of macroeconomic policies. Such a welfare analysis is implicit in all the vast literature on policy and regime choice but, surprisingly, it is almost never done in open-economy macroeconomics at a level of rigor that would be acceptable to, say, public-finance or pure-trade theorists.

Now, some suggestions on how to use this book. We stress that it is by no means necessary to read the book in sequence. Even though the overarching goal of our approach has been to unify the material in different chapters, we have also gone to great lengths to make chapters reasonably self-contained. We do so in part by using appendixes and supplements for material that may be helpful in more than one chapter. We also repeat ourselves a bit in explaining how to solve certain problems. (Hopefully, most readers will find this occasional repetition more useful than tiresome. In any case, there is free disposal.)

Our goal throughout has been to make the book as easy as possible for the serious reader.[2] We warn, however, that some material is intrinsically harder than the rest. The *starred* (*) sections include some of the most technically challenging subject matter, as well as topics that represent nonessential digressions. All starred sections can be skipped on a first reading without loss of continuity.

Another strategic choice was to use discrete-time models wherever possible. This approach should take some of the mystery out of many topics that have traditionally been taught using continuous time models (for example, growth theory).

---

1. With much else of value along the way, as surveyed by Kenen (1985).

2. Albert Einstein once observed that anyone who reads scientific material without a pencil and paper at hand can't seriously care about understanding it.

We use continuous time in a couple of instances where the resulting model is much more elegant and easier to comprehend than it would be in discrete time. (Speculative attacks on fixed exchange rates and target zones are the two main examples.)

We also take pains to solve dynamic maximization problems in the simplest and most intuitive way. Most of the time we use straightforward substitution to eliminate budget constraints, thereby turning constrained into unconstrained maximization problems. We forgo substitution mainly in instances, such as in our analysis of Tobin's q, where a Lagrangian approach yields more economic insight. The reader is not compelled to use our methods. Supplements to Chapters 2 and 8 summarize alternative dynamic optimization techniques.

Though we have written this book with second-year graduate students in mind, our approach is basic enough that the main body of material can easily be understood by first-year graduate macroeconomics students or advanced undergraduates. One might want to skip most or all of Chapters 4, 6, and 10 in such a course, since this material is more difficult and is more central to advanced international finance than to basic core macroeconomics. On the other hand, most of Chapter 5, which looks at global capital market integration under complete markets, probably *should* be part of the core macroeconomics curriculum, even if it isn't now at many schools. (Macro readers might skip the somewhat more advanced material on nontraded goods in section 5.5 though even this should be accessible.)

You won't have to read the book very long before you see that it is replete with empirical examples and boxes of a sort rather unconventional in advanced graduate texts. These digressions encompass a wide variety of concrete applications meant to illustrate and deepen understanding of material in the exposition's main body. Like the starred sections, this illustrative material can be skipped without loss of continuity. However, we view it as very important. Applications give substance to theoretical points, helping readers make the connection between an abstract model and the real-world question it is trying to capture. We treat the reader as a skeptic, and we try to offer evidence that there is life to these mathematical representations of stylized economic actors. In the empirical "application" sections and boxes we generally do not attempt to reach the technical standards of a paper in *Econometrica*. Rather, the examples are meant to *illustrate*, more than decisively to *prove*, a point. That said, we have generally tried to assemble the most compelling supporting evidence we know or were able to think of.

Finally, a word on notation. The choice of symbols is designed to minimize overlap across the various chapters, without going outside the Greek and Roman alphabets. But the lower and upper cases of those alphabets are finite, and in a book this size it was impossible entirely to avoid overlap. For example, the Greek letter θ is now standard as the parameter in a Dixit-Stiglitz constant-elasticity-of-substitution utility function. But θ is also traditionally used to denote factor shares in trade theory. We use μ for that purpose instead, but μ is standard for denoting money-supply growth in monetary theory. You get the idea. On the whole, we think we have been quite successful in avoiding notational ambiguity either within a chapter or within a group of chapters covering common ground. If chapters are far removed from each other and cover disparate material, we worry less. Throughout the first seven chapters, for example, k denotes per capita (or per worker) capital. In Chapters 8 through 10, capital no longer enters the picture, and so we do not refrain from giving k other minor roles. A symbol glossary explains the notation and lists how the different letters are used. We hope our conventions are clear enough that the reader will never have to consult it.

Timing of asset stocks is another issue. The problem could have been finessed entirely had we used a continuous-time assumption throughout, but to us, the greater clarity and simplicity of a discrete-time approach, as well as its broader applicability without advanced mathematics, seemed decisive advantages. In the growth literature, it is natural to denote by K_t the capital stock set aside in period $t - 1$ for use in period t production; this convention becomes particularly appealing once we start to look at capital-labor ratios K_t/L_t. But in the asset-pricing litera- ture, the convention is to define V_t as the market price at time t of a claim to the firm's output for periods $t + 1$ and beyond. In a model of Solow-style "shmoo" capital this notation gives rise to the somewhat jarring (but correct) result that $V_t = K_{t+1}$, which we could write more appealingly as $V(t) = K(t)$ in continuous time. We wanted Chapter 7 on growth to flow naturally for those conversant with the literature, but we also wanted Chapter 5 on asset pricing to look familiar. Our compromise is to use the growth-literature convention for the timing of capital and riskless bonds (including government debt) and the asset-pricing convention for market asset prices. A similar issue arose in our dating convention for money, as we discuss in Chapter 8. Again, this should be clear enough that it does not cause confusion. If not, the notation supplement is available.

Open-economy macroeconomics is a fascinating subject. No one book, even a very long one, can cover every issue. Nor can any single treatment of a field so big hope to treat even the issues it does take up in comprehensive detail, capturing every nuance and contending viewpoint. We do hope, however, that this book conveys both the excitement of international macroeconomics and the unifying economic principles underlying many of its seemingly disparate aspects.

FOUNDATIONS OF INTERNATIONAL MACROECONOMICS

1 Intertemporal Trade and the Current Account Balance

One fundamental way open and closed economies differ is that an open economy can borrow resources from the rest of the world or lend them abroad. With the aid of loans from foreigners, an economy with a temporary income shortfall can avoid a sharp contraction of consumption and investment. Similarly, a country with ample savings can lend and participate in productive investment projects overseas. Resource exchanges across time are called *intertemporal trade*.

Much of the macroeconomic action in an open economy is connected with its intertemporal trade, which is measured by the current account of the balance of payments. The purpose of this chapter is to illustrate the basic economic principles that govern intertemporal trade patterns: when are countries foreign borrowers, when do they lend abroad, what role do government policies play, and what are the welfare implications of international capital-market integration? In the process, we take a first look at the key factors behind aggregate consumption and investment behavior and at the determination of world interest rates. We assume throughout that only one good exists on each date, the better to focus attention on aggregate international resource flows without introducing considerations related to changing intratemporal prices. A large part of international economics is, of course, concerned with relative domestic and international prices. As several later chapters illustrate, however, the macroeconomic roles these prices play are understood most easily if one starts off by abstracting from the complications they create.

1.1 A Small Two-Period Endowment Economy

You probably are familiar with the standard two-period microeconomic model of saving, due to Irving Fisher (1930). We begin by adapting Fisher's model to the case of a small open economy that consumes a single good and lasts for two periods, labeled 1 and 2. Although the model may seem simple, it is a useful building block for the more realistic models developed later. Our main goal in this section is to describe how a country can gain from rearranging the timing of its consumption through international borrowing and lending.

1.1.1 The Consumer's Problem

An individual i maximizes lifetime utility, U_1^i, which depends on period consumption levels, denoted c^i:

$$U_1^i = u(c_1^i) + \beta u(c_2^i), \qquad 0 < \beta < 1. \tag{1}$$

In this equation β is a fixed preference parameter, called the subjective discount or time-preference factor, that measures the individual's impatience to consume.

As usual, we assume that the period utility function $u(c^i)$ is strictly increasing in consumption and strictly concave: $u'(c^i) > 0$ and $u''(c^i) < 0$.[1]

Let y^i denote the individual's output and r the real interest rate for borrowing or lending in the world capital market on date 1. Then consumption must be chosen subject to the lifetime budget constraint

$$c_1^i + \frac{c_2^i}{1+r} = y_1^i + \frac{y_2^i}{1+r}. \tag{2}$$

This constraint restricts the present value of consumption spending to equal the present value of output. Output is perishable and thus cannot be stored for later consumption.[2]

We assume, as we shall until we introduce uncertainty about future income in Chapter 2, that the consumer bases decisions on *perfect foresight* of the future. This is an extreme assumption, but a natural one to make whenever the complexities introduced by uncertainty are of secondary relevance to the problem being studied. Perfect foresight ensures that a model's predictions are driven by its intrinsic logic rather than by ad hoc and arbitrary assumptions about how people form expectations. Unless the focus is on the economic effects of a particular expectational assumption per se, the deterministic models of this book therefore assume perfect foresight.[3]

To solve the problem of maximizing eq. (1) subject to eq. (2), use the latter to substitute for c_2^i in the former, so that the individual's optimization problem reduces to

$$\max_{c_1^i} u(c_1^i) + \beta u[(1+r)(y_1^i - c_1^i) + y_2^i].$$

The first-order condition for this problem is

---

1. Until further notice, we also assume that

$$\lim_{c^i \to 0} u'(c^i) = \infty.$$

The purpose of this assumption is to ensure that individuals always desire at least a little consumption in every period, so that we don't have to add formal constraints of the form $c^i \geq 0$ to the utility maximization problems considered later.

Whenever we refer to the subjective time-preference *rate* in this book, we will mean the parameter δ such that $\beta = 1/(1 + \delta)$, that is, $\delta = (1 - \beta)/\beta$.

2. At a positive rate of interest r, nobody would want to store output in any case. In section 1.2 we will see how this intertemporal allocation problem changes when output can be invested, that is, embodied in capital to be used in producing future output.

3. Even under the perfect foresight assumption we may sometimes loosely refer to an individual's "expectation" or (worse) "expected value" of a variable. You should understand that in a nonstochastic environment, these expectations are held with subjective certainty. Only when there is real uncertainty, as in later chapters, are expected values averages over nondegenerate probability distributions.

$$u'(c_1^i) = (1+r)\beta u'(c_2^i), \tag{3}$$

which is called an *intertemporal Euler equation*.[4] This Euler equation, which will recur in many guises, has a simple interpretation: at a utility maximum, the consumer cannot gain from feasible shifts of consumption between periods. A one-unit reduction in first-period consumption, for example, lowers U_1 by $u'(c_1^i)$. The consumption unit thus saved can be converted (by lending it) into $1+r$ units of second-period consumption that raise U_1 by $(1+r)\beta u'(c_2^i)$. The Euler equation (3) thus states that at an optimum these two quantities are equal.

An alternative and important interpretation of eq. (3) that translates it into language more closely resembling that of static price theory is suggested by writing it as

$$\frac{\beta u'(c_2^i)}{u'(c_1^i)} = \frac{1}{1+r}. \tag{4}$$

The left-hand side is the consumer's marginal rate of substitution of present (date 1) for future (date 2) consumption, while the right-hand side is the price of future consumption in terms of present consumption.

As usual, individual i's optimal consumption plan is found by combining the first-order condition (3) [or (4)] with the intertemporal budget constraint (2). An important special case is the one in which $\beta = 1/(1+r)$, so that the subjective discount factor equals the market discount factor. In this case the Euler equation becomes $u'(c_1^i) = u'(c_2^i)$, which implies that the consumer desires a flat lifetime consumption path, $c_1^i = c_2^i$. Budget constraint (2) then implies that consumption in both periods is $\bar{c}^i$, where

$$\bar{c}^i = \frac{[(1+r)y_1^i + y_2^i]}{2+r}. \tag{5}$$

1.1.2   Equilibrium of the Small Open Economy

We assume that all individuals in the economy are identical and that population size is 1. This assumption allows us to drop the individual superscript i and to identify per capita quantity variables with national aggregate quantities, which we denote by uppercase, nonsuperscripted letters. Thus, if C stands for aggregate consumption and Y for aggregate output, the assumption of a homogeneous population of size 1 implies that $c^i = C$ and $y^i = Y$ for all individuals i. Our assumed demographics simplify the notation by making the representative individual's first-order conditions describe aggregate dynamic behavior. The Euler equation (3), to take

---

4. The Swiss mathematician Leonhard Euler (1707–1783) served at one time as the court mathematician to Catherine the Great of Russia. The dynamic equation bearing his name arose originally in the problem of finding the so-called *brachistochrone*, which is the least-time path in a vertical plane for an object pulled by gravity between two specified points.

one instance, will also govern the motion of *aggregate* consumption under our convention.

We must keep in mind, however, that our notational shortcut, while innocuous in this chapter, is not appropriate in every setting. In later chapters we reintroduce individually superscripted lowercase quantity variables whenever consumer heterogeneity and the distinction between per capita and total quantities are important.

Since the only price in the model is the real interest rate r, and this is exogenously given to the small economy by the world capital market, national aggregate quantities are equilibrium quantities. That is, the small economy can carry out any intertemporal exchange of consumption it desires at the given world interest rate r, subject only to its budget constraint. For example, if the subjective and market discount factors are the same, eq. (5), written with C in place of c^i and Y in place of y^i, describes aggregate equilibrium consumption.

The idea of a representative national consumer, though a common device in modern macroeconomic modeling, may seem implausible. There are, however, three good reasons for taking the representative-consumer case as a starting point. First, several useful insights into the macroeconomy do not depend on a detailed consideration of household differences. An instance is the prediction that money-supply changes are neutral in the long run. Second, there are important cases where one can rigorously justify using the representative-agent model to describe aggregate behavior.[5] Finally, many models in international macroeconomics are interesting precisely because they assume differences between residents of different countries. Sometimes the simplest way to focus on these cross-country differences is to downplay differences within countries.

We have seen [in eq. (5)] that when $\beta = 1/(1 + r)$, the time path of aggregate consumption is flat. This prediction of the model captures the idea that, other things the same, countries will wish to *smooth* their consumption. When the subjective time-preference rate and the market interest rate differ, the motivation to smooth consumption is modified by an incentive to *tilt* the consumption path. Suppose, for example, that $\beta > 1/(1 + r)$ but $C_1 = C_2$. In this case the world capital market offers the country a rate of return that more than compensates it for the postponement of a little more consumption. According to the Euler equation (3), $u'(C_1)$ should exceed $u'(C_2)$ in equilibrium; that is, individuals in the economy maximize utility by arranging for consumption to rise between dates 1 and 2. The effects of a rise in

---

5. One does not need to assume literally that all individuals are identical to conclude that aggregate consumption will behave as if chosen by a single maximizing agent. Under well-defined but rather stringent preference assumptions, individual behavior can be aggregated exactly, as discussed by Deaton and Muellbauer (1980, ch. 6). We defer a formal discussion of aggregation until Chapter 5. For a perspective on ways in which the representative-agent paradigm can be misleading, however, see Kirman (1992).

r on initial consumption and on saving are rather intricate. We postpone discussing them until later in the chapter.

1.1.3   International Borrowing and Lending, the Current Account, and the Gains from Trade

Let's look first at how intertemporal trade allows the economy to allocate its consumption over time.

1.1.3.1   Defining the Current Account

Because international borrowing and lending are possible, there is no reason for an open economy's consumption to be closely tied to its current output. Provided all loans are repaid with interest, the economy's intertemporal budget constraint (2) is respected. In the special case $\beta = 1/(1 + r)$, consumption is flat at the level $C_1 = C_2 = \bar{C}$ in eq. (5), but output need not be. If, for example, $Y_1 < Y_2$, the country borrows $\bar{C} - Y_1$ from foreigners on date 1, repaying $(1 + r)(\bar{C} - Y_1)$ on date 2. Whenever date 2 consumption equals output on that date less the interest and principal on prior borrowing—that is, $C_2 = Y_2 - (1 + r)(C_1 - Y_1)$—the economy's intertemporal budget constraint obviously holds true.

A country's *current account balance* over a period is the change in the value of its net claims on the rest of the world—the change in its net foreign assets. For example, in our initial simple model without capital accumulation, a country's first-period current account is simply national saving. (In section 1.2 we will see that in general a country's current account is national saving less domestic investment.) The current account balance is said to be in surplus if positive, so that the economy as a whole is lending, and in deficit if negative, so that the economy is borrowing.

Our definition of a country's current account balance as the increase in its net claims on foreigners may puzzle you if you are used to thinking of the current account as a country's *net exports* of goods and services (where "service" exports include the services of domestic capital operating abroad, as measured by interest and dividend payments on those assets). Remember, however, that a country with positive net exports must be acquiring foreign assets of equal value because it is selling more to foreigners than it is buying from them; and a country with negative net exports must be borrowing an equal amount to finance its deficit with foreigners. Balance-of-payments statistics record a country's net sales of assets to foreigners under its *capital account balance*. Because a payment is received from foreigners for any good or service a country exports, every positive item of its net exports is associated with an equal-value negative item in its capital account— namely, the associated payment from abroad, which is a foreign asset acquired. Thus, as a pure matter of accounting, the net export surplus and the capital account surplus sum identically to zero. Hence, the capital account surplus preceded by a minus sign—the net *increase* in foreign asset holdings—equals the current account balance.

Despite this accounting equivalence, there is an important reason for focusing on the foreign asset accumulation view of the current account. It plainly shows that the current account represents trade *over* time, whereas the net exports view draws attention to factors determining gross exports and imports *within* a single time period. Those factors are far more than unimportant details, as we shall see in subsequent chapters, but to stress them at the outset would only obscure the basic principles of intertemporal trade.

To clarify the concept of the current account, let B_{t+1} be the value of the economy's net foreign assets at the end of a period t. The current account balance over period t is defined as $CA_t = B_{t+1} - B_t$. In general, the date t current account for a country with no capital accumulation or government spending is

$$CA_t = B_{t+1} - B_t = Y_t + r_t B_t - C_t, \tag{6}$$

where $r_t B_t$ is interest earned on foreign assets acquired previously. (This convention makes r_t the one-period interest rate that prevailed on date $t - 1$.)

1.1.3.2   Gross National Product and Gross Domestic Product

Equation (6) shows that a country's current account (or net export surplus) is the difference between its *total income* and its consumption. The national income of an economy is also called its *gross national product* (GNP) and is measured as the sum of two components: the value of the final output produced within its borders *and* net international factor payments. Here, these factor payments consist of interest and dividend earnings on the economy's net foreign assets, which are viewed as domestic capital operating abroad.[6] (In line with the definition of net exports given earlier, a country's earnings on its foreign assets are considered part of its national product despite the fact that this product is generated abroad.) In terms of our formal model, GNP over any period t is $Y_t + r_t B_t$, as just indicated.

The first component of national product, output produced within a country's geographical borders, is called *gross domestic product* (GDP). In the present model

---

6. Strictly speaking, national income equals national product plus net unrequited transfer payments from abroad (including items like reparations payments and workers' remittances to family members in other countries). Workers' remittances, which represent a payment for exported labor services, are not truly unrequited and are completely analogous to asset earnings, which are payments for capital services. We will treat them as such in section 1.5. In practice, however, national income accountants usually don't treat remittances as payments for service exports. The term "gross" in GNP reflects its failure to account for depreciation of capital—a factor absent from our theoretical model. When depreciation occurs, *net* national product (NNP) measures national income less depreciation. Empirical economists prefer to work with GNP rather than NNP data, especially in international comparisons, because actual national account estimates of depreciation are accounting measures heavily influenced by domestic tax laws. Reported depreciation figures therefore are quite unreliable and can differ widely from country to country. For the United States, a ballpark estimate of annual depreciation would be around 10 percent of GNP.

Table 1.1
GNP versus GDP for Selected Countries, 1990 (dollars per capita)

Country	GDP	GNP	Percent Difference
Australia	17,327	17,000	−1.9
Brazil	2,753	2,680	−2.7
Canada	21,515	20,470	−4.9
Saudi Arabia	5,429	7,050	29.9
Singapore	11,533	11,160	−3.2
United Arab Emirates	17,669	19,860	12.4
United States	21,569	21,790	1.0

Source: World Bank, *World Development Report 1992.*

GDP is Y_t. Typically the difference between national and domestic product is a rather small number, but for some countries, those which have amassed large stocks of foreign wealth or incurred substantial foreign debts, the difference can be significant. Table 1.1 shows several of these cases.

1.1.3.3   The Current Account and the Budget Constraint in the Two-Period Model

Our formulation of budget constraint (2) tacitly assumed that $B_1 = 0$, making $CA_1 = Y_1 - C_1$ on the formal model's date 1 (but not in general). By writing constraint (2) as a strict equality, we have also assumed that the economy ends period 2 holding no uncollected claims on foreigners. (That is, $B_3 = 0$. Obviously foreigners do not wish to expire holding uncollected claims on the home country either!) Thus,

$$CA_2 = Y_2 + rB_2 - C_2 = Y_2 + r(Y_1 - C_1) - C_2$$
$$= -(Y_1 - C_1) = -B_2 = -CA_1,$$

where the third equality in this chain follows from the economy's intertemporal budget constraint, eq. (2). Over any stretch of time, as over a single period, a country's cumulative current account balance is the change in its net foreign assets, but in our two-period model with zero initial and terminal assets, $CA_1 + CA_2 = B_3 - B_1 = 0$.

Figure 1.1 combines the representative individual's indifference curves with the intertemporal budget constraint (2), graphed as

$$C_2 = Y_2 - (1 + r)(C_1 - Y_1).$$

It provides a diagrammatic derivation of the small economy's equilibrium and the implied trajectory of its current account. (The figure makes no special assumption about the relation between β and $1 + r$.) The economy's optimal consumption choice is at point **C**, where the budget constraint is tangent to the highest

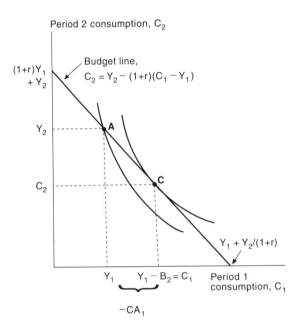

Figure 1.1
Consumption over time and the current account

attainable indifference curve. The first-period current account balance (a deficit in Figure 1.1) is simply the horizontal distance between the date 1 output and consumption points. As an exercise, the reader should show how to read from the figure's vertical axis the second-period current-account balance.

Economic policymakers often express concern about national current account deficits or surpluses. Our simple model makes the very important point that an unbalanced current account is not necessarily a bad thing. In Figure 1.1, for example, the country clearly does better running an unbalanced current account in both periods than it would if forced to set $C_1 = Y_1$ and $C_2 = Y_2$ (the autarky point **A**). Intertemporal trade makes possible a less jagged time profile of consumption. The utility gain between points **A** and **C** illustrates the general and classic insight that countries gain from trade.

Application: Consumption Smoothing in the Second Millennium B.C.

An early anecdote concerning the consumption-smoothing behavior underlying this chapter's model comes from the story of Joseph in the Book of Genesis. Scholars of the biblical period place the episode somewhere around 1800 B.C.

The Pharaoh of Egypt summoned Joseph, then an imprisoned slave, to interpret two dreams. In the first, seven plump cattle were followed and devoured by seven lean, starving cattle. In the second, seven full ears of corn were eaten by seven thin ears. After hearing these dreams, Joseph prophesied that Egypt would enjoy seven years of prosperity, followed by seven of famine. He recommended a consumption-smoothing strategy to provide for the years of famine, under which Pharaoh would appropriate and store a fifth of the grain produced during the years of plenty (Genesis 41:33–36). According to the Bible, Pharaoh embraced this plan, made Joseph his prime minister, and thereby enabled Joseph to save Egypt from starvation.

Why did Joseph recommend storing the grain (a form of domestic investment yielding a rate of return of zero before depreciation) rather than lending it abroad at a positive rate of interest? Cuneiform records of the period place the interest rate on loans of grain in Babylonia in a range of 20 to 33 percent per year and show clear evidence of international credit transactions within Asia Minor (Heichelheim 1958, pp. 134–135). At such high interest rates Egypt could have earned a handsome return on its savings. It seems likely, however, that, under the military and political conditions of the second millennium B.C., Egypt would have found it difficult to compel foreign countries to repay a large loan, particularly during a domestic famine. Thus storing the grain at home was a much safer course. The model in this chapter assumes, of course, that international loan contracts are always respected, but we have not yet examined mechanisms that ensure compliance with their terms. We will study the question in Chapter 6.   ■

1.1.4   Autarky Interest Rates and the Intertemporal Trade Pattern

Diagrams like Figure 1.1 can illuminate the main factors causing some countries to run initial current account deficits while others run surpluses. The key concept we need for this analysis is the *autarky real interest rate*, that is, the interest rate that would prevail in an economy barred from international borrowing and lending.

Were the economy restricted to consume at the autarky point **A** in Figure 1.1, the only real interest rate consistent with the Euler eq. (3) would be the autarky interest rate r^A, defined by eq. (4) with outputs replacing consumptions:

$$\frac{\beta u'(Y_2)}{u'(Y_1)} = \frac{1}{1 + r^A}. \tag{7}$$

This equation also gives the autarky price of future consumption in terms of present consumption.

Figure 1.1 shows that when the latter autarky price is below the *world* relative price of future consumption—which is equivalent to r^A being above r—future consumption is relatively cheap in the home economy and present consumption relatively expensive. Thus the home economy will "import" present consumption from abroad in the first period (by running a current account deficit) and "export" future consumption later (by repaying its foreign debt). This result is in accord with the *principle of comparative advantage* from international trade theory, which states that countries tend to import those commodities whose autarky prices are high compared with world prices and export those whose autarky prices are comparatively low.[7] It is the opportunity to exploit these pretrade international price differentials that explains the gains from trade shown in Figure 1.1.

A rise in present output or a fall in future output lowers the autarky real interest rate: either event would raise desired saving at the previous autarky interest rate, but since the residents of a closed endowment economy cannot save more in the aggregate without lending abroad, r^A must fall until people are content to consume their new endowment. Similarly, greater patience (a rise in β) lowers r^A. By modifying Figure 1.1, you can check that when r^A is below the world interest rate r, the country runs a first-period current account surplus followed by a deficit, but still gains from trade.

It may come as a surprise that the existence of gains from intertemporal trade does not depend on the sign of the country's initial current account balance. The reason is simple, however. What produces gains is the chance to trade with someone different from oneself. Indeed, the greater is the difference, the greater the gain. The only case of no gain is the one in which, coincidentally, it happens that $r^A = r$.

This reasoning also explains how changes in world interest rates affect a country's welfare. In Figure 1.1 the economy reaps trade gains by borrowing initially because its autarky interest rate is above the world rate, r. Notice, however, that, were the world interest rate even lower, the economy's welfare after trade would be higher than in Figure 1.1. The basic reason for this welfare gain is that a fall in the world interest rate accentuates the difference between the home country and the rest of the world, increasing the gains from trade. A small rise in the world interest rate (one that doesn't reverse the intertemporal trade pattern) therefore harms a first-period borrower but benefits a first-period lender.

1.1.5 Temporary versus Permanent Output Changes

A suggestive interpretation of the preceding ideas leads to a succinct description of how alternative paths for output affect the current account.

The natural benchmark for considering the effects of changing output is the case $\beta = 1/(1+r)$. The reason is that, in this case, eq. (7) becomes

$$\frac{u'(Y_2)}{u'(Y_1)} = \frac{1+r}{1+r^A},$$

which implies that the *sole* factor responsible for any difference between the world and autarky interest rates is a changing output level.

---

7. For a detailed discussion, see Dixit and Norman (1980).

Imagine an economy that initially expects its output to be constant over time. The economy will plan on a balanced current account. But suppose Y_1 rises. If Y_2 does not change, the economy's autarky interest rate will fall below the world interest rate: a date 1 current account surplus will result as people smooth their consumption by lending some of their temporarily high output to foreigners. If Y_2 rises by the same amount as Y_1, however, the autarky interest rate does not change, and there is no current account imbalance. Alternatively, consumption automatically remains constant through time if people simply consume their higher output in both periods.

One way to interpret these results is as follows: *permanent* changes in output do not affect the current account when $\beta = 1/(1+r)$, whereas *temporary* changes do, temporary increases causing surpluses and temporary declines producing deficits. Likewise, a change in future expected output affects the sign of the current account in the same qualitative manner as an opposite movement in current output. We will generalize this reasoning to a many-period setting in the next chapter.

1.1.6 Adding Government Consumption

So far we have not discussed the role of a government. Government consumption is, however, easy to introduce.

Suppose government consumption per capita, G, enters the utility function additively, giving period utility the form $u(C) + v(G)$. This case is, admittedly, a simple one, but it suffices for the issues on which we focus. For now, it is easiest to suppose that the government simply appropriates G_t in taxes from the private sector for $t = 1, 2$. This policy implies a balanced government budget each period (we will look at government deficits in Chapter 3). The representative private individual's lifetime budget constraint is thus

$$C_1 + \frac{C_2}{1+r} = Y_1 - G_1 + \frac{Y_2 - G_2}{1+r}. \tag{8}$$

Government spending also enters the date t current account identity, which is now

$$CA_t = B_{t+1} - B_t = Y_t + r_t B_t - C_t - G_t.$$

The new feature here is that both government and private consumption are subtracted from national income to compute the current account. (Plainly we must account for *all* domestic expenditure—public as well as private—to reckon how much a country as a whole is saving.)

Since G is beyond the private sector's control we can follow the same steps as in section 1.1.1 to conclude that the Euler equation (3) remains valid. Indeed, introducing government consumption as we have done here is equivalent to relabeling the private sector's endowment Y as output net of government consumption, $Y - G$.

How do government consumption decisions affect the current account? A natural benchmark once again is the case in which $\beta = 1/(1 + r)$, and output is constant at $Y_1 = Y_2 = \bar{Y}$. Absent government consumption, private consumption would be constant in this case at $\bar{C} = \bar{Y}$, with the current account balanced. Suppose, however, that $G_1 > 0$ while $G_2 = 0$. Now the private sector will want to borrow against its relatively high second-period after-tax income to shift part of the burden of the temporary taxes to the future. The country therefore will run a deficit in period 1 and a surplus in period 2.

Replacing Y with $Y - G$ in eq. (5) implies that in the preceding example

$$\bar{C} = \frac{[(1 + r)(\bar{Y} - G_1) + \bar{Y}]}{2 + r} = \bar{Y} - \frac{(1 + r)G_1}{2 + r}.$$

Government consumption in period 1 lowers private consumption, but by an amount *smaller* than G_1. The reason is that the government consumption is temporary: it drops to zero in period 2. Thus the current account equation presented earlier in this subsection (recall that $B_1 = 0$ here) implies that

$$CA_1 = \bar{Y} - \bar{C} - G_1 = -\frac{G_1}{2 + r} < 0.$$

In contrast, suppose that $G_1 = G_2 = \bar{G}$. Then consumption is constant at $\bar{C} = \bar{Y} - \bar{G}$ in both periods, and the current account is balanced always. Government consumption affects the current account here only to the extent that it tilts the path of private *net* income.

*1.1.7 A Digression on Intertemporal Preferences

Equation (1) assumes the representative individual's preferences are captured by a very particular lifetime utility function rather than an unrestricted function $U_1 = U(C_1, C_2)$. In eq. (1) consumption levels for different dates enter additively; moreover, the *period* utility function $u(C)$ is constant over time. With consumption occurring over T rather than just two periods, the natural generalization of utility function (1) is

$$U_1 = \sum_{t=1}^{T} \beta^{t-1} u(C_t). \tag{9}$$

Preferences that can be represented by an additive lifetime utility function are called *intertemporally additive preferences*. The key property implied by intertemporal additivity is that the marginal rate of substitution between consumption on any two dates t and s [equal to $\beta^{s-t} u'(C_s)/u'(C_t)$ for the preferences described by eq. (9)] is independent of consumption on any third date. This property is restrictive (provided $T > 2$, of course). It rules out certain kinds of intertemporal consumption dependencies, such as complementarity between total consumption levels in different periods. Such dependencies are at the heart of recent models of habit persistence in aggregate consumption.[8]

Although we will discuss particular alternative assumptions on tastes at several points in the book, the assumption of intertemporally additive preferences with an unvarying period utility function will form the backbone of our formal analysis. There are several reasons for this choice:

1. It is true that some types of goods, such as refrigerators and automobiles, are *durable* goods typically consumed over many periods rather than just one. This type of consumption linkage, however, is fundamentally technological. By defining utility over the flow of services from durables, and by imputing their rental cost, one can easily incorporate such goods within the umbrella of intertemporally additive preferences. (We show this in Chapter 2.)

2. For some types of goods, consumption at one point in time clearly does influence one's utility from consuming in closely neighboring periods. After eating a large meal, one is less inclined to want another an hour later. The time intervals of aggregation we look at in macroeconomic data, however, typically are measured in months, quarters, or years, periods over which many types of intertemporal dependencies fade.

3. Admittedly, even over long periods, habit persistence can be important. Drug addiction is an extreme example; watching television is a closely related one. In macroeconomics, however, one should think of preferences as being defined over consumption variables that really represent aggregate spending on a wide array of different goods. While we may have some intuition about the persistence effects of consuming certain items, it is harder to see obvious and quantitatively significant channels through which the *totality* of consumption has long-lived persistence effects.

4. One can think of some types of goods that most individuals would prefer to consume only once, such as marriage services. But even though consumption of such services is lumpy for an individual, it is relatively smooth in the aggregate.

---

8. If $G(\cdot)$ is any monotonically increasing function, then the utility function

$$G\left[\sum_{t=1}^{T} \beta^{t-1} u(C_t)\right]$$

naturally represents the same preferences as U_1 does, i.e., a monotonically increasing transformation of the lifetime utility function does not affect the consumer's underlying preference ordering over different consumption paths. Intertemporally additive preferences take the general form $G\left[u_1(C_1) + \cdots + u_T(C_T)\right]$ (with period utility functions possibly distinct). They also go by the name *strongly intertemporally separable* preferences. For further discussion of their implications, see Deaton and Muellbauer (1980, ch. 5.3).

People get married all the time. Similarly, people may take vacation trips only at infrequent intervals, but this is not the case in the aggregate. (Seasonality can be important in either of these examples, but such effects are easily dealt with.)

5. Fundamentally, a very general intertemporally nonadditive utility function would yield few concrete behavioral predictions. If consumptions on different dates are substitutes, one gets dramatically different results from the case in which they are complements. Because maximal generality would lead to an unfalsifiable macroeconomic theory with little empirical content, macroeconomists have found it more fruitful to begin with a tractable basic setup like eq. (9), which has very sharp predictions. The basic setup can then be amended in parsimonious and testable ways if its implications seem counterintuitive or counterfactual.

6. In any event, while empirical research has raised interesting questions about the simplest time-additive preference model, it does not yet clearly point to a superior nonadditive alternative.

1.2   The Role of Investment

Historically, one of the main reasons countries have borrowed abroad is to finance productive investments that would have been hard to finance out of domestic savings alone. In the nineteenth century, the railroad companies that helped open up the Americas drew on European capital to pay laborers and obtain rails, rolling stock, and other inputs. To take a more recent example, Norway borrowed extensively in world capital markets to develop its North Sea oil resources in the 1970s after world oil prices shot up.

So far we have focused on consumption smoothing in our study of the current account, identifying the current account with national saving. In general, however, the current account equals saving minus investment. And because, in reality, investment usually is much more volatile than saving, to ignore investment is to miss much of the action.

1.2.1   Adding Investment to the Model

Let's modify our earlier model economy to allow for investment. We now assume that output is produced using capital, which, in turn, can be accumulated through investment. The production function for new output in either period is

$$Y = F(K). \tag{10}$$

As usual production is strictly increasing in capital but subject to diminishing marginal productivity: $F'(K) > 0$ and $F''(K) < 0$. Furthermore, output cannot be produced without capital: $F(0) = 0$. We will think of the representative consumer as having the additional role of producer with direct access to this technology.[9]

A unit of capital is created from a unit of the consumption good. This process is reversible, so that a unit of capital, after having been used to produce output, can be "eaten." You may find these assumptions unrealistic, but they help us sidestep some technical issues that aren't really central here. One key simplification due to our assumptions is that the relative price of capital goods in terms of consumption always equals 1.

Introducing investment requires that we rethink the budget constraints individuals face, because now saving can flow into capital as well as foreign assets. Total domestic private wealth at the end of a period t is now $B_{t+1} + K_{t+1}$, the sum of net foreign assets B_{t+1} and the stock of domestic capital K_{t+1}.[10]

How is capital investment reflected in the date t current account? The stock of capital K_{t+1} accumulated through the end of period t is the sum of preexisting capital K_t and new investment during period t, I_t (we ignore depreciation of capital):

$$K_{t+1} = K_t + I_t. \tag{11}$$

Nothing restricts investment to be nonnegative, so eq. (11) allows people to eat part of their capital.

Next, the change in total domestic wealth, national saving, is

$$B_{t+1} + K_{t+1} - (B_t + K_t) = Y_t + r_t B_t - C_t - G_t.$$

Finally, rearranging terms in this equation and substituting (11) shows that the current account surplus is

$$CA_t = B_{t+1} - B_t = Y_t + r_t B_t - C_t - G_t - I_t. \tag{12}$$

A very useful way to interpret the preceding current account identity is to label national saving as S_t:

$$S_t \equiv Y_t + r_t B_t - C_t - G_t. \tag{13}$$

---

9. As we discuss in later chapters, it is reasonable to think of labor as being an additional production input alongside capital. A production function of the form (10) still is valid as long as labor is supplied inelastically by the individual producer. We assume

$$\lim_{K \to 0} F'(K) = \infty$$

to ensure a positive capital stock.

10. It is simplest to suppose that all domestic capital is owned by domestic residents. The statement that total domestic wealth equals $B + K$ is true even when foreigners own part of the domestic capital stock, however, because domestic capital owned by foreigners is subtracted in calculating *net* foreign assets B. As long as perfect foresight holds, so that the ex post returns to assets are equal, the ownership of the domestic capital stock is irrelevant. The ownership pattern is not irrelevant, as we see later, when unexpected shocks can occur.

Fraction of GDP

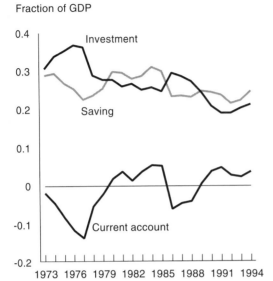

Figure 1.2
Norway's saving-investment balance, 1973–94. (*Source:* OECD)

Then eq. (12) states that in an economy with investment,

$$CA_t = S_t - I_t. \tag{14}$$

National saving in excess of domestic capital formation flows into net foreign asset accumulation.

The saving-investment identity (14) discloses that the current account is fundamentally an *intertemporal* phenomenon. Simple as it is, the identity $CA = S - I$ is vital for analyzing how economic policies and disturbances change the current account. Will a protective tariff, often imposed to improve the current account, succeed in its aim? The answer cannot be determined from partial-equilibrium reasoning, but ultimately depends instead on how the tariff affects saving and investment.

Figure 1.2 returns to the Norwegian case mentioned at the start of this section, graphing recent data on saving, investment, and the current account. In the mid-1970s, the Norwegian current account registered huge deficits, touching -14 percent of GDP in 1977. In an accounting sense, higher energy-sector investment is "responsible" for much of the deficit, although saving simultaneously fell in the mid-1970s, possibly in anticipation of higher future oil revenues. Subsequent surpluses through 1985, reflecting higher saving and lower investment, enabled Norway to repay much of the debt incurred in the 1970s.

The Norwegian data illustrate an important point. The saving-investment identity is a vital analytical tool, but because CA, S, and I are jointly determined endogenous variables that respond to common exogenous shocks, it may be misleading to identify a specific ex post investment or saving shift as the "cause" of a current account change. Our model with investment will show how various exogenous shocks can simultaneously affect all three variables in the saving-investment identity.

1.2.2   Budget Constraint and Individual Maximization

To derive the intertemporal budget constraint analogous to eq. (8) when there is both government spending and investment, we simply add the asset-accumulation identities for periods 1 and 2. For period 1, current account eq. (12) gives

$$B_2 = Y_1 - C_1 - G_1 - I_1$$

(recall that $B_1 = 0$). For period 2, eq. (12) gives

$$-B_2 = Y_2 + rB_2 - C_2 - G_2 - I_2$$

(recall that $B_3 = 0$). Solve this equation for B_2, and substitute the result into the equation that precedes it. One thereby arrives at the intertemporal budget constraint

$$C_1 + I_1 + \frac{C_2 + I_2}{1 + r} = Y_1 - G_1 + \frac{Y_2 - G_2}{1 + r}. \tag{15}$$

Now it is the present value of consumption *plus* investment that is limited by the present value of output.

In this economy with investment, a representative individual maximizes $U_1 = u(C_1) + \beta u(C_2)$ subject to eq. (15), where eq. (10) replaces Y with $F(K)$ and eq. (11) is used to replace I with the change in K. To simplify further, observe that people will never wish to carry capital past the terminal period 2. Thus capital K_2 accumulated in period 1 will be consumed at the end of period 2 and K_3 will be zero, implying that

$$I_2 = K_3 - K_2 = 0 - K_2 = -K_2.$$

Using eq. (15) to eliminate C_2 from U_1 therefore transforms the individual's problem to

$$\max_{C_1, I_1} u(C_1)$$

$$+ \beta u \left\{ (1 + r) \left[F(K_1) - C_1 - G_1 - I_1 \right] + F(I_1 + K_1) - G_2 + I_1 + K_1 \right\}. \tag{16}$$

(K_1 is given by history and is not subject to choice on date 1.) The two corresponding first-order conditions are the Euler equation (3) and

$$F'(K_2) = r, \tag{17}$$

where we have used the identity $K_2 = K_1 + I_1$.

An extra unit of output invested on date 1 can be fully consumed, together with its marginal contribution to output, $F'(K_2)$, on date 2. Equation (17) says that

Box 1.1
Nominal versus Real Current Accounts

Our use in Figure 1.2 of data from official national income and product accounts raises an important measurement problem that you should recognize as you read this book. Unfortunately, the problem is easier to understand than to cure, so in most cases we reluctantly continue to rely on the official data.

Ideally, the current account should measure the change in an economy's net *real* claims on foreigners. In practice, however, government statistical agencies measure the current account and GDP by adding up the values of transactions measured in *nominal* terms, that is, in units of domestic money. This practice poses no conceptual hazards when money has a stable value in terms of real output, but, for reasons we will understand better after learning about monetary economics in Chapters 8–10, real-world economies are almost always afflicted by at least some *price-level infla-tion*, a tendency for the money prices of all goods and services to rise over time. Such inflation would not be a problem if all international borrowing and lending involved the exchange of output-indexed bonds, as our theoretical model assumes. But most bonds traded between countries have returns and face values that are contracted in terms of currencies, implying that inflation can affect their real values.

A hypothetical example illustrates the problem. Suppose United States GDP is $7 trillion dollars and the U.S. net foreign debt is $700 billion. Suppose also that all international debts are linked to dollars, that the interest rate on dollar loans is 10 percent per year, and that U.S. GDP equals the sum of consumption, investment, and government spending. Under these assumptions the U.S. Department of Commerce would report the current account balance as the nominal interest outflow on net foreign assets, or $(0.1) \times (\$700 \text{ billion}) = \$70$ billion. So measured, the current account deficit is 1 percent of GDP.

Suppose, however, that all dollar prices are rising at 5 percent per year. Over the course of the year, the U.S. external debt declines in real value by $(0.05) \times (\$700 \text{ billion}) = \$35$ billion as a result of this inflation. Thus the dollar value of the change in U.S. *real* net foreign assets is not $70 billion, but $70 billion $-\$35$ billion $= \$35$ billion. This smaller number divided by GDP, equal to 0.5 percent, shows the change in the economy's real net foreign assets as a fraction of real output. Naive use of nominal official numbers makes the deficit look twice as large relative to GDP as it really is!

While it was easy to measure the current account correctly in our example, doing so in practice is much harder. International financial transactions are denominated in many currencies. Changes in currency exchange rates as well as in national money price levels therefore enter into the real current account, but, because the currency composition of a country's net foreign debt is difficult to monitor, accurate correction is problematic. Many internationally held assets, such as stocks, long-term bonds, and real estate, can fluctuate sharply in value. Accounting for these price changes involves similar problems.

Caveat emptor. Unless otherwise stated, the ratios of the current account to output that you encounter in this book are the rough approximations one gleans from official national accounts. The same is true of related wealth flows, such as saving-to-output ratios.

period 1 investment should continue to the point at which its marginal return is the same as that on a foreign loan. A critical feature of eq. (17) is its implication that the desired capital stock is *independent* of domestic consumption preferences! Other things equal, wouldn't a less patient country, one with a lower value of β, wish to invest less? Not necessarily, if it has access to perfect international capital markets. A country that can borrow abroad at the interest rate r never wishes to pass up investment opportunities that offer a net rate of return above r.

Several key assumptions underpin the separation of investment from consumption decisions in this economy. First, the economy is *small*. The saving decisions of its residents don't change the interest rate at which investment projects can be financed in the world capital market. Second, the economy produces and consumes a single tradable good. When the economy produces nontraded goods, as in some of Chapter 4's models, consumption shifts can affect investment. Third, capital markets are free of imperfections that might act to limit borrowing. We shall see later (in Chapter 6) that when factors such as default risk restrict access to international borrowing, national saving can influence domestic investment.[11]

In the present setup, investment is independent of government consumption as well. In particular, government consumption does not crowd out investment in a small open economy facing a perfect world capital market.

1.2.3   Production Possibilities and Equilibrium

Let's assume temporarily that government consumption is zero in both periods. Then Figure 1.3 shows how the current account is determined when there is investment. To the information in Figure 1.1, Figure 1.3 adds an *intertemporal production possibilities frontier* (PPF) showing the technological possibilities available in autarky for transforming period 1 consumption into period 2 consumption. The PPF is described by the equation

$$C_2 = F\left[K_1 + F(K_1) - C_1\right] + K_1 + F(K_1) - C_1. \tag{18}$$

What does this equation imply about the PPF's position and shape? If the economy chose the lowest possible investment level on date 1 by eating all its inherited capital immediately (setting $I_1 = -K_1$), it would enjoy the highest date 1 consumption available in autarky, $C_1 = K_1 + F(K_1)$. In this case date 2 consumption

---

11. Once we allow for uncertainty, as in Chapters 2 and 5, restrictions on the tradability of certain assets also can upset the separation of investment from consumption. We have not yet introduced labor as an explicit factor of production, but if the supply of labor influences the marginal product of capital, the separation can also fail when consumption and labor effort enter the period utility function in a nonadditive manner.

Even if consumption shifts don't alter investment, the converse proposition need *not* be true! As budget constraint (15) shows, investment enters the consumer's budget constraint in equilibrium, so in general factors that shift domestic investment can affect national saving too.

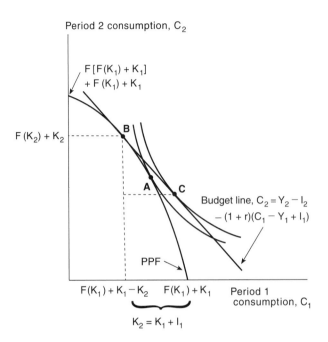

Figure 1.3
Investment and the current account

would be at its lowest possible level, $C_2 = F(0) + 0 = 0$. The resulting point is the PPF's horizontal intercept in Figure 1.3. At the other extreme, the economy could invest all output on date 1 and eat no inherited capital K_1. This decision would set $C_1 = 0$, $I_1 = F(K_1)$, $K_2 = K_1 + F(K_1)$, and $C_2 = F[K_1 + F(K_1)] + K_1 + F(K_1)$, the last being the highest date 2 consumption available in autarky. The PPF's vertical intercept in Figure 1.3 shows the allocation just described. In between, the PPF's slope is obtained from (18) by differentiation:

$$\frac{dC_2}{dC_1} = -[1 + F'(K_2)].$$

Capital's diminishing marginal productivity makes the PPF strictly concave, as shown.[12]

Point **A** in Figure 1.3 is the autarky equilibrium. There, the PPF is tangent to the highest indifference curve the economy can reach without trade. The common slope of the two curves at **A** is $-(1 + r^A)$, where r^A, as earlier, is the autarky real interest rate. All three closed-economy equilibrium conditions hold at point **A**. First, producer maximization: investment decisions are efficient, given r^A [that

---

12. To test your understanding, show that the second derivative $d^2C_2/dC_1^2 = F''(K_2) < 0$.

is, condition (17) holds for r^A]. Second, consumer maximization: the intertemporal Euler condition holds, again given r^A. Third, output-market clearing: consumption and investment sum to output in both periods. You can see that markets clear at **A** by observing that in autarky K_2 equals the distance between C_1 and $Y_1 + K_1$ along the horizontal axis, so that $C_1 + I_1 = Y_1$, whereas eq. (18) can be written as $C_2 = Y_2 + K_2 = Y_2 - I_2$.

In Figure 1.3, the economy faces a *world* interest rate, r, lower than the autarky rate r^A implied by the dual tangency at point **A**. Thus, at **A**, the marginal domestic investment project offers a rate of return above the world cost of borrowing. The opportunity to trade across periods with foreigners lets domestic residents gain by investing more and producing at point **B**, through which the economy's new budget line passes. Production at **B** maximizes the present value of domestic output (net of investment) by placing the economy on the highest feasible budget line at world prices. Consuming at point **C** gives the economy the highest utility level it can afford.

The horizontal distance between points **A** and **B** is the extra investment generated by opening the economy to the world capital market. The horizontal distance between points **A** and **C** shows the extra first-period consumption that trade simultaneously allows. Since total first-period resources $Y_1 + K_1$ haven't changed, the sum of these two horizontal distances—the distance from **B** to **C**—is the first-period current account deficit.

The utility curve through point **C** lies above the one through point **A**. The distance between them measures the gains from trade. In Figure 1.1, trade gains were entirely due to smoothing the time path of consumption. In Figure 1.3 there is an additional source of gain, the change in the economy's production point from **A** to **B**.

Had the world interest rate r been *above* r^A rather than below it, the country would have run a first-period current account surplus but still enjoyed gains from intertemporal trade, as in the pure endowment case studied earlier.

1.2.4   The Model with Government Consumption

In section 1.2.3 we assumed away government consumption. Now we reinstate it in our graphical analysis.

A glance at eqs. (15) (for the individual's intertemporal budget constraint) and (18) (for the PPF) shows how changes in government consumption affect the graphs of these two relations between C_2 and C_1: both are shifted vertically downward by the amount of the increase in G_2 and horizontally leftward by the amount of the increase in G_1.

In understanding the difference that government consumption can make, it helps intuition to begin with an economy in which government consumption is always zero and the current account is in balance, so that consumption and production are

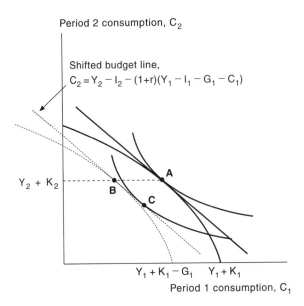

Figure 1.4
Government consumption and the current account

at point **A** in Figure 1.4. Compare this economy with an otherwise identical one in which $G_1 > 0$ while G_2 remains at zero. In the second economy, both the PPF and the budget constraint have shifted to the left by an amount G_1, and the economy's production point is **B**, implying the same investment level as at **A**.[13] Notice, however, that as long as consumption is a *normal* good on both dates, consumers will not wish to consume at **B**, for this choice would imply an unchanged C_2. Instead, they respond to a lower lifetime income level by reducing consumption on *both* dates and choosing consumption point **C**, which is southeast of **B** on the new budget constraint.

We conclude from Figure 1.4 that, other things equal, an economy with disproportionately high period 1 government consumption will have a current account deficit in that period. When government consumption is expected to occur on the future date 2 instead, the current account will be in surplus on date 1. Both predictions are explained by individuals' efforts to spread the burden of higher taxes over both periods of life through borrowing or lending abroad.

---

13. It may seem odd at first glance that in autarky a rise in G_1 alone reduces the maximal output available for private consumption on date 2 as well as on date 1. Recall, however, that when private consumption is zero on date 1, investment is lower by G_1 in autarky, so the maximal date 2 consumption available to the autarkic economy is only $F(K_1 + Y_1 - G_1) + K_1 + Y_1 - G_1$.

1.3   A Two-Region World Economy

Until now we have focused on a country too small to affect the world interest rate. In this section we show how the world interest rate is determined and how economic events in large regions are transmitted abroad.

1.3.1   A Global Endowment Economy

Let us start by abstracting from investment again and assuming a world of two regions or countries, called Home and Foreign, that receive exogenously determined endowments on dates 1 and 2. The two economies have parallel structures, but symbols pertaining to Foreign alone are marked by asterisks. We also omit government spending, which operates precisely as a reduction in output in our model.

Equilibrium in the global output market requires equal supply and demand on each date $t = 1, 2$,

$$Y_t + Y_t^* = C_t + C_t^*.$$

Equivalently, subtracting world consumption from both sides in this equation implies world saving must be zero for $t = 1, 2$,

$$S_t + S_t^* = 0.$$

Since there is so far no investment in the model, this equilibrium condition is the same as $CA_t + CA_t^* = 0$. We can simplify further by recalling that when there are only two markets, output today and output in the future, we need only check that one of them clears to verify general equilibrium (Walras's law). Thus the world economy is in equilibrium if

$$S_1 + S_1^* = 0. \tag{19}$$

Figure 1.5 shows how the equilibrium world interest rate is determined for given present and future endowments. In this case a country's date 1 saving depends only on the interest rate it faces. Curve **SS** shows how Home saving depends on r and curve **S*S*** does the same for Foreign. We will probe more deeply into the shapes of the saving schedules in a moment, but for now we ask you to accept them as drawn in Figure 1.5.

In Figure 1.5, the equilibrium world interest rate makes Home's lending, measured by the length of segment **AB**, equal to Foreign's borrowing, measured by the length of **B*A***. The equilibrium world interest rate r must lie between the two autarky rates:

$$r^A < r < r^{A*}.$$

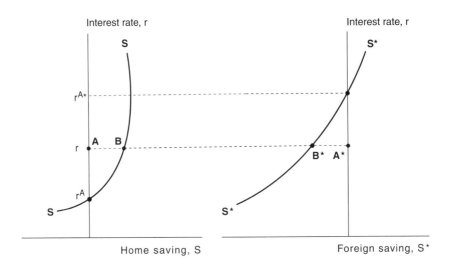

Figure 1.5
Global exchange equilibrium

In Home, the rise in the interest rate from its autarky level encourages saving, leading to positive Home saving of **AB**. Home's first-period current account surplus also equals **AB**. Foreign's situation is the reverse of Home's, and it runs a current account deficit of **B*A***. (Because Home and Foreign face the same world interest rate, we do not mark it with an asterisk.) The intertemporal trade pattern naturally conforms to the comparative advantage principle.

It is easy to see in Figure 1.5 how changes in exogenous variables alter the world interest rate and international capital flows. A ceteris paribus increase in Home's date 1 output, as we know, leads the country to raise its saving at a given rate of interest. As a result, **SS** shifts to the right. Plainly, the new equilibrium calls for a lower world interest rate, higher Home lending on date 1, and higher Foreign borrowing. Other things equal, higher date 2 output in Home shifts **SS** leftward, with opposite effects. Changes in Foreign's intertemporal endowment pattern work similarly, but through a shift of the Foreign saving schedule **S*S***.

An important normative issue concerns the international distribution of the benefits of economic growth. Is a country helped or hurt by an increase in trading partners' growth rates? To be concrete, suppose Home's date 2 output Y_2 rises, so that **SS** shifts leftward and the world interest rate rises. Because Foreign finds that the terms on which it must borrow have worsened, Foreign is actually worse off. Home, conversely, benefits from a higher interest rate for the same reason: the terms on which it lends to Foreign have improved. Thus, alongside the primary gain due to future higher output, Home enjoys a secondary gain due to the induced change in the intertemporal relative price it faces.

An interest-rate increase improves the *intertemporal terms of trade* of Home, which is "exporting" present consumption (through a date 1 surplus), while worsening those of Foreign, which is "importing" present consumption (through a date 1 deficit). In general, a country's terms of trade are defined as the price of its exports in terms of its imports. Here, $1 + r$ is the price of present consumption in terms of future consumption, that is, the price of a date 1 surplus country's export good in terms of its import good. As in static trade theory, a country derives a positive welfare benefit when its terms of trade improve and a negative one when they worsen.

It may seem reasonable to suppose that if Home's date 1 output Y_1 rises Home must benefit. In this case, however, the last paragraph's reasoning works in reverse. Because the world interest rate falls, Home's terms of trade worsen and counteract the primary benefit to Home of higher date 1 output. (Part of Home's benefit is exported abroad, and Foreign's welfare unambiguously rises.) Indeed, the terms-of-trade effect can be so big that higher date 1 output for Home actually worsens its lot. This paradoxical outcome has been dubbed *immiserizing growth* by Bhagwati (1958).

Application: War and the Current Account

Nothing in human experience is more terrible than the misery and destruction caused by wars. Their high costs notwithstanding, wars do offer a benefit for empirical economists. Because wars have drastic consequences for the economies involved, usually are known in advance to be temporary, and, arguably, are exogenous, they provide excellent "natural experiments" for testing economic theories.

Wartime data can have drawbacks as well. During wars, market modes of allocation may be supplemented or replaced by central economic planning. Because price controls and rationing are common, data on prices and quantities become hard to interpret in terms of market models. Matters are even worse when it comes to testing open-economy models, as wars inevitably bring tighter government control over capital movements and trade. Sometimes the normal data collecting and processing activities of statistical agencies are disrupted.

One way to reduce some of these problems is to focus on data from before the 1930s, when governments decisively turned away from laissez-faire in attempts to shield their economies from the worldwide Great Depression. Although pre-1930s data can be of uneven quality compared with modern-day numbers, they have been surprisingly useful in evaluating modern theories. We illustrate the use of historical data by looking briefly at the effects on both bystanders and participants of some early twentieth-century wars.

Sweden did not directly participate in World War I, while Japan took part only peripherally. Current-account data for the war's 1914–18 span are available

Figure 1.6
Current accounts of Japan and Sweden, 1861–1942

for both countries. What does our model predict about the effect of a foreign war on nonbelligerents? Return to Figure 1.5, interpreting "Home" as the warring portion of the world. For inhabitants of Home the war represents a situation in which the output available for private consumption has exogenously become much lower in the present than in the future. In response, Home lowers its saving at every interest rate, causing **SS** to shift to the left. Home's current account surplus falls (and may become a deficit), and the world interest rate rises. In Foreign, the region still at peace, the rise in the world interest rate causes a rise in saving and an improved current account balance (perhaps even a surplus).

Figure 1.6, which graphs current account data for Japan and Sweden, is consistent with the prediction that nonparticipants should run surpluses during large foreign wars. In both countries there is an abrupt shift from secular deficit toward a massive surplus reaching 10 percent of national product. The huge surpluses disappear once the war is over.

What is the evidence that belligerents do wish to borrow abroad? Foreign financing of wars has a long history; over the centuries, it has helped shape the institutions and instruments of international finance. From the late seventeenth century through the end of the Napoleonic Wars, lenders in several other continental countries underwrote Britain's military operations abroad. As far back as the first half of the fourteenth century, Edward III of England invaded France with the help of

Table 1.2
Japan's Gross Saving and Investment During the Russo-Japanese War (fraction of GDP)

Year	Saving/GDP	Investment/GDP
1903	0.131	0.136
1904	0.074	0.120
1905	0.058	0.168
1906	0.153	0.164

loans from Italian bankers. Edward's poor results in France and subsequent refusal to honor his foreign debts illustrate a potential problem for tests of the hypothesis that wars worsen the current account. Even though a country at war may wish to borrow, why should lenders respond when a country's ability to repay may be impaired even in the event of victory? The prospect that borrowers default can limit international capital flows, as we discuss in greater detail in Chapter 6. But intergovernment credits often are extended in wartime, and private lenders may stay in the game, too, if the interest rates offered them are high enough to compensate for the risk of loss.

Japan's 1904–1905 conflict with Russia offers a classic example of large-scale borrowing to finance a war. In February 1904, tensions over Russia's military presence in Manchuria and its growing influence in Korea erupted into open hostilities. Public opinion on the whole favored Japan, but Russia's superiority in manpower and other resources led more sober commentators to predict that the great power would beat its upstart challenger in the long run. These predictions quickly faded as Japan's naval prowess led to a string of victories that helped lay bare the fragility of tsarist Russia's social, political, and economic fabric.

The Russian surrender of Port Arthur in January 1905 decisively gave Japan the upper hand. Over the war's course Japan's government borrowed tens of millions of pounds sterling in London, New York, and Berlin. In 1904, Japan had to pay an interest rate of around $7\frac{1}{2}$ percent per year on its borrowing, but by 1905, with the war's ultimate outcome no longer in doubt, lenders were charging Japan only around $5\frac{1}{2}$ percent. The Japanese neutralized Russia's naval forces in June 1905, and peace was concluded the following September.

The Russo-Japanese War offers an unusually good testing ground for the model we have developed: it caused no disruption of global financial markets and there was a fair amount of certainty as to the eventual winner. Figure 1.6 shows that Japan's current account moved sharply into deficit during the war, with foreign borrowing topping 10 percent of GDP in 1905. Also consistent with the our model, national saving dropped sharply in the years 1904 and 1905, as shown in Table 1.2.

■

1.3.2 Saving and the Interest Rate

We now justify the shapes of the saving schedules drawn in Figure 1.5. This reasoning requires an understanding of the complex ways a change in the interest rate affects the lifetime consumption allocation.

1.3.2.1 The Elasticity of Intertemporal Substitution

The key concept elucidating the effects of interest rates on consumption and saving is the elasticity of intertemporal substitution, which measures the sensitivity of the intertemporal consumption allocation to an interest-rate change.

To see the role of intertemporal substitutability in determining the demands for consumption on different dates, take natural logarithms of the across-date first-order condition (4) and compute the total differential

$$d \log (1 + r) = \frac{u''(C_1)}{u'(C_1)} dC_1 - \frac{u''(C_2)}{u'(C_2)} dC_2$$

$$= \frac{C_1 u''(C_1)}{u'(C_1)} d \log C_1 - \frac{C_2 u''(C_2)}{u'(C_2)} d \log C_2. \tag{20}$$

Define the inverse of the elasticity of marginal utility by

$$\sigma(C) = -\frac{u'(C)}{C u''(C)}. \tag{21}$$

The parameter defined in eq. (21) is called the *elasticity of intertemporal substitution*. When σ is constant, eq. (20) becomes

$$d \log \left(\frac{C_2}{C_1} \right) = \sigma d \log(1 + r).$$

Intuitively, a gently curving period utility function (a high σ) implies a sensitive relative consumption response to an interest-rate change.

The class of period utility functions characterized by a constant elasticity of intertemporal substitution is

$$u(C) = \frac{C^{1 - \frac{1}{\sigma}}}{1 - \frac{1}{\sigma}}, \qquad \sigma > 0. \tag{22}$$

We refer to this class of utility functions as the *isoelastic* class. For $\sigma = 1$, the right-hand side of eq. (22) is replaced by its limit, $\log(C)$.[14]

---

14. We really have to write the isoelastic utility function as

$$u(C) = \frac{C^{1 - \frac{1}{\sigma}} - 1}{1 - \frac{1}{\sigma}}$$

1.3.2.2   The Shape of the Saving Schedule

To determine the date 1 consumption response to an interest-rate change, use Home's intertemporal budget constraint, $C_2 = (1+r)(Y_1 - C_1) + Y_2$, to eliminate C_2 from its Euler equation, $u'(C_1) = (1+r)\beta u'(C_2)$. (We are assuming $B_1 = 0$.) The result is

$$u'(C_1) = (1+r)\beta u'\left[(1+r)(Y_1 - C_1) + Y_2\right].$$

Implicitly differentiating with respect to r gives

$$\frac{dC_1}{dr} = \frac{\beta u'(C_2) + \beta(1+r)u''(C_2)(Y_1 - C_1)}{u''(C_1) + \beta(1+r)^2 u''(C_2)}. \tag{23}$$

Let's assume for simplicity that $u(C)$ is isoelastic with constant intertemporal substitution elasticity σ. We can then divide the numerator and denominator of the last equation by $u'(C_2)/C_2$ and, using definition (21) and the Euler equation (3), express the derivative as

$$\frac{dC_1}{dr} = \frac{(Y_1 - C_1) - \sigma C_2/(1+r)}{1 + r + (C_2/C_1)}. \tag{24}$$

The numerator shows that a rise in r has an ambiguous effect on Home's date 1 consumption. The negative term proportional to σ represents substitution away from date 1 consumption that is entirely due to the rise in its relative price. But there is a second term, $Y_1 - C_1$, that captures the terms-of-trade effect on welfare of the interest rate change. If Home is a first-period borrower, $C_1 > Y_1$, the rise in the interest rate is a terms-of-trade deterioration that makes it poorer. As eq. (24) shows, this effect reinforces the pure relative-price effect in depressing C_1. But as r rises and Home switches from borrower to lender, the terms-of-trade effect reverses direction and begins to have a positive influence on C_1. For high enough interest rates, C_1 could even become an increasing function of r. If $Y_1 - C_1 > 0$, we can be sure that $dC_1/dr < 0$ only if r is not too far from the Home autarky rate.

Since date 1 output is given at Y_1, these results translate directly into conclusions about the response of saving S_1, which equals $Y_1 - C_1$. The result is a saving schedule **SS** such as the one in Figure 1.5. (Of course, the same principles govern an analysis of Foreign, from which the shape of **S*S*** follows.)

---

if we want it to converge to logarithmic as $\sigma \to 1$. To see convergence, we now can use L'Hospital's rule. As $\sigma \to 1$, the numerator and denominator of the function both approach 0. Therefore, we can differentiate both with respect to σ and get the answer by taking the limit of the derivatives' ratio, $C^{1-\frac{1}{\sigma}} \log(C)$, as $\sigma \to 1$.

Subtracting the constant $1/(1 - \frac{1}{\sigma})$ from the period utility function does not alter economic behavior: the utility function in eq. (22) has exactly the same implications as the alternative function. To avoid burdening the notation, we will always write the isoelastic class as in eq. (22), leaving it implicit that one must subtract the appropriate constant to derive the $\sigma = 1$ case.

The possibility of a "perverse" saving response to the interest rate means that the world economy could have multiple equilibria, some of them unstable. Provided the response of total world saving to a rise in r is positive, however, the world market for savings will be stable (in the Walrasian sense), and the model's predictions still will be intuitively sensible. Introducing investment, as we do later, reduces the likelihood of unstable equilibria. Further analysis of stability is left for the chapter appendix. Our diagrammatic analysis assumes a unique stable world equilibrium.

1.3.2.3 The Substitution, Income, and Wealth Effects

A closer look at the consumption behavior implied by isoelastic utility leads to a more detailed understanding of how an interest rate change affects consumption.

Consider maximizing lifetime utility (1) subject to (2) when the period utility function is isoelastic. Since $u'(C) = C^{-1/\sigma}$ now, Euler equation (3) implies the dynamic consumption equation $C_1^{-1/\sigma} = (1+r)\beta C_2^{-1/\sigma}$. Raising both sides to the power $-\sigma$ yields

$$C_2 = (1+r)^{\sigma} \beta^{\sigma} C_1. \tag{25}$$

Using the budget constraint, we find that consumption in period 1 is

$$C_1 = \frac{1}{1 + (1+r)^{\sigma-1}\beta^{\sigma}} \left(Y_1 + \frac{Y_2}{1+r} \right). \tag{26}$$

This consumption function reflects three distinct ways in which a change in the interest rate affects the individual:

1. *Substitution effect.* A rise in the interest rate makes saving more attractive and thereby induces people to reduce consumption today. Alternatively, a rise in r is a rise in the price of present consumption in terms of future consumption; other things the same, it should cause substitution toward future consumption.

2. *Income effect.* A rise in the interest rate also allows higher consumption in the future given the present value of lifetime resources. This expansion of the feasible consumption set is a positive income effect that leads people to raise present consumption and curtail their saving. The tension between this income effect and the substitution effect is reflected in the term $(1+r)^{\sigma-1}$ appearing in consumption eq. (26). When $\sigma > 1$ the substitution effect dominates because consumers are relatively willing to substitute consumption between periods. When $\sigma < 1$ the income effect wins out. When $\sigma = 1$ (the log case), the fraction of lifetime income spent on present consumption doesn't depend on the interest rate: it is simply $1/(1+\beta)$.

3. *Wealth effect.* The previous two effects refer to the fraction of lifetime income devoted to present consumption. The wealth effect, however, comes from the change in lifetime income caused by an interest rate change. A rise in r low-

ers lifetime income $Y_1 + Y_2/(1+r)$ (measured in date 1 consumption units) and thus reinforces the interest rate's substitution effect in lowering present consumption and raising saving.

As we have seen, the conflict among *substitution, income,* and *wealth effects* can be resolved in either direction: theory offers no definite prediction about how a change in interest rates will change consumption and saving. Section 1.3.4 will examine the interplay of these three effects in detail, for general preferences. A key conclusion of the analysis is that the income and wealth effects identified in this subsection add up to the *terms-of-trade effect* discussed in section 1.3.2.2's analysis of saving.

1.3.3   Investment, Saving, and the Metzler Diagram

We now introduce investment into the two-country model. Saving and investment can differ for an individual country that participates in the world capital market. In equilibrium, however, the world interest rate equates global saving to global investment. That equality underlies our adaptation of a classic diagram invented by Metzler (1960), updated to incorporate intertemporally maximizing decision makers.

1.3.3.1   Setup of the Model

Figure 1.7 graphs first-period saving and investment for Home and Foreign. Because we wish to study changes in investment productivity, let us now write the Home and Foreign production functions as

$$Y = AF(K), \qquad Y^* = A^*F^*(K^*),$$

where A and A^* are exogenously varying productivity coefficients. Home's investment curve (labeled **II**) traces out the analog of eq. (17), $A_2 F'(K_1 + I_1) = r$ (where we remind you that K_1 is predetermined). Still marking Foreign symbols with asterisks, we write the corresponding equation for Foreign, which defines its investment curve (**I*I***), as $A_2^* F^{*'}(K_1^* + I_1^*) = r$. Because production functions are increasing but strictly concave, both investment curves slope downward.

Saving behavior appears somewhat trickier to summarize than in the endowment model of section 1.3.1. The reason is that investment now enters a country's budget constraint [recall eq. (15)], so interest rate effects on investment affect saving directly. To explore the saving schedules **SS** and **S*S*** we proceed as in the pure endowment case. Use Home's intertemporal budget constraint, which now is $C_2 = (1+r)[A_1 F(K_1) - C_1 - I_1] + A_2 F(K_1 + I_1) + K_1 + I_1$ [in analogy with the maximand (16)], to eliminate C_2 from its Euler equation, $u'(C_1) = (1+r)\beta u'(C_2)$. (We are assuming $B_1 = 0$.) The result is

$$u'(C_1) = (1+r)\beta u' \left\{ (1+r)[A_1 F(K_1) - C_1 - I_1] + A_2 F(K_1 + I_1) + K_1 + I_1 \right\}.$$

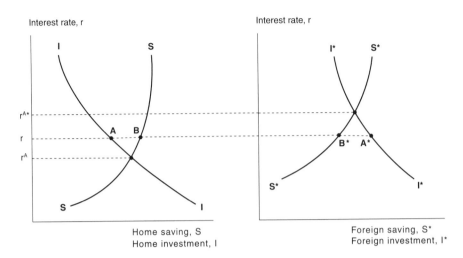

Figure 1.7
Global intertemporal equilibrium with investment

Implicitly differentiating with respect to r gives

$$\frac{dC_1}{dr} =$$

$$\frac{\beta u'(C_2) + \beta(1+r)u''(C_2)\left\{[A_1 F(K_1) - C_1 - I_1] + [A_2 F'(K_1 + I_1) - r]\frac{\partial I_1}{\partial r}\right\}}{u''(C_1) + \beta(1+r)^2 u''(C_2)},$$

where $\partial I_1/\partial r$ represents the (negative) date 1 investment response to a rise in r. If we assume that saving decisions are based on profit-maximizing output and investment levels, as is natural, then the equality of the marginal product of capital and r, $A_2 F'(K_1 + I_1) = r$, implies that the last derivative is precisely the same as eq. (23) in section 1.3.2.2, but with $Y_1 - C_1$ replaced by the date 1 current account for an investment economy with $B_1 = 0$, $A_1 F(K_1) - C_1 - I_1$. For isoelastic utility, we have the analog of eq. (24),

$$\frac{dC_1}{dr} = \frac{(Y_1 - C_1 - I_1) - \sigma C_2/(1+r)}{1 + r + (C_2/C_1)},$$

which means that, given current account balances, the slopes of the saving schedules are the same as for pure endowment economies!

How can this be? The answer turns on a result from microeconomics that is useful at several points in this book, the *envelope theorem*.[15] The first-order condition for investment ensures that a small deviation from the optimum doesn't alter the

---

15. For a description, see Simon and Blume (1994, p. 453).

present value of national output, evaluated at the world interest rate. When we compute the consumer's optimal response to a small interest rate change, it therefore doesn't matter whether production is being adjusted optimally: at the margin, the investment adjustment $\partial I_1 / \partial r$ has no effect on net lifetime resources, and hence no effect on the consumption response.

Now consider the equilibrium in Figure 1.7. If Home and Foreign could not trade, each would have its own autarky interest rate equating country saving and investment. In Figure 1.7, Home's autarky rate, r^A, is below Foreign's, r^{A*}.

What is the equilibrium with intertemporal trade? Equilibrium requires

$$Y_1 + Y_1^* = C_1 + C_1^* + I_1 + I_1^*$$

(still omitting government spending). An alternative expression of this equilibrium condition uses eq. (13):

$$S_1 + S_1^* = I_1 + I_1^*.$$

The world as a whole is a closed economy, so it is in equilibrium when desired saving and investment are equal. Because $CA_1 = S_1 - I_1$, however [recall eq. (14)], the equilibrium world interest rate also ensures the mutual consistency of desired current accounts:

$$CA_1 + CA_1^* = 0.$$

The equilibrium occurs at a world interest rate r above r^A but below r^{A*}, as indicated by the equal lengths of segments **AB** and **B*A***. Home has a current account surplus in period 1, and Foreign has a deficit, in line with comparative advantage. The equilibrium resource allocation is *Pareto optimal*, or efficient in the sense that there is no way to make everyone in the world economy better off. (This was also true in the pure endowment case, of course.) Since both countries face the same world interest rate, their intertemporal optimality conditions (4) imply equal marginal rates of substitution of present for future consumption. The international allocation of capital also is efficient, in the sense that capital's date 2 marginal product is the same everywhere: $A_2 F'(K_2) = A_2^* F^{*\prime}(K_2^*) = r$.

1.3.3.2   Nonseparation of Investment from Saving

Having derived a Metzler diagram, we are ready for applications. Consider first an increase in Home's impatience, represented by a fall in the parameter β. In Figure 1.7 this change would shift Home's saving schedule to the left, raising the equilibrium world interest rate and reducing Home's date 1 lending to Foreign.

Notice that investment falls everywhere as a result. Unlike in the small country case, a shift in a large country's consumption preferences can affect investment by moving the world interest rate. In the present example, saving and investment move in the same direction (down) in Home but in opposite directions (saving up, investment down) in Foreign.

1.3.3.3   Effects of Productivity Shifts

In section 1.3.1 we asked how exogenous output shocks affect the global equilibrium. For small changes, the envelope theorem implies that the saving curves here will respond to shifts in the productivity factors A_2 and A_2^* as if these were purely exogenous output changes not warranting changes in investment. (Shifts in A_1 and A_1^* plainly are of this character because K_1 can't be adjusted retroactively!) Thus shifts in productivity affect **SS** and **S*S*** precisely as the corresponding output shifts in section 1.3.1 did.

The investment schedules, however, also shift when capital's future productivity changes. At a constant interest rate, the (horizontal) shift in **II** due to a rise in A_2 comes from differentiating the condition $A_2 F'(K_1 + I_1) = r$:

$$\left.\frac{dI_1}{dA_2}\right|_{r \text{ constant}} = -\frac{F'(K_2)}{A_2 F''(K_2)} > 0.$$

A rise in A_2^* has a parallel effect on **I*I***.

Let's use the model first to consider a rise in date 1 Home productivity A_1. As in the endowment model, Home saving increases at every interest rate. Thus **SS** in Figure 1.7 shifts to the right, pushing the world interest rate down, as before. What is new is the response of investment, which rises in both countries. Home's date 1 current account surplus rises, as does Foreign's deficit.

Next think about a rise in A_2, which makes Home's capital more productive in the second period. In Figure 1.8, which assumes zero current accounts initially, Home's investment schedule shifts to the right. At the same time, Home's saving schedule shifts to the left because future output is higher while first-period output is unchanged. The world interest rate is unambiguously higher. Since Foreign's curves haven't shifted, its saving is higher and its investment is lower. The result is a current account surplus for Foreign and a deficit for Home.

In Figure 1.8 the ratio of Home to Foreign investment is higher as a result of A_2 rising, but since the level of Foreign investment is lower, it isn't obvious that Home investment actually rises. Perhaps surprisingly, it is theoretically possible for Home investment to *fall* because of the higher world interest rate. Predictions as to what might occur in practice therefore must rest on empirical estimates of preference parameters and production functions. The next application illustrates the underlying reasoning by considering the related question of how total world investment responds to a change in expected future productivity.

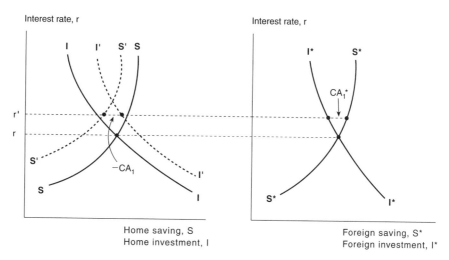

Figure 1.8
A rise in future Home productivity

Application: Investment Productivity and World Real Interest Rates in the 1980s

In the early 1980s world real interest rates suddenly rose to historically high levels, sparking a lively debate over the possible causes. Figure 1.9 shows a measure of global real interest rates since 1960.[16]

An influential paper by Blanchard and Summers (1984) identified anticipated future investment profitability as a prime explanatory factor. In support of their view, they offered econometric equations for the main industrial countries showing that investment in 1983 and early 1984 was higher than one would have predicted on the basis of factors other than the expected future productivity of capital.

Subsequent empirical work by Barro and Sala-i-Martin (1990) showed that a stock-market price proxy for expected investment profitability had a positive effect on both world investment and the world real interest rate. This evidence, suggesting that a rise in expected investment profitability could indeed have caused the world-wide increase in investment and interest rates observed in 1983–84, lent retroactive support to the Blanchard-Summers thesis.

The issue is easily explored in our global equilibrium model. Since the main points do not depend on differences between Home and Foreign, it is simplest to assume that the two countries are completely identical. In this case, one can think

---

16. The data shown are GDP-weighted averages of ten OECD countries' annual average real interest rates. Real interest rates are defined as nominal long-term government bond rates less actual consumer-price index inflation over the following year.

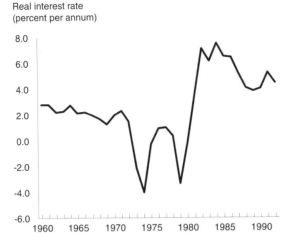

Real interest rate
(percent per annum)

Figure 1.9
World ex post real interest rates, 1960–92

of the world as a single closed economy populated by a single representative agent and producing output according to the single production function $Y = AK^\alpha, \alpha < 1$. Consider now the effects of an increase in the date 2 productivity parameter A_2 that characterizes Home and Foreign industry alike. Figure 1.10 supplies an alternative way to picture global equilibrium. It shows that the productivity disturbance raises world investment demand, which we continue to denote by $I_1 + I_1^*$, at every interest rate. We also know, however, that a rise in future productivity lowers world saving, $S_2 + S_2^*$, at every interest rate. The move from equilibrium **A** to equilibrium **B** in the figure appears to have an ambiguous effect on world investment.

To reach a more definite answer, we compare the vertical distances by which the two curves shift. A proof that the world saving schedule shifts further upward than the world investment schedule is also a proof that world investment must fall.

As a first step, we compute the shift in the investment curve. For the production function we have assumed, the optimal second-period capital stock is $K_2 = (A_2\alpha/r)^{1/(1-\alpha)}$, as end-of-chapter exercise 3 asks you to show. As a result, the world investment schedule is defined by

$$I_1 + I_1^* = (A_2\alpha/r)^{1/(1-\alpha)} - K_1.$$

The vertical shift induced by a rise dA_2 in A_2 is the change in r, dr, consistent with $d(I + I^*) = 0$. Since world investment clearly remains constant if r rises precisely in proportion to A_2,

$$dr|_{I+I^* \text{ constant}} = r\frac{dA_2}{A_2} = r\hat{A}_2,$$

where a "hat" denotes a small percentage change.

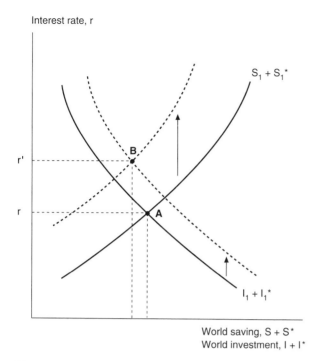

Interest rate, r

$S_1 + S_1{}^*$

r'

B

r

A

$I_1 + I_1{}^*$

World saving, S + S*
World investment, I + I*

Figure 1.10
A rise in world investment productivity

To compare this shift with that of the world saving schedule, let's assume temporarily that Home and Foreign residents share the logarithmic lifetime utility function $U_1 = \log C_1 + \beta \log C_2$. End-of-chapter exercise 3 implies that date 1 world saving can be expressed as

$$S_1 + S_1^* = \frac{\beta}{1+\beta} A_1 F(K_1) + \frac{1}{1+\beta}\left[K_2 - K_1 - \frac{A_2 F(K_2) + K_2}{1+r}\right].$$

Differentiate this schedule with respect to r and A_2, imposing $d(S_1 + S_1^*) = 0$. The envelope theorem permits omission of the induced changes in K_2, so the result of differentiation is

$$\frac{-1}{1+\beta}\left[\frac{F(K_2)}{1+r}dA_2 - \frac{A_2 F(K_2) + K_2}{(1+r)^2}dr\right]$$

$$= \frac{-1}{1+\beta}\left[\frac{A_2 F(K_2)}{1+r}\hat{A}_2 - \frac{A_2 F(K_2) + K_2}{(1+r)^2}dr\right]$$

$$= d(S_1 + S_1^*) = 0.$$

The solution for dr is

$$dr|_{S+S^* \text{ constant}} = (1+r) \frac{A_2 F(K_2)}{A_2 F(K_2) + K_2} \hat{A}_2$$

$$= (1+r) \frac{A_2^{\frac{1}{1-\alpha}} \left(\frac{\alpha}{r}\right)^{\frac{\alpha}{1-\alpha}}}{A_2^{\frac{1}{1-\alpha}} \left(\frac{\alpha}{r}\right)^{\frac{\alpha}{1-\alpha}} + A_2^{\frac{1}{1-\alpha}} \left(\frac{\alpha}{r}\right)^{\frac{1}{1-\alpha}}} \hat{A}_2$$

$$= \frac{1+r}{1+\frac{\alpha}{r}} \hat{A}_2 > r \hat{A}_2 = dr|_{I+I^* \text{ constant}} \cdot$$

Thus, as Figure 1.10 shows, world investment really is lower at the new equilibrium **B** than at **A**.

The preceding result obviously flows from assuming logarithmic preferences, which imply an intertemporal substitution elasticity $\sigma = 1$. How would the outcome in Figure 1.10 be affected by making σ smaller? Making σ smaller would only make it more likely that rises in future investment productivity push world investment down. The factor driving the seemingly perverse result of the log-utility case is a wealth effect: people want to spread the increase in period 2 income over both periods of life, so they reduce period 1 saving, pushing the real interest rate so high that investment actually falls. But if $\sigma < 1$, the desire for smooth consumption is even stronger than in the log case. Thus the interest rate rises and investment falls even more sharply.

We conclude that while an increase in expected investment profitability can in principle explain a simultaneous rise in real interest rates and current investment, as Blanchard and Summers (1984) argued, this outcome is unlikely unless individuals have relatively high intertemporal substitution elasticities. Economists disagree about the likely value of σ, but while there are many estimates below 0.5, few are much higher than 1. We are left with a puzzle. Without positing a rise in expected investment profitability, it is hard to explain the comovement of investment and real interest rates in 1983–84. But if the consensus range of estimates for σ is correct, this change probably should have lowered, not raised, world investment.

Can the simultaneous rise in investment and real interest rates be explained if both *current* capital productivity *and* future profitability rose together? Under that scenario, the fall in saving is reduced, but so is the accompanying rise in the interest rate. This would only leave a greater portion of the sharp increase in real interest rates unexplained.

The empirical record would seem to bear out our theoretical skepticism of the view that expected future productivity growth caused the high real interest rates of the early 1980s. World investment actually turned out to be lower on average after

1983. The fact that *future* investment (as opposed to current investment) dropped suggests that, ex post, productivity did not rise. We will look at the real interest rate puzzle again from the angle of saving at the end of the chapter.   ∎

---

*1.3.4   Real Interest Rates and Consumption in Detail

This section examines the substitution, income, and wealth effects of section 1.3.2.3 in greater detail. As a notational convenience, we define the market discount factor

$$R \equiv \frac{1}{1+r}$$

as the price of future consumption in terms of present consumption. We simplify by holding $G_1 = G_2 = 0$ and assuming exogenous output on both dates.

1.3.4.1   The Expenditure Function and Hicksian Demands

The easiest way to understand substitution, income, and wealth effects is to use the *expenditure function*, denoted by $E(R, U_1)$. It gives the minimal lifetime expenditure, measured in date 1 output, that enables a consumer to attain utility level U_1 when the price of future consumption is R. In Chapter 4 we will use the expenditure function to construct price indexes.[17]

We will need one main result on expenditure functions. Define the *Hicksian consumption demands* as the consumption levels a consumer chooses on the two dates when lifetime utility is U_1. We write the Hicksian demands as $C_1^H(R, U_1)$ and $C_2^H(R, U_1)$. The result we need states that the partial derivative of the expenditure function with respect to R is the Hicksian demand for date 2 consumption:[18]

$$C_2^H(R, U_1) = E_R(R, U_1). \tag{27}$$

This result and the budget constraint imply that $C_1^H(R, U_1) = E(R, U_1) - RE_R(R, U_1)$.

---

17. Dixit and Norman (1980) provide the classic treatise on the use of expenditure functions in static international trade theory.

18. The Hicksian demands satisfy $C_1^H(R, U_1) + RC_2^H(R, U_1) = E(R, U_1)$. Differentiating partially with respect to R gives us

$$\frac{\partial C_1^H}{\partial R} + R\frac{\partial C_2^H}{\partial R} + C_2^H = E_R.$$

These partial derivatives are taken with the utility level U_1 held constant. But along a fixed utility curve, the ratio $\frac{\partial C_1^H}{\partial R} / \frac{\partial C_2^H}{\partial R}$ is just minus the marginal rate of substitution of C_1^H for C_2^H, which equals $-R$. The equality $E_R = C_2^H$ follows. (This is another example of the envelope theorem.)

1.3.4.2   Income and Wealth Effects

The income and wealth effects of a change in R reflect its impact on lifetime utility, U_1. The expenditure function yields a slick derivation of this impact. The equilibrium lifetime utility level of a maximizing representative individual is given implicitly by

$$E(R, U_1) = Y_1 + RY_2.$$

Totally differentiating with respect to R gives us

$$E_R dR + E_U dU_1 = Y_2 dR,$$

which, using eq. (27), can be solved to yield the income-cum-wealth effect

$$E_U \frac{dU_1}{dR} = Y_2 - C_2^H(R, U_1) = Y_2 - C_2. \tag{28}$$

This equation formalizes the basic intuition about terms-of-trade effects mentioned in section 1.3.1. When $Y_2 > C_2$, a country is repaying past debts incurred through a current account deficit on date 1. A rise in the price of future consumption, R, is a fall in the interest rate, r, and an improvement in the country's terms of intertemporal trade. Thus a rise in R has a positive welfare effect in this case, but a negative effect when the country is an importer of future consumption.

1.3.4.3   Substitution Effect and Slutsky Decomposition

Hicksian demand functions are useful for a decomposition of interest-rate effects because their price derivatives show the pure substitution effects of price changes, that is, the effects of price changes after one controls for income and wealth effects by holding the utility level constant. In this chapter, however, we have focused on *Marshallian* demand functions that depend on wealth rather than utility. Define wealth on date 1, W_1, as the present value of the consumer's lifetime earnings:

$$W_1 \equiv Y_1 + RY_2.$$

Then eq. (26), for example, implies the Marshallian demand function for date 1 consumption,

$$C_1(R, W_1) = \frac{W_1}{1 + \beta^\sigma R^{1-\sigma}} = \frac{Y_1 + RY_2}{1 + \beta^\sigma R^{1-\sigma}},$$

which expresses date 1 consumption demand as a function of the interest rate and wealth.

As we now show, the total derivative dC_1/dR of this Marshallian demand is the sum of a Hicksian substitution effect, an income effect, *and* a wealth effect.

The proof relies on an important identity linking Marshallian and Hicksian demands: the Marshallian consumption level, given the minimum lifetime expenditure needed to reach utility U_1, equals its Hicksian counterpart, given U_1 itself. Thus, for date 1 consumption,

$$C_1[R, E(R, U_1)] = C_1^{\mathrm{H}}(R, U_1). \tag{29}$$

With the machinery we have now developed, it is simple to show how substitution, income, and wealth effects together determine the response of consumption and saving to interest-rate changes. Partially differentiate identity (29) with respect to R (holding U_1 constant) and use eq. (27). The result is the famous Slutsky decomposition of partial price effects,

$$\frac{\partial C_1(R, W_1)}{\partial R} = \frac{\partial C_1^{\mathrm{H}}(R, U_1)}{\partial R} - \frac{\partial C_1}{\partial W_1} C_2. \tag{30}$$

The two terms on the right-hand side of this equation are, respectively, the substitution effect and the income effect.

The interest-rate effect analyzed in section 1.3.2.3 was, however, the *total* derivative of C_1 with respect to R. The total derivative is, using eq. (30) and the wealth effect $dW_1/dR = Y_2$,

$$\frac{dC_1(R, W_1)}{dR} = \frac{\partial C_1(R, W_1)}{\partial R} + \frac{\partial C_1(R, W_1)}{\partial W_1} \frac{dW_1}{dR}$$

$$= \frac{\partial C_1^{\mathrm{H}}(R, U_1)}{\partial R} + \frac{\partial C_1(R, W_1)}{\partial W_1}(Y_2 - C_2). \tag{31}$$

This equation shows that the total effect of the interest rate on present consumption is the sum of the pure substitution effect and a term that subtracts the income from the wealth effect. Looking again at eq. (28), we see that the latter difference is none other than the consumption effect of a change in wealth equivalent to the intertemporal terms-of-trade effect. Together, the income and wealth effects push toward a rise in consumption on both dates and a fall in saving for a country whose terms of intertemporal trade improve, and the opposite effects for one whose terms of intertemporal trade worsen.

1.3.4.4   The Isoelastic Intertemporally Additive Case

All the results in this subsection have been derived without reference to a specific utility function: we have not even assumed intertemporal additivity. When the lifetime utility function is additive and the period utility functions are isoelastic [recall eq. (22)], closed-form solutions for the Hicksian demands can be derived. For example, it is a good homework problem to show that the Hicksian demand function for date 1 consumption is

$$C_1^H(R, U_1) = \left[\frac{\left(1 - \frac{1}{\sigma}\right) U_1}{1 + \beta^\sigma R^{1-\sigma}} \right]^{\frac{\sigma}{\sigma-1}}.$$

You can also show that decomposition (31) takes the form

$$\frac{dC_1}{dR} = \sigma \frac{\beta^\sigma R^{-\sigma}}{1 + \beta^\sigma R^{1-\sigma}} C_1 + \frac{1}{1 + \beta^\sigma R^{1-\sigma}} (Y_2 - C_2).$$

Here, the first term on the right is the pure substitution effect and the second is the difference between the wealth and income effects. Applying the Euler equation (25) to this expression transforms the derivative into

$$\frac{dC_1}{dR} = (\sigma - 1) \frac{\beta^\sigma R^{-\sigma}}{1 + \beta^\sigma R^{1-\sigma}} C_1 + \frac{1}{1 + \beta^\sigma R^{1-\sigma}} Y_2.$$

This version makes apparent that the sign of $\sigma - 1$ determines whether the substitution or income effect is stronger. You can verify that the last equation is equivalent to eq. (24) derived in section 1.3.2.2.

1.4   Taxation of Foreign Borrowing and Lending

Governments sometimes restrict international borrowing and lending by taxing them. In this section we look at the taxation of international capital flows in a two-country world and produce a possible nationalistic rationale for taxation.

Government intervention in the international loan market potentially can raise *national* welfare while reducing that of trading partners and pushing the world economy as a whole to an inefficient resource allocation. The mechanism is the one at work in the classic "optimal tariff" argument in trade theory: through taxation, a government can exploit any collective monopoly power the country has to improve its intertemporal terms of trade and, thereby, to raise national welfare.

For simplicity we return to the pure endowment case with logarithmic utility, which is the subject of a detailed end-of-chapter exercise. Suppose initially that Home is a command economy in which the government chooses C_1 and C_2. Both Home and Foreign are large enough to influence world prices, but individual Foreign actors continue to be competitive price takers. There is therefore a supply schedule for Foreign savings,

$$S_1^*(r) = Y_1^* - C_1^*(r) = \frac{\beta^*}{1 + \beta^*} Y_1^* - \frac{1}{(1 + \beta^*)(1 + r)} Y_2^*.$$

Home's government sees matters differently from competitive individuals. It knows that changes in its consumption choices affect the world interest rate and that the world interest rate is determined by the equilibrium condition $Y_1 + Y_1^* =$

$C_1 + C_1^*(r)$. By combining this condition with the Foreign saving schedule, Home's government can calculate how the world interest rate rises as C_1 rises,

$$1 + r = \frac{Y_2^*}{(1 + \beta^*)(Y_1 - C_1) + \beta^* Y_1^*}.$$

Putting this equation and the Home budget constraint, $C_2 = Y_2 - (1 + r)(C_1 - Y_1)$, together, we get the trade-off between present and future consumption as perceived by Home's government,

$$C_2 = Y_2 + \frac{Y_2^*}{(1 + \beta^*)(Y_1 - C_1) + \beta^* Y_1^*}(Y_1 - C_1). \tag{32}$$

This trade-off describes, of course, the Foreign *offer curve* of trade theory.

Figure 1.11 illustrates Home's position in the case $r^A > r^{A*}$. The heavier straight line passing through the endowment point **A** has slope $-(1 + r^L)$, where r^L is the equilibrium world interest rate that would prevail were both governments to follow laissez-faire principles and allow free trade. The curve **TT** passing through **A** is the graph of eq. (32); it shows the consumption possibilities open to Home when Foreign residents are price takers while Home's government sets domestic consumption taking into account its influence on the world interest rate.

The key feature to notice about Figure 1.11 is that part of **TT** lies *strictly outside* the laissez-faire budget line. How can we be sure this is the case?

Differentiation of eq. (32) shows that the slope of **TT** at **A** is

$$\left.\frac{dC_2}{dC_1}\right|_{C_1 = Y_1} = -\frac{Y_2^*}{\beta Y_1^*} = -(1 + r^{A*})$$

[recall eq. (7), which parallels the second equality in this expression]. The interpretation of this derivative is intuitive. At their autarky consumption allocation, Foreign residents are willing to lend or borrow a small amount at their autarky interest rate, r^{A*}, which we know is below the laissez-faire equilibrium rate, r^L. Since Home's laissez-faire consumption choice at **B** certainly remains feasible when Home's government internalizes the country's market power, point **B** lies on **TT**, and that locus therefore has the shape shown in Figure 1.11.

Point **B** is not the preferred consumption point of a Home planner bent on maximizing national welfare. The planner would instead pick point **C**, which is feasible and yields higher national utility.

In a decentralized economy, the Home government can use a tax on foreign borrowing to induce price-taking residents to choose point **C** on their own. Notice first that if **C** is to be chosen by price-taking individuals, the slope of their indifference curves at **C** must equal $-(1 + r^\tau + \tau)$, where τ is the tax an individual pays the government for each unit of output borrowed from abroad and r^τ is the equilibrium world interest rate when the tax is in place.

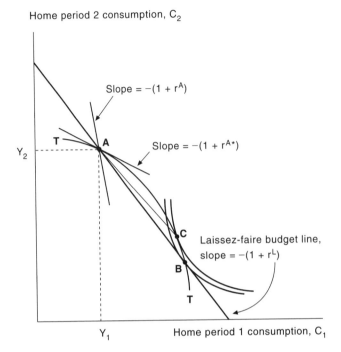

Figure 1.11
The optimal tax on foreign borrowing

We can read r^τ off of Figure 1.11 by noting that the economy's trade must be intertemporally balanced at the world rate of interest, that is, $Y_2 - C_2 = (1 + r^\tau)(C_1 - Y_1)$. (We are assuming here that the government rebates tax proceeds to its citizens in the form of lump-sum transfer payments.) Because points **A** and **C** both are feasible given the borrowing tax, this budget constraint implies that $-(1 + r^\tau)$ must equal the slope of the segment **AC**. Therefore, the optimal tariff τ is simply the wedge between the slope of **AC** and the slope of the indifference curve passing through **C**.[19]

Methods other than taxation can similarly enable the government to maximize Home's welfare. Most simply, the government could impose a quota to limit residents' borrowing to the amount corresponding to point **C** in Figure 1.11.

Observe that government policy drives the world interest rate below its laissez-faire level: $r^\tau < r^L$. Thus the Home government's exercise of monopoly power drives down the interest rate Foreign earns on its loans to Home: Home's intertemporal terms of trade improve. Correspondingly, Foreign is impoverished. Home's

---

19. As a test of understanding, reproduce the argument in the text for the case $r^A < r^{A*}$, and show that the optimal policy is a tax on foreign lending.

advantage comes from appropriating some of Foreign's potential gains from trade. Home's borrowing tax thus is a beggar-thy-neighbor policy, one that benefits a country at its trading partners' expense. Although Home also forgoes some trade gains, this loss is more than offset by the better borrowing terms its tax artificially creates.

Finally, Home's policy, by reducing the volume of intertemporal trade, moves the world as a whole away from an efficient, or Pareto-optimal, resource allocation. Because of this global inefficiency, Foreign's government could, in principle, bribe Home's not to impose the tax, while still leaving its own residents better off than under the tax.

Alternatively, Foreign's government, which we have assumed passively to follow a laissez-faire policy, could retaliate by imposing a tax on international lending. How would the world economy fare if the two governments ended up having a trade war? Alternatively, could they reach a negotiated solution that avoids such a confrontation? These possibilities are at the heart of everyday conflicts over trade and macroeconomic policies, an area we revisit in Chapter 9.

Notice that a *small* country, one whose output and consumption are dwarfed by foreign output, has no scope to influence the trade-off schedule (32): it faces the rest-of-world gross interest rate $Y_2^*/\beta^*Y_1^*$ no matter what it does. For a small country there is thus no terms-of-trade gain to offset the tax's distorting effect on trade. As a result, a small country's optimal tax on foreign borrowing is zero.

1.5   International Labor Movements

A central assumption in most models of international trade and finance is that labor is much less mobile internationally than either commodities or capital. Language and cultural barriers, family and ethnic ties, and political barriers all work to make international migration difficult. And, with only a few major exceptions such as Australia, Canada, and the United States, industrial countries have experienced low levels of immigration over the past twenty years. Table 1.3's figures for 1974–87 illustrate the magnitudes of industrial countries' recent net inflows of foreign workers.

For developing countries and countries of the former Soviet bloc, however, outward migration of workers is substantial. Even in more developed countries like Greece, where workers' remittances from abroad were 3 percent of GDP in 1992, international labor mobility has important economic consequences. Up until World War I, footloose labor flowed in massive waves from Europe to former European colonies in North America and Oceania (again see Table 1.3), as well as to Latin America. As recently as 1950–73, Germany and Switzerland let in numerous "guest workers" from Mediterranean countries, while France welcomed

Table 1.3
Industrial Country Net Immigration (average per year, as a percent of labor force)

Country	1870–1913	1914–49	1950–73	1974–87
Australia	0.96	0.74	2.06	1.14
Belgium	0.15	0.16	0.34	−0.02
Canada	1.08	0.15	1.35	0.50
France	0.11	−0.03	0.75	0.11
Germany	−0.48	−0.08	1.12	0.26
Italy	−0.64	−0.25	−0.41	0.17
Japan	n.a.	0.02	−0.01	−0.02
Netherlands	−0.18	−0.03	0.04	−0.02
Norway	−1.63	−0.33	0.00	0.30
Sweden	−0.92	0.06	0.38	0.28
Switzerland	0.07	−0.15	1.15	0.00
United Kingdom	−0.97	−0.24	−0.10	0.00
United States	1.38	0.35	0.47	0.51

Source: Maddison (1991) and OECD, *Labor Force Statistics*. The figures were calculated by dividing Maddison's average net immigration series by labor force membership as of 1890, 1929, 1960, and 1981.

immigrants from its former African colonies. These experiences justify a close examination of the causes and effects of international labor movements.

Though immigration usually is a much more emotion-charged issue than capital mobility is, labor mobility can yield similar efficiency benefits by equalizing marginal products of labor across countries.[20] To illustrate this point we develop a two-period small-country model in which there is no international borrowing or lending (perhaps the result of prohibitive barriers to international capital movements). International emigration and immigration are, however, completely free. How should we think about the gains from trade in such a world?

1.5.1 Capital, Labor, and the Production Function: A Digression

Since an analysis of labor flows must account for the impact of labor on output, we now make explicit that produced output is a function of capital *and* labor inputs,

$$Y = F(K, L). \tag{33}$$

The production function $F(K, L)$ shows *constant returns to scale* in the two factors; that is, for any number ξ, $F(\xi K, \xi L) = \xi F(K, L)$. Some properties of constant-returns (also known as linear homogeneous) production functions figure

20. With internationally identical production technologies, labor and capital marginal products could be equalized even without factor mobility across borders. This factor-price equalization can occur in a multigood model with free and costless trade, along the lines of the classic Heckscher-Ohlin model (see Dixit and Norman, 1980). All empirical evidence suggests that even when capital is somewhat mobile, equalization of real wages applies, if at all, only to the very long run.

prominently in the present model and in later chapters. We digress briefly to remind you of them.

First, output equals the sum of factor marginal products multiplied by factor inputs:

$$Y = F(K, L) = F_K(K, L)K + F_L(K, L)L. \tag{34}$$

Second, the marginal products of capital and labor depend only on the capital-labor ratio, $k \equiv K/L$. Because $F(K, L) = LF(K/L, 1)$,

$$F_K(K, L) = f'(k), \tag{35}$$

where $f(k) \equiv F(K/L, 1)$ is the "intensive" or per-worker production function.[21] From these two results we derive a third,

$$F_L(K, L) = f(k) - f'(k)k. \tag{36}$$

1.5.2 A Two-Period, Small-Country Model

Now we can get on with the model. On date 2 (the model's second period), the home economy's output is

$$Y_2 = F(K_2, L_2),$$

where K_2 is the capital that domestic residents accumulate during period 1. For simplicity, we assume that output on date 1, Y_1, is exogenous, and that the starting capital stock, K_1, is zero. Thus production takes place only on date 2.

Our small country faces a given world wage rate, w, at which it can export or import labor services on date 2. The representative resident has an inelastically supplied labor endowment of L^H on date 2, but the economy employs a total of L_2 labor units, where L_2 can be greater or less than L^H as a result of trade in labor services.[22] There is no government consumption. Because neither international borrowing nor lending is possible, the representative home-country individual maximizes $U_1 = u(C_1) + \beta u(C_2)$ subject to the constraints

---

21. Totally differentiate the equation $F(\xi K, \xi L) = \xi F(K, L)$ with respect to ξ and evaluate the result at $\xi = 1$; the implication is $F(K, L) = F_K(K, L)K + F_L(K, L)L$, a special case of Euler's theorem on homogeneous functions. To derive the second result mentioned in the text, observe that

$$F_K(K, L) = \lim_{\Delta K \to 0} \frac{F(K + \Delta K, L) - F(K, L)}{\Delta K}$$

$$= \lim_{\Delta K \to 0} \frac{F[k + (\Delta K)/L, 1] - F(k, 1)}{(\Delta K)/L} = f'(k).$$

22. If $L^H > L_2$, one can think of the representative individual as working abroad part-time or, equivalently, of some domestic workers emigrating to work abroad.

$$C_1 = Y_1 - K_2,$$

$$C_2 = L_2 f(K_2/L_2) - w(L_2 - L^H) + K_2.$$

The first of these constraints is self-explanatory; it differs from the first-period constraint under capital mobility in that borrowing from abroad can't be used to supplement first-period resources.[23] The second constraint states that date 2 consumption equals domestic product (a function of the economy's total employment), less the net wage payments on imported labor services, less investment (where we remind you that, as explained in section 1.2.2, $I_2 = -K_2$).

Using the two constraints to eliminate C_1 and C_2 from the utility function, we can write the representative individual's problem as

$$\max_{K_2, L_2} u(Y_1 - K_2) + \beta u \left[L_2 f(K_2/L_2) - w(L_2 - L^H) + K_2 \right].$$

First-order conditions with respect to K_2 and L_2 are

$$u'(C_1) = \beta[1 + f'(k_2)]u'(C_2), \tag{37}$$

$$w = f(k_2) - f'(k_2)k_2, \tag{38}$$

where we have defined $k_2 \equiv K_2/L_2$ as the capital-labor ratio in production during period 2. The first of these equations is the Euler equation when the domestic real interest rate equals the marginal product of capital [recall eq. (35)]. The second states that under free international labor mobility, the marginal product of labor [recall eq. (36)] must equal the world wage rate.

Notice that eq. (38) ties down $k_2 = K_2/L_2$ as a function of the world wage rate, so we can write the production capital-labor ratio as a function $k(w)$, with $k'(w) = -1/k(w)f''[k(w)] > 0$. By implication, the domestic interest rate also is a function of w alone: it is given by $r(w) = f'[k(w)]$, so that $r'(w) = f''[k(w)]k'(w) = -1/k(w) < 0$. The model's negatively sloped functional relation between r and w is called the *factor-price frontier*. A rise in the world wage raises the optimal capital intensity of production, lowering the domestic marginal product of capital. As long as w doesn't change, however, neither k nor r can change, no matter what else in the economy *does* change (other than the production function itself). Given w, net labor exports adjust to ensure that k and r remain constant.

1.5.3   Pattern of Trade and Gains from Trade

Figure 1.12 illustrates the economy's equilibrium in a way that parallels our earlier discussion of capital mobility. The concave locus is the autarky PPF, which describes the home economy's intertemporal production (and consumption) trade-off when the labor used in second-period production is restricted to the domestic

---

23. To ensure that the nonnegativity constraint on capital doesn't bind, the appropriate condition on the production function is now $\lim_{K \to 0} F_K(K, L) = \infty$.

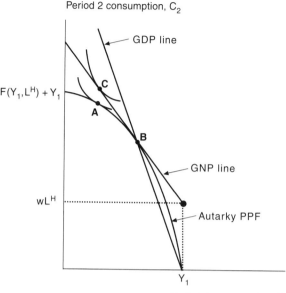

Figure 1.12
Trade in labor services

endowment, L^H. The autarky PPF is described by

$$C_2 = F\left(Y_1 - C_1, L^H\right) + Y_1 - C_1.$$

Its slope is (minus) $1 + F_K(K_2, L^H)$, its horizontal intercept is at $C_1 = Y_1$, and its vertical intercept is at $C_2 = F(Y_1, L^H) + Y_1$. Point **A** is the economy's autarky equilibrium.

The straight line tangent to the autarky PPF at **B** is the representative domestic resident's intertemporal budget constraint when there is trade in labor services. It is described by the equation

$$C_2 = [1 + r(w)](Y_1 - C_1) + wL^H,$$

and its linearity is due to the constancy of $r(w)$, given w. We call this line the *GNP line* because it equates second-period consumption plus investment to domestic output plus net factor payments from abroad. Point **B** is generated by an investment level at which the marginal product of capital is $r(w)$ when employment L_2 equals L^H.

The economy does not have to consume and produce at point **B**, however. By importing labor services from abroad [and doing enough extra investment to maintain $f'(k_2) = r(w)$], residents can move consumption up and to the left along the GNP line from **B**; by exporting labor services (and investing less) they can move down and to the right. Because K_2 can't be less than zero (and by assumption there is no foreign borrowing), C_2 can never be less than wL^H. At this lowest point on the GNP line, the country consumes all its first-period output, has a domestic product of zero in the second period, and exports all its labor services abroad to generate a GNP of wL^H.

In Figure 1.12 the economy's preferred consumption point is **C**. At **C**, the economy is investing more than it would at **B**. To hold the marginal product of capital at $r(w)$, the economy imports labor services from abroad, raising L_2 above L^H.

Also passing through point **B** on the autarky PPF is the *GDP line*, which shows how the sum of second-period GDP and K_2 changes with first-period consumption decisions. (Remember that K_2 is eaten after date 2 production.) Recalling eq. (34) and noting that $L_2 = K_2/k(w)$, we see that the GDP line is described by

$$Y_2 + K_2 = F(K_2, L_2) + K_2 = [1 + r(w)]K_2 + wL_2$$

$$= \left[1 + r(w) + \frac{w}{k(w)}\right](Y_1 - C_1).$$

The GDP line passes through point **B** because there, net labor imports are zero and GDP = GNP. The GDP line is steeper than the GNP line, however. As investment rises, so does immigration, and net payments to foreigners place a wedge between GDP and GNP. Thus GDP exceeds GNP above **B** but is less than GNP below **B**.

At the autarky point **A** in Figure 1.12, the marginal product of capital is less than $r(w)$. The factor-price frontier therefore implies that the autarky wage rate, w^A, is greater than the world wage, w. It is straightforward to show that any country with $w^A > w$ will recruit foreign workers abroad, as in Figure 1.12. Countries with $w^A < w$ will export labor instead. The autarky wage depends on a number of factors. For example, an increase in a country's labor endowment, L^H, lowers its autarky wage rate and raises its net exports of labor. Countries that save more in the first period will tend to have higher autarky wages and higher net immigration.

The usual gains from trade are apparent in the figure: the GNP line lies above the autarky PPF except at **B**, where it is tangent. This result is based, however, on a representative-agent setup in which international labor-market integration has no distributional effects. When the real wage falls as a result of trade, for example, the representative agent gains more in his role as a capitalist than he loses in his role as a laborer.

Even in an economy of heterogenous individuals, everyone can gain from trade provided lump-sum side payments are made to redistribute its benefits. Such side payments are rarely made in reality, so some economic groupings are likely to lose from international labor movements. These losses explain the fierce opposition immigration usually arouses in practice. We will return to immigration again in Chapter 7.

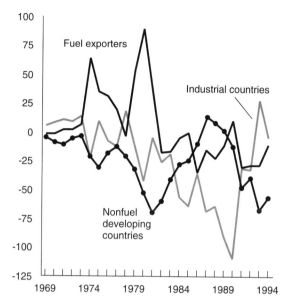

Figure 1.13
Global current account patterns, 1969–94

Application: Energy Prices, Global Saving, and Real Interest Rates

To conclude this chapter we revisit—not for the last time—the vexing question of explaining the wide swings in real interest rates of recent decades. An earlier application gave reasons to doubt the hypothesis that increases in actual or anticipated investment productivity were the primary factor behind the sharp rise in real interest rates in the early 1980s. A glance at Figure 1.9 shows that while real interest rates have been high since the 1980s in comparison with the 1960s, they were unusually low from 1974 to 1979. We can get clues about the key factors moving real interest rates by looking at their behavior, not just in the early 1980s, but over the entire period starting in the early 1970s.

A striking feature of Figure 1.9 is the sharpness with which rates decline in the early 1970s. The major shock to the world economy in that period was the decision by the world oil cartel, the Organization of Petroleum Exporting Countries (OPEC), to quadruple the dollar price of oil. Figure 1.13 shows the immediate impact of this event on the current accounts of three major country groups, the fuel exporters, other developing countries, and the industrial countries. The industrial countries ran a small and temporary deficit, the nonfuel developing countries ran a larger (relative to their GDPs) and more persistent deficit, and the fuel-exporting group moved to a massive surplus.

The major beneficiaries of the oil shock included countries like Kuwait and Saudi Arabia, which were unable to raise their spending quickly in line with the massive increase in their wealth. This inability explains the fuel exporters' current account surplus, and also suggests an explanation for the initial decline in real interest rates. OPEC's price hike, by worsening the rest of the world's terms of trade, caused a transfer of current income from its customers to itself. It caused a similar transfer of lifetime wealth. Since the OPEC countries as a group had a lower marginal propensity to spend out of wealth, their consumption rose by less than the fall in non-OPEC consumption. As a result, the world saving curve pictured in Figure 1.10 shifted to the right. To the extent that the oil price increase discouraged investment outside OPEC, the investment curve shifted to the left. Both shifts helped push the world interest rate down.[24]

The fuel exporters' external surplus shot up again in 1979 when a second OPEC shock followed the Iranian revolution. They were able to raise their spending more rapidly this time. As Figure 1.13 shows, fuel exporters as a group had a roughly balanced current account by 1981, the year real interest rates rose above their levels of the 1960s.

The conclusive disappearance of the OPEC surplus is not the only new trend that begins in 1981. Also, the industrial economies go into a protracted current account deficit (much of which is accounted for by the United States). The coincidence of these events with the rise in real interest rates is intriguing, and suggests that a look at the saving trends underlying the current account patterns could throw light on the real interest rate mystery.

Table 1.4 suggests that differences and shifts in countries' saving patterns might go a long way toward explaining the broad swings in world real interest rates. Saving rates in the industrial world declined substantially between the 1970s and 1980s. Furthermore, the saving rate of the fuel-exporting group, initially much higher than that of the rest of the world, dropped precipitously between the same two decades. Finally, other developing countries, which are smaller actors in the world capital market than the industrial group, register only a minor rise in saving in the early 1980s followed by a bigger increase later on. In terms of Figure 1.10, a leftward shift of the world saving schedule in the early 1980s would help explain the simultaneous reduction in global saving and high real interest rates of the decade. The exceptionally high saving rate of the fuel-exporting group during the 1970s helps explain why unusually low real interest rates followed the first oil shock. Other factors to be discussed later in this book, notably shifts in monetary policies, were at work, too, particularly in determining the year-to-year interest-

---

24. This effect on the intertemporal trade terms of income redistribution between economies with different intertemporal spending patterns is an example of the classical *transfer problem* of trade theory, which we revisit in detail in Chapter 4. Sachs (1981) reviews international adjustment to the oil shocks of the 1970s.

Table 1.4
Gross Saving as a Percent of GDP (period average)

Country Group	1973–80	1981–87	1988–94
Industrial	23.5	20.9	20.5
Fuel exporting	42.0	20.2	19.7
Nonfuel developing	22.4	22.9	26.2

Source: International Monetary Fund, *World Economic Outlook*, October 1995.

rate movements in Figure 1.9. One must always be cautious in interpreting simple correlations, and we do not mean the analysis here as anything more than suggestive. Nevertheless, long-term movements correspond surprisingly well to a story based on inter-country and intertemporal variation in the supply of savings.

What are the underlying causes of the secular decline in world saving shown in Table 1.4? That is a topic we will examine in considerable detail in Chapter 3. ∎

Appendix 1A   Stability and the Marshall-Lerner Condition

A market is stable in the Walrasian sense if a small increase in the price of the good traded there causes excess supply while a small decrease causes excess demand. This simple definition of stability is obviously inapplicable to a general-equilibrium, multimarket context: the meaning of stability and its significance are the subject of a large literature, see Arrow and Hahn (1971). In the two-country model of section 1.3, however, where only a single price—the interest rate—needs to be determined, the simple Walrasian stability condition is easily interpreted in a general-equilibrium setting. That condition, as we show here, is equivalent to an elasticity inequality with a long history in static international trade theory, the *Marshall-Lerner* condition.[25]

With saving and investment written as functions of the world interest rate, the global equilibrium condition is

$$S_1(r) + S_1^*(r) = I_1(r) + I_1^*(r).$$

The condition defining Walrasian stability in the market for world savings is that a small rise in r should lead to an excess supply of savings:

$$S_1'(r) + S_1^{*'}(r) - I_1'(r) - I_1^{*'}(r) > 0. \tag{39}$$

To relate this inequality to the Marshall-Lerner elasticity condition, let's assume for the moment that Home is an importer of first-period consumption and an exporter of second-period consumption. (Home has a current account deficit, followed by a surplus. An equilibrium with zero current accounts always is stable.) Home's imports are denoted by $IM_1 \equiv C_1 + I_1 - Y_1 = I_1 - S_1 > 0$, its exports by $EX_2 \equiv Y_2 - C_2 - I_2 > 0$. The condition of "balanced trade" in this model, that the value of imports equal that of exports, is

---

25. For a detailed discussion of stability conditions in international trade, see R. Jones (1961).

$$IM_1 = \left(\frac{1}{1+r}\right) EX_2,$$

where trade-flow values are in units of date 1 consumption. This condition always holds because it is nothing more than a rearrangement of Home's intertemporal budget constraint. For Foreign, $IM_2^* \equiv C_2^* + I_2^* - Y_2^* > 0$ and $EX_1^* \equiv Y_1^* - C_1^* - I_1^* = S_1^* - I_1^* > 0$.

Foreign's intertemporal budget constraint implies its current account is $S_1^* - I_1^* = IM_2^*/(1+r)$. We therefore can express stability condition (39) as

$$\frac{d}{dr}\left[\left(\frac{1}{1+r}\right) IM_2^*(r) - IM_1(r)\right] > 0. \tag{40}$$

To express this inequality in terms of import elasticities, define

$$\zeta \equiv -\frac{(1+r)IM_1'(r)}{IM_1(r)}, \qquad \zeta^* = \frac{(1+r)IM_2^{*\prime}(r)}{IM_2^*(r)}$$

(The elasticity ζ is defined to be positive when a rise in r reduces Home's date 1 current account deficit.) Since the initial interest rate is an equilibrium rate such that $IM_1 = IM_2^*/(1+r)$, eq. (40) can be rewritten as

$$\zeta + \zeta^* > 1. \tag{41}$$

The Walrasian stability condition holds if and only if the sum of the Home and Foreign price elasticities of import demand exceeds 1. International trade theorists call condition (41) the Marshall-Lerner condition. When Home happens to be the exporter of date 1 consumption, rather than the importer, (41) still characterizes the Walras-stable case, but with import elasticities defined so that Home's and Foreign's roles are interchanged.

Exercises

1. *Welfare and the terms of trade.* Let the representative individual in a small open economy maximize $U(C_1, C_2)$ subject to $C_1 + C_2/(1+r) = Y_1 + Y_2/(1+r)$, where Y_1 and Y_2 are fixed.

   (a) Show that the intertemporal Euler equation takes the form $\partial U(C_1, C_2)/\partial C_1 = (1+r)\partial U(C_1, C_2)/\partial C_2$.

   (b) Use the Euler condition together with the (differentiated) budget constraint to compute the total derivative

   $$\frac{dU(C_1, C_2)}{dr} = \frac{\partial U(C_1, C_2)}{\partial C_2}(Y_1 - C_1).$$

   (c) Explain why the answer in b implies that a country benefits from a rise in the world interest rate if and only if its terms of intertemporal trade improve.

   (d) Let $W_1 \equiv Y_1 + Y_2/(1+r)$ (that is, W_1 is lifetime wealth in units of date 1 consumption). Show that a small percentage gross interest rate increase of $\hat{r} = dr/(1+r)$ has the same effect on lifetime utility as a lifetime wealth change of $dW_1 = \hat{r}(Y_1 - C_1)$.

2. *Logarithmic case of the two-country endowment model.* Consider the pure endow-
    ment model, in which equilibrium holds when $S_1 + S_1^* = 0$. Home's utility function
    is

    $$U_1 = \log C_1 + \beta \log C_2. \tag{42}$$

    Foreign has an analogous log utility function, with its consumption levels and time-
    preference factor distinguished by asterisks. Governments consume no resources.

    (a) Home receives perishable endowments Y_1 and Y_2 in the two periods. Show that
    the Home date 1 consumption function is a function of r,

    $$C_1(r) = \frac{1}{1+\beta} \left(Y_1 + \frac{Y_2}{1+r} \right).$$

    [This equation shows a general property of logarithmic preferences that we will use
    many times in this book: expenditure shares on the available goods are constants that
    correspond to the relative weights on the logarithmic summands in U_1. Thus spending
    on date 1 consumption, C_1, is a fraction $1/(1+\beta)$ of lifetime income (measured
    in date 1 consumption units), and spending on date 2 consumption, $C_2/(1+r)$,
    is a fraction $\beta/(1+\beta)$ of lifetime income. This property follows from the unitary
    intertemporal substitution elasticity.]

    (b) Show that Home saving is

    $$S_1(r) = Y_1 - C_1(r) = \frac{\beta}{1+\beta} Y_1 - \frac{1}{(1+\beta)(1+r)} Y_2.$$

    (c) Compute the equilibrium world interest rate.

    (d) Check that it lies between the autarky rates r^A and r^{A*}.

    (e) Confirm that the country with an autarky interest rate below r will run a current
    account surplus on date 1 while the one with an autarky rate above r will run a deficit.

    (f) How does an increase in Foreign's rate of output growth affect Home's welfare?
    Observe that a rise in the ratio Y_2^*/Y_1^* raises the equilibrium world interest rate. Then
    show that the derivative of U_1 with respect to r is

    $$\frac{dU_1}{dr} = \frac{\beta}{1+r} \left[\frac{r - r^A}{(1+r) + \beta(1+r^A)} \right].$$

    What is your conclusion?

3. *Adding investment to the last exercise.* Assume date 2 Home output is a strictly
    concave function of the capital stock in place multiplied by a productivity parameter,

    $$Y_2 = A_2 K_2^\alpha$$

    ($\alpha < 1$), with a parallel production function in Foreign. (Date 1 outputs are exoge-
    nous because they depend on inherited capital stocks.)

    (a) Investment is determined so that the marginal product of capital equals r. Show
    that this equality implies

$$K_2 = \left(\frac{\alpha A_2}{r}\right)^{\frac{1}{1-\alpha}}.$$

(b) Show that Home's **II** schedule can be written as

$$I_1(r) = K_2 - K_1 = \left(\frac{\alpha A_2}{r}\right)^{\frac{1}{1-\alpha}} - K_1.$$

(c) Derive Home's date 1 consumption function, and show it can be written as

$$C_1(r) = \frac{1}{1+\beta}\left(Y_1 - I_1 + \frac{Y_2 - I_2}{1+r}\right).$$

(d) Using $I_2 = -K_2$ and the results of parts a–c, explain why

$$C_1(r) = \frac{1}{1+\beta}\left[K_1 + Y_1 + \frac{(1-\alpha)}{1+r}\left(\frac{\alpha}{r}\right)^{\frac{\alpha}{1-\alpha}}A_2^{\frac{1}{1-\alpha}}\right],$$

and conclude that the equation for **SS** is the upward-sloping curve

$$S_1(r) = Y_1 - \frac{1}{1+\beta}\left[K_1 + Y_1 + \frac{(1-\alpha)}{1+r}\left(\frac{\alpha}{r}\right)^{\frac{\alpha}{1-\alpha}}A_2^{\frac{1}{1-\alpha}}\right].$$

4.   *Problem on $\sigma = 0$.* The individual has an isoelastic period utility function and exogenous endowments. This exercise considers the limit as $\sigma \to 0$.

(a) Show that the Euler equation (25) approaches $C_2 = C_1$, so that a flat consumption path is chosen irrespective of the market interest rate r.

(b) Derive the consumption function for this case,

$$C_1 = \left(\frac{1+r}{2+r}\right)Y_1 + \left(\frac{1}{2+r}\right)Y_2.$$

Show that $C_2 = C_1$ using this consumption function and the current account identity.

(c) Calculate that

$$\frac{dC_1}{dr} = \frac{Y_1 - Y_2}{(2+r)^2}.$$

What is your interpretation?

(d) Does zero intertemporal substitutability necessarily imply a literally constant consumption path, as in parts a–c, under all possible preference assumptions? [Hint: Suppose lifetime utility is

$$U_1 = \frac{1}{1-1/\sigma}\left(C_1^{1-1/\sigma} + \beta^{1/\sigma}C_2^{1-1/\sigma}\right).$$

Show that as $\sigma \to 0$, we approach $C_2 = \beta C_1$, which corresponds to the consumption pattern chosen under the Leontief utility function $U_1 = \min\{\beta C_1, C_2\}$.]

5. *Endowment shifts and world interest rates.* In the two country endowment model of borrowing and lending, show algebraically that a rise in Y_1 or Y_1^* lowers r, whereas a rise in Y_2 or Y_2^* raises r.

6. *Future productivity shocks when current accounts are initially unbalanced.* Let Home have the production function $Y = AF(K)$, and Foreign the function $Y^* = A^*F^*(K^*)$, on each of two dates. Let the corresponding lifetime utility functions of residents be $U_1 = u(C_1) + \beta u(C_2)$ and $U_1^* = u(C_1^*) + \beta u(C_2^*)$, where $u(\cdot)$ is isoelastic. On date 1 the countries may borrow (lend) at the world interest rate r, determined by $S_1 + S_1^* = I_1 + I_1^*$. A Walras-stable world market with a single equilibrium is assumed.

(a) Suppose date 2 Home investment productivity, A_2, rises slightly. If Home has a date 1 surplus on current account and Foreign a date 1 deficit before the productivity rise, how does the change affect date 1 current accounts?

(b) Do the same exercise for a rise in A_2^* (Foreign's date 2 productivity), still assuming Home has a positive current account on date 1. Is the effect on Home's current account simply a mirror image of the answer to part a?

7. *Interest rates and saving with exponential period utility.* A country's representative individual has the exponential period utility function

$$u(C) = -\gamma \exp(-C/\gamma)$$

$(\gamma > 0)$ and maximizes $U_1 = u(C_1) + \beta u(C_2)$ subject to

$$C_1 + RC_2 = Y_1 + RY_2 = W_1$$

[where $R \equiv 1/(1+r)$].

(a) Solve for C_2 as a function of C_1, R, and β using the consumer's intertemporal Euler equation.

(b) What is the optimal level of C_1, given W_1, R, and β?

(c) By differentiating this consumption function C_1 (including differentiation of W_1) with respect to R, show that

$$\frac{dC_1}{dR} = -\frac{C_1}{1+R} + \frac{Y_2}{1+R} + \frac{\gamma}{1+R}\left[1 - \log(\beta/R)\right].$$

(d) Calculate the inverse elasticity of marginal utility, $-u'(C)/Cu''(C)$, for the exponential utility function. [It is a function $\sigma(C)$ of consumption, rather than being a constant.]

(e) Show that the derivative dC_1/dR calculated in part c above can be expressed as

$$\frac{dC_1}{dR} = \frac{\sigma(C_2)C_2}{1+R} - \frac{C_2}{1+R} + \frac{Y_2}{1+R}.$$

Interpret the three additive terms that make up this derivative.

8. *The optimal borrowing tax.* Return to section 1.5's model of the optimal tax on foreign borrowing, but assume a general utility function $U(C_1, C_2)$.

(a) Show that the optimal ad valorem borrowing tax [such that $(1 + \tau)(1 + r^\tau)$ is the gross interest rate domestic residents face when the world rate is $1 + r^\tau$] is given by $\tau = 1/(\zeta^* - 1)$, where ζ^* is the elasticity with respect to $1 + r$ of Foreign's demand for imports of date 2 consumption. (The elasticity ζ^* is defined formally in the chapter appendix.)

(b) Explain why $\zeta^* - 1 > 0$ at the world interest rate associated with the optimal tax.

Dynamics of Small Open Economies

The last chapter's two-period model illuminates the basic economics of international borrowing and lending. Despite its important lessons, it misses many important issues that cannot easily be condensed within a two-period horizon. What are the limits on a growing country's foreign debt? What if capital-stock changes must take place over several time periods, or if consumption includes durable goods? How do expected movements in future short-term interest rates affect the current account? Perhaps most importantly, the theories we have developed so far cannot meaningfully be adapted to real-world data without extending them to a multiperiod environment.

In most of the chapter we will simplify by assuming not only that there are many time periods, but that there is no definite end to time. This abstraction may seem extreme: after all, cosmologists have developed theories predicting that the universe as we know it will end in 60 to 70 billion years! That grim prophecy notwithstanding, there are two defenses for an infinite-horizon assumption. First, there is genuine uncertainty about the terminal date. The relevant cosmological theories yield only approximations, and theories, after all, are revised in light of ongoing scientific discovery. Second, other things being the same, the behavior of an infinite-horizon economy will differ only trivially from that of a finite-horizon one when the terminal date is very distant.

It is quite another matter to assume, as we do in this chapter, that *individuals* live forever. Once again, two defenses are offered. First, uncertainty about length of life can act much like an infinite horizon in blurring one's terminal planning date. Second, when people care about their offspring, who, in turn, care about theirs, an economy of finite-lived individuals may behave just like one peopled by immortals. Chapter 3 explores this possibility rigorously.

In this chapter we focus on the case of a small open economy inhabited by a representative individual with an infinite horizon. The economy is small in the sense that it takes the path of world interest rates as exogenous. Abstracting from global general-equilibrium considerations makes sense here, since they are not important for many questions and would unnecessarily complicate the analysis. Besides, for the vast majority of countries in the world, the small-country assumption is the right one. There are really only a few economies large enough that their unilateral actions have a first-order impact on world interest rates. However, in studying the small-country case, one does have to be on guard against scenarios that strain the paradigm. For example, if a small country's Gross Domestic Product were perpetually to grow faster than world GDP, the country would eventually become large! Similarly, if the country is a high saver with ever-growing net foreign assets, the assumption that it always faces a fixed world interest rate may again become strained. We will alert the reader on occasions where such issues arise, though we defer full general equilibrium analysis of the particular class of models considered here until we take up global growth in Chapter 7.

The first part of the chapter looks at perfect foresight models. Later, we show how the same insights extend to explicitly stochastic models, which are more appropriate for testing and empirical implementation of the modeling approach.

2.1   A Small Economy with Many Periods

In this section we revisit the last chapter's analysis of the small open economy, but in a many-period setting. This extension allows some first results on how well our models match the complicated dynamics in actual macroeconomic data.

2.1.1   Finite Horizons

As an initial step we extend the model of section 1.1 by assuming that the economy starts on date t but ends on date $t + T$, where T can be any number greater than zero. Ultimately, we hope to understand the infinite-horizon case by taking the limit of the T-period economy as $T \to \infty$. As in the last chapter, we will normalize population size to 1, so that we can think of individual quantity choices as economy-wide aggregates.

Generalizing the time-separable utility function to a T-period setting is simple: the representative individual maximizes

$$U_t = u(C_t) + \beta u(C_{t+1}) + \beta^2 u(C_{t+2}) + \dots + \beta^T u(C_{t+T}) = \sum_{s=t}^{t+T} \beta^{s-t} u(C_s). \quad (1)$$

As for the individual's budget constraint, let's simplify by assuming that the world interest rate r is constant over time. This assumption allows us to focus initially on the role of productivity fluctuations. Output on any date s is determined by the production function $Y = AF(K)$, where $F(K)$ has the same properties as in Chapter 1. Again, the economy starts out on date t with predetermined stocks of capital K_t and net foreign assets B_t, both accumulated on prior dates.

To derive the T-period budget constraint, we proceed by an iterative argument based on the one-period current account identity [Chapter 1, eq. (12)]. The current account identity (assuming a constant interest rate) states that

$$CA_t = B_{t+1} - B_t = Y_t + rB_t - C_t - G_t - I_t \quad (2)$$

for any date t, where $I_t = K_{t+1} - K_t$. Rearranging terms, we have

$$(1 + r)B_t = C_t + G_t + I_t - Y_t + B_{t+1}. \quad (3)$$

Forward this identity by one period and divide both sides of the result by $1 + r$. This step yields

$$B_{t+1} = \frac{C_{t+1} + G_{t+1} + I_{t+1} - Y_{t+1}}{1 + r} + \frac{B_{t+2}}{1 + r},$$

which we use to eliminate B_{t+1} from eq. (3):

$$(1+r)B_t = C_t + G_t + I_t - Y_t + \frac{C_{t+1} + G_{t+1} + I_{t+1} - Y_{t+1}}{1+r} + \frac{B_{t+2}}{1+r}.$$

We can repeat the foregoing process to eliminate $B_{t+2}/(1+r)$ here. Forward eq. (3) by two periods and divide both sides of the result by $(1+r)^2$. This operation gives the equation

$$\frac{B_{t+2}}{1+r} = \frac{C_{t+2} + G_{t+2} + I_{t+2} - Y_{t+2}}{(1+r)^2} + \frac{B_{t+3}}{(1+r)^2},$$

which we use to substitute for $B_{t+2}/(1+r)$ in the equation preceding it.

By now our iterative substitution method is clear. Repeating it, we successively eliminate B_{t+3}, B_{t+4}, and so on. This sequence of steps leads to the constraint we seek:

$$\sum_{s=t}^{t+T} \left(\frac{1}{1+r}\right)^{s-t} (C_s + I_s) + \left(\frac{1}{1+r}\right)^T B_{t+T+1}$$

$$= (1+r)B_t + \sum_{s=t}^{t+T} \left(\frac{1}{1+r}\right)^{s-t} (Y_s - G_s). \tag{4}$$

To find the consumption/investment plan maximizing U_t in eq. (1) subject to eq. (4), we first use the current account identity, written as

$$B_{s+1} - B_s = rB_s + A_s F(K_s) - C_s - (K_{s+1} - K_s) - G_s,$$

to substitute for the consumption levels in eq. (1). Thus, U_t is expressed as

$$U_t = \sum_{s=t}^{t+T} \beta^{s-t} u\left[(1+r)B_s - B_{s+1} + A_s F(K_s) - (K_{s+1} - K_s) - G_s\right].$$

One finds necessary first-order conditions for our problem by maximizing U_t with respect to B_{s+1} and K_{s+1}. (Supplement A to this chapter outlines some alternative but equivalent solution procedures that sometimes are used in this book.) For every period $s \geq t$, two conditions must hold:

$$u'(C_s) = (1+r)\beta u'(C_{s+1}), \tag{5}$$

$$A_{s+1} F'(K_{s+1}) = r. \tag{6}$$

We have already met these conditions: they are the consumption Euler equation and the equality between the marginal product of capital and the world interest rate. They correspond to eqs. (3) and (17) from our two-period model in Chapter 1.

As in the two-period case, we simplify by observing that the terminal condition

$$B_{t+T+1} = 0 \tag{7}$$

must always hold for a maximizing individual: lenders will not permit the individual to die with unpaid debts (that is, with $B_{t+T+1} < 0$), nor can it be optimal for the individual to leave the scene with unused resources (that is, with $B_{t+T+1} > 0$). (Since the economy is assumed to end after T periods, there are no descendants around to inherit a positive B_{t+T+1}.) As a result, the economy's unique optimal consumption path satisfies eq. (5) and eq. (4) with $B_{t+T+1} = 0$,

$$\sum_{s=t}^{t+T} \left(\frac{1}{1+r}\right)^{s-t} (C_s + I_s) = (1+r)B_t + \sum_{s=t}^{t+T} \left(\frac{1}{1+r}\right)^{s-t} (Y_s - G_s), \qquad (8)$$

where all investment and output levels are determined by eq. (6), given initial capital K_t.

One important example assumes $\beta = 1/(1+r)$. The consumption Euler equation shows that optimal consumption must be constant in this special case. You can calculate that the maximum constant consumption level satisfying eq. (8) is[1]

$$C_t = \left[\frac{1}{1-(1+r)^{-(T+1)}}\right]\left(\frac{r}{1+r}\right)$$

$$\cdot \left[(1+r)B_t + \sum_{s=t}^{t+T} \left(\frac{1}{1+r}\right)^{s-t} (Y_s - G_s - I_s)\right]. \qquad (9)$$

We will not linger over such complicated-looking consumption functions, which often arise in finite-horizon models, because by moving directly to the infinite-horizon case we can reduce their complexity and make them easier to interpret. For example, letting $T \to \infty$ in eq. (9), we obtain the simpler equation

$$C_t = \frac{r}{1+r}\left[(1+r)B_t + \sum_{s=t}^{\infty} \left(\frac{1}{1+r}\right)^{s-t} (Y_s - G_s - I_s)\right]. \qquad (10)$$

With this consumption function, the private sector consumes the *annuity value* of its total discounted wealth net of government spending and investment. The idea is associated with the "permanent income hypothesis" advanced and tested by Friedman (1957).[2]

---

1. In doing this calculation, use the fact that for any number ξ, the sum $1 + \xi + \xi^2 + \dots + \xi^T = (1 - \xi^{T+1})/(1 - \xi)$. (To verify the formula, multiply both sides by $1 - \xi$.)

2. The annuity value of wealth is the amount that can be consumed while leaving wealth constant. If we define date t wealth, W_t, to be the term in square brackets on the right-hand side of eq. (10), then that equation reads

$$C_t = \frac{r}{1+r}W_t.$$

Consumption on date t is therefore equal to the interest on end-of-period $t - 1$ wealth, $W_t/(1 + r)$; as a result, W_t remains constant over time. As an alternative motivation, notice that eq. (5) in Supplement A to this chapter shows that $W_{t+1} = (1 + r)(W_t - C_t)$. From this equation, only $C_t = rW_t/(1 + r)$ is consistent with an unchanging wealth level.

2.1.2   An Infinite-Horizon Model

It is not always convenient to solve infinite-horizon optimization problems, as we just have, by first solving a finite-horizon problem and then seeing what happens when the horizon becomes very distant. In most cases it is simpler to solve the infinite-horizon problem directly; this subsection describes how to do so.

Our interest in solving infinite-horizon problems goes beyond mere convenience, though. For one thing, we would like to know how the relevant constraints and preferences look when there is no fixed end to time. Does the absence of a definite end point for economic activity raise any new possibilities? For example, can debts be rolled over perpetually without ever being repaid?

The utility function we use is the obvious generalization of eq. (1):

$$U_t = \lim_{T \to \infty} \left[u(C_t) + \beta u(C_{t+1}) + \beta^2 u(C_{t+2}) + \dots \right] = \sum_{s=t}^{\infty} \beta^{s-t} u(C_s). \tag{11}$$

The only new question that arises concerning this function is a mathematical one. The limit in eq. (11) need not exist for all feasible consumption paths, possibly implying that there is no feasible consumption path that cannot be improved on. While we shall see such a case shortly, the possibility that the individual's maximization problem has no solution will not trouble us in practice. One generally can avoid the issue by assuming that the period utility function $u(C)$ is bounded from above; this type of boundedness can assure the existence of a solution because it implies U_t cannot be arbitrarily large. Restricting oneself to bounded-from-above utility functions would, however, be inconvenient. Many of our simplest algebraic examples are based on $u(C) = \log(C)$, which lacks an upper bound, as do all other members of the isoelastic class with $\sigma \geq 1$. Fortunately, it will turn out that in most standard applications a utility maximum exists even without bounded period utility.

Let's therefore assume an optimum exists and look at necessary conditions for maximizing U_t in eq. (11). As in the finite-horizon case, we substitute for the consumption levels in eq. (11) using the current account identity and obtain the same maximand as earlier, but with $T = \infty$:

$$U_t = \sum_{s=t}^{\infty} \beta^{s-t} u \left[(1+r)B_s - B_{s+1} + A_s F(K_s) - (K_{s+1} - K_s) - G_s \right].$$

Maximization with respect to B_{s+1} and K_{s+1} once again yields eqs. (5) and (6), which must hold now, as in the finite-horizon case.

As before, we need to combine these necessary first-order conditions with the intertemporal budget constraint to determine the optimal consumption level for each date. But what form does the budget constraint now take? For the case of an economy lasting only T periods, in which the intertemporal budget constraint was eq. (4), we know that eq. (7), $B_{t+T+1} = 0$, always holds. For the T period case, there was thus no harm in assuming that the consumer maximized subject to eq. (8).

Your first guess might be that the proper way to generalize this reasoning is to assume $\lim_{T\to\infty} B_{t+T+1} = 0$ always must hold. But that guess would be wrong!

The easiest way to see this is to imagine an economy with a constant and exogenous output level $\bar{Y}$ and no government spending, in which $\beta = 1/(1+r)$. Recall eq. (5)'s implication that in this case, optimal consumption must be constant at some level $\bar{C}$. As a result, the current account identity implies that the economy's net foreign assets follow

$$B_{t+T+1} = (1+r)B_{t+T} + \bar{Y} - \bar{C}$$
$$= (1+r)\left[(1+r)B_{t+T-1} + \bar{Y} - \bar{C}\right] + \bar{Y} - \bar{C}$$
$$= \ldots = (1+r)^{T+1}B_t + \sum_{s=0}^{T}(1+r)^s\left(\bar{Y} - \bar{C}\right)$$
$$= (1+r)^{T+1}B_t - \frac{1 - (1+r)^{T+1}}{r}\left(\bar{Y} - \bar{C}\right)$$
$$= B_t + \left(rB_t + \bar{Y} - \bar{C}\right)\left[\frac{(1+r)^{T+1} - 1}{r}\right]. \tag{12}$$

The last equation implies that, unless $\bar{C} = rB_t + \bar{Y}$, $\lim_{T\to\infty} B_{t+T+1} = +\infty$ (for consumption below initial income) or $-\infty$ (for consumption above initial income). Even if the individual consumes exactly initial income forever, so that $B_{t+T+1} = B_t$ for all T, foreign assets will not obey $\lim_{T\to\infty} B_{t+T+1} = 0$ unless it accidentally happens that initial net foreign assets are zero. So the naive "limits" version of condition (7) doesn't appear useful in characterizing optimal plans.

The *right* condition comes from inspecting eq. (4) and noting that the terminal condition leading to eq. (8) is actually $(1+r)^{-T}B_{t+T+1} = 0$ (which holds if, and only if, $B_{t+T+1} = 0$). Taking *this* term's limit yields

$$\lim_{T\to\infty}\left(\frac{1}{1+r}\right)^T B_{t+T+1} = 0. \tag{13}$$

Condition (13) is called the *transversality condition*. It implies that the relevant infinite-horizon budget constraint is the limit as $T \to \infty$ of eq. (8), which is the same as the limit of eq. (4) with eq. (13) imposed:

$$\sum_{s=t}^{\infty}\left(\frac{1}{1+r}\right)^{s-t}(C_s + I_s) = (1+r)B_t + \sum_{s=t}^{\infty}\left(\frac{1}{1+r}\right)^{s-t}(Y_s - G_s). \tag{14}$$

Why is eq. (13) the condition we seek? Think about how eq. (4) behaves as T gets very large. If $\lim_{T \to \infty} (1+r)^{-T} B_{t+T+1} < 0$, the present value of what the economy is consuming and investing exceeds the present value of its output by an amount that never converges to zero. The economy is continually borrowing to meet the interest payments on its foreign debt rather than transferring real resources to its creditors by reducing $C + I$ below $Y - G$. As a result, its debt grows at the rate of interest (at least), which is why $\lim_{T \to \infty} (1+r)^{-T} B_{t+T+1}$ is strictly negative. But foreigners will never allow such a Ponzi scheme at their expense: that would amount to providing another economy with free resources, and they would prefer to consume those resources themselves.[3] (For this reason, the requirement $\lim_{T \to \infty} (1+r)^{-T} B_{t+T+1} \geq 0$ is called the *no-Ponzi-game* condition.)

In the opposite case, $\lim_{T \to \infty} (1+r)^{-T} B_{t+T+1} > 0$ (a strict inequality), the present value of the resources the home economy uses never converges up to the present value of its output. In that case, domestic residents are making an unrequited gift to foreigners. Plainly they could raise their lifetime utility by consuming a little more. Only when $\lim_{T \to \infty} (1+r)^{-T} B_{t+T+1} = 0$ is the economy, asymptotically, using up exactly the resources its budget constraint allows, no more and no less. Thus, for the present problem, conditions (13), (2), (5), and (6) are necessary and sufficient for optimality. [Implicitly we are still assuming nonbinding nonnegativity constraints on C and K. The nonnegativity constraints imply that a country's foreign debt must be bounded from above by the market value of a claim to its entire future net output, that is, by $\sum_{s=t}^{\infty} (1+r)^{-(s-t)} (Y_s - G_s - I_s)$.][4]

Before going on we mention an existence problem analogous to the one caused by positing, as in eq. (11), that utility accrues over infinitely many time periods. Because of the lack of a definite end to time, the budget constraint (14) may not be well defined. For example, one can easily devise model economies with *negative* real interest rates. (Can you write one down?) In such models neither side of eq. (14) has meaning. If you think about it for a few minutes, you will see the economics of this mathematical oddity: in a world with negative interest rates, debts shrink over time even when no payments to creditors ever are made, so people do

---

3. In the 1920s, Boston swindler Charles Ponzi duped investors by offering high returns that he was able to pay, for a time, using money provided by new clients. Once the flow of new money dried up, however, Ponzi could no longer meet his obligations and his fraud was exposed.

4. To avoid misunderstanding, we reiterate the reasoning we have followed to conclude that transversality condition (13) can be imposed on the individual's maximization from the start. (We followed parallel logic in imposing $B_{t+T+1} = 0$ on finite-horizon problems.) The no-Ponzi-game condition $\lim_{T \to \infty} (1+r)^{-T} B_{t+T+1} \geq 0$ is the true constraint on the consumer, who is certainly free not to consume all lifetime resources if he wishes. The transversality condition $\lim_{T \to \infty} (1+r)^{-T} B_{t+T+1} = 0$ states that it cannot be *optimal* to do so (provided the marginal utility of consumption is positive). The transversality condition thus is not a constraint, but since it must hold for (virtually) all the problems we consider, nothing is lost by imposing it from the start and thereby assuming that intertemporal budget equality (14) has to hold. Appendix 2B and Supplement A to this chapter develop alternative motivations for the transversality condition. In the rare cases when it need not hold, we will warn you.

not face meaningful budget constraints.[5] A somewhat more plausible situation in which eq. (14) is problematic arises when r is positive but output grows at a net rate above r. In such cases, the present value of the economy's resources is unbounded! As Chapter 7 will show, we need not worry about this troublesome possibility in representative agent economies with subjective discounting of the future and investment, but the issue may arise in economies with overlapping generations such as those discussed in the next chapter. We return to the topic there. For the balance of this chapter, we assume that the interest rate is positive and all economic variables whose present values we need to compute grow at net rates strictly *below* the rate of interest.

Application: When Is a Country Bankrupt?

Both government policymakers and private actors in world capital markets spend a good deal of time analyzing the "sustainability" of indebted countries' current-account deficits. Their purpose is to detect situations in which countries might become bankrupt, that is, unable to pay off foreign obligations at their face values. In such a situation, constraint (14) would not hold with foreign debts valued at par.

Assessing the possibility of national bankruptcy is a very subjective matter. In reality, it is hard to forecast future national outputs, and, perhaps more importantly, there may be limits to the share of GDP that a country is willing to devote to repaying foreign creditors. (We look at the latter issue in great detail in Chapter 6.) Notwithstanding the large subjective element involved, assessments of creditworthiness are made all the time and motivate both the course of economic policy and the decisions of private international investors. It has happened repeatedly, most recently in the decade starting in 1982, that groups of countries are cut off from world capital markets because potential creditors perceive them to be bad risks. It is therefore useful to know whether current account data offer any rough-and-ready indicators of national bankruptcy.

A useful framework for thinking about this question is provided by rearranging constraint (14) to read

$$-(1+r)B_t = \sum_{s=t}^{\infty} \left(\frac{1}{1+r}\right)^{s-t} (Y_s - C_s - I_s - G_s).$$

Define the quantity $TB_s \equiv Y_s - C_s - I_s - G_s$ as the economy's *trade balance*. The trade balance is the net amount of output the economy transfers to foreigners each period. The preceding constraint states simply that the present value of an

---

5. For this reason, we would not expect the transversality condition (13) to hold in a model with a zero or negative interest rate. A famous example in which the condition fails to hold is Ramsey's (1928) famous model of optimal economic growth, which assumes no discounting of the future ($\beta = 1$) and thus has a zero long-run rate of interest.

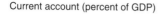

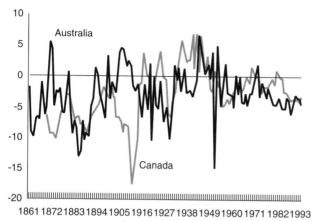

Figure 2.1
Current accounts of Australia and Canada, 1861–1994

economy's resource transfers to foreigners must equal the value of the economy's initial debt to them. Thus the intertemporal budget constraint holds if, and only if, a country pays off any initial foreign debt through sufficiently large future surpluses in its balance of trade.

Figure 2.1, which shows the current accounts of Australia and Canada over the entire historical span for which data are available, illustrates why this way of look-ing at national solvency is helpful. Policymakers often view persistently large cur-rent account deficits as a portent of future borrowing problems. Both Australia and Canada have run persistent and, at times, immense deficits, especially during their periods of settlement and development prior to World War I. But both countries' strong tendency to run deficits has remained pronounced in the postwar period. Between 1950 and 1994, Australia's current account was in deficit in all but four years, while Canada's was in deficit in all but five. And even these postwar deficits have been substantial, as Figure 2.1 makes apparent.

Does it follow that Australia and Canada are about to go broke? On the con-trary, they have been able to finance their external borrowing with remarkably little difficulty. Figure 2.2 shows clearly why Canada's credit has remained good: even though the country has run *current account* deficits, its *trade balance* has registered substantial surpluses over 1976–93. The reasons for Australia's continuing cred-itworthiness are less obvious from Figure 2.2, which shows that, despite a 1993 debt-GDP ratio of 54 percent, the country has had persistent trade deficits since 1976. Perhaps Australia's creditors, reassured by recent economic reforms, expect trade surpluses to emerge in the relatively close future.

Indeed, an economy with growing output can run perpetual current account deficits and still maintain a constant ratio of foreign debt to both output and wealth.

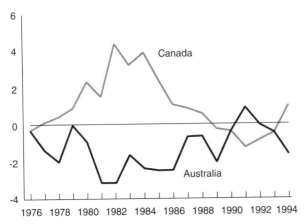

Figure 2.2
Trade balances of Australia and Canada, 1976–94. (*Source:* OECD)

Suppose that $Y_{s+1} = (1 + g)Y_s$, where $g > 0$ is the output growth rate, and that the economy maintains a steady debt-output ratio B_s/Y_s, so that $B_{s+1} = (1 + g)B_s$. The current account identity implies a steady imbalance of

$$B_{s+1} - B_s = g B_s = r B_s + T B_s,$$

which shows that

$$\frac{T B_s}{Y_s} = \frac{-(r - g)B_s}{Y_s} = \frac{-B_s}{Y_s/(r - g)}.$$

The first equality above shows that to maintain a constant debt-GDP ratio, the country need pay out only the excess of the interest rate over the growth rate. The second equality shows that the necessary trade balance surplus is a fraction of GDP equal to the ratio of debt to the world market value of a claim to the economy's entire future GDP. Thus, the ratio $-(r - g)B/Y$ measures the burden a foreign debt imposes on the economy. The higher this burden, the greater the likelihood that the debt is unsustainable, in the sense that the debtor country finds itself unable or unwilling to repay.[6]

Table 2.1 reports values of this measure for a sample of economies. For r we use a real interest rate of 8 percent per year.[7] For g we use estimates based on average

---

6. For an interesting and related attempt to construct an index number measuring national solvency, see Cohen (1985). Notice that we assume $r > g$, in line with the assumption made earlier on p. 66.

7. Since the real world is stochastic, practical application of our debt burden measure requires addressing the subtle question of what interest rate should be used in discounting a country's future output. Clearly, a riskless real interest rate is inappropriate, since the country's future growth rate g is highly uncertain. The rate of return on equities is probably a better approximation, and this tends to be much

Table 2.1
Real External Debt Burdens of Selected Countries, 1970–91 (percent of GDP per year)

Country	1970	1983	1991
Argentina	0.5	2.9	3.9
Australia	1.7	1.3	2.4
Brazil	0.0	1.3	0.8
Canada	1.2	1.6	1.6
Chile	1.7	1.5	3.1
Hungary	0.0	2.3	3.8
Mexico	0.1	3.1	1.5
Nigeria	0.1	1.1	4.8
Thailand	0.0	0.0	0.2

Source: Authors' calculations based on data from World Bank, *World Development Report,* various issues.

output growth for each individual country. The average growth rate of real GDP over 1970–91 enters the calculation of the 1991 debt burden; to calculate the 1970 and 1983 burdens, we use average GDP growth rates over 1970–80 and 1980–91, respectively. According to our measure, external debt burdens vary widely across countries. The 1991 burdens were greatest for slow-growing Argentina and highly indebted Nigeria (its debt-GDP ratio exceeded 100 percent), and smallest for fast-growing Thailand. Note also that the demands of foreign debt service generally tend to be relatively small. In many cases the trade surplus needed to service the 1991 debt amounts to less than 2 percent of GDP, and it is far lower than that figure in rapidly growing economies. Thus, even though some of these countries had sizable ratios of debt to GDP in the early 1990s (Mexico's ratio was 36 percent, Thailand's 38 percent, for example), it would be hard to describe these levels as unsustainable based purely on ability-to-pay criteria.

As mentioned earlier, a decade-long international lending slowdown started in 1982; its greatest effect was in Latin America. Table 2.1 generally does show a sharp rise in debt burdens for the countries in this region between 1970 and 1983, notably in Mexico, where the debt crisis began. But while Mexico's 1983 burden is significant, those of countries like Brazil and Chile seem too moderate to have pushed these countries into crisis too. Two factors not evident from the table are part of the explanation. First, short-term real interest rates increased sharply in the 1980s. If investors expected these rates to be sustained, such expectations could have sharply increased estimated debt burdens. Second, by preventing countries from borrowing against expected future growth, a cutoff of lending can, itself, heighten the pain of servicing existing debts. That is, a foreign debt crisis can have self-fulfilling elements.

---

higher; thus our choice of 8 percent for these developing country claims. We defer a rigorous discussion of how to price a claim on a country's future output until Chapter 5.

Still, Canada's immunity to the post-1982 debt crisis and Australia's avoidance of a crisis in the early 1990s suggest that additional factors influenced international lenders when they decided to reduce their lending to developing countries. In particular, lenders feared that the political and legal institutions in those countries would be too weak to ensure compliance with even moderately higher debt obligations. As we have already noted, Chapter 6 will examine how the prospect of national default affects international credit markets.   ∎

2.1.3   Consumption Functions: Some Leading Examples

The characterization of optimal consumption plans derived in section 2.1.2 leads to a number of useful examples.

1. As a first case, return to the economy for which $\beta = 1/(1+r)$, the government uses no resources, and output is exogenous and constant at $\bar{Y}$. Equation (12) can be used to show that the only solution for consumption satisfying the Euler equations (5) and the transversality condition is

$$C_t = \bar{C} = r B_t + \bar{Y}.$$

Economic actors choose a constant consumption level equal to the economy's income, which, in the absence of variation in output, is also constant over time. We could, alternatively, have derived this consumption function directly from the Euler equation and the intertemporal budget constraint. We illustrate how to do this in our second, more complex, example.

2. Retain the assumption $\beta = 1/(1+r)$, which implies that consumption is constant at some level $\bar{C}$, but allow for time-varying investment, government consumption, and output. To solve for $\bar{C}$, substitute it into the intertemporal budget constraint (14),

$$\sum_{s=t}^{\infty} \left(\frac{1}{1+r}\right)^{s-t} (\bar{C} + I_s) = (1+r)B_t + \sum_{s=t}^{\infty} \left(\frac{1}{1+r}\right)^{s-t} (Y_s - G_s).$$

Solving for $\bar{C}$, we obtain

$$\bar{C} = C_t = \frac{r}{1+r} \left[(1+r)B_t + \sum_{s=t}^{\infty} \left(\frac{1}{1+r}\right)^{s-t} (Y_s - G_s - I_s) \right].$$

This is the same as eq. (10).

3. Suppose the period utility function is isoelastic, $u(C) = C^{1-1/\sigma}/(1 - 1/\sigma)$. Euler equation (5) takes the form

$$C_{s+1} = (1+r)^\sigma \beta^\sigma C_s. \tag{15}$$

Use it to eliminate C_{t+1}, C_{t+2}, ... from budget constraint (14). Under the assumption that $(1+r)^{\sigma-1}\beta^{\sigma} < 1$, so that consumption grows at a net rate below r according to eq. (15), the result is the consumption function

$$C_t = \frac{(1+r)B_t + \sum_{s=t}^{\infty} \left(\frac{1}{1+r}\right)^{s-t}(Y_s - G_s - I_s)}{\sum_{s=t}^{\infty} \left[(1+r)^{\sigma-1}\beta^{\sigma}\right]^{s-t}}.$$

Defining $\vartheta \equiv 1 - (1+r)^{\sigma}\beta^{\sigma}$, we rewrite this as

$$C_t = \frac{r+\vartheta}{1+r}\left[(1+r)B_t + \sum_{s=t}^{\infty} \left(\frac{1}{1+r}\right)^{s-t}(Y_s - G_s - I_s)\right]. \tag{16}$$

Given r, consumption is a decreasing function of β. Notice that when the expression $(1+r)^{\sigma-1}\beta^{\sigma}$ is *above* 1, the denominator of the expression preceding eq. (16) is a nonconvergent series and the consumption function is not defined. This nonsensical mathematical outcome reflects a possibility mentioned earlier, that no utility maximum exists.[8]

It is easy to check using eq. (5) that, regardless of the utility function, a small country's consumption grows forever when $\beta > 1/(1+r)$ and shrinks forever when $\beta < 1/(1+r)$. The fixed discrepancy between β and $1/(1+r)$ *tilts* the desired consumption path, upward if the consumer is patient enough that $\beta > 1/(1+r)$, downward in the opposite case. Only when it happens that $\beta = 1/(1+r)$ is a constant, steady-state consumption path optimal. (A steady state for a variable is a level that will be maintained indefinitely unless there is some external shock to the system determining the variable.) Note that if somehow the time-preference factor β could be made to depend on consumption, this type of knife-edge behavior would be avoided. Supplement B to this chapter shows one way of achieving this result. In the next chapter you will see that a small economy populated by diverse overlapping generations can have a steady state for aggregate per capita consumption even when all individuals share a constant time-preference factor β different from $1/(1+r)$.

The possibility that there is no steady state when $(1+r)\beta \neq 1$ is more than a mere curiosity. It shows that some of the very-long-run implications of the infinitely-lived, representative-agent, small-country model must be interpreted

---

8. Why? The intertemporal budget constraint could not be satisfied in any usual sense were C to grow at a gross rate of $1+r$ or more—the present value of consumption would be infinite. But optimality requires consumption to grow at the gross rate $(1+r)^{\sigma}\beta^{\sigma} > 1+r$. Thus the best the consumer can do is to get the consumption growth rate as close to $1+r$ as possible, without ever actually reaching $1+r$. That is a maximization problem with no solution, since it is always possible to do a little better! It is easy to check that, because β is assumed to be strictly less than 1, $(1+r)^{\sigma-1}\beta^{\sigma} > 1$ can happen only when $\sigma > 1$. (The assumption that consumption grows more slowly than $1+r$ is consistent with our assumption on p. 66 restricting the net growth rates of real quantities to values below r.)

with caution. Another case in which the small-country model strains believability is that of trend domestic output or productivity growth at a rate exceeding the rest of the world's. For example, with trend growth in its endowment and $(1+r)\beta = 1$, the country will wish to maintain perfectly constant consumption by borrowing against future output gains. But with consumption constant and output growing, the ratio of consumption to output must eventually go to zero! We explore the implications of trend productivity growth for long-run debt-GDP ratios in appendix 2A.

2.1.4   Dynamic Consistency in Intertemporal Choice

A question that arises once an economy exists longer than two periods is whether consumers, having made consumption plans for all future periods on the initial date t, will find it optimal to abide by those original plans as the future actually unfolds.

On date t the consumer maximizes U_t subject to the intertemporal budget constraint, given B_t. In solving his date t problem of maximizing U_t, the consumer chooses an optimal initial consumption level, C_t, and, via the Euler equation (5), optimal consumption levels for dates $t+1, t+2$, and so on. On date $t+1$, he maximizes

$$U_{t+1} = \sum_{s=t+1}^{\infty} \beta^{s-(t+1)} u(C_s),$$

given a new lifetime budget constraint with starting assets $B_{t+1} = (1+r)B_t + Y_t - C_t - G_t - I_t$. But do the values of C_{t+1}, C_{t+2}, and so on, chosen on date t solve the date $t+1$ maximization problem? If so, we say the consumer's initial optimal plan has the property of *dynamic consistency*.

For a two-period problem, consumption in the second—and final—period is determined entirely by the intertemporal budget constraint: preferences have no role. Thus the second-period consumption level planned in the first period *must* be implemented. There is no possibility of dynamic inconsistency.

With more than two periods, the answer requires more work, but not much more. Since C_t has already been implemented in accordance with the date t optimal plan, the date $t+1$ starting asset stock B_{t+1} inherited from date t is exactly the one the consumer originally intended to bequeath. Under the original optimal plan, consumptions from date $t+1$ forward satisfy the Euler equation (5) and the date $t+1$ intertemporal budget constraint. The consumption plan maximizing U_{t+1} follows the same Euler equation and must satisfy the same budget constraint, so it cannot differ from the continuation of the plan that maximized U_t.

In a famous article, Strotz (1956) claimed to have shown that certain intertemporal utility functions could give rise to dynamically inconsistent plans. For example, suppose an individual maximizes

$$U_t = (1 + \gamma)u(C_t) + \sum_{s=t+1}^{\infty} \beta^{s-t}u(C_s),$$

where $\gamma > 0$, on every date t. Such a consumer places an especially high weight on current enjoyment. From the standpoint of date t, the marginal rate of substitution of date $t + 1$ for date $s > t + 1$ consumption is $\beta^{s-t-1}u'(C_s)/u'(C_{t+1})$. At a constant interest rate the consumer will optimally equate the latter to $(1 + r)^{-(s-t-1)}$.

On date $t + 1$, Strotz argues, a consumer with these preferences will maximize

$$U_{t+1} = (1 + \gamma)u(C_{t+1}) + \sum_{s=t+2}^{\infty} \beta^{s-(t+1)}u(C_s)$$

and will reckon the marginal rate of substitution of date $t + 1$ for date $s > t + 1$ consumption to be $\beta^{s-t-1}u'(C_s)/(1 + \gamma)u'(C_{t+1})$. If the consumer equates *this* rate to $(1 + r)^{-(s-t-1)}$, his optimal consumption plan will be different from the one desired on date t.

Economists have debated whether Strotz's examples pose a deep problem for intertemporal choice theory, or instead are only a sophisticated rendering of the mundane observation that people's plans change if their preferences aren't stable over time.[9] Strotz's critics argue that what a consumer with stable preferences maximizes on date $t + 1$ is not U_{t+1}, but U_t itself, subject to the new budget constraint and the *additional* constraint that C_t is historically given. In terms of the earlier example, the individual would maximize

$$(1 + \gamma)u(\bar{C}_t) + \sum_{s=t+1}^{\infty} \beta^{s-t}u(C_s)$$

on date $t + 1$, with $\bar{C}_t$ the historical date t consumption level. If we look at the problem this way, it is apparent immediately that lifetime consumption plans can never be dynamically inconsistent. This observation is true even if U_t is of the general form $U(C_t, C_{t+1}, \ldots)$.

As we have shown, the time-additive utility function that we assumed in eq. (1) is not subject to the Strotz phenomenon. Thus it makes no difference whether you think of the consumer as maximizing U_{t+1} on date $t + 1$, or as maximizing U_t on date $t + 1$ given the historical value of C_t. We have adopted the former interpretation in this book, not because we disagree with Strotz's critics, but because it allows more compact notation while making no substantive difference to the results.

---

9. Deaton (1992) espouses the latter view.

2.2   Dynamics of the Current Account

This section derives and analyzes a neat and testable characterization of the current account based on the distinction between current flows and capitalized values of future output, government spending, investment, and interest rates.[10]

2.2.1   A Fundamental Current Account Equation

For a constant interest rate r, define the *permanent* level of variable X on date t by

$$\sum_{s=t}^{\infty}\left(\frac{1}{1+r}\right)^{s-t}\tilde{X}_t = \sum_{s=t}^{\infty}\left(\frac{1}{1+r}\right)^{s-t}X_s$$

so that

$$\tilde{X}_t \equiv \frac{r}{1+r}\sum_{s=t}^{\infty}\left(\frac{1}{1+r}\right)^{s-t}X_s. \tag{17}$$

A variable's permanent level is its annuity value at the prevailing interest rate, that is, the hypothetical constant level of the variable with the same present value as the variable itself.

Let's assume initially that $\beta = 1/(1+r)$. Substitute the consumption function (10) for that case into the current account identity, eq. (2), and make use of definition (17). The result is a fundamental equation for the current account,

$$CA_t = B_{t+1} - B_t = (Y_t - \tilde{Y}_t) - (I_t - \tilde{I}_t) - (G_t - \tilde{G}_t). \tag{18}$$

This simple equation yields a number of vital predictions. Output above its permanent level contributes to a higher current account surplus because of consumption smoothing. Rather than raising consumption point for point when output rises temporarily above its long-run discounted average, individuals choose to accumulate interest-yielding foreign assets as a way of smoothing consumption over future periods.

Similarly, people use foreign borrowing to cushion their consumption in the face of unusually high investment needs. Rather than financing extraordinarily profitable opportunities entirely out of domestic savings, countries wish to avoid sharp temporary drops in consumption by borrowing foreign savings.

Finally, abnormally high government spending needs have the same effect as abnormally low output. A higher current account deficit enables people to minimize such a shock's impact in any given period by spreading that impact over the entire

---

10. In its simplest form the characterization comes from Sachs (1982).

future. Chapter 1's application to the current-account implications of wars provides some good examples of this effect.

Even though eq. (18) assumes perfect foresight about the future, it is often used to understand the current account's response to one-time, unanticipated events that jolt the economy to a new perfect-foresight path. For example, suppose that initially Y, I, and G are expected to be constant through time, so that $CA = 0$. Suddenly and unexpectedly, people learn that the new perfect foresight path for output is one along which output falls over time. Equation (18) implies that the current account will immediately move from balance to a surplus.[11]

A model that assumes perfect foresight except for initial shocks should leave you somewhat uneasy. In reality the future is always uncertain. Wouldn't it be better to introduce uncertainty explicitly and model its effects on individual decisions? Emphatically, the answer is yes. In section 2.3, however, we develop an explicitly stochastic model of international borrowing and lending in which the effects of random shocks are exactly as described in the last paragraph. Thus there is nothing seriously wrong about the perfect foresight cum initial shocks mode of analysis, provided we accept one restriction: countries must trade only riskless bonds, as they do here, and not assets with payoffs indexed to uncertain events. Chapter 5 will go more deeply into the ramifications of uncertainty when countries trade a richer menu of assets.

What replaces eq. (18) when $\beta \neq 1/(1+r)$? The question is readily answered when utility is isoelastic and consumption is given by eq. (16). Here, as well as in several other places in the book, it is convenient to employ the construct:

$$W_t \equiv (1+r)B_t + \sum_{s=t}^{\infty} \left(\frac{1}{1+r}\right)^{s-t} (Y_s - I_s - G_s). \tag{19}$$

Note that as we have defined it, W_t is a *beginning-of-period-t* measure of "wealth" that includes financial assets accumulated through period $t-1$ as well as current and future expected income as of date t. (Use of W_t rather than our usual end-of-period asset-stock notation allows us to express certain formulas more simply.)

By logic similar to that leading to eq. (18), eq. (16) then implies

$$CA_t = (Y_t - \tilde{Y}_t) - (I_t - \tilde{I}_t) - (G_t - \tilde{G}_t) - \frac{\vartheta}{1+r} W_t, \tag{20}$$

where, we remind you, $\vartheta = 1 - (1+r)^{\sigma} \beta^{\sigma}$.

---

11. A word of caution about applying eq. (18): be sure to remember that the paths of output and investment are not generally independent. Investment behavior can be inferred from eq. (6). The country will be increasing its capital stock in periods s such that $A_{s+1} > A_s$, and running capital down in the opposite case. Equation (18) thus shows that when A_{s+1} is unusually high the current account for date s is in greater deficit both because current investment is expected to be unusually productive and because output is expected to rise.

Box 2.1
Japan's 1923 Earthquake

At 11:58 A.M. on September 1, 1923, Japan suffered one of recorded history's most devastating earthquakes. Damage was spread over 6,000 square miles. A large part of Tokyo was destroyed; most of Yokohama, the principal port, was reduced to rubble. More than 150,000 people were killed or injured. Property destroyed by the quake and the fires, aftershocks, and tidal waves that followed it was valued at more than a third of Japan's 1922 GDP.

Japan's earthquake is the example par excellence of an exogenous economic shock whose effects are widely understood to be temporary. Output growth slowed, reconstruction needs stimulated investment, and government disaster relief swelled public expenditures—but only for a time. Equations (18) and (20) alike predict sharply higher current account deficits in 1923 and 1924.

That prediction is borne out. The current account deficit rose from 1.2 percent of GDP in 1922 to 3.6 percent in 1923 and 4.4 percent in 1924, before falling back to 1.6 percent in 1925.

The new feature in eq. (20) is the presence of a consumption-tilt factor, ϑ, when $\beta \neq 1/(1+r)$. This generalization of (18) shows that the current account is driven by two distinct motives, the pure smoothing motive [just as in the case $\beta = 1/(1+r)$] and a tilting motive related to any discrepancy between the subjective discount factor β and the world market discount factor $1/(1+r)$. For $\vartheta > 0$ (the country is relatively impatient) the current account is reduced, but it is raised for $\vartheta < 0$ (the country is relatively patient).

* 2.2.2   Effects of Variable Interest Rates

Real interest rates are rarely constant for very long. Variation in real interest rates, particularly when anticipated, can have economic effects that the fixed-rate model we've been using obviously can't encompass. An extended model that incorporates changing interest rates brings the economy's intertemporal prices to center stage.

Let r_{s+1} denote the real interest rate the market offers for loans between periods s and $s + 1$. Define $R_{t,s}$ as the *market discount factor* for date s consumption on date $t \leq s$, that is, as the relative price of date s consumption in terms of date t consumption. Only if intertemporal prices obey

$$R_{t,s} = \frac{1}{\prod_{v=t+1}^{s}(1+r_v)} \tag{21}$$

are arbitrage possibilities ruled out. Here, $R_{t,t}$ is interpreted as 1, $R_{t,t+1} = 1/(1+r_{t+1})$, $R_{t,t+2} = 1/(1+r_{t+1})(1+r_{t+2})$, and so on. If the interest rate happens to be constant at r, $R_{t,s} = 1/(1+r)^{s-t}$, as before.

The individual's accumulation of net foreign claims between periods s and $s + 1$ is

$$B_{s+1} - B_s = Y_s + r_s B_s - C_s - G_s - I_s. \tag{22}$$

Retracing the steps leading to budget constraint (14), which assumed a constant interest rate, we now derive the date t budget constraint

$$\sum_{s=t}^{\infty} R_{t,s}(C_s + I_s) = (1 + r_t)B_t + \sum_{s=t}^{\infty} R_{t,s}(Y_s - G_s). \tag{23}$$

The derivation of this constraint assumes that the generalized transversality condition

$$\lim_{T \to \infty} R_{t,t+T} B_{t+T+1} = 0$$

always holds.

Let's follow our usual method of eliminating consumption from the lifetime utility function U_t via the current account identity. Also, express output as a function of capital using the production function. The first-order conditions for the individual's problem are the (by now) familiar:

$$u'(C_s) = (1 + r_{s+1})\beta u'(C_{s+1}), \tag{24}$$

$$A_{s+1} F'(K_{s+1}) = r_{s+1}.$$

Given an isoelastic period utility function with $u'(C) = C^{-1/\sigma}$, Euler equation (24) implies $C_s = R_{t,s}^{-\sigma} \beta^{\sigma(s-t)} C_t$ for $s \geq t$. Together with eq. (23), this evolution of consumption implies the optimal consumption level

$$C_t = \frac{(1 + r_t)B_t + \sum_{s=t}^{\infty} R_{t,s}(Y_s - I_s - G_s)}{\sum_{s=t}^{\infty} R_{t,s}\left[R_{t,s}^{-\sigma} \beta^{\sigma(s-t)}\right]}. \tag{25}$$

You will recognize eq. (25) as a close cousin of eq. (16), which assumed a constant interest rate.[12] Rather than exploring its full range of implications, we concentrate on generalizing the fundamental equation of the current account, eq. (20).

With variable interest rates, the *permanent* level of a variable is found by solving

$$\sum_{s=t}^{\infty} R_{t,s} \tilde{X}_t = \sum_{s=t}^{\infty} R_{t,s} X_s$$

so that

---

12. The family resemblance is easy to spot if you look at the unnumbered equation directly preceding eq. (16).

$$\tilde{X}_t \equiv \frac{\sum_{s=t}^{\infty} R_{t,s} X_s}{\sum_{s=t}^{\infty} R_{t,s}}.$$

By the Euler equation, the gross growth rate of consumption between dates t and s, C_s/C_t, equals $R_{t,s}^{-\sigma} \beta^{\sigma(s-t)}$. Define $\tilde{\Gamma}_t$ to be the discount-rate-weighted average of consumption growth rates between date t and later dates:

$$\tilde{\Gamma}_t \equiv \frac{\sum_{s=t}^{\infty} R_{t,s} \left[R_{t,s}^{-\sigma} \beta^{\sigma(s-t)} \right]}{\sum_{s=t}^{\infty} R_{t,s}}.$$

By substituting eq. (25) into the current account identity (22) (for $s = t$), we learn (after a fair bit of algebraic manipulation) that[13]

$$CA_t = (r_t - \tilde{r}_t) B_t + (Y_t - \tilde{Y}_t) - (I_t - \tilde{I}_t) - (G_t - \tilde{G}_t)$$

$$+ \left(\frac{\tilde{\Gamma}_t - 1}{\tilde{\Gamma}_t} \right) \left(\tilde{r}_t B_t + \tilde{Y}_t - \tilde{I}_t - \tilde{G}_t \right). \tag{26}$$

This generalized fundamental equation has a new and important implication that was masked by eq. (20)'s assumption of a constant interest rate. If the economy is a net foreign claimant and the world interest rate currently being earned exceeds its permanent level, the current account surplus is unusually high as people save to smooth into the future their unusually high asset income. Matters are reversed if the economy is a net foreign debtor.

Notice the form consumption tilting takes. In the current account equation we have derived, the annuity value $\tilde{r}_t B_t + \tilde{Y}_t - \tilde{I}_t - \tilde{G}_t$ is the consumption of a hypothetical consumer for whom intertemporal substitution is intolerable ($\sigma = 0$).[14] Consumption is always constant through time for this consumer, but for nonpathological consumers with $\sigma > 0$, consumption can, on average, be growing ($\tilde{\Gamma}_t > 1$) or shrinking ($\tilde{\Gamma}_t < 1$) over time, depending on the time path of interest rates in relation to β. Consumption tilting adds to the current account the product of a consumption growth coefficient and the consumption of a $\sigma = 0$ individual.

---

13. There is only one tricky part of the derivation. As a preliminary step, make sure you see why

$$\sum_{s=t+1}^{\infty} R_{t,s} r_s = 1.$$

(The left-hand side is the discounted stream of payoffs from one unit of output invested and rolled over in perpetuity, while the right-hand side is the price of that asset.) Now use the preceding fact to verify the chain of equalities:

$$\frac{1 + r_t}{\sum_{s=t}^{\infty} R_{t,s}} = \frac{r_t + \sum_{s=t+1}^{\infty} R_{t,s} r_s}{\sum_{s=t}^{\infty} R_{t,s}} = \frac{\sum_{s=t}^{\infty} R_{t,s} r_s}{\sum_{s=t}^{\infty} R_{t,s}} = \tilde{r}_t.$$

This hint should be enough to guide you to the following equation without too much trouble.

14. To see why, set $\sigma = 0$ in eq. (25) and use the final result in the last footnote.

2.3   A Stochastic Current Account Model

Thus far we have looked at perfect-foresight economies, but it is time now to think more carefully about the inherent uncertainties that always underlie consumption and investment decisions. People plainly do *not* foresee perfectly the random economic events that can affect their future wage income or the payoffs on investments. Decisions today must be based on informed guesses about what is likely to happen later on; as new information comes in, people revise previous plans. Modeling this process should lead to more realistic empirical predictions about the short-run behavior of economic aggregates. In this section we discuss a particularly simple way of introducing uncertainty that leads to a model very similar in spirit to the ones we have been studying.

The main difference uncertainty makes here is that individuals can now be surprised by unexpected events, not just in a hypothetical initial period, but repeatedly. While we previously endowed individuals with perfect foresight concerning their future consumption possibilities, in a stochastic setting we can only make the weaker assumption that individuals have *rational expectations*. A rational expectation is a mathematical conditional expectation based on an accurate model of the economy's structure and on all the information about current economic variables that the individual has available. Rational expectations of future events need not be correct, but rational forecasts are unbiased, and rational forecast errors are uncorrelated with the information on which the forecast was conditioned.[15]

2.3.1   Uncertainty and Consumption in a Small Infinite-Horizon Economy

We now allow future levels of output, investment, and government consumption all to be random variables. In this setting, individuals can only choose contingency plans for future consumption, rather than definite future consumption levels. Future consumptions therefore are random variables. We assume that the representative individual, faced with this uncertainty, maximizes the *expected value* of lifetime utility,

$$U_t = E_t \left\{ \sum_{s=t}^{\infty} \beta^{s-t} u(C_s) \right\}.$$

The operator $E_t\{\cdot\}$ is a mathematical conditional expectation—a probability-weighted average of possible outcomes, in which probabilities are conditioned on all information available to the decision maker up to and including date t.

---

15. The classic original reference on rational expectations is Muth (1961). Lucas (1976) discusses implications of the rational expectations hypothesis in macroeconomics.

A riskless bond is still the only internationally traded asset in this model.[16] For simplicity we assume that the world interest rate is constant at r, so that the same current account identity (2) as in the certainty model holds for each period. In this stochastic setting, the same iterative argument that led to the certainty model's intertemporal budget constraint (14) leads to the apparently identical equation

$$\sum_{s=t}^{\infty} \left(\frac{1}{1+r}\right)^{s-t} (C_s + I_s) = (1+r)B_t + \sum_{s=t}^{\infty} \left(\frac{1}{1+r}\right)^{s-t} (Y_s - G_s).$$

Now there is a subtle difference, however. The preceding equation involves random variables, and its derivation requires that Ponzi game outcomes in which debt grows at the rate of interest never occur, regardless of what shocks hit the economy. This restriction means that the random intertemporal budget constraint must be obeyed with probability one.[17]

The current account identity (2) can be used as in the certainty case to eliminate consumption levels from U_t, turning the consumer's problem into the unconstrained maximization of

$$U_t = E_t \left\{ \sum_{s=t}^{\infty} \beta^{s-t} u \left[(1+r)B_s - B_{s+1} + Y_s - G_s - I_s \right] \right\} \tag{27}$$

with respect to the sequence of contingency plans for net foreign asset holdings. The first-order condition with respect to an unconditional change in B_{s+1} is

$$E_t \left\{ u'(C_s) \right\} = (1+r)\beta E_t \left\{ u'(C_{s+1}) \right\}, \tag{28}$$

which implies for date $s = t$ that

$$u'(C_t) = (1+r)\beta E_t \left\{ u'(C_{t+1}) \right\}. \tag{29}$$

This stochastic Euler equation generalizes the deterministic equation (5).

2.3.2 The Linear-Quadratic "Permanent Income" Model

A variant of this model that has been extensively applied in the empirical literature is the *linear-quadratic utility model* in which the period utility function is

---

16. Enlarging the menu of traded assets to include assets with risky payoffs has important consequences for the model's dynamics. We study this question at length in Chapter 5, and in Chapter 6 consider theoretical reasons why the bonds-only economy of this chapter may be a reasonable approximation for empirical purposes. Our assumption of expected-utility maximization also receives further discussion in Chapter 5.

17. We continue to assume that there are nonnegativity constraints on consumption and capital stocks which are nonbinding with probability one. The consumption assumption implies that a country will never let its foreign debt get so large that an adverse output shock allows it to remain solvent (with probability one) only by setting $C \leq 0$. Under mild restrictions on output growth, this precautionary behavior implies that the transversality condition on foreign assets will hold with probability one.

$$u(C) = C - \frac{a_0}{2}C^2, \qquad a_0 > 0. \tag{30}$$

With quadratic utility, one can actually solve for the optimal level of consumption in much the same manner as in the perfect-foresight case. In order to constrain consumption to follow a trendless long-run path, we specify that $(1 + r)\beta = 1$, although this restriction could easily be relaxed.

Notice first that the marginal utility of consumption, $u'(C) = 1 - a_0 C$, is linear in C. Substituting this marginal utility into the Euler equation (29), we obtain Hall's (1978) famous result

$$E_t C_{t+1} = C_t; \tag{31}$$

that is, consumption follows a random walk.[18]

We can use the random-walk Euler equation to derive a reduced form for the level of consumption as a function of current and expected future values of output, government spending, and investment. The intertemporal budget constraint holds with probability one, so it plainly holds in expectation:

$$E_t \left\{ \sum_{s=t}^{\infty} \left(\frac{1}{1+r} \right)^{s-t} (C_s + I_s) \right\} = E_t \left\{ (1+r)B_t + \sum_{s=t}^{\infty} \left(\frac{1}{1+r} \right)^{s-t} (Y_s - G_s) \right\}.$$

In the case of quadratic utility, the Euler equation (28) implies that for any $s > t$, $E_t C_s = E_t C_{s-1} = E_t C_{s-2} = \cdots = E_t C_{t+1} = C_t$. Substituting C_t for $E_t C_s$ in the expected-value budget constraint and rearranging yields

$$\sum_{s=t}^{\infty} \left(\frac{1}{1+r} \right)^{s-t} C_t = E_t \left\{ (1+r)B_t + \sum_{s=t}^{\infty} \left(\frac{1}{1+r} \right)^{s-t} (Y_s - G_s - I_s) \right\}.$$

The solution for C_t is simply an expected-value rendition of the permanent income consumption function (10):

$$C_t = \frac{r}{1+r} \left[(1+r)B_t + \sum_{s=t}^{\infty} \left(\frac{1}{1+r} \right)^{s-t} E_t \{Y_s - G_s - I_s\} \right]. \tag{32}$$

With quadratic utility, consumption is determined according to the *certainty equivalence principle*. People make decisions under uncertainty by acting as if future stochastic variables were sure to turn out equal to their conditional means. Certainty equivalence is rarely a rational basis for decisions. It is appropriate here because the special quadratic utility function in eq. (30) makes the marginal utility

---

18. More precisely, consumption follows a *martingale*, meaning that the expected value of C_{t+1} conditional on *all* available information (not just the history of consumption) is C_t. Hall (1978) found that U.S. per capita consumption data did follow an approximate random walk, but that stock-market prices added significantly to the predictive power of past consumption for future consumption.

of consumption linear in C, eliminating all moments of $Y - G - I$ higher than the first from the consumption function (32).

Note that the derivation of eq. (32) did not exclude the level of C becoming negative, or C growing so large that the marginal utility of consumption, $u'(C) = 1 - a_0 C$, becomes negative. These problems could be confronted explicitly, but the neat linearity of the certainty equivalence framework would then be lost. For these reasons, the consumption function (32) is best viewed as an approximation that captures the spirit of consumption-smoothing hypotheses like Friedman's (1957).[19] Again, as we warned in our perfect-foresight analysis, this highly tractable model gives useful insights about the effect of short- to medium-run fluctuations, but its long-run implications must be interpreted with caution.

2.3.3 Output Shocks, Consumption, and the Current Account

As a simple application of the linear-quadratic model, forget temporarily about government consumption and investment and suppose that output Y follows the exogenous stochastic process

$$Y_{t+1} - \bar{Y} = \rho \left(Y_t - \bar{Y} \right) + \epsilon_{t+1}, \tag{33}$$

where ϵ_t is a serially uncorrelated disturbance, $E_t \epsilon_{t+1} = 0$, and $0 \leq \rho \leq 1$.

Because $E_t \epsilon_s = 0$ for all $s > t$ (by the law of iterated conditional expectations) the preceding stochastic difference equation for output implies

$$E_t \left\{ Y_s - \bar{Y} \right\} = \rho^{s-t} (Y_t - \bar{Y}), \tag{34}$$

as you can check by iterated forward substitutions.[20] Note that when $G = I = 0$, eq. (32) can be written

$$C_t = r B_t + \bar{Y} + \frac{r}{1+r} \sum_{s=t}^{\infty} \left(\frac{1}{1+r} \right)^{s-t} E_t \left\{ Y_s - \bar{Y} \right\}.$$

---

19. The approximation view of eq. (32) raises two questions. First, what ensures that wealth does not randomly walk arbitrarily far from the approximation point? Second, given the absence of a natural expected steady state for wealth, around which wealth level is an approximation to be taken? One answer comes from precautionary saving theory (see section 2.3.6). Clarida (1990) proposes a general-equilibrium model of borrowing and lending by a continuum of stochastic endowment economies, each subject to a nonnegativity constraint on consumption and a condition precluding bankruptcy with probability one. If there is no aggregate uncertainty, the model predicts that at a constant world interest rate below the rate of time preference, the equilibrium distribution of foreign assets among countries is described by an invariant (or steady-state) distribution. (An invariant distribution is one that perpetuates itself once reached, see Stokey and Lucas, 1989, p. 21.) Clarida's result, while special, suggests that an approximation like the one behind the permanent income hypothesis is justifiable in a general-equilibrium setting. Other justifications could be based on an underlying overlapping generations structure (see Chapter 3) or an endogenous time preference rate (see Supplement B to this chapter).

20. Our shock specification assumed that $E_{s-1} \epsilon_s = 0$ for any s. The law of iterated conditional expectations assures us that for $t < s$, $E_t \left\{ E_{s-1} \epsilon_s \right\} = E_t \epsilon_s = 0$ also. With rational expectations, what you expect today to expect tomorrow must be the same as what you expect today!

Substituting in for $E_t \{Y_s - \bar{Y}\}$ here using eq. (34) yields:

$$C_t = r B_t + \bar{Y} + \frac{r(Y_t - \bar{Y})}{1 + r - \rho}. \tag{35}$$

This simple example yields a "Keynesian" consumption function in the sense that higher current output Y_t raises consumption C_t less than dollar for dollar (except in the special case $\rho = 1$, in which they rise by the same amount). Why? Under stochastic process (33), output can be written as

$$Y_t = \bar{Y} + \sum_{s=-\infty}^{t} \rho^{t-s} \epsilon_s, \tag{36}$$

so that shocks' effects decay geometrically over time provided $\rho < 1$ (they are permanent only if $\rho = 1$).[21] As a result, unexpected shifts in current output cause smaller unexpected shifts in permanent output, so that consumption-smoothing makes consumption respond less than fully to output shocks.

To see implications for the current account, write the consumption function (35) in terms of the unexpected shock to output, the *innovation* ϵ_t :

$$C_t = r B_t + \bar{Y} + \frac{r\rho}{1 + r - \rho}(Y_{t-1} - \bar{Y}) + \frac{r}{1 + r - \rho}\epsilon_t.$$

Substituting this formula into the current account identity $CA_t = r B_t + Y_t - C_t$ gives

$$CA_t = \rho \left(\frac{1 - \rho}{1 + r - \rho} \right)(Y_{t-1} - \bar{Y}) + \left(\frac{1 - \rho}{1 + r - \rho} \right)\epsilon_t. \tag{37}$$

An unexpected positive shock to output ($\epsilon_t > 0$) causes an unexpected rise in the current account surplus when the shock is temporary ($\rho < 1$), because people smooth expected consumption intertemporally through asset accumulation. A permanent shock ($\rho = 1$) has no current account effect because consumption remains level (in expectation) if people simply adjust consumption by the full innovation to output. As we suggested in section 2.2.1, these effects are the same as in a "perfect-foresight" model that permits initial unexpected changes. The latter interpretation corresponds to the dynamic impulse-response profile of the present stochastic model.

Equation (37) shows that the current account also has a predictable component coming from the previous period's expected future output profile. On date $t - 1$,

---

21. To derive eq. (36), use the *lag operator* L (defined so that $LX_t = X_{t-1}$ for any variable X) to write eq. (33) (lagged by one period) as $(1 - \rho L)(Y_t - \bar{Y}) = \epsilon_t$. Its solution is $Y_t - \bar{Y} = (1 - \rho L)^{-1}\epsilon_t$, which is the same as eq. (36). (Supplement C to this chapter reviews the properties of lag operators.) Equation (39) is derived the same way.

people expected the deviation between date t output and its "permanent" level to be

$$E_{t-1} \left\{ Y_t - \frac{r}{1+r} \sum_{s=t}^{\infty} \left(\frac{1}{1+r} \right)^{s-t} Y_s \right\}$$

$$= \rho (Y_{t-1} - \bar{Y}) - \frac{r}{1+r} \sum_{s=t}^{\infty} \left(\frac{1}{1+r} \right)^{s-t} \rho^{s-t+1}(Y_{t-1} - \bar{Y})$$

$$= \rho \left(\frac{1-\rho}{1+r-\rho} \right) (Y_{t-1} - \bar{Y}).$$

Absent the shock ϵ_t, which leads to a revision of expectations on date t, the preceding difference would equal the date t current account, just as in the deterministic current account equation (18) from section 2.2.1.

Now suppose that, rather than following eq. (33), output follows

$$Y_{t+1} - Y_t = \rho \left(Y_t - Y_{t-1} \right) + \epsilon_{t+1} \tag{38}$$

with $0 < \rho < 1$. This process makes output a nonstationary random variable,

$$Y_t = Y_{t-1} + \sum_{s=-\infty}^{t} \rho^{t-s} \epsilon_s. \tag{39}$$

There is only one difference between eqs. (36) and (39), but it is critical. The first equation has $\bar{Y}$ on its right side, the second Y_{t-1}. This difference means that under eq. (38), an output surprise ϵ_t raises Y_{t+1} by $(1+\rho)\epsilon_t$, Y_{t+2} by $(1+\rho+\rho^2)\epsilon_t$, and so on [whereas under eq. (33) the corresponding increases are only $\rho\epsilon_t$, $\rho^2\epsilon_t$, ...]. Because eq. (38) makes all future output levels rise by more than ϵ_t, permanent output fluctuates *more* than current output (except in the special case $\rho = 0$, in which their fluctuations are the same). Consumption smoothing now implies that an unexpected increase in output causes an even greater increase in consumption. As a result, a positive output innovation now implies a current account *deficit*, in sharp contrast to what eq. (37) for the stationary case predicts.[22]

Application: Deaton's Paradox

Deaton (1992) points out that in United States data, the hypothesis that output *growth* is positively serially correlated is difficult to reject statistically. If so, then it is a puzzle why consumption does not move more dramatically in response to output changes than it does. Put differently, given that output appears to be mean reverting in growth rates rather than levels, as in eq. (38), it is a puzzle that standard Keynesian consumption functions match the data at all!

---

22. Exercise 4 at the end of the chapter asks you to verify these claims.

There are several potential answers to "Deaton's paradox." One is that the present model is partial equilibrium and treats the interest rate as exogenous. Even a small country's output is likely to be positively correlated with world productivity, in which case world interest rates can rise along with home output, damping the consumption response. Perhaps the most likely explanation is simply that it is very hard to discriminate empirically between the processes of eqs. (33) and (38) using the relatively short sample of postwar time series data. Thus output shocks may indeed dampen over time, but at such a slow rate that it is difficult to distinguish the true stationary process from a nonstationary one such as eq. (38).

Unfortunately, for ρ near 1 even tiny differences in estimates can imply very big differences in the predicted consumption effect of output shocks. We have already seen that if eq. (33) holds and $\rho = 1$, eq. (35) predicts that output and consumption will move one for one. If instead ρ is very close to 1, say $\rho = 0.96$, and $r = 0.04$, then $r/(1 + r - \rho) = 0.04/(1 + 0.04 - 0.96) = 0.5$, and the consumption response is halved! Intuitively, at a real interest rate of $r = 0.04$, output fifteen years hence has a weight equal to more than half that of current output in permanent output. Thus the consumption response can be quite sensitive to the rate at which output shocks die out.   ∎

2.3.4   Investment

Suppose output is given by the production function $Y_t = A_t F(K_t)$, where the productivity parameter A_t is now a random variable. Since investment is $I_s = K_{s+1} - K_s$, the constrained expected utility function that the representative domestic individual now maximizes, eq. (27), can be written as

$$U_t = \mathrm{E}_t \left\{ \sum_{s=t}^{\infty} \beta^{s-t} u \left[(1+r)B_s - B_{s+1} + A_s F(K_s) - (K_{s+1} - K_s) - G_s \right] \right\}.$$

The first-order condition with respect to B_{t+1} is still the bond Euler equation (29). Differentiating with respect to K_{t+1} yields

$$u'(C_t) = \mathrm{E}_t \left\{ \left[1 + A_{t+1} F'(K_{t+1}) \right] \beta u'(C_{t+1}) \right\}.$$

To interpret this condition, note that $u'(C_t)$ is nonrandom on date t so that dividing it into both sides above gives

$$1 = \mathrm{E}_t \left\{ \left[1 + A_{t+1} F'(K_{t+1}) \right] \frac{\beta u'(C_{t+1})}{u'(C_t)} \right\}$$

$$= \mathrm{E}_t \left\{ 1 + A_{t+1} F'(K_{t+1}) \right\} \mathrm{E}_t \left\{ \frac{\beta u'(C_{t+1})}{u'(C_t)} \right\} + \mathrm{Cov}_t \left\{ A_{t+1} F'(K_{t+1}), \frac{\beta u'(C_{t+1})}{u'(C_t)} \right\},$$

where $\text{Cov}_t\{\cdot, \cdot\}$ denotes the conditional covariance.[23] By using eq. (29) we reduce this expression to

$$E_t\left\{A_{t+1}F'(K_{t+1})\right\} = r - \text{Cov}_t\left\{A_{t+1}F'(K_{t+1}), \frac{u'(C_{t+1})}{u'(C_t)}\right\} \tag{40}$$

after imposing $(1+r)\beta = 1$.

This equation differs from the certainty-equivalence version of eq. (6) only because of the covariance term on its right-hand side. We have assumed that all domestic capital is held by domestic residents, so the covariance is likely to be negative: when capital is unexpectedly productive (A_{t+1} is above its conditional mean), domestic consumption will be unusually high and its marginal utility unexpectedly low [$u'(C_{t+1})$ below its conditional mean]. As a result, the expected marginal product of capital on the left-hand side of eq. (40) must be higher than r, so that the capital stock is lower than in the corresponding certainty-equivalence model. Intuitively, the riskiness of capital discourages investment.

We will say more about investment under uncertainty in Chapter 5. For now we will simply ignore the covariance in eq. (40), assuming that investment is determined according to the certainty-equivalence principle. Implicitly, we are treating the covariance term as a constant. Thus our discussion of investment in the rest of this section captures only part (but probably the main part) of how productivity shocks affect the current account. Empirically, changes in the covariance in eq. (40) are likely to be small compared to changes in the expected productivity of capital or in the real interest rate.

Suppose that the stochastic process governing productivity shocks is

$$A_{t+1} - \bar{A} = \rho(A_t - \bar{A}) + \epsilon_{t+1}, \tag{41}$$

where $0 \le \rho \le 1$ and ϵ_{t+1} is a serially uncorrelated shock with $E_t\epsilon_{t+1} = 0$. When $\rho > 0$, positive productivity shocks not only raise the expected path of future output directly, but they also induce investment (by raising the anticipated return to domestic capital), thereby raising expected future output even further.

An unanticipated productivity increase on date t ($\epsilon_t > 0$) affects the date t current account via two channels, assuming eq. (32) holds. First, it raises investment, tending to worsen the current account as domestic residents borrow abroad to finance additional capital accumulation. Second, the productivity increase affects saving. The magnitude of ρ influences whether date t saving rises, and, if so, by

---

23. The covariance between X and Y, $\text{Cov}\{X, Y\}$, is defined as $E\{(X - EX)(Y - EY)\} = E\{XY\} - E\{X\}E\{Y\}$. (The number $\text{Cov}\{X, X\} \equiv \text{Var}\{X\}$ is called the variance of X. *Conditional* variances and covariances are defined in the same way, but with conditional in place of unconditional expectations operators.) In deriving the covariance in the immediately preceding equation, we made use of the fact that for any constant a_0, $\text{Cov}\{a_0 + X, Y\} = \text{Cov}\{X, Y\}$.

more or less than investment. With reasonable generality, the more persistent productivity shocks are, the lower is $CA_t = S_t - I_t$.

If $\rho = 1$, the current account must fall. Why? The capital stock takes a period to adjust to its new, higher level, so expected future output rises by more than current output on date t. At the same time, current investment rises but expected future investment doesn't change. Saving therefore falls, while investment rises.[24]

On the other hand, if ρ is sufficiently far below 1, future output rises by less than current output, even taking account of any increases in future capital. Since, in addition, the present discounted value of current and expected future investment rises on date t, saving rises; see eq. (32). Saving may rise by even more than investment. In the extreme case $\rho = 0$, there is no investment response at all because a surprise date t productivity increase does not imply that productivity is expected to be any higher on date $t + 1$. The $\rho = 0$ case thus is just like the case of exogenous output. The country runs a higher current account surplus on date t to spread over time the benefits of its temporarily higher output. For four different degrees of persistence ($\rho = 0, 0.25, 0.75$, and 1), Figure 2.3 shows the current account's dynamic response to an unexpected 1 percent rise in productivity on date $t = 0$. (The examples assume that $r = 0.05$ and that $Y = AK^{0.4}$.)[25]

Application: The Relative Impact of Productivity Shocks on Investment and the Current Account

Empirically, productivity shocks for most countries appear to be very highly correlated over time and indeed, it is not easy to reject the hypothesis that $\rho = 1$ in specification (41). As we have just shown, our model predicts that in this case positive productivity shocks cause investment to rise and the current account surplus to fall. Moreover, because saving also falls, the current account effect is larger in absolute value than the investment effect. How does this prediction fare empirically?

Glick and Rogoff (1995) test this hypothesis using annual time series data on productivity shocks, investment, and the current account for the "Group of Seven"

---

24. Why does initial saving fall, or, equivalently, why does consumption initially rise more than output when $\rho = 1$? Assume a pre-shock steady state with $A = \bar{A}$. If the economy did no additional investing in response to the permanent productivity rise, it would be able to raise its consumption permanently by exactly the initial change in output. Saving would not change in this hypothetical case. Since profitable investment raises the economy's intertemporal consumption possibilities, however, an even higher constant consumption path actually is feasible. So saving must fall. For a small shock this further consumption increase is second order, by the envelope theorem.

25. Notice that if $\rho = 0$ or 1 the current account returns to its prior level immediately after date t absent further unexpected productivity shocks. For intermediate ρ values, the current account moves into greater surplus on date $t + 1$ as a result of $\epsilon_t > 0$. (See Figure 2.3.) Output on date $t + 1$ exceeds its permanent level by more, and investment (which is lower than if the shock hadn't occurred) is below its permanent level by more; see eq. (42) below. The dynamics of the current account are quite different when capital installation is costly, as in section 2.5.2. See, for example, Baxter and Crucini (1995).

Change in current account
(percent of initial GDP)

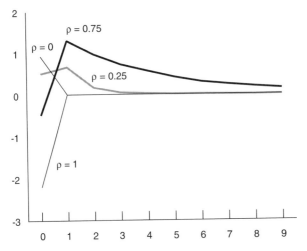

Figure 2.3
Dynamic current-account response to a 1 percent productivity increase

(G-7) countries (the United States, Japan, Germany, France, Italy, the United Kingdom, and Canada). Their analysis allows for partial adjustment in investment (see
section 2.5.2), but this does not alter the model's basic prediction about the relative size of the current-account and investment responses to permanent productivity
shocks.

Glick and Rogoff derive and estimate equations of the form

$$\Delta I_t = a_0 + a_1 \Delta A_t^C + a_2 \Delta A_t^W + a_3 I_{t-1},$$

$$\Delta C A_t = b_0 + b_1 \Delta A_t^C + b_2 \Delta A_t^W + b_3 I_{t-1},$$

where A^W is a shock to global productivity and A^C is the country-specific (idiosyncratic) component of productivity shocks; the lagged I terms arise from costs
of adjustment in investment. The distinction between global and country-specific
productivity shocks is essential for any sensible empirical implementation of the
model. Our theoretical analysis has implicitly treated all productivity shocks as
affecting only the small country in question, but in reality there is likely to be a
common component to such shocks across countries.

Why is the local-global distinction so important? If a shock hits all countries in
the world symmetrically, the current account effect will be much smaller (under
some conditions zero) than if it hits just the one small country. If all countries try
to dissave at once, the main effect will be for global interest rates to rise. There
are a number of approaches for trying to decompose shocks into local and global
components. In the results reported here, global productivity shocks are simply a

Table 2.2
Pooled Time-Series Regressions for the G-7 Countries, 1961–90

Dependent Variable	a_1	a_2	a_3
ΔI	0.35	0.53	−0.10
	(0.03)	(0.06)	(0.04)
	b_1	b_2	b_3
ΔCA	−0.17	0.01	0.04
	(0.03)	(0.02)	(0.03)

Standard errors in parentheses. Regressions include a time trend.
Source: Glick and Rogoff (1995).

GNP-weighted average of total productivity shocks for each of the seven countries, and country-specific shocks are formed taking the difference between the total productivity shock hitting each country and the global shock.

Assuming A^C (but not necessarily A^W) follows a random walk (a hypothesis the data do not reject), then the model predicts that $a_1 > 0$, $b_1 < 0$, and $|b_1| > a_1$. The model also predicts that $a_2 > 0$ and $b_2 = 0$: global shocks raise investment in all countries leaving the world current account pattern unchanged. The econometric results, reported in Table 2.2, use labor-productivity measures to proxy total productivity A.

The data do not reject the hypothesis $b_2 = 0$, that is, that global productivity shocks do not affect current accounts. The same finding emerges from virtually all the individual-country regressions, and it appears to be robust to various changes in specification. As predicted by the model, a_1, which measures the impact of country-specific productivity shocks on investment, is positive, and b_1, which measures the impact of country-specific productivity shocks on the current account, is negative. However, the estimated absolute value of b_1 is consistently smaller than the estimate of a_1. Results for the individual-country specifications are generally similar to the pooled cross-country regressions shown in Table 2.2.

Why does investment respond much more sharply to productivity shocks than the current account does? Glick and Rogoff argue that the most likely explanation is the same as the one suggested earlier for the Deaton paradox. Even if the true process $A_t^C = \rho A_{t-1}^C + \epsilon_t^C$ has ρ only slightly less than 1, the current account effect of a country-specific productivity change can be greatly muted. For $\rho = 0.96$ (in annual data), Glick and Rogoff show that theoretically, a_1 can be more than eight times as large as $|b_1|$. Thus the fact that current accounts appear less sensitive than investment to country-specific productivity shocks is not necessarily evidence against integrated G-7 markets for borrowing and lending.   ■

*2.3.5   A Test of the Stochastic Small-Country Current Account Model

The certainty equivalence consumption function (32) implies that an equation fully parallel to eq. (18) governs the current account in a stochastic setting, with the present discounted sums in the deterministic equation simply replaced by their conditional expected values. Thus, eq. (18) is replaced by

$$CA_t = B_{t+1} - B_t = (Y_t - E_t \tilde{Y}_t) - (I_t - E_t \tilde{I}_t) - (G_t - E_t \tilde{G}_t) \tag{42}$$

where, for any variable X,

$$E_t \tilde{X}_t = \frac{r}{1+r} \sum_{s=t}^{\infty} \left(\frac{1}{1+r} \right)^{s-t} E_t X_s.$$

Several econometric studies have tested implications of stochastic current account models like the one in eq. (42). Here we describe an approach, suggested by Campbell's (1987) work on saving, that makes full use of the model's structure to derive testable hypotheses.[26]

Define *net output* Z as output less government consumption and investment,

$$Z \equiv Y - G - I.$$

This definition gives eq. (42) the simple form $CA_t = Z_t - E_t \tilde{Z}_t$. Campbell's approach starts by rearranging the terms in eq. (42) as

$$CA_t = - \sum_{s=t+1}^{\infty} \left(\frac{1}{1+r} \right)^{s-t} E_t \Delta Z_s, \tag{43}$$

where $\Delta Z_s = Z_s - Z_{s-1}$. Equation (43) shows that the current account is in deficit when the present discounted value of future net output changes is positive, and it is in surplus in the opposite case. Put briefly, the current account deficit is a predictor of future increases in net output.[27]

How might we test eq. (43)? Ideally we would posit a model allowing us to estimate the right-hand side of eq. (43), and then compare its prediction to actual current account data.

Even to get started, however, we need some proxy for the expected values eq. (43) contains. Current and lagged net output changes are useful in predicting future net output changes (as our discussion of Deaton's paradox has suggested), but consumers plainly have more information than that available. One way to capture

---

26. The extension of Campbell's methodology to the current account is due to Sheffrin and Woo (1990), Otto (1992), and Ghosh (1995). Ghosh and Ostry (1995) apply the test to a sample of developing countries. (Exercise 5 at the end of the chapter describes an alternative way to do the test.) The same methodology is applied to stock prices by Campbell and Shiller (1987). For a survey of other empirical tests of consumption-smoothing current account theories, see Obstfeld and Rogoff (1995b).

27. You are asked to derive eq. (43) in exercise 6 at the end of the chapter.

the additional information of consumers is to have them base forecasts on the current and lagged *current account* in addition to current and lagged net output changes. Indeed, under the null hypothesis of eq. (43), the current account itself should incorporate all of consumers' information on future net output changes.

These considerations lead us to assume that consumers' forecasts of ΔZ_s for $s > t$ are based on the first-order vector autoregressive (VAR) model

$$\begin{bmatrix} \Delta Z_s \\ CA_s \end{bmatrix} = \begin{bmatrix} \psi_{11} & \psi_{12} \\ \psi_{21} & \psi_{22} \end{bmatrix} \begin{bmatrix} \Delta Z_{s-1} \\ CA_{s-1} \end{bmatrix} + \begin{bmatrix} \epsilon_{1s} \\ \epsilon_{2s} \end{bmatrix}, \tag{44}$$

where ϵ_1 and ϵ_2 are errors with conditional means of zero and where ΔZ and CA are now expressed as deviations from unconditional means. (At the cost of additional complexity, a higher-order VAR could be analyzed.) It is easy to forecast future output changes using eq. (44). In analogy with the one-variable case,

$$E_t \begin{bmatrix} \Delta Z_s \\ CA_s \end{bmatrix} = \begin{bmatrix} \psi_{11} & \psi_{12} \\ \psi_{21} & \psi_{22} \end{bmatrix}^{s-t} \begin{bmatrix} \Delta Z_t \\ CA_t \end{bmatrix}.$$

Premultiplication by the 1×2 vector $[\,1 \quad 0\,]$ yields $E_t \Delta Z_s$:

$$E_t \Delta Z_s = [\,1 \quad 0\,] \begin{bmatrix} \psi_{11} & \psi_{12} \\ \psi_{21} & \psi_{22} \end{bmatrix}^{s-t} \begin{bmatrix} \Delta Z_t \\ CA_t \end{bmatrix}.$$

To calculate the right-hand side of eq. (43), substitute this formula. If we define Ψ to be the matrix $[\psi_{ij}]$, the result is our model's prediction of the current account, $\widehat{CA}_t$. Let $\mathbf{I}$ be the 2×2 identity matrix. Then[28]

$$\widehat{CA}_t = -[\,1 \quad 0\,] \left(\frac{1}{1+r} \Psi \right) \left(\mathbf{I} - \frac{1}{1+r} \Psi \right)^{-1} \begin{bmatrix} \Delta Z_t \\ CA_t \end{bmatrix}$$

$$\equiv [\, \Phi_{\Delta Z} \quad \Phi_{CA} \,] \begin{bmatrix} \Delta Z_t \\ CA_t \end{bmatrix}. \tag{45}$$

This is the predicted current account that we compare to actual data.

The comparison is very easy. The variable CA_t is included in the date t information set upon which consumers base date t consumption. Furthermore, current account equation (43) equates CA_t to the same variable that equation (45) is supposed to be estimating. Thus, if our model and forecasting equation are valid, $\widehat{CA}_t$ should equal CA_t up to the sampling error in the econometrician's estimate of VAR

---

28. The following formula is derived by summing the matrix geometric series

$$\left(\frac{1}{1+r} \Psi \right) \sum_{s=t}^{\infty} \left(\frac{1}{1+r} \right)^{s-t} \Psi^{s-t}$$

via the matrix analog of the same formula that applies in the scalar case.

(44). To evaluate the model, we therefore test the hypothesis that $[\, \Phi_{\Delta Z} \quad \Phi_{CA} \,] = [\, 0 \quad 1 \,]$ in eq. (45), so that $CA_t = \widehat{CA}_t$.[29]

Figures 2.4 through 2.8 graph both CA_t and $\widehat{CA}_t$ for Belgium, Canada, Denmark, Sweden, and the United Kingdom. For each of these industrial countries, the VAR (44) is estimated with annual data, and an annual real interest rate of $r = 0.04$ is used to form the 1×2 matrix $[\, \Phi_{\Delta Z} \quad \Phi_{CA} \,]$ in (45).[30] The VAR characterizing the Belgian data, for example, is

$$\begin{bmatrix} \Delta Z_t \\ CA_t \end{bmatrix} = \begin{bmatrix} 0.20 & -0.09 \\ -0.03 & 0.83 \end{bmatrix} \begin{bmatrix} \Delta Z_{t-1} \\ CA_{t-1} \end{bmatrix} + \begin{bmatrix} \epsilon_{1t} \\ \epsilon_{2t} \end{bmatrix}.$$

Given how rudimentary the model is, there is no surprise in its failure to track current accounts exactly. (In Belgium's case, for example, the model yields the estimate $[\, \widehat{\Phi}_{\Delta Z} \quad \widehat{\Phi}_{CA} \,] = [\, -0.26 \quad 0.54 \,]$ and a formal test rejects the [0, 1] null hypothesis.) The empirical implementation ignored the distinction between global and country-specific shocks. Also contradicting the model's basis, the four European countries under study limited residents' access to world capital markets over much of the sample period. The model fares especially poorly in United Kingdom data (Figure 2.8): the near random-walk followed by U.K. net output implies little variability in $\widehat{CA}_t$, yet CA_t is very variable.

---

29. Perhaps surprisingly, the restriction $CA_t = \widehat{CA}_t$ must hold even when the assumed forecasting eq. (44) represents only *part* of the information consumers use to predict future net output. We have already noted the reason. Under the null hypothesis, $-CA_t$ represents the consumer's best forecast of the present discounted value of future net output changes *no matter what other information he has*. To see this formally, let $\mathfrak{I}_t$ denote the full date t information set of consumers, which contains past and current realizations of ΔZ and CA, and possibly more. Under the theory, eq. (43) can be written

$$CA_t = -\mathrm{E} \left\{ \sum_{s=t+1}^{\infty} \left(\frac{1}{1+r} \right)^{s-t} \Delta Z_s \,\bigg|\, \mathfrak{I}_t \right\},$$

where $\mathrm{E}\{\cdot \mid \mathfrak{I}_t\}$ is an expectation conditional on information set $\mathfrak{I}_t$. Notice, however, that if we apply conditional expectations with respect to ΔZ_t and CA_t on both sides of this equation, the result is

$$\mathrm{E}\{CA_t \mid \Delta Z_t, CA_t\} = CA_t = -\mathrm{E} \left\{ \mathrm{E} \left\{ \sum_{s=t+1}^{\infty} \left(\frac{1}{1+r} \right)^{s-t} \Delta Z_s \,\bigg|\, \mathfrak{I}_t \right\} \bigg| \Delta Z_t, CA_t \right\}$$

$$= -\mathrm{E} \left\{ \sum_{s=t+1}^{\infty} \left(\frac{1}{1+r} \right)^{s-t} \Delta Z_s \,\bigg|\, \Delta Z_t, CA_t \right\},$$

where the last equality follows from the law of iterated conditional expectations. If conditional expectations are linear projections on past information, however, the last term in this string of equalities simply equals $\widehat{CA}_t$, the conditional expectation based on the VAR in eq. (44).

30. Data are drawn from International Monetary Fund, *International Financial Statistics*. Data sample periods for the five countries are 1954–90 (Belgium), 1952–90 (Canada), 1951–90 (Denmark, Sweden), and 1949–90 (United Kingdom).

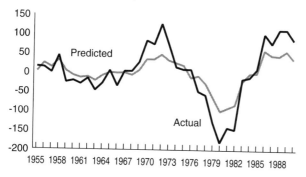

Figure 2.4
Belgium: Actual and predicted current accounts

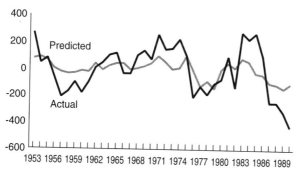

Figure 2.5
Canada: Actual and predicted current accounts

What *is* surprising, in view of the model's many simplifying assumptions, is the visual evidence in Figures 2.4 through 2.7. Graphically, the model does quite well in capturing shifts in the current accounts of Belgium, Canada, Denmark, and, especially, Sweden. This success suggests that, in the case of industrial countries experiencing short-run fluctuations in net output, current-account models based on consumption smoothing can have significant explanatory power.[31]

---

31. Campbell's (1987) original application of the preceding test was to financial saving in the United States. In analogy with the arguments we have made, the permanent income theory of consumption implies that total financial saving is (minus) the present value of future changes in labor income. The open-economy test explored in this section focuses on changes in a narrower asset category—foreign assets—and, correspondingly, involves expected future changes in a broader income measure. Direct comparison of the results of our tests with Campbell's results therefore is difficult. (However, for the version of the permanent-income model that he tested, Campbell reached conclusions very similar to those we reached concerning the consumption-smoothing current-account model.)

1985 kroner per capita

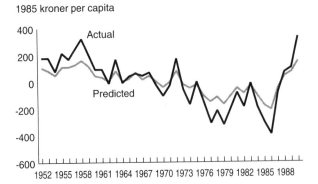

Figure 2.6
Denmark: Actual and predicted current accounts

1985 kronor per capita

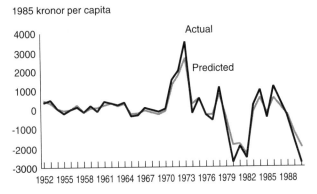

Figure 2.7
Sweden: Actual and predicted current accounts

2.3.6   Precautionary Saving

The permanent income consumption formula (32) overstates a country's consumption if individuals engage in *precautionary saving* that depends on the *variability* of future net output and not just expected values.

The extent of precautionary saving depends in part on the third derivative of the utility function, $u'''(C)$, which equals zero for quadratic utility. To see how the third derivative matters, look at the stochastic Euler equation (29). If $u'''(C) > 0$, marginal utility $u'(C)$ is a convex function of C. By Jensen's inequality, a rise in uncertainty about period $t + 1$ income that causes C_{t+1} to be more variable also raises $E_t\{u'(C_{t+1})\}$. In order for the Euler condition to continue holding, C_t must fall. That is, the consumer will respond to increased income uncertainty by

1985 pounds sterling per capita

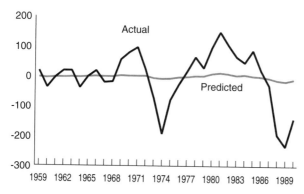

Figure 2.8
United Kingdom: Actual and predicted current accounts

saving more. For many commonly used utility functions such as isoelastic utility, $u'''(C) > 0$, implying a positive motive for precautionary saving.[32]

We have already observed (on p. 82) that consumption could become negative under a certainty-equivalence theory of consumption. If negative consumption levels are ruled out (as they would be with isoelastic period utility, for example), consumers with low wealth will be reluctant to borrow even in the face of temporarily low income. Borrowing might leave them vulnerable to further negative income shocks that force them to consume nothing in order to respect the intertemporal budget constraint with probability one. Instead, consumers will wish to accumulate a buffer of assets to be run down in case of negative income shocks. Greater uncertainty will increase the propensity to acquire such a buffer.

Thus precautionary behavior may dominate consumption behavior at low wealth levels, becoming less important as wealth rises. Even if consumers have constant discount rates equal to the interest rate r, their consumption and wealth will tend to rise over time (but at a declining rate) if wealth initially is low. In this respect, the predictions of models with precautionary saving are similar to those of models with endogenous rates of time preference such as the one in Supplement B to this chapter.

---

32. For isoelastic utility, $u'(C) = C^{-1/\sigma}$ so

$$u'''(C) = \frac{1}{\sigma}\left(1 + \frac{1}{\sigma}\right)C^{-(1/\sigma)-2} > 0.$$

Leland (1968), Zeldes (1989b), Caballero (1991), and Deaton (1992) discuss the theory of precautionary saving. United States evidence on its importance is presented by Carroll (1992) and Gourinchas and Parker (1995).

Having shown how to extend our analysis to incorporate uncertainty, we will revert to the perfect-foresight case for the remainder of the chapter.

2.4   Consumer Durables and the Current Account

A significant portion of measured consumption spending reflects purchases of *consumer durables*—long-lived items such as furniture, autos, televisions, and home computers. As we noted in Chapter 1, if all durables were rented in perfect rental markets, the durable-nondurable distinction would be unimportant. Empirically, however, consumer purchases of durable items are substantial. In the United States, for example, 18.1 percent of 1994 consumption spending was devoted to durables (including clothing and shoes). In this section we present a modified consumption theory and explore how consumer durables change our view of the current account.[33]

2.4.1   A Simple Model with Consumer Durables

Let C_s stand in this section for the individual's consumption of *non*durables on date s, and let D_s be the stock of durable goods the consumer owns as date s ends. A stock of durables yields its owner a proportional service flow each period it is owned. The representative consumer in a small country has perfect foresight and maximizes

$$U_t = \sum_{s=t}^{\infty} \beta^{s-t} \left[\gamma \log C_s + (1 - \gamma) \log D_s \right], \tag{46}$$

subject to an intertemporal budget constraint. Notice our convention that durables begin to yield services in the same period they are first purchased.[34]

Let p be the price of durable goods in terms of nondurable consumption; we assume that p is determined in the world market and taken as given by the small country. Assuming that bonds are indexed to nondurables consumption and that the durables stock depreciates at rate δ, the period-to-period finance constraint of the consumer is

$$B_{s+1} - B_s = r_s B_s + Y_s - C_s - p_s[D_s - (1 - \delta)D_{s-1}] - (K_{s+1} - K_s) - G_s,$$

---

33. For a closed-economy model with durables, see Mankiw (1987a). Burda and Gerlach (1992) conduct an empirical study of durables in U.S. international trade flows.

34. In contrast, our assumption on producer durables (i.e., capital) has been that the service flow commences a period after the capital is "purchased" with forgone consumption. A parallel treatment of consumer durables would not alter our main points. It is because durables, unlike capital, begin to yield services (and to depreciate) in the same period they are acquired that we label durables accumulated through period s as D_s rather than D_{s+1}.

where $p_s[D_s - (1 - \delta)D_{s-1}]$ is the cost of durable goods purchases in period s. After using the finance constraint to eliminate C_s from eq. (46) and the production function $Y_s = F(K_s)$ to eliminate Y_s, we can derive first-order conditions for the individual's maximization problem by differentiating with respect to B, K, and D.

The necessary conditions include the usual condition that equates the marginal product of capital to r_{s+1} and

$$C_{s+1} = (1 + r_{s+1})\beta C_s,$$

$$\frac{\gamma p_s}{C_s} = \frac{1 - \gamma}{D_s} + \beta(1 - \delta)\frac{\gamma p_{s+1}}{C_{s+1}}.$$

The first of these conditions looks just like the usual consumption Euler equation when the elasticity of intertemporal substitution is 1. It holds here for nondurables consumption because the period utility function is additive in nondurables and durables. The second of the preceding conditions is new. This intertemporal Euler equation emphasizes that the purchase of a durable item is partly an investment. For the path of durables to be optimal, the marginal utility cost of acquiring a durable must equal its immediate service yield plus the discounted marginal utility of the revenue from selling what is left of the durable next period.

A useful perspective on the solution comes from combining the two Euler conditions into one by eliminating C_{s+1}:

$$\frac{(1 - \gamma)C_s}{\gamma D_s} = p_s - \frac{1 - \delta}{1 + r_{s+1}}p_{s+1} \equiv \iota_s. \tag{47}$$

The variable ι_s above is the implicit date s rental price, or *user cost*, of the durable good. Given a resale market with no transaction costs, user cost equals the net expense of buying the durable in one period, using it in the same period, and selling it the next. Equation (47) states that, at an optimum, the marginal rate of substitution of nondurables consumption for the services of durables equals the user cost of durables in terms of nondurables consumption.

To derive solutions for expenditure levels, we must write down the intertemporal budget constraint corresponding to the finance constraint we used earlier. There are several ways to represent the intertemporal constraint: one that is particularly useful is

$$\sum_{s=t}^{\infty} \left(\frac{1}{1+r}\right)^{s-t} (C_s + \iota_s D_s)$$

$$= (1 + r)B_t + (1 - \delta)p_t D_{t-1} + \sum_{s=t}^{\infty} \left(\frac{1}{1+r}\right)^{s-t} (Y_s - G_s - I_s), \tag{48}$$

where we have simplified by assuming a constant interest rate. This constraint states that the present value of expenditures—the sum of nondurables purchases plus the implicit rental cost of the durables held—equals initial financial assets (including durables) plus the present value of net output.

Combining (47) and (48) and assuming $\beta = 1/(1+r)$ (as in the permanent income theory), one can solve for the consumption of nondurables as

$$C_t = \frac{\gamma r}{1+r} \left[(1+r)B_t + (1-\delta)p_t D_{t-1} + \sum_{s=t}^{\infty} \left(\frac{1}{1+r} \right)^{s-t} (Y_s - G_s - I_s) \right], \quad (49)$$

while consumption of durables services is

$$D_t = \frac{(1-\gamma)r}{\iota_t(1+r)} \left[(1+r)B_t + (1-\delta)p_t D_{t-1} + \sum_{s=t}^{\infty} \left(\frac{1}{1+r} \right)^{s-t} (Y_s - G_s - I_s) \right].$$

Let's assume for simplicity that p_t and hence the user cost ι_t also are constant. Then C_t and D_t always move in proportion, and the consumer smooths the paths of both. By smoothing D_t, the consumer smooths the service flow of durable services. Note that the consumer does not smooth the path of expenditures $p[D_s - (1 - \delta)D_{s-1}]$ on durables. In the special case where r and p are both fixed and where durables do not deteriorate ($\delta = 0$), the consumer makes all planned durable goods purchases in one lump sum in the first period, and, absent shocks, makes no further purchases thereafter. In a linear-quadratic variant of this same simple case where income is stochastic, the level of durable goods holdings follows a random walk (as does nondurable goods consumption). *Expenditures* on durable goods, however, are serially uncorrelated.

2.4.2   Implications for the Current Account

To see how durables can affect the current account, we continue to take the world price of durable goods, p, as constant. With p constant, eq. (47) implies that, for all $s \geq t$,

$$p = \left(\frac{1+r}{r+\delta} \right) \left(\frac{1-\gamma}{\gamma} \right) \frac{C_s}{D_s}. \quad (50)$$

Let $Z = Y - G - I$ again. The current account in period t can be written

$$CA_t = B_{t+1} - B_t = r B_t + Z_t - \frac{C_t}{\gamma} + \frac{(1-\gamma)C_t}{\gamma} - p[D_t - (1-\delta)D_{t-1}].$$

Use eq. (49) to substitute for the first occurrence of C_t in this equation and get

$$CA_t = \left\{ Z_t - \frac{r}{1+r} \sum_{s=t}^{\infty} \left(\frac{1}{1+r} \right)^{s-t} Z_s \right\}$$

$$- \frac{r}{1+r}(1-\delta)p D_{t-1} + \frac{(1-\gamma)C_t}{\gamma} - p D_t + (1-\delta)p D_{t-1},$$

Equation (50) allows us to get rid of C_t in this expression, so that we can combine the last four additive terms. What results is a modified version of the fundamental current account equation (18),

$$CA_t = (Y_t - \tilde{Y}_t) - (I_t - \tilde{I}_t) - (G_t - \tilde{G}_t) + (\iota - p)\Delta D_t. \tag{51}$$

When the demand for durables changes, consumers spend p to purchase them outright rather than renting their services period-by-period at cost ι. Equation (51) shows that, aside from this factor, the current account is determined exactly as it would be in an economy with no durables. As the depreciation rate for durables, δ, approaches 1, ι approaches p [see eq. (47)], and the final term disappears. Qualitatively, when durable goods are an important component of demand, the current account may become more variable, since agents tend to lump their purchases of durable goods. Of course, if durable goods could be rented instead of purchased, this issue would disappear.

2.5   Firms, the Labor Market, and Investment

So far in this book we have usually thought of producers as self-employed "yeoman farmers" who invest with the goal of maximizing their lifetime consumption opportunities. That paradigm has allowed us to cut quickly to many key results. We have asked the reader to accept on faith (and by analogy with Chapter 1) that the results would be exactly the same as if we had explicitly allowed for markets in capital and labor.

It is now time, however, to introduce those markets and to verify the claimed parallels. In taking this step, we are motivated by more than a desire to check a special case of the second welfare theorem of economics. Vital topics in macroeconomics, such as labor supply and the theory of investment, require one to think about the way in which wages and stock prices are determined. Introducing factor markets will prove very helpful in developing our economic intuition about economies with more than one industry. Finally, we will have to abandon the yeoman farmer paradigm if we want to study economies where individuals are asymmetrically endowed with factors and productive opportunities. In this case, market-driven reallocation of factors among employers is a prerequisite for productive efficiency. Furthermore, changes in the economy will generally have redistributive effects that are best understood through an examination of how factor prices change.

This section will illustrate a number of advantages of analyzing the economy in terms of its capital and labor markets. Other advantages are illustrated in succeeding chapters. Our discussion will draw heavily on the results about homogeneous production functions reviewed in section 1.5.1. We do not introduce uncertainty explicitly into the theoretical development, but instead assume perfect foresight except for initial shocks.

2.5.1   Financial Wealth and Human Wealth

We now assume that output is given by the aggregate production function $Y = AF(K, L)$, where L is the amount of labor employed and $F(K, L)$ is homogeneous of degree one. We also assume initially that the representative individual's labor supply is constant at a level which we also denote by (a nonsuperscripted) L. Under the assumption that there is no international labor mobility, the fixed domestic supply of labor makes the aggregate production function the same as the one we have been analyzing in representative yeoman farmer economies.

Given our assumption of constant returns, we can think of output as being produced by a single representative domestic firm that behaves competitively and is owned entirely by domestic residents. The firm hires labor at wage w and makes investment decisions, producing output according to the aggregate production function. Anyone can buy a share of the firm's future profits in the stock market. Our convention is to denote the date t price of a claim to the firm's entire *future* profits (starting on date $t + 1$) by V_t.

We could, alternatively, imagine an economy organized so that firms rent capital from consumers who directly own it and make investment decisions on their own. It is a good exercise to convince yourself that all the results we will derive in this section would carry through in that alternative setup.

2.5.1.1   The Consumer's Problem

Let x_{s+1} be the share of the domestic firm owned by the representative consumer at the end of date s and d_s the dividends the firm issues on date s. The individual enters a period holding foreign assets and shares purchased the period before. He receives interest and dividends on those assets, may earn capital gains or losses on shares, earns labor income, and consumes. Savings are divided between increases in foreign assets and in the value of shares to be carried into the next period. The consumer thus solves the problem of maximizing U_t, given in eq. (11), subject to the finance constraints

$$B_{s+1} - B_s + V_s x_{s+1} - V_{s-1} x_s = r B_s + d_s x_s$$
$$+ (V_s - V_{s-1}) x_s + w_s L - C_s - G_s, \qquad (52)$$

where we have assumed all taxes to be personal rather than corporate. (We also assume a constant interest rate, although nothing depends on this assumption.)

Following our usual modus operandi, we substitute for consumption in lifetime utility and maximize

$$U_t = \sum_{s=t}^{\infty} \beta^{s-t} u \left[(1 + r) B_s - B_{s+1} - V_s (x_{s+1} - x_s) + d_s x_s + w_s L - G_s \right].$$

Differentiation with respect to B_{s+1} and x_{s+1} gives the familiar Euler equation (5) plus the new first-order condition

$$V_s u'(C_s) = (V_{s+1} + d_{s+1})\beta u'(C_{s+1}).$$

Comparing this with eq. (5), we see that under perfect foresight, consumers will be indifferent on the margin between foreign assets and shares provided the gross rate of return on shares equals the gross real interest rate:

$$1 + r = \frac{d_{s+1} + V_{s+1}}{V_s}. \tag{53}$$

We can use this equality to reformulate the individual's budget constraint in a useful way. Let Q_{s+1} denote the value of the individual's *financial wealth* at the end of period s, the sum of foreign assets and domestic shares:

$$Q_{s+1} = B_{s+1} + V_s x_{s+1}.$$

Equation (53), which always holds in the future along a perfect-foresight path, implies

$$d_s x_s + (V_s - V_{s-1})x_s = r V_{s-1} x_s \tag{54}$$

when lagged a period. We thus can write the constraints (52) for $s > t$ as

$$Q_{s+1} - Q_s = r Q_s + w_s L - C_s - G_s.$$

This version of the budget constraint holds only in the absence of unexpected shocks that might force an ex post departure from the arbitrage condition (53). It therefore does not apply on the initial date t, since we are allowing for the possibility that an unanticipated shock occurs between $t - 1$ and t.

For the initial date $s = t$, we must use eq. (52),

$$Q_{t+1} = (1+r)B_t + d_t x_t + V_t x_t + w_t L - C_t - G_t.$$

Applying to eq. (52) the forward iteration argument that we have already used several times yields the individual intertemporal budget constraint

$$\sum_{s=t}^{\infty} \left(\frac{1}{1+r}\right)^{s-t} C_s$$

$$= (1+r)B_t + d_t x_t + V_t x_t + \sum_{s=t}^{\infty} \left(\frac{1}{1+r}\right)^{s-t} (w_s L - G_s). \tag{55}$$

The constraint limits the present value of consumption to beginning-of-period financial wealth plus the present value of after-tax labor income. In writing eq. (55) we have imposed the individual's transversality condition,

$$\lim_{T \to \infty} \left(\frac{1}{1+r} \right)^T Q_{t+T+1} = 0,$$

which can be justified by the same argument that led to eq. (13).

2.5.1.2   The Stock Market Value of the Firm

We have now developed the individual Euler equations and budget constraint. To compare equilibrium outcomes with those we found for the yeoman farmer economy, we must take a detailed look at the behavior of asset prices and firms, and then combine what we learn with the consumer's demand functions.

Equation (53) implies that, on date t,

$$V_t = \frac{d_{t+1}}{1+r} + \frac{V_{t+1}}{1+r}.$$

Since the corresponding expression for the following date holds, it also is true that

$$V_t = \frac{d_{t+1}}{1+r} + \frac{d_{t+2}}{(1+r)^2} + \frac{V_{t+2}}{(1+r)^2}.$$

Continuing in this way, we find that

$$V_t = \sum_{s=t+1}^{\infty} \left(\frac{1}{1+r} \right)^{s-t} d_s \tag{56}$$

provided a condition ruling out self-fulfilling speculative asset-price bubbles,

$$\lim_{T \to \infty} \left(\frac{1}{1+r} \right)^T V_{t+T} = 0, \tag{57}$$

holds true. We simply assume condition (57), deferring extended discussion until appendix 2B. Given this assumption, eq. (56) shows that a firm's market value on date t is the present discounted value of the dividends it will pay shareholders over the future, starting on date $t+1$. For this reason, we will sometimes call V_t the firm's *ex dividend* market value on date t.[35]

2.5.1.3   Firm Behavior

The dividends a firm pays out in a period are its current profits, equal to earnings, $Y_s - w_s L_s$, less investment expenditures.[36] Thus, eq. (56) implies

---

35. The expression "ex dividend" signifies that the share price V_t is paid by a buyer on date t only after the firm has issued its dividend for the period.

36. Nothing in the model precludes negative dividends. If the unrealism of this possibility bothers you, you may assume that the firm borrows to cover any excess of investment over earnings. Exercise (the Modigliani-Miller theorem): Show that allowing firms to borrow and lend does not affect any of the results that follow.

$$V_t = \sum_{s=t+1}^{\infty} \left(\frac{1}{1+r}\right)^{s-t} \left[A_s F(K_s, L_s) - w_s L_s - (K_{s+1} - K_s)\right]. \tag{58}$$

The firm makes current hiring and investment decisions to maximize the present value of current *and* future dividends, equal to $d_t + V_t$, given K_t:

$$d_t + V_t = \sum_{s=t}^{\infty} \left(\frac{1}{1+r}\right)^{s-t} \left[A_s F(K_s, L_s) - w_s L_s - (K_{s+1} - K_s)\right].$$

(Notice that the preceding infinite sum starts at $s = t$ instead of $s = t + 1$.) By differentiating the last expression, we find that the firm's maximizing first-order conditions for capital and labor are the familiar

$$A_s F_K(K_s, L_s) = r$$

for $s > t$, and, for $s \geq t$, the equality of the wage and the marginal product of labor,

$$A_s F_L(K_s, L_s) = w_s.$$

Again, capital can be adjusted only after a period, so an unexpected date t shock could cause $A_t F_K(K_t, L_t)$ to differ from r ex post. Labor input, however, can be adjusted immediately, so the labor first-order condition holds exactly even in the initial post-shock period t.

Since the marginal product of capital will equal the interest rate (for $s > t$), investment in the present economy is the same as in the yeoman farmer economy. What about consumption? We have already verified that eq. (5) holds, so consumption will be exactly the same if consumers face the same budget constraint in equilibrium. To see that they do, use the definition $d_t = Y_t - w_t L_t - I_t$, impose the equilibrium conditions that

$$x_s = 1, \qquad L_s = L$$

on all dates s, and use eq. (58) to substitute for V_t in eq. (55). The result is eq. (14), the same constraint the yeoman farmer faced.

2.5.1.4   Intertemporal Budget Constraints in Terms of Financial and Human Wealth

An alternative representation of the equilibrium intertemporal budget constraint often proves useful, so we pause to mention it now. Recall that by Euler's theorem $AF(K, L) = AF_K K + AF_L L = rK + wL$ (see section 1.5).[37] Using this information, you can show that eq. (58) for V_t implies

---

37. The results of section 1.5 also show that w is determined by r and A.

$$V_t = \sum_{s=t+1}^{\infty} \left(\frac{1}{1+r}\right)^{s-t} \left[rK_s - (K_{s+1} - K_s)\right]$$

$$= \sum_{s=t+1}^{\infty} \left(\frac{1}{1+r}\right)^{s-t} \left[(1+r)K_s - K_{s+1}\right] = K_{t+1}. \tag{59}$$

Thus the maximizing firm's ex dividend market value equals the capital in place for production next period. A consequence is that, in equilibrium, $Q = B + K$: the economy's end-of-period financial wealth is the sum of its net foreign assets and capital.

These results and eq. (54) reduce the representative individual budget constraint (55) to

$$\sum_{s=t}^{\infty} \left(\frac{1}{1+r}\right)^{s-t} C_s = \left[(1+r)B_t + (1+r)K_t\right] + \sum_{s=t}^{\infty} \left(\frac{1}{1+r}\right)^{s-t} (w_s L - G_s)$$

$$= (1+r)Q_t + \sum_{s=t}^{\infty} \left(\frac{1}{1+r}\right)^{s-t} (w_s L - G_s) \tag{60}$$

in equilibrium, provided the ex post rate of return to capital between periods $t-1$ and t was r.[38] Constraint (60) distinguishes between two sources of lifetime income, financial wealth and *human wealth*, the latter defined as the present value of after-tax labor income. The distinction will have important ramifications in several subsequent chapters.

Constraint (60) also leads to an alternative representation of the consumption function. For example, if $\beta = 1/(1+r)$, consumption is

$$C_t = rQ_t + \frac{r}{1+r} \sum_{s=t}^{\infty} \left(\frac{1}{1+r}\right)^{s-t} (w_s L - G_s). \tag{61}$$

It is a stochastic version of this consumption function, rather than eq. (32), that most closed-economy tests of the permanent income hypothesis examine.

Equation (61) leads, in turn, to an alternative version of the fundamental current account equation, eq. (18), which assumes $1 + r$ is fixed and equal to $1/\beta$. In deriving it we relax the assumption that labor supply is constant. Recall from eq. (14) of Chapter 1 that the current account CA equals national saving, S, less investment, I. Since $S_t = rQ_t + w_t L_t - G_t - C_t$, eq. (61) shows that the current account is

$$CA_t = \left[w_t L_t - \left(\widetilde{w_t L_t}\right)\right] - (G_t - \tilde{G}_t) - I_t,$$

---

38. More generally, date t capital income rK_t would be replaced by $Y_t - w_t L$ in eq. (60) to allow for initial surprises.

where tildes denote "permanent" values. Permanent investment and the terms involving capital's present and future output shares drop out. Adding investment to both sides gives an equivalent equation,

$$S_t = \left[w_t L_t - \left(\widetilde{w_t L_t} \right) \right] - (G_t - \tilde{G}_t),$$

which is the saving function typically assumed in closed-economy tests of the permanent income hypothesis, such as Campbell (1987). As before, these simple expressions can be modified when the world interest rate is variable.

2.5.2   Investment When Capital Is Costly to Install: Tobin's q

Until now, our treatment of investment has assumed that capital will be adjusted in a single period up to the point where its marginal product equals the interest rate. Thus firms always plan to maintain a capital stock such that $A F_K = r$ in every period. This simple modeling device, while perhaps not too misleading when the "period" is fairly long, seems strained even for annual data. In reality capital cannot be installed, or dismantled and moved into a different line of work, without incurring frictional costs. And these costs are typically higher the more dramatic is the capital-stock change considered: management becomes spread more thinly, there is greater disruption to current production, and so on.

The last section's conclusion that a firm's value is precisely equal to the capital it owns need not be true when there are costs to moving capital among alternative uses. In a more realistic model in which capital is costly to move, we would expect a favorable shock to an industry's fortunes to raise the market value of capital located there, perhaps for some time, because new capital cannot immediately rush in to drive capital's marginal product back down to r.

The *Tobin's q* model of investment explicitly accounts for the adjustment costs borne when a firm changes the amount of capital it is using. This modification alters not only investment behavior, but also the response of the current account even to permanent shifts in factor productivity. We can appreciate these points better by working through a particular example of the q model.[39]

2.5.2.1   The Model

Once again, firms maximize the present value of current and future profits. Now, however, a firm's profit flow is not given simply by

---

39. The model gets its name from Tobin's (1969) suggestion that investment is a positive function of a variable q, which he defined as the ratio of the market value of capital to the capital's replacement cost. The model is based on capital adjustment costs that are internal to the firm. An alternative model assumes a two-sector economy producing nontraded capital goods and traded consumption goods, such that adjustment costs appear at the level of the economy because of a concave aggregate production possibilities frontier. Obstfeld and Stockman (1985, section 4.2) analyze a model in this class. The basic idea of modeling investment adjustment costs for the economy as a whole was introduced into macroeconomics by Foley and Sidrauski (1970) (who built on earlier work in growth theory).

$$A_s F(K_s, L_s) - w_s L_s - (K_{s+1} - K_s).$$

The particular assumption we make is that, to change the capital stock by the amount $K_{s+1} - K_s = I_s$ between dates s and $s + 1$, the firm must pay a deadweight installation cost of $\chi I_s^2 / 2K_s$ over and above the actual cost I_s of purchasing the new capital goods. As a result, the firm's output net of adjustment costs is only $Y = A F(K, L) - \chi I^2 / 2K$. Other things being the same, the more rapidly the firm adjusts its stock of capital, the lower its output is.

The specific cost function we have chosen shows an increasing marginal cost of investment (or, symmetrically, disinvestment). This assumption captures the observation that a faster pace of change requires a greater than proportional rise in installation costs. These costs depend negatively on the amount of capital already in place. A larger manufacturing establishment can absorb a given influx of new capital at lower cost.

The sum of the firm's present and discounted future profits on date t is thus

$$d_t + V_t = \sum_{s=t}^{\infty} \left(\frac{1}{1+r}\right)^{s-t} \left[A_s F(K_s, L_s) - \frac{\chi}{2}(I_s^2 / K_s) - w_s L_s - I_s\right], \tag{62}$$

which the firm maximizes, for a given K_t, subject to

$$K_{s+1} - K_s = I_s.$$

From an economic viewpoint, it will turn out that the most transparent setup of the firm's maximization problem is based on the Lagrangian expression

$$\mathcal{L}_t = \sum_{s=t}^{\infty} \left(\frac{1}{1+r}\right)^{s-t} \left\{A_s F(K_s, L_s) - \frac{\chi}{2}(I_s^2 / K_s) - w_s L_s - I_s \right.$$

$$\left. -q_s \left(K_{s+1} - K_s - I_s\right)\right\}.$$

(You'll see in a moment why we've labeled the Lagrange multiplier q.)[40] Differentiate with respect to labor, investment, and capital. Since labor can be adjusted without cost, the condition $A F_L(K, L) = w$ still describes the firm's demand for labor, given the capital in use.

However, the firm may no longer plan to maintain the capital it uses at the point where $A F_K(K, L) = r$. The adjustment cost of pushing the capital stock toward that level acts as a brake that slows the optimal pace of adjustment. This braking effect is reflected in the first-order conditions for investment and capital. The first-order condition for investment is $\partial \mathcal{L}_t / \partial I_s = 0$, which implies

$$-\frac{\chi I_s}{K_s} - 1 + q_s = 0.$$

---

40. In the preceding Lagrangian formulation, there is a separate multiplier q_s for each period s.

Because q_s has an interpretation as the shadow price of capital in place at the end of s, this condition states that the shadow price of capital equals the marginal cost of investment (including installation costs), $1 + \chi(I_s/K_s)$. The condition can be rewritten as a version of the investment equation posited by Tobin (1969),

$$I_s = \frac{q_s - 1}{\chi} K_s.$$ (63)

Equation (63) shows that investment is positive only when the shadow price q of installed capital exceeds 1, the price of new, uninstalled capital.

The first-order condition for capital is $\partial \mathcal{L}_t / \partial K_s = 0$, equivalent to

$$-q_s + \frac{A_{s+1} F_K(K_{s+1}, L_{s+1}) + \frac{\chi}{2}(I_{s+1}/K_{s+1})^2 + q_{s+1}}{1 + r} = 0.$$ (64)

This condition is an investment Euler equation. It states that, at an optimum for the firm, the date s shadow price of an extra unit of capital is the discounted sum of

1. the capital's marginal product next period;

2. the capital's marginal contribution to lower installation costs next period [the term $\frac{\chi}{2}(I_{s+1}/K_{s+1})^2$]; and

3. the shadow price of capital on the next date, $s + 1$.

Intuitively, eq. (64) states that if a firm's planned investment path is optimal, it will not benefit from raising its installed capital above plan by a unit on date s [at marginal cost $q_s = 1 + \chi(I_s/K_s)$], enjoying a higher marginal product and lower investment costs [$A_{s+1} F_K(K_{s+1}, L_{s+1}) + (\chi/2)(I_{s+1}/K_{s+1})^2$] on date $s + 1$, and then disinvesting the above-plan unit of capital at the end of $s + 1$ [to reap a net marginal revenue of $q_{s+1} = 1 + \chi(I_{s+1}/K_{s+1})$].

Provided bubbles in the shadow price of capital are ruled out, so that $\lim_{T\to\infty}(1 + r)^{-T} q_{t+T} = 0$ (see appendix 2B for details), the usual iterative substitution argument, here applied to eq. (64), leads to

$$q_t = \sum_{s=t+1}^{\infty} \left(\frac{1}{1+r}\right)^{s-t} \left[A_{s+1} F_K(K_{s+1}, L_{s+1}) + \frac{\chi}{2}(I_{s+1}/K_{s+1})^2\right].$$ (65)

The shadow price of installed capital equals its discounted stream of future marginal products plus the discounted stream of its marginal contributions to the reduction in future capital installation costs.

2.5.2.2   A Phase Diagram

We can gain more insight into the investment dynamics eqs. (63) and (64) represent by developing a *phase diagram* for the implied behavior of q and K. Assume temporarily that the productivity coefficient A is constant, that the economy's labor force L is constant, and that the wage continually adjusts in the background to ensure that the firm wishes to employ exactly L workers every period. The last assumption means we can analyze the economy's equilibrium in terms of its representative firm. Equation (63) implies that the change in the capital stock between the beginnings of periods $t + 1$ and t is

$$K_{t+1} - K_t = \left(\frac{q_t - 1}{\chi} \right) K_t, \tag{66}$$

while this equation and eq. (64) imply that the change in q between the same two periods is

$$q_{t+1} - q_t = rq_t - AF_K \left[K_t \left(1 + \frac{q_t - 1}{\chi} \right), L \right] - \frac{1}{2\chi} (q_{t+1} - 1)^2. \tag{67}$$

The economy's *steady state* is defined by levels $\bar{q}$ and $\bar{K}$ of the endogenous variables which, once they are simultaneously reached, both remain constant through time. Equations (66) and (67) show that $\bar{q} = 1$ (so that capital is constant in the steady state) and that $\bar{K}$ satisfies $AF_K(\bar{K}, L) = r$. Only in the steady state does the marginal product of capital necessarily equal r, as in the investment model with no installation costs.[41]

The simplest way to analyze the dynamic system described by eqs. (66) and (67) is to study their linear approximations near the steady-state point, $K = \bar{K}, q = \bar{q}$.[42] The approximate linear system is

$$K_{t+1} - K_t = \frac{\bar{K}}{\chi} (q_t - 1), \tag{68}$$

$$q_{t+1} - q_t = \left[r - \frac{A\bar{K} F_{KK}(\bar{K}, L)}{\chi} \right] (q_t - 1) - AF_{KK}(\bar{K}, L)(K_t - \bar{K}). \tag{69}$$

Figure 2.9 represents the dynamics of this system. The schedule labeled $\Delta K = 0$ shows points in the plane at which the capital stock is stationary. Equation (68) shows that this schedule, given by $\bar{K}(q - 1)/\chi = 0$, is horizontal at $q = \bar{q} = 1$. For $q > 1$ the capital stock is rising, as indicated by the small arrows parallel to the horizontal axis, and the capital stock is falling when $q < 1$.[43]

---

41. In a model with trend productivity or labor-force growth, steady-state q can differ from 1 and the steady-state marginal product of capital can differ from r.

42. Let $G(X_1, X_2)$ be a differentiable function of two variables. Its linear approximation in the neighborhood of $X_1 = \bar{X}_1, X_2 = \bar{X}_2$ is $G(X_1, X_2) \approx G(\bar{X}_1, \bar{X}_2) + G_{X_1}(\bar{X}_1, \bar{X}_2)(X_1 - \bar{X}_1) + G_{X_2}(\bar{X}_1, \bar{X}_2)(X_2 - \bar{X}_2)$. In the next equation, we present linear approximations for the functions describing ΔK_{t+1} and Δq_{t+1}, both of which depend on the two variables K_t and q_t.

43. Of course, the $\Delta K = 0$ schedule looks the same even if we do not work with the linear approximation to eq. (66). Thus the representation of this schedule in Figure 2.9 is globally, and not just locally, valid.

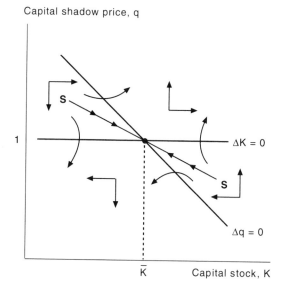

Capital shadow price, q

Figure 2.9
Dynamics of the q investment model

The schedule labeled $\Delta q = 0$ shows points at which Tobin's q is stationary. By inspecting the equation for this schedule implied by eq. (69),

$$0 = \left[r - \frac{A\bar{K}F_{KK}(\bar{K}, L)}{\chi} \right] (q - 1) - AF_{KK}(\bar{K}, L)(K - \bar{K}),$$

you can see that it has the negative slope

$$\frac{dq}{dK}\bigg|_{\Delta q = 0} = \frac{AF_{KK}(\bar{K}, L)}{r - A\bar{K}F_{KK}(\bar{K}, L)/\chi} < 0$$

(because $F_{KK} < 0$). For q above the $\Delta q = 0$ schedule, eq. (69) shows that q must be rising, as indicated by the small vertical arrows in the figure. Symmetric reasoning justifies the small arrows pointing downward below the $\Delta q = 0$ schedule.

The system shown in Figure 2.9 is an example of a *saddle-point-stable* system. This description means that the system has a *unique* path, denoted **SS**, that converges to the steady state. Specifically, for any starting capital stock K_t, there is one and only one value of q_t that places the firm on the stable adjustment path **SS**. Only on **SS** does the equation excluding bubbles in q, eq. (65), hold. As a result, **SS** *is* the path q and K will follow for an optimizing firm. The unstable paths in Figure 2.9 are paths that satisfy the *necessary* conditions for optimality, but, because they contain bubbles, are not really optimal. The reason bubble paths appear in the figure is that the $\Delta q = 0$ schedule is derived from eq. (67), and that equation does not incorporate the bubble-excluding condition $\lim_{T\to\infty}(1+r)^{-T}q_{t+T}=0$ that we imposed in deriving eq. (65).

How can we see that paths other than **SS** are suboptimal bubble paths? Paths starting in Figure 2.9's northeast quadrant, say, call for both q and K to rise forever at accelerating rates. Clearly, the ever-increasing capital stock is supported entirely by self-fulfilling expectations of a rising shadow price, notwithstanding the objective fact that the capital's marginal product is declining over time, never to recover. In the southwest quadrant, q and K are falling ever more quickly. In fact, both variables would have to turn negative in finite time—an economic impossibility—to continue satisfying eqs. (66) and (67). None of these unstable paths maximizes the firm's discounted profits, as appendix B rigorously shows.

In contrast, the dynamics implied by the saddle path **SS** are intuitive. If the firm starts with a capital stock below $\bar{K}$, for example, the marginal product of its capital in place exceeds the interest rate. Attempting to raise its capital all the way to $\bar{K}$ in an instant is ruled out by the high adjustment costs so rapid an investment rate would entail. Instead, the capital stock rises gradually toward its steady-state level. But the high (relative to r) marginal product of capital in place will be reflected in a high (relative to 1) value of q, as well as in an expectation that q will fall in the future as the capital stock expands. As q falls toward 1 along **SS**, investment, initially high, declines to zero.

Figure 2.10 illustrates these dynamics in the case of a permanent unanticipated rise in the interest rate from r to r'. The interest rate enters only into the $\Delta q = 0$ locus, and it shifts to the left, as shown. The new steady-state capital stock is $\bar{K}'$, which is below $\bar{K}$ because the required rate of return on capital has risen. Correspondingly, the saddle path shifts leftward to **S'S'**. The capital stock is a predetermined variable that cannot change in the short run. On the other hand, the shadow price of capital is free to adjust immediately. Thus the rise in r causes the initial equilibrium to shift from point **A** to point **B** on the new saddle path. At point **B**, however, capital's marginal product is too low and $q < 1$; the firm disinvests until reaching its new long-run position, point **C**.

An advantage of our diagram is that it can be used to investigate the response to *anticipated* shocks. Take the example of a foreseen future permanent rise in the interest rate. Figure 2.11 shows the implied adjustment path. Suppose that on date $t = 0$ people suddenly learn the interest rate will rise from r to r' on date T in the future. We can find the resulting equilibrium path by working backward from date T. A key observation underlies the solution. Since no further change in the interest rate is expected to occur after date T, the economy must be on the new saddle path **S'S'** by that date.

Let us first dispose of the possibility that the firm simply ignores information about the future and remains at its initial steady state until date T. If this were the equilibrium, the marginal product of capital would remain at r through date T and eq. (69) could be satisfied on date $T - 1$ only if $q_T = 1$ were expected. But q would

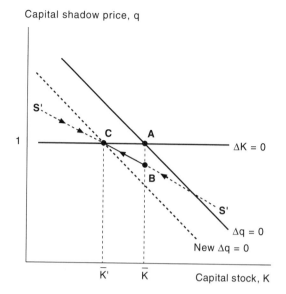

Figure 2.10
An unexpected permanent rise in the interest rate

have to fall between dates $T - 1$ and T to place the firm on $S'S'$. The counterfactual scenario therefore contradicts the assumption that the rise in r is anticipated.[44]

   This contradiction implies that the economy actually moves away from its initial position *prior* to date T. Since its motion before date T has to conform to eqs. (66) and (67) (with the original value of r in the latter), the economy must travel along an unstable path of the predisturbance system up to date T. Thus the initial response to the news of a future increase in the interest rate is a drop in capital's shadow price to q_0 in Figure 2.11, followed by a gradual process of disinvestment that allows the firm to smooth the reduction in its capital stock over time. After its initial sharp drop, q continues falling until it just equals q_T on $S'S'$. That shadow price is reached precisely when the expected interest-rate jump occurs. Subsequently, q rises back to 1 as $K = \bar{K}'$ is approached. The bigger is T—the longer in advance the firm foresees the rise in r—the smaller the initial fall in q.

2.5.2.3   Marginal and Average q

We now tackle an important question that may have occurred to you already: what is the relationship between q, which is the firm's internal shadow price of capital, and the *stock-market value* of a unit of the firm's capital, given by V/K. When

---

44. One can also show that the original nonlinear eq. (67) wouldn't be satisfied, but the argument is a bit more intricate.

Capital shadow price, q

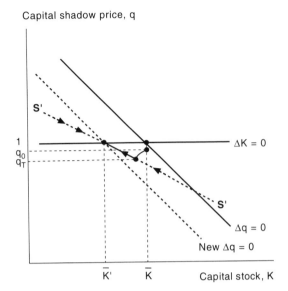

Figure 2.11
A foreseen permanent rise in the interest rate

there are no capital-installation costs, $q = 1$ and $V = K$, so the market value of a unit of the firm's capital, V/K, trivially equals $q = 1$. As we now show, the property $q = V/K$ also holds in the more general adjustment-cost model.

The proof is relatively painless and is valid for arbitrary paths of the exogenous variables. Multiply eq. (64) for date $s = t$ by K_{t+1} and use the capital-accumulation identity $K_{t+2} - K_{t+1} = I_{t+1}$ to write

$$q_t K_{t+1}$$

$$= \frac{A_{t+1} F_K(K_{t+1}, L_{t+1}) K_{t+1} + (\chi/2)(I_{t+1}^2/K_{t+1}) - q_{t+1} I_{t+1} + q_{t+1} K_{t+2}}{1 + r}.$$

Since $q_{t+1} = 1 + \chi(I_{t+1}/K_{t+1})$ [this is eq. (63) for $s = t + 1$ rearranged],

$$q_t K_{t+1} = \frac{A_{t+1} F_K(K_{t+1}, L_{t+1}) K_{t+1} - (\chi/2)(I_{t+1}^2/K_{t+1}) - I_{t+1} + q_{t+1} K_{t+2}}{1 + r}.$$

Because the production function is linear homogeneous, the (by now) familiar forward iteration on the variable $q_s K_{s+1}$ above, combined with Euler's theorem and a no-bubbles condition on that variable, shows that

$$q_t K_{t+1} = \sum_{s=t+1}^{\infty} \left(\frac{1}{1+r}\right)^{s-t} \left[A_s F(K_s, L_s) - \frac{\chi}{2}(I_s^2/K_s) - w_s L_s - I_s\right] = V_t; \quad (70)$$

recall eq. (62). Thus $q_t = V_t/K_{t+1}$ (or, as it often is put, "marginal" q equals "average" q).[45]

This result is illuminating for two reasons. First, it implies that eq. (64), rewritten as

$$r = \frac{A_{t+1}F_K(K_{t+1}, L_{t+1}) - (\chi/2)(I_{t+1}/K_{t+1})^2 - (I_{t+1}/K_{t+1}) + q_{t+1}(K_{t+2}/K_{t+1}) - q_t}{q_t},$$

can be identified with the asset-market equilibrium condition equating the rate of return on a unit of the firm's capital to r. (The numerator on the right-hand side of this equation equals dividends paid out per unit of date $t + 1$ capital plus capital gains. These gains are computed recognizing that an owner of K_{t+1} units of capital at the end of date t automatically owns K_{t+2}/K_{t+1} units once date $t + 1$ investment is complete.)[46]

A second inference from the equality of marginal and average q concerns the consumption function. The individual's intertemporal budget constraint can now be expressed as

$$\sum_{s=t}^{\infty} \left(\frac{1}{1+r}\right)^{s-t} C_s = \left[(1+r)B_t + (1+r)q_{t-1}K_t\right]$$

$$+ \sum_{s=t}^{\infty} \left(\frac{1}{1+r}\right)^{s-t} (w_s L_s - G_s) \tag{71}$$

if perfect foresight holds between dates $t - 1$ and t. [The derivation follows upon using eqs. (53), (55), and (70).] Equation (71) differs from eq. (60) only because investment adjustment costs can make the price of capital q differ from 1.

2.5.2.4 Investment and Current Account Dynamics

One dramatic difference between the q model and our earlier investment model without installation costs is in the current account's response to a permanent increase in factor productivity.

Assume, for simplicity, that $\beta = 1/(1 + r)$. Then it is straightforward to show that eq. (18) still holds. That is,

$$CA_t = (Y_t - \tilde{Y}_t) - (I_t - \tilde{I}_t) - (G_t - \tilde{G}_t),$$

with Y interpreted as output net of capital-installation costs.

---

45. Hayashi (1982) established the equality of marginal and average q under the following assumptions: the firm is a price taker, the production function is linear homogeneous in K and L, and the installation-cost function is linear homogeneous in K and I. (Note that Hayashi's conditions all hold in the example in the text.) Applications of the q model in open-economy contexts include Blanchard (1983) and Matsuyama (1987).

46. The reason is that the firm is financing its investment out of the potential earnings of existing shareholders, rather than selling additional shares.

Suppose that in period t the productivity coefficient in the production function rises unexpectedly and permanently from its previously constant level A to a higher level A'. For illustration, let labor supply and government spending be constant. In either of the investment models we have studied, a current account deficit emerges in period t as consumption rises above income in anticipation of permanently higher future output and as investment shoots up.

When there are *no* costs of adjusting the capital stock to its optimal long-run level, however, the capital stock needs only period t to reach the steady-state $\bar{K}$ at which $A'F_K(\bar{K}, L) = r$. Thus, from period $t + 1$ on, output and investment are at their permanent levels, and there is no further current account imbalance. (Recall Figure 2.3.)

With capital installation costs, however, the permanent rise in A causes a current-account deficit that converges to zero only in the long run. These dynamics follow immediately from the gradual adjustment of the capital stock to its new steady state. Because the capital stock no longer adjusts in a single period, the deficit is drawn out over the entire future. Capital is rising and investment falling, both at decreasing rates. Output net of installation costs is rising also, but at a decreasing rate, and therefore saving is rising to zero over time. The combination of gradually rising saving and gradually declining investment implies a current account deficit that converges to zero only in the long run.

2.5.3   Endogenous Labor Supply

This section has drawn a distinction between financial and human wealth. The distinction is important, in part, because it helps us understand how economic events impinge on the distribution of income when the representative-agent paradigm is not appropriate. In addition, financial and human wealth are determined in very different ways and pose different levels of income risk for their owners: distinct subfields of economics study in detail how these different forms of wealth are generated. By endogenizing the supply of labor as it depends on the real wage, we now take a first step in understanding an economy's level of human wealth. Future chapters will probe that important question more deeply insofar as it is important for understanding international macroeconomics. Here, our main concern is to understand how an endogenous supply of labor can change our previous conclusions about current-account behavior.

Suppose the individual is endowed with $\bar{L}$ hours of time each period, and chooses how to divide that time between work, L, and leisure, $\bar{L} - L$. The individual's lifetime utility depends positively on consumption and leisure,

$$U_t = \sum_{s=t}^{\infty} \beta^{s-t} u(C_s, \bar{L} - L_s),$$

and the individual maximizes it subject to[47]

$$\sum_{s=t}^{\infty} \left(\frac{1}{1+r}\right)^{s-t} C_s = (1+r)Q_t + \sum_{s=t}^{\infty} \left(\frac{1}{1+r}\right)^{s-t} (w_s L_s - G_s).$$

As you can verify on your own, the consumption Euler equation still holds with $u'(C)$ replaced by the partial derivative $u_C(C, \bar{L} - L)$:

$$u_C(C_s, \bar{L} - L_s) = (1+r)\beta u_C(C_{s+1}, \bar{L} - L_{s+1}). \tag{72}$$

In addition, on every date s, the allocation of time between work and leisure satisfies the standard equation of the marginal utility of leisure to the wage's marginal consumption value,

$$u_{\bar{L}-L}(C_s, \bar{L} - L_s) = u_C(C_s, \bar{L} - L_s)w_s. \tag{73}$$

To draw out some implications of an endogenous labor supply for the current account, it is convenient to specialize to the isoelastic period utility function

$$u(C, \bar{L} - L) = \frac{1}{1 - 1/\sigma} \left[C^\gamma (\bar{L} - L)^{1-\gamma} \right]^{1-1/\sigma}.$$

Under this utility function, eq. (73) can be solved explicitly to show how leisure depends on consumption and the real wage:

$$\bar{L} - L = \frac{1 - \gamma}{\gamma w} C.$$

This expression, when combined with our assumed isoelastic utility function and Euler equation (72), implies the dynamic consumption equation

$$C_{s+1} = \left(\frac{w_s}{w_{s+1}}\right)^{(1-\gamma)(\sigma-1)} (1+r)^\sigma \beta^\sigma C_s.$$

Compare this with eq. (15), in which leisure did not interact with consumption in the period utility function. Unless $\sigma = 1$, in which case consumption and leisure enter utility separably (because utility is logarithmic), the rate of consumption growth depends on the rate of real wage growth, something that was not true before.

An important implication of a labor-leisure trade-off is that, even when $\beta = 1/(1 + r)$, a flat consumption path may no longer be optimal. For example, if $\sigma < 1$ and real wages are growing over time, the path of consumption will have an upward tilt when $\beta = 1/(1 + r)$. With internationally immobile labor, this case

---

47. The obvious constraints $L_s \leq \bar{L}$, for all s, are handled in the same way as the nonnegativity constraint on consumption.

might be relevant for an economy in which output is given by $Y = AF(K, L)$ and productivity A is secularly increasing.

Another important feature of this type of economy is that investment can no longer be decoupled from consumption behavior in general. Changes in consumption typically will change the marginal utility of leisure and thus alter the amount of labor residents wish to supply at every wage. As a result, the marginal product of capital will change, with investment effects that depend on the technology for installing capital.

We have presented the preceding example merely to indicate that realistic extensions of the consumption-smoothing model explored in this chapter can change some of its basic predictions. Further analysis is deferred, however, until Chapter 4, where we will see how to fit models with several goods into the basic framework of this chapter.

Appendix 2A   Trend Productivity Growth, Saving, and Investment: A Detailed Example

We have already emphasized the knife-edge long-run behavior of the fixed discount rate, infinitely-lived representative agent model. In this appendix we explore this issue further by looking at the small-country model's implications for long-run debt-GDP ratios in the presence of trend productivity growth. The example is interesting because it highlights the large debt-GDP ratios implied by the model for fast-growing developing countries. We warn you in advance that this example strains the small-country paradigm—which is precisely what it is intended to do.

2A.1   Deriving the Steady-State Debt-Output Ratio

A model with trend productivity growth provides an important application of the fixed real interest rate version of the fundamental equation for the current account, eq. (20).

Suppose the production function is

$$Y = AF(K) = AK^\alpha$$

($\alpha < 1$), where the productivity coefficient A grows so that

$$A_{s+1} = (1+g)^{1-\alpha} A_s$$

and $0 < g < r$. In a steady state with growth the marginal product of capital, $AF'(K) = \alpha AK^{\alpha-1}$, always equals r. Thus the capital stock is $K = (\alpha A/r)^{1/(1-\alpha)}$, and investment is

$$I_s = K_{s+1} - K_s = \left(\frac{\alpha A_s}{r}\right)^{1/(1-\alpha)} g.$$

Because output is

$$Y = AK^\alpha = A\left[\left(\frac{\alpha A}{r}\right)^{1/(1-\alpha)}\right]^\alpha = A^{1/(1-\alpha)}\left(\frac{\alpha}{r}\right)^{\alpha/(1-\alpha)},$$

investment can be expressed as

$$I = \left(\frac{\alpha A}{r}\right)^{1/(1-\alpha)} g = \frac{\alpha}{r}\left(\frac{\alpha}{r}\right)^{\alpha/(1-\alpha)} A^{1/(1-\alpha)} g = \left(\frac{\alpha g}{r}\right) Y.$$

Output and investment therefore both grow at the net rate g. Assume that government spending is always a constant fraction, $\varsigma < 1 - (\alpha g/r)$, of output. Output net of investment and government spending for dates $s \geq t$ is

$$Y_s - I_s - G_s = (1 + g)^{s-t}\left(1 - \frac{\alpha g}{r} - \varsigma\right) Y_t.$$

Equation (20) gives the optimal current account,

$$CA_t = Y_t - I_t - G_t - \frac{r}{1+r}\sum_{s=t}^{\infty}\left(\frac{1}{1+r}\right)^{s-t}(Y_s - I_s - G_s) - \frac{\vartheta}{1+r} W_t$$

$$= -\vartheta B_t - \frac{g + \vartheta}{r - g}\left(1 - \frac{\alpha g}{r} - \varsigma\right) Y_t. \tag{74}$$

[In deriving the second equality we used eq. (19).] This balance is decreasing in the growth rate g. A higher growth rate causes higher investment and lower saving.

What does this optimal current account deficit imply for the economy's ratio of foreign assets or debt to output? Notice that, by eq. (74) together with the definition $CA_s = B_{s+1} - B_s$,

$$\frac{B_{s+1}}{Y_{s+1}} = \left[\frac{(1+r)^{\sigma}\beta^{\sigma}}{1+g}\right]\frac{B_s}{Y_s} - \frac{1 + g - (1+r)^{\sigma}\beta^{\sigma}}{(1+g)(r-g)}\left(1 - \frac{\alpha g}{r} - \varsigma\right) \tag{75}$$

for $s \geq t$ [we have made the substitution $\vartheta = 1 - (1+r)^{\sigma}\beta^{\sigma}$]. This relationship is a linear *difference equation* in B_s/Y_s, the ratio of net foreign assets to output. The equation will be our main tool in a diagrammatic analysis of the dynamics of foreign assets. (Supplement C to this chapter explains how to solve linear difference equations algebraically.)

Figure 2.12 superimposes a graph of the linear eq. (75) on a diagram indicating the 45° line. Equation (75) has a slope of $(1 + r)^{\sigma}\beta^{\sigma}/(1 + g)$. We saw earlier that $(1 + r)^{\sigma-1}\beta^{\sigma}$ must be below 1, and thus $(1 + r)^{\sigma}\beta^{\sigma}$ below $1 + r$, for the consumer's problem to have a well-defined maximum. Let's temporarily add the stronger assumption that $(1 + r)^{\sigma}\beta^{\sigma} < 1 + g$, which guarantees that the slope of eq. (75) is less than 1 and that its vertical-axis intercept is negative, as shown in the figure. (Recall that $g < r$, by assumption.)

Starting from the date t asset-output ratio B_t/Y_t indicated on the horizontal axis, we find the date $t + 1$ ratio, B_{t+1}/Y_{t+1}, as the point on the vertical axis directly to the left of point **A** on eq. (75). Using the 45° line (point **B**), we reflect B_{t+1}/Y_{t+1} onto the horizontal axis so that we can visualize its position relative to the previous period's ratio, B_t/Y_t. Continuing in this way, we can plot B_{t+2}/Y_{t+2}, B_{t+3}/Y_{t+3}, etc., on the horizontal axis.

The intersection of the two schedules at point **C** defines an asset-output ratio $\overline{B/Y}$ that, absent some exogenous shock, would be maintained indefinitely if ever attained. Point **C** therefore is a steady state.

To derive an algebraic expression for the steady state, just set $B_{s+1}/Y_{s+1} = B_s/Y_s = \overline{B/Y}$ in eq. (75) and solve:

$$\overline{B/Y} = -\frac{1 - \varsigma - (\alpha g/r)}{r - g}. \tag{76}$$

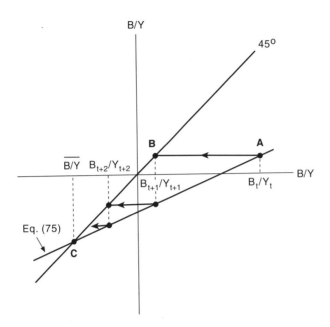

Figure 2.12
Dynamics of a small economy's debt-output ratio

Because $\alpha g/r = I/Y$ under perfect foresight, the long-run ratio of foreign debt to output equals $1/(1+r)$ times the ratio to current output of the *entire present value* of current and future output net of government spending and investment:

$$\frac{1}{(1+r)Y_t}\sum_{s=t}^{\infty}\left(\frac{1+g}{1+r}\right)^{s-t}(Y_t - G_t - I_t) = \frac{Y_t - G_t - I_t}{(r-g)Y_t}$$

$$= \frac{1 - \varsigma - (\alpha g/r)}{r-g} = -\overline{B/Y}.$$

The root cause of this finding is easy to understand. Since the gross rate of private consumption growth, $(1+r)^\sigma\beta^\sigma$, is constant and below the constant gross rate of output growth, $1+g$, the private consumption-output ratio must approach zero asymptotically. (This is the price the economy pays for cashing in on future growth early on.) But eq. (16) implies that, because $Y - G - I$ grows at rate g,

$$\frac{C}{Y} = \frac{r+\vartheta}{1+r}\left[(1+r)\frac{B}{Y} + \frac{1+r}{(r-g)}\left(\frac{Y-G-I}{Y}\right)\right] = (r+\vartheta)\left[\frac{B}{Y} + \frac{Y-G-I}{(r-g)Y}\right]$$

on any date. As a consequence, $C/Y \to 0$ implies that $B/Y \to -(Y-G-I)/(r-g)Y$.[48] We now see why the limiting debt-output ratio is independent of the taste parameters β and σ (although the current account and, hence, the rate of approach to the steady state, are not).

---

48. Because Y grows at rate g, this convergence does *not* imply that $B \to -(Y - I - G)/(r - g)$. That is, C itself need not converge to zero.

In Figure 2.12 the asset-output ratio initially is above $\overline{B/Y}$, and thereafter falls monoton-ically toward the steady state. Asset-output ratios below $\overline{B/Y}$, however, are not consistent with the intertemporal budget constraint. Below $\overline{B/Y}$, the interest and principal on debt, $-(1+r)B$, exceed the present value of current and future net output. Thus consumption would have to be negative, which is infeasible. Point **C** is *stable* in the sense that the econ-omy converges toward it starting from any feasible initial position.

If $(1+r)^\sigma \beta^\sigma > 1 + g$, steady-state net foreign assets are still negative and given by eq. (76). But the steady state is unstable. Starting from any point to the right of the steady state (the only debt levels for which the economy is solvent), the ratio of foreign assets to output would shoot off toward infinity (straining the small-country assumption). If it so happens that $(1+r)^\sigma \beta^\sigma = 1 + g$, eq. (75) boils down to $B_{s+1} = (1+g)B_s$, and the economy maintains its initial asset-output ratio forever. Because we wish to compare the model's predictions with the experience of countries that have accumulated debt to finance development, we focus henceforth on the stable case $(1+r)^\sigma \beta^\sigma < 1 + g$.

What size debt-output ratio does eq. (76) imply in the stable case? Suppose the world real interest rate r is 8 percent per year, g is 5 percent per year, $\alpha = 0.4$, and $\varsigma = 0.3$. Then $\overline{B/Y} = -15$. What is the steady-state trade surplus? In the long run, $CA = \Delta B = gB$ (because the economy is maintaining a constant ratio of net foreign assets to output); thus, the long-run trade surplus is $TB = CA - rB = -(r-g)B$. As a consequence, the economy's steady-state trade balance surplus each period must amount to $-(r-g)\overline{B/Y} = 45$ percent of GDP!

2A.2   Some Important Qualifications

Such large debt levels and debt burdens are never observed in practice: economies that must borrow at market interest rates rarely have debts much bigger than a single year's GDP. What explains our model's unrealistic prediction? The answer is fourfold:

1. Although it may not be obvious, our partial equilibrium model assumes that the small economy grows forever at a rate exceeding the world rate. To see this, suppose that all of the many countries in the world economy look exactly like the small economy, except for diverse net foreign asset stocks and a different shared growth rate, g^*. Since the small economy is a negligible actor in the global economy, we can calculate the world interest rate as if the rest of the world were a *closed* economy. For a closed economy, however, the current account and net foreign assets B both are zero, so, by eq. (16),

$$C = Y - G - I = \frac{r+\vartheta}{1+r}\left[\frac{1+r}{r-g^*}(Y-G-I)\right]$$

when Y, G, and I all grow at rate g^*. Solving for the equilibrium world interest rate, we find that $\vartheta + g^* = 1 - (1+r)^\sigma \beta^\sigma + g^* = 0$, or,

$$1 + r = \frac{(1+g^*)^{1/\sigma}}{\beta}. \tag{77}$$

Because $1 + g > (1+r)^\sigma \beta^\sigma$, g must exceed g^*. If, for example, we take $\beta = 0.96$ and $\sigma = 1$, then the assumption of a world real interest rate r of 8 percent per year implies, according to eq. (77), that the world outside our small economy is growing at rate $g^* = (0.96) \times (1.08) - 1 = 3.68$ percent per year. Economists believe, however, that fast-growing developing economies eventually *converge* to the growth rates of industrialized economies. (We take a closer look at the theory and evidence on convergence in Chapter 7.) If g does not converge to g^*, then in the long run the country will become very large relative to the rest of the world and the assumption of a fixed interest rate is no longer tenable.

2. If g does converge down to g^*, the economy's long-run debt level will be lower. Convergence in growth rates thus implies that the economy is likely to near a constant debt-output ratio long before that ratio gets too large. To see why, let's continue to assume internationally uniform preferences and look more closely at the dynamic implications of international growth disparities. Use eq. (76) and the fact that the world growth rate, g^*, satisfies $1 + g^* = (1 + r)^\sigma \beta^\sigma$ [see eq. (77)] to write difference equation (75) as

$$\frac{B_{s+1}}{Y_{s+1}} - \frac{\bar{B}}{Y} = \left(\frac{1 + g^*}{1 + g} \right) \left(\frac{B_s}{Y_s} - \frac{\bar{B}}{Y} \right).$$

This version of eq. (75) implies that a fraction

$$1 - \frac{1 + g^*}{1 + g} = \frac{g - g^*}{1 + g}$$

of the distance between the current asset-output ratio and $\overline{B/Y}$ is eliminated each period. For example, in an economy that has converged to the world level (so that $g = g^*$), *none* of the distance is eliminated: the existing asset-output ratio, whatever its level, is the long-run ratio too. In the last paragraph's example with $g = 0.05$, $g^* = 0.0368$, and the time period equal to a year, a developing economy starting from zero foreign debt would travel only 1.26 percent of the distance to the steady-state debt-output level each year if g did not converge to g^*. At that rate, it would take the economy 55 years to get halfway to the steady state. A domestic growth rate g converging downward to g^* over time would extend this half-life dramatically. Given the slow approach to a steady state, g would very likely near g^*, allowing the debt-output ratio to stabilize, before too much debt had been built up.

3. Even these considerations leave the theoretical implication that fast-growing developing economies have foreign debts larger than those we observe.[49] A third factor explaining the small size of observed debt-output ratios, one we have alluded to on several occasions, is the limited scope for writing enforceable international financial contracts. The problem is especially severe for poorer countries with little collateral to offer and little to lose from sanctions in the event of default.

4. We have been pushing the assumption of infinitely lived decision makers very hard in a setting where its empirical application could be particularly misleading. Individuals with finite lives wouldn't be able to borrow against the economy's immense but distant future output. Cutting off that possibility sharply reduces the long-run ratio of debt to output.

An important moral of the analysis is that a small-country model can be misleading for analyzing long-run trends in current accounts. General equilibrium considerations that may be secondary for analyzing short- to medium-run fluctuations may become important when examining the very long run.

---

49. Blanchard's (1983) simulation analysis of Brazil illustrates the magnitudes one would obtain.

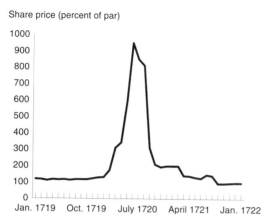

Share price (percent of par)

Figure 2.13
South Sea Company shares, January 1719 to January 1722

Appendix 2B   Speculative Asset Price Bubbles, Ponzi Games, and Transversality Conditions

The saddle-point stability property of the q investment model (section 2.5.2) is typical of macroeconomic models in which agents price assets on the basis of perfect foresight or, in a stochastic setting, rational expectations of future events. In our discussion of firm behavior, we argued that neither explosive stock-market prices nor explosive shadow prices of capital make economic sense. More specifically, in eq. (57) we assumed that the present value of a firm's stock-market price on a future date must converge to zero as the future date becomes more and more distant. In other words, the firm's market value cannot rise at a rate equal to, or above, the rate of interest. Similarly, in deriving eq. (65) we claimed that a firm cannot be maximizing profits if it is following a plan in which the shadow price of its installed capital, q, rises at a rate above or equal to the rate of interest. This sort of phenomenon would reflect a speculative bubble driven by self-fulfilling price expectations.[50]

What guarantee is there that a market economy won't generate the speculative price frenzies we have assumed away? Figure 2.13 shows the price of South Sea Company shares in London during a celebrated eighteenth-century episode of explosive asset-price behavior, the so-called South Sea bubble.[51] Isn't it possible in theory, as some argue was the case during the South Sea bubble, for expectations of future price increases to become self-validating as investors bid prices ever higher in the expectation of growing capital gains?

The short answer is that some fairly compelling arguments rule out speculative bubbles in the class of infinite-horizon models studied in this chapter. This appendix presents those arguments and shows how they are related to the transversality requirements for optimality

---

50. Recall our assumption on p. 66 that economic quantity variables grow at rates below r and thus have finite present values.

51. The South Sea bubble and other historical cases of financial-market turbulence are discussed by Kindleberger (1978) and Garber (1990). The data in Figure 2.13 are taken from Neal (1990).

at the level of individual decision makers. However, the appendix to Chapter 3 shows that there are alternative models in which speculative bubbles can arise. Ultimately, therefore, one must appeal to empirical as well as theoretical arguments to rule out bubbles entirely.[52]

2B.1 Ruling Out Asset-Price Bubbles

Let V_t be the date t price of an asset that yields the dividend d_{t+1} on date $t + 1$. The consumption Euler equation for this asset, which must hold provided the consumer can increase or decrease holdings of the asset by a small amount, is

$$V_t u'(C_t) = \beta(d_{t+1} + V_{t+1})u'(C_{t+1}).$$

As always, this equation states that an optimizing consumer cannot gain by lowering holdings of the asset by a unit on date t, consuming the proceeds, $V_t u'(C_t)$, forgoing the consumption allowed by the dividend, worth $\beta d_{t+1}u'(C_{t+1})$ in terms of date t utility, and then lowering consumption on date $t + 1$ to repurchase the asset ex dividend at a date t cost of $\beta V_{t+1}u'(C_{t+1})$.

Consider what happens when we iterate this Euler equation forward into time. By successive substitutions into the last term on the right-hand side below, we deduce that

$$V_t u'(C_t) = \beta d_{t+1}u'(C_{t+1}) + \beta V_{t+1}u'(C_{t+1})$$

$$= \beta d_{t+1}u'(C_{t+1}) + \beta^2 d_{t+2}u'(C_{t+2}) + \beta^2 V_{t+2}u'(C_{t+2}),$$

and so on. The intuitive interpretation of these iterated Euler equations is that, along an optimal path, an individual cannot gain by transforming a unit of the asset into consumption at time t, reducing consumption by the amount of the dividends forgone over the next T periods, and then repurchasing the unit of the asset at the end of period $t + T$. Taking the limit as $T \to \infty$ yields:

$$V_t u'(C_t) = \sum_{s=t+1}^{\infty} \beta^{s-t} u'(C_s)d_s + \lim_{T \to \infty} \beta^T u'(C_{t+T})V_{t+T}. \tag{78}$$

We have assumed our consumer to be in a position to reduce holdings of the asset on date t and to reverse that reduction on date $t + T$, where T is a *finite* number. Let us now make the slightly stronger assumption that the consumer is in a position to reduce holdings of the asset *permanently* on date t.[53] If the consumer reduces his subsequent consumption by the forgone dividend flow, his utility loss is

$$\sum_{s=t+1}^{\infty} \beta^{s-t} u'(C_s)d_s.$$

---

52. For alternative theoretical models in which bubbles can be excluded, see the discussion of real asset pricing in Obstfeld and Rogoff (1983) and Tirole (1982). A capsule summary of the literature is given by O'Connell and Zeldes (1992).

53. Only rarely does this assumption fail in economic models. Its failure is rare because most assets can be held in *negative* quantities: an individual can issue a liability offering the same stream of dividends as a positive position in the asset. Thus, even if the individual's holdings of the asset are falling toward zero, a unit reduction in holdings still is always feasible. A leading case in which a reduction in asset holdings is not always feasible involves holdings of money, which can never fall below zero. We discuss monetary issues further in Chapters 8–10.

Suppose, however, that the term $\lim_{T\to\infty} \beta^T u'(C_{t+T})V_{t+T}$ in eq. (78) is strictly positive.[54] Then the current utility gain from consuming the proceeds of the asset sale, $V_t u'(C_t)$, is strictly greater than the loss in utility due to forgone dividends. So when the limit in eq. (78) is positive, all consumers will try to reduce their holdings of the asset, and their collective efforts will drive its price down to the present value of dividends,

$$V_t = \sum_{s=t+1}^{\infty} \beta^{s-t} \frac{u'(C_s)}{u'(C_t)} d_s = \sum_{s=t+1}^{\infty} \left(\frac{1}{1+r}\right)^{s-t} d_s,$$

where the second equality comes from iterating Euler equation (5). Thus the price path we were looking at cannot be an equilibrium: the equilibrium price path is characterized by

$$\lim_{T\to\infty} \beta^T u'(C_{t+T})V_{t+T} = 0.$$

Since $u'(C_t) > 0$, and, by eq. (5), $\beta^T u'(C_{t+T}) = u'(C_t)(1+r)^{-T}$, the preceding condition is equivalent to the no-bubbles condition imposed in eq. (57),

$$\lim_{T\to\infty} (1+r)^{-T} V_{t+T} = 0.$$

Before concluding, it is worth noting that this condition, which rules out equilibrium bubbles, bears a family resemblance to the transversality condition we have imposed on individual asset holdings. (For this reason, the no-bubbles condition often is itself referred to as a transversality condition.) This resemblance is no coincidence, since both follow from the exclusion of Ponzi schemes.[55] Prior to imposing the transversality condition on total assets for this economy, one would write the individual's intertemporal budget constraint (55) as

$$\sum_{s=t}^{\infty} \left(\frac{1}{1+r}\right)^{s-t} C_s + \lim_{T\to\infty} \left(\frac{1}{1+r}\right)^T (B_{t+T+1} + V_{t+T}x_{t+T+1})$$

$$= (1+r)B_t + d_t x_t + V_t x_t + \sum_{s=t}^{\infty} \left(\frac{1}{1+r}\right)^{s-t} (w_s L - G_s).$$

In a hypothetical situation where $\lim_{T\to\infty}(1+r)^{-T}V_{t+T} > 0$, any individual would be able to increase the present value of consumption above that of lifetime resources simply by going short and maintaining forever a constant negative value of the asset holding x. But if $\lim_{T\to\infty}(1+r)^{-T}V_{t+T} > 0$, no one would wish to hold the counterpart *positive* position in x indefinitely for the reason we have seen: the price of the position equals the present value of its payouts only if one liquidates the position in finite time. Indeed, everyone would wish to maintain a negative x because all agents are identical and to hold a portfolio such that $\lim_{T\to\infty}(1+r)^{-T}V_{t+T}x_{t+T+1} \geq 0$ is to pass up or, even worse, be the victim of a profitable Ponzi scheme. Viewed from this alternative perspective, it is again clear that bubble paths cannot be equilibrium. As noted earlier, however, we will revisit the topic of bubbles for a different class of economies in the next chapter.

---

54. The case in which this limit is negative is excluded by the free disposability of the asset.

55. For additional discussion of this point, see Supplement A to this chapter.

2B.2   Ruling Out Bubbles in the q Model

The argument that disposes of divergent paths for the shadow price of capital parallels the one just given for asset prices.

Forward iteration of eq. (64) leads to

$$q_t =$$

$$\sum_{s=t+1}^{\infty} \left(\frac{1}{1+r}\right)^{s-t} \left[A_{s+1}F_K(K_{s+1}, L_{s+1}) + \frac{\chi}{2}(I_{s+1}/K_{s+1})^2\right] + \lim_{T\to\infty} \left(\frac{1}{1+r}\right)^T q_{t+T}.$$

Suppose that the limit term on the right-hand side is positive. In this case,

$$q_t > \sum_{s=t+1}^{\infty} \left(\frac{1}{1+r}\right)^{s-t} \left[A_{s+1}F_K(K_{s+1}, L_{s+1}) + \frac{\chi}{2}(I_{s+1}/K_{s+1})^2\right],$$

where the right-hand side is the stream of earnings that a marginal unit of capital permanently in place will generate for the firm. But, by eq. (63), q_t equals $1 + \chi(I_t/K_t)$, which is the value to the firm of dismantling the marginal unit of capital and selling it on the market. Thus the strict inequality shown here says that the firm cannot be optimizing. Its capital stock is too high, since discounted profits can be raised by a permanent reduction in capital (which certainly is feasible, given that installed capital is exploding; see Figure 2.9). A symmetric argument rules out the possibility that $\lim_{T\to\infty}(1+r)^{-T}q_{t+T} < 0$. The conclusion is that $\lim_{T\to\infty}(1+r)^{-T}q_{t+T} = 0$, as claimed in section 2.5.2.

Exercises

1. *Current account sustainability and the intertemporal budget constraint.* Suppose that a country has negative net foreign assets and adopts a policy of running a trade balance surplus sufficient to repay a constant small fraction of the interest due each period. It rolls over the remaining interest. That is, suppose it sets its trade balance according to the rule $TB_s = -\xi r B_s, \xi > 0$.

    (a) Using the current account identity and the definition of the trade balance, show that under this policy, net foreign assets follow the equation

    $$B_{s+1} = \left[1 + (1-\xi)r\right] B_s.$$

    (b) Show directly that the intertemporal budget constraint is satisfied for *any* $\xi > 0$. [Hint: Show why

    $$\sum_{s=t}^{\infty} \left(\frac{1}{1+r}\right)^{s-t} TB_s = -\sum_{s=t}^{\infty} \left(\frac{1}{1+r}\right)^{s-t} \xi r B_s = -(1+r)B_t.]$$

    Note that even if ξ is very small, so that trade balance surpluses are very small, debt repayments grow over time as B_s grows more negative.

    (c) Have you now proved that current account sustainability requires only that countries pay an arbitrarily small constant fraction of interest owed each period, rolling over the remaining debt and interest? [Hint: Consider the case of an endowment economy with $G = I = 0$ and constant output Y. How big can B get before the country owes *all* its future output to creditors? Will this bound be violated if ξ is not large enough? If so, how can the intertemporal budget constraint have held in part b?]

2.   *Uncertain lifetimes and infinite horizons.* One way to motivate an infinite individual planning horizon is to assume that lives, while finite in length, have an uncertain terminal date. In this case, the terminal period $t + T$ of section 2.1.1 becomes a random variable. Let $E_t U_t$ denote the individual's *expected utility* over all possible lengths of life, that is, the weighted average over different life spans with weights equal to survival probabilities. Assume that individuals maximize expected utility.

(a) In any given period, an individual lives on to the next period with probability $\varphi < 1$ but dies with probability $1 - \varphi$ after consuming. In the following period, the individual faces the same probabilities of survival and death. Show that expected utility is the weighted average

$$E_t U_t = \sum_{T=0}^{\infty} \varphi^T (1 - \varphi) \left[\sum_{s=t}^{t+T} \beta^{s-t} u(C_s) \right].$$

(b) Notice that one's consumption conditional on reaching date s, C_s, cannot be a function of one's eventual longevity, since the ultimate date of death is unknown when date s consumption occurs. Rewrite $E_t U_t$ by collecting all the terms involving $u(C_t)$, then collecting all those involving $u(C_{t+1})$, and so on. Show the result implies

$$E_t U_t = \sum_{s=t}^{\infty} (\varphi \beta)^{s-t} u(C_s).$$

The uncertain lifetime thus gives the consumer a utility function with an infinite horizon and a subjective discount factor that equals the product of the "pure" time-preference factor and the survival probability for each date. (For more on this model, including the implications in general equilibrium, see Yaari, 1965, which is the original reference; Blanchard, 1985; and Frenkel and Razin, 1992.)

3.   *Another form of Hall's random walk.* Show that if consumption has a conditional log-normal distribution and $u(C)$ is isoelastic, then the natural logarithm of consumption follows a random walk with constant drift when $(1 + r)\beta = 1$.

4.   *Details on Deaton's paradox.* Consider the linear-quadratic stochastic consumption model, in which $(1 + r)\beta = 1$ and $G = I = 0$ on all dates.

(a) Use the current account identity together with consumption equation (32) in the text to show that the change in consumption is the present value of changes in expected future output levels,

$$C_{t+1} - C_t = \frac{r}{1+r} \sum_{s=t+1}^{\infty} \left(\frac{1}{1+r} \right)^{s-(t+1)} (E_{t+1} - E_t) Y_s.$$

In this equation, for any variable X_s, $(E_{t+1} - E_t) X_s$ denotes the amount by which expectations of X_s are revised as a result of information that arrives between dates t and $t + 1$. (Here, the change in consumption automatically equals the *unexpected change* or innovation in consumption, due to Hall's random walk result.)

(b) Suppose output follows a nonstationary stochastic process like eq. (38) in the text,

$$Y_{t+1} - Y_t = \rho(Y_t - Y_{t-1}) + \epsilon_{t+1}$$

where $0 < \rho < 1$. Show that for $s > t$,

$$(E_{t+1} - E_t)Y_s = (1 + \rho + \ldots + \rho^{s-(t+1)})\epsilon_{t+1} = \frac{1 - \rho^{s-t}}{1 - \rho}\epsilon_{t+1}.$$

(c) Conclude that for the permanent-income consumption equation (32), the consumption innovation on date $t + 1$ is

$$C_{t+1} - C_t = \frac{1 + r}{1 + r - \rho}\epsilon_{t+1} = \frac{1 + r}{1 + r - \rho}(Y_{t+1} - E_t Y_{t+1}).$$

Because $\rho > 0$, consumption innovations now are *more* variable than output innovations when individuals desire smooth consumption.

(d) Compute the current account response to output innovations in this case. Verify the claim at the end of section 2.3.3.

5. *An alternative form of the Campbell (1987) saving test.* Show that eq. (43) in the text holds if and only if the variable $CA_{t+1} - \Delta Z_{t+1} - (1 + r)CA_t$ is statistically uncorrelated with date t (or earlier) variables.

6. *Derivation of eq. (43).* Equation (42) in the text implies that $CA_t = Z_t - E_t \tilde{Z}_t$, where Z is net output, $Y - G - I$. Show that an equivalent equation is eq. (43),

$$CA_t = -\sum_{s=t+1}^{\infty} \left(\frac{1}{1+r}\right)^{s-t} E_t \Delta Z_s.$$

[Hint: Define the *lead operator*, L^{-1}, by $L^{-1}E_t X_t = E_t X_{t+1}$ for any variable X, and use the methodology described in Supplement C to this chapter, noting that $E_t \tilde{Z}_t = \frac{r}{1+r}(1 - \frac{1}{1+r}L^{-1})^{-1}E_t Z_t$.]

7. *Unstable debt-output ratios and transversality.* In the unstable case of the model of a small country's debt-output ratio (appendix 2A), why is the transversality condition not violated as $B/Y \to \infty$?

8. *The business cycle and the current account.* In the simplest static Keynesian models of undergraduate macroeconomics texts, higher current income Y may be associated with a current account deficit as imports mY rise. Thus the current account can be countercyclical. In actual industrial-country data, current accounts do tend to be countercyclical (see, for example, Baxter 1995). Early critics of the intertemporal approach to the current account (e.g., models such as those in this chapter) argued that a major empirical flaw of the approach is its inability to yield countercyclical current accounts. Are they right?

9. *A simplified q model.* Suppose that a firm facing a market interest rate $1 + r$ has a production function given by $Y_t = A_t F(K_t)$, where A is a productivity parameter and we treat L as fixed. The firm's objective function is to maximize the present discounted value of profits. However, the firm faces adjustment costs to changing its capital stock. Specifically, it must pay $\chi I^2/2$ in adjustment costs in any period where

it invests (or disinvests) at rate I ($-I$). [Note: In contrast to the text formulation, we are not normalizing adjustment costs by K.] Thus the firm maximizes

$$\sum_{s=t}^{\infty}(1+r)^{-(s-t)}\left[A_s F(K_s) - I_s - \frac{\chi I_s^2}{2}\right]$$

subject to the usual capital accumulation equation

$$K_{t+1} = K_t + I_t.$$

Denote by q_t the Lagrange multiplier for the capital accumulation equation in period t, so that the first-order conditions for the firm's maximization problem come from solving

$$\max_{I,K}\sum_{s=t}^{\infty}(1+r)^{-(s-t)}\left[A_s F(K_s) - I_s - \frac{\chi I_s^2}{2} - q_s\left(K_{s+1} - K_s - I_s\right)\right].$$

(a) Differentiate the firm's objective function with respect to I_s and K_s to find the first-order conditions characterizing efficient investment.

(b) Show that the first-order conditions imply the following system in q and K:

$$K_{t+1} - K_t = \frac{q_t - 1}{\chi},$$

$$q_{t+1} - q_t = rq_t - A_{t+1}F'\left(K_t + \frac{q_t - 1}{\chi}\right).$$

(c) Assume that the productivity parameter is constant at A, and draw the phase diagram of the system with q on the vertical axis and K on the horizontal axis. Find the steady state. Does it depend on adjustment costs?

(d) Using your graph, show what happens when there is an unanticipated permanent rise in A to A'. Show the new steady state and the transition to the new steady state.

(e) Now suppose that the system is initially in a steady state corresponding the productivity level A, but the firm learns (by surprise) on date t that A will rise permanently to A' at some future date T. (Perhaps the firm learns that it will be able to use a new invention that aids productivity but not until the patent expires at time T.) Show, using your K, q graph, what happens at time t and thereafter.

(f) In the model of the text, we showed that marginal q equals average q. Is that true in this formulation?

The Life Cycle, Tax Policy, and the Current Account

From the representative-agent models of the preceding chapter, one might infer that fast-growing countries tend to have lower saving rates and larger current-account deficits than slow-growing countries. Clearly this is not always true in practice. Over the period 1983–92, for example, Japan's annual GDP growth averaged nearly 4 percent while that of the United States averaged only 2.7 percent. Yet Japan's saving rate was more than twice that of the United States, and it ran immense current account surpluses while the United States ran deficits. Although there are several stories that might reconcile the representative-agent model with these facts, it is worthwhile considering alternative theoretical approaches.

The most important alternative approach is based on the *overlapping generations model*, first introduced by Allais (1947) and Samuelson (1958). Consistent with the celebrated analysis of life cycle saving due to Modigliani and Brumberg (1954, 1980), the overlapping generations model allows for heterogeneity across young and old consumers. It implies that demographic trends and the generational incidence of taxes can be important determinants of national saving and the current account.

An overlapping generations framework suggests, for example, that the large government budget deficits of the 1980s and the concomitant increases in old-age entitlement programs may have contributed to the United States' low saving rate and high current account deficits. Japan's high saving rate and large current account surpluses, on the other hand, may have been due partly to the saving behavior of a relatively young labor force. If so, Japan's external surpluses may well drop dramatically or even turn to deficits as the large cohort of current workers begins to retire en masse early in the twenty-first century. These explanations plainly are simplistic, but they suggest important factors that are entirely absent from the representative-individual framework of Chapter 2.

The chapter starts with a discussion of government budget deficits and debt, which can have important effects in overlapping generations models, as Diamond (1965) first showed. It then looks at how growth and demographic trends influence the current account in those models.

As in the last chapter, we are able to bring out many of the main ideas in the context of a small-country model, though we also consider a two-country model of global equilibrium. In addition to the most basic overlapping generations model with two-period lives, we study another variant, based on work by Blanchard (1985) and Weil (1989a), in which agents have potentially unbounded lifetimes. We also explore how the strength and nature of intergenerational linkages affects the answers overlapping generations models give compared with those of representative-agent models.

3.1   Government Budget Policy in the Absence of Overlapping Generations

The first step in a more detailed examination of national saving behavior is to distinguish between its two components, *private* saving and *government* saving. Although this distinction is important in general, as we shall see, there are prominent special cases in which it is irrelevant for understanding national saving. The basic model underlying Chapters 1 and 2, which assumes a single representative type of national individual, provides one such case; those chapters didn't worry about public deficit finance. To set the stage for an analysis of government saving in models with richer demographic structures, we first show why government budget deficits are neutral in the representative-agent setting of the first two chapters.

As in those chapters, we assume that population size is constant and normalized to 1, so that the quantity variables entering the representative individual's utility function and budget constraint correspond to economy-wide totals. Starting with the simplest two-period case, we consider in turn the intertemporal budget constraints of individuals and of the government.

If initial private bond holdings are zero, the individual's constraint is derived in the same way as eq. (15) in Chapter 1. Now, however, we want to relax the assumption that the government's budget is balanced in every period. In the individual's budget constraint, taxes, T, which are lump-sum in nature, thus appear in place of government spending, G:

$$C_1 + I_1 + \frac{C_2 + I_2}{1 + r} = Y_1 - T_1 + \frac{Y_2 - T_2}{1 + r}. \tag{1}$$

The corresponding constraint for the government (assuming a zero initial government debt) is

$$G_1 + \frac{G_2}{1 + r} = T_1 + \frac{T_2}{1 + r}, \tag{2}$$

which limits the present value of the government's consumption to the present value of its revenues.

Substituting eq. (2) into eq. (1) yields

$$C_1 + I_1 + \frac{C_2 + I_2}{1 + r} = Y_1 - G_1 + \frac{Y_2 - G_2}{1 + r},$$

which is identical to eq. (15) in Chapter 1. Thus, given the interest rate r, individuals will make the same consumption decisions that they would were the government's budget balanced each period. Since unbalanced government budgets leave individual consumption and investment schedules (expressed as functions of r) unchanged, they have no impact on resource allocation, given G_1 and G_2.

This neutrality of the timing of lump-sum taxes, given government spending levels, should be no surprise. Every dollar of taxes postponed today must be paid with interest tomorrow by the exact same group of taxpayers alive today. Thus all that matters for the consumption choices of these identical individuals is the *present value* of government spending, as in Chapters 1 and 2. As a result, a government deficit, say, cannot affect consumer choices.

Observe that even though a change in the timing of taxes changes government saving, the national saving schedule doesn't change. Private saving is

$$S^P = Y - T - C,$$

whereas government saving is the public budget surplus,

$$S^G = T - G.$$

National saving, the sum of private and government saving, thus is $S^P + S^G = S = Y - C - G$ [as in eq. (13) of Chapter 1, which, however, allows for nonzero initial net foreign assets]. As we have just seen, C is the same, given r. Thus national saving does not change. The reason is that a private saving change exactly offsets any change in government saving. If the government lowers taxes by dT on date 1 and therefore raises them by $(1 + r)dT$ on date 2, the private sector will simply raise its own date 1 saving by dT so that it can pay its higher date 2 tax bill without disturbing the optimal consumption plan it is following.[1]

The assertion that government budget imbalances are irrelevant to resource allocation is called the *Ricardian equivalence* of debt and taxes.[2] In sections 3.2 and 3.7, we shall examine a number of theoretical frameworks in which Ricardian equivalence fails. Even within the confines of the present model, however, a number of very strong assumptions underpin the Ricardian result. It may fail to hold if individuals can't borrow at the same interest rate as the government (or, in the

---

1. The reader may have noticed that we didn't use the small-country assumption to show that the timing of taxes is irrelevant. Indeed, no small-country assumption is needed. Provided national saving and investment schedules do not change—and they do not in this case—equilibria are not altered.

Size does matter for a separate issue, the effects of a change in the timing of government consumption. For a large economy, though not for a negligibly small economy facing a given r, the individual values of the government spending levels G_1 and G_2, and not just the present value, do affect the equilibrium. A small economy can perfectly offset government spending changes through international borrowing or lending if the present value of government spending doesn't change. But the world economy as a whole cannot offset government spending changes through borrowing and lending. Thus a shift in government spending toward the present, even one causing no change in the present value of world government spending at the *initial* world interest rate, will raise the world interest rate.

2. Although the English economist David Ricardo (1772–1823) reviewed theoretical arguments for equivalence in his *Principles of Political Economy and Taxation* (1817), he did not believe the result applied in practice and warned against the dangers of high public debt levels. He feared, in particular, that labor and capital might migrate abroad to avoid the taxes needed to service national debt. See Ricardo (1951, pp. 247–249).

extreme, if their borrowing is capped).[3] And Ricardian equivalence generally fails when taxes are distorting. In this case, changes in the time path of taxes have real effects by changing the severity of tax distortions in different periods. Our current assumption that individuals have finite lives is quite inessential, however: Ricardian equivalence holds in the infinite-horizon model of Chapter 2 provided Ponzi schemes are ruled out.

To see why, write the asset-accumulation identity for a private individual as

$$B_{t+1}^P - B_t^P = Y_t + r_t B_t^P - T_t - C_t - I_t, \tag{3}$$

where B_t^P stands for individual holdings of financial assets other than capital at the end of period $t - 1$. Notice that eq. (3) is the same as eq. (12) of Chapter 1, except for two changes: net *private* assets, B_t^P, appear in place of the overall economy's net foreign assets, B_t, and taxes appear in place of government spending. The same argument that led to lifetime budget constraint (14) of Chapter 2 shows that, under a constant interest rate r,

$$\sum_{s=t}^{\infty} \left(\frac{1}{1+r}\right)^{s-t} (C_s + I_s) = (1+r)B_t^P + \sum_{s=t}^{\infty} \left(\frac{1}{1+r}\right)^{s-t} (Y_s - T_s). \tag{4}$$

A similar argument, based on the government asset-accumulation identity

$$B_{t+1}^G - B_t^G = T_t + r_t B_t^G - G_t \tag{5}$$

leads to the government's intertemporal budget constraint (under a constant interest rate),

$$\sum_{s=t}^{\infty} \left(\frac{1}{1+r}\right)^{s-t} G_s = (1+r)B_t^G + \sum_{s=t}^{\infty} \left(\frac{1}{1+r}\right)^{s-t} T_s, \tag{6}$$

where B_t^G denotes the government's net financial *assets* at the end of period $t - 1$. (The government's assets can include claims on or debts to both domestic residents and foreigners.) As in the two-period case, the present discounted value of government consumption equals the present discounted value of government revenues (including any net asset income). (The government's initial net asset position on date t, B_t^G, may be negative, of course, in which case the government has a debt.)

Notice that B_t, the net foreign asset stock of the economy *as a whole*, is the sum of private assets and government assets,

$$B = B^P + B^G, \tag{7}$$

since the government's net debt vis-à-vis its own citizens cancels out when the private and public sectors are consolidated.

---

3. For further discussion, see Hayashi (1987) and Yotsuzuka (1987).

Once again, the validity of Ricardian equivalence for this economy can be seen by merging the individual and government budget constraints, eqs. (4) and (6), and applying eq. (7):

$$\sum_{s=t}^{\infty} \left(\frac{1}{1+r} \right)^{s-t} (C_s + I_s) = (1+r) B_t + \sum_{s=t}^{\infty} \left(\frac{1}{1+r} \right)^{s-t} (Y_s - G_s). \tag{8}$$

Constraint (8), which is *exactly* constraint (14) of Chapter 2, has two important implications. First (as before), the time path of taxes does not affect individual consumption or investment demands, expressed as functions of the interest rate. Thus mere rearrangement of the time path of lump-sum taxes can't change the world economy's equilibrium. Second, since private individuals fully internalize their government's budget constraint, it doesn't matter how a representative-agent economy's net foreign assets are divided between its private sector and government. Given the path of government spending, a transfer of foreign assets from a country's private sector to its government, say, would cause tax cuts just sufficient to leave the present value of private disposable income unchanged.

3.2   Government Budget Deficits in an Overlapping Generations Model

This section introduces a model that breaks the link between the horizon of private individuals and that of the government. The modification creates a channel through which lump-sum tax policy can alter the economy's equilibrium. Furthermore, the model's predictions about the determinants of private saving are quite different from those of representative-agent models.

3.2.1   A Small Endowment Economy

Consider first a small open endowment economy in which each generation of individuals lives for two periods, and a new generation is born each period. For convenience, we normalize population so that each generation consists of exactly one person. A person born on date t is assumed to have the utility function

$$U \left(c_t^Y, c_{t+1}^O \right) = \log \left(c_t^Y \right) + \beta \log \left(c_{t+1}^O \right). \tag{9}$$

In this equation c_t^Y denotes consumption during youth of someone born on date t and c_{t+1}^O denotes the consumption of the same person while old in period $t + 1$. For simplicity we have assumed that the utility function is logarithmic, though none of the main results that follow depends on this assumption.[4] We assume

---

4. Indeed, since we fix the foreign interest rate throughout the next few sections, it would be sufficient for most of our results to assume that $U \left(c_t^Y, c_{t+1}^O \right)$ is *homothetic* in first- and second-period consumption (so that the optimal ratio c_t^Y/c_{t+1}^O depends only on the interest rate). With homothetic preferences and an unchanging interest rate, the consumer always spends a constant fraction $1 - s$ of lifetime wealth on first-period consumption. For the two-period logarithmic utility function, this fraction $1 - s =$

perfect foresight, although many of the results would have analogs in an explicitly stochastic setting.

Much more complicated overlapping generations models, involving longer life spans, alternative utility functions, and more complicated demographic evolution, are used in both theoretical and applied work. (Indeed, Samuelson's original contribution assumed three periods of life.) The particular case we scrutinize here is a natural one to build on, and it is rich enough to illustrate effects that also are present in more elaborate models.

Let τ_t^Y denote net lump-sum taxes paid by an individual who is young on date t and τ_{t+1}^O the individual's net lump-sum tax bill when old. (Negative values represent net transfer receipts.) This notation allows for the possibility that the government imposes differential taxation on the young and old within the *same* period. (Thus, unlike in a representative-individual model, τ_t^Y is not necessarily equal to τ_t^O even though both taxes apply to the same date.) Ruling out inheritances for the time being, the individual's budget constraint is

$$c_t^Y + \frac{c_{t+1}^O}{1+r} = y_t^Y - \tau_t^Y + \frac{y_{t+1}^O - \tau_{t+1}^O}{1+r}, \tag{10}$$

where the interest rate r is given by the world capital market and assumed to be constant.

The individual's problem is the same one solved in the two-period model of Chapter 1. Maximizing eq. (9) subject to eq. (10) yields the intertemporal Euler equation,

$$c_{t+1}^O = (1+r)\,\beta c_t^Y. \tag{11}$$

Every individual's consumption path over the two periods of life is upward tilting if $1 + r$ exceeds $1/\beta$, and downward tilting in the opposite case. Together, Euler equation (11) and budget constraint (10) imply the consumption demands:

$$c_t^Y = \left(\frac{1}{1+\beta}\right)\left(y_t^Y - \tau_t^Y + \frac{y_{t+1}^O - \tau_{t+1}^O}{1+r}\right), \tag{12}$$

$$c_{t+1}^O = (1+r)\left(\frac{\beta}{1+\beta}\right)\left(y_t^Y - \tau_t^Y + \frac{y_{t+1}^O - \tau_{t+1}^O}{1+r}\right). \tag{13}$$

$1/(1+\beta)$. For isoelastic period utility,

$$1 - s = \frac{1}{1 + (1+r)^{\sigma-1}\beta^\sigma}.$$

(Recall section 1.3.2.3.) We choose log utility for ease of exposition and the reader should have no trouble generalizing the results.

Although the *individual's* problem is the same as in previous chapters, there is no longer a single representative individual. Instead, two different individuals coexist on each date. Thus, to study the economy's *aggregate* behavior, we have to add up over the two generations alive each period. Aggregate consumption C_t in period t is the sum of consumption by the young and consumption by the old:

$$C_t = c_t^Y + c_t^O. \tag{14}$$

Careful attention to the government's intertemporal budget constraint is critical in what follows. The constraint is no different from the one that applies in the representative-agent economy, but it recognizes now that different demographic groups may face different tax rates. Let G denote aggregate government consumption (*not* government consumption in per capita terms, which equals $G/2$). The increase in government assets between the ends of dates t and $t-1$ is the difference between government net revenues (including public asset income) and government consumption. Thus,

$$B_{t+1}^G - B_t^G = \tau_t^Y + \tau_t^O + r B_t^G - G_t. \tag{15}$$

(Notice that now B^G denotes aggregate, not per capita, government assets. This distinction was not important in the representative-agent model.) Coupled with a prohibition on Ponzi games, constraint (15) leads, in the usual way, to the government's intertemporal budget constraint,

$$\sum_{s=t}^{\infty} \left(\frac{1}{1+r} \right)^{s-t} G_s = (1+r)B_t^G + \sum_{s=t}^{\infty} \left(\frac{1}{1+r} \right)^{s-t} \left(\tau_s^Y + \tau_s^O \right). \tag{16}$$

This equation is exactly the same as eq. (6), of course, because aggregate taxes T equal $\tau^Y + \tau^O$.[5]

To understand the implications of eqs. (12) and (13) for the economy's overall equilibrium, it is helpful to spend a moment on the special case in which y_t^Y, y_t^O, τ_t^Y, τ_t^O, and G_t are constant over time at y^Y, y^O, τ^Y, τ^O, and G. In this case, each young individual is identical with the young of prior generations, and the consumption of the economy's representative young and old residents is constant period after period at the levels c^Y and c^O implied by eqs. (12) and (13). Adding, we find that aggregate consumption also is constant at

$$C = \left[\frac{1 + (1+r)\beta}{1+\beta} \right] \left(y^Y - \tau^Y + \frac{y^O - \tau^O}{1+r} \right).$$

Because government spending and (age-specific) tax levels are constant through time, the government's budget constraint (16) reduces to

---

$$G = rB^G + \tau^Y + \tau^O,$$

where we omit the subscript on B^G because it must be constant over time if spending and taxes are. Using this constraint to eliminate τ^O from the preceding expression for aggregate consumption yields

$$C = \left[\frac{1 + (1+r)\beta}{1+\beta}\right]\left(y^Y + \frac{y^O - G - r\tau^Y + rB^G}{1+r}\right).$$

Notice that we do not require the assumption that $(1+r)\beta = 1$ to achieve stable aggregate consumption, as we did in the models of Chapters 1 and 2. Even though every *individual's* consumption may rise or fall over his life cycle, he dies off after two periods of life, and his place is taken by an identical member of the generation following his. Therefore the *cross-sectional* profile of consumption in the economy remains constant. An implication is that a small open economy's consumption will reach a steady state even when $(1+r)\beta \neq 1$, in sharp contrast to the case in which all individuals share the same life span. Also in sharp contrast to the models of the last two chapters is the feature that aggregate consumption can depend not only on government spending, but also on tax policy (represented by the presence of τ^Y in the aggregate consumption equation) and on the level of government assets. Thus this is a model in which the Ricardian equivalence of debt and taxes does not hold.

3.2.2   Government Saving, Private Saving, and the Current Account

How do changes in the government's budget deficit affect the nation's current account balance? The current account is the change in the economy's total net foreign assets. In an economy without investment, all of an economy's *net* assets are claims on foreigners—claims of domestic entities on other domestic entities net out. By eq. (7), a country's total net assets are the sum of private and government assets. Thus,

$$CA_t = B_{t+1} - B_t = B_{t+1}^P + B_{t+1}^G - \left(B_t^P + B_t^G\right)$$

$$= \left(B_{t+1}^P - B_t^P\right) + \left(B_{t+1}^G - B_t^G\right). \tag{17}$$

This equation says that the current account is the sum of net saving by the private sector, $S_t^P = B_{t+1}^P - B_t^P$, and net saving by the government, $S_t^G = B_{t+1}^G - B_t^G$. Of course, the current account here is still also given by $CA_t = rB_t + Y_t - C_t - G_t$, as usual, but it is often instructive to view the problem from the perspective of eq. (17).

For a given government budget policy, how is aggregate private saving determined? The economy's private financial assets at the end of period t equal the savings of the period t young (because the old consume all their wealth and therefore hold no assets at the period's end). The young of period t start out with no assets, so their saving is

$$S_t^Y = B_{t+1}^P. \tag{18}$$

The old of period t simply decumulate the assets B_t^P they accumulated in youth (or repay youthful debts if B_t^P is negative),[6]

$$S_t^O = -S_{t-1}^Y = -B_t^P. \tag{19}$$

As a result, total net private saving,

$$S_t^P = S_t^Y + S_t^O = B_{t+1}^P - B_t^P, \tag{20}$$

is the sum of saving by the young and saving by the old.

Notice a key implication of eqs. (7) and (18). In our overlapping generations model, the economy's net foreign assets at the end of period t equal the savings of the young plus the government's assets at the end of the period:

$$B_{t+1} = B_{t+1}^P + B_{t+1}^G = S_t^Y + B_{t+1}^G. \tag{21}$$

In the special case $\beta(1+r) = 1$, individual consumption profiles are flat [see eqs. (12) and (13)], and the solution for saving by the young generation simplifies to

$$S_t^Y = y_t^Y - \tau_t^Y - c_t^Y = \left(\frac{\beta}{1+\beta}\right)\left[(y_t^Y - \tau_t^Y) - (y_{t+1}^O - \tau_{t+1}^O)\right] = B_{t+1}^P. \tag{22}$$

Consolidating eq. (22) and eq. (19), which describes the saving of the old, we see that total private saving on date t, S_t^P, is

$$S_t^P = B_{t+1}^P - B_t^P = S_t^Y - S_{t-1}^Y = \left(\frac{\beta}{1+\beta}\right)\left[\Delta\left(y_t^Y - \tau_t^Y\right) - \Delta\left(y_{t+1}^O - \tau_{t+1}^O\right)\right], \tag{23}$$

where, for any variable X, $\Delta X_t \equiv X_t - X_{t-1}$.[7] Equation (23) emphasizes that aggregate private saving depends on how the economy's age-earnings profile is changing over time, an interpretation we shall return to later on in section 3.3.2.

3.2.3   The Timing of Taxes: An Example

In overlapping generations models, the timing of taxes can have significant implications for aggregate consumption, the economy's net foreign assets, and the

---

6. The old consume all of their disposable income, including the interest on their earlier savings, but that interest is part of their income. Their saving thus is $S_t^O = rS_{t-1}^Y + y_t^O - \tau_t^O - c_t^O$. By the intertemporal budget constraint,

$$y_t^O - \tau_t^O - c_t^O = -(1+r)\left(y_{t-1}^Y - \tau_{t-1}^Y - c_{t-1}^Y\right) = -(1+r)S_{t-1}^Y.$$

The conclusion is that $S_t^O = -S_{t-1}^Y$.

7. This definition means, for example, that

$$\Delta\left(y_t^Y - \tau_t^Y\right) = y_t^Y - \tau_t^Y - \left(y_{t-1}^Y - \tau_{t-1}^Y\right),$$

that is, the change in the disposable income of a young person between dates $t-1$ and t.

intergenerational welfare distribution. To understand the economic forces at work, we consider a simple illustrative example in which the government issues debt to finance a one-time transfer payment, divided equally between the current young and old. In the representative-agent model of the last two chapters, a bond-financed transfer would have no effect on consumption, the economy's net foreign asset position, or anyone's welfare. Individuals would anticipate the higher future taxes needed to pay off the debt and would simply save the entire transfer to cover those taxes. As we now see, matters are not so simple in the overlapping generations model.

Suppose that in period $t = 0$, the government lowers the per capita taxes paid by both the young and the old by $d/2$, financing its higher budget deficit in period 0 by selling bonds worth d to each of the current young. That is, the current tax bill of the young falls to $\tau_0^Y - (d/2)$ and the current tax bill of the old falls to $\tau_0^O - (d/2)$, but the government's net end-of-period assets B_1^G decline to $B_1^G - d$ as a result. Assume further that the tax burden due to future interest payments on the added debt, rd, is split evenly between young and old generations. That is, for all $t \geq 1$, per capita taxes on the young and old rise to $\tau_t^Y + (rd/2)$ and $\tau_t^O + (rd/2)$, respectively.[8] This policy always has the government changing the net taxes of contemporaneous generations by identical amounts, thus offering a close parallel to our earlier treatment of bond financing in the representative agent case.

Here, however, unlike in the representative-agent model, aggregate consumption rises in the short run and falls in the long run. Let variables with primes ($'$) denote the economy's path after the fiscal policies we have described are implemented. The period 0 old obviously consume their entire windfall transfer, so

$$c_0^{O\prime} = c_0^O + \frac{d}{2}. \tag{24}$$

The young of period 0 receive the same windfall $d/2$, but, for two reasons, do not consume it all at once. First, they want to spread the consumption benefits of their windfall over both periods of their lives. Second, the net benefit to them is not quite as large as that to the date 0 old; the young will face added taxes $rd/2$ in their old age. Thus, by eq. (12), the consumption change for the period 0 young is

$$c_0^{Y\prime} = c_0^Y + \frac{1}{1+\beta}\left(1 - \frac{r}{1+r}\right)\frac{d}{2} = c_0^Y + \frac{1}{1+\beta}\left(\frac{1}{1+r}\right)\frac{d}{2}. \tag{25}$$

---

8. Under the scheme in the text, the government never pays off the principal on the added debt [although, as you can confirm, the intertemporal budget constraint (16) is still satisfied if it already held before the added period 0 deficit]. The short-term effects would be qualitatively similar if the government were to pay off the new debt in full in period 1. By period 3, however, the economy would return to its original path.

Adding eqs. (24) and (25), we see that aggregate date 0 consumption C_0 rises, but by

$$c_0^{O\,\prime} + c_0^{Y\,\prime} - (c_0^O + c_0^Y) = \left[1 + \frac{1}{(1+\beta)(1+r)}\right]\frac{d}{2}, \tag{26}$$

an amount less than d.

What happens in following periods? Now we use eq. (13). The period 1 old, who were young in period 0, still have higher consumption, equal to

$$c_1^{O\,\prime} = c_1^O + (1+r)\frac{\beta}{1+\beta}\left(1 - \frac{r}{1+r}\right)\frac{d}{2} = c_1^O + \left(\frac{\beta}{1+\beta}\right)\frac{d}{2}. \tag{27}$$

The period 1 young generation, and all generations born afterward, are the losers, of course. For all these generations, lifetime income changes by

$$-\left(1 + \frac{1}{1+r}\right)\left(\frac{rd}{2}\right) = -\left(\frac{2r + r^2}{1+r}\right)\left(\frac{d}{2}\right).$$

As a result, their consumption while young falls to

$$c_t^{Y\,\prime} = c_t^Y - \left(\frac{1}{1+\beta}\right)\left(\frac{2r + r^2}{1+r}\right)\left(\frac{d}{2}\right), \tag{28}$$

and their consumption while old falls to

$$c_t^{O\,\prime} = c_t^O - \left(\frac{\beta}{1+\beta}\right)(2r + r^2)\left(\frac{d}{2}\right). \tag{29}$$

Combining eqs. (27) and (28) (the latter for $t = 1$), we see that aggregate period 1 consumption changes by

$$c_1^{O\,\prime} + c_1^{Y\,\prime} - (c_1^O + c_1^Y) = \left[\left(\frac{\beta}{1+\beta}\right) - \left(\frac{1}{1+\beta}\right)\left(\frac{2r + r^2}{1+r}\right)\right]\left(\frac{d}{2}\right), \tag{30}$$

which has an ambiguous sign.[9] As addition of eqs. (28) and (29) confirms, aggregate consumption is unambiguously lower from period 2 on.[10]

---

9. The ambiguity necessarily remains for more general homothetic preferences. Follow the same steps as in the text, replacing $1/(1+\beta)$ by $1 - s$ and $\beta/(1+\beta)$ by s. The condition for first-period consumption to rise is

$$\frac{s}{1-s} > \frac{2r + r^2}{1+r},$$

where $1 - s$ is the share of lifetime wealth devoted to first-period (youth) consumption.

10. In the special case $\beta(1+r) = 1$, steady-state aggregate consumption falls by rd. More generally,

The changed government budget deficit has real effects in this example because the transfer and tax policies that accompany it shift income among generations. Generations living at time 0 receive a net positive transfer (paid for by all future generations) and raise their consumption accordingly. The reactions of the future generations hurt by the budget deficit don't affect date 0 aggregate consumption for the simple reason that those generations haven't yet been born! Ricardian equivalence fails under the overlapping generations demographics we have assumed because government borrowing can shift current taxes from today's population to unrelated individuals who will be born later.[11]

We can solve for the path of the current account in the preceding example either by summing government and private savings as in eq. (17) or by subtracting aggregate expenditure from GNP, $Y_t + rB_t - C_t - G_t$. Since output and government spending are constant throughout (there is no investment), the latter approach is slightly simpler. Note that in period 0, net foreign assets are given, so the only element of the current account identity to change is consumption. Therefore, the period 0 current account change is simply

$$CA_0' - CA_0 = -\left[c_0^{O\,\prime} + c_0^{Y\,\prime} - (c_0^O + c_0^Y)\right] = -\left[1 + \frac{1}{(1+\beta)(1+r)}\right]\frac{d}{2} \tag{31}$$

by eq. (26). As we have already seen, the far-right-hand-side term is less than d in absolute value because the period 0 young save more. To find the period 1 current account change, we note that the rise in net foreign assets entering period 1 is equal simply to the change in the period 0 current account. Therefore, to find $CA_1' - CA_1$, we must add the interest on $CA_0' - CA_0$ to the period 1 change in consumption:

$$CA_1' - CA_1 = r\left(CA_0' - CA_0\right) - \left[c_1^{O\,\prime} + c_1^{Y\,\prime} - (c_1^O + c_1^Y)\right].$$

Use of eqs. (31) and (30) yields

$$CA_1' - CA_1 = -\left(\frac{\beta}{1+\beta}\right)(1+r)\left(\frac{d}{2}\right). \tag{32}$$

The current account thus remains negative in period 1. It is easy to check that there is no change for dates $t > 1$ because all generations living on dates $t > 1$ bear the debt burden equally. Thus the current account temporarily worsens, returning to its original path after two periods.

---

when there is a consumption-tilting effect, it falls by

$$\left(1 + \frac{\beta r}{1+\beta}\right)\left(\frac{2r + r^2}{1+r}\right)\left(\frac{d}{2}\right).$$

11. In section 3.7.1 we will look into a question that may have occurred to you, namely, what happens when current generations, who presumably beget the generations that follow, care about their welfare?

Nonetheless, the period 0 fiscal deficit has *permanent* effects. The consumption equations for those born in or after period 1, eqs. (28) and (29), show that consumption is lower in both periods of life for all future generations. The higher current account deficits for dates 0 and 1 imply that increased government indebtedness has reduced the net foreign asset position of the economy. Higher consumption by those alive in period 0 thus is financed through the accumulation of a foreign debt that future generations must service.

In our example we assumed an initial government deficit and a specific, arbitrary rule for splitting the resulting government interest burden between the young and the old. However, intergenerational redistributions can alter the economy's consumption, saving, and net foreign assets even when no public budget imbalance is involved. Consider, for example, a one-time tax-financed transfer from young to old. On the date the transfer (unexpectedly) is made, the young, who smooth consumption, do not reduce it by as much as the old increase theirs. Thus there is no government budget deficit, but the country nonetheless runs a current account deficit. Conversely, one can easily think up fiscal policies that involve deficits yet have no non-Ricardian real effects. (For an example see Box 3.1, which discusses "generational accounting" as an alternative to the conventionally measured government deficit.)

The general point is that it makes no sense to ask about the impact of fiscal changes, whether they entail government debt issue or not, without carefully specifying how the associated future tax changes affect the budget constraints of current and future generations.

3.2.4 Evidence on Ricardian Equivalence

Does the available empirical evidence support or refute the Ricardian view of tax policy? As often in economics, the data are difficult to interpret without ambiguity. History contains few, if any, Ricardian experiments in which taxes are changed independently of other events that might simultaneously influence consumption and saving. Moreover, many of the tests one might conduct require strong maintained assumptions about the nature of the aggregate consumption function, interest-rate and income expectations, and other features of the economic environment. Such assumptions are necessary because the econometrician cannot know all the coincidental influences on consumption that ideally should be controlled to isolate the pure effects of government deficits and debts.

Bernheim (1987) offers a catalog of the econometric difficulties along with a vigorous critique of the empirical work supporting Ricardian equivalence. Barro's (1989) alternative discussion finds more empirical support for equivalence. A particularly striking piece of contrary evidence is Wilcox's (1989) discovery that, in monthly 1965–85 United States data, changes in social security benefits are

Box 3.1
Generational Accounting

Generational accounting is a convenient methodology for summarizing how tax changes alter the intertemporal budget constraints facing different generations. The basic insight of the approach is that the government's intertemporal budget constraint can be expressed in terms of the present-value net lifetime tax burdens that enter individual budget constraints.

In the context of our overlapping generations model with two-period lifetimes, observe that the government's intertemporal budget constraint, eq. (16), can be rewritten as

$$\sum_{s=t}^{\infty} \left(\frac{1}{1+r} \right)^{s-t} G_s - (1+r) B_t^G = \tau_t^O + \sum_{s=t}^{\infty} \left(\frac{1}{1+r} \right)^{s-t} \left(\tau_s^Y + \frac{\tau_{s+1}^O}{1+r} \right).$$

All we have done above is to regroup the government's tax receipts according to the generation that pays them, not the date on which the taxes are paid. The term

$$\tau_s^Y + \frac{\tau_{s+1}^O}{1+r}$$

is called the *generational account* for the generation born on date s. It is the same present value of net lifetime taxes determining the generation's intertemporal consumption possibilities. Thus the government's budget constraint equates the present value of government spending, net of initial government assets, to the present value of the generational accounts. (The generational account of a generation that has already been born is simply the current present value of its *remaining* net tax liabilities.)*

The generational accounting perspective emphasizes that, for a given path of government spending, a reduction in one generation's account can only be achieved through expanding other generations' accounts in a way that respects the government's intertemporal budget constraint.

The generational accounting perspective also shows how misleading the government deficit can be as an indicator of intergenerational redistributions. Take the example of an unfunded, pay-as-you-go social security scheme, which lowers the net taxes of the old while raising those of the young by an equal amount, thus avoiding the need for government borrowing on any date. Despite the complete absence of any government deficit, the introduction of social security has effects analogous to those of the public-sector borrowing analyzed in section 3.2.3. The generational account of the current old falls, but that of every younger generation rises. As a result, the consumption of the current old is enhanced, but that of subsequent generations is diminished. Furthermore, future generations, having less after-tax income in youth but expecting social security payments in old age, lower their saving. Even though there has been no government deficit, the economy's net foreign assets decline.

Box 3.1 *(continued)*

An alternative fiscal policy that lowers each τ_s^Y ($s \geq t$) by a unit while simultaneously raising the corresponding τ_{s+1}^O by $1 + r$ units does not change any generation's account and thus does not affect any generation's consumption. Nor do national saving or the country's net foreign asset stock change on any date. (Why?) The policy does, however, increase the government fiscal deficit by 1 on date t (while leaving the deficit unchanged for dates after t). Although perhaps unrealistic, this fiscal policy package provides an example of a deficit that has no resource-allocation effects, the overlapping-generations structure of the population notwithstanding. In reality, government deficits normally do transfer at least some income from future generations to those currently alive.

Advocates of generational accounting argue that conventionally measured fiscal deficits are essentially meaningless, as gauges either of macroeconomic policy or of the intergenerational fairness of government policy. In their view, conventional deficit measures should effectively be banished from policy debate and replaced by generational accounts. Given the importance of old-age entitlement programs (for example, social security) in the industrialized world, it is certainly true that conventional government debt-burden measures miss a major part of the action in fiscal policy. On the other hand, there are some practical obstacles to making a wholesale switch to newer, theoretically sounder measures of fiscal policy. For one thing, generational accounts are typically very sensitive to the interest rate chosen to discount future government taxes and transfers, and they require heroic projections on the future growth of national productivity. This sensitivity raises the concern that politicians would have too much freedom in making fiscal projections, rendering them essentially meaningless. Nevertheless, generational accounts are clearly a useful tool for thinking about fiscal policy, both for policymakers and for researchers interested in the effects of budget deficits.[†]

---

[*] For a discussion of generational accounting, see Auerbach, Gokhale, and Kotlikoff (1991). Calvo and Obstfeld (1988) show how the government in a closed overlapping generations economy can vary generational accounts so as to attain socially preferred equilibrium paths for generational consumption levels and the capital stock.

[†] Conventional, cash-flow-based deficit measures can be relevant when individuals are borrowing constrained (see the application on p. 146) or when taxes are distorting (Bohn, 1992).

---

strongly positively correlated with contemporaneous changes in aggregate consumption expenditures. Except in the unlikely case that increases in benefits coincide with cuts in future government spending, the pattern Wilcox finds is hard to rationalize if consumers currently alive internalize the future taxes needed to pay for higher social security benefits.[12]

---

12. Since the increases in social security benefits are always announced more than a month in advance of their payment, Wilcox's finding that the (anticipated) payments themselves seem to affect consumption goes against the spirit of forward-looking consumption theories. However, some social security recipients are liquidity constrained and, as Deaton (1992, p. 162) suggests, some may not keep informed about future changes in their benefits.

Difficulties of interpretation notwithstanding, both time-series and cross-section data indicate a generally positive correlation between consumption and measures of government deficits; see Bernheim (1987). The government deficit captures the intergenerational impact of tax policy imperfectly, as we saw in the discussion of generational accounting. Nonetheless, the regularity Bernheim reports suggests that current accounts might be negatively related to government deficits, as in our overlapping generations model, rather than being completely unrelated as Ricardian equivalence implies. The next application takes the question to data from industrial countries.

Application: Do Government Budget Deficits Cause Current Account Deficits?

Overlapping generations models suggest that in realistic cases, government budget deficits will induce current account deficits by redistributing income from future to present generations. Is any such tendency apparent in data from those countries with the easiest access to international capital markets?

An unsophisticated but transparent way to organize the data is simply as a cross-section regression of the current account surplus (expressed as a percent of GDP) on the general government surplus (similarly expressed). For a sample of 19 OECD countries, a regression with each country's data averaged over the 1981–86 period yields a positive and statistically significant coefficient:

$$CA/Y = -3.55 + 0.78(T - G)/Y, \qquad R^2 = 0.24.$$
$$(4.06) \ \ (0.33)$$

Figure 3.1 shows the data underlying this regression.[13]

The 1981–86 period seems to be somewhat atypical, however. Similar regressions over other five-year spans after 1970 yield insignificant slope estimates. One should not attach too much weight to the regressions because they omit important variables that potentially affect current accounts. Further, as we have seen, conventionally measured deficits may not capture adequately the intergenerational transfers that feed into saving and the current account.

A different approach is to look for drastic shifts in tax policy that may approximate the Ricardian experiment of a ceteris paribus tax cut. There are two reasonably good recent examples among major industrial countries, the United States tax cuts of the early 1980s and the large government transfer program from the western to the eastern parts of reunified Germany starting in 1990. Figure 3.2 shows that in both cases, the fiscal shift widened the government budget and current ac-

---

13. The countries included are Australia, Austria, Belgium, Canada, Denmark, Finland, France, Germany, Greece, Ireland, Italy, Japan, the Netherlands, Norway, Portugal, Spain, Sweden, the United Kingdom, and the United States.

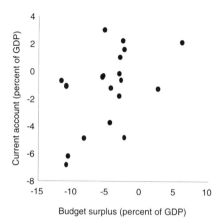

Figure 3.1
Current accounts and fiscal surpluses of industrial countries, 1981–86

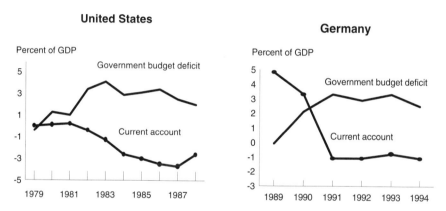

Figure 3.2
Government and foreign borrowing: United States and Germany

count deficits simultaneously. Interpretation of the German data is complicated by their coverage of reunified Germany after 1990, but of only western Germany up to the end of 1990. One robust implication of the Ricardian proposition, however, is that western Germans should have increased their saving after 1990 in the face of mounting evidence that the huge deficit-financed transfers to the east would continue for some time. Private saving in the west did not appear to increase, however.

∎

Application: Overlapping Generations and Econometric Tests of the Euler Equation

Despite their differences, the overlapping generations model and the infinite-horizon representative-consumer model share a common prediction: an individual's lifetime consumption path satisfies the consumption Euler equation. Using the more general utility function $U\left(c_t^Y, c_{t+1}^O\right) = u(c_t^Y) + \beta u(c_{t+1}^O)$ and allowing for a variable real interest rate, we would write the individual Euler equation that figures in the overlapping generations model as

$$u'(c_t^Y) = (1 + r_{t+1})\beta u'(c_{t+1}^O).$$

As we have seen, however, the two models can lead to very different descriptions of the economy's aggregate consumption despite containing similar-looking individual Euler equations.

   These differences also affect attempts to test empirically whether actual individual consumption levels and asset returns are jointly generated according to the stochastic Euler equation

$$u'(c_t) = \beta E_t \left\{(1 + r_{t+1})u'(c_{t+1})\right\},$$

in which the notation suggests that the real interest rate to be earned on date t investments may be uncertain.[14] Econometric tests of Euler equations using aggregate per capita United States consumption data for c have tended to reject it.[15]

   But such tests involve potential aggregation problems that are fatal for reliable statistical inference. If the economy indeed has an overlapping generations structure, a major problem is that aggregate consumption is being carried out by different groups of people on different dates. In this case we wouldn't necessarily expect aggregate consumption on a particular date to be related in any special way to aggregate consumption on other dates. For example, the consumption of the young on date $t + 1$ need bear no particular relationship to that of the old on date t, even though the Euler equation does link the consumption of the date t young to that of the date $t + 1$ old (who are the same, one-period older, people).

---

14. The stochastic Euler equation of Chapter 2 assumed a known, riskless real interest rate. The Euler equation in this application, which encompasses assets with random returns, will be rigorously derived and analyzed in Chapter 5.

15. See, for example, Mankiw, Rotemberg, and Summers (1985). These tests are based on the idea that the ex post forecast error $\beta(1 + r_{t+1})u'(c_{t+1}) - u'(c_t)$ must be statistically uncorrelated with any information the consumer knows as of date t. Given a specific parametric class of utility functions $u(c)$ and data on a sufficiently large number of economic variables from the consumer's date t information set, one can estimate the parameters of $u(c)$, form estimated forecast errors, and test whether the latter are uncorrelated with lagged information. Obviously the test is based on important maintained hypotheses about the form of the utility function.

Tests on micro-level data can in principle avoid this aggregation problem, but have led to ambiguous results. In one important paper, Zeldes (1989a) presents evidence that a significant fraction of the U.S. families tracked by the time-series/cross-section Panel Study on Income Dynamics (PSID) behave as if they are unable to borrow as much as they would like. Since the PSID covers food consumption only, interpretation of Zeldes' results requires strong maintained assumptions, such as the separability in preferences of food consumption and other forms of consumption. A study of the British Family Expenditure Survey by Attanasio and Weber (1993) presents results more favorable to the Euler equation for the average consumption of the age cohort born in the decade 1930–40. Attanasio and Weber (1995) likewise find that data from the U.S. 1980–90 Consumer Expenditure Survey do not contradict the validity of a generalized Euler equation at the household level.

Many of the problems that prevent individuals and countries from borrowing as much as they would like in international markets (see Chapter 6) also limit to some degree households' borrowing even from lenders of the same nationality. Casual observation suggests that borrowing constraints do affect many households, especially those with low incomes and little collateralizable wealth.[16] Thus Euler equations are unlikely to hold exactly for all individuals. This departure from the theory does not imply, however, that it yields a poor approximation in practice, or that the basic insight that consumers look forward in planning consumption is anything less than an important and even central feature of the macroeconomy. ∎

3.3   Output Fluctuations, Demographics, and the Life Cycle

The overlapping generations approach captures the essence of the *life-cycle theory* of consumption and saving introduced by Modigliani and Brumberg (1954). According to that view, individuals or families with finite horizons arrange their saving so as to maintain a more or less constant consumption level through youth, middle age, and retirement. Despite a similar spirit in assuming forward-looking consumers, the life-cycle account should be distinguished from Friedman's (1957) *permanent income theory*, as set out in Chapter 2. The permanent-income consumer effectively lives forever, and an economy peopled by a representative permanent-income consumer yields very different predictions about aggregate saving than one peopled by overlapping generations of life-cycle consumers. We have already seen one difference in our discussion of Ricardian equivalence. The overlapping generations model also makes distinct predictions about the response of aggregate saving

---

16. See Jappelli and Pagano (1989) for a discussion of international evidence, Guiso, Jappelli, and Terlizzese (1992) for a detailed look at the case of Italy.

to output changes, and these provide a potentially powerful empirical basis for distinguishing between the permanent-income and life-cycle theories.

3.3.1   Effects of Transitory Output Movements

In the infinite-horizon representative consumer model of Chapter 2, a temporary unanticipated rise in output led to a smaller, but permanent, increase in the path of aggregate consumption. Overlapping generations models tell a different story, as the simple economy developed in the last section illustrates.

Suppose that on date $t = 0$ the per capita endowments of the young and old alike rise temporarily and unexpectedly by an amount dy, returning to their initial paths on date $t = 1$. The path of the government budget is unaffected, as is the path of saving for all generations born on or after date 1. Nor does the shock change the saving of the date 0 old, who simply consume all of their additional income. Therefore, to track the current account effect of the shock, we need only look at the path of saving for the period 0 young. Equation (12) implies that the date 0 young will save the portion $\beta/(1 + \beta)$ of their additional income dy, in order to smooth consumption. As a result, there is an equal rise in the period 0 external surplus. Then, at date 1, the formerly young spend the entire principal plus interest. The current account deficit for period 1 is higher by an amount exactly equal to the extra principal consumed.

Summarizing (in the notation of section 3.2.3), we see that the temporary surprise increase dy in date 0 endowments shifts the date 0 and 1 current accounts by

$$CA_0' - CA_0 = \left(\frac{\beta}{1 + \beta}\right) dy,$$

$$CA_1' - CA_1 = -\left(\frac{\beta}{1 + \beta}\right) dy,$$

but leaves the current account unchanged for dates $t \geq 2$. The current account temporarily improves, as in the infinite-horizon representative consumer model, but then, in contrast, it worsens, canceling the previous period's gain in net foreign assets. Although the very short-run effects of the shock are broadly similar in the two models, the effects in subsequent periods are not. In the overlapping generations model, temporary income shocks have *no* long-run effects.

3.3.2   Trend Output Growth and Saving

An overlapping generations model's predictions about how long-term output changes affect the current account also generally differ from those of the infinite-horizon consumer model. These predictions are intimately connected with trends in the size and age structure of the population.

We have been abstracting from demographic change by assuming that each generation—hence, the aggregate population—is of constant size. Let us continue to do so initially in order to focus on the pure effects of output growth in our simple model economy.

Equation (23), which is based on our logarithmic example with $\beta(1 + r) = 1$, captures these effects. We rewrite it here for convenience:

$$S_t^P = B_{t+1}^P - B_t^P = S_t^Y - S_{t-1}^Y = \left(\frac{\beta}{1 + \beta}\right)\left[\Delta\left(y_t^Y - \tau_t^Y\right) - \Delta\left(y_{t+1}^O - \tau_{t+1}^O\right)\right]. \tag{23}$$

It is sometimes argued that countries with rapid trend growth in per capita incomes (Japan is an example) will also have high saving rates, and, if other things are equal, larger current account surpluses. This outcome does not occur in the infinite-horizon representative-consumer model, where higher expected future income *reduces* the need for current saving. Equation (23) shows, however, that higher per capita output growth will raise *aggregate* private saving if the growth in the output young people produce rises more than the growth in that of old people. Why? The basic reason is that one's saving when young depends positively on contemporaneous earnings and negatively on old-age earnings. Total private saving equals the saving of this period's young less that of last period's young. Thus total saving rises whenever the saving of this period's young rises relative to that of last period's young; and, in the present logarithmic model, this occurs when earnings while young rises more than earnings while old. We can see this connection clearly by rearranging the terms in eq. (23) so that it reads

$$S_t^P = \left(\frac{\beta}{1 + \beta}\right)\left\{\underbrace{\left(y_t^Y - \tau_t^Y\right) - \left(y_{t+1}^O - \tau_{t+1}^O\right)}_{(1+\beta)S_t^Y/\beta} - \underbrace{\left[\left(y_{t-1}^Y - \tau_{t-1}^Y\right) - \left(y_t^O - \tau_t^O\right)\right]}_{(1+\beta)S_{t-1}^Y/\beta}\right\}.$$

To understand more fully the two competing effects of growth on a country's saving and current account, we turn to a special case of the overlapping-generations model with two-period lives.

In intercountry or intertemporal comparisons of saving behavior, the *level* of a country's saving is not a very informative variable: it is much easier to interpret variations in the saving *rate*, that is, the fraction of GNP that is saved. For the same reason, we focus below on how changes in the percentage *rate* of GDP growth affect saving.

Take government taxes and spending to be zero for simplicity, and assume that, over any individual's lifetime, earnings growth is given by

$$y_{t+1}^O = (1 + e)y_t^Y,$$

where the possibly negative number e (we assume $e \geq -1$) is the growth rate of an individual's lifetime earnings. On the other hand, let g denote the (nonnegative) growth rate of a young person's endowment across generations,

$$y_{t+1}^Y = (1+g)y_t^Y.$$

Since y_{t+1}^O and y_t^Y stand in a constant ratio to each other (given by $1+e$), g is also the growth rate of an old person's endowment *and* of aggregate output, $Y_t = y_t^Y + y_t^O$. To visualize what is going on, observe that all generations have identically-sloped age-earnings profiles, while the starting point for the profiles of successive generations grows at rate g.

Given the preceding data about the economy, eq. (23) shows that the private saving rate (relative to total GDP) is

$$\frac{S_t^P}{Y_t} = -\frac{\beta}{1+\beta}\left(\frac{eg}{2+e+g}\right).$$

In this simple model, saving will be positive or negative depending on whether earnings fall ($e < 0$) or rise ($e > 0$) over an individual's life cycle. A rise in e causes every individual's saving while young to fall. What is the effect on aggregate saving? Assuming (realistically) that the growth rate g of total output is positive, the share in output of youthful saving (dissaving) must be greater than the share of old dissaving (saving). Thus, a rise in lifetime earnings growth, e, which lowers saving by the young and raises saving by the old, lowers aggregate private saving:

$$\frac{d(S_t^P/Y_t)}{de} = -\frac{\beta}{1+\beta}\left[\frac{g(2+g)}{(2+e+g)^2}\right] < 0.$$

Consider next the effects of a rise in the aggregate output growth rate, g. The change in the saving rate is

$$\frac{d(S_t^P/Y_t)}{dg} = -\frac{\beta}{1+\beta}\left[\frac{e(2+e)}{(2+e+g)^2}\right],$$

the sign of which depends on that of e. If $e < 0$ (the case we would need to get a positive aggregate saving rate), a rise in g, unlike a rise in e, raises the aggregate private saving rate. The reason: young people save a positive amount, and when income growth accelerates, the scale of their saving in GDP rises compared to that of dissaving by the old. Reversing the signs, the same reasoning shows why a rise in g would lower the aggregate private saving rate were e positive.

A rise in expected aggregate output growth raises the aggregate saving rate here when the young are net savers because the growth accrues to a succession of different generations. No single decision maker's budget constraint incorporates all the future benefits of growth. Higher growth influences the overall saving rate through a scale effect that raises the wealth accumulated by young savers relative to the wealth decumulated by the old. This effect explains the contrast with the representative-individual model of aggregate saving.

It is easy to imagine more complicated scenarios than the one just analyzed, in which aggregate productivity growth affects the young and old uniformly. To know how faster income growth will affect saving and the current account, we must know the shape of the expected age-earnings profile and the precise phase of the life cycle at which the faster income growth is concentrated. The dependence of aggregate saving on life-cycle factors obviously leads to a much richer range of possibilities than the simple representative-agent model. Consider, for example, an economy in which generations have three-period life spans—encompassing youth, middle age, and old age—and in which earnings increase through middle age but then fall off in old age. Thus saving is concentrated in middle age, with the old dissaving and the young saving little or, perhaps, borrowing. Productivity growth that primarily affects middle-aged workers leads to a sharper peak in the age-earnings profile, raising the saving of the middle-aged and lowering that of the young and the old, while, on balance, tending to lower the aggregate private saving rate unless the young are borrowing-constrained. Productivity growth concentrated on the young could, in contrast, raise or lower the overall saving rate. The latter outcome is particularly likely if the young have a relatively high propensity to consume that is due, for example, to the cost of rearing children.[17]

3.3.3   Demographic Change

So far we have abstracted from demographic factors by holding both population and its composition between young and old constant. The life-cycle perspective on saving suggests, however, that demographic changes and trends have important effects on aggregate saving rates and hence on current accounts. Nothing in what follows requires that $\beta(1 + r) = 1$, so, until further notice, we drop that assumption.

As an illustration, suppose that the young generation born at the start of date t has N_t members and that N_t can change over time. Now it is useful to make a notational distinction between aggregate and individual saving flows, and we use a lowercase letter to signify the latter. Let s^Y therefore denote the saving of a typical member of a young generation. To focus on the pure effects of population growth, we assume that s^Y and the per capita endowments y^Y and y^O of the young and old are constant through time. If Y_t is total date t GDP, then eqs. (19) and (20) show that the aggregate private saving rate is

$$\frac{S_t^P}{Y_t} = \frac{(N_t - N_{t-1}) s^Y}{N_t y^Y + N_{t-1} y^O} = \frac{n s^Y}{(1 + n) y^Y + y^O},\tag{33}$$

---

17. Tobin (1967) explores some of the possibilities through simulation analysis.

where $N_t = (1 + n)N_{t-1}$, so that n is the growth rate of generations and also of total population, $N_t + N_{t-1}$. To see the effect of higher population growth on the saving rate, differentiate the last expression and note that if s^Y is positive,

$$\frac{d\left(S^P/Y\right)}{dn} = \frac{s^Y\left(y^Y + y^O\right)}{\left[(1+n)y^Y + y^O\right]^2} > 0.$$

Provided the young save a strictly positive amount, higher population growth raises a country's private saving rate by increasing the proportion of young savers relative to old dissavers. This scale effect is analogous to the one whereby productivity growth affects aggregate saving.

Once again, more elaborate demographic considerations can alter this simple story. For example, saving sometimes is found to be positively correlated with labor-force growth but not with population growth, because higher population growth may raise the proportion of dependent children and divert some family members' time from labor outside the home into home child care.

Application: How Are Saving and Growth Related?

Our theoretical model has shown that the growth rates of output and population can be positively related to a country's aggregate saving rate. We have noted theoretical conditions under which the relationship could be negative, but these probably are not typical. As an empirical matter, productivity gains are reflected disproportionately in the earnings of prime-age workers, and young workers who might wish to borrow are discouraged to some extent by high loan rates or outright credit limits. Thus plausible versions of the life-cycle model predict a definite positive association between saving and growth.

Modigliani (1970) provided some early confirmation of this basic prediction. Let z be the net rate of total output growth, defined by $(1 + z) = (1 + n)(1 + g)$, where n is the population growth rate and g the per capita output growth rate. Using data from the 1950s on 36 developing and developed countries, Modigliani found the following significant cross-sectional regression relationship between average private saving rates, S^P/Y, and average rates of total output growth, z:

$$S^P/Y = 4.5 + 1.42z.$$
$$\quad\quad (1.3)\ \ (0.25)$$

(Standard errors appear in parentheses.) According to this equation, a 1 percent rise in output growth is associated with a 1.42 percent increase in the aggregate saving rate.

This relationship between saving and growth is apparently confirmed by more recent data. Table 3.1 shows decade-by-decade changes in average total output growth and private saving rates for the seven largest industrial countries. Between

Table 3.1
Growth and Saving in the Seven Largest Industrial Countries, 1960–87

Period	GNP Growth Rate	Net Private Saving Rate
1960–70	4.9	12.3
1971–80	3.3	11.1
1981–87	2.6	9.1

Source: Guiso, Jappelli, and Terlizzese (1992). Growth rates are a simple average of period average growth rates for Canada, France, Italy, West Germany, Japan, the United Kingdom, and the United States, expressed in percent per year. Saving rates are a simple average of period average ratios of inflation-adjusted net private saving to net national product, expressed in percent.

the 1960s and 1980s, the ratio of the fall in the average private saving rate to the fall in the average growth rate is $3.2/2.3 = 1.39$, virtually the same ratio as Modigliani's regression would predict. We note also that, generally speaking, average government budget surpluses—public saving—also fell steadily over the period covered in Table 3.1.[18] To the extent that consumers are even partially "Ricardian," their saving fell less than it would have in the absence of growing government deficits. Thus, the private savings reduction in the table could understate the true impact of growth.

Figure 3.3 shows data for a sample of 100 individual countries in the Penn World Table, Mark 5.5, constructed by Robert Summers and Alan Heston.[19] A scatter plot of average total output growth data for 1970–90 against 1990 gross national saving rates out of GDP shows a positive relationship. The line plotted in Figure 3.3 comes from the cross-section regression equation for the 100-country sample,

$$S/Y = 7.93 + 0.99z, \qquad R^2 = 0.03.$$
$$\quad (1.90) \ (0.47)$$

This equation is not significantly different from Modigliani's (1970) and likewise shows a positive and statistically significant saving-growth relationship.

That relationship is not, however, a robust one. The R^2 of the last equation is very low, indicating substantial unexplained intercountry variation in saving rates. When the dependent variable is average 1970–90 saving (in analogy with Modigliani's study) rather than 1990 saving, the slope coefficient becomes insignificant and slightly negative. Furthermore, the data underlying the last regression are, in many cases, quite undependable, a fact Summers and Heston recognize by assigning a letter grade to each country's data quality. When countries with data of quality below C− are excluded (leaving us with a sample of only 65 countries), the coefficient on z again becomes insignificant and slightly negative.

---

18. See Table 3.2 on p. 173 below.

19. An earlier version of the Penn World Table is described by Summers and Heston (1991).

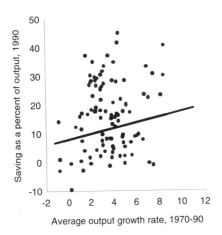

Figure 3.3
Saving and growth, 1970–90

There is another problem in interpreting the evidence. Many countries impose restrictions on private international borrowing and lending, effectively limiting the size of the current account. In this circumstance, private saving and investment may be closely correlated. If so, might regressions like the one we have reported here simply be reflections of the joint determination of investment and output growth rates? Indeed, in Chapter 7 we will examine models with imperfect capital mobility in which domestic saving is a key determinant of investment and growth.

On balance, the econometric evidence suggests that the life-cycle "growth rate effect" on the composition of aggregate saving does play a role, particularly in industrial-country data. But the "pure" life-cycle theory, as exposited in the last section, is unable to explain fully the intercountry and intertemporal variation in saving rates. Several types of evidence point to this conclusion:

1. Life-cycle consumption smoothing is unable to explain the totality of wealth held in the United States, the United Kingdom, and other countries. Direct evidence indicates that, contrary to the pure life-cycle model in which retired people consume all of their wealth before death, a significant proportion of the old either continue accumulating into old age or run their wealth down very slowly. This finding can be rationalized in part by a desire to leave bequests to loved ones, to beloved institutions, or to worthy charities. Another rationale is uncertainty over the date of death: some individuals guard against the possibility of living "too long" by holding substantial wealth well into old age.[20] The fraction of aggregate sav-

---

20. In principle, people could insure against that contingency by annuitizing their wealth, thereby earning a higher return while alive in return for giving up ownership rights upon death. (This is what happens in the Blanchard, 1985, model, see exercise 3 at the chapter's end.) In reality, however, annuity

ing explicable in terms of life cycle factors is difficult to estimate precisely, and seemingly reasonable estimates can diverge dramatically. The exchange between Modigliani (1988) and Kotlikoff (1988) illustrates the range of uncertainty that has prevailed. Recent estimates by Gale and Scholz (1994) suggest 51 percent of net wealth accumulation in the United States represents intended transfers and bequests.

2. One can attempt to calculate the component of national wealth due to life-cycle consumption smoothing by estimating individual cohorts' lifetime consumption and earnings profiles. Data from the limited set of countries for which such estimates are feasible suggest that consumption growth closely parallels income growth early in working life, whereas systematic saving for retirement begins not too long before retirement. Public pension programs may contribute to the phenomenon. In any case, if this saving dynamic prevails at the household level, one might not observe a strong positive association between aggregate saving and growth, depending on the age-incidence of productivity gains.

3. Carroll and Summers (1991) have used consumption data disaggregated by age to question the basic premise of the life-cycle hypothesis, that saving decisions depend on lifetime resources. In effect, they compare the per capita consumption of the young and the old on a given date, showing that the ratio c_t^Y/c_t^O does not appear to be systematically higher in fast-growing economies than in slow-growing ones. On the assumption that growth differentials have been steady and predictable, the young in high-growth economies should have relatively greater lifetime resources, compared to their parents, than those in low-growth economies.[21] Our failure to observe a corresponding relative consumption difference would seem to contradict the forward-looking spirit of the life-cycle idea, although explicit allowance for the stochastic properties of output growth can change this assessment.

4. Bosworth, Burtless, and Sabelhaus (1991) study household survey data on saving in the United States, Canada, and Japan. These data allow them to track changes over time in the saving rates of particular age groups. They conclude that, for all three countries, recent aggregate saving changes are the result of parallel changes in the propensity to save by *all* age groups. They find little in their data to support the idea that the slowdown in industrial-country growth shown in Table 3.1 has reduced saving rates by altering the relative weight of different age groups in determining aggregate savings. Rather, they suggest, slower growth can lower the saving of all groups in society if individuals seek to maintain "target" ratios

---

markets are not perfect, in part because of an adverse selection problem: those most likely to buy private annuities are also those with private information that their longevity is above average.

21. Trend growth differences between countries could lead to different bequest behavior, but this would be unlikely to reverse the preceding argument.

of wealth to income—a type of behavior that does not emerge from the relatively simple consumption models we have concentrated on thus far.

The foregoing evidence shows that the simplest life-cycle models offer an incomplete picture of observed saving behavior. Additional factors must be considered to explain saving rates, one of which certainly is precautionary saving in the face of uncertainty.[22] Nonetheless, the general life-cycle approach of analyzing aggregate saving data in terms of the individual decisions of separate and heterogeneous household groupings has proved powerful and successful. By sticking with the pure life-cycle model for now, we will be able to explore some further implications of the general approach in a relatively transparent theoretical setting. Later in this chapter we shall see how these implications stand up when our basic life-cycle model is extended in a number of different ways.   ∎

3.4   Investment and Growth

By adding production and investment we achieve a complete parallel with the representative-agent production economies introduced in Chapter 2. The predictions about current account behavior often are quite different, however. To avoid issues of policy-induced intergenerational redistribution, we assume in this section that there is no government. We simplify further by ignoring any installation costs for capital equipment. Thus a unit of date t consumption can be converted into a unit of capital on date $t + 1$, and capital can be fully consumed.

3.4.1   Firms and Factors of Production

In the representative-consumer model of Chapter 2, it did not matter whether we thought of production as being carried out by firms or by individual self-employed investor/producers. But the intrinsic heterogeneity in asset holdings assumed by the overlapping generations model forces us to distinguish carefully between labor and capital income.

Competitive domestic firms combine capital and labor to produce output according to the Cobb-Douglas production function

$$Y_t = A_t F(K_t, L_t) = A_t K_t^\alpha L_t^{1-\alpha}, \tag{34}$$

where A_t is a total factor-productivity shift. As usual, firm size is indeterminate under constant returns, so we can think of production as being carried out by a single representative firm. Capital does not depreciate, and so the capital stock follows $K_{t+1} = K_t + I_t$, where I_t is investment during period t.

---

22. See, for example, Caballero (1991), Carroll (1992), Hubbard, Skinner, and Zeldes (1994), and Gourinchas and Parker (1995). All these studies point to the potential importance of precautionary saving in explaining several of the empirical shortcomings of the simplest life-cycle models.

As in section 2.5.1, the firm hires workers up to the point where the marginal product of labor equals the wage, and it invests to the point where the marginal product of capital equals the world interest rate. We hold the real interest rate fixed at r in the present small-country model. As an additional simplification, we abstract from the labor-supply decision and assume that each individual inelastically supplies 1 unit of labor when young and none when old. (We thus view the young as prime-age workers, the old as retired workers.) The labor force on date t is therefore $L_t = N_t$, where, as before, N_t is the size of the cohort born on date t. The assumption of an exogenous supply of labor means that the capital stock and investment, as in Chapter 1 and most of Chapter 2, are determined independently of the economy's consumption side. Finally, assume that the number of young and hence the total population grow at rate n:

$$N_t = (1+n)N_{t-1}. \tag{35}$$

For the Cobb-Douglas production function in eq. (34), the perfect-foresight capital-labor ratio and the wage are given by

$$r = A_t F_K(K_t, L_t) = \alpha A_t k_t^{\alpha-1}, \tag{36}$$

$$w_t = A_t F_L(K_t, L_t) = (1-\alpha)A_t k_t^{\alpha}, \tag{37}$$

where k_t denotes the capital-labor ratio K_t/L_t.[23] As a result, the economy's total demand for capital takes the form

$$K(r, A_t, N_t) = L_t k(r, A_t) = N_t k(r, A_t),$$

where $k(r, A_t)$ is given implicitly by eq. (36). The perfect-foresight capital stock is

$$K(r, A_t, N_t) = N_t k(r, A_t) = N_t \left(\frac{\alpha A_t}{r}\right)^{1/1-\alpha}, \tag{38}$$

and the corresponding real wage is

$$w_t = (1-\alpha)A_t k(r, A_t)^{\alpha} = (1-\alpha)A_t \left(\frac{\alpha A_t}{r}\right)^{\alpha/1-\alpha}. \tag{39}$$

3.4.2 Saving, Investment, and Total Output Growth in Steady State

Although investment is determined independently of saving in this small, open economy, supply shifts such as productivity shocks or changes in labor-force growth (as well as changes in the world interest rate) can cause the two variables to move simultaneously. As preparation for our next application on the empirical

---

23. Recall the demonstration in section 1.5.1 that with constant returns in production the marginal products of capital and labor depend on K and L only through the capital-labor ratio $k = K/L$. Notice that if r varied with time, then eq. (36) would be $r_t = \alpha A_t k_t^{\alpha-1}$, where r_t is the interest rate on loans between dates $t-1$ and t. This relationship follows from eq. (24) of Chapter 2.

correlation between long-run saving and investment rates, we explore this point in detail. It is easiest to make our main points through a comparison of steady states.

How does total output growth affect saving and the current account in an investment economy? In contrast to an endowment economy, the saving of the young has two components, net foreign assets and the capital that will be used in production next period. (As in section 2.5.1, it makes no difference whether we view savers as purchasing claims on firms' profits or, alternatively, physical capital that they lease to firms at a competitive rental equal to the world interest rate.) Recall this section's assumption that there is no government, hence no government assets or debt. Then the net foreign assets of the young at the end of a period, t, are also the net foreign assets of the economy as a whole, and the aggregate saving of the young therefore satisfies

$$S_t^Y = B_{t+1}^P + K_{t+1} = B_{t+1} + K_{t+1}. \tag{40}$$

The validity of this equation does *not* require that domestic firms be owned entirely by home residents: foreign claims on domestic firms are subtracted from B_{t+1}, which measures *net* claims on foreigners.

Assume for now that the productivity parameter, A, is constant. In this case, aggregate output growth is driven entirely by domestic labor-force growth, and it is natural to look for a steady state in which the ratios of all aggregate variables to the labor force, L, are constant. Notice that perfectly anticipated labor-force growth does not affect the wage, according to eq. (39). The economy can borrow abroad to finance the capital-labor ratio k at which the marginal product of capital equals r; and that equality ties down w as well in a perfect-foresight equilibrium. Because the productivity parameter, A, is constant, the wage and lifetime income of each generation are constant as well. From eq. (38) the capital stock grows at the same rate, n, as the labor force, so the capital-labor ratio is constant at the steady-state level $\bar{k}$.

With individual saving by the young constant (because r and w which determine lifetime income are constant) the aggregate savings of the young grow at rate n. Dividing both sides of eq. (40) by the date t labor force yields

$$s_t^Y = (1+n)(b_{t+1} + k_{t+1}), \tag{41}$$

where s_t^Y is the saving of a typical young person and $b_t \equiv B_t/N_t$. Since, as we have already argued, s^Y is constant at $\bar{s}^Y$ in a steady state, and k is constant at $\bar{k}$, eq. (41) implies that b is constant as well in a steady state, at

$$\bar{b} = \frac{\bar{s}^Y}{1+n} - \bar{k}. \tag{42}$$

In the pure endowment cases of sections 3.2 and 3.3, an economy's stock of net foreign assets was determined entirely by the saving of the young, being positive if the young were savers and negative if they were borrowers. Now, however, an economy's net foreign assets equal the savings of the young less the capital stock required for efficient domestic production in the following period.

Equation (42) implies that, in a steady state with per capita net foreign assets constant but population and labor force growing, the economy must be running a perpetual current account surplus or deficit depending on whether $\bar{b}$ is, respectively, positive or negative. Since net foreign assets or debts grow at the same rate n as does the labor force and output, such a steady state poses no solvency problem.

Let's return to the question with which we started this subsection, the effect of output growth shifts on saving and the current account. The home country's aggregate per capita saving rate in a steady state is

$$\frac{S_t^Y + S_t^O}{N_t + N_{t-1}} = \left(\frac{1+n}{2+n}\right)\bar{s}^Y + \left(\frac{1}{2+n}\right)\bar{s}^O.$$

Thus, when the young save a positive amount (as they must in the present model, since they have no old-age income source other than their savings), a rise in the population growth rate, n, will raise saving through the same mechanism we discussed in section 3.3.3: higher population growth raises the number of young savers relative to old dissavers, raising aggregate saving per capita.[24]

Investment in the steady state equals the flow of new capital needed to keep k at $\bar{k}$ in the face of labor-force growth. This requirement means that $K_{t+1} = (1+n)K_t$; alternatively, investment per capita is

$$\frac{K_{t+1} - K_t}{N_t + N_{t-1}} = \frac{(1+n)n}{2+n}\bar{k}.$$

A rise in n raises not only steady-state saving, but also steady-state investment per capita.[25] In summary, increases in labor-force growth will cause saving and investment per capita to move together in the long run.

If the productivity parameter A rises at a constant positive rate through time, say

$$A_{t+1} = (1+g)^{1-\alpha}A_t, \tag{43}$$

the capital-labor ratio will no longer be constant in a steady state, per eq. (38).[26] But a steady state can still be constructed by scaling all key variables by output. The Cobb-Douglas production function of eq. (34) and eq. (38) imply the simple

---

24. The derivative with respect to n of steady-state aggregate per capita saving is $(\bar{s}^Y - \bar{s}^O)/(2+n)^2 > 0$. If the old had some labor income and β were sufficiently low relative to $1/(1+r)$, the young could be net borrowers. If we view the "young" of the model as prime-age workers, this case is implausible.

25. The derivative with respect to n of investment per capita is $(n^2 + 4n + 2)\bar{k}/(2+n)^2 > 0$.

26. The growth parameter g will turn out to be the growth rate of young workers' incomes and thus corresponds to the growth rate g in the endowment model of section 3.3.2. Since the old supply no labor and thus have no labor income, $e = -1$ in the present model.

steady-state relation

$$\frac{\overline{K}}{Y} = \frac{\alpha}{r}$$

(which will also hold out of steady state, given the assumed absence of adjustment costs, provided investors make no forecasting mistakes).[27] Again invoking eq. (38), we therefore see that the steady-state share of investment in current output is

$$\frac{\overline{I}}{Y} = \left(\frac{N_{t+1}A_{t+1}^{\frac{1}{1-\alpha}}}{N_t A_t^{\frac{1}{1-\alpha}}}\right)\frac{\overline{K}}{Y} - \frac{\overline{K}}{Y} = (n + g + ng)\frac{\alpha}{r}. \tag{44}$$

Notice that n and g affect the steady state in symmetrical fashion; a rise in either obviously raises investment. The same statements apply to steady-state saving. With logarithmic utility, eq. (9), the consumption plan of a date t young person is

$$c_t^Y = \frac{w_t}{1+\beta}, \qquad c_{t+1}^O = \frac{(1+r)\beta w_t}{1+\beta}. \tag{45}$$

As a consequence, a typical date t young person saves the amount

$$s_t^Y = w_t - \frac{w_t}{1+\beta} = \frac{\beta w_t}{1+\beta} = \frac{\beta(1-\alpha)A_t^{\frac{1}{1-\alpha}}}{1+\beta}\left(\frac{\alpha}{r}\right)^{\frac{\alpha}{1-\alpha}},$$

where we have used the solution for the wage in eq. (39) and the assumption of zero earnings in old age. From this last equation, the production function, the fact that $s_t^O = -s_{t-1}^Y$, and eq. (38), the aggregate saving rate out of GDP is

$$\frac{N_t s_t^Y + N_{t-1}s_t^O}{Y_t} = \frac{\overline{S}}{Y} = \frac{\beta(1-\alpha)}{1+\beta}\left[1 - \frac{1}{(1+n)(1+g)}\right]. \tag{46}$$

Clearly net saving rises when n or g rises, for now-familiar life-cycle reasons.

The net stock of foreign assets, measured as a fraction of output, is $B_{t+1}/Y_{t+1} = (N_t s_t^Y/Y_{t+1}) - (K_{t+1}/Y_{t+1})$, by condition (40). Observe that in the steady state, $N_t s_t^Y/Y_{t+1} = \beta(1-\alpha)/(1+\beta)(1+n)(1+g)$: the share of the current young's saving in the *following* period's GDP is the marginal propensity to save times labor's GDP share, scaled down by the gross output growth rate $(1+n)(1+g)$. Thus, the steady-state ratio of beginning-of-period foreign assets to GDP is

---

27. Substitution of eq. (38) for K_t in the production function yields the useful intermediate result that

$$Y_t = N_t A_t^{1/(1-\alpha)}\left(\frac{\alpha}{r}\right)^{\alpha/(1-\alpha)}.$$

This equation clearly shows that $Y_{t+1} = (1+n)(1+g)Y_t$ in the steady state we are considering.

$$\frac{\overline{B}}{Y} = \frac{\beta(1-\alpha)}{(1+\beta)(1+n)(1+g)} - \frac{\alpha}{r}.$$

The steady-state current account balance follows from eqs. (44) and (46) as the asset flow needed to keep this ratio constant,

$$\frac{\overline{CA}}{Y} = \frac{\overline{S}}{Y} - \frac{\overline{I}}{Y} = (n+g+ng)\frac{\overline{B}}{Y}.$$

The economy may be either debtor or creditor in the steady state: more impatient countries (low β) tend to have bigger debt-output ratios, and (with log utility) the debt-output ratio falls as the world interest rate r rises. Notice that the growth rate g doesn't even enter the formula for per capita saving of the young. The productivity growth implied by $g > 0$ accrues to successive generations and thus has no influence on any generation's saving out of output. In the present model, we therefore do not observe the very large debt-output ratios implied by the representative-consumer model of appendix 2A.

Application: Feldstein and Horioka's Saving-Investment Puzzle

In a closed economy, national saving equals domestic investment, and the current account is always zero. Furthermore, any observed increase in national saving will automatically be accompanied by an equal rise in domestic investment. This prediction contrasts strongly with the behavior we expect when capital is internationally mobile. Under capital mobility, saving and investment can diverge, even over protracted periods, as countries with opportunities to gain from intertemporal trade run unbalanced current accounts.

In a well-known paper, Feldstein and Horioka (1980) claimed that, even among industrial countries, capital mobility is sufficiently limited that changes in national saving rates ultimately change domestic investment rates by the same amount. As evidence, they reported cross-sectional regressions of gross domestic investment rate averages (I/Y) on gross national saving rate averages (S/Y). For a sample of 16 OECD countries over 1960-74, Feldstein and Horioka found the following least-squares regression result:

$$I/Y = 0.04 + 0.89 S/Y, \qquad R^2 = 0.91.$$
$$ (0.02) \ \ (0.07)$$

Over the 1960–74 period, capital was not as mobile internationally as it is today. Figure 3.4, however, shows the cross-sectional saving-investment association in the OECD sample over the decade 1982–91, with Luxembourg, which is an outlier, and developing Turkey both omitted. The estimation result for this 22-country sample is

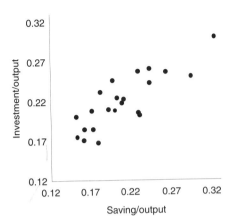

Figure 3.4
Industrial-country saving and investment rates, 1982–91

$$I/Y = 0.09 + 0.62S/Y, \qquad R^2 = 0.69.$$
$$\quad\;\,(0.02)\ \ (0.09)$$

This equation shows a weakening, but still very significant, positive association.

Feldstein and Horioka argued that if capital indeed were highly mobile among industrial countries, slope coefficients like this one should be much smaller than 1, as a country's savings would then be free to seek out the most productive investment opportunities worldwide. If one accepts this argument, these regression results pose a puzzle. They contradict other evidence that capital is quite mobile within the developed world, notably, the remarkable closeness of the interest rates that comparable assets offer despite being located in different industrial countries.[28]

Our models advise a skeptical approach to Feldstein and Horioka's interpretation of their results. Even when domestic investment is determined independently of the economy's consumption side, a number of common factors might simultaneously influence countries' saving and investment rates. Furthermore, there are plausible cases (the case of endogenous factor-market conditions. is one) in which shifts in national saving behavior could exert a direct influence on investment by altering factor-market conditions. There are many potential explanations of the Feldstein-Horioka results. Here are some that have been suggested:

1. Governments sometimes adjust fiscal or monetary policies to avoid large and protracted current-account imbalances. The evidence on this current account targeting hypothesis is mostly anecdotal, however, and there are prominent instances

---

28. For surveys of this evidence, see Obstfeld (1986, 1995).

(for example, the United States in the early 1980s) in which macroeconomic policies have instead instigated major external imbalances.

2. Developed countries may be sufficiently well endowed with capital to be near steady states for their external debt or asset levels. In this situation the intertemporal budget constraint of the economy would imply that long averages of saving-investment differences are small. Developing countries, which presumably could realize greater gains from intertemporal trade through borrowing for investment purposes, are likely to be more distant from a stationary distribution of foreign debt. This interpretation seems borne out by cross-sectional results for developing countries prior to 1982, a year that initiated a near-decade-long reduction in developing-country access to the industrial world's savings. For pre-1982 developing countries, the cross-sectional saving-investment association is much looser than for the OECD sample.

3. If corporations, like some individuals, have limited access to markets for finance, then investment may respond positively to higher corporate saving (in the form of retained earnings), even when international capital markets are as well integrated as domestic markets. Corporate saving typically is a substantial component of total saving, so it seems plausible that shifts in corporate saving might induce a strong saving-investment relationship in the data. Although there is some evidence in favor of this hypothesis, an account of how corporate saving and investment are related need not have strong implications for the relationship between total private saving and investment. For example, the household sector ultimately owns much of the corporate sector; households therefore may pierce the "corporate veil" and nullify the effect of corporate saving shifts on total saving through their own offsetting saving decisions.[29] Moreover, to the extent that the investing firms are owned by foreigners, their decision to retain earnings increases foreign rather than domestic saving, other things equal.

4. In the life-cycle theory of consumption, sustained demographic and productivity changes that increase a country's long-term investment rate also may increase its saving rate. Equations (44) and (46) show a case in which higher trend growth in total output causes long-run saving and investment to rise in tandem. Alan Taylor (1994) revisits the Feldstein-Horioka equation, controlling for (a) measures of domestic relative prices, (b) the age structure of the population, and (c) the interaction of the age structure with the growth rate of domestic output. He finds that for a number of country samples the cross-sectional saving-investment association disappears.

As we discussed earlier, there is reason to question whether saving and growth are related through the life cycle or some other mechanism. Thus, despite Taylor's

---

29. The mechanism is entirely analogous to the one underlying the Ricardian equivalence proposition.

(1994) findings, controversy over the Feldstein-Horioka puzzle is likely to continue. In all likelihood, no single one of the mechanisms we have outlined fully explains the behavior of every industrial country.   ∎

3.5 Aggregate and Intergenerational Gains from Trade

In this section we revisit a central result of Chapter 1 on the gains from intertemporal trade. We saw in Chapter 1 that, the greater the difference between a representative-consumer economy's autarky interest rate and the world interest rate, the more it gains from opening its capital market to international borrowing and lending. Here we show that this result can be extended to overlapping generations economies, but with an important qualification. Opening the capital market can have divergent welfare impacts across the current young and old, and across those currently alive and those to be born in the future. Absent side payments to redistribute domestic income, everyone may not gain from integration into the world capital market. The winners gain more than the losers lose, however, so Chapter 1's result on trade gains reemerges, in the sense that feasible side payments can make everyone in the economy better off after trade. As before, the aggregate gains from trade are greater when the difference between the initial autarky interest rate and the world rate is greater.[30]

Consider a small economy, initially in autarky, that carries out a permanent opening of its capital market at the start of period t.[31] We continue to assume that generations work only when young, and retain the logarithmic utility function in eq. (9). With this utility function, and maintaining the simplifying assumption that there is initially no government economic activity, the consumption choices of young and old individuals are described by eq. (45). To simplify we assume there is no trend productivity or labor-force growth. The economy's initial position is a steady state with a constant real wage and interest rate.

A useful starting assumption is that the world interest rate $r > 0$ differs only marginally from the domestic autarky interest rate, r^A. In this case the *aggregate* gains the economy reaps from opening up to trade are of second-order importance,

---

30. There is another important qualification to the presumption that there are positive aggregate gains from trade: the world interest rate must be above the rate of total output growth. (See exercise 2 at the end of the chapter for a counterexample.) The issue does not arise in this section because we assume a positive interest rate and zero growth. Appendix 3A discusses anomalies that arise when the economy's scale grows at a proportional rate in excess of the real interest rate. The appendix also discusses evidence suggesting that this case is empirically irrelevant.

31. For similar welfare analyses, see Fried (1980), Persson (1985), Fried and Howitt (1988), and Ruffin and Yoon (1993). Eaton (1988) and Matsuyama (1988) develop related models with nonreproducible factors of production (such as land).

but, as we now show, the associated redistribution effects are of first-order importance.

Consider first the impact of a small interest rate change—an increase, say—on those young on dates t (the initial date of opening) and after. (This group comprises all of the economy's current and prospective residents other than the date t old.) Substituting the consumption plans in eq. (45) into the utility function (9), we find that

$$U = (1 + \beta) \log(w) + \beta \log(1 + r)$$

(apart from an irrelevant additive constant). Differentiation yields

$$\frac{dU}{dr} = \frac{1 + \beta}{w} \left(\frac{dw}{dr} \right) + \frac{\beta}{1 + r},$$

where dr refers to the infinitesimal rise of r^A up to the world rate, r. The interest-rate rise increases the rate of return required on domestic investment and so lowers the capital-labor ratio in production; hence, the wage falls. How large is its fall? Because the interest-rate rise is infinitesimal and the initial factor allocation was optimal (given autarky factor prices), the envelope theorem tells us that the gain to capital is simply $K\,dr$, which must correspond to labor's loss of $-K\,dr = L\,dw$. Thus $dw/dr = -K/L = -k$,[32] and we therefore can write the preceding lifetime utility change as

$$\frac{dU}{dr} = \frac{-(1 + \beta)}{w} k + \frac{\beta}{1 + r} = -\beta + \frac{\beta}{1 + r} = \frac{-\beta r}{1 + r} < 0. \tag{47}$$

[We have used the fact that, in the initial autarky equilibrium, $k = \beta w/(1 + \beta)$, the per-person saving of the young.]

Equation (47) implies that the current young and every generation that follows them suffer a utility loss as a result of opening to trade. To transform the young's utility loss into its first-period income equivalent, we divide the first equality in eq. (47) by the initial marginal utility of first-period income, $\partial U/\partial c^Y = 1/c^Y = (1 + \beta)/w$, to infer that the first-period income loss of a young person amounts to

$$-k\,dr + \frac{\beta w\,dr}{(1 + \beta)(1 + r)} = -k\,dr + \frac{k\,dr}{1 + r} = \frac{-rk\,dr}{1 + r}.$$

The intuition behind this result is simple: each person born on or after date t loses $dw = -k\,dr$ in first-period wage income but gains $k\,dr$ in second-period capital income, this pattern of loss and gain having a net present value of $-k\,dr + k\,dr/(1 +$

---

32. You may recall that the relation $dw/dr = -k$ follows from the efficient *factor-price frontier* that we derived in section 1.5.2.

$r) = -rkdr/(1+r)$. On date t, the combined *present discounted value* of the per capita income losses to the young and all future generations is

$$\frac{-rkdr}{(1+r)}\left[1 + \left(\frac{1}{1+r}\right) + \left(\frac{1}{1+r}\right)^2 + \cdots\right] = -kdr.$$

Someone must gain from the opening to world markets. The only domestic residents we have not considered are those who are already old in period t, when opening occurs. They earn the higher, postintegration return on the saving they did in period $t - 1$: their per capita income gain is exactly kdr, the opposite of the present discounted value lost by all other agents in the economy. The government would ensure that no one was hurt by the opening to world markets if it levied a tax of kdr on each of the period t old and, starting with the period t young, gave each newly born generation a per capita transfer payment of $rkdr/(1+r)$.

A rise in the domestic interest rate due to integration with world markets benefits owners of capital and, because the wage and the return to capital are inversely related, harms owners of labor. Because these opposite effects are equal in the present example, and because generations born on date t or after are labor owners early in life and capital owners late in life, the interest-rate rise hurts those generations while benefiting the date t old. If the world interest rate is marginally below the autarky rate, of course, the redistribution of income works in the opposite direction. The current old are hurt, but the current young and all subsequent generations gain.

In the preceding example, the *net* societal gains from opening to trade are of second-order importance because the world interest rate differs only marginally from the autarky interest rate. When the world interest rate exceeds the autarky rate by a finite amount, however, capital's gains outweigh labor's losses. In this case, an appropriate government tax-and-transfer scheme can make everyone better off.

Similar reasoning applies in analyzing how world interest-rate changes affect economies already open to trade. In that case, the saving of each young person, $\beta w/(1+\beta)$, is equal to $k + b$, the sum of the economy's per-worker stocks of capital and net foreign assets. As a result, eq. (47) becomes

$$\frac{dU}{dr} = \frac{-(1+\beta)}{w}k + \frac{\beta}{1+r} = \frac{-\beta k}{k+b} + \frac{\beta}{1+r}.$$

The lifetime income change for each newly born young generation is now

$$-kdr + \frac{(k+b)dr}{1+r},$$

so, if b is sufficiently positive, all generations can gain from a positive dr. The gain to the economy as a whole is $(1+r)bdr/r$, equal to the present value of income effects less wealth effects on the aggregate economy's intertemporal budget constraint.[33] This is a loss if $b < 0$. The key determinant of the welfare effect is how the interest-rate change alters the gap between the world interest rate and the economy's domestic autarky rate. When b is positive, for example, the domestic autarky interest rate is below the world rate. Thus a rise in the world rate enhances the economy's gains from trade by expanding the relevant set of feasible aggregate consumption levels.

3.6   Public Debt and the World Interest Rate

Up to now this chapter has focused on the case of a small economy facing an exogenous world interest rate. The small country paradigm can be very useful, but, as we saw in Chapter 1, there are important practical applications for which it is inadequate. The discussion in section 3.2 showed how lump-sum tax policy can affect saving in a small economy populated by overlapping generations. Now we explore how large economies' tax policies affect the world economy. In the process, we shall see how the world interest rate and capital stock are determined in an overlapping generations model.[34]

3.6.1   A Two-Country Global-Equilibrium Model

There are two countries, Home and Foreign. Since our main points do not depend on differences between the two countries, we shall impose a great deal of symmetry, assuming that the two countries have access to identical Cobb-Douglas production technologies and that residents have identical logarithmic preferences, given by eq. (9).

Once again, everyone lives for two periods, supplying 1 unit of labor in youth but none in old age. Foreign counterparts of Home variables are marked with asterisks. In Home (Foreign), the young generation born on date t has N_t (N_t^*) members. The levels of the two young populations may differ, but we assume that their net growth rates are both n [as in eq. (35)].

Since we think of the young generation as consisting of prime-age workers, it is an empirically reasonable simplification to assume that all taxes fall on the young. (We abstract from social security programs that result in transfers to the old.) Under log utility, a typical Home resident's savings in youth are

$$s_t^Y = \frac{\beta}{1+\beta}\left(w_t - \tau_t^Y\right).$$

(48)

There is a corresponding saving function for young Foreign residents.

---

33. On the income and wealth effects of interest-rate changes, see section 1.3.

34. For models related to the one taken up next, see Buiter (1981, 1989), Persson (1985), Eaton (1988), and Frenkel and Razin (1992).

A country's wage is the domestic equilibrium marginal product of labor according to eq. (37). Abstracting from trend productivity growth and normalizing $A = 1$, this equation can be written as

$$w_t = (1 - \alpha)k_t^\alpha. \tag{49}$$

A parallel relationship determines w_t^*.

With Home and Foreign linked by an integrated world capital market, investment will equate the date t marginal products of capital in both countries to the interest rate on loans between dates $t - 1$ and t, so that

$$\alpha k_t^{\alpha-1} = \alpha k_t^{*\alpha-1} = r_t = \alpha(k_t^W)^{\alpha-1}, \tag{50}$$

where $k^W = k = k^*$ is the common capital-labor ratio across the two economies with identical production technologies. [Equation (50) holds continuously in this model if there are no unexpected shocks.]

3.6.2   Equilibrium Dynamics and Steady State

We are now in a position to characterize world equilibrium. For simplicity we assume away government economic activity, an assumption we relax in the next subsection when we examine the effects of government debt. In the absence of government debt, global equilibrium requires that saving by the world's young must equal the total world supply of capital available for production the following period. On any date t, therefore,

$$K_{t+1} + K_{t+1}^* = N_t s_t^Y + N_t^* s_t^{Y*}. \tag{51}$$

Since labor is immobile internationally, market clearing also requires

$$L_t = N_t, \qquad L_t^* = N_t^*.$$

Equations (48) and (49) allow us to write equilibrium saving by a young Home resident as

$$s_t^Y = \frac{\beta(1 - \alpha)}{1 + \beta}(k_t^W)^\alpha,$$

with a corresponding saving function for Foreign's young. (Remember: we've assumed temporarily that τ^Y and τ^{Y*} are zero.) With this substitution, the world capital-market equilibrium condition (51) becomes

$$K_{t+1} + K_{t+1}^* = \frac{\beta(1 - \alpha)}{1 + \beta}(N_t + N_t^*)(k_t^W)^\alpha.$$

Dividing both sides by the world labor force $N_t + N_t^*$ and noting that

$$\frac{K_{t+1} + K_{t+1}^*}{N_t + N_t^*} = (1 + n)\frac{K_{t+1} + K_{t+1}^*}{N_{t+1} + N_{t+1}^*} = (1 + n)k_{t+1}^W,$$

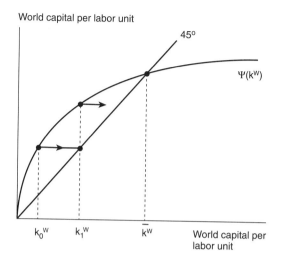

Figure 3.5
Stability of the world capital-labor ratio

we get a very simple difference equation in the world capital-labor ratio:

$$k_{t+1}^{W} = \frac{\beta(1-\alpha)}{(1+n)(1+\beta)}(k_t^{W})^{\alpha} \equiv \Psi(k_t^{W}).$$

(52)

Figure 3.5 shows the adjustment path for the world capital ratio, starting from an initial positive level k_0^{W}. As you can see, the world economy always converges to a unique positive steady-state capital ratio, $\bar{k}^{W}$, which is found by setting $k_{t+1}^{W} = k_t^{W} = \bar{k}^{W}$ in eq. (52) and solving

$$\bar{k}^{W} = \left[\frac{\beta(1-\alpha)}{(1+n)(1+\beta)}\right]^{\frac{1}{1-\alpha}}.$$

There is a second steady state with a zero capital stock, but it is unstable. The steady-state marginal product of capital is

$$\alpha(\bar{k}^{W})^{\alpha-1} = \bar{r} = \frac{\alpha(1+n)(1+\beta)}{\beta(1-\alpha)}.$$

(53)

3.6.3   Deficits, Debt, and Crowding Out

One vitally important question the present framework can address is the *global* effect of government deficits and debts.

Assume that the Home government, starting from a zero net asset position, issues as a gift to the current old a positive quantity of claims on itself. In addition, Home's government taxes the current and all future young generations so as to hold constant at the positive level $\bar{d}$ the ratio $-B_t^G/N_t$ of government debt to the labor force. (Recall our assumption, stated at the start of section 3.6.1, that the young pay all the taxes.) In the present setting (which assumes zero government consumption), the government finance constraint corresponding to eq. (5) is

$$B_{t+1}^G = (1 + r_t)B_t^G + N_t\tau_t^Y,$$

where τ^Y is the tax per unit of labor. Note that we must allow r_t to vary here since the interest rate is endogenous. Dividing both sides of the above equation by N_{t+1}, we observe that constancy of $-B^G/N$ at $\bar{d}$ requires that

$$\bar{d} = \frac{-B_{t+1}^G}{N_{t+1}} = (1 + r_t)\frac{N_t}{N_{t+1}}\bar{d} - \frac{N_t}{N_{t+1}}\tau_t^Y = \frac{(1 + r_t)\bar{d} - \tau_t^Y}{1 + n}.$$

Solving for the taxes a young worker must pay to maintain $-B^G/N$ at $\bar{d}$, we find

$$\tau_t^Y = (r_t - n)\bar{d}. \tag{54}$$

Substitute this expression for taxes into eq. (48). The saving of the Home young now will be

$$s_t^Y = \frac{\beta}{1 + \beta}\left[w_t - (r_t - n)\bar{d}\right].$$

The saving function of the Foreign young, who are not taxed, is unchanged. Use of eqs. (49) and (50) to eliminate w_t and r_t in the preceding equation results in

$$s_t^Y = \frac{\beta}{1 + \beta}\left\{(1 - \alpha)\left(k_t^W\right)^\alpha - \left[\alpha\left(k_t^W\right)^{\alpha-1} - n\right]\bar{d}\right\}. \tag{55}$$

The introduction of government debt changes the world asset market-clearing condition in a fundamental way. Now young savers must acquire the Home government debt, $-B_{t+1}^G$, in addition to the world capital stock. The condition for world capital-market equilibrium is therefore changed from eq. (51) to

$$K_{t+1} + K_{t+1}^* - B_{t+1}^G = N_t s_t^Y + N_t^* s_t^{Y*}.$$

Use eq. (55) together with the unchanged saving function of the Foreign young to eliminate the per-worker saving levels. Then divide the result by the world labor force $N_t + N_t^*$ to obtain

$$k_{t+1}^W = \frac{\beta\left\{(1 - \alpha)(k_t^W)^\alpha - x\left[\alpha(k_t^W)^{\alpha-1} - n\right]\bar{d}\right\}}{(1 + n)(1 + \beta)} - x\bar{d} \equiv \Psi\left(k_t^W, \bar{d}\right),$$

where

$$x \equiv \frac{N_t}{N_t + N_t^*}$$

is the home country's share of the world labor force (and population).

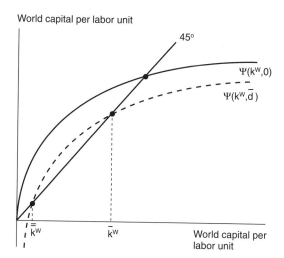

World capital per labor unit

$45°$

$\Psi(k^W,0)$

$\Psi(k^W,\bar{d})$

$\underline{\bar{k}}^W$ $\bar{k}^W$ World capital per
labor unit

Figure 3.6
Steady-state effect of public debt

Figure 3.6 shows the dynamics of world capital after the introduction of the public debt by Home's government. The stable steady-state capital ratio, $\bar{k}^W$, is lower than in the absence of the debt. By reducing the saving of the domestic young and diverting world saving into paper assets, higher Home government debt reduces steady-state capital intensity in Home *and* in Foreign, thereby raising the world interest rate. It is not hard to see that the dynamics of adjustment involve a rise in the world interest rate and an immediate fall in world investment. When a large country runs a fiscal deficit and capital markets are internationally integrated, capital accumulation is crowded out abroad as well as at home. Notice in Figure 3.6 that there is again a second steady state at the lower capital ratio $\underline{\bar{k}}^W$, but it is unstable and we ignore it.

3.6.4   Dynamic Inefficiency and Welfare

In an overlapping generations model, government debt not only affects the *division* of the economic pie across generations, it can affect the *size* of the pie by changing the capital stock. A full analysis of the welfare impact of higher public debt, however, is somewhat subtle. With $n > 0$, we confront the possibility that the steady-state world interest rate $\bar{r} = \alpha(\bar{k}^W)^{\alpha-1}$, which is determined endogenously in global equilibrium, may lie at or below the growth rate n of total output. The possibility can be seen from eq. (53) just by making α sufficiently small.

The consequence of having $\bar{r} \leq n$ initially follows from eq. (54). In that case, a small rise in $\bar{d}$ not only benefits the current old, but also appears to allow a *low-*

ering of taxes on future generations of Home young! Indeed, one can go further and show that all generations, in Foreign as well as in Home, can benefit! There is clearly something very wrong here, a free lunch. The problem is due to a phenomenon known as *dynamic inefficiency*. The behavior of dynamically inefficient economies wreaks havoc with much of our intuition about the laws of economics. Because dynamic inefficiency appears to be more a theoretical than a practical problem, however, we postpone a detailed discussion until appendix 3A.[35] There we also extend our analysis to allow for steady-state productivity growth at rate g, leading to the generalized condition for dynamic inefficiency $1 + r < (1 + n)(1 + g)$.

So, assume that the economy is dynamically efficient; that is, the world interest rate exceeds the growth rate of the economy. In that case, the fully anticipated introduction of a (small) public debt $\bar{d}$ in Home, as in the last subsection, confers the primary benefit of a transfer on the initial Home old, but imposes the primary cost of higher taxes on all successor generations.

The accompanying rise in the world interest rate entails secondary welfare effects, however. ("Secondary" does not necessarily mean small here!) Home gains in the aggregate if it is initially a net foreign creditor, and Foreign, correspondingly, loses. In case Home initially is a net foreign debtor, Foreign benefits in the aggregate from the intertemporal terms-of-trade change.

These secondary gains and losses at the country level need not accrue uniformly to different generations. Generally, a country as a whole gains, for example, only in the sense that its government *could* use lump-sum transfers to make all generations better off.

How are individual Home and Foreign generations affected by the rise in the world interest rate? Since the initial old in both countries receive asset income only (and in positive amounts), they necessarily gain from the interest rate increase. In both countries, the initial young (and all future generations) suffer lower wages because of the factor-price-frontier effect discussed in section 3.5. As explained there, this wage loss in the first period of life can be more than offset by higher interest earnings later if the savings of the young exceed domestic capital needs by a sufficient amount. Thus in at least one country, and possibly in both, the initial young and all future generations must lose absolutely. If the Foreign government itself holds net claims on the private sector (that is, has a negative debt), the Foreign young, whose transfers rise when the interest rate rises, are more likely to be better off.

---

35. In the model of Chapter 2, we always assumed that interest rates exceeded growth rates. Was that assumption wrong? No. We reiterate a promise we made in the last chapter: in Chapter 7 we will prove that dynamic inefficiency cannot arise for the representative-consumer model.

Table 3.2
Government Saving in the Main Industrial Countries

Country	1960s	1970s	1980s
Canada	3.6	2.7	−1.6
France	n.a.	3.6	1.3
West Germany	6.2	3.9	2.0
Italy	2.1	−5.6	−6.7
Japan	6.2	4.8	4.6
United Kingdom	3.6	2.6	0.1
United States	2.0	0.4	−2.1

Source: Shafer, Elmeskov, and Tease (1992). Government budget surpluses are expressed as a percent of GNP.

Application: Government Debt and World Interest Rates since 1970

The government budget surpluses that the largest industrial countries tended to run in the 1960s have declined steadily since then and, in some cases, have given way to large and persistent deficits. Table 3.2 shows the decade-by-decade evolution of public-sector balances for the seven largest industrial countries. Our overlapping generations model suggests that these fiscal shifts are likely to have reduced total world saving and to have pushed world real interest rates upward.

In the application on global saving and interest rates at the end of Chapter 1, we noted that gross world saving has declined since the 1970s. We can now see part of the reason: a fall in government saving that non-Ricardian households failed to offset fully through a rise in their own saving. Indeed, for reasons that still are not fully understood, gross private saving has declined somewhat.[36]

The overlapping generations model implies that, even in the absence of continuing government deficits, higher public debt levels can reduce private saving and crowd capital out of private portfolios, thus raising interest rates. Figure 3.7 provides direct evidence of that mechanism in post-1970 data. The first series plotted in the figure is the ratio of world public debt to world GDP, computed as a GDP-weighted average of 15 industrial countries' public debt-GDP ratios. The second series is a measure of the world real interest rate, based on data from the same 15 countries. Clearly, the two series are highly correlated. While changing public-debt levels cannot explain all recent movements in world real interest rates, they certainly appear to be an important part of the story.   ∎

---

36. Table 3.1 reported the behavior of net private saving in the largest industrial countries. But recall that the capital depreciation estimates underlying net saving figures can be quite unreliable.

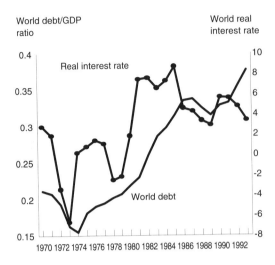

Figure 3.7
World public debt and ex post real interest rates, 1970–93

3.7   Integrating the Overlapping Generations and Representative-Consumer Models

Though similar in some respects, the overlapping generations model and the representative-consumer, infinite-horizon model of aggregate consumption give fundamentally different answers to some key questions. Does a temporary output shock leave per capita domestic consumption unchanged in the long run? Can higher trend output growth raise private saving and the current account balance? Does the economy reach a steady state in per capita consumption when individuals' time-preference rate differs from the world interest rate? Can changes in the timing of lump-sum taxes have real effects? To all of these questions the overlapping generations model answers yes while the representative-agent model answers no. These are fundamental differences. Which approach is more nearly right?

This section tries to unify the two approaches within more general frameworks that serve to highlight similarities as well as differences. We consider two alternative unifying frameworks. The first introduces a bequest motive into the overlapping generations model. A bequest motive can arise when individuals care about future generations' welfare, not just their own consumption, but it may also be motivated by considerations other than kindheartedness, as we shall see. The second framework we look at is based on a model that incorporates both infinitely-lived consumers and overlapping generations. That framework yields a straightforward synthesis of the representative-agent and overlapping generations approaches.

While purely theoretical exercises such as these cannot, in themselves, determine the empirical validity of a particular aggregate consumption theory, they can help to isolate key, and perhaps testable, assumptions behind competing visions of the economy.

3.7.1   Intergenerational Altruism and Bequests

The overlapping generations model we have been studying assumes that each generation is completely selfish, with no regard for the welfare of future generations. This assumption is not very realistic: future generations are the offspring of individuals currently alive, and few people seem completely indifferent about their children's welfare. This simple observation has far-reaching implications. Indeed, an economy of finite-lived individuals who care about their children may, in some respects, mimic the behavior of an economy peopled by infinite-lived individuals.

To see the role of intergenerational altruism most simply, let's think about an endowment economy peopled by "nonoverlapping" generations, each of which lives only one period but cares about the welfare of its immediate descendant. In this setting, we will refer to the succession of individuals making up a family line as a *dynasty*. We also assume that the economy is inhabited by a single representative dynasty, whose consumption corresponds to aggregate consumption.

The date t member of the representative dynasty (who lives only during period t), maximizes the utility function

$$U_t = u(C_t) + \beta U_{t+1}, \tag{56}$$

where $0 < \beta < 1$. The notation means that an individual alive during period t derives utility from two sources: his own consumption, C_t, and the welfare of a child whose utility will be U_{t+1}. The utility function (56) therefore implies that each agent shows altruism toward his child. Notice that reproduction here takes the form of parthenogenesis. More realistic models based on marriage (which implies economic not to mention genetic mixing) will be taken up later on.

The individual alive on date t has the lifetime budget constraint

$$(1+r)H_t + Y_t - T_t = C_t + H_{t+1}, \tag{57}$$

where $Y_t - T_t$ is the date t generation's after-tax income and H_{t+1} is the bequest the date t dynasty member makes to his immediate successor. According to eq. (57), the dynasty's date t resources include the principal and interest on the bequest that the date t individual's own parent left.

A realistic constraint on the individual's maximization problem is

$$H_{t+1} \geq 0. \tag{58}$$

People can receive neither *inter vivos* gifts nor bequests from unborn children. Furthermore, the legal system exempts children from responsibility for parental debts.[37]

For the moment, we will assume constraint (58) holds as a strict inequality, and focus on the case where optimal bequests are always positive. In that case, we think about an individual's optimal consumption problem as follows. First, perform iterated forward substitutions for H_{t+1}, H_{t+2}, etc., in eq. (57) to derive the dynasty's intertemporal budget constraint

$$\sum_{s=t}^{\infty} \left(\frac{1}{1+r} \right)^{s-t} C_s = (1+r)H_t + \sum_{s=t}^{\infty} \left(\frac{1}{1+r} \right)^{s-t} (Y_s - T_s), \tag{59}$$

in which we have ruled out the possibility that bequests grow at or above the rate of interest.[38] This is the same constraint that the representative infinitely-lived consumer faced in Chapter 2.

Next, lead eq. (56) by a period to obtain

$$U_{t+1} = u(C_{t+1}) + \beta U_{t+2}.$$

After using this to eliminate U_{t+1} from eq. (56), we have

$$U_t = u(C_t) + \beta u(C_{t+1}) + \beta^2 U_{t+2}.$$

Repeated forward substitutions of this kind transform eq. (56) into

$$U_t = \sum_{s=t}^{\infty} \beta^{s-t} u(C_s) + \lim_{s \to \infty} \beta^{s-t} U_s.$$

Provided $\lim_{s \to \infty} \beta^{s-t} U_s = 0$, a date t individual acts so as to maximize

$$U_t = \sum_{s=t}^{\infty} \beta^{s-t} u(C_s) \tag{60}$$

subject to eq. (59).[39] The objective function (60) is the same one maximized by a single infinite-horizon decision maker.

---

37. Later we will touch briefly on the implications of resource transfers from children to parents.

38. Thus we require $\lim_{s \to \infty} (1+r)^{-(s-t)} H_{s+1} = 0$. The next footnote suggests that, while this condition is correct when the lifetime objective function is eq. (60) below, it might fail in other cases.

39. The limit condition leading to eq. (60) is not innocuous, as pointed out by Gale (1983). To take his example, consider a dynasty whose members are misers: suppose that the date t member has the alternative lifetime utility function

$$U_t = \sum_{s=t}^{\infty} \beta^{s-t} u(C_s) + \mu \lim_{s \to \infty} \beta^{s-t} H_{s+1},$$

according to which a positive utility weight μ is attached to the limiting value of the subjectively discounted future bequest. In such cases the dynasty generally won't consume all its lifetime resources. Leading the preceding lifetime objective a period yields

Thus, aside from the fact that intergenerational transfers can never be negative [recall constraint (58), which we have temporarily set aside], the present overlapping generations model based on eqs. (56) and (59) leads to the same predictions about consumption as the single representative-agent model.[40] Even though each individual cares directly only about his *immediate* descendant, this is enough to link him to *all* future generations!

Plainly, Ricardian equivalence can prevail in the overlapping generations model with bequests even though each individual is mortal. This point was first made in an insightful paper by Barro (1974). Suppose that initially parents wish to leave strictly positive bequests to their children. In this situation, parents will vary their bequests to undo any (sufficiently small) government attempt to transfer income across generations. For example, a bond-financed transfer payment to the current generation, coupled with higher taxes on the next generation, leads the current generation to increase its bequest by the amount of the transfer. On balance, no intergenerational redistribution occurs, the reason being that the dynasty's budget constraint (59) is not altered.[41]

In certain cases, however, the nonnegativity constraints will bind, implying behavior different from what we saw in Chapter 2. Suppose, for example, that output is growing rapidly. The individual alive on date t, knowing that his descendants will be far better off than he, would like to consume future dynasty income by borrowing today and leaving the resulting debt to his child, who in turn will bequeath debt to his, ad infinitum. Negative bequests of this sort are, however, impossible: the best the date t dynasty member can do is to consume $Y_t - T_t$ and leave the bequest $H_{t+1} = 0$.

This case of a growing economy with binding nonnegativity constraints on bequests is one in which Ricardian equivalence does *not* hold. By making bond-financed payments to the current generation and requiring its descendants to repay

---

$$U_{t+1} = \sum_{s=t+1}^{\infty} \beta^{s-(t+1)} u(C_s) + \mu \lim_{s \to \infty} \beta^{s-(t+1)} H_{s+1},$$

from which it is readily verified that the alternate solution for U_t satisfies eq. (56). Notice that now $\lim_{s \to \infty} \beta^{s-t} U_s = \mu \lim_{s \to \infty} \beta^{s-t} H_{s+1}$, which may be strictly positive. Thus it is not true that eq. (56) automatically leads to eq. (60). The recursion in eq. (56) is consistent with eq. (60); because the constant μ is arbitrary, however, eq. (56) is, strictly speaking, also consistent with a vast multiplicity of other intertemporal objective functions. While this indeterminacy matters for predicting the level of consumption, it has little bearing on other issues, e.g., Ricardian equivalence.

40. Observe that there can never be intergenerational conflict about consumption, despite the existence of a different decision maker at each date. Intergenerational conflict would imply a problem of *dynamic inconsistency* in intertemporal preferences. As we saw in Chapter 2, however, the preference scheme of eq. (60) isn't subject to dynamic inconsistency.

41. Interestingly, a similar argument shows that Ricardian equivalence could hold without bequests if altruistic children make positive gifts to their parents. A formal demonstration requires a model in which children and parents coexist over some time interval; see, for example, Drazen (1978).

the loan, the government can do what private individuals would like to do, but cannot: pass on debt to future generations.

*3.7.2   Further Theoretical Problems with Ricardian Equivalence

Barro's (1974) demonstration that Ricardian equivalence can hold in an economy populated by a succession of finite-lived individuals is remarkable. The observation of substantial intentional bequests and *inter vivos* parent-to-child gifts in industrialized economies has lent added force to the theoretical argument. But that argument is based on a counterfactual account of dynastic propagation, on special assumptions about utility functions, and on a too-narrow view of how parents provide for their offspring. The examples that follow illustrate what can happen when these assumptions are relaxed.

3.7.2.1   Implications of Sexual Reproduction

New human beings (generally) result from a pooling of genes by people with different parents. Once we combine this fact of life with the assumption that people care about the utility of their offspring, a troubling implication arises: virtually *every* change in taxes, even in distorting taxes, may become neutral! Recall, for example, the tax on foreign borrowing analyzed in Chapter 1. With intermarriage between different family groups, the consumption-distorting effect of this tax may disappear.

How is this possible? Bernheim and Bagwell (1988) first explained the mechanism. In an economy with sexual reproduction and altruism toward offspring, all the private budget constraints in the economy can become interlinked. For example, A may not care about B directly, but if A and B share a common descendant, C, about whom they both care, then government income redistributions from A to B can become less costly for A than they otherwise would be. The reason is that such transfers are likely to benefit C and thus to generate utility for A. In fact, it is entirely possible that government *intra*generational redistribution from A to B is neutral, just like *inter*generational redistribution between A and C or B and C. Let the government tax A by τ and hand the proceeds to B. If, in response, A reduces his bequest to C by τ, and B increases his own bequest to C by τ, then the original consumption allocation is restored.

This basic mechanism can render even usually distorting redistributive taxes neutral. Loosely speaking, if any individual A looks far enough into the future, it becomes increasingly likely that he and any other individual B will have a common descendant whose utility will affect theirs even if they care directly only about their immediate children. Because the proceeds of any tax thus are perceived as a benefit for one's future descendants, individuals cease to view the tax as a private cost.

Bernheim and Bagwell (1988) argue that the absurdity of this conclusion invalidates the premises from which it follows, notably the assumption of unselfish intergenerational altruism vital to the Barro result.[42]

3.7.2.2 Intrafamily Exchange

Barro (1974) noted that Ricardian equivalence might fail if bequests are not motivated solely by altruism, but instead represent a payment for some service offspring provide (for example, housing services, nursing care, or just attention). Bernheim, Shleifer, and Summers (1985) develop a model along these lines and marshall supporting evidence. The basic idea is illustrated by a simple three-period example in which the parent lives on dates 0 and 1 while the child lives on dates 1 and 2.

The parent's concave utility function is $U^{\mathrm{P}}(c_1, a_1)$ and the child's is $U^{\mathrm{C}}(c_2, a_1)$, where a_1 ("attention") is the level of a service that children can provide to parents on date 1. To make the sharpest contrast with the altruistic model, we make the two coldhearted assumptions that (a) the parent doesn't care about his child's welfare at all, and (b) more attention, while raising the parent's utility, does not raise the child's. Assumption (a) is built into the parental utility function we have assumed; adding altruism toward the child wouldn't change the gist of our analysis. Assumption (b) can be summarized as

$$\frac{\partial U^{\mathrm{P}}}{\partial a_1} > 0, \qquad \frac{\partial U^{\mathrm{C}}}{\partial a_1} \leq 0.$$

Finally, we suppose (c) that $\partial U^{\mathrm{C}}/\partial a_1 < 0$ unless $a_1 = 0$, in which case $\partial U^{\mathrm{C}}/\partial a_1 = 0$. Assumption (c) implies that it is painless for the child to provide the first unit of attention, but not subsequent units.

Observe first that if the parent doesn't bribe the child in some way, the child will provide no attention [assumption (b)]. But the parent would, in general, like to "consume" some of both the model's goods, consumption and filial attention. The parent can do so by purchasing attention from the child through a date 1 gift or through a bequest placed in an irrevocable trust fund until date 2.[43] The child, in turn, is happy to provide some attention if compensated [assumption (c)]. Because of these initial gains from trade, we observe a positive resource flow from parent to child.

Figure 3.8 illustrates the intrafamily equilibrium under the temporary simplifying assumption that the interest rate, r, is zero. The horizontal axis in the figure has length equal to total family resources, $y^{\mathrm{P}} + y^{\mathrm{C}}$. The vertical axis measures amounts of attention, a_1. The parent's consumption, c_1, is measured horizontally starting

---

42. Laitner (1991) shows that when individuals marry others of similar wealth, rather than mating randomly, the extreme Bernheim-Bagwell neutrality results may not hold.

43. An irrevocable trust fund would prevent the selfish parent from reneging on the promised bequest after attention had been provided.

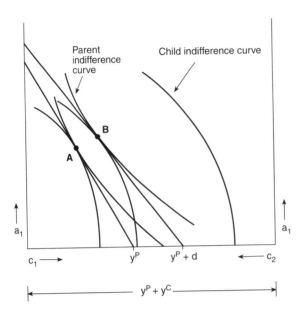

Figure 3.8
Non-Ricardian equivalence with contingent bequests

from the left-hand origin, and the child's is measured horizontally starting from the right-hand origin. At point **A**, where the parent and child indifference curves are tangent to a line passing through the income endowment point y^P, gains from trade are fully exploited.[44] Notice that the parent's consumption is strictly below his endowment y^P.

Notwithstanding the positive transfer from parent to child, Ricardian equivalence does not hold. Suppose that on date 1 the government makes a payment d to the parent and raises the child's future taxes by d. This policy shifts the equilibrium to point **B** in Figure 3.8. The Ricardian parental response would leave both family members' consumption levels intact. But this outcome is not what the figure shows. At point **B**, the parent is enjoying more consumption and more attention; the child has lower consumption. Thus the government policy has been successful in redistributing income between the generations.

3.7.2.3   Investment in Human Capital

A large share of (altruistic) parental expenditure on children takes the form of educational expenses, which may be viewed as investment in human capital. Drazen (1978) showed how this factor could invalidate Ricardian equivalence unless there is a perfect market for human capital.

---

44. The tangent line's slope is the equilibrium "price" of consumption in terms of attention.

Suppose an altruistic two-period-lived parent has optimally divided second-period resources between his own consumption, investment in his child's human capital, and a bequest. Suppose also that the child cannot borrow to finance fully his own education. Then it may well happen that the return to further investment in the child's human capital exceeds the interest rate r, but that no resources are available to exploit this excess return. (In that case, bequests are zero: the child benefits more from extra education than from financial assets that earn only r.)

If the government pays the parent a transfer d, imposing a tax of $d(1 + r)$ on the child next period, the parent normally will increase his own consumption as well as his investment in the child's education, in such a way that parent and child are both better off. The reason is that the transfer actually has expanded the family's intertemporal budget constraint by mitigating the negative effect of personal borrowing constraints on the child's lifetime income.

The larger point raised by models like Drazen's concerns the definition of saving. Like most of the literature on life-cycle saving, we have used a narrow definition in which saving refers to the accumulation of financial assets. Human capital accumulation is also a form of saving, however: just like investment in physical capital, investment in human capital expands the stock of a long-lived factor of production and thus is another way people can provide for the future. A complete picture of the household's (and nation's) intertemporal allocation process must account for human-capital investments.[45] We will return to the subject of human capital later in this book, in Chapter 7.

3.7.3   Infinitely Lived Overlapping Generations

An alternative way to integrate the overlapping generations and representative-consumer models is to follow Philippe Weil (1989a), who assumes an economy of distinct infinitely lived dynasties that come into being on different dates.[46] To highlight the main distinctions between the present model and the overlapping generations model with two-period lives, we abstract from investment and focus on the small country case. (We examine a global equilibrium version of the model in Chapter 7.)

Imagine again an economy with a single consumption good facing a given world interest rate r. An individual born on date v (the individual's "vintage") lives forever and, on any date t, maximizes

---

45. For an attempt to adjust national saving rates accordingly, see Shafer, Elmeskov, and Tease (1992).

46. Weil's model builds on the Blanchard (1985) uncertain-horizons framework, which itself builds on Yaari (1965). The Blanchard model yields results similar to those of Weil's but is slightly more intricate (see exercise 3 at the end of the chapter). For related alternative approaches, see Frenkel and Razin (1992) and Matsuyama (1987), who assume constant populations and uncertain lifetimes, as well as Buiter (1988, 1989) and Abel (1989).

$$U_t^v = \sum_{s=t}^{\infty} \beta^{s-t} \log(c_s^v), \tag{61}$$

the same lifetime objective studied in Chapter 2's representative-consumer model. Now, however, the number of individuals in the economy, N_t, grows at rate $n < r$, $N_t = (1+n)N_{t-1}$. It is convenient to assume that there is a date $t = 0$ on which the economy starts, and that $N_0 = 1$.

As before, we could interpret eq. (61) as the objective function of an immortal dynasty consisting of successive agents with one-period lives. In that case, positive dynastic wealth would be transmitted between generations in the form of bequests. As we shall see, however, Ricardian equivalence fails to hold in this model—providing another example in which the timing of nondistorting taxes matters despite an important role for bequests in accounting for the economy's financial wealth.

The budget constraint for individual v at time $t \geq v$ is

$$\sum_{s=t}^{\infty} \left(\frac{1}{1+r} \right)^{s-t} c_s^v = (1+r)b_t^{\mathrm{P},v} + \sum_{s=t}^{\infty} \left(\frac{1}{1+r} \right)^{s-t} \left(y_s^v - \tau_s^v \right), \tag{62}$$

where we index individual bond holdings, $b^{\mathrm{P},v}$, the output endowment, and lump-sum taxes, like consumption, by vintage as well as calendar time. A central assumption of the model is that

$$b_v^{\mathrm{P},v} = 0. \tag{63}$$

Since newly born individuals aren't linked by altruism to individuals of earlier vintage, they are born owning no *financial* wealth. They are, however, born owning the present discounted value of after-tax endowment income, which we refer to as *human* wealth.[47]

Maximization of eq. (61) subject to eq. (62) leads to the individual consumption function

$$c_t^v = (1-\beta) \left[(1+r)b_t^{\mathrm{P},v} + \sum_{s=t}^{\infty} \left(\frac{1}{1+r} \right)^{s-t} \left(y_s^v - \tau_s^v \right) \right], \tag{64}$$

which follows from Chapter 2's eq. (16) upon setting $\sigma = 1$.

As in the model with overlapping two-period lives, we are interested in the behavior of *aggregate* consumption. To calculate its value, we must sum the consumptions of all vintages born since $t = 0$. Vintage $v = 0$, born at $t = 0$, has $N_0 = 1$ members. Total population on date $t = 1$ is N_1; of this population, $N_1 - N_0 =$

---

47. A question that naturally arises is, where do new individuals come from? They could be poor immigrants. Alternatively, dynasties, following a practice like primogeniture, could feel selective altruism and leave bequests only to some children.

$(1+n) - 1 = n$ are of vintage $v = 1$. Similarly, vintage $v = 2$ contains $N_2 - N_1 = (1+n)^2 - (1+n) = n(1+n)$ members. Continuing with this reasoning, we see that any vintage $v > 0$ is $n(1+n)^{v-1}$ strong. The economy's *aggregate per capita consumption* on date t therefore is

$$c_t = \frac{c_t^0 + nc_t^1 + n(1+n)c_t^2 + \cdots + n(1+n)^{t-1}c_t^t}{(1+n)^t}, \tag{65}$$

which is simply total consumption divided by the total population $N_t = (1+n)^t$. (Our notation for aggregate per capita variables simply drops the vintage superscript.)

The preceding linear aggregation procedure can be applied to any other variable. Aggregating the individual consumption functions (64) shows that aggregate per capita consumption is related in a simple way to aggregate per capita financial and human wealth:

$$c_t = (1 - \beta)\left[(1+r)b_t^P + \sum_{s=t}^{\infty}\left(\frac{1}{1+r}\right)^{s-t}(y_s - \tau_s)\right]. \tag{66}$$

Similarly, the equation governing individual asset accumulation,

$$b_{t+1}^{P,v} = (1+r)b_t^{P,v} + y_t^v - \tau_t^v - c_t^v,$$

can be aggregated up into an equation of aggregate private asset accumulation. To accomplish this aggregation, apply the weighting in eq. (65) to both sides of the last equation. The result is

$$\frac{b_{t+1}^{P,0} + nb_{t+1}^{P,1} + \cdots + n(1+n)^{t-1}b_{t+1}^{P,t}}{(1+n)^t} = (1+r)b_t^P + y_t - \tau_t - c_t,$$

where the right-hand variables all are per capita aggregates with respect to the date t population.[48] The left-hand side can similarly be expressed in per capita aggregate terms once we remember that the missing term $b_{t+1}^{P,t+1} = 0$ [by eq. (63)]: a newly born generation has no financial wealth. Thus we can express the left-hand side of the preceding equation as

$$(1+n)\frac{\left[b_{t+1}^{P,0} + nb_{t+1}^{P,1} + \cdots + n(1+n)^{t-1}b_{t+1}^{P,t} + n(1+n)^t b_{t+1}^{P,t+1}\right]}{(1+n)^{t+1}} = (1+n)b_{t+1}^P.$$

Combining this expression with the immediately preceding one yields the result we are after:

---

48. This includes b_t^P, which is the average per capita value on date t of the net financial assets private individuals carry over from date $t - 1$. In other words, b_t^P equals total assets accumulated during period $t - 1$ divided by the following period's population.

$$b_{t+1}^P = \frac{(1+r)b_t^P + y_t - \tau_t - c_t}{1+n}. \tag{67}$$

By using eq. (66) to eliminate c_t from eq. (67), we obtain a single difference equation that completely characterizes private asset accumulation:

$$b_{t+1}^P = \left[\frac{(1+r)\beta}{1+n}\right]b_t^P + \left[\frac{y_t - \tau_t - (1-\beta)\sum_{s=t}^{\infty}\left(\frac{1}{1+r}\right)^{s-t}(y_s - \tau_s)}{1+n}\right]. \tag{68}$$

Specific predictions about private asset accumulation will follow from assumptions concerning the time paths of output and taxes.

3.7.4 Dynamics and Steady State

With the help of some simplifying assumptions, we develop a diagram that helps in visualizing the dynamics implied by eq. (68). Consider first the case in which there is no government economic activity. Thus, $\tau = 0$ on all dates and, since there are no government assets or debt, the net assets of the private sector as a whole also are the country's net foreign assets, $b^P = b$. We also assume that y is constant at $\bar{y}$, thereby excluding, at least for now, trend productivity growth.

In this special case, the dynamic equilibrium condition (68) simplifies to

$$b_{t+1} = \left[\frac{(1+r)\beta}{1+n}\right]b_t + \left[\frac{(1+r)\beta - 1}{r(1+n)}\right]\bar{y}. \tag{69}$$

The dynamic behavior implied by eq. (69) is shown in Figure 3.9.

Starting from any initial net foreign asset stock b_0, the economy converges to a steady state in which the per capita aggregate stock of net foreign assets is $\bar{b}$. Thus the steady state is dynamically stable. Existence and stability of the steady state follow from the assumption made in drawing Figure 3.9 that $(1+r)\beta/(1+n) < 1$, so that the slope of eq. (69) is less than that of the 45° line. Recall that the product $(1+r)\beta$ determines the "tilt" of an individual's consumption path. If $(1+r)\beta > 1$, for example, each infinitely-lived individual is accumulating financial assets over time. (Because y is constant at $\bar{y}$, consumption and wealth can grow over time only if financial assets do.) But if $(1+r)\beta < 1+n$, new individuals with no inherited financial assets are entering the economy sufficiently quickly that per capita *aggregate* foreign assets can reach a stable steady state.[49] That steady state involves a positive level of foreign assets, of course, since the assumption

---

49. If $(1+r)\beta > (1+n)$, existing consumers are accumulating assets at such a rapid clip that per capita aggregate assets are always rising despite population growth. The "steady state" that the diagram implies in this case is an illusion, since it occurs at a net foreign debt so large that consumption would have to be negative! [See eq. (70).] Any initial foreign asset level consistent with positive consumption thus implies that $b \to \infty$ over time.

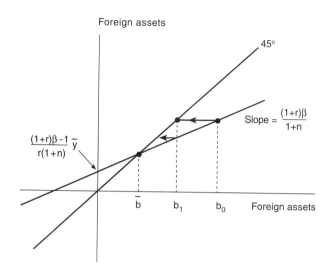

Figure 3.9
Steady state with infinitely-lived overlapping generations

$(1 + r)\beta > 1$ implies that there are no individuals with negative financial asset holdings. This is the case illustrated in Figure 3.9.

Suppose, however, that $(1 + r)\beta < 1$, so that all consumers dissave over their lifetimes. This assumption would make the vertical intercept of eq. (69) negative in Figure 3.9, shifting the intersection of the two schedules to the diagram's southwest quadrant. This is the case in which $\bar{b} < 0$, so that the economy is a steady-state debtor. Stability is now assured if the population growth rate n is nonnegative.

Setting $b_t = b_{t+1} = \bar{b}$ in eq. (69), we find the steady-state foreign asset level to be

$$\bar{b} = \left[\frac{(1 + r)\beta - 1}{(1 + n) - (1 + r)\beta} \right] \frac{\bar{y}}{r}. \tag{70}$$

Look at the fraction in square brackets on the right-hand side of eq. (70). The existence/stability condition $(1 + n) > (1 + r)\beta$ determines the sign of the denominator, while the consumption-tilt factor, $(1 + r)\beta - 1$, determines the sign of the numerator.

The preceding solution for $\bar{b}$ leads immediately to a solution for steady-state per capita consumption, $\bar{c}$. Since there is no government, $b^P = b$ and the private finance constraint (67) coincides with the overall current-account constraint

$$b_{t+1} = \frac{(1 + r)b_t + y_t - c_t}{1 + n}.$$

In a steady state with $y_t = \bar{y}$ and $b_{t+1} = b_t = \bar{b}$, c_t must be constant at

$$\bar{c} = (r - n)\bar{b} + \bar{y}. \tag{71}$$

Let us continue to assume that the world economy is dynamically efficient (which means, in the present context, that $r > n$). Then a positive (negative) net foreign asset level implies that steady-state consumption is above (below) output.[50]

We stress that in interpreting these results, it is important to remember that the economy under study here is small, and its small size is what allows one to treat the world interest rate as being independent of the country's rate of time preference or population growth rate. If this were a closed global economy, as in the version of the model we develop in Chapter 7, the interest rate would be determined endogenously and would, in general, rise when n rises or β falls.

3.7.5   Output Changes and Productivity Growth

As a first application of the model, consider an unanticipated permanent rise in the per capita output endowment, from $\bar{y}$ to $\bar{y}'$. In Figure 3.10 we show the case $(1 + r)\beta < 1$, implying a steady state at point **A** with $\bar{b} < 0$.[51] The increase of $\bar{y}$ to $\bar{y}'$ shifts down the intercept of eq. (69), lowering $\bar{b}$ to $\bar{b}'$ at point **B**. [The same conclusion follows from eq. (70).] On the assumption that the economy was at **A** before the favorable surprise, it will converge gradually to **B** afterward. Why do long-run foreign assets become even more negative? When $(1 + r)\beta < 1$, individuals are impatient to consume; higher human wealth allows them to borrow more early in life. Substitution of eq. (70) into eq. (71) shows that $\bar{c}$ rises even though $\bar{b}$ falls.[52]

Turn next to the case of a *transitory* rise in output. Specifically, assume the economy is initially in a steady state with per capita output $\bar{y}$ and foreign assets $\bar{b}$ when output rises unexpectedly to $\bar{y}' > \bar{y}$ for one period only. That is, starting on date t, output follows the new path:

$$y_s = \begin{cases} \bar{y}' & (s = t), \\ \bar{y} & (s > t). \end{cases} \tag{72}$$

---

50. It may seem paradoxical that, in the dynamically inefficient case $(r < n)$, eq. (71) implies the economy permanently consumes more than its per capita income despite a foreign debt. But, when $n > r$, new, debt-free consumers are entering the economy so rapidly that their high initial consumption—the factor generating the steady-state debt—outweighs the low consumption of their debt-burdened elders. Obviously, each *individual* will eventually have to lower consumption below $\bar{y}$ to remain within his intertemporal budget constraint.

51. As an exercise, the reader should work through the case $(1 + r)\beta > 1$.

52. The result of the substitution is

$$\bar{c} = \frac{n(1 + r)(1 - \beta)\bar{y}}{\left[(1 + n) - (1 + r)\beta\right]r}.$$

Because the denominator is positive (the existence/stability condition) and $\beta < 1$, $d\bar{c}/d\bar{y} > 0$.

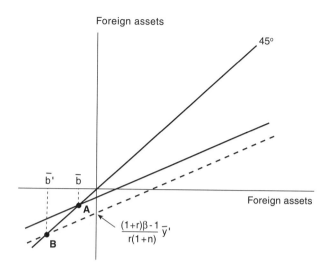

Figure 3.10
An unexpected permanent rise in output

Let's tackle this exercise algebraically. Since initial foreign assets $b_t = \bar{b}$, eq. (68) (with b^p still equal to b and all taxes still zero) implies that per capita foreign assets at the start of date $t + 1$ are

$$
b_{t+1} = \left[\frac{(1+r)\beta}{1+n}\right]\bar{b} + \left\{\frac{\bar{y}' - (1-\beta)\left[\bar{y}' + \sum_{s=t+1}^{\infty}\left(\frac{1}{1+r}\right)^{s-t}\bar{y}\right]}{1+n}\right\}
$$

$$
= \left[\frac{(1+r)\beta}{1+n}\right]\bar{b} + \left[\frac{(1+r)\beta - 1}{r(1+n)}\right]\bar{y} + \frac{\beta}{1+n}(\bar{y}' - \bar{y})
$$

$$
= \bar{b} + \frac{\beta}{1+n}(\bar{y}' - \bar{y}) > \bar{b},
$$

where the last equality follows most easily from eq. (69) and the definition of a steady state. Thus the economy has a current account surplus on date t: consumers at time t save a fraction β of any transitory output rise, and per capita foreign assets at the start of period $t + 1$ equal the implied rise in total foreign assets divided by the new, n percent higher population. Starting on date $t + 1$, however, output is back at its original level, and so the original transition equation (69), which has the steady state $\bar{b}$, applies once again. Since $b_{t+1} > \bar{b}$, net foreign assets fall monotonically back to their starting level. Thus a temporary output shock has a transitory effect but no long-run effect, just as in the overlapping-generations model with two-period lives (section 3.3.1).

The model can also be used to study trend productivity growth. In our discussion of productivity growth in models with two-period lives (especially section 3.3.2), we saw that the saving effect of higher productivity growth depends on the distribution of the resulting earnings gains across groups at different stages of the life cycle. Here we make the very simple assumption that per capita output y grows at the constant rate g,

$$y_{t+1} = (1+g)y_t,$$

where $(1+n)(1+g) < 1+r$. The per capita aggregate consumption function (66) (again with $b^P = b$ and taxes zero) yields

$$c_t = (1-\beta)\left[(1+r)b_t + \left(\frac{1+r}{r-g}\right)y_t\right]$$

in this case. Substitution of this equation into eq. (67) (for the case with no government) leads to the following generalization of eq. (69):

$$b_{t+1} = \left[\frac{(1+r)\beta}{1+n}\right]b_t + \left[\frac{(1+r)\beta - (1+g)}{(1+n)(r-g)}\right]y_t.$$

To convert this equation to stationary form (since y_t is growing), we divide both sides by y_{t+1} to obtain

$$\frac{b_{t+1}}{y_{t+1}} = \left[\frac{(1+r)\beta}{(1+n)(1+g)}\right]\frac{b_t}{y_t} + \left[\frac{(1+r)\beta - (1+g)}{(1+n)(1+g)(r-g)}\right], \tag{73}$$

where we have made use of the fact that $y_{t+1} = (1+g)y_t$. Note that the condition for the economy to have positive net foreign assets is now $\beta(1+r) > 1+g$, since each cohort can borrow against growing output. This difference equation can be graphed analogously to eq. (69) in Figure 3.9, but with the ratio of net foreign assets to output in place of per capita aggregate net foreign assets. One can easily show that a rise in the growth rate g always lowers the economy's long-run net foreign-asset-to-output ratio. Intuitively, faster output growth encourages all generations to save less. In section 3.3.2 we found that productivity growth that accrues disproportionately toward the end of individual life cycles tends to lower aggregate saving. Here we find the same result because of the assumption that ever-greater output gains are always expected to occur later in life.

3.7.6 Overlapping Generations and Representative-Agent Models: A Synthesis

Having outlined the basics of Weil's (1989a) overlapping generations model, we are now ready to deliver the synthesis with the representative-agent model promised at the start of this section. We consider two questions, the response to temporary output shocks and the effects of government debt issue.

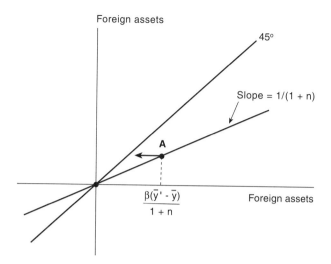

Figure 3.11
A transitory rise in output

3.7.6.1   Temporary Output Shocks

In the last subsection we studied an economy in a steady state with constant output $\bar{y}$ whose residents suddenly learn, at the start of date t, that output will follow eq. (72) rather than remaining constant. We saw that b_{t+1} rose above its initial level, $\bar{b}$, by the amount $\beta(\bar{y}' - \bar{y})/(1 + n)$ because each household in the economy on date t wished to save a fraction β of its temporary income increase. For dates $s > t$, eq. (69) again governed the economy's dynamics. To simplify our discussion we assume that $(1 + r)\beta = 1$, so that $\bar{b} = 0$ and difference equation (69) becomes

$$b_{t+1} = \frac{b_t}{1 + n},$$

which is graphed in Figure 3.11.

The graph reinforces a point made earlier: the transitory endowment shock, which initially shifts the economy to point **A**, has effects that damp out over time. With $(1 + r)\beta = 1$, consumers already on the scene permanently increase their foreign asset holdings and permanently raise consumption by the interest on those additional foreign assets. Over time, however, new individuals are born, and per capita consumption returns to its original level. As the population growth rate, n, falls, the rate of convergence slows. In the limit of *zero* population growth ($n = 0$), b no longer converges to $\bar{b} = 0$. The equation of motion for net foreign assets becomes $b_{t+1} = b_t$; there is no tendency at all for foreign assets to revert to a well-defined long-run level. In Figure 3.11, as $n \to 0$, the flatter schedule overlaps the $45°$ line, and all foreign asset changes become permanent.

In this example the initial per capita consumption increase is $(1 - \beta)(\bar{y}' - \bar{y})$ *regardless* of the value of n. The population growth rate affects only the speed of convergence to the steady state, which is lower the smaller n is. As a result, for realistic values of n, the short- to medium-term prediction of this overlapping generations model will be very close to that of the representative-consumer model of Chapter 2. It is primarily the long-run implications of transitory output changes that differ.

3.7.6.2   Government Deficits and Debt

The Ricardian equivalence of debt and taxes fails in the present model with positive population growth n. By understanding why it fails, and seeing how it is reestablished in the limit as $n \to 0$, we can sharpen our appreciation of how economies inhabited by overlapping generations are related to representative-agent economies.

To study government deficits and debt, we reintroduce taxes and the distinction between private and national net asset holdings. Let's assume that the government levies a uniform tax, τ_t, on every person alive on date t. The government finance constraint, eq. (5), is transformed into aggregate per capita terms through division by the date $t + 1$ population. The result is

$$b_{t+1}^G = \frac{(1 + r)\, b_t^G + \tau_t - g_t}{1 + n}, \tag{74}$$

where we now use g to denote government consumption per capita (and *not*, as earlier in this chapter, the output growth rate).

Suppose that, initially, $b^G = 0$ at the start of period t when the government decides to lower b^G to $-\bar{d}$ by giving every individual currently alive a claim on the government paying $r\bar{d}$ each period, starting in period t. The government then maintains the per capita public debt level at $\bar{d}$ forever by the appropriate combination of new borrowing and uniform taxes on all of those alive. What we will show is that Ricardian equivalence breaks down for this experiment: the initial gift of debt has a positive consumption effect when $n > 0$, despite the fact that the gift is financed by additional future taxes of equal present value.

Equation (74) shows that, to maintain $b^G = -\bar{d}$, per capita taxes in each period $s \geq t$ must be set at

$$\tau_s = (r - n)\bar{d} + g_s. \tag{75}$$

Equation (75) implies that for an *individual* who receives the government gift, the present value of taxes to be paid in period t and after is

$$\sum_{s=t}^{\infty} \left(\frac{1}{1+r}\right)^{s-t} \tau_s = \sum_{s=t}^{\infty} \left(\frac{1}{1+r}\right)^{s-t} (r - n)\bar{d} + \sum_{s=t}^{\infty} \left(\frac{1}{1+r}\right)^{s-t} g_s.$$

Since, now, $b^P = b - b^G = b + \bar{d}$, the per capita consumption function (66) becomes

$$c_t = (1 - \beta) \left[(1 + r)(b_t + \bar{d}) + \sum_{s=t}^{\infty} \left(\frac{1}{1+r} \right)^{s-t} (y_s - g_s) - \frac{(1+r)(r-n)}{r} \bar{d} \right]$$

$$= (1 - \beta) \left[(1 + r) \left(b_t + \frac{n\bar{d}}{r} \right) + \sum_{s=t}^{\infty} \left(\frac{1}{1+r} \right)^{s-t} (y_s - g_s) \right].$$

Notice that per capita consumption depends, as in Chapter 2's representative-consumer model, on the per capita national stock of net foreign assets, b, as well as on the present value of per capita output net of per capita government spending. In the present setting, however, consumption *also* depends on the government debt, $\bar{d}$. Only as $n \to 0$ does government debt become irrelevant.

Government debt is net wealth in this model, even though individuals live forever, because some fraction of the taxes that service the debt will fall on new entrants to the economy who are not linked by ties of altruism to existing consumers. Only when $n = 0$, so that new individuals are never born, does Ricardian equivalence apply.

Appendix 3A   Dynamic Inefficiency

Section 3.6.4 noted that in the general equilibrium of an overlapping generations model, the steady-state interest rate, $\bar{r}$, can be below the growth rate of total output. This appendix explores some important (and surprising) consequences of that dynamically inefficient case.[53] The discussion that follows assumes two-period lives, but similar results hold in the model with immortal overlapping generations (see Weil, 1989a).

3A.1   Pareto Inefficiency

To allow our results to incorporate the possibility of steady-state productivity growth, we work with the general linear-homogeneous production function

$$Y = F(K, EL), \tag{76}$$

where E is a parameter that captures the level of *labor-enhancing* productivity. We assume that E grows at rate g:

$$E_{t+1} = (1 + g)E_t,$$

which implies that "efficiency labor," EL, grows at rate $(1 + n)(1 + g)$:

$$E_{t+1}L_{t+1} = (1 + n)E_t(1 + g)L_t = (1 + z)E_t L_t,$$

---

53. A complete theoretical treatment of conditions under which dynamic inefficiency can arise is in Cass (1972).

where

$$1 + z \equiv (1+n)(1+g).$$

For the Cobb-Douglas production function we have been using, thinking of productivity as labor-enhancing amounts to no more than a sleight of hand. Simply define $E \equiv A^{1/(1-\alpha)}$ and write the production function $Y = AK^\alpha L^{1-\alpha}$ as $Y = K^\alpha(EL)^{1-\alpha}$. For more general production functions, as will become apparent in Chapter 7 on growth, modeling productivity as labor-enhancing is necessary to ensure the existence of a steady state.

If we now define $k^E \equiv K/EL$ and $y^E \equiv Y/EL$, we can write the constant-returns-to-scale production function (76) in intensive (per efficiency labor unit) form as

$$y^E = F(K/EL, 1) \equiv f(k^E).$$

We now ask the following question (as did Phelps, 1961, and, in the overlapping generations model, Diamond, 1965): what steady-state capital stock is consistent with the maximal steady-state level of consumption per person? It is simplest to treat the world economy as if it were a single closed economy.

The first step in finding the answer is to write the economy's capital-accumulation equation as

$$K_{t+1} - K_t = F(K_t, E_t L_t) - C_t,$$

where C denotes total (not per capita) consumption by both young and old. Transform this equation into intensive form by invoking the equilibrium condition $L = N$ and dividing through by $E_{t+1}N_{t+1}$; the result is

$$k_{t+1}^E = \frac{k_t^E + f(k_t^E) - c_t^E}{1+z},$$

where $c_t^E \equiv C_t/E_t N_t$. In a steady state, $k_{t+1}^E = k_t^E = \bar{k}^E$. Therefore, the last equation shows that the steady-state ratio of total consumption to the productivity-adjusted labor force, $\bar{c}^E$, is related to $\bar{k}^E$ by

$$\bar{c}^E = f(\bar{k}^E) - z\bar{k}^E. \tag{77}$$

The intuition is easy. In a steady state, consumption per labor efficiency unit equals output per labor efficiency unit less the investment, $z\bar{k}^E$, needed to maintain $\bar{k}^E$ steady in the face of a growing effective labor input.

Step two in finding maximal per capita consumption is to observe that maximizing $\bar{c}^E$ is the same as maximizing consumption per member of the population. Why? The growth of both E and N is exogenous, so by finding a steady state with maximal $c^E = C/EN$, we also find the steady state that maximizes total consumption, given population.

Finally, differentiate eq. (77) to find that the optimal capital ratio is defined by

$$\frac{d\bar{c}^E}{d\bar{k}^E} = 0 \iff f'(\bar{k}^E) = \bar{r} = z. \tag{78}$$

Equation (78) is called the *golden rule of capital accumulation*. It states that steady-state consumption per head is maximized when the marginal product of capital is precisely equal to the economy's growth rate. In dynamically inefficient economies, those with $\bar{r} < z$, people are saving too much. A lower capital-stock ratio reduces output per head. But when

$\bar{r} < z$, this cost is less than the output saved by maintaining a lower ratio of capital to adjusted labor forever.

This feature of the steady-state allocation actually implies Pareto inefficiency. Suppose the economy is taken over by an all-powerful economic planner who orders everyone to reduce saving. This reduction obviously results in a lower steady-state capital stock and higher potential steady-state consumption for everyone. Even in the *transition* to the new steady state, however, everyone can enjoy higher lifetime consumption: after all, total consumption is higher on every date than in the original steady state. It follows that, when the economy is dynamically inefficient, it is feasible to make everyone better off. Notice that this argument fails if, initially, $f'(\bar{k}^E) = \bar{r} > z$. A planner could raise steady-state consumption, but only at the cost of forcing earlier generations to sacrifice utility by consuming less.

A complete proof that the immortal-representative-consumer economies of Chapter 2 aren't subject to dynamic inefficiency must await Chapter 7. But the essential idea is easy to grasp. Since aggregate and individual consumption basically coincide in Chapter 2, consumers, despite their selfishness, never forgo a costless opportunity to expand *aggregate* intertemporal consumption possibilities. Individuals in an overlapping generations economy, similarly, do not care directly about aggregate consumption possibilities. Absent altruism (and, perhaps, even in its presence), however, there is no longer any assurance that aggregate consumption inefficiencies will be avoided.[54] To achieve a Pareto improvement, the hypothetical economic planner must allocate resources in a way that the unaided market cannot.

One way for the government of a dynamically inefficient economy to achieve a Pareto improvement is to issue and maintain a steady-state level of government debt, as in section 3.6.3. We observed in section 3.6.4 that, in the dynamically inefficient case, this scheme never requires that taxes be levied. Further, as Figure 3.6 suggests, the scheme lowers the steady-state capital stock: less capital is accumulated because part of the saving of the young now flows into government paper. In a dynamically inefficient economy, debt issue leads to an efficiency gain.

3A.2 Ponzi Games and Bubbles

Many other anomalies arise in dynamically inefficient economies. These include Ponzi games and asset-price bubbles, both of which can be ruled out when $r > z$. To make the main points, it is easiest to think about a closed economy in which, initially, $r < z$. We consider "small" Ponzi games and bubbles, such that it is a reasonable approximation to assume that the interest rate remains fixed.

3A.2.1 Ponzi Games

Suppose that on date $t = 0$ the government makes a debt-financed transfer D to current generations and subsequently rolls over both principal and interest on that debt. If we simplify by assuming that this is the only reason for debt issuance, then the government's assets, B^G, will thereafter follow

$$B^G_{t+1} = -(1+r)^t D.$$

---

54. Interestingly, dynamic inefficiency *can* arise in economies whose decision-making units are dynasties that consist of overlapping generations with altruistic feelings toward grandchildren as well as children. See Ray (1987). This is another instance in which intergenerational altruism is insufficient to replicate the allocation produced by infinitely-lived individuals.

The economy's growth rate, at z, is higher than r, however. It follows that the ratio of D to output must go to zero asymptotically. And this consequence occurs without the government ever needing to levy taxes. Because the economy's growth rate is so high, the government can, in effect, run a Ponzi game: enough new, richer people are continually entering the economy that initial debt holders can be fully paid off using the growing savings that younger people willingly provide to the government at interest rate r. If r were greater than z, the new demand for government debt would be insufficient to keep up with the growth of debt, and the Ponzi scheme would sooner or later collapse. (A noncollapsing Ponzi scheme would plainly be inconsistent with a fixed interest rate.)

3A.2.2   Bubbles in Asset Prices

Assets without intrinsic value may trade at strictly positive prices in a dynamically inefficient economy. Bubbles are analogous to Ponzi games: they are supported as equilibria only by the continuous arrival of enough new agents that intrinsically worthless assets can be sold at a price that yields the previous owners a rate of return equal to r.

To illustrate, suppose the government issues a fixed supply D of a paper asset that yields no dividend. Provided the price of the asset, p, rises at the rate of interest,

$$\frac{p_{t+1}}{p_t} = 1 + r,$$

people will willingly hold it in place of foreign assets that pay r. Further, the total amount the young have to pay to buy the outstanding stock of the asset each period, $p_t D$, will grow more slowly than the supply of savings (which grows at rate z). Thus the young will always be able to afford the entire supply of the paper asset. Indeed, *any* price path that rises at rate $1 + r$ is an equilibrium path provided the asset's initial price p_0 is not so high that $p_0 D$ exceeds the savings of the period 0 young. This is a case in which price is positive and rising only because all generations believe that it should be.[55] (If, in contrast, r is greater than z, there is a finite time t, for any $p_0 > 0$, at which $p_t D$ overtakes the maximum feasible savings of the young. Thus bubbles are not possible when $r > z$.)

Notice that there can be bubbles on useful as well as useless assets in the dynamically inefficient case. For example, there is no reason interest-bearing government debt must trade at any particular price: a self-validating price bubble could raise the debt's current price while adding a capital-gains term to the interest component of its total return.

3A.3   Dynamic Inefficiency in Practice

How serious a concern is dynamic inefficiency in practice? We could try to compare growth rates with interest rates, but it isn't obvious which of many possible interest rates to use, or how to control for risk.

An alternative approach is to observe that $r > z$ is equivalent to

$$\frac{rK}{Y} > \frac{zK}{Y}.$$

Thus eq. (78) implies that a steady state is dynamically inefficient if and only if the share of profits in output is less than that of investment. A dynamically efficient economy does not

---

55. Tirole (1985) explores this type of bubble.

invest more than 100 percent of its profits simply to maintain a constant ratio of capital to effective labor.

This criterion is readily generalized to the stochastic case. International evidence marshaled by Abel, Mankiw, Summers, and Zeckhauser (1989) suggests that dynamic inefficiency is not a problem in practice. For the United States, France, Germany, Italy, Japan, and Canada, gross profits exceeded investment by a wide margin in every year from 1960 to 1984.

Exercises

1.   *Saving and growth in a three generation model.* Consider a pure endowment economy facing a given world interest rate $r = 0$. Residents' lifetimes last three periods, and on any date three distinct generations of equal size (normalized to 1) coexist. The young cannot borrow at all, and must save a positive amount or consume their income, y^Y. The middle-aged are endowed with y^M and can borrow or save. Finally, the old have the endowment y^O and either run down prior savings or repay what they owe before death. Everyone has the same lifetime utility function, $U(c^Y, c^M, c^O) = \log c^Y + \log c^M + \log c^O$ (so $\beta = 1$ here).

   (a) Suppose $y^M = (1 + e)y^Y$ and $y^O = 0$, where $e > 0$. Calculate the saving of all three generations as functions of y^Y and e.

   (b) Let the growth rate of total output be $g > 0$, where $y_{t+1}^Y = (1 + g)y_t^Y$. What is the aggregate saving rate out of total output Y_t?

   (c) Suppose e rises. What is the effect on the saving rate? How does your answer change when the young can borrow against future earnings?

   (d) Suppose that the young can borrow and their endowment grows according to $y_{t+1}^Y = (1 + g)y_t^Y$. However $y^O = 0$ and y^M remain constant over time. How does the date t saving rate depend on g? Do the same exercise assuming it is the endowment of the middle aged that grows at rate g while those of the young and old stay constant.

2.   *Dynamic inefficiency and trade.* Consider an overlapping-generations economy (as in section 3.5) that is open to trade. Now, however, the world interest rate r lies *below* the population growth rate n, which is positive

   (a) Suppose that the world interest rate r equals the autarky rate, r^A. Show that a small permanent rise in the world interest rate that occurs on date t benefits not only the date t old, but also the young on dates t, $t + 1$, $t + 2$, and so on. What is the intuition for this result? [Hint: The capital-labor ratio now satisfies $k = \beta w/(1 + \beta)(1 + n)$.]

   (b) Suppose $n > r^A > r$. Show that opening to trade makes everyone in the economy worse off. Interpret this result in terms of the second-best principle of trade theory (we are removing one distortion, trade barriers, while leaving dynamic inefficiency uncorrected).

3.   *Government debt in the Blanchard (1985) model.* Exercise 2 of Chapter 2 provided an example in which the expected utility function for a consumer with a constant (age-independent) probability $1 - \varphi$ of dying at the end of each period has the form $E_t U_t = \sum_{s=t}^{\infty} (\varphi \beta)^{s-t} u(c_t)$. The present exercise embeds that consumer in a general-equilibrium overlapping generations model. We assume a small open economy that

faces a given world interest rate r on riskless loans. There is no capital accumulation, so output is exogenous.

(a) Suppose that at the start of every period t a new generation of size 1 is born, where a generation consists of a continuum of ex ante identical individuals who die or survive independently of one another. A fraction $1 - \varphi$ of those born in period t dies off at the end of period t, a fraction $1 - \varphi$ of the survivors from period t dies off at the end of $t + 1$, and so on. (The idea is that even though there is survival uncertainty at the level of the individual, there is no uncertainty at the aggregate level because of the law of large numbers.) Show that total population size in the economy at the start of any period is $1/(1 - \varphi)$.

(b) Suppose a competitive "insurance" industry sells annuity contracts that pay a domestic saver a gross interest rate of $(1 + r)/\varphi$ as long as he lives, but that become null and void when he dies. Insurance companies also lend to individuals, charging them the gross rate $(1 + r)/\varphi$. Show that if the insurance industry holds all of domestic residents' gross assets and finances all of their gross borrowing, itself earning or paying the world interest rate r on riskless loans, then it must break even with zero profits.

(c) Since we assume there is no bequest motive, individuals will use any wealth they accumulate to purchase annuities rather than earning the lower market return r. (As in the Weil model, people are born with zero financial wealth.) Domestic borrowers cannot borrow from anyone at a lower rate. [If they could, they would have a pure arbitrage opportunity to borrow at the low rate and buy annuities paying the higher rate $(1 + r - \varphi)/\varphi$. Since nothing prevents them from dying in debt, they simply would reap the interest difference until death, and thus would have an incentive to borrow unlimited amounts.] Argue that under this circumstance, an individual of vintage v faces the date t budget constraint

$$\sum_{s=t}^{\infty} \left(\frac{\varphi}{1+r}\right)^{s-t} c_s^v = \left(\frac{1+r}{\varphi}\right) b_t^{P,v} + \sum_{s=t}^{\infty} \left(\frac{\varphi}{1+r}\right)^{s-t} (y_t^v - \tau_t^v)$$

(where the notation parallels that in section 3.7.3).

(d) For $u(c_t^v) = \log(c_t^v)$, calculate *aggregate* total private consumption as a function of aggregate net private foreign assets B_t^P, aggregate output Y_t, and aggregate taxes T_t. (Aggregate consumption C_t here is just the weighted sum of c_t^v from $v = t$ to $v = -\infty$, with the weight on c_t^v equal to the number of vintage v individuals still alive; similarly for other aggregates.) Show that B_t^P follows the (usual) difference equation

$$B_{t+1}^P = (1 + r)B_t^P + Y_t - T_t - C_t,$$

and explain why it holds. (Remember that the economy's net foreign assets at the beginning of period $t + 1$ equals the savings of *all* those alive in period t, even those who died at the end of t.)

(e) Assume that Y and T are constants. Show that B_t^P obeys the difference equation

$$B_{t+1}^P = \varphi\beta(1+r)B_t^P + \varphi\left[\frac{(1+r)\beta - 1}{1+r-\varphi}\right](Y - T).$$

Can you show the dynamics it implies in a diagram analogous to Figure 3.9?

(f) Aggregate government assets follow $B_{t+1}^G = (1 + r)B_t^G + T_t - G_t$ (the government never dies and thus borrow and lends at the interest rate r). Suppose G is constant at zero but that the government maintains a steady state debt of $D = -B^G$ through a uniform tax of $\tau = rD(1 - \varphi)$ on everyone alive. How do changes in D affect the economy's steady state net foreign assets? How do they affect its steady state consumption?

4.   *Public debt and the intertemporal terms of trade.* In the global-equilibrium model of section 3.6, can the initial young and future generations ever benefit when the government introduces a steady state public debt financed entirely by taxes on the young?

5.   *Debt and deficits in the Weil (1989a) model.* Suppose the public debt follows an arbitrary (non-Ponzi) path in Weil's overlapping generations model. Show that aggregate per capita consumption satisfies

$$c_t = (1 - \beta) \left\{ (1 + r)\frac{n}{r}d_t + \sum_{s=t}^{\infty} \left(\frac{1}{1+r}\right)^{s-t} \left(\frac{1+r}{r}\right) n(d_{s+1} - d_s) \right.$$

$$\left. + (1 + r)b_t + \sum_{s=t}^{\infty} \left(\frac{1}{1+r}\right)^{s-t} (y_s - g_s) \right\},$$

so that current and future *deficits* as well as the current debt level affect consumption. Explain this result intuitively. [Hint: Analyze a representative vintage's generational account.]

6.   *Tax smoothing and deficits à la Barro (1979).* Consider a small, open representative-consumer economy with an infinite-horizon (on the lines of Chapter 2). The subjective time preference factor satisfies $\beta = 1/(1 + r)$. Suppose that the output of the economy is not Y_t, but $Y_t - aT_t^2/2$, where T_t represents taxes. Assume the government maximizes the lifetime utility of the representative individual, but (exogenously) must spend $G_t < Y_t$ in resources per period on projects that yield no benefits. Will the government be indifferent as to the path of taxes that finance its expenditures? Will it ever run fiscal deficits or surpluses? Can you discern any rule by which the government should set taxes?

4 The Real Exchange Rate and the Terms of Trade

The first three chapters of this book focused on models with a single commodity on every date, thereby assuming implicitly that the relative prices of different goods and services never change. Of course that strong assumption, while useful in highlighting some important features of intertemporal trade and fiscal policy, is flatly contradicted by the data. Both relative costs of living in different countries and the relative prices of countries' exports and imports often display dramatic short-term and long-term shifts. Not surprisingly, therefore, international relative prices have long been at the heart of open-economy analysis. This chapter shows how the models we have explored can be extended to encompass changing *intra*temporal relative prices. The chapter's main goals are three: to explain the determinants of relative international price movements, to show how such price movements affect economic activity, and to provide a basis for judging when it is safe to abstract from intratemporal price changes as we did in Chapters 1 through 3.

Actual economies produce and consume tens of thousands of commodities and services, many of which have prices that differ from country to country because of transport costs, tariffs, and other trade barriers. A realistic model that incorporated *all* goods' relative prices would be hopelessly complicated. A better strategy is to focus on the relative prices of a small set of aggregate output groups. This chapter concentrates on two relative prices in particular: the ratio of national price levels—*the real exchange rate*—and the relative price of exports in terms of imports—*the terms of trade*. Both of these relative prices play central roles, as we shall see, in an open economy's adjustment to economic shocks.

It will prove easiest to incorporate relative prices in steps. The first step is to abstract from changes in the terms of trade but allow for real exchange rate changes that result from the existence of *nontraded goods*, goods that are so costly to ship that they do not enter international trade. We then study the causes and effects of terms-of-trade changes while abstracting from the existence of nontradables. The chapter concludes by integrating the real exchange rate and the terms of trade within a single model.

We emphasize that the theoretical analysis of this chapter focuses entirely on the *relative* prices of different goods or consumption baskets, not on *money* prices. Thus, for example, one can think of the prices here as describing the cost of apples in terms of oranges or perhaps a broad-based consumption basket, but not the cost of apples in terms of dollars or yen. Implicitly, we are assuming that there are no nominal rigidities and no feedback from the monetary to the real side of the economy. We will introduce money in Chapter 8 and the possibility of nominal rigidities in Chapters 9 and 10. Because short-run nominal rigidities appear to be important in practice, the models here are probably best suited to capturing medium- to long-run movements in the real exchange rate and terms of trade, rather than very short-term fluctuations.

4.1   International Price Levels and the Real Exchange Rate

Given some fixed numeraire, a country's *price level* is defined as the domestic purchase price, in terms of the numeraire, of a well-defined basket of commodities. Price level indexes can differ according to both the basket used to define them and the item used as a numeraire. For most of the models in this book, the reference basket usually represents a bundle of "typical" consumer purchases, with a weighting scheme that can be rigorously rationalized in terms of an underlying utility maximization problem. (Section 4.4 shows how.) As for the numeraire, it could be a currency such as "dollars" (in which case we would refer to the index as a *nominal* price index) but it could also be a good. Indeed, there are no nominal prices in any of the theoretical models in the first seven chapters of this book. Throughout the theoretical analyses in this chapter, we typically use a traded good as the numeraire.

The *real exchange rate* between two countries is the relative cost of the common reference basket of goods, where the baskets' costs in the two countries are compared after conversion into a common numeraire. For two countries 1 and 2 with price levels P_1 and P_2 (measured in some *common* numeraire), we say that country 1 experiences a *real appreciation*, and country 2 a *real depreciation*, when P_1/P_2 rises. The theory of *purchasing power parity* (PPP) predicts that real exchange rates should equal 1, or at least have a tendency to return quickly to 1 when that long-run ratio is disturbed for some reason. Sometimes this version of PPP is called *absolute* PPP. *Relative* PPP is the weaker statement that changes in national price levels always are equal or, at least, tend to equality over sufficiently long periods.[1]

Unfortunately, the measures of consumer prices published by national statistical agencies are of little use in constructing measures of absolute PPP, because they are typically reported as indexes relative to a base year (say, $1995 = 100$). Thus they only measure the rate of change of the price level from the base year, not its absolute level. For this reason, they can only be used to measure relative PPP, or, equivalently, *changes* in real exchange rates. (Another failing of standard

---

1. If you have studied international finance before, you may be used to seeing (absolute) PPP between two countries 1 and 2 written as

$$P_1 = \mathcal{E} P_2^*,$$

where P_1 is country 1's price level in terms of its national currency, P_2^* is country 2's price level in its own currency, and $\mathcal{E}$ is the nominal exchange rate, defined as the price of country 2 currency in terms of country 1 currency. Since $P_2 = \mathcal{E} P_2^*$ is country 2's price level *in terms of country 1's currency*, the familiar formulation of PPP as $P_1 = \mathcal{E} P_2^*$ is equivalent to the definition in the text, $P_1 = P_2$ (where the chosen numeraire is country 1 currency). Similarly, the text's definition of the real exchange rate as P_1/P_2 is equivalent to the perhaps more familiar expression $P_1/\mathcal{E} P_2^*$.

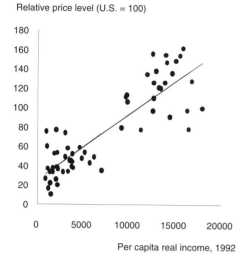

Relative price level (U.S. = 100)

Per capita real income, 1992

Figure 4.1
Real per capita incomes and price levels, 1992. (*Source:* Penn World Table)

published CPIs is that they typically involve somewhat different baskets of commodities across countries, though their constructions usually are similar enough that comparisons of changes are still useful.)

The best evidence we have on absolute PPP comes from the Penn World Table (PWT), the culmination of a sequence of studies, starting with Gilbert and Kravis (1954), and described more recently by Summers and Heston (1991). The PWT endeavors to compare, in levels, the U.S. dollar prices of identical, quality-adjusted output baskets for a large sample of countries. The vertical axis of Figure 4.1 shows 1992 PWT price levels for countries with data quality above a specified cutoff. As you can see, there is an enormous range of national price levels, with the highest and lowest differing by a factor of about 20!

Having such dollar price indexes for comparable baskets of goods can be very useful in comparing countries' real incomes. Consider, for example, a Japanese worker whose yen income is equal to that of an American worker when yen are converted to dollars at the prevailing nominal exchange rate. The Japanese worker has lower real income, because the price of the comparison basket (again converted to dollars) is higher in Japan than in the United States.

Annual per capita 1992 real incomes are plotted along the horizontal axis of Figure 4.1. The clear positive association between price levels and incomes implies that international comparisons of dollar incomes tend to overstate (the still-large) differences in real incomes. Later in this chapter we say more about the positive relation between national incomes and price levels.

Why do national price levels differ? The basic building block of the absolute PPP theory is the *law of one price*, which states that, absent natural or government-imposed trade barriers, a commodity should sell for the same price everywhere (when prices are measured in a common numeraire). The mechanism supposedly enforcing the law of one price is arbitrage. If such arbitrage were pervasive, not only would gold bars sell for the same price in Tokyo and Miami, so would golf lessons. A large body of empirical evidence shows, however, that the law of one price fails dramatically in practice, even for products that commonly enter international trade.[2] The reasons include transport costs, official trade barriers, and noncompetitive market structures.[3]

Transport costs are so high for some commodities that they become *nontraded goods*. Many personal services are nontradable because of the high cost of travel compared to the value of the service provided. Thus haircuts are a nontraded good, open-heart surgery a tradable good. The high cost of transporting some commodities—for example, housing—makes them nontraded as well. For modern industrial economies, the share of services and construction in GDP tends to be around 60 percent. But the role of nontradability is surely more important than even that figure indicates, because the retail prices of virtually all goods reflect some nontradable production inputs. As Kravis and Lipsey (1983, p. 5) put it:

Indeed, it is not easy to think of a tradable good that reaches its final purchaser without the addition of nontradable services such as distribution and local transport. This substantially widens the possible gap for differences in national price levels.

As we shall see in this chapter, nontraded goods have important implications for our thinking on a whole range of questions in international macroeconomics.

4.2   The Price of Nontraded Goods with Mobile Capital

Our first task is to understand the factors that influence the prices of nontraded goods. The problem has many facets: we begin by focusing on an extreme case in which economies produce and consume only two goods, a composite traded good that can be shipped between countries free of taxes or transport costs, and a composite nontraded good so costly to ship that it never leaves the country in which it is produced. In reality, the dividing line between traded and nontraded goods is

---

2. See Froot and Rogoff (1995) for a survey of the empirical evidence on PPP.

3. Federal Reserve Chairman Alan Greenspan has argued that transport costs are dropping because GNP is effectively getting lighter. For example, goods once produced with steel now use aluminum, and information-intensive goods such as computer software (that weigh virtually nothing) are becoming a greater and greater share of total output. Therefore, the importance of nontraded goods is becoming ever smaller; see Greenspan (1989). That view notwithstanding, there is considerable evidence that transport costs still play a significant role in determining trade patterns.

Box 4.1
Empirical Evidence on the Law of One Price

Tariffs, nontariff trade barriers, and nontraded inputs can drive a substantial wedge between the prices across countries of seemingly homogeneous goods. Consider, for example, McDonald's "Big Mac" hamburgers. Many of the components of Big Macs, such as frozen beef patties, cooking oil, and special sauce can be traded, but many cannot, including restaurant space and labor inputs. As a result of nontraded inputs and other factors such as differences in value-added taxes and the degree of local competition, cross-country price disparities can be large. The following table, drawn from the annual *Economist* magazine survey of Big Mac prices, illustrates the point dramatically.

Country	Price of Big Mac (in dollars)
China	1.05
Germany	3.48
Japan	4.65
Russia	1.62
Switzerland	5.20
United States	2.32

Source: Economist, April 15, 1995.

A number of studies have shown that price differentials can be surprisingly large even for heavily traded goods. Isard (1977) finds large deviations from the law of one price for a broad group of manufactures including glass and paper products, apparel, and chemicals. Giovannini (1988) finds substantial price differences between the United States and Japan even for standardized commodity manufactures such as nuts, bolts, and screws. Part of the explanation for these results is the one offered by Kravis and Lipsey cited earlier. Even a seemingly highly traded good, such as a banana at the supermarket, comes bundled with a large component of nontraded inputs: local transportation, supermarket space, check-out clerks, and so on.

a shifting one that depends on market conditions and government policies. Moreover, relative price changes occur within the commodity groups generally classified as traded and nontraded. In section 4.5 we will develop a model that accounts for these real-world complexities, but the simple traded-nontraded dichotomy we adopt at the outset is a useful vehicle for developing some basic intuition.

The model we initially employ is one in which capital is mobile, both internationally and between sectors of an economy, and in which labor is free to migrate between sectors of an economy but not between countries. Thus the model is best thought of as a portrayal of *long-run* relative-price determination. An important implication of this long-run model is that, for a small country, the relative price of tradables and nontradables is *independent* of consumer demand patterns (assuming, as we shall, that the economy actually produces traded as well as nontraded goods). This fact allows us to defer to later sections our consideration of the demand side.

4.2.1 The Relative Price of Nontraded and Traded Goods

In an economy with exogenous output supplies, the relative price of nontraded and traded goods would be determined by the interaction of supply and demand. As usual, increases in the relative supply of nontradeds would drive down their relative price, and increases in the relative demand for nontradeds would drive that price upward. Endogenous supply responses, however, tend to dampen the price effects of economic disturbances: the migration of labor and capital into nontraded production following an increase in demand, for example, leads to a smaller increase in the price of nontraded goods than the one that occurs when supply is fully price-inelastic. What we now show is that when productive factors are mobile domestically and capital can be freely imported or exported, supply is so elastic that demand shifts do not affect the relative price of nontraded goods at all!

Consider a small economy that produces two composite goods, tradables and nontradables. Outputs are given by constant-returns production functions of the capital and labor employed,

$$Y_\mathrm{T} = A_\mathrm{T} F(K_\mathrm{T}, L_\mathrm{T}), \qquad Y_\mathrm{N} = A_\mathrm{N} G(K_\mathrm{N}, L_\mathrm{N}), \tag{1}$$

where subscript T denotes the traded sector, subscript N the nontraded sector, and the A's are productivity shifters. Labor is internationally immobile but can migrate instantaneously between sectors within the economy. Labor mobility insures that workers earn the same wage w in either sector, where the numeraire is the traded good. (We will use tradables as the numeraire until further notice.)

The total domestic labor supply is fixed at $L = L_\mathrm{T} + L_\mathrm{N}$. There is, however, no economy-wide resource constraint for capital comparable to the labor constraint. Because capital is internationally mobile, resources can always be borrowed abroad and turned into domestic capital. As usual, it does not matter whether we model capital as being accumulated by individuals and allocated through a rental market, or as being accumulated by firms for their own use.

Assume that one unit of tradables can be transformed into a unit of capital at zero cost. The reverse transformation is, similarly, assumed to be costless. *Nontradables cannot be transformed into capital*, however. Only tradable goods are usable for capital formation. (This is an inessential but helpful simplifying assumption.) Consistent with the timing assumption maintained in the first three chapters, we assume that capital (whether owned by firms or rented) must be put in place a period before it is actually used. And, as before, capital can be used for production and then consumed (as a tradable) at the end of the same period.

As in previous chapters, the assumption of perfect international capital mobility ties capital's domestic rate of return to the world interest rate. If r is the world interest rate *in terms of tradables*, then, under perfect foresight, r must also be the marginal product of capital *in the traded-goods sector*. At the same time, r must be the value, measured in tradables, of capital's marginal product in the nontraded-goods sector.[4]

To establish these equalities formally, consider the maximization problems of representative firms producing traded and nontraded goods. Let p be the relative price of nontradables in terms of tradables. Assuming (for simplicity) a constant world interest rate, firms' present-value profits measured in units of tradables are

$$\sum_{s=t}^{\infty} \left(\frac{1}{1+r}\right)^{s-t} \left[A_{T,s}F(K_{T,s}, L_{T,s}) - w_s L_{T,s} - \Delta K_{T,s+1}\right]$$

in the tradable sector and

$$\sum_{s=t}^{\infty} \left(\frac{1}{1+r}\right)^{s-t} \left[p_s A_{N,s}G(K_{N,s}, L_{N,s}) - w_s L_{N,s} - \Delta K_{N,s+1}\right]$$

in the nontradable sector. (As usual, $\Delta K_{i,s+1} = K_{i,s+1} - K_{i,s}$, $i = $ T, N. There is no depreciation.) As you can easily show, the firms' first-order conditions for profit maximization equate marginal value products of labor and capital to the current wage and real interest rate, respectively. Let us define the capital-labor ratios in traded and nontraded goods production as $k_T \equiv K_T/L_T$ and $k_N \equiv K_N/L_N$, and express outputs per employed worker as $y_T = A_T f(k_T) \equiv A_T F(k_T, 1)$ and $y_N = A_N g(k_N) \equiv A_N G(k_N, 1)$. Referring back to the discussion in section 1.5.1, we can write firms' first-order conditions for capital and labor, respectively, as

$$A_T f'(k_T) = r \tag{2}$$

and

$$A_T \left[f(k_T) - f'(k_T)k_T\right] = w \tag{3}$$

in the tradable sector, and as

$$p A_N g'(k_N) = r \tag{4}$$

and

$$p A_N \left[g(k_N) - g'(k_N)k_N\right] = w \tag{5}$$

in the nontradable sector.

---

4. The rate r corresponds to the *own-rate of interest* on tradables, as defined, for example, by Bliss (1975). That is, someone who borrows (lends) a unit of tradables on the world capital market makes (receives) repayment of $1 + r$ units of tradables next period. Alternatively, $1/(1 + r)$ is the price of tradables delivered next period in terms of tradables available today. Under the present assumptions, r is, additionally, the rental rate (or user cost) of capital, measured in traded goods.

We stress that if *unanticipated* shocks to productivity can occur, eq. (2) or (4) can fail to hold ex post, because we've assumed that capital must be installed a period ahead of its use. In contrast, eqs. (3) and (5) always hold, ex post as well as ex ante, because firms can adjust labor forces and workers can move between jobs instantaneously. For now we will assume that unanticipated shocks cannot occur.

We can now proceed to the main result of this subsection: given the interest rate r presented by the world capital market, eqs. (2)–(5) are enough to fully determine the relative price of nontradables, p. An implication is that demand (including government expenditure patterns) has *no* role in determining p in the present long-run, perfect-foresight setting.

Mechanically speaking, this last result follows from the observation that eqs. (2)–(5) constitute four independent equations in the four unknowns k_T, w, k_N, and p. But an alternate chain of reasoning better conveys the intuition. Notice first that eq. (2) makes the capital-labor ratio in tradables, k_T, a function $k_T(r, A_T)$ of r and A_T: we can write $k_T(r, A_T) = f'^{-1}(r/A_T)$, where $\partial k_T(r, A_T)/\partial r = 1/A_T f''[k_T(r, A_T)] < 0$. Substituting $k_T(r, A_T)$ for k_T in eq. (3) makes w a function $w(r, A_T)$ of r and A_T:

$$w(r, A_T) = A_T f[k_T(r, A_T)] - r k_T(r, A_T). \tag{6}$$

This *factor-price frontier* relationship, first discussed in section 1.5.2, defines a negative relationship between the marginal products of labor and capital in an industry: $\partial w(r, A_T)/\partial r = -k_T(r, A_T) < 0$.[5] Finally, eqs. (4) and (5), the latter with the factor-price frontier $w(r, A_T)$ from eq. (6) substituted for w, jointly determine k_N and p. Figure 4.2 is a graphical display of the solution, which can be denoted $(k_N(r, A_T, A_N), p(r, A_T, A_N))$. The schedule labeled **MPK** graphs eq. (4). It slopes upward because a rise in the price of nontradables raises the marginal value product of capital and, given r, the optimal capital intensity of production. The schedule labeled **MPL** can be written as

$$p A_N \left[g(k_N) - g'(k_N)k_N\right] = w(r, A_T),$$

which follows from eq. (5). **MPL** has a negative slope because, given r and, hence, w, a higher k_N raises the marginal physical product of labor, equal to $A_N \left[g(k_N) - g'(k_N)k_N\right]$. The price p must therefore fall to keep labor's marginal *value* product equal to its level $w(r, A_T)$ in the traded sector.

A perhaps obvious but nevertheless important implication of our analysis is that absolute PPP may well hold between two countries even when both produce a

---

5. Section 1.5.2 analyzed a model with international labor mobility in which the world wage, w, was given. The factor-price frontier relation for that model therefore was written as $r = r(w)$. Now it is the world interest rate that is given, so we write the factor-price frontier as a mapping from the interest rate to the domestic wage. This function is, of course, just the inverse of the one defined in Chapter 1.

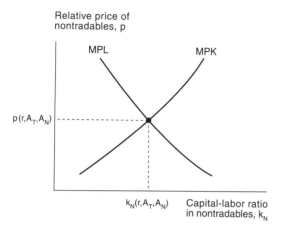

Figure 4.2
Determination of the price of nontradables

nontradable good. If the two countries have identical production functions and capital is perfectly mobile, their nontradables will have the same price in terms of tradables. While the assumption of identical technologies may not seem very plausible as a short-run assumption, there is a stronger case to be made that it holds in the long run. (We return to the issue of productivity convergence in Chapter 7.)

There is a caveat, theoretically if not practically important, to our results. The optimal employment conditions we have used to derive the preceding results need not hold in both sectors unless *both* goods actually are being produced. If the economy produces only nontraded goods, the world interest rate alone no longer determines the wage via the factor-price frontier for tradables. Thus p and w, while still functionally dependent upon r, also depend on demand considerations. When we invoke the preceding results subsequently, we implicitly continue to assume an economy that produces both types of good.

Is this implicit assumption strong? Because they cannot be imported, nontraded goods are always produced (provided the marginal utility of nontraded consumption grows without bound as consumption goes to zero). But in theory a country can consume traded goods even if it produces none. Kuwait, once its oil reserves have been exhausted, may produce little in the way of tradables. Nonetheless, the wealth it is accumulating through its oil exports will finance tradables *consumption* long after the last drop of oil has been pumped. While a logical possibility, this type of case is very unusual, and we will ignore it.

4.2.2   Price Effects of Anticipated Productivity and Interest Rate Shifts

An important application of Figure 4.2 is to show the effects of anticipated productivity shifts (that is, productivity shifts that are anticipated in $t - 1$ when agents choose the capital stock for production in period t). Consider first a rise in A_T, which measures total factor productivity in the traded-goods sector. The variable A_T enters Figure 4.2 only through its effect on w, which rises because the rise in A_T and the attendant rise in k_T both push up the marginal product of labor in tradables. Accordingly, the **MPL** schedule shifts upward along the original **MPK**, giving higher equilibrium values of p and k_N.

What about an anticipated rise in total factor productivity in nontraded goods, A_N? The **MPK** and **MPL** schedules both shift downward in exact proportion to the rise in A_N. As a result, k_N is unchanged but p falls by the same percentage as the percentage rise in A_N—so that the marginal value products of capital and labor remain constant.

We summarize these results on productivity algebraically. Recalling eq. (34) of Chapter 1 and eqs. (2)–(5), we derive the zero-profit conditions

$$A_T f(k_T) = rk_T + w, \quad pA_N g(k_N) = rk_N + w, \tag{7}$$

which hold as long as no unexpected shocks occur. Taking natural logs of the first of these equalities and differentiating (remembering to hold r constant) yields

$$\frac{dA_T}{A_T} + \frac{rk_T}{A_T f(k_T)}\frac{dk_T}{k_T} = \frac{rk_T}{A_T f(k_T)}\frac{dk_T}{k_T} + \frac{w}{A_T f(k_T)}\frac{dw}{w},$$

where we have made use of the first-order condition for investment in the traded goods sector, eq. (2). Let a "hat" above a variable denote a small percentage change or logarithmic derivative: $\hat{X} \equiv d\log X = dX/X$ for any variable X restricted to assume positive values. Let $\mu_{LT} \equiv wL_T/Y_T$ and $\mu_{LN} \equiv wL_N/pY_N$ be labor's share of the income generated in the traded and nontraded goods sectors, respectively. Then the last equation reduces to

$$\hat{A}_T = \mu_{LT}\hat{w}. \tag{8}$$

Similarly, log-differentiation of the zero-profit condition for nontradables, making use of eq. (4), gives

$$\hat{p} + \hat{A}_N = \mu_{LN}\hat{w}.$$

Substituting $\hat{w} = \hat{A}_T/\mu_{LT}$ from eq. (8) here yields

$$\hat{p} = \frac{\mu_{LN}}{\mu_{LT}}\hat{A}_T - \hat{A}_N \tag{9}$$

along a perfect-foresight path.

Provided the inequality $\mu_{LN}/\mu_{LT} \geq 1$ holds, faster productivity growth in tradables than in nontradables will push the price of nontradables upward over time. Because the rate of increase in p depends on wage growth, the effect is greater the more labor-intensive are nontradables relative to tradables.

A similar argument shows how a rise in the world interest rate affects p. Let $\mu_{KT} \equiv r K_T / Y_T = 1 - \mu_{LT}$ be capital's share of the income generated in the traded goods sector, and $\mu_{KN} \equiv r K_N / p Y_N = 1 - \mu_{LN}$ be capital's share in the nontraded sector. Log-differentiating the equalities in eq. (7) holding A_T constant, we find

$$\hat{p} = \frac{1}{\mu_{LT}} (\mu_{KN} - \mu_{KT}) \hat{r} = \frac{1}{\mu_{LT}} (\mu_{LT} - \mu_{LN}) \hat{r}.$$

Provided nontradables are relatively labor intensive (the assumption $\mu_{LN}/\mu_{LT} \geq 1$ again), a rise in the interest rate lowers their relative price by lowering the wage. This result is a converse to the famous *Stolper-Samuelson theorem*, which states that a change in relative product prices benefits the factor used intensively in the industry that expands.[6] Here, instead, an increase in capital's reward raises the relative price of the product that uses capital intensively. But the underlying logic is the same as in the Stolper-Samuelson analysis.

Application: Sectoral Productivity Differentials and the Relative Prices of Nontradables in Industrial Countries

If the theory we have been discussing is a reasonable description of the long run, we would expect to see a rising trend in national ratios of nontradables to tradables prices. Empirically, nontraded goods tends to be at least as labor-intensive as traded goods, so the condition $\mu_{LN}/\mu_{LT} \geq 1$ holds in practice. Furthermore, productivity growth in nontradables historically has been lower than in tradables.

One reason for relatively low productivity growth in the nontradables sector is its substantial overlap with services, which are inherently less susceptible to standardization and mechanization than are manufactures or agriculture. This is not to say that there cannot be substantial technical advance in services. To use an example from Baumol and Bowen (1966), the hourly output of a string quartet has changed dramatically since Haydn's day. Through modern audiovisual and communications technology, the music that once entertained at most a roomful of listeners (hence the name "chamber music") now can be brought instantly to millions worldwide. This remarkable progress notwithstanding, the efficiency gains in manufactures and agriculture have been even more impressive.

The "Baumol-Bowen effect" of a rising relative price of services comes through very clearly in the data, as time-series evidence for industrial countries shows; see Figure 4.3. Across industrial countries, there is also a positive cross-sectional relation between long-run tradables-nontradables productivity-growth differentials

---

6. See Stolper and Samuelson (1941) and Dixit and Norman (1980).

Price index of services relative to GDP deflator
(1985 = 100)

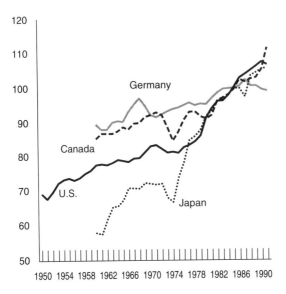

Figure 4.3
The relative price of services

and long-run rates of increase in p. Figure 4.4 shows that relation and furthermore confirms that productivity growth in tradable goods has indeed been higher than in nontradables.[7]   ∎

4.2.3   Productivity Differences and Real Exchange Rates: The Harrod-Balassa-Samuelson Effect

A country's price level is increasing in the prices of both tradables and nontradables. Thus international productivity differences can have implications for relative international price levels, that is, for real exchange rates. Balassa (1964), Samuelson (1964), and, earlier, Harrod (1933) used this observation to explain the international pattern of deviations from PPP. The *Harrod-Balassa-Samuelson effect* is a tendency for countries with higher productivity in tradables compared with nontradables to have higher price levels.[8]

---

7. For econometric studies, see Asea and Mendoza (1994) and De Gregorio, Giovannini, and Wolf (1994), from which Figure 4.4 is drawn. (For the figure, services other than transportation services, along with construction, electricity, gas, and water, are classified as nontradable.) Baumol (1993) discusses disaggregated time-series data on service prices for several countries.

8. The basic idea was known to David Ricardo.

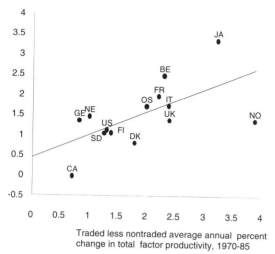

Average annual percent change in relative
price of nontradables, 1970-85

Figure 4.4
Differential productivity growth and the price of nontradables. (*Source:* De Gregorio, Giovannini, and Wolf, 1994)

To illustrate the Harrod-Balassa-Samuelson effect. let us assume that traded goods are a composite with a uniform price in each of two countries, Home and Foreign. Nontraded goods have possibly distinct Home and Foreign prices in terms of tradables, denoted p and p^*. For illustrative purposes, we assume a particular functional form to describe how the price level, or cost of living, depends on the prices of traded and nontraded goods. (Formal derivation of such cost-of-living indexes from utility functions is deferred until section 4.4.1.1. Suffice it to say for now that the results we derive next hold for any well-behaved price index.) We assume that the price level is a geometric average, with weights γ and $1 - \gamma$, of the prices of tradables and nontradables. Since we take tradables as the numeraire, with a common price of 1 in both countries, the Home and Foreign price indexes are

$$P = (1)^{\gamma} p^{1-\gamma} = p^{1-\gamma}, \qquad P^* = (1)^{\gamma}(p^*)^{1-\gamma} = (p^*)^{1-\gamma}.$$

Thus the Home-to-Foreign price level ratio is

$$\frac{P}{P^*} = \left(\frac{p}{p^*}\right)^{1-\gamma}.$$

We see that in the present model, Home's real exchange rate against Foreign depends only on the internal relative prices of nontraded goods.

By log-differentiating this ratio and using eq. (9), one can see how relative productivity shifts cause real exchange rates to change systematically. For simplicity, let both countries' sectoral outputs be proportional to the same functions $F(K_T, L_T)$ and $G(K_N, L_N)$, but with possibly different factor productivities. Then

$$\hat{P} - \hat{P}^* = (1 - \gamma)(\hat{p} - \hat{p}^*) = (1 - \gamma)\left[\frac{\mu_{LN}}{\mu_{LT}}\left(\hat{A}_T - \hat{A}_T^*\right) - \left(\hat{A}_N - \hat{A}_N^*\right)\right].$$

If we assume again the plausible condition $\mu_{LN}/\mu_{LT} \geq 1$, it follows that Home will experience real appreciation (a rise in its relative price level) if its productivity-growth advantage in tradables exceeds its productivity-growth advantage in nontradables.

We remind you of an important feature of this result: it holds regardless of any assumptions about the model's demand side and, in particular, is robust to international differences in consumption tastes.

We argued earlier that the scope for productivity gain is more limited in nontradables than in tradables. If so, then rich countries should have become rich mainly through high productivity in tradables. Although they are also likely to have achieved higher productivity in nontradables than poorer countries, the difference tends to be less pronounced. This reasoning leads to a famous prediction of the Harrod-Balassa-Samuelson proposition, that price levels tend to rise with country per capita income. Referring back to Figure 4.1 on p. 201, we see that 1992 Penn World Table data are indeed consistent with this prediction.

Application: Productivity Growth and Real Exchange Rates

Rapid manufacturing productivity growth in Japan has contributed to a secular real appreciation of the yen that began with postwar reconstruction. Figure 4.5 shows Japan's Penn World Table price level divided by an (unweighted) average of PWT price levels in other major industrial countries. The largely relentless process depicted has better than doubled Japan's price level relative to that of other countries since 1950. An important part of the story is "catch-up." World War II left Japan's economy in ruins, and productivity growth there was bound to exceed that in the United States for some time afterward as Japan's economy returned to its prewar growth path. (We revisit this question in Chapter 7.)

There is more to the story, however. Total factor productivity is difficult to measure, but simpler measures of labor productivity (calculated as output per hour worked) indicate that by the 1990s, Japan had pulled significantly ahead of the United States in several manufacturing sectors. A study by the McKinsey Global Institute (1993) showed that Japan's 1990 labor productivity was 16 percent higher than America's in autos, 24 percent higher in auto parts, 19 percent higher in metalworking, 45 percent higher in steel, and 15 percent higher in consumer elec-

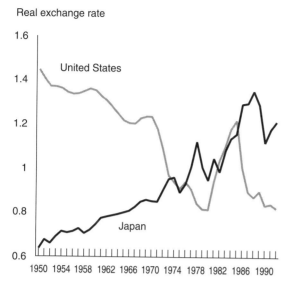

Figure 4.5
Real exchange rates for Japan and the United States, 1950–92. (*Source:* Penn World Table)

tronics, but lower in computers, food, beer, and soap and detergent. In contrast, the sketchy data available suggest that the United States remains far more productive than Japan in services. In the light of its relatively high productivity in traded goods and low productivity in nontraded goods, Japan's sky-high price level comes as no surprise.

One caveat is that labor-productivity differences in manufacturing exaggerate true differences in *total* factor productivity—which corresponds to the ratio A_T/A_T^* in our model. Recall that Japan's saving rate is much higher than that of the United States, as is its capital stock. Extra capital raises output, holding other factor inputs constant, and therefore raises measured output per hour worked. The resulting bias is likely to be greater for relatively capital-intensive tradables than for nontradeds. Nonetheless, data that attempt to control for capital inputs (as in Figure 4.4) still show Japan having one of the highest rates of increase in traded- relative to nontraded-goods production efficiency.

The flip side of productivity "catch-up" in countries devastated by World War II has been a secular decline in the United States price level relative to those of industrial trading partners. Figure 4.5 shows the secular real depreciation for the United States, one that has driven its relative price level to half its 1950 value. Again, mere catch-up is only part of the story. International differences in government regulations, trade policies, and market structure also seem to be relevant. As Table 4.1 shows, even as late as 1979–93, manufacturing labor productivity growth abroad often outstripped that in the United States. Many of the countries shown have had

Table 4.1
Average Annual Labor Productivity Growth in Manufacturing, 1979–93

Country	Productivity Growth (percent per year)
Belgium	4.3
Canada	1.7
Denmark	1.5
France	2.8
Germany	1.9
Italy	4.1
Japan	3.8
Netherlands	2.6
Norway	2.3
Sweden	3.2
United Kingdom	4.1
United States	2.5

Source: Dean and Sherwood (1994). Data for Italy cover 1979–92 only.

rapid productivity growth in services, too, but as Figure 4.4 suggests, in most of them productivity growth has been more sharply biased toward tradables than in the United States.[9]   ∎

*4.2.4   More Factors, More Goods, and International Capital Immobility

We have derived the Harrod-Balassa-Samuelson result from a very special model that assumes, among other things, two productive factors, perfect capital mobility, and no possibility for changes in the relative prices of different traded goods (and hence in the terms of trade). This restrictive structure has permitted us to make strong inferences without assumptions concerning the economy's demand side. Interestingly, several of these inferences receive empirical support. Yet for many countries, particularly the poorer ones underlying Figure 4.1, international capital mobility remains severely restricted, and sharp terms-of-trade movements are a way of life. Further, there certainly exist productive factors other than labor and capital—for example, land, livestock, inventories of finished goods, and the skills and knowledge that make up part of human capital. The reader should find it reassuring, therefore, to know that even without supplementary assumptions on consumer demand, the basic Harrod-Balassa-Samuelson prediction is much more general than our special model makes it seem. So is the result on which it is based, that the relative price of nontradables is determined independently of demand. We sketch two generalizations, leaving the detailed analysis to you.

---

9. Froot and Rogoff (1995, section 3) survey the econometric literature relating relative productivity trends to real exchange rates.

1. MORE FACTORS.   Suppose there is a third factor of production—call it skilled labor, S—that is used to produce tradables and nontradables. It is easy to see that the arguments of section 4.2.1, which allowed us to derive the wage, and hence p, from r and the production functions, no longer go through. Let w_L denote the wage of unskilled labor, L, and w_S the wage of skilled labor. Then the factor-price relationship in tradables is no longer a two-dimensional frontier linking r and w_L, but a more complicated three-dimensional surface involving all three factor rewards. In general, demand conditions therefore play a role in determining p, w_L, and w_S. We can derive a Harrod-Balassa-Samuelson result without invoking demand restrictions, however, if we recognize there is typically a multiplicity of individual tradable goods. Suppose two traded goods labeled 1 and 2 are produced domestically out of capital, unskilled labor, and skilled labor. Both traded-goods industries show constant returns to scale and share a common rate of total factor productivity change, $\hat{A}_T$. Choose tradable 1 as numeraire, with p the price of the nontraded good and p_T the price of the second tradable, both prices expressed in terms of tradable 1. Let p_T be given by world markets, as is r. Log-differentiating the zero-profit conditions corresponding to eq. (7) for the two traded goods, and remembering that $\hat{p}_T = \hat{r} = 0$, we obtain a system of two linear equations in $\hat{w}_L$ and $\hat{w}_S$, which can be solved to determine the rate of increase in these factor rewards and hence, from the zero-profit condition for nontradables, $\hat{p}$. Although the answer depends on factor intensities in all three industries in a rather complicated way, a very definite prediction results from assuming that both traded-goods industries have the same share of capital income in output, μ_{KT}, but different shares for skilled and unskilled labor. In this special case, the tradables zero-profit conditions give

$$\hat{w}_L = \hat{w}_S = \frac{\hat{A}_T}{1 - \mu_{KT}},$$

and so, by the nontradables zero-profit condition,

$$\hat{p} = \mu_{LN}\hat{w}_L + \mu_{SN}\hat{w}_S - \hat{A}_N = \left(\frac{\mu_{LN} + \mu_{SN}}{1 - \mu_{KT}} \right) \hat{A}_T - \hat{A}_N.$$

As before, it is likely that $(\mu_{LN} + \mu_{SN})/(1 - \mu_{KT}) \geq 1$, so we get the Harrod-Balassa-Samuelson result [cf. eq. (9)].[10]

2. INTERNATIONALLY IMMOBILE CAPITAL.   Without capital mobility, we can no longer take r as given by the outside world. But, once again, the existence of several distinct tradable goods with prices determined in world markets can pin down

---

10. The preceding result is based on the kind of reasoning leading to the famous *factor-price equalization* idea of trade theory (see Dixit and Norman, 1980, and Ethier, 1984, both of whom entertain the possibility of some international factor mobility). The generalization in the next paragraph is based on similar arguments. Factor prices aren't necessarily being internationally equalized in the models under discussion because we are allowing international differences in the production technologies for tradables.

all factor prices. For example, assume there are two tradables (with a common rate of productivity growth) and two factors, capital and labor. Except in degenerate cases, zero-profit conditions for the tradable goods uniquely determine domestic factor prices. Both factor prices rise at the rate of technical advance in the tradable goods sector, $\hat{A}_T$, so that $\hat{p} = \hat{A}_T - \hat{A}_N$.

There are, of course, other theories that predict lower price levels in poorer countries but depend on assumptions about demand. Not all of these require international productivity differences. Kravis and Lipsey (1983) and Bhagwati (1984) propose a model with two internationally immobile factors. In their model, poor countries are abundantly endowed with labor relative to capital, while rich countries are in the opposite situation. If consumption tastes are the same in rich and poor countries and factor endowments so dissimilar that they specialize in different tradables, then wages will be relatively lower in poor countries, as will the prices of the relatively labor-intensive nontradable goods.[11]

The Kravis-Lipsey-Bhagwati effect is, no doubt, part of the story underlying Figure 4.1. Productivity differences and some degree of capital mobility are essential, however, to explain why wage differences between rich and poor countries seem so much greater than differences in the return to capital.[12]

4.3   Consumption and Production in the Long Run

The last section led us to conclude that in the long run, the relative price of nontradables is independent of the economy's demand side under a range of assumptions. Nonetheless, the mix of output that an economy produces does depend on demand. In this section we explain this dependence and explore some implications for a prominent political concern, the secular shrinkage in manufacturing employment that many industrial countries, including the United States, have been experiencing in recent decades. Throughout this section we focus on steady-state results.

4.3.1   How Demand Determines Output

We first develop a useful diagram for visualizing how demand determines the economy's mix of tradable and nontradable production in the long run.

To simplify the derivations, we assume that individual preferences over consumption within a period are *homothetic*. This assumption implies that a person's desired ratio between tradable and nontradable consumption depends only on the

---

11. Why do we need similarity in tastes? If poor countries were disproportionately fond of nontradables, these preferences could raise wages enough to offset the effect of the international factor-proportion disparity.

12. The data on the latter point are fragmentary. See, for example, Harberger (1980).

relative price of nontradables, p, and not on his spending level.[13] We also assume that the economy is in a steady state with national consumption spending equal to income and thus with a constant level $\bar{Q}$ of national financial wealth measured in tradable goods.[14] In analogy to the analysis in section 2.5.1,

$$Q \equiv B + K_T + K_N = B + K.$$

We assume a constant labor force, L, and, for the moment, abstract from productivity trends and government consumption.

A simple diagram illustrates how consumption patterns determine production in the long run. We cannot use the standard autarky production possibilities frontier (PPF) for this purpose, because capital is free to enter or exit the economy so as to hold marginal value products of capital at the given world interest rate, r. Instead, we introduce a diagram, Figure 4.6, analogous to one with which we studied international migration in section 1.5.3.

As we saw in section 4.2.1, the world interest rate r determines the capital-labor ratios, $k_T(r)$ and $k_N(r)$, the wage $w(r)$, and the relative price $p(r)$ of nontradables in terms of tradables. (The notation here suppresses the dependence of k_T, k_N, w, and p on the constant values of A_T and A_N.) The steeper of the two negatively sloped schedules in Figure 4.6 is the *GDP line*, defined as the locus of efficient long-run output combinations, given the availability of capital flows. You can think of the GDP line as the PPF that applies when profit-maximizing international capital movements are allowed. The GDP line is constructed from the zero-profit conditions in traded and nontraded goods, the equations in (7), written as

$$\bar{Y}_T = r\bar{K}_T + w\bar{L}_T = \left[rk_T(r) + w(r)\right]\bar{L}_T,$$

$$p(r)\bar{Y}_N = r\bar{K}_N + w\bar{L}_N = \left[rk_N(r) + w(r)\right]\left(L - \bar{L}_T\right).$$

---

13. As one example of homothetic preferences, suppose the period utility function is of the form $u(C_T, C_N) = G\left(C_T^\gamma C_N^{1-\gamma}\right)$ for some strictly concave and increasing function $G\left(\cdot\right)$. Optimal consumption demands satisfy

$$\frac{\partial u/\partial C_N}{\partial u/\partial C_T} = p = \frac{(1-\gamma)G'\left(C_T^\gamma C_N^{1-\gamma}\right)(C_T/C_N)^\gamma}{\gamma G'\left(C_T^\gamma C_N^{1-\gamma}\right)(C_T/C_N)^{\gamma-1}} = \frac{(1-\gamma)}{\gamma}\frac{C_T}{C_N},$$

so the desired consumption ratio depends only upon p.

14. Implicit in our assumption that the economy's consumption profile is flat is the condition that residents' subjective discount factor β satisfies $\beta = 1/(1+r)$. See section 4.4 for a general discussion of the consumption time profile in models with traded and nontraded goods. As in previous chapters, B denotes the economy's net foreign assets and K the domestic capital stock. Recall that through international borrowing, a rise in K, say, can be financed by an equal fall in B without any change in total financial wealth Q. This fact is central to the analysis of this section.

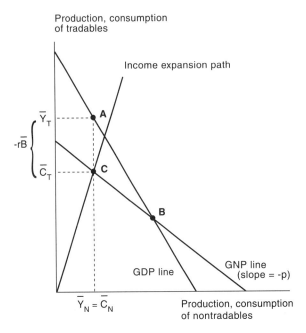

Figure 4.6
Long-run GDP and GNP

(Overbars denote equilibrium values associated with a steady state in consumption.) Use the second of these equations to solve for $\bar{L}_T$ and substitute to eliminate $\bar{L}_T$ from the first. The algebraic description of the GDP line results:[15]

$$\bar{Y}_T = -\left[\frac{rk_T(r) + w(r)}{rk_N(r) + w(r)}\right] p(r)\bar{Y}_N + \left[rk_T(r) + w(r)\right] L. \tag{10}$$

Notice that the (absolute value) slope of the GDP line is strictly *above* p if, as we have been assuming, nontraded goods are relatively labor-intensive [$k_T(r) > k_N(r)$]. A reduction in nontradables output raises tradables output by more than p (the marginal rate of transformation in an autarky equilibrium) because additional capital must be borrowed from abroad if the economy is to expand its capital-intensive traded sector with no rise in the rental-to-wage ratio.[16]

The flatter, negatively sloped line in Figure 4.6, the *GNP line*, shows the economy's steady-state budget constraint, that is, the locus of best feasible steady-state

---

15. In the standard Heckscher-Ohlin model of trade theory, with two outputs and two factors in fixed economy-wide supply, it is the need to vary production techniques as the economy varies its output mix that is responsible for diminishing returns. Thus the lack of international factor mobility gives the PPF its concave shape in that familiar model.

16. Trade theorists will recognize the GDP line as the Rybczynski line. On Rybczynski's theorem, see Dixit and Norman (1980).

consumptions of tradables and nontradables, $\bar{C}_T$ and $\bar{C}_N$. Since the economy has been assumed stationary with unchanging financial wealth, steady-state consumption expenditure equals GNP, that is, wage income plus the return on financial (nonhuman) wealth [as in eq. (61) of Chapter 2]:

$$\bar{C}_T + p(r)\bar{C}_N = w(r)L + r\bar{Q}. \tag{11}$$

Solving this constraint for $\bar{C}_T$ yields the GNP line, which has slope $-p(r)$.

The last ingredient in Figure 4.6 is the upward-sloping *income expansion path* for the relative price $p(r)$. This is the steady-state Engel curve, which shows desired consumption of the two goods at various income levels when saving is zero and $p = p(r)$. [By definition, the representative consumer's indifference curves have slope $-p(r)$ where they intersect the income expansion path.] The path is a straight line through the origin because of the assumption of homothetic demand.[17]

The diagram is read as follows. Consumers are simultaneously on their income expansion path and on their budget line, the GNP line. The intersection of the two, shown at **C**, therefore determines the steady-state consumptions $\bar{C}_T$ and $\bar{C}_N$. Domestic supply and demand for nontradeds must be equal, so $\bar{Y}_N = \bar{C}_N$. As a result, however, the economy's actual output mix, which the GDP line describes, is vertically above point **C**, at point **A**. Notice that $\bar{Y}_T > \bar{C}_T$ in the figure, implying a positive balance of trade. (Once the economy has reached a given steady state, its subsequent investment is zero, given that there is neither growth nor depreciation. Since steady-state saving is zero, the current account also is zero.)

To produce at **A** given its total financial wealth $\bar{Q}$, the economy must borrow capital from abroad, creating a GDP-GNP gap equal to the flow of interest payments to foreigners. We can read this gap off of the tradables axis in Figure 4.6. The vertical distance between the GDP and GNP lines, which equals $\bar{Y}_T - \bar{C}_T$, must also equal the steady-state interest on foreign debt [since $\bar{Y}_T$ is given by eq. (10) and $\bar{C}_T$ is given by eq. (11)].[18] Thus, for example, if steady-state foreign assets, $\bar{B}$, are negative, as at point **A**, then $\bar{Y}_T$ exceeds $\bar{C}_T$ by the positive quantity $-r\bar{B}$.

At point **B** in Figure 4.6 the GDP and GNP lines cross, giving a point at which GDP and GNP are equal. Were the income expansion path to pass through point **B**

---

17. If the period utility function is $u(C_T, C_N)$, the income expansion path for p is the locus of C_T and C_N that satisfy the static consumption optimality condition given in footnote 13,

$$\frac{\partial u(C_T, C_N)/\partial C_N}{\partial u(C_T, C_N)/\partial C_T} = p.$$

Homothetic preferences, by their definition, make the ratio C_T/C_N dependent on p only, so that as income changes the proportional consumption mix does not. This feature implies linear income expansion paths that pass through the origin, as in Figure 4.6.

18. Remembering that $\bar{Y}_N = \bar{C}_N$ and invoking, yet again, the nontraded goods zero-profit condition, we see that

on the GNP line instead of point **C**, the economy could produce the desired steady-state consumption bundle without borrowing abroad at all. With $\bar{Q} = \bar{K}$ and $\bar{B} = 0$, the economy's factor supplies would equal factor demands, which depend on the production techniques implied by r and $w(r)$ and consumption demands.[19]

As consumption demands move down from **B** along the GNP line, the economy sends capital abroad, which brings GDP below GNP. Moves down along the GNP line shrink the capital-intensive traded sector and expand the labor-intensive non-traded sector. If capital did not migrate abroad in response, full employment of the capital stock could be maintained only if both sectors adopted production techniques that combined more capital with each unit of labor. But this course of action would push the marginal value product of capital below r, creating powerful incentives for overseas investment. Similarly, moves of desired consumption upward along the GNP line cause capital inflows from abroad. These head off incipient excess demand for capital and excess supply of labor.

Let us consider two comparative steady-state exercises with the model. A rise in national financial wealth, $d\bar{Q}$, causes a parallel upward shift in the GNP line (of size $r d\bar{Q}$) while leaving the GDP line and the income expansion path in place. Consumption of both goods rises along the income expansion path, and production of tradables falls. But to produce more nontradables and fewer tradables at unchanged factor prices, the economy must reduce its total capital stock by sending some capital abroad. The GDP-GNP gap in Figure 4.6 therefore falls by more than $r d\bar{Q}$.

As a second application, we can look at the long-run effects of government spending patterns. Compare the steady state of the economy in Figure 4.6 with that of an economy in which the government spends G_T on tradables, paying the bill through equal lump-sum taxes on residents. Compared with Figure 4.6, the GNP line, now viewed as the after-tax private-sector budget constraint, is shifted downward by the amount G_T. Private consumption of both goods falls and domestic production of tradables expands with the help of a capital inflow. The GDP-GNP gap rises. If the government spending fell on nontradables rather than tradables,

$$\bar{Y}_T - \bar{C}_T = -\left[\frac{rk_T(r) + w(r)}{rk_N(r) + w(r)}\right] p(r)\bar{Y}_N + \left[rk_T(r) + w(r)\right]L - \left[w(r)L + r\bar{Q} - p(r)\bar{C}_N\right]$$

$$= \left[\frac{rk_N(r) - rk_T(r)}{rk_N(r) + w(r)}\right] p(r)\bar{Y}_N + rk_T(r)L - r\bar{Q}$$

$$= \left[\frac{rk_N(r) - rk_T(r)}{rk_N(r) + w(r)}\right]\left[rk_N(r) + w(r)\right]\bar{L}_N + rk_T(r)L - r\bar{Q}$$

$$= rk_N(r)\bar{L}_N + rk_T(r)\bar{L}_T - r\bar{Q} = r(\bar{K} - \bar{Q}) = -r\bar{B}.$$

19. To test your understanding, make sure you see why the *autarky* PPF—the set of efficient ouput combinations given L and $\bar{K} = \bar{Q}$—lies strictly within the GNP line except for a tangency at point **B.**

however, we would find a different result. Compared with Figure 4.6, nontradables output would expand at the expense of tradables output, and capital would flow abroad.

4.3.2   Productivity Trends and the Size of the Traded Goods Sector

Figure 4.4 showed that productivity tends to grow more rapidly in tradables than in nontradables; we have seen how this fact helps explain the rising prices of services like schooling and medical care. There is another fact that many observers tie to the faster growth of productivity in traded goods: employment in the manufacturing sectors of many developed countries, sectors that produce largely tradable output, has been declining over time. In 1950 nonservice, nonagricultural production accounted for 33.3 percent of total employment in the United States and 46.5 percent in the United Kingdom; by 1987 the corresponding percentages had dropped to 26.6 and 29.8.[20]

The economic argument often made to rationalize this decline seems plausible at first glance. With fewer workers able to produce a higher volume of manufactures, some will have to switch jobs to satisfy the economy's higher demand for nonmanufactures as national income grows. But is this reasoning correct? It does not take account of the fact that the demand for manufactures may rise if their relative price falls, nor does it account for any general-equilibrium effects of the relative price change on the marginal value product of capital in the labor-intensive nonmanufacturing sector.

To analyze the relationship between productivity change and manufacturing employment, we turn to our long-run model. For simplicity, we consider a change of $\hat{A}_T$ percent in traded goods productivity assuming constant productivity in nontradables ($\hat{A}_N = 0$). Our goal is to determine the sign of $\hat{L}_N$, the percent change in steady-state employment in nontradables. (Since the aggregate labor supply is fixed, a flow of labor into nontradables must, of course, imply a flow out of manufacturing.)

Let us write the production function for nontradables in the special Cobb-Douglas form

$$Y_N = A_N K_N^{\alpha} L_N^{1-\alpha} = A_N k_N^{\alpha} L_N.$$

The Cobb-Douglas form implies that the factor shares we defined in section 4.2.2, $\mu_{KN} \equiv r K_N / p Y_N$ and $\mu_{LN} \equiv w L_N / p Y_N$, are constant at α and $1 - \alpha$, respectively.[21]

---

20. The numbers come from Maddison (1991, pp. 248–249). They actually apply to an employment category he labels "industry," which includes the (largely nontradable) construction sector.

21. For example, eq. (4) implies $r = p \alpha A_N (L_N/K_N)^{1-\alpha}$ under perfect foresight, so

$$\mu_{KN} = \frac{r K_N}{p Y_N} = \frac{p \alpha A_N (L_N/K_N)^{1-\alpha} K_N}{p Y_N} = \frac{\alpha A_N K_N^{\alpha} L_N^{1-\alpha}}{Y_N} = \alpha.$$

Log-differentiating the production function, we find that $\hat{L}_N$ satisfies

$$\hat{L}_N = \hat{Y}_N - \alpha \hat{k}_N;$$

that is, higher nontraded output requires a proportionally higher labor input (in or out of a steady state) except to the extent that the capital intensity of nontradables production rises. Since domestic demand and supply are equal in nontradables, the last equation implies

$$\hat{L}_N = \hat{C}_N - \alpha \hat{k}_N. \tag{12}$$

To determine the sign of $\hat{L}_N$ from eq. (12), we must calculate $\hat{C}_N$ and $\hat{k}_N$. We tackle these jobs one at a time.

1. CALCULATING $\hat{C}_N$.   On the consumption side, we have seen that *total* steady-state expenditure is determined by eq. (11); but what determines its division between tradables and nontradables? To answer this question, we assume that in each period, the representative agent maximizes a constant-elasticity-of-substitution (CES) function

$$\left[\gamma^{\frac{1}{\theta}} C_T^{\frac{\theta-1}{\theta}} + (1-\gamma)^{\frac{1}{\theta}} C_N^{\frac{\theta-1}{\theta}} \right]^{\frac{\theta}{\theta-1}}, \qquad \gamma \in (0, 1), \ \theta > 0, \tag{13}$$

given total expenditure measured in traded goods,

$$Z \equiv C_T + p C_N. \tag{14}$$

Maximizing the function (13) subject to constraint (14) yields

$$\frac{\gamma C_N}{(1-\gamma) C_T} = p^{-\theta}, \tag{15}$$

showing that consumption preferences are homothetic (relative demand depends only on relative price) and that θ (a constant) is the *elasticity of substitution* between tradables and nontradables. [As θ approaches 1, function (13) becomes proportional to the Cobb-Douglas function, $C_T^\gamma C_N^{1-\gamma}$.][22] Combining eq. (15) with eq.

---

22. The elasticity of substitution in consumption can be defined as

$$\frac{d \log (C_T/C_N)}{d \log p} = \theta.$$

To see why the consumption index (13) is Cobb-Douglas for $\theta = 1$, note that the *logarithm* of formula (13) can be written as

$$\frac{\theta \log \left[\gamma^{\frac{1}{\theta}} C_T^{\frac{\theta-1}{\theta}} + (1-\gamma)^{\frac{1}{\theta}} C_N^{\frac{\theta-1}{\theta}} \right]}{\theta - 1},$$

the numerator and denominator of which both approach 0 as $\theta \to 1$. So we may invoke L'Hospital's rule to examine instead the limit of the derivative (with respect to θ) ratio, which turns out to be:

(14), we obtain the demand functions for tradables and nontradables,

$$C_{\mathrm{T}} = \frac{\gamma Z}{\gamma + (1 - \gamma)p^{1-\theta}}, \qquad C_{\mathrm{N}} = \frac{p^{-\theta}(1 - \gamma)Z}{\gamma + (1 - \gamma)p^{1-\theta}}. \qquad (16)$$

Let us define units of nontradables so that $p = 1$ initially. Then log-differentiation of the second equation in (16) gives

$$\hat{C}_{\mathrm{N}} = \hat{Z} - [\gamma\theta + (1 - \gamma)]\hat{p}. \qquad (17)$$

If other things are equal, a rise in spending measured in traded goods raises the demand for nontradables in proportion. Given Z, however, a rise in the price of nontradables reduces demand, through both a direct substitution effect and a reduction in the real purchasing power of Z.[23]

Equation (11) implies that the change in the log of *steady-state* expenditure, $\bar{Z} = wL + r\bar{Q}$, is

$$\widehat{\bar{Z}} = \frac{wL}{wL + r\bar{Q}}\hat{w} \equiv \psi_{\mathrm{L}}\hat{w},$$

where ψ_{L} is the share of labor income in total GNP at the initial steady state. (Remember: we are assuming $\bar{Q}$ is constant across steady states.) Equation (8) now implies the steady-state expenditure change:

$$\widehat{\bar{Z}} = \frac{\psi_{\mathrm{L}}}{\mu_{\mathrm{LT}}}\hat{A}_{\mathrm{T}}.$$

To compute $\hat{p}$ in eq. (17), we invoke eq. (9) with $\hat{A}_{\mathrm{N}} = 0$, which has the form

$$\hat{p} = \frac{1 - \alpha}{\mu_{\mathrm{LT}}}\hat{A}_{\mathrm{T}}$$

given the Cobb-Douglas production function for nontradables. Substituting this equation and the one preceding it into eq. (17), which holds even when consumption is not in a steady state, we finally have expressed the change in steady-state nontradables consumption in terms of the single exogenous change, $\hat{A}_{\mathrm{T}}$:

$$\widehat{\bar{C}}_{\mathrm{N}} = \{\psi_{\mathrm{L}} - (1 - \alpha)[\gamma\theta + (1 - \gamma)]\}\frac{\hat{A}_{\mathrm{T}}}{\mu_{\mathrm{LT}}}.$$

2. CALCULATING $\hat{k}_{\mathrm{N}}$.   A glance back at eq. (12) shows that we are halfway home. All that remains is to calculate $\hat{k}_{\mathrm{N}}$, which is easy compared with the ground already

---

$\gamma \log C_{\mathrm{T}} + (1 - \gamma)\log C_{\mathrm{N}} - \gamma\log\gamma - (1 - \gamma)\log(1 - \gamma).$

(To crunch this, you will have to use the calculus formula $da^x/dx = a^x \log a$.) Since this positive quantity is the limit of the *log* of formula (13) as $\theta \to 1$, the limit of (13) itself is proportional to $C_{\mathrm{T}}^{\gamma}C_{\mathrm{N}}^{1-\gamma}$ [with proportionality constant $1/\gamma^{\gamma}(1 - \gamma)^{1-\gamma}$], as claimed.

23. We return to the last effect in the next section when we derive the price index associated with the consumption index (13).

covered! Log-differentiation of eq. (4) under our example's production-technology assumption yields

$$(1 - \alpha)\hat{k}_N = \hat{p} = \frac{1 - \alpha}{\mu_{LT}} \hat{A}_T,$$

where the second equality again follows from eq. (9).

With reduced-form expressions for both $\widehat{C}_N$ and $\hat{k}_N$ in hand at last, we use eq. (12) to derive the solution for $\widehat{L}_N$ that we seek:

$$\widehat{L}_N = \{\psi_L - (1 - \alpha)[\gamma\theta + (1 - \gamma)] - \alpha\} \frac{\hat{A}_T}{\mu_{LT}}. \tag{18}$$

Observe that the sign of $\widehat{L}_N$ is ambiguous. It depends on the sum of the three terms in the braces in eq. (18). The first term, ψ_L (labor's share of GNP), captures the effect mentioned on page 221: as wages rise, incomes rise and people demand more nontradables. But there are two additional effects, both of which pull labor *into* tradables. First, the rise in the relative price of nontradables implied by eq. (9) reduces the demand for them at a given spending level. Second, the same rise in price raises the capital-intensity of nontradables production [recall eq. (4)], also pushing labor into tradables. (We saw this effect in discussing Figure 4.2.)

Which effects are likely to dominate in reality? If θ were equal to 1 (the case of a Cobb-Douglas consumption index), eq. (18) would simply be

$$\widehat{L}_N = (\psi_L - 1) \frac{\hat{A}_T}{\mu_{LT}}.$$

Now ψ_L, labor's share in GNP, is always below 1 unless a country has negative financial wealth, that is, foreign debts exceeding its capital stock. Thus a unit elasticity of consumption substitution very likely implies that employment in nontradables falls (and therefore employment in tradables *rises*) as a result of an increase in tradables productivity. (If $\widehat{L}_N$ is negative, $\widehat{L}_T$ must be positive.)

This result could be reversed for θ very low, implying little substitutability in consumption between tradables and nontradables. It would also be mitigated by a large foreign debt (which raises ψ_L), by restrictions on capital inflows that prevent the capital-intensity of nontradables production from rising as p rises, or by a lower elasticity of substitution in nontradables production between capital and labor.[24] Overall, however, one must conclude that differential productivity gains

---

24. Our Cobb-Douglas production function for nontradables makes the elasticity of substitution in production, defined as

$$\frac{d \log k_N}{d \log(w/r)},$$

equal to 1.

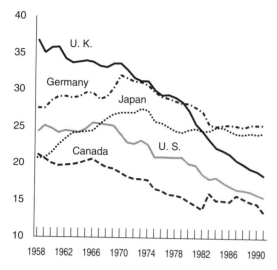

Manufacturing employment as a
percent of total employment

Figure 4.7
Employment in manufacturing

in manufacturing do not necessarily explain observed declines in manufacturing employment in countries like the United States and United Kingdom. The popular explanation that the decline is due to increased productivity in manufacturing is not compelling.

Recent international data confirm this message, showing that steadily declining manufacturing employment is not a universal phenomenon. Figure 4.7 shows the evolution of manufacturing employment (as a percent of total employment, for 1958–91) in five industrial countries. True, a declining trend is very pronounced for the United Kingdom over the entire period, for Canada and the United States since the mid-1960s, and for Germany from the early 1970s to the early 1980s. Germany's manufacturing employment share levels off in the mid-1980s, however, and Japan's has been roughly level since the mid-1970s. Considering that Japan has had exceptionally high productivity growth in manufacturing relative to services, its experience is especially hard to square with productivity-based theories of manufacturing employment decline.

4.4 Consumption Dynamics, the Price Level, and the Real Interest Rate

In the last section we assumed a stationary consumption level equal to national income. While steady-state consumption analysis provides useful intuition about the effects of demand on production and capital flows, it does not allow us to analyze the effects of anticipated future economic events. In this section, we therefore extend to a multicommodity setting the dynamic consumption analysis that we pursued in the first three chapters.

A lesson of those chapters is that a major driving force behind international borrowing and lending is the individual's desire to smooth consumption in the face of output fluctuations. In the aggregate, however, it is simply infeasible for a country to smooth its consumption of nontraded goods, which cannot be imported or exported. In this section, we will explore various mechanisms that can clear the market for nontradables, including endogenous real-interest-rate changes that may temper individuals' desire for smooth consumption paths. The interactions involved are complex, and we will have to extend our conceptual framework in order to understand them.

We shall assume, as in Chapter 2, that the economy is inhabited by an infinitely-lived representative resident, whose demands and asset holdings we identify with aggregate national counterparts. Why do we return to that assumption, having presented so much evidence against it already? The same simplicity that renders the framework of Chapter 2 empirically inaccurate for some purposes makes it a good vehicle for highlighting some subtle theoretical concepts whose applicability is much more general. Much of the remaining analysis of this chapter can be read as applying at the individual level. The results could be aggregated over heterogeneous individuals, as in Chapter 3. Other ingredients of our analysis, including the budget constraints we derive, apply at the aggregate level regardless of intertemporal preferences or demographics. On all of these grounds, the material that follows is a necessary component of more complex and realistic theories.

4.4.1   The Consumer's Problem

We first look at the problem of individual intertemporal optimization when total consumption spending includes nontradables as well as tradables.

Rather than tackling the consumer's problem head-on, we simplify it in ways that will make its solution comparable to the ones derived in the single-good models of Chapter 2. As is often the case, the cost of ultimate simplicity is some upfront investment in conceptual equipment. That investment will have a handsome payoff throughout the balance of this book.

4.4.1.1   The Consumption-Based Price Index

Since we are working with a representative-consumer economy, we identify individual variables with national aggregates from the outset, and we therefore use uppercase letters to denote them. The representative consumer maximizes a lifetime utility function of the special form

$$U_t = \sum_{s=t}^{\infty} \beta^{s-t} u\left(C_s\right), \tag{19}$$

where $C = \Omega\,(C_T, C_N)$ is a linear-homogenous function of C_T and C_N. The function C is interpreted as an index of total consumption, which we shall sometimes call *real consumption*.

We specialize the form of the period utility function in eq. (19), rather than working with a general concave function $u\,(C_T, C_N)$, so that we can introduce the *consumption-based price index* that was alluded to in section 4.2.3. A price index can be expressed in any unit of measurement; we choose our current numeraire, tradable goods. We are interested in the price index because it will tell us how much real consumption C the consumer derives from a given expenditure of tradables.

DEFINITION   The consumption-based price index P is the minimum expenditure $Z = C_T + pC_N$ such that $C = \Omega\,(C_T, C_N) = 1$, given p.

So defined, the consumption-based price index measures the least expenditure of tradables that buys a unit of the consumption index, on which period utility depends. Of course, P is an increasing function of p.

To make the discussion less abstract, we assume the specific CES consumption index already encountered in eq. (13):

$$C = \Omega\,(C_T, C_N) = \left[\gamma^{\frac{1}{\theta}} C_T^{\frac{\theta-1}{\theta}} + (1-\gamma)^{\frac{1}{\theta}} C_N^{\frac{\theta-1}{\theta}} \right]^{\frac{\theta}{\theta-1}}, \qquad \gamma \in (0,1),\ \theta > 0.$$

What is the price index P under this assumption? The equations in (16) shows the demands that maximize C given spending, Z. The highest value of the index C, given Z, thus is found by substituting those demands into the last expression:

$$\left\{ \gamma^{\frac{1}{\theta}} \left[\frac{\gamma Z}{\gamma + (1-\gamma)p^{1-\theta}} \right]^{\frac{\theta-1}{\theta}} + (1-\gamma)^{\frac{1}{\theta}} \left[\frac{p^{-\theta}(1-\gamma)Z}{\gamma + (1-\gamma)p^{1-\theta}} \right]^{\frac{\theta-1}{\theta}} \right\}^{\frac{\theta}{\theta-1}}.$$

Since P is defined as the minimum expenditure such that $C = 1$,

$$\left\{ \gamma^{\frac{1}{\theta}} \left[\frac{\gamma P}{\gamma + (1-\gamma)p^{1-\theta}} \right]^{\frac{\theta-1}{\theta}} + (1-\gamma)^{\frac{1}{\theta}} \left[\frac{p^{-\theta}(1-\gamma)P}{\gamma + (1-\gamma)p^{1-\theta}} \right]^{\frac{\theta-1}{\theta}} \right\}^{\frac{\theta}{\theta-1}} = 1,$$

from which the solution

$$P = \left[\gamma + (1-\gamma)p^{1-\theta} \right]^{\frac{1}{1-\theta}} \tag{20}$$

follows.[25]

---

25. Observe that, because $C = \Omega(C_T, C_N)$ is linear-homogeneous, P is simply $E(p, C)/C = E(p, 1)$, where $E(p, C)$ is the expenditure function defined in section 1.3.4. The statement that C is the highest

Observe that Z/P is the ratio of spending, measured in units of tradables, to the minimum price, in tradables, of a single unit of the consumption index. Thus Z/P equals the level of the total real consumption index C that an optimizing consumer enjoys:

$$C = \frac{Z}{P}. \tag{21}$$

As promised, the price index P translates consumption spending measured in tradables into real consumption, C. For example, after the relative price of nontradables, p, rises, a given expenditure of tradables obviously yields less real consumption and utility; eq. (20) tells us exactly how much less.

Formula (20) may appear messy. In truth, it leads to enormous simplifications. Equality (21) lets us write the complicated demand functions in eq. (16) as

$$C_{\mathrm{T}} = \gamma \left(\frac{1}{P}\right)^{-\theta} C, \qquad C_{\mathrm{N}} = (1-\gamma) \left(\frac{p}{P}\right)^{-\theta} C. \tag{22}$$

The preceding formulas simply state that the demand for a good is proportional to real consumption, with a proportionality coefficient that is an isoelastic function of the ratio of the good's price (in terms of the numeraire) to the price index (calculated in the same numeraire). We shall encounter these convenient demand functions again at several points in this book.

To handle the Cobb-Douglas case ($\theta = 1$), observe that the price index [eq. (20)] converges to

$$P = (1)^{\gamma} p^{1-\gamma} = p^{1-\gamma}$$

as $\theta \to 1$.[26] (We now have formal justification for the formula used in section 4.2.3.)

4.4.1.2   Reformulating the Consumer's Problem

The formulas in eq. (22) solve the consumer's *intra*temporal maximization problem, given the real consumption level, C. We now show how to reformulate the consumer's *inter*temporal allocation problem in terms of the one variable C alone rather than two separate variables, C_{T} and C_{N}. Notice that this reformulation does

---

consumption-index level one can reach by spending $E(p, C)$ worth of tradables (given p) is just a statement of the inverse relationship between the expenditure function and the indirect utility function (Dixit and Norman, 1980, p. 60).

26. You can establish this, as in similar cases we've looked at, by taking logs and invoking L'Hospital's rule as $\theta \to 1$. (Compare footnote 22.) Notice that if the starting point is one at which $p = 1$, then eq. (20) implies $\hat{P} = (1-\gamma)\hat{p}$ as in section 4.2.3, even for $\theta \neq 1$.

not require the function $C = \Omega (C_T, C_N)$ to have the CES form we've assumed: any linear-homogeneous function will do.

To recast the intertemporal problem, we need only rewrite the lifetime budget constraint in terms of C. The obvious extension of the perfect-foresight constraint (60) of Chapter 2, derived in a single-good setting in section 2.5.1.4, likewise forces the present value of consumption expenditure to equal the sum of financial and human wealth:

$$\sum_{s=t}^{\infty} \left(\frac{1}{1+r}\right)^{s-t} (C_{T,s} + p_s C_{N,s}) = (1+r)Q_t + \sum_{s=t}^{\infty} \left(\frac{1}{1+r}\right)^{s-t} (w_s L_s - G_s).$$

(23)

Here, G denotes total government spending on tradables and nontradables, which is assumed to equal tax payments. Tradables are the numeraire in eq. (23), and the (constant, by assumption) own-interest rate on tradables, r, must be used to discount future tradables flows. When written in terms of C using eqs. (14) and (21), eq. (23) boils down to

$$\sum_{s=t}^{\infty} \left(\frac{1}{1+r}\right)^{s-t} P_s C_s = (1+r)Q_t + \sum_{s=t}^{\infty} \left(\frac{1}{1+r}\right)^{s-t} (w_s L_s - G_s).$$

(24)

The consumer's intertemporal problem is to maximize eq. (19) with respect to $\{C_s\}_{s=t}^{\infty}$, subject to eq. (24).[27]

4.4.1.3   The Real-Consumption Euler Equation and the Real Consumption-Based Interest Rate

The consumer's financial asset-accumulation identity, written as

$$Q_{s+1} - Q_s = rQ_s + w_s L_s - G_s - P_s C_s,$$

can be used to substitute for C_s in eq. (19), yielding

$$U_t = \sum_{s=t}^{\infty} \beta^{s-t} u \left[\frac{(1+r)Q_s - Q_{s+1} + w_s L_s - G_s}{P_s}\right].$$

Necessary conditions for intertemporal optimality come from differentiating with respect to Q_{s+1}, $s \geq t$. The resulting intertemporal Euler condition on total real consumption is

---

27. It is simplest to think of foreign assets as being indexed to tradables, so that B bonds are a claim to rB tradables per period in perpetuity. Different schemes for bond indexation yield identical results barring unanticipated shocks, because, under perfect foresight, all assets must yield equal real returns however measured. We will use a slightly different scheme for indexing bonds in section 4.5.

$$\frac{u'(C_s)}{P_s} = (1+r)\beta\frac{u'(C_{s+1})}{P_{s+1}}.$$

An illuminating way to look at this last Euler equation is to rewrite it in terms of the *consumption-based real interest rate*, defined by

$$1 + r^C_{s+1} \equiv \frac{(1+r)P_s}{P_{s+1}}. \tag{25}$$

The interest rate r^C_{s+1} is the own rate of interest on the consumption index C; that is, a loan of one unit of C on date s is worth $1 + r^C_{s+1}$ units on date $s + 1$.[28] In the present model, r^C differs from r whenever people expect changes in the relative price of nontradables and, hence, in the overall price level, P. With the definition of r^C, the Euler equation becomes

$$u'(C_s) = \frac{(1+r)P_s}{P_{s+1}}\beta u'(C_{s+1}) = \left(1 + r^C_{s+1}\right)\beta u'(C_{s+1}). \tag{26}$$

The only difference between eq. (26) and the entirely analogous equation (24) in Chapter 2 is that consumption now is explicitly an index, and the relevant interest rate is the own-rate on that index.[29]

4.4.1.4 Optimal Consumption

The analogy with the results of Chapter 2 goes much deeper and leads to very similar predictions about optimal individual consumption behavior. To see why, let us start by rewriting constraint (24) in terms of the consumption-based real interest rate.

Observe that eq. (24) is an equality between two quantities measured in terms of date t traded goods. We can express the constraint in terms of date t real consumption by dividing both sides by P_t. The left-hand side becomes

$$\sum_{s=t}^{\infty}\left(\frac{1}{1+r}\right)^{s-t}\frac{P_s C_s}{P_t} = \sum_{s=t}^{\infty}\left[\frac{P_{t+1}}{(1+r)P_t}\right]\left[\frac{P_{t+2}}{(1+r)P_{t+1}}\right]\cdots\left[\frac{P_s}{(1+r)P_{s-1}}\right]C_s$$

$$= \sum_{s=t}^{\infty}\frac{C_s}{\prod_{v=t+1}^{s}(1+r^C_v)},$$

(where the $s = t$ summand is simply C_t). The right-hand side becomes

---

28. One unit of date s real consumption buys P_s units of date s tradables and $(1+r)P_s$ units of date $s + 1$ tradables, which are worth $(1+r)P_s/P_{s+1} = 1 + r^C_{s+1}$ units of date $s + 1$ real consumption. Note that $1/(1 + r^C_{s+1})$ has the dimensions of units of C_s per unit of C_{s+1}. Thus it is the price of future real consumption in terms of present real consumption.

29. With a variable own interest rate on tradables, the Euler equation is the same once r in eq. (25) is replaced by r_{s+1}, the rate on loans of tradables between periods s and $s + 1$.

$$\frac{(1+r)Q_t}{P_t} + \sum_{s=t}^{\infty} \left(\frac{1}{1+r}\right)^{s-t} \frac{P_s(w_sL_s - G_s)}{P_sP_t}$$

$$= \frac{(1+r)Q_t}{P_t} + \sum_{s=t}^{\infty} \frac{(w_sL_s - G_s)/P_s}{\prod_{v=t+1}^{s}(1+r_v^C)}.$$

In analogy with eq. (21) in Chapter 2, let the date t market discount factor for date s real consumption be

$$R_{t,s}^C = \frac{1}{\prod_{v=t+1}^{s}(1+r_v^C)},$$

with $R_{t,t}^C = 1$. This discount factor is the price of date s real consumption in terms of date t real consumption. By combining our preceding manipulations of the two sides of eq. (24), we express that budget constraint in the familiar form

$$\sum_{s=t}^{\infty} R_{t,s}^C C_s = \frac{(1+r)Q_t}{P_t} + \sum_{s=t}^{\infty} R_{t,s}^C \frac{w_sL_s - G_s}{P_s}. \tag{27}$$

This rendition of eq. (24) shows that the present value of lifetime real consumption, discounted at the real interest rate, equals the present real-consumption value of financial plus human wealth.

Euler equation (26) and budget constraint (27) lead to an optimal consumption function very similar to those derived in previous chapters. For concreteness, let us again assume the isoelastic period utility function in eq. (22) of Chapter 1, which implies a constant *inter*temporal substitution elasticity, σ. Then eq. (26) implies that $C_s = \left(R_{t,s}^C\right)^{-\sigma} \beta^{\sigma(s-t)} C_t$ (as in section 2.2.2). Optimal consumption is

$$C_t = \frac{\frac{(1+r)Q_t}{P_t} + \sum_{s=t}^{\infty} R_{t,s}^C \frac{w_sL_s - G_s}{P_s}}{\sum_{s=t}^{\infty} \left(R_{t,s}^C\right)^{1-\sigma} \beta^{\sigma(s-t)}}. \tag{28}$$

Given this total consumption level C_t, demands for the two individual consumer goods are given by intratemporal maximization, as in eq. (22). Had we generalized eq. (61) of Chapter 2 to the case of variable interest rates (as you are invited to do now), we would have obtained this same consumption function in the isoelastic-utility case, with quantity variables and real interest rates in terms of the single output good rather than a consumption index.

Equation (28) exhibits the usual substitution, income, and wealth effects of changes in real interest rates. We must be cautious in interpreting these at the aggregate level, however, because changes in real interest rates due to changes in the relative price of nontradables generally are accompanied by simultaneous changes in other components of the numerator in eq. (28). In equilibrium, some of the effects cancel. For example, reversal of the reasoning at the beginning of this subsection shows that eq. (28) can be written

$$C_t = \frac{(1+r)Q_t + \sum_{s=t}^{\infty} \left(\frac{1}{1+r}\right)^{s-t}(w_s L_s - G_s)}{P_t \sum_{s=t}^{\infty}\left[(1+r)^{s-t}\left(\frac{P_t}{P_s}\right)\right]^{\sigma-1}\beta^{\sigma(s-t)}}. \tag{29}$$

Notice that, for a given P_t, ceteris paribus changes in real interest rates due to changes in future P_s have no wealth effect on C_t. [That is, P_s doesn't enter the numerator in eq. (29).] A rise in P_s, say, lowers the real interest rate between dates t and s, raising the present real value of real income to be received later; but it also lowers the real consumption value of net date s income in proportion. The result is a wash, analogous to the effect of higher expected CPI inflation on the value of a CPI-indexed bond.

To understand better the role of expected changes in the price of nontraded goods, we proceed to examine the economy's equilibrium.

*4.4.2   The Current Account in Equilibrium

The analysis up until now has shown close similarities between the behavior of individual real consumption in this model and its behavior in the one-good model of Chapter 2. Because the current account reflects output exchanges with other countries, however, it is most naturally measured in terms of *tradable* goods rather than in real consumption units. We now rewrite the model in terms of tradable output, investment, and foreign assets to see its current-account implications. Most importantly, this perspective clarifies the economy's behavior in equilibrium, when the nontraded goods market clears.

Both of the economy's industries produce with constant returns to scale. Thus, the result in eq. (59) of Chapter 2 applies to each industry separately. That is, each industry's capital, measured at its price of 1 in tradables, equals the industry's future discounted profits, also measured in tradables. At the aggregate level, therefore,

$$K_t = K_{T,t} + K_{N,t}$$

$$= \sum_{s=t}^{\infty} \left(\frac{1}{1+r}\right)^{s-t+1}\left[r\left(K_{T,s} + K_{N,s}\right) - \Delta K_{T,s+1} - \Delta K_{N,s+1}\right]$$

$$= \sum_{s=t}^{\infty} \left(\frac{1}{1+r}\right)^{s-t+1}(rK_s - I_s).$$

The economy's capital stock at the end of date $t-1$ equals the present value of future capital income less investment (assuming investment is set optimally by competitive firms).[30] Since $Y_T = rK_T + w_s L_T$ and $pY_N = rK_N + wL_N$, total GDP

---

30. To refresh your memory, work backward. The asserted equality can be written in terms of the lead operator L^{-1} as

(in units of tradables) is $Y_T + pY_N = rK + wL$. Using these relations, we rewrite eq. (24) as

$$\sum_{s=t}^{\infty} \left(\frac{1}{1+r}\right)^{s-t} P_s C_s$$

$$= (1+r)\,(B_t + K_t) + \sum_{s=t}^{\infty} \left(\frac{1}{1+r}\right)^{s-t} (w_s L_s - G_s)$$

$$= (1+r)B_t + \sum_{s=t}^{\infty} \left(\frac{1}{1+r}\right)^{s-t} (Y_{T,s} + p_s Y_{N,s} - I_s - G_s) \tag{30}$$

(presuming capital yields the ex post rate of return r on date t as well as subsequently).

Budget constraint (30) isn't quite what we want for understanding the current account because it incorporates nontradable consumption and output. But these are easily netted out. By eq. (21) and the definition (14) of Z, $PC = C_T + pC_N$. Furthermore, since we have assumed that nontradeds cannot be invested, only consumed, consumption of nontradeds equals their supply in equilibrium. Let us divide total government spending into its constituent parts: $G = G_T + pG_N$. Then the market for nontraded goods is in equilibrium when

$$C_N + G_N = Y_N. \tag{31}$$

Thus nontradable consumption and production drop out from eq. (30), leaving us with

$$\sum_{s=t}^{\infty} \left(\frac{1}{1+r}\right)^{s-t} (C_{T,s} + I_s + G_{T,s}) = (1+r)B_t + \sum_{s=t}^{\infty} \left(\frac{1}{1+r}\right)^{s-t} Y_{T,s}. \tag{32}$$

The reason the economy's budget constraint vis-à-vis the rest of the world takes this form should be clear after a moment's reflection. By definition, all of the economy's trade with the outside world consists of exchanges of tradable goods. Thus a more stringent intertemporal budget constraint holds at the national level than at that of the individual (who has the opportunity to purchase tradables with nontradables from other domestic residents). The present value of the economy's *tradable* expenditure must equal the present value of its *tradable* income.

$$K_t = \left(\frac{1}{1+r}\right)\left(1 - \frac{1}{1+r} L^{-1}\right)^{-1} (rK_t - I_t)$$

(see Supplement C to Chapter 2). Multiplying through by the inverted lag polynomial, we find

$$K_t - \frac{1}{1+r} K_{t+1} = \left(\frac{1}{1+r}\right)(rK_t - I_t),$$

which is equivalent to the identity $K_t - K_{t+1} = -I_t$.

Together with an Euler equation for tradable consumption, constraint (32) determines the current account. Let us again assume that $u(C)$ is isoelastic with intertemporal substitution elasticity σ. The Euler equation for C, eq. (26), therefore is

$$C_{s+1} = \left[\frac{(1+r)P_s}{P_{s+1}}\right]^{\sigma} \beta^{\sigma} C_s. \tag{33}$$

To derive the Euler equation for C_T that we seek, we need, for the first time since introducing it in section 4.4.1.1, the assumption that the consumption index C has a CES form. When combined with the last Euler equation, the equation for C_T in eq. (22) implies that

$$C_{T,s+1} = \left(\frac{P_s}{P_{s+1}}\right)^{\sigma-\theta} (1+r)^{\sigma} \beta^{\sigma} C_{T,s}. \tag{34}$$

We see from this equation that tradables consumption conforms to the predictions of the Euler equation of the one-good model, except insofar as the price index P changes over time. Only when $\sigma = \theta$ do price changes have no influence on consumption growth.

The reason the difference $\sigma - \theta$ figures into eq. (34) isn't hard to grasp. If other things are equal, a falling P, for example, raises the gross real interest rate; this increase raises the optimal gross growth rate of *real* consumption, C, with elasticity σ. But as P falls, tradables consumption C_T becomes relatively dearer and falls as a fraction of C with elasticity θ [recall eq. (22)]. These intertemporal and intratemporal substitution effects on C_T pull in opposite directions.

We can combine Euler equation (34) with budget constraint (32) to calculate the optimal consumption of tradables:

$$C_{T,t} = \frac{(1+r)B_t + \sum_{s=t}^{\infty} \left(\frac{1}{1+r}\right)^{s-t} (Y_{T,s} - I_s - G_{T,s})}{\sum_{s=t}^{\infty} \left[(1+r)^{\sigma-1}\beta^{\sigma}\right]^{s-t} \left(\frac{P_t}{P_s}\right)^{\sigma-\theta}}. \tag{35}$$

This equation reduces to eq. (16) of Chapter 2 when P is constant (although here it involves only tradables). The current account is the difference between total income and absorption; in equilibrium, it is the difference between *tradable* income and *tradable* absorption:

$$CA_t = B_{t+1} - B_t = rB_t + Y_{T,t} + p_t Y_{N,t} - C_{T,t} - p_t C_{N,t} - I_t - G_t$$

$$= rB_t + Y_{T,t} - C_{T,t} - I_t - G_{T,t}. \tag{36}$$

Thus the presence of nontradables affects the current account, given current and future net outputs of tradables, *only* by influencing the path of the consumer price index P. For example, if P is constant (or if $\sigma = \theta$), eqs. (35) and (36) together can be used to deduce the tradables analog of fundamental current-account equation

(20) of Chapter 2, which we derived in section 2.2.1. The current account behavior studied in Chapter 2 therefore provides the natural benchmark against which to understand the effects of nontraded goods.

If P is rising over time, for example, eq. (35) shows that initial consumption of tradables exceeds its Chapter 2 level if $\sigma > \theta$. The initial current account balance thus is below the level consistent with the tradables version of consumption function (16) in Chapter 2. The reason is that the relevant real interest rate is below $1 + r$ and intertemporal substitution is strong enough to raise tradables consumption. If $\theta > \sigma$ the intratemporal substitution effect wins out: initial consumption is lower and the initial current account stronger so that consumption of tradables can rise more rapidly as P (and hence the price of nontradables, p) rises.

The preceding analysis illuminates how the interplay between σ and θ influences the current account response to alternative disturbances, including endowment changes and productivity shocks. We leave the details as (advanced) exercises.[31] When nontradables arrive in the economy as a pure endowment, the current account behaves much as in a tradables-only model provided the net supply of nontradables is constant through time. But that case, in which nontradables effectively become an unchanging parameter of the utility function, is very special.

Appendix 4A takes a detailed look at labor supply and its relation to the current account. Because leisure can be thought of as a nontraded good, real wage variation (which affects labor supply and therefore the supply of leisure) can have current account effects analogous to those of variation in the relative price of nontraded goods.

Appendix 4B analyzes the effects of output changes in a model with costly investment in the nontraded goods sector. Convex capital installation costs slow the economy's response to productivity and demand shocks, making their effects more persistent.

4.5   The Terms of Trade in a Dynamic Ricardian Model

So far in this chapter we have simplified by assuming that there is a single composite traded good. This assumption has usefully focused attention on the factors determining the relative price of nontradables and tradables taken as a group. In reality, however, the goods a country exports tend to differ in at least some respects from those it imports, and the relative price of imports and exports—the terms of trade—change as a result of shifts in demand and supply. These terms-of-trade changes affect private consumption decisions, induce the creation and extinction of

---

31. See also Dornbusch (1983), who focuses on the $\theta = 1$ case.

entire industries, and are a major channel for the global transmission of macroeconomic shocks. Importantly, intratemporal terms of trade changes also affect a country's welfare—in the same way as did the *intertemporal* terms of trade changes on which we focused in the one-good-per-date models of Chapters 1 through 3. The reason is basic: a country whose terms of trade fall receives less in return for each unit of the good it exports.

To capture these important effects, we turn in this section to the explicit incorporation of the terms of trade.[32] Our dynamic model, inspired by a classic paper of Dornbusch, Fischer, and Samuelson (1977), simultaneously determines the range of goods a country produces and its current account. The basic source of static comparative advantage in the model is a Ricardian production structure based on international differences in labor productivity.[33]

An ultimate goal of this section is to understand how the set of nontradable goods is endogenously determined by international transport costs. Our extended model addresses some time-honored and much-debated questions in international economics that cannot even be asked in models with only a single good. One of these concerns the macroeconomic factors that cause some countries to lose industries while others gain them.

4.5.1 A Model with a Continuum of Goods

It proves convenient to assume that the world economy can potentially produce a *continuum* of goods, indexed by $z \in [0, 1]$. There are two countries, Home and Foreign, and only one factor of production, labor, available in fixed quantities L in Home and L^* in Foreign. In line with Ricardo's famous account of comparative advantage, the countries have different technologies for producing goods out of labor. In Home a unit of good z can be made out of $a(z)$ units of labor, while in Foreign a unit of good z can be made out of $a^*(z)$ units of labor. Our neglect of an explicit role for capital in production reflects a desire to focus on medium-term dynamics.

On the consumption side, there is a representative individual in each country who maximizes

$$U_t = \sum_{s=t}^{\infty} \beta^{s-t} \log C_s, \tag{37}$$

where C is a consumption index that depends on consumption of every good $z \in [0, 1]$ through the formula

32. The large literature on the dynamic effects of terms-of-trade shocks started with Obstfeld (1982), Sachs (1981), and Svensson and Razin (1983). See Sen (1994) for an overview.

33. Since MacDougall's (1951) classic study, researchers have consistently found relative labor costs to be a powerful explanatory variable for trade flows. The many follow-up studies include Balassa (1963) and Golub and Hsieh (1995).

$$C = \exp\left[\int_0^1 \log c(z)\mathrm{d}z\right].\tag{38}$$

As usual, Foreign consumptions are denoted by asterisks.

Take good $z = 1$ as the numeraire, so that the wage rates w and w^* and commodity prices $p(z)$ are expressed in units of good 1. [Of course, $p(1) = 1$ in this case.] The consumption-based price index in terms of the numeraire is defined (as in section 4.4.1.1) as the lowest possible cost, measured in units of good 1, of purchasing a unit of C. Here, the price index is

$$P = \exp\left[\int_0^1 \log p(z)\mathrm{d}z\right].\tag{39}$$

Its derivation yields the individual's consumption demands, and therefore merits a digression.

Consider the problem of finding

$$\min_{\{C(z)|z\in[0,1]\}} \int_0^1 p(z)c(z)\mathrm{d}z$$

subject to the constraint

$$C = \exp\left[\int_0^1 \log c(z)\mathrm{d}z\right] = 1.$$

Because the latter constraint is equivalent to

$$\int_0^1 \log c(z)\mathrm{d}z = 0,$$

we can find first-order conditions by differentiating [with respect to $c(z)$] the Lagrangian expression

$$\mathcal{L} = \int_0^1 p(z)c(z)\mathrm{d}z - \lambda \int_0^1 \log c(z)\mathrm{d}z,$$

where λ is a multiplier, and equating the result to zero. The resulting condition, which holds for all z, is

$$p(z)c(z) = \lambda,$$

so that every good receives an equal weight in expenditure. To find the value of λ when consumption expenditure is allocated optimally, substitute the above relation into the constraint $\int_0^1 \log c(z)\mathrm{d}z = 0$ and derive

$$\lambda = \exp\left[\int_0^1 \log p(z)\mathrm{d}z\right].$$

The index P is thus given by

$$\int_0^1 p(z)c(z)\mathrm{d}z = \int_0^1 \lambda \mathrm{d}z = \lambda = \exp\left[\int_0^1 \log p(z)\mathrm{d}z\right],$$

as eq. (39) states.

Since $P = \lambda$ in the preceding problem, consumption of good z is given by $c(z) = P/p(z)$ when $C = 1$. Therefore, because the intratemporal preferences specified in (38) are homothetic, the demand for good z when $C \neq 1$ is the corresponding fraction of C,

$$c(z) = \left[\frac{P}{p(z)}\right]C. \tag{40}$$

According to eq. (40), individual expenditure on any interval $[z_1, z_2] \subset [0, 1]$ of goods is given by $\int_{z_1}^{z_2} p(z)c(z)\mathrm{d}z = (z_2 - z_1)PC$. We will make use of this demand function shortly.[34]

4.5.2 Costless International Trade: Determining Wages, Prices, and Production

The easiest case to start with is one in which there are no costs of transporting goods internationally. Since we will later derive nontradability explicitly from the assumption of transport costs, we think of the present, frictionless, case as one in which all goods are traded. In that setting it is easy to derive the international trade pattern.

A useful tool for understanding the pattern of trade is the *relative Home labor productivity schedule* $A(z)$, which gives ratios of Foreign to Home required unit labor inputs:

$$A(z) \equiv \frac{a^*(z)}{a(z)}. \tag{41}$$

On the assumption that goods have been ordered along $[0, 1]$ so that the relative Foreign labor requirement falls as z rises, $A(z)$ is a downward-sloping schedule,

$$A'(z) < 0.$$

The $A(z)$ schedule helps to determine international specialization. Any good z such that $wa(z) < w^*a^*(z)$ can be produced more cheaply in Home than in Foreign, whereas Foreign has a cost advantage over Home for any good satisfying the reverse inequality. Consequently, any good such that

$$\frac{w}{w^*} < A(z) = \frac{a^*(z)}{a(z)}$$

is produced in Home, while goods for which

---

34. You may recognize eq. (40) as the special case of eq. (22) corresponding to $\theta = 1$.

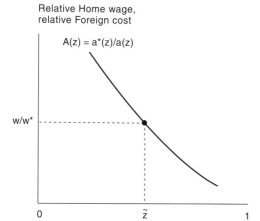

Figure 4.8
Determining the pattern of specialization

$$\frac{w}{w^*} > A(z)$$

are produced in Foreign. We arbitrarily allocate production of the marginal "cut-off" good $\tilde{z}$, defined by

$$\frac{w}{w^*} = A(\tilde{z}),$$

to Home. Given the international wage ratio, Home therefore produces the goods in the range $[0, \tilde{z}]$ while Foreign produces the rest. Figure 4.8 is a graphic depiction of the determination of $\tilde{z}$.

Equilibrium relative wages depend, however, on the range of products a country produces. When the range of goods produced in Home expands, world demand for Home labor services rises while world demand for Foreign labor falls. The result is a rise in the relative Home wage. This positively sloped relationship between production range and relative Home wages, when added to the negatively sloped one shown in Figure 4.8, closes the model of product and factor markets.

To derive this second schedule formally, notice that in a world equilibrium, total world consumption measured in any numeraire (good 1, say) must equal world output, which, in turn, equals world labor income. (There is no capital in the model.) Thus

$$P(C + C^*) = wL + w^*L^*. \tag{42}$$

In equilibrium the supply of Home output, equal to Home labor income, must also equal the demand for it. Equation (40) implies that if Home produces the goods in $[0, z]$ itself, its demand for its own goods (measured in good 1) is zPC, and

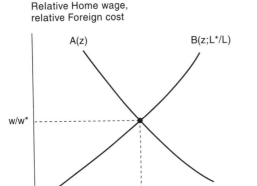

Figure 4.9
Joint determination of wages and industry location

Foreign's demand for Home goods (similarly measured) is zPC^*. By eq. (42), clearing of the Home goods market therefore requires

$$wL = zP(C + C^*) = z(wL + w^*L^*),$$

which can be solved to yield

$$\frac{w}{w^*} = \frac{z}{1-z}\left(\frac{L^*}{L}\right) \equiv B\left(z; \frac{L^*}{L}\right). \tag{43}$$

This upward-sloping schedule, which has been added in Figure 4.9, shows that the relative Home wage rises with an increase in the derived demand for Home labor. Both w/w^* and $\tilde{z}$ are uniquely determined by the intersection of the $A(z)$ and $B(z; L^*/L)$ schedules in Figure 4.9.

4.5.3   Labor-Supply and Productivity Changes and the Terms of Trade

Some exercises help in building intuition about the model. Consider a rise in the relative Foreign labor supply, L^*/L, to $L^{*\prime}/L'$. In Figure 4.10, this change shifts the $B(z; L^*/L)$ schedule inward (why?), resulting in a rise in the relative Home wage to $w'/w^{*\prime}$ and a fall in the range of goods produced at Home, from $\tilde{z}$ to $\tilde{z}'$. The interval $(\tilde{z}', \tilde{z}]$ gives the range of industries that Home loses to Foreign.

How does the increase in relative Foreign labor affect *real* wages? Let us continue to use primes (') to denote the values of variables after the Foreign labor supply increase.

For all goods produced by Home both before and after (that is, for all $z \leq \tilde{z}'$), $w'/p(z)'$ remains unchanged at $w/p(z)$, since the price of any Home-produced good z is

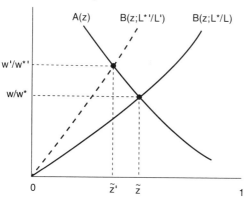

Relative Home wage,
relative Foreign cost

Figure 4.10
A rise in relative Foreign labor supply

$$p(z) = a(z)w \tag{44}$$

and the technological coefficient $a(z)$ has not changed. That is, the purchasing power of Home wages in terms of Home-produced goods remains constant. By the same argument, $w^{*\prime}/p(z)' = w^*/p(z)$ for all $z > \tilde{z}$, since the price of any Foreign-produced good is

$$p(z) = a^*(z)w^*. \tag{45}$$

Foreign real wages therefore remain constant in terms of goods that Foreign continues to produce.

What about Home real wages in terms of the goods *Foreign* produces before as well as after its labor-supply increase? For these goods $z > \tilde{z}$, the zero-profit condition (45) holds both before and after the change. Thus the inequality $w'/w^{*\prime} > w/w^*$ shows that

$$\frac{w'}{p(z)'} = \frac{w'}{a^*(z)w^{*\prime}} > \frac{w}{a^*(z)w^*} = \frac{w}{p(z)},$$

implying that Home's real wage must rise in terms of these consistent Foreign products. A parallel argument shows that Foreign's real wage must fall in terms of the initial Home goods $z \leq \tilde{z}'$ whose production sites remain in Home.

Finally, consider the industries that Home loses to Foreign. These $z \in (\tilde{z}', \tilde{z}]$ can now be produced more cheaply in Foreign than in Home, so $p(z)' = w^{*\prime}a^*(z) < w'a(z)$, which implies that

$$\frac{w'}{p(z)'} > \frac{1}{a(z)} = \frac{w}{p(z)}.$$

Home's real wage rises in terms of those goods that have become imports, precisely because foreign costs now are lower than domestic costs. At the same time, it must be true that

$$\frac{w^{*\prime}}{p(z)'} = \frac{1}{a^*(z)} < \frac{w^*}{p(z)}$$

for Foreign's new export goods. Foreign's real wage in terms of these goods has fallen enough to make Foreign the lower-cost production location.

Our unsurprising conclusion is that, overall, a rise in Foreign relative labor supply lowers its own real wage and raises Home's. What this means, though, is that Home is better off and Foreign worse off (per unit of labor) despite the migration of industries from Home to Foreign! The example shows that, contrary to popular notions, there is no intrinsic connection between a country's "competitiveness"—its ability to undercut rivals in international markets—and its per capita living standards.

Another way to represent the improvement in Home's relative welfare is as an improvement in its *terms of trade*, the price of its exports in terms of its imports from Foreign.

To evaluate how the terms of trade move, we look at the change in the average price of Home's exports relative to the change in the average price of Foreign's (which are Home's imports). For any good $z \le \tilde{z}'$ that Home still exports after the rise in Foreign labor supply, the log change in its price is given by $\log p(z)' - \log p(z) = \log w' - \log w$. The log prices of goods $z > \tilde{z}$ that originally were Foreign exports rise by the smaller percentage $\log w^{*\prime} - \log w^* < \log w' - \log w$. If no industries at all relocated in Foreign, Home's average export prices would simply rise by $\log w' - \log w - (\log w^{*\prime} - \log w^*) > 0$ relative to Foreign's. The overall rise in Foreign's export prices is an average, however, of the rises in the prices of its prior exports and in those of the new export goods it actually does capture from Home. The log prices of the latter goods $z \in (\tilde{z}', \tilde{z}]$ must change by strictly *less* than $\log w' - \log w$ as a result of their move to Foreign; otherwise Foreign would have no cost advantage over Home for those goods. As a result, Home's average export prices still rise relative to Foreign's even after we account for industrial relocation. Thus Home's terms of trade improve while Foreign's worsen.

Consider next a proportional fall in Foreign unit labor requirements for all goods, so that $a^*(z)' = a^*(z)/v$, $v > 1$. The change induces a proportional downward shift in the $A(z)$ schedule in Figure 4.9. The Home relative wage falls, but its decline is less than proportionate to the decline in relative Home productivity [because $B(z; L^*/L)$ has a finite positive slope]. Home loses some industries, but this fact does not imply that Home is worse off. Indeed, Home *gains* from the Foreign productivity increase because its workers' real wage, like that of Foreign's workers, rises. (Show this result.) Foreign's productivity gain is shared with Home because Foreign's terms of trade fall (and Home's correspondingly improve) as a result of a more productive Foreign labor force. To see why, observe that the prices of goods that consistently remain Home exports rise relative to those that consistently remain Foreign exports because the percent fall in Home's relative wage is less than the percent fall in Foreign unit labor requirements. Goods that shift production from Home to Foreign experience proportional price rises below those for consistent Home exports. Thus Home's terms of trade must rise. The example shows that when higher productivity raises a country's relative wage, the relative price of its exports may fall. The result is not general, however. In models that allow countries to produce the same goods that they import, higher productivity in a country's import-competing sector can raise its terms of trade and have a negative impact abroad.[35]

4.5.4   Costless International Trade: The Current Account

As developed so far, the model determines relative wages and the international specialization pattern without reference to saving behavior. This property comes from the assumptions of identical international tastes and zero transport costs, without which the division of world aggregate demand between Home and Foreign would influence the demand for particular commodities or supply conditions. Even in the present simple model, however, temporary economic changes influence saving and the current account, leading to persistent changes in national welfare. We now examine these effects.

4.5.4.1   Saving

The first step is to take a detailed look at saving behavior. Suppose individuals in the two countries can borrow and lend through bonds denominated in units of the real consumption index given in eq. (38). (That is, a bond with face value 1 costs 1 unit of C today and is a claim on $1 + r$ units of C tomorrow, where r is the real consumption-based interest rate.) The Home current-account identity (expressed in units of the consumption index) is

$$CA_t = B_{t+1} - B_t = \frac{w_t L}{P_t} + r_t B_t - C_t, \tag{46}$$

while the corresponding Foreign identity is

$$CA_t^* = B_{t+1}^* - B_t^* = \frac{w_t^* L^*}{P_t} + r_t B_t^* - C_t^*. \tag{47}$$

Of course, $CA = -CA^*$ and $B = -B^*$. As always, we can combine eq. (46) with the appropriate no-Ponzi condition on foreign assets to derive Home's intertemporal budget constraint (similarly for Foreign).

---

35. For a classic analysis, see Johnson (1955).

The intertemporal Euler equation is derived by maximizing U_t in eq. (37) subject to eq. (46). Substituting eq. (46) into eq. (37) gives the maximand

$$U_t = \sum_{s=t}^{\infty} \beta^{s-t} \log \left[(1 + r_t) B_t - B_{t+1} + \frac{w_t L}{P_t} \right],$$

which, upon differentiation with respect to B_{t+1}, yields the intertemporal Euler condition

$$C_{t+1} = (1 + r_{t+1}) \beta C_t. \tag{48}$$

The corresponding (and identical) Euler equation for C^* follows similarly.

To carry out our dynamic analysis, we assume the world economy starts out in a steady state. Equation (48) implies that the steady-state world real interest rate is

$$\bar{r} = \frac{1 - \beta}{\beta}.$$

(Steady-state variables are marked with overbars.) Steady-state Home and Foreign total consumption levels are

$$\bar{C} = \bar{r} \bar{B} + \frac{\bar{w} L}{\bar{P}}, \qquad \bar{C}^* = -\bar{r} \bar{B} + \frac{\bar{w}^* L^*}{\bar{P}}. \tag{49}$$

The steady-state wages, international production pattern, and prices are those determined by Figure 4.9 and eqs. (44) and (45), given unchanging technologies and labor forces. Consumption levels for individual commodities are determined by eq. (40).

4.5.4.2   Current-Account Effects of Temporary Changes

Unexpected permanent changes, such as a permanent rise in Foreign productivity, have no current-account effects in the model. Consumption levels adjust immediately to those given by eq. (49). Temporary changes can induce changes in current accounts and the world interest rate, however. To analyze these, we make two simplifying assumptions. First, the world economy is initially (before the unexpected, temporary shock occurs) in a symmetric steady state, denoted by zero subscripts, in which $\bar{B}_0 = -\bar{B}_0^* = 0$. Second, the temporary shock is reversed after a single period. The second assumption means that the world economy reaches its new steady state in only one period. We refer to the initial, preshock steady state as the world economy's "baseline" path, and we compute deviations from that reference path.

To illustrate the workings of the model, we consider an unexpected, one-period increase in Foreign productivity—the same proportional fall in $a^*(z)$ (across all z) that we studied in section 4.5.3. To parameterize the change, we suppose that, for every z, $a^*(z)$ falls to $a^*(z)/\nu$, where $\nu > 1$ *for one period only* before reverting to its prior level. The easiest way to compute the short-run impact is to work backward from the new steady state that is reached the period after the temporary Foreign productivity drop.

The productivity shock is temporary, and wages and prices do not depend on the international distribution of wealth. Furthermore, the steady-state interest rate $\bar{r}$ doesn't change. Thus, eq. (49) implies that percent changes in steady-state consumption levels are simply

$$\widehat{\bar{C}} = \frac{\bar{r}\,d\bar{B}}{\bar{C}_0}, \qquad \widehat{\bar{C}^*} = \frac{-\bar{r}\,d\bar{B}}{\bar{C}_0^*}. \tag{50}$$

In general, "hats" over variables with overbars will denote percent changes in steady-state values, for example, $\widehat{\bar{C}} = d\bar{C}/\bar{C}_0$.

For infinitesimal changes, a logarithmic approximation to the Euler equation (48) shows the relationship between short-run and long-run consumption changes and the world interest rate. (Since we rely heavily on logarithmic approximations in what follows, we will refresh your memory and present the first derivation in detail.) Taking natural logarithms of the Euler equation yields

$$\log C_{t+1} = \log(1 + r_{t+1}) + \log \beta + \log C_t,$$

the differential of which is

$$\frac{dC_{t+1}}{C_{t+1}} = \frac{dr_{t+1}}{1 + r_{t+1}} + \frac{dC_t}{C_t}.$$

If the economy is initially (on date t) on a baseline steady-state path with $C_{t+1} = C_t = \bar{C}_0$ and $r_{t+1} = \bar{r} = (1 - \beta)/\beta$, and will reach its new steady state in period $t + 1$, the preceding equation becomes

$$\widehat{\bar{C}} = (1 - \beta)\hat{r} + \hat{C}, \tag{51}$$

where hatted variables without overbars refer to short-run (i.e., date t) deviations from the baseline path. The corresponding Foreign equation is

$$\widehat{\bar{C}^*} = (1 - \beta)\hat{r} + \hat{C}^*. \tag{52}$$

To economize on notation, let's assume that, initially,

$$L = L^* \quad \text{and} \quad A(1/2) = 1,$$

so that

$$\tilde{z}_0 = 1/2$$

and the two countries initially have equal wage, real-output, and consumption levels. Under these assumptions, we compute the short-run real interest rate change. Since the new steady-state output levels equal the original ones, the long-run change in *world* consumption is nil:

$$\frac{d\bar{C} + d\bar{C}^*}{\bar{C} + \bar{C}^*} = \left(\frac{\bar{C}}{\bar{C} + \bar{C}^*}\right)\widehat{\bar{C}} + \left(\frac{\bar{C}^*}{\bar{C} + \bar{C}^*}\right)\widehat{\bar{C}^*} = \frac{\widehat{\bar{C}} + \widehat{\bar{C}^*}}{2} = 0.$$

Thus, adding eqs. (51) and (52) and making use of the last result, we have

$$\hat{r} = \frac{-1}{(1-\beta)}\left(\frac{\hat{C} + \hat{C}^*}{2}\right),$$

which shows that a temporary expansion of world consumption must be associated with a fall in the world real interest rate. To determine $\hat{r}$, we next want to solve for the percentage short-run change in world consumption, $\frac{1}{2}\left(\hat{C} + \hat{C}^*\right)$. Log-differentiating eq. (42) yields

$$\frac{\hat{C} + \hat{C}^*}{2} = \frac{\hat{w} + \hat{w}^*}{2} - \hat{P}. \tag{53}$$

Price equations (44) and (45), together with the definition of the price index P in eq. (39), show that, while Foreign productivity is temporarily high,

$$P = \exp\left[\int_0^{\tilde{z}} \log wa(z)dz + \int_{\tilde{z}}^1 \log \frac{w^*a^*(z)}{v}dz\right].$$

Log-differentiating with respect to v and evaluating at the initial symmetric steady state (where $v = 1$), we get[36]

$$\hat{P} = \frac{\hat{w} + \hat{w}^*}{2} - \frac{\hat{v}}{2}. \tag{54}$$

Combination of this with eq. (53) leads to the simple result that world consumption rises by the percentage increase in world productivity,

$$\frac{\hat{C} + \hat{C}^*}{2} = \frac{\hat{v}}{2},$$

which implies a fall in the world interest rate equal to

$$\hat{r} = \frac{-\hat{v}}{2(1-\beta)}. \tag{55}$$

---

36. To derive the following, notice that because the wages and $\tilde{z}$ are functions of v but the technological coefficients $a(z)$ and $a^*(z)$ do not change,

$$dP = P\left\{\left[\log \bar{w}_0 a(1/2) - \log \bar{w}_0^* a^*(1/2)\right]d\tilde{z} + \int_0^{1/2} \hat{w}dz + \int_{1/2}^1 (\hat{w}^* - \hat{v})dz\right\}.$$

But $\bar{w}_0 a(1/2) = \bar{w}_0^* a^*(1/2)$ at the initial steady state, by our assumption of initial symmetry.

We next use the preceding real interest rate change to figure out short- and long-run consumption changes and the current account. Log-differentiation of eq. (46) shows that[37]

$$\frac{d\bar{B}}{\bar{C}_0} = \hat{w} - \hat{P} - \hat{C} = -\frac{d\bar{B}^*}{\bar{C}_0^*}.$$

Use of eq. (54) to eliminate $\hat{P}$ in this expression shows, however, that

$$\frac{d\bar{B}}{\bar{C}_0} = \frac{\hat{w} - \hat{w}^* + \hat{v}}{2} - \hat{C}. \tag{56}$$

Let's find the change in relative international wages. From the fact that $w/w^* = A(\tilde{z})/v$, we see that, starting from the initial steady state,

$$\hat{w} - \hat{w}^* = -\hat{v} + A'(1/2)d\tilde{z}$$

[recall we've assumed $A(1/2) = 1$ and $\tilde{z}_0 = 1/2$]. But now go back to eq. (43): log-differentiation of that relationship and evaluation at the initial steady state yields

$$\hat{w} - \hat{w}^* = 4d\tilde{z},$$

which allows us to solve for $\hat{w} - \hat{w}^*$ as

$$\hat{w} - \hat{w}^* = \frac{-\hat{v}}{1 - \frac{1}{4}A'\left(\frac{1}{2}\right)}. \tag{57}$$

Home's relative wage falls temporarily, but less than in proportion to the increased average productivity differential (just as in the static analysis of section 4.5.3).

To find the equilibrium current-account effect of the productivity disturbance, substitute eqs. (51) and (57) into eq. (56) to obtain

---

37. Equation (46) is

$$B_{t+1} - B_t = \frac{w_t L}{P_t} + r_t B_t - C_t.$$

Since the economy goes from one zero-saving steady state to a new one between dates t and $t + 1$, the left-hand side above is $d\bar{B}$. Taking the differential of the right-hand side, and noting that $d(r_t B_t) = 0$ because date t interest earnings are determined in period $t - 1$, we have

$$d\bar{B} = \frac{dw}{\bar{w}_0} \cdot \frac{\bar{w}_0 L}{\bar{P}_0} - \frac{dP}{\bar{P}_0} \cdot \frac{\bar{w}_0 L}{\bar{P}_0} - dC.$$

Initial foreign assets are zero by assumption, so eq. (49) states that $\bar{C}_0 = \bar{w}_0 L/\bar{P}_0$. Division by $\bar{C}_0$ thus yields the next equation in the text.

$$\frac{d\bar{B}}{\bar{C}_0} = \frac{-A'\left(\frac{1}{2}\right)\hat{v}}{8 - 2A'\left(\frac{1}{2}\right)} - \widehat{C} + (1 - \beta)\hat{r}.$$

Then substitute eqs. (50) and (55) into the last expression to conclude that

$$\frac{d\bar{B}}{\bar{C}_0} = \frac{-A'\left(\frac{1}{2}\right)\hat{v}}{8 - 2A'\left(\frac{1}{2}\right)} - \frac{\bar{r}d\bar{B}}{\bar{C}_0} - \frac{\hat{v}}{2},$$

which simplifies to

$$\frac{d\bar{B}}{\bar{C}_0} = \frac{-\hat{v}}{(1 + \bar{r})\left[2 - \frac{1}{2}A'\left(\frac{1}{2}\right)\right]} < 0. \tag{58}$$

Obviously, Foreign's current account surplus has to balance Home's deficit,

$$\frac{d\bar{B}^*}{\bar{C}_0} = \frac{\hat{v}}{(1 + \bar{r})\left[2 - \frac{1}{2}A'\left(\frac{1}{2}\right)\right]} > 0.$$

Correspondingly, eq. (50) yields the long-run consumption changes

$$\widehat{C}^* = \frac{\bar{r}\hat{v}}{(1 + \bar{r})\left[2 - \frac{1}{2}A'\left(\frac{1}{2}\right)\right]} = -\widehat{C}. \tag{59}$$

   The last equation has a clear and intuitive interpretation. The temporary productivity rise in Foreign opens up a one-period real wage differential given by eq. (57). Given the fall in the world interest rate, eq. (55), implied by our symmetry assumptions, Foreign's current-account surplus is only large enough to raise long-run consumption by *half* the annuity value of its temporary income gain relative to Home. Without the short-run interest rate fall, Home would actually desire a surplus, too. Why? As in the static analysis of section 4.5.3, despite the loss of some industries, Home's real income rises temporarily when Foreign productivity does.

   In this dynamic setting, Home regains its lost industries in the long run but its welfare is lower after the initial period due to the permanent debt it has incurred to Foreign. Foreign is better off in the long as well as in the short run. One can also show (as we ask you to do in end-of-chapter exercise 7) that Home's first-period welfare gain outweighs its subsequent losses. The intuition is that Home's optimizing residents would, by the envelope theorem, incur only a second-order welfare loss were they to spend exactly their income in the first period. Thus the logic of the static case applies: Foreign's good fortune indirectly benefits Home by raising its terms of trade.

4.5.5   Transport Costs and Nontraded Goods

So far we have abstracted from costs of shipping goods between countries, but consideration of international transport costs shows how some of the goods countries produce can become nontraded.

4.5.5.1   Transport Costs and International Specialization

Imagine that a fraction κ of any good shipped between countries evaporates in transit. (Think of melting ice cream.) Under this assumption, it is no longer true that countries will produce only those goods they can produce more cheaply than foreign competitors. It costs Home $wa(z)$ to produce a unit of good z, but the cost of importing a unit of the good from Foreign is no longer $w^*a^*(z)$: instead it costs a total of $w^*a^*(z)/(1 - \kappa)$ to import a unit of good z from Foreign. Given wages, those goods such that $wa(z) < w^*a^*(z)/(1 - \kappa)$, that is,

$$\frac{w}{w^*} < \frac{A(z)}{1 - \kappa} = \frac{a^*(z)}{(1 - \kappa)a(z)},$$

are produced in Home. Similarly, Foreign produces goods such that $w^*a^*(z) < wa(z)/(1 - \kappa)$. Foreign therefore produces when

$$\frac{w}{w^*} > (1 - \kappa)A(z) = (1 - \kappa)\frac{a^*(z)}{a(z)}.$$

Figure 4.11 depicts the pattern of international specialization for a given international wage ratio w/w^* and a given proportional international transport cost κ. Home produces all z to the left of the cutoff z^H, which is defined by

$$\frac{w}{w^*} = \frac{A(z^H)}{1 - \kappa}.$$

To be definitive, we assume, arbitrarily, that Home does not produce good z^H. Similarly, Foreign produces all z to the right of z^F, which is defined by

$$\frac{w}{w^*} = (1 - \kappa)A(z^F),$$

but we assume Foreign does not produce good z^F. Goods $z \in [0, z^F]$ are produced exclusively in Home and exported, since Home's inherent cost advantage in these products is high enough to outweigh the transport costs. At the same time, Foreign's cost advantage in goods $z \in [z^H, 1]$ is so great that those goods are produced exclusively there and exported.

Goods $z \in (z^F, z^H)$ are produced in *both* countries—something that could not occur without positive transport costs—and do *not* enter international trade. Why? If $z \in (z^F, z^H)$, then, as Figure 4.11 shows,

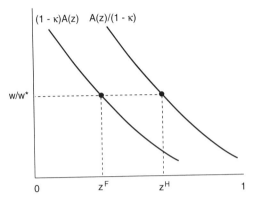

Figure 4.11
Specialization with transport costs

$$wa(z) < \frac{w^*a^*(z)}{1 - \kappa},$$

but

$$w^*a^*(z) < \frac{wa(z)}{1 - \kappa},$$

meaning that each country can obtain the good more cheaply through domestic production than through importation.

Since the goods in (z^F, z^H) are nontraded, they may have distinct prices $p(z) = wa(z)$ and $p^*(z) = w^*a^*(z)$ in Home and in Foreign. But traded goods—those in $[0, z^F] \cup [z^H, 1]$—are no longer subject to the law of one price either. The price of a traded good must be κ percent higher in the importing than in the exporting country. An implication of these cross-border price differentials, of course, is that each country will have its own consumer price index in terms of the numeraire, which we can take to be units of good 1 delivered in Foreign. Formula (39) implies that the Home and Foreign price levels now are given, respectively, by

$$P = \exp\left\{\int_0^{z^H} \log\left[wa(z)\right] dz + \int_{z^H}^1 \log\left[\frac{w^*a^*(z)}{1 - \kappa}\right] dz\right\},$$

$$(60)$$

$$P^* = \exp\left\{\int_0^{z^F} \log\left[\frac{wa(z)}{1 - \kappa}\right] dz + \int_{z^F}^1 \log\left[w^*a^*(z)\right] dz\right\}.$$

From these expressions follows the real exchange rate,

$$\frac{P}{P^*} = \exp\left\{\int_{z^F}^{z^H} \log\left[\frac{wa(z)}{w^*a^*(z)}\right]dz + \left[z^F - \left(1 - z^H\right)\right]\log(1 - \kappa)\right\}.$$

This ratio depends on the ratio of nontraded goods' prices in the two countries. But in the present model P/P^* is not a function simply of the ratio of Home to Foreign prices for nontraded goods. More subtly, the real exchange rate also depends on the international specialization pattern. If z^F rises, say, the range of goods Foreign must import from Home expands (other things being the same). Because the prices of these goods include transport costs, Foreign's consumer price index rises relative to Home's [recall that $\log(1 - \kappa) < 0$].

4.5.5.2   Joint Determination of Relative Wages and International Specialization

We now develop a diagram to illustrate the joint determination of z^F, z^H, and w/w^*. For that purpose, we need, as earlier, to analyze the linkage between world spending patterns and international relative wages. The global equality of income and consumption spending corresponding to eq. (42) is[38]

$$PC + P^*C^* = wL + w^*L^*. \tag{61}$$

Moreover, the equilibrium supply of Home output, equal to wL, must balance the equilibrium global demand for it:

$$wL = z^H PC + z^F P^*C^*$$

$$= z^H PC + z^F \left(wL + w^*L^* - PC\right). \tag{62}$$

To simplify this expression, recall that Home's *trade balance* TB is the excess of output over spending:

$$TB = wL - PC. \tag{63}$$

[Observe that TB, equal to the current account less the interest earnings on Home's claims on Foreign, is the net transfer of currently available resources to Foreign from Home, or the excess of output exports over imports. Clearly, eq. (61) implies $TB = -TB^*$.] Using eq. (63) to eliminate PC from the second line of eq. (62) yields the present model's analog of eq. (43):

---

38. Because some portion of a traded good dissipates in transit, it is no longer the case that world consumption equals world output. The price indexes P and P^* in eq. (60), however, explicitly account for transport costs by recognizing that people must pay CIF (cost, insurance, and freight) prices for imports, not FOB (free on board) prices. Equation (61) below therefore states that world output equals world consumption spending inclusive of spending on transport costs. Equations (62) and (63) have similar interpretations.

$$\frac{w}{w^*} = \left\{ \frac{-\left(z^H - z^F\right)TB}{\left[L^*/a^*(1)\right]} + z^F \right\} \frac{L^*/L}{(1 - z^H)}, \tag{64}$$

where we have used the fact that, since the numeraire is good 1 delivered in Foreign, $w^* = p^*(1)/a^*(1) = 1/a^*(1)$.[39]

So far our analysis is very similar to that in section 4.5.2. The main complication is that, instead of simply determining w/w^* and the single cutoff commodity $\tilde{z}$, there are now two separate cutoffs, z^H and z^F, to be determined. We simplify our problem by observing that we can write one of these, z^H, say, as a function of the other. Notice from Figure 4.11 that, whatever the wage ratio, z^F and z^H must satisfy the relationship[40]

$$(1 - \kappa)A(z^F) = A(z^H)/(1 - \kappa).$$

Because the $A(z)$ function is strictly decreasing over $[0, 1]$, it has an inverse, denoted $A^{-1}(z)$. The preceding equation can be solved for z^H in terms of that inverse: $z^H = A^{-1}\left[(1 - \kappa)^2 A\left(z^F\right)\right]$. Purely to cut down on notation, we now assume a specific functional form for $A(z)$,

$$A(z) = \exp(1 - 2z),$$

which corresponds, for example, to the assumptions $a(z) = \exp(z)$ and $a^*(z) = \exp(1 - z)$. Under the functional form above, z^H and z^F are related by the equation $(1 - \kappa)\exp(1 - 2z^F) = \left[\exp(1 - 2z^H)\right]/(1 - \kappa)$, or, taking natural logs,

$$z^H = z^F - \log(1 - \kappa). \tag{65}$$

This last equation lets us write eq. (64) in terms of z^F alone:

$$\frac{w}{w^*} = \left\{ \frac{\log(1 - \kappa)TB}{\left[L^*/a^*(1)\right]} + z^F \right\} \frac{L^*/L}{\left[1 + \log(1 - \kappa) - z^F\right]}. \tag{66}$$

We write this last schedule, viewed as a function of z, as $w/w^* = \tilde{B}(z)$. To summarize, $\tilde{B}(z)$ shows the market-clearing international wage ratio given any z^F, taking account of the implied value of z^H.

Figure 4.12 (the analog of Figure 4.9) shows the determination of z^F, z^H, and w/w^*, given $TB = 0$. The intersection of the schedule $(1 - \kappa)A(z)$ with $\tilde{B}(z)$ determines z^F and w/w^*. From the schedule $A(z)/(1 - \kappa)$ we then read off z^H.[41]

---

39. Of course, eq. (64) reduces to eq. (43) when there are no transport costs and, therefore, $z^H = z^F$.

40. Recall how this condition follows from the two conditions $wa(z^H) = w^*a^*(z^H)/(1 - \kappa)$, which equates the domestic production cost of Home's cutoff good to the cost of importing that good from Foreign, and the corresponding condition for Foreign's cutoff good, $w^*a^*(z^F) = wa(z^F)/(1 - \kappa)$.

41. We have drawn $\tilde{B}(z)$ as positively sloped. You can verify from eq. (66) that this is correct. Of course, we assume κ is small enough that there actually is some trade.

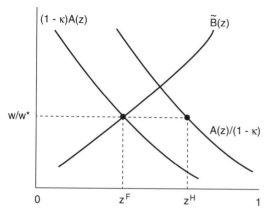

Relative Home wage,
relative Foreign cost

$(1 - \kappa)A(z)$ $\tilde{B}(z)$

w/w*

$A(z)/(1 - \kappa)$

0   z^F z^H 1

Figure 4.12
Endogenous determination of nontradability

4.5.5.3   Permanent Shocks and Relative Prices

Figure 4.12 allows straightforward extension of the exercises carried out in the case of zero transport costs. One major difference between the present case and the earlier one, however, is that demand conditions now affect international wages and the pattern of global specialization through the trade balance term in eq. (66), which shifts the $\tilde{B}(z)$ schedule. Permanent changes of the sort we discuss next, however, do not alter a stock of net foreign claims that initially is zero or create a current-account imbalance. They accordingly leave the trade balance unchanged. The term TB in eq. (66) therefore can be held fixed at $TB = 0$. In this special case $\tilde{B}(z)$ reduces to

$$\frac{z^F}{1 - z^H}\left(\frac{L^*}{L}\right)$$

and thus is simply a steeper leftward-shifted version of the function $B\left(z; L^*/L\right)$ introduced in eq. (43).

Consider first a rise in the relative Foreign labor supply, illustrated in Figure 4.13. The function $\tilde{B}(z)$ shifts inward, leading to a rise in Home's relative wage, a reduction in the range of goods produced in Home, and an expansion in the range produced in Foreign. The fall in Foreign's relative wage allows it to export some goods, those in $[z^{H\prime}, z^H)$, that previously were nontraded. For the same reason, some goods previously exported by Home, those in $(z^{F\prime}, z^F]$, become

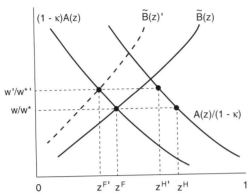

Figure 4.13
A rise in relative Foreign labor supply

nontraded. Home benefits at Foreign's expense from the resulting change in the terms of trade, just as in the case of zero transports costs.[42]

Furthermore, Home's real exchange rate, P/P^*, rises. To see why, we refer to eq. (60) and argue that for every $z \in [0, 1]$, $p(z)'/p^*(z)' \geq p(z)/p^*(z)$. Figure 4.13 shows that $[0, 1]$ is made up of four disjoint categories:

1. For goods that were and remain nontraded, those in $(z^F, z^{H'})$, the rise in w/w^* obviously implies a rise in the Home price relative to that in Foreign.

2. Goods in $(z^{F'}, z^F]$ are newly nontraded goods that Home previously exported to Foreign. For these goods, the new Home-Foreign price ratio exceeds its prior value $1 - \kappa$ because

$$\frac{w'a(z)}{1 - \kappa} > w^{*'}a^*(z).$$

3. Goods in $[z^{H'}, z^H)$ are formerly nontraded goods that Foreign now exports to Home. Because these goods satisfied

$$wa(z) < \frac{w^*a^*(z)}{1 - \kappa}$$

before the change, the new Home-Foreign price ratio, $1/(1 - \kappa)$, also exceeds its prior level.

---

42. This is left as an exercise, which you should not attempt until completing exercise 7 at the end of this chapter.

4. Finally, goods in $[0, z^{F'}] \cup [z^H, 1]$ were and remain traded. These goods continue at the same international price ratio, which is determined entirely by transport costs.

What is the effect of a proportional fall in Foreign's unit labor requirements for all goods? You can verify that, as in the $\kappa = 0$ case, Home's wage falls relative to Foreign's, but its real wage and terms of trade rise. Home's terms-of-trade increase allows it to pay for the wider range of exports Foreign now produces despite the shift of more of the Home labor force into nontraded goods. Finally, P^* rises relative to P, so that Foreign's relative productivity gain leads to a rise in its real exchange rate.

4.5.5.4   The Classical Transfer Problem

The Versailles Treaty that ended World War I required Germany to make large reparations payments to the victors. In the late 1920s, John Maynard Keynes and Bertil Ohlin carried on a famous debate over the effects of such payments on the terms of trade.[43] Keynes argued that the paying country would suffer a deterioration in its terms of trade that would aggravate the primary harm of making a foreign tribute. Ohlin took a different view, pointing out that the payer's terms of trade would not need to deteriorate if the recipient spent the transfer on the payer's goods. Ohlin's case seems to be borne out by the model of section 4.5.2, in which international wages and the production pattern are determined independently of national consumption levels. In that model, a pure redistribution of income between countries has no effects.

The model with transport costs, however, does incorporate a transfer effect of the sort Keynes predicted: it enters through the term TB in eq. (66). A positive Home trade balance, for example, implies that Home's production exceeds its consumption in value, so that Home is making a transfer of resources to Foreign. Suppose that TB rises from an initial value of zero. In Figure 4.12, the effect is to lower the $\tilde{B}(z)$ schedule, lowering Home's relative wage and increasing the range of goods Home produces for export. Accompanying this change is a fall in Home's real wage, a fall in its real exchange rate, and, as Keynes asserted, a fall in its terms of trade.

What explains the Keynesian transfer effect here? Foreign spends part of any transfer from Home on its own nontraded goods, and this additional demand draws labor out of Foreign's export sector, whose output contracts. The relative scarcity of Foreign exports raises their price compared with Home exports, and, by implication, raises the relative Foreign wage. The wage change turns some of Home's initial nontraded goods into exports and some of Foreign's initial exports

---

43. See Keynes (1929) and Ohlin (1929).

Box 4.2
The Transfer Effect for Industrial Countries

For industrial countries, the Keynesian transfer effect receives confirmation from the cross-sectional relation between changes in countries' net external assets and changes in their real exchange rates and terms of trade vis-à-vis trading partners. Figure 4.14 shows the positive association between the 1981–90 change in net foreign assets (measured as a percent of GDP) and the change in a trade-weighted real exchange rate measure based on wholesale price indexes, which contain fewer nontradables than CPIs. Changes are calculated as 1986–90 averages less 1981–85 averages.

   Least squares regression yields a significantly positive slope estimate, the magnitude of which suggests that a 1 percent of GDP rise in net foreign wealth is associated with a 1 percent real appreciation. The precise structural mechanism generating the statistical association between these two endogenous variables is, however, uncertain. Our Ricardian model with transport costs suggests one, but others are possible.*

* For alternative models, see Buiter (1989) and Obstfeld and Rogoff (1995b).

into nontradables. Box 4.2 provides some evidence consistent with this transfer effect.

4.5.6 Temporary Productivity Shocks and the Current Account

The model with transport costs provides a richer setting in which to investigate temporary shocks, such as the temporary foreign productivity rise we thought about earlier. Such shocks not only have current account effects, but those effects now *permanently* alter the terms of trade, the relative prices of traded and nontraded goods, and the international location of industries.[44] As in section 4.5.4.2, we illustrate the model's dynamics by considering an unexpected temporary (one-period) Foreign productivity increase, modeled once again as a uniform fall in $a^*(z)$ to $a^*(z)/v$, $v > 1$, lasting one period only.

   While conceptually straightforward, a complete algebraic analysis of the model is lengthy, and therefore we provide only a verbal description of what happens. Home runs a current account deficit (and Foreign runs a surplus) while Foreign's productivity is temporarily high. Thus, $d\bar{B} < 0$. Even though Home experiences a transitory increase in its terms of trade, a fall in the world interest rate induces it to raise first-period consumption beyond the first-period increase in its real income. Foreign also raises its consumption, but initially does so by less than its short-run income increase. Home experiences a short-run real appreciation, and Foreign, a

---

44. As usual, effects that are permanent in the present model might erode over time in models with alternative demographic structures.

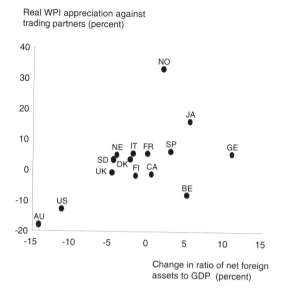

Figure 4.14
Net foreign assets and the terms of trade, 1981–90

real depreciation, as the relative prices of nontraded goods are bid up in Home and fall in Foreign.

The other factor contributing to Home's real appreciation is a short-run shift in the international production pattern. Home's relative wage does not fall in proportion to its greater productivity disadvantage, so its traded-goods sector contracts (z^H falls) while Foreign's expands (z^F falls). Perhaps surprisingly, these effects are *reversed* in the long run. In the steady state Home is making a transfer of $-\bar{r}d\bar{B} > 0$ to Foreign and productivity has returned to initial levels, so Home's relative wage is lower than before the shock. In terms of Figure 4.12, the $\tilde{B}(z)$ curve has shifted outward along unchanged $A(z)$ curves. The reduction in Home's relative wage allows it to run a wider range of industries in the long run.

This expansion of the traded-goods sector is no cause for joy, however. Home's greater competitiveness comes from the lower real wages at which its labor force works. Starting from the new long-run position, Home is worse off because of the primary and secondary effects of the transfer it must make to Foreign. It can be shown, however, that Home's first-period gain outweighs its subsequent losses. In a present-value sense Home benefits from Foreign's temporarily high productivity. So, of course, does Foreign. As we noted in discussing the similar welfare effects of productivity changes when there are no transport costs, the proposition that all countries gain from a productivity increase anywhere in the world need not always be true.

Appendix 4A   Endogenous Labor Supply, Revisited

In section 2.5.3, we introduced a period utility function of the form $u(C, \bar{L} - L)$, where C was consumption of the single available good, $\bar{L}$ the individual's time endowment, L his labor supply, and $\bar{L} - L$, therefore, leisure. The results of that section can be readily understood and extended now, because leisure is an example of a nontraded good. Our previous results go through with $C = C_T$, $\bar{L} - L = C_N$, and w, the wage in terms of tradables, interpreted as p. In section 2.5.3 we implicitly assumed a CES-isoelastic period utility function such that $\theta = 1$, but now we are less restrictive. For an arbitrary $\theta > 0$, Euler equation (34) governs the behavior of consumption, with P given by

$$P = \left[\gamma + (1 - \gamma)w^{1-\theta}\right]^{\frac{1}{1-\theta}}.$$

The number of hours in a day, $\bar{L}$, cannot change, but several other factors, notably shifts in productivity, can change the wage and the consumption-based real interest rate. Accordingly, the current account will not be determined the same way as in a model with no leisure, except in special cases.

This is apparent from the consumption function, which we derive by working backward from eq. (35). (We retain T subscripts on consumptions and outputs to avoid confusion, even though all consumption goods are now tradable.) Reasoning similar to that used in eq. (30) lets us rewrite eq. (35) (under perfect foresight) as

$$C_{T,t} = \frac{(1+r)Q_t + \sum_{s=t}^{\infty} \left(\frac{1}{1+r}\right)^{s-t} (w_s L_s - G_{T,s})}{\sum_{s=t}^{\infty} \left[(1+r)^{\sigma-1}\beta^\sigma\right]^{s-t} \left(\frac{P_t}{P_s}\right)^{\sigma-\theta}}.$$

This form is somewhat inconvenient as an analytical tool, however, because labor supply L_s is now an *endogenous* variable. To get around this inconvenience, we note that $L_s = \bar{L} - (\bar{L} - L_s)$, and, using the implication of eq. (22) that

$$\bar{L} - L_s = C_{T,s} \left(\frac{1-\gamma}{\gamma}\right) w_s^{-\theta},$$

we transform the last version of the consumption function into

$$C_{T,t} = \frac{(1+r)Q_t + \sum_{s=t}^{\infty} \left(\frac{1}{1+r}\right)^{s-t} \left[w_s\bar{L} - \left(\frac{P_s^{1-\theta}}{\gamma} - 1\right)C_{T,s} - G_{T,s}\right]}{\sum_{s=t}^{\infty} \left[(1+r)^{\sigma-1}\beta^\sigma\right]^{s-t} \left(\frac{P_t}{P_s}\right)^{\sigma-\theta}}.$$

In deriving this equation we have manipulated the price index to write $w^{1-\theta} = (P^{1-\theta} - \gamma)/(1 - \gamma)$. Now use Euler equation (34) to write the future consumption levels $C_{T,s}$ on the right-hand side of the preceding equation in terms of the date t value $C_{T,t}$. Simplification yields

$$0 = (1+r)Q_t + \sum_{s=t}^{\infty} \left(\frac{1}{1+r}\right)^{s-t} (w_s\bar{L} - G_{T,s})$$

$$- \sum_{s=t}^{\infty} \left(\frac{P_s^{1-\theta}}{\gamma}\right) \left[(1+r)^{\sigma-1}\beta^\sigma\right]^{s-t} \left(\frac{P_t}{P_s}\right)^{\sigma-\theta} C_{T,t}.$$

Observe that we can rewrite the summation that multiplies $C_{\mathrm{T},t}$ as

$$
\sum_{s=t}^{\infty} \left(\frac{P_t^{1-\theta}}{\gamma} \right) \left[(1+r)^{\sigma-1} \beta^{\sigma} \right]^{s-t} \left(\frac{P_s}{P_t} \right)^{1-\theta} \left(\frac{P_t}{P_s} \right)^{\sigma-\theta}
$$

$$
= \left(\frac{P_t^{1-\theta}}{\gamma} \right) \sum_{s=t}^{\infty} \left[(1+r)^{s-t} \left(\frac{P_t}{P_s} \right) \right]^{\sigma-1} \beta^{\sigma(s-t)}.
$$

Solving for $C_{\mathrm{T},t}$ therefore gives

$$
C_{\mathrm{T},t} = \gamma \left(\frac{1}{P_t} \right)^{-\theta} \left\{ \frac{(1+r)Q_t + \sum_{s=t}^{\infty} \left(\frac{1}{1+r} \right)^{s-t} \left[w_s \bar{L} - G_{\mathrm{T},s} \right]}{P_t \sum_{s=t}^{\infty} \left[(1+r)^{s-t} \left(\frac{P_t}{P_s} \right) \right]^{\sigma-1} \beta^{\sigma(s-t)}} \right\} = \gamma \left(\frac{1}{P_t} \right)^{-\theta} C_t, \quad (67)
$$

where $C_t = \Omega(C_{\mathrm{T},t}, \bar{L} - L_t)$ is the CES consumption index given in eq. (13). The second equality in eq. (67) follows from reinterpreting the exogenous labor endowment variables in eq. (29) as being equal to $\bar{L}$. It is the same as eq. (22).

To complete the picture of equilibrium, we recall how wages are determined. Let output (all of which is tradable here) be given by the production function $Y_{\mathrm{T}} = Af(k)L$. Then w depends on r and A through the factor-price frontier (6): $w = w(r, A)$. Equilibrium consumption therefore is

$$
C_{\mathrm{T},t} = \gamma \left\{ \frac{1}{P[w(r, A_t)]} \right\}^{1-\theta} \left[\frac{(1+r)Q_t + \sum_{s=t}^{\infty} \left(\frac{1}{1+r} \right)^{s-t} \left[w(r, A_s) \bar{L} - G_{\mathrm{T},s} \right]}{\sum_{s=t}^{\infty} \left\{ (1+r)^{s-t} \frac{P[w(r, A_t)]}{P[w(r, A_s)]} \right\}^{\sigma-1} \beta^{\sigma(s-t)}} \right], \quad (68)
$$

where the price index P has been written in a way that exhibits its dependence on the current wage. The associated optimal demand for leisure is just $\bar{L} - L_t = \left[(1-\gamma) C_{\mathrm{T},t}/\gamma \right] w(r, A_t)^{-\theta}$. International capital flows ensure that, given the wage, this demand for leisure plus the demand for labor by firms equals $\bar{L}$.

To see some implications of the model, assume consumers come to expect a future rise in the productivity parameter A, an event that will raise the wage w and, with it, the price level P. Even though the current wage and price level are unchanged, the anticipated wage changes represented in the numerator of eq. (68) work to raise current consumption as well as leisure. If $\sigma > 1$, the foregoing positive effects on consumption and leisure are reinforced by long-term real interest rates that are below r. But if $\sigma < 1$, the real interest rate changes dampen the rises in consumption and leisure.

The current-account effects of the anticipated productivity rise mirror these consumption and leisure effects. The higher is σ, the greater is the fall in the current account. This happens for two reasons: the consumption increase is greater, and since the increase in leisure also is greater, output falls more. See Bean (1986) for discussion of terms-of-trade shocks.

Macroeconomic theories seeking to explain business-cycle fluctuations in terms of market-clearing models rely heavily on the effect of wage movements on leisure. Consider a variant of the problem we've just analyzed, an unanticipated temporary fall in the productivity parameter A, which temporarily depresses the wage. The effect on leisure is ambiguous: the income effect of lower lifetime wealth calls for less leisure, the substitution effect of a lower current wage, for more. If $\sigma > 1$, however, the real interest rate effect of the expected future rise in w (and hence in P) pulls in the direction of *more* leisure.

The *intertemporal-substitution theory of employment fluctuations* holds that these mechanisms can rationalize observed business-cycle fluctuations in employment. In theory, a transitory negative productivity shock, even if it leads to a wage decline as small as those typically observed, could elicit a large negative labor-supply response through its effect on the consumption-based real interest rate. Some (though by no means all) economists believe, however, that actual intertemporal substitution elasticities are too low (somewhere below $\sigma = 0.5$) to make this story plausible.[45] Furthermore, an important role for real interest rates makes it harder to explain the negative correlation between leisure and consumption that we see in the data.

Appendix 4B   Costly Capital Mobility and Short-Run Relative Price Adjustment

The chapter has so far assumed that capital can move without cost both across national borders and within different sectors of an economy. This assumption is patently unrealistic: while it may apply in the long run, it obscures the short-run response of relative prices to demand and productivity shocks, as well as the concurrent transitional consumption effects. To give an idea of the effects of costly capital mobility, this appendix develops a simple model with costly capital installation, along the lines of the q model introduced in Chapter 2. The resulting short-run "stickiness" in capital gives demand-side factors a prominent and persistent role in determining the relative price of tradables.[46] This role is in sharp contrast to our analysis in section 4.2.1, where demand factors did not affect p.

4B.1   Assumptions of the Model

The model assumes that there is a speed-of-adjustment differential between the sectors producing traded and nontraded goods. The traded-goods sector can adjust its entire capital stock in a single period, as in the chapter, whereas the nontraded-goods sector faces increasing marginal costs of capital installation, as in the q model. Thus the representative producer of nontradables maximizes

$$\sum_{s=t}^{\infty} \left(\frac{1}{1+r} \right)^{s-t} \left[p_s A_{N,s} K_{N,s}^{\alpha} L_{N,s}^{1-\alpha} - \frac{\chi}{2} \left(I_{N,s}^2 / K_{N,s} \right) - w_s L_{N,s} - I_{N,s} \right],$$

given $K_{N,t}$, subject to $I_{N,s} = \Delta K_{N,s+1}$, where the notation is as in section 2.5.2 except that we assume a specific Cobb-Douglas form for the production function. The "short run" we will refer to considers the variable $K_{N,t}$ as predetermined. We are assuming that the installation costs $\frac{\chi}{2} \left(I_{N,s}^2 / K_{N,s} \right)$ are "paid" in terms of tradables and do not reduce net output

---

45. For a review of micro-data estimates of intertemporal substitution elasticities relating to labor supply, see Heckman (1993). It is hard in any case to detect any definite cyclical pattern in aggregate measures of United States real wages, except perhaps after 1970 (see Abraham and Haltiwanger, 1995). Ostry and Reinhart (1992) present aggregate Euler equation estimates of σ for developing countries in the range of $\sigma = 0.4$ to 0.8.

46. Alternative models with nontradables and costly investment are studied by McKenzie (1982), P. Brock (1988), and Gavin (1990).

of nontradables. This assumption is irrelevant at the level of the firm, but it does affect the way we specify the economy's equilibrium.

Our assumption on differential adjustment speeds reflects the idea that the outward-oriented tradables sector is relatively flexible and dynamic. Otherwise, the production side of the model is exactly as in section 4.2.1. In particular, labor can migrate instantaneously between sectors, ensuring a unique economy-wide wage.

Letting q denote the shadow price of installed capital in nontradables, we record the first-order conditions for profit maximization by firms as

$$L_{N,s} = \left[\frac{(1-\alpha)p_s A_{N,s}}{w_s} \right]^{1/\alpha} K_{N,s}, \tag{69}$$

$$K_{N,s+1} - K_{N,s} = \frac{q_s - 1}{\chi} K_{N,s}, \tag{70}$$

$$q_{s+1} - q_s = rq_s - p_{s+1} A_{N,s}\alpha \left(\frac{L_{N,s+1}}{K_{N,s+1}} \right)^{1-\alpha} - \frac{1}{2\chi}(q_{s+1} - 1)^2. \tag{71}$$

The first of these equations results from equating the marginal value product of labor to the wage, and the second and third are derived exactly as in Chapter 2, eqs. (63) and (64). As in this chapter's body, the wage is given by the factor-price frontier for tradables [eq. (6)], with costless capital mobility in that sector ensuring a cleared national labor market at the technologically determined wage.

Now we make some simplifying assumptions on demand. The period utility function has constant, unitary elasticities of inter- and intratemporal substitution ($\sigma = \theta = 1$). Further, $\beta(1+r) = 1$. Accordingly, equilibrium consumption of tradables is constant along perfect-foresight paths, and is given by eq. (35), modified to reflect the deadweight cost of installing capital in the nontraded sector:

$$C_{T,t} = \bar{C}_T$$

$$= \frac{r}{1+r} \left\{ (1+r)B_t + \sum_{s=t}^{\infty} \left(\frac{1}{1+r} \right)^{s-t} \left[Y_{T,s} - I_s - G_{T,s} - \frac{\chi}{2}\left(I_{N,s}^2/K_{N,s} \right) \right] \right\}. \tag{72}$$

4B.2   Short-Run Equilibrium

Equilibrium in the nontradables market holds when

$$C_N + G_N = Y_N = A_N K_N^\alpha L_N^{1-\alpha}$$

(we omit time subscripts until they are needed again). Assume that each period the government fixes its expenditure of tradables on nontraded goods at $\tilde{G}_N = pG_N$. Because eq. (22) implies that $C_N = (1-\gamma)\bar{C}_T/\gamma p$, the equilibrium condition for nontradeds becomes

$$\frac{(1-\gamma)\bar{C}_T}{\gamma p} + \frac{\tilde{G}_N}{p} = A_N K_N^\alpha L_N^{1-\alpha}.$$

Putting this together with eq. (69), we find short-run equilibrium values of p and L_N:

$$p = \frac{w^{1-\alpha}\left[(1-\gamma)\bar{C}_T/\gamma + \tilde{G}_N \right]^\alpha}{(1-\alpha)^{1-\alpha}A_N K_N^\alpha}, \tag{73}$$

$$L_N = \frac{(1-\alpha)\left[(1-\gamma)\bar{C}_T/\gamma + \tilde{G}_N\right]}{w}. \tag{74}$$

Notice that when K_N is given in the short run, eq. (73) makes p a function of the demand variable $\left[(1-\gamma)\bar{C}_T/\gamma + \tilde{G}_N\right]$, in contrast to the long-run result of section 4.2.1.

As you can verify, however, eq. (74), even though valid in the short run, is the same as in a model without investment costs. Indeed, L_N does not depend on K_N at all! If K_N rises by n percent, other things being the same, output of nontradables rises by αn percent, and their price therefore falls by αn percent to generate a market-clearing αn percent rise in demand. So the nontradables market is restored to equilibrium with no reallocation of labor between sectors. This remarkable result, which is not in the least general, comes from our assumption of unitary intratemporal substitution elasticities in production and consumption. Despite its knife-edge nature, we can use this special case to shed light on the price dynamics that result when K_N adjusts only gradually to its long-run position.

4B.3   Equilibrium Dynamics and Long-Run Equilibrium

The easiest case to consider is one in which the productivity parameters A_T and A_N (as well as the world interest rate) are expected to remain constant in the future, so that the wage w and labor input L_N also are constant along a perfect-foresight path. As in Chapter 2, we can develop a two-equation phase diagram in q and K_N depicting the economy's dynamics. Equation (70) provides one equation. The other comes from substituting eqs. (73), (74), and (70) into eq. (71) to obtain

$$q_{t+1} - q_t = rq_t - \frac{\alpha\left[(1-\gamma)\bar{C}_T/\gamma + \tilde{G}_N\right]}{K_{N,t}\left[1 + (q_t - 1)/\chi\right]} - \frac{1}{2\chi}(q_{t+1} - 1)^2. \tag{75}$$

The stationary position of the system of eqs. (75) and (70) is denoted by

$$\bar{q} = 1, \qquad \bar{K}_N = \frac{\alpha\left[(1-\gamma)\bar{C}_T/\gamma + \tilde{G}_N\right]}{r}.$$

Notice that $\bar{K}_N/L_N = \alpha w/(1-\alpha)r$, which implies that in the long run, the marginal value product of capital in the nontraded sector is restored to r.

As in section 2.5.2, it is simplest to analyze the dynamics of eqs. (75) and (70) by linearizing those equations around the steady state $\bar{q} = 1$, $\bar{K}_N$. The approximate linear system is

$$K_{N,t+1} - K_{N,t} = \frac{\bar{K}_N}{\chi}(q_t - 1),$$

$$q_{t+1} - q_t = \left\{ r + \frac{\alpha\left[(1-\gamma)\bar{C}_T/\gamma + \tilde{G}_N\right]}{\chi \bar{K}_N} \right\}(q_t - 1)$$

$$+ \frac{\alpha\left[(1-\gamma)\bar{C}_T/\gamma + \tilde{G}_N\right]}{\bar{K}_N^2}(K_{N,t} - \bar{K}_N).$$

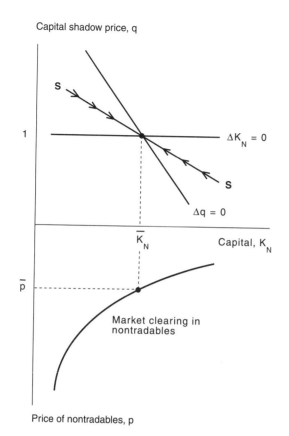

Figure 4.15
Nontradables and gradual capital adjustment

The dynamics of this system are of the usual saddle-point variety, as illustrated in the upper panel of Figure 4.15, where **SS** is the unique convergent path. The lower panel is drawn so that the relative price of nontradables, p, rises as one moves downward along the vertical axis. Graphed there is the short-run equilibrium condition (73), which shows how p depends on K_N for given values of w, A_N, $\bar{C}_T$, and $\tilde{G}_N$. Since these four variables are constant during the transition process (if no unforeseen shocks occur), eq. (73) shows how p will fall as K_N rises over time and shifts the economy's supply curve for nontradables to the right.

4B.4   Shocks to Government Spending and Productivity

We now have a framework allowing us to analyze in detail the dynamic impact of demand factors. Consider what happens on date t, for example, when the government unexpectedly and permanently increases $\tilde{G}_N$, the total amount of tradable goods budgeted for public spending on nontradables. Equation (72) can be used to show that a fall in $\bar{C}_T$ to a permanently lower level results from the rise in $\tilde{G}_N$. The reasoning is as follows. There is an immediate shift of labor into nontradables production and, after a period, a further labor outflow from tradables to balance the reduction ΔK_T in the tradable sector's capital at the end of period t. The capital thus released flows abroad to maintain at r the domestic marginal product of capital in tradables. The intersectoral allocation of the labor force remains steady absent further surprises [recall eq. (74)], so neither K_T nor Y_T changes again after the initial period of the public spending shift. But the increase in demand for nontradables sets off a period of costly investment in that sector. Let ΔL_T denote the total (negative) change in tradables employment between dates $t - 1$ and $t + 1$ that occurs in response to the initial shock. Adding up all of the relevant effects shows that the date t present value of net tradables output falls by the positive amount:

$$(Y_{T,t} \text{ loss}) - \sum_{s=t+1}^{\infty} \left(\frac{1}{1+r}\right)^{s-t} w \Delta L_T + (\text{present value of } I_N, \text{ including installation losses}).$$

As a result, $\bar{C}_T$ also falls.

Notice that the sum $(1 - \gamma)\bar{C}_T/\gamma + \tilde{G}_N$, which equals total spending on nontradables measured in units of tradables, necessarily rises; otherwise, the factors causing $\bar{C}_T$ to fall in the first place would be reversed. Equation (73) therefore shows that p rises for every value of K_N, making the locus in the lower panel of Figure 4.15 shift toward the bottom of the page. In the upper panel of Figure 4.15, the $\Delta q = 0$ schedule and SS both shift to the right because of the rise in the steady-state capital stock in nontradables, $\bar{K}_N$. Thus, p and q both rise in the short run as investment in nontradables commences. Over time, q falls back toward 1 and p falls toward the long-run value described in section 4.2.1. We know p cannot remain above that level permanently because the investment process relentlessly drives the marginal value product of K_N toward r.

In contrast to the effect of an increase in $\tilde{G}_N$, an increase in G_T, which also lowers $\bar{C}_T$, causes a short-run fall in p and starts a process of gradual disinvestment in the nontraded sector.

Like demand shocks, other shocks to the economy can set off protracted adjustment periods, but need not. For example, an unexpected permanent rise in nontradables productivity, A_N, causes a proportional fall in p, see eq. (73), but has no further effects given our assumptions on tastes and technology.

A rise in tradables productivity, A_T, has quite different effects. The wage w rises as does $\bar{C}_T$ and, with it, the demand for nontradables. In the short run labor leaves the nontraded sector (why?), but K_N rises over time as production there shifts toward a long-run production technique that economizes on labor. The rise in w means that p is higher in the long run. It is higher in the short run, too. Indeed, because supply initially falls as demand rises, the price of nontradables overshoots in the short run, rising more than in the long run. Countries that liberalize their foreign trade, thereby raising traded-sector productivity, often experience sharp increases both in real wages and in the relative price of nontradables. The model of this appendix provides one explanation for that phenomenon.

Exercises

1. *Labor-saving technical change and the manufacturing sector.* In eq. (1) we assumed that productivity growth is "Hicks-neutral," raising the marginal products of capital and labor in the same proportion. If the constant-returns production function in tradables now takes the form

    $$Y_T = F(K_T, E_T L_T),$$

so that technological progress $\hat{E}_T$ is labor-saving, how does this assumption affect the result of section 4.3.2? (Assume the production function in nontradables is the same as in that section.) Does it become more likely that faster productivity growth in tradables causes a labor exodus from that sector?

2.   *The world interest rate and long-run resource allocation.* In the long-run GDP-GNP diagram of section 4.3, explain the effects of a rise in the world interest rate r.

3.   *The current account in terms of real consumption.* Retrace the steps that led to eq. (27), using eq. (30) instead of eq. (24) (these last two budget constraints are equivalent under perfect foresight). You will obtain another version of eq. (27),

$$\sum_{s=t}^{\infty} R_{t,s}^C C_s = \frac{(1+r_t^c)B_t}{P_{t-1}} + \sum_{s=t}^{\infty} R_{t,s}^C \frac{Y_{T,s} + pY_{N,s} - I_s - G_s}{P_s}.$$

Deduce from this an alternative rendition of eq. (28) that parallels eq. (25) of Chapter 2:

$$C_t = \frac{\frac{(1+r_t^c)B_t}{P_{t-1}} + \sum_{s=t}^{\infty} R_{t,s}^C \frac{Y_{T,s} + pY_{N,s} - I_s - G_s}{P_s}}{\sum_{s=t}^{\infty} \beta^{\sigma(s-t)} \left(R_{t,s}^C\right)^{1-\sigma}}.$$

Finally, compute the change in B_t/P_t, the stock of foreign assets measured in real consumption units. Show that this change is given by an equation exactly parallel to eq. (26) in section 2.2.2.

4.   *The supply of nontradables and the current account.* Consider an economy in which consumer choice is as in section 4.4, $\beta(1+r) = 1$, and the outputs of tradables and nontradables are exogenous endowments.

(a) Show that if the net endowment $Y_N - G_N$ of nontradables is constant, consumption of tradables is constant too. What is the constant consumption level for tradables, and how does it compare to that predicted by eq. (10) of Chapter 2?

(b) Suppose that the economy is in a steady state with a zero current account balance when its suddenly becomes known that the constant nontradable supply $Y_N - G_N$ will rise permanently to $Y_N' - G_N'$ in T periods. Describe the responses of consumption and the current account, and explain how they depend on the sign of $\sigma - \theta$.

5.   *Another derivation of eq. (67).* Give an alternative derivation of eq. (67), based on eqs. (29), (22), and (33).

6.   *Endogenous labor productivity and the real exchange rate.* The economy has two sectors, tradables and nontradables. Tradables are produced out of capital K and skilled labor S, which earn factor rewards of r and h, respectively. Nontradables are produced out of capital and raw labor L, which earns the factor reward w. All factor rewards are expressed in terms of tradables. Let both sectors have linear-homogeneous production technologies, so that $h = h(r)$, $h'(r) < 0$, according to the factor-price frontier in tradables. Individuals have uncertain lifetimes with a constant death probability $1 - \varphi$ each period. We will assume a continuous-time version of the Blanchard (1985) model of Chapter 3, exercise 3, under which the effective market discount factor was $\varphi/(1 + r)$. In continuous time, however, we shall denote the discount *rate* by $r + \pi$, where π is an *instantaneous* death probability (see Blanchard, 1985). The economy is in a steady state with constant factor rewards. (If you are uncomfortable

with continuous-time mathematics, you may wish to return to this problem after covering models based on those methods in Chapter 8.)

(a) Consider the human-capital accumulation decision. Each individual has a unit endowment of labor time that can be used for unskilled or (after schooling) skilled employment, or be devoted to schooling. If a person spends a time interval T in school, he accumulates an amount of human capital equal to AT^α, $0 < \alpha \leq 1$. (During that period, of course, all employment income is foregone; however, there is no charge for attending school.) Show that at birth ($t = 0$) the individual selects T to maximize

$$\int_T^\infty \exp\left[-(r+\pi)t\right] AT^\alpha h\, dt - \frac{w}{r+\pi}.$$

(b) For an interior solution, of course, there must be some T such that the integral exceeds $w/(r+\pi)$. Assuming an interior solution, calculate the necessary first-order condition for T. Show that the condition implies an optimal choice of $T^* = \alpha/(r + \pi)$. Is this answer sensible?

(c) Show that the lifetime earnings of the educated (discounted at the rate $r + \pi$), equal $(r+\pi)^{-1} \exp\left[-(r+\pi)T^*\right] AT^{*\alpha}h$. In equilibrium this must equal $w/(r+\pi)$ if there are to be any unskilled workers to produce nontradables. Show that the implied relative wage of skilled and unskilled workers is

$$\frac{h}{w} = A^{-1} \exp(\alpha) \left(\frac{r+\pi}{\alpha}\right)^\alpha.$$

(Of course $AT^{*\alpha}h$, the hourly earnings of a worker schooled for the optimal length of time, must exceed w.)

(d) Using the solution for h/w above, show that w rises with α and with A, and falls with higher r or π. Explain intuitively. (You may assume the inequality $\alpha > r + \pi$.)

(e) Show that given r, the relative price of nontradables, p, is higher in countries where more schooling is sought (because of high α, high A, or low mortality π). Note that if we measure labor input simply by man-hours, more human capital translates into higher measured relative productivity in tradables.

7.   *Intertemporal welfare effects in the Ricardian model.* In the setting of section 4.5.4.2, show that a transitory increase in Foreign productivity makes Home better off in terms of its lifetime utility.

8.   *The current account and the terms of trade (following Obstfeld 1996a).* In a small open economy the representative individual maximizes

$$\sum_{s=t}^\infty \beta^{s-t} \frac{(X_s^\gamma M_s^{1-\gamma})^{1-1/\sigma}}{1-1/\sigma},$$

where X is consumption of an export good and M consumption of an import good. The country is specialized in production of the export good (the endowment of which is constant at Y) and faces the fixed world interest rate $r = (1-\beta)/\beta$ in terms of the real consumption index $C = X^\gamma M^{1-\gamma}$. (In section 4.5.4.1 we similarly assumed that the bonds countries trade are indexed to real consumption, so that a loan of 1 real consumption unit today returns $1+r$ real consumption units next period.) There is no investment or government spending.

(a) Let p be the price of exports in terms of imports. (A rise in p is an improvement in the terms of trade.) Show directly that the consumption-based price index in terms of imports is $P = p^\gamma / \gamma^\gamma (1 - \gamma)^{1-\gamma}$.

(b) Show that the home country's current account identity is

$$B_{t+1} - B_t = r B_t + \frac{p_t (Y - X_t)}{P_t} - \frac{M_t}{P_t}.$$

What is the intertemporal budget constraint corresponding to this finance identity?

(c) Derive necessary first-order conditions for the consumer's problem. (You may wish to reformulate the utility function and budget constraint in terms of real consumption C.) What are the optimal time paths for X and M?

(d) Suppose initially p is expected to remain constant over time. What is the effect on the current account (measured as in part b) of a sudden temporary fall in the terms of trade to $p' < p$?

(e) Suppose bonds are indexed to the *import good* rather than to real consumption, and let r now denote the own-rate of interest on imports. On the assumption that r is constant at $(1 - \beta)/\beta$, how does a temporary fall in p affect the current account? If there are differences compared to your answer in part d, how do you explain them?

Until now, we have limited our discussion of uncertainty mainly to economies that trade riskless real bonds in an environment of unexpected output, government spending, and productivity shocks. Our earlier framework is a useful one for many purposes, but it has at least two important drawbacks. First, it prevents study of the nature, pricing, and economic role of the increasingly wide array of assets traded in today's international financial markets. Second, it obscures the channels through which prior asset trades influence an economy's reaction to unexpected events.

This chapter is based on the idea that people often have sufficient foresight to make asset trades that protect them, at least partially, against future contingencies affecting their economic well-being. An individual can guard against such risks by buying assets with payoffs that are themselves uncertain, but tend to be unexpectedly high when the individual has unexpected bad economic luck elsewhere. Some types of hedges, such as health, disability, homeowner's, and auto insurance, are familiar. But other types of risky assets, such as currencies, stocks, long-term bonds, and their derivatives, can also play an insurance role. Indeed, the market value of any asset with uncertain returns depends in part on its effectiveness as a means of insurance. Asset pricing in general equilibrium will be one important application of our analysis.

International trade in risky assets can dramatically alter the way an economy's consumption, investment, and current account respond to unanticipated shocks. Consider the simple example of a small endowment economy in which the representative citizen faces uncertainty over the future path of gross domestic product. Suppose further, for the sake of illustration, that the representative individual lays off 100 percent of his output risk in international markets. He might accomplish this purpose either by selling off all local industries to foreign investors in exchange for riskless international bonds, or simply by purchasing an insurance policy that guarantees an income level. Now think about the current-account effect of a temporary rise in the country's gross domestic product. In the bonds-only framework of our earlier chapters, a temporary productivity shock causes a current-account surplus motivated by residents' desire to smooth consumption. But if foreigners have taken on all the country's output risk, a shock to its *GDP* does not affect its *GNP*. The fall in domestic output is matched exactly by a higher net inflow of asset income from abroad. Neither income, consumption, nor the current account changes.

This simple example sidesteps many issues. What price will a country pay to insure its income, and will it choose full insurance at that price? Will countries invest in riskless bonds or buy instead a portfolio of risky foreign assets? The point is clear enough, though. The presence of international markets for risky assets weakens and may sever the link between shocks to a country's output or factor productivity and shocks to its residents' incomes. Sophisticated international financial markets thus force us to rethink the channels through which macroeconomic shocks impinge on the world economy.

In reality, factors such as moral hazard or imperfect international contract enforcement make it impossible for any country fully to insure itself against all the risks it faces. For much of the analysis in this chapter, however, we suspend skepticism over the scope and efficiency of international financial markets and consider a world with no practical limitations on the kinds of contracts people (and countries) can write with one another. As in the classic models of complete contingent claims markets developed by Kenneth Arrow (1964) and Gerard Debreu (1959), we assume that there is a market for insuring *any* type of risk. While admittedly extreme, this assumption provides an indispensable starting point for clear thinking about the economic effects of risks and markets for risks.

The Arrow-Debreu paradigm of complete markets allows us to think about risk allocation in the same way we think about the allocation of standard commodities at a point in time and over time. Thus, despite more elaborate notation, the maximization problems individuals solve in complete-markets models are no more difficult mathematically than those of our earlier chapters. In addition, standard principles of trade theory apply to the international sharing of risks, allowing us to analyze asset trade in terms of the familiar principle of comparative advantage.

Because it is a straightforward generalization of dynamic macroeconomic analysis under certainty, the Arrow-Debreu setup is easier to analyze than intermediate cases with partially complete markets, one of which we take up toward the end of this chapter. Yet the intuition that a complete-markets benchmark yields also provides critical help in inferring and interpreting the predictions of models with incomplete financial markets.

A final advantage of complete-markets analysis derives from its very strong empirical predictions concerning a host of issues, including global portfolio diversification, asset pricing, and patterns of international consumption growth (to name just a few). In many cases these predictions do not stand up to careful empirical testing, as we shall see, but by looking at the complete-markets model's empirical failures we gain important clues about the kinds of asset-market imperfections most likely to be important in practice.

5.1   Trade across Random States of Nature: The Small-Country Case

We introduce trade in risky assets within the simplest possible setting: a small open endowment economy that exists for two periods (labeled 1 and 2) and produces and consumes a single tradable good.[1] To simplify further, we assume for most of this section that on date 2 only two "states of nature" are possible. The two states occur randomly according to a specified probability distribution and differ only in their associated output levels.

5.1.1   Uncertainty and Preferences

As usual when population size is constant, we will normalize population to 1 and identify the consumption and endowment of a representative individual with national aggregate consumption and output. The representative individual has known first-period income Y_1 and starts out with zero net foreign assets. From the perspective of date 1, however, output on date 2 is uncertain. Either of two states of nature may occur on date 2. In state s, which occurs with probability $\pi(s)$, the economy's output equals $Y_2(s)$, $s = 1, 2$.

An individual with uncertain future income cannot predict his future optimal consumption level exactly. In general, the best he can do is predict a range of consumption levels, each contingent on the state of nature that occurs. In analyzing how an individual plans consumption under uncertainty, we therefore focus on a set of desired *contingency plans* for consumption. Exactly which plan is brought into play on a future date will depend on the history of economic outcomes up to then. In terms of our simple two-period, two-state example, we denote by $C_2(s)$, $s = 1, 2$, the two state-contingent consumption plans for date 2.

How does an individual evaluate lifetime utility when future consumption prospects are uncertain? Our usual assumption will be that satisfaction is measured on date 1 by lifetime *expected utility*, that is, by average lifetime utility given the chosen contingency plans for future consumption.[2] Let C_1 denote consumption on date 1, which must be chosen before the uncertainty is resolved and thus cannot depend on the state of nature that occurs on date 2. The individual's lifetime expected utility on date 1 is

$$U_1 = \pi(1)\{u(C_1) + \beta u[C_2(1)]\} + \pi(2)\{u(C_1) + \beta u[C_2(2)]\},$$

which, because $\pi(1) + \pi(2) = 1$, implies

$$U_1 = u(C_1) + \pi(1)\beta u[C_2(1)] + \pi(2)\beta u[C_2(2)]. \tag{1}$$

---

1. For related models of international asset trade, see Cole (1988) and Svensson (1988).

2. We also took this approach in the stochastic model of Chapter 2. The assumption that individuals maximize expected utility can be justified by appealing to the standard Savage (1954) axioms on individual preferences over state-contingent commodities. As with the assumption of intertemporally additive preferences that we discussed in Chapter 1, the assumption of expected utility has the advantages that it is analytically tractable and delivers sharp predictions. However, the framework can be restrictive for some purposes (as we shall illustrate soon) and is subject to some well-known anomalies; see Machina (1987). Section 5.1.8 will briefly consider a richer preference setup.

Notice the tacit assumption that the utility function $u(C)$ in eq. (1) does not depend in any way on the realized state of nature. This need not be the case in general: an individual who unexpectedly falls ill, for example, may well experience a shift in his relative preference for various commodities. We will discuss this possibility in section 5.5.2, but we assume throughout most of this chapter that $u(C)$ is stable across states of nature.

5.1.2 Arrow-Debreu Securities and Complete Asset Markets

The asset-market structure that the Arrow-Debreu paradigm posits makes the choice of consumption in different *states* completely analogous to the choice of consumption on different *dates* or, for that matter, to the choice of different consumption goods on a single date. We assume that there is a worldwide market in which people can buy or sell contingent claims. These contingent claims have period 2 payoffs that vary according to the exogenous shocks that actually occur in period 2; that is, their payoffs depend on the state of nature.

Specifically, suppose that on date 1 people can buy or sell securities with the following payoff structure: the owner (seller) of the security receives (pays) 1 unit of output on date 2 if state s occurs then, but receives (pays) nothing in all other states. We call this security the *Arrow-Debreu security* for state of nature s and assume that there is a competitive market in Arrow-Debreu securities for every state s.[3]

Of course, we will continue to allow people to borrow and lend, that is, to sell and buy *noncontingent* (or riskless) assets, bonds, that pay $1 + r$ per unit on date 2 regardless of the state of nature, where r is the riskless real rate of interest. If there exist Arrow-Debreu securities for every state, however, the bond market is redundant, in the sense that its elimination would not affect the economy's equilibrium. With only two states, for example, the simultaneous purchase of $1 + r$ state 1 Arrow-Debreu securities and $1 + r$ state 2 Arrow-Debreu securities assures a payoff of $1 + r$ output units next period regardless of the economy's state, just as a bond does. Bonds thus add nothing to the trading opportunities people have once a full set of Arrow-Debreu claims can be traded. This example provides a very simple illustration of how prices for more complicated assets (such as options) can easily be constructed once one knows the primal Arrow-Debreu prices.[4] When we

---

3. One possible interpretation of the model's initial date 1 is as the date on which securities markets first open. From a multiperiod perspective, however, there is a more sophisticated interpretation: the current and future endowments as of date 1 could be the endogenous result of contingent securities trade *prior* to that date. Our discussion of dynamic consistency in appendix 5D shows that the economy's equilibrium on dates 1 and 2 will be the same (given the same endowments as of date 1) regardless of which interpretation is adopted.

4. By analogy, any T-period bond can be viewed as a collection of T pure "discount" bonds, each of which makes a payment in a single period only. (A one-period discount bond makes a payoff after one period, a two-period discount bond makes a single payoff after two periods, etc. In contrast, a standard

say an economy has *complete asset markets*, we mean that people can trade an Arrow-Debreu security corresponding to every future state of nature.[5]

It may seem unrealistic to assume that markets in Arrow-Debreu securities exist—no price quotations for such assets are reported in the *Wall Street Journal* or *Financial Times!* Virtually all assets, however, have state-contingent payoffs. Some of these assets, such as stocks and stock options, are traded in organized markets, while others, such as various types of insurance contracts, are not. Later in this chapter (section 5.3 and appendix 5A) we shall see that repeated trading in familiar securities such as stocks can sometimes replicate the allocations that arise when a complete set of Arrow-Debreu securities is traded. Thus, even though Arrow-Debreu securities may seem to be stylized theoretical constructs, thinking about them helps to clarify the economic roles of the more complex securities tracked daily in the financial press.

5.1.3   Budget Constraints with Arrow-Debreu Securities

We now turn to analyzing a country's budget constraint under uncertainty and complete asset markets. Let $B_2(s)$ be the representative individual's net purchase of state s Arrow-Debreu securities on date 1. [Thus, $B_2(s)$ is the stock of state s Arrow-Debreu securities the individual holds at the end of date 1 and the start of date 2.] Let $p(s)/(1+r)$ denote the world price, quoted in terms of date 1 consumption, of one of these securities—that is, of a claim to one output unit to be delivered on date 2 if, and only if, state s occurs.[6] Since this price is determined in a world market, it is exogenously given from the standpoint of the small country.

As usual in an exchange economy, the value of a country's net accumulation of assets on date 1 must equal the difference between its income and consumption:

$$\frac{p(1)}{1+r}B_2(1) + \frac{p(2)}{1+r}B_2(2) = Y_1 - C_1. \tag{2}$$

(We need not explicitly consider purchases of bonds because, as we have seen, bonds are redundant given the two Arrow-Debreu securities available.) When date 2 arrives, the state of nature s is observed, and the country will be able to consume

---

T-period bond makes interest payments in all T periods, and repays principal in the last period.) In the same way, analyzing simple assets that pay off only in a single state of nature allows one to construct the price of any more complex asset.

5. Scholars of Islamic banking have long emphasized that the ban in the Qur'an (holy book) on *riba*, or interest, does not rule out profit-sharing or other arrangements where the lender takes on risk; see Khan and Mirakhor (1987). When there are complete markets for Arrow-Debreu securities, a ban on noncontingent debt contracts alone would not interfere with the efficiency of the economy.

6. Thus $p(s)$ is the price of date 2 consumption *conditional* on state s in terms of *certain* date 2 consumption. We adopt this notation for two reasons: to remind the reader that transactions in Arrow-Debreu securities transfer purchasing power across time as well as states, and to render the resulting budget constraints and Euler equations in a form that is easily compared with their certainty analogs.

Box 5.1
Lloyd's of London and the Custom Market for Risks

If the world truly had complete markets, one would be able to insure against virtually any of life's vicissitudes. The typical college student would have access to insurance covering the risk of an unsuccessful career.* Homeowners or prospective home buyers would be able to hedge against changes in real estate values. Taxpayers might purchase insurance against unanticipated tax increases. Indeed, the kinds of risks one would be able to insure in a true complete-markets environment are limited only by one's imagination.

Not surprisingly, there *are* markets for insuring exotic risks—at a price. The leading provider of unusual insurance policies over the past three centuries has been Lloyd's of London.[†] Lloyd's consists of a group of wealthy individuals—the famous "names"—who accept unlimited liability for the insurance their underwriters provide. Lloyd's origins are in maritime insurance, an area in which it has remained active. The company made a fortune insuring merchant vessels and gold cargoes during the Napoleonic Wars, but paid more than $1 billion in claims during the 1991 Persian Gulf war. In addition to its core shipping and reinsurance businesses, Lloyd's has long stood ready to quote rates for singular contingencies. Lloyd's was a pioneer in nuclear power plant insurance (although its share of the U.S. market had fallen to 7 percent by the time of the 1979 Three Mile Island accident). At Lloyd's, star baseball pitchers can insure their arms, top opera singers can insure their voices, and thoroughbred racehorse owners can insure their prize stallions. Need insurance on a commercial satellite? It's big business at Lloyd's. A store owner can buy riot insurance, and Lloyd's will tailor certain kinds of political risk insurance contracts. Worried about being kidnapped and ransomed? "K&R" insurance, as it is known in the trade, peaked during the terrorism sprees of late of 1970s when world premiums exceeded $75 million, but it is still available.**

Most of the world's insurance business, of course, deals with more mundane matters such as life, fire, and auto insurance. Lloyd's accounts for only a very small fraction of the overall OECD market for standard insurance policies. The table below gives total gross insurance premiums as a percent of GDP for the entire OECD and for the five large countries that account for more than four-fifths of the total.[‡]

Total Gross Insurance Premiums Paid by Country, 1993

Country	Total Premiums (as percent of GDP)	Life Insurance Only (as percent of GDP)
France	8.6	4.7
Germany	7.9	2.8
Japan	8.8	6.5
United Kingdom	12.9	7.6
United States	10.6	4.3
OECD	8.2	4.0

Source: Organization for Economic Cooperation and Development, *Insurance Statistics Yearbook, 1985–1993* (Paris: OECD, 1995).

Box 5.1 *(continued)*

It must be emphasized that the figures in the table refer only to the conventional definition of the insurance industry. Therefore, while significant, these figures grossly understate the true overall level of insurance in the world economy according to the much broader concept used in this chapter. Nevertheless, the rarity of exotic contracts of the type Lloyd's of London writes suggests we are making a considerable leap of faith in assuming complete contingent-claims markets. As with other scientific abstractions—for example, the perfect-competition paradigm in economics or the frictionless surface of physics—bold simplification pays off by providing a conceptual framework without which complex real-world situations would be impossible to grasp. As we proceed, we will look closely at the empirical evidence on complete markets.

* In this spirit, several universities (including Yale) have experimented with loan programs in which repayments are indexed to future income.

† Lloyd's has suffered severe financial setbacks in recent years, especially because of uncertainty over settlements on U.S. lawsuits involving asbestos and pollution. But even if Lloyd's the institution does not survive, it is likely that other insurers will fill its place.

** For further reading on Lloyd's, see Hodgson (1984).

‡ On a per capita basis, Switzerland was the most heavily insured country in the OECD in the early 1990s, followed by (in order) Japan, the United States, and the United Kingdom. Although a substantial fraction of all insurance policies is resold through the reinsurance market, foreign holdings of domestic insurance policies are small in most OECD countries (less than 10 percent). This is an example of the home bias phenomenon that we discuss below.

the sum of its endowment and any payments on its state s contingent assets,[7]

$$C_2(s) = Y_2(s) + B_2(s), \qquad s = 1, 2. \tag{3}$$

Using eqs. (3) to eliminate $B_2(1)$ and $B_2(2)$ in the asset-accumulation identity (2), we derive the intertemporal budget constraint for this Arrow-Debreu economy:

$$C_1 + \frac{p(1)C_2(1) + p(2)C_2(2)}{1+r} = Y_1 + \frac{p(1)Y_2(1) + p(2)Y_2(2)}{1+r}. \tag{4}$$

Equation (4) is a slight variation on the usual present-value constraint. It says that the date 1 present value of the country's uncertain consumption stream must equal the date 1 present value of its uncertain income, where contingent quantities are evaluated at world Arrow-Debreu prices. Here international markets allow the country to smooth consumption not only across time but across states of nature. Suppose that the country's output is extremely low in state 1 and extremely

---

7. In the present setting a person's period 2 income can fall short of required payments on the state-contingent securities issued in period 1 only if this shortfall is planned. Such a plan would be fraudulent, and, as in previous chapters, we continue to assume that people do not plan to violate their intertemporal budget constraints.

high in state 2. Then by going "short" in state 2 securities [choosing $B_2(2) < 0$] and "long" in state 1 securities [$B_2(1) > 0$], the country can smooth consumption across states. Indeed, a consumer could assure himself of a completely *nonrandom* period 2 consumption level by, for example, selling his future state 1 output for $p(1)Y_2(1)/(1+r)$ in bonds and his future state 2 output for $p(2)Y_2(2)/(1+r)$ in bonds. That strategy guarantees the safe date 2 consumption level

$$C_2 = p(1)Y_2(1) + p(2)Y_2(2).$$

But, as we now see, a strategy of full insurance is not necessarily optimal.

5.1.4 Optimal Behavior

The country's optimal saving and portfolio allocations maximize expected utility (1) subject to constraint (4). To accomplish that end we use eqs. (2) and (3) to express the consumption levels in eq. (1) as functions of asset choices, by analogy with the procedure followed in earlier chapters. The resulting problem is to maximize over $B_2(1)$ and $B_2(2)$ the unconstrained expected utility

$$U_1 = u\left[Y_1 - \frac{p(1)}{1+r}B_2(1) - \frac{p(2)}{1+r}B_2(2)\right] + \sum_{s=1}^{2}\pi(s)\beta u[Y_2(s) + B_2(s)].$$

The necessary first-order conditions are

$$\frac{p(s)}{1+r}u'(C_1) = \pi(s)\beta u'[C_2(s)], \qquad s = 1, 2. \tag{5}$$

Equation (5) is closely related to the intertemporal Euler equation introduced in Chapter 1, although it pertains to an Arrow-Debreu security rather than a riskless bond. The left-hand side of eq. (5) is the cost, in terms of date 1 marginal utility, of acquiring the Arrow-Debreu security for state s. After referring back to eq. (1), you will see that the right-hand side of eq. (5) is the *expected* discounted benefit from having an additional unit of consumption in state s on date 2. As usual, eq. (5) can be rearranged to show that the marginal rate of substitution between C_1 and $C_2(s)$ is equal to the two goods' relative price:

$$\frac{\pi(s)\beta u'[C_2(s)]}{u'(C_1)} = \frac{p(s)}{(1+r)}, \qquad s = 1, 2. \tag{6}$$

One can use eqs. (5) to derive the intertemporal Euler conditions for more complex securities that pay off in more than one state of nature. The first such asset that comes to mind is probably a riskless bond, which pays $1+r$ output units on date 2 for every one output unit worth of bonds bought on date 1. As we have already noted, one can create a synthetic bond by buying $1+r$ units of the state 1 Arrow-Debreu security on date 1 at price $p(1)/(1+r)$ per unit and $1+r$ units of the state 2 Arrow-Debreu security at price $p(2)/(1+r)$ per unit. Since this "portfolio" assures delivery of $1 + r$ output units on date 2 regardless of which state occurs, it must have the same date 1 price as a bond paying $1 + r$ output units next period (that is, it must cost 1 output unit). Thus,

$$\frac{(1+r)p(1)}{1+r} + \frac{(1+r)p(2)}{1+r} = 1,$$

or equivalently,

$$p(1) + p(2) = 1. \tag{7}$$

[For $\mathcal{S} > 2$ states, the obvious generalization of eq. (7) is $\sum_{s=1}^{\mathcal{S}} p(s) = 1$.]

We derive the bond Euler equation by adding eqs. (5) over the two states:

$$[p(1) + p(2)]u'(C_1) = (1+r)\{\pi(1)\beta u'[C_2(1)] + \pi(2)\beta u'[C_2(2)]\}.$$

Using the definition of a mathematical expectation and eq. (7), we can write this last equality as the *stochastic Euler equation for riskless bonds*,

$$u'(C_1) = (1+r)\beta E_1\{u'(C_2)\}, \tag{8}$$

where $E_t\{\cdot\}$ is the expectation operator conditioned on information known on date t. This Euler equation is identical to the stochastic Euler equation (29) in Chapter 2. Its intuitive meaning is the same. Equation (8) can be rewritten as

$$\frac{\beta E_1\{u'(C_2)\}}{u'(C_1)} = \frac{1}{1+r}.$$

The *expected* marginal rate of substitution of present for future consumption equals $1/(1+r)$, the price of certain future consumption in terms of present consumption.

Another critical implication of eq. (5) is

$$\frac{\pi(1)u'[C_2(1)]}{\pi(2)u'[C_2(2)]} = \frac{p(1)}{p(2)}. \tag{9}$$

That is, the marginal rate of substitution of state 2 for state 1 consumption must equal the relative price of state 1 in terms of state 2 consumption. (This equality is an incarnation of the familiar static optimality condition from consumer theory.) Observe that only when

$$\frac{p(1)}{p(2)} = \frac{\pi(1)}{\pi(2)} \tag{10}$$

does condition (9) imply that $C_2(1) = C_2(2)$, so that it is optimal to equate consumption in different states of nature. We say that Arrow-Debreu security prices are *actuarially fair* when eq. (10) holds. At actuarially fair prices, a country trading in complete asset markets will fully insure against *all* future consumption fluctuations. If prices aren't actuarially fair, however, the country will chose to "tilt" its consumption across states. Given two equiprobable states, for example, the country will plan for relatively lower consumption in the state for which consumption insurance is relatively expensive. Similarly, if other things are equal, individuals confronted with a higher relative price of auto insurance buy less of it (lower coverage limits, higher deductible, and so on).

5.1.5 The Role of Risk Aversion

As you will recall from studying microeconomics, it is the strict concavity of the period utility function $u(C)$ that makes an expected-utility maximizer risk averse and, thus, interested in purchasing insurance. Concavity implies that individuals strictly prefer the expected value of a finite gamble to the gamble itself. The main point we make in this subsection is that, loosely speaking, the degree of concavity of the utility function, which measures the extent of risk aversion, is an inverse measure of the individual's portfolio response to changes in Arrow-Debreu prices.

To see the role of risk aversion in determining the demands for state-contingent consumptions, take natural logarithms of the across-state first-order condition (9), and then totally differentiate it (holding probabilities constant, of course, since they are fixed). The result is

$$d \log \left[\frac{p(1)}{p(2)} \right] = \frac{u''[C(1)]}{u'[C(1)]} dC(1) - \frac{u''[C(2)]}{u'[C(2)]} dC(2)$$

$$= \frac{C(1)u''[C(1)]}{u'[C(1)]} d \log C(1) - \frac{C(2)u''[C(2)]}{u'[C(2)]} d \log C(2). \qquad (11)$$

The ratio

$$\rho(C) = -\frac{Cu''(C)}{u'(C)} \qquad (12)$$

is the celebrated Arrow-Pratt *coefficient of relative risk aversion*. If we assume that $\rho(C)$ is a constant, denoted ρ, for all consumption levels, then eq. (11) simplifies to

$$d \log \left[\frac{C(2)}{C(1)} \right] = \frac{1}{\rho} d \log \left[\frac{p(1)}{p(2)} \right].$$

This equation shows that the inverse of the coefficient of relative risk aversion is also the elasticity of substitution between state-contingent consumption levels with respect to relative Arrow-Debreu prices. Intuitively, high risk aversion produces an inelastic response of consumption-insurance demands to relative insurance prices.

The *constant relative risk aversion* (CRRA) class of utility functions is given by

$$u(C) = \begin{cases} \dfrac{C^{1-\rho}}{1-\rho} & (\rho > 0, \rho \neq 1) \\ \log(C) & (\rho = 1), \end{cases} \tag{13}$$

a description that also fits the familiar isoelastic class if σ, the intertemporal substitution elasticity, equals $1/\rho$! This example illustrates a shortcoming of the expected utility framework: it does not permit us to vary the consumer's aversions to risk and intertemporal substitution (two very different things) independently of each other. Notwithstanding this drawback, the need for tractability leads us to retain the expected-utility assumption in most of what follows, and we continue to specialize to CRRA (or isoelastic) preferences when it is helpful to do so.[8] (In section 5.1.8 it will prove illuminating to relax the expected-utility assumption briefly.)

A consumer is said to be *risk neutral* when $u''(C) = 0$, implying that ρ, as defined previously, is 0. As $\rho \to 0$ and the demand elasticity $1/\rho$ grows without bound, individuals respond by concentrating all of their consumption in states s with $\pi(s) > p(s)$. As we will see in the next section, in a world equilibrium the date 2 output market must clear state by state. Thus the only price vector consistent with general equilibrium as $\rho \to 0$ is $p(s) = \pi(s)$ (in which case risk-neutral agents are indifferent as to the allocation of their consumption across states of nature).

5.1.6 Consumption Demands and the Current Account: A Log Utility Example

Thus far we have focused on the first-order conditions characterizing a country's equilibrium. For log utility, it is straightforward to derive closed-form solutions for the current account.

With $u(C) = \log(C)$, the lifetime utility function that the representative individual maximizes subject to lifetime budget constraint (4) is

$$U_1 = \log(C_1) + \pi(1)\beta \log[C_2(1)] + \pi(2)\beta \log[C_2(2)]. \tag{14}$$

Let W_1 be the present value of lifetime resources on date 1:

$$W_1 = Y_1 + \frac{p(1)Y_2(1) + p(2)Y_2(2)}{1+r}.$$

From earlier encounters with logarithmic utility we know that a country whose representative resident has the preferences in eq. (14) will spend $W_1/(1+\beta)$,

---

8. These preferences have the advantage that they are consistent with a steady long-run rate of consumption growth, a factor that will be important in Chapter 7. The reason risk aversion and intertemporal substitutability are indistinguishable with CRRA expected-utility preferences is that utility is additive across states as well as time, with probabilities weighting the period utility function as applied to different states in the same multiplicative fashion that the temporal discount factor weights the value of period utility on different dates.

$\pi(1)\beta W_1/(1+\beta)$, and $\pi(2)\beta W_1/(1+\beta)$ on C_1, $C_2(1)$, and $C_2(2)$, respectively.[9] Thus consumption demands are

$$C_1 = \frac{1}{1+\beta}\left[Y_1 + \frac{p(1)Y_2(1) + p(2)Y_2(2)}{1+r}\right], \tag{15}$$

$$\frac{p(s)}{1+r}C_2(s) = \frac{\pi(s)\beta}{1+\beta}\left[Y_1 + \frac{p(1)Y_2(1) + p(2)Y_2(2)}{1+r}\right], \qquad s = 1, 2. \tag{16}$$

The date 1 consumption demand (15) is completely parallel to that for the non-stochastic case with log preferences, but in place of a known Y_2, eq. (15) has $p(1)Y_2(1) + p(2)Y_2(2)$, the date 1 value of random date 2 output at world market prices.[10]

Using the solution for C_1, one can thus express the date 1 current account balance as

$$CA_1 = Y_1 - C_1 = \frac{\beta}{1+\beta}Y_1 - \frac{1}{1+\beta}\left[\frac{p(1)}{1+r}Y_2(1) + \frac{p(2)}{1+r}Y_2(2)\right]. \tag{17}$$

Again, this expression is parallel to the nonstochastic log case.

In the two-date certainty model of Chapter 1, we showed how a country's current account can be interpreted as depending on comparative advantage in trade across time, by analogy with comparative advantage in trade across different goods at the same point in time in classic international trade theory. In particular, the sign of CA_1 depended on the difference between the world and autarky interest rates, r and r^A. As we show in appendix 5B, this simple form of comparative advantage does not apply here.[11] The basic difficulty is that there are three goods in this model: consumption on date 1, and consumption on date 2 in each of two states of nature. In standard trade theory, the law of comparative advantage generally holds only in a weaker form when there are more than two goods, and such is the case here.

5.1.7   A General Result on Comparative Advantage

Even though comparative advantage does not hold in its simplest and strongest form here, it still holds in a weaker but more general form. As we shall see, the more general form does not require any strong restrictions either on the utility function or on the number of states of nature, S.

---

9. Be sure you can show these conclusions.

10. In general, the world market value in terms of sure date 2 consumption of the country's date 2 output, $p(1)Y_2(1) + p(2)Y_2(2)$, is not the same as its expected output, $E(Y_2) = \pi(1)Y_2(1) + \pi(2)Y_2(2)$. That equality holds only in the actuarially fair case with $p(1) = \pi(1)$ and $p(2) = \pi(2)$.

11. Appendix 5B also derives closed-form solutions for the country's optimal portfolio allocation and shows that gross asset flows can be large even when the net flow (i.e., the current account) is small.

We begin by defining the autarky price $p(s)^A/(1+r^A)$ as the price for the Arrow-Debreu security corresponding to state s that would obtain if the country could not engage in any type of asset trade with the rest of the world. From the first-order Euler condition (5) corresponding to state s, we see that for the general case of additive preferences

$$\frac{p(s)^A}{1+r^A} = \frac{\pi(s)u'[Y_2(s)]}{u'(Y_1)},$$

where we have imposed the autarky market-clearing conditions that $C_1^A = Y_1$, $C_2^A(s) = Y_2(s)$.

Now let C_1 and $C_2(s)$, $s = 1, 2, \ldots, S$, be the country's consumption choices under free trade. They must satisfy the country's intertemporal budget constraint at free-trade prices, which is the obvious generalization of eq. (4) to S possible states on date 2:

$$C_1 - Y_1 + \sum_{s=1}^{S} \frac{p(s)}{1+r}[C_2(s) - Y_2(s)] = 0. \tag{18}$$

Of course, the country must be made (weakly) better off by the opportunity to trade. Thus its consumption choices under free trade must be (weakly) more valuable than its endowment at autarky prices:

$$C_1 - Y_1 + \sum_{s=1}^{S} \frac{p(s)^A}{1+r^A}[C_2(s) - Y_2(s)] \geq 0. \tag{19}$$

(If the preceding inequality failed, the country would be able to buy its free-trade consumption bundle, and then some, at autarky prices, contradicting the presence of gains from trade.)

Subtracting eq. (18) from eq. (19) and using the second-period budget constraint (3) yields the principle of comparative advantage,

$$\sum_{s=1}^{S} \left[\frac{p(s)^A}{1+r^A} - \frac{p(s)}{1+r} \right][C_2(s) - Y_2(s)] = \sum_{s=1}^{S} \left[\frac{p(s)^A}{1+r^A} - \frac{p(s)}{1+r} \right] B_2(s) \geq 0.$$

This fundamental inequality states that, on average, a country's net imports of date 2, state s consumption tend to be high when the date 1 autarky price of state s consumption is high compared with the world price.

The deterministic case of Chapter 1 corresponds to the standard two-good case of classical trade theory: the two goods are date 1 consumption and (sure) date 2 consumption, so $S = 1$ and the last inequality states merely that countries with low autarky interest rates import date 2 consumption and, by the budget constraint, run current account surpluses on date 1. In general, for $S > 1$ one cannot link net imports of any one specific commodity to the difference between its world and autarky prices. Comparative advantage applies only in the average sense given by the last inequality.[12]

Because the preceding result requires only the weakest assumptions about preferences (e.g., that more consumption is preferred to less), it is quite general. Indeed, the result holds true for nonexpected- as well as expected-utility preferences.

*5.1.8   Risk Aversion and Intertemporal Substitution in a General Characterization of the Current Account

The analysis has simplified the problem of choice under uncertainty by treating consumption in each possible date 2 state as a distinct commodity. In this section we draw out further implications of this abstraction, making use of the general analytical approach to multicommodity intertemporal models developed in Chapter 4. A small amount of notational translation permits a straightforward transplant of Chapter 4's framework to complete-markets models of uncertainty. The analogy with Chapter 4 is most transparent if we temporarily relax the assumption of expected utility maximization. Thus this subsection yields as a by-product a quick look at how recent research on choice under uncertainty has attempted to decouple risk aversion and intertemporal substitutability.

We continue to assume that there are $s = 1, 2, \ldots, S$ possible date 2 states of nature. Suppose, by analogy with section 4.4.1.1, that we can write lifetime utility as

$$U_1 = u(C_1) + \beta u\{\Omega[C_2(1), \ldots, C_2(S); \pi(1), \ldots, \pi(S)]\}, \tag{20}$$

where the consumption index $\Omega[C_2(1), \ldots, C_2(S); \pi(1), \ldots, \pi(S)]$ is homogeneous of degree 1 in $C_2(1), \ldots, C_2(S)$. Let Z_2 be total spending on date 2 goods, measured in terms of *sure* (that is, noncontingent) date 2 consumption. Furthermore, define the date 2 consumption-based price index P as the minimal expenditure, measured in terms of sure date 2 consumption, necessary to achieve $\Omega[C_2(1), \ldots, C_2(S); \pi(1), \ldots, \pi(S)] = 1$. Then, since the consumption index is linear homogeneous, we write lifetime utility as

$$U_1 = u(C_1) + \beta u(Z_2/P) \tag{21}$$

and the lifetime budget constraint as

$$C_1 + \frac{Z_2}{1+r} = Y_1 + \frac{1}{1+r} \sum_{s=1}^{S} p(s) Y_2(s) \tag{22}$$

---

12. This version of the comparative advantage theorem is offered by Deardorff (1980) and Dixit and Norman (1980). Svensson (1988), who explores a framework similar to the one in this section, notes the application to trade in risky assets. Svensson's model and results cover cases of incomplete asset markets.

[recalling that $1/(1+r)$ is the date 1 price of sure date 2 consumption, the unit in which Z_2 is measured]. Given these preliminaries, one can, as in Chapter 4, envision individuals performing a two-stage maximization process:

1. Maximize eq. (21) subject to eq. (22) to find the optimal division of lifetime spending across *dates*, C_1 and Z_2.

2. Then, to find the optimal division of date 2 spending Z_2 across *states*, maximize the consumption index $\Omega[C_2(1), \ldots, C_2(S); \pi(1), \ldots, \pi(S)]$ subject to $\sum_{s=1}^{S} p(s)C_2(s) = Z_2$.

To highlight the close parallel with section 4.4.1.1, we take $\Omega[C_2(1), \ldots, C_2(S); \pi(1), \ldots, \pi(S)]$ to be of the constant elasticity of substitution (CES) form proposed in eq. (13) of Chapter 4. Section 5.1.5 showed that in the CRRA utility case described by the present chapter's eq. (13), $1/\rho$ is the constant elasticity of substitution between state-contingent consumptions. Our view of state-contingent consumptions as distinct commodities suggests that we replace the intratemporal substitution elasticity θ in eq. (13) of Chapter 4 by $1/\rho$ and choose

$$\Omega[C_2(1), \ldots, C_2(S); \pi(1), \ldots, \pi(S)] = \left[\sum_{s=1}^{S} \pi(s)C_2(s)^{1-\rho} \right]^{\frac{1}{1-\rho}}. \qquad (23)$$

Under this choice, date 2 contingent consumption demands are given by the analog of eq. (22) in Chapter 4 [with θ replaced by $1/\rho$ and the weights of the form γ replaced by $\pi(s)^{1/\rho}$],

$$C_2(s) = \left[\frac{p(s)/\pi(s)}{P} \right]^{-1/\rho} \frac{Z_2}{P}, \qquad (24)$$

where [the analog of eq. (20) in Chapter 4]

$$P = \left[\sum_{s=1}^{S} \pi(s)^{\frac{1}{\rho}} p(s)^{\frac{\rho-1}{\rho}} \right]^{\rho/(\rho-1)}. \qquad (25)$$

The postulate that $u(C)$ in eq. (20) is itself isoelastic, together with eq. (23), leads to an intertemporal utility function that generalizes both isoelastic and CRRA utility by allowing σ, the intertemporal substitution elasticity, to differ from $1/\rho$:

$$U_1 = \frac{C_1^{1-1/\sigma}}{1 - \frac{1}{\sigma}} + \beta \frac{\left\{ \left[\sum_{s=1}^{S} \pi(s)C_2(s)^{1-\rho} \right]^{\frac{1}{1-\rho}} \right\}^{1-1/\sigma}}{1 - \frac{1}{\sigma}}. \qquad (26)$$

Notice that the contingent consumption demand (24) confirms that $1/\rho$ is the price elasticity of substitution, so that ρ is the coefficient of relative risk aversion (recall section 5.1.5). However, σ, the intertemporal substitution elasticity, is a distinct parameter.[13] Only when $\sigma = 1/\rho$ does eq. (26) reduce to the expected lifetime utility

$$U_1 = \frac{C_1^{1-\rho}}{1-\rho} + \beta \sum_{s=1}^{S} \pi(s) \frac{C_2(s)^{1-\rho}}{1-\rho}.$$

To see the current-account implications of this framework, maximize eq. (21) subject to eq. (22) when P is given by eq. (25). The resulting intertemporal Euler equation for bonds is

$$u'(C_1) = (1+r)\beta \left(\frac{1}{P}\right) u' \left(\frac{Z_2}{P}\right).$$

When $u(C)$ is isoelastic with substitution elasticity σ, this Euler equation becomes

$$Z_2 = (1+r)^{\sigma} \beta^{\sigma} \left(\frac{1}{P}\right)^{\sigma-1} C_1, \tag{27}$$

which implies that date 1 consumption equals

$$C_1 = \frac{W_1}{1 + \left(\frac{1+r}{P}\right)^{\sigma-1} \beta^{\sigma}}.$$

[As before, W_1 is date 1 lifetime resources, the right-hand side of eq. (22).]

Euler equation (27) differs from those we saw in deterministic one-good models only through the presence of the date 2 price index P. Absent this factor, expenditure on the two dates, measured in noncontingent output units, would be determined by the same consumption smoothing and tilting factors explained in Chapter 1. [Compare the last equation giving optimal C_1 with eq. (26) in Chapter 1.] Indeed, there are some special cases in which it actually is legitimate to extrapolate from the deterministic results in Chapter 1 simply by treating the country's date 2 endowment $\sum p(s)Y_2(s)$ as if it were derived from a deterministic date 2 output level:

1. $\sigma = 1$. In this case the real interest rate effect associated with $P \neq 1$ has exactly offsetting income and substitution effects. The logarithmic expected-utility example of section 5.1.6 has this property, but so do the cases in which $\sigma = 1$ but $\rho \neq 1$.

2. $\pi(s) = p(s)$. For actuarially fair prices, eq. (25) implies that $P = 1$. The current account of a country that has laid off all of its second-period risk in world

---

13. Multiperiod versions of the preferences described by eq. (26) are proposed by Epstein and Zin (1989) and Weil (1989b, 1990). As usual, the special cases with $\rho = 1$ or $\sigma = 1$ are handled by L'Hospital's rule. (Recall Chapter 1, footnote 14.)

markets is, quite intuitively, the same as in a deterministic model. More formally, in this case the date 2 consumption index (23) corresponds to noncontingent date 2 consumption.

What do we make of cases in which P can differ from 1? Notice first that P can only be *below* 1, never above. The reason is that by choosing $C_2(s) = 1$ for all s, one can set the consumption index in eq. (23) equal to 1 at an expenditure of $\sum p(s) C_2(s) = 1$, *regardless* of the prices $p(s)$. We have seen that for actuarially fair prices this is the best one can do. For $p(s) \neq \pi(s)$, one therefore does strictly better, implying that $P < 1$.

More intuitively, an economy facing prices that are not actuarially fair *could* finance a noncontingent date 2 consumption level of $Z_2 = (1+r)(Y_1 - C_1) + \sum p(s) Y_2(s)$ by selling date 2 output forward on date 1 and investing the proceeds in bonds that mature on date 2. The date 2 output expenditure required is, of course, just Z_2. This strategy is suboptimal, however, when prices aren't actuarially fair, meaning that the consumption index Ω could have been set to Z_2 at a price $P Z_2$ strictly below Z_2.

When $P < 1$, the consumption-based real interest rate is above $1 + r$. For $\sigma > 1$, date 1 consumption therefore is lower, and CA_1 higher, than in a parallel certainty model with $Y_2 = \sum p(s) Y_2(s)$. When $\sigma < 1$ the effect of a real interest rate above $1 + r$ is reversed. Thus, even if $\beta(1+r) = 1$ and $Y_1 = \sum p(s) Y_2(s)$, eq. (27) implies that for $P < 1$, the country will have a first-period current account surplus when $\sigma > 1$ and a deficit when $\sigma < 1$.[14]

5.2   A Global Model

The last section showed how a small country allocates its consumption across dates and across uncertain states of nature, given world prices of contingent securities. While the small-country case is a useful starting point for thinking about intertemporal trade under uncertainty, several important implications of the complete markets approach becomes clear only in a world general-equilibrium setting.

In this section, we extend the two-period small-country analysis to the global case. Our model highlights the difference between global and country-specific risk and discloses the conditions under which Arrow-Debreu prices are actuarially fair.

---

14. Equation (27) implies that the "current account autarky" interest rate defined in appendix 5B is given here by

$$1 + r^{CA} = \frac{1}{\beta} \left[\frac{\sum p(s) Y_2(s)}{P^{1-\sigma} Y_1} \right]^{1/\sigma}.$$

As in appendix 5B, if $r > r^{CA}$ the country has a date 1 current account surplus, and it has a date 1 deficit if $r < r^{CA}$.

It also illustrates the very strong restrictions that a complete markets model can place on international consumption-growth comovements.

5.2.1 The CRRA Case

As an aid to intuition, we begin by developing a CRRA example. Discussion of more general utility functions is deferred until later in this section.

The world economy consists of two countries, Home and Foreign, with output levels that fluctuate across S states of nature. Foreign's necessary Euler equations are of the same forms as Home's were in section 5.1.4, with due allowance for the possibility that $S > 2$. As usual, Foreign quantities corresponding to Home's are marked with an asterisk ($*$). Home and Foreign consumers have the same degree of risk aversion.

5.2.1.1 Equilibrium Prices

Global general equilibrium requires that supply and demand balance in $S + 1$ markets: the market for date 1 output and those for date 2 output delivered in each of the S states of nature:

$$C_1 + C_1^* = Y_1 + Y_1^*, \tag{28}$$

$$C_2(s) + C_2^*(s) = Y_2(s) + Y_2^*(s), \qquad s = 1, 2, \ldots, S. \tag{29}$$

Equilibrium prices are found by combining these market-clearing conditions with the national representatives' Euler equations. Define $Y^W \equiv Y + Y^*$ as total world output. For a common CRRA period utility function [recall the definition in eq. (13)], Euler equation (5) for state s securities (which holds for any number of states S) shows that $C_2(s) = [\pi(s)\beta(1+r)/p(s)]^{1/\rho}C_1$ in Home and $C_2^*(s) = [\pi(s)\beta(1+r)/p(s)]^{1/\rho}C_1^*$ in Foreign. Adding these and applying equilibrium conditions (28) and (29) gives

$$Y_2^W(s) = \left[\frac{\pi(s)\beta(1+r)}{p(s)}\right]^{\frac{1}{\rho}} Y_1^W, \qquad s = 1, 2, \ldots, S,$$

which implies that the date 1 price of the state s contingent security is

$$\frac{p(s)}{1+r} = \pi(s)\beta \left[\frac{Y_2^W(s)}{Y_1^W}\right]^{-\rho}, \qquad s = 1, 2, \ldots, S. \tag{30}$$

Notice the key role of our assumption that Home and Foreign have *the same* risk aversion coefficient, ρ. Without this simplification, the model would not necessarily yield a closed-form solution in terms of aggregate output alone.

The preceding results throw light on the conditions under which securities prices will be actuarially fair. Write down eq. (30) for any two states s and s' and conclude by dividing the two equations that

$$\frac{p(s)}{p(s')} = \left[\frac{Y_2^W(s)}{Y_2^W(s')}\right]^{-\rho} \times \frac{\pi(s)}{\pi(s')}. \tag{31}$$

For $\rho > 0$, contingent claims' prices all will be actuarially fair [that is, satisfy eq. (10)] if and only if total *world* output is the same in all states of nature. The requirement for actuarial fairness, then, is absence of output uncertainty *at the aggregate level*. If there is no aggregate uncertainty, it is feasible for both countries to have state-independent date 2 consumption levels. As a result, equilibrium prices need not provide an incentive for people to "tilt" consumption in favor of states with relatively abundant world output. If, however, world output in state s' exceeds that in state s, prices must induce countries to consume relatively more in state s'. As eq. (31) shows, state s consumption therefore will command a premium over its actuarially fair price, while state s' consumption will sell at a discount.

With equilibrium Arrow-Debreu prices for date 1 in hand, we can easily find the real interest rate. As an intermediate step, we solve for the date 2 prices $p(s)$. For any state s', the arbitrage condition $\sum p(s) = 1$ and eq. (31) imply

$$p(s') = 1 - \sum_{s \neq s'} p(s) = 1 - p(s') \sum_{s \neq s'} \left[\frac{Y_2^W(s)}{Y_2^W(s')}\right]^{-\rho} \frac{\pi(s)}{\pi(s')},$$

an equation that can be solved for $p(s')$:

$$p(s') = \frac{\pi(s')[Y_2^W(s')]^{-\rho}}{\sum_{s=1}^{S} \pi(s)[Y_2^W(s)]^{-\rho}}. \tag{32}$$

This equation and eq. (30) give the world interest rate:

$$1 + r = \frac{(Y_1^W)^{-\rho}}{\beta \sum_{s=1}^{S} \pi(s)[Y_2^W(s)]^{-\rho}}. \tag{33}$$

Equation (33) is intuitive. Higher world output on date 1 implies a lower real interest rate (raises the price of date 2 consumption relative to date 1 consumption). Similarly, higher future output in any state (that is, higher expected future output) raises the real interest rate.

5.2.1.2   Equilibrium Consumption Levels

The complete-markets model has strong implications concerning correlations in international consumption levels across time and across states of nature. These strong predictions arise because complete markets allow all individuals in Home and

Foreign to equate their marginal rates of substitution between current consumption and state-contingent future consumption to the same state-contingent security prices.

The many-state analogs of eqs. (5) and (9) imply

$$\frac{\pi(s)\beta u'[C_2(s)]}{u'(C_1)} = \frac{p(s)}{(1+r)} = \frac{\pi(s)\beta u'[C_2^*(s)]}{u'(C_1^*)} \tag{34}$$

and

$$\frac{\pi(s)u'[C_2(s)]}{\pi(s')u'[C_2(s')]} = \frac{p(s)}{p(s')} = \frac{\pi(s)u'[C_2^*(s)]}{\pi(s')u'[C_2^*(s')]}$$

for all states s and s'. You will recognize these as fundamental necessary conditions for efficient resource allocation: all individuals' marginal rates of substitution in consumption—over time and across states—are equal, so no potential gains from trade remain to be exploited.[15] These equations relate only marginal utilities of consumption, but specific utility functions yield implications for consumption levels.

With CRRA utility, for example, $u'(C) = C^{-\rho}$, so the last two equations, combined with the equations for state-contingent prices (30), imply

$$\frac{C_2(s)}{C_2(s')} = \frac{C_2^*(s)}{C_2^*(s')} = \frac{Y_2^W(s)}{Y_2^W(s')} \tag{35}$$

and

$$\frac{C_2(s)}{C_1} = \frac{C_2^*(s)}{C_1^*} = \frac{Y_2^W(s)}{Y_1^W} \tag{36}$$

for all states. Equation (35) implies the equalities

$$\frac{C_2(s)}{Y_2^W(s)} = \frac{C_2(s')}{Y_2^W(s')}, \qquad \frac{C_2^*(s)}{Y_2^W(s)} = \frac{C_2^*(s')}{Y_2^W(s')},$$

meaning that Home consumption is a constant fraction μ of world date 2 output regardless of the state. (Foreign's state-invariant share, correspondingly, is $1 - \mu$.) Equation (36) says that consumption *growth rates* are the same across countries in every state and are equal to the growth rate of world output.

Equation (36) implies the equalities (for all s)

---

15. As usual, efficiency means *Pareto optimality*: any rise in one country's welfare would have to come at the other country's expense. This property of the equilibrium follows because preferences are quasi-concave, there is complete information, and there are no increasing returns to scale in production (production is exogenous), no nonpecuniary externalities in production or consumption, and no limitations on the kinds of contracts that can be enforced. Furthermore, all consumers can participate in all markets (in contrast to the overlapping generations model of section 5.6).

$$\frac{C_2(s)}{Y_2^W(s)} = \mu = \frac{C_1}{Y_1^W}, \qquad \frac{C_2^*(s)}{Y_2^W(s)} = 1 - \mu = \frac{C_1^*}{Y_1^W},$$

meaning that the countries' date 1 consumption shares in world output are the *same* as their date 2 shares. A country's share in world consumption, one can easily show, is the country's share of the world's present discounted output on date 1, evaluated at equilibrium Arrow-Debreu prices.[16]

Note that when date 2 world output is uncertain, *at equilibrium prices* neither Home nor Foreign arranges for constant consumption across states. Each country's consumption is internationally diversified, however, in the sense that any consumption risk it does absorb is entirely due to *systematic* output uncertainty, that is, uncertainty in global output.[17]

Date 2 equilibrium is illustrated in Figure 5.1 for the case $S = 2$. The diagram is a familiar Edgeworth box in which the two goods are state-contingent consumptions and world output is assumed higher in state 1 than in state 2 . At the endowment point **A**, Home has higher output in both states, but it is *relatively* better endowed with state 1 output. Equilibrium point **E** is therefore achieved through Home sales of claims to state 1 output in return for state 2 output claims issued by Foreign. The equilibrium relative price of the two contingent securities, equal to the absolute slope of line **EA**, is $p(1)/p(2)$. Under identical CRRA preferences the fraction of world output each country consumes is constant across states, but this would not necessarily be the case for more general utility functions or with differing national degrees of risk aversion.

---

16. In equilibrium, Home's budget constraint implies

$$Y_1 + \sum_{s=1}^{S} \frac{p(s)Y_2(s)}{1+r} = C_1 + \sum_{s=1}^{S} \frac{p(s)C_2(s)}{1+r}$$

$$= \mu \left[Y_1^W + \sum_{s=1}^{S} \frac{p(s)Y_2^W(s)}{1+r} \right],$$

an equation readily solved for μ to verify the text's claim. By substituting equilibrium prices [eq. (30)] for $p(s)/(1+r)$ in the resulting solution, one derives the following reduced-form expression for μ:

$$\mu = \frac{Y_1(Y_1^W)^{-\rho} + \beta \sum_{s=1}^{S} \pi(s)Y_2(s)[Y_2^W(s)]^{-\rho}}{(Y_1^W)^{1-\rho} + \beta \sum_{s=1}^{S} \pi(s)[Y_2^W(s)]^{1-\rho}}.$$

17. The first theorem of welfare economics implies that the equilibrium resource allocation corresponds to the choice of a benevolent social planner who allocates output by command. It is a good exercise to show that here, the equilibrium allocation results if the social welfare function $\kappa U_1 + (1 - \kappa)U_1^*$ is maximized subject to resource constraints, where

$$\kappa = \frac{\mu^\rho}{\mu^\rho + (1 - \mu)^\rho}.$$

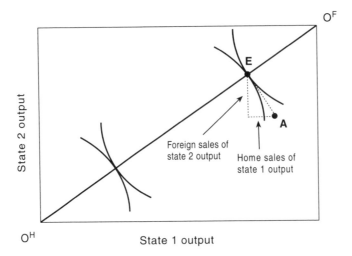

Figure 5.1
Efficient risk pooling

Application: Comparing International Consumption and Output Correlations

One of the most powerful predictions of the one-good complete-markets model is that different countries' per capita consumption growth rates should be highly correlated even if growth rates in per capita output are not. We have seen that when two countries have identical CRRA preferences, their shares of world consumption are constant across time, so that their rates of consumption growth must always be equal ex post. However, even for two countries n and m with different constant coefficients of risk aversion, ρ_n and ρ_m, and different subjective discount factors, β_n and β_m, the model still yields a very strong empirical prediction. If we use lowercase c and y to denote *per capita* consumption and output, then eq. (34) implies

$$\log\left[\frac{c_2^n(s)}{c_1^n}\right] = \left(\frac{\rho_m}{\rho_n}\right)\log\left[\frac{c_2^m(s)}{c_1^m}\right] + \frac{1}{\rho_n}\log\left(\frac{\beta_n}{\beta_m}\right). \tag{37}$$

This equation shows that any two countries' ex post consumption growth rates, although individually random, are perfectly statistically correlated (they have a correlation coefficient of 1).[18]

Does this perfect-correlation implication match the data? Embarrassingly for the

---

18. The *correlation coefficient* between two random variables X and Y, $\mathrm{Corr}\{X, Y\}$, is defined as

Table 5.1
Consumption and Output: Correlations between Domestic and World Growth Rates, 1973–92

Country	Corr $(\hat{c}, \hat{c}^w)$	Corr $(\hat{y}, \hat{y}^w)$
Canada	0.56	0.70
France	0.45	0.60
Germany	0.63	0.70
Italy	0.27	0.51
Japan	0.38	0.46
United Kingdom	0.63	0.62
United States	0.52	0.68
OECD average	0.43	0.52
Developing country average	−0.10	0.05

Note: The numbers Corr$(\hat{c}, \hat{c}^w)$ and Corr$(\hat{y}, \hat{y}^w)$ are the simple correlation coefficients between the annual change in the natural logarithm of a country's real per capita consumption (or output) and the annual change in the natural logarithm of the rest of the world's real per capita consumption (or output), with the "world" defined as the 35 benchmark countries in the Penn World Table (version 5.6). Average correlations are population-weighted averages of individual country correlations. The OECD average excludes Mexico.

simplest one-good version of the complete markets model, it does not. Table 5.1 presents 1973–92 estimates of correlation coefficients between national per capita consumption growths and world per capita consumption growth. These are compared with correlation coefficients between national per capita output growths and world per capita output growth. [The Penn World Table data used in Table 5.1 allow a meaningful international comparison of real income and consumption levels by correcting for price-level differences among countries (recall Chapter 4).]

For the seven largest industrial countries (the Group of Seven, or G-7), the correlation between domestic and world consumption growth is lower in almost every case than the correlation between domestic and world output growth; the only exception is for Britain where the two correlations are almost equal. When smaller OECD countries are included, the puzzle remains. For developing countries, the average correlation between domestic and world consumption growth is actually slightly negative.[19] In section 5.5 we will consider some possible explanations of

---

$$\text{Corr}\{X, Y\} = \frac{\text{Cov}\{X, Y\}}{\sqrt{\text{Var}\{X\}}\sqrt{\text{Var}\{Y\}}}.$$

If X and Y are linearly related, so that $Y = a_0 + a_1 X$ for some constants a_0 and $a_1 > 0$, then these random variables are *perfectly correlated*, by which we mean that Corr$\{X, Y\} = 1$. Perfect *negative* correlation means that Corr$\{X, Y\} = -1$, and occurs when $a_1 < 0$. The Cauchy-Schwarz inequality implies that $-1 \leq \text{Corr}\{X, Y\} \leq 1$ always.

19. The observation that consumptions are less correlated internationally than outputs has been made in various ways and for various data samples by Backus, Kehoe, and Kydland (1992), Devereux, Gregory,

the "paradox" that outputs are more correlated than consumptions, as well as more formal econometric tests.   ∎

5.2.2 A Rationale for the Representative-Agent Assumption

Throughout much of this book we maintain the convenient fiction that each country is inhabited by a single representative agent. This assumption has allowed us to analyze each country's aggregate per capita consumption as if it were decided by a composite individual endowed with the economy's per capita economic resources. Having introduced an explicit stochastic general equilibrium model, we are now able to present a deeper rationale for the representative-agent approach than the preliminary one we offered in Chapter 1. This subsection shows that if asset markets are complete and agents face the same prices, then, for a broad class of period utility functions, prices and aggregate per capita consumption behave *as if* there were a single representative agent despite substantive differences across individuals.

To take a simple example, consider a complete markets environment in which I agents with possibly different wealth levels have identical discount factors and period utility functions given by the following generalization of the CRRA case,

$$u(c^i) = \frac{(a_0 + a_1 c^i)^{1-\rho}}{1 - \rho}, \tag{38}$$

where a_0, a_1, and ρ all are constants. We know from eq. (5) that individual i's consumption choices for all states s satisfy the Euler equation

$$(a_0 + a_1 c_1^i)^{-\rho} = \frac{\beta(1 + r)\pi(s)[a_0 + a_1 c_2^i(s)]^{-\rho}}{p(s)}, \qquad i = 1, 2, \dots, I.$$

The preceding equation becomes

$$a_0 + a_1 c_1^i = \left[\frac{\beta(1 + r)\pi(s)}{p(s)}\right]^{-1/\rho} [a_0 + a_1 c_2^i(s)], \qquad i = 1, 2, \dots, I,$$

if both sides are raised to the power $-1/\rho$. Sum this equation over all agents, divide by I, and then raise both sides of the resulting equality to the power $-\rho$. The result

---

and Smith (1992), Tesar (1993, 1995), Obstfeld (1994a), and Stockman and Tesar (1995). Time-series structural studies of consumption risk sharing include Obstfeld (1989, 1994a), Canova and Ravn (1994), Bayoumi and MacDonald (1995), and Kollmann (1995). Lewis's (1996) related panel estimates are the subject of an application in section 5.5. Baxter (1995) evaluates the success of simulated dynamic general-equilibrium models with complete markets in matching international consumption and output correlations (as well as other business-cycle regularities). The connection between complete markets and international aggregate consumption correlations was first made by Leme (1984) and Scheinkman (1984).

shows that for all s, *per capita* aggregate consumption $c = \sum_i c^i / I$ satisfies the Euler equation

$$(a_0 + a_1 c_1)^{-\rho} = \frac{\beta(1+r)\pi(s)[a_0 + a_1 c_2(s)]^{-\rho}}{p(s)}. \tag{39}$$

Because the individual budget constraints are also linear, of course, one can similarly average these to show that per capita individual consumptions must equal per capita individual resources in value. Equation (39) thus implies the result claimed: the economy's per capita consumption behaves as if chosen by a representative individual who owns the economy's average endowment. This result actually holds for a broader class of utility functions than we have analyzed here.[20] We emphasize, however, that aggregation usually is impossible absent a complete-markets allocation.[21]

Another approach to aggregation is sometimes useful under complete markets even when there are I individuals with *distinct* CRRA utility functions in the restricted class of eq. (13). Now we define the representative consumer to have wealth and consumption equal, respectively, to the geometric averages of all individuals' wealth and consumption levels. The (unweighted) geometric average of individual consumptions is

$$\tilde{c} \equiv \prod_{i=1}^{I} (c^i)^{1/I}.$$

For individual i the Euler equation (5) is equivalent to

---

20. That class of utility functions is the hyperbolic absolute risk aversion (HARA) class, which includes functions of the form

$$u(c) = -a_0 \exp(-c/a_0),$$

$$u(c) = \log(a_0 + a_1 c),$$

or

$$u(c) = (1 - \rho)^{-1}(a_0 + a_1 c)^{1-\rho},$$

see M. Rubinstein (1974). Milne (1979) observes that for utility functions that are additive over commodities (the case here), the HARA class is also the class of *quasi-homothetic* utility functions such that demand functions are linear in lifetime resources.

21. Suppose, for example, that there are two states of nature ($S = 2$) but that the only asset is a risk-free bond. The individual bond Euler equations imply

$$a_0 + a_1 c_1^i = [\beta(1+r)]^{-1/\rho} \left\{ \sum_{s=1}^{2} \pi(s)[a_0 + a_1 c_2^i(s)]^{-\rho} \right\}^{-1/\rho},$$

but the right-hand side doesn't aggregate over agents unless their marginal rates of substitution between the two states happen to be the same.

$$c_2^i(s) = \left[\frac{\pi(s)(1+r)\beta}{p(s)}\right]^{1/\rho_i} c_1^i.$$

Taking both sides to the power $1/I$ and multiplying over all agents i gives

$$\tilde{c}_2(s) = \prod_{i=1}^{I}\left[\frac{\pi(s)(1+r)\beta}{p(s)}\right]^{1/I\rho_i}\tilde{c}_1,$$

or

$$\frac{p(s)}{1+r} = \pi(s)\beta\left[\frac{\tilde{c}_2(s)}{\tilde{c}_1}\right]^{-\tilde{\rho}},$$

where $\tilde{\rho}$ is the harmonic mean of the countries' risk-aversion coefficients,

$$\tilde{\rho} \equiv \frac{1}{\frac{1}{I}\sum_{i=1}^{I}\frac{1}{\rho_i}}.$$

The representative's period utility function $u(\tilde{c})$ therefore is of the CRRA class with risk-aversion coefficient equal to the harmonic mean of the possibly distinct individual coefficients.

There are some important situations where perfect aggregation is infeasible, for example, in an overlapping generations framework. (People who haven't yet been born obviously can't participate in markets for future output.) Even there, we may be able to aggregate within generations that have coterminous lifetimes. Nevertheless, our examples show that the representative-agent assumption is a somewhat less restrictive paradigm for analyzing consumption behavior and asset prices than might appear at first glance. It is also apparent that our practice throughout most of this book of assuming a representative agent at the national level but not necessarily at the international level implicitly assumes that national markets are more complete and better integrated than international markets.

5.2.3 Dynamic Implications of Complete Markets with an Infinite Horizon

The infinite-horizon case allows a dynamic analysis of the current account's response to unexpected shocks that is impossible in the two-period paradigm, where random events occur only in the second and final period. In this subsection, we contrast how output shocks affect the current account in complete-markets versus bonds-only models with infinite horizons. The discussion is mostly intuitive. Appendix 5C formally extends the two-period Arrow-Debreu model to allow for an infinite horizon. Except for greater notational complexity the extension is straightforward, with results about risk sharing and global consumption correla-

Box 5.2
Are Markets More Complete within than among Countries?

Many of this book's models assume representative national residents in order to focus on country-specific sources of individual heterogeneity. A possible justification for this approach is that markets seem to be better integrated within than between countries. Crucini (1992), for example, finds that for 1971–90 data, the consumption growth rates of different Canadian provinces are more highly correlated than are cross-province output growth rates or different countries' consumption growth rates. Atkeson and Bayoumi (1993), looking at regions within the United States, also find support for the view that risk sharing is higher within countries than among them, as do Bayoumi and Klein (1995) in another study of Canadian provinces. For a discussion of some of the difficulties in making comparisons between regional and international consumption correlations, see Obstfeld (1995).

One major reason to expect higher consumption correlations within than across countries is fiscal federalism. In most countries, federal taxes and transfers are effectively indexed to income, so that government policy plays a substantial role in pooling risks. Sachs and Sala-i-Martin (1992) estimate that in the United States, federal taxes and transfers offset roughly one-third of deviations of regional from national income. Other studies have arrived at somewhat lower estimates of 10 to 25 percent, but as we shall see, even these lower numbers may be large relative to the risk sharing that appears to take place through international capital markets.*

In discussing sovereign risk in Chapter 6, we shall identify another major reason why risk sharing is greater within countries than across them: the relative ease of intranational compared with international contract enforcement. Even if domestic capital markets allow more efficient risk pooling than international markets, they still appear to leave large opportunities for intranational pooling unexploited (see the studies of U.S. microeconomic data by Cochrane, 1991, and Mace, 1991). Indeed, Altonji, Hayashi, and Kotlikoff (1992) find evidence of unexploited risk-sharing opportunities even within U.S. families.

* See Bayoumi and Masson (1994) and the references therein. Bayoumi and Masson estimate that the U.S. federal fiscal system reduces long-term income differentials by 22 cents out of every dollar. They obtain a substantially larger estimate for Canada.

tions closely parallel to those of the two-period model.[22] With regard to the current account, however, the infinite-horizon model yields important new insights.

Assume a world of two pure endowment economies, Home and Foreign, identical in every respect on the first date t of economic activity. Not only are they alike in preferences (which are intertemporally additive), but they also have identical outputs $\bar{Y} = \bar{Y}^*$ in all periods except for period $t + 1$. On date $t + 1$, the countries'

---

22. This similarity should not be surprising, because one can think of all trade taking place in the initial period of the Arrow-Debreu model, regardless the economy's time horizon (see appendix 5D). As noted by Arrow (1964), however, periodic trading opportunities can lead to efficient risk sharing without the full complement of securities that would be needed were trading restricted to a single date.

outputs are subject to identically and independently distributed mean-zero shocks ϵ_{t+1} and ϵ^*_{t+1}, so that

$$Y_{t+1} = \bar{Y} + \epsilon_{t+1},$$

$$Y^*_{t+1} = \bar{Y} + \epsilon^*_{t+1},$$

with $E_t\epsilon_{t+1} = E_t\epsilon^*_{t+1} = 0$. Thus the only uncertainty is about period $t + 1$ output. Moreover, shocks to $t + 1$ output are purely temporary and don't affect outputs in period $t + 2$ and beyond.

First consider a world analogous to the infinite-horizon models of Chapter 2, in which there is borrowing and lending in riskless one-period bonds, but no trade in contingent claims. Since the two countries are identical as of period t, there are initially no gains from intertemporal trade and the period t current account will be zero. Now suppose that in period $t + 1$, the Home output shock is greater than the Foreign output shock, $\epsilon_{t+1} > \epsilon^*_{t+1}$. Since the shock is purely temporary, Home smooths its consumption by lending to Foreign and running a current account surplus. In all future periods, current accounts are zero (the two countries have equal discount rates and, by assumption, there are no further shocks). Home consumption thus remains permanently higher than Foreign consumption.

Now suppose that there are complete markets, so that agents can trade Arrow-Debreu securities on date t for all the possible date $t + 1$ states of nature [that is, all possible realizations of the random pair $(\epsilon_{t+1}, \epsilon^*_{t+1})$]. In this case, by the time period $t + 1$ arrives both countries will already have pooled their output risks and insured each other against any future country-specific output shocks by effectively trading a 50 percent equity share in the domestic output stream for a 50 percent share in foreign output. If it now turns out that $\epsilon_{t+1} > \epsilon^*_{t+1}$, *absolutely no* current account imbalances result. Realized Home *output* (GDP) Y_{t+1} is higher than realized foreign output Y^*_{t+1}, but under complete markets, Home *income* (GNP), equal to GDP plus net dividend payments from abroad, $Y_{t+1} + \frac{1}{2}Y^*_{t+1} - \frac{1}{2}Y_{t+1} = \frac{1}{2}(Y_{t+1} + Y^*_{t+1})$, remains equal to Foreign income. Because Home and Foreign consumption both equal $\frac{1}{2}(Y_{t+1} + Y^*_{t+1})$ as well on date $t + 1$, both national current accounts remain at zero. On dates after $t + 1$, both Home and Foreign consumption revert to average world output, $\bar{Y}$.

If the date $t + 1$ output shocks are *permanent*, the current account remains at zero in the bonds-only case too: Home consumption changes permanently by the change in Home output and Foreign consumption changes permanently by the change in Foreign output. The only difference under complete markets is that Home and Foreign consumption both change by equal amounts (half the change in world output).

While the current account implications of the two asset structures differ when productivity shocks are short-lived, the two models' implications for world interest rates are quite similar. With complete markets, a permanent rise in world output leaves the world interest rate unchanged, regardless of its incidence. This is the same as in the bonds-only model. Similarly, regardless of the asset structure, a temporary rise in world output incipiently raises saving and thus lowers the world interest rate. Thus complete markets remove the relative asymmetric income effects shocks would cause in the absence of risk sharing, but not the relative price effects.[23]

When investment is possible (as in the next section), a country with a persistent positive productivity shock experiences a current account deficit even in an infinite-horizon complete-markets setting.[24] The country's saving increases only partially to match higher domestic investment, and foreign capital flows in to buy up the rest of the expanded productive capacity. Even in this case, however, the current account is merely an accounting device for tracking the international distribution of the new equity claims foreigners must buy to maintain the efficient global pooling of national output risks.

5.2.4   Efficient Investment under Uncertainty

Although so far we have considered only endowment economies, it is simple to extend the complete markets model to incorporate investment.[25] All the main issues can be explained within a two-period framework. We continue to take Home's date 1 endowment Y_1 as exogenous, but we now assume that the country's date 2 output is produced by a competitive individual or "firm" using the production function

$$Y_2(s) = A(s)F(K_2),$$

where K_2 is capital accumulated during period 1 and invested in Home. As in Chapter 1 we abstract from the labor market, and we assume that producers can sell claims to their future outputs. For convenience $K_1 = K_1^* = 0$ and depreciation is zero, so that date 1 investment equals the date 2 capital stock.

The (representative) Home firm chooses investment K_2 in period 1 to maximize the present value of profits, just as in earlier models. Here, however, profits earned in a state s are valued using the Arrow-Debreu security price for output delivered in that state. The present value of the Home firm's state-contingent profits, measured in terms of date 1 output, therefore is

---

23. This point is emphasized by Stockman (1988a). The basic idea is that asset-market structure affects how shocks' income effects are distributed among countries, but with restrictions on preferences (e.g., homotheticity), international price effects can be unaffected by asset-market structure. This result is less likely to hold when investment is possible (see the following discussion). International differences in time preference or deterministic fluctuations in output growth can generate perfectly anticipated current-account imbalances even under complete markets, but not unexpected imbalances.

24. See, for example, Stockman and Svensson (1987) and Cantor and Mark (1988).

25. The text's discussion abstracts from some interesting and important issues, such as nonconvexities, that would considerably complicate the analysis. For an interesting partial-equilibrium analysis (and references), see Abel, Dixit, Eberly, and Pindyck (1995).

$$\sum_{s=1}^{S} \frac{p(s)}{1+r} [A(s)F(K_2) + K_2] - K_2,$$

and it is maximized (with respect to net investment K_2) when

$$\sum_{s=1}^{S} \frac{p(s)}{1+r} [A(s)F'(K_2) + 1] = 1. \tag{40}$$

Since the analogous condition holds in Foreign, the date 2 marginal value product of investment is the same everywhere in the world and equal to the world interest rate,

$$\sum_{s=1}^{S} p(s)A(s)F'(K_2) = \sum_{s=1}^{S} p(s)A^*(s)F^{*'}(K_2^*) = r.$$

Equations (5) and (40) imply that profit-maximizing investment decisions satisfy

$$u'(C_1) = \sum_{s=1}^{S} \pi(s)\beta u'[C_2(s)][A(s)F'(K_2) + 1]$$

$$= \sum_{s=1}^{S} \pi(s)\beta u'[C_2(s)][A^*(s)F^{*'}(K_2^*) + 1], \tag{41}$$

which states that the marginal utility of current Home consumption equals the expected Home marginal utility due to investing anywhere in the world. Because eq. (5) holds with C replaced by C^*, the preceding relationship also holds for C replaced by C^*. These two investment Euler equations are necessary conditions for efficient resource allocation.

5.2.4.1   An Example of a Two-Country Global Equilibrium with Investment

An example of a global equilibrium is based on the model of section 5.2.1, with $\rho = 1$ (log preferences) and $F(K_2) = K_2$. When some resources are invested, the market-clearing conditions become

$$Y_1 + Y_1^* = C_1 + C_1^* + K_2 + K_2^*,$$

$$Y_2(s) + Y_2^*(s) + K_2 + K_2^* = C_2(s) + C_2^*(s), \qquad s = 1, 2, \ldots, S.$$

As a result, the price equation (30) for state s is replaced by

$$\frac{p(s)}{1+r} = \frac{\pi(s)\beta(Y_1^W - K_2 - K_2^*)}{Y_2^W(s) + K_2 + K_2^*} = \frac{\pi(s)\beta(Y_1^W - K_2 - K_2^*)}{A(s)F(K_2) + A^*(s)F^*(K_2^*) + K_2 + K_2^*}.$$

Using these relationships, we eliminate $p(s)/(1+r)$ from the firms' profit-maximization condition (40) and find [for our linear production function with

$F'(K_2) \equiv 1]$ that the Home and Foreign firms' profit-maximization conditions are

$$\sum_{s=1}^{S} \left[\frac{\pi(s)\beta(Y_1^W - K_2 - K_2^*)}{A(s)K_2 + A^*(s)K_2^* + K_2 + K_2^*} \right] [A(s) + 1] = 1,$$

$$\sum_{s=1}^{S} \left[\frac{\pi(s)\beta(Y_1^W - K_2 - K_2^*)}{A(s)K_2 + A^*(s)K_2^* + K_2 + K_2^*} \right] [A^*(s) + 1] = 1.$$

These two equations in the unknowns K_2 and K_2^* can be solved for equilibrium investment levels. We can solve for total world investment, $K_2 + K_2^*$, by multiplying the first of the immediately preceding equations by K_2, the second by K_2^*, and adding. The result is

$$K_2 + K_2^*$$

$$= \sum_{s=1}^{S} \left[\frac{\pi(s)\beta(Y_1^W - K_2 - K_2^*)}{A(s)K_2 + A^*(s)K_2^* + K_2 + K_2^*} \right] \{[A(s) + 1]K_2 + [A^*(s) + 1]K_2^*\}$$

$$= \sum_{s=1}^{S} \pi(s)\beta[Y_1^W - (K_2 + K_2^*)] = \beta Y_1^W - \beta(K_2 + K_2^*),$$

from which $K_2 + K_2^* = \beta Y_1^W/(1 + \beta)$ follows. As a result of risk sharing, each country's consumption now is a date- and state-invariant share of world output *net* of world investment.

5.2.4.2   Reprise: The Independence of Investment from Saving for a Small Country

We close with two further remarks about investment. First, eq. (40) shows that, just as in Chapter 1, a small country's investment is independent of its domestic consumption behavior. Given the production function and the statistical distribution of its productivity shock, world securities prices determine a country's equilibrium investment level. Equation (41) may make it appear as if a small country's consumption preferences affect investment decisions. But that interpretation of eq. (41) would be misleading. With complete markets, all country-specific output risk has been diversified away, which is why eq. (41) also holds with Foreign in place of Home consumption. The relation between consumption and a country's investment productivity in eq. (41) is really a relationship that involves *world* consumption.

Second, we've said nothing about the *ownership* of firms. In a complete-markets world, the nationality of a firm's owners clearly has no bearing on optimal investment decisions. But what determines how people actually do allocate their wealth among firms in various countries? We now turn to a model that can answer that question, and we will explain in detail its relationship to the complete-markets model of this section.

5.3   International Portfolio Diversification

By studying a world economy that trades a complete set of Arrow-Debreu securities, we have been able to understand the basic determinants of international trade across states of nature and the requirements for efficient economic allocation under uncertainty. As mentioned earlier, however, real-world international asset trade typically consists of exchanges of much more familiar securities, such as equity shares and risky bonds. How does a world that trades only these familiar assets compare to a complete-markets Arrow-Debreu world?

In this section we explore a world economy in which the only risky assets traded are claims to countries' uncertain outputs—essentially, shares of stock in national economies. We ask how the predictions of this more realistic model compare to those of the Arrow-Debreu model, and we examine various aspects of international portfolio diversification. Lucas (1982) explores a two-country, two-good version of this model. His solution approach, however, is valid only when the equilibrium yields asset prices such that initial wealth is equal across countries. The analysis that follows relaxes this restriction and shows how to derive the international distribution of wealth endogenously.

5.3.1   A Model of Portfolio Allocation

There are two dates (1 and 2), N countries in the world, and S states of nature on date 2. People throughout the world have the same preferences.

Let V_1^n be the date 1 market value of country n's uncertain date 2 output—that is, V_1^n is the price of an asset that pays its owner $Y_2^n(s)$ in state s. One can think of V_1^n as the value of a mutual fund that owns the totality of country n's productive units. Obviously no single investor is likely to be rich enough to own an entire country's future output, but residents of different countries can exchange fractional shares. Indeed, we assume that the N ownership claims on national outputs, along with a risk-free bond offering a net real interest rate of r, are the *only* assets traded on date 1.

A representative resident of country n must divide date 1 income Y_1^n between consumption C_1^n and saving. Given the menu of assets assumed, country n's saving takes the form of net bond purchases B_2^n and net purchases of fractional shares x_m^n in country m's future output, $m = 1, 2, \ldots, N$. [Country n net sales to foreigners of shares in future domestic output, Y_2^n, equal $(1 - x_n^n)V_1^n$, that is, the market value of country n's future output less the share of it that country n's own residents desire to retain in their portfolio, x_n^n.] The constraint linking consumption and saving on date 1 therefore takes the form

$$Y_1^n + V_1^n = C_1^n + B_2^n + \sum_{m=1}^{N} x_m^n V_1^m. \tag{42}$$

Country n's date 2 consumption depends on how its assets perform between periods 1 and 2, which depends, in turn, on the realized state of nature s:

$$C_2^n(s) = (1+r)B_2^n + \sum_{m=1}^{N} x_m^n Y_2^m(s). \tag{43}$$

In interpreting the budget constraint (43), it is worth stressing the distinction between the country mutual fund shares people trade here and the Arrow-Debreu forward contracts considered in previous sections. A standard Arrow-Debreu claim entitles the agent to a payoff in only one state of nature. Here, an investor holding x_m shares of country m's mutual fund is entitled to x_m percent of country m's date 2 output in *every* state of nature.

Country n's representative resident maximizes the S-state analog of eq. (1) subject to eqs. (42) and (43). Substituting the constraints into the expected utility function gives

$$U_1 = u\left[Y_1^n + V_1^n - B_2^n - \sum_{m=1}^{N} x_m^n V_1^m \right]$$

$$+ \beta \sum_{s=1}^{S} \pi(s) u\left[(1+r)B_2^n + \sum_{m=1}^{N} x_m^n Y_2^m(s) \right].$$

The necessary conditions for a maximum are, with respect to B_2^n,

$$u'(C_1^n) = (1+r)\beta \sum_{s=1}^{S} \pi(s) u'[C_2^n(s)] = (1+r)\beta E_1\{u'(C_2^n)\}$$

[which is the same as the bond Euler equation (8)], and, with respect to portfolio shares x_m^n,

$$V_1^m u'(C_1^n) = \beta \sum_{s=1}^{S} \pi(s) u'[C_2^n(s)] Y_2^m(s)$$

$$= \beta E_1\{u'(C_2^n) Y_2^m\}, \qquad m = 1, 2, \dots, N. \tag{44}$$

The intuition underlying eq. (44) is similar to that for other Euler conditions we have encountered. The left-hand side of eq. (44) is the marginal utility cost to a country n resident who purchases country m's risky future output on date 1, and the right-hand side is his expected marginal utility gain. In equilibrium these must be equal.[26]

---

26. Supplement A to this chapter looks at the individual's problem when the horizon is infinite, and derives consumption functions using dynamic programming.

5.3.2   Solving the Model with CRRA Utility

To illustrate the model's implications we assume that people in every country n have identical CRRA period utility functions; see eq. (13). To solve the model we take an educated guess at the equilibrium allocation and find equilibrium portfolios and prices that support it. Our conjecture is that the equilibrium allocation is Pareto efficient (even though there is trade only in bonds and country mutual funds), and that equilibrium allocations therefore take the same general form as for the two-country, CRRA complete-markets example in section 5.2.1.

Defining country n's share of initial world wealth as

$$\mu^n = \frac{Y_1^n + V_1^n}{\sum_{m=1}^{N}(Y_1^m + V_1^m)}, \tag{45}$$

we guess that its share of world consumption in each period and state is also μ^n, just as in section 5.2.1:

$$C_1^n = \mu^n \sum_{m=1}^{N} Y_1^m = \mu^n Y_1^W, \tag{46}$$

$$C_2^n(s) = \mu^n \sum_{m=1}^{N} Y_2^m(s) = \mu^n Y_2^W(s), \qquad s = 1, \dots, S. \tag{47}$$

For any country n the date 2 budget constraint (43) is consistent with eq. (47) if the representative national holds μ^n percent of a global mutual fund that encompasses all countries' second-period outputs,

$$x_m^n = \mu^n, \qquad m = 1, \dots, N, \tag{48}$$

and if bond holdings are zero, $B_2^n = 0$. These consumption and portfolio plans are globally feasible if chosen simultaneously by every country n. To establish that they characterize the economy's equilibrium, we must find prices at which they maximize any country n's intertemporal utility subject to satisfying its date 1 budget constraint. (We already know the date 2 constraint holds.)

For CRRA utility, the bond Euler equation (8) is equivalent to

$$1 + r = \frac{(C_1^n)^{-\rho}}{\beta \sum_{s=1}^{S} \pi(s) C_2^n(s)^{-\rho}}.$$

It is simple to check that the consumption plans posited in eqs. (46) and (47) satisfy this Euler equation, for all countries n, if the equilibrium real interest rate is

$$1 + r = \frac{(Y_1^W)^{-\rho}}{\beta \sum_{s=1}^{S} \pi(s) Y_2^W(s)^{-\rho}}. \tag{49}$$

Similarly, the CRRA case of eq. (44) holds for all countries n when consumption plans follow eqs. (46) and (47) if equilibrium share prices are

$$
V_1^m = \sum_{s=1}^{S} \pi(s)\beta \left[\frac{Y_2^W(s)}{Y_1^W} \right]^{-\rho} Y_2^m(s)
$$

$$
= \beta E_1 \left\{ \left(\frac{Y_2^W}{Y_1^W} \right)^{-\rho} Y_2^m \right\}, \qquad m = 1, 2, \ldots, N. \tag{50}
$$

It remains to check that every country's date 1 budget constraint (42) holds in the hypothesized equilibrium. But this task is easy. By definition (45), country n's date 1 resources, $Y_1^n + V_1^n$, make up a fraction μ^n of total world wealth—the sum of current output and capitalized future output. Thus it is certainly consistent with eq. (42) for country n to consume a fraction μ^n of world output [as in eq. (46)], to purchase the same share μ^n of the global mutual fund [as in eq. (48)], and to choose $B_2^n = 0$.[27]

5.3.3 Efficiency of the Allocation

The close parallel between the equilibrium we have just described and the complete-market equilibrium of section 5.2.1 points to a remarkable result. Even when the assets traded are limited to riskless bonds and shares in each of the N countries' future outputs, the equilibrium allocation is efficient. Indeed, it is *identical* to the equilibrium reached through trade in a full set of S Arrow-Debreu securities, even when S is much greater than N.

To see what is going on, observe by comparing eqs. (50) and (30) that a country n's stock-market value, V_1^n, is also the value of the country's uncertain future output evaluated at the date 1 Arrow-Debreu prices that would prevail were a complete set of contingent claims markets in operation. Thus the consumption share μ^n defined in eq. (45) is the same date- and state-invariant share of world consumption the country would enjoy with complete markets. (We pointed out in section 5.2.1.2 that a country's consumption share under complete markets is its share of wealth in world wealth when uncertain future outputs are evaluated at Arrow-Debreu prices.) Of course, the equilibrium interest rate is the same in the two economies; compare eq. (49) with eq. (33).

---

27. When people in different countries have different degrees of risk aversion, they may still hold the same mutual fund of *risky* assets, but those who are more risk-averse will hold some of their wealth in safe assets while those who are less risk-averse will go short in safe assets (take negative positions in bonds). As a result, the risk-sharing condition (37) can hold, with countries' consumption growth rates perfectly correlated but with the less risk-averse countries having a higher variance of consumption growth. For one model along these lines, see the continuous-time analysis of Obstfeld (1994c). For an example with exponential period utility, see exercise 5.

The economy behaves *as if* there were complete markets because all agents choose to hold equities in the same proportions, *regardless of their wealth levels.* The resulting equilibrium makes everyone's date 2 consumption move in proportion to the return on a single global mutual fund of risky assets. This common diversification strategy eliminates the gains from any further mutual consumption insurance between countries. We have demonstrated this result for identical CRRA preferences, but the same result can be obtained for a broader preference class.[28]

With other utility functions, or with international differences in preferences, people in different countries around the world might choose different portfolios of risky assets.[29] In this situation we can be certain that trade in equities is a perfect substitute for trade in a complete set of Arrow-Debreu securities only under much more restrictive assumptions. Specifically, Pareto efficiency can be ensured only when the number of states of nature S is no greater than $N + 1$, the number of countries plus 1. The intuition behind this "spanning condition" (which appendix 5A proves formally) is simple. With one state of nature on date 2 (the case of certainty), trade in riskless bonds is sufficient to achieve an efficient allocation. If one adds a second state of nature, efficient allocation can be achieved provided a single risky asset is traded in addition to the bond: the two primal Arrow-Debreu securities can be constructed as linear combinations of the bond (which, as we have seen, is itself a linear combination of the Arrow-Debreu securities) and the risky asset. But adding more uncertain states without a corresponding addition of independent risky assets may compromise the economy's ability to achieve an efficient allocation of all risks. In general, spanning requires as many independent assets as states of nature.

Application: International Portfolio Diversification and the Home Bias Puzzle

In section 5.3.2's simple model investors throughout the world all hold the same globally diversified portfolio of stocks. Even in richer settings, the logic of diversification suggests that people should hold a substantial fraction of their stock portfolios abroad. In practice, however, residents of most countries seem to hold a very large share of their equity wealth at home. A number of studies (for example, Grauer and Hakansson, 1987) suggest that an individual's gains from international stock-portfolio diversification are large, especially when emerging markets are included.

The contradiction between the obvious benefits of holding a globally dispersed set of equities and the apparent reluctance to do so is known as the *home bias*

---

28. That class is the HARA class noted in section 5.2.2, footnote 20. See M. Rubinstein (1974) for a proof.

29. But in some special cases they might not (see footnote 27).

Table 5.2
Share of Domestic Equities in Total Equity Portfolio, End 1989

United States	United Kingdom	Japan
0.96	0.82	0.98

Source: French and Poterba (1991).

puzzle. Table 5.2, based on figures reported by French and Poterba (1991), gives the share of domestic equities in the equity holdings of the United States, the United Kingdom, and Japan at the end of 1989. Tesar and Werner (1995) find similar results for 1990 data.[30]

Several considerations cloud the interpretation of Table 5.2, however. First, residents who hold shares of domestic-based multinationals obtain some degree of global portfolio diversification, and taking it into account goes a small way toward resolving the puzzle (see Mitra-Stiff, 1995). A second and closely related point is that Table 5.2 only gives equity holdings and does not give direct foreign investment or bond holdings. (The sharp distinction between corporate stocks and bonds becomes blurred once default and exchange rate risk are taken into account.) Direct foreign investment holdings are difficult to measure because there are no data on the market values of historical capital investments abroad. Tesar and Werner (1995) estimate that in 1990, U.S., Canadian, German, and Japanese direct foreign investment holdings stood at 11, 13, 6, and 6 percent of GNP, respectively. These numbers are substantial but not enough to erase home bias. However, home bias in bond holdings is smaller than that for stocks. The International Monetary Fund estimates that the share of public debt held by nonresidents now exceeds 20 percent for the seven major industrial countries. For Germany and France, nonresidents now hold more than 30 percent of negotiable public debt (Folkerts-Landau and Goldstein, 1994).

A number of possible explanations of the home bias puzzle have been presented; we will consider two of the most important (nontraded goods and small utility gains to diversification) later in this chapter. One obvious explanation is relatively high costs connected with foreign stock acquisition or ownership. Tesar and Werner (1995), noting that the turnover rate on nonresident holdings of equities is greater than the turnover rate for resident owners, argue that trading costs are unlikely to be the answer. Trading cost, however, is only one of several possible costs that might inhibit global diversification.[31]

---

30. Home bias seems to be present but somewhat less extreme for some smaller economies.

31. Kang and Stulz (1995) find that Japanese investors hold a disproportionate share of their foreign assets in large firms. They argue that this practice can be explained by fixed information costs in learning about individual foreign investment opportunities.

Whatever the cause of the current home bias, a growing share of portfolio investment is being channeled abroad today, so that the puzzle may be considerably reduced 25 years from now. American individual investors and mutual funds, for example, substantially increased their foreign equity holdings in the early 1990s. Bohn and Tesar (1995) estimate that the share of foreign equity in U.S. residents' equity portfolios had risen to 8 percent by the end of 1994.   ∎

5.4   Asset Pricing

When the set of assets traded is sufficient to produce a Pareto optimal equilibrium allocation, the price of any asset can be calculated as a linear combination of the underlying Arrow-Debreu prices. The calculation is valid even if the economy does not literally trade Arrow-Debreu securities, provided it *behaves* as if they did exist. In this section we apply this logic to explore asset pricing and the determinants of relative asset returns. Not surprisingly in light of our analysis so far, the less useful an asset is as a consumption hedge, the higher the rate of return that asset must offer investors in equilibrium.

5.4.1   The Consumption-Based Capital Asset Pricing Model

5.4.1.1   Essentials of Asset Pricing

Let us begin within the two-period multicountry framework we used in the last section. Because date 1 Arrow-Debreu prices are the marginal rates of substitution of present consumption for future consumption in various states of nature—recall this interpretation of eq. (6)—they can be used to value the totality of state-contingent payoffs that defines any particular asset. For example, the market price of a country m mutual fund that pays off $Y_2^m(s)$ in date 2 state of nature s is simply

$$V_1^m = \sum_{s=1}^{S} \frac{p(s)Y_2^m(s)}{1+r}.$$

The country m fund's payoffs can be perfectly replicated by a portfolio containing $Y_2^m(s)$ state s Arrow-Debreu securities for every state s, so a price other than this one would create an arbitrage opportunity. The same argument can be applied to price all other assets.

When countries face the same Arrow-Debreu prices, we may substitute any country n's marginal rate of substitution, given by eq. (6), for $p(s)/(1+r)$ in the preceding formula for V_1^m. The result is

$$V_1^m = \sum_{s=1}^{S} \left\{ \frac{\pi(s)\beta u'[C_2^n(s)]}{u'(C_1^n)} \right\} Y_2^m(s).$$

An alternative way to express this equation is as

$$V_1^m = E_1 \left\{ \frac{\beta u'(C_2)}{u'(C_1)} Y_2^m \right\}. \tag{51}$$

In eq. (51) we suppress the country superscript on consumption, n, since it does not matter which country's intertemporal marginal rate of substitution is used to price the asset: all are equal in complete markets. This is another sense in which the complete-markets assumption rationalizes a representative-agent perspective. We have seen that when countries have identical CRRA utility functions, C_1 and C_2 in eq. (51) could be replaced by world consumption levels. [This reasoning inspired our "guess" in section 5.3.2 that eq. (50) was the equilibrium value of V_1^m.]

5.4.1.2   Asset Returns

We now derive a formula that explains asset prices in terms of expected payoffs and the riskiness of those payoffs. Notice that eq. (51) is equivalent to

$$V_1^m = E_1 \left\{ \frac{\beta u'(C_2)}{u'(C_1)} \right\} E_1\{Y_2^m\} + \text{Cov}_1 \left\{ \frac{\beta u'(C_2)}{u'(C_1)}, Y_2^m \right\}.$$

Equation (8) permits the substitution $1/(1+r) = E_1\{\beta u'(C_2)/u'(C_1)\}$ here. The result is

$$V_1^m = \frac{E_1\{Y_2^m\}}{1+r} + \text{Cov}_1 \left\{ \frac{\beta u'(C_2)}{u'(C_1)}, Y_2^m \right\}. \tag{52}$$

According to this equation, the date 1 price of country m's uncertain date 2 output is the sum of two terms. The first is the asset's expected payout, discounted at the riskless rate of interest. The second is the covariance between the relative marginal utility of date 2 consumption and the payout. This covariance reflects the asset's value as consumption insurance. Other things being equal, an asset that tends to pay off unexpectedly well on date 2 when the marginal utility of consumption is unexpectedly high (meaning that consumption itself is unexpectedly low) has value as a consumption hedge and therefore will command a price above its "risk-neutral" or actuarially fair price.

Define the *ex post net real rate of return* to a share in country m's output, r^m, by

$$r^m = \frac{Y_2^m - V_1^m}{V_1^m}.$$

Multiplying both sides of eq. (52) by $(1+r)/V_1^m$ yields

$$E_1\{r^m\} - r = -(1+r)\text{Cov}_1 \left\{ \frac{\beta u'(C_2)}{u'(C_1)}, 1 + r^m \right\}$$

$$= -(1+r)\text{Cov}_1 \left\{ \frac{\beta u'(C_2)}{u'(C_1)}, r^m - r \right\}. \tag{53}$$

Equation (53) is called the *consumption-based capital asset pricing model* (or consumption-based CAPM).[32] It says that the expected premium an asset must yield over the riskless rate of return (called the asset's risk premium or excess return) depends negatively on the covariance of the asset's excess return with the rate of growth of the marginal utility of consumption. Put differently, the excess return depends *positively* on the correlation of the asset's return with world consumption growth.[33]

Our discussion of how the covariance on the right-hand side of eq. (53) affects the asset's *price* also explains how that factor influences the asset's equilibrium *expected return*. A positive covariance means that the asset tends to yield unexpectedly high returns in states of nature when the marginal utility of world consumption is unexpectedly high or, equivalently, when the level of world consumption is unexpectedly low. Because the asset therefore provides a hedge against world output fluctuations, it offers an expected rate of return below the riskless rate of interest in equilibrium. Conversely, if an asset is more likely to have high returns when world output is high (that is, when the marginal utility of consumption is low), the covariance term in eq. (53) is negative and the asset's expected return will include a positive risk premium. Because individual national outputs sum to world output, the "typical" country stock's payoff is likely to be high when global output is high (and therefore to covary negatively with the marginal utility of world consumption).

5.4.1.3   Market Incompleteness, Asset Pricing, and Investment

We have derived the consumption-based CAPM under the assumption that sufficiently many assets are traded to replicate complete markets. In fact, however, when riskless bonds are traded, eq. (53) holds for any internationally traded risky asset, *even if asset markets are not complete*. Equation (44), derived in section 5.3 without any assumptions on the completeness of markets, implies that eq. (51) holds true for the intertemporal marginal rate of substitution $\beta u'(C_2^n)/u'(C_1^n)$ of any country n that can freely trade the country m mutual fund.[34] If riskless bonds are traded, expected intertemporal rates of substitution will be equal across coun-

---

32. In deriving it we have used the fact that for any constant a_0,

$$\text{Cov}_1\left\{\frac{\beta u'(C_2)}{u'(C_1)}, r^m + a_0\right\} = \text{Cov}_1\left\{\frac{\beta u'(C_2)}{u'(C_1)}, r^m\right\}.$$

33. It is worth emphasizing that the present model is a general equilibrium model, in contrast to the older partial equilibrium capital asset pricing model (as in Sharpe, 1964, for example). In the older (international) CAPM model, assets whose returns are positively correlated with the world market portfolio must offer a higher expected return, a risk premium. There is a substantial empirical literature devoted to testing whether a global or national portfolio is more suitable for measuring an asset's risk premium. See Dumas (1994) and Lewis (1995) for surveys of partial equilibrium asset-pricing models.

34. This statement must be qualified if short sales are prohibited and some countries do not hold positive amounts of the fund. A deep issue concerns sufficient conditions under which a global equilibrium

tries [see eq. (8)]. Thus, even if ex post intertemporal rates of substitution are not internationally equal (so that risks are not allocated efficiently), the first-order conditions for utility maximization nonetheless ensure equality among the *covariances* of countries' intertemporal marginal rates of substitution with the return on *any* risky asset they all trade.

This point also has implications for investment under incomplete markets. As we saw in eq. (40), under complete markets the investment decision maximizes the market value of the country m firm's future dividends net of date 1 investment,

$$V_1^m - K_2^m = \sum_{s=1}^{S} \frac{p(s)}{1+r}[A^m(s)F^m(K_2^m) + K_2^m] - K_2^m$$

$$= \sum_{s=1}^{S} \frac{\pi(s)\beta u'[C_2^n(s)]}{u'(C_1^n)}[A^m(s)F^m(K_2^m) + K_2^m] - K_2^m$$

$$= E_1\left\{\frac{A^m(s)F^m(K_2^m) + K_2^m}{1+r}\right\}$$

$$+ \text{Cov}_1\left\{\frac{\beta u'[C_2^n(s)]}{u'(C_1^n)}, A^m(s)\right\}F^m(K_2^m) - K_2^m,$$

where the consumption of any country n gives the same value. If markets are incomplete but people trade bonds and shares in the firm, the covariance term in the last equation must still be the same for all national consumptions n, for any K_2^m. (Again, this equality is true because the same Euler condition corresponding to the asset holds for individuals in all countries.) Thus all owners of the firm, regardless of nationality, will agree that it should raise its investment slightly whenever $d(V_1^m - K_2^m)/dK_2^m > 0$, for the derivative

$$\frac{d(V_1^m - K_2^m)}{dK_2^m} =$$

$$E_1\left\{\frac{A^m(s)F^{m'}(K_2^m) + 1}{1+r}\right\} + \text{Cov}_1\left\{\frac{\beta u'[C_2^n(s)]}{u'(C_1^n)}, A^m(s)\right\}F^{m'}(K_2^m) - 1$$

does *not* depend on which consumption n is used. As a result, optimal investment will still be governed by the condition $d(V_1^m - K_2^m)/dK_2^m = 0$, which is equivalent to eq. (41) and will hold for any shareholder's consumption.[35]

---

is guaranteed to *exist* without complete markets. For theoretical discussion, see Magill and Quinzii (1996).

35. Our assumption of multiplicative production uncertainty plainly is critical to the argument. For a general discussion, see Ekern and Wilson (1974).

5.4.2 The Equity Premium Puzzle

One of the most striking mysteries in empirical finance is the enormous observed average rate of return differential between stocks and bonds. Over the past seventy years, the annual rate of return on stocks has exceeded that on government bonds by more than 5 percent across most major stock markets of the world (see Siegel, 1995). Plainly it is no puzzle that the expected return on stocks is higher than on safer assets. It is the *size* of the differential that perplexes researchers. For seemingly reasonable parameterizations of a general equilibrium complete markets model, premiums of more than 1 or 2 percent cannot easily be rationalized. This problem is the *equity premium puzzle*, first pointed out by Mehra and Prescott (1985) for annual 1889–1978 United States data. As we shall see, the great riskiness of equities that the equity premium puzzle implies only deepens the home bias puzzle.

To see the basic problem, look at the CRRA case of eq. (53), which gives the excess expected return on an equity share of country m's output:

$$E_1\{r^m\} - r = -(1+r)\text{Cov}_1\left\{\beta\left(\frac{C_2}{C_1}\right)^{-\rho}, r^m - r\right\}. \tag{54}$$

Because annual consumption growth is fairly stable and the annual variability of major stock market returns relatively moderate, the covariance of consumption growth with returns, while positive, is too low to explain the huge equity premium unless the risk-aversion coefficient ρ is extremely high.

To get a better feel for the magnitudes involved we consider an approximate version of eq. (54). The approximation is based on a second-order Taylor expansion of the function

$$G\left(\frac{C_2}{C_1}, r^m\right) \equiv \beta\left(\frac{C_2}{C_1}\right)^{-\rho}(r^m - E_1 r^m),$$

the expected value of which equals the covariance entering the equity premium in eq. (54).[36] Near the points $C_2/C_1 = 1$ and $r^m = E_1 r^m$ the approximation is

---

36. The second-order approximation to $G(X_1, X_2)$ in the neighborhood of $X_1 = \bar{X}_1$, $X_2 = \bar{X}_2$ is

$$G(X_1, X_2) \approx G(\bar{X}_1, \bar{X}_2) + G_{X_1}(\bar{X}_1, \bar{X}_2)(X_1 - \bar{X}_1) + G_{X_2}(\bar{X}_1, \bar{X}_2)(X_2 - \bar{X}_2)$$

$$+ \tfrac{1}{2}G_{X_1X_1}(\bar{X}_1, \bar{X}_2)(X_1 - \bar{X}_1)^2 + \tfrac{1}{2}G_{X_2X_2}(\bar{X}_1, \bar{X}_2)(X_2 - \bar{X}_2)^2$$

$$+ G_{X_1X_2}(\bar{X}_1, \bar{X}_2)(X_1 - \bar{X}_1)(X_2 - \bar{X}_2)$$

(assuming the listed derivatives exist). In omitting any higher-order Taylor-expansion terms when we equate expectations of this approximation's two sides (as we will do), we are implicitly assuming that higher-order moments of the joint distribution of X_1 and X_2 are negligible compared to the first and

$$G\left(\frac{C_2}{C_1}, r^m\right) \approx \beta(r^m - E_1 r^m) - \beta\rho\left(\frac{C_2}{C_1} - 1\right)(r^m - E_1 r^m).$$

Taking conditional expectations of both sides above yields

$$E_1 G\left(\frac{C_2}{C_1}, r^m\right) = \text{Cov}_1\left\{\beta\left(\frac{C_2}{C_1}\right)^{-\rho}, r^m - r\right\}$$

$$\approx -\beta\rho\,\text{Cov}_1\left\{\frac{C_2}{C_1} - 1, r^m - r\right\}$$

(recall footnote 32). Using this estimate to eliminate the covariance term in eq. (54) yields the approximation we seek,

$$E_1\{r^m\} - r = (1 + r)\beta\rho\,\text{Cov}_1\left\{\frac{C_2}{C_1} - 1, r^m - r\right\}$$

$$= (1 + r)\beta\rho\kappa\,\text{Std}_1\left\{\frac{C_2}{C_1} - 1\right\}\text{Std}_1\{r^m - r\},$$

where $\kappa \equiv \text{Corr}_1(C_2/C_1, r^m - r)$ is the conditional correlation coefficient between consumption growth and the excess return on equity, and the conditional standard deviation, Std_1, is the square root of the conditional variance.[37]

Mankiw and Zeldes (1991) point out that, taking averages over the entire Mehra-Prescott data set, $\kappa = 0.4$, the standard deviation of per capita consumption growth is 0.036 per year, and that of the excess equity return is 0.167 per year. If we assume that $(1 + r)\beta = 1$, then the model fits the excess average annual 1889–1978 equity return of

$$E\{r^m\} - r = 0.0698 - 0.0080 = 0.0618$$

only if ρ is roughly 26![38] As Mankiw and Zeldes (1991) also observe, the equity premium puzzle is even more severe in postwar U.S. data than in the original

---

second moments. Ingersoll (1987, pp. 259–262) describes the class of "compact" distributions for which this will be the case if the trading interval is sufficiently small.

37. When variables are jointly lognormally distributed, one can obtain an exact expression for the equity premium that closely parallels this one. See, for example, Aiyagari (1993).

38. Another way to see the puzzle is to let mrs_2 be the ex post marginal rate of intertemporal substitution realized on date 2 and rewrite eq. (51) as

$$1 = E_1\{mrs_2, 1 + r^m\}$$

$$= \text{Cov}_1\{mrs_2, 1 + r^m\} + E_1\{mrs_2\}E_1\{1 + r^m\},$$

which implies that

$$1 - E_1\{mrs_2\}E_1\{1 + r^m\} = \text{Cov}_1\{mrs_2, 1 + r^m\}.$$

Observe that $\text{Std}_1\{mrs_2\}\text{Std}_1\{1 + r^m\} = \text{Cov}_1\{mrs_2, 1 + r^m\}/\text{Corr}_1\{mrs_2, 1 + r^m\}$, where $\text{Corr}_1\{mrs_2, 1 + r^m\}$, the correlation coefficient, is below 1 in absolute value. Thus,

Mehra-Prescott sample, with values of ρ as high as 100 needed to justify the observed premium on stocks. Most economists feel that such high levels of risk aversion are unrealistic.[39]

If agents are really so risk averse, it is all the more puzzling that they do not take greater advantage of opportunities to diversify their equity portfolios internationally. From this perspective there is an intimate connection between the home bias and equity premium puzzles: if equity risk is so significant, why isn't much more of it laid off on foreign investors?

Several possible solutions of the equity premium puzzle have been proposed. One factor, stressed by Aiyagari and Gertler (1991), is that transaction costs on stock trades may be higher than on bond trades.[40] The cost difference leads to a liquidity premium on bonds that can explain the high equity premium. Transaction costs must be very high, however, to explain a significant portion of it. Aiyagari and Gertler (1991) and Weil (1992) argue that the presence of nondiversifiable labor-income risk also can help to resolve the puzzle. [With nondiversifiable income eq. (54) won't generally hold for aggregate per capita consumption, only for the individual consumptions of those who can trade equities.] Heaton and Lucas (1995) show how the interaction of several market frictions and imperfections can explain asset-pricing puzzles.

Another line of explanation, due to Constantinides (1990), abandons time-additive utility. Consider a period utility function with *habit persistence*,

$$u(C_t, D_t) = \frac{(C_t - D_t)^{1-\rho}}{1 - \rho},$$

where D_t is a stock of "consumption experience" that evolves according to

---

$\text{Std}_1\{mrs_2\}\text{Std}_1\{1 + r^m\} \geq 1 - \text{E}_1\{mrs_2\}\text{E}_1\{1 + r^m\},$

or

$$\text{Std}_1\{mrs_2\} \geq \frac{1 - \text{E}_1\{mrs_2\}\text{E}_1\{1 + r^m\}}{\text{Std}_1\{1 + r^m\}}.$$

This inequality, due to Hansen and Jagannathan (1991), uses only observable data on returns to define combinations of the mean and standard deviation of mrs_2 (which is not directly observable) that are consistent with an Euler equation like eq. (51). The rationale for this approach, which does not rely on estimating the marginal rate of substitution in consumption, is that the econometrician may be unsure of the underlying utility function or else the consumption data may be measured with error. For $mrs_2 = \beta(C_2/C_1)^{-\rho}$ and low values of ρ, U.S. equity returns violate the Hansen-Jagannathan bound.

39. Kandel and Stambaugh (1991) argue that risk aversion as high as $\rho = 30$ should not be ruled out, but even that high value would be insufficient to match the model to postwar data. The prewar-postwar difference may be due in part to spurious volatility in prewar U.S. national income data; see C. Romer (1989).

40. In this spirit, He and Modest (1995) show that even for low degrees of risk aversion, transaction costs and trading constraints can make aggregate consumption data appear consistent with modified Hansen-Jagannathan bounds.

$$D_t = (1 - \delta)D_{t-1} + \delta\zeta C_{t-1}, \qquad 0 < \zeta, \delta < 1.$$

(Supplement B to Chapter 2 shows a different way of relaxing time additivity.) With habit persistence, accumulated consumption experience D_t tends to make $C_t - D_t$ a small number if ζ is close to 1, allowing realistic consumption fluctuations to have a very large effect on the marginal rate of substitution between current and future consumption even when ρ is not large. Since a more volatile ex post intertemporal marginal rate of substitution raises the warranted equity premium [by analogy to what eq. (54) would predict], habit persistence can help resolve the puzzle. But the attendant increase in the volatility of expected intertemporal marginal substitution rates [by analogy to what eq. (8) would predict] makes real interest rates counterfactually volatile.

A related asset-pricing puzzle, raised by Mehra and Prescott (1985) and emphasized by Weil (1989b), is the "low riskless interest rate puzzle." With CRRA utility, eq. (8) can be written

$$1 + r = \frac{1}{E_1\left\{\beta\left(\frac{C_{t+1}}{C_t}\right)^{-\rho}\right\}}.$$

To illustrate the riskless rate puzzle we assume that C is lognormally distributed.[41] Then the last equation yields the approximation

$$r \approx \log(1 + r) = \rho E_1\left\{\log\left(\frac{C_{t+1}}{C_t}\right)\right\} - \frac{\rho^2}{2}\text{Var}\left\{\log\left(\frac{C_{t+1}}{C_t}\right)\right\} - \log(\beta).$$

In the Mehra-Prescott sample the mean annual per capita consumption growth rate is 0.018 per year, with a variance of 0.0013. Thus for a reasonable ρ value such as 2, even with $\beta = 1$, the model predicts a yearly riskless rate of 3.34 percent, more than four times the 0.80 percent that Mehra and Prescott estimated.

Some of the same factors that help explain the equity premium puzzle—for example, transaction costs and uninsured labor income—also imply a low riskless rate. In the early 1980s real interest rates rose globally, largely erasing the riskless rate conundrum from recent data. As the next application shows, several other historical epochs have been characterized by quite high real interest rates.

---

41. If X is a normally distributed random variable with mean μ_X and variance σ_X^2, then $\exp X$ is lognormal with mean

$$E\{\exp X\} = \exp\left(\mu_X + \tfrac{1}{2}\sigma_X^2\right).$$

Notice that $E\{\exp X\} > \exp \mu_X$ is consistent with Jensen's inequality [the function $\exp(\cdot)$ is strictly convex].

Application: The Equity Premium Puzzle over the Very Long Run

Mehra and Prescott (1985) calculated that the average annual real return on a market portfolio of U.S. stocks exceeded that on U.S. Treasury securities by 6.18 percent over the period 1889–1978.[42] Table 5.3 reports data on real equity and bond returns over subperiods of the years 1802–1992, a span of nearly two centuries.

Despite its year-to-year variability, the real return on the U.S. stock market over long periods has been remarkably stable. Real bond returns, in contrast, were much lower after 1925 than earlier. (A major reason for these low average returns was that bonds yielded negative real returns during the high-inflation 1970s.) Thus there is some sense in which the equity premium puzzle becomes less severe when one looks at longer time periods. Still, even the period 1926–92 is a very long one.

One might conjecture that the high ex post long-term returns on U.S. equities simply reflect the fact the United States has been one of the world's great economic success stories. The equity premium phenomenon, however, while not universal, certainly has characterized several other industrial-country financial markets. Over the 1926–92 period, annual real yields of 5.71 percent on British stocks and of 5.43 percent on German stocks far exceeded bond returns in those countries. (British bond yields averaged below comparable U.S. yields while German bonds suffered the ravages of postwar inflation.) Twentieth-century Britain is hardly an example of unalloyed economic dynamism. German stocks performed well despite the nearly total destruction or dismantling of the country's physical capital stock during and just after World War II. Thus the equity premium puzzle seems to have arisen in several countries despite disparate economic circumstances. This finding is not totally surprising: to the extent that international capital markets have been integrated since 1926, relative average asset returns over long periods should reflect global rather than country-specific factors.

Some researchers suggest that the equity premium is simply a historical anomaly of the post-Depression period. Blanchard (1993) develops ex ante measures of the equity premium for a number of OECD countries (the numbers in Table 5.3 are based on ex post returns) and contends that the equity premium has become much smaller since 1980. Brown, Goetzmann, and Ross (1995) argue for an international investing perspective that accounts for survival bias, which appears to be more important when one looks at very long time periods. They point out that in 1792, investors could buy stocks in markets in Holland, France, Austria, and Germany

---

42. Over 1889–1919 they used a commercial paper rate, as the first Treasury certificates were issued only in 1920.

Table 5.3
Real U.S. Stock and Government Bond Returns (annual geometrically compounded percent rate of return)

Period	Stocks	Short Bonds	Long Bonds
1802–1992	6.7	2.9	3.4
1871–1992	6.6	1.7	2.6
1802–70	7.0	5.1	4.8
1871–1925	6.6	3.2	3.7
1926–92	6.6	0.5	1.7
1946–92	6.6	0.4	0.4

Source: Siegel (1995).

in addition to the United States and Britain. But only the U.S. and British markets have operated continuously since then. When market casualties are taken into account, Brown, Goetzman, and Ross argue, the equity premium becomes much smaller.

∎

5.4.3   The Infinite-Horizon Consumption-Based CAPM

The model we have been exploring in this section and section 5.3 is easily extended to encompass an infinite horizon. The representative resident of country n now maximizes the expected utility function

$$U_t = E_t \left\{ \sum_{s=t}^{\infty} \beta^{s-t} u(C_s^n) \right\} \tag{55}$$

on any date t, where the conditional expectation operator averages over all possible future contingency plans for consumption. The country n individual's period-by-period finance constraint is

$$B_{s+1}^n + \sum_{m=1}^{N} x_{m,s+1}^n V_s^m = (1 + r_s) B_s^n + \sum_{m=1}^{N} x_{m,s}^n (Y_s^m + V_s^m) - C_s^n, \tag{56}$$

where V_s^m now denotes the *ex dividend* date s market price of a claim to the entire income stream of country m in *all* future periods, $x_{m,s}^n$ denotes the fractional share of country m's security purchased by agent n in period $s - 1$, and r_s is the one-period real interest rate between periods $s - 1$ and s. Maximizing the utility function (55) subject to the constraints (56) shows that on every date s the first-order conditions

$$u'(C_s^n) V_s^m = \beta E_s \{ u'(C_{s+1}^n)(Y_{s+1}^m + V_{s+1}^m) \}, \tag{57}$$

$$u'(C_s^n) = (1 + r_{s+1})\beta E_s\{u'(C_{s+1}^n)\}$$ (58)

will hold.[43]

To derive asset prices take the $s = t + 1$ Euler condition (57) and use it to eliminate V_{t+1}^m from the $s = t$ condition. The result is

$$V_t^m = E_t\left\{\frac{\beta u'(C_{t+1})}{u'(C_t)} Y_{t+1}^m\right\} + E_t\left\{\frac{\beta u'(C_{t+1})}{u'(C_t)} E_{t+1}\left\{\frac{\beta u'(C_{t+2})}{u'(C_{t+1})}(Y_{t+2}^m + V_{t+2}^m)\right\}\right\}$$

(where we have dropped the country superscript n on consumption because the equilibrium asset price does not depend on which nation's consumption we use to value future payoffs). Because $\beta u'(C_{t+1})/u'(C_t)$ is in the set of information upon which date $t + 1$ expectations are conditioned, we may pass that marginal rate of substitution through the expectations operator $E_{t+1}\{\cdot\}$ and express the second summand on the right-hand side of the preceding equation as

$$E_t\left\{\frac{\beta u'(C_{t+1})}{u'(C_t)} E_{t+1}\left\{\frac{\beta u'(C_{t+2})}{u'(C_{t+1})}(Y_{t+2}^m + V_{t+2}^m)\right\}\right\}$$

$$= E_t\left\{E_{t+1}\left\{\frac{\beta^2 u'(C_{t+2})}{u'(C_t)}(Y_{t+2}^m + V_{t+2}^m)\right\}\right\}.$$

By the law of iterated conditional expectations, $E_t\{E_{t+1}\{X\}\} = E_t\{X\}$ for any random variable X, so we obtain the simplified formula for V_t^m:

$$V_t^m = E_t\left\{\frac{\beta u'(C_{t+1})}{u'(C_t)} Y_{t+1}^m\right\} + E_t\left\{\frac{\beta^2 u'(C_{t+2})}{u'(C_t)}(Y_{t+2}^m + V_{t+2}^m)\right\}.$$

The usual process of iterative forward substitution, coupled with the condition

$$\lim_{T\to\infty} E_t\left\{\beta^T[u'(C_{t+T})/u'(C_t)]V_{t+T}^m\right\} = 0$$

to exclude speculative bubbles, shows the date t price of the country m equity to be

$$V_t^m = E_t\left\{\sum_{s=t+1}^{\infty}\frac{\beta^{s-t}u'(C_s)}{u'(C_t)} Y_s^m\right\}$$

$$= \sum_{s=t+1}^{\infty} R_{t,s}E_t\{Y_s^m\} + \sum_{s=t+1}^{\infty} \text{Cov}_t\left\{\frac{\beta^{s-t}u'(C_s)}{u'(C_t)}, Y_s^m\right\}.$$ (59)

---

43. Just solve eq. (56) for C_s^n, substitute the result into eq. (55), and differentiate with respect to $x_{m,s+1}^n$ and B_{s+1}^n. Alternatively, Supplement A to this chapter gives a dynamic programming approach and also shows how to derive the optimal consumption function in special cases.

The second equality is derived in the same fashion as eq. (52), where $R_{t,s}$ (as usual) is the date t market discount factor for noncontingent date $s > t$ consumption,

$$R_{t,s} = E_t \left\{ \frac{\beta^{s-t} u'(C_s)}{u'(C_t)} \right\}, \tag{60}$$

that is, the inverse of the gross interest rate on a riskless $s - t$ period discount bond.[44] Equation (59) is a very natural extension of the two-period pricing equation (52). It states that an asset's price is the expected present value of payouts (discounted at riskless rates) plus a sum of risk adjustments, each of which reflects the asset's contribution to consumption insurance on a different future date.

All the results on the efficiency of equity trade in a two-period model carry over to an infinite horizon. For CRRA utility the results of section 5.3.2 generalize immediately. In particular, each country holds a fixed share of the world equity portfolio, each country's consumption is a constant fraction of world output Y_t^W on every date t, and the multiperiod analog of eq. (50) holds:

$$V_t^m = E_t \left\{ \sum_{s=t+1}^{\infty} \beta^{s-t} \left(\frac{Y_s^W}{Y_t^W} \right)^{-\rho} Y_s^m \right\}, \qquad m = 1, 2, \ldots, N. \tag{61}$$

Application: GDP-Linked Securities and Estimates of V^m

If claims to countries' entire future outputs were traded, how big would V^m be in practice? Shiller (1993) has advocated creation of such securities on the grounds that they would facilitate hedging against fluctuations in currently nontradable income components, notably much of labor income. (Labor income is largely uninsurable because it depends on the worker's effort and thus is subject to moral hazard absent some harsh enforcement mechanism such as slavery.) Shiller estimates the market value of a perpetual claim to a county's entire GDP, along with the standard deviation of the return on that asset. His measures of a country's worth far exceed those produced by standard financial wealth calculations, in part because roughly two-thirds of output in most countries goes to labor, and payment streams earned by labor are not securitized. Positing a common, constant market discount rate of 6.8 percent per annum (which is assumed to incorporate an appropriate risk correction), Shiller calculates the dollar market value of a claim to all future U.S.

---

44. The same reasoning behind Euler equations (8) or (58) shows that when there is a riskless long-term discount bond that pays 1 output unit after $s - t$ periods in return for $R_{t,s}$ output units invested today, individual consumption optimality requires

$R_{t,s} u'(C_t) = \beta^{s-t} E_t\{u'(C_s)\}$.

Equation (60) for $R_{t,s}$ follows.

Table 5.4
Measures of V^m, the Securitized Value of a Claim to a Country's Entire Future GDP, 1992 (billions of U.S. dollars)

Country	V^m	$\text{Std}(r^m)$	Country	V^m	$\text{Std}(r^m)$
Argentina[a]	2,460	9.86	Nigeria	2,019	10.06
Australia	4,340	3.88	Pakistan	2,894	2.45
Brazil	10,032	8.88	Philippines[a]	1,602	3.68
Canada	7,663	4.22	South Africa	1,722	8.98
France	12,901	5.38	Spain	6,721	6.30
Germany (West)	16,796	4.47	Sweden	1,972	5.70
India	20,378	4.32	Switzerland	1,911	5.30
Italy	11,540	4.68	Thailand	4,007	3.99
Japan	31,762	8.41	Turkey	3,868	3.38
Kenya	418	4.34	United Kingdom	13,495	1.46
Mexico	9,583	5.33	United States	82,075	2.03
Netherlands	3,607	4.68	Venezuela	2,501	6.87

Source: Methodology is based on Shiller (1993, ch. 4). Underlying annual real GDP data are from Penn World Table, version 5.6. Standard deviations are on annual return (income plus appreciation) of a perpetual claim to GDP.
[a] 1990 value based on 1950–90 data.

output at $81 trillion as of 1990, or more than 14 times that year's GDP. By contrast, standard measures of wealth (real estate, stocks and bonds, and so on) arrive at a 1990 figure of $18 trillion, just over three times GDP.

In Table 5.4 we update Shiller's V^m calculations to 1992; also presented are estimates of the standard deviations of annual net returns r^m on the perpetual GDP claims, defined by

$$r_t^m = \frac{Y_t^m}{V_{t-1}^m} + \frac{V_t^m - V_{t-1}^m}{V_{t-1}^m},$$

the sum of the GDP "dividend" and the capital gain, per dollar invested. (In the two-period model of this section, we could omit a term containing the future asset price in defining returns because assets had no resale value after paying their date 2 dividends.) The V^m estimates are constructed using simple univariate time series processes for each country's GDP, estimated over 1950–92. The parameter estimates are then used to construct the forecasts of future GDP growth that enter into the present value formula for V^m; see Shiller (1993, ch. 4) for details.

Though the market value of Japanese financial wealth (including stocks, bonds, and land) frequently exceeds that of the United States, a perpetual claim to Japan's entire output, including labor's product, is estimated to be worth less than half as much. The standard deviation of the yearly return on a claim to U.S. output is only 2.03 percent; the perpetual Japanese claim's annual return volatility, at 8.41 percent, is more than four times higher. Note that because the claims are present values of current and all expected future GDPs, routine rate-of-return fluctuations can imply very large international wealth redistributions.

These present-value calculations can be questioned on a number of grounds: they depend on the discount factor chosen and on the assumption that it is constant, and they can be sensitive to the time series processes used to represent expectations of future GDP. Moreover, the discount factor for future outputs is not explicitly linked to a risk premium, either of the consumption-based CAPM variety or a covariance with financial-market returns as in Sharpe (1964). But Shiller's basic point that existing asset markets are not nearly complete enough to substitute for perpetual claims on national GDPs probably is robust.

Shiller goes on to argue that markets in perpetual GDPs are feasible and that policymakers should be actively working to facilitate them. A number of practical obstacles would have to be surmounted, however, before this step could be taken. One is moral hazard. If the claims are indexed to government reports on GDP, and if a country is short in its own stock (as it would be in the models considered thus far), one can envision large incentives for governments to underreport output. Another problem, enforceability, will be central in Chapter 6. How would other countries enforce a trillion-dollar claim against Japan, much less against the United States? Individuals would still be subject to idiosyncratic nontradable risks. Finally, as section 5.5 will discuss in detail, there are limits to a country's ability to insure against fluctuations in the nontraded component of its GDP, even when problems of contract enforceability or moral hazard are absent. Despite these causes for caution, Shiller's plan raises interesting and important questions about the possibility of more efficient global risk sharing.   ∎

5.5   The Role of Nontradables

Chapter 4 pointed out that many goods, especially service-intensive goods, are never traded across national borders. Since nontraded goods constitute a large share of total output in most countries, it is important to ask how their presence modifies our analysis of international diversification and portfolio choice. We shall see that even when there are no restrictions on trade in assets, the existence of nontraded goods can lead to lower international consumption correlations and to a home preference in asset holdings.

5.5.1   Trade in Contingent Securities

The effects of nontradable goods can be illustrated by introducing them into a two-period, S state complete markets model. Assume again N countries, with a representative country n resident maximizing a function of tradable and nontradable consumption levels,

$$U_1 = u(C_{T,1}^n, C_{N,1}^n) + \beta \sum_{s=1}^{S} \pi(s) u[C_{T,2}^n(s), C_{N,2}^n(s)]. \tag{62}$$

For simplicity we consider the case of a pure endowment economy, in which country n's per capita endowments of tradable and nontradable goods are denoted by Y_T^n and Y_N^n, respectively. We assume it is costless to ship tradables.

What types of securities can be traded if some goods are not tradable? People from any country can still promise to deliver specified amounts of *tradable* output in the various states of nature. But securities promising the delivery of *nontradable* output can be traded only among residents of the same country. Nonetheless, international trade is possible in claims that are *indexed* to random nontradable endowments but *payable* in traded goods.

Now $p(s)/(1+r)$ stands for the price, in terms of date 1 tradables, of a unit of tradables delivered on date 2 if and only if the state is s. Under free trade, countries face common prices $p(s)/(1+r)$. The relative price of nontradables in terms of tradables, however, is country specific (because international arbitrage is not possible for nontradables). We denote by $p_{N,1}^n$ the country n price of nontradables in terms of tradables on date 1, and by $p_{N,2}^n(s)$ the same relative price on date 2 *in state s*. Thus, $p_{N,2}^n(s)p(s)/(1+r)$ is the price of date 2, state s, *non*tradables in terms of date 1 tradables. Given these prices, a typical resident of country n faces the budget constraint

$$C_{T,1}^n + p_{N,1}^n C_{N,1}^n + \sum_{s=1}^{S} \frac{p(s)C_{T,2}^n(s) + p_{N,2}^n(s)p(s)C_{N,2}^n(s)}{1+r}$$

$$= Y_{T,1}^n + p_{N,1}^n Y_{N,1}^n + \sum_{s=1}^{S} \frac{p(s)Y_{T,2}^n(s) + p_{N,2}^n(s)p(s)Y_{N,2}^n(s)}{1+r}. \tag{63}$$

Necessary first-order conditions for maximization of the lifetime utility function (62) subject to the constraint (63) are derived in the usual way. These conditions show that on date 1 and for each state s on date 2, the marginal rate of substitution between traded and nontraded goods is equal to their relative price

$$\frac{\partial u(C_T^n, C_N^n)/\partial C_N^n}{\partial u(C_T^n, C_N^n)/\partial C_T^n} = p_N^n, \tag{64}$$

where the relevant date subscripts and state indexes are understood. Similarly, Euler equations analogous to eq. (5) also follow for every $s = 1, \ldots, S$,

$$\frac{p(s)}{1+r} \cdot \frac{\partial u(C_{T,1}^n, C_{N,1}^n)}{\partial C_T^n} = \pi(s)\beta \frac{\partial u[C_{T,2}^n(s), C_{N,2}^n(s)]}{\partial C_T^n},$$

$$\frac{1}{p_{N,1}^n} \cdot \frac{p_{N,2}^n(s)p(s)}{1+r} \cdot \frac{\partial u(C_{T,1}^n, C_{N,1}^n)}{\partial C_N^n} = \pi(s)\beta \frac{\partial u[C_{T,2}^n(s), C_{N,2}^n(s)]}{\partial C_N^n}. \tag{65}$$

The second, less familiar, Euler condition states that at an optimum, the date 1 marginal utility cost of a unit of date 2, state s nontradables must equal the expected date 2 marginal utility benefit.

Nontraded goods have to be consumed domestically, so equilibrium in nontradables within country n requires that on date 1 and in every date 2 state,

$$C_N^n = Y_N^n. \tag{66}$$

Since agents throughout the world face a common set of Arrow-Debreu prices for state-contingent payments of tradables, Euler equation (65) and the market-clearing condition (66) imply that for any two countries m and n,

$$\frac{\pi(s)\beta\partial u[C_{T,2}^m(s), Y_{N,2}^m(s)]/\partial C_T^m}{\partial u(C_{T,1}^m, Y_{N,1}^m)/\partial C_T^m} = \frac{\pi(s)\beta\partial u[C_{T,2}^n(s), Y_{N,2}^n(s)]/\partial C_T^n}{\partial u(C_{T,1}^n, Y_{N,1}^n)/\partial C_T^n}. \tag{67}$$

This condition generalizes eq. (34); it implies that ex post growth rates in the marginal utility of tradables are equal when countries are able to transact in a complete set of state-contingent claims on future tradable goods.

For national consumptions of nontradables there is no simple condition on marginal utilities analogous to eq. (67). Because forward contracts for nontradables can be traded only domestically, no common relative prices force equality across countries in marginal rates of intertemporal substitution for nontradables. Condition (67) implies that further international exchanges of tradables across time and across states of nature yield no efficiency gains, but further exchanges of nontradables could—if only nontradables could be traded! As a result, the allocation of world resources is only *constrained* Pareto efficient, not Pareto efficient *tout court*.

It is important to avoid a semantic trap here. Is the allocation that the market produces inefficient in any meaningful sense? To answer, one must determine if a utilitarian planner could improve on it. In this case the answer is *no*, unless the planner somehow has the technological capacity to move goods across national borders when the market will not. If, for example, goods are nontraded because they are prohibitively costly to transport, then a planner cannot usefully ship them across borders either, and has no advantage over the market. If, on the other hand, a good is nontraded in part because of an artificial government restriction, such as a licensing requirement that allows only French electricians to wire houses in France, then a planner able to shift electrician services around internationally can improve on the market. We say that the market equilibrium is *constrained* Pareto efficient if a benevolent economic planner facing the same technological and information constraints as the market cannot Pareto-improve on the market outcome (that is, cannot make one country better off without making at least one other country worse off). In practice, there are nontraded goods in both categories, those that are literally impossible to transport and those that would be traded except for government restrictions. For purposes of clarity, the reader should assume in the following analysis that nontraded goods are internationally immobile for technological reasons. Because most of the analysis is positive rather than normative, however, which way we choose to interpret nontradability is not essential.

In the presence of nontraded goods, it is generally no longer possible to derive neat relationships such as eq. (37) between countries' total real per capita consumption growth rates as conventionally measured. However, in the special case where utility within a period is additive in tradeds and nontradeds and of the form

$$u(C_T, C_N) = \frac{C_T^{1-\rho}}{1-\rho} + v(C_N),$$

eq. (67) does imply that national growth rates of *tradables* consumption are perfectly correlated with each other. In the more general case of nonadditive period utility, nontradable consumption affects marginal rates of substitution for tradable consumption and prevents any simple general relationship analogous to eq. (37) from holding even for tradable consumption.

It is nonetheless straightforward to extend the consumption-based CAPM, even when individuals' marginal utility of tradables is not independent of their nontradable consumption. Claims to a country's nontradable endowment are priced in the same way as claims to its tradable endowment. However, nontradable output must be converted into tradables locally, and at the local relative price, before foreign shareholders can be paid. For a claim to country m's tradable date 2 output,

$$V_{T,1}^m = \sum_{s=1}^{S} \frac{p(s) Y_{T,2}^m(s)}{1+r} = \sum_{s=1}^{S} \frac{\pi(s) \beta \partial u[C_{T,2}^n(s), Y_{N,2}^n(s)]/\partial C_T^n}{\partial u(C_{T,1}^n, Y_{N,1}^n)/\partial C_T^n} Y_{T,2}^m(s), \qquad (68)$$

where $1/(1+r)$ is the date 1 tradables price of sure date 2 tradables. By the marginal equality (67) implied by complete markets for future tradables, $V_{T,1}^m$ is independent of the country n whose residents' consumptions are used to evaluate that price. For a claim to country m's nontradable date 2 output, again independently of n,

$$V_{N,1}^m = \sum_{s=1}^{S} \frac{p(s) p_{N,2}^m(s) Y_{N,2}^m(s)}{1+r}$$

$$= \sum_{s=1}^{S} \frac{\pi(s) \beta \partial u[C_{T,2}^n(s), Y_{N,2}^n(s)]/\partial C_T^n}{\partial u(C_{T,1}^n, Y_{N,1}^n)/\partial C_T^n} p_{N,2}^m(s) Y_{N,2}^m(s). \qquad (69)$$

5.5.2   Preference Shocks

Throughout the chapter, we have assumed that $u(C)$ is stable across states of nature. What if there are unanticipated shocks to national health, weather patterns, birth rates, and so on, that affect a country's marginal rates of substitution across various market goods? A model with preference shocks can be interpreted as a special case of the nontraded goods model.

Let us assume that all goods are traded internationally and all countries n have utility functions of the form

$$u(C_1^n) + \beta \sum_{s=1}^{S} \pi(s)u[C_2^n(s); \varepsilon^n(s)], \tag{70}$$

where $\varepsilon^n(s)$ is a country-specific, state-specific preference shock in period 2. Since preference shocks don't affect endowments, the budget constraint is the same as in the traded-goods-only case. The intertemporal state-specific Euler equations for representatives from countries m and n imply an efficiency condition completely analogous to eq. (67) for the model with nontradables,

$$\frac{\pi(s)\beta u'[C_2^m(s); \varepsilon^m(s)]}{u'(C_1^m)} = \frac{\pi(s)\beta u'[C_2^n(s); \varepsilon^n(s)]}{u'(C_1^n)}. \tag{71}$$

Just as in the case of nontraded goods, the presence of preference shocks rules out any exact relationship between consumption growth rates across countries. In particular, equations as simple as eq. (37) generally won't hold. By putting additional structure on the stochastic processes governing differentials in shocks across countries, one can sometimes derive predictions about consumption correlations. In any case, complete Arrow-Debreu contracts still yield a Pareto efficient allocation provided preference shocks are fully observable. (An omnipotent benevolent planner could not improve upon the market outcome.) When preference shocks aren't observable, the question of efficiency becomes more subtle; see Atkeson and Lucas (1992) and Lucas (1992).

Preference shocks that are large and erratic present a problem for empirical work, since it may be hard to control for such shocks using observable variables (see the next application). Nevertheless, many of our results can be generalized to allow for preference shocks (though we do not treat the issue in detail here). The remaining theoretical development in this section focuses on nontraded goods rather than preference shocks, but which factor is more important in practice ultimately is an empirical question.

Application: Nontradability and International Consumption Correlations

The earlier application on international consumption correlations (p. 290) implicitly assumed that all output is tradable. But if a significant share of output cannot be traded, a country's consumption growth could be more highly correlated with domestic output growth than with world consumption growth, despite complete markets in claims on future tradables, simply because it is technologically infeasible for countries to pool nontraded consumption risks. If the period utility function is additive over tradables and nontradables, then efficiency condition (67) implies for internationally identical CRRA preferences that consumption growth rates for *tradables* are equalized in a constrained-efficient equilibrium. But without intraperiod additivity, even that simple prediction of the model doesn't follow. Nevertheless, Lewis (1996) shows that one can still test the complete-market model's predictions about international consumption correlations by controlling for nontradable consumption levels.

To illustrate, assume that the period utility function takes the CES-CRRA form

$$
u(C_T, C_N) = \frac{\left\{ \left[\gamma^{\frac{1}{\theta}} C_T^{\frac{\theta-1}{\theta}} + (1-\gamma)^{\frac{1}{\theta}} C_N^{\frac{\theta-1}{\theta}} \right]^{\frac{\theta}{\theta-1}} \right\}^{1-\rho}}{1-\rho},
\tag{72}
$$

where $\rho > 0$ continues to denote the risk aversion coefficient and $\theta > 0$ is the intratemporal substitution elasticity between traded and nontraded goods. Efficiency condition (67) implies that on any date t, the ex post intertemporal marginal rate of substitution for tradables is a constant λ_t that is the same for any country n,

$$
\frac{\partial u(C_{T,t}^n, Y_{N,t}^n)/\partial C_T^n}{\partial u(C_{T,t-1}^n, Y_{N,t-1}^n)/\partial C_T^n} = \lambda_t.
$$

Using the functional form (72), let's logarithmically differentiate with respect to the date t variables, starting at their date $t-1$ values. With "hats" denoting log derivatives (infinitesimal percent changes), we arrive at the equation

$$
\widehat{C}_T^n = \frac{-\theta}{1 - [\phi(1-\theta\rho)]} \widehat{\lambda} + \frac{(1-\phi)(1-\theta\rho)}{1 - [\phi(1-\theta\rho)]} \widehat{Y}_N^n,
\tag{73}
$$

where

$$
\phi \equiv \frac{\gamma^{\frac{1}{\theta}} (C_T^n)^{\frac{\theta-1}{\theta}}}{\gamma^{\frac{1}{\theta}} (C_T^n)^{\frac{\theta-1}{\theta}} + (1-\gamma)^{\frac{1}{\theta}} (C_N^n)^{\frac{\theta-1}{\theta}}} < 1.
$$

Equation (73) shows that in a constrained-efficient equilibrium, the evolution of country n's traded-goods consumption depends on both the change in the "global" factor λ_t (which is higher the scarcer world tradable resources are) and the change in the domestic endowment of nontradeds. Only when $\theta\rho = 1$ is the function (72) additive, so that growth rates of traded-goods consumption are perfectly correlated across countries.

Lewis (1996) tests eq. (73) econometrically by estimating an equation of the form

$$\Delta \log(C^n_{\mathrm{T},t} - Y^n_{\mathrm{D},t})$$

$$= \upsilon_t + \psi_1 \Delta \log Y^n_{\mathrm{N},t} + \psi_2 \Delta \log Y^n_{\mathrm{D},t} + \psi_3 \Delta \log(Y^n_{\mathrm{T},t} - Y^n_{\mathrm{D},t}) + \epsilon^n_t$$

for a panel of countries, where $Y^n_{\mathrm{D},t}$ is a proxy for the services of durables, υ_t is a global consumption shock common to all countries on date t, $Y^n_{\mathrm{N},t}$ is nontradable output as conventionally measured, $Y^n_{\mathrm{T},t}$ is tradable output, and the composite error ϵ^n_t incorporates measurement error as well as random preference shocks.[45] Under constrained-efficient risk sharing, the coefficient $\psi_3 = 0$: tradable consumption growth can depend on domestic nontraded output growth but not on domestic traded output growth, as shocks to the latter have been internationally pooled and influence $\Delta \log(C^n_{\mathrm{T},t} - Y^n_{\mathrm{D},t})$ only through their effect on the common time-varying intercept υ_t.

Lewis finds in her full sample of countries that ψ_3 is significantly positive, so that idiosyncratic nondurable tradable output growth has a detectable positive correlation with nondurable tradable consumption growth even after possible correlations with nontradable supply shocks have been controlled for. However, a split of her sample into countries with severe official foreign exchange restrictions and others reveals that ψ_3 is significant only for the former group. Lewis concludes that after corrections for nontradability and durability are made, constrained-efficient risk sharing cannot be rejected for the group of countries with relatively low government barriers to asset trade.

Lewis's results are based on a number of maintained hypotheses and data compromises, and therefore warrant cautious interpretation. Further, her tests do not examine risks other than output risks. Nonetheless, the Lewis study suggests that the low international correlations between aggregate national consumptions may in fact be compatible with substantial use of feasible opportunities for pooling output risks by the more developed economies. The nature of the assets countries trade to achieve such risk pooling is an open question, since even trade in noncontingent bonds can facilitate partial sharing of risks.[46] ∎

5.5.3   International Diversification with Nontraded Goods

As noted earlier, the significant shares of nontradables in most countries' consumption baskets may help explain the puzzlingly low international diversification of

---

45. Lewis argues that the services consumer durables provide are likely to be nontradable, despite the tradability of the durable goods themselves. Her paper provides a detailed discussion of the data, which are drawn from 1970–85 studies underlying the Penn Word Table.

46. Baxter and Crucini's (1995) simulations of a two-country model economy suggest that, for industrial-country levels of uncertainty, consumption in a complete-markets world behaves much like it does in a world with only bond trade when productivity shocks are transitory. When a shock is permanent, however, the country in which it occurs adjusts its consumption more or less fully in a bonds-only regime, in sharp contrast to what would happen if the shock's effects had been shared ex ante.

private equity portfolios (see Table 5.2). To illustrate, we continue to assume a global endowment economy with the preferences of a country n resident described by eq. (62).

Assume now, however, that people can trade only shares of future national outputs (and bonds) as in section 5.3 rather than the Arrow-Debreu securities of the last subsection. We continue to denote by $V_{T,1}^m$ the price in terms of date 1 tradables of the claim to country m's random output of tradables on date 2. People also can trade claims on any country m's output of nontradables, but as we have seen, because nontradables cannot cross national borders, a *foreign* owner of such a claim must be paid in tradables. Again, $V_{N,1}^m$ denotes the price (in terms of date 1 tradables) of the claim to $p_{N,2}^m(s)Y_{N,2}^m(s)$ units of the tradable in state s on date 2.

Section 5.3.2 showed that for an important class of period utility functions, international trade in output equity claims can bring about an efficient resource allocation when all output is tradable. When some output is nontradable, however, the conditions leading to efficiency are more stringent. To illustrate, we start by following Stockman and Dellas (1989) in considering a period utility function that is *additive* in C_T and C_N. More specifically, suppose any country's expected utility function takes the form

$$U_1 = \frac{C_{T,1}^{1-\rho}}{1-\rho} + v(C_{N,1}) + \beta \sum_{s=1}^{\mathcal{S}} \pi(s) \left\{ \frac{C_{T,2}(s)^{1-\rho}}{1-\rho} + v[C_{N,2}(s)] \right\}.$$

This case is relatively simple because the additivity of period utility allows the results of section 5.3 to carry through with minimal modification.

Following the same steps as in section 5.3.2, one easily shows that the equilibrium for tradables here parallels the one described there. All agents hold shares in a single global mutual fund of tradable output processes: for any country n, share holdings $x_{T,m}^n$ in country m tradables and all consumption shares C_T^n/Y_T^W equal n's initial equilibrium share in world tradable wealth. Each country's net bond holdings are zero. The reader can confirm that the traded-goods equilibrium is characterized by equations identical to eqs. (45)–(50), except that consumption, output, portfolio-share, and share-price variables all have T subscripts. [Equation (49), so modified, gives the world own interest rate on tradables.] Equation (67) holds and implies ($\forall m, n$)

$$\frac{C_{T,2}^m(s)}{C_{T,1}^m} = \frac{C_{T,2}^n(s)}{C_{T,1}^n} = \frac{Y_{T,2}^W(s)}{Y_{T,1}^W}, \tag{74}$$

so that the equilibrium is constrained-efficient.[47]

---

47. As usual, this efficiency result generalizes to utility-of-tradables functions in the HARA class. (Recall footnote 28.)

What about investors' holdings of shares in foreign *nontradable* output streams? The answer is surprisingly simple. It is an equilibrium for all claims to a country n's risky *nontraded* output to be held *only* by residents of country n: for all n,

$$x^n_{N,m} = \begin{cases} 1 & (m = n) \\ 0 & (m \neq n). \end{cases}$$

Thus overall stock portfolios can exhibit a home bias, containing all of the claims to domestic nontradables industries despite being diversified among all the world's tradable industries. The larger the total share of nontradable output in world output, the larger the home bias.

How can we be sure that investors will not avail themselves of the opportunity to hold claims indexed to foreign countries' nontraded endowments? There is no benefit from doing so: with an additive period utility function, diversification among the world's tradable endowments exhausts all available gains from trade. To see this point formally, note the implication of eqs. (69) and (74) that the price in terms of tradables of a claim indexed to country m's nontraded goods is valued at

$$V^m_{N,1} = \sum_{s=1}^{S} \pi(s)\beta \left[\frac{Y^W_{T,2}(s)}{Y^W_{T,1}} \right]^{-\rho} p^m_{N,2}(s) Y^m_{N,2}(s),$$

in every country n, independently of its residents' portfolio of nontradables. This convergence of valuations tells us that once people have fully diversified their portfolios of claims to tradables, they cannot gain further by diversifying their holdings of nontradables.[48]

Unfortunately, this explanation at best goes only partway toward explaining the facts. One reason is empirical. The portfolio bias observed through the mid-1990s was too extreme to be due entirely to nontradables. For a small country, even if half of all output is nontradable, the model still implies that roughly half of agents' portfolios should be held abroad. Nothing near this proportion was observed.

Furthermore, a *nonadditive* intraperiod utility function can imply that individuals should hold shares in foreign industries that produce nontradables. This case is difficult to analyze because an equilibrium with trade in bonds and equity only (rather than Arrow-Debreu contracts) need not be constrained-efficient. Nonetheless, provided an equilibrium exists, we can develop some intuition about it. Suppose, for example, that the period utility function is of the nonadditive CES-CRRA form in eq. (72). Since the nontradables equilibrium condition (66) must hold in each country, date 2 shocks to nontradables output, like preference shocks, cause the marginal utility of tradables consumption to move idiosyncratically across

---

48. Recall the meaning of the Euler condition that this pricing equation satisfies in equilibrium. It implies that when $x^n_{N,n} = 1$, $x^n_{N,m} = 0$ $(m \neq n)$, a country n resident (for any n) has no positive incentive to alter his portfolio of risky claims to nontradable outputs.

countries ex post even when all countries' portfolios are fully diversified among tradables industries. Differentiation of the period utility function shows that the cross-partial derivative

$$\frac{\partial^2 u(C_T, C_N)}{\partial C_N \partial C_T}$$

has the same sign as $1 - \theta\rho$. Thus when $\theta > 1/\rho$, a higher date 2 endowment of nontradables *lowers* the marginal utility of date 2 tradables consumption. If a rise in nontradables output raises industry revenue measured in tradables, $p_{N,2} Y_{N,2}$ (this requires $\theta > 1$), then when $\theta > 1/\rho$ all countries may be able simultaneously to achieve a better allocation of risks by swapping ownership claims to their nontradables industries. Afterward, any country with unexpectedly high nontradables output will ship additional dividends, payable in tradables, abroad, reducing the incipient discrepancy between the domestic and foreign ex post marginal rates of intertemporal substitution of tradables. Thus trade in nontraded industry shares can enable all countries to hedge against fluctuations in the marginal utility of tradables consumption caused by output shocks in nontradables. This conclusion also follows when $\theta < 1/\rho$, but in that case investors may hold more than 100 percent of domestic nontraded industries and assume a negative position (that is, "go short") in foreign nontraded industries. (Someone with a short position in an asset pays rather than receives its ex post return. In the aggregate the market must hold the entire existing supply of any asset, but some individuals can take negative positions if others demand more than the total supply.)[49]

There is another problem with the view that nontradables explain home portfolio bias. Even though individuals are content to concentrate their nontradables portfolios domestically in the case of additive intraperiod utility, they might have no positive reason to do so. One special but interesting case occurs when the period utility function for the representative agent (of any country) is given by

$$u(C_T, C_N) = \gamma \log C_T + (1 - \gamma) \log C_N,$$

making the intratemporal elasticity of substitution between tradables and nontradables 1. In this case, payoffs on all countries' nontradable equities are perfectly

49. Eldor, Pines, and Schwartz (1988), Tesar (1993), Feeney and Jones (1994), Pesenti and van Wincoop (1994), and Baxter, Jermann, and King (1995) all stress the interplay between ρ and θ in determining international diversification patterns under nonadditive period utility. Tesar and Pesenti-van Wincoop explore the possibility of a home bias in portfolios of traded-goods industries when shares in nontraded-goods industries cannot be traded. Baxter, Jermann, and King study a static model of risk allocation with infinitesimal uncertainty and trade in claims to nontradable outputs. They show that the complete-markets allocation may be attainable through trade in shares, and argue that it remains optimal for investors to hold the global mutual fund of traded-goods industries. Their conclusions do not hold generally for noninfinitesimal uncertainty, however. Stulz (1981) develops a very general dynamic analysis of portfolio choice and asset pricing when residents of different countries face different consumption opportunity sets. He does not, however, model the source of international discrepancies in consumption opportunities.

correlated with the mutual fund of world tradables and, as a result, are perfectly correlated with each other. (The reason stochastic variation in nontradable outputs plays no role is that a rise in nontradable output, for example, causes a proportional fall in price, leaving the nontradable endowment's value in terms of tradables unchanged.) But perfect correlation in payoffs makes any nontradable equity a *perfect substitute* for the world tradable portfolio, a fact that renders countries' portfolios *indeterminate*. As a result, we can no longer make predictions about home bias purely on the basis of some part of output being nontradable.

Cole (1988), Golub (1994), Brainard and Tobin (1992), Baxter and Jermann (1993), and Ghosh and Pesenti (1994) discuss models in which all goods are traded, but in which, realistically, there are forward markets only in income earned by capital, not in income earned by labor. If nontradable labor income is positively correlated with the returns on domestic equities, then individuals should go short in the domestic stock market to hedge labor-income risk. In this case, recognizing that labor income is nontraded would seem to make the home bias puzzle even deeper. Bottazzi, Pesenti, and van Wincoop (1996) argue that empirically, domestic labor and capital income actually tend to be negatively correlated in most OECD countries; that is, the relative share of labor and capital income in output is quite volatile. They suggest that domestic rather than foreign equity may provide the better hedge against redistributive shocks, although the quantitative significance of this effect is unlcear. In most countries, of course, fixed transaction costs and borrowing constraints result in equity holdings being concentrated disproportionately among a relatively small number of better-off individuals, many of whom derive a substantial fraction of their total income from financial wealth (see, for example, Mankiw and Zeldes, 1991). For such individuals, the correlation between aggregate labor and capital income might be a comparatively minor factor in portfolio decisions.

Application: How Large Are the Gains from International Risk Sharing?

International financial markets aid in allocating risks more efficiently among countries, but are the welfare benefits they confer in theory substantial in practice? One school of thought holds that the benefits are actually quite minimal—a view that could throw light on the home bias diversification puzzle, since it implies that small transaction costs could go far to discourage trade in risky assets.

An influential estimate by Lucas (1987) of the welfare cost of variability in United States consumption conveys intuitively the grounds for believing that the gains from risk sharing are small. Lucas considers a representative individual whose lifetime utility is

$$U_t = E_t \left\{ \sum_{s=t}^{\infty} \beta^{s-t} \frac{C_s^{1-\rho}}{1-\rho} \right\},$$

where $C_s = (1+g)^{s-t} \bar{C} \exp[\epsilon_s - \frac{1}{2} \text{Var}(\epsilon_s)]$ and ϵ_s is a normal, i.i.d., mean-zero shock. By direct calculation,

$$E_t\{C_s^{1-\rho}\} = (1+g)^{(1-\rho)(s-t)} \bar{C}^{1-\rho} \exp\left[-\frac{1}{2}(1-\rho)\rho\text{Var}(\epsilon)\right]$$

(where we have used the fact that $\exp[1-\rho]\epsilon_s$ is lognormally distributed with mean $\exp\left\{\frac{1}{2}[1-\rho]^2\text{Var}[\epsilon]\right\}$). Thus, prior to observing ϵ_t,

$$U_t = \frac{\bar{C}^{1-\rho}}{1-\rho}\left[\frac{1}{1-\beta(1+g)^{1-\rho}}\right]\exp\left[-\frac{1}{2}(1-\rho)\rho\text{Var}(\epsilon)\right]$$

[assuming $\beta(1+g)^{1-\rho} < 1$].

Lucas asks us to imagine that all consumption uncertainty could be eliminated, resulting in the expected-value consumption path $\bar{C}_s \equiv E_t C_s = (1+g)^{s-t}\bar{C}$. The associated lifetime utility is

$$\bar{U}_t = \frac{\bar{C}^{1-\rho}}{1-\rho}\left[\frac{1}{1-\beta(1+g)^{1-\rho}}\right].$$

What percent increase τ in annual consumption has the same positive utility effect as the total elimination of consumption uncertainty? This equivalent variation is given by

$$\frac{[(1+\tau)\bar{C}]^{1-\rho}}{1-\rho}\exp\left[-\frac{1}{2}(1-\rho)\rho\ \text{Var}(\epsilon)\right] = \frac{\bar{C}^{1-\rho}}{1-\rho},$$

which can be solved to yield

$$\tau = \left\{\exp\left[\frac{1}{2}(1-\rho)\rho\ \text{Var}(\epsilon)\right]\right\}^{1/(1-\rho)} - 1.$$

A first-order Taylor approximation in the neighborhood of $\text{Var}(\epsilon) = 0$ yields

$$\tau \approx \frac{1}{2}\rho\ \text{Var}(\epsilon). \tag{75}$$

Thus we end up with a remarkably simple approximation to the cost of consumption variability, expressed as a perpetual percent tax on consumption.

For annual 1950-90 U.S. data on total per capita consumption, $\text{Var}(\epsilon) = 0.000708$, which corresponds to a standard deviation slightly below 2.7 percent per year. Thus, even if $\rho = 10$, the total elimination of consumption variability would be worth only about a third of a percent of consumption per year to a representative U.S. consumer, a surprisingly small amount. (The reader may note the strong parallels with our earlier discussion of the equity risk premium. Here, too, the low measured variability of U.S. aggregate consumption makes it difficult to assign a large role to consumption risk.)

One might conclude that if the gain from *eliminating* unpredictable consumption variability altogether is so small, then the gain from perfect international pooling of risks, which still leaves people facing systematic global consumption risk, must be even smaller. However, a closer look at Lucas's reasoning suggests that caution is warranted:

1. Lucas's assumption that consumption fluctuates randomly around a fixed time trend has been questioned by many economists. That setup makes all consumption fluctuations temporary; but if permanent shocks to consumption sometimes occur, the welfare cost of incomplete insurance is potentially much more severe.

2. The United States is atypical in the relative stability of its aggregate per capita consumption and output. Some industrial countries and many developing countries have substantially greater variability. The numbers in Table 5.4 are suggestive of the disparity across different countries. Since the measure in eq. (75) depends on the square of variability, it rises sharply as variability rises.

3. Lucas's calculations do not allow for individual heterogeneity—that is, they abstract altogether from uninsurable idiosyncratic risks and look only at the cost of systematic risk. Thus Lucas's numbers are relevant at best to the *marginal* benefit that global risk pooling may yield once domestic risk pooling possibilities have been exhausted.

Cole and Obstfeld (1991) assessed the gains from international risk sharing in a version of the Lucas (1982) model with representative national agents and permanent as well as transitory output shocks. Assuming output innovations comparable in variance to those of the United States, they found small gains from perfect pooling of output risks, on the order of a fifth of a percent of output per year even for $\rho = 10$. Backus, Kehoe, and Kydland (1992) find that essentially for this reason, even small transactions costs can seriously limit international asset trade. Introducing fairly minor trade restrictions into their calibrated dynamic general equilibrium model leads to an equilibrium close to autarky.

Mendoza (1995) and Tesar (1995) look at calibrated world-economy models with nontraded goods, endogenous labor supply, and investment, allowing for different degrees of persistence in (statistically stationary) productivity shocks but no nondiversifiable risks. Their general conclusion is that the gains from risk pooling are of the order of those found by Cole and Obstfeld (or smaller), in part because domestic investment possibilities offer greater scope for self-insurance through intertemporal domestic reallocations. Obstfeld (1995) argues that for many developing countries, the gains from international risk sharing are nonetheless likely to be large (a point we reexamine in the next chapter).

When output shocks are persistent, with effects that propagate over time, utility functions that make risk aversion high only when intertemporal substitutability is low may understate the cost of uncertainty (see Obstfeld, 1994b). Van Wincoop (1994) evaluates gains from risk pooling among the OECD economies in a model with a random walk assumed for log per capita consumption, nonexpected-utility preferences, and an idiosyncratic component of consumption risk that cannot be diversified away domestically or internationally. He finds much larger average benefits than did Cole and Obstfeld, averaging as high as 5.6 percent of GDP per year for the OECD when risk aversion $\rho = 3$ and the intertemporal substitution elasticity $\sigma = 1$. The wide divergence in estimates shows how sensitive answers can be to seemingly minor differences in assumptions.

In reality, uninsurable risks seem to be potentially important determinants of what countries gain from pooling insurable risks globally. Similarly, research on the equity premium puzzle suggests that uninsurable risks greatly increase the price people will pay to lay off insurable risks. By implication, uninsurable risks raise the welfare benefit of feasible risk reduction.

More detailed and explicit modeling of consumer heterogeneity would shed light on both the effects of international financial integration and on the domestic distribution of risk-sharing gains. The noninsurability of much labor-income risk plainly is related to another puzzle: the contrast between the often slim apparent gains from pooling aggregate national consumption risks, and the finding in the finance literature that global diversification of equity portfolios can yield large benefits to consumers whose incomes come entirely from financial wealth (for example, Grauer and Hakansson, 1987).

Even if the gains from risk pooling are small in conventional dynamic models with representative national individuals, they may be much larger in models where investment rises in response to expanded diversification opportunities and where higher investment endogenously generates a higher rate of long-run economic growth. We will return to this idea in Chapter 7.   ■

---

*5.6   A Model of Intragenerational Risk Sharing

Models of incomplete risk sharing have aggregate implications that can differ from those of models with complete markets. In this section we explore a model in which an overlapping generations structure prevents all people alive on a given date from pooling endowment risks for that date. The reason complete risk sharing fails is not the adverse incentives full insurance might create. (Such models are the topic of the next chapter.) Here markets fail to pool all consumption risks efficiently simply because those who have not yet been born cannot sign contracts. Interpreted broadly, the model shows how aggregate consumption can behave when some, but not all, individuals have access to insurance markets.

The world consists of two countries, Home and Foreign, whose residents consume a single consumption good on each date. The world economy has an infinite horizon but people do not: every period a new generation with a two-period lifetime is born in each country. A Home resident born on date t maximizes lifetime expected utility,

$$U_t = \log c_t^Y + \beta E_t \log c_{t+1}^O.$$

In Foreign, expected utility is the same function of c_t^{Y*} and c_{t+1}^{O*}. The size of a generation (in either country) is constant and normalized to 1.

The only uncertainty concerns the values of individuals' exogenous endowments. Everyone in Home, whether young or old, receives the same endowment $y_t(s)$ on date t, where s is one of S possible states of nature. Similarly, everyone in Foreign receives $y_t^*(s)$. The probability distribution of the states $s = 1, \ldots, S$ occurring on a date t is described by the probability density function denoted $\pi_{t-1}(s)$.

In this model, someone born on date t cannot insure date t consumption because the initial-period endowment is revealed before there is a chance to transact in asset markets. (If populations formed immortal dynasties, parents could transact on behalf of their offspring, but that is not the case here.) After the date t state is revealed, however, those born on date t can trade on a complete set of markets for contingent claims to date $t + 1$ consumption. Only *intra*generational asset trade is possible: the young do not sign contracts with the old because the old will not be around tomorrow to fulfill commitments made today. (Nor is there any long-lived asset in the model, such as capital or government debt, for the old to sell to the young, though even this would not generally result in an efficient allocation.) Clearly the young of a given date t could attain higher unconditional expected utility (expected utility conditional on no information about endowments) if they could trade claims contingent on the date t state *before* it became known.

To see the model's implications for international consumption covariation and the distribution of wealth, consider how a Home resident, young on date t, chooses current and future consumption. This person maximizes

$$U_t = \log c_t^Y + \beta \sum_{s=1}^{S} \pi_t(s) \log c_{t+1}^O(s)$$

subject to the constraint

$$c_t^Y + \frac{1}{1+r_{t+1}} \sum_{s=1}^{S} p_t(s) c_{t+1}^O(s) = y_t + \frac{1}{1+r_{t+1}} \sum_{s=1}^{S} p_t(s) y_{t+1}(s),$$

where $p_t(s)/(1 + r_{t+1})$ is the date t price of the Arrow-Debreu security for state s occurring on date $t + 1$. This is the same type of problem analyzed in section 5.2.1. Now retrace the steps taken there, remembering that all trade occurs within age cohorts. You can confirm that *equilibrium* consumption levels for the young on date t are

$$c_t^Y = \mu_t(y_t + y_t^*), \qquad c_t^{Y*} = (1 - \mu_t)(y_t + y_t^*),$$

and, for this same cohort when old on date $t + 1$, they are

$$c_{t+1}^O(s) = \mu_t[y_{t+1}(s) + y_{t+1}^*(s)], \qquad c_{t+1}^{O*}(s) = (1 - \mu_t)[y_{t+1}(s) + y_{t+1}^*(s)],$$

where (set $\rho = 1$ in footnote 16, section 5.2.1.2)

$$\mu_t = \frac{1}{1 + \beta}\left[\frac{y_t}{y_t + y_t^*} + \beta\sum_{s=1}^{S}\pi_t(s)\frac{y_{t+1}(s)}{y_{t+1}(s) + y_{t+1}^*(s)}\right]$$

$$= \frac{1}{1 + \beta}\left[\frac{y_t}{y_t + y_t^*} + \beta E_t\left\{\frac{y_{t+1}}{y_{t+1} + y_{t+1}^*}\right\}\right].$$

For example, if Home's output is exactly half of world output today and expected to be half tomorrow, the current Home young will consume exactly half of their generation's world output [that is, $\frac{1}{2}(y + y^*)$] in both periods of life, regardless of the state of nature when they are old. As in section 5.2.1, the equilibrium prices associated with the preceding consumption allocation are

$$1 + r_{t+1} = \frac{\dfrac{1}{y_t + y_t^*}}{\beta E_t\left\{\dfrac{1}{y_{t+1} + y_{t+1}^*}\right\}}$$

and, for all states s,

$$p_t(s) = \frac{\dfrac{\pi_t(s)}{y_{t+1}(s) + y_{t+1}^*(s)}}{E_t\left\{\dfrac{1}{y_{t+1} + y_{t+1}^*}\right\}}.$$

Turn next to the model's implications for *aggregate* national consumption levels. Aggregate Home per capita consumption, c_t, is

$$c_t = \tfrac{1}{2}(c_t^Y + c_t^O) = \tfrac{1}{2}(\mu_t + \mu_{t-1})(y_t + y_t^*)$$

$$= \frac{y_t + y_t^*}{2(1 + \beta)}\left[\frac{y_t}{y_t + y_t^*} + \beta E_t\left\{\frac{y_{t+1}}{y_{t+1} + y_{t+1}^*}\right\}\right.$$

$$\left. + \frac{y_{t-1}}{y_{t-1} + y_{t-1}^*} + \beta E_{t-1}\left\{\frac{y_t}{y_t + y_t^*}\right\}\right]. \tag{76}$$

Box 5.3
A Test of Complete Markets Based on Consumption Divergence within Age Cohorts

> The model of this section suggests that if the only major departure from complete markets were the inability of future generations to write contracts today, the consumption levels of individuals within the *same* cohort would still be highly correlated. What does the evidence suggest?
>
> Deaton and Paxson (1994) analyze cohort survey data on consumer income and expenditure for three countries—the United States, Britain, and Taiwan. They use the data to track income and consumption dispersion among individuals born in a specific year (an age cohort) within a given country. (They do not compare consumptions across countries.) While Deaton and Paxson's data do not permit them actually to track the exact same group of individuals for the entire sample period, they are able to make comparisons across time by using random sampling techniques. The results, Deaton and Paxson argue, provide a compelling rejection of the complete-markets model. In all three countries, consumption inequality within a cohort tends to rise sharply over time.
>
> On the other hand, the divergence of cohort consumptions over time is consistent with the bonds-only model of Chapter 2, which allows individual shares in the economy's total consumption to drift arbitrarily far apart. Evidence such as Deaton and Paxson's is one compelling reason not to assume automatically that the complete-markets model of this chapter is necessarily a closer approximation to reality than the models of Chapters 2 and 3. However, it would be much more satisfying from a theoretical standpoint to justify market incompleteness rigorously rather than simply assuming it. Deepening our understanding of the reasons for incompleteness in international financial markets will be the main goal of the next chapter.

A parallel formula holds for Foreign per capita consumption. With complete markets and a representative infinitely-lived consumer with log utility in each country, the ratio of national to world per capita consumption would be constant through time. In the present model, however, consumption aggregates do not behave as if chosen by infinitely-lived representative consumers, despite the access of all agents to state-contingent claims on second-period-of-life output.

Equation (76) shows that here, instead, the distribution of world consumption changes over time, even with time-invariant probability distributions for outputs, because of the dependence of domestic consumption on current and lagged idiosyncratic components of domestic output. This conclusion is reminiscent of models in which countries trade only noncontingent claims to future outputs.

Appendix 5A   Spanning and Completeness

In the N-country diversification model of section 5.3, we saw that trade in country-fund equities may lead to the same resource allocation that trade in a complete set of Arrow-Debreu claims would produce. That remarkable result holds only under a restricted class of utility functions. This appendix makes precise and derives a result that is weaker but does not depend on utility functions: given a sufficient number of assets with independently varying returns, investors can synthesize a complete set of derivative Arrow-Debreu securities.

Recall (see p. 307) that in a two-period model the state s net real rate of return on shares in country m, $r^m(s)$, is output in state s divided by the date 1 price of a claim to the output, less 1:

$$r^m(s) = \frac{Y_2^m(s) - V_1^m}{V_1^m}.$$

Next define the $S \times (N + 1)$ matrix $\mathbf{R}$ of gross ex post returns:

$$\mathbf{R} \equiv \begin{bmatrix} 1+r & 1+r^1(1) & \dots & 1+r^N(1) \\ 1+r & 1+r^1(2) & \dots & 1+r^N(2) \\ \cdot & \cdot & \cdot & \cdot \\ \cdot & \cdot & \cdot & \cdot \\ \cdot & \cdot & \cdot & \cdot \\ 1+r & 1+r^1(S) & \dots & 1+r^N(S) \end{bmatrix}.$$

Each column of $\mathbf{R}$ is a state-by-state list of returns on a different asset, with the first column corresponding to the riskless bond.

If $S \leq N + 1$, the rank of the return matrix $\mathbf{R}$ is at most S. The *spanning condition* states that

$$\text{Rank}(\mathbf{R}) = S. \tag{77}$$

Condition (77) means that $\mathbf{R}$ contains a set of S linearly independent columns; that is, there is a set of S assets such that no member's state-by-state return vector can be replicated by a linear combination (or *portfolio*) of the $S - 1$ other assets. Notice that eq. (77) couldn't possibly hold were $N + 1 < S$, because then the rank of $\mathbf{R}$ could be at most $N + 1$.

The spanning condition allows international diversification to lead to the same Pareto-optimal resource allocation that would occur with complete Arrow-Debreu securities markets, regardless of what the utility functions are. The existence of S assets with linearly independent return vectors provides market risk-sharing opportunities as rich as those provided by S Arrow-Debreu securities with linearly independent return vectors.

In showing why the Arrow-Debreu equilibrium results if eq. (77) holds, we restrict attention to the special case of $N + 1 = S$ assets, in which $\mathbf{R}$ is a square matrix. (More assets can never reduce insurance possibilities.) To see why condition (77) allows us to form a portfolio paying 1 unit of output in exactly one state s and 0 in all the others, let a_{0s} be the value of the safe asset in the hypothesized portfolio and a_{ns} (for $n = 1, \dots, N$) the value of the country n output claim. Thus, the portfolio contains a share a_{ns}/V_1^n of claim n. If

$$\mathbf{a}_s = [\, a_{0s} \quad a_{1s} \quad \dots \quad a_{Ns} \,]^{\mathsf{T}}$$

(where T denotes matrix transposition) and $\mathbf{1}_s$ is the $S \times 1$ vector with 1 as its sth row entry and 0 elsewhere, then by choosing $\mathbf{a}_s = \mathbf{R}^{-1}\mathbf{1}_s$, we form a portfolio with the state-by-state return vector $\mathbf{R}\mathbf{a}_s = \mathbf{1}_s$. [The spanning condition (77) tells us that the inverse $\mathbf{R}^{-1}$ exists.] But $\mathbf{1}_s$ is simply the payoff vector for a state s Arrow-Debreu security. Thus the S portfolios described by the vectors $\mathbf{a}_1$ through $\mathbf{a}_S$ are indistinguishable from the primal Arrow-Debreu securities.

The circumstances under which the spanning condition is met might seem implausible, but the issue is more subtle in richer dynamic settings. In models with continuous trading, dynamic hedging strategies (strategies involving continual rebalancing of portfolios) can, under certain conditions, lead to a complete markets outcome even when the number of securities available is small relative to the number of states of nature. Interested readers should consult Duffie and Huang (1985).

Appendix 5B   Comparative Advantage, the Current Account, and Gross Asset Purchases: A Simple Example

In section 5.1.6, we derived the current account under log period utility in a two-period, two-state, small-country model with complete markets. The current account is given by eq. (17),

$$CA_1 = Y_1 - C_1 = \frac{\beta}{1+\beta} Y_1 - \frac{1}{1+\beta} \left[\frac{p(1)Y_2(1) + p(2)Y_2(2)}{1+r} \right].$$

In this appendix, we explore further the role of comparative advantage in determining the current account. The extended example illustrates why the strong results on comparative advantage in Chapter 1 extend only weakly to the stochastic case. In addition to studying net capital flows, we also derive closed-form solutions for gross capital flows in the log case.

5B.1   The Autarky Interest Rate and the Current Account

To interpret the current account balance in terms of the relationship between relative autarky prices and world prices, let us begin by temporarily assuming that $\beta(1 + r) = 1$. Equation (17) then shows that if the value of output is the same on both dates—that is, if $Y_1 = p(1)Y_2(1) + p(2)Y_2(2)$—then the current account balance CA_1 will be zero, just as in Chapter 1's model. With $Y_1 < p(1)Y_2(1) + p(2)Y_2(2)$, CA_1 is negative, and it is positive in the opposite case.

The intuition behind this result is easy to grasp. Observe that in the log case, the Euler equation for the state s security, eq. (5), reads

$$\frac{p(s)}{(1+r)C_1} = \frac{\pi(s)\beta}{C_2(s)}.$$

Multiply both sides by $(1+r)C_1 C_2(s)$ and sum over states s. The result is

$$p(1)C_2(1) + p(2)C_2(2) = \beta(1+r)C_1 = C_1,$$

where the last equality follows from our assumption that $\beta(1 + r) = 1$. People seek a level (across time) expenditure path, and if their first-period income is below (above) the constant expenditure level consistent with the intertemporal budget constraint, they will shift purchasing power to the present (future) through a current account deficit (surplus). In short, the current account is determined just as in the certainty case, but with the date 2 endowment's *value* at world Arrow-Debreu prices in place of the nonstochastic date 2 endowment. (Section 5.1.8 of the text showed the very limited extent to which this result generalizes beyond the log case.)

If the country were somehow forbidden from altering the timing of its overall spending through the current account, but could still trade date 2 risks at world prices $p(s)$, it would have no choice but to consume $C_1 = Y_1$, and it would then set $C_2(s) = \pi(s)[p(1)Y_2(1) + p(2)Y_2(2)]/p(s)$. The (gross) domestic real interest rate in the resulting circumstance of "current account autarky" would be

$$
1 + r^{CA} = \frac{u'(Y_1)}{\beta \left(\sum_{s=1}^{2} \pi(s)u' \{\pi(s)[p(1)Y_2(1) + p(2)Y_2(2)]/p(s)\} \right)}
$$

$$
= \frac{1}{\beta Y_1}[p(1)Y_2(1) + p(2)Y_2(2)], \tag{78}
$$

which is simply the interest rate consistent with the intertemporal Euler condition (8). The autarky interest rate when the country has access to *no* financial markets at all is, however,

$$
1 + r^A = \frac{u'(Y_1)}{\beta \sum_{s=1}^{2} \pi(s)u'[Y_2(s)]} = \frac{1}{\beta Y_1} \left[\frac{\pi(1)}{Y_2(1)} + \frac{\pi(2)}{Y_2(2)} \right]^{-1} \tag{79}
$$

[because consumption levels necessarily are $C_1 = Y_1$ and $C_2(s) = Y_2(s)$ in complete autarky]. Plainly, r^{CA} and r^A coincide only in very special circumstances, for example, when $Y_2(1) = Y_2(2)$, so that the country has no output uncertainty.[50] But since $\beta = 1/(1 + r)$ in the present example, eq. (78) and the discussion in the two paragraphs preceding it show that CA_1 has the same sign as $r - r^{CA}$, not $r - r^A$.[51] This is a good example of how the textbook 2×2 comparative advantage theorem is inapplicable with more than two goods.

Now relax the assumption that $\beta(1 + r) = 1$. An alternative way to characterize the current account in the logarithmic case is in terms of the autarky date 1 prices of Arrow-Debreu securities. Using condition (5) with log utility, we read off the equilibrium autarky price ratios

$$
\frac{p(s)^A}{1 + r^A} = \frac{\pi(s)\beta Y_1}{Y_2(s)}, \qquad s = 1, 2. \tag{80}
$$

If one rewrites the current account equation (17) as

$$
CA_1 = \frac{1}{1 + \beta} \left[\pi(1)\beta Y_1 - \frac{p(1)Y_2(1)}{1 + r} + \pi(2)\beta Y_1 - \frac{p(2)Y_2(2)}{1 + r} \right],
$$

then the formula for autarky prices, eq. (80), shows that

---

50. When $Y_2(1) = Y_2(2) = Y_2$, $r^{CA} = r^A$ because

$$
p(1)Y_2 + p(2)Y_2 = Y_2 = \frac{Y_2}{\pi(1) + \pi(2)} = \left[\frac{\pi(1)}{Y_2} + \frac{\pi(2)}{Y_2} \right]^{-1}.
$$

The date 1 current account is simply

$$
CA_1 = \frac{Y_2}{1 + \beta} \left(\frac{1}{1 + r^A} - \frac{1}{1 + r} \right).
$$

Even in this case, the country opts for different consumption levels in states 1 and 2 if world prices $p(s)$ aren't actuarially fair.

51. The latter result holds even when $\beta(1 + r) \neq 1$, as eqs. (17) and (78) show.

$$CA_1 = \frac{Y_2(1)}{1+\beta}\left[\frac{p(1)^A}{1+r^A} - \frac{p(1)}{1+r}\right] + \frac{Y_2(2)}{1+\beta}\left[\frac{p(2)^A}{1+r^A} - \frac{p(2)}{1+r}\right]. \tag{81}$$

According to eq. (81) the current account balance depends positively on the difference between the autarky and world market prices of Arrow-Debreu securities. If other things are equal, the higher are the autarky prices of assets relative to world prices on date 1, the greater will be the country's date 1 net asset purchases from abroad, the sum of which equals the date 1 current account surplus. (This is reminiscent of—but distinct from—the result in standard two-good trade theory, that a country imports the good with an autarky price above the world price.) An alternative (and equivalent) interpretation of eq. (81) is that countries with relatively high autarky prices for future state-contingent consumption will tend to import future consumption, and export current consumption, through a date 1 current account surplus.[52]

5B.2   Understanding Gross Capital Flows

Equation (81) explains the economy's *net* asset purchases or sales from the rest of the world. In special cases the simple form of the comparative advantage principle can be useful in understanding *gross* imports or exports of Arrow-Debreu securities, which may be quite large even when the current account is small.

By eq. (80), the autarky relative price of state 1 in terms of state 2 consumption is

$$\frac{p(1)^A}{p(2)^A} = \frac{\pi(1)/Y_2(1)}{\pi(2)/Y_2(2)}.$$

Let us suppose that the country desires a balanced current account, so that [by eqs. (17) and (78)] its interest rate in "current account autarky" equals the world rate, $r^{CA} = r$. In that case the country will spend a total of $p(1)Y_2(1) + p(2)Y_2(2)$ on date 2, choosing state-contingent consumption levels by $C_2(s) = \pi(s)[p(1)Y_2(1) + p(2)Y_2(2)]/p(s)$, as we have seen. The date 2 budget constraint (3) now gives the country's demand for state 1 securities as

$$B_2(1) = C_2(1) - Y_2(1)$$

$$= \frac{\pi(1)[p(1)Y_2(1) + p(2)Y_2(2)]}{p(1)} - Y_2(1)$$

$$= \frac{p(2)\pi(1)}{p(1)}Y_2(2) - \pi(2)Y_2(1)$$

$$= \frac{\pi(2)p(2)Y_2(1)}{p(1)}\left[\frac{\pi(1)/Y_2(1)}{\pi(2)/Y_2(2)} - \frac{p(1)}{p(2)}\right]$$

$$= \frac{p(2)}{p(1)}\pi(2)Y_2(1)\left[\frac{p(1)^A}{p(2)^A} - \frac{p(1)}{p(2)}\right].$$

---

52. By combining eqs. (79) and (80) you can compute the autarky prices or Arrow-Debreu securities in terms of date 2 output. Equation (81) implies that when $p^A(s) = p(s)$ for $s = 1, 2$, we have another case in which CA_1 depends only on the difference between r and r^A. [International equality of absolute state-contingent prices, $p^A(s) = p(s)$, follows from equality of relative prices because the prices sum to 1.]

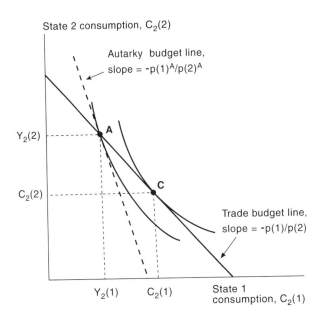

Figure 5.2
Trade across states of nature

The assumption of a zero current account implies that the demand for state 2 securities must be

$$B_2(2) = -\pi(2)Y_2(1)\left[\frac{p(1)^A}{p(2)^A} - \frac{p(1)}{p(2)}\right].$$

When the current account is zero, so that the country's international trade consists entirely of trade across date 2 states of nature, it imports the asset with the relatively high autarky price and exports the one with the relatively low autarky price. These opposite but equal (in value) gross capital flows allow the country to use output from the relatively prosperous state to hedge against the low consumption level that would prevail in the other state in the absence of asset trade. Figure 5.2 illustrates how this pure trade across states of nature maximizes expected second-period utility, $\pi(1)\log[C_2(1)] + \pi(2)\log[C_2(2)]$, given total spending of $p(1)Y_2(1) + p(2)Y_2(2)$ on date 2 consumption.

The preceding asset-trade pattern is consistent with the simplest version of the comparative advantage principle. If the country had an unbalanced current account, however, it might import or export both assets irrespective of their relative autarky prices. End-of-chapter exercise 1 considers that more general case.

Appendix 5C   An Infinite-Horizon Complete-Markets Model

In this appendix, we extend to an infinite horizon the chapter's two-period Arrow-Debreu model. The extension, discussed informally in section 5.2.3, is quite straightforward with the help of some additional notation.

5C.1   Dynamic Uncertainty

Our two-period model involved uncertainty on one future date only. Thus we were able to summarize the future state of the economy by the outcome of only one set of random events, those occurring "tomorrow." With many periods, random events occur not only tomorrow, but also the day after tomorrow, the day after that one, and so on. The *history* of these random events up to and including a date t determines the state of nature the economy occupies on date t.

More formally, denote by $\mathbf{h}_t$ the history of the world economy on date t, that is, the set whose elements are a list of how events that were not predictable with certainty before they occurred actually turned out. The set of positive-probability random events whose outcomes become known on date t itself is denoted by $S(\mathbf{h}_{t-1})$: this set is a function of past history $\mathbf{h}_{t-1}$ because the history of the economy through date $t-1$ determines the set of events that can occur on date t. (For example, U.S. President Kennedy's death in 1963 precluded his reelection in 1964.) If event $s_t \in S(\mathbf{h}_{t-1})$ occurs on date t, then $\mathbf{h}_t$ is given recursively by $\mathbf{h}_t = \{s_t\} \cup \mathbf{h}_{t-1}$. More generally, we will say that $\mathbf{h}_{t'}$, $t' > t$, is a *continuation of* $\mathbf{h}_t$ *through date* t' if there are events $s_{t+1} \in S(\mathbf{h}_t)$, $s_{t+2} \in S(\{s_{t+1}\} \cup \mathbf{h}_t)$, ..., $s_{t'} \in S(\{s_{t'-1}, \ldots, s_{t+1}\} \cup \mathbf{h}_t)$ such that $\mathbf{h}_{t'} = \{s_{t'}, \ldots, s_{t+1}\} \cup \mathbf{h}_t$.

In a dynamic model, it is natural for contingent contracts to specify payoffs for a date as a function of the economy's realized *future* history through that date, which is not known with certainty when contracts are signed. We therefore assume that on an initial date 1 (and only then) agents can trade Arrow-Debreu securities of the following form: a history $\mathbf{h}_t$ security pays its owner one unit of output on date $t > 1$ if the economy's history through that date turns out to be $\mathbf{h}_t$, but it pays zero otherwise. We denote by $p(\mathbf{h}_t \mid \mathbf{h}_1)$ the date 1 price of this security, measured in terms of sure date t output. Correspondingly, $\pi(\mathbf{h}_t \mid \mathbf{h}_1)$ is the conditional probability that the economy's history on date t turns out to be $\mathbf{h}_t$, given what has happened through date 1. The set $H_t(\mathbf{h}_1)$ is defined to consist of all positive-probability continuations of $\mathbf{h}_1$ through date t.

5C.2   Individual Optimality

Given these notational conventions, the analysis of a representative country n individual's behavior goes through much as in section 5.1. The individual from country n maximizes expected utility,

$$U_1 = u(C_1^n) + \sum_{t=2}^{\infty} \beta^{t-1} \left\{ \sum_{\mathbf{h}_t \in H_t(\mathbf{h}_1)} \pi(\mathbf{h}_t \mid \mathbf{h}_1) u[C^n(\mathbf{h}_t)] \right\}, \tag{82}$$

subject to

$$C_1^n + \sum_{t=2}^{\infty} R_{1,t} \left[\sum_{\mathbf{h}_t \in H_t(\mathbf{h}_1)} p(\mathbf{h}_t \mid \mathbf{h}_1) C^n(\mathbf{h}_t) \right]$$

$$= Y_1^n + \sum_{t=2}^{\infty} R_{1,t} \left[\sum_{\mathbf{h}_t \in H_t(\mathbf{h}_1)} p(\mathbf{h}_t \mid \mathbf{h}_1) Y^n(\mathbf{h}_t) \right], \tag{83}$$

where $R_{1,t}$ is the multiperiod discount factor for sure date t consumption defined in eq. (60), section 5.4.3. Constraint (83) generalizes constraint (4) from the two-period, two-state model of the text. You can easily check that the necessary conditions for individual optimality imply

$$R_{1,t}p(\mathbf{h}_t \mid \mathbf{h}_1)u'(C_1^n) = \pi(\mathbf{h}_t \mid \mathbf{h}_1)\beta^{t-1}u'[C^n(\mathbf{h}_t)] \tag{84}$$

for all dates t and histories $\mathbf{h}_t$. [Compare this with eq. (5) for the two-period model.] From this equation, we derive the analog of eq. (9) for any two date t histories $\mathbf{h}_t^1$ and $\mathbf{h}_t^2$,

$$\frac{\pi(\mathbf{h}_t^1 \mid \mathbf{h}_1)u'[C^n(\mathbf{h}_t^1)]}{\pi(\mathbf{h}_t^2 \mid \mathbf{h}_1)u'[C^n(\mathbf{h}_t^2)]} = \frac{p(\mathbf{h}_t^1 \mid \mathbf{h}_1)}{p(\mathbf{h}_t^2 \mid \mathbf{h}_1)},$$

along with Euler equations for noncontingent bonds that generalize eq. (8),

$$u'(C_1^n) = \frac{\beta^{t-1}}{R_{1,t}}E_1\{u'(C_t^n)\} = \frac{\beta^{t-1}}{R_{1,t}}E\{u'[C^n(\mathbf{h}_t)] \mid \mathbf{h}_1\}. \tag{85}$$

Equation (85) follows from the observation that for any date t,

$$\sum_{\mathbf{h}_t \in H_t(\mathbf{h}_1)} p(\mathbf{h}_t \mid \mathbf{h}_1) = 1$$

[a generalization of the no-arbitrage condition (7)]. Notice that the conditional expectation $E_1\{\cdot\}$ in eq. (85) is a function of the conditioning information $\mathbf{h}_1$, consistent with our notation for conditional probabilities and securities prices.

5C.3   Equilibrium in the CRRA Case

With CRRA utility, $u(C) = C^{1-\rho}/(1 - \rho)$, it is easy to build on these relationships to obtain closed-form solutions for asset prices and interest rates in a global equilibrium. Prices are determined so that aggregate output demands and supplies are equal on every date, for every history. In equilibrium, as in the two-period case, country n's consumption on any date, and for any history, will be an unchanging fraction μ^n of world output,

$$C^n(\mathbf{h}_t) = \mu^n Y^W(\mathbf{h}_t),$$

where μ^n equals country n's share in the date 1 present value of current and future world output. By eq. (85), the equilibrium long-term interest rate is given by

$$R_{1,t} = \frac{\beta^{t-1} \sum_{\mathbf{h}_t \in H_t(\mathbf{h}_1)} \pi(\mathbf{h}_t \mid \mathbf{h}_1)Y^W(\mathbf{h}_t)^{-\rho}}{(Y_1^W)^{-\rho}}.$$

The history-contingent securities prices $p(\mathbf{h}_t \mid \mathbf{h}_1)$ are similarly derived (we leave this as an exercise).

Notice why the current account always is zero after period 1 in this infinite-horizon economy. World saving is zero, and since countries differ only in their scale (measured by μ^n), each country's saving is zero as well. With investment, countries' saving rates relative to income still would always be identical, but not necessarily their investment rates. Stochastic investment opportunities localized in individual countries would thus open up the possibility of random current-account imbalances.

The formalism we have developed in this appendix can be applied to the bonds-only economy studied in Chapter 2. Naturally the present approach leads to identical results.

Appendix 5D   Ongoing Securities Trade and Dynamic Consistency

In the many-period Arrow-Debreu model as presented in appendix 5C, agents commit on date 1 to a sequence of contingent consumption plans for all dates $t > 1$. They do this by trading contingent claims to future outputs in a market that meets on date 1 *only*. After date 1 there is no further asset trade: as the economy evolves stochastically over time, individuals have only to execute the sequence of history-dependent output transfers they contracted to make on date 1.

There is no reason, however, not to consider *continuing* asset trade over time. Indeed, this is how asset markets work in real economies, and such trade would arise endogenously if it offered opportunities for mutual gain. On date 2, for example, after execution of contracts written contingent on $\mathbf{h}_2$, people will still be holding securities for contingencies occurring on dates 3, 4, and so on. The arrival of new information makes some of these securities more valuable than when purchased on date 1, some less. If the remaining contingent securities could be bought and sold again on date 2, won't individuals sometimes wish to recontract and thus alter the contingent consumption levels they selected on date 1?

The answer, it turns out, is no. We will prove this result by showing that after we allow for continuing security-market activity, the solution to maximizing eq. (82) subject to eq. (83) is *dynamically consistent*: contingency plans that appear optimal on date 1 remain so as the dates and states in which they are supposed to be implemented arrive.

In section 2.1.4, we raised the potential problem of dynamic inconsistency in individual intertemporal plans. The question is a bit more subtle in models with uncertainty because as time passes, individuals update the probabilities entering the expected utility function (82) in light of new information. This updating appears to make preferences change over time, but in reality preferences are stable here. Because this stability may not be completely obvious to you, we include a formal proof of dynamic consistency.

To prove dynamic consistency in an economy with ongoing securities trade, we first make a useful notational economy. Let $\widetilde{p}(\mathbf{h}_t \mid \mathbf{h}_1)$ denote the price of the Arrow-Debreu security for history $\mathbf{h}_t$ *in terms of date 1 output*; that is, $\widetilde{p}(\mathbf{h}_t \mid \mathbf{h}_1) \equiv p(\mathbf{h}_t \mid \mathbf{h}_1)R_{1,t}$. Similarly, $\widetilde{p}(\mathbf{h}_t \mid \mathbf{h}_2)$ denotes the price of the same security on date 2 measured in date 2 output units. Using this convention we can, for example, rewrite eq. (84) as

$$\widetilde{p}(\mathbf{h}_t \mid \mathbf{h}_1)u'(C_1) = \pi(\mathbf{h}_t \mid \mathbf{h}_1)\beta^{t-1}u'[C(\mathbf{h}_t)], \tag{86}$$

where we drop the country superscripts, which are superfluous for current purposes.

To begin, consider the position on date 2 of an individual who learns s_2 (and therefore $\mathbf{h}_2$) after having maximized eq. (82) subject to eq. (83) on date 1 and planned for history-contingent consumption levels $C(\mathbf{h}_t)$, $\forall t > 1$. In contrast to appendix 5C, securities markets reopen on date 2 so that people can recontract, if they wish, on the basis of their new information about the economy's state. Individuals are legally bound to make the payments they contracted for on date 1, but they are not bound to stick with their original consumption plans for dates $t \geq 2$. To establish dynamic consistency, we have to show that the consumption contingency plans chosen on date 1 remain feasible and optimal on date 2.

Let's take feasibility first. Given a realized history $\mathbf{h}_2$ on date 2, the consumption levels contracted on date 1 determine the individual's endowment. So he faces the date 2 budget constraint:

$$C_2' + \sum_{t=3}^{\infty} \left[\sum_{h_t \in H_t(h_2)} \widetilde{p}(h_t \mid h_2)C(h_t)' \right]$$

$$= C(h_2) + \sum_{t=3}^{\infty} \left[\sum_{h_t \in H_t(h_2)} \widetilde{p}(h_t \mid h_2)C(h_t) \right],$$

where primes indicate new consumption levels that could be picked on date 2. Clearly the original consumption plans $C(h_t)$ are still feasible given this constraint.

But are they optimal? They are provided they satisfy the date 2 versions of the first-order conditions in eq. (86),

$$\widetilde{p}(h_t \mid h_2)u'[C(h_2)] = \pi(h_t \mid h_2)\beta^{t-2}u'[C(h_t)], \tag{87}$$

for all histories $h_t \in H_t(h_2)$ [recall that in eq. (87), $\widetilde{p}$ is a date 2 present value].

Consumption was planned on date 1 to satisfy eq. (84) for all $t > 1$; in particular,

$$\widetilde{p}(h_2 \mid h_1)u'(C_1) = \pi(h_2 \mid h_1)\beta u'[C(h_2)].$$

Combining this with eq. (86) to eliminate $u'(C_1)$, we find that the date 1 plan sets

$$\frac{\widetilde{p}(h_t \mid h_1)}{\widetilde{p}(h_2 \mid h_1)}u'[C(h_2)] = \left[\frac{\pi(h_t \mid h_1)}{\pi(h_2 \mid h_1)} \right] \beta^{t-2}u'[C(h_t)] \tag{88}$$

By the properties of conditional expectations (Bayes's rule),[53]

$$\frac{\pi(h_t \mid h_1)}{\pi(h_2 \mid h_1)} = \pi(h_t \mid h_2).$$

Furthermore, because history $h_t \in H_t(h_2)$ can only occur if h_2 does, a simple arbitrage argument shows that

$$\frac{\widetilde{p}(h_t \mid h_1)}{\widetilde{p}(h_2 \mid h_1)} = \widetilde{p}(h_t \mid h_2).$$

On date 1 one can buy a unit of date t output contingent on h_t in two ways: pay $\widetilde{p}(h_t \mid h_1)$ directly, or buy $\widetilde{p}(h_t \mid h_2)$ units of h_2-contingent date 2 output at date 1 cost $\widetilde{p}(h_2 \mid h_1)\widetilde{p}(h_t \mid h_2)$, using the proceeds (if h_2 is realized) to buy a unit of h_t-contingent date t output on date 2. These two strategies must entail the same sacrifice of date 1 output.

The last two equalities show, however, that eq. (88) reduces to eq. (87), completing our proof that to continue the date 1 optimal plan always remains optimal on date 2.

---

53. In general, for all $s \geq t + 1$,

$$\pi(h_s \mid h_{t+1}) = \pi(h_s \mid h_t)/\pi(h_{t+1} \mid h_t).$$

Proof: Let $h_{t+1} = \{s_{t+1}\} \cup h_t$ and $h_s \in H_s(h_{t+1})$. Then by the definition of conditional expectation,

$$\pi(h_s \mid h_{t+1}) = \pi(h_s \mid s_{t+1} \text{ and } h_t)$$

$$= \pi(h_s \text{ and } s_{t+1} \mid h_t)/\pi(s_{t+1} \mid h_t)$$

$$= \pi(h_s \mid h_t)/\pi(h_{t+1} \mid h_t).$$

Exercises

1.   *More on the logarithmic small-country example.* Consider the small-country Arrow-Debreu model with log preferences of section 5.1.6 and appendix 5B. Show that in general, when the current account need not be zero, the country's *gross* purchases of the individual Arrow-Debreu security purchases, $B_2(1)$ and $B_2(2)$ satisfy

$$\frac{p(1)}{1+r}B_2(1) = \frac{p(2)\pi(2)Y_2(1)}{1+r}\left[\frac{p(1)^A}{p(2)^A} - \frac{p(1)}{p(2)}\right] + \pi(1)CA_1,$$

$$\frac{p(2)}{1+r}B_2(2) = \frac{-p(2)\pi(2)Y_2(1)}{1+r}\left[\frac{p(1)^A}{p(2)^A} - \frac{p(1)}{p(2)}\right] + \pi(2)CA_1.$$

Provide an intuitive interpretation. [Hint: Any date 2 expenditure $(1+r)CA_1$ above (below) $p(1)Y_2(1) + p_2(2)Y_2(2)$ goes to increase (reduce) state s consumption in the proportion $\pi(s)/p(s)$ with log preferences. The country then does any additional portfolio rebalancing it desires by a pure swap between state 1 and state 2 securities, as in the text.]

2.   *An example with risk neutrality.* Consider the two-country, two-period, two-state Arrow-Debreu endowment economy in section 5.2.1. Suppose the utility function at home and abroad is given by

$$U_1 = \log(C_1) + \pi(1)\beta C_2(1) + \pi(2)\beta C_2(2),$$

so that countries are risk-neutral with respect to second-period consumption. Determine equilibrium Arrow-Debreu prices $p(1)$ and $p(2)$ for this world economy. Are they actuarially fair? Also describe equilibrium Home and Foreign consumption levels, and determine the interest rate $1+r$.

3.   *Comparing optimal consumption with complete and incomplete markets.* Consider a two-period small open endowment economy facing the world interest rate r for riskless loans. Date 1 output is Y_1. There are S states of nature on date 2 that differ according to the associated output realizations $Y_2(s)$ and have probabilities $\pi(s)$ of occurring. The representative domestic consumer maximizes the expected lifetime utility function

$$U_1 = C_1 - \frac{a_0}{2}(C_1)^2 + (1+r)^{-1}E_1\left\{C_2 - \frac{a_0}{2}(C_2)^2\right\}, \qquad a_0 > 0,$$

in which period utility is quadratic. The relevant budget constraints when markets are *incomplete* can be written as

$$B_2 = (1+r)B_1 + Y_1 - C_1,$$

$$C_2(s) = (1+r)B_2 + Y_2(s), \qquad s = 1, 2, \dots, S,$$

where B_1 is given. The last constraint is equivalent to the S constraints: for all states s,

$$C_1 + \frac{C_2(s)}{1+r} = (1+r)B_1 + Y_1 + \frac{Y_2(s)}{1+r}.$$

(You may assume that all output levels are small enough that the marginal utility of consumption $1 - a_0 C$ is safely positive.)

(a) Start by temporarily ignoring the nonnegativity constraints $C_2(s) \geq 0$ on date 2 consumption. Compute optimal date 1 consumption C_1. What are the implied values of $C_2(s)$? What do you think your answer for C_1 would be with an infinite horizon and output uncertainty in each future period? [Hint: Recall Chapter 2.]

(b) Now let's worry about the nonnegativity constraint on C_2. Renumber the date 2 states of nature (if necessary) so that $Y_2(1) = \min_s\{Y_2(s)\}$. Show that if

$$(1 + r)B_1 + Y_1 + \frac{2 + r}{1 + r} Y_2(1) \geq E_1 Y_2,$$

then the C_1 computed in part a (for the two-period case) is still valid. What is the intuition? Suppose the preceding inequality does not hold. Show that the optimal date 1 consumption is lower (a precautionary saving effect) and equals

$$C_t = (1 + r)B_1 + Y_1 + \frac{Y_2(1)}{1 + r}.$$

[Hint: Apply the Kuhn-Tucker theorem.] Explain the preceding answer. Does the bond Euler equation hold in this case?

(c) Now assume the consumer faces *complete* global asset markets with $p(s)$, the state s Arrow-Debreu security price, equal to $\pi(s)$. Find the optimal values of C_1 and $C_2(s)$ now. Why can nonnegativity constraints be disregarded in the complete-markets case?

4.   *An alternative solution of the diversification model.* This problem illustrates an alternative approach to solving the model in section 5.3.1 when period utility is logarithmic. Note that eq. (42) implies that a representative individual from country n has a lifetime income equal to $Y_1^n + V_1^n$, the sum of current output and the market value on date 1 of uncertain future output. Given the agent's log utility function, a reasonable guess is that optimal date 1 consumption will be

$$C_1^n = \frac{1}{1 + \beta}(Y_1^n + V_1^n). \tag{89}$$

Let us further guess that the agent invests savings $\frac{\beta}{1+\beta}(Y_1^n + V_1^n)$ in the global mutual fund that gives the agent an equal share in every country's output:

$$C_2^n(s) = \frac{\beta}{1 + \beta}(Y_1^n + V_1^n)\frac{\sum_{m=1}^N Y_2^m(s)}{\sum_{m=1}^N V_1^m}. \tag{90}$$

Use these guesses to find asset prices consistent with individual agents' first-order conditions and with global equilibrium.

5.   *Consequences of exponential period utility.* Suppose we have the two-country, two-period, S state endowment setup of section 5.2 and of the $N = 2$ case from section 5.3. Now, however, in both Home and Foreign, agents have the exponential period utility function $u(C) = -\exp(-\gamma C)/\gamma$, $\gamma > 0$, rather than CRRA period utility.

[The parameter $\gamma = -u''(C)/u'(C)$ is called the coefficient of *absolute* risk aversion.]

(a) For the case of complete markets (paralleling section 5.2), calculate equilibrium prices and consumption levels.

(b) Suppose that instead of complete markets, people are restricted to trading riskless bonds and shares in Home and Foreign period 2 outputs. Show that the resulting allocation is still efficient (paralleling section 5.3), and that Home and Foreign consumptions on both dates are given by $C = \frac{1}{2}Y^W - \mu$, $C^* = \frac{1}{2}Y^W + \mu$, where Y^W is world output and μ is a time-invariant constant. Show that to support this equilibrium, both countries purchase equal shares in the risky world mutual fund on date 1 and one country makes riskless loans to the other.

(c) How does your answer to part b change when Home and Foreign have distinct coefficients of absolute risk aversion, $\gamma \neq \gamma^*$?

6.   *The Lucas (1982) two-good model.* There are two countries, Home and Foreign, with exogenous stochastic endowments of *distinct* goods, the outputs of which we denote by X and Y. Residents of the two countries have identical tastes, such that for the representative Home resident, say,

$$U_t = \mathrm{E}_t \left\{ \sum_{s=t}^{\infty} \beta^{s-t} u(C_{X,s}, C_{Y,s}) \right\}.$$

We also assume that the countries start out endowed with equal and perfectly-pooled portfolios of risky claims, such that each country owns exactly half the Home output process and half the Foreign output process. Thus, either country's initial endowment each period is $\frac{1}{2}(X + pY)$, where p denotes the price of good Y (Foreign's output) in terms of good X (Home's output). As usual, countries are free to trade away from these initial endowments.

(a) Paralleling section 5.3, let $V_{X,t}$ be the ex dividend price on date t of the claim to Home's entire future output process (where asset prices are measured in terms of current units of good X). Correspondingly, let $V_{Y,t}$ be the ex dividend date t price (in units of good X) of the claim to Foreign's future output process. Write down the finance constraints corresponding to eq. (56) in section 5.4.3, but with two risky assets. Derive a representative consumer's first-order Euler conditions corresponding to the two risky assets and the riskless bond.

(b) Show that the equilibrium consumption allocation is $C_{X,t} = C^*_{X,t} = \frac{1}{2}X_t$, $C_{Y,t} = C^*_{Y,t} = \frac{1}{2}Y_t$, in every period. (People find it optimal to hold initial endowments.) In particular, the distribution of world wealth is constant. Show that in equilibrium,

$$p_t = p(X_t, Y_t) = \frac{\partial u\left(\frac{1}{2}X_t, \frac{1}{2}Y_t\right)/\partial Y}{\partial u\left(\frac{1}{2}X_t, \frac{1}{2}Y_t\right)/\partial X}.$$

(c) Calculate the equilibrium levels of $V_{X,t}$ and $V_{Y,t}$ as expected present values.

(d) What is the date t price of a unit of X to be delivered with certainty on date $t + 1$? Similarly, what is the own-rate of interest on good Y?

6 Imperfections in International Capital Markets

The last chapter explored models in which there are virtually no restrictions on the range of financial contracts people can sign, and where contracts are always honored. In reality, difficulties in enforcing contracts ex post limit the range of contracts agents will agree to ex ante. Without doubt, enforcement problems are a major reason why financial trading falls far short of producing the kind of efficient global equilibrium that the Arrow-Debreu model of complete asset markets portrays.

The problem of contract enforcement is particularly severe in an international setting. The sanctions that foreign creditors can impose on a country that defaults are limited and often fairly indirect. The first part of our analysis considers how such limitations may or may not reduce a country's ability to tap international capital markets for consumption insurance, and the following section looks at how they can curtail efficient investment. Among the questions we address are the "debt overhang" problem that some observers hold responsible for the Latin American recession of the 1980s and the implications of various types of financial restructuring. The third and fourth sections of the chapter assume that the binding constraint on contracts is private information rather than the limited ability of creditors to impose penalties. We first look at an environment where countries are free to misrepresent domestic economic conditions in order to increase their insurance payments from abroad. We then show how investment and international capital flows can be dampened by moral hazard problems at the firm level.

It is important to contrast the capital market imperfections studied here with the stochastic bonds-only model of Chapter 2. The earlier model simply assumed without any explicit justification that some markets are closed to trade (specifically, international markets for risky assets). Here, the nature of any limitations on asset trade is determined *endogenously* based on underlying information or enforcement problems. A central lesson of the analysis is that endogenous imperfections in international capital markets will not necessarily cause those markets to collapse completely. Instead, capital markets usually will still be able to facilitate risk sharing and intertemporal trade, but only to a limited extent.

6.1 Sovereign Risk

Perhaps the most fundamental reason why international capital markets may be less integrated than domestic capital markets is the lack of a supranational legal authority, capable of enforcing contracts across borders. In the first part of this chapter, we will study some of the implications of "sovereign risk," which, broadly interpreted, can refer to any situation in which a government defaults on loan contracts with foreigners, seizes foreign assets located within its borders, or prevents domestic residents from fully meeting obligations to foreign creditors. We have already mentioned the developing-country debt crisis of the 1980s, in which a large number of countries, especially in Latin America and Africa, renegotiated debt obligations to foreign creditors. (See Chapter 2.) Eastern Europe followed in the 1990s. This recent experience is hardly unique. Some of the same countries defaulted on their debts during the 1930s and during the 1800s. Indeed, countries have been defaulting on debts to foreign creditors periodically since the inception of international lending. It is important to understand, though, that in the vast majority of cases, sovereign default has been *partial* rather than complete. A country may stand in default for years if not decades, but it generally reaches some type of accommodation with its creditors before reentering capital markets.

Because foreign lenders have only limited powers directly to punish sovereign borrowers, especially governments, the binding constraint on debt repayments is generally a country's *willingness to pay* rather than simply its *ability to pay*. This fundamental distinction was first emphasized in a classic paper by Eaton and Gersovitz (1981). In this section, we will look at two different mechanisms by which foreign creditors can enforce repayment, at least up to a certain level. The first consists of direct punishments. Generally speaking, we think of these as being based on rights that the creditors have within their own borders, rights which allow them to impede or harass the international trade and commerce of any borrower that unilaterally defaults. (Gone are the days when gunboats would steam into third-world harbors to protect the financial claims of American or European investors.) Thus, although creditors may not be able to seize plant and equipment within a defaulting country's borders, they can often prevent it from fully enjoying its gains from trade.[1] The second motive for repayment we shall consider is reputation: a country may be willing to repay loans to foreigners in order to ensure access to international capital markets in the future. Creditors' legal rights of direct punishment can also make it difficult for a country in default to gain access to new international loans. There are many subtle issues here, and the legal framework is complex (see Box 6.1 on the legal doctrine of foreign sovereign immunity). But as we shall emphasize later, there is a fundamental level at which creditors must have some legal or political rights to enforce repayment or international capital markets would collapse.

Throughout our analysis, we will treat each sovereign borrower as a single unified entity, "the country." We will not distinguish between government and private borrowers. In many developing countries, government and government-guaranteed debt accounts for the bulk of foreign borrowing, and in this section we will generally be thinking of the government as the borrower.[2] We recognize that the costs

---

1. In earlier days countries might pledge specified future customs revenues to debt service. (See Box 6.1.) Such pledges, which themselves are revocable, would offend nationalistic sensibilities today.

2. Even if a domestic firm wants to repay foreign creditors, it can be prevented from doing so by a government that blocks its access to the necessary foreign exchange. Sometimes creditors have been able to pressure borrowing governments to take responsibility for private domestic debts to them. Díaz-

and benefits of default typically fall very unevenly across groups within a country, but we do not explore the implications of this issue. Instead we focus on the overall gains and losses to a country of sovereign borrowing and default.

6.1.1   Sovereign Default and Direct Creditor Sanctions

The topic of sovereign risk raises a host of interesting but difficult modeling issues. A simple starting point is to assume that a sovereign's creditors can impose direct sanctions with a current cost proportional to the sovereign's output. Broadly interpreted, we have in mind trade sanctions, including the confiscation of exports or imports in transit and the seizure of trade-related foreign assets.[3] Concern over access to short-term trade credits has often been an especially important consideration for modern borrowers contemplating default. Good relations with international financial intermediaries, who specialize in gathering and processing information on creditworthiness, have become increasingly essential to international trade in complex modern economies.

Just as we do not model the tensions across different groups within debtor countries, we will not place too much emphasis in this chapter on tensions across various creditors (see Eaton and Fernandez, 1995). In practice, cross-default clauses in loans from banks and provisions for the organization of bondholders' committees serve to coordinate the actions of lenders in the event of default.[4] We assume, however, that lenders behave competitively in making loans, so that they cannot extract monopoly rents from a borrowing country. This assumption is realistic, since a country in good standing on its debt is generally free to pay off one lending consortium with a new loan from another one. Foreign claim holders have no legal rights to apply sanctions unless a country violates its contract with them.

The present section (section 6.1) focuses on insurance aspects of international capital markets. Throughout, unless otherwise noted (as in section 6.1.3), we will assume a fundamental asymmetry between foreign providers of insurance and country recipients. In particular, we will assume that foreign insurers can credibly make commitments to a future state-contingent payment stream whereas the

---

Alejandro (1985) discusses one prominent case, that of Chile in the early 1980s. In other cases, by assuming private debts, governments may have actually made default easier. This is especially the case in countries where foreign creditors might have some hope of pressing claims in domestic courts against private companies, but not against the government.

3. Generally, the net gain to creditors from sanctions will be much less than the cost to the debtor. This point is not central to the analysis of this section, but can be important in a broader bargaining context, such as the one we consider in appendix 6A. The assumption that the pain of sanctions is proportional to output is proposed by Sachs (1984) and by Cohen and Sachs (1986). It is far from innocuous, as we shall see. Nor is it obviously valid—the marginal cost of trade disruption, say, might sometimes be higher for a poorer economy.

4. For further discussion, see Bulow and Rogoff (1989a, appendix).

Box 6.1
Sovereign Immunity and Creditor Sanctions

The legal doctrine of sovereign immunity would appear to exempt the property of foreign governments from the jurisdiction of domestic courts. (In most countries, foreign diplomats generally cannot even be forced to pay parking tickets.) Historically, sovereign immunity has sometimes limited the direct sanctions creditors can apply in cases of sovereign default. Over the years, however, as a result of considerable evolution, the practical application of the doctrine has increasingly given creditors leverage to retaliate against defaulting sovereigns. In modern times, the ability of countries expressly to waive sovereign immunity in their commercial contracts has strengthened the rights of their creditors, thereby paving the way for an expansion of international lending.

The idea of sovereign immunity is an old one. Chief Justice John Marshall of the United States Supreme Court invoked it as early as 1812 in a famous decision. The American schooner *Exchange*, seized at sea in 1810 in the name of the French Emperor Napoleon, later docked in Philadelphia. When its previous owners tried to recover the *Exchange* in federal district court, their case was dismissed on the grounds that the ship was a state vessel of France employed in the pursuit of national objectives. The circuit court reversed this decision, but the Supreme Court overturned the reversal and affirmed the district court's original judgment leaving the ship in France's hands. Chief Justice Marshall argued that by welcoming a friendly nation's "public armed ship" into its port, the United States had implicitly exempted the ship from its jurisdiction, that is, extended sovereign immunity. In general, Marshall stated,

[F]ull and absolute territorial jurisdiction being alike the attribute of every sovereign, and being incapable of conferring extra-territorial power, would not seem to contemplate foreign sovereigns nor their sovereign rights as its objects. One sovereign being in no respect amenable to another, and being bound by obligation of the highest character not to degrade the dignity of his nation, by placing himself or its sovereign rights within the jurisdiction of another, can be supposed to enter a foreign territory only under an express license, or in the confidence that the immunities belonging to his independent sovereign station, though not expressly stipulated, are reserved by implication, and will be extended to him. (Quoted in Bishop, 1971, p. 660)

Where courts showed some reluctance to help creditors in pursuing claims on sovereign debtors before World War I, national governments could be more compliant. Political pressure and even military force might be deployed on behalf of aggrieved domestic creditors (though usually when creditor interests matched their government's foreign-policy goals). Examples abound. Britain, France, and Spain intervened in Mexico on behalf of creditors during the years 1859–61. When Egypt, a province of the Ottoman Empire, repudiated its debts in 1879, Britain and France induced the Ottoman sultan, a heavy borrower himself, to turn control of Egypt's finances over to British and French functionaries. (Turkey itself put foreign creditors in charge of important revenues in 1881 in return for debt reduction and continued access to foreign loans.) Invasions by U.S. Marines gave the United States control over the Dominican Republic's customs revenues in 1905 and over Nicaragua's during 1911–12. Britain sent a battleship to Guatemala's waters in 1913 to persuade the country to continue servicing debt held by British subjects.*

Box 6.1 *(continued)*

In the postimperialist era after 1945, a middle ground has emerged between jurists' respect for sovereign rights and politicians' willingness to disregard them. Starting in 1952, the United States adopted a policy of restricted sovereign immunity, which distinguished between governmental activities sui generis (for example, diplomatic missions) and governmental activities (including commercial activities) that private persons also can conduct. The latter, but not the former, can be subject to standard domestic commercial law. This doctrine was formalized in the United States by the Foreign Sovereign Immunities Act (FSIA) of 1976, and in Britain by the State Immunity Act of 1978.

By strengthening creditors' rights, these legal changes made sovereign borrowing easier. A key feature of the FSIA is that it permits countries to waive sovereign immunity in many commercial transactions. Most developing-country government debt contracts after 1976 have contained explicit waivers of sovereign immunity, with the details of the waiver an important bargaining point. The waivers have made it more difficult for sovereigns that repudiate their debts to engage in international trade, and their existence supports the assumption that creditors can impose direct sanctions on a reneging sovereign debtor.

[*] For details, see Feis (1930), Lindert and Morton (1989), and the latter authors' references to the intervening literature.

country may or not be able to do so (as we shall illustrate). One can think of justifying this asymmetry in two ways. First, many of the basic models here can easily be reformulated as models of equity investment or lending with state-contingent repayments rather than pure insurance. If the foreign investors provide cash up front, their credibility is not at issue. Indeed, we generally have in mind this interpretation of the models, and we use the example of pure insurance contracts to highlight the analogies with the complete-markets models of Chapter 5. Second, interpreting the country as a developing economy, one can think of foreign insurers as having access to a stronger legal system that allows them to make financial commitments. Thus, if a British bank legally promises to make a payment to a small country, the country can generally enforce the claim in British courts. This asymmetry seems quite realistic in the developing-country context, although we will not attempt to model the broader underpinnings of the industrialized-country legal system.

6.1.1.1   The Model

Some central points about sovereign risk's impact can be made in a bare-bones model. Consider a small endowment economy inhabited by a risk-averse representative agent who lives for two periods, labeled 1 and 2, in which date 1 consumption yields no utility and the country's date 1 endowment is zero. These assumptions together imply that the country can neither save nor dissave on date 1: its only economic activity on that date is to enter into contracts with foreign insurers so as to reduce the consumption risks posed by an uncertain date 2 output level.

There is a single good on date 2, and the representative agent's lifetime utility equals the date 1 expected utility of date 2 consumption

$$U_1 = Eu(C_2),$$

where we now follow our usual notation that identifies individual with aggregate domestic consumption when there is a single representative agent.[5] Date 2 output is uncertain as of date 1 and is given by

$$Y_2 = \bar{Y} + \epsilon,$$

where $E\{Y_2\} = \bar{Y}$ and the mean-zero shock ϵ can take any of N values $\underline{\epsilon} = \epsilon_1 < \epsilon_2 < \ldots < \epsilon_N = \bar{\epsilon}$, $\bar{Y} + \underline{\epsilon} > 0$. The shock ϵ is the only source of potential consumption uncertainty for the small country. The term $\pi(\epsilon_i)$ denotes the probability that $\epsilon = \epsilon_i$, and $\sum_{i=1}^{N} \pi(\epsilon_i) = 1$.

On date 1, the country contracts with foreign insurers to pay them the shock-contingent amount $P(\epsilon)$ on date 2. (The value that ϵ takes on date 2 is observed by everyone.) A negative value of $P(\epsilon)$ means that the insurers make a payment to the country in state ϵ, a positive value that the country pays an insurance "premium." Insurers compete against each other in offering contracts, and they are risk-neutral. (One could equivalently assume that insurers are risk-averse but that the country's output shock ϵ can be completely diversified away in international capital markets.) Because insurers put no money down on date 1, they are willing to sign any contract under which the sovereign can credibly promise to make payments $P(\epsilon)$ satisfying the zero-expected-profit condition:

$$\sum_{i=1}^{N} \pi(\epsilon_i) P(\epsilon_i) = 0. \tag{1}$$

Of course, the sovereign's credibility is only ever an issue when $P(\epsilon) > 0!$[6]

---

5. Lifetime utility could, alternatively, be of the discounted form $U_1 = \beta Eu(C_2)$, but the multiplicative constant β is inconsequential for the analysis and therefore can be omitted. The conditional expectations operator will be denoted throughout by $E\{\cdot\}$ rather than $E_1\{\cdot\}$ when there can be no confusion surrounding the information on which expectations are conditioned.

6. It will sometimes prove convenient to interpret $\pi(\epsilon)$ as the probability density function for a continuously distributed ϵ, in which case eq. (1) becomes

$$\int_{\underline{\epsilon}}^{\bar{\epsilon}} \pi(\epsilon) P(\epsilon) d\epsilon = 0.$$

Condition (1) would not hold if a single insurer or a small collusive group could extract monopoly rents from the country.

6.1.1.2   A Benchmark Case: Full Insurance

Let's initially assume away any risk of default, so as to obtain a benchmark case against which we can later compare our main results. Thus the country can commit itself to any schedule $P(\epsilon)$ of date 2 payments such that $P(\epsilon) \le Y_2$. In this case we get an equilibrium familiar from the discussion of complete markets in Chapter 5. The payments schedule $P(\epsilon) = \epsilon$ satisfies (1)—because the shock ϵ has mean zero—and results in a date 2 consumption level that is *independent* of ϵ,

$$C_2(\epsilon) = Y_2 - P(\epsilon) = Y_2 - \epsilon = \bar{Y}.$$

Stabilizing consumption across all states of nature is the best the country can do; so, in equilibrium, the country will diversify away its output risk completely.[7] We will refer to the contract with payments schedule $P(\epsilon) = \epsilon$ as the *full insurance* contract.

The full insurance contract solves the problem of maximizing expected utility given the availability of binding Arrow-Debreu contracts at the actuarially fair prices for consumption contingent on the state ϵ. Alternatively, one can think of the country as selling its uncertain endowment forward to the outside world at the risk-neutral equity price (measured in date 2 consumption units)

$$\sum_{i=1}^{N} \pi(\epsilon_i) Y_2 = \sum_{i=1}^{N} \pi(\epsilon_i) \bar{Y} + \sum_{i=1}^{N} \pi(\epsilon_i)\epsilon_i = \bar{Y}.$$

This forward sale guarantees the consumption level $\bar{Y}$ on date 2. On any interpretation, the country receives $-\epsilon$ from insurers when $\epsilon < 0$, but must hand over to insurers any $\epsilon > 0$.

This last part of the full insurance contract is troublesome. We have assumed away the possibility that the insurers themselves fail to make scheduled payments when $P(\epsilon) < 0$. (Exercise 1 shows how to relax this assumption.) But when $P(\epsilon) > 0$, a sovereign that maximizes its citizens' welfare will choose not to pay ex post unless it perceives some cost to default. If the sanctions foreign creditors can impose in the event of default cost the country only a fraction $\eta \in (0, 1)$ of its output, there is no guarantee that the country will always honor its end of the full insurance contract. Indeed, the country would prefer to default and pay nothing if $P(\epsilon) = Y_2 - \bar{Y} > \eta Y_2$. Thus, unless repudiation is ruled out by sufficiently strong sanctions, the full insurance contract would never be offered in the first place.[8]

---

7. It is straightforward to check that this allocation describes the solution to maximizing $Eu(C_2) = \sum_{i=1}^{N} \pi(\epsilon_i)u[C_2(\epsilon_i)]$ subject to eq. (1) and $C_2(\epsilon_i) = Y_2 - P(\epsilon_i)$.

8. Assuming that the country repays in cases of indifference, a default occurs whenever $\eta Y_2 < Y_2 - \bar{Y} = \epsilon$, that is, whenever $\epsilon > \eta \bar{Y}/(1 - \eta)$.

6.1.1.3 Optimal Incentive-Compatible Contracts

What type of contracts would we see instead? Since the foreign insurers themselves never default, these contracts will have three features. First, the contract can never call on the sovereign to make a payment to foreign creditors in excess of the sanction cost. Thus the payments schedule $P(\epsilon)$ satisfies (for every $i = 1, \ldots, N$) the *incentive-compatibility constraint*,

$$P(\epsilon_i) \leq \eta(\bar{Y} + \epsilon_i). \tag{2}$$

Second, competition among the risk-neutral insurers must result in an equilibrium that yields them expected profits of zero. Third, competition will ensure that the contract is optimal for the sovereign, subject to eqs. (2) and (1)—otherwise, the sovereign would offer to pay insurers slightly positive expected profits for a contract slightly more favorable to itself.

Together, these three features imply that the optimal incentive-compatible insurance contract solves the problem:

$$\max_{C_2(\epsilon), P(\epsilon)} \sum_{i=1}^{N} \pi(\epsilon_i) u[C_2(\epsilon_i)]$$

subject to the incentive-compatibility constraint (2), the zero-profit condition (1), and the N budget constraints

$$C_2(\epsilon_i) = \bar{Y} + \epsilon_i - P(\epsilon_i). \tag{3}$$

To solve, we substitute eq. (3) into the maximand and set up the Lagrangian

$$\mathcal{L} = \sum_{i=1}^{N} \pi(\epsilon_i) u[\bar{Y} + \epsilon_i - P(\epsilon_i)] - \sum_{i=1}^{N} \lambda(\epsilon_i)[P(\epsilon_i) - \eta(\bar{Y} + \epsilon_i)]$$

$$+ \mu \sum_{i=1}^{N} \pi(\epsilon_i) P(\epsilon_i),$$

as directed by the Kuhn-Tucker theorem for problems with inequality constraints (see Supplement A to Chapter 2). Differentiate the Lagrangian with respect to $P(\epsilon_i)$, for each ϵ_i. Along with eqs. (1) and (2), necessary conditions for an optimal $P(\epsilon)$ schedule are (for all ϵ, dropping the i subscripts)

$$\pi(\epsilon) u'[C_2(\epsilon)] + \lambda(\epsilon) = \mu \pi(\epsilon), \tag{4}$$

$$\lambda(\epsilon)[\eta(\bar{Y} + \epsilon) - P(\epsilon)] = 0, \tag{5}$$

for nonnegative multipliers $\lambda(\epsilon)$. The first of these conditions, eq. (4), shows how positive multipliers on the incentive constraint, $\lambda(\epsilon) > 0$, may induce unequal consumption across different realizations of ϵ. The second, eq. (5), is the complementary slackness condition, which implies that $\lambda(\epsilon) = 0$ for ϵ values at which eq. (2) holds as a *strict* inequality.

How does the optimal incentive-compatible contract look? For simplicity, let us assume that the distribution of ϵ is *continuous*. A plausible guess is that incentive inequality (2) will not hold as an equality for the lowest values of ϵ: these are states in which insurers make net payments to the country, or where the country's payments to insurers are strictly smaller than the costs of punishment.[9] Across these states $\lambda(\epsilon) = 0$ according to eq. (5), so eq. (4) reduces to $u'[C_2(\epsilon)] = \mu$, implying that consumption is constant irrespective of ϵ. From eq. (3), it follows that across states where $\lambda(\epsilon) = 0$, $P(\epsilon) = P_0 + \epsilon$ for some constant P_0. This repayment function makes $C_2(\epsilon)$ equal to $\bar{Y} + \epsilon - P(\epsilon) = \bar{Y} - P_0$, which is independent of ϵ. We will know P_0's value only at the end of our calculation of the optimal repayment schedule. The reason is that the level of consumption the country can assure itself in the "bad" (low ϵ) states of nature depends on how much it can credibly promise to repay creditors in the good states.

Since the last paragraph's analysis shows that P_0 satisfies $u'(\bar{Y} - P_0) = \mu$, eqs. (3) and (4) tell us that in states of nature such that the incentive constraint (2) holds with equality, it must be true that

$$u'(\bar{Y} - P_0) - u'[C_2(\epsilon)] = u'(\bar{Y} - P_0) - u'[\bar{Y} + \epsilon - P(\epsilon)]$$

$$= u'(\bar{Y} - P_0) - u'[(1 - \eta)(\bar{Y} + \epsilon)]$$

$$= \frac{\lambda(\epsilon)}{\pi(\epsilon)} \geq 0. \tag{6}$$

Notice that the left-hand side of the last equality falls as ϵ falls. Consider the critical value of ϵ, denoted by e, such that $u'(\bar{Y} - P_0) - u'[(1 - \eta)(\bar{Y} + e)] = 0$, and, therefore, $\lambda(e) = 0$.[10] For ϵ above e, eq. (6) shows that $\lambda(\epsilon)$ is strictly positive, so that, by eq. (5), $P(\epsilon) = \eta(\bar{Y} + \epsilon)$. For ϵ below e, the country is not constrained by eq. (2): since Kuhn-Tucker forbids a negative $\lambda(\epsilon)$, $\lambda(\epsilon) = 0$ and $P(\epsilon) = P_0 + \epsilon$ in this region. Our definition of e therefore implies that

$$\bar{Y} - P_0 = (1 - \eta)(\bar{Y} + e), \tag{7}$$

which can be rewritten as

$$P_0 + e = \eta(\bar{Y} + e). \tag{8}$$

Equation (8) implies that $P_0 = \eta\bar{Y} - (1 - \eta)e$, which shows that the repayment schedule is

---

9. Note that $\epsilon - \eta(\bar{Y} + \epsilon) = (1 - \eta)\epsilon - \eta\bar{Y}$, the difference between the full insurance payment and the cost of default, is an increasing function of ϵ.

10. We assume that e lies in the interior of $[\underline{\epsilon}, \bar{\epsilon}]$. If $e = \bar{\epsilon}$, the certain component of the country's output $\bar{Y}$ is large enough, given η, to make full insurance feasible.

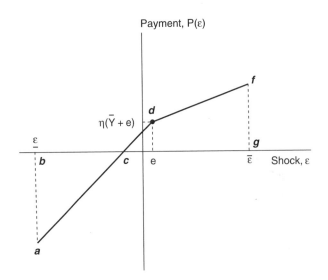

Figure 6.1
The optimal incentive-compatible contract

$$P(\epsilon) = \begin{cases} \eta\bar{Y} - (1-\eta)e + \epsilon = \eta(\bar{Y}+e) + (\epsilon - e), & \epsilon \in [\underline{\epsilon}, e), \\ \eta(\bar{Y}+e) = \eta(\bar{Y}+e) + \eta(\epsilon - e), & \epsilon \in [e, \bar{\epsilon}]. \end{cases} \quad (9)$$

Thus at $\epsilon = e$, as elsewhere on $[\underline{\epsilon}, \bar{\epsilon}]$, the repayment schedule $P(\epsilon)$ is continuous, as shown in Figure 6.1. Note that $P(\epsilon)$ rises dollar for dollar in states of nature where $\epsilon < e$. As ϵ rises above e, $P(\epsilon)$ rises only at rate η since the incentive constraint is binding.

To complete the derivation of the optimal repayment schedule, we have only to tie down e [and hence, by eq. (8), P_0] through the zero-profit condition (1). In Figure 6.1, we assume that ϵ is uniformly distributed over $[\underline{\epsilon}, \bar{\epsilon}]$ (implying $\underline{\epsilon} = -\bar{\epsilon}$, since $E\epsilon = 0$). The condition that the optimal incentive-compatible contract must yield insurers zero expected profits is represented by the equality of the areas of triangle **abc** and quadrilateral **cdfg**.

6.1.1.4 An Example

The assumption that ϵ is continuous and uniformly distributed allows explicit computation of the optimal repayment schedule, that is, of the parameter e. Since this exercise serves to make our discussion more concrete, we describe it in detail. All that we need do is ensure that e makes the contract in eq. (9) consistent with zero expected profits. When ϵ is uniformly distributed over $[-\bar{\epsilon}, \bar{\epsilon}]$, its probability density function is $\pi(\epsilon) = 1/2\bar{\epsilon}$, and so eq. (1) can be written

$$\int_{-\bar{\epsilon}}^{e} [\eta(\bar{Y}+e) + (\epsilon - e)]\frac{d\epsilon}{2\bar{\epsilon}} + \int_{e}^{\bar{\epsilon}} [\eta(\bar{Y}+e) + \eta(\epsilon - e)]\frac{d\epsilon}{2\bar{\epsilon}} = 0.$$

By evaluating these two integrals, we find (after some algebra) that the foregoing equation in e reduces to the quadratic equation

$$e^2 + 2\bar{\epsilon}e + \left(\bar{\epsilon}^2 - \frac{4\eta\bar{\epsilon}\bar{Y}}{1-\eta}\right) = 0.$$

The quadratic has two roots, one of which is less than $-\bar{\epsilon}$ and is disregarded. The economically relevant solution is

$$e = -\bar{\epsilon} + 2\sqrt{\frac{\eta\bar{\epsilon}\bar{Y}}{1-\eta}}. \tag{10}$$

You can verify that $e < \bar{\epsilon}$, giving a range over which the incentive-compatibility constraint actually does bind, provided $\bar{\epsilon} > \eta(\bar{Y} + \bar{\epsilon})$. The last inequality means the country would rather default at $\epsilon = \bar{\epsilon}$ than make the full-insurance payment $\bar{\epsilon}$ to creditors. It is simply the condition that sanctions are not severe enough to support full insurance.

6.1.1.5   Discussion

With this example under our belts, it is easier to grasp the intuition behind the optimal incentive-compatible contract in Figure 6.1. For sufficiently low realizations of ϵ, there is no enforcement problem. As a result, the country can smooth consumption across these states. For higher values of ϵ, though, the temptation to default would be too great under full insurance. So the optimal contract calls on the country to transfer only a fraction η of any unexpected output increase to creditors, which is the most they can extract through the threat of sanctions. This provision has two effects. First, limitations on how much the country can promise to repay in good states of nature reduce the level of consumption its insurers can afford to guarantee it in bad states of nature. Second, the country is limited in how much it can smooth consumption across the good states. Figure 6.2 shows the constrained consumption locus compared with the full insurance locus $C_2(\epsilon) = \bar{Y}$.

Consider the first contract feature described in the preceding paragraph: given the contract's asymmetric treatment of low and high ϵ values, insurers can earn zero expected profits only if the contract guarantees them higher net payments than the full insurance contract over a range of the lowest ϵ values. This observation implies that $(1-\eta)(\bar{Y} + e) < \bar{Y}$ (as shown in Figure 6.2), which is equivalent, by eq. (7), to $P_0 > 0$ (as in Figure 6.1).[11] The optimal contract therefore requires the country to make positive transfers to insurers even for some negative values of ϵ. Interestingly, this prediction of the model matches the observation that economies with temporarily low outputs often have made positive transfers to creditors.

---

11. The form of the constrained consumption locus in Figure 6.2 implies that the country in effect exchanges its risky output Y_2 for the asset with date 2 payoff $(1-\eta)Y_2$ and a put option.

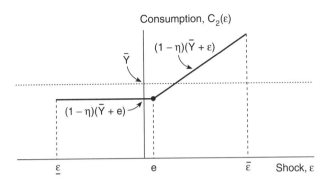

Figure 6.2
Optimal incentive-compatible consumption

Equation (10) illustrates the effects of higher sanctions, η. These raise e, allowing consumption stabilization over a higher range of shocks. Notice that e could well be negative (just take η low enough); as $\eta \to 0$, so that sanctions become powerless, $e \to \underline{\epsilon} = -\bar{\epsilon}$ and contracting becomes altogether infeasible in this model.

Because insurers earn zero expected profits, the optimal contract under default risk still sets the country's expected consumption to equal $\bar{Y}$. However, the contract's failure to equalize consumption across states of nature leaves the country worse off than it would be were full insurance possible. Perhaps surprisingly, it is in the country's interest for sanctions to be as dire as possible! As η rises, consumption can be stabilized across more states of nature, to the country's benefit. The sanctions are never exercised in equilibrium anyway, so their only role here is the positive one of enhancing the credibility of the country's promise to repay. Only if there were some contingencies that could bring the sanctions into play might higher potential punishments be a mixed blessing.

We have assumed that creditors are precommitted to imposing their maximal sanctions ηY_2 in the event of any default. How would the analysis change if creditors might somehow be bargained into settling for less than they are owed? Appendix 6A discusses a model of this type. The main impact on the preceding analysis is quantitative. The country will still obtain partial insurance, but only through contracts inferior to those it could get were creditors truly committed to applying maximal sanctions after any infraction.

The reader may find the pure risk-sharing contracts we have considered rather unrealistic. After all, most international capital-account transactions take the form of noncontingent money loans, equity purchases, or direct foreign investment. All we have done in our analysis, though, is to separate out two features that these more standard contracts typically combine: a riskless intertemporal loan and a pure risk-sharing contract. For example, if a home firm were to sell equity to a foreign investor, it would be receiving money up front in return for a share of a risky future profit stream. Funds obtained by issuing bonds or by borrowing from foreign banks are technically noncontingent, but the long history of sovereign lending shows that the payments may be rescheduled, renegotiated, or even changed unilaterally when the borrower's economy falters. Lenders as well as borrowers almost certainly anticipate such possibilities, so that interest rates on loans contain a premium to compensate for states of nature in which scheduled payments are not made in full. Thus *implicit* lending contracts involve risk sharing even if the *explicit* contracts do not.

"Stripping out" the pure risk-sharing component of a foreign investment from its lending component makes the analysis simpler and cleaner, and this advantage will become increasingly apparent as we move to explicitly dynamic models. In interpreting the results, however, it is important to bear in mind that in reality the two components typically come as a package. With pure risk-sharing contracts, the danger of the country's "defaulting" appears only in the good states of nature because in bad states the country receives resources from abroad rather than having to pay. If sovereign lending takes the form of equity arrangements, this still makes sense. If, however, one reinterprets the analysis as a model of loans, then the binding constraint becomes the country's willingness to meet its obligations in bad states of nature (where the lender's leverage to enforce repayment is lowest). Though the bond or bank-loan interpretation would seem to give very different results, in fact, it does not, as we illustrate in end-of-chapter exercise 2. By either interpretation, the implicit contract calls for the country to make relatively larger net payments when output is high and relatively smaller payments when output is low.[12]

This hyperrational interpretation of sovereign borrowing may seem strained given the experience of the developing-country debt crisis in the 1980s. Many borrowers that paid relatively modest interest rate premiums prior to 1982 fell into serious debt-servicing difficulties thereafter, and world secondary market prices for their government-guaranteed debt plummeted. In some cases (for example, Bolivia and Peru), discounts relative to face value exceeded 90 percent. Some have argued that lenders could not possibly have foreseen even the possibility that the debt crisis would be so severe.[13] Of course, many sovereign debtors in western Europe and Asia also seemed potentially risky in the 1970s, but loans to these countries

---

12. Bulow and Rogoff (1989a) argue that many contingencies, even though observable by both parties in the event of default, may be difficult to write contracts on. Therefore, lenders and borrowers write noncontingent loans, fully anticipating that they may have to be renegotiated. See also H. Grossman and Van Huyck (1988).

13. Bulow and Rogoff (1988a) argue that banks in industrial countries made loans recognizing that their governments, out of concern for the stability of world trade and the world financial system, could be gamed into making side payments to avoid a creditor-debtor showdown. See Dooley (1995) for a retrospective on the debt crisis of the 1980s.

generally paid off handsomely. One cannot evaluate overall investor returns just on the basis of the countries that ran into difficulties.

6.1.1.6   The Role of Saving

The last "two-period" model made the unrealistic assumption that there is no consumption or saving in the first period. What happens if the small country maximizes

$$U_1 = u(C_1) + \beta E u(C_2), \qquad \beta < 1,$$

receives the endowment $Y_1 = \bar{Y}$ in the first period, and starts out with neither foreign assets nor debt? We again assume that $Y_2 = \bar{Y} + \epsilon$ and that risk-neutral insurers compete on date 1 to offer the country zero-expected-profit contracts for date 2, but we also allow the country to borrow or lend at a given world interest rate $r > 0$, where $\beta(1 + r) = 1$.

To see how things change, we have to be very precise about what happens in the event of default. First, we assume that if the country defaults on its contracts with insurers, it forfeits any repayments on savings it may have invested abroad, up to the amount in default.[14] This provision amounts to assuming that aggrieved creditors can seize a defaulting sovereign's foreign assets as compensation. Second, we assume that default on an amount that exceeds the sovereign's own foreign claims triggers sanctions that cost the country a fraction η of its output.[15]

We reserve a detailed analysis of this model for appendix 6B, but its main predictions are easily grasped. Absent default risk there is no saving and the country fully eliminates its second-period consumption risk, as in section 6.1.1.2. With default risk, however, the country recognizes that its own saving effectively gives creditors collateral to seize in case of default. Thus, by saving, the country expands its access to insurance. (Indeed, through this mechanism the country can get partial insurance even when $\eta = 0$, something that wasn't possible in the last model.) But insurance is incomplete, and the repayment schedule still has slope $\eta < 1$ once ϵ reaches a cutoff analogous to e in Figure 6.1. In the extended model, the country distorts its intertemporal consumption profile, consuming less than it otherwise would on date 1, in order to reduce its date 2 consumption variability.

---

14. It will be in the interest of the country to put its first-period savings into assets that can be seized, since in this way it can expand its insurance opportunities.

15. Technically, in states of nature where the cost of maximal sanctions exceeds the shortfall in repayment, sanctions could be imposed at the minimal level required to ensure repayment. Indeed, this is the natural outcome predicted by bargaining models such as the one considered in appendix 6A. In the absence of private information, default does not take place in equilibrium.

6.1.1.7   Observability and Loan Contracts

One way in which models such as the previous one can be misleading is the tacit assumption that creditors (insurers) can fully observe all the contracts the country engages in. If they cannot, insurers may have no way to be sure that incentive-compatibility constraints like eq. (2) actually are being respected. Their doubts would seriously limit the sovereign's ability to enter into any agreements at all. Problems of observability raise fascinating and important questions, but we shall continue to place them aside until we discuss the consequences of hidden borrower actions in sections 6.3 and 6.4.[16]

6.1.2   Reputation for Repayment

The preceding analysis assumed that a sovereign in default faces sanctions proportional to its income. One of the most severe punishments a defaulting country can face, however, would seem to be a long-term cutoff from foreign capital markets. History furnishes many examples of countries that were largely shut out of private world capital markets for long periods after defaults, for example, much of Latin America for roughly four decades starting in the early 1930s. Certainly, the idea that a country with a bad "reputation" loses access to further credit is intuitively appealing—as anyone who has gone through a thorough credit check can attest. Thus much of the literature on sovereign debt focuses on the question: How much net uncollateralized lending can be supported by the threat of a capital-market embargo? As we shall see, the answer depends in sometimes subtle ways on a detailed specification of the economic environment.[17]

6.1.2.1   A Reputational Model with Insurance

To isolate the role of reputation, we now deprive creditors of any ability to interfere actively with a defaulting debtor's trade or to seize its output. Instead the *only* cost of default is a loss of reputation that brings immediate and permanent exclusion from the world capital market, including the abrogation of current creditor financial obligations to the debtor. We will assume for now, as before, that creditors as a group can precommit to carry out this threat if the country does not make promised payments. (All the results below are easily modified when defaulters suffer only temporary exclusion from capital markets, although less severe penalties naturally can support only more limited sovereign borrowing.) We remind the reader of our continuing assumption that creditors never repudiate their own commitments to the sovereign unless the sovereign defaults first.

---

16. For a model that explicitly considers hidden actions by a sovereign in a model with default risk, see Atkeson (1991).

17. Surveys of sovereign borrowing that focus on this issue include Eaton and Fernandez (1995) and Kletzer (1994).

A small country has stochastic output $Y_s = \bar{Y} + \epsilon_s$ for dates $s \geq t$. Importantly, the mean-zero shock ϵ_s is i.i.d. As before, it takes values $\epsilon_1, \ldots, \epsilon_N \in [\underline{\epsilon}, \bar{\epsilon}]$, and $\pi(\epsilon_i)$ is the probability that $\epsilon = \epsilon_i$. On date t the country's infinitely-lived representative resident maximizes

$$U_t = E_t \left\{ \sum_{s=t}^{\infty} \beta^{s-t} u(C_s) \right\} \tag{11}$$

subject to the constraints that[18]

$$B_{s+1} = (1+r)B_s + \bar{Y} + \epsilon_s - C_s - P_s(\epsilon_s), \tag{12}$$

where B denotes national holdings of noncontingent claims on foreigners, $B_t = 0$, and, for every date s, insurance payments $P_s(\epsilon_i)$ satisfy

$$\sum_{i=1}^{N} \pi(\epsilon_i) P_s(\epsilon_i) = 0. \tag{13}$$

The world interest rate r satisfies $\beta(1+r) = 1$. It is easy to verify that full insurance contracts, which set $P_s(\epsilon) = \epsilon$, will be equilibrium contracts if the country can precommit to meet its obligations to creditors. (In particular, the full insurance contracts are time independent.) Under full insurance, consumption is $C_s = \bar{Y}$ in every period, and B remains steady at 0.

If the country cannot precommit to pay, is the threat of being cut off from world capital markets enough to support full insurance? We answer the question by comparing the country's short-run gain from default to its long-run loss from financial autarky.

Suppose that on date t a country contemplates default on the full insurance contract. Its short-run gain is the extra utility on date t from avoiding repayment:

$$\text{Gain}(\epsilon_t) = u(\bar{Y} + \epsilon_t) - u(\bar{Y}). \tag{14}$$

The punishment for default (even partial default) is that the country loses access to world markets forever after, and is consigned to consuming its random endowment rather than $\bar{Y}$. The date t cost associated with default therefore is

$$\text{Cost} = \sum_{s=t+1}^{\infty} \beta^{s-t} u(\bar{Y}) - \sum_{s=t+1}^{\infty} \beta^{s-t} E_t u(\bar{Y} + \epsilon_s).$$

By the economy's stationarity, we can drop all time subscripts and write Cost as the time-invariant quantity:

---

18. As is implicit in the following constraint, we consider only contracts making the country's payment a function of the current shock (rather than of current and past shocks). In the applications that follow, this assumption does not restrict the generality of the conclusions.

$$\text{Cost} = \frac{\beta}{1-\beta}[u(\bar{Y}) - Eu(\bar{Y} + \epsilon)].\tag{15}$$

Because $u(C)$ is strictly concave, $u(\bar{Y}) > Eu(\bar{Y} + \epsilon)$, so there is a positive penalty for defaulting.[19] That cost does not depend on how small or large an infraction the country has committed. Because of this knife-edge property, a punishment such as the one reflected in eq. (15) is called a *trigger strategy*. Notice also that the cost in eq. (15) becomes unboundedly large as $\beta \to 1$.

The gain from defaulting, eq. (14), is highest when ϵ_t assumes its maximum possible value, $\bar{\epsilon}$. As a result, the full insurance contract is sustainable in all states of nature (and on all dates) only if

$$\text{Gain}(\bar{\epsilon}) \leq \text{Cost},$$

that is, when

$$u(\bar{Y} + \bar{\epsilon}) - u(\bar{Y}) \leq \frac{\beta}{1-\beta}[u(\bar{Y}) - Eu(\bar{Y} + \epsilon)].\tag{16}$$

If this last inequality holds (as it will if β is close enough to 1), then the country has a strong enough interest in maintaining its reputation for repayment that it will always honor the full insurance contract, even when the temptation to renege is highest.

Note that the reputational equilibrium we have just described would collapse if the country had a *finite* horizon. Let T be the model's last period. Then a debtor has nothing whatsoever to lose by defaulting completely on date T, and will do so if it owes money. Potential creditors understand this fact, and thus will not enter into unsecured contracts on date $T - 1$. But then the threat of a future cutoff carries no weight on date $T - 2$: since it will happen in any case, debtors will certainly default beforehand, on date $T - 2$. By backward induction, you can see that on no date will creditors ever be paid a penny of what they are owed. Thus they won't lend in the first place. Reputational considerations can never support repayment in this model if there is a known finite date beyond which access to international capital markets offers no further gains. However, one should not think of reputational arguments as narrowly applying to infinite-horizon models. Equilibria in which reputation

---

19. A second-order Taylor approximation around $\epsilon = 0$ gives

$$u(\bar{Y} + \epsilon) \approx u(\bar{Y}) + u'(\bar{Y})\epsilon + \tfrac{1}{2}u''(\bar{Y})\epsilon^2,$$

implying that $Eu(\bar{Y} + \epsilon) \approx u(\bar{Y}) + (1/2)u''(\bar{Y})E\epsilon^2$, and thus that

$$\text{Cost} \approx \frac{-\beta}{2(1-\beta)}u''(\bar{Y})\text{Var}(\epsilon) > 0,$$

where $\text{Var}(\epsilon) = E\epsilon^2$ is the variance of ϵ.

is important can occur in finite-horizon models where the borrowing country has private information, for example, about its direct costs of default. Our focus on the preceding infinite-horizon trigger-strategy equilibrium is in part due to its relative analytical tractability.

Application: How Costly Is Exclusion from World Insurance Markets?

Even when the world capital market allows a country fully to insure its output, is the fear of future permanent exclusion from that market likely to suffice to deter default? To answer the question, we calculate empirical measures of the long-term cost of a capital-market embargo, using data from a selection of developing countries.

In our calculations we return to the framework used in Chapter 5 (pp. 329–332) to discuss the gains from international risk sharing. By analogy with that application, the stochastic process generating a country's GDP is assumed to be

$$Y_s = (1 + g)^{s-t} \bar{Y} \exp[\epsilon_s - \tfrac{1}{2} \text{Var}(\epsilon)],$$

where $\bar{Y}$ is the trend level of output on the initial date t and where the shock ϵ_s is i.i.d. and distributed normally with mean zero and constant variance $\text{Var}(\epsilon)$.

The representative resident's period utility function takes the isoelastic form

$$u(C) = \frac{C^{1-\rho}}{1 - \rho},$$

where $\rho > 0$ is the coefficient of relative risk aversion (here equal to the inverse of the intertemporal substitution elasticity, see Chapter 5). To take a polar but tractable case, we assume that under a full insurance contract the country would completely diversify its output risk in world capital markets before date t. (The country's GDP risk is purely idiosyncratic.) In this case consumption, C_s, equals mean output, $(1 + g)^{s-t} \bar{Y}$, on every date $s \geq t$.[20] Accordingly, the compo-

---

20. Recall that if X is a normally distributed random variable with mean μ_X and variance σ_X^2, then $\exp X$ is lognormal with mean

$$E\{\exp X\} = \exp\left(\mu_X + \tfrac{1}{2}\sigma_X^2\right).$$

Thus, in the case at hand,

$$E_t Y_s = (1 + g)^{s-t} \bar{Y} \exp\left[-\tfrac{1}{2}\text{Var}(\epsilon)\right] E_t \exp(\epsilon_s)$$

$$= (1 + g)^{s-t} \bar{Y} \exp\left[-\tfrac{1}{2}\text{Var}(\epsilon)\right] \exp\left[\tfrac{1}{2}\text{Var}(\epsilon)\right]$$

$$= (1 + g)^{s-t} \bar{Y}.$$

nent of the representative national resident's lifetime date t utility accruing after date t is

$$\beta\bar{U}_{t+1} = \frac{1}{1-\rho} \sum_{s=t+1}^{\infty} \beta^{s-t}(1+g)^{(1-\rho)(s-t)}\bar{Y}^{1-\rho} = \frac{\bar{Y}^{1-\rho}}{1-\rho} \times \frac{\beta(1+g)^{1-\rho}}{1-\beta(1+g)^{1-\rho}}$$

[assuming $\beta(1+g)^{1-\rho} < 1$]. In autarky, however, the country must consume its random endowment instead of mean output. On date t expected utility accruing from date $t+1$ onward therefore is

$$\beta E_t U_{t+1}^A = \frac{1}{1-\rho} \sum_{s=t+1}^{\infty} \beta^{s-t} E_t Y_s^{1-\rho}$$

$$= \frac{\bar{Y}^{1-\rho}}{1-\rho} \sum_{s=t+1}^{\infty} \beta^{s-t}(1+g)^{(1-\rho)(s-t)} E_t \exp\left\{(1-\rho)\left[\epsilon_s - \tfrac{1}{2}\mathrm{Var}(\epsilon)\right]\right\}$$

$$= \frac{\bar{Y}^{1-\rho}}{1-\rho} \sum_{s=t+1}^{\infty} \beta^{s-t}(1+g)^{(1-\rho)(s-t)} \exp\left\{\tfrac{1}{2}[(1-\rho)^2 - (1-\rho)]\mathrm{Var}(\epsilon)\right\}$$

$$= \frac{\bar{Y}^{1-\rho}}{1-\rho} \times \frac{\beta(1+g)^{1-\rho}}{1-\beta(1+g)^{1-\rho}} \exp\left[-\tfrac{1}{2}\rho(1-\rho)\mathrm{Var}(\epsilon)\right] < \beta\bar{U}_{t+1}.$$

Exclusion from world capital markets will support full insurance in the present case if and only if inequality (16) holds for all output realizations Y_t, on all dates t. Since the left-hand side of inequality (16) is strictly increasing in date t output, an equivalent condition is

$$\lim_{Y_t \to \infty} [u(Y_t) - u(\bar{Y})] \leq \beta(\bar{U}_{t+1} - E_t U_{t+1}^A).$$

Invoking the isoelastic form of the period utility function and dividing the preceding inequality through by $\bar{Y}^{1-\rho}$, we see that full insurance will be feasible if and only if the following time-invariant inequality holds:

$$\frac{\lim_{\epsilon_t \to \infty} \exp\{(1-\rho)[\epsilon_t - \tfrac{1}{2}\mathrm{Var}(\epsilon)]\} - 1}{1-\rho}$$

$$\leq \frac{\beta(1+g)^{1-\rho}}{(1-\rho)[1-\beta(1+g)^{1-\rho}]}\left\{1 - \exp\left[-\tfrac{1}{2}\rho(1-\rho)\mathrm{Var}(\epsilon)\right]\right\}.$$

Notice first that when $\rho \leq 1$, this inequality never holds: because marginal period utility falls off relatively gently as consumption rises, there is always some finite output realization high enough that inequality (16) is violated. Thus, concern for reputation can support full insurance in the present model only when the risk aversion coefficient ρ exceeds 1.[21]

When $\rho > 1$, $\lim_{\epsilon_t \to \infty} \exp(1 - \rho)[\epsilon_t - \frac{1}{2}\text{Var}(\epsilon)] = 0$ and the last inequality therefore reduces to

$$1 \le \beta(1 + g)^{1-\rho} \exp\left[\frac{1}{2}\rho(\rho - 1)\text{Var}(\epsilon)\right].$$

Intuitively, higher values of β and $\text{Var}(\epsilon)$ make it more likely that a full-insurance equilibrium is sustainable. A higher trend growth rate, g, makes the full-insurance equilibrium less likely by making future output uncertainty progressively less costly in utility terms.

For eight developing countries, Table 6.1 presents estimates of g and $\text{Var}(\epsilon)^{1/2}$, the mean and standard deviation in the growth rate of real per capita GDP. The table assumes that $\rho = 4$ and $\beta = 0.95$. Also reported are two measures of the cost of capital-market exclusion. The column labeled Cost/Y shows the total cost of reputation loss as a ratio to *current* mean output. That ratio can be measured by the solution κ to the equation

$$u[(1 + \kappa)\bar{Y}] - u(\bar{Y}) = \beta(\bar{U}_{t+1} - \text{E}_t U_{t+1}^\Lambda),$$

which is, in the present example,

$$\kappa = \left[\frac{1 - \beta(1 + g)^{1-\rho} \exp\left[\frac{1}{2}\rho(\rho - 1)\text{Var}(\epsilon)\right]}{1 - \beta(1 + g)^{1-\rho}}\right]^{-\frac{1}{\rho - 1}} - 1.$$

Notice that for $\rho > 1$, Cost/$Y \to \infty$ as $\beta(1 + g)^{1-\rho} \exp\left[\frac{1}{2}\rho(\rho - 1)\text{Var}(\epsilon)\right] \to 1$ from below, so Cost/Y is undefined (effectively infinite) for countries such that full insurance is sustainable by reputation. The column Cost per Year reports the permanent fractional increase in GDP equivalent to access to full insurance. This number is the same as the "cost of consumption variability" τ calculated on p. 330, and it is therefore given by $\tau = \{\exp[\frac{1}{2}(1 - \rho)\rho\text{Var}(\epsilon)]\}^{1/(1-\rho)} - 1$.

For the preference parameters underlying Table 6.1, only Venezuela, with the lowest per capita growth rate in the group, would never default on a full in-surance contract if the penalty were future exclusion from the world capital market. For the other countries, the total cost of exclusion in terms of current output, κ, is a finite number equivalent to anywhere from 4 (for Colombia) to 53 (for Lesotho) percent of one year's GDP. Thus, positive output shocks of the same size would be enough to induce default on a full-insurance con-tract, implying that the lenders would never offer the contract in the first place. Remember however, that we have unrealistically assumed the possibility of un-

---

21. This peculiar feature of the model stems from the assumption that output shocks are potentially unbounded from above. We assumed a lognormal distribution for output, however, purely to facilitate the exact calculations in the text. For more reasonable probability distributions making output bounded on every date, we wouldn't necessarily be able to rule out full-insurance equilibria when $\rho \le 1$.

Table 6.1
Output Processes and Cost of Capital-Market Exclusion, 1950–92

Country	g	$\mathrm{Var}(\epsilon)^{1/2}$	Cost/Y (κ)	Cost per Year (τ)
Argentina	0.015	0.099	0.36	0.020
Brazil	0.040	0.117	0.24	0.028
Colombia	0.023	0.050	0.04	0.005
Lesotho	0.053	0.160	0.53	0.052
Mexico	0.030	0.088	0.13	0.016
Philippines	0.023	0.100	0.24	0.020
Thailand	0.043	0.081	0.08	0.013
Venezuela	0.011	0.118	Undefined	0.028

Source: Penn World Table, version 5.6. The calculations assume $\beta = 0.95$ and $\rho = 4$.

bounded positive output shocks. With a more realistic bounded distribution, positive output shocks as much as 53 percent of GDP would be zero-probability events, so a country with Lesotho's high output-growth variability around trend (16 percent per year) might well be deterred from default by its fear of reputation loss. The final column of Table 6.1, showing the cost of consumption variability τ as an annuitized flow, reports estimates substantially larger than those applicable to most industrialized countries (recall Chapter 5). Since τ is not a present value, it does not depend on the economy's growth rate or discount rate.

The trend-stationary stochastic process used to capture output variability underestimates the cost of exclusion from the world capital market if output shocks are persistent, and especially if there is a unit root in output.[22] For several reasons, however, Table 6.1 is more likely to convey an exaggerated picture of the deterrent power of reputation loss. First, countries usually cannot eliminate *all* output risk through financial contracts. Second, the results are quite sensitive to the assumed taste parameters. (Were β equal to 0.85 rather than 0.95—imagine that a somewhat myopic government, one facing some probability of losing office, makes the default decision—Argentina would reckon the cost of reputation loss as equivalent to only 11 percent of current GDP, not 36 percent.) Third, the possibilities of investment or disinvestment at home, absent in the preceding model, create self-insurance possibilities that reduce the gains from external risk sharing. Finally, it could occur in reality that a country can still lend in international markets, even when it can no longer borrow. As discussed in section 6.1.2.4 below, this possibility, along with domestic investment possibilities, can facilitate self-insurance and thereby reduce the cost of losing one's reputation as a good borrower. ■

22. See Obstfeld (1994b, 1995).

6.1.2.2   The Feasibility of Partial Insurance

What if eq. (16) does not hold? Can the country still obtain partial insurance, as in our two-period analyses? The answer, first illustrated by Eaton and Gersovitz (1981), is yes. It simplifies presentation of the main points to begin by adopting a setup analogous to the one in section 6.1.1.1. In that spirit, we assume that the country can neither save nor dissave, and can sign only one-period contracts to share the following period's output risk with competitive, risk-neutral foreign insurers.[23] (We discuss how to relax the somewhat artificial no-saving assumption in the next section.) Thus the country maximizes the function (11) subject to

$$C_s(\epsilon_s) = \bar{Y} + \epsilon_s - P_s(\epsilon_s) \tag{17}$$

(which is the same constraint as in section 6.1.1.1, for every period s), the zero-profit condition for foreign insurers, eq. (13), and an incentive-compatibility constraint that guarantees payment for all $P_s(\epsilon_s) > 0$. Our setup precludes the accumulation of any collateral to secure risk-sharing contracts, as in section 6.1.1.6, and ensures that expected consumption always equals $\bar{Y}$. This loss of generality is harmless for present purposes, as it is only when debts are at least partially unsecured that there can be a meaningful default.

The form of the incentive compatibility constraint can be derived by modifying our analysis of the full insurance case. A major simplifying factor is the time-independent or stationary nature of the country's problem (recall there is no saving or dissaving and ϵ is i.i.d.). Stationarity implies that the optimal incentive-compatible contract covering any date s (given that no default has occurred) will be time-independent, that is, $P_s(\epsilon_s) = P(\epsilon_s)$. If the country defaults on this contract on date t after observing ϵ_t, its short-term gain is

$$\text{Gain}(\epsilon_t) = u(\bar{Y} + \epsilon_t) - u[\bar{Y} + \epsilon_t - P(\epsilon_t)].$$

The cost of future exclusion from the world capital market (given that an optimal incentive-compatible one-period insurance contract otherwise would have been signed in every future period) is the time-independent quantity

$$\text{Cost} = \frac{\beta}{1 - \beta} \left\{ Eu[\bar{Y} + \epsilon - P(\epsilon)] - Eu(\bar{Y} + \epsilon) \right\}.$$

Thus the incentive-compatibility constraint, $\text{Gain}(\epsilon_t) \leq \text{Cost}$, has the form

$$u(\bar{Y} + \epsilon_t) - u[\bar{Y} + \epsilon_t - P(\epsilon_t)] \leq \frac{\beta}{1 - \beta} \left\{ Eu[\bar{Y} + \epsilon - P(\epsilon)] - Eu(\bar{Y} + \epsilon) \right\}$$

$$= \frac{\beta}{1 - \beta} \sum_{j=1}^{N} \pi(\epsilon_j) \left\{ u[\bar{Y} + \epsilon_j - P(\epsilon_j)] - u(\bar{Y} + \epsilon_j) \right\}. \tag{18}$$

---

23. Grossman and Van Huyck (1988) base their analysis on a similar assumption.

Consider the country's position on any arbitrary date. Since the country is sign-
ing a contract covering next-period consumption only, and since its problem is
stationary, the best it can do is to choose the schedule $P(\epsilon)$ to maximize

$$\sum_{i=1}^{N} \pi(\epsilon_i) u[\bar{Y} + \epsilon_i - P(\epsilon_i)]$$

subject to constraints (18) (one for each state $i = 1, \ldots N$) and eq. (1). The Lagrangian (which does not depend on the date) therefore is

$$\mathcal{L} = \sum_{i=1}^{N} \pi(\epsilon_i) u[\bar{Y} + \epsilon_i - P(\epsilon_i)]$$

$$- \sum_{i=1}^{N} \lambda(\epsilon_i) \left(u(\bar{Y} + \epsilon_i) - u[\bar{Y} + \epsilon_i - P(\epsilon_i)] \right.$$

$$\left. - \frac{\beta}{1-\beta} \sum_{j=1}^{N} \pi(\epsilon_j) \left\{ u[\bar{Y} + \epsilon_j - P(\epsilon_j)] - u(\bar{Y} + \epsilon_j) \right\} \right)$$

$$+ \mu \sum_{i=1}^{N} \pi(\epsilon_i) P(\epsilon_i).$$

The associated Kuhn-Tucker necessary conditions (which must hold for all ϵ) are

$$\left[\pi(\epsilon) + \lambda(\epsilon) + \frac{\beta \pi(\epsilon)}{1-\beta} \sum_{j=1}^{N} \lambda(\epsilon_j) \right] u'[C(\epsilon)] = \mu \pi(\epsilon) \tag{19}$$

and the complementary slackness condition

$$\lambda(\epsilon) \left(\frac{\beta}{1-\beta} \sum_{j=1}^{N} \pi(\epsilon_j) \left\{ u[\bar{Y} + \epsilon_j - P(\epsilon_j)] - u(\bar{Y} + \epsilon_j) \right\} \right.$$

$$\left. - u(\bar{Y} + \epsilon) + u[\bar{Y} + \epsilon - P(\epsilon)] \right) = 0, \tag{20}$$

for nonnegative $\lambda(\epsilon)$.[24]

Equations (19) and (20) look more forbidding than their analogs in the sanctions
model of section 6.1.1, eqs. (4) and (5), but their implications are pretty much the
same. For relatively low values of ϵ, incentive-compatibility constraint (18) doesn't

---

24. In taking the partial derivatives leading to eq. (19), recall that we are seeking the optimal $P(\epsilon)$
schedule, which requires that we maximize for every $P(\epsilon_i), i = 1, \ldots, N$. To compute a specific partial
$\partial \mathcal{L}/\partial P(\epsilon_i)$, for example, $\partial \mathcal{L}/\partial P(\epsilon_2)$, simply write out $\mathcal{L}$ term by term and differentiate with respect to
$P(\epsilon_2)$. You should end up with eq. (19) for $\epsilon = \epsilon_2$. Notice that in eq. (19), the time subscript attached to
$C(\epsilon)$ can be suppressed thanks to the problem's stationarity.

bind and $\lambda(\epsilon) = 0$. For these states, eq. (19) implies that

$$u'[C(\epsilon)] = \frac{\mu}{1 + \frac{\beta}{1-\beta}\sum_{j=1}^{N}\lambda(\epsilon_j)}. \tag{21}$$

Because the right-hand side of eq. (21) is the same for *all* ϵ, consumption is again stabilized in the face of the worst downside risks. As before, this fact means that $P(\epsilon) = P_0 + \epsilon$ for some constant P_0, and therefore that $C(\epsilon) = \bar{Y} - P_0$ as long as $\lambda(\epsilon) = 0$.

When $\lambda(\epsilon) > 0$, constraint (18) holds as an equality and fully determines the functional dependence of $P(\epsilon)$ upon ϵ. Implicit differentiation of the equality constraint corresponding to eq. (18) gives the slope

$$\frac{dP(\epsilon)}{d\epsilon} = \frac{u'[\bar{Y} + \epsilon - P(\epsilon)] - u'(\bar{Y} + \epsilon)}{u'[\bar{Y} + \epsilon - P(\epsilon)]}.$$

Because constraint (18) never binds unless $P(\epsilon)$ is positive, the strict concavity of $u(C)$ implies that $0 < dP(\epsilon)/d\epsilon < 1$. By eq. (17), $C(\epsilon)$ must therefore increase with ϵ when eq. (18) binds in order to deter debt repudiation.

Now we tie together the two portions of $P(\epsilon)$—over the range of relatively low ϵ where $\lambda(\epsilon) = 0$ and over the range of higher ϵ where $\lambda(\epsilon) > 0$. (We took an analogous step in the model of section 6.1.1.) Equation (21) holds for ϵ such that $\lambda(\epsilon) = 0$, and for such ϵ, $C(\epsilon) = \bar{Y} - P_0$, as we saw a moment ago. Thus, eq. (21) implies that

$$\mu = \left[1 + \frac{\beta}{1-\beta}\sum_{j=1}^{N}\lambda(\epsilon_j)\right]u'(\bar{Y} - P_0).$$

Using this expression to eliminate μ from eq. (19), we get

$$\left[1 + \frac{\beta}{1-\beta}\sum_{j=1}^{N}\lambda(\epsilon_j)\right]\{u'(\bar{Y} - P_0) - u'[C(\epsilon)]\} = \frac{\lambda(\epsilon)u'[C(\epsilon)]}{\pi(\epsilon)},$$

which holds for all ϵ.

Assume for simplicity that ϵ has a continuous distribution function. We have seen that $C(\epsilon)$ falls as ϵ falls over the range of ϵ with $\lambda(\epsilon) > 0$. Thus the left-hand side of the preceding equation also falls as ϵ falls until ϵ reaches $e \in (\underline{\epsilon}, \bar{\epsilon})$, where $u'(\bar{Y} - P_0) = u'[C(e)]$ and $\lambda(e) = 0$.[25] Since $C(e)$ therefore equals $\bar{Y} - P_0$, the consumption schedule is continuous at $\epsilon = e$, where constraint (18) switches from nonbinding to binding as ϵ rises. Because consumption thus is continuous

---

25. As in section 6.1.1, cases with $e = \bar{\epsilon}$ imply that full insurance is feasible.

over states, the two portions of $P(\epsilon)$ must coincide at $\epsilon = e$, where the incentive-compatibility constraint first starts to bite.

A picture similar to Figure 6.1 illustrates the optimal incentive-compatible contract, but now the constrained arm of $P(\epsilon)$ will not in general be linear.

6.1.2.3   The Fully Dynamic Case

What happens when full insurance is not initially possible, but the country can save or dissave according to eq. (12)? Equivalently, what if we relax constraint (13) and require instead only that foreign lenders offer contracts with expected present values of zero? This case has been analyzed formally by Worrall (1990); here we offer an intuitive sketch.

As in the two-period model of section 6.1.1.6, a partially binding incentive-compatibility constraint gives the country an additional motive for saving: by accumulating a positive foreign asset position that creditors can seize in the event of default, the country provides a hostage that modifies its own incentive to withhold payment. This, in turn, allows the country fully to insure its income over more states of nature.

In a dynamic setting, the country continues to accumulate foreign assets as long as the incentive-compatibility constraint binds in any state of nature. But the marginal return to those extra assets falls as the country's foreign wealth increases, so mean consumption rises over time. The country stops saving once it owns just enough foreign wealth that default no longer pays even in the highest state of nature, $\bar{\epsilon}$. This occurs when the full insurance contract is completely collateralized, that is, when the foreign asset stock reaches the value $\bar{B}$ at which $(1+r)\bar{B} = \bar{\epsilon}$. At this point the country can credibly promise always to fulfill the full insurance contract, and consumption thus occupies the steady state $\bar{C} = \bar{Y} + r\bar{B}$ thereafter.

The country's long-run consumption is higher than in the full insurance case, but to earn its collateral it has had to distort the flat first-best intertemporal consumption profile it would have preferred. While saving allows the country fully to insure its output in the long run, it is still worse off than if it had been able to commit to full repayment at the outset.

6.1.2.4   The Significance of Reputation

Concern over maintaining a reputation for creditworthiness can support some uncollateralized international lending between sovereign nations. But one should not conclude that reputation alone, absent *any* legal rights for creditors at home or abroad other than the right not to lend in the future, can support a significant level of sovereign lending. Indeed, the deterrent effect of reputation loss depends critically on our implicit assumptions regarding creditor rights and incentives.

The preceding models assumed that defaulting countries are simply cut off from world capital markets. While it is plausible that potential lenders would shun a country with a past record of nonrepayment, it is much less plausible that foreign banks would worry about a reputation for repayment when *accepting* the country's deposits, or that foreign firms would worry about it when selling the country shares. Of course, if the country tried to place deposits, for example, in the same banks it had borrowed from, the banks might, with legal justification, confiscate the country's funds. But what about other banks, possibly even banks in other countries? Throughout this section we have relied on the assumption that lenders throughout the world will present a united front, either in imposing direct trade sanctions or in enforcing a total capital-market embargo on an offending sovereign borrower. For this to be a reasonable assumption, even as an approximation, creditors must have rights at home and abroad that go far beyond the right simply to stop lending.

Why does a debtor's ability to accumulate assets make any difference? Perhaps surprisingly, the threat that a transgression will be punished by loss of future borrowing possibilities does not deter a country from default when its lending opportunities are not simultaneously curtailed. To see how a candidate reputational equilibrium can unravel when creditors cannot touch a sovereign's foreign assets, let us revisit the simple model of section 6.1.2.1. There, the threat of financial market autarky could be sufficient to support complete insurance, provided the borrower did not discount the future too much.

Suppose we now relax the implicit assumption that creditors can seize assets held abroad. In fact, we assume that after defaulting a country is free to hold any type of asset and write any type of *fully collateralized* insurance contract. (A fully collateralized insurance contract is one where the country posts a large enough bond to cover any possible payment it might be called upon to make.)

With this option, will the country still have an incentive to honor its reputation contract? As before, it is sufficient to consider its incentive to default in the most favorable state of nature, $\bar{\epsilon}$, in which the reputation contract calls upon the country to make the maximum payment, $P(\bar{\epsilon})$. Let us imagine now that state $\bar{\epsilon}$ occurs, but that instead of paying $P(\bar{\epsilon})$ to creditors, the country defaults on its reputation contract. Rather, it takes the money it would have paid to its creditors and invests it abroad in a riskless bond paying the world interest rate r. At the same time, the country writes an explicit insurance contract with a new group of foreign insurers, providing it with the *exact same* payout function $P(\epsilon)$, as in its original (possibly implicit) reputation contract. Crucially, the new insurers do not need to rely on the country's (now defunct) reputation because it can put up its bond as collateral. Under this scheme, the country must come out ahead. Its new insurance contract fully duplicates its old insurance contract. At the same time, the country can consume the interest on its bond in each future period while still maintaining the necessary amount of collateral. (As an alternative to writing a new insurance contract, the country could invest in a portfolio of foreign stocks and bonds having a return that covaries negatively with its output.)

Why does it matter if the reputation contract fails in state $\bar{\epsilon}$? If one node on the equilibrium tree fails, the whole reputation contract cannot be an equilibrium, since foreign insurers must be able to break even on average. Might there not be another reputation contract, providing perhaps a bit less insurance, that still works? The answer is no. For any reputation contract, there must always be some state of nature in which the country's payment is higher than (or at least as high as) the payment in any other state of nature. The country will always default in that state. Therefore, *no* level of reputation-based insurance is possible!

The foregoing argument assumed a stationary endowment economy, but it is in fact quite general and requires virtually no assumptions on the production or utility functions (see Bulow and Rogoff, 1989b). The main nuance in extending the result to more general environments is that in a growing economy, the largest possible reputation payment may also be growing over time. The proof involves noting that the world market value of a claim to all the expected future payments by a country can never exceed the world market value of a claim to its entire future net output.

The no-reputation result we have just derived is quite remarkable but, as Bulow and Rogoff note, there are some important qualifications. For example, the country may not be able to construct an asset portfolio that exactly mimics its reputation contract, and this consideration may sustain a limited amount of reputation insurance. Countries that default on debt may lose reputation in other areas (e.g., trade agreements).[26] A limited amount of reputation lending may also be possible if creditors cannot perfectly observe a country's actions or preferences. The overall conclusion from this analysis, however, is that if countries with poor credit histories can safely lend abroad, the threat of reputation loss becomes much weaker as a lever to deter default.[27]

So far in this section we have ignored the possibility that creditors (insurers), rather than being unfailingly honest themselves, may break their financial promises. The more general question is whether creditors' threats and promises are credible. To think about answers, we need a framework in which borrowers and lenders are treated symmetrically.

6.1.3   A General-Equilibrium Model of Reputation

We turn to a setup in which no country can effectively commit itself to pay uncollateralized debts. Thus the positions of all participants in the world capital market are symmetrical. In this context, there do exist equilibria in which the cost of losing reputation is sufficient to support international contracts.

---

26. See also Cole and P. Kehoe (1995, 1996).

27. Remember that throughout this chapter, we have presented a very simplistic notion of default. Real world default is complex and generally involves bargaining between debtors and creditors of the nature sketched in appendix 6A.

Consider a world composed of a very large number of small countries j, all of which share the utility function

$$U_t^j = E_t \left\{ \sum_{s=t}^{\infty} \beta^{s-t} u(C_s^j) \right\}.$$

Country j's endowment is

$$Y_t^j = \bar{Y} + \epsilon_t^j + \omega_t,$$

where ω_t is a mean-zero global shock common to all countries, and ϵ_t^j is a mean-zero idiosyncratic country shock such that

$$\sum_j \epsilon_t^j = 0. \tag{22}$$

Shocks are assumed to be i.i.d. and bounded within $[\underline{\epsilon}, \bar{\epsilon}]$ and $[\underline{\omega}, \bar{\omega}]$, respectively, so that every country's output is always positive.

Given assumption (22), the efficient (Arrow-Debreu) allocation for this economy sets

$$C_t^j = \bar{Y} + \omega_t, \qquad \forall j, t.$$

To attain this first-best (full insurance) allocation through the market, countries sell off their positive idiosyncratic shocks and insure themselves against negative realizations, all at actuarially fair prices. Can this equilibrium be supported if countries have no direct sanctions to punish a sovereign that breaches its insurance contract? The answer is yes, provided countries follow the right kind of trigger strategy in response to a default.

Specifically, suppose that any country j that defaults on its contract is completely and permanently cut off from world markets. This exclusion requires (a) that country j lose its reputation for repayment, so that everyone believes it will always default in the future if given the opportunity; *and* (b) that all other countries lose their own reputations for repaying country j. [Part (b) is needed to prevent country j from purchasing bonded insurance contracts in favorable states of nature, thereby eliminating its dependence on foreign insurers by analogy with the example in section 6.1.2.4.]

Under these assumptions about expectations, no country will lend to a defaulting country j. Nor will the defaulter itself lend abroad, because after defaulting, country j believes that any potential insurer i will default at the first opportunity. (Hence country j would confirm country i's beliefs by again defaulting were country i nevertheless to sign a contract with j. Similarly, country i, believing country j will never make promised payments, would perceive no loss from seizing any assets j foolishly entrusted to i.) Thus the punishments on a defaulter are self-enforcing. In terminology from game theory, the equilibrium is subgame perfect because the threats that support it are credible.

The short-term gain to country j from repudiating the first-best insurance contract on date t is

$$\text{Gain}(\epsilon_t^j, \omega_t) = u(\bar{Y} + \epsilon_t^j + \omega_t) - u(\bar{Y} + \omega_t),$$

while the expected future cost is

$$\text{Cost} = \text{E}_t \sum_{s=t+1}^{\infty} \beta^{s-t}[u(\bar{Y} + \omega_s) - u(\bar{Y} + \epsilon_s^j + \omega_s)]$$

$$= \frac{\beta}{1-\beta}[\text{E}u(\bar{Y} + \omega) - \text{E}u(\bar{Y} + \epsilon^j + \omega)].$$

(We can drop time subscripts in the final expression thanks to the problem's stationarity.) The foregoing formulas for gain and cost are analogous to the ones we derived in eqs. (14) and (15), except for the presence of the global shock ω. Note especially that the world shock causes the gain from default to fluctuate over time. The temptation is greatest when the world is in an extreme recession ($\omega = \underline{\omega}$) and country j in a relative boom ($\epsilon^j = \bar{\epsilon}$). As we have noted, the cost of default is constant (because of the i.i.d. shocks). Thus the first-best allocation can be supported by reputation if

$$\text{Gain}(\bar{\epsilon}, \underline{\omega}) \leq \text{Cost}.$$

This condition can always be met if β is close enough to 1 (that is, if countries place high enough weight on continued capital-market access). If not, partial insurance may still be possible, as in the small-country case.

The model shows that reputation *may* support international lending, not that it will. There is a vast multiplicity of trigger-strategy equilibria supporting different degrees of international risk sharing, including none. We have not provided any argument to show why countries should coordinate on the particular expectations assumed.

An obvious shortcoming of the permanent exclusion scheme we have examined is that, after a transgression by one party, countries willingly forgo potential gains from trade forever. Might they not find it mutually advantageous to reopen asset trade at a later date? In the parlance of game theory, the equilibrium on which our example focuses is subgame perfect but not obviously *renegotiation-proof*: it is conceivable that after a default on a first-best insurance contract, all players would wish to interrupt the defaulter's punishment and proceed with insurance restrictive enough to deter default in the future. Here we note only that for high enough discount factors β, renegotiation-proof equilibria that support the first-best allocation can be constructed.[28]

---

28. See Kletzer (1994) for a detailed discussion of renegotiation- and coalition-proof equilibria in debt models.

Application: How Have Prior Defaults Affected Countries' Borrowing Terms?

A basic tenet of reputational models of sovereign borrowing is that default reduces a sovereign's future gains from the international capital market. What is the historical record?

Many sovereign borrowers of the 1920s defaulted in the 1930s and weren't able to return to world capital markets until the 1970s. It would be misleading, however, to view these exclusions as independent cases in which individual defaulters were shut out of an otherwise well-functioning world financial system. In reality, the defaults were a symptom of a much larger contraction of world capital markets and trade, in which even some countries that continuously met their foreign obligations suffered denial of new loans. The situation could be modeled using the last subsection's general-equilibrium default model, modified to allow even honest borrowers who did not default to lose reputation.[29]

Exclusion from capital markets is virtually never permanent. As documented by Lindert and Morton (1989), fewer than a third of borrowers with some default history over 1820–1929 fully repaid foreign debts in the 1930s. Seventy percent of those with payments problems over 1940–79 fell into arrears or rescheduled on concessional terms in the first half of the 1980s (a period of generalized debt crisis that we will discuss further in section 6.2.3). Even Mexico, Turkey, and the Soviet Union, all of which lost access to foreign credits in the 1920s after new revolutionary governments repudiated *ancien régime* debts in the 1910s, eventually regained private market access in the 1970s (only to experience renewed debt problems in the 1980s).

Elements of an explanation are suggested by the fact that many defaulting borrowers eventually settled with creditors. In many of the defaults that took place over the first part of the twentieth century, the terms of the final settlements tended to be generous enough so that, on average, British and U.S. investors ended up earning rates of return slightly above what they could have earned on U.S. or British government debt (see Eichengreen, 1991, for a survey of estimates).[30] Thus creditors may have viewed many defaults as "excusable" and been willing to accept, at least ex post, the implicit state contingency of their prior loans. Alterna-

---

29. Why, contrary to such a model, did some debtors continue to repay after the world capital market dried up? The answer may be that creditors had additional sanctions to deploy in these cases. Argentina, which had borrowed extensively from Britain, had an important export surplus with that country and feared commercial retaliation. It therefore continued to service debt through the 1930s even after most other Latin American countries defaulted (see Díaz-Alejandro, 1983).

30. Loans to prerevolutionary Mexico, Turkey, and Russia were not settled quickly and yielded low rates of return after the fact, a circumstance that may help explain why the successor governments were kept from borrowing in the 1920s.

tively, settlement of old debts may have represented a renegotiation process by which defaulting debtors restored their standing in world capital markets.

Experience also suggests that lenders face considerable uncertainty about borrower characteristics and preferences. As a result, changes in a borrowing country's political regime or economic prospects can have a big impact on its capital-market access, despite past sins. Peru's development of guano exports aided the country in settling prior foreign claims and reentering world capital markets in 1849 (see Fishlow, 1985). More recently, radical economic liberalization and macroeconomic stabilization in Argentina, Chile, and Mexico returned those countries to world capital markets around 1990 after the debt crisis of the 1980s (although investors in Mexico were soon burned in a financial crisis sparked by the country's 1994 currency devaluation).

Econometric studies indicate that lenders typically base their country risk assessments on past debt-servicing behavior as well as on newer information. After controlling for current economic and political determinants of default risk, Özler (1993) finds that among countries with borrowing histories, those with earlier debt problems faced higher commercial-bank interest rates in the 1970s. Lenders apparently do take default histories into account, at least to some extent.   ∎

6.2   Sovereign Risk and Investment

Because sovereign debt problems have been most acute for low- and middle-income countries, concerns about their economic effects have centered more on possible harm to investment and growth than on limited risk sharing. These areas of concern are not unrelated, of course. But a number of interactions between sovereigns' borrowing and investment decisions are most easily understood in a setting without uncertainty. Indeed, several main points can be made most simply in a framework based on the two-period model of Chapter 1.

While a certainty setting serves well to illustrate some basic concepts, such as the importance of borrower commitments, it is inadequate for a realistic account of other issues, notably the pricing of sovereign debt in world secondary markets. Uncertainty therefore reappears in the latter part of this section when we discuss the interaction between investment and the market value of sovereign debt. One of the robust conclusions that will emerge is that international capital flows do not necessarily equalize countries' marginal rates of return on investment when creditors fear sovereign default.

6.2.1   The Role of Investment under Direct Sanctions

The small country is inhabited by a representative agent with utility function

$$U_1 = u(C_1) + \beta u(C_2).$$

On date 1 the country receives the endowment Y_1, but no capital is inherited from the past ($K_1 = 0$). Date 2 output depends on date 1 investment, $I_1 = K_2 - K_1 = K_2$, according to the production function

$$Y_2 = F(K_2).$$

As usual, $F'(K) > 0$ and $F''(K) < 0$.

In deference to the conventions of the vast literature on international debt, we depart from our usual notation for a country's foreign *assets*, B, and instead throughout the remainder of this chapter refer to D, its foreign *debt*. (Clearly, $D = -B$.) Using this notation, let D_2 be the country's borrowing from foreign lenders on date 1, and $\Re$ the amount of loan repayment the country makes on date 2.

The first-period finance constraint is

$$K_2 = Y_1 + D_2 - C_1,$$

whereas that for the second period is

$$C_2 = F(K_2) + K_2 - \Re,$$

assuming that capital does not depreciate and can be "eaten" at the end of the second period. We do not presume that the sum of interest and principal, $(1+r)D_2$, is repaid in full. Thus we interpret $\Re$ broadly, as the lesser of the face value owed to creditors and the sanctions they impose in the event of default, which here (as in section 6.1.1) take the form of a proportional reduction in the country's date 2 resources. Specifically, we assume creditor sanctions reduce the country's date 2 resources by the fraction η in case of default, so that

$$\Re = \min \{(1+r)D_2, \eta[F(K_2) + K_2]\}, \tag{23}$$

with full repayment in case of a tie.

If the country could commit to repay in full we would be in the world of Chapter 1, in which investment continues up to the point at which

$$F'(K_2) = r$$

and consumption obeys the Euler equation

$$u'(C_1) = (1+r)\beta u'(C_2).$$

Suppose, however, that the country cannot commit to repay, so that its repayment never exceeds the cost of sanctions

$$\Re \leq \eta[F(K_2) + K_2].$$

There are two cases to consider, which differ in allowing the country to commit to an investment strategy before receiving any loans. Investment is significant for lenders because by raising date 2 output, it raises the power of their sanctions to deter default. (The assumption that the cost of sanctions is a fixed *fraction* of output, rather than a constant amount, is crucial in giving investment this strategic role.)

6.2.1.1   Discretion over Investment: Calculating the Debt Ceiling

Perhaps more realistic is the case in which the country is free to choose any investment strategy it wants after borrowing. Here potential creditors must ask themselves, "If we lend D_2 today, will the country choose to invest enough to make $\eta[F(K_2) + K_2] \geq (1 + r)D_2$?" If not, lenders won't be repaid in full. Their task, therefore, is to figure out how much they can safely lend. We denote by $\bar{D}$ the most they can lend without triggering default. The first part of the present problem is to calculate this credit limit.

This problem turns out to be surprisingly tricky, though quite instructive. The basic issue is that lenders must calculate their returns under each of two scenarios, depending on whether the borrower chooses investment with the intent of repaying or chooses it intending to default. We find that the equilibrium debt level has a knife-edge quality, such that a small increase in debt could lead to very large decreases in both investment and payments to creditors. (On a first pass, the reader may choose to skip to section 6.2.1.2, where we treat $\bar{D}$ as given and look at the implications. However, skipping the intermediate step of calculating $\bar{D}$, though conventional in the literature, obscures some fundamental issues.)

To calculate $\bar{D}$, let's put ourselves in the sovereign's position after lenders have given it money. Given date 1 borrowing of D_2, it is free to choose C_1 and K_2 and then set repayments according to eq. (23). Substituting the relevant finance constraints into U_1, we formulate the country's problem as

$$\max_{K_2} u(Y_1 + D_2 - K_2) + \beta u \left[F(K_2) + K_2 - \min\{(1+r)D_2, \eta[F(K_2) + K_2]\} \right].$$

$$(24)$$

Its solution tells us whether the sovereign defaults, and $\bar{D}$ is the largest value of D_2 such that full repayment is the sovereign's preferred action.

The simplest way to see what is going on is through a diagram. Figure 6.3 graphs the country's production and consumption possibilities over C_1 and C_2, both for a *given* debt D_2, in analogy to the PPFs for GDP and GNP that we saw in Chapter 1.

In Figure 6.3, the **GDP** PPF is indicated by the broken line. It intersects the horizontal axis at $Y_1 + D_2$, a sum equal to the total resources the country has available for consumption or investment on date 1. **GDP** plots date 2 resources, $F(K_2) + K_2$, against $K_2 = I_1$, where K_2 is measured from right to left starting at $Y_1 + D_2$. There are two other transformation loci in the figure. The one labeled **GNP**^{D} (the D stands for "default") plots $(1 - \eta)[F(K_2) + K_2]$, the output the country can consume on date 2 after it defaults and suffers sanctions, against K_2. The one labeled **GNP**^{N} (the N stands for "nondefault") plots $F(K_2) + K_2 - (1+r)D_2$, the output the economy can consume on date 2 if it repays in full. **GNP**^{N} is simply **GDP** shifted vertically downward by the distance $(1 + r)D_2$. According to eq. (23), the outer

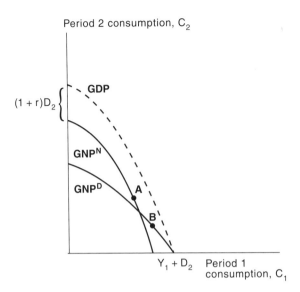

Figure 6.3
Post borrowing consumption possibilities

envelope of **GNP**^{D} and **GNP**^{N}, the locus of maximal consumption possibilities, is what constrains utility. Unless contracted debt repayments are very big, there will be some investment levels high enough that repayment is optimal.

But what investment level will the sovereign choose, given D_2? The optimal value of K_2 is given by the tangency of the consumption-possibilities locus with the highest consumption indifference curve. The unusual feature of the present problem is that the **GNP**^{D}-**GNP**^{N} outer envelope is nonconcave, meaning that the sovereign's optimal investment decision may *not* be uniquely determined as a function of D_2! The kink, it is important to note, occurs precisely where $\eta[F(K_2) + K_2] = (1+r)D_2$, at the intersection of **GNP**^{D} and **GNP**^{N}. It is possible in Figure 6.3 that two different investment levels, such as those at points **A** and **B**, yield equal utility. This seemingly peculiar feature of the problem is the key to solving for $\bar{D}$.

Since we have a badly behaved (nonconvex) problem on our hands, it is prudent to work out thoroughly a simple example that conveys the intuition behind more general cases. The utility function we assume is $U_1 = \log C_1 + \beta \log C_2$, and the production function, $Y_2 = \alpha K_2$, where $\alpha > r$.[31] A critical inequality assumption is needed to make what follows interesting:

---

31. This case would not make sense, of course, absent default risk: without that risk, all the world's savings would flow into the country's capital stock until r was driven up to α. Think of the present example as one in which the marginal domestic product of capital is approximately constant over the small scale on which the country can invest.

$$1 + r > \eta(1 + \alpha). \tag{25}$$

This inequality—which holds for any empirically plausible values of r, η, and α—ensures that a higher debt makes default more attractive even when all additional borrowing is invested.[32]

We see how the sovereign's investment and repayment decisions depend on D_2 by solving two maximization problems, one of which assumes full repayment and the other default. The utility maxima for these problems, U^N and U^D, respectively, are compared to see whether the sovereign actually defaults.

To find U^N, solve the problem of maximizing U_1 subject to $K_2 = Y_1 + D_2 - C_1$ and $C_2 = (1 + \alpha)K_2 - (1 + r)D_2$, which, when combined, imply the intertemporal constraint

$$C_1 + \frac{C_2}{1 + \alpha} = Y_1 + \frac{(\alpha - r)}{1 + \alpha} D_2. \tag{26}$$

(This equation describes **GNP**^{N}.) Optimal consumption levels are

$$C_1 = \frac{1}{1 + \beta} \left[Y_1 + \frac{(\alpha - r)}{1 + \alpha} D_2 \right], \qquad C_2 = \frac{(1 + \alpha)\beta}{1 + \beta} \left[Y_1 + \frac{(\alpha - r)}{1 + \alpha} D_2 \right], \tag{27}$$

implying a maximized lifetime utility of

$$U^N = (1 + \beta) \log \left\{ \frac{1}{1 + \beta} \left[Y_1 + \frac{(\alpha - r)}{1 + \alpha} D_2 \right] \right\} + \beta \log \left[(1 + \alpha)\beta \right].$$

To find U^D, maximize lifetime utility U_1 subject to $K_2 = Y_1 + D_2 - C_1$ and $C_2 = (1 - \eta)(1 + \alpha)K_2$, which, when combined, imply the equation for **GNP**^{D},

$$C_1 + \frac{C_2}{(1 - \eta)(1 + \alpha)} = Y_1 + D_2. \tag{28}$$

Optimal consumptions in this case are

$$C_1 = \frac{1}{1 + \beta}(Y_1 + D_2), \qquad C_2 = \frac{(1 - \eta)(1 + \alpha)\beta}{1 + \beta}(Y_1 + D_2), \tag{29}$$

so that

$$U^D = (1 + \beta) \log \left[\frac{1}{1 + \beta}(Y_1 + D_2) \right] + \beta \log[(1 - \eta)(1 + \alpha)\beta].$$

Now calculate the utility difference between default and nondefault as a function of the debt-output ratio at the end of period 1, D_2/Y_1:

---

32. Even with $r = 0.05$, $\alpha = 1$, and $\eta = 0.5$, so that α is absurdly large relative to r and creditors are endowed with overwhelming retaliatory power, eq. (25) is still satisfied.

$$U^D - U^N = (1 + \beta) \log \left[\frac{1 + \dfrac{D_2}{Y_1}}{1 + \dfrac{(\alpha - r)}{1 + \alpha} \left(\dfrac{D_2}{Y_1} \right)} \right] + \beta \log(1 - \eta).$$

For D_2 close to zero, this difference is close to $\beta \log(1 - \eta) < 0$; but it rises as D_2/Y_1 rises. Thus a higher debt incurred on date 1 makes default a relatively more attractive strategy on date 2. The point at which the sovereign is indifferent between default and full repayment (but, in a tie, repays) occurs when $U^D - U^N = 0$, or, exponentiating this equality, when

$$1 = \left[\frac{1 + \dfrac{D_2}{Y_1}}{1 + \dfrac{(\alpha - r)}{1 + \alpha} \left(\dfrac{D_2}{Y_1} \right)} \right]^{1+\beta} (1 - \eta)^\beta.$$

Solving for D_2/Y_1, we find that the limit beyond which lenders will not extend credit is

$$\bar{D} = \left[\frac{\left(\dfrac{1}{1 - \eta} \right)^{\beta/(1+\beta)} - 1}{1 - \dfrac{(\alpha - r)}{(1 + \alpha)} \left(\dfrac{1}{1 - \eta} \right)^{\beta/(1+\beta)}} \right] Y_1, \tag{30}$$

a positive number in view of inequality (25).[33] They will not extend credit beyond this point because they do not wish to forfeit full repayment. As you can see, making the force of sanctions greater (raising η) increases the borrowing limit, as does greater patience (higher β) and more productive domestic capital (higher α). A higher world interest rate r, by making default more attractive, lowers $\bar{D}$.

A better understanding of the debt limit comes from looking directly at the investment incentives of higher debt. Provided the sovereign is not going to default, its preferred investment level is given by eq. (27) as

$$K_2 = Y_1 + D_2 - C_1 = \frac{\beta}{1 + \beta}(Y_1 + D_2) + \frac{(1 + r)D_2}{(1 + \beta)(1 + \alpha)}.$$

Once debt is high enough that default is the preferred option, eq. (29) shows that investment is lower, at only

---

33. Inequality (25) holds if and only if

$$\frac{1 + r}{1 + \alpha} > \eta \Leftrightarrow 1 - \frac{1 + r}{1 + \alpha} < 1 - \eta \Leftrightarrow \frac{\alpha - r}{1 + \alpha} < 1 - \eta.$$

Because $\beta/(1 + \beta) < 1$, however, $1 - \eta < (1 - \eta)^{\beta/(1+\beta)}$.

$$K_2 = \frac{\beta}{1 + \beta}(Y_1 + D_2).$$

Thus, in deciding investment when default is planned, the sovereign treats the initial debt as "owned" resources that need not be repaid.

Were lenders to allow the country's borrowing to rise beyond $\bar{D}$, the point at which it is indifferent between default and repayment, investment would crash discontinuously as the sovereign moved to reduce its vulnerability to the anticipated creditor sanctions. Figures 6.4a and 6.4b convey the discontinuity graphically.[34] In Figure 6.4a, debt is initially at a level where full repayment is optimal, the utility maximum is at point **A**, and the associated investment level is denoted K^A.[35] An increase in D_2 causes both **GNP^D** and **GNP^N** to shift upward, but the flatter **GNP^D** schedule takes the relatively larger vertical upward shift.[36] The differentially shifting curves move the economy to a position at which $U^N = U^D$ (the same indifference curve has tangencies at **B** and **B'**), and investment is determined at K^B rather than $K^{B'}$ only because we've assumed repayment in case of ties. Thus the debt level associated with this second equilibrium must be the debt ceiling $\bar{D}$. A further small increase in D_2, as in Figure 6.4b, moves the optimum to point **C**, where default is preferred, and causes a sharp investment decline from K^B to K^C. (Notwithstanding these discontinuous shifts in action, higher borrowing raises the sovereign's utility level continuously.)

One further point is noteworthy: the kink in the solid **GNP^D-GNP^N** outer envelope in Figure 6.4b has the property that if $\bar{K}$ is investment at that point, the cost of sanctions equals the gain from default, that is, $\eta[F(\bar{K}) + \bar{K}] = (1 + r)\bar{D}$. Thus, at point **B**, we find the surprising result that $\eta[F(K^B) + K^B]$ is *strictly* greater than $(1 + r)\bar{D}$: although the country really is on the verge of default, creditor sanctions appear superficially more than sufficient to discourage it. Nonetheless, an

---

34. As we shall discuss later, the discontinuity could be removed by sufficient uncertainty over period 2 investment productivity.

35. To avoid cluttering the diagram, we do not actually show K^A, which corresponds to the distance between the horizontal-axis intercept of **GNP^D** and the point on the horizontal axis vertically below point **A**. Similarly, the investment levels associated with other labeled points in Figure 6.4 are not shown explicitly but can be inferred. The investment level marked $\bar{K}$ will be brought in momentarily.

36. The equation of **GNP^N** follows from eq. (26) as

$$C_2 = -(1 + \alpha)C_1 + (1 + \alpha)Y_1 + (\alpha - r)D_2.$$

That of **GNP^D** follows from eq. (28) as

$$C_2 = -(1 - \eta)(1 + \alpha)C_1 + (1 - \eta)(1 + \alpha)(Y_1 + D_2).$$

Thus higher D_2 shifts the vertical intercept of **GNP^N** upward by $(\alpha - r)\Delta D$ and shifts that of **GNP^D** upward by $(1 - \eta)(1 + \alpha)\Delta D$. As we saw in footnote 33, however, inequality (25) implies that $\alpha - r < (1 - \eta)(1 + \alpha)$.

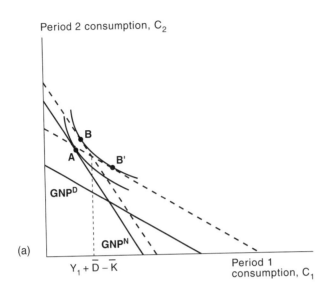

Figure 6.4
Investment effects of growing debt: (a) full repayment is optimal; (b) default is preferred

extra penny of foreign borrowing causes a default. The reason, of course, is the catastrophic investment decline that the extra penny of borrowing sets off.[37]

The discontinuity in investment with respect to debt can, as we have noted, be removed if there is sufficient uncertainty over second-period investment productivity. (Sections 6.2.3 through 6.2.5 will rely on such models.) With enough uncertainty, the country doesn't know for sure whether it will default on date 2: given date 1 borrowing D_2, the ex post repayment decision depends not only on today's investment choice K_2, but also on the realized value of domestic productivity. Even when the country would be sure of repaying under certainty, there is a chance output will turn out so low that default is preferred. Thus, other things being equal, the country reduces the prospective force of creditor sanctions by investing somewhat less than it would under certainty. Conversely, a country that would be sure to default under certainty will invest somewhat more under uncertainty to cover the possibility of

---

37. As the similar aspect of Figure 6.3 makes clear, this "bang-bang" behavior can occur even when production functions aren't linear.

We urge you to approach the relevant published literature on the foregoing problem with caution, as much of it is incorrect. The usual treatment argues that the sovereign's investment K_2 is a function $K(D_2)$ of debt, with $\bar{D}$ determined so as to equate the output cost of default to the gain from nonrepayment: $\eta\{F\left[K(\bar{D})\right] + K(\bar{D})\} = (1+r)\bar{D}$. You can now see the flaws in this line of argument. First, investment is not necessarily a well-defined function of debt under certainty. Second, because the condition $\eta[F(K) + K] = (1+r)D$ occurs at the kink in the **GNP^D-GNP^N** outer envelope, it generally *cannot* characterize any kind of optimum for the sovereign, let alone an optimum where it is indifferent between default and nondefault. (The preceding statement assumes standard preferences with strictly convex indifference curves. An exception would be the case of Leontief preferences over C_1 and C_2.)

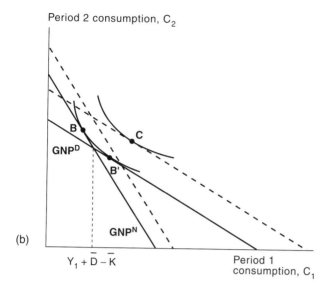

Figure 6.4 *(continued)*

unexpectedly high ex post productivity values. In general, a small increase in D_2 is likely to have only a small negative effect on the probability of full repayment, and thus dictate only a small optimal change in current investment. Future production uncertainty therefore can make investment a single-valued continuous function of first-period borrowing. The investment effect of uncertain future productivity is illustrated in Figure 6.5, which compares the preceding model's investment response to debt under certainty (solid line) with investment under uncertainty (broken line).

6.2.1.2   Optimal Investment and Consumption Given the Debt Limit

The sovereign takes the upper borrowing limit $\bar{D}$, which we have just calculated, as a given constraint. As our previous discussion has shown, creditors set $\bar{D}$ so that for any $D_2 \le \bar{D}$, $\min\{(1+r)D_2, \eta[F(K_2)+K_2]\} = (1+r)D_2$ when the sovereign chooses K_2 optimally after the loan has been extended. So the maximand in eq. (24) simplifies to

$$U_1 = u(Y_1 + D_2 - K_2) + \beta u[F(K_2) + K_2 - (1+r)D_2], \tag{31}$$

which the sovereign maximizes over K_2 and D_2 subject to the constraint

$$D_2 \le \bar{D}. \tag{32}$$

If λ is the nonnegative Kuhn-Tucker multiplier on this inequality constraint and the Lagrangian is

$$\mathcal{L} = u(Y_1 + D_2 - K_2) + \beta u[F(K_2) + K_2 - (1+r)D_2] - \lambda(D_2 - \bar{D}),$$

necessary conditions for an optimum are

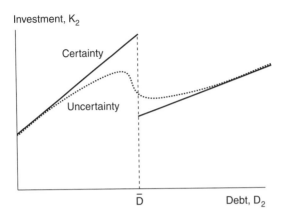

Figure 6.5
Uncertainty and the investment response to debt

$$u'(C_1) = (1+r)\beta u'(C_2) + \lambda,$$

$$u'(C_1) = [1 + F'(K_2)]\beta u'(C_2),$$

$$\lambda(\bar{D} - D_2) = 0.$$

When $\lambda = 0$, these conditions reduce to those governing the model of Chapter 1 with no default risk. This situation might occur if the sanctions η are very powerful, or if the country needs to borrow only a little to attain the Chapter 1 optimum. But when constraint (32) binds so that λ is positive, the domestic interest rate $F'(K_2)$ exceeds the world rate r, and if $\beta(1+r) = 1$, consumption is tilted upward, that is, $u'(C_1) > u'(C_2)$. The tilt reflects a domestic "shadow" rate of interest above the world rate r. Despite consumption's upward tilt, the country's inability to push investment all the way to the efficient point can result in second-period consumption being below its unconstrained level.

6.2.1.3 Precommitment in Investment

An alternative setup assumes the country can commit to an investment strategy *before* creditors lend it any money. One can think of this as a case of partial commitment: the country can commit to an investment strategy but not to repaying loans. For example, the government could prepay some of the cost of a major investment project or subscribe to an International Monetary Fund program that placed credible limits on government consumption.

If the country actually can choose K before lenders extend credit, the latter are always willing to lend any amount up to $\eta[F(K) + K]$. The borrower's problem therefore is to maximize U_1 as given by eq. (31) subject to

$$(1+r)D_2 \le \eta[F(K_2) + K_2]. \tag{33}$$

The associated Kuhn-Tucker Lagrangian is

$$\mathcal{L} = u(Y_1 + D_2 - K_2) + \beta u[F(K_2) + K_2 - (1+r)D_2]$$
$$- \lambda\{(1+r)D_2 - \eta[F(K_2) + K_2]\}.$$

Notice the difference between the country's problem here and the one it faced with an inflexible upper bound $\bar{D}$ for D_2. Here, the country can always borrow more by committing to invest more. Before, such promises were empty, since lenders knew exactly how much the borrower would wish to invest once the loan had been disbursed.

Differentiating $\mathcal{L}$ with respect to D_2 and K_2 and invoking complementary slackness, we have

$$u'(C_1) = (1+r)[\beta u'(C_2) + \lambda], \tag{34}$$

$$u'(C_1) = [\beta u'(C_2) + \lambda\eta][1 + F'(K_2)], \tag{35}$$

$$\lambda\{\eta[F(K_2) + K_2] - (1+r)D_2\} = 0,$$

where the multiplier λ is nonnegative. Condition (34) shows that if the inequality constraint is binding (and, consequently, $\lambda > 0$), consumption will have an upward tilt when $\beta(1+r) = 1$, as in the discretionary investment model. Condition (35) shows that, contrary to the latter model, $1 + F'(K_2) < u'(C_1)/\beta u'(C_2)$, that is, the marginal gross return to investment is below the marginal rate of substitution of future for present consumption. This policy is optimal because the country expands its borrowing possibilities by $\eta[1 + F'(K_2)]$ for every additional date 1 output unit it invests. However, $F'(K_2)$ must exceed r in order for λ to be strictly positive.

Although the ability to commit investment in advance does not do the country as much good as being able to commit to repay, the ability to tie its hands even in a limited way helps it. The country must benefit, since it can always commit to the investment level that would arise under complete discretion.

6.2.1.4 Dynamic Inconsistency in Policy

The two contrasting models we have just sketched are useful vehicles for a first look at the general problem of *dynamic inconsistency* in economic policymaking. A future policy that the government finds optimal today, taking account of its influence over the actions of others, may no longer be optimal once those actions have been taken. Policymaking is subject to dynamic inconsistency when the optimal policy rule for a *given* date changes as time passes. Unlike the dynamic inconsistency problem in intertemporal consumer choice (Chapter 2), policy choice can be dynamically inconsistent with unchanging policymaker preferences: at bottom, the phenomenon is due to constraints on policy that change over time as an initially optimal plan is implemented.

The preceding two subsections illustrate the problem nicely. The policy the sovereign finds optimal when investment influences lenders' decisions (section 6.2.1.3) is different from the one it finds optimal after the loans have been made (section 6.2.1.1).

To demonstrate the point in detail, let us return to the specific case underlying Figure 6.4, in which $u(C) = \log C$ and $F(K) = \alpha K$, with $\alpha > r$. In the last subsection we derived in general terms the optimal *precommitment* investment level, call it K^P. This is simply the investment level the government finds it optimal to promise when it is constrained by eq. (33). Combining eqs. (34) and (35) by solving for λ, we find that

$$\frac{u'(C_1)}{\beta u'(C_2)} = \frac{C_2}{\beta C_1} = \frac{(1+r)(1+\alpha)(1-\eta)}{1+r-\eta(1+\alpha)} > 1 + \alpha.$$

[Be sure to verify the asserted inequality using eq. (25).] In Figure 6.6, the precommittment consumption ratio C_2/C_1 lies along the ray **OC**.[38] The maximum loan D^P lenders are willing to make under precommitted investment is linked to K^P by the repayment constraint (33) (which we assume binds),

$$\eta(1+\alpha)K^P = (1+r)D^P.$$

Figure 6.6 shows the equilibrium that results, with consumption at point **P**, if the government's investment commitment is carried out.[39] What if the government cannot be held to its commitment? In that case, once credit D^P has been extended, eq. (33) no longer is relevant for the country. This result gives rise to dynamic inconsistency: the country can do better for itself after it has borrowed if it is not actually forced to follow its initial plan. In Figure 6.6, it chooses the lower investment level K^D, defaults, and consumes at point **D**, which is on a higher indifference curve than **P**.

Rational lenders understand the dynamic inconsistency of the optimal plan the government adopts before loans are made. Unless the government can somehow precommit its future actions, lenders therefore won't consider the investment level specified in the plan to be *credible*. Instead of believing that the government will implement it once loans have been made, lenders will do the calculation described in section 6.2.1.1 and offer no more than the amount $\bar{D}$ in eq. (30). The government

---

38. The slope of **OC** is

$$\frac{\beta(1+r)(1+\alpha)(1-\eta)}{1+r-\eta(1+\alpha)}.$$

39. How does the constraint $\eta(1+\alpha)K = (1+r)D$ prevent the government from raising without limit borrowing, investment, and (since $\alpha > r$) date 2 consumption? Because $1 + r > \eta(1 + \alpha)$ [inequality (25) again], $D/K < 1$ along the repayment constraint. Thus the country must cut current consumption every time it raises investment. The increasing marginal utility of current consumption as D and K rise in proportion thus places a limit on borrowing in the precommitment optimum.

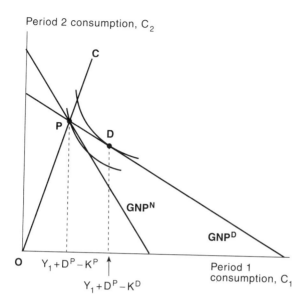

Period 2 consumption, C_2

Figure 6.6
Dynamic inconsistency in investment plans

thus will have no choice but to optimize taking $\bar{D}$ as given, as in the equilibrium of section 6.2.1.1.[40]

6.2.2   Reputation and Investment

In the preceding two-period model, countries are able to borrow only if creditors can impose direct sanctions. As in the consumption insurance case of section 6.1.2, one can dispense with direct sanctions and rely on reputation arguments if the horizon is infinite. There is an important sense, however, in which it is the consumption-smoothing rather than the investment motive that underpins reputation-for-repayment models of sovereign debt. Even in the two-period case, a country with enough first-period output could self-finance the efficient investment level with no utility loss if it did not care about smoothing consumption across periods. In fact, the analysis of section 6.1.2.4, which suggested that the scope for *purely* reputation-based lending is limited, applies with even greater force to the investment case.

As a simple example of a more general problem, think of a borrowing country in a deterministic environment: it has the production function $Y = AF(K)$, where both A and the world interest rate r are constant. Once the country reaches the

---

40. The seminal references on dynamically inconsistent policy problems are Kydland and Prescott (1977) and Calvo (1978). A lucid survey is Persson and Tabellini (1990). Of course, a very basic example of a dynamically inconsistent policy is at the heart of the sovereign debt problem: a country promises to repay lenders but, once loans have been made, would rather not!

steady-state capital stock $\bar{K}$ at which $AF'(\bar{K}) = r$, it no longer needs the world capital market. Fear that it will lose reputation therefore will not deter repudiation of its foreign debt, which makes the country better off in every subsequent period. Lender anticipation of this eventual default leaves the country unable to borrow even when its capital stock is far below $\bar{K}$. If lenders cannot deploy direct sanctions, there will be no sovereign borrowing.[41]

6.2.3 Debt Overhang

During the 1980s many developing countries, notably in Latin America, found it hard to pay their foreign creditors. The booming growth these countries had experienced in the 1970s—growth aided in large part by low world real interest rates and ready foreign credit—came to a screeching halt as both the intertemporal terms of trade (the real interest rate) and the intratemporal terms of trade dramatically and simultaneously worsened.[42] These developments led in many cases to severe debt-servicing problems.

Many have argued that the causality between debt problems and the growth slowdown was bidirectional. That is, the huge foreign debt borrowers had run up by the early 1980s itself made a direct contribution to slower growth. The channel for this effect is that a legacy of foreign debt effectively generates a tax on investment. The following example illustrates the claim.

On date 1, the first of two periods, a country has an inherited debt of face value D that will come due on date 2. (We are not going to be concerned here with how the debt was acquired.) The country's income is Y_1 in period 1 and $AF(K_2)$ in period 2, where the productivity shock A now is a random variable with mean $E(A) = 1$, distributed over $[\underline{A}, \overline{A}]$ with probability density function $\pi(A)$. It is convenient here to assume that capital depreciates by 100 percent in use. Thus, the only capital available for date 2 production is the amount the economy invested on date 1, that is, $K_2 = I_1$. Similarly, because K_2 dissipates entirely in production, $AF(K_2)$ equals the economy's total resources available for consumption or debt repayment on date 2.

To focus squarely on the problem's investment aspect, we assume the country is risk-neutral with expected utility function

$$U_1 = C_1 + E(C_2)$$

(which we have simplified further by setting the subjective discount factor, β, to 1). Purely as a notational simplification, the world interest rate, r, is set to 0. This is a direct sanctions model, in which creditors penalize the country in the amount

---

41. If capital depreciates rapidly enough, the incentive to repudiate may be altered. Thomas and Worrall (1994) examine such a case under the assumption that capital must be provided by a foreign direct investor, for example, a multinational firm.

42. See Bulow and Rogoff (1990).

$\eta A F(K_2)$ (a random quantity from the perspective of date 1) should it default. We will assume in that case that creditors actually *gain* the same fraction η of total debtor output $AF(K_2)$. (It is simple to modify the model so that seizure of debtor goods or curtailment of its trade involves deadweight costs that drive a wedge between what the country pays and what its creditors gain.)

Eliminating consumption levels by using the constraints

$$C_1 = Y_1 - K_2, \quad C_2 = AF(K_2) - \min[\eta A F(K_2), D],$$

we write the country's utility as a function of its investment choice, K_2:

$$U_1 = U(K_2) = Y_1 - K_2 + E\{AF(K_2) - \min[\eta A F(K_2), D]\}.$$

The assumption $E\{A\} = 1$, which implies $E\{AF(K_2)\} = F(K_2)$, converts the country's maximization problem to

$$\max_{K_2} U(K_2) = Y_1 - K_2 + F(K_2) - V(D, K_2), \tag{36}$$

where $V(D, K_2)$ is the payment creditors actually expect to receive on date 2. (This sum is the debt's *market* value.) Since the borrower will default for A realizations such that $\eta A F(K_2) < D$, that is, when $A < D/\eta F(K_2)$, we see that

$$V(D, K_2) = \eta F(K_2) \int_{\underline{A}}^{\frac{D}{\eta F(K_2)}} A\pi(A)dA + D \int_{\frac{D}{\eta F(K_2)}}^{\bar{A}} \pi(A)dA. \tag{37}$$

The first of the two summands on the right-hand side of eq. (37) captures payments in default states, the second, payments in nondefault states. In default states, creditors cannot collect in full but in effect can levy a "tax" equal to η percent of output. Only when A is sufficiently high are creditors fully repaid (in which event the sum they are paid is independent of output). Importantly, the probability of default is *not* exogenous: it depends on how much the country invests.

How does an increase in its inherited debt affect the country's optimal investment choice? Substituting eq. (37) into eq. (36), differentiating with respect to K_2, and equating the resulting derivative to zero, we get the first-order condition

$$F'(K_2)\left[1 - \eta \int_{\underline{A}}^{\frac{D}{\eta F(K_2)}} A\pi(A)dA\right] = 1. \tag{38}$$

This condition[43] states that the debtor will invest up to a point where the expected marginal product of investment, net of expected additional penalty payments to creditors, equals the current consumption cost of investing (that is, 1). We denote the optimal investment choice by $K(D)$, and assume sufficient uncertainty that it

---

43. Contrary to first appearances, we have not forgotten to differentiate the integration limits in eq. (37) in deriving eq. (38). The derivative of $U(K_2)$ with respect to K_2 is

is uniquely defined. At first glance, it might appear that raising D can move investment either way: a rise in D raises the effective creditor tax on investment, and while a fall in K_2 raises $F'(K_2)$, it also widens the range of A realizations over which losses to creditors rise with total output. One can show, however, that $K'(D) < 0$ using the fact that the second-order condition for the country's maximization problem is met at an interior optimum. Thus an inherited liability to foreigners may indeed have a negative, *debt overhang effect* on the debtor's investment.[44,45]

6.2.4 The Debt Laffer Curve

Krugman (1989) and Sachs (1989) have argued that a severe enough debt overhang may enable creditors as a group to *raise* expected debt repayments $V(D, K_2)$ simply by forgiving (that is, canceling) a portion of what they are owed. Let us differentiate eq. (37) with respect to D, taking account of the dependence of K_2 on D. The total derivative is

$$\frac{dV[D, K(D)]}{dD} = \int_{\frac{D}{\eta F(K_2)}}^{\bar{A}} \pi(A)dA + \left[\eta F'(K_2) \int_{\underline{A}}^{\frac{D}{\eta F(K_2)}} A\pi(A)dA \right] K'(D). \quad (39)$$

$$U'(K_2) = -1 + F'(K_2) \left[1 - \eta \int_{\underline{A}}^{\frac{D}{\eta F(K_2)}} A\pi(A)dA \right]$$

$$+ \left\{ \eta F(K_2) \frac{D}{\eta F(K_2)} - D \right\} \pi \left[\frac{D}{\eta F(K_2)} \right] \frac{DF'(K_2)}{\eta F(K_2)^2}.$$

But the last term, which comes from differentiating the integration limits in $U(K_2)$, is 0. (Because the integration limits are chosen optimally, this is another example of the envelope theorem.) Equation (38) shows that a high enough value of $\lim_{K \to 0} F'(K)$ guarantees that K_2 will be chosen strictly positive.

44. Differentiating $U(K_2)$ twice with respect to K_2, we see that the second-order condition for a maximum is

$$U''(K_2) = F''(K_2) \left[1 - \eta \int_{\underline{A}}^{\frac{D}{\eta F(K_2)}} A\pi(A)dA \right] + \frac{D^2 F'(K_2)^2 \pi \left[\frac{D}{\eta F(K_2)} \right]}{\eta F(K_2)^3} < 0.$$

[This inequality need not hold globally (for all K_2), but it must hold at the optimal (interior) investment level.] Implicit differentiation of eq. (38) gives

$$\frac{dK_2}{dD} = K'(D) = \frac{DF'(K_2)\pi \left[\frac{D}{\eta F(K_2)} \right]}{U''(K_2)\eta F(K_2)^2},$$

which is negative if $U''(K_2) < 0$. Interestingly, eq. (38) also implies that the sign of $dK_2/d\eta$ is ambiguous. A higher η raises the creditor "tax" on investment in default states, but also lowers the probability that a default state occurs. Second-order conditions do not rule out the possibility that $dK_2/d\eta > 0$; see Bulow, Rogoff, and Zhu (1994).

45. With concave utility, it is no longer true that higher debt necessarily reduces investment. (This effect can be seen in Figure 6.5.) Imagine a small country that is excluded from new international borrowing on date 1 but that nonetheless becomes liable then to pay a very small transfer to foreign creditors on date 2. For the usual consumption-smoothing reasons, the country will cut current as well as future consumption, and invest more on date 1. (Helpman, 1989, emphasizes this point.) Notice that this example is predicated on the upward tilt in the stream of expected transfer obligations to foreigners.

Market value of debt, V

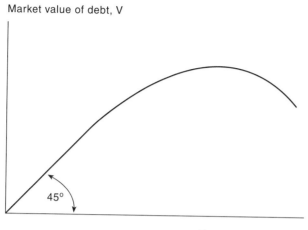

45°

Face value of debt, D

Figure 6.7
The debt Laffer curve

The first term on the right-hand side is the probability of full repayment and clearly is nonnegative. Conditional on the country repaying in full, creditors do better if the face value of its obligations is higher. The second term is negative, however, because a higher face value of debt depresses investment and thus makes default more probable.[46] In principle the second term can dominate the first for D sufficiently large. Thus, if we graph $V[D, K(D)]$ against D (as in Figure 6.7), V may be declining with D for large D, as shown. Krugman (1989) has dubbed Figure 6.7 the *debt Laffer curve*, by analogy with the usual tax Laffer curve showing how the revenue from a tax first rises and then falls as the tax is progressively raised from zero.

Because a rise in D both depresses investment and raises the chances of default, V rises less than in proportion to D (except for D small enough that full repayment is assured). The Laffer curve therefore is concave, as drawn.

If a country has so much debt that it is on the wrong side of the Laffer curve, creditors can make themselves better off as a group by unilaterally writing down the debt's face value. This result occurs because $V(D, K_2)$, the payment they expect to receive, rises. (The debtor naturally is better off as well.)

If this free lunch is readily available, why is voluntary debt forgiveness rarely observed in practice? Sachs (1989) argues that it may be difficult to *coordinate* debt forgiveness among a large group of creditors: each has an incentive to hold out for full repayment on its own claims and watch their value rise when others forgive.

---

46. It has been argued, more generally, that external debt discourages governments from needed but harsh economic reform efforts, since most of the short-term benefits would accrue to creditors (in the form of higher secondary-market prices for sovereign debt). This is another possible factor behind the debt Laffer curve's eventual negative slope.

The free-rider problem can be solved if a very large buyer purchases most of a country's debt and forgives some of it. The buyer would thereby internalize the externalities that prevent numerous small holders from coordinating on forgiveness. The problem with this idea, however, is the same free-rider problem that prevents coordination on forgiveness: why should any of the existing small debt holders sell, except at the higher postforgiveness price? The result is that the large buyer will not realize profits and therefore won't undertake the deal.[47]

Some observers have concluded that the inability of private debtors to negotiate deals for debt forgiveness is prima facie evidence that there is scope for Pareto-improving intervention by some public entity such as a multilateral lending agency. This is debatable. While there is some evidence that debt indeed impedes investment, the effect generally seems to be fairly weak [see, for example, Bulow and Rogoff (1990), Warner (1992), or Cohen (1993)]. And even if large debt levels do act as a tax on investment, this fact does not prove that any countries have actually been on the wrong side of the debt Laffer curve. Cohen's (1990) evidence, for example, suggests that the far side of the debt Laffer curve was not relevant for highly indebted countries even during the peak of the 1980s developing-country debt crisis. Of course, one might still argue that even if public intervention is not literally Pareto improving, the costs (to private creditors and to industrialized-country taxpayers) are still relatively small compared to the potential benefits for highly indebted developing countries. This remains an important and unresolved question.

6.2.5 Debt Buybacks

As Figure 6.8 illustrates, secondary-market prices for developing-country debt fell to deep discounts during the 1980s. These discounts inspired proposals that countries buy back their own debt on the open market at seemingly bargain-basement prices. Despite some legal obstacles, many countries did carry out such debt buybacks. It may seem obvious that a country benefits if it can effectively cancel a dollar of its debt by paying much less than one dollar. But a closer look using the model we have developed shows that the problem is harder than it appears at first glance. In truth, when buybacks are not accompanied by negotiated creditor concessions, they are likely to harm a highly indebted country while helping its creditors.

Let us write the market price of the country's debt on date 1, p, as the ratio of total expected repayments to total face value outstanding:

$$p = \frac{V(D, K_2)}{D}.$$

---

47. A similar free-rider problem can discourage even socially productive corporate takeover attempts, as shown in a classic paper by S. Grossman and Hart (1980).

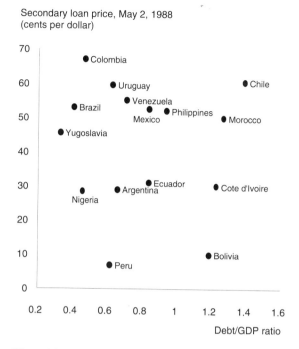

Secondary loan price, May 2, 1988
(cents per dollar)

Figure 6.8
Market price of debt for 15 highly indebted developing countries

We assume that buybacks occur before investment and that buybacks are publicized before they are executed. On the assumption of rational expectations, debt owners understand that the function $K(D)$ defined in section 6.2.3 determines how the country's investment decision will be altered by the reduction in its debt's face value. This point is important because the country will have to pay the higher *post*buyback price for every unit of debt repurchased. No rational seller who knew that the price was about to jump up to a new equilibrium would sell at a lower price.

Suppose the country uses some of its first-period endowment Y_1 to buy back an amount Q of its debt on date 1 at a market price p, where p is the postbuyback price and incorporates rational expectations of the buyback's investment effect. Based on eq. (36) the country's expected utility after the buyback is

$$U_1 = Y_1 - pQ - K_2 + F(K_2) - V(D - Q, K_2)$$

$$= Y_1 - \frac{V[D - Q, K(D - Q)]}{D - Q} Q - K(D - Q) + F[K(D - Q)]$$

$$- V[D - Q, K(D - Q)],$$

where the second line reflects the optimal dependence of investment on debt implicit in the function $K(D)$. To assess the effects of a small buyback, observe that

$$\left.\frac{dU_1}{dQ}\right|_{Q=0} = -\left\{F'[K(D)] - 1\right\} K'(D) - \left\{\frac{V[D, K(D)]}{D} - \frac{dV[D, K(D)]}{dD}\right\}.$$

(40)

The foregoing derivative can be split into two terms.[48] The first of these, $-\{F'[K(D)] - 1\}K'(D)$, is an unambiguous gain for the country. By eq. (38), the debt-overhang investment effect makes $F'[K(D)] > 1$; because the buyback reduces debt and spurs investment [remember that $K'(D) < 0$], it moves the economy closer to a first-best investment allocation.

However, the second term in eq. (40),

$$-\left\{\frac{V[D, K(D)]}{D} - \frac{dV[D, K(D)]}{dD}\right\},$$

represents a net loss for the country. This term is the difference between what the country pays to repurchase its discounted debt, which is the debt's *average* price, and the reduction in total expected future debt payments, which one can think of as the debt's *marginal* price.[49] By eq. (39), the debt's marginal price is the slope of the debt Laffer curve in Figure 6.7, and the curve's concavity implies that marginal price is below average price. The buyback is costly because the country is paying average price for marginal debt units that have a below-average effect on what the country expects to repay.[50] Notice that this loss to the country is a pure gain to creditors, who are paid the debt's average price on each unit they sell and lose only the reduction in expected country repayments, equal to the debt's marginal price.

Contrary to appearances, therefore, the buyback's effect on debtor welfare need not be positive (although creditors always gain). Only if the buyback provides an investment stimulus strong enough to overcome the effect of the gap between average and marginal debt prices will the debtor gain. But is this outcome even possible? Remember that the debt Laffer curve's bowed shape is related to the strength of the investment effect: it is precisely when the investment effect is strong

---

48. For arbitrary $Q > 0$ the derivative is

$$\frac{dU_1}{dQ} = \left[\frac{(D-Q)(V_D + V_K K') - V}{(D-Q)^2}\right] Q - \frac{V}{D-Q} + K' - F'K' + V_D + V_K K'.$$

Equation (40) is obtained by evaluating at $Q = 0$ and noting that the total derivative dV/dD equals $V_D + V_K K'$. The proof that even large buybacks are also detrimental to debtors is fairly straightforward for the proportional seizure technology assumed here. It can, in fact, be generalized to allow for more general (possibly nonlinear) seizure technologies, under fairly mild restrictions. See Bulow and Rogoff (1991).

49. The distinction is discussed in greater detail by Bulow and Rogoff (1988b).

50. Having a little more debt outstanding raises the country's payments only in nondefault states. However, the totality of debt yields payoffs in default as well as nondefault states.

that the gap between average and marginal debt price is also high. So there is no presumption, after all, that a strong investment effect makes the debtor more likely to come out ahead.

We settle the question by using eq. (38) to eliminate $F'[K(D)] - 1$, eq. (37) to eliminate $V[D, K(D)]$, and eq. (39) to eliminate $dV[D, K(D)]/dD$ from eq. (40). The result is the surprisingly simple expression

$$\left.\frac{dU_1}{dQ}\right|_{Q=0} = -\frac{\eta F(K_2)}{D} \int_{\underline{A}}^{\frac{D}{\eta F(K_2)}} A\pi(A)dA < 0.$$

The country's investment gains go entirely into increased expected payments to creditors; on balance the country therefore must *lose* when it repurchases its discounted debt.

There is a more intuitive way to see why investment stimulus cannot make a buyback helpful in this model. Because the country is continuously optimizing its investment, investment changes can have only second-order welfare effects for the country. Thus the envelope theorem implies that the change in debtor utility is approximately the same as in the case of unchanged investment.[51]

Application: Debt Buybacks in Practice

During the late 1980s and early 1990s, heavily indebted countries throughout the world, but especially in Latin America, engaged heavily in various forms of debt buybacks. The case of Bolivia provides a much-discussed example.

Like many other countries in the developing world, Bolivia accumulated large foreign debts during the years after the 1973 oil-price shock. In the early 1980s, however, facing plummeting terms of trade for its commodity exports, a sharp rise in world real interest rates, and worldwide recession, Bolivia allowed its debt to fall into arrears. By September 1986, when discussions of a buyback first began, Bolivian debt traded on world secondary markets at a mere 6 cents on the dollar. Using money largely contributed by foreign donors (including the Netherlands, Spain, and Brazil), Bolivia spent $34 million in March 1988 to repurchase debt with a face value of $308 million—nearly half of the country's $670 million privately held debt. After the buyback, the country's remaining debt was priced at 11 cents on the dollar, a fact many contemporary observers interpreted as evidence that the buyback had sharply improved Bolivia's economic prospects.

---

51. For further analysis, including cases of buybacks beneficial to the debtor, see Bulow and Rogoff (1991) and the following application. Alternative discussions include Detragiache (1994) and Diwan and Rodrik (1992).

Table 6.2
Bolivia's March 1988 Debt Buyback

	Prebuyback	Postbuyback
Face value of debt, D	$670 million	$362 million
Price, p (fraction of a dollar)	0.06	0.11
Total market value, $p \times D$	$40.2 million	$39.8 million

Table 6.2 suggests a very different interpretation, however. Bolivia spent $34 million = $308 million × 0.11 on debt reduction, the product of the face value of repurchased debt and the debt's postbuyback secondary-market price. As a result, the total *market* value of Bolivia's debt (expected repayments to creditors in our model) fell only $40.2 million − $39.8 million = $400, 000. Bolivia thus recouped less than 1.2 percent of the money it spent. Why did the country gain so little? Our model suggests the answer.

With an average debt price of only 6 cents on the dollar, the marginal value of Bolivian debt was nearly zero. The repurchase nearly doubled p mainly because the face value of debt outstanding, D, fell by just under a half without significantly affecting the country's expected future trade balance surpluses. It is possible, of course, that other factors contributed to the rise in Bolivia's debt price, but related evidence strongly suggests that this was not the case; see Bulow and Rogoff (1988b). For example, over the same period where Bolivian debt rose sharply in price, secondary-market prices for the debts of all other heavily indebted countries fell by a weighted average of 30 percent.

Bolivia did not bear the cost of the buyback, but the donors who contributed the bulk of the funds used presumably had no intention that the main beneficiaries of their largesse be American, British, and Japanese banks. Of course, one can equate creditors' gain with Bolivia's loss only when the transaction does not produce pure efficiency gains. If debt reduction ameliorates debt overhang, for example, then a buyback might no longer be a zero-sum game. Our theoretical analysis has shown that efficiency considerations are unlikely to reverse the overall conclusion that the cost of a straight buyback exceeds the benefit. At a more pragmatic level, the efficiency gains from a buyback come mainly from a higher probability of full repayment, and since Bolivian debt traded at only 11 cents after the repurchase, it is hard to imagine that any efficiency gains were large.[52]

---

52. Table 6.2 ignores official debts (such as money owed to the IMF and the World Bank), which nominally are senior to private debts. If some of the funds used to pay off private creditors might have ended up instead being used to repay official debts, then the benefit to Bolivia of the buyback is higher. Bulow and Rogoff (1988b) and Bulow, Rogoff, and Bevilaqua (1992) argue that in practice private debt is, if anything, de facto senior to official debt, so that the calculations in Table 6.2 would not be affected by incorporating official debt into the analysis.

The basic problem illustrated here extends to many other popular buyback schemes. These include debt-for-equity swaps, in which shares in debtor-country firms are used to repurchase debt, and "debt-for-nature" swaps, in which contributions from "green" organizations finance the buyback in return for the country's promise to preserve endangered natural habitats. Not all debt-reduction schemes are necessarily inefficient for the debtor, however. As part of an overall debt reduction deal with creditors, countries can sometimes negotiate repurchase prices much closer to the marginal rather than average value of debt. The key to such plans is usually an agreement by all creditors that those who hold on to their debt must make concessions (say, agree to a lower interest rate). Such concessions push down the postbuyback price of the debt and, therefore, lower the price at which creditors are willing to sell. Creditors as a group may agree to such buybacks if their best alternative option is the status quo. Mexico's early 1990 debt reduction under the "Brady plan" (named for former U.S. Treasury secretary Nicholas Brady) is a good example of a negotiated repurchase. Subsequent calculations generally suggest that the leakage of donated funds to creditors was much smaller than it would have been under a straight buyback.[53]

Postscript: In May 1993, Bolivia conducted another large buyback, although this time at a negotiated rather than market-determined price. Total principal extinguished was $170 million, at a price of 16 cents on the dollar. This buyback followed a concessional refinancing in March 1993 that covered roughly $500 million including arrears, in which Bolivia was granted a 67 percent reduction in its stock of officially held debt. As of this writing, the country has not yet been able to return to private capital markets.   ∎

*6.3   Risk Sharing with Hidden Information

In the risk-sharing models we have analyzed so far, we have assumed that the events upon which payments are conditioned (explicitly or implicitly) are observable by the country, its creditors, and all potential lenders. This section briefly considers how risk sharing is compromised when key contingencies upon which agents would like to contract are private information, directly observed by only one of the parties. Here the focus is not on willful default, as in the case of sovereign debt; rather, it is on the adverse incentives caused by informational asymmetries.

---

53. For analyses of Mexico's 1990 Brady plan debt reduction, see Bulow and Rogoff (1991) and van Wijnbergen (1991).

In the case we examine, a country's output cannot be observed perfectly, perhaps because of incomplete, inaccurate, or falsified data on its economy.[54] The country would like to share output risk with other countries through Arrow-Debreu contracts, making insurance payments when output is above the world average and receiving them when it is below. But if other countries cannot check the country's reports about its own output, the country has an irresistible incentive to misrepresent its output as being lower than it really is, so as to receive insurance payments to which it is not entitled.

Potential trading partners understand this incentive, of course, and the nature of the contracts they will sign therefore is limited. Is there any scope at all for trade in state-contingent assets in this situation? Perhaps surprisingly there may be, although the conditions supporting trade are fragile.

6.3.1   The Model

The world economy produces and consumes on two dates and consists of a continuum of very small countries, indexed by [0, 1], that receive exogenous output endowments each period. On the first date, date 1, half the countries receive low output, $\underline{Y}$, and half receive high output, $\overline{Y}$, where average output is denoted by

$$Y = \frac{\underline{Y} + \overline{Y}}{2}.$$

On the second date, date 2, everyone receives the same output, equal to average date 1 output, Y. So only date 1 output is risky. The 50 percent of countries that receive low date 1 output are chosen randomly and independently—for example, through a simultaneous toss of fair coins for every country in [0, 1].

Let us imagine that, *prior* to date 1, countries can sign contracts to diversify the risk of their date 1 output.[55] Each country knows it will have low (high) output with probability $\frac{1}{2}$ and wishes to maximize expected utility

$$EU_1 = E\{\log(C_1) + \log(C_2)\},$$

where the discount factor β has again been set to 1 for simplicity. It is easy to see the Arrow-Debreu equilibrium for this simple world economy. Since there is no *world* output risk on date 1, actuarially fair full consumption insurance will be available. Each country agrees to deliver the amount $\overline{Y} - Y$ to insurers on date 1 in the event its output is high, and to receive $Y - \underline{Y}$ if its output is low.

---

54. While we assume unobservability, the results for the two-period model of this section really only require that there is no way for a third party (say, a court of law) to *verify* the private information upon which countries would like to write contracts. In a multiperiod setting, this would not necessarily be the case.

55. You can think of this prior date as date 0 and view the model as describing a three-period economy in which only date 1 endowments are uncertain and in which consumption occurs only on dates 1 and 2.

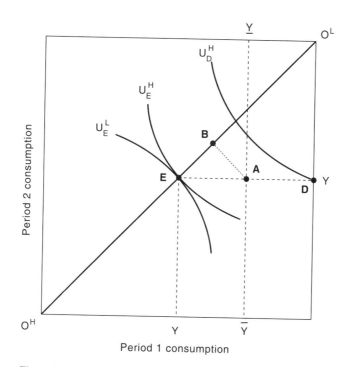

Figure 6.9
Efficient and borrowing solutions

In this way each country can be sure of consuming $C_1 = Y$ with certainty: all consumption risk can be diversified. Since everyone's consumption is also constant over time and $\beta = 1$, the equilibrium world interest rate r is zero.[56] Indeed the constancy over time of total world output implies that the world interest rate is zero in *any* equilibrium allowing riskless borrowing and lending, as you can see by aggregating individual countries' consumption Euler equations. We shall refer to this fact again.

Figure 6.9 is an Edgeworth box diagram showing intertemporal endowments and consumption allocations for high date 1 output (type H) and low date 1 output (type L) countries. (We measure type H quantities starting from the southwest corner of the box and type L quantities starting from the northeast corner. Each side's length equals $2Y$, the sum of the two types' incomes.) Point **A** is the autarky point and **E** represents the Arrow-Debreu equilibrium, where both types achieve equal consumption and utility levels, U_E^H and U_E^L ex post.

---

56. Let $p(\underline{Y}^j)$ be the price of a unit of date 1 output contingent on country j's output being low, and $p(\overline{Y}^j)$ the price contingent on country j's output being high. Since $p(\underline{Y}^j) = p(\overline{Y}^j) = \frac{1}{2}$ (there is no global uncertainty), it is optimal for the country to choose equal consumption levels across possible date 1 states.

If outputs cannot be observed, then simple Arrow-Debreu contracts will not be traded and markets will not be able to reach point **E**. Consider the situation of a type H country on date 1 given the efficient Arrow-Debreu contingent consumption trades just described. Since its output cannot be observed, it will claim it is a low-output type, hoping to receive $Y - \underline{Y}$ rather than paying $\overline{Y} - Y$. This ploy, if successful, would place the type H country's consumption at point **D** and raise its utility to U_D^H. But potential insurers, aware of the incentive to claim falsely that output is low, will refuse to promise insurance in the first place.

International debt contracts are noncontingent here and thus do not require revelation of hidden information. If we assume these are enforceable, the world economy will reach consumption point **B** in Figure 6.9 through borrowing and lending. Point **B** is on the diagonal contract curve, along which both types' ex post marginal rates of intertemporal substitution are equal. Why does trade in riskless bonds produce the ex post efficient allocation described by **B**?

At **B** a type H country consumes

$$C_1^H = C_2^H = \tfrac{1}{2}(\overline{Y} + Y)$$

by lending $\tfrac{1}{2}(\overline{Y} - Y)$ to foreigners on date 1 and receiving a repayment of the same amount on date 2. Similarly, a type L country consumes

$$C_1^L = C_2^L = \tfrac{1}{2}(\underline{Y} + Y)$$

by borrowing exactly what a type H country wishes to lend on date t,

$$\tfrac{1}{2}(\overline{Y} - Y) = \tfrac{1}{2}(Y - \underline{Y}),$$

and repaying that amount on date 2. It is simple to check that $r = 0$ is indeed the equilibrium interest rate.

Trade in bonds thus brings the world economy to the diagonal contract curve in Figure 6.9. The intertemporal marginal rates of substitution of country types H and L are equalized at **B**, so the bond-intermediated allocation welfare-dominates **A** ex post. Using the concavity of utility, you can easily show that allocation **B** also guarantees higher *expected* utility to a country that does not know ex ante what type it will be. Because the two types end up with different lifetime consumption levels at **B**, however, consumption uncertainty is not eliminated as in the Arrow-Debreu allocation. Trade in bonds cannot replicate the allocation that trade in Arrow-Debreu securities achieves.

6.3.2   Incentive-Compatible Risk Sharing

An interesting question is whether there exist feasible state-contingent contracts that bring the world economy to allocations better than point **B**. The answer is a qualified yes. These contracts are structured in such a way that, even though date 1 endowments are unobservable, no country can gain through deception.

The basic idea is simple.[57] We have seen that a type H certainly lies when covered by full Arrow-Debreu insurance: lying brings a positive payment on date 1 without any cost on date 2, moving consumption from point **A** to point **D** in Figure 6.9. Suppose, however, that contracts could be structured so that any country reporting low output on date 1 were penalized by having to make a payment on date 2. (We assume away problems of enforcing that payment.) If the gain from reporting low output were made small enough and the subsequent penalty large enough, a type H country might be deterred from pretending to be of type L.

Formally, a feasible incentive-compatible contract satisfies market-clearing and incentive-compatibility or "truth-telling" constraints that deter each type of country from posing as the other. Suppose that a country reporting high output on date 1 makes payments P_1 on date 1 and P_2 on date 2 while a country reporting low output on date 1 pays $-P_1$ and $-P_2$ on dates 1 and 2, respectively. (Payments can be negative.) Clearly such a contract satisfies resource constraints and is incentive-compatible if it induces both types to report honestly. Expected utility is the average utility of types H and L,

$$EU_1 = \tfrac{1}{2}[\log(\overline{Y} - P_1) + \log(Y - P_2)] + \tfrac{1}{2}[\log(\underline{Y} + P_1) + \log(Y + P_2)].$$

The constraint that a type H does not gain from posing as a type L is

$$\log(\overline{Y} - P_1) + \log(Y - P_2) \geq \log(\overline{Y} + P_1) + \log(Y + P_2), \tag{41}$$

and the constraint that a type L does not gain from posing as a type H is

$$\log(\underline{Y} + P_1) + \log(Y + P_2) \geq \log(\underline{Y} - P_1) + \log(Y - P_2). \tag{42}$$

Notice that both constraints cannot simultaneously hold with equality: this would imply $\overline{Y} = \underline{Y}$, a contradiction.

It is easy to give examples of incentive-compatible contracts that produce allocations Pareto-superior to **B**. Consider, for example, setting

$$P_1 = \frac{\overline{Y}}{\overline{Y} + Y}(\overline{Y} - Y), \qquad P_2 = \frac{-Y}{\overline{Y} + Y}(\overline{Y} - Y), \tag{43}$$

so that a country of type H makes a positive payment in period 1 but receives a transfer in period 2. As the reader can confirm, the preceding payment schedule implies that in both periods, a type H consumes

---

57. The initial reference is Green (1987). Related papers include Thomas and Worrall (1990), Green and Oh (1991), and Taub (1990). Atkeson and Lucas (1992) and Lucas (1992) consider insurance for unobservable preference shocks, as well as implications for the distribution of wealth.

$$\left(\frac{\overline{Y}}{\overline{Y} + \underline{Y}}\right) 2Y,$$

while a type L consumes

$$\left(\frac{\underline{Y}}{\overline{Y} + \underline{Y}}\right) 2Y.$$

This allocation is denoted by point $\mathbf{C}$ in Figure 6.10. Because $P_1 > (\overline{Y} - \underline{Y})/2$ and $-P_2 < (\overline{Y} - \underline{Y})/2$, the proposed payment scheme involves a net present-value transfer to type L. Thus point $\mathbf{C}$ is closer to $\mathbf{E}$ than $\mathbf{B}$ is and yields higher expected utility than $\mathbf{B}$.[58] You can verify algebraically that eq. (41) holds with equality at $\mathbf{C}$ whereas eq. (42) holds as a strict inequality: the operative constraint here is to prevent the high-income country from posing as poor, not the reverse. In Figure 6.10, a false claim of poverty would place type H at point $\mathbf{C}'$, which is on the same utility contour $U_{\mathbf{C}}^H$ as the truthful allocation $\mathbf{C}$. (When indifferent, agents tell the truth.)

Allocation $\mathbf{C}$ is not the *best* that can be done through a truth-telling mechanism. The optimal incentive-compatible allocation lies to the northwest of $\mathbf{C}$ in Figure 6.10. Since the derivation of the optimal contract is not particularly edifying, we leave it as an exercise. We note, however, that the optimal incentive-compatible contract does *not* lie on the contract curve.[59]

This last observation suggests it may be hard to make the preceding ideas work in a market setting. Our discussion has implicitly assumed that the incentive-compatible contract is the only financial commitment agents can make. But what happens if countries can borrow and lend freely after they announce their type and receive the endowment specified in the contract? Return to the contract that led to allocation $\mathbf{C}$. If a type H announces it is poor, receiving the endowment $\mathbf{C}'$ in Figure 6.10 thanks to the contract, it can then smooth its consumption by lending until it reaches point $\mathbf{C}''$ on utility contour $U_{\mathbf{C}''}^H > U_{\mathbf{C}}^H$. Thus type H countries will no longer tell the truth.

The contract penalizes lying through the "punishment" of an uneven intertemporal consumption path, but that punishment is empty if transgressors can always turn to the international bond market to smooth out their consumption. In this case, the best the market can do is indeed the borrowing-lending allocation, point $\mathbf{B}$. The

---

58. The closer we get to $\mathbf{E}$ along the contract curve, the smaller is the ex post consumption difference between the two types on both dates. This unambiguous reduction in consumption variability implies a higher expected utility level ex ante. (We know $\mathbf{C}$ is on the contract curve in Figure 6.10 because $\overline{Y} - P_1 = \underline{Y} - P_2$ and $\underline{Y} + P_1 = Y + P_2$.)

59. It may seem restrictive to limit the search for an optimal contract to ones in which each country truthfully reveals its type. The revelation principle of Myerson (1979) and Harris and Townsend (1981) assures us that we cannot do better by allowing for nontruthful revelation.

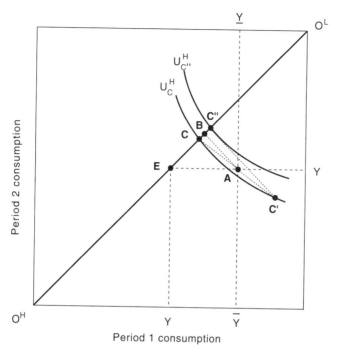

Figure 6.10
Incentive-compatible risk sharing

model thus provides some justification for the prevalence of bond-intermediated lending that we assumed in the stochastic models of Chapter 2.

Limited risk-sharing through incentive contracts is possible only if insurers can monitor and control countries' *other* financial trades, perhaps using some sort of credit-rationing scheme. But as we saw in section 6.1.2.4, these things are extremely hard to do. Indeed, the point here is quite analogous to the one we made in connection with reputation in the sovereign-debt context. The power of an explicit or implicit penalty to support financial trades is crucially dependent on the inability of a country to enter into financial agreements with others that would undo the penalty's effects.

6.4   Moral Hazard in International Lending

In the last section we saw how international risk sharing is restricted when the output risks that countries wish to diversify are not directly observable. Even when final outputs are observable and verifiable, and even if the terms of international contracts are enforceable by a supranational legal body, hidden information about borrower investment or work effort may still limit the scope for intertemporal trade and risk sharing. We illustrate these points using a model in which a firm's foreign creditors cannot observe how it allocates borrowing between investment and disguised consumption.[60]

6.4.1   Moral Hazard in Investment

A small country facing the world interest rate r is populated by a large number of two-period-lived entrepreneurs who invest on date 1 and consume only on date 2. To abstract, for now, from consumption insurance aspects, we assume the representative individual has the linear utility function

$$U_1 = U(C_1, C_2) = C_2.$$

On date 1 an individual entrepreneur receives an exogenous endowment Y_1 that can be converted into date 2 income either by investing abroad at the riskless rate of return r or by investing at home in a risky "family firm." Home investment at level I yields a random output Y_2 distributed as follows:

$$Y_2 = \begin{cases} Z & \text{with probability } \pi(I) \\ 0 & \text{with probability } 1 - \pi(I). \end{cases}$$

We assume that $\pi'(I) > 0$, $\pi''(I) < 0$, $\pi(0) = 0$, and $\pi'(0)Z > 1 + r$.[61] As more traditional production functions imply, higher investment raises expected output at a decreasing marginal rate. Firms' outputs are mutually independent.

The efficient (full information) investment level $\bar{I}$ occurs at the maximum of expected profits

$$-I + \frac{\pi(I)Z}{1+r},$$

that is, where the expected marginal product of investment equals the gross world interest rate:

$$\pi'(\bar{I})Z = 1 + r. \tag{44}$$

We shall assume that

$$\bar{I} > Y_1,$$

so that domestic entrepreneurs cannot finance their optimal investment levels without foreign loans.

In our earlier models of intertemporal trade there was no need to look separately at gross borrowing and lending levels. That is not the case here. Let L denote *gross*

---

60. The model is based on Gertler and Rogoff (1990), which relaxes some of the simplifying assumptions we will make here.

61. The last assumption implies that a positive investment level is efficient under symmetric information.

foreign lending by the small country on date 1 and D its *gross* foreign borrowing. A domestic individual's date 1 finance constraint is

$$I + L = Y_1 + D, \tag{45}$$

where

$$L \geq 0, \qquad D \geq 0.$$

We are allowing for gross foreign lending to capture the idea that domestic entrepreneurs may covertly invest borrowed funds abroad rather than at home, a round-tripping strategy reminiscent of "capital flight." (Similar results obtain if we introduce the possibility of secret first-period consumption.)

Foreign lenders are risk-neutral and competitive, so they will earn the expected return r on any loan to an entrepreneur. If borrowers could *commit* to investing $\bar{I}$, they would borrow $D = \bar{I} - Y_1$ and choose $L = 0$ (since the expected return to domestic investment is higher than r until $\bar{I}$ is reached).[62] However, no repayment would be possible in the bad (zero-output) state of nature. Thus promised payments on securities issued against family-firm output have to be of the state-contingent form $P(Y_2)$, with $P(0) = 0$ and $P(Z)$ determined by the lenders' zero-profit condition, in this case

$$\pi(\bar{I})P(Z) = (1 + r)(\bar{I} - Y_1).$$

This is the first-best borrowing contract.

Under asymmetric information, however, the borrower might be unable to commit credibly to an investment of $\bar{I}$. Suppose the information structure is as follows: lenders directly observe the borrower's first-period endowment Y_1, gross borrowing D, and second-period output Y_2, but not first-period investment I or the gross foreign assets L that the borrower may secretly accumulate on date 1.[63] Moreover, the borrower doesn't choose I and L until after lenders set the amount and terms of the loan, D and $P(Y_2)$. The timing assumption alone wouldn't be a problem if repayments could be indexed to I, but as lenders can't observe investment, the best they can do is index to Y_2. This *is* problematic because if an entrepreneur's investment goes sour, creditors have no way to prove if he has failed to act in good faith.

Let's look at the borrower's problem in this private information setting. The borrower maximizes

---

62. In this model, there would be no point in borrowing more than $\bar{I} - Y_1$ at rate r, investing $\bar{I}$, and sending the balance of what had been borrowed back abroad to earn r. Thus we can safely assume $L = 0$ under full information.

63. The assumption $L \geq 0$ rules out secret borrowing from abroad. An alternative model would have lenders unable to observe final output, in the spirit of the last section's model. Greenwood and Williamson (1989) consider a model of that type in which there is *costly state verification*; that is, lenders can observe the output realization at some cost.

$$EC_2 = \pi(I)[Z - P(Z)] - [1 - \pi(I)]P(0) + (1 + r)L$$
$$= \pi(I)[Z - P(Z)] - [1 - \pi(I)]P(0) + (1 + r)(Y_1 + D - I), \qquad (46)$$

where eq. (45) was used to eliminate L. For the borrower the contract terms $[P(Z), P(0), D]$ are given. The first-order condition for a maximum is

$$\pi'(I)\{Z - [P(Z) - P(0)]\} = 1 + r. \qquad (47)$$

Now recall the features of the investment contract under commitment, which sets $P(Z) = (1 + r)(\bar{I} - Y_1)/\pi(\bar{I})$ and $P(0) = 0$. Comparing eq. (47) with eq. (44), we see that the borrower will actually choose an investment level $I < \bar{I}$ if he can take up the first-best contract despite freedom to choose investment ex post. Because the lender agrees to share in the risk of a bad outcome whenever $P(Z) > P(0)$, the borrower has less incentive to invest in a good outcome; he would rather secretly lend some money abroad and earn the sure return r, which, when $I = \bar{I}$, exceeds the net return given by the left-hand side of eq. (47) [see eq. (44)]. This moral hazard problem, which is reminiscent of the sovereign debt overhang problem we studied earlier, implies that if lenders offer the full information first-best contract, they will earn an expected rate of return strictly below r. Understanding the borrower's incentives, they therefore will not offer that contract.

There is, however, an optimal incentive-compatible contract, one that earns lenders r *given* the borrower's proclivity to underinvest in a successful outcome. The contract provisions $[P(Z), P(0), D]$ maximize eq. (46) subject to the lender's zero-profit condition,

$$\pi(I)P(Z) + [1 - \pi(I)]P(0) = (1 + r)D, \qquad (48)$$

given that investment is determined by eq. (47), which we interpret as an incentive-compatibility constraint. We shall also assume that $P(0) = 0$. The only way for the borrower to pay a positive amount when $Y_2 = 0$ is by drawing on his own assets abroad; but since these are unobservable by lenders, the borrower could always feign bankruptcy.[64] Thus the incentive-compatibility constraint (47) reduces to

$$P(Z) = Z - \frac{1 + r}{\pi'(I)},$$

which is graphed as the downward-sloping curve **IC** in Figure 6.11. The curve has a negative slope because a reduction in the amount $P(Z)$ that lenders appropriate in the event of success stimulates the borrower to invest more. Notice that **IC** intersects the horizontal axis at $\bar{I}$, because only when the repayment in the good

---

64. Alternatively, the borrower could ensure bankruptcy in the bad state by raising C_1 if we relaxed the assumption that first-period consumption yields no utility.

Borrower repayment, P(Z)

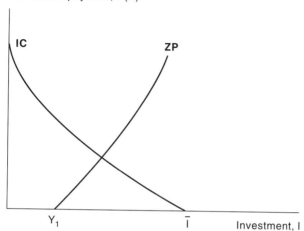

Figure 6.11
Small-country equilibrium

state equals that in the bad state, $P(Z) = P(0) = 0$, is investment not distorted [consult eq. (47)].

It is straightforward to show that the optimal contract induces the borrower to choose $L = 0$. If the contract led to $L > 0$ instead, $P(Z)$ would have to be higher for lenders to break even, which would reduce the incentive to invest.[65]

---

65. The Lagrangian for the borrower's problem is

$$\mathcal{L} = \pi(I)[Z - P(Z)] + (1 + r)(Y_1 + D - I)$$

$$+ \psi[\pi(I)P(Z) - (1 + r)D] + \mu \left\{\pi'(I)[Z - P(Z)] - (1 + r)\right\}$$

$$- \lambda(I - Y_1 - D).$$

Here, ψ is the Lagrange multiplier on the zero-profit constraint, μ that on the incentive-compatibility constraint $\pi'(I)[Z - P(Z)] - (1 + r) = 0$, and λ that on the constraint $L = Y_1 + D - I \geq 0$. The Kuhn-Tucker necessary conditions can be written [after using the incentive-compatibility condition to eliminate $Z - P(Z)$] as

$$\psi\pi'(I)P(Z) + \mu[(1 + r)\pi''(I)/\pi'(I)] - \lambda = 0, \qquad \text{(i)}$$

$$(1 + r)(1 - \psi) + \lambda = 0, \qquad \text{(ii)}$$

$$(\psi - 1)\pi(I) - \mu\pi'(I) = 0, \qquad \text{(iii)}$$

$$\lambda(Y_1 + D - I) = 0, \qquad \text{(iv)}$$

where (i)–(iii) are the first-order conditions for I, D, and $P(Z)$, and (iv) is a complementary slackness condition. We wish to show that $\lambda > 0$, which, by (iv), implies $L = 0$.
Proof: We reason by contradiction. If a positive amount D is borrowed, then, given $P(0) = 0$, $P(Z)$ must be positive for eq. (48) to hold. (If $D = 0$, all output would be invested domestically, leaving $L = 0$.) Suppose $\lambda = 0$. Then (ii) implies $\psi = 1$. Because $P(Z)$ and $\pi'(I)$ are strictly positive, (i), $\psi = 1$, and $\pi''(I) < 0$ imply $\mu > 0$. But this means that (iii) can't be satisfied unless $\pi'(I) = 0$, which is ruled out. We see that the assumption $\lambda = 0$ leads to a contradiction.

(Notice that even though the borrower *chooses* to place no covert funds abroad when offered the optimal incentive-compatible contract, it is precisely his option of doing so that constrains borrowing.) Using eq. (45) to eliminate D from eq. (48) and remembering that $P(0) = 0$ and $L = 0$, we rewrite the zero-profit condition for lenders as

$$P(Z) = \frac{(1+r)(I - Y_1)}{\pi(I)}. \tag{49}$$

This equation defines the upward-sloping **ZP** locus in Figure 6.11. Since Y_1 is fixed, a rise in I implies a rise in borrowing which means $P(Z)$ must go up.[66] This second locus intersects the horizontal axis at Y_1.

Figure 6.11 shows that equilibrium investment is strictly below $\bar{I}$. It also allows us to do some comparative statics exercises. A rise in first-period income Y_1, for example, shifts **ZP** to the right: any given $P(Z)$ is consistent with a higher I. Thus a rise in Y_1 lowers $P(Z)$ and raises investment. Investment clearly rises by less than Y_1, however, and because $L = Y_1 + D - I = 0$, capital inflows D decline. A rise in Z shifts **IC** upward, raising $P(Z)$, investment, and borrowing. A rise in the world interest rate shifts both curves leftward, lowering investment.

Because the number of firms is large and their date 2 output realizations independent, per capita aggregate output on date 2 equals $\pi(I)Z$, and, like investment, is lower than under full information. But countries with higher date 1 wealth, Y_1, enjoy higher investment and higher date 2 output.

One interesting implication of the model is that even when international capital markets are perfectly integrated with *riskless* rates of return equal across countries, expected marginal products of capital exceed riskless interest rates and depend on country characteristics. The expected (gross) marginal product of capital is

$$\pi'(I)Z > 1 + r.$$

Since I is an increasing function of the initial endowment Y_1, the model predicts that initially richer countries will have higher investment and lower gaps between the expected marginal products of capital and the risk-free rate, other things being equal.

We have worked so far with a representative entrepreneur, but an interesting question concerns the effect of inequality in initial endowments on aggregate in-

---

66. The slope of **ZP** is

$$\frac{dP(Z)}{dI}\bigg|_{\textbf{ZP}} = (1+r)\frac{\pi(I) - (I - Y_1)\pi'(I)}{\pi(I)^2}.$$

But since $\pi(I)$ is strictly concave with $\pi(0) = 0$, $\pi(I)/I > \pi'(I)$ for any I. Furthermore, because $I > Y_1$, $\pi(I)/(I - Y_1) > \pi(I)/I > \pi'(I)$, implying $\pi(I) > (I - Y_1)\pi'(I)$. Thus the numerator in the slope is positive. Investing an extra dollar of borrowing cannot raise the probability of a good outcome enough to warrant a lower repayment in the event of a good outcome.

vestment and date 2 output. Under plausible conditions capital-market imperfections make I a strictly concave function of Y_1, in which case greater wealth inequality within a country lowers average per capita investment and, with it, date 2 output.

6.4.2   A Two-Country Model

A general-equilibrium version of the model confirms that richer countries will tend to have lower expected marginal returns to capital. It also yields some surprising predictions concerning the possible direction of international capital flows between rich and poor countries.

Two countries, Home and Foreign, have equal populations. A fraction s of each population comprises savers, the rest being entrepreneurs. Savers do not have access to investment projects and can save only by acquiring the securities entrepreneurs issue. By diversifying across a large number of independent firms, savers can assure themselves a riskless (gross) return of $1 + r$, which will now be endogenously determined. Home savers and Home entrepreneurs both have a date 1 endowment y_1; both types of Foreign agent have an endowment y_1^*. (We switch to lower-case quantity variables here because populations within each country are heterogeneous. As a result, per capita quantity variables are no longer interchangeable with aggregates.) Preferences and technologies are the same as in the small-country case and identical across countries, with productivity outcomes statistically independent between as well as within countries. We assume that Home is the richer country, so that $y_1 > y_1^*$. (What really matters in determining the global allocation of investment is that Home entrepreneurs have higher wealth than Foreign entrepreneurs.)

As before, everyone has the utility function $U(c_1, c_2) = c_2$, so all of the world's first-period output is invested in equilibrium.

Absent informational asymmetries, investment levels in Home and Foreign would be governed by

$$\pi'(I)Z = 1 + r, \qquad \pi'(I^*)Z = 1 + r,$$

where $Z = Z^*$ because both countries' technologies are the same. Under full information we therefore would have $\bar{I} = \bar{I}^*$, with the world interest rate equal to the common expected marginal product of capital,

$$\pi'(\bar{I})Z = \pi'(\bar{I}^*)Z = \pi'\left[\frac{y_1 + y_1^*}{2(1 - s)}\right]Z.$$

(Please note that in this section we interpret I and I^* as *per entrepreneur* investment in each country; similarly for Z and Z^*. Since only $1 - s$ percent of all agents are entrepreneurs, one must divide world per capita income by $1 - s$ to convert to investment funds per entrepreneur.)

Let us assume that in equilibrium both $y_1 < \bar{I}$ and $y_1^* < \bar{I}^*$, so that neither Home nor Foreign entrepreneurs can finance the first-best equilibrium investment levels without drawing on the resources of savers. Under asymmetric information, the loan contracts entrepreneurs in the two countries are offered therefore will have to satisfy the incentive-compatibility constraints

$$P(Z) = Z - \frac{1+r}{\pi'(I)}, \qquad P(Z)^* = Z - \frac{1+r}{\pi'(I^*)}, \tag{50}$$

and the zero-profit conditions

$$P(Z) = \frac{(1+r)(I - y_1)}{\pi(I)}, \qquad P(Z)^* = \frac{(1+r)(I^* - y_1^*)}{\pi(I^*)}. \tag{51}$$

If we knew $1 + r$, we could use these conditions, as before, to calculate repayments in case of investment success, investment levels, and borrowing for each country.

To calculate investment levels and the world interest rate, substitute for $P(Z)$ in eq. (50) using eq. (51); then solve the result for $1 + r$ to get the Home interest rate equation,

$$1 + r = \frac{\pi'(I)Z}{1 + \frac{\pi'(I)(I - y_1)}{\pi(I)}} \equiv \rho(I, y_1). \tag{52}$$

(There is a parallel definition for Foreign.) Notice that $\partial \rho / \partial I < 0$ and $\partial \rho / \partial y_1 > 0$.[67] The locus of investment pairs along which Home and Foreign face a common risk-free interest rate is given by

$$\rho(I, y_1) = \rho(I^*, y_1^*), \tag{53}$$

and it has a positive slope, as the corresponding $\rho\rho$ locus in Figure 6.12 shows. Curve **IS** graphs the equality of world saving and investment,

$$\frac{y_1 + y_1^*}{1 - s} = I + I^*.$$

Curve **IS** has slope -1. A key observation is that $\rho\rho$ cannot intersect **IS** at point **A**, the first-best allocation given the identical Home and Foreign technologies. Because $y_1 > y_1^*$, eq. (52) shows that $\rho(I, y_1) > \rho(I^*, y_1^*)$ at **A**, creating an incentive

---

67. To see the negative relationship between I and r, recall that in Figure 6.11, a rise in r shifts both curves to the left and lowers I. If you prefer a calculus proof, compute

$$\frac{\partial \rho}{\partial I} = \frac{\pi''(I)\pi(I)^2 Z + \pi'(I)^2[\pi'(I)(I - y_1) - \pi(I)]Z}{[\pi(I) + \pi'(I)(I - y_1)]^2}.$$

In the numerator of this fraction, $\pi''(I) < 0$ by the strict concavity of $\pi(I)$. As shown in footnote 66 $\pi'(I)(I - y_1) - \pi(I) < 0$. So $\partial \rho / \partial I < 0$, as claimed.

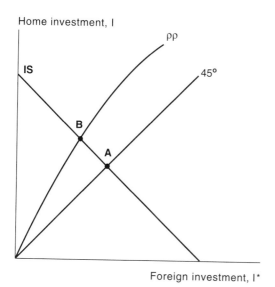

Home investment, I

Foreign investment, I*

Figure 6.12
Two-country world equilibrium

for world savings to flow from Foreign to the richer country, Home. Thus $\rho\rho$ and **IS** must intersect at a point like **B**, with investment higher in the richer country (just as the partial-equilibrium model suggested). Only with an equal distribution of initial wealth among entrepreneurs worldwide would the world economy attain efficient investment. With unequal entrepreneurial wealth, expected world output therefore is lower than under full information.

Home's higher income implies that it saves more, but, as we have seen, it also invests more. Thus it is by no means clear that richer Home lends to poorer Foreign. Instead, a seemingly perverse flow of savings from Foreign to Home can occur. The model therefore suggests an explanation of the phenomenon that capital sometimes flows from low-income to high-income countries.

It is easy to show that if Foreign's government has a debt to Home, and taxes Foreign firms (on either date) to service it, Foreign investment is depressed. (As Foreign's debt rises, $\rho\rho$ in Figure 6.12 shifts upward.) This effect, a variant of the debt overhang effect, has implications for the transfer problem analyzed in Chapter 4. When one country transfers income to another, credit-market imperfections may magnify the direct costs. (See end-of-chapter exercise 4.)

Given initial wealth distributions, however, the equilibrium is constrained Pareto optimal. Despite the higher rate of return on marginal investment in the poor country, there is no way for a world planner to engineer a Pareto-improving allocation unless the planner has access to more information than do lenders. (See end-of-chapter exercise 5.)

6.4.3   Implications for Consumption Insurance

Under risk aversion, informational asymmetries may lead to suboptimal insurance, with repercussions on investment. To see this relationship we modify the small-country model of section 6.4.1 so that the representative entrepreneur's utility function is strictly concave in date 2 consumption,

$$U_1 = U(C_1, C_2) = u(C_2).$$

To focus squarely on insurance considerations, we make the entrepreneur's date 1 endowment more than sufficient to finance the first-best investment level: $Y_1 > \bar{I}$, where, as before, $\pi'(\bar{I})Z = 1 + r$. The entrepreneur's sole reason for using capital markets is to reduce consumption variability.

Now the entrepreneur's date 2 consumption is

$$C_2 = \begin{cases} Z - P(Z) + (1+r)(Y_1 - I) & \text{with probability } \pi(I) \\ -P(0) + (1+r)(Y_1 - I) & \text{with probability } 1 - \pi(I). \end{cases}$$

The first-best insurance contract would be

$$P(Z) = [1 - \pi(\bar{I})]Z, \qquad P(0) = -\pi(\bar{I})Z,$$

which stabilizes consumption at its expected value of $\pi(\bar{I})Z + (1+r)(Y_1 - \bar{I})$ and satisfies the zero-profit condition for insurers,

$$\pi(\bar{I})P(Z) + [1 - \pi(\bar{I})]P(0) = 0.$$

Under asymmetric information, however, the entrepreneur has no reason to invest anything at all once insurers have guaranteed his date 2 consumption. The precise form of the optimal incentive-compatible contract is messy, but it is analogous to those analyzed earlier. The contract involves a trade-off between efficient production and efficient risk sharing, one that leaves domestic consumption subject to domestic production uncertainty and investment below its first-best level.

6.4.4   Discussion

The possibility of moral hazard is clearly an important reason why the complete-markets model of Chapter 5 squares so poorly with the data. We have explored moral hazard in the context of physical capital investment, but it arises in many other contexts, for example, investment in human capital. A graduate student who could buy full insurance on his future lifetime income would face a diminished incentive to study hard!

The preceding models also illustrate how moral hazard in *government* investment may interfere with international (or interregional) insurance markets. Suppose one interprets investment in the last model as tax-financed public investment in infrastructure, schools, and so on. If a government can commit to the first-best investment level, it may be able to obtain full insurance. But if commitment is impossible, full insurance would give voters an ex post incentive to elect a government that invests (and taxes) at levels below the ex ante optimum. This is another example of dynamic inconsistency in government policy.[68]

More generally, asymmetric information has broad ramifications for the functioning of credit markets, domestically as well as in an international context, although informational distortions are likely to be even more severe in the latter setting. Transactions may be limited not only by moral hazard, as in the models just examined, but also by adverse selection problems—the tendency for "bad" borrowers (those with a low likelihood of repayment) to drive out "good" borrowers when lenders cannot observe borrower quality. If sufficiently severe, adverse selection may lead to a collapse of the market, as shown in a pioneering paper by Akerlof (1970). Gertler (1988) provides a good survey of the roles of moral hazard and adverse selection problems in models of financial intermediation.

One theme of the moral hazard model is that a rise in initial borrower wealth can mitigate the dampening effects on investment—recall how an increase in the borrower's initial endowment, Y_1, shifted the locus **ZP** outward in Figure 6.11. In an economy where the value of wealth is endogenous and depends on expectations about future economic conditions, a collapse in economic confidence can reduce borrower wealth, depressing investment and consumption and inducing self-fulfilling cycles of bust and boom. Kiyotaki and Moore (1995) present a theoretical model of credit cycles.

Mishkin (1978), Bernanke (1983), and others have argued that a general credit collapse linked to declining asset values helped deepen the Great Depression of the 1930s. A body of more recent evidence points to similar effects of borrower net worth on economic activity, as the following application illustrates.

Application: Financing Constraints and Investment

If there are no impediments to borrowing at the firm level—as, for example, in the q investment model of Chapter 2—then it should not matter whether a firm finances additions to physical capital out of retained earnings or out of borrowed funds. The logic is closely analogous to that for the small country model of Chapters 1 and 2, where the efficient level of national investment is independent of national savings. In the neoclassical investment model, firm-level savings (or, more generally, firm financial structure) should be irrelevant for investment allocations.

When informational problems constrain firm borrowing, however, the firm's current financial condition can have a critical effect on its investment. Firms with high current cash flow (high current income net of wages, taxes, and interest payments)

---

68. Persson and Tabellini (1996) discuss a different model of moral hazard in government investment.

have the means to self-finance a greater proportion of their investment. One strong empirical implication of the class of models we have just studied is that firms with high cash flow actually should invest more. A substantial body of research suggests that this is indeed the case.

In an early and influential study, Fazzari, Hubbard, and Peterson (1988) showed that cash flow can help explain firm-level investment empirically, even after one controls for a firm's q ratio and other factors suggested by standard neoclassical models of investment. They study a large panel data set consisting of publicly-traded United States manufacturing firms for the years 1970–84. Reasoning that borrowing constraints are likely to be more severe for rapidly growing firms than for mature firms, and that mature firms tend to pay the highest dividends, they divided their sample into three groups. Class I firms consist of those with dividend-earnings ratios less than 0.1 for at least 10 years, Class II firms consist of those with dividend-earnings ratios greater than 0.1 but less than 0.2, and Class III consists of all other firms. They then ran panel regressions of the general form

$$\left(\frac{I}{K}\right)^i_t = a_0 + a_1 q^i_t + a_2 \left(\frac{cashflow}{K}\right)^i_t + \epsilon^i_t,$$

where q^i is a measure of Tobin's q for firm i (see Chapter 2) and *cashflow* is a measure of firm i's cash flow.[69] Theoretically, once one controls for q, the cash flow variable should not have any explanatory power absent borrowing constraints. However, Fazzari, Hubbard, and Peterson found that cash flow is consistently significant in their regressions, and it is significant for all three firm groups. Interestingly, the coefficient is much larger for Class I firms (those most likely to be constrained) than for the other two classes, with the Class III firms having the lowest coefficient. The authors emphasize that this last result is their most important. It is possible that all three groups face a differential cost between external and external finance, but it is also possible that the cash flow variable is simply proxying for other factors. If the Class II and III firms are viewed as control groups, one can (loosely) think of the differential between the cash flow coefficients for these firms versus the Class I firms as measuring the importance of cash flow.

Similar results have been found by other researchers using different time periods and different methods of classifying firms.[70] Smaller firms, for example, might be expected to have less access to equity financing and therefore be more reliant on bank loans and other forms of intermediated credit. Gertler and Gilchrist (1993)

---

69. Recall that q measures the ratio of the shadow value of a unit of capital in place to the cost (not including installation cost) of new investment. In practice, q is sometimes measured by the ratio of the market value of a firm to the book value of its assets, but this measure is very crude because it can be very sensitive to accounting conventions. Also, technically, the right variable to include in the regression is *marginal q* rather than *average q*. In Chapter 2 we demonstrated conditions under which marginal and average q are equal, but these conditions might not always be met in practice.

70. For a recent survey of the evidence, see Bernanke and Gertler (1995).

find that small U.S. firms are indeed more sensitive to general financial conditions and argue that the differential cost of internal versus external financing is a plausible explanation. Further confirming evidence comes from studies based on countries outside the United States; see, for example, Devereux and Schiantarelli (1990) on the United Kingdom and Hoshi, Kashyap, and Scharfstein (1991) on Japan. (The latter study tests for an internal-external financing differential by classifying firms according to whether or not they belong to an industrial group.)

Unquestionably the biggest problem plaguing this literature is the difficulty in measuring Tobin's q. If q is badly measured, it is hard to be sure that the cash flow variable is capturing the effects of credit constraints rather than say, expected future earnings. (Expectations would be fully embodied in q if that variable were correctly measured.) One interesting approach to dealing with this problem has been suggested by Gilchrist and Himmelberg (1995). They measure q by using vector autoregressions to forecast a firm's expected future earnings, including cash flow as one of the predictive variables. Then, in their second-stage regressions, they include only the part of cash flow that is orthogonal to q. Cash flow remains a consistently important variable in their investment regressions, even after controlling for its predictive power for future earnings.

None of the tests described is foolproof, in the sense that one can construct models with perfect asset markets that generate the same empirical regularities. Given the uniformity of the empirical results and the lack of convincing positive documentation for alternative explanations, however, it is hard to deny some role to asset market imperfections in limiting both flows of outside funds to firms and investment.

■

Appendix 6A   Recontracting Sovereign Debt Repayments

In the models of sections 6.1.1 and 6.2.1, we assumed that if creditors could threaten a country with ηY in default costs (where Y is output), they could force it to make up to ηY in debt payments. For two reasons, this magnitude probably overstates creditors' power to enforce repayment. First, imposing sanctions is costly for creditors and does not necessarily yield them any direct benefits—other than the satisfaction of revenge! Second, a country may be able temporarily to avoid sanctions or seizure and buy time for negotiation with creditors by delaying and rerouting goods shipments.

If either of these channels is important (or if both are), creditors will be unable to make credible take-it-or-leave-it offers to debtors, such as "Pay in full or we will annihilate a fraction η of your output." Instead, actual debt repayments will be the outcome of a bargaining process. Consider, for example, the following very stylized infinite-horizon model of a small endowment economy, which is specialized in producing an exportable but consumes only an importable.[71]

The sovereign maximizes the intertemporal utility function

---

71. The model is based on Bulow and Rogoff (1989a).

$$U_t = \sum_{s=0}^{\infty} \frac{hC_{t+hs}}{(1+\delta h)^s}, \tag{54}$$

where C is consumption of the import good. The length of a period here is h; we leave this as a parameter so as to be able to consider the limit of continuous bargaining ($h \to 0$). Because the length of period is not fixed, we have written the discount factor as $1/(1+\delta h)$ instead of β as we usually do, and we interpret δ as the subjective *rate* of time preference. We assume that $\delta > r$, where $1 + rh$ is the fixed exogenous gross world rate of interest on importable goods. Finally, notice the assumption of a linear period utility function; this feature simplifies our analysis of bargaining considerably.

Each period, the country is endowed with Yh units of its export good, each of which is worth P units of the imported good on the world market. (P is constant.) While the country does not consume the export good, it cannot be forced to export it in any given period. Instead, the country may avail itself of a storage technology whereby S_t stored in period t yield $(1 - \theta h)S_t$ units after a period,

$$S_{t+h} = (1 - \theta h)S_t,$$

where $\theta > 0$ and $1 > \theta h$.[72] Storage is inefficient, but may nevertheless be relevant in situations where the country is trying to renegotiate its international debts. Think of a debtor country as producing bananas that may be seized by creditors once they are shipped abroad, but cannot be seized while they are still in the country. Thanks to the storage technology, the country can credibly threaten creditors with delayed payment if they are unwilling to reschedule or simply write down debts.

Because period utility is linear in eq. (54), there is no consumption-smoothing motive for borrowing here. Instead, the country's sole motive for borrowing is that its subjective discount rate exceeds the world interest rate ($\delta > r$). Thus the country will do all its consuming on the initial date, date t, by immediately borrowing the entire present discounted value of its future income and spending the rest of eternity repaying PYh per period. In this case the initial amount borrowed (measured in terms of imports) would be

$$D = \frac{PYh}{rh} = \frac{PY}{r}. \tag{55}$$

Let us suppose that the country actually did borrow and consume this much in the initial period. Could it actually be forced to repay PYh to lenders in each ensuing period? In general, the answer is no, even if lenders can seize 100 percent of any international shipments ($\eta = 1$ in terms of the text's model, with creditors obtaining an equal benefit). If the country has absolutely nothing to gain by shipping its goods, it will put them in storage and bargain with its creditors for repayments below the sum PYh that it owes.

Exactly how much of a reduction in its contracted payment PYh the country can get depends on the nature of the bargaining process, but the country clearly should be able to get something. After all, creditors are impatient: their discount rate is r and the goods they would otherwise seize are deteriorating at rate θ in storage. Thus creditors have something to gain by making an immediate concession that induces the sovereign to ship its output and pay at least partially what it owes.

---

72. Without affecting the results we could allow for a storage technology yielding a nonnegative return ($\theta \leq 0$), provided $-\theta < r$.

One simple model of how the country's income is divided each period draws on A. Rubinstein (1982). (Here, though, bargaining is over a flow rather than a stock.) It predicts that a key factor governing actual repayments is the relative impatience of the two countries. For the creditors, the effective discount rate (in the continuous-time limit) is $r + \theta$. (Any delay in reaching an agreement costs the creditors both because they must wait to relend any repayments they receive and because the sum being bargained over shrinks in storage.) For the debtor country, the effective discount rate is $\delta + \theta$.

Imagine first that the country simply cannot sell any of its output until it has reached an agreement with creditors (that is, $\eta = 1$). Absent private information, a Rubinstein-type model predicts that in the continuous-time limit ($h \to 0$), the two parties will reach an agreement *immediately*, with creditors receiving at most a fraction

$$\frac{\delta + \theta}{(\delta + \theta) + (r + \theta)} = \frac{\delta + \theta}{\delta + r + 2\theta} \tag{56}$$

of the country's output PY and the country receiving at least

$$\frac{r + \theta}{(\delta + \theta) + (r + \theta)} = \frac{r + \theta}{\delta + r + 2\theta}. \tag{57}$$

Of course, creditors will be repaid in full if debtors initially borrowed a fraction of PY no greater than expression (56), but only then. Anticipating that the country will try to bargain over repayments, creditors therefore will never make an initial loan bigger than

$$D = \left[\frac{\delta + \theta}{(\delta + \theta) + (r + \theta)} \right] \frac{PY}{r},$$

which is strictly below the amount in (55).[73]

More realistic assumptions might allow the country to consume the good it produces, or allow creditors to seize only a fraction $\eta < 1$ of exported goods. Either of these possibilities can create an "outside option" for the country that may influence the outcome of bargaining. For example, if the fraction of shipments creditors can seize, η, is less than the share in

---

73. The Rubinstein (1982) solution assumes an alternating offers framework in which the debtor and its creditors take turns making offers each period (so that the exogenous component of bargaining power is equal). When it is the country's turn to make an offer, its best strategy is to offer creditors a share just large enough so that they would rather reach an agreement immediately than wait a period to make a counteroffer. The reverse holds when it is the creditors' turn to make an offer. Thus, on its turn, the debtor will offer creditors

$$x_t = \frac{1 - \theta h}{1 + rh} x'_{t+h},$$

where x_t is the share of output and goods in storage the country offers the creditors on date t and x'_{t+h} is the share the creditors will offer themselves if they wait a period. When it is the creditors' turn, they offer the country

$$1 - x'_t = \frac{1 - \theta h}{1 + \delta h} (1 - x_{t+h}).$$

The creditors' equilibrium share, eq. (56), is found by solving for the stationary state of these two difference equations (that is, remove time subscripts and solve for x and x'), and then taking the limit as $h \to 0$. A recent exposition is contained in Mas-Colell, Whinston, and Green (1995).

eq. (56), the sovereign will be able to borrow only η percent of the present discounted value of his output, and the bargaining factors highlighted in eq. (56) may no longer be relevant. If $\eta > (\delta + \theta)/(\delta + r + 2\theta)$, however, improvements in creditors' power to seize a country's goods abroad may do little to enhance their bargaining position or, accordingly, the debtor's ability to borrow. Also, the present model endows neither creditors nor borrowers with any type of private information. Kletzer (1989) shows that with private information, debtors and creditors may reach agreement only after some delay, so that bargaining results in inefficiencies. It is also easy to make the model stochastic. In a stochastic setting, Bulow and Rogoff (1989a) reinterpret the bargaining model as an account of debt-rescheduling agreements. If shocks are observable to the two parties in the rescheduling agreement but difficult to verify in a court of law, the optimal loan contract may involve a high face value of debt, with both parties anticipating the likelihood of debt rescheduling later.

At one level, the main results derived earlier in this chapter are easily modified to incorporate the possibility of bargaining. We can then reinterpret the parameter η as the outcome of a bargaining process rather than simply an exogenous seizure-technology parameter. However, a bargaining perspective raises other important issues that are somewhat obscured by the more mechanical repayment model of the text. Perhaps the most important is the possibility that creditor-country governments might be drawn into the bargaining process and gamed into making side payments. Think of the sovereign's foreign creditors as private agents representing only a small fraction of creditor-country taxpayers. By interfering in trade with the debtor country, private creditors inflict damage on their compatriots as well as on debtor-country citizens. Therefore, creditor-country governments may be willing to make side payments to "facilitate" rescheduling agreements. This view assumes that creditor-country governments will not simply abrogate international loan contracts and deprive creditors of their legal right of retribution. The creditor country may be reluctant to do so if it is concerned that such abrogation will undermine the reputation of its constitution and its legal system.

Bulow and Rogoff (1988a) develop a model of three-way bargaining among debtor-country governments, creditor-country governments, and private creditors. They show that expected future government side payments may increase the borrowing limits of small debtor countries. They also show that from an ex ante perspective, debtors facing competitive lenders capture the entire surplus from anticipated side payments. In practice, side payments can take many forms, ranging from trade concessions to subsidized loans channeled through multilateral lenders or bilateral export-import banks.

Appendix 6B   Risk Sharing with Default Risk and Saving

This appendix derives the results summarized in section 6.1.1.6. Recall the assumptions made there, that a small country maximizes

$$U_1 = u(C_1) + \beta E\{u(C_2)\}, \qquad \beta < 1,$$

receives an endowment $Y_1 = \bar{Y}$ in the first period, and begins that period without foreign assets or debt. In the second period the (stochastic) endowment is

$$Y_2 = \bar{Y} + \epsilon.$$

The mean-zero shock ϵ can take any of the values $\epsilon_1, \ldots, \epsilon_N$ in the closed interval $[\underline{\epsilon}, \bar{\epsilon}]$, where $\bar{Y} + \underline{\epsilon} > 0$. Risk-neutral insurers compete on date 1 to offer the country zero-expected-profit contracts covering uncertain date 2 output, and on date 1 the country can borrow or lend at a given world interest rate $r > 0$, where $\beta(1 + r) = 1$.

The full insurance allocation is essentially the same as in the model without date 1 consumption and saving. If the country could somehow credibly forswear default, it would be able to obtain a riskless date 2 consumption level of $\bar{Y}$ by committing to the insurance-payment schedule $P(\epsilon) = \epsilon$. Given that $C_2 = \bar{Y}$ is feasible (for all ϵ) and that $\beta(1 + r) = 1$, the optimal choice for C_1 is $\bar{Y}$, making optimal date 1 saving zero.

With default risk, however, the full-insurance contract is not incentive compatible. The optimal incentive-compatible contract maximizes U_1 subject to the intertemporal budget constraints (which must hold for each ϵ)

$$C_2(\epsilon) = \bar{Y} + \epsilon - P(\epsilon) + (1 + r)(\bar{Y} - C_1),$$

the zero-profit condition (1), which requires that $E\{P(\epsilon)\} = 0$, and the incentive compatibility constraints, which, in the present context, are (for each ϵ)

$$P(\epsilon) \leq \eta(\bar{Y} + \epsilon) + (1 + r)(\bar{Y} - C_1) \tag{58}$$

instead of eq. (2). These incentive constraints reflect the assumption of section 6.1.1.6 that a sovereign defaulting on payments to insurers forfeits any interest and principal on its date 1 foreign investment. (Foreign creditors can compensate themselves by seizing the sovereign's own foreign assets if it defaults.)[74]

The Lagrangian for this problem is

$$\mathcal{L} = u(C_1) + \sum_{i=1}^{N} \pi(\epsilon_i)\beta u[\bar{Y} + \epsilon_i - P(\epsilon_i) + (1 + r)(\bar{Y} - C_1)]$$

$$- \sum_{i=1}^{N} \lambda(\epsilon_i)[P(\epsilon_i) - \eta(\bar{Y} + \epsilon_i) - (1 + r)(\bar{Y} - C_1)] + \mu \sum_{i=1}^{N} \pi(\epsilon_i)P(\epsilon_i).$$

The Kuhn-Tucker necessary conditions for C_1 and $P(\epsilon)$ are

$$u'(C_1) = \beta(1 + r) \sum_{i=1}^{N} \pi(\epsilon_i)u'[C_2(\epsilon_i)] + (1 + r) \sum_{i=1}^{N} \lambda(\epsilon_i), \tag{59}$$

$$\pi(\epsilon)\beta u'[C_2(\epsilon)] + \lambda(\epsilon) = \mu\pi(\epsilon), \tag{60}$$

and the complementary slackness condition is

$$\lambda(\epsilon)[\eta(\bar{Y} + \epsilon) + (1 + r)(\bar{Y} - C_1) - P(\epsilon)] = 0, \tag{61}$$

where $\lambda(\epsilon) \geq 0$, for all ϵ.

The first of these conditions differs from the standard Euler equation in that higher date 1 consumption lowers the amount of insurance available next period by raising the benefit of default relative to its cost. This effect tends to encourage saving. The second and third conditions are analogous to eqs. (4) and (5).

To proceed, sum both sides of eq. (60) over $i = 1, \ldots, N$ and infer from eq. (59) that

---

74. In case $C_1 > \bar{Y}$, the constraint says that the total sum owed to foreign creditors in state ϵ, $P(\epsilon) + (1 + r)(C_1 - \bar{Y})$, must be no greater than the cost of their sanctions in that state.

$$u'(C_1) = \beta(1+r) \sum_{i=1}^{N} \pi(\epsilon_i) u'[C_2(\epsilon_i)] + (1+r) \sum_{i=1}^{N} \lambda(\epsilon_i) = (1+r)\mu.$$

Let's simplify the problem as before by dividing $[\underline{\epsilon}, \bar{\epsilon}]$ into the disjoint intervals $[\underline{\epsilon}, e)$, on which constraint (58) does *not* bind [and where $\lambda(\epsilon) = 0$ by eq. (61)], and $[e, \bar{\epsilon}]$, on which constraint (58) holds with equality. Combining the preceding equation $u'(C_1) = (1+r)\mu$ with eq. (60) for $\epsilon \in [\underline{\epsilon}, e)$ yields

$$u'(C_1) = (1+r)\beta u'[C_2(\epsilon)] = u'[C_2(\epsilon)] \qquad (62)$$

[recall $\beta(1+r) = 1$], which implies that the country equates consumption across dates for those states in which sanctions more than suffice to compel compliance with loan contracts. For ϵ such that $\lambda(\epsilon) > 0$, however, constraint (58) holds as an equality. But in these cases we can solve for $P(\epsilon)$ and $C_2(\epsilon)$ from constraint (58) and the intertemporal budget constraint:

$$P(\epsilon) = \eta(\bar{Y} + \epsilon) - (1+r)(C_1 - \bar{Y}), \qquad C_2(\epsilon) = (1-\eta)(\bar{Y} + \epsilon). \qquad (63)$$

The implications thus are similar to those of the simpler case worked out in the text. Where the repayment constraint is binding, a small unexpected drop in output increases net payments to the country by only a fraction η of the output decline. On the other hand, where the constraint is not binding, net payments to creditors rise one-for-one with ϵ, which is the only way $C_2(\epsilon)$ can be maintained at C_1 ex post in that region, as eq. (62) requires.

It is straightforward to solve for the shape of the optimal $P(\epsilon)$ schedule. Observe that at the critical value $\epsilon = e$ when $\lambda(\epsilon)$ first becomes zero, the last two eqs. (62) and (63) both hold, implying that

$$C_1 = (1-\eta)(\bar{Y} + e). \qquad (64)$$

This equation leads to part of the solution for $P(\epsilon)$. For $\epsilon \in [\underline{\epsilon}, e)$,

$$C_2(\epsilon) = \bar{Y} + \epsilon - P(\epsilon) + (1+r)(\bar{Y} - C_1) = C_1$$

by eq. (62), so substituting eq. (64) for C_1, one can infer the equation for $P(\epsilon)$ on the unconstrained region $[\underline{\epsilon}, e)$. Similarly, eq. (64) and the first equation in (63) give an equation describing $P(\epsilon)$ over the constrained region $[e, \bar{\epsilon}]$. The results are

$$P(\epsilon) = \begin{cases} \epsilon + (2+r)[\eta\bar{Y} - (1-\eta)e], & \epsilon \in [\underline{\epsilon}, e) \\ \eta\epsilon + (2+r)\left[\eta\bar{Y} - \dfrac{1+r}{2+r}(1-\eta)e\right], & \epsilon \in [e, \bar{\epsilon}]. \end{cases} \qquad (65)$$

A figure similar to Figure 6.1 shows the implied $P(\epsilon)$ schedule.

Solution is straightforward when ϵ is uniformly distributed. We leave the general case as an exercise, and restrict ourselves to solving the interesting special case $\eta = 0$. Under these assumptions $\underline{\epsilon} = -\bar{\epsilon}$, and eq. (65) becomes

$$P(\epsilon) = \begin{cases} \epsilon - (2+r)e, & \epsilon \in [-\bar{\epsilon}, e) \\ -(1+r)e, & \epsilon \in [e, \bar{\epsilon}]. \end{cases} \qquad (66)$$

This implies that the zero-profit condition (1) is

$$\int_{-\bar{\epsilon}}^{e} [\epsilon - (2+r)e] \frac{d\epsilon}{2\bar{\epsilon}} - \int_{e}^{\bar{\epsilon}} (1+r)e \frac{d\epsilon}{2\bar{\epsilon}} = 0,$$

which reduces to the quadratic

$$e^2 + [2(3 + 2r)\bar{e}]e + \bar{e}^2 = 0.$$

The relevant root of this equation is

$$e = -\bar{e}[3 + 2r - \sqrt{(3 + 2r)^2 - 1}] \in (-\bar{e}, 0).$$

What explains the availability of partial insurance ($e > -\bar{e}$) despite the total inefficacy of sanctions ($\eta = 0$)? By eq. (64), the country's date 1 saving when $\eta = 0$ is $\bar{Y} - (\bar{Y} + e) = -e > 0$. Thus creditors are in a position to confiscate $-(1 + r)e$ on date 2 should the country renege on its contract. For realizations of $\epsilon \in [-\bar{e}, e)$, eq. (66) calls for the country to pay insurers an amount $P(\epsilon) = \epsilon - (2 + r)e$ strictly below the amount of country principal and interest that insurers could seize.[75] For $\epsilon \in [-\bar{e}, e)$, date 2 consumption therefore is stabilized at

$$C_2(\epsilon) = \bar{Y} + \epsilon - P(\epsilon) - (1 + r)e$$

$$= \bar{Y} + \epsilon - [\epsilon - (2 + r)e] - (1 + r)e$$

$$= \bar{Y} + e.$$

In contrast, for $\epsilon \in [e, \bar{e}]$, eq. (66) has the country pay out an amount exactly equal to its own claims on foreigners. In this constrained region of $[-\bar{e}, \bar{e}]$, the country thus is restricted to the autarky consumption level $C_2(\epsilon) = \bar{Y} + \epsilon$.

The result is that by saving $-e$ on date 1, the country can credibly promise to comply with a zero-profit contract that insures it against shocks $\epsilon < e$.

Exercises

1.   *Two-sided default risk.* Consider the following one-period, two-country version of the model in section 6.1.1, in which Home and Foreign agents have identical utility functions $u(C)$ [$u(C^*)$]. Home's endowment is given by $Y = \bar{Y} + \epsilon$, while Foreign's is given by $Y^* = \bar{Y} - \epsilon$, where ϵ is zero-mean random shock that is symmetrically distributed around 0 on the interval $[-\bar{e}, \bar{e}]$. Home and Foreign agents write insurance contracts prior to the realization of the relative output shock, which specify a payment by Home to Foreign of $P(\epsilon)$ [$= -P^*(\epsilon)$]. Obviously, in the absence of default risk, $P(\epsilon) = \epsilon$, and $C = C^* = \bar{Y}$: there is perfect risk-sharing. Assume, however, that due to enforcement limitations, any equilibrium contract must obey the incentive compatibility constraints:

$$P(\epsilon) \le \eta Y, \qquad P^*(\epsilon) \le \eta Y^*.$$

The questions below refer to the efficient symmetric incentive-compatible contract. (You may answer using a graph.)

(a) Show that there is a range $[-e, e]$ such that $C = C^*$ for $\epsilon \in [-e, e]$. Solve for e. (This is not hard.)

(b) Characterize $C(\epsilon)$ and $C^*(\epsilon)$ for ϵ outside the interval $[-e, e]$.

---

75. The inequality $\epsilon - (2 + r)e < -(1 + r)e$ is equivalent to $\epsilon < e$.

2. *Indexed debt contracts in lieu of insurance.* Again reconsider the small-country model of section 6.1.1, where consumption takes place only in period 2. Now, instead of being able to write insurance contracts, the country is only able to borrow in the form of equity or output-indexed debt contracts. In particular, it borrows D in period 1 and makes *nonnegative* payments $P(\epsilon) \geq 0$ in period 2 subject to the zero-profit condition

$$\sum_{i=1}^{N} \pi(\epsilon_i) P(\epsilon_i) = (1+r)D$$

and the incentive compatibility constraint

$$P(\epsilon_i) \leq \eta[\bar{Y} + (1+r)D + \epsilon_i], \qquad \forall i.$$

We justify this last constraint as follows. As in the text, the country receives a second-period endowment of $\bar{Y}$ and has no first-period endowment (nor inherited capital stock). In addition, it has access to a linear local production technology such that $F(K) = (1+r)K$. Thus the country can invest borrowed funds locally and still earn the world market rate of return. Note that K will equal D, given our assumptions. Observe also that in this formulation, creditors pay cash up front so their credibility is never at issue.

(a) Treating D as given, characterize the optimal incentive-compatible $P(\epsilon)$ schedule. [Hint: $C(\underline{\epsilon}) = \bar{Y} + \underline{\epsilon} + (1+r)D$.] Draw a diagram illustrating your answer.

(b) If the country has access only to equity contracts, is it equally well off as in the text's case of pure insurance contracts? (Consider how large η must be to achieve full insurance in each of the two cases.)

3. *A problem on reputational equilibrium.* This problem places a number of restrictions on contracts and investment which you should take as given for now; we will allow you to critique them at the end. Suppose that the infinitely lived representative agent in a small country has utility function given by

$$U_t = E_t \left\{ \sum_{s=t}^{\infty} \beta^{s-t} u(C_s) \right\},$$

where $\beta(1+r) = 1$. The country cannot lend abroad or obtain pure insurance contracts. It can borrow but exclusively in the form of one-period bonds that must pay risk-neutral foreign lenders the expected return $1+r$. Repayments $P(\epsilon_t)$ may, however, be indexed to ϵ_t (explicitly or implicitly). Consumption each period is given by

$$C_t = F(D_t) + \epsilon_t - P(\epsilon_t),$$

where $P(\epsilon_t) \geq 0$ and $\epsilon_t \in [\underline{\epsilon}, \bar{\epsilon}]$ is a positive ($\epsilon > 0$), serially uncorrelated shock such that $E_{t-1}\{\epsilon_t\} = e > 0$. The term $F(D_t)$ comes from the assumption that only fresh foreign capital may be used for investment; capital depreciates by 100 percent in production. The production function satisfies $F'(D) > 0$ and $F''(D) < 0$ for $D < \tilde{D}$, and $F'(D) = 1 + r$ for $D \geq \tilde{D}$, where $\tilde{D}$ is a constant.

(a) Assume that the country can commit to any feasible repayment schedule. Characterize the optimal contract. Under what conditions can this contract be enforced as a trigger-strategy equilibrium where the only penalty to default is that the country is excluded from all future borrowing?

(b) Briefly: How reasonable is the assumption here that the country cannot use its own income to finance investment, even though its income can be used to make debt repayments to foreigners? Recall the discussion of the text in section 6.2.2.

(c) Briefly: How important is the assumption that the country is prohibited from lending money abroad? Recall the discussion of section 6.1.2.4.

4.   *Collateralizable second-period endowment.* Take the small-country model with moral hazard in investment of section 6.4.1. Assume now that in addition to receiving first-period endowment Y_1, each entrepreneur receives *exogenous* second-period endowment income E_2. This income is in addition to any income received from the investment project or from secret lending abroad. E_2 is fully observable and can be used either for second-period consumption or to help pay off loans.

(a) How does the introduction of collateralizable future income change the analysis? You need not make your answer self-contained; you can just show how the **IC** and **ZP** curves are modified, and why.

(b) Suppose now that there is only first-period endowment, but that in the second period, the government must pay off a per capita debt D^G. It finances the debt by placing a second-period tax of τ on successful entrepreneurs. (Obviously, unsuccessful entrepreneurs cannot be made to pay any tax in the second period, as they have no observable income.) Show how the overhang of government debt reduces investment.

5.   *Fiscal policy with moral hazard.* Consider again the model of section 6.4.1 (with only a first-period endowment), but now assume that for every entrepreneur, there is a "saver." Savers have the same utility function and initial endowment Y_1 as entrepreneurs, but do not have access to any investment project. They can either lend their money to local entrepreneurs or lend abroad at rate $1 + r$. Note that the presence of local savers does not change the determination of equilibrium investment, since they do not affect the world interest rate. Assume that Y_1 is sufficiently small so that in market equilibrium, investment is below its full-information efficient level.

   Can you think of any way a home social planner can make some agents better off without making any others worse off? Assume that the social planner faces the same information constraints as other agents; that is, the planner is not able directly to observe an individual entrepreneur's choice of I, only final project output Y_2 (which equals either Z if successful or 0 if not). Consider a scheme whereby the planner makes each saver pay a first-period tax of τ_1, transferring the income to entrepreneurs. Then, in the second period, the planner places a tax τ_2 on successful entrepreneurs, transferring the money back to savers.

6.   *Debt overhang and debt forgiveness.* Consider a small open economy that inherits a very large (effectively infinite) debt, D, which is scheduled to be paid off in the second period. The representative agent in the country has the utility function

$$U_1 = \log C_1 + \beta \log C_2.$$

First-period endowment income is Y_1. Capital depreciates by 100 percent in production and second-period output is $Y_2 = I^\alpha$, where $I = K_2$ is date 1 investment. In the second period, creditors will be able to force the country to pay ηY_2 in debt repayments. (Assume that the debt is so large that the country cannot fully repay its debt even if it invests all its resources.)

(a) Solve for the country's optimal choice of investment, I^D, and the implied level or repayments to creditors, $\eta(I^D)^\alpha$.

(b) Now assume that entering period 1, creditors decide partly to forgive the country's debt, writing down the face value to $\eta(I^D)^\alpha$, the amount they expect to be repaid if they do nothing. Does this cost the creditors anything? Can the debtor country benefit?

(c) Assume that creditors have no interest in the welfare of the country and care only about maximizing debt repayments. How far should they write down the country's debt, if at all? You may find it convenient to answer this part with a graph.

It is often claimed that long-run per capita output growth is the only measure of economic performance that really matters. While this is a gross overstatement, it is certainly true that over long horizons, growth differentials can swamp the temporary effects of recessions and booms. Over the period 1950–92, the increase in Japan's real per capita GDP outstripped that of the United States by an average of 1.5 percent per year. It is exceedingly unlikely that this growth differential will be maintained indefinitely, but if it were, per capita income in Japan would be more than four times that of the United States by the end of the twenty-first century.

In earlier chapters of this book we examined many key determinants of long-run growth—investment, population expansion, and productivity improvements, to name a few. But until now we have not analyzed growth in any systematic fashion. What determines international growth rate differences? Do countries' living standards tend to converge over long periods, or can per capita output differences persist indefinitely? How do government policies affect long-run growth? What is the role of integration into the world capital market and trading system? In this chapter we consider a number of different approaches to analyzing these issues.

We begin by looking at the rudimentary but justly celebrated closed-economy neoclassical growth model of Solow (1956) and Swan (1956), which highlights the effects of saving, technological advance, and population expansion.[1] Despite its primitive static demand structure and neglect of international borrowing and lending, this simple model yields vital insights and intuition. Many of the results can be preserved in models with more fully specified microfoundations, although some turn out to be sensitive to how current generations weigh the welfare of future generations. One fairly robust prediction of these closed-economy neoclassical growth models is that steady-state output per worker can differ across countries because of differences in nontechnological factors such as saving rates and population growth. Another prediction is that convergence to the steady-state growth path is gradual, since all new capital construction must be financed out of domestic savings.

In a fully integrated global economy, cross-country differences in (risk-adjusted) rates of return on capital are eliminated, even in the short run. For a Solow-type economy, this fact implies that the equalization of all countries' per worker output levels is immediate (given common production technologies worldwide). Why, then, does the Solow model seem to have some degree of predictive power? Motivated by our analyses in Chapter 6, we look at how frictions in international capital markets can impede absolute convergence in incomes, both in the short run and in the long run.

Regardless of whether they yield absolute convergence, a major limitation of all neoclassical growth models is that they treat technological progress as exogenous.

---

1. For an excellent discussion of the intellectual history of first-generation growth theory, see Wan (1971).

So we also consider models of *endogenous growth* that attempt to explain the pace of research and development. Because these models typically feature externalities and monopolistic firms, they often imply a role for government intervention (at least in theory). As we shall see, endogenous growth models also point to a number of subtle channels through which economic integration can affect trading partners' welfare levels and rates of GDP growth.

The reader will note we revert to perfect-foresight models for a significant portion of this chapter's analysis. The main reason for this modeling choice is that many of the key topics we want to examine center around long-run trends rather than short-term fluctuations. Nevertheless, there are some important questions, involving international business cycles and investment flows, that require integrating short-term fluctuations into long-run growth analysis. Therefore, we close the chapter by taking up some explicitly stochastic growth models.

7.1   The Neoclassical Growth Model

The neoclassical model of long-run economic growth is built around a standard production function with constant returns to scale in capital and labor. It is really just a straightforward extension of models we looked at in earlier chapters, except that it allows for steady-state growth in both labor force and productivity.

7.1.1   A Model with Fixed Saving Rates: Solow and Swan

The most influential of the early neoclassical growth models is due to Solow (1956) and Swan (1956). Their framework marries a neoclassical supply side to a rudimentary Keynesian aggregate demand specification. Though neoclassical growth models with more sophisticated microfoundations have come to supplant it in modern theoretical analyses, the Solow-Swan model still provides a good vehicle for introducing some of the main concepts and issues in growth economics. We will focus on the more popular Solow variant of the model, though Swan's version is closely related.

7.1.1.1   The Model

For the reader who has made it this far into the book, the only feature of the Solow model that might give pause is the way technological progress is introduced. Typically, we have found it convenient to model technological shocks as "Hicks neutral," so that the production function can be written $Y_t = A_t F(K_t, L_t)$, where A_t is an exogenous productivity parameter and $F(K, L)$ exhibits constant returns to scale in capital and labor together. Technological progress of this form is "neutral" in the sense that it does not directly affect the marginal rate of substitution between capital and raw labor. In a growth context, however, it is more convenient to look at models with well-specified steady states, and this approach turns out to require having trend productivity growth be purely labor-augmenting, or "Harrod neutral." In this case, the production function takes the form

$$Y_t = F(K_t, E_t L_t),\tag{1}$$

where E is now the labor-augmenting technological shift parameter, so that EL may be thought of as the supply of *efficiency units* of labor. As we shall see, the Harrod-neutral specification of technological progress admits a convenient transformation of variables that would not be possible in general with the Hicks-neutral specification. For the case of a Cobb-Douglas production function, however, the two are equivalent since $K^\alpha (EL)^{1-\alpha} = AK^\alpha L^{1-\alpha}$ if $A = E^{1-\alpha}$.[2]

On the demand side, the economy is closed, and there is no government. Private saving S_t is assumed to be a fixed fraction s of current income Y_t (equal to output here), regardless of interest rates, expectations of future productivity shifts, and so on. Thus,

$$Y_t - C_t = S_t = sF(K_t, E_t L_t).\tag{2}$$

In analyzing short-run dynamics or in trying to ascertain welfare results, it is by no means innocuous to assume this simple mechanical saving function in place of one derived from individual maximization. But as we have already said, Solow's shortcut is still useful for introducing some basic growth concepts.

Because domestic saving must equal domestic investment in a closed economy, capital accumulation is given by

$$K_{t+1} - K_t = sF(K_t, E_t L_t) - \delta K_t,\tag{3}$$

where δ is the rate of depreciation.

The two key engines of growth in this model are exogenous technological change and labor-force expansion. The level of Harrod-neutral productivity E is assumed to grow at rate

$$E_{t+1} = (1 + g)E_t,\tag{4}$$

while the labor force L (which equals the population) grows at rate

$$L_{t+1} = (1 + n)L_t.\tag{5}$$

Because E and L are growing over time, it will help us visualize the economy's dynamics to use Solow's (1956) device of normalizing all the variables by the "efficiency labor supply" EL so that, for example, the capital-to-efficiency-labor ratio is given by

---

2. Recall appendix 3A. This equivalence fails to hold when the production function implies a nonunitary elasticity of substitution between capital and labor.

$$k_t^E = K_t/E_tL_t. \tag{6}$$

By using this normalization, we will be able to write the system in terms of variables that have constant instead of trending steady states.

In order to rewrite the capital accumulation equation (3) in terms of k_t^E, we divide both sides by E_tL_t to obtain

$$\frac{K_{t+1}}{E_tL_t} - \frac{K_t}{E_tL_t} = \frac{sF(K_t, E_tL_t)}{E_tL_t} - \delta\frac{K_t}{E_tL_t}. \tag{7}$$

Noting that

$$\frac{K_{t+1}}{E_tL_t} = \frac{K_{t+1}}{E_{t+1}L_{t+1}} \cdot \frac{E_{t+1}L_{t+1}}{E_tL_t} = k_{t+1}^E(1+z),$$

where $1 + z \equiv (1+n)(1+g)$, we can write eq. (7) as

$$k_{t+1}^E - k_t^E = \frac{1}{1+z}\left[sf(k_t^E) - (z+\delta)k_t^E\right], \tag{8}$$

where $f(k^E) \equiv F(K/EL, 1)$ is the intensive form of the production function.[3] Equation (8) is the central equation of the Solow growth model. The first term inside the brackets on the right-hand side gives gross saving per efficiency worker in period t. The second term reflects the downward pull on k^E caused by depreciation and growth in the efficiency labor force. Both terms are multiplied by $1/(1+z)$ because any net investment in period t must be spread over a larger number of efficiency workers in period $t+1$. Figure 7.1, with k^E on the horizontal axis, is a discrete-time version of the familiar Solow diagram. The output curve $f(k^E)$ is strictly concave because the production function is strictly concave in capital. The saving curve $sf(k^E)$ is also concave because saving is proportional to output. The vertical distance between the two curves gives consumption per efficiency worker. The linear ray $(z+\delta)k^E$ gives the savings needed to maintain any given level of k^E; it may be thought of as the $\Delta k^E = 0$ schedule. The vertical distance between the saving curve and the linear $\Delta k^E = 0$ schedule is proportional (by a factor of $1+z$) to the net increase in capital per efficiency worker, $k_{t+1}^E - k_t^E$. When the capital stock is high, $sf(k^E) < (z+\delta)k^E$, and savings are inadequate to maintain the current level of k^E. Thus the capital stock (per EL) is falling ($k_{t+1}^E - k_t^E < 0$). The opposite occurs when the capital stock is low. Therefore, over time, the economy must converge to the steady-state level $\bar{k}^E$ where

---

3. Note that by constant returns to scale,

$$\frac{1}{EL}F(K, EL) = F\left(\frac{K}{EL}, 1\right) \equiv f(k^E).$$

(Recall section 1.5.1.)

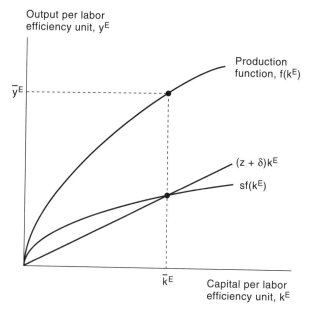

Figure 7.1
The Solow-Swan model

$$sf(\bar{k}^E) = (z+\delta)\bar{k}^E.\tag{9}$$

When the economy reaches this long-run equilibrium, $k^E = K/EL$ is constant. Thus K and Y must be growing at the gross rate $1 + z = (1+n)(1+g)$, since EL is growing at that rate. Steady-state per capita output, Y/L, grows at the rate of technological advance, $1 + g$.

We can use Figure 7.1 to consider how various parameters affect the economy's steady-state capital stock. First, consider the effect of decline in the saving rate s to s', as illustrated in Figure 7.2. In the long run, the capital-efficiency labor ratio declines and therefore so does per capita income. However, once the economy adjusts to its new lower *level* of capital, it resumes its former rate of *growth*. The fact that changes in saving rates have only temporary effects on growth is one of the most powerful and universal predictions of the Solow model. A country willing to invest more of its output can enjoy a temporary growth spurt, but this strategy cannot raise growth indefinitely. Eventually diminishing returns to capital set in. The Solow model does not predict that technologically identical closed economies necessarily converge *absolutely* to the same per capita output levels. It only predicts absolute convergence conditional on the saving rate and population growth, as well as technology.

Another implication of the model is that a rise in a country's population growth rate will lower steady-state per capita output. A rise in n causes the $(z+\delta)\bar{k}^E$

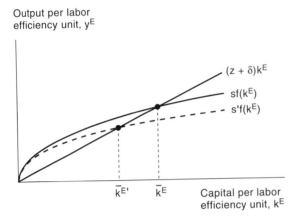

Output per labor
efficiency unit, y^E

$(z + \delta)k^E$

$sf(k^E)$

$s'f(k^E)$

$\bar{k}^{E'}$ $\bar{k}^E$ Capital per labor
efficiency unit, k^E

Figure 7.2
A decline in the saving rate

schedule to rotate upward in Figure 7.1 [since $1 + z = (1 + n)(1 + g)$], leading to a lower value of $\bar{k}^E$. Given the economy's fixed saving rate, higher population growth dilutes capital resources. The message from these exercises, of course, is that countries with faster growing populations and lower saving rates will be poorer than countries with low population growth and high saving rates.

In appendix 3A we discussed the *golden-rule* ratio of capital to efficiency labor, at which steady-state consumption per efficiency laborer, $\bar{c}^E \equiv \overline{C/EL}$, is maximized. Since $\bar{c}^E = f(\bar{k}^E) - (z + \delta)\bar{k}^E$, the golden-rule capital stock is given here by $f'(\bar{k}^{E\star}) = z + \delta$. The golden-rule steady state is generally suboptimal for a society with a positive discount rate. But capital stocks above the golden-rule level are inefficient, regardless of society's rate of time preference. The reason is that raising the capital-labor ratio above its golden-rule level adds more in replacement costs (due to depreciation and the need to equip the growing workforce) than it adds in higher output. Is there any guarantee that the steady-state $\bar{k}^E$ produced by the Solow model will be efficient? Plainly the answer is no. Saving decisions do not reflect intertemporal trade-offs, so inefficiency cannot be ruled out. To say anything meaningful about dynamic efficiency, or any welfare question for that matter, we must turn to a model that specifies individual preferences.

7.1.1.2   Cross-Country Tests of the Solow Model's Steady-State Predictions

Though informal evidence on cross-country differences in capital accumulation is suggestive (see Box 7.1), much more systematic tests of the Solow model are possible. For example, if one is prepared to make a number of ancillary assumptions, one can develop a direct cross-country test of the steady-state relationship (9). We begin by assuming a Cobb-Douglas production function, $F(K, EL) = K^\alpha (EL)^{1-\alpha}$, in which case $f(k^E) = (k^E)^\alpha$ and eq. (9) can be solved to yield

Box 7.1
Capital-Output Ratios since World War II

One simple and powerful prediction of the Solow model is that if a country suffers a sudden decline in its capital stock, say, because of an earthquake or a war, it will eventually return to the former predisaster path for its capital-output ratio. The re-building of Europe after World War II is a dramatic example of this phenomenon. Figure 7.3 graphs data, taken from Maddison (1991), on six industrialized countries' capital-output ratios in the years 1950 and 1987. (These capital stock data do not cover residential structures.) For the United States, which suffered relatively little destruction during the war, this ratio has stayed virtually constant. France, the Nether-lands, Germany, Japan, and the United Kingdom have all experienced pronounced capital deepening since 1950. Note that by Maddison's measure, the capital-output ratio in high-saving Japan was 1.9 for 1987 versus roughly 1.3 for the United States. (Because of difficulties in reconciling different national accounting conventions, one must be somewhat guarded in making cross-country capital stock comparisons.)

$$\bar{k}^{\mathrm{E}} = \left(\frac{s}{z+\delta}\right)^{\frac{1}{1-\alpha}}.$$ (10)

Of course, the level of productivity E is not observed directly, and capital stocks are difficult to measure. Thus it is more helpful to solve for steady-state output per worker. Because $Y/EL = y^{\mathrm{E}} = (k^{\mathrm{E}})^\alpha$, eq. (10) implies

$$\frac{Y_t}{L_t} = E_t \left(\frac{s}{z+\delta}\right)^{\frac{\alpha}{1-\alpha}}.$$

Taking natural logs of both sides of this equation yields

$$\log \frac{Y_t}{L_t} = \log E_0 + t \log(1+g) + \frac{\alpha}{1-\alpha}\log s - \frac{\alpha}{1-\alpha}\log(z+\delta).$$

Here we have made use of the solution to difference equation (4), which implies that $E_t = E_0(1+g)^t$ if E_0 is the level of technology in the initial year of the data sample.

Mankiw, Romer, and Weil (1992) (henceforth MRW) estimate a continuous-time version of the steady-state output per worker relationship, which we derive in ap-pendix 7A. In continuous time, $z = n + g$ (the second-order term ng disappears) and $\log(1+g)$ becomes g [because $\log(1+X) \approx X$ for small X]. Thus the pre-ceding equation becomes

$$\log \frac{Y_t}{L_t} = \log E_0 + gt + \frac{\alpha}{1-\alpha}\log s - \frac{\alpha}{1-\alpha}\log(n+g+\delta).$$ (11)

MRW estimate eq. (11) on a cross-section of 98 industrialized and developing countries, with each country taken as one observation. They set Y_t/L_t equal to

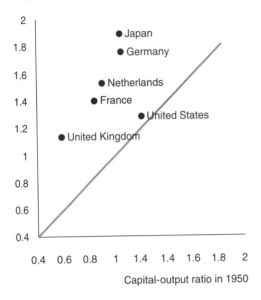

Capital-output ratio in 1987

Capital-output ratio in 1950

Figure 7.3
Industrial country capital-output ratios

end-of-sample (1985) GDP per *worker*, and use the 1960–85 average ratio of investment to GDP as a proxy for the saving rate s. (Remember, the relationship
being tested governs the long-run steady state, so it is reasonable to look at long-
run averages.) Population growth n is set equal to the 1960–85 average rate of
population growth for each country, and g and δ are both assumed to be the same
across countries, with $g + \delta = 0.05$. Finally, any differences across countries in
initial technology E_0 are assumed uncorrelated with the explanatory variables, and
are absorbed into the cross-section error term. Given these assumptions, MRW obtain the following estimates using ordinary least squares:

$$\log \frac{Y_t}{L_t} = 5.48 + 1.42 \log s - 1.97 \log(n + g + \delta), \quad R^2 = 0.59. \tag{12}$$
$$\quad (1.59) \ (0.14) \qquad (0.56)$$

(Standard errors are reported in parentheses.)

Regression (12) appears quite supportive of some of the main qualitative predictions of the Solow model: the higher a country's saving rate and the lower its
rate of population growth, the richer it is. Interestingly, MRW find they cannot reject the hypothesis that the coefficients on $\log s$ and on $\log (n + g + \delta)$ are equal in
absolute value but of opposite sign, as the model [see eq. (11)] predicts.

Whereas the empirical results are qualitatively consistent with the Solow model, MRW argue that some of eq. (12)'s quantitative implications appear, at first glance, to be quite unrealistic. In particular, the implied value for α, which equals capital's share in GDP, seems quite high. Even if one takes the lower of the two estimates for $\alpha/(1 - \alpha)$ in eq. (12) (that is, if one takes the point estimate on $\log s$), one still arrives at an implied value for α of 0.59. MRW regard this as very high, since for the United States, capital's share of output tends to be around 35 percent. [Taking the United States as representative probably exaggerates the problem, since capital's measured share tends to be higher in many other countries (especially developing countries).][4]

It is not hard to see why a high estimated value for α is needed to fit the data. The continuous-time version of eq. (10) gives the steady-state capital stock as $\bar{k}^E = [s/(n + g + \delta)]^{1/(1-\alpha)}$; output is therefore $\bar{y}^E = [s/(n + g + \delta)]^{\alpha/(1-\alpha)}$. Since MRW's specification constrains $g + \delta$ to be the same across countries, all differences in income per capita must be explained by differences in the saving rate s and the population growth rate n. But with $\alpha = 1/3$, the elasticity of output per worker with respect to these parameters is very small. Suppose for the sake of argument that the saving rate s is four times higher in the United States than in India but that population growth rates are the same. Then, if capital's share is $\alpha = 1/3$, eq. (10) puts the U.S. capital stock at 8 ($= 4^{3/2}$) times that of India. But because the exponent on capital in the production function is $1/3$ [recall that $\bar{y}^E = (\bar{k}^E)^\alpha$], the *eightfold* difference in capital stocks translates into only a *twofold* difference in per capita outputs. This is nowhere near the actual difference in income between the two countries, which was about tenfold in 1992. Differentials in birth rates similarly cannot go very far in explaining the observed income differences.

The crux of the problem is that with $\alpha = 1/3$, there are sharply decreasing returns to capital accumulation. Thus a model that ultimately relies on differences in capital-labor ratios to explain international income differentials cannot easily be reconciled with the data. If, however, one assumes that capital's share is $\alpha = 2/3$, diminishing returns set in more slowly and the model becomes much more plausible. The same calculation as before shows that a four-fold difference in saving rates translates into a sixteenfold difference in per capita incomes (4^2). The only problem is that it is difficult to justify so high a value for α when capital's share of income appears to be well under 50 percent for most countries.[5]

---

4. A value of $\alpha = 1/3$ is sometimes taken as a universal constant, but in fact internationally there appears to be a wide range of variation in capital's share of output. OECD estimates for other industrialized countries range, for example, from 0.50 in Italy to 0.35 in Canada; see Stockman and Tesar (1995, p. 171).

5. It is also sometimes argued that without a high value of α, the Solow model predicts real interest differentials that are much too large to be plausible. Suppose, for example, that the intensive production function is $A(k^E)^\alpha$ everywhere in the world, so that real interest rates are given by

$$r = \alpha A(k^E)^{\alpha-1} - \delta.$$

MRW offer an insightful rationale for viewing a high value of α as plausible. They point out that conventional measures of capital include only physical capital. If one adds human capital, the share of total capital in output becomes much larger.[6] MRW reformulate their model using a more general production function of the form

$$Y_t = K_t^\alpha H_t^\phi (E_t L_t)^{1-\alpha-\phi},$$

where H is human capital. Normalizing by efficiency (raw) labor EL turns this equation into

$$y_t^E = (k_t^E)^\alpha (h_t^E)^\phi, \tag{13}$$

where $h^E \equiv H/EL$. For simplicity, MRW treat human and physical capital symmetrically. Society is assumed to invest s_H percent of its total income Y in human capital each period, and human capital is assumed to depreciate at the same rate δ as physical capital. (See exercise 6, Chapter 4, for an alternative human-capital model.) Given these assumptions, the accumulation equation for human capital is given by

$$H_{t+1} - H_t = s_H[K_t^\alpha H_t^\phi (E_t L_t)^{1-\alpha-\phi}] - \delta H_t$$

or, in terms of ratios to efficiency labor, by

$$h_{t+1}^E - h_t^E = \frac{1}{1+z}\{s_H[(k^E)^\alpha (h^E)^\phi] - (z+\delta)h_t^E\}. \tag{14}$$

Similarly, the accumulation equation for physical capital is

Suppose that the ratio of the United States capital stock to India's is 8. Then if $\delta = 0$ and $\alpha = 1/3$, the ratio of the U.S. real interest rate to India's should be approximately $8^{-2/3} = 1/4$. (Taking depreciation into account does not substantially change the answer.) Differentials of this magnitude seem highly implausible. With $\alpha = 2/3$, the real interest rate ratio increases to $1/2$, which is still small but more reasonable.

The sensitivity of interest rates to the aggregate capital-labor ratio is, however, a special feature of the one-sector model. Suppose that there are two goods instead of one, and that one good is more capital-intensive than the other. Under specific conditions (instantaneous factor mobility across sectors and sufficiently similar initial proportions of labor and capital among trading partners), trade in the two goods will lead to factor price equalization and, therefore, real interest rate equality. As Ventura (1994) and Obstfeld (1995) point out, this result holds even without capital mobility and without international equality of capital-labor ratios. Admittedly, the condition that capital is instantly mobile across sectors within a country is quite unrealistic, but still the two-sector example shows that simple calculations based on an assumed one-sector structure can be quite misleading. (Even if factor proportions are so different that trade alone can't equalize factor prices, the Stolper-Samuelson theorem implies that international factor-price differences are reduced by trade. The key point is that technologically efficient factor reallocations within a multisector economy can alter the marginal products of labor and capital. Comparisons based on one-sector models miss this possibility.)

6. See Barro (1991) on the importance of allowing for differences in human capital in explaining cross-country growth differentials.

$$K_{t+1} - K_t = s_K[K_t^\alpha H_t^\phi (E_t L_t)^{1-\alpha-\phi}] - \delta K_t$$

or

$$k_{t+1}^E - k_t^E = \frac{1}{1+z}\{s_K[(k^E)^\alpha (h^E)^\phi] - (z+\delta)k_t^E\}. \tag{15}$$

One can easily solve eqs. (14) and (15) for the steady-state values of k^E and h^E,

$$\bar{k}^E \equiv \left[\frac{(s_K)^{1-\phi}(s_H)^\phi}{z+\delta}\right]^{\frac{1}{1-\alpha-\phi}}, \tag{16}$$

$$\bar{h}^E \equiv \left[\frac{(s_H)^{1-\alpha}(s_K)^\alpha}{z+\delta}\right]^{\frac{1}{1-\alpha-\phi}}. \tag{17}$$

Substituting eqs. (16) and (17) into the production function (13), multiplying both sides by E_t, and taking logs yields the revised estimating equation:

$$\log \frac{Y_t}{L_t} = \log E_0 + gt + \frac{\alpha}{1-\alpha-\phi}\log s_K + \frac{\phi}{1-\alpha-\phi}\log s_H$$

$$- \log \frac{\alpha+\phi}{1-\alpha-\phi}(n+g+\delta),$$

where we have again used the approximations $z \approx n + g$ and $\log(1+g) \approx g$ for ease of comparison with eq. (11). Fitting a variant of the preceding equation, in which s_H is proxied by the fraction of the working-age population in secondary school, MRW obtain estimates for both α and ϕ close to 1/3. Thus, while the estimated share for physical capital in GNP is in line with what MRW take as representative, the total share of a broader concept of capital is much higher. Note that MRW's point estimate for ϕ suggests that roughly half of labor's total share of national income may be viewed as a return to human capital.

   Though supportive of a modified Solow model, the MRW results are potentially vulnerable to several criticisms. Some or all of the right-hand side variables in the last equation surely are endogenous. For example, there can be feedback from income to family size, and there is some empirical evidence to this effect; see Razin and Sadka (1995). Also, MRW use investment as a share of GDP to proxy for saving, but investment is itself an endogenous variable. As G. Grossman and Helpman (1994) point out, investment is an important determinant of technological progress in some of the new growth literature considered later in this chapter. It is therefore difficult to believe that the growth rate of technological efficiency is exogenous and equal across countries. One might expect countries with low initial levels of technology (low E_0) to enjoy faster technology growth due to catch up, other things being equal.

Finally, the preceding regression equation is valid only in the *steady state* of the Solow model. There is no reason to presume that over much of the 1960–85 sample period countries were in a steady state. Figure 7.3 on the growth of capital-output ratios indeed suggests that even the major industrialized countries (except perhaps for the United States) were sharply increasing capital-to-effective-labor ratios over most of the postwar period.

7.1.2 Neoclassical Growth Models with Microfoundations for Aggregate Demand

From a theoretical perspective, the most unattractive feature of the Solow model is that the saving function, the model's only behavioral equation, is ad hoc. In the next two sections, we look at two fully specified closed-economy growth models, one based on a representative-agent framework, and one based on overlapping generations. Though the maximizing models yield short-run dynamics that are substantially different from the Solow model, their long-run steady states are, for the most part, qualitatively similar. Some key results, however—for example, the effects of population growth on steady-state output—turn out to be quite sensitive to how parents weigh their children's welfare.

7.1.2.1 The Ramsey-Cass-Koopmans Model of Growth with an Infinitely-Lived Representative Dynasty

In this section, we analyze a closed-economy growth model with intertemporally maximizing, infinitely-lived dynasties. Ramsey (1928), Cass (1965), and Koopmans (1965) were the first to analyze models of this type; our analysis follows Koopmans' variant. Imagine a world populated by identical infinitely-lived dynasties, each having a size L that grows at the exogenous rate $1+n$: $L_{t+1} = (1+n)L_t$. Dynasty planners are assumed to be egalitarian, weighting the consumption of each generation in proportion to its size. Thus on each date t, the representative dynasty maximizes

$$U_t = L_t \sum_{s=t}^{\infty} \beta^{s-t}(1+n)^{s-t} u\left(c_s\right), \qquad (18)$$

where c_t is consumption of the representative dynasty member alive at time t. To insure bounded dynasty utility, it is necessary to assume $\beta\left(1+n\right) \leq 1$. (Actually, as we shall clarify shortly, a somewhat stronger assumption is needed to insure that utility is bounded in the presence of technological progress leading to growing dynasty consumption.)

It is important to stress how this model differs from the P. Weil (1989a) overlapping generations model we looked at in Chapter 3. In that model, population expansion resulted in new families that received no bequests from existing families. Here new births are additions to existing families, each consisting of members who are mutually connected by intergenerational altruism.

As in the Solow model, labor-augmenting technological advance E proceeds exogenously at rate g: $E_{t+1} = (1 + g)E_t$. As a shortcut to solving the model, we will assume that each dynasty runs its own constant-returns-to-scale production function. From earlier chapters we know that an identical equilibrium allocation would be reached if there were a decentralized market for capital and labor, thanks to the symmetry of the model. As a further (and equally innocuous) simplifying assumption, we set depreciation $\delta = 0$. The period budget constraint of the representative dynasty is therefore given by

$$K_{t+1} = K_t + F(K_t, E_t L_t) - C_t.$$

Since we have written the dynasty utility function in per capita terms, it is convenient to express the dynasty budget constraint in per capita terms also. Dividing both sides of the preceding equation by L_t yields

$$k_{t+1} - k_t = \frac{F(k_t, E_t) - c_t}{1 + n} - \frac{nk_t}{1 + n}, \tag{19}$$

where $k_t \equiv K_t / L_t$. Note that $F(k_t, E_t)$ is the per worker (as opposed to the per efficiency worker) production function; that is, $F(k, E) = F(K, EL)/L$. We will later normalize by efficiency units EL as in the Solow model, but only after deriving the first-order conditions for the dynasty problem.

The first-order Euler equation obtained by maximizing eq. (18) subject to eq. (19) is

$$u'(c_t) = [1 + F_K(k_{t+1}, E_{t+1})]\beta u'(c_{t+1}). \tag{20}$$

To clarify the conditions needed for steady-state growth in the presence of technological progress, we specialize to the isoelastic class of utility functions,

$$u(c) = \frac{c^{1-\frac{1}{\sigma}}}{1 - \frac{1}{\sigma}}, \tag{21}$$

in which case the Euler condition (20) becomes

$$c_{t+1}/c_t = \beta^\sigma \left[1 + F_K(k_{t+1}, E_{t+1})\right]^\sigma. \tag{22}$$

With isoelastic utility, existence of a steady-state growth path requires the parameter restriction

$$\beta(1 + n)(1 + g)^{(\sigma - 1)/\sigma} < 1, \tag{23}$$

as otherwise the objective function (18) is not bounded. The need for this restriction is easily understood by imposing isoelastic period utility on the objective function (18), and guessing (correctly) that c_t must grow at rate $1 + g$ in the steady state. When $g = 0$, restriction (23) reduces to $\beta(1 + n) < 1$.

The equilibrium of the system is characterized by the Euler equation (22) and the resource constraint (19). To transform the model so that we can visualize its dynamics using a phase diagram, it is once again helpful to normalize by EL rather than simply by L. To do so, we divide both sides of eqs. (19) and (22) by E_t to obtain

$$k_{t+1}^{E} - k_t^{E} = \frac{f(k_t^{E}) - c_t^{E}}{1+z} - \frac{z}{1+z}k_t^{E}, \tag{8'}$$

$$\frac{c_{t+1}^{E}}{c_t^{E}} = \frac{\beta^{\sigma}[1 + f'(k_{t+1}^{E})]^{\sigma}}{1+g}, \tag{24}$$

where, as in the Solow model, $(1+z) \equiv (1+n)(1+g)$, $c_t^{E} \equiv C_t/E_tL_t$, $k_t^{E} \equiv K_t/E_tL_t$, and $f(k^{E})$ is the intensive form of the production function.

In Figure 7.4 the vertical $c_{t+1}^{E}/c_t^{E} = 1$ schedule (or equivalently, the $\Delta c^{E} = 0$ schedule) intersects the k^{E} axis at the unique steady-state value of capital per efficiency labor units, $\bar{k}^{E}$, such that consumption per efficiency labor unit is constant. Equation (24) shows that the steady-state value of k^{E} is given by

$$f'(\bar{k}^{E}) = \frac{(1+g)^{1/\sigma}}{\beta} - 1. \tag{25}$$

In the absence of technology growth ($g = 0$), eq. (25) simply states that the steady-state marginal product of capital equals the rate of time preference, $(1 - \beta)/\beta$. If $g > 0$, however, then dynasty planners will wish to convert some portion of expected future efficiency gains into present consumption. This desire to tilt consumption toward the present will push the steady-state interest rate above the rate of time preference. Note that, as drawn, the steady-state capital stock lies below its golden-rule level, defined by $1 + f'(\bar{k}^{E*}) = (1+g)(1+n)$. In fact, eq. (23) [a restriction necessary for lifetime utility (18) to be finite in the steady state] and eq. (25) together imply that the long-run equilibrium must be dynamically efficient.

The hump-shaped $\Delta k^{E} = 0$ schedule is the locus of points such that there is no tendency for k^{E} to rise or fall. It is given by $f(k_t^{E}) - c_t^{E} - zk_t^{E} = 0$, so that steady-state consumption per efficiency unit of labor equals

$$\bar{c}^{E} = f(\bar{k}^{E}) - z\bar{k}^{E}. \tag{26}$$

Since consumption per efficiency labor is constant in the steady state, consumption per capita must be growing at $1 + g$, the growth rate of technological efficiency.

Figure 7.4 also shows the economy's adjustment to the steady state. To the right of the steady-state capital stock, the marginal product of capital is below its steady-state level, so by eq. (24), c^{E} is falling. It is rising when $k^{E} < \bar{k}^{E}$. Equation (8') shows that k^{E} is falling whenever c^{E} is greater than $f(k^{E}) - zk^{E}$ and is rising in the opposite case. Thus for any initial level of k^{E} there is a unique optimal consumption level c^{E} placing the economy on the saddle path **SS** converging to

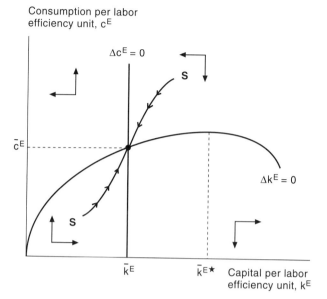

Figure 7.4
The Ramsey-Cass-Koopmans model

the steady state. (In section 7.4.3, we will illustrate in a closely related model how to solve analytically for the dynamics in the neighborhood of the steady state.)

How do the predictions of the Koopmans growth model compare with those of the Solow model? Let's think first about a decline in the saving rate which, in the Solow model, leads to a new steady state with lower output and capital. In the Koopmans framework, saving will decline if people become more impatient to consume. Thus the perturbation most analogous to an exogenous decline in the saving rate is a fall in the subjective discount factor β. Equation (25) shows that a rise in impatience leads to a lower steady-state level of capital per efficiency labor unit, just as does a fall in the saving rate in the Solow model.[7]

Figure 7.5 illustrates the dynamics on the assumption that the economy is in a steady state before β falls. An increase in impatience leads to an immediate *upward* jump in consumption to the new saddle path S'S'. As the economy's capital stock is run down, however, output and consumption per efficiency labor unit both fall until the economy settles at its new long-run position, in which consumption is lower than in the initial steady state.

Consider next a rise in the population growth rate n. The $\Delta k^E = 0$ schedule shifts downward as in Figure 7.6. With higher population growth, more investment is

---

7. From eq. (25) $d\bar{k}^E/d\beta = -[1 + f'(\bar{k}^E)]/\beta f''(\bar{k}^E)$, which is positive because the production function is strictly concave.

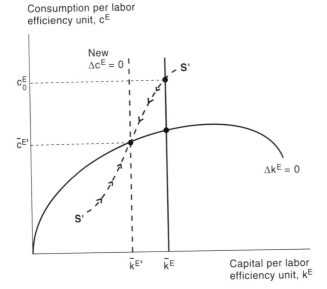

Figure 7.5
An increase in subjective impatience

required to equip newly born efficiency labor units. The $\Delta c^E = 0$ schedule does not shift, however, and therefore $\bar{k}^E$ does not move. The economy therefore adjusts immediately to the new steady state, in which output per efficiency labor unit is unchanged but consumption is lower. Why doesn't the path of output fall as in the Solow model? In the Koopmans model, dynastic planners are forward looking and weigh the utility of future generations in making today's consumption and investment decisions. When the dynasty expects more progeny, it provides for them by cutting current consumption today, thereby maintaining the same path of capital per dynasty member as before the rise in the birth rate. In the Solow model, by contrast, the saving rate is assumed fixed, so there can be no rise in saving to accommodate a higher number of descendants. This contrast suggests that one might be more likely to obtain Solow-Swan-type population-growth-rate results in a forward-looking framework where the utility of future generations is somehow down weighted.

One such variant of the neoclassical model that has been widely utilized in the literature is based on the dynasty utility function

$$U_t = L_t \sum_{s=t}^{\infty} \left(\frac{\beta}{1+n} \right)^{s-t} (1+n)^{s-t} u(c_s) = L_t \sum_{s=t}^{\infty} \beta^{s-t} u(c_s). \tag{27}$$

In this dynasty utility function, it is assumed that the utilities of individual future progeny are weighted inversely to the size of their cohort. It isn't hard to see that in this model, steady-state k^E satisfies

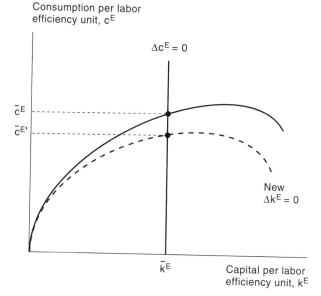

Figure 7.6
Effects of faster population growth

$$f'(\bar{k}^E) = \frac{(1+g)^{1/\sigma}}{\beta/(1+n)} - 1 \tag{28}$$

instead of eq. (25).[8] Now a rise in n changes the capital stock in the same way as a "pure" increase in impatience (a fall in β), so the results are analogous to those of the Solow model.

An alternative way to reduce the influence of future generations on today's saving decisions is to adopt an overlapping generations framework, which we turn to next.

7.1.2.2   An Overlapping Generations Growth Model

We next look at a closed-economy version of the overlapping generations Weil (1989a) model from section 3.7.3. Recall that in Weil's model, all agents are infinitely-lived, but newborns form their own households and do not receive any bequests. In deriving the equilibrium, we can't use the shortcut of assuming autarkic production, as in the previous section. Here, agents of different vintages will

---

8. You can derive this equation by following the steps in the text, starting with the Euler equation

$$u'(c_t) = [1 + F_K(k_{t+1}, E_{t+1})] \left(\frac{\beta}{1+n} \right) u'(c_{t+1}),$$

which replaces eq. (20) when eq. (27) rather than eq. (18) is the maximand.

turn out to own different amounts of capital in equilibrium, so efficient production requires trade in factor services. To simplify, we abstract from productivity growth (setting $g = 0$) and assume log utility. Both assumptions are easily relaxed.

An individual born on date v (the individual's vintage) maximizes the utility function

$$U_t^v = \sum_{s=t}^{\infty} \beta^{s-t} \log(c_s^v) \qquad (29)$$

on date t. Total population (equals labor supply) grows at rate n as given by eq. (5). Here, of course, it is the number rather than the size of households that is growing at rate n. We normalize the size of the initial vintage $v = 0$ (also the initial population) at $L_0 = 1$.

Each period, agents earn income from wages and from renting out capital. The period budget constraint for a family of vintage v is given by

$$k_{t+1}^v = (1 + r_t)k_t^v + w_t - c_t^v, \qquad (30)$$

where r_t is the market return on capital held between $t - 1$ and t, and w_t is the period t wage rate.[9] Maximizing utility (29) subject to the budget constraint (30) yields the Euler condition for the vintage v dynasty as

$$\frac{c_{t+1}^v}{c_t^v} = (1 + r_{t+1})\beta. \qquad (31)$$

We next need to aggregate the Euler and capital accumulation equations across the different vintages to derive the dynamic equations governing aggregate per capita consumption and capital. Remember from Chapter 3, eq. (65), that the aggregate per capita value of any variable X_t can be found by aggregating over agents from all vintages from 0 through t and then dividing by total population:

$$x_t = \frac{x_t^0 + nx_t^1 + n(1 + n)x_t^2 + \ldots + n(1 + n)^{t-1}x_t^t}{(1 + n)^t}.$$

Aggregate per capita variables are lowercase but naturally carry no vintage superscripts.[10] Following the same aggregation procedure as for the asset accumulation condition in the Weil model [eq. (67) of Chapter 3], we can write budget equation

---

9. Compared to the model of Chapter 3, the economy here is closed, so foreign bonds are not a component of aggregate wealth. Individual vintages can, however, lend to other vintages. To reduce the notational burden, we avoid a separate symbol for such domestic bond holdings; one can instead interpret k^v in eq. (30) as vintage v's total financial wealth. Of course, private bond holdings will net out when we aggregate financial wealth across the whole population. The model of section 3.7.3 did not allow for capital accumulation. Obviously, we abstract from government here.

10. Recall from Chapter 3 that if *total* population is growing at rate n, and if the size of the initial population, L_0 (also vintage $v = 0$), is 1, then vintage $v = 1$ has n members, vintage $v = 2$ has $(1 + n)^2 - (1 + n) = n(1 + n)$ members, $v = 3$ has $(1 + n)^3 - (1 + n)^2 = n(1 + n)^2$ members, etc.

(30) in average per capita terms:

$$k_{t+1} - k_t = \frac{f(k_t) - c_t}{1+n} - \frac{nk_t}{1+n}. \tag{32}$$

The derivation uses the fact $k_{t+1}^{t+1} = 0$ and equates $r_t k_t + w_t$ to $f(k_t)$ by Euler's theorem. (Recall section 1.5.1.)[11] The aggregate capital accumulation equation (32) is, of course, exactly the same as the corresponding eqs. (8') for the Koopmans model (p. 442) and (8) for the Solow model (except that $g = 0$ and $\delta = 0$, since we have abstracted from technological progress and depreciation here). The capital accumulation equation is merely an accounting identity and does not depend on the behavioral assumptions of the model.

We next turn to translating the Euler condition (31) into per capita terms. Aggregating eq. (31) across all agents born through date t yields

$$\frac{c_{t+1}^0 + nc_{t+1}^1 + \ldots + n(1+n)^{t-1}c_{t+1}^t}{(1+n)^t} = (1 + r_{t+1})\beta c_t.$$

Notice that the left-hand side of this expression equals $(1+n)\left(c_{t+1} - \frac{n}{1+n}c_{t+1}^{t+1}\right)$. Thus the expression implies

$$c_{t+1} = (1 + r_{t+1})\beta c_t - n\left(c_{t+1} - c_{t+1}^{t+1}\right).$$

To write this equation in terms of per capita variables only, we use a shortcut to eliminate c_{t+1}^{t+1} (the consumption of one newly born in $t + 1$). We know from several models in earlier chapters that an agent with log utility will always consume a fixed fraction $1 - \beta$ of total wealth, broadly defined to include the present discounted value of labor income. But since all agents have identical labor income, the difference between average per capita consumption and the consumption of a newly born person must be simply

$$c_{t+1} - c_{t+1}^{t+1} = (1 - \beta)(1 + r_{t+1})k_{t+1}.$$

Combining the preceding two expressions yields

$$c_{t+1} = (1 + r_{t+1})\beta c_t - n(1 - \beta)(1 + r_{t+1})k_{t+1}.$$

---

11. Averaging k_{t+1}^v on the left-hand side of eq. (30) over the date t population yields

$$\frac{k_{t+1}^0 + nk_{t+1}^1 + n(1+n)k_{t+1}^2 + \ldots + n(1+n)^{t-1}k_{t+1}^t}{(1+n)^t},$$

which equals $(1+n)k_{t+1}$. This conclusion follows from the definition

$$k_{t+1} \equiv \frac{k_{t+1}^0 + nk_{t+1}^1 + n(1+n)k_{t+1}^2 + \ldots + n(1+n)^{t-1}k_{t+1}^t + n(1+n)^t k_{t+1}^{t+1}}{(1+n)^{t+1}}$$

and from the fact that $k_{t+1}^{t+1} = 0$, since new vintages are born without financial wealth.

Finally, by substituting the equilibrium relationship $r_{t+1} = f'(k_{t+1})$ into the preceding equation, we obtain the second key aggregate per capita dynamic equation of our closed-economy overlapping generations model:

$$c_{t+1} = [1 + f'(k_{t+1})][\beta c_t - n(1 - \beta)k_{t+1}]. \tag{33}$$

Except for the fact we have made the simplifying assumptions that $\sigma = 1$ and $g = 0$ here, eq. (33) differs from eq. (24) of the Koopmans model only by an additional term proportional to the population growth rate n.

Figure 7.7 illustrates the phase diagram for the system governed by eqs. (32) and (33). A rise in population growth shifts the $\Delta k = 0$ schedule downward as before. In the present model, however, the $\Delta c = 0$ schedule, governed by eq. (33), also shifts, moving upward.[12] Clearly the equilibrium capital-labor ratio falls as in the Solow model. Qualitatively, of course, the model here is very similar to the two-period, two-country overlapping generations model we studied in section 3.6. Here, as in that model, if one were to introduce government budget deficits, they would lead to a reduction of $\bar{k}$ ("crowding out"). Similarly, because there is no altruistic link between unborn generations and the present, one cannot rule out the possibility that the steady-state capital stock will be inefficiently high.[13]

Aside from providing a deeper perspective on the positive predictions of the neoclassical growth model, introducing maximizing behavior allows one to understand the welfare implications of some important policy questions. The next section provides an example.

7.1.2.3   The Benefits of Immigration: Skilled versus Unskilled Labor

We took a first look at international labor migration as an alternative to capital flows in Chapter 1, but the growth models developed in this chapter offer a dynamic perspective that was not available in a two-period framework. We now use them to address the popular view that countries lose by admitting immigrants with little human capital, and that only foreigners with substantial skills should be encouraged to immigrate.

---

12. Removing time subscripts and dividing both sides of eq. (33) by c yields the $\Delta c = 0$ locus,

$$1 = [1 + f'(k)]\left[\beta - n(1 - \beta)\frac{k}{c}\right].$$

Thus a rise in n must be offset by a rise in c, and the $\Delta c = 0$ schedule shifts up as stated in the text. Notice that for a capital stock k such that $[1 + f'(k)]\beta = 1$, c would have to be infinite for $\Delta c = 0$ to hold. This reasoning justifies the shape of the $\Delta c = 0$ schedule shown in Figure 7.7.

13. Since $g = \delta = 0$, the golden rule level of the capital stock, k^*, is defined by

$$f'(k^*) = n.$$

It is easy to check that this condition is not necessarily met in the steady state of the system governed by eqs. (32) and (33). See also Weil (1989a).

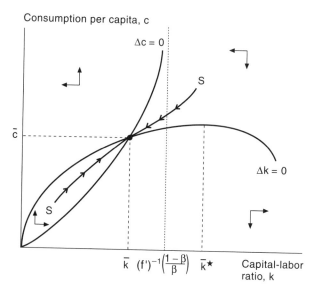

Consumption per capita, c

$\Delta c = 0$

S

S

$\bar{c}$

$\Delta k = 0$

$\bar{k}$ $(f')^{-1}\left(\dfrac{1-\beta}{\beta}\right)$ $\bar{k}\star$

Capital-labor
ratio, k

Figure 7.7
Growth with overlapping generations

Consider a closed economy that is inhabited by a constant number N of "natives" with the common utility function

$$U_t = \sum_{s=t}^{\infty} \beta^{s-t} \log c_s^N, \tag{34}$$

where c_s^N is the consumption at time s of the representative native. We will abstract from physical capital entirely and assume that the inputs to production are (raw) labor L and human capital H. The production function $F(H, L)$ is assumed to exhibit constant returns to scale. Following the Mankiw, Romer, and Weil (1992) setup in section 7.1.1.2, we posit that human capital accumulation is entirely analogous to physical capital accumulation. Thus an agent must sacrifice current consumption in order to increase the human capital he has available for production in the following period. Perhaps because of difficulties in enforcement, there is no international borrowing or lending.

On date t every person inelastically supplies one unit of raw labor and receives w_t, the national wage for unskilled labor. An agent also brings h_t^N units of human capital into period t, for which he receives income $w_{s,t}h_t^N$, where $w_{s,t}$ is the period t wage for human capital. (Think of skilled labor as a package including both raw labor and the skills embodied in human capital. Separating the returns to each is simply a useful accounting convention.) Finally, parallel to our treatment of physical capital, we assume that h can be freely converted back into the consumption good so that its relative price is always 1. (This is a minor technical convenience; note that human capital can be reduced simply through depreciation.) The period budget constraint for the representative individual thus is

$$h_{t+1}^N = (1 + w_{s,t} - \delta)h_t^N + w_t - c_t^N, \tag{35}$$

where δ is the depreciation rate of human capital.

Maximizing utility (34) subject to constraint (35) leads to the Euler condition

$$\frac{c_{t+1}^N}{c_t^N} = (1 + w_{s,t+1} - \delta)\beta \tag{36}$$

for a representative native. Denote the intensive form of the production function by $f(h) \equiv F(h, 1)$, where h is the human-capital to raw-labor ratio. Let h_t be the economy-wide ratio of human capital to raw labor on date t. Since we have not yet introduced any immigrants, the economy-wide per capita level of human capital h is still equal to h^N, the per capita human capital level of the natives. Then, assuming competitive domestic firms, we infer from Euler's theorem that

$$w_t = f(h_t) - h_t f'(h_t), \tag{37}$$

$$w_{s,t} = f'(h_t), \tag{38}$$

in equilibrium.

Substituting the factor payment equations (37) and (38) into eq. (35) yields the economy-wide per capita human capital accumulation equation:

$$h_{t+1} - h_t = f(h_t) - \delta h_t - c_t. \tag{39}$$

Substituting the equation for skilled wages (38) into the individual Euler equation (36) yields the corresponding equation governing consumption growth:

$$\frac{c_{t+1}}{c_t} = [1 + f'(h_{t+1}) - \delta]\beta. \tag{40}$$

[We have dropped the N superscript on consumption because eqs. (39) and (40) will still hold for aggregate per capita consumption even after we allow immigration.]

Figure 7.8 graphs the equilibrium path of the economy, with per capita consumption c on the vertical axis and per capita human capital h on the horizontal axis. The system is isomorphic to the one for the Koopmans model when productivity and population growth are zero. The steady-state level of h [governed by eq. (40) with $c_{t+1}/c_t = 1$] is given by

$$\bar{h} = (f')^{-1}\left(\frac{1-\beta}{\beta} + \delta\right).$$

The figure also indicates the dynamic behavior of the system and the saddle path leading to the long-run steady state.

Let us now consider the effects of an influx of unskilled workers. Suppose that the economy is initially in a steady state when it admits M immigrants who are identical to natives except that they have *no* initial endowment of human capital. The representative immigrant's utility function and capital accumulation equation

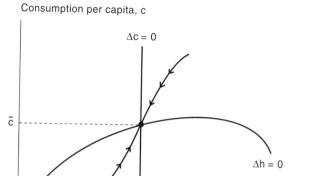

Figure 7.8
Human capital accumulation with immigration

are the same as eqs. (34) and (35), with h^N and c^N replaced by h^M and c^M. Similarly, his first-order Euler condition for consumption is the same as eq. (36).

Linear aggregation across the native and immigrant Euler and human capital accumulation equations is straightforward with log utility. Define the country's per capita consumption level

$$c = \frac{Nc^N + Mc^M}{N + M},\tag{41}$$

and define other per capita variables similarly. Next, note that the individual human capital accumulation and Euler equations, (35) and (36), can be aggregated, since both immigrants and natives face the same wages.[14] Finally, note that since the production function is linear-homogeneous, w and w_s are functions of the economy-wide human-capital to raw-labor ratio h. Thus we conclude that the aggregate per capita variables h and c are governed by eqs. (39) and (40), after as well as before immigration.

---

14. To aggregate, note that the individual native and immigrant Euler equations are

$$c^N_{t+1} = (1 + w_{s,t+1} - \delta)\beta c^N_t,$$

$$c^M_{t+1} = (1 + w_{s,t+1} - \delta)\beta c^M_t.$$

Multiplying the native equation by N and the immigrant equation by M, summing the resulting equations, and then dividing both sides by $N + M$ yields the aggregate per capita consumption Euler condition.

Since the same dynamic equations govern per capita aggregates before and after immigration, we see immediately that the influx of unskilled immigrants does not affect steady-state *per capita* levels of consumption or human capital. There is, however, a short-run impact: the average per capita human capital stock h drops to $h_0 = \frac{N}{N+M}\bar{h}$, denoted by point **A** in Figure 7.8. Afterward, the economy converges back to the original steady state along the saddle path, as illustrated.

Figure 7.8 describes only the economy-wide average values of consumption and human capital. How is the welfare of individual natives affected? Wages for unskilled workers must initially fall (since h falls), and, conversely, the rate of return to human capital must rise. Since natives supply both unskilled labor and human capital, what is their net benefit? First, consider the impact effect. If the unskilled immigrants are paid their marginal product $F_L(N\bar{h}, N+M)$ when they arrive, then the initial impact on the total income of natives is

$$F(N\bar{h}, N+M) - F(N\bar{h}, N) - MF_L(N\bar{h}, N+M).$$

This expression must be positive. Why? Holding H constant, the production function $F(H, L)$ is strictly concave in L, which implies that

$$\frac{F(N\bar{h}, N+M) - F(N\bar{h}, N)}{M} > F_L(N\bar{h}, N+M).$$

Thus the total rise in output in period zero exceeds payments to immigrants. (A diagrammatic proof would parallel the famous exposition of the benefits of foreign capital inflows by MacDougall, 1960.)

Can later developments reverse the initial impact on native welfare and make natives worse off overall? A simple argument shows that such a reversal can't happen. The basic point is that with constant returns to scale, any native who chooses can insulate himself from any further effects of immigration by consuming the entire initial windfall and then going into production autarky at the steady-state level of h, $\bar{h}$. By doing so, he ensures that his welfare after the initial period will be exactly the same as if the immigrants had never come. He will only choose to do something different if that makes him at least as well off. Since there is a clear benefit in the initial period, natives therefore must gain.

The fact that aggregate per capita consumption and human capital eventually return to their original steady-state levels does *not* imply that unskilled immigrants will eventually catch up with natives. In fact, the steady state will have $\bar{h}^N > \bar{h} > \bar{h}^M$. This conclusion follows from the Euler condition (36), which is the same for both immigrants and natives. Given that both groups face the same net rate of return to human capital accumulation ($w_s - \delta$), they both will tilt their consumption paths by the same degree. Along any transition path where immigrants are accumulating capital, natives will be accumulating capital as well. Clearly this strong result that immigrants never catch up is an artifact of our assumption that agents are infinitely-lived. In an overlapping generations setup (with no bequests), immigrant children would catch up in one generation. The truth most likely lies somewhere in between.

Should we conclude from the preceding analysis that unskilled immigration is preferable to skilled immigration? Not necessarily. Suppose that immigrants came in with a *higher* level of human capital than natives, $h_0^M > \bar{h}$. Then a similar argument again shows that the rise in total GDP exceeds factor payments to immigrants.[15] Indeed, the only case where natives do not gain is when the immigrants bring the *same* skill level as natives, so that $h_0^M = \bar{h}$. In this case, since output is produced with constant returns to scale in H and L, there is no effect. The familiar point is that from a purely economic perspective, the greater are the differences between natives and immigrants, the larger are the benefits of immigration—the gains from trade.

What kinds of factors are missing that might reverse the conclusion of this model that immigration is never undesirable? The issues are similar to those we raised in the two-period model of section 1.5. First of all, we have abstracted from distributional effects among natives. Suppose that the native population consisted of unconnected overlapping generations. Then, an argument identical to the preceding one shows that the country as a whole benefits from an influx of unskilled labor. But the newborn generation, which holds no capital and sees its wage rate drop, clearly loses. Indeed, one can show that the distributional effect is generally large compared to the overall welfare gain, which takes the form of a Harberger triangle. Another important issue is that there may be public goods that are shared equally by all residents of a country, new and old. Thus when foreign residents enter, they immediately become full co-owners of public bridges, roads, and the like. If congestion effects are sufficiently strong, they can outweigh the direct beneficial effects of immigration.

Our model also abstracts from the effects of international trade and capital mobility. If physical capital were perfectly mobile with no costs of adjustment, then the optimal world allocation of labor would be indeterminate. In addition, as we have emphasized earlier, trade in goods may also lead to some degree of factor price equalization which, in the extreme, can imply that immigration has no effect

---

15. **Proof:** Think of the skilled-labor immigration as occurring in two stages. In the first stage, immigrants bring only $\bar{h}$ per person. This stage has no effect on the welfare of domestic residents, since production exhibits constant returns to scale. In the second stage, immigrants bring over their remaining $h_0^M - \bar{h}$ per person in skilled labor. The total benefit to the economy, less the payments for the second-stage import of human capital, is

$$F\left[(N + M)\bar{h} + M(h_0^M - \bar{h}), N + M\right] - F\left[(N + M)\bar{h}, N + M\right]$$

$$- M(h_0^M - \bar{h})F_H\left[(N + M)\bar{h} + M(h_0^M - \bar{h}), N + M\right],$$

which is necessarily greater than zero because $F(H, L)$ is strictly concave in H, given L.

on native wages. Under conditions of factor price equalization, the only effect of immigration is to shift domestic production toward the labor-intensive good, either reducing imports or increasing exports of that good. But this case involves many extreme assumptions such as perfect factor mobility within countries and nonspecialization in production.

Certainly immigration is an emotional and complex issue, and our model is a very simple one. It nonetheless gives a useful dynamic perspective on immigration that is different from the usual static one. Our model of immigration again illustrates the advantages of introducing fully specified microfoundations for demand into the Solow model.

7.2   International Convergence

Following the evolution of growth theory, our discussion thus far has ignored international borrowing and lending. With perfectly integrated global capital markets, however, there can be no intercountry differences in (risk-adjusted) returns to capital, regardless of differences in birth rates, rates of time preference, and so on. Indeed, absent costs of adjustment in investment, cross-country differences in marginal products of capital disappear instantly as capital flows to the country where the rate of return is highest. With identical technologies in all countries, per worker output levels are immediately equalized internationally in this case.

As we shall see, the empirical evidence on productivity convergence agrees with other evidence we have reviewed in suggesting a reality somewhere between the two extremes of a world of closed economies and a world of perfectly integrated capital markets. Even across regions within the same country, per worker output differentials appear to damp out roughly at a rate of only 2 percent per year. After studying the empirical evidence, we will turn to various explanations of why the international convergence in output per worker is relatively slow, and why deviations may persist even in the long run. We show that the possible failure of long-run absolute convergence, especially between rich and developing countries, can easily be understood if there are international capital market imperfections of the type we studied in Chapter 6.

7.2.1   Absolute Convergence: The Empirical Evidence

In a world of fully integrated markets for goods, capital, and ideas, one would expect to observe *absolute* convergence, regardless of countries' saving rates or demographics. (By absolute convergence we mean convergence by different countries to the same level of output per worker. Remember that the closed-economy Solow model does not predict absolute convergence in general unless countries have identical saving and labor-force-growth rates as well as identical technologies.) Absent capital market imperfections, rates of return on capital will be equalized across countries in the long run. If production technologies are the same, as they ultimately will be if innovations diffuse internationally, then steady-state outputs per worker must also be equalized.[16] What is the evidence? One test, analogous to our earlier Figure 7.3 on the rebuilding of capital stocks after World War II, is to see whether countries that started with relatively low incomes after World War II experienced faster growth thereafter. For the group of rich OECD economies, Figure 7.9 plots the difference between 1990 log GDP per worker and 1950 log GDP per worker (vertical axis) against the log of GDP per worker in 1950 (horizontal axis).[17] As the figure shows, OECD economies that were poor after the war indeed tended to grow faster than initially richer OECD economies.[18] Indeed, a regression involving the two variables in the figure yields a statistically significant negative correlation:

$$\log\left(\frac{Y_{1990}}{L_{1990}}\right) - \log\left(\frac{Y_{1950}}{L_{1950}}\right) = 6.47 - 0.58 \log\left(\frac{Y_{1950}}{L_{1950}}\right), \quad R^2 = 0.83.$$
$$(0.54) \quad (0.06)$$

The estimated coefficient of -0.58 on 1950 GDP per worker means that somewhat more than half the absolute difference in initial country per capita incomes had dissipated by the end of the sample period.

When one looks at income differentials across regions within a given country, there appears to be an even stronger tendency toward long-run absolute convergence. Barro and Sala-i-Martin (1991, 1992a, 1992b, 1994) have examined convergence among states in the United States, prefectures in Japan, and regions within Europe (90 regions across 8 countries). In all cases, they find a strong tendency toward absolute convergence, albeit at very slow rates typically in the neighborhood of 2 percent per year. At this rate of convergence—which Barro and Sala-i-Martin claim to be almost a universal constant—it takes roughly 35 years for half the gap in two countries' per capita incomes to close. (Solving the half-life equation $0.98^X = 0.5$ yields $X \approx 35$.) This rate is consistent with the one implied by the preceding regression for the OECD group of countries.

In data samples covering more heterogeneous economic groupings, it is much harder to demonstrate absolute convergence at *any* speed. Figure 7.10 graphs per worker output growth versus initial output per worker for a broad set of 55 countries, including developing as well as rich countries. There is no obvious relationship between the two series, and a regression yields no evidence of a significant

---

16. Note that equality of output per worker does not imply equality in output per capita unless all countries have identical labor force participation rates. Moreover, equal output only implies equal *income* if net foreign assets are zero.

17. GDP per worker is calculated by dividing real GDP (the Penn World Table, version 5.6, measure) by the population of working age, defined as ages 15–64 (from the World Bank, *World Tables* and *World Development Report*).

18. See Dowrick and Nguyen (1989) for further discussion of the evidence on OECD countries.

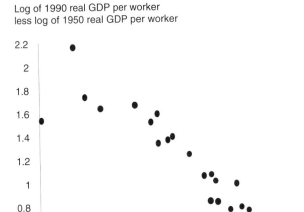

Log of 1990 real GDP per worker
less log of 1950 real GDP per worker

Log of 1950 GDP per worker
(thousands of 1985 dollars)

Figure 7.9
Absolute convergence in the OECD

statistical correlation. Indeed, the failure of the third world to catch up with the developed world is stunning. Baumol, Blackman, and Wolf (1989) argue that if one looks separately at low-income, medium-income, and high-income countries, there is evidence of convergence within each group. But this finding does not explain the larger question of why one does not observe convergence across groups.[19] Whether this failure of absolute convergence should be regarded as a great puzzle is a matter of some debate. One perspective, which we have already discussed, is that there is no puzzle at all. The *closed-economy* neoclassical model does not predict absolute convergence, and differences in cross-country saving and population growth rates go a long way toward explaining differences in output per worker. However, the world is not made up of closed economies. After looking more closely at the nonconvergence phenomenon in very long-run data, we will examine how various impediments to international capital mobility can slow or prevent absolute convergence.

19. Bernard and Durlauf (1994) argue that cross-section evidence of the type discussed in the text is limited by sensitivity to the choice of the initial comparison year, and that time series evidence is ultimately more informative. (See also the discussion of measurement error in the following application on the long-run convergence controversy.)

Log of 1990 real GDP per worker
less log of 1950 real GDP per worker

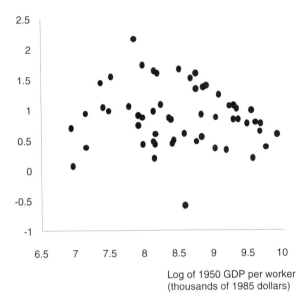

Log of 1950 GDP per worker
(thousands of 1985 dollars)

Figure 7.10
Nonconvergence for developing and developed countries

Application: Productivity Convergence, 1870–1979: The Baumol–De Long–Romer Debate

If convergence is slow, then even the entire postwar period may be too short to detect it. Maddison (1982) has constructed data over a longer period, 1870–1979, for sixteen advanced economies. The data, subject to revisions discussed in De Long (1988), are listed in Table 7.1.

As Table 7.1 shows, the countries that had relatively high per capita incomes in 1870 tended to have slower growth in income per person over the ensuing century. A regression yields (standard errors are in parentheses)

$$\log\left(\frac{Y_{1979}}{N_{1979}}\right) - \log\left(\frac{Y_{1870}}{N_{1870}}\right) = 8.46 - \underset{(0.09)}{1.00}\log\left(\frac{Y_{1870}}{N_{1870}}\right), \quad R^2 = 0.88.$$

Over this 110-year sample, one cannot reject the hypothesis that the slope coefficient is −1, implying complete convergence. (A slope of −1 implies that for every percent a country's per capita income was below average in 1870, its cumulative growth rate was 1 percent higher over the next 110 years.) Thus these data for the

Table 7.1
Convergence in Output Per Capita, 1870–1979

Country	Per Capita 1870 Income (1975 dollars)	Growth in Per Capita Income (1870–1979, log difference × 100)
Australia	1,922	116
United Kingdom	1,214	145
Switzerland	1,118	174
Belgium	1,137	168
Netherlands	1,104	166
United States	1,038	207
Denmark	883	201
Canada	881	214
France	847	207
Austria	751	203
Italy	746	178
West Germany	731	223
Norway	665	228
Sweden	557	247
Finland	506	241
Japan	328	286

Sources: De Long (1988) and Maddison (1982).

very long term appear to give even more striking evidence of convergence than the postwar OECD data. Baumol (1986) looks at a similar regression and concludes that the Maddison data provide very strong support for the hypothesis of absolute convergence. His interpretation emphasizes the forces that lead to convergence in technologies.

P. Romer (1986) and De Long (1988) offer some persuasive criticisms of Baumol's interpretation.[20] They point out that there is a natural sample-selection bias problem that tends to overstate the case for convergence. The countries studied by Maddison are all relatively wealthy today. Almost by definition, then, the sixteen countries in Table 7.1 are countries that have converged. De Long pursues this point by trying to compare the performance of countries that were rich in 1870, rather than in 1979. He adds seven countries that seemed poised for success in 1870 but have since performed relatively poorly (see Table 7.2).

If one redoes Baumol's regressions of growth on initial output levels including the seven countries in Table 7.2 but throwing out Japan (whose subsequent growth performance is unrepresentative of other countries that were very poor in 1870), the estimated slope coefficient falls dramatically (in absolute value) to −0.57. Given the standard error of 0.14, one can reject the hypothesis that the coefficient is −1 at

---

20. The last regression is taken from De Long (1988).

Table 7.2
The Once Rich Seven

Country	Per Capita 1870 Income (1975 dollars)	Growth in Per Capita Income (1870–1979, log difference × 100)
New Zealand	981	157
Argentina	762	141
East Germany	741	199
Spain	728	176
Ireland	656	167
Portugal	637	150
Denmark	519	150

Source: De Long (1988).

the 5 percent significance level. A slope of -0.57 implies a tendency to converge, but one so slow as to be far from complete even after 110 years.

De Long points to a further econometric problem with the Baumol regression. It is likely that income for 1870 is measured with greater error than income for 1979, since much less information is available for the earlier period. If so, this measurement error would strongly bias the results toward exhibiting convergence. It is easy to see why. If there is no measurement error for a country's 1979 income, and a high positive one for its 1870 income, then estimates of the country's growth rate will be biased downward. Similarly, if measurement error causes a country's 1870 income to appear very low, estimates of its growth rate will be biased upward. Either way, regressions of the type we have been considering will overstate the degree of convergence; that is, the estimated slope coefficient will be biased toward -1. De Long considers some procedures to adjust for measurement-error bias and shows that an appropriate correction can even reverse the sign on the slope coefficient, implying that incomes actually diverged instead of converging.

A reasonable conclusion to draw from the Baumol–De Long–Romer debate is that if there is convergence in output per worker across countries, the rate is likely to be very slow, probably no faster than the 2 percent per year one seems to find for regions within the same country.   ∎

7.2.1.1   Taxes and Absolute Convergence

What factors might be able to explain the failure of absolute convergence in productivity levels across countries? One obstacle to convergence by otherwise identical economies, even under perfect international capital mobility, is government tax policy. Suppose, for example, that a small country taxes the gross outputs of all firms at rate τ. From the viewpoint of a profit-maximizing firm, this is exactly equivalent to a τ percent decrease in total factor productivity. Let r^W be the world real interest rate. With a Cobb-Douglas production function of the form $K^\alpha (EL)^{1-\alpha}$ (and assuming zero depreciation), the condition $(1 - \tau) f'(k^E) = r^W$ implies that the steady-state capital-to-effective-labor ratio must be

$$\bar{k}^E = \left[\frac{(1 - \tau) \alpha}{r^W} \right]^{1/(1-\alpha)} \tag{42}$$

Given that the elasticity of $\bar{k}^E$ with respect to $(1 - \tau)$ is $\frac{1}{1-\alpha} > 1$, differences in marginal tax rates could conceivably explain substantial differences in capital-labor ratios. [If in truth $\alpha \approx 2/3$, as Mankiw, Romer, and Weil (1992) argue, then $1/(1 - \alpha) \approx 3$.] And though marginal tax rates are quite difficult to compare across countries, it is certainly true that average tax rates range widely. King and Fullerton (1984, p. 307), for example, find that by their "fixed-p" measure, average effective 1980 tax rates on capital ranged from 4 percent for the United Kingdom to 37 percent for the United States to 48 percent for Germany. If one interprets τ more broadly as incorporating variation in the strength of property rights across countries, then differences probably become even larger. Of course, if eq. (42) is correct, then the right variables to condition on in cross-country growth regressions are marginal tax rates rather than population growth rates and saving rates.

7.2.1.2   Openness and Nonconvergence

Another theory of absolute convergence holds that countries that are relatively open achieve higher growth rates than countries that are not. More open economies presumably are better at absorbing foreign technology and are likely to suffer less from credit constraints that limit investment. Levine and Renelt (1992) find that the degree of openness, typically proxied by exports plus imports over GDP, is one of the two variables that have the most robust correlation with growth in cross-country regressions. (The other variable is the investment-GDP ratio, which appeared as a saving proxy in the Solow model regressions of section 7.1.1.2.)[21] Figure 7.11 looks at the correlation between 1960 GDP per capita and growth over the period 1960–90 for a group of 31 countries that Sachs and Warner (1995) classify as open.[22] As the reader can see, the negative correlation for this group is almost as striking as that for the OECD group in Figure 7.9. The slope coefficient in a growth regression with the log of 1960 GDP per capita on its right-hand side is

---

21. Ben-David (1993) finds that liberalized trade within the European Community accelerated the rate of income convergence.

22. Sachs and Warner classify a country as closed if it exhibits at least one of the following five characteristics: (1) nontariff barriers cover more than 40 percent of trade; (2) average tariff rates exceed 40 percent; (3) the economy has a socialist economic system (as defined by Kornai, 1992); (4) the state has a monopoly on major exports; (5) the black market exchange rate was depreciated by 20 percent or more relative to the official rate during either the 1970s or 1980s.

Log of 1990 real GDP per capita
less log of 1960 real GDP per capita

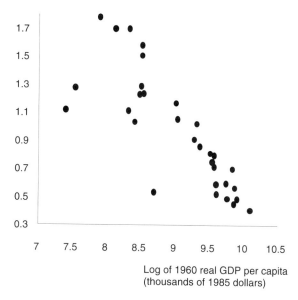

Figure 7.11
Absolute convergence for open economies

−0.44 (with a standard error of 0.06), very similar to the result for the OECD country sample over the period 1950–1990. (Part of the reason for this similarity, of course, is that the OECD countries constitute two-thirds of Sachs and Warner's "open" economies.)

7.2.2   Convergence Dynamics

Even within groups of countries showing evidence of absolute convergence, the process appears to be very slow. Indeed, for two regions of the same country it seems to take roughly 35 years to close half of a per capita income gap. Costs of adjusting the physical capital stock (as in Chapter 2's *q* model) can generate slow convergence even under free capital mobility, but it is difficult to believe that these costs are sufficiently large or long-lasting to explain the long-term data. (Admittedly, the gestation period for *human* capital is quite possibly longer.) In this section, we focus on how various international capital market imperfections can impede convergence, and see whether such models yield quantitatively plausible explanations of slow convergence. The reader may find the models of this subsection quite crude by comparison with the more sophisticated models of capital market imperfection considered in Chapter 6. We have chosen to work with rather mechanical models of imperfections here in order to obtain analytically tractable dynamics, but the basic insights should extend to more sophisticated models.

7.2.2.1 Transition Dynamics in the Closed Economy

Even in the absence of international capital mobility, per capita incomes will converge across countries with like population growth rates, technologies, and saving rates. Thus, as a benchmark for understanding the convergence speed of identical open economies with incomplete access to world capital markets, it is useful to consider the transition dynamics of a closed-economy model. We will focus here on the simple Solow model rather than more sophisticated models based on intertemporal maximization; both yield similar results. (We will take up linearization techniques for studying convergence speeds in maximizing models in section 7.4.3.)

One can easily check how fast a Solow economy converges to its steady state by examining the equilibrium capital accumulation relationship, eq. (8). Assuming a Cobb-Douglas production function as we did in section 7.1.1.2, that equation becomes

$$k_{t+1}^E - k_t^E = \frac{s(k_t^E)^\alpha}{1+z} - \frac{z+\delta}{1+z}k_t^E, \tag{43}$$

where $1 + z \equiv (1+g)(1+n)$. Recall that setting $k_{t+1}^E = k_t^E = \bar{k}^E$ yields the steady state given in eq. (10),

$$\bar{k}^E = \left(\frac{s}{z+\delta}\right)^{\frac{1}{1-\alpha}}.$$

Equation (43) is a stable nonlinear difference equation in k^E. By inspection, one can see that the higher is k^E above $\bar{k}^E$, the faster k^E falls. This must be the case because the positive first term on the right-hand side of eq. (43) rises less than proportionately with rises in k^E, while the negative second term is linear. By the same logic, when k^E lies below $\bar{k}^E$, its rate of increase must be larger when the gap is larger. If we restrict our attention to values of k^E close to the steady state, it is possible to say more. Linearizing eq. (43) in the neighborhood of the steady state yields

$$k_{t+1}^E - \bar{k}^E = \mu(k_t^E - \bar{k}^E), \tag{44}$$

where

$$\mu \equiv \left[1 + \frac{s\alpha(\bar{k}^E)^{\alpha-1}}{1+z} - \frac{z+\delta}{1+z}\right] = \frac{1+\alpha z + (\alpha-1)\delta}{1+z}. \tag{45}$$

[The second equality in eq. (45) is obtained by substituting for $\bar{k}^E$ using eq. (10)].[23] The rate at which the economy converges to the steady state is $1 - \mu$; that is, $1 - \mu$ of any difference between k^E and $\bar{k}^E$ tends to disappear each period, absent further shocks.[24]

According to the closed-economy Solow model, what rate of convergence would one expect to observe in per worker capital stocks across countries? For the United States over the past thirty years, the rate of growth in population has been about 1 percent per year, and the rate of growth in output per person about 2 percent. We will assume a depreciation rate δ of 3 percent, which roughly equals the capital depletion allowance in the GNP accounts divided by the capital stock. If we use these parameters and set $\alpha = 1/3$, then

$$\mu = \frac{1 + (1/3)\left[(1.02)(1.01) - 1\right] - (2/3)(0.03)}{(1.02)(1.01)} \approx 0.96.$$

This result implies that the economy converges toward the steady state at a rate of 0.04 (4 percent) per year. This is more than twice as fast as the 2 percent per year speed of convergence that typifies the empirical results we have discussed. The relatively fast speed of convergence implied by the theory is puzzling, since we have not even introduced international capital mobility yet, which will presumably increase the predicted speed of convergence. (Indeed, the puzzle is compounded if one recalls that the predicted speed of convergence is faster when the economy lies farther from its steady state, and our 4 percent estimate applies only to small deviations.) Interestingly, one way to address the convergence-speed puzzle is by assuming a larger value of α. One can see from eq. (45) that the higher the value of α, the slower the rate $1 - \mu$ at which k_t^E converges to $\bar{k}^E$. Intuitively, the higher α, the slower the rate at which diminishing returns set in as k^E rises. For example,

---

23. For the continuous-time version of the model in appendix 7A, it is actually possible to find a closed-form solution for the path of k^E without linearization. Divide both sides of eq. (8)'s continuous-time analog by $(k_t^E)^\alpha$ to obtain

$$\frac{dk_t^E}{dt}(k_t^E)^{-\alpha} = s - (n + g + \delta)(k_t^E)^{1-\alpha}.$$

Defining $x \equiv (k^E)^{1-\alpha}$, this equation can be written

$$\dot{x}_t = (1 - \alpha)s - (1 - \alpha)(n + g + \delta)x_t,$$

which is a first-order linear differential equation in x_t with solution

$$x_t \equiv (k_t^E)^{1-\alpha} = \bar{x} + (x_0 - \bar{x})\exp[-(1 - \alpha)(n + g + \delta)t], \quad \bar{x} = s/(n + g + \delta).$$

Since x converges to $\bar{x}$ at a constant rate, the rate of convergence of k^E to $\bar{k}^E$ must decrease as the differential becomes smaller. [This trick is pointed out by Barro and Sala-i-Martin (1994), who attribute it to Jaume Ventura.]

24. We note that our speed of convergence estimate is for the *level* of k^E, but a logarithmic approximation yields the same result. This claim may be confirmed by dividing both sides of eq. (44) by $\bar{k}^E$, and noting that in the neighborhood of $\bar{k}^E$, $(k^E/\bar{k}^E) - 1 \approx \log(k^E) - \log(\bar{k}^E)$.

when $\alpha = 2/3$ instead of $1/3$, μ becomes 0.98 and the half-life for convergence rises to 35 years.

*7.2.2.2   Transition Dynamics in an Open Economy with Impediments to Financing Human Capital Formation

In a world of identical closed economies, the transition dynamics we described in the last subsection also would underlie the process of absolute convergence. If, on the other hand, there were no impediments to international borrowing and lending, transnational investment would quickly force convergence across countries in net marginal products of capital. True, there would still be slow convergence in *global* output per worker toward its steady state, but, abstracting from costs of adjustment in investment, cross-country per worker output differentials would disappear immediately. As we have seen, the data suggest that this scenario is totally unrealistic, even for regions within the same country. How can one reconcile the theory with the empirical evidence?

One obvious potential explanation is based on capital-market imperfections of the sort we studied in Chapter 6. Most of the analysis in Chapter 6 focused on two-period models or on models without investment, but here we try to incorporate credit-market imperfections into the more fully dynamic models of this chapter.

The first model we take up is based on the small-country formulation of Barro, Mankiw, and Sala-i-Martin (1995). It assumes that all market imperfections stem from moral hazard problems associated with inalienability of human capital, and makes that assumption operative by stipulating that creditors can seize physical capital but not human capital.

Whether the dichotomy Barro, Mankiw, and Sala-i-Martin stress is useful is debatable. Even if investors cannot seize human capital, they may be able to garnishee the income stream it produces. Nor is it clear that any part of a sovereign debtor's domestic physical capital stock could be seized with substantially greater ease than its human capital stock. Furthermore, as we saw in Chapter 6, when borrowers cannot commit future investment levels prior to accepting loans, the credibility and moral hazard problems in implicitly using new physical capital investment as collateral can be quite severe.

Despite these shortcomings, however, the model of Barro, Mankiw, and Sala-i-Martin has illustrative value because it leads to a speed-of-convergence calculation closely parallel to that for the simple Solow model. (Earlier macroeconomic models emphasizing imperfections in the market for human capital include Loury, 1981, and Ljungqvist, 1993.[25])

---

25. Ljungqvist solves a general equilibrium two-period overlapping generations model in which families must bear fixed education costs to raise their children's human capital. The critical assumptions in his framework are that future labor earnings cannot be used as collateral for borrowing and that there

Assume, as in the extended Mankiw, Romer, and Weil model of section 7.1.1.2, that the production function is given by

$$Y_t = K_t^\alpha H_t^\phi (E_t L_t)^{1-\alpha-\phi},$$

where H is human capital and L is raw labor. Recall that the intensive form of this production function, found by normalizing by EL, can be written as eq. (13),

$$y_t^E = (k_t^E)^\alpha (h_t^E)^\phi.$$

Before, when we considered this production function, we did so in the context of a closed economy. Now assume that the economy is open, but that an agent can borrow in world markets only up to the level of the physical capital he owns. The rationale for this assumption, as we have noted, is that creditors can seize physical capital if a debtor defaults but cannot seize human capital.

If a country can borrow as much as k_t^E per efficiency worker on date $t-1$, then it will always borrow at least enough to drive the net marginal product of physical capital down to the level of the world interest rate.[26] If the country initially owns capital in excess of its foreign debts, it can use the difference to finance some immediate additional human capital accumulation, too. It is helpful to simplify matters slightly by assuming zero depreciation for physical capital while allowing human capital to depreciate at rate δ. In this case, eq. (13) implies

$$r = \alpha (k_t^E)^{\alpha-1} (h_t^E)^\phi.$$

Combining eq. (13) with the preceding rate-of-return condition, one can confirm that

$$k_t^E = \frac{\alpha y_t^E}{r}. \qquad (46)$$

Thus the ratio k_t^E / y_t^E (and hence K_t / Y_t) is constant along the adjustment path. Substituting eq. (46) into the production function eq. (13) yields

$$y_t^E = \chi (h_t^E)^\nu, \qquad (47)$$

where

$$\nu \equiv \frac{\phi}{1-\alpha},$$

---

are indivisibilities in education. He shows that in such a world it is possible to have developed and underdeveloped countries coexist, even in the steady state.

26. Implicitly, the country can commit to k_{t+1}^E before borrowing on date t, effectively putting up an equal collateral on its loan. This case is slightly simpler analytically than allowing the country to borrow up to k_t^E in period t. Notice that this model provides another example in which rates of return to capital can be equal internationally despite disparate capital-output ratios.

$$\chi \equiv \left(\frac{\alpha}{r}\right)^{\frac{\alpha}{1-\alpha}}.$$

Given these transformations, the model behaves very much like the standard physical-capital-only version of Solow's model. The economy's wealth-accumulation identity is

$$H_{t+1} - H_t + K_{t+1} - K_t + B_{t+1} - B_t = Y_t + r B_t - C_t - \delta H_t,$$

where B_t, as usual, stands for net claims on foreigners accumulated through the end of date $t - 1$. As we have already noted, as long as capital stocks are below the levels at which their net marginal products both equal the world interest rate r, it will be profitable for domestic residents to borrow at the world rate and use the proceeds for higher-yielding domestic investments. As a result, the constraint that $B_t \geq -K_t$ will bind on every date t at which h^E and k^E are still rising, and thus

$$B_t = -K_t.$$

Combining this equality with the preceding wealth-accumulation identity yields

$$H_{t+1} - H_t = Y_t - r K_t - C_t - \delta H_t$$

as the accumulation equation for human capital, where the term $-r K_t$ on the right captures repayments on borrowing from abroad.[27]

One could derive consumption from intertemporal maximization, but we will instead make the Solovian simplifying assumption that a country consumes $1 - s$ percent of its current income, here given by $Y_t - r K_t$. Thus human capital accumulation is given by

$$H_{t+1} - H_t = s(Y_t - r K_t).$$

Dividing both sides of this equation by $E_t L_t$, and making use of eq. (46) to substitute for k^E and eq. (47) to substitute for y^E, one arrives at

$$h^E_{t+1} - h^E_t = \frac{s'(h^E_t)^\nu}{1 + z} - \frac{z + \delta}{1 + z} h^E_t, \tag{48}$$

where

$$s' \equiv s(1 - \alpha) \left(\frac{\alpha}{r}\right)^{\frac{\alpha}{1-\alpha}}.$$

Equation (48) is isomorphic to eq. (43). Thus the long-run equilibrium $\bar{h}^E$ is given by

---

27. Note that again we have implicitly assumed that human capital can be cannibalized in the same way as physical capital. This should be thought of as a small analytical convenience, not a grand anthropological assertion.

$$\bar{h}^{E} = \left(\frac{s'}{z+\delta}\right)^{1/(1-\nu)},\tag{49}$$

and the equation of adjustment in the neighborhood of $\bar{h}^{E}$ is approximately

$$h_{t+1}^{E} - \bar{h}^{E} = \mu'(h_{t}^{E} - \bar{h}^{E}),\tag{50}$$

where, as in eq. (45) with $\alpha = \nu$,

$$\mu' \equiv \left[1 + \frac{s'\nu(\bar{h}^{E})^{\nu-1}}{1+z} - \frac{z+\delta}{1+z}\right] = \frac{1+\nu z+(\nu-1)\delta}{1+z}.\tag{51}$$

We find that the speed of convergence $1 - \mu'$ in this two-capital-good economy is exactly the same as in a closed-economy model with only physical capital and a capital share of $\nu \equiv \phi/(1-\alpha)$. Convergence is slower than in a one-capital-good closed-economy model where capital's share is ϕ (here the share of human capital) but faster than in a closed economy where capital's share is $\phi + \alpha$ (here the sum of the shares of physical and human capital). This model is interesting because it implies that impediments to borrowing against human capital slow down the accumulation of physical capital. The reason is that the two factors are complements in the production process. In sum, the model shows that borrowing constraints on financing human capital can potentially explain slow absolute convergence in per capita outputs, even across regions linked by highly integrated financial markets. These results also follow in the optimizing version of the model analyzed by Barro, Mankiw, and Sala-i-Martin (1995).

We have already emphasized some weaknesses in the model's assumptions. These include the maintained hypothesis that physical capital or its income can be seized by foreigners more readily than the income from human capital. One might also quarrel with the model's stipulation that human capital formation requires only a minimal gestation lag. Realistically, such lags could be quite important even in the absence of credit-market imperfections.

Application: Public Capital Accumulation and Convergence

Clarida (1993) presents a model that is similar in some respects to the preceding one. In his framework, however, it is gradual adjustment of public capital that impedes convergence. Suppose that public capital enters the private-sector production function

$$Y_{t} = (K_{t}^{G})^{\phi} K^{\alpha} (E_{t} L_{t})^{1-\alpha-\phi},$$

where K^{G} is public-sector capital and K is private-sector capital, as before. This specification seems plausible: public investment in roads, telephone lines, schools, sewers, and such is likely to be an essential input into production, especially in the early stages of development. Suppose further that public-sector investment adjusts very sluggishly, say, because of political inertia in choosing projects. Clarida models this sluggishness by assuming costs of adjustment in public investment. By analogy with the previous model, slow adjustment of public capital can slow down accumulation of other types of capital that are complements to public capital in the production process.

One prediction of the model is that public-sector capital should be correlated with standard measures of multifactor private-sector productivity that ignore the contribution of public capital. A standard measure of productivity growth is the percent increase in output that cannot be explained by increases in physical capital and labor,

$$\Delta y_t - \alpha \Delta k_t - (1 - \alpha) \Delta l_t,$$

where lowercase sans serif letters denote logs of uppercase aggregates. (This measure of productivity is sometimes referred to as the *Solow residual*, since it is the portion of output growth that cannot be explained by changes in measured inputs.) According to Clarida's model, part of this residual can be explained by changes in the public capital stock. To test his theory, Clarida asks if public-sector investment is "cointegrated" with private-sector productivity in data for the United States, United Kingdom, France, and Germany. Loosely speaking, he tries to show that any random-walk component in productivity disappears once one controls for public investment. The first step is to show that the two variables have unit roots, which he finds to be the case for all four countries. The only exception is in Britain, where the hypothesis of a unit root in public capital can be rejected at the 10 percent, but not the 5 percent, level. The next step is to test whether there exist linear combinations of public capital and private-sector productivity measures that are stationary (that is, combinations that do not have a unit root component, implying that the two variables are cointegrated). For the United States, France, and Germany, Clarida finds that he can reject the hypothesis of no cointegration at the 5 percent level; for Britain rejection is at the 10 percent level. The empirical results thus tend to confirm one salient implication of the theory.

Clarida emphasizes that evidence of this type is very weak. In his model, exogenously determined increases in public-sector capital raise private-sector productivity. But a perfectly plausible alternative hypothesis is that high private-sector productivity leads to increases in tax receipts that in turn lead to higher public investment expenditures on completely unproductive projects. Clarida attempts to test which variable is exogenous, but the results are inconclusive.

While the broader empirical evidence on the productivity effects of public-sector capital investment is mixed, the issue is clearly an important one in understanding growth dynamics.   ∎

7.2.2.3   An Overlapping Generations Model of Convergence in the Presence of Credit Market Imperfections

The assumption of section 7.2.2.2 that agents can borrow to finance physical capital but not human capital is analytically convenient but rather ad hoc. Certainly in an international setting, foreign debtors can no more seize physical capital than they can seize human capital. As we saw in Chapter 6, the main weapons of foreign creditors in the event of default are to impede a country's trade and to cut it off from future borrowing. Both of these sanctions would appear to be no more or less effective in dealing with a borrower whose income is generated by physical capital than a borrower whose income is generated by human capital. Even in a closed-economy context, the assumption that one cannot borrow against future income is very strong, though in some situations bankruptcy procedures may shield future earnings without shielding financial wealth.

In this section, we look at an overlapping generations model in which borrowing is limited to a fraction of current output. Unlike in the model of section 7.2.2.2, saving here is based on maximizing individual choices instead of being simply a constant fraction of current income. We also admit the possibility that countries have different autarky interest rates despite sharing the same production technology, perhaps because national preferences differ. As a consequence, absolute convergence need not take place, even in the long run. Whether convergence ultimately is complete depends on a simple and intuitive inequality, as we shall see. Since our main points do not require them, we abstract entirely from population and productivity growth. Also, human capital is not needed for our example, so we focus on a world in which there is only physical capital.

Again, think of a small country facing a fixed world interest rate r. Individuals live two periods and work only in the first period of life when they earn wage w_t. They may use their savings either to invest in domestic capital k_{t+1} or to lend in world markets at rate r. They can also borrow in world markets, but net borrowing is limited to a maximum of ηw_t.[28] Since w_t is a function of k_t, this constraint may seem exactly the same as in section 7.2.2.2. This analogy is not quite right. Here the operative constraint on borrowing is a function of current income, not of investment that the borrower promises to undertake in the future.

We again assume that the domestic production function is Cobb-Douglas,

$$y_t = k_t^\alpha.$$

We also assume that a fraction δ of the capital stock depreciates each period. In equilibrium, the domestic interest rate r^D must equal the net marginal return to

---

28. The reader may observe that in the models of Chapter 6, the borrowing constraint did not typically depend on current income but on expectations of future income. In equilibrium, however, expected future income depends on current income, so the text formulation may be considered a reduced form of a more complete model.

domestic investment,

$$r^{D} = f'(k) - \delta = \alpha k^{\alpha-1} - \delta. \tag{52}$$

The domestic interest rate r^{D} can exceed the world rate r when the borrowing constraint is binding.

An individual's budget constraints while young and old are given by

$$k_{t+1} + b_{t+1} = w_t - c_t^{Y}, \tag{53}$$

$$c_{t+1}^{O} = (1 + r_{t+1}^{D})k_{t+1} + (1 + r)b_{t+1}, \tag{54}$$

where b_{t+1} denotes individual asset holdings abroad (there is no government). There is also a constraint on how negative net foreign assets can be,

$$b_{t+1} \geq -\eta w_t. \tag{55}$$

A young individual maximizes the utility function

$$U_t = \log(c_t^{Y}) + \beta \log(c_{t+1}^{O})$$

subject to eqs. (53)–(55). To understand optimal saving behavior, combine eqs. (53) and (54) by eliminating k_{t+1}. One obtains the intertemporal constraint

$$c_t^{Y} + \frac{c_{t+1}^{O}}{1 + r_{t+1}^{D}} = w_t - \frac{(r_{t+1}^{D} - r)}{1 + r_{t+1}^{D}}b_{t+1}. \tag{56}$$

The right-hand side of eq. (56) is the present value of a young person's income, evaluated at the domestic interest rate. It depends on the wage plus the pure profit that can be made by borrowing abroad at rate r and investing in home capital.

We will skip the details of the individual's maximization problem, since these are by now familiar, and instead take a more heuristic approach to characterizing the equilibrium path for the economy. There are three possible cases to consider, depending on whether and when the domestic interest rate r^{D} exceeds the world rate r.[29] We will assume that in each case the country starts out at its *autarky* steady-state capital stock and then opens itself to the world capital market.

CASE 1: r^{D} *is equal to r after one period.*   If the net marginal product of capital is less than r at the country's autarky steady state, the country will be a net creditor in the international capital market. Even if the country needs to borrow

---

29. All three cases are based on a young individual's constrained maximization problem, with Lagrangian

$$\mathcal{L} = \log(c_t^{Y}) + \beta \log(c_{t+1}^{O}) + \lambda \left[w_t - \frac{(r_{t+1}^{D} - r)}{1 + r_{t+1}^{D}}b_{t+1} - c_t^{Y} - \frac{c_{t+1}^{O}}{1 + r_{t+1}^{D}} \right] + v[\eta w_t + b_{t+1}].$$

The Kuhn-Tucker necessary conditions are

to reach the efficient capital stock such that $f'(k) - \delta = r$, the amount it needs to borrow may be small enough that it doesn't hit its borrowing constraint. (We will make this statement precise in discussing Case 3.) In these cases, the domestic interest rate moves from its autarky level to r in a single period.

CASE 2: r^D *is always above* r.   Clearly individuals will always choose the highest possible level of borrowing, setting $-b_{t+1} = \eta w_t$, whenever $r^D_{t+1} > r$. In this case, the country's borrowing constraint will always bind. As usual with log utility and two periods of life, first-period consumption is a fraction $1/(1 + \beta)$ of lifetime income, and thus the per capita saving of the young is

$$s^Y_t = w_t - c^Y_t = \frac{\beta w_t}{1 + \beta} - \frac{\left(r^D_{t+1} - r\right)\eta w_t}{(1 + \beta)\left(1 + r^D_{t+1}\right)}.$$

Since additions to the capital stock are enhanced by foreign borrowing of $-b_{t+1} = \eta w_t$, the per-young-person capital stock k_{t+1} is therefore given by

$$k_{t+1} = s^Y_t - b_{t+1} = \left[\frac{\beta(1 + \eta)}{1 + \beta} + \frac{(1 + r)\eta}{(1 + \beta)(1 + r^D_{t+1})}\right] w_t \tag{57}$$

as long as the country's borrowing constraint is binding.

In equilibrium, $r^D_{t+1} = \alpha k^{\alpha-1}_{t+1} - \delta$ [by eq. (52)], and the wage is given by the marginal product of labor, $w_t = (1 - \alpha) k^\alpha_t$. Therefore, eq. (57) can be written as a difference equation that describes how the per capita capital stock changes through time under a binding borrowing constraint. To simplify matters a bit (without affecting the qualitative results), let us assume that capital depreciates by 100 percent in one period, so that $\delta = 1$.[30] Equation (57) can then be written

$$k_{t+1} = (1 - \alpha)\left[\frac{\beta(1 + \eta)}{1 + \beta} + \frac{(1 + r)\eta}{(1 + \beta)\alpha k^{\alpha-1}_{t+1}}\right]k^\alpha_t. \tag{58}$$

$\partial\mathcal{L}/\partial c^Y_t = 1/c^Y_t - \lambda = 0,$

$\partial\mathcal{L}/\partial c^O_{t+1} = \beta/c^O_{t+1} - \lambda/\left(1 + r^D_{t+1}\right) = 0,$

$\partial\mathcal{L}/\partial b_{t+1} = -\lambda\dfrac{(r^D_{t+1} - r)}{1 + r^D_{t+1}} + v = 0,$

the budget constraint (56), and the complementary slackness condition

$v[\eta w_t + b_{t+1}] = 0.$

The last condition tells us that the borrowing constraint must be binding ($\eta w_t + b_{t+1} = 0$) unless the multiplier v is zero, in which event the condition $\partial\mathcal{L}/\partial b_{t+1} = 0$ implies that r^D_{t+1} and r must be equal.

30. One hundred percent depreciation may seem like an extreme assumption, but remember that each of the two periods of life lasts around 25 years.

The case in which $\eta = 0$ is closely analogous to a closed-economy Solow model with the saving rate $s = (1 - \alpha)\beta/(1 + \beta)$ (together with zero technological change and population growth, and 100 percent depreciation). It is easy to see from eq. (57) that because an easing of the borrowing constraint lowers the domestic interest rate, the growth rate of the capital stock will be higher to the extent that η is higher (assuming k_t lies below the unconstrained steady state). Loosely speaking, greater capital inflows from abroad foster convergence.

We are now ready to ask under what conditions the domestic interest rate will converge to the world level. Note that if the capital stock is growing, the wages of young savers will rise over time, and by eq. (55) the country will be allowed to borrow increasing amounts. Will this be enough to drive the net marginal product of capital to the world interest rate r?

Let $\bar{k}^D$ denote the steady-state capital stock with constrained borrowing. We can find it in the usual way by setting $k_{t+1} = k_t = \bar{k}^D$ in eq. (58) and solving to yield

$$
\bar{k}^D = \left[\frac{\alpha\beta(1 - \alpha)(1 + \eta)}{\alpha(1 + \beta) - \eta(1 - \alpha)(1 + r)} \right]^{\frac{1}{1-\alpha}}
\tag{59}
$$

If $\bar{k}^U$ is the steady state that would be reached absent a borrowing constraint, one can show (after a bit of algebra) that the condition $\bar{k}^D < \bar{k}^U$ is the same as

$$
\frac{\beta\bar{w}}{1 + \beta} + \eta\bar{w} < \bar{k}^U,
\tag{60}
$$

where $\bar{w}$ is the wage of the young in the unconstrained steady state.[31]

Equation (60) has a simple interpretation. It says that an economy is unable to reach the unconstrained steady state $\bar{k}^U$ if, given $\bar{w}$, the saving of the young out of wages plus their maximum borrowing from abroad isn't enough to finance $\bar{k}^U$. Thus we find that a credit constraint can not only slow down absolute convergence, but can also prevent it from occurring even in the long run.

Clearly, a low saving rate (as captured by a low β) will make nonconvergence more likely. The economy's wage income serves as a collateral against foreign borrowing, but this may not be enough if residents are too impatient.

CASE 3: r^D *starts above* r, *but then converges to* r.   If the nonconvergence condition (60) is reversed, the economy will converge in the long run to $\bar{k}^U$. If the initial wage w_0 satisfies

$$
\frac{\beta w_0}{1 + \beta} + \eta w_0 \geq \bar{k}^U,
$$

---

31. To derive eq. (60), you will have to use the facts that $\bar{w} = (1 - \alpha)(\bar{k}^U)^\alpha$ and $r = \alpha(\bar{k}^U)^{\alpha-1} - 1$. Using eq. (60), one can show that the difference $\alpha(1 + \beta) - \eta(1 - \alpha)(1 + r)$ in eq. (59) is positive if the borrowing constraint is never slack.

convergence will take place in one period; saving out of wages plus the maximum allowable borrowing from abroad are sufficient to achieve the efficient capital stock. Otherwise, convergence will take several periods. Thus, in the setup of this section, absolute convergence may be achieved even if the country's autarky interest rate differs from that of the rest of the world. It will occur if the country is not too impatient and the credit constraint is not too strict.

The model we have presented is for a small country that faces an exogenously given world interest rate r. What happens in a two-country general equilibrium model in which the world interest rate is determined endogenously? Clearly, if the two countries are identical except for their initial capital stocks, convergence will eventually occur even in the absence of borrowing and lending. Trivially, both countries are heading toward identical steady states. Suppose, however, they differ in their rates of time preference. Then one can show that they will not converge if η is small enough and the difference in rates of time preference is large enough. Absolute convergence occurs only if countries are not too different from each other.

The models of this section give some interesting insights on convergence dynamics, but as we have emphasized, they are somewhat limited by their failure to endogenize market incompleteness. These models do not, for example, capture the possibility that moral hazard problems in investment may cause capital to flow from poor countries to rich countries, as we illustrated in section 6.4. The reader should note that the models developed here rely entirely on cross-country differences in capital stocks (physical and human) to explain income differentials. In practice, technologies are probably not identical across countries, and slow technology diffusion contributes to slow convergence.

7.3   Endogenous Growth

The neoclassical growth model provides important insights about growth, but it also has some serious limitations. The model tells us that in the long run, technological progress is the central factor driving changes in per capita income. But it says nothing about the factors that drive technological progress itself. Do larger economies innovate faster? How will international trade and capital-market integration promote growth? Can government subsidies to research and development raise a country's growth rate? Also, the neoclassical growth model is arguably limited in its ability to explain the magnitude and persistence of the real income gaps between poor and rich countries.

In recent years, a "new growth theory" has evolved that extends neoclassical growth theory to incorporate market-driven innovation and that therefore allows for endogenously driven growth. The pioneer in this new research was Paul Romer (1986, 1987, 1990). Other influential theoretical contributions include Lucas

(1988), Aghion and Howitt (1992), and G. Grossman and Helpman (1991). In this section, we will look at a couple of core models underlying this research, and we will also examine the empirical case for new growth theory.

It is helpful to think of new growth theory as consisting of two pieces. One is a "macro" piece that shows how an economy can sustain indefinite growth in per capita income even in the absence of exogenous technological change. The other is a "micro" piece that attempts to endogenize changes in technology by introducing an explicit research and development sector. We begin with the macro side.

7.3.1   The *AK* Model

In the Solow model, there are diminishing returns to scale in capital, holding efficiency labor constant. It is precisely for this reason that the economy eventually settles down to a steady-state growth path in which the capital-labor ratio is constant, and where the only source of growth in output per capita is exogenous technological progress. The *AK* model takes its name from the assumption that, at the aggregate level, output is linear in capital so that there are constant rather than diminishing returns to raising the capital-labor ratio. While fundamentally mechanical—it is really a model of perpetual growth through capital deepening rather than innovation—the *AK* model nonetheless provides a good introduction to the macro mechanics of new growth models.

Consider a closed economy in which the standard engines of neoclassical growth are absent: there is no technological progress, and the population's size is constant. The infinitely-lived representative consumer-manager has time-additive isoelastic preferences given by

$$U_t = \sum_{s=t}^{\infty} \beta^{s-t} \frac{c_s^{1-\frac{1}{\sigma}}}{1 - \frac{1}{\sigma}}, \qquad \sigma > 0. \tag{61}$$

As usual, equilibrium per capita consumption obeys

$$1 + r_{t+1} = \frac{1}{\beta} \left(\frac{c_{t+1}}{c_t} \right)^{\frac{1}{\sigma}}, \tag{62}$$

which is the familiar first-order Euler condition for the isoelastic case, rearranged in a way that will prove convenient. Each worker manages his own firm, the production technology of which is

$$y_t = Ak_t, \tag{63}$$

where k_t is the capital-to-(managerial)-labor ratio. Thus, in this example, there are constant returns to scale for capital at the firm level. As usual, we assume that capital can be transformed costlessly into consumption, and for simplicity we assume that depreciation is impounded into the productivity coefficient A.

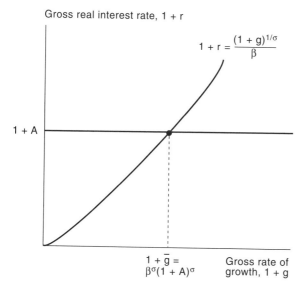

Figure 7.12
The *AK* model

In each period t, firms invest up to the point where the net marginal product of capital equals the interest rate, or

$$r_{t+1} = A. \tag{64}$$

At any interest rate other than A, firms would want to invest either an infinite amount or zero. Finally, the model is closed by the goods-market equilibrium condition,

$$c_t + i_t = y_t = Ak_t,$$

where $i = k_{t+1} - k_t$ denotes per capita investment.

The determination of the equilibrium is illustrated in Figure 7.12, which gives the gross real interest rate on the vertical axis and the gross growth rate of the economy, $1 + g = c_{t+1}/c_t$, on the horizontal axis. The curve parallel to the horizontal axis is technological condition (64) which governs the interest rate, and the upward-sloping curve is the Euler equation (62): for each interest rate the consumer faces, there is a corresponding desired rate of consumption growth. Equilibrium growth is constant through time (because the interest rate is) and is determined by the intersection of the two curves, where

$$\frac{c_{t+1}}{c_t} = [\beta(1 + A)]^\sigma = 1 + \bar{g}. \tag{65}$$

For eq. (61) to converge, we must assume that $\bar{r} = A > \bar{g}$ (recall section 2.1.3). We also assume that $\beta(1 + A) > 1$; otherwise, in equilibrium, the economy gradually runs down its capital in much the same way as an impatient small country facing a fixed world interest rate. Given these parameter restrictions, the steady state in Figure 7.12 has perpetual consumption growth at a positive net rate $\bar{g}$! Such a steady state is feasible provided the capital stock and output grow at rate $\bar{g}$ as well. To solve for the share of investment in GDP, note that if the capital stock is growing at rate $\bar{g}$, then per capita investment must equal

$$i_t = k_{t+1} - k_t = \bar{g}k_t = \frac{\bar{g}}{A}y_t,$$

where the final equality makes use of production function (63). Since $y_t = c_t + i_t$, this expression implies that

$$c_t = \frac{A - \bar{g}}{A}y_t.$$

A striking difference between the present model and the neoclassical growth model is that a change in the saving rate now has a *permanent* effect on the rate of growth of the economy. For example, eq. (65) shows that the more patient consumers are—the higher is β—the higher will $\bar{g}$ be. A second difference (one that is not a feature of all new growth models) is that the economy reaches its steady-state growth path immediately, as we have seen. There is no transition period. Intuitively, the reason for this instantaneous adjustment is that the production function is linear in k, and so ties down the interest rate independently of the economy's capital stock. Finally, observe that the market outcome is Pareto optimal here since there isn't any type of externality creating a wedge between the private and social marginal products of capital.[32]

Consider now a "learning by doing" variant of the model (due to P. Romer, 1986). Suppose that consumption is still characterized by Euler equation (62), but that each firm's j's output is given by

$$y_t^j = A\left(k_t^j\right)^\alpha k_t^{1-\alpha}, \tag{66}$$

where k^j is the individual firm's level of capital per worker, and k is the *economy-wide average* level of capital per worker. In this model each individual firm faces diminishing returns to its own investment, but the production function exhibits constant returns to scale in k^j and k taken together. The rationale for eq. (66), a variant of which was first proposed by Arrow (1962), is that the pro-

---

32. The formulation for the planner's problem involves maximizing eq. (61) subject to eq. (63) and the capital accumulation equation

$$k_{t+1} = k_t + y_t - c_t.$$

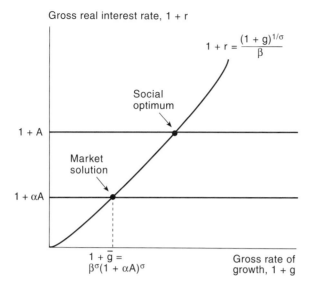

Figure 7.13
Learning by doing in the AK model

duction process generates knowledge externalities. The higher the average level of capital intensity in the economy, the greater the incidence of technological spillovers that raise the marginal productivity of capital throughout the economy. Given eq. (66), an individual firm views the marginal product of its own investment as

$$\frac{dy^j}{dk^j} = \alpha A \left(\frac{k}{k^j}\right)^{1-\alpha}. \tag{67}$$

In equilibrium, of course, $k^j = k$, so

$$\frac{dy}{dk} = \alpha A = r. \tag{68}$$

An individual's intertemporal optimal consumption allocation is still characterized by eq. (62), so that the market equilibrium is now given as in Figure 7.13.[33] The steady-state rate of growth of the economy is

$$\frac{c_{t+1}}{c_t} = [\beta(1 + \alpha A)]^\sigma = 1 + \bar{g}.$$

---

33. The similarity of the equilibrium for the learning-by-doing model to the one for the straight AK model obscures an important difference between the two. In the first model we considered, nontraded managerial labor received no income; if capital is paid its marginal product there is nothing left over for labor. In the learning-by-doing variant [characterized by production function (66)], payments to capital no longer exhaust output, since, at the *firm* level, there are diminishing returns to capital. The remaining share of income goes to labor. After modifying the individual's budget constraint to include labor income, one still obtains the usual first-order condition (62).

As before, the economy adjusts immediately to its steady-state equilibrium growth path. [Here, positive steady-state growth requires the restriction $\beta(1 + \alpha A) > 1$.]

Note that the market interest rate and the equilibrium growth rate are lower here than in our earlier example. Why? Because individual firms do not internalize the "learning-by-doing" externality their investment produces for other firms. The presence of the externality implies that, absent government intervention, the rate of growth of the economy is suboptimally low. The market equilibrium growth rate is suboptimally low because the planner faces the production function

$$y_t = Ak_t,$$

so that the socially optimal rate of growth is the same as in our earlier example. The government could try to step in and alleviate this problem by a subsidy that raises the perceived private return on investment to A from αA; a subsidy on gross output at rate $(1 - \alpha)/\alpha$ would produce the desired result. (The revenue could be raised by a constant proportional tax on consumption, which would be nondistorting here as there is no labor-leisure choice.)

Note that in the AK model, two closed economies that are alike except for their initial capital-labor ratios *do not* converge to identical per capita output levels. Only their growth rates converge. The early endogenous-growth literature viewed this as a major advantage of the model, arguing that it could thus potentially explain why the convergence evidence appears to be so mixed. Whether the data really demand an assumption of constant returns to scale in capital alone is now considered highly debatable, as we shall see in the application starting on p. 481 below.

For further refinements of the AK model, see, for example, Barro (1990), L. Jones and Manuelli (1990), and Rebelo (1991).

7.3.2   International Capital Market Integration and the AK Model

International capital market integration can raise the level of world output by allowing capital to migrate toward its most productive global uses. In this section, we use a stochastic version of the AK model to illustrate how world capital market integration can raise steady-state growth, even when countries have identical riskless autarky interest rates. The simple intuition is that the possibility of world portfolio diversification induces individuals to place a larger fraction of their wealth in high-yielding but risky capital investments. We begin with the closed economy in investment autarky.[34]

---

34. The analysis here is a simplified variant of the model in Obstfeld (1994c), who shows how the results extend to more general utility functions. That paper also illustrates that the growth effects of international portfolio diversification may be quite important empirically.

7.3.2.1   Technology and Preferences

Suppose that the representative agent has an infinite-horizon expected utility function given by

$$U_t = E_t \left\{ \sum_{s=t}^{\infty} \beta^{s-t} \log C_s \right\},$$

$$(69)$$

where we normalize the population to 1. As in the simplest AK model, we assume a linear technology with constant returns to scale in capital at the firm level. Now, however, there are two types of capital instead of one. The first offers a constant riskless gross return $1 + A$ per unit invested, as in the model of section 7.3.1. By the earlier logic, provided the stock of riskless capital is positive (which we assume), the gross riskless interest rate is $1 + r = 1 + A$. The other type of capital offers a risky return $1 + \tilde{r}_{t+1}$ per unit of capital invested on date t, where $\tilde{r}_{t+1}$ is an i.i.d. random variable such that $E_t\{\tilde{r}_{t+1}\} > r$. Capital can be moved from risky to riskless production, and vice versa, instantaneously and with no frictional costs.

Let K_t denote the *total* amount of capital (safe as well as risky) accumulated by the end of period $t - 1$. Capital is the only source of income in the model, so the representative agent's period budget constraint is

$$K_{t+1} = \left[x_t(1 + \tilde{r}_t) + (1 - x_t)(1 + r) \right] K_t - C_t,$$

$$(70)$$

with x_t denoting the end-of-period $t - 1$ share of capital invested in the risky asset.

This two-sector model generates endogenous steady-state growth in the same manner as are our earlier perfect-foresight model. The novel twist here is that the expected growth rate of the economy is an increasing function of the share of wealth invested in the risky asset. How is this share determined?

7.3.2.2   Optimal Consumption and Portfolio Shares

Supplement A to Chapter 5 shows how to solve stochastic intertemporal maximization problems of the type we have here. The first-order conditions for this problem imply the usual stochastic Euler conditions for the log case,

$$1 = (1 + r)\beta E_t \left\{ \frac{C_t}{C_{t+1}} \right\}$$

$$(71)$$

and

$$1 = \beta E_t \left\{ (1 + \tilde{r}_{t+1}) \frac{C_t}{C_{t+1}} \right\}.$$

$$(72)$$

The *level* of consumption is

$$C_t = (1 - \beta) \left[x_t(1 + \tilde{r}_t) + (1 - x_t)(1 + r) \right] K_t.$$

$$(73)$$

In our discussion of the equity premium puzzle in section 5.4.2, we showed that the first-order condition (72) can be linearized and combined with eq. (71) to yield the approximation

$$E_t(\tilde{r}_{t+1}) - r \approx (1+r)\beta \text{Cov}_t \left\{ \frac{C_{t+1}}{C_t} - 1, \tilde{r}_{t+1} - r \right\}. \tag{74}$$

(With log utility, the relative risk aversion coefficient $\rho = 1$.)

We can combine eqs. (70), (73), and (74) to solve for x_t, the share of total capital allocated to the risky activity. First, use eq. (73) to substitute out K_t and K_{t+1} in eq. (70) and derive

$$\frac{C_{t+1}}{C_t} - 1 = \beta \left[1 + r + x(\tilde{r}_{t+1} - r) \right] - 1, \tag{75}$$

where we have dropped the time subscripts on the share variable x. (With i.i.d. returns, shares will turn out to be constant over time in equilibrium.) Substituting eq. (75) into eq. (74) yields

$$E_t(\tilde{r}_{t+1} - r) \approx (1+r)\beta \text{Cov}_t \left\{ \beta[1 + r + x(\tilde{r}_{t+1} - r)] - 1, \tilde{r}_{t+1} - r \right\}$$

$$= x(1+r)\beta^2 \text{Var}_t(\tilde{r}_{t+1} - r).$$

Solving for x yields

$$x = \frac{E_t(\tilde{r}_{t+1} - r)}{\beta^2(1+r)\text{Var}_t(\tilde{r}_{t+1} - r)}. \tag{76}$$

Naturally, the share of risky capital in portfolios is positively related to the expected return differential $E_t(\tilde{r}_{t+1} - r)$ and negatively related to the variance of the risky return.

7.3.2.3 Expected Growth of Consumption and Output in the Closed Economy versus the Open Economy

Having solved for x, we can find the economy's expected gross rate of consumption growth by plugging eq. (76) into eq. (75):

$$E_t \left\{ \frac{C_{t+1}}{C_t} \right\} = \frac{\left[E_t(\tilde{r}_{t+1} - r) \right]^2}{\beta(1+r)\text{Var}_t(\tilde{r}_{t+1} - r)} + \beta(1+r). \tag{77}$$

The key implication of this approximate equation is that the expected consumption growth rate is a decreasing function of the variance of the risky return.

So far we have merely extended our nonstochastic AK model to a case with risky as well as riskless investment. Now let's extend the analysis to an open-economy setting. Assume that all countries throughout the world have the same preferences and technologies as before, but that the returns to risky projects are imperfectly correlated internationally. Since individuals in all countries have the same log preferences, they will hold the same portfolio consisting of the riskless asset and a single mutual fund of risky assets.[35] Denote the date $t+1$ realized rate of return on the world mutual fund by $\tilde{r}^W_{t+1}$. Risky capital is assumed to have the same mean rate of return in all countries, $E_t\{\tilde{r}^W_{t+1}\} = E_t\{\tilde{r}^n_{t+1}\}$ for all countries n. Following the same steps as previously, we find that

$$E_t\left\{\frac{C^n_{t+1}}{C^n_t}\right\} = \frac{[E_t(\tilde{r}^W_{t+1} - r)]^2}{\beta(1+r)\mathrm{Var}_t(\tilde{r}^W_{t+1} - r)} + \beta(1+r) \tag{78}$$

for every n. Since the world portfolio of risky capital is globally diversified, however, $\mathrm{Var}_t(\tilde{r}^W_{t+1}) < \mathrm{Var}_t(\tilde{r}^n_{t+1})$ for every n. It follows immediately that expected consumption growth under capital market integration [characterized by eq. (78)] is higher than under autarky [characterized by eq. (77)]. Because of the symmetry of the model, expected output growth is higher in each country as well.

The logic here is simple: the opportunity to diversify their portfolios induces people to allocate a larger share of wealth to high-expected-return, risky assets. Therefore, expected growth rises. We have derived this result in a model where there are constant returns to capital. In a model with decreasing returns, international portfolio diversification has a positive level effect on expected world output, but not a growth effect.

Having developed the theory of *AK* models in both an open- and closed-economy context, we now turn to some of the empirical evidence.

Application: Can Capital Deepening Be an Engine of Sustained High Growth Rates: Evidence from Fast-Growing East Asia

Many observers throughout the industrialized and developing world have cast a jealous eye toward the fast-growing economies of East Asia. Over sustained periods, these economies have achieved rates of per capita income growth that are simply remarkable. Between 1966 and 1990, growth in real GDP per capita averaged 5.7 percent per year in Hong Kong, 6.7 percent in Taiwan, and 6.8 percent in both Singapore and South Korea. Over the same period, growth in the OECD countries averaged only around 2 percent. In many parts of the developing world, growth has been even slower. It is well known that the East Asian "tigers" have very high rates of investment in both physical capital and education. Is their ability to sustain exceptionally high growth evidence in favor of an *AK*-type learning-by-doing model? It might seem so, since at first glance the Asian tigers appear to have

---

35. We assume again that in equilibrium, holdings of riskless capital are positive. Otherwise the world interest rate could be below r and financial integration might lower growth (while still raising welfare). See Devereux and Smith (1994) and Obstfeld (1994c).

sustained high growth rates without experiencing diminishing returns for an extraordinarily long period.

In a series of papers, Young (1992, 1994, 1995) has argued that *nothing* in the East Asian growth experience contradicts the lessons of the basic neoclassical growth model with diminishing returns to capital. Young finds no compelling evidence that these countries have enjoyed any sort of learning-by-doing externality. Rather, Young argues, the East Asian countries have been able to sustain their high growth rates only through steadily increasing rates of labor force participation and through phenomenally high, and often increasing, rates of investment.

The approach underlying Young's calculations is *growth accounting*, a methodology for decomposing growth into the component due to higher inputs and the component due to higher productivity. (We introduced this concept earlier in the application on public capital investment and growth, but we explain it again here to make the present discussion self-contained.) Suppose, for example, that a country's production function is $Y_t = A_t K_t^\alpha L_t^{1-\alpha}$. Taking the natural logarithm of this equation and subtracting the corresponding equation for $t - 1$, one obtains

$$y_t - y_{t-1} = a_t - a_{t-1} + \alpha(k_t - k_{t-1}) + (1 - \alpha)(l_t - l_{t-1}),$$

where lowercase sans serif letters denote logs, for example, $y_t \equiv \log Y_t$. Because $\alpha < 1$, the equation shows that there are diminishing returns to increasing capital alone. The rate of growth of total factor productivity, $a_t - a_{t-1}$, is measured by forming an estimate of α and calculating measures of $k_t - k_{t-1}$ and $l_t - l_{t-1}$. Any residual that cannot be explained by measured factor inputs is assumed to be attributable to total factor productivity growth.

Young's approach actually involves a more general translog production function, and it also attempts to adjust for the quality of physical capital and labor inputs. This adjustment is especially important because improvements in the education system in East Asia have sharply increased the overall level of human capital.

Young's growth accounting reveals that high rates of growth in factor inputs, rather than extraordinary productivity gains, can explain most of East Asia's rapid output growth. Aside from increased educational attainment, these countries have generally experienced sharp increases in labor force participation (especially due to increased participation of women in labor forces) and very high rates of investment. Adjustment for labor-force growth alone already shows that output per worker has grown much less rapidly than output as a ratio to total population. At the same time, many East Asian countries have engaged in levels of physical capital investment that are exceptionally high. Singapore's investment in physical capital has consistently exceeded 30 percent of GDP since the 1970s, reaching levels as high as 47 percent in 1984 and 40 percent in 1990. South Korea's investment also approached 40 percent of GDP by 1990. As Table 7.3 illustrates, East Asian

Table 7.3
Average Annual Total Factor Productivity Growth in East Asia and the G-7 Countries

Country	Period	Annual Growth (percent)
Hong Kong	1966–91	2.3
Singapore	1966–90	0.2
South Korea	1966–90	1.7
Taiwan	1966–90	2.1
Canada	1960–89	0.5
France	1960–89	1.5
Germany	1960–89	1.6
Italy	1960–89	2.0
Japan	1960–89	2.0
United Kingdom	1960–89	1.3
United States	1960–89	0.4

Source: Young (1995).

productivity growth rates seem less impressive once one controls for the region's high level of factor input growth.

Overall, the East Asian countries have generally enjoyed strong gains in to-tal factor productivity but not supernormal gains (though productivity growth in high-investment Singapore has actually been only 0.2 percent per year). Young concludes that there is nothing of importance in the East Asian growth experience that cannot be accounted for by a model with constant returns to scale in physical capital, human capital, and raw labor taken jointly, and diminishing returns in each input taken individually. One inference that might be drawn from Young's results is that the period of booming growth in East Asia—growth that has been achieved largely through sacrifice of current consumption—must eventually come to an end, just as the basic neoclassical model insists.   ∎

7.3.3   A Model of Endogenous Innovation and Growth

The *AK* models are of theoretical interest, but, as we have seen, the empirical evidence doesn't support the view that a country can sustain indefinite growth in per capita income through physical and human capital deepening alone. In this section, we turn to the alternative endogenous growth model of P. Romer (1990), in which invention is a purposeful economic activity that requires real resources. This is the "micro" side of new growth theory. By explicitly modeling the research and development process, one can gain important insights into the effects of both government policy and international integration on growth.

The trickiest problem in introducing an R&D sector is deciding how to deal with the fact that ideas are *nonrival*. A unit of physical capital can only be used by one firm at a time. In contrast, there are no technological barriers preventing more than one firm from simultaneously using the same idea. Indeed, if firms are to have an incentive to innovate, there must exist some type of institutional mechanism that allows an inventor to appropriate rents from his discovery. The Romer model, following Judd (1985), handles this problem by assuming that inventors can obtain patent licenses on the "blueprints" for their inventions.

There are a number of ways to model how innovation affects production. Inventions might expand the variety or improve the quality of consumer products. Alternatively, research and development might lead to new methods for achieving more efficient production. Both of these channels are important in practice, but to maintain comparability with our earlier treatment of exogenous technological progress, we will focus on the production efficiency channel.[36] Specifically, we will assume that inventions lead to the development of new *types* of intermediate goods ("capital") that enhance the productivity of labor in the production of a single, homogenous consumption good. It will be convenient to think of the economy as having three sectors, one producing final consumer goods, one producing blueprints for new capital goods, and an intermediate goods sector that produces capital goods that are sold to producers of consumer goods. There is free entry into each of the sectors.

7.3.3.1 Final Goods Production

Consider a closed economy in which "final goods" production function is given by

$$Y_t = L_{Y,t}^{1-\alpha} \sum_{j=1}^{A_t} K_{j,t}^{\alpha}, \tag{79}$$

where $j \in \{1, 2, \ldots, A_t\}$ indexes the different types of capital goods K_j that can be used in production. The parameter A_t captures the number of types of capital that have been invented as of date t. The variable L_Y denotes labor used in final goods production. The economy's total labor supply is L, but some portion of it may be allocated to research and development.[37]

The production function (79) is familiar in that it exhibits constant returns to scale in L_Y and the K_j's taken jointly. In other ways, though, it is radically different from our usual one. Until now, we have implicitly treated different types of capital as perfect substitutes that can be aggregated into a summary measure K. In eq. (79), however, production is an additively separable function of the differ-

---

36. See G. Grossman and Helpman (1991) and Barro and Sala-i-Martin (1994) for treatments of the different channels by which invention can have an impact on the economy.

37. The original P. Romer (1990) model has human capital as a third factor of production. The present, more streamlined model, is actually closer to the continuous time formulation in G. Grossman and Helpman (1991, ch. 5).

ent types of capital goods, so that an increase in K_j has no effect on the marginal productivity of K_i, $i \neq j$. That is,

$$\frac{\partial Y}{\partial K_j} = \alpha L_Y^{1-\alpha} K_j^{\alpha-1} \tag{80}$$

is independent of the level of all other capital goods i.

Despite the more general form of the production function, the model here would give qualitatively similar results to those of our earlier growth models if the range of capital goods A (the level of technology) were determined exogenously. The only difference would be that the economy would spread investment resources among the different types of capital. Our assumption of endogenous R&D seems quite compelling, though, given the strong economic incentive for developing new products in this model. As eq. (80) shows, there are decreasing returns to investment in any type of capital already in use. But the marginal product of a *new* capital good is

$$\alpha L_Y^{1-\alpha} K_j^{\alpha-1} |_{K_j=0} = \infty.$$

It is infinite.

7.3.3.2   The Production of Blueprints

Production in the R&D sector is assumed to depend on the amount of labor employed L_A, and on the current technology, captured by the range of existing blueprints for capital goods, A,

$$A_{t+1} - A_t = \theta A_t L_{A,t}, \tag{81}$$

where θ is a productivity shift parameter. In order to ensure a steady-state growth path where interest rates are constant, we will assume that the total labor force available for employment in the consumption and R&D sectors is constant, so that

$$L = L_A + L_Y. \tag{82}$$

Equation (81) embodies two important assumptions. First, it assumes that the greater the body of existing knowledge, A_t, the lower the labor cost of generating new knowledge. Even if inventors can ration the use of their creations in final goods production, there is generally little they can do to prevent other inventors from drawing on their ideas to create new blueprints. Our assumption of learning by doing in research and development may be extreme, but it is plausible.[38] Second, specification (81) implicitly embodies the assumption that there are constant

---

38. Rivera-Batiz and Romer (1991) and Barro and Sala-i-Martin (1994) look at models where invention requires paying a fixed cost. The "lab equipment" model of invention yields results generally similar to those of the model in the text, though there are slight differences in prescriptions for government intervention to promote growth.

returns to scale in A taken alone. If the right-hand side of eq. (81) were $\theta A^{\psi} L_A$, with $\psi < 1$, we would find that this model would not generate steady-state growth, absent labor supply growth. The question of whether there is steady-state growth should not concern us too much, since most of the model's central insights on the role of research and development in the economy apply equally to the case where output per capita converges to a constant.

Once developed, a blueprint shows how to combine raw material (in the form of final output) to produce quantities of the new capital good. One unit of the final good input in period t yields one unit of $K_{j,t+1}$.[39] To keep the algebra tractable, it is convenient to assume that a blueprint can be put into production immediately during the same period it is developed, and that capital goods produced in period t depreciate by 100 percent when used in production in period $t + 1$. The 100 percent depreciation assumption insures that the rental and sales prices for a machine are the same.[40]

7.3.3.3 Pricing and Production of Intermediate Capital Goods

How are blueprints allocated after being invented? A variety of institutional mechanisms are possible, but a simple approach is to assume a third sector that intermediates between the R&D sector and the final goods production sector. In particular, we will assume that firms in the R&D sector sell blueprints to an intermediate capital goods sector that manufactures the designs in period t, and then sells the machines to firms in the final goods production sector in period $t + 1$. Obviously, it would also be possible to have the R&D sector manufacture and license machines, or to assume that the intermediate capital goods sector is vertically integrated into the final goods sector. In our specification, once an intermediate goods producer buys the blueprint to produce capital good j, it becomes the monopoly supplier of that type of capital to the final goods sector.

Because some goods are allocated monopolistically, solving the Romer model involves a few more steps than did solving the AK model. Ultimately we have to find what percent of the economy's labor supply is allocated to R&D and how final output is divided between investment and consumption. But first we must tackle the intermediate step of figuring out the prices at which the R&D sector sells its

---

39. It does not really matter whether we view final output as being directly converted to the intermediate good, or instead think of the final goods sector as producing both types of good using the same production function. What matters is that the resources diverted to production of intermediate capital goods subtract from the resources available to produce final consumption goods.

40. If the capital machines did not depreciate by 100 percent each period and if there were no rental market, manufacturers of intermediate capital goods would face credibility problems. In particular, they would have an incentive to announce low future values of production in order to raise current sales prices (if the machines are durable, future implicit rents will be higher if fewer machines are in existence). But once the machines have been sold, there will in general be an incentive to renege and produce more machines than promised. An analysis of credibility problems in durable goods monopoly is Bulow (1982).

blueprints and the prices the intermediate goods sector charges for its machines. The two are interrelated, of course, because the price of blueprints, p_A, depends on the profits the intermediate sector can expect to earn for producing and selling machines.

To solve the model, we will guess that its equilibrium involves a constant real interest rate, constant relative prices, and a constant allocation of labor across the two sectors. (We will later confirm that this guess is correct.) Then, given the production function (79) and the assumption that there is 100 percent depreciation of intermediate capital goods, one can easily derive the demand for intermediate capital goods by the final goods sector as the solution to the static maximization problem

$$\max_{\{K_j\}} L_Y^{1-\alpha} \sum_{j=1}^{A_t} K_j^\alpha - \sum_{j=1}^{A_t} p_j K_j, \tag{83}$$

where p_j is the price of capital good K_j in terms of final goods. Because production is separable among the capital goods K_j, the demand for each capital good is separable as well. [Note that if our stationarity conjecture is correct, A_t is the only variable in eq. (83) that is changing over time.] Maximizing eq. (83) with respect to K_j yields

$$p_j = \alpha L_Y^{1-\alpha} K_j^{\alpha-1}. \tag{84}$$

Thus each intermediate goods producer faces a constant-price-elasticity demand curve, so that a 1 percent rise in price leads to a $1/(1-\alpha)$ percent fall in demand. To maximize current profits, the intermediate goods producer sets K_j to maximize

$$\Pi_j = \frac{p_j K_j}{1+r} - K_j = \frac{\alpha L_Y^{1-\alpha} K_j^\alpha}{1+r} - K_j. \tag{85}$$

This equation embodies the assumption that capital sold in period t must be produced in period $t-1$; hence future sales must be discounted by $1+r$. Maximizing profits (85) with respect to K_j and solving implies that

$$\bar{K} = \left(\frac{\alpha^2}{1+r}\right)^{1/(1-\alpha)} L_Y, \tag{86}$$

where we have dropped the j subscripts since the solution is symmetric across intermediate goods producers. (Overbars denote values associated with the economy's steady-state growth path.) Substituting eq. (86) into eq. (84) yields

$$\bar{p} = \frac{1+r}{\alpha}. \tag{87}$$

Given that the cost of producing the capital good is $1 + r$ (in terms of the final consumption good), we see that eq. (87) implies a price that is a constant markup over cost. This is just the usual formula for a monopolist facing a constant price elasticity of demand. Note that the price of capital does not depend on the range or the quantity of capital goods being produced; this again comes from the assumption of separability in the production function. Finally, substituting eqs. (86) and (87) into eq. (85) implies that the present-value profit on capital produced in period $t - 1$ for sale in period t is

$$\bar{\Pi} = \frac{\bar{p}\bar{K}}{1+r} - \bar{K} = \left(\frac{1-\alpha}{\alpha}\right)\left(\frac{\alpha^2}{1+r}\right)^{\frac{1}{1-\alpha}} L_Y. \tag{88}$$

We now know what the blueprint for a new capital good is worth to an intermediate goods producer in terms of profits per period. Thus we can turn to asking what a blueprint will sell for, a price we have denoted by p_A. Since there is free entry into the intermediate goods sector, the value of a blueprint must equal the entire present discounted value of the profit stream an intermediate goods producer will enjoy after purchasing it:

$$\bar{p}_A = \sum_{s=t}^{\infty} \frac{\bar{\Pi}}{(1+r)^{s-t}} = \frac{(1+r)\bar{\Pi}}{r}. \tag{89}$$

(Remember that a blueprint developed and sold in period t can be put into production in the same period.)

7.3.3.4 Solving for the Equilibrium Rate of Growth

Having solved for the prices of blueprints and of intermediate capital goods, it is now a simple matter to find the steady-state growth path of the economy. If L_A is constant over time, then by eq. (81), the growth rate of A is

$$\bar{g} = \frac{A_{t+1} - A_t}{A_t} = \theta \bar{L}_A. \tag{90}$$

In a steady state, the number of capital good types grows at rate $\bar{g}$, whereas the quantity of each type of capital good remains constant at $\bar{K}$.

The final key step in solving the supply side of the model is to determine the allocation of human capital between the R&D sector and the final goods sector. Equating the marginal product of labor in the two sectors implies

$$\frac{\partial(\bar{p}_A \theta A L_A)}{\partial L_A} = \bar{p}_A \theta A = (1-\alpha)L_Y^{-\alpha} A\bar{K}^\alpha = \frac{\partial Y}{\partial L_Y}, \tag{91}$$

where the far left-hand expression is the marginal product of labor in the R&D sector and we have made use of the fact that in the symmetric equilibrium,

$\sum_{j=1}^{A} \bar{K}_j^{\alpha} = A\bar{K}^{\alpha}$.[41] After substituting for $\bar{p}$, $\bar{K}$, and $\bar{p}_A$ in eq. (91) using eqs. (86), (88), and (89), one obtains

$$\bar{L}_Y = \frac{r}{\theta\alpha},$$

(92)

which is consistent with our steady-state assumption that L_Y is constant. Combining eq. (90) with eqs. (82) and (92) implies a technology-determined relationship between the rate of growth of the economy and the interest rate:

$$\bar{g} = \theta L - \frac{r}{\alpha}.$$

Written in terms of gross interest rates and growth rates this becomes:

$$1 + \bar{g} = \left(\theta L + \frac{1+\alpha}{\alpha}\right) - \frac{1+r}{\alpha}.$$

(93)

Equation (93) is analogous to the marginal product of capital equations in our earlier AK model, except that it is downward-sloping as illustrated by the **TT** curve in Figure 7.14.

So far, we have only dealt with the supply side of the model. To close it, we need to specify demand. We again assume infinitely-lived consumers with isoelastic period utility,

$$U_t = \sum_{s=t}^{\infty} \beta^{s-t} \frac{c_s^{1-\frac{1}{\sigma}}}{1 - \frac{1}{\sigma}},$$

so that the individual's Euler condition is again given by eq. (62). (Because population size turns out to be quite important here, we do not adopt the convention of normalizing the population to 1.) We can aggregate across the identical agents to derive the Euler equation for aggregate consumption,

$$1 + g = \frac{C_{t+1}}{C_t} = [(1+r)\beta]^{\sigma},$$

or

$$1 + r = \frac{1}{\beta}(1+g)^{\frac{1}{\sigma}}.$$

(94)

---

41. Given that $K_j = \bar{K}$ is the same across firms, in a steady state one can rewrite the production function (79) as

$$Y = L^{1-\alpha} \sum_{j=1}^{A} K_j^{\alpha} = L^{1-\alpha} A\bar{K}^{\alpha}.$$

If A were exogenous, this function would be exactly the same as in a standard Solow model.

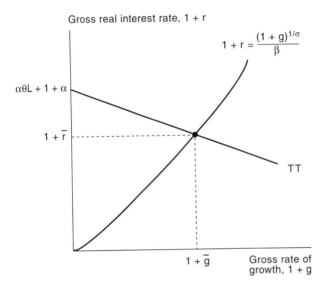

Figure 7.14
Paul Romer's growth model

Equation (94) is drawn as the upward-sloping curve in Figure 7.14. Because capital depreciates by 100 percent in production, the economy jumps immediately to a steady state in which K, Y, C, and A grow at the same constant rate, determined by the intersection of the two curves in the figure. (If capital were durable as in P. Romer, 1990, there would be a transition period if the initial ratio A/K differed from that along the steady-state path.) Our assumption that equilibrium interest rates, relative prices, and labor allocations are constant over time thus is confirmed.

For the case of log utility ($\sigma = 1$), eqs. (93) and (94) imply that the equilibrium interest rate is given by

$$\bar{r} = \frac{\alpha(1 + \theta L - \beta)}{1 + \alpha\beta}, \tag{95}$$

$$\bar{g} = \frac{\alpha\beta\theta L - (1 - \beta)}{1 + \alpha\beta}. \tag{96}$$

Note that since negative growth is not possible in this model (assuming ideas cannot be forgotten), we require the condition

$$\theta L > \frac{1 - \beta}{\alpha\beta}$$

for an interior equilibrium in the log case. If the initial size of the economy is too small for this condition to be met, the profits from invention are insufficient to pay for the labor costs, and there will be no innovation or growth.

We observe that the growth rate given by eq. (96) is an increasing function of the total labor supply L. Graphically, a rise in L shifts the **TT** technology curve upward, implying an increase in the rate of technology growth. Why? Basically, the more people there are in the economy, the more new processes are discovered, and the faster the rate of growth. The model embodies the perfectly plausible assumption that the same discovery can be spread out across a larger economy without any decreasing returns.

7.3.3.5   Government Policy and the Socially Optimal Rate of Growth

The "learning-by-doing" version of the AK model admitted the possibility of welfare-enhancing government intervention. Beneficial intervention was possible because individual firms didn't internalize the effects of their investments on the productivity of other firms. In the Romer model, there are two sources of inefficiency. One, coming from the R&D sector, is analogous to the learning-by-doing externality: R&D firms do not take into account that their inventions will lower the amount of labor required to create inventions in the future. Second, firms producing intermediate capital goods assume a monopoly position once they buy rights to a blueprint. As monopolists, they tend to produce less than the socially efficient quantities of capital. A social planner would instead maximize the lifetime utility function of the representative agent subject to the R&D production function (81), the aggregate labor constraint (82), the final output production function

$$Y_t = L_{Y,t}^{1-\alpha} A_t K_t^{\alpha}$$

[which is derived from eq. (79)], and the budget constraint

$$Y_t = C_t + A_{t+1} K_{t+1}.$$

In both these equations, we have taken advantage of the model's inherent symmetry to impose the assumption that the planner will produce equal quantities of all the intermediate capital goods. (There is no intertemporal constraint involving capital because we have assumed that there is 100 percent depreciation and that therefore all capital used in tomorrow's production is produced today.) The solution for the planner's problem with log utility ($\sigma = 1$) is given by[42]

---

42. The solution to the planner's problem is found by differentiating the Lagrangian

$$\sum_{s=t}^{\infty} \beta^{s-t} \{\log[A_s K_s^{\alpha}(L - L_{A,s})^{1-\alpha} - A_{s+1}K_{s+1}] + \lambda_s(A_{s+1} - A_s - \theta A_s L_{A,s})\}$$

with respect to $L_{A,s}$, A_{s+1}, and K_{s+1}, and solving for the steady state where $C_{s+1}/C_s = 1 + \bar{g}$. One can show that the steady level of K under the planner's problem is given by

$$\bar{K}^{\mathrm{PLAN}} = \alpha^{\frac{1}{1-\alpha}} \left(\frac{1-\beta}{\theta}\right)(1+\theta L)^{\frac{\alpha}{\alpha-1}}.$$

$$\bar{g}^{\text{PLAN}} = \beta\theta L - (1 - \beta). \tag{97}$$

Comparing eqs. (97) and (96), we see that the growth rate for the planner's problem is unambiguously higher. Again, there are two distortions. First, firms in the R&D sector do not internalize the fact that their inventions will lower the cost of producing future inventions. Second, for any given allocation of labor, monopolistic suppliers set K lower than a planner would. That is, they underutilize inventions, creating a static inefficiency (albeit one that affects R&D employment).

Suppose the government subsidizes the production of intermediate goods, financing the subsidy by lump-sum taxes. The subsidy is set so that for every dollar of sales, the intermediate-goods-producing firm receives $1/\alpha$ dollars. [This return would require an ad valorem subsidy rate of $(1 - \alpha)/\alpha$.] Then, retracing the steps in section 7.3.3.3, we see that intermediate goods suppliers would set $\bar{p} = 1 + r$ and $\bar{K} = [\alpha/(1 + r)]^{1/(1-\alpha)} L_Y$. Such a policy would eliminate the static inefficiency problem caused by monopoly supply of intermediate goods, but would do nothing about the externality resulting from the fact that additions to the stock of blueprints lower the cost of future inventions. In this case, the growth rate of output is given by

$$\bar{g} = \frac{\beta\theta L - (1 - \beta)}{1 + \beta},$$

which is intermediate between the growth rate chosen by a planner and the market growth rate in the absence of a subsidy, eq. (96). To eliminate the remaining distortion, the planner must also subsidize R&D.

Lest the unwary reader get too excited about the possibilities for government intervention to promote growth, we note that the predictions of new growth models concerning intervention can be quite sensitive to specification as, for example, G. Grossman and Helpman (1991) show. In some models, a policy that raises growth may decrease welfare. In practice, moreover, a government must decide what kind of research and development to subsidize.

Application: Population Size and Growth

A straightforward corollary of the Romer model is that as a country's population grows, its rate of per capita income growth will increase. The more people there are around to invent things and the bigger the market for inventions, the greater the rate at which inventions will be discovered. At first blush, this seems to be a rather embarrassing prediction for an endogenous growth model, since some of the countries with the world's largest populations rank among its poorest. Tiny Luxembourg has a per capita income more than ten times that of behemoth India. Kremer (1993) argues that perhaps we should take the population size predictions of new growth models seriously anyway. But, as Kremer points out, the best measure of size for gauging the pace of innovation is *world* population. His argument assumes that over long enough horizons, technology advances diffuse across borders.

Kremer's basic framework combines a very simple version of the Romer model with a Malthusian model of population growth. Its main elements are as follows. Technology growth is assumed to be positively related to the overall size of the population,

$$A_{t+1} - A_t = \theta A_t L_t, \tag{98}$$

as in the Romer model. Kremer does not worry about the nuances of how market forces determine the pace of innovation. He simply assumes that invention is proportional to population, reasoning that this is the equilibrium outcome of some process that governs R&D allocation.

Output is given by

$$Y_t = A_t L_t^{1-\alpha}. \tag{99}$$

Think of the decreasing returns to labor as resulting from some fixed factor such as land.[43] Finally, the level of population—which until now we have treated as exogenous—is assumed to increase endogenously up to the point where everyone is living at a subsistence level governed by the Malthusian relationship

$$\bar{C}^{\text{MIN}} = \frac{Y_t}{L_t}, \tag{100}$$

where $\bar{C}^{\text{MIN}}$ is subsistence consumption. Using eq. (100) to substitute for Y in eq. (99) yields

$$A_t = \bar{C}^{\text{MIN}} L_t^{\alpha}. \tag{101}$$

Finally, substituting eq. (101) into eq. (98) gives a difference equation in L,

$$L_{t+1}^{\alpha} - L_t^{\alpha} = \theta L_t^{1+\alpha},$$

which can be written as

$$\frac{L_{t+1}}{L_t} = (\theta L_t + 1)^{\frac{1}{\alpha}}. \tag{102}$$

Equation (102) is the fundamental equation of the Kremer model. Its key prediction is that a higher *level* of population L_t implies a faster rate of population *growth*

---

43. In the neoclassical growth models we studied earlier in this chapter, the long-run marginal product of labor was independent of the *level* of the labor supply. As long as the production function exhibits constant returns to scale in capital and labor taken jointly, there are no diminishing returns to labor in the long run. With a fixed factor such as land, this is no longer the case.

Table 7.4
World Population Growth, 1,000,000 B.C. to 1990

Start of Period	Population (millions)	Population Growth Rate (percent per year)	Major Calamities
−1,000,000	0.125	0.0003	
−25,000	3.34	0.0020	
−5000	5	0.0562	
−2000	27	0.0873	
−500	100	0.1062	
1	170	0.0559	
200	190	0.0	
400	190	0.0256	
600	200	0.0477	
800	220	0.0931	
1000	265	0.1533	
1200	360	0.0	Mongol invasions
1300	360	−0.0282	Black Death
1400	350	0.2217	
1600	545	0.1127	Thirty Years War, Ming dynasty fall
1700	610	0.3897	
1800	900	0.5926	
1900	1625	1.0125	
1980	4450	1.8101	

L_{t+1}/L_t. Basically, the model says that the more people there are around to innovate, the faster the rate at which mankind develops technologies to support higher population.[44]

Since the Malthusian relationship (100) is one that presumably holds only over the very long term, Kremer tests eq. (102) on global population data from the year 1 million B.C. through 1990! Table 7.4, taken from Kremer (1993), reports world population growth alongside the world population level. (The early data points are based on archaeologists' estimates.) Except for a few outliers attributable to wars and plagues, the long-run data show a remarkable correlation between the level of population and the rate of population growth over very long periods.

Kremer offers a second piece of prehistoric evidence in favor of his hypothesis. The last ice age led to a breakup of the land bridges that connected the Eurasian-African, North American, Australian, and Tasmanian continents. Kremer argues that technology may be assumed to have evolved rather independently across these land masses until about 1500 when communication was reestablished. Assuming that initial populations were proportional to land area, Kremer's theory predicts that the larger land masses would have experienced faster population growth during

---

44. Kremer also considers some more general variants of his model that allow for research productivity as a function of income and as a function of the general level of technology.

the periods of autarky. He finds that the data support this hypothesis. Tiny Tasmania, for example, grew far more slowly than the larger continents.

A skeptic could argue that one can find other explanations for the exponential rise in population growth over time, and that the evidence on population size and technological advance is much thinner. Also, there have clearly been periods, such as the Dark Ages in Europe, when the stock of ideas, if anything, seemed to decrease. Nevertheless, Kremer's evidence points to a fascinating stylized fact about growth deserving more detailed study.   ∎

7.3.3.6   Implications of Global Integration

We have already seen the Romer model's prediction that a rise in population leads to a higher steady-state growth rate. An immediate implication is that when two identical economies merge, their steady-state growth rates will rise. An integrated global economy can better exploit scale economies. (Rivera-Batiz and Romer, 1991, emphasize this result.)

A related implication of the model is that when two economies merge, the resulting world interest rate does not have to lie between the two autarky interest rates! Suppose that the home and foreign economies are identical except that the home economy has a larger labor supply. The Romer model [see eq. (95)] implies that the larger economy will have the higher autarky interest rate. By the same logic, it is easy to see that when the two economies merge, the resulting steady-state interest rate will be higher than either country's autarky rate. It is important to stress that this result really stems from the integration of the two countries' goods markets and not the integration of their capital markets. Allowing for trade in goods (and blueprints) while continuing to keep capital markets in autarky would lead to the same outcome.

While the result that greater integration promotes growth is a sensible one, it is possible to come up with examples where opening an economy to trade lowers the rate of growth. Consider the following simple example based on G. Grossman and Helpman (1990). A small two-sector economy produces two consumption goods, Y and X, using inputs of land Z and labor L that are fixed in total supply. The constant-returns-to-scale production functions for the two goods are

$$Y_t = A_t F(Z_{Y,t}, L_{Y,t}),$$

$$X_t = A_t F(Z_{X,t}, L_{X,t}),$$

where Z_Y and L_Y are land and labor inputs to production of good Y, and Z_X and L_X are the inputs to X production. There is no investment. Aggregate resource constraints are:

$$L_X + L_Y = \bar{L},$$

$$Z_X + Z_Y = \bar{Z}.$$

Finally, consumers have time-additive preferences, and the period utility function is homothetic in consumption of Y and X.

It is easy to check that the static allocation in this economy is independent of the level of technology A. That is, factor allocations and the relative price of good X in terms of Y are both independent of A. The reason, of course, is that the level of technology affects productivity in both sectors proportionately.

Suppose now there is a "learning-by-doing" externality arising only from the production of good X:

$$A_{t+1} - A_t = \theta X_t A_t.$$

Assume, however, that there is no way for producers in the X sector to capture the benefits of the knowledge externality they generate, despite the fact that it raises productivity equally in both sectors. Because X-sector firms ignore the effects of their actions on productivity growth, both the allocations of factors across sectors and the relative price of good X will be the same as in a static economy with no productivity growth. The economy will grow over time at a rate that depends on the equilibrium share of factors employed in the sector with knowledge spillovers.

Now assume that the economy opens itself up to trade in goods. Production takes place independently at home and abroad, with no knowledge externalities across national borders. It is easy to check that the effect of opening on growth depends on whether the world price of good X lies above or below the autarky price. If the world price of X is higher, factors will flow into the X sector and growth will rise. But if the world price is lower, factors will flow out of the X sector and the rate of productivity growth will fall. This simple example embodies many special assumptions, but it shows that it is possible to come up with counterexamples to the proposition that more open economies necessarily grow faster.[45]

7.4   Stochastic Neoclassical Growth Models

When discussing international portfolio diversification in Chapter 5, we focused largely on endowment economies. In this section, we extend the analysis to incorporate investment in general equilibrium. For the purpose of portfolio diversification issues, incorporating capital adds little to our earlier analysis. However, stochastic general equilibrium growth models have become quite popular as a framework for trying to understand business cycles. The *real business cy-*

---

45. In Chapter 6, we looked at a model with moral hazard in investment at the microeconomic level. There we showed that the poorer country may actually see a decline in investment when it merges with the richer country. In a growth setting, this phenomenon could also produce the result that a country's growth rate falls upon integration into global capital markets.

cle (RBC) approach, first clearly articulated by Kydland and Prescott (1982) and Prescott (1986), argues that one cannot separate growth from business cycle issues as the postwar Keynesians tried to do. Rather, growth and business cycles must be treated within an integrated theory. Today, the canonical RBC analysis is based on a stochastic growth model with complete markets in which productivity shocks are the main force behind business cycles.

We have already seen that the simplest versions of complete-markets models are seriously at odds with some important properties of international business cycle data. They predict that consumption will be more correlated across countries than output, but the opposite is closer to the truth. The home bias puzzle in portfolio allocation also seems to contradict the complete-markets model. Nevertheless, we pursue the models further because they are important methodologically and because efforts to reconcile RBC models with the data remain an active area of research. (For alternative evaluations of the approach, see the papers by Hansen and Heckman, 1996, Kydland and Prescott, 1996, and Sims, 1996.)

7.4.1   A Closed Economy with Immediate Capital Depreciation

We begin by looking at a simplified closed-economy model in which capital depreciates by 100 percent each period. Though not terribly realistic, the model has a simple closed-form solution and is therefore useful in highlighting some key issues. To simplify further, we posit a constant population and zero trend technology growth, two assumptions that are easily relaxed. The main conclusions about fluctuations would not be changed by explicitly allowing for growth.

The representative consumer has the utility function

$$U_t = E_t \left\{ \sum_{s=t}^{\infty} \beta^{s-t} \log C_s \right\}, \tag{103}$$

and the production function is Cobb-Douglas,

$$Y_t = A_t K_t^{\alpha}.$$

Here A_t is random and the constant population L is normalized to 1. Given our assumption that capital depreciates by 100 percent per period, the aggregate budget constraint is simply

$$K_{t+1} = A_t K_t^{\alpha} - C_t. \tag{104}$$

Assuming a decentralized market for capital and labor, and following by now very familiar steps, we can obtain the first-order Euler condition for individual utility maximization

$$\frac{1}{C_t} = \beta E_t \left\{ \frac{1 + \tilde{r}_{t+1}}{C_{t+1}} \right\}. \tag{105}$$

Combining this with the equation defining the (random) after-depreciation marginal product of capital on date $t + 1$,

$$\tilde{r}_{t+1} = \alpha A_{t+1} K_{t+1}^{\alpha-1} - 1, \tag{106}$$

we obtain

$$1 = \beta E_t \left\{ \alpha A_{t+1} K_{t+1}^{\alpha-1} \left(\frac{C_t}{C_{t+1}} \right) \right\}, \tag{107}$$

which is our usual equation for pricing risky assets. Here the current price of a unit of capital is always one (since it is fungible with consumption), so it is the expected marginal return on capital in terms of utility that must adjust to maintain equilibrium.

Equations (104) and (107) constitute a system of two first-order nonlinear stochastic difference equations. In general, one must analyze such systems either by numerical simulation techniques or by linearizing the model in the neighborhood of the steady state as in section 7.4.3. However, this special case with log utility, Cobb-Douglas production, and 100 percent depreciation is one for which a closed-form solution can be found without resort to linearization. We solve the model by conjecturing that the solution takes the form

$$C_t = \omega A_t K_t^{\alpha} \tag{108}$$

and then check to see whether we can find a constant value of ω that works.[46] (This approach is, unfortunately, not algorithmic. It is akin to the "art" of dynamic programming as described in Supplement A to Chapter 2.)[47] Note that in the conjectured solution, it is assumed that equilibrium consumption each period remains in constant proportion to *output*. (Consumption is proportional to wealth for the log case, see Supplement A to Chapter 5 and exercise 4, so for our conjecture to be correct, the output-wealth ratio must be constant in equilibrium.)

If we plug our guess, eq. (108), into eq. (107), we get

$$\frac{1}{A_t K_t^{\alpha}} = \frac{\beta \alpha}{K_{t+1}},$$

so that all $t + 1$ dated variables factor out except K_{t+1} which is known as of date t. Conveniently, the expectation operator therefore disappears. Next use eqs. (104) and (108) to substitute for K_{t+1} in the preceding expression. Solving yields

$$\omega = 1 - \alpha\beta. \tag{109}$$

---

46. By restricting our attention to paths along which consumption is proportional to output, we are implicitly imposing saddle path stability.

47. Long and Plosser (1983), who appear to have been the first to point out the closed-form solution for this class of stochastic growth models, attribute their finding to "dumb luck."

Thus the conjectured solution, eq. (108), indeed works. Note that our method did not require strong restrictions on the probability distribution governing the productivity shock A.

Substituting eq. (109) into eq. (108) and the resulting expression into eq. (104) yields

$$K_{t+1} = \alpha \beta A_t K_t^{\alpha}.$$

Substituting for K using the production function $Y_t = A_t K_t^{\alpha}$ and then taking logs of the resulting expression yields a first-order stochastic linear difference equation in the log of output,

$$y_t = \chi_0 + \alpha y_{t-1} + a_t, \tag{110}$$

where $\chi_0 \equiv \alpha \log \alpha \beta$. (As usual, lowercase sans serif letters denote logs, that is, $y_t \equiv \log Y_t$, and so on.)

Assuming that the unconditional mean of $a = \bar{a}$ (that is, $\lim_{T \to \infty} E_t \{a_{t+T}\} = \bar{a}$), then the long-run steady state (unconditional mean) of the log of output is given by

$$\bar{y} = \frac{\chi_0 + \bar{a}}{1 - \alpha}. \tag{111}$$

Subtracting the steady relationship

$$\bar{y} = \chi_0 + \alpha \bar{y} + \bar{a}$$

from eq. (110) yields

$$y_t - \bar{y} = \alpha(y_{t-1} - \bar{y}) + (a_t - \bar{a}), \tag{112}$$

which, iterating backward (see Supplement C to Chapter 2), implies the reduced-form solution[48]

$$y_t - \bar{y} = \sum_{s=1}^{t} \alpha^{t-s}(a_s - \bar{a}) + (y_0 - \bar{y})\alpha^t. \tag{113}$$

Equations (111) and (113) reveal some straightforward but important insights. First, a permanent change in $\bar{a}$ raises $\bar{y}$ more than proportionately: $d\bar{y} = d\bar{a}/(1 - \alpha)$. But a purely transitory (one-period) shock to date t output raises date $t + 1$ output by only α as much. Thus this very simple model suggests that in order to explain the substantial persistence of output shocks one observes in the data, the

---

48. That is, lag eq. (112) by one period to obtain

$$y_{t-1} - \bar{y} = \alpha(y_{t-2} - \bar{y}) + (a_{t-1} - \bar{a})$$

and substitute the result into eq. (112) to eliminate $y_{t-1} - \bar{y}$. Repeat the procedure to eliminate $y_{t-2} - \bar{y}$, and so on.

productivity shocks must themselves be very persistent. Put another way, the "internal dynamics" of the model are fairly weak because α tends to be far below 1. The 100 percent depreciation assumption makes this model quite unrealistic, of course. But even when we look at more realistic depreciation assumptions later in section 7.4.3, we will still find it is difficult to generate any strong dynamics beyond those already embodied in the underlying productivity shocks.

7.4.2 A Two-Country Model with 100 Percent Capital Depreciation

The preceding closed-economy example extends to a two-country global model. A neat closed-form solution is available, however, only when the country-specific component of productivity shocks is serially uncorrelated.[49] The model assumes that countries effectively trade a complete set of Arrow-Debreu securities.

Suppose that the utility function of the Foreign representative consumer is identical to that of the Home consumer, given in (103). Home and Foreign production levels are

$$Y_t = A_t^W \cdot A_t K_t^\alpha, \qquad Y_t^* = A_t^W \cdot A_t^* \left(K_t^* \right)^\alpha, \qquad \alpha < 1,$$

where A^W is the common global component of productivity shocks and A_t and A_t^* are the respective country-specific components. The random variables A^W, A, and A^* are all distributed independently of each other, and the two country-specific shock components are assumed to be distributed independently over time. Implicitly, production in each country uses (alongside capital) a fixed supply of internationally immobile labor. With a 100 percent capital depreciation rate, global goods-market equilibrium requires

$$K_{t+1} + K_{t+1}^* = A_t^W \left[A_t K_t^\alpha + A_t^* (K_t^*)^\alpha \right] - \left(C_t + C_t^* \right). \tag{114}$$

We restrict attention to a benevolent planner's problem since it is simpler and we know that it yields that same solution as the decentralized market problem with complete markets. (Different planner weights on Home and Foreign correspond to different initial world wealth distributions.) To each type of individual and capital corresponds a distinct first-order Euler condition—giving four conditions in all. In Chapter 5 we saw how to derive first-order conditions within this type of stochastic model. The conditions take the form

---

49. Long and Plosser's (1983) many-sector closed-economy model does not require an analogous restriction on relative productivity shocks. Their model represents a closed economy in which labor is instantaneously mobile among sectors. As a result, ex post marginal products of capital are always the same in different industries. This equality doesn't hold in the next model because it assumes labor is internationally immobile. The closest antecedent of the two-country model that follows is in Cantor and Mark (1988). For an overlapping-generations variant of the Long-Plosser closed-economy model, see appendix 7B. An open-economy variant is in Cole and Obstfeld (1991).

$$\frac{1}{C_t^i} = \beta E_t \left\{ \alpha A_{t+1}^w \cdot A_{t+1}^j (K_{t+1}^j)^{\alpha-1} \left(\frac{1}{C_{t+1}^i} \right) \right\},$$

where i alternately denotes the Home or Foreign consumer and j alternately denotes the Home or Foreign marginal product of capital. Let Y^w be total world output. Drawing on our intuition from the closed-economy model, we conjecture a solution of the form

$$C_t = \kappa(1 - \alpha\beta)Y_t^w, \tag{115}$$

$$K_{t+1} = \Psi\alpha\beta Y_t^w, \tag{116}$$

where $\kappa < 1$ is the weight assigned to Home by the planner and Ψ is defined by

$$\Psi \equiv E_t \left\{ \frac{Y_{t+1}}{Y_{t+1}^w} \right\} = \frac{K_{t+1}}{K_{t+1}^w}.$$

(The investment share Ψ is a constant because of the i.i.d. nature of the country-specific shocks.) The Foreign equations corresponding to (115) and (116) have $1 - \kappa$ and $1 - \Psi$ in place of κ and Ψ. It is easy to check that the conjectured solutions satisfy all the various Euler conditions and that $C_{t+1}/C_t = C_{t+1}^*/C_t^*$.

In this simple setup, a positive Home productivity disturbance unambiguously raises investment in both countries. Higher current income leads to higher global savings, which are invested in constant relative proportion in the two countries. When relative productivity disturbances are serially correlated, however, investment shares are not necessarily constant. With positive serial correlation, for example, world saving still rises after a positive Home productivity shock but it flows disproportionately into Home investment. To look further into this phenomenon, and to understand better the dynamics of RBC models, we turn to a richer structure.

7.4.3   A More General Stochastic Growth Model

In this section, we look at a model identical to that of section 7.4.1, except that we drop the assumption of 100 percent depreciation. In this case, it is no longer possible to obtain a general closed-form solution, but it is still possible to solve the model analytically by log-linearizing in the neighborhood of the nonstochastic steady state.[50] It would also be possible to solve the model numerically as Kydland and Prescott (1982) do. As a general rule, however, having an analytical approach is helpful for aiding one's intuition and sometimes reveals the effects of opposing

---

50. The log-linearization approach we follow here is based on Campbell (1994). See also King, Plosser, and Rebelo (1988a,1988b), who log-linearize as an intermediate step toward numerical simulation. Linearization in levels is another possibility, but log-linearization has a number of advantages, not the least of which is a more attractive empirical specification.

forces that might be obscured in a simulation. Of course, in more complex models, closed-form analytical solutions usually are not available.

7.4.3.1   Technology and Preferences in a Closed-Economy Model

We will retain the assumption of Cobb-Douglas production, a constant population equal to 1, and no trend productivity growth. These special assumptions simplify the algebra somewhat but they are not strictly necessary, and the log-linearization approach illustrated here can readily be extended to study significantly more general models (for examples, see Campbell, 1994; Campbell and Cochrane, 1995; and Ludvigson, 1995).

Again the representative agent has time-separable log utility,

$$U_t = \mathrm{E}_t \left\{ \sum_{s=t}^{\infty} \beta^{s-t} \log C_s \right\},$$

and the capital accumulation equation is that of a closed economy,

$$K_{t+1} - K_t = Y_t - C_t. \tag{117}$$

Equation (117) assumes that capital does not depreciate at all.

It will make our notation slightly easier if we specify the technology shock as Harrod neutral rather than Hicks neutral (they are of course equivalent in the Cobb-Douglas case),

$$Y_t = K_t^{\alpha} E_t^{1-\alpha}, \tag{118}$$

where we have normalized $L = 1$. In anticipation of our later log-linearization, we will assume that the productivity shock E_t is lognormally distributed.

The conditions characterizing market equilibrium are

$$\frac{1}{C_t} = \beta \mathrm{E}_t \left\{ \frac{1 + \tilde{r}_{t+1}}{C_{t+1}} \right\}, \tag{119}$$

$$1 + \tilde{r}_{t+1} = 1 + \alpha \left(\frac{K_{t+1}}{E_{t+1}} \right)^{\alpha-1}, \tag{120}$$

where now, since we are assuming 0 depreciation instead of 100 percent depreciation, $\alpha(K_{t+1}/E_{t+1})^{\alpha-1}$ is the *net* marginal product of capital in period $t + 1$.

7.4.3.2   The Nonstochastic Steady State

To solve the dynamic system characterized by eqs. (117), (118), (119), and (120), we first characterize the long-run steady state that would obtain if the shock process could be shut down. This hypothetical long-run equilibrium turns out to be a convenient point around which to linearize the model.

In the deterministic long run, C_{t+1}/C_t must be unity when there is no productivity or population growth. Therefore, in the steady state, eq. (119) implies

$$\frac{1}{\beta} = 1 + \bar{r}, \tag{121}$$

which together with eq. (120) implies that

$$\frac{\bar{E}}{\bar{K}} = \left(\frac{1 - \beta}{\beta\alpha}\right)^{\frac{1}{1-\alpha}}, \tag{122}$$

where $\bar{E}$ is the mean value of E. Equations (118) and (122) imply that

$$\frac{\bar{Y}}{\bar{K}} = \frac{1 - \beta}{\beta\alpha}. \tag{123}$$

Finally, since K is constant in the steady state, eq. (117) implies

$$\frac{\bar{C}}{\bar{Y}} = 1. \tag{124}$$

7.4.3.3   Log-Linear Approximation

We now log-linearize the model around the nonstochastic state to obtain a linear difference equation system in the logs of K, C, and the exogenous productivity shock E. The Cobb-Douglas production function (118) is linear in logs and therefore needs no approximation:

$$y_t = \alpha k_t + (1 - \alpha)e_t. \tag{125}$$

To log-linearize the capital accumulation equation (117) near the nonstochastic steady state, we first use the production function (118) to substitute for Y and then totally differentiate the result:

$$dK_{t+1} - dK_t = \alpha \left(\frac{\bar{E}}{\bar{K}}\right)^{1-\alpha} dK_t + (1 - \alpha)\left(\frac{\bar{E}}{\bar{K}}\right)^{-\alpha} dE_t - dC_t.$$

To convert to log deviations, we will make use of the fact that $(X - \bar{X})/\bar{X} \approx d\log X$ in the neighborhood of $\bar{X}$. After dividing both sides of the preceding equation by $\bar{K}$, it can be written as

$$\frac{dK_{t+1}}{\bar{K}} = \left[1 + \alpha\left(\frac{\bar{E}}{\bar{K}}\right)^{1-\alpha}\right]\frac{dK_t}{\bar{K}} + (1 - \alpha)\left(\frac{\bar{E}}{\bar{K}}\right)^{1-\alpha}\frac{dE_t}{\bar{E}} - \frac{\bar{C}}{\bar{K}} \cdot \frac{dC_t}{\bar{C}}.$$

Making use of eqs. (122)–(124), this equation implies that in a neighborhood of the steady state

$$k_{t+1} = \frac{1}{\beta} k_t - \frac{1-\beta}{\beta\alpha} c_t + \frac{(1-\alpha)(1-\beta)}{\beta\alpha} e_t, \tag{126}$$

where we now use sans serif letters to denote log deviations from the steady state.

The trickiest equation to linearize is the Euler equation (119). It contains the expected value of a nonlinear function of random future consumption. Therefore, because of Jensen's inequality, a first-order Taylor series approximation is inadequate. We dealt with this problem before in our analysis of the equity premium puzzle in section 5.4.2. Here we adopt the approach we used in the same subsection to analyze the riskless rate puzzle.

Assume that the random variable $(1+\tilde{r})/C$ on the right hand side of Euler equation (119) is lognormally distributed, with a conditional variance that is constant over time. Lagged by one period, the Euler equation can be written

$$\frac{1}{C_{t-1}} = \beta E_{t-1}\left\{\exp\left[\log\left(\frac{1+\tilde{r}_t}{C_t}\right)\right]\right\}$$

$$= \beta \exp\left\{E_{t-1}[\log(1+\tilde{r}_t) - \log(C_t)] + \tfrac{1}{2}\mathrm{Var}\left[\log\left(\frac{1+\tilde{r}_t}{C_t}\right)\right]\right\}$$

by the properties of lognormal random variables. Taking logs of both sides gives

$$E_{t-1}\{\log C_t\} - \log C_{t-1} = \log\beta + \tfrac{1}{2}\mathrm{Var}\left[\log\left(\frac{1+\tilde{r}_t}{C_t}\right)\right] + E_{t-1}\log(1+\tilde{r}_t).$$

Since $\tfrac{1}{2}\mathrm{Var}\left\{\log\left[(1+\tilde{r}_t)/C_t\right]\right\} \equiv \chi_0$ is a constant and the steady-state interest rate $1+\bar{r}$ equals $1/\beta$, the foregoing equation can be expressed in terms of deviations from the steady state as

$$E_{t-1}\{\log C_t - \log\bar{C}\} - (\log C_{t-1} - \log\bar{C}) = E_{t-1}\{\log(1+\tilde{r}_t) - \log(1+\bar{r})\} + \chi_0.$$

The preceding linear equation plainly holds for small deviations, and it thus implies

$$E_{t-1}c_t - c_{t-1} = E_{t-1}\tilde{r}_t + \chi_0,$$

where $\tilde{r}_t \equiv \log(1+\tilde{r}_t) - \log(1+\bar{r})$. We are interested in the system's dynamic response to shocks rather than in trend movements, so we henceforth omit the constant χ_0 and write the approximate Euler equation as

$$E_{t-1}c_t - c_{t-1} = E_{t-1}\tilde{r}_t. \tag{127}$$

Finally, linearly approximating eq. (120) yields

$$1 + \tilde{r}_t = 1 + \bar{r} + \alpha(\alpha - 1)\left(\frac{\bar{K}}{\bar{E}}\right)^{\alpha-1}\left(\frac{dK_t}{\bar{K}} - \frac{dE_t}{\bar{E}}\right),$$

or, after dividing both sides by $1 + \bar{r}$ ($= 1/\beta$) and using eq. (122),

$$\tilde{r}_t = (1-\alpha)(1-\beta)\left(e_t - k_t\right).\tag{128}$$

If we combine eqs. (127) and (128), we obtain the second key equation governing the linearized dynamic system:

$$E_{t-1}c_t - c_{t-1} = (1-\alpha)(1-\beta)(E_{t-1}e_t - k_t).\tag{129}$$

7.4.3.4   Solution

Equations (126) and (129) constitute a system of two linear stochastic difference equations with exogenous forcing variable e. They can be solved using the general approach developed in Supplement C to Chapter 2. Instead, following Campbell (1994), we illustrate a frequently used alternative solution approach, the *method of undetermined coefficients*. This approach is less algorithmic but also slightly less cumbersome for our application (since it implicitly assumes a saddle-path equilibrium). To apply the method of undetermined coefficients, we first close the system by assuming a specific process for the exogenous productivity shock,

$$e_t = \rho e_{t-1} + \epsilon_t,\tag{130}$$

where ϵ is a normally distributed white noise disturbance with mean zero. We then conjecture a solution of the form

$$c_t = a_{ck}k_t + a_{ce}e_t,\tag{131}$$

where a_{ck} and a_{ce} are unknown parameters that are assumed to be constant. (This conjecture is reasonable because we know from nonstochastic saddle-point-stable systems that, in the neighborhood of long-run equilibrium, all variables remain in constant proportion as they move along the saddle path.) Substituting the conjectured solution (131) into the linearized capital accumulation equation (126) yields

$$k_{t+1} = \left[\frac{1}{\beta} - \frac{(1-\beta)a_{ck}}{\beta\alpha}\right]k_t + \left[\frac{(1-\alpha)(1-\beta)}{\beta\alpha} - \frac{(1-\beta)a_{ce}}{\beta\alpha}\right]e_t.\tag{132}$$

Similarly, forwarding eq. (129) by one period and substituting in the conjectured solution (131) yields

$$a_{ck}(k_{t+1} - k_t) + a_{ce}(E_t e_{t+1} - e_t) = (1-\alpha)(1-\beta)(E_t e_{t+1} - k_{t+1}).\tag{133}$$

Substituting eq. (132) into eq. (133) and noting that by eq. (130), $E_t e_{t+1} = \rho e_t$, we find that

$$a_{ck}\left[\frac{1-\beta}{\beta} - \frac{(1-\beta)a_{ck}}{\beta\alpha}\right]k_t$$

$$+ a_{ck}\left[\frac{(1-\alpha)(1-\beta)}{\beta\alpha} - \frac{(1-\beta)a_{ce}}{\beta\alpha}\right]e_t + a_{ce}(\rho - 1)e_t$$

$$= \rho(1-\alpha)(1-\beta)e_t - (1-\alpha)(1-\beta)\left[\frac{1}{\beta} - \frac{(1-\beta)a_{ck}}{\beta\alpha}\right]k_t$$

$$- (1-\alpha)(1-\beta)\left[\frac{(1-\alpha)(1-\beta)}{\beta\alpha} - \frac{(1-\beta)a_{ce}}{\beta\alpha}\right]e_t. \tag{134}$$

To solve this equation, equate coefficients on k_t to solve for a_{ck} (given a_{ce}) and then similarly equate coefficients on e_t to find a_{ce}. Equating the coefficients on k_t and simplifying gives the quadratic equation

$$-a_{ck}^2 + [2\alpha - 1 + \beta(1-\alpha)]a_{ck} + \alpha(1-\alpha) = 0. \tag{135}$$

Note that this equation implies that a_{ck} does *not* depend on ρ, the degree of persistence of the productivity shock. From eq. (131), we see that this statement is true because a_{ck} is the partial elasticity of c_t with respect to k_t, holding the level of technology constant. Similarly, a_{ce} has the interpretation of the partial elasticity of c_t with respect to e_t, holding the level of capital constant.

As Campbell (1994), shows, for reasonable parameter values, eq. (135) has one positive and one negative root. Choosing the positive root is necessary to insure that the coefficient on k_t in eq. (132) is less than one.

Solving eq. (134) for a_{ce} yields

$$a_{ce} = \frac{-a_{ck}(1-\alpha) + (1-\alpha)\left[\rho\beta\alpha - (1-\alpha)(1-\beta)\right]}{\frac{\beta\alpha}{1-\beta}(\rho-1) - \left[a_{ck} + (1-\alpha)(1-\beta)\right]}.$$

With a bit of algebra, one can show that an increase in ρ leads to a rise in a_{ce}. The more persistent the productivity shock, the greater the effect on consumption, since expected future income rises by more. (This result is sensitive to our assumption here that the intertemporal elasticity of substitution is 1; see Campbell, 1994.)

Campbell shows that for reasonable parameter values, a temporary shock to current productivity has only a very small effect on next period's output. That is, the internal dynamics of the model are fairly weak. This conclusion seems plausible. For most countries, the capital stock is considerably greater than a year's GNP. [For the United States, if we count only physical capital (including consumer durables and residential structures) and land, the ratio is about 3.] An unanticipated temporary productivity shock that raises period t output by 1 percent leads to a rise in the period $t+1$ capital stock of well under 1 percent. (If $K/Y = 3$, the rise would be less than 0.2 percent even if half of the increment to income is saved. Even if the marginal product of capital were 20 percent, the effect on period $t+1$ output would be less than 0.04 percent.) The potential for internally generated persistence is somewhat greater when labor supply is allowed to vary endogenously, though one can obtain a significant effect only if labor supply is highly wage-elastic. (See also Cogley and Nason, 1995.) We conclude that a realistically parameterized RBC model is capable of only slightly amplifying the dynamic effects of productivity shocks on output. This conclusion brings somewhat into question the view that capital accumulation is central to the propagation of short-run business cycles.

7.4.3.5   A Two-Country Model

If we maintain the complete-markets assumption, then extending the model to a two-country (or n-country) global economy is quite straightforward. Assuming the same utility and production functions at home and abroad, the behavior of global output, consumption, and investment is exactly as in the closed-economy model. Consumption growth rates are identical across countries. The only issue is determining the optimal allocation of investment each period. The first-order conditions for either the market or planner's problem imply

$$1 = \beta E_t \left\{ \left[1 + \alpha \left(\frac{E_{t+1}}{K_{t+1}} \right)^{1-\alpha} \right] \left(\frac{C_t}{C_{t+1}} \right) \right\},$$

$$1 = \beta E_t \left\{ \left[1 + \alpha \left(\frac{E^*_{t+1}}{K^*_{t+1}} \right)^{1-\alpha} \right] \left(\frac{C_t}{C_{t+1}} \right) \right\}.$$

Note that it does not matter whether we use Home or Foreign (or global) per capita consumption levels in these two Euler equations, since under complete markets ex post consumption growth rates are equalized. The two Euler equations can be linearized in the same manner as in section 7.4.3.3 to yield

$$E_{t-1}c_t - c_{t-1} = (1 - \alpha)(1 - \beta)(E_{t-1}e_t - k_t),$$

$$E_{t-1}c_t - c_{t-1} = (1 - \alpha)(1 - \beta)(E_{t-1}e^*_t - k^*_t)$$

(where we have suppressed constant terms) or, combining these two equations,

$$E_{t-1}(e_t - k_t) = E_{t-1}(e^*_t - k^*_t). \tag{136}$$

Holding global investment constant, higher expected productivity at home shifts investment toward the home country.[51] Empirically, investment is highly positively correlated across countries (see Baxter, 1995). This fact implies that if the model is correct, Home and Foreign productivity shocks must be highly correlated. As in the closed-economy model, the internal dynamics of the two-country model are quite weak. Even if a rise in Home productivity raises investment abroad, the effects on Foreign output will be relatively small. Most of the action occurs in the exogenously specified productivity factors; that is, it occurs outside the model.[52]

---

51. Remember that in general there is a constant term in the preceding equation that depends on the stochastic properties of the output shocks in the two countries; see section 7.4.3.3.

52. Obviously, the model analyzed here is special in that it contains only one sector. Kraay and Ventura (1995) argue that expansions in foreign output transmit to the home country by raising the relative prices of labor-intensive commodities. (The effect is stronger when countries do not trade financial assets, since when they do, foreign expansions tend to raise income at home and lower work effort.)

Appendix 7A   Continuous-Time Growth Models as Limits of Discrete-Time Models

In this appendix, we derive continuous-time versions of the Solow and Ramsey-Cass-Koopmans models as limits of discrete-time versions. Let each period be of arbitrary (small) length h. Then the equilibrium dynamics of the general discrete-time Solow model can be written

$$K_{t+h} - K_t = sh F(K_t, E_t L_t) - \delta h K_t, \tag{3'}$$

$$E_{t+h} - E_t = gh E_t, \tag{4'}$$

$$L_{t+h} - L_t = nh L_t. \tag{5'}$$

In eqs. (4') and (5'), it is assumed that changes in productivity and the labor force are proportional to the length of the time period. In (3'), production and depreciation are proportional to period length. Note that when $h = 1$, we have the discrete-time model of the text.

Dividing through both sides of eq. (3') by $h E_t L_t$, and (as usual) defining $k_t^E \equiv K_t / E_t L_t$, one obtains

$$\frac{k_{t+h}^E - k_t^E}{h} = \frac{sf(k_t^E)}{(1 + nh)(1 + gh)} - \frac{(n + g + \delta) + ngh}{(1 + nh)(1 + gh)} k_t^E,$$

so that, in the steady state,

$$sf(\bar{k}^E) = [(n + g + \delta) + ngh]\bar{k}^E.$$

The two preceding equations are the same as eqs. (8) and (9) in the discrete-time model of the text when $h = 1$. As $h \to 0$, we obtain the steady state for the continuous-time model

$$sf(\bar{k}^E) = (n + g + \delta)\bar{k}^E, \tag{9'}$$

as we claimed in section 7.1.1.2.

One could, of course, infer this solution directly from the continuous-time version of the model. The key equations are found by dividing eqs. (3'), (4'), and (5') by h, and taking the limit as $h \to 0$:

$$\dot{K}_t = s F(K_t, E_t L_t) - \delta K_t, \tag{3''}$$

$$\frac{\dot{E}_t}{E_t} = g, \tag{4''}$$

$$\frac{\dot{L}_t}{L_t} = n, \tag{5''}$$

where a dot over a variable indicates a time derivative:

$$\dot{X}_t \equiv \frac{dX_t}{dt} = \lim_{h \to 0} \frac{X_{t+h} - X_t}{h}.$$

Dividing both sides of eq. (3'') by $E_t L_t$, one obtains

$$\frac{\dot{K}_t}{E_t L_t} = \frac{sF(K_t, E_t L_t)}{E_t L_t} - \frac{\delta K_t}{E_t L_t}.$$

Noting that $(1/EL)F(K, EL) = F(K/EL, 1)$ (by constant returns to scale) and that

$$\dot{k}_t^{\mathrm{E}} = \frac{\dot{K}_t}{E_t L_t} - \frac{K_t}{E_t L_t}\left(\frac{\dot{E}_t}{E_t} + \frac{\dot{L}_t}{L_t}\right) = \frac{\dot{K}_t}{E_t L_t} - k_t^{\mathrm{E}}(g + n),$$

we can write eq. (3″) as

$$\dot{k}_t^{\mathrm{E}} = sf(k_t^{\mathrm{E}}) - (n + g + \delta)k_t^{\mathrm{E}}.$$

Setting $\dot{k}_t^{\mathrm{E}} = 0$ and solving for steady-state $\bar{k}^{\mathrm{E}}$ yields eq. (9′), the limiting answer for the discrete-time case.

In section 7.1.1.2, we used the fact that the solution to differential equation (4″) is $\log E_t = \log E_0 + gt$, where E_0 is the level of technology in the initial year of the sample. Note that the corresponding discrete-time equation (4′) implies that

$$E_t = (1 + gh)^{t/h} E_0,$$

since there are t/h periods between time 0 and time t. In the limit,

$$\lim_{h \to 0} E_t = \lim_{h \to 0}(1 + gh)^{t/h} E_0 = \lim_{n \to \infty}\left(1 + \frac{g}{n}\right)^{tn} E_0 = \exp(gt) E_0.$$

Taking logs of both sides yields the claimed solution for the continuous-time case.

One similarly obtains the continuous-time version of the Ramsey-Cass-Koopmans maximizing model (see section 7.1.2.1) as a limit of discrete-time models. For simplicity, we assume that population and technology growth are zero ($n = g = 0$) and normalize the size of the representative dynasty to 1. For an arbitrary time interval h, the analog of the dynasty utility function (18) is

$$U_t = \sum_{s=t}^{\infty}\left(\frac{1}{1 + \delta h}\right)^{(s-t)/h} u(C_s)h,$$

where $\delta > 0$ now stands for the rate of time preference (*not* the depreciation rate of capital, which is zero) and the summation is over $t, t + h, t + 2h$, etc. Note that $u(C_s)$ is multiplied by h because the period utility flow derived from any consumption flow is proportional to the period's length. The dynasty capital accumulation equation becomes

$$K_{t+h} = K_t + hF(K_t) - hC_t$$

(recall that $L = 1$). Substituting this equation into U_t yields the problem

$$\max_{\{K_s\}} \sum_{s=t}^{\infty}\left(\frac{1}{1 + \delta h}\right)^{(s-t)/h} u\left[\frac{K_s - K_{s+h}}{h} + F(K_s)\right]h, \quad K_t \text{ given.}$$

Maximizing with respect to K_{s+h} gives the necessary first-order condition

$$u'(C_s) = \left(\frac{1}{1 + \delta h}\right)\left[1 + hF'(K_{s+h})\right]u'(C_{s+h}).$$

For $h = 1$, this is equivalent to eq. (20) of the text. To find the first-order condition for the continuous-time limit, divide by h and rearrange the preceding equation as

$$\frac{u'(C_{s+h}) - u'(C_s)}{h} = \left[\frac{\delta}{1 + \delta h} - \frac{F'(K_{s+h})}{1 + \delta h}\right] u'(C_{s+h}).$$

Taking the limit of both sides as $h \to 0$ yields (by the chain rule)

$$\frac{du'(C_s)}{dC_s} \cdot \frac{dC_s}{ds} = u''(C_s)\dot{C}_s = [\delta - F'(K_s)] u'(C_s).$$

This first-order condition also follows directly from continuous-time maximization methods (see Supplement A to Chapter 8). In continuous time, the dynasty's objective function becomes

$$U_t = \int_t^\infty u(C_s) \exp[-\delta(s - t)]ds$$

and the capital accumulation equation becomes

$$\dot{K}_s = F(K_s) - C_s.$$

The Hamiltonian for the corresponding maximization problem is

$$\mathcal{H}(C_s, K_s, s) = u(C_s) + \lambda_s \left[F(K_s) - C_s\right],$$

where C is the "control" variable and K is the "state" variable. The necessary first-order conditions are

$$\frac{\partial \mathcal{H}}{\partial C_s} = u'(C_s) - \lambda_s = 0, \quad \dot{\lambda}_s = \delta \lambda_s - \frac{\partial \mathcal{H}}{\partial K_s} = \lambda_s[\delta - F'(K_s)].$$

Taking the time derivative of both sides of the first-order condition for C yields $du'(C_s)/ds = \dot{\lambda}_s$, or $u''(C_s)\dot{C}_s = \dot{\lambda}_s$. Thus

$$\dot{\lambda}_s = u''(C_s)\dot{C}_s = [\delta - F'(K_s)]u'(C_s),$$

which is the same answer we reached by taking the limit of the discrete-time case.

Appendix 7B   A Simple Stochastic Overlapping Generations Model with Two-Period Lives

In this appendix, we look at a stochastic closed-economy version of the symmetric global model of investment and growth considered in section 3.4. The model yields results very similar to the RBC model in section 7.4.1 with infinitely-lived representative agents and 100 percent depreciation. Agents live for two periods, earning wage income while young and living off of savings when old. Assume that the production function is given by

$$Y_t = A_t K_t^\alpha L_t^{1-\alpha}, \tag{137}$$

where A_t is a lognormally distributed random productivity shock. To simplify, we abstract from trend productivity growth and also assume no depreciation. There is no government spending or taxes.

The labor force of young people, and therefore the total population, both grow at rate $1 + n$. Agents have log utility

$$U_t = \log(c_t^Y) + \beta E_t \log(c_{t+1}^O), \tag{138}$$

and can invest their period t savings either in a riskless bond that pays the net real interest rate r_{t+1} or in shares of capital that pay the risky net return $\tilde{r}_{t+1}$. The return on capital investment is risky because the Hicks-neutral productivity parameter A_{t+1} is unknown at time t. If x_{t+1} denotes the share of a person's saving going to the riskless bond on date t, then the budget constraint of a date t young agent can be written as

$$c^o_{t+1} = (w_t - c^Y_t)[x_{t+1}(1 + r_{t+1}) + (1 - x_{t+1})(1 + \tilde{r}_{t+1})]. \tag{139}$$

The solution to the agent's maximization problem, with which the reader is by now well familiar, yields

$$c^Y_t = \frac{w_t}{1 + \beta}.$$

That is, the agent with log utility consumes $1/(1 + \beta)$ percent of wealth in the first period. Saving per young person is given by $s^Y = w - c^Y$, so

$$s^Y_t = \frac{\beta w_t}{1 + \beta}. \tag{140}$$

In the symmetric equilibrium of this closed economy with identical young agents, individual bond holdings must be zero (there is no government), and the share of capital $1 - x$ in the portfolios the young acquire must equal 1. Therefore, the period $t + 1$ aggregate capital stock equals the savings of the young (as in Chapter 3):

$$K_{t+1} = L_t s^Y_t.$$

Dividing both sides of this equation by L_{t+1} and making use of eq. (140) yields

$$k_{t+1} = \frac{\beta w_t}{(1 + \beta)(1 + n)}.$$

Finally, noting that the production function (137) implies $w_t = \partial Y_t / \partial L_t = (1 - \alpha) A_t k^\alpha_t$, we find that capital accumulation is governed by

$$k_{t+1} = \frac{\beta(1 - \alpha) A_t k^\alpha_t}{(1 + \beta)(1 + n)}. \tag{141}$$

Equation (141) is a nonlinear first-order difference equation in the capital-labor ratio, which can be transformed into a linear equation by taking logs of both sides to yield

$$\mathsf{k}_{t+1} = \log\left[\frac{\beta(1 - \alpha)}{(1 + \beta)(1 + n)}\right] + \alpha\mathsf{k}_t + \mathsf{a}_t. \tag{142}$$

(Here $\mathsf{k}_t \equiv \log k_t$ and $\mathsf{a}_t \equiv \log A_t$.) Since we are interested in looking at the business-cycle properties of the model, it is useful to transform it into an equation for the log of output. The production function (137) implies that $y_t = A_t k^\alpha_t$, so that in logs

$$\mathsf{k}_t = \frac{\mathsf{y}_t - \mathsf{a}_t}{\alpha}.$$

Using this equation to substitute for k_{t+1} and k_t in eq. (142) yields

$$\mathsf{y}_t = \chi_0 + \alpha\mathsf{y}_{t-1} + \mathsf{a}_t, \tag{143}$$

where

$$\chi_0 \equiv \alpha \log \frac{\beta(1-\alpha)}{(1+\beta)(1+n)}.$$

This difference equation for output is isomorphic to that for the 100 percent depreciation model of section 7.4.1, so that the results are essentially the same.

It should not be surprising that the two models give such similar results. In an overlapping generations model, the current savings of the young on date t must be sufficient to finance the entire date $t+1$ capital stock. This is the same situation as in an infinitely-lived representative agent model when capital depreciates by 100 percent each period.

Exercises

1. *Government spending.* Consider the Weil (1989a) model of section 7.1.2.2. Assume now that there is government consumption spending of g per capita, financed by an equiproportionate tax on all those currently alive.

   (a) How does the introduction of tax-financed government spending affect eqs. (30) and (32)?

   (b) What is the phase diagram corresponding to Figure 7.7? Assuming the economy is initially in a steady state, analyze an unanticipated permanent rise in g.

   (c) The economy is in a steady state with $g = 0$, when it is announced that per capita government spending will permanently rise to g at a future time T. Analyze the impact effect of the announcement and the transition path of the economy.

2. *Dynamics of the borrowing-constrained overlapping generations model.* Take the model with credit constraints analyzed in section 7.2.2.3. Assume that the parameters of the model are such that the economy's autarky interest rate r^A equals the world interest rate r, in which case $r^D = r$ as well. (Thus, when the country becomes integrated into world capital markets, the credit constraint is not binding.)

   At time 0, there is an unanticipated permanent productivity rise, so that $y_t = A k_t$ where $A > 1$ (given that $A = 1$ initially as in the text). Analyze the path of the economy. Does the economy eventually return to a long-run steady state with $r^D = r$?

3. *Efficient allocation in the P. Romer (1990) model.* In the model of section 7.3.3, derive eq. (97), which gives the growth rate of output a planner would choose.

4. *Consumption and wealth in the Long-Plosser (1983) model.* In the model of section 7.4.1, where the period utility function is $u(C) = \log(C)$, show that equilibrium consumption satisfies

   $$C_t = (1-\beta)\left[(1+\tilde{r}_t)K_t + \sum_{s=t}^{\infty} E_t \left\{ \frac{\beta^{s-t}u'(C_s)}{u'(C_t)} w_s L \right\} \right],$$

   where w_s is the date s marginal product of labor and L is the representative individual's labor endowment. What is your interpretation? [Hint: Consult Supplement A to Chapter 5.]

Many of the most intriguing and important questions in international finance involve money. But until now we have put monetary issues aside, assuming implicitly that transactions on the economy's real side can be carried out frictionlessly without the aid of money. With this chapter, we turn to more realistic models in which money serves as a *medium of exchange* that reduces real transaction costs, as well as a store of value and a nominal unit of account. By introducing money we can address a number of interesting and important problems, including the determinants of seignorage, the mechanics of exchange rate systems, and the long-run effects of money-supply changes on prices and exchange rates. We can also see that the real-asset pricing models of Chapter 5 extend readily to price risky nominal assets.

Nominal prices—prices quoted in money terms—are perfectly flexible in all the models of this chapter. Thus they adjust immediately to clear product, factor, and asset markets. Admittedly, this extreme "classical" assumption is not realistic for short-run analysis. The abstraction of fully flexible prices is invaluable, however. It helps us think clearly about the long run and about other situations, such as hyperinflations, in which nominal price inflexibility is unimportant. But flexible price models have another, less obvious, role. When we turn to models with nominal rigidities in Chapters 9 and 10, we will find that the market-clearing benchmark this chapter provides will deepen our understanding of the differences that price stickiness makes.

This chapter begins with the deceptively simple empirical model of money and inflation due to Phillip Cagan (1956). Cagan's model offers a remarkably rich range of insights into inflation dynamics and seignorage. An open-economy extension provides a natural starting point for thinking about *nominal exchange rates*, which are relative prices of different currencies.

Next we look into the microfoundations of money demand, though this proves quite challenging. Most of our discussion assumes that each national government is a monopoly issuer of the currency used in domestic transactions. Unless a government somehow backs up the value of its currency in terms of real commodities, the currency is a *fiat money* with no intrinsic value aside from its usefulness in facilitating trade. This feature of money makes its valuation very different from that of other assets. The value of money is acutely tied to social convention. Paper currency is worth virtually nothing to an individual unless he knows that it is valued by others. Consequently, reaching an equilibrium in which money is used raises a *coordination* problem. Perhaps because of the difficulty of capturing the frictions and social conventions underpinning money, there is no universally accepted framework for understanding the microfoundations of money demand. Though debates over the "right" model of money sometimes seem to reflect almost religious zeal, we prefer to take an eclectic view. The chapter considers several alternatives, including models in which money enters the utility function and models with "cash-in-advance" constraints on consumers.

For some countries and epochs the assumption of a government monopoly over currency issue is unrealistic. Thus we also consider the phenomenon of *dollarization* or *currency substitution*, in which a more stable foreign currency circulates (perhaps illegally) alongside local currency. The assumption of pure fiat money is generally applicable today, but it has not always been so. The chapter briefly considers the gold standard, a type of a commodity money system used widely in the past. The flexible-price monetary model proves vital not only for the preceding applications, but also for understanding the basic functioning of present-day international monetary systems. One perennially topical question is whether fixed-exchange-rate regimes are sustainable for long in a world of highly mobile international capital. We therefore cover the basic model of how a fixed-exchange-rate regime can be terminated by a speculative attack. The final part of this chapter introduces uncertainty, describes exchange rate target zones, and integrates the model of international money markets with our broader analysis of international financial markets in Chapter 5.

8.1   Assumptions on the Nature of Money

Before diving into the mechanics of various monetary models, it is useful to clarify terminology and put the topic of money and monetary regimes in perspective.

First, unless otherwise stated, *money* means currency in our formal models. Thus the theoretical discussion will abstract from the banking system and from any devices such as checks and credit cards that may be used to ease transactions. Plainly other transactions media are important in the real world. But by focusing on a narrow interpretation of money, we can make our models simpler and their implications more transparent. Furthermore, currency must have a central role in a theory of money. The nominal price level is the value of goods in terms of currency, and a nominal exchange rate is the value of one currency in terms of another. While introducing a richer transaction technology may affect the demand for currency, it can never negate currency's central role. Most of the results in this chapter extend easily to models with richer transaction frameworks.

A second assumption we make is that currency does not bear interest. Historically, this has usually been the case. In principle, there is no reason why paper money cannot pay some interest, and there is historical precedent.[1] The possibility of interest-bearing money is likely to become much more important if and when electronic forms of currency replace paper currency. But interest-bearing money can still retain the basic characteristics of money as we study it here if there re-

---

1. How might interest on currency be paid? Before the 1991 monetary reform, one Argentinian state paid interest on bonds by holding lotteries based on their serial numbers.

mains a liquidity premium (that is, if people willingly hold a money even though it pays a lower interest rate than bonds denominated in the same money).

Paper currency is a relatively modern invention. In earlier eras, some form of commodity typically served as the medium of exchange. At one time or another, rice, seashells, beads, and cigarettes have all served as money. Silver and gold coins were used as money starting in antiquity. One might think that commodity monies protect citizens from the inflation tax, but that has never been the case. Governments can always lower the metal content of coinage, taking in existing coins and replacing them with debased ones. For example, when Henry VIII of England began a series of debasements in 1542, the mint value of one pound was 6.4 troy ounces of gold. By the time his son Edward VI stopped shaving the currency, the value of a pound had dropped below 1 troy ounce. Other European countries underwent similar experiences.[2] The invention of modern paper money, which has become predominant in the last two centuries, has simply made the process of currency debasement easier.

Finally, it is an open secret among central bankers that a very large percentage of all currency is held by the underground economy. We will discuss some of the evidence on this phenomenon and its consequences when we turn to dollarization.

8.2   The Cagan Model of Money and Prices

In his classic paper, Cagan (1956) studied seven *hyperinflations*. Cagan defined hyperinflations as periods during which the price level of goods in terms of money rises at a rate averaging at least 50 percent per month. With compounding, this corresponds to an annual inflation rate of almost 13,000 percent! Cagan's study encompassed episodes from Austria, Germany, Hungary, Poland, and Russia after World War I, and from Greece and Hungary after World War II. Few recent inflations quite match Hungary's record rate of 19,800 percent *per month* (July 1945 and February 1946), but the reader should not think of these monetary aberrations as a thing of the past. Bolivia's price level, for example, rose by 23,000 percent between April 1984 and July 1985, and inflations of several hundred percent or more per year are veritably commonplace.

8.2.1   The Cagan Model as a Special Case of the *LM* Curve

Let M denote a country's money supply and P its price level, defined as the price of a specified basket of consumption goods in terms of money. A stochastic discrete-time version of Cagan's model posits that the demand for *real* money

---

2. See Rolnick, Velde, and Weber (1994). Over this period, international (market) exchange rates reflected approximately the metal content of the various currencies. See Froot, Kim, and Rogoff (1995) for a discussion of the guilder-pound rate.

balances M/P depends entirely on expected future price-level inflation, and that higher expected inflation lowers the demand for real balances by raising the opportunity cost of holding money. Let lowercase sans serif letters denote natural logarithms of the corresponding uppercase variables. We write Cagan's model in the conveniently log-linear form

$$\mathsf{m}_t^d - \mathsf{p}_t = -\eta \mathrm{E}_t\{\mathsf{p}_{t+1} - \mathsf{p}_t\}, \tag{1}$$

where $\mathsf{m} \equiv \log M$, $\mathsf{p} \equiv \log P$, and η is the semielasticity of demand for real balances with respect to expected inflation. In eq. (1), m_t^d denotes (the log of) nominal money balances held at the end of period t. The analysis assumes rational expectations in the sense of Muth (1961).[3]

Cagan's equation (1) is a simplified form of the standard Keynes (1936)–Hicks (1937) *LM* curve appearing in intermediate macroeconomics texts. In the conventional *LM* curve, real money demand on date t depends positively on aggregate real output Y_t and negatively on the nominal interest rate i_{t+1} between dates t and $t+1$,

$$\frac{M_t^d}{P_t} = L(Y_t, i_{t+1}). \tag{2}$$

Familiar logic underlies eq. (2). A rise in aggregate real output, Y, raises the transaction demand for real balances. In contrast, a rise in the nominal interest rate raises the opportunity cost of holding money. The nominal interest rate is the net nominal rate of return on currency loans, that is, the amount of money one earns by lending out a currency unit for a period. By reducing money holdings by a dollar and lending it (buying a bond) instead, one could earn the nominal return i_{t+1} on the dollar instead of nothing.

Cagan argued that during a hyperinflation, expected future inflation swamps all other influences on money demand. Thus one can ignore changes in real output Y and the real interest rate r, which will not vary much compared with monetary factors.[4] Note that under perfect foresight the real interest rate links the nominal interest rate to inflation through the *Fisher parity* equation

---

3. As explained in Chapter 2, agents with rational expectations forecast in a way that is internally consistent with the model generating the variable they seek to predict. At the time of Cagan's writing, both the concept of rational expectations and the necessary mathematics to implement it were not well understood by economists. Cagan actually based his analysis on an *adaptive* forecasting scheme making expectations of future inflation depend on lagged inflation. We follow the modern literature in using the internally consistent rational expectations approach.

4. Cagan actually made the stronger assumption that real variables are in effect exogenous during hyperinflation because price level adjustments take place so frequently that money is essentially neutral. But even small temporary price rigidities can imply large nonneutralities in a hyperinflation. During the peak of the post–World War I German hyperinflation, children would meet their parents at the factory gate on payday to take their parents' money and rush to town by bicycle in order to make purchases before inflation rendered the pay worthless.

$$1 + i_{t+1} = (1 + r_{t+1})\frac{P_{t+1}}{P_t}. \tag{3}$$

The Fisher equation implies that in equilibrium, the gross real rates of return on real and on nominal bonds must be the same.[5] Thus the nominal interest rate and expected inflation will move in lockstep if the real interest rate is constant, which explains Cagan's simplification of making money demand a function of expected inflation.

We shall see later that the Fisher relationship (3) does not hold exactly, even in expectation, in an explicitly stochastic model. This nuance, like changes involving real variables, is ignored by the Cagan model.

8.2.2　Solving the Model

Having motivated Cagan's money demand equation, we study its implications for the relationship between money and the price level. Assume that the supply of money m is set exogenously. In equilibrium, demand equals supply:

$$m_t^d = m_t.$$

Equation (1) therefore becomes the monetary equilibrium condition

$$m_t - p_t = -\eta E_t\{p_{t+1} - p_t\}. \tag{4}$$

Equation (4) is a first-order stochastic difference equation explaining price-level dynamics in terms of the money supply, which is an exogenous "forcing" variable here. We show how to solve equations of this general type in Supplement C to

---

5. This equality can be seen by rewriting Fisher parity as

$$1 + r_{t+1} = (1 + i_{t+1})\frac{P_t}{P_{t+1}}.$$

Alternatively, rewrite eq. (3) as

$$\frac{1}{1 + i_{t+1}} = \frac{1}{1 + r_{t+1}} \cdot \frac{P_t}{P_{t+1}}.$$

The left-hand side is the price in terms of date t currency of a unit of currency delivered on date $t + 1$. The right-hand side is the cost of buying the future currency unit a different way. Investing $\frac{1}{1+r_{t+1}} \cdot \frac{1}{P_{t+1}}$ date t output units in real bonds yields

$$P_{t+1} \cdot (1 + r_{t+1}) \cdot \left(\frac{1}{1 + r_{t+1}} \cdot \frac{1}{P_{t+1}}\right) = 1$$

unit of currency next period. The cost of this strategy in terms of date t currency is

$$P_t \cdot \left(\frac{1}{1 + r_{t+1}} \cdot \frac{1}{P_{t+1}}\right) = \frac{1}{1 + r_{t+1}} \cdot \frac{P_t}{P_{t+1}}.$$

Under perfect foresight, eq. (3) therefore must hold to preclude an arbitrage opportunity.

Chapter 2. Nonetheless, we solve the model from first principles here to build intuition about its predictions.

We first tackle the nonstochastic perfect foresight case, where eq. (4) becomes

$$m_t - p_t = -\eta(p_{t+1} - p_t). \tag{5}$$

Start by rewriting eq. (5) as

$$p_t = \frac{1}{1+\eta}m_t + \frac{\eta}{1+\eta}p_{t+1}, \tag{6}$$

so that today's price level depends on the foreseen future price level. Lead eq. (6) by one period to obtain

$$p_{t+1} = \frac{1}{1+\eta}m_{t+1} + \frac{\eta}{1+\eta}p_{t+2};$$

then use this expression to eliminate p_{t+1} in eq. (6),

$$p_t = \frac{1}{1+\eta}\left(m_t + \frac{\eta}{1+\eta}m_{t+1}\right) + \left(\frac{\eta}{1+\eta}\right)^2 p_{t+2}.$$

Repeating this procedure successively to eliminate p_{t+2}, p_{t+3}, and so on, we get

$$p_t = \frac{1}{1+\eta}\sum_{s=t}^{\infty}\left(\frac{\eta}{1+\eta}\right)^{s-t} m_s + \lim_{T \to \infty}\left(\frac{\eta}{1+\eta}\right)^T p_{t+T}. \tag{7}$$

Let's tentatively assume that the second term on the right-hand side of (7) is zero:

$$\lim_{T \to \infty}\left(\frac{\eta}{1+\eta}\right)^T p_{t+T} = 0. \tag{8}$$

This limit is indeed zero unless the absolute value of the log price level grows exponentially at a rate of at least $(1+\eta)/\eta$ (which implies that the *level* of prices changes at an ever-increasing proportional rate).[6] We impose condition (8) to eliminate self-generating *speculative bubbles* in the price level, as we explain in the next subsection. The condition implies that the equilibrium price level is

$$p_t = \frac{1}{1+\eta}\sum_{s=t}^{\infty}\left(\frac{\eta}{1+\eta}\right)^{s-t} m_s. \tag{9}$$

Notice that the sum of coefficients on the money-supply terms in eq. (9) is

---

6. To ensure convergence of the first term on the right-hand side of eq. (7), we need to impose the restriction that the logarithm of the money supply does not grow indefinitely at an exponential rate of $(1+\eta)/\eta$ or above. Notice that because p is the logarithm of the price level P, $p \to -\infty$ means that $P \to 0$.

$$\frac{1}{1+\eta}\left[1+\frac{\eta}{1+\eta}+\left(\frac{\eta}{1+\eta}\right)^2+\cdots\right]=\frac{1}{1+\eta}\left(\frac{1}{1-\frac{\eta}{1+\eta}}\right)=1.$$

Thus the price level depends on a weighted average of future expected money supplies, with weights that decline geometrically as the future unfolds. The fact that these weights sum to 1 implies that money is fully *neutral*. Changing the level of the money supply or the nominal unit of account by the same proportion on all dates leads to an immediate equal proportional change in the price level. This property of monetary neutrality characterizes all models that lack nominal rigidities and money illusion. A stronger property than neutrality, which does not always hold in the models of this chapter, is *real-monetary dichotomy*, under which the economy's real resource allocation is totally independent of monetary variables. In this case, money is a "veil," the removal of which would leave the underlying real resource allocation unchanged.[7]

To check the reasonableness of solution (9), consider some cases so simple that we can guess the solution. For example, if the money supply is expected to remain constant at $\bar{m}$ forever, then it is logical to think that inflation should be zero too, $p_{t+1}-p_t=0$. But in this case eq. (5) implies that the price level is constant at $\bar{p}=\bar{m}$, which is the solution (9) also implies. As a second case, suppose that the money supply is growing at a constant percentage rate μ per period,

$$m_t=\bar{m}+\mu t.$$

(If the *log* of a variable is growing linearly at rate μ, then the *level* of the variable must be growing at μ percent per year.) In this case, it makes sense to think that the price level is also growing at rate μ, $p_{t+1}-p_t=\mu$. Substituting this guess into the Cagan equation (5) yields

$$p_t=m_t+\eta\mu. \tag{10}$$

This, too, is the answer eq. (9) implies.[8]

---

7. In general, even if money is neutral in the sense that once-off changes in the money supply's *level* have no real effects, it is not necessarily true that changes in the expected rate of money-supply *growth* have no real effects.

8. Verifying this claim requires some computation. As one can confirm through term-by-term multiplication of the product in the second equality below, eq. (9) implies that

$$p_t=\frac{1}{1+\eta}\sum_{s=t}^{\infty}\left(\frac{\eta}{1+\eta}\right)^{s-t}[m_t+\mu(s-t)]$$

$$=m_t+\frac{\mu}{1+\eta}\left[\left(\frac{\eta}{1+\eta}\right)+\left(\frac{\eta}{1+\eta}\right)^2+\cdots\right]\sum_{s=t}^{\infty}\left(\frac{\eta}{1+\eta}\right)^{s-t}$$

$$=m_t+\left(\frac{\mu}{1+\eta}\right)\eta(1+\eta)=m_t+\eta\mu.$$

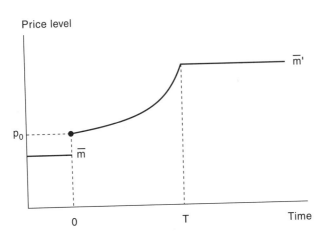

Figure 8.1
A perfectly anticipated rise in the money supply

Solution (9) covers more general money supply processes. Consider the effects of an unanticipated announcement on date $t = 0$ that the money supply is going to rise sharply and permanently on a future date T. Specifically, suppose

$$m_t = \begin{cases} \bar{m} & t < T, \\ \bar{m}' & t \geq T. \end{cases}$$

Given this money-supply path, eq. (9) gives the path of the price level as

$$p_t = \begin{cases} \bar{m} + \left(\frac{\eta}{1+\eta}\right)^{T-t} (\bar{m}' - \bar{m}), & t < T, \\ p_t = \bar{m}', & t \geq T. \end{cases}$$

This path is graphed in Figure 8.1. Notice how the log price level jumps up at time 0 and accelerates over time until it reaches its new steady-state value on date T.

8.2.3 The Assumption of No Speculative Bubbles

Our proposed solution for the path of the price level is predicated, of course, on the assumption of no speculative bubbles. Otherwise, there might be solutions to eq. (5) of the form

$$p_t = \frac{1}{1+\eta} \sum_{s=t}^{\infty} \left(\frac{\eta}{1+\eta}\right)^{s-t} m_s + b_0 \left(\frac{1+\eta}{\eta}\right)^t, \tag{11}$$

where b_0 is the initial deviation of p_0 from its *fundamental* value, that is

$$b_0 = p_0 - \frac{1}{1+\eta} \sum_{s=0}^{\infty} \left(\frac{\eta}{1+\eta}\right)^s m_s.$$

Chapter 2 showed that when individual preferences and constraints are specified in full, one often can rule out nonmonetary asset price bubbles that violate conditions resembling eq. (8). A natural question is whether there is a similar basis for believing eq. (8) once we introduce explicitly maximizing agents, as we do in the next section. For now we simply assume away speculative bubbles, so that $b_0 = 0$ and the equilibrium price level depends only on fundamentals as in eq. (9).

8.2.4   The Stochastic Cagan Model

Because the Cagan equation is *linear*, extending it to a stochastic environment is simple. When the future money supply is uncertain, the no-bubbles solution to the Cagan model [the solution to eq. (4)] is

$$p_t = \frac{1}{1+\eta} \sum_{s=t}^{\infty} \left(\frac{\eta}{1+\eta}\right)^{s-t} E_t\{m_s\}, \tag{12}$$

as you can check by substitution. This solution differs from the perfect-foresight solution (9) only in the replacement of perfectly foreseen future money supplies by their expected values. Suppose, for example, that the money supply process is governed by

$$m_t = \rho m_{t-1} + \epsilon_t, \qquad 0 \le \rho \le 1, \tag{13}$$

where ϵ_t is a serially uncorrelated white-noise money-supply shock such that $E_t\{\epsilon_{t+1}\} = 0$. Substitute this money-supply process into price equation (12) and note that $E_t\{\epsilon_{t+s}\} = 0$ for $s > t$. The result is

$$p_t = \frac{m_t}{1+\eta} \sum_{s=t}^{\infty} \left(\frac{\eta\rho}{1+\eta}\right)^{s-t} = \left(\frac{m_t}{1+\eta}\right) \frac{1}{1 - \frac{\eta\rho}{1+\eta}} = \frac{m_t}{1+\eta-\eta\rho}. \tag{14}$$

In the limiting case $\rho = 1$ (in which money shocks are expected to be permanent), the solution reduces to $p_t = m_t$, in analogy with the nonstochastic case.

8.2.5   The Cagan Model in Continuous Time

For some problems, such as modeling exchange-rate crises as we do later in this chapter, it is dramatically easier and neater to work in a continuous-time setting. Before proceeding, we therefore pause to describe a continuous-time version of the Cagan model. For simplicity we assume perfect foresight.

In continuous time, the Cagan money demand function (5) becomes

$$m_t - p_t = -\eta \dot{p}_t, \tag{15}$$

where $d(\log P)/dt = \dot{P}/P$ is the anticipated inflation rate in continuous time. Using conventional differential equation methods (see, for example, Sargent, 1987, ch. 1), one finds that the general solution to eq. (15) is

$$p_t = \frac{1}{\eta} \int_t^\infty \exp[-(s-t)/\eta] m_s ds + b_0 \exp(t/\eta), \tag{16}$$

which strongly resembles the discrete-time solution, eq. (11).[9] Speculative bubbles are ruled out by setting the arbitrary constant b_0 to zero. If we assume $b_0 = 0$, then the remaining integral term shows that the price level depends on a discounted value of future money supplies with weights summing to one, as in eq. (9).

The most instructive way to derive these results is as the limit, for a very small trading interval, of the discrete-time Cagan model. Let the time interval between dates be of arbitrary length h. Then the perfect-foresight Cagan equation (5) becomes

$$m_t - p_t = -\frac{\eta}{h}(p_{t+h} - p_t). \tag{17}$$

We divide η by h because a given price-level increase lowers the real rate of return to holding money in inverse proportion to the time interval over which it occurs. Taking the limit of this equation as $h \to 0$ yields the differential equation (15) that governs the continuous-time Cagan model.[10]

Solving eq. (17) forward as before (with $h = 1$) results in a generalization of eq. (11),

$$p_t = \frac{1}{1 + \eta/h} \sum_{s=t}^\infty \left(\frac{\eta/h}{1+\eta/h}\right)^{(s-t)/h} m_s + b_0 \left(\frac{1+\eta/h}{\eta/h}\right)^{t/h},$$

where the preceding summation is over $s = t$, $t + h$, $t + 2h$, etc. Rewriting this expression as

$$p_t = \frac{1}{h+\eta} \sum_{s=t}^\infty \left(1 + \frac{h}{\eta}\right)^{-(s-t)/h} m_s h + b_0 \left(1 + \frac{h}{\eta}\right)^{t/h}$$

---

9. The reader can differentiate eq. (16) with respect to t to confirm that it indeed solves differential equation (15). It will help to remember the calculus formula

$$\frac{d}{dt} \int_{a(t)}^{b(t)} f(z,t)dz = f[b(t),t]b'(t) - f[a(t),t]a'(t) + \int_{a(t)}^{b(t)} \frac{\partial f(z,t)}{\partial t} dz$$

(where all relevant derivatives are assumed to exist).

10. The anticipated inflation term $\dot{p}$ in the continuous-time Cagan equation (15) should be interpreted as a "right-hand" derivative, that is, as the price level's rate of change over the immediate future,

$$\dot{p}_t = \lim_{h \downarrow 0} \frac{p_{t+h} - p_t}{h}.$$

This rate of change need not equal the inflation rate over the immediate past, because the *derivative* of the price level can be discontinuous along a perfect foresight path. In contrast, solution (16) implies that the perfect-foresight path for the *level* of prices cannot be discontinuous. That is, the price level must be a continuous function of time when there are no unanticipated shocks.

and taking its limit as the time interval $h \to 0$ gives the solution to the continuous-time model, eq. (16).

As a simple example of applying eq. (16), suppose that the money supply is growing at the constant rate $\dot{m} = \mu$. Assuming no speculative bubbles ($b_0 = 0$) and applying integration by parts to eq. (16) yields[11]

$$p_t = \frac{1}{\eta} \int_t^\infty e^{-(s-t)/\eta} m_s ds = m_t + \int_t^\infty e^{-(s-t)/\eta} \dot{m}_s ds = m_t + \eta\mu. \tag{18}$$

[For this simple case it would have been easier to solve the model directly by guessing that $\dot{p} = \mu$ and substituting that guess into eq. (15).] For future reference, we note that if one does not impose the no-speculative-bubbles assumption, the price level for the case of constant money growth is given by

$$p_t = m_t + \eta\mu + b_0 e^{t/\eta}, \tag{19}$$

where, as usual, $b_0 = p_0 - m_0 - \eta\mu$ is the gap between the initial price level and its fundamental, no-bubbles value.

8.2.6 Seignorage

Seignorage represents the real revenues a government acquires by using newly issued money to buy goods and nonmoney assets.[12] Most hyperinflations stem from the government's need for seignorage revenue, so it is natural to introduce the concept in the context of the Cagan model.

A government's real seignorage revenue in period t is

$$\text{Seignorage} = \frac{M_t - M_{t-1}}{P_t}. \tag{20}$$

The numerator in eq. (20) is the increase in the nominal money supply between periods t and $t - 1$. The denominator P_t converts this nominal increase into a flow of real resources to the government.[13]

---

11. A general statement of the principle of integration by parts is that for differentiable functions $f(s)$ and $g(s)$,

$$\int_a^b \frac{df(s)}{ds} g(s) ds = [f(b)g(b) - f(a)g(a)] - \int_a^b f(s) \frac{dg(s)}{ds} ds.$$

12. In many economies, the branch of the government in charge of monetary policy is separate from the one in charge of fiscal policy, so one must consolidate the branches' balance sheets to understand seignorage. In the United States, for example, the Treasury issues debt and uses the proceeds to make the government's purchases of goods and services. If the central bank so chooses, it can *monetize* the debt by printing money and buying it back from the public. Since the transfer of debt from the Treasury to the central bank has no effect on the consolidated government balance sheet, the net effect is the same as if the government had simply printed money and purchased goods.

13. Note the distinction between seignorage revenue and the proceeds of the *inflation tax*, which are given by

What are the limits to the real resources a government can obtain by printing money? If high inflation leads to a reduction in holdings of real money balances, it shrinks the effective tax base. So in principle, the marginal revenue from money growth can be negative, at least for sufficiently high levels of inflation. To see this point, rewrite eq. (20) as

$$\text{Seignorage} = \frac{M_t - M_{t-1}}{M_t} \cdot \frac{M_t}{P_t}. \tag{21}$$

If higher money growth raises expected inflation, the demand for real balances M/P will fall, so that a rise in money growth does not necessarily augment seignorage revenues.

The problem of finding the seignorage-revenue-maximizing rate of inflation is relatively straightforward if we limit ourselves to looking at steady states with constant rates of money growth. Suppose that the demand for real balances is isoelastic as in the perfect-foresight Cagan model. Exponentiating eq. (5) yields

$$\frac{M_t}{P_t} = \left(\frac{P_{t+1}}{P_t}\right)^{-\eta}.$$

Denote the constant gross rate of money growth as

$$1 + \mu = \frac{M_t}{M_{t-1}} = \frac{P_t}{P_{t-1}},$$

where the second equality follows from eq. (10), which was the price-level solution in this case. Substituting the two preceding expressions into the seignorage equation (21) yields

$$\text{Seignorage} = \frac{\mu}{1 + \mu} \cdot (1 + \mu)^{-\eta} = \mu (1 + \mu)^{-\eta - 1}. \tag{22}$$

Maximizing with respect to μ gives the first-order condition

$$(1 + \mu)^{-\eta - 1} - \mu(\eta + 1)(1 + \mu)^{-\eta - 2} = 0,$$

or

$$\frac{M_{t-1}}{P_{t-1}} - \frac{M_{t-1}}{P_t} = \frac{P_t - P_{t-1}}{P_t} \cdot \frac{M_{t-1}}{P_{t-1}},$$

or the total capital loss that inflation inflicts on holders of real money balances. Seignorage equals inflation-tax proceeds plus the change in the economy's real money holdings,

$$\frac{M_t - M_{t-1}}{P_t} = \left(\frac{M_t}{P_t} - \frac{M_{t-1}}{P_{t-1}}\right) + \left(\frac{M_{t-1}}{P_{t-1}} - \frac{M_{t-1}}{P_t}\right).$$

In a growing economy, seignorage revenue typically exceeds inflation tax revenue, as the government can print money to accommodate a rising demand for real transactions balances without generating inflation.

$$\mu^{\text{MAX}} = \frac{1}{\eta}. \tag{23}$$

The revenue-maximizing net rate of money growth depends inversely on the semielasticity of real balances with respect to inflation. This formula, which Cagan (1956) appears to have been the first to derive, is the standard pricing formula for a monopolist with zero marginal cost of production.[14]

A question that puzzled Cagan is how governments could ever let money growth exceed the rate given by eq. (23), as they seemed to do over at least some portion of each hyperinflation he studied. Desperate governments sometimes rely excessively on seignorage when their ability to collect tax revenues through other means is very limited. But why would any government ever choose to be on the wrong side of the "inflation Laffer curve"?[15] Cagan reasoned that if expectations of inflation are adaptive, and therefore backward-looking, then there may be a short-run benefit to a government of temporarily exceeding the revenue-maximizing rate. Contemporary researchers are skeptical of any explanation that relies on adaptive expectations, since it implies that the government can systematically fool the public.

Even under forward-looking rational expectations, however, Cagan's reasoning still points to a subtle problem with a steady-state analysis of the seignorage-maximizing rate of inflation. By assuming the government can choose a point on the real money demand schedule $(P_{t+1}/P_t)^{-\eta}$, we implicitly assumed that it can *commit* itself to follow a particular future growth path for money. To see why this might be a problem, consider the following scenario. Suppose the government announces on date 0 that it will stick forever to the revenue-maximizing rate of money growth $1/\eta$. If the public believes the government, it will hold real balances $M/P = [(1+\eta)/\eta]^{-\eta}$. What then if, on date 1, the government suddenly sets money growth greater than $1/\eta$, promising this will never happen again? If the public is gullible enough to believe this promise, the government will have succeeded in obtaining higher period 1 revenues at no future cost. If the public is not gullible, it will anticipate the government's temptation to cheat even at the outset. In that case, the public's holdings of real balances will almost certainly be below

---

14. A small detail is that the *cost* of producing paper money is not actually zero. The United States Treasury recently estimated that the cost of printing a paper one dollar bill is 3.8 cents and that the average lifespan of a bill is roughly one and a half years (*Federal Reserve Bulletin,* September 1995). Many developing countries have their currency printed abroad, since very high-quality production is required to discourage counterfeiters. With a positive marginal cost of producing currency, eq. (23) must be modified to yield the result that marginal revenue equals marginal cost. In truth, the problem is more complicated because the production function for producing money is not smoothly convex. It costs little more to produce a hundred dollar bill than a one dollar bill. (The marginal cost of printing the new "counterfeit-proof" United States $100 bill is about 4.7 cents.)

15. Cukierman, Edwards, and Tabellini (1992) argue that very few economies have had money growth in excess of the seignorage-maximizing rate in recent decades. This assertion is debatable, since estimates of the inflation elasticity of the demand for real balances vary widely.

$[(1 + \eta)/\eta]^{-\eta}$. Thus, unless a government can establish credibility for its money-growth announcements, its maximum seignorage revenue in reality may well be less than the maximum implied by our analysis. Furthermore, one could easily observe cases in which governments set monetary growth above $1/\eta$.

One admittedly impractical solution is for the government legally to bind itself in perpetuity to a given rate of money growth. Even if feasible, such rigidity may be ill-advised if there is a risk that future changes in the economy's transactions technology will drastically alter the demand for money. Another solution, possible under some conditions, is for the government to develop a reputation for sticking to its monetary growth announcements, perhaps with the aid of a trigger-strategy punishment mechanism of the type we studied in Chapter 6.[16] In Chapter 9 we will return to this idea.

8.2.7 A Simple Monetary Model of Exchange Rates

A variant of the log-linear Cagan model leads to a simple monetary model of the nominal exchange rate. Since we wish to apply the model in conditions of moderate inflation, we reintroduce the dependence of money demand on the nominal interest rate and real income.[17]

Consider a small, open economy in which real output is exogenous and the demand for money is given by

$$m_t - p_t = -\eta i_{t+1} + \phi y_t, \tag{24}$$

where $i \equiv \log(1 + i)$. As before, p is the log price level, and y is the log of real output.

One of the key building blocks of the flexible-price monetary model is the assumption of purchasing power parity (PPP), introduced in Chapter 4.[18] Recall that under PPP, countries have identical price levels when prices are measured in a common numeraire. Let $\mathcal{E}$ be the nominal exchange rate, defined as the price of foreign

---

16. The credibility problems inherent in seignorage extraction were first raised by Auernheimer (1974), and later studied by Calvo (1978), H. Grossman and Van Huyck (1986), and others. One simple trigger-strategy mechanism is for the public to form expectations of money growth such that $E_t\{\mu_{t+1}\} = \mu^{MAX}$ if $\mu_s \leq \mu^{MAX} \; \forall s \leq t$, and $E_t\{\mu_{t+1}\} = \infty$ otherwise. Under these "grim trigger strategy" expectations, the price level on date t will immediately and permanently rise to infinity if date t money growth exceeds μ^{MAX}. That is, the public will cease holding or accepting the currency. Faced with such expectations, the government will never have any incentive to set money growth above μ^{MAX} because there is not even a *short-term* gain. The assumption sometimes made in the literature (e.g., Grossman and Van Huyck) is that there is a short lag in expectations formation so that the government can indeed get a short-run gain from unanticipated excess inflation. In this case, in analogy to the trigger-strategy model of Chapter 6, the seignorage-maximizing rate may not be sustainable as a trigger-strategy equilibrium if the government discounts the future too heavily.

17. The monetary model was introduced by Frenkel (1976) and Mussa (1976).

18. It is easy to modify the flexible-price monetary model to incorporate exogenous deviations from PPP. In Chapter 9 we will introduce models where deviations from PPP arise endogenously in response to monetary shocks.

Box 8.1
How Important Is Seignorage?

The following table shows average 1990–94 seignorage revenues for a select group of industrialized countries. Seignorage is scaled in two ways, as a percent of government spending and as a percent of GDP.

Country	Percent of Government Spending	Percent of GDP
Australia	0.95	0.31
Canada	0.84	0.09
France	−0.83	−0.23
Germany	2.89	0.56
Italy	3.11	0.32
New Zealand	0.04	0.01
Sweden	3.22	1.52
United States	2.19	0.44

Source: International Monetary Fund, *International Financial Statistics.*

For all countries in the table except Sweden, seignorage revenues amounted to less than 1 percent of GDP. Seignorage is more important as a fraction of total government spending, amounting to more than 2 percent for the United States and Germany, and more than 3 percent for Italy and Sweden. (Seignorage revenues can be much higher for developing countries, though sustained rates above 5 percent of GDP are rare; see Fischer, 1982.)

currency in terms of home currency, and let P^* denote the world foreign-currency price of the consumption basket with home-currency price P. Purchasing power parity implies that

$$P_t = \mathcal{E}_t P_t^*$$
(25)

or, in logs with e denoting $\log \mathcal{E}$,

$$p_t = e_t + p_t^*.$$
(26)

The second building block of the monetary model is *uncovered interest parity.* Let i_{t+1} be the date t interest rate on bonds denominated in home currency, and let i_{t+1}^* be the interest rate on foreign-currency bonds. Then uncovered interest parity holds when

$$1 + i_{t+1} = (1 + i_{t+1}^*)E_t\left\{\frac{\mathcal{E}_{t+1}}{\mathcal{E}_t}\right\}.$$
(27)

In a world of perfect foresight, uncovered interest parity must hold via a simple arbitrage argument. An investor can take one unit of home currency and buy $1/\mathcal{E}_t$ units of foreign bonds that each pay principal and interest $1 + i^*_{t+1}$. This sum can then be converted back into home currency at the date $t + 1$ exchange rate, $\mathcal{E}_{t+1}$. The gross home-currency return is the right-hand side of eq. (27) which, of course, must equal the gross return on the left-hand side, $1 + i_{t+1}$. In a stochastic world, exchange rate risk (among other factors) can drive a wedge into the uncovered interest parity relationship, as we shall see later. In effect, the monetary model treats this wedge as constant.[19]

Written in logs, the uncovered interest parity relationship (27) is approximated by

$$i_{t+1} = i^*_{t+1} + E_t e_{t+1} - e_t. \tag{28}$$

Equation (28) is only an approximation under uncertainty because of Jensen's inequality, which implies $\log E_t\{\mathcal{E}_{t+1}\} > E_t\{\log \mathcal{E}_{t+1}\}$. (The log function is strictly concave.) We will say much more about this approximation toward the end of the chapter.

Substitute PPP, eq. (26), and the uncovered interest parity approximation, eq. (28), into the money demand equation (24). The result is

$$(m_t - \phi y_t + \eta i^*_{t+1} - p^*_t) - e_t = -\eta(E_t e_{t+1} - e_t). \tag{29}$$

Formally, eq. (29) is the same as the stochastic Cagan hyperinflation model, eq. (4), except that e appears in place of p and the exogenous variable is now the compound term $m_t - \phi y_t + \eta i^*_{t+1} - p^*_t$ instead of just m_t. In analogy to solution (12) for the stochastic Cagan model, the solution for the exchange rate is

$$e_t = \frac{1}{1+\eta} \sum_{s=t}^{\infty} \left(\frac{\eta}{1+\eta}\right)^{s-t} E_t\{m_s - \phi y_s + \eta i^*_{s+1} - p^*_s\}. \tag{30}$$

In this monetary model, raising the path of the home money supply raises the domestic price level and forces e up through the PPP mechanism. This is a *depreciation* of the home currency against foreign currency. Changes in real domestic income, the foreign interest rate, and the foreign price level have the qualitative effects indicated by the signs in eq. (30). For example, a rise in the path of home output raises money demand. Because the domestic price level falls to produce an accommodating increase in real balances, PPP implies an *appreciation* of domestic currency in the foreign exchange market, that is, a fall in e.

As we shall see in Chapter 9, the data are not very kind to this monetary model of exchange rates outside hyperinflationary environments. The model is more useful

---

19. A related parity concept is *covered interest parity*, which we will discuss in greater detail in section 8.7.

empirically as a long-run relationship. Nevertheless, the simple monetary model yields some important insights that are preserved in much more general contexts. One very important and quite robust insight is that *the nominal exchange rate must be viewed as an asset price*. Like other assets, the exchange rate depends on expectations of future variables, as eq. (30) shows.

The following example provides an illustration of how sensitive the exchange rate can be to expectations. It also illustrates how to apply eq. (30) in practice. Let y, p, and i* be constant with $\eta i^* - \phi y - p^* = 0$, and suppose that the money supply follows the process

$$m_t - m_{t-1} = \rho(m_{t-1} - m_{t-2}) + \epsilon_t, \qquad 0 \le \rho \le 1, \tag{31}$$

where ϵ is a serially uncorrelated mean-zero shock such that $E_{t-1}\{\epsilon_t\} = 0$. For $\rho > 0$, the process (31) differs from the one we considered for the Cagan model, eq. (13). Here, ϵ_t is a shock to the growth rate of the money supply rather than to its level.[20] With the above specification for the exogenous variables, the easiest way to evaluate the solution (30) is to lead it by one period, take date t expectations of both sides, and then subtract the original equation. That procedure leads to

$$E_t e_{t+1} - e_t = \frac{1}{1+\eta} \sum_{s=t}^{\infty} \left(\frac{\eta}{1+\eta} \right)^{s-t} E_t\{m_{s+1} - m_s\} \tag{32}$$

(remember that $\eta i^* - \phi y - p^* = 0$). Substituting eq. (31) into eq. (32) yields

$$E_t e_{t+1} - e_t = \frac{\rho}{1+\eta - \eta\rho}(m_t - m_{t-1}).$$

Substituting this expression into eq. (29) yields the solution for the exchange rate:

$$e_t = m_t + \frac{\eta\rho}{1+\eta - \eta\rho}(m_t - m_{t-1}).$$

This equation shows that an unanticipated shock to m_t may have two impacts. It always raises the exchange rate directly by raising the current nominal money supply. When $\rho > 0$, it also raises expectations of future money growth, thereby pushing the exchange rate even higher. Thus this simple monetary model provides one story of how instability in the money supply could lead to proportionally greater variability in the exchange rate.

While the models we have studied in this section capture a number of important and robust insights, they nonetheless have serious limitations. They do not embody intertemporal budget constraints, either for individuals or for the government. Nor do they show how changes in wealth affect money demand. Finally, the models of

---

20. The reader may recognize eqs. (13) and (31) as formally identical to the two stochastic processes we compared in Chapter 2 to illustrate Deaton's paradox.

this section can provide no rigorous basis for ruling out speculative bubbles. To go further, we need to look at models with more fully articulated microfoundations.

8.3   Monetary Exchange Rate Models with Maximizing Individuals

This section is devoted to models that derive money demand from individual utility maximization. As we remarked earlier, at present there is no completely satisfactory or universally accepted approach to modeling the microfoundations of money. The very nature of money as a good that has value thanks to social convention raises many subtle modeling issues, especially when it comes to welfare analysis. These problems are only compounded in an international environment with multiple currencies. Beware of articles that claim to have found the "right" way to model money. The literature is strewn with inflated claims that subsequently prove ill-founded. The particular choice-theoretic models we present below plainly have their limitations. Such is the state of the art. We would argue, however, that these models based on maximization represent a clear advance over the Cagan model and its relatives. Their advantage lies in building on the firmer foundation of individual choice without sacrificing the central empirically motivated features of the last section's models.

Here we look only at small-country versions of the models. Stochastic general equilibrium versions are presented later in section 8.7 (see also appendix 8A).

8.3.1   Money in the Utility Function

In this section we assume people hold money because real balances are an argument of the utility function. Underpinning this approach is the implicit assumption that agents gain utility from both consumption and leisure. Real money balances enter the utility function indirectly because they allow agents to save time in conducting their transactions. While unsatisfactory in assuming much of what we would like to explain, the approach does capture money's role as a store of value and a medium of exchange, and it yields empirically realistic money demand equations. Last but not least, the resulting model is highly tractable. The first fully dynamic applications of this approach are due to Sidrauski (1967) and Brock (1974), who assumed closed economies.

Most of the main ideas can be illustrated in the context of a small, open, endowment economy that produces and consumes one perishable good. To focus on the basic mechanics of introducing money, we assume perfect foresight.

The utility function of the representative agent is

$$U_t = \sum_{s=t}^{\infty} \beta^{s-t} u\left(C_s, \frac{M_s}{P_s}\right),$$

(33)

where M_t denotes the nominal money stock that the individual acquires at the beginning of period t and then holds through the end of the period.[21] We assume that u_C, $u_{M/P} > 0$ and that $u(C, M/P)$ is strictly concave. As usual, population size is normalized to 1. Since this is a one-good model, PPP holds,

$$P_t = \mathcal{E}_t P^*,$$

where $\mathcal{E}_t$ is the domestic-currency price of foreign currency and P^* is the constant foreign price level measured in foreign currency. Since P^* is constant, PPP implies that we can identify the domestic price level P with the exchange rate $\mathcal{E}$.

Equation (33) can be viewed as a *derived* utility function that includes real balances because they economize on time spent transacting.[22] Suppose, for example, that the individual's true period utility function depends on consumption and leisure rather than consumption and real balances,

$$\alpha \log C + (1 - \alpha) \log(\bar{L} - L_t),$$

where $\bar{L} - L_t$ is leisure. Assume further that time available for leisure is an increasing function of the ratio of real balances to consumption

$$\bar{L} - L_t = \bar{L} \left(\frac{M_t/P_t}{C_t} \right)^{\varepsilon},$$

where $0 < \varepsilon < \frac{\alpha}{1-\alpha}$.[23] Combining these two equations shows that (apart from an irrelevant constant)

$$\alpha \log C + (1 - \alpha) \log(\bar{L} - L_t) = [\alpha - \varepsilon(1 - \alpha)] \log C_t + \varepsilon(1 - \alpha) \log \frac{M_t}{P_t},$$

which is the same form as the period utility function in eq. (33). The money-in-the-utility-function approach is thus simply a convenient shorthand.

In an autarkic closed economy, this might be enough discussion of our setup, but an open economy raises additional questions. Our formulation assumes that only domestic currency is used in transactions and that foreign currency cannot serve the same purpose. What could possibly justify this asymmetry? While one

---

21. Note that our timing convention for money (which the Cagan model also implicitly uses) may seem inconsistent with our timing convention for other asset stocks. Money acquired in period t is labeled M_t, whereas, for example, capital acquired in period t is labeled K_{t+1}. Our timing convention for money is natural though, since, as with the durable goods of Chapter 2, we assume that money starts to yield services in the period in which it is acquired.

22. An alternative approach that gives very similar results involves assuming that money economizes on transaction costs: the higher real balances are, the greater is the fraction of income that is left over for consumption. In this case, real balances enter the budget constraint rather than the utility function. Feenstra (1986) describes alternative ways to derive a specification like eq. (33).

23. The preceding function must be regarded as an approximation that applies only in a relevant region where L_t is much lower than $\bar{L}$. We don't literally think that someone who held zero real balances would use up his entire leisure endowment conducting transactions! Nor can L_t ever be negative.

can advance elaborate explanations, the most realistic one is to assume that the government imposes severe legal restrictions on the use of other types of currencies, foreign or private. Without such restrictions, the government's monopoly on currency would be severely compromised, and it might have great difficulty collecting seignorage revenues or controlling the domestic price level. Our analysis does not require that the ban on foreign currency use be absolute. One can think of domestic agents as being allowed to swap domestic currency for foreign currency (within a period) as needed to purchase instantly *foreign* goods or bonds. Similarly, foreign residents can acquire domestic currency to buy instantly domestic goods or bonds. Later on, we will look at models of currency substitution in which legal obstacles do not fully prevent the use of foreign currency even in domestic transactions.

8.3.2 The Budget Constraint and Individual Maximization

To simplify, we assume that the domestic government issues no interest-bearing debt and holds no interest-bearing assets, so that the representative individual is confined to holding home money and interest-bearing claims on foreigners. (Ricardian equivalence holds in the model, so we will not sacrifice substantial generality by abstracting from domestic government debt.) The individual's financing constraint for any date t is then given by

$$B_{t+1} + \frac{M_t}{P_t} = (1+r)B_t + \frac{M_{t-1}}{P_t} + Y_t - C_t - T_t, \tag{34}$$

since date t trades are made at the date t price level. In this equation, T stands for lump-sum net taxes paid to the government, r is the world real rate of interest, and B denotes net private holdings of bonds issued by foreigners, which are denominated in output. Recall that our timing convention for money has M_t as the quantity of nominal balances accumulated during period t and carried over into period $t + 1$. Our assumption that bonds are real instruments is relatively innocuous in this perfect-foresight model. In this case, Fisher parity assures that all bonds, regardless of currency denomination, pay the same real rate of interest (when measured in a common consumption basket). Currency of denomination becomes a more interesting issue later when we turn to a stochastic version of the model.[24]

To derive the first-order conditions for the individual's problem, we use the financing constraint (34) to substitute for C_s in utility function (33):

---

24. If the bonds traded were nominally denominated instead of real, then the domestic individual's budget constraint (written in terms of home currency) would be replaced by

$$\mathcal{E}_t B_{F,t+1} + B_{H,t+1} + M_t = \mathcal{E}_t(1+i_t^*)B_{F,t} + (1+i_t)B_{H,t} + M_{t-1} + P_t(Y_t - C_t - T_t).$$

Here, B_F denotes holdings of foreign-currency-denominated bonds and B_H denotes holdings of domestic-currency-denominated bonds.

$$U_t = \sum_{s=t}^{\infty} \beta^{s-t} u \left[-B_{s+1} - \frac{M_s}{P_s} + (1+r)B_s + \frac{M_{s-1}}{P_s} + Y_s - T_s, \frac{M_s}{P_s} \right].$$

By differentiating this expression with respect to B_{t+1} and M_t we arrive at

$$u_C \left(C_t, \frac{M_t}{P_t} \right) = (1+r)\beta u_C \left(C_{t+1}, \frac{M_{t+1}}{P_{t+1}} \right), \tag{35}$$

$$\frac{1}{P_t} u_C \left(C_t, \frac{M_t}{P_t} \right) = \frac{1}{P_t} u_{M/P} \left(C_t, \frac{M_t}{P_t} \right) + \frac{1}{P_{t+1}} \beta u_C \left(C_{t+1}, \frac{M_{t+1}}{P_{t+1}} \right). \tag{36}$$

From an individual's perspective, money may be thought of here as a nontraded durable good, and the two first-order conditions highlight this analogy. Equation (35) is the standard first-order Euler condition in the presence of a nontraded good that enters additively into period utility (recall section 4.4). Condition (36) is familiar from our analysis of durable goods in section 2.4. On the left-hand side, $1/P_t$ is the quantity of current consumption a person must forgo to raise real balances by one unit, and $u_C(C_t, M_t/P_t)$ is the marginal utility of that consumption. On the right-hand side, the first term is the marginal (derived) utility the individual gets from having one extra currency unit to conduct transactions (the utility flow from holding the durable good). Breaking down the second term on the right of eq. (36), $1/P_{t+1}$ is the quantity of consumption the individual will be able to buy in period $t+1$ with the extra currency unit, and $\beta u_C(C_{t+1}, M_{t+1}/P_{t+1})$ is the marginal utility of date $t+1$ consumption, discounted to date t.

The durable goods analogy is sharpened by combining eqs. (35) and (36) into

$$\frac{u_{M/P} \left(C_t, \frac{M_t}{P_t} \right)}{u_C \left(C_t, \frac{M_t}{P_t} \right)} = 1 - \frac{P_t/P_{t+1}}{1+r} = \frac{i_{t+1}}{1+i_{t+1}}, \tag{37}$$

where the second equality follows from the Fisher parity equation (3). (We have not formally introduced nominal bonds into this model yet, but one can think of i as a shadow nominal interest rate.) The far left-hand side of eq. (37) is the marginal rate of substitution of consumption for real balances. The far right-hand side is the user or *rental* cost, in terms of the consumption good, of holding an extra unit of real balances for one period. Why? Think about the net consumption cost of buying a unit of real balances on date t and selling it on date $t+1$. By giving up a unit of consumption on date t, the individual acquires P_t units of currency equal to 1 unit of real balances. A unit of real balances carried over into period $t+1$ is devalued to only P_t/P_{t+1} units by inflation. The present value of the remaining P_t/P_{t+1} units of real balances is $(P_t/P_{t+1})/(1+r)$. On date t, the net cost of holding an extra unit of real balances for a period therefore is $1 - (P_t/P_{t+1})/(1+r)$.

Yet another way to highlight the durable goods interpretation of the model comes from the individual's intertemporal budget constraint. Forward the period budget constraint (34) by one period and divide both sides by $1 + r$. The result is

$$\frac{B_{t+2}}{1+r} + \frac{M_{t+1}}{P_{t+1}(1+r)} = B_{t+1} + \frac{M_t}{P_{t+1}(1+r)} + \frac{Y_{t+1} - C_{t+1} - T_{t+1}}{1+r}.$$

Now rewrite this expression as

$$\frac{B_{t+2}}{1+r} + \frac{M_{t+1}}{P_{t+1}(1+r)}$$

$$= \left(B_{t+1} + \frac{M_t}{P_t} \right) - \frac{M_t}{P_t} \left[1 - \frac{P_t}{P_{t+1}(1+r)} \right] + \frac{Y_{t+1} - C_{t+1} - T_{t+1}}{1+r},$$

and use the result to substitute out for $B_{t+1} + (M_t/P_t)$ in eq. (34). Iterating this process, and making use of the fact that

$$1 - \frac{P_t}{P_{t+1}(1+r)} = \frac{i_{t+1}}{1+i_{t+1}}$$

(by Fisher parity), we see that the individual's intertemporal budget constraint is given by

$$\sum_{s=t}^{\infty} \left(\frac{1}{1+r} \right)^{s-t} \left[C_s + \frac{i_{s+1}}{1+i_{s+1}} \left(\frac{M_s}{P_s} \right) \right]$$

$$= (1+r)B_t + \frac{M_{t-1}}{P_t} + \sum_{s=t}^{\infty} \left(\frac{1}{1+r} \right)^{s-t} (Y_s - T_s). \tag{38}$$

[In passing to this limiting constraint we have assumed a transversality condition

$$\lim_{T \to \infty} \left(\frac{1}{1+r} \right)^T \left(B_{t+T+1} + \frac{M_{t+T}}{P_{t+T}} \right) = 0$$

on total financial assets.] Initial financial wealth plus the present discounted value of disposable income must equal the present discounted value of expenditure on consumption and on "renting" real balances.

One can think of eq. (37), which relates the marginal rate of substitution between real balances and consumption to the nominal interest rate, as the money demand equation for this model. To illustrate, suppose that the period utility function has the isoelastic form

$$u \left(C, \frac{M}{P} \right) = \frac{[C^\gamma (M/P)^{1-\gamma}]^{1-\frac{1}{\sigma}}}{1 - \frac{1}{\sigma}}, \tag{39}$$

which assumes a unitary intratemporal substitution elasticity between consumption and real balances. Then the money demand equation implied by eq. (37) is

$$\frac{M_t^d}{P_t} = \left(\frac{1-\gamma}{\gamma} \right) \left(1 + \frac{1}{i_{t+1}} \right) C_t. \tag{40}$$

Equation (40) has the same general form as the Keynes-Hicks *LM* curve (2), except that consumption rather than income captures the transactions demand for money.

*8.3.3   Closed-Form Solutions for Optimal Consumption

The problem of maximizing lifetime utility criterion (33) subject to constraint (34) [or (38)] is exactly the same as the corresponding problem with nontraded goods that we solved in section 4.4. Here, the relative price of nontradables is replaced by the price of monetary services, which we have assumed to be nontradable. Following Chapter 4's analysis, we can once again derive closed-form solutions for certain utility functions.

Suppose the period utility function takes the CES-isoelastic form

$$
u\left(C, \frac{M}{P}\right) = \frac{\left\{\left[\gamma^{\frac{1}{\theta}} C^{\frac{\theta-1}{\theta}} + (1-\gamma)^{\frac{1}{\theta}} \left(\frac{M}{P}\right)^{\frac{\theta-1}{\theta}}\right]^{\frac{\theta}{\theta-1}}\right\}^{1-\frac{1}{\sigma}}}{1 - \frac{1}{\sigma}},
$$

where $\theta > 0$ is the intratemporal substitution elasticity. The consumption-based price index P^C (measured in units of the consumption good), an index that here depends on the nominal interest rate, is given by eq. (20) of Chapter 4, with the user cost $i/(1 + i)$ in place of the relative price of nontradables, p:

$$
P_t^C \equiv \left[\gamma + (1-\gamma)\left(\frac{i_{t+1}}{1 + i_{t+1}}\right)^{1-\theta}\right]^{\frac{1}{1-\theta}}.
$$

The consumption-based real interest rate is defined as in eq. (25) of Chapter 4,

$$
1 + r_{t+1}^C = (1+r)\frac{P_t^C}{P_{t+1}^C}.
$$

Imposing CES-isoelastic preferences on first-order condition (37) yields a generalization of money demand equation (40):

$$
\frac{M_t^d}{P_t} = \left(\frac{1-\gamma}{\gamma}\right)\left(1 + \frac{1}{i_{t+1}}\right)^\theta C_t.
$$

Recall that the consumption-based price index P^C is the minimal cost (in terms of consumption) of setting the linear-homogeneous CES "real consumption" index

$$
\Omega\left(C, \frac{M}{P}\right) = \left[\gamma^{\frac{1}{\theta}} C^{\frac{\theta-1}{\theta}} + (1-\gamma)^{\frac{1}{\theta}} \left(\frac{M}{P}\right)^{\frac{\theta-1}{\theta}}\right]^{\frac{\theta}{\theta-1}}
$$

equal to 1. Therefore, if $Z_t \equiv C_t + [i_{t+1}/(1 + i_{t+1})](M_t/P_t)$ is total expenditure measured in consumption units, $Z_t/P_t^C = \Omega(C_t, M_t/P_t)$. Equation (29) of

Chapter 4 then gives the optimal value of "real consumption" Ω in that chapter's model.[25] Translating that equation into this section's setup (where money services are the "nontradable" and financial wealth includes real money balances) gives

$$\frac{Z_t}{P_t^C} = \frac{(1+r)B_t + \frac{M_{t-1}}{P_t} + \sum_{s=t}^{\infty} \left(\frac{1}{1+r}\right)^{s-t} (Y_s - T_s)}{P_t^C \sum_{s=t}^{\infty} \left[(1+r)^{s-t} \left(\frac{P_t^C}{P_s^C}\right)\right]^{\sigma-1} \beta^{\sigma(s-t)}}.$$

The first demand function in eq. (22) of Chapter 4 shows that in this section's model, optimal consumption C_t is equal to $\gamma (1/P_t^C)^{-\theta} \Omega(C_t, M_t/P_t) = \gamma (1/P_t^C)^{-\theta} (Z_t/P_t^C)$. Thus, using the definition of the consumption-based real interest rate, we see that

$$C_t = \frac{\gamma}{(P_t^C)^{-\theta}} \cdot \frac{(1+r)B_t + \frac{M_{t-1}}{P_t} + \sum_{s=t}^{\infty} \left(\frac{1}{1+r}\right)^{s-t} (Y_s - T_s)}{P_t^C \sum_{s=t}^{\infty} \left[\prod_{v=t+1}^{s}(1+r_v^C)\right]^{\sigma-1} \beta^{\sigma(s-t)}}.$$

For the special case $\sigma = \theta = 1$, this solution reduces to

$$C_t = \gamma(1-\beta) \left[(1+r)B_t + \frac{M_{t-1}}{P_t} + \sum_{s=t}^{\infty} \left(\frac{1}{1+r}\right)^{s-t} (Y_s - T_s) \right].$$

Outside of this special case, the path of nominal interest rates can influence consumption and therefore the current account. We thus have a first example of a flexible-price model in which the real-monetary dichotomy fails. The question is probed further in exercise 3 and in Supplement A to this chapter.

8.3.4 The Equilibrium Path for Prices and Exchange Rates

The individual takes nominal prices as given and chooses a desired path of nominal money holdings. In the aggregate, though, the nominal money supply is exogenous, and the path of the price level adjusts to equate money supply and demand. To proceed to general equilibrium, we must close the model by specifying the government budget constraint.

8.3.4.1 Government Budget Constraint

We have assumed that the government balances its budget each period, which is not restrictive because Ricardian equivalence holds here. Therefore, the government's budget constraint is

$$G_t = T_t + \frac{M_t - M_{t-1}}{P_t}, \tag{41}$$

---

25. In the notation of section 4.4, $C = \Omega$. Here, however, consumption C plays the role tradables consumption C_T did in Chapter 4, whereas the services of real money balances M/P here play the role of nontradables consumption C_N.

where the second term on the right-hand side is seignorage.[26] Using the government budget constraint to substitute out for conventional taxes T in the individual's budget constraint (34), one obtains the aggregate economy's budget constraint vis-à-vis the rest of the world

$$B_{t+1} = (1+r)B_t + Y_t - G_t - C_t. \tag{42}$$

Note that currency, which is a nontraded good, does not enter into the economy-wide consolidated budget constraint.

In the case where government spending is zero, the government budget constraint is

$$-T_t = \frac{M_t - M_{t-1}}{P_t}. \tag{43}$$

In this case the government simply makes net transfer payments to the public that it finances by printing money. Even though the government is handing the seignorage revenues back to the public here, inflation still discourages money holding because each competitive individual perceives his transfer receipts as a lump sum unrelated to his own money demand decisions.

8.3.4.2   Solving for the Price Level

We now proceed to solve for the equilibrium path of prices under perfect foresight. (Recall that because purchasing power parity holds, this is equivalent to solving for the path of the exchange rate.) We focus on a relatively simple case with $(1+r)\beta = 1$ and the gross rate of money-supply growth constant at $1 + \mu$. As one can easily confirm from the individual's first-order conditions (35) and (37), there exists an equilibrium in which the gross inflation rate is $P_{t+1}/P_t = 1 + \mu$,

---

26. It is instructive to derive the intertemporal government budget constraint. Lead eq. (41) by one period and divide both sides by $1 + r$. The result can be written as

$$\frac{G_{t+1} - T_{t+1}}{1 + r} = \frac{M_{t+1}/P_{t+1}}{1 + r} - \frac{M_t}{P_t}\left(\frac{P_t}{P_{t+1}(1 + r)}\right)$$

or

$$\frac{M_t}{P_t} = \frac{(M_{t+1}/P_{t+1}) - G_{t+1} + T_{t+1}}{1 + r} + \frac{M_t}{P_t}\left(\frac{i_{t+1}}{1 + i_{t+1}}\right).$$

Next, use this result to substitute for M_t/P_t in eq. (41). Iterating this procedure and assuming no speculative price bubbles, the present-value government budget constraint emerges:

$$\sum_{s=t}^{\infty}\left(\frac{1}{1+r}\right)^{s-t}(G_s - T_s) = -\frac{M_{t-1}}{P_t} + \sum_{s=t}^{\infty}\left(\frac{1}{1+r}\right)^{s-t}\left(\frac{i_{s+1}}{1 + i_{s+1}}\right)\frac{M_s}{P_s}.$$

One can think of the government as renting the money supply to the private sector for a charge of $i_{t+1}/(1 + i_{t+1})$. The present value of the excess of government spending over conventional taxes equals the present value of real rental receipts on the total money supply, less the initial real money stock that the public owns and need not rent.

and in which both consumption C and real balances M/P are constant. The constant equilibrium level of consumption $\bar{C}$ can be determined by integrating the economy-wide budget constraint (42) (which incorporates both the individual and government budget constraints) in the usual way to obtain

$$\bar{C} = rB_t + \frac{r}{1+r} \sum_{s=t}^{\infty} \left(\frac{1}{1+r}\right)^{s-t} (Y_s - G_s). \tag{44}$$

The price level on any date can be found from condition (37) with $C = \bar{C}$ and $P_{t+1}/P_t = 1 + \mu$ imposed. As in section 8.3.3, however, consumption wouldn't necessarily be constant if the money growth rate, and therefore the nominal interest rate, were fluctuating.

8.3.5   Ruling Out Speculative Bubbles

The preceding discussion assumes that the economy indeed goes to the steady state. We saw in the ad hoc Cagan model that in addition to the steady-state path for the price level, numerous speculative bubble paths also satisfy the difference equation that characterizes equilibrium. We ruled out these bubbles as unreasonable but offered no rigorous justification. Related issues arise in a maximizing model of money demand but, armed with microfoundations, we are able to say much more.

8.3.5.1   Saddle-Path Stability of the Steady State

We begin by showing that the model has saddle-path stability properties similar to those of the Cagan model. To make our main points, it is convenient to continue assuming that $(1+r)\beta = 1$ and to give the period utility the additive form

$$u\left(C, \frac{M}{P}\right) = \log C + v\left(\frac{M}{P}\right), \tag{45}$$

where $v(M/P)$ is strictly concave. One convenient aspect of additive period utility is that when $(1+r)\beta = 1$, consumption is constant at $\bar{C}$ in eq. (44) regardless of what is happening to nominal interest rates. (The reason is that money holdings do not affect marginal rates of intertemporal substitution for consumption.) Under functional form (45), money demand equation (37) becomes

$$\frac{v'\left(\frac{M_t}{P_t}\right)}{1/\bar{C}} = 1 - \frac{P_t/P_{t+1}}{1+r}$$

or, using $(1+r)\beta = 1$ and assuming that $M_{t+1}/M_t = 1 + \mu$ is constant,

$$\frac{M_{t+1}}{P_{t+1}} \left(\frac{\beta}{1+\mu}\right) = \frac{M_t}{P_t} \left[1 - \bar{C}v'\left(\frac{M_t}{P_t}\right)\right]. \tag{46}$$

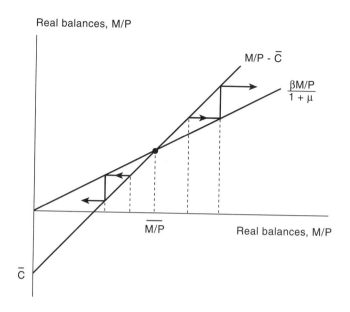

Figure 8.2
Saddle-path dynamics of the price level

Figure 8.2 illustrates the dynamics for real money balances, M/P, that eq. (46) implies in the special case $v(M/P) = \log(M/P)$. The left-hand side of eq. (46) is graphed as a straight line through the origin with slope $\beta/(1 + \mu)$. The right-hand side becomes the line $(M/P) - \bar{C}$. It is clear that as long as $1 + \mu > \beta$, as we shall assume, there is a unique steady-state level of real balances,

$$\frac{\overline{M}}{P} = \bar{C}\left(\frac{1}{1 - \frac{\beta}{1+\mu}}\right).$$

From the diagram, it is apparent that the steady state is unstable. That is, the steady state has the same type of saddle-point dynamics we saw in the Cagan model and in other perfect-foresight models. Unless the price level jumps immediately to place the economy at the steady-state level of real balances, the price level diverges.[27] (The mathematical analogy with the Cagan model is imperfect, however, since the present system is not linear in the log of the price level.)

The reason for the saddle-point property is easiest to grasp when the money supply is constant at $\bar{M}$. At the steady-state price level $\bar{P}$, the marginal cost of

---

27. The assumption $1 + \mu > \beta$ ensures that the steady-state net nominal interest rate is positive. [Given our assumption that $1 + r = 1/\beta$, the steady-state nominal interest rate $\bar{i}$ in this model is given by Fisher parity as $(1 + \mu)/\beta - 1$.] If the nominal interest rate were zero (or lower), there would be no cost to holding money (or a negative cost). Since money gives a positive transactions benefit at the margin, money would always be in excess demand, and no steady-state equilibrium would exist.

increasing nominal balances by one dollar exactly offsets the marginal benefit. A lower price level—and a higher level of real money holdings—can be an equilibrium only if people expect to earn capital gains on money. That is, they must foresee deflation. But deflation raises real balances further, which is consistent with equilibrium only if people foresee even faster deflation for the following period. The same argument generating an unstable downward path for prices works in reverse for a small rise in P from $\bar{P}$. Difference equation (46), like Cagan's model, thus has a plethora of unstable "bubble" solutions.[28]

8.3.5.2   Why Hyperinflationary Equilibria Can Occur

In appendix B to Chapter 2, we saw that for a wide class of real models, one can rule out speculative bubbles for real asset prices.[29] Do similar arguments apply to fiat money? It turns out that under mild restrictions one can rule out hyperdeflationary paths in which the value of money rises explosively. The logic is close to that behind the transversality condition derived in Chapter 2. But ruling out hyperinflationary paths, in which the real value of money goes to zero, is more problematic. The basic reason is one we alluded to in this chapter's introduction. Assets that yield flows of physical goods or services have intrinsic value. Their usefulness to individuals does not depend on what society thinks about their market values. In contrast, the real service a unit of fiat currency yields depends on the nominal price level, which depends, in turn, on people's beliefs about the current and future value of money.

Consider a real asset such as land. A deflationary bubble that drives the land's real price toward zero must eventually be punctured. Land yields tangible services each period independently of its market valuation, so there is some positive level below which its value cannot fall. Because people realize that any bubble path requiring land's real price to fall increasingly below the present value of its services cannot be an equilibrium, no point on a deflationary bubble path can be an equilibrium. This argument, upon which we relied in Chapter 2, fails for fiat money, which, unlike land, has no intrinsic value. Thus there is no positive level below

---

28. Many writers, for example, Tirole (1982, 1985), define a bubble as any deviation of an asset's price from the present value of the dividends it yields. (A bubble in this sense does not necessarily exhibit explosive or implosive behavior.) In the present model, money's marginal "dividend" stream consists of liquidity services worth $\beta^{s-t} v'(M_s/P_s)/P_s u'(C_t)$ on date t. These dividends depend on future price levels and therefore are endogenous to the monetary sector. Even along hyperinflationary paths such that $P \to \infty$, $1/P_t$ equals the present value of such dividends. [See eq. (49).] Thus one could argue that explosive price paths are not bubbles at all, just examples of potential multiple equilibria generated by alternative self-validating expectations. The semantic question of whether such paths are labeled bubbles has no substantive bearing on our analysis of their sustainability as equilibria. (In the overlapping generations model of Tirole, 1985, money does not even offer a convenience yield, so *any* equilbrium in which money has value is considered a bubble.)

29. In Chapter 3 we saw real models in which bubbles are theoretically possible. We observed, however, that empirical evidence seems to argue against the relevance of such bubbles in practice.

which fiat money's real value cannot fall. That is, there is no limit to how high the nominal price level can rise even if the aggregate money supply is constant. If the general public decides for any reason to stop using a paper currency, no individual agent can derive liquidity services from holding it. Unless the government takes some action to back the currency (so that it is worth something to individuals even when all others reject it), there is no way to rule out hyperinflations in which the money sooner or later passes out of use.

8.3.5.3 Ruling Out Speculative Deflations by a Transversality Condition

We now turn to a formal analysis.[30] The main points are again made most easily when the quantity of nominal currency is fixed at $\bar{M}$. In this case, as we've seen, the no-bubbles equilibrium is a steady state with a constant price level $\bar{P}$.

To begin, let's eliminate bubble paths making the real price of money rise explosively. These correspond to points in Figure 8.2 where M/P starts out above $\overline{M/P}$. The argument for ruling out these hyper*deflationary* paths is essentially the same for money as for real assets, since the problem is that money is becoming worth too much rather than too little. The argument in appendix 2B involved deriving a transversality condition from an iterated Euler condition. We apply the argument to real balances, returning to a general (not necessarily logarithmic) $v(M/P)$ function.

For the period utility function (45), the individual Euler equation for real balances, eq. (36), is

$$\frac{1}{P_t}\left(\frac{1}{C_t}\right) = \frac{1}{P_t}v'\left(\frac{M_t}{P_t}\right) + \frac{1}{P_{t+1}}\left(\frac{\beta}{C_{t+1}}\right).$$

(47)

By forwarding this equation one period, we can substitute for $1/P_{t+1}C_{t+1}$ in eq. (47):

$$\frac{1}{P_t}\left(\frac{1}{C_t}\right) = \frac{1}{P_t}v'\left(\frac{M_t}{P_t}\right) + \frac{\beta}{P_{t+1}}v'\left(\frac{M_{t+1}}{P_{t+1}}\right) + \frac{1}{P_{t+2}}\left(\frac{\beta^2}{C_{t+2}}\right).$$

Continuing this process through $T-1$ iterations and imposing the equilibrium conditions $M_t = \bar{M}$ and $C_t = \bar{C}$, we find

$$\frac{1}{P_t}\left(\frac{1}{\bar{C}}\right) = \sum_{s=t}^{t+T-1} \beta^{s-t}\frac{1}{P_s}v'\left(\frac{\bar{M}}{P_s}\right) + \frac{1}{P_{t+T}}\left(\frac{\beta^T}{\bar{C}}\right).$$

(48)

---

30. For a more complete treatment of speculative nominal price bubbles in models with money entering the utility function, see Obstfeld and Rogoff (1983, 1986). For a general treatment of multiple equilibria in monetary models, see Woodford (1994).

Equation (48) ensures that along an equilibrium path, there is no net advantage to holding one less (more) dollar during periods t through $T - 1$, and then raising (lowering) nominal balances by a dollar on date T.

It must also be the case, however, that there is no advantage to converting a dollar into consumption (or vice versa) in period t and *never* undoing that shift. We write that requirement as

$$\frac{1}{P_t} \left(\frac{1}{\bar{C}} \right) = \sum_{s=t}^{\infty} \beta^{s-t} \frac{1}{P_s} v' \left(\frac{\bar{M}}{P_s} \right), \tag{49}$$

the right-hand side of which is the marginal utility cost of having one less unit of real money balances in all future periods. But eq. (49) follows as the limit of eq. (48) if and only if the *transversality condition*

$$\lim_{T \to \infty} \frac{1}{P_{t+T}} \cdot \frac{\beta^T}{\bar{C}} = 0 \tag{50}$$

holds.[31]

The transversality condition can be used to rule out speculative deflationary paths, though there is one nuance. For a constant money supply, eq. (46) implies that the price level follows the nonlinear difference equation

$$\frac{1}{P_{t+1}} = \frac{1}{\beta P_t} - \frac{\bar{C} v'(\bar{M}/P_t)}{\beta P_t}. \tag{51}$$

Observe that even if $\lim_{P \to 0} v'(\bar{M}/P) = 0$, as is reasonable, the denominator of the term $\bar{C} v'(\bar{M}/P)/\beta P$ in eq. (51) also goes to zero as $P \to 0$. So we cannot automatically infer that all paths with $P_0 < \bar{P}$ violate condition (50) without a further assumption. Fortunately, the necesssary assumption is rather weak. Assume there is a limit to the utility one can derive from holding money, so that $v(M/P)$ is bounded from above. Then if M/P starts out above $\overline{M/P}$, one can show that $1/P$ will eventually grow at rate $1/\beta$. [This conclusion is true even for some standard cases in which $v(M/P)$ isn't bounded from above, for example, the logarithmic case.][32] But in this case,

---

31. At the *individual* level the appropriate condition actually is $\lim_{T \to \infty} \beta^T (M_{t+T}/P_{t+T})/C_{t+T} = 0$. (Because it is infeasible to reduce nominal balances below zero, we have a complementary slackness condition.) But in a symmetric equilibrium with a constant money supply $\bar{M}$, the representative agent can always contemplate permanently reducing money holdings by one unit. Thus we get the condition in the text.

32. In the log case eq. (51) is

$$\frac{1}{P_{t+1}} = \frac{1}{\beta P_t} - \frac{\bar{C}}{\beta \bar{M}},$$

which plainly implies that $1/P$ eventually grows at rate $1/\beta$ if $P_0 < \bar{P}$. Note that if $v(\bar{M}/P)$ is bounded from above, then $\lim_{P \to 0} v'(\bar{M}/P)/P$ in eq. (51) also is bounded by a constant, as in the log case just

$$\lim_{T \to \infty} \frac{1}{P_{t+T}} \cdot \frac{\beta^T}{\bar{C}} > 0$$

and transversality condition (50) fails, so eq. (48) implies

$$\frac{1}{P_t} \left(\frac{1}{\bar{C}} \right) > \sum_{s=t}^{\infty} \frac{1}{P_s} \beta^{s-t} v' \left(\frac{\bar{M}}{P_s} \right).$$

This inequality means that along any *incipient* path starting at $P_0 < \bar{P}$, people would wish *immediately* to reduce their nominal balances. Efforts to do so would reduce real balances in the aggregate by driving the price level all the way up to its steady-state value.[33]

8.3.5.4   The Possibility of Speculative Hyperinflations

While transversality condition (50) generally rules out deflationary paths, it clearly does not preclude inflationary price bubbles where the initial price level P_0 is *above* $\bar{P}$. To rule out hyperinflationary paths, we must appeal to some other argument. Figure 8.3 is similar to Figure 8.2, which graphically depicts eq. (46). In contrast to Figure 8.2, however, Figure 8.3 assumes that

$$\lim_{M/P \to 0} \frac{M}{P} v' \left(\frac{M}{P} \right) = 0, \tag{52}$$

so that the two curves intersect at the origin. Inspection of eq. (46) shows that condition (52) implies that an infinite price level can be an equilibrium. That is, there is an equilibrium where the public refuses to hold currency and conducts trade by barter. This is clearly not an *efficient* equilibrium. Welfare is unambiguously higher in the steady-state monetary equilibrium. But if condition (52) holds, the nonmonetary equilibrium with $\bar{\bar{P}} = \infty$ also is a steady-state. As Figure 8.3 illustrates, it is easy to work backward from the origin to construct hyperinflationary paths that lead to the barter equilibrium. Along such paths (assuming for simplicity M is constant at $\bar{M}$) there comes some period $T - 1$ such that

---

considered. To see why, notice that the strict concavity of $v(M/P)$ means that for any two real balance levels $\bar{M}/P > \bar{M}/P_0$,

$$v \left(\frac{\bar{M}}{P} \right) - v \left(\frac{\bar{M}}{P_0} \right) > v' \left(\frac{\bar{M}}{P} \right) \left(\frac{\bar{M}}{P} - \frac{\bar{M}}{P_0} \right).$$

But if the left-hand side of this inequality is bounded as $P \to 0$, so must be the right-hand side, which has the limit $\bar{M} \cdot \lim_{P \to 0} v'(\bar{M}/P)/P$.

33. In some models, paths along which real asset values spiral upward can be eliminated by the boundary condition that an asset's price cannot exceed the present discounted value of world output. In such cases, it may not be necessary to appeal to the individual transversality condition.

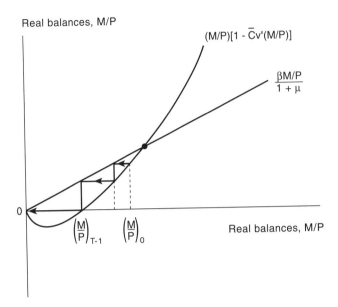

Figure 8.3
Speculative hyperinflationary equilibrium

$$\frac{1}{\bar{C}} = v'\left(\frac{\bar{M}}{P_{T-1}}\right) \tag{53}$$

and such that in period T, $P_T = \infty$ (money becomes worthless). Condition (53) states that in the penultimate period, the derived transactions utility from an additional unit of real balances must just equal the marginal utility of consumption. This equality implies that agents willingly hold money in $T-1$, even though they know it will become worthless in T, because it still yields liquidity services in $T-1$. One possible equilibrium path for the economy, of course, is for the price level to jump immediately to $P_0 = \infty$. In this case the public rejects the currency immediately.

The existence of speculative bubble equilibria hinges crucially on condition (52). In Figure 8.2, we assumed that $v(M/P) = \log(M/P)$, so that $(M/P)v'(M/P)$ is constant at 1. That example therefore shows a case in which

$$\lim_{M/P \to 0} \frac{M}{P} v'\left(\frac{M}{P}\right) > 0. \tag{54}$$

When condition (54) holds, the origin cannot be a steady state as in Figure 8.3. Consequently, it is not possible to construct hyperinflationary equilibria as we did using that figure. Which assumption is more reasonable, eq. (52) or (54)? Obstfeld and Rogoff (1983) show that a necessary (but not sufficient) condition for eq. (54) to hold is that $\lim_{M/P\to 0} v(M/P) = -\infty$.[34] This behavior is implausible, as it implies that no finite quantity of the consumption good can compensate an individual for not having a medium of exchange. An absolute necessity for money seems inconsistent with money's role of merely reducing frictions in the economy. Thus a utility-of-money function such as log utility may provide a good approximation for studying interior equilibria but may give misleading results near corners.

Our discussion of hyperinflations may seem very special to the money-in-the-utility-function model, but the main points are quite general. If there is no intrinsic value to paper currency and if society can survive without it, there is nothing to rule out hyperinflationary price bubbles that completely wipe out money's value. This central result of modern monetary theory is fascinating. Because the use of money is grounded in social convention, free market forces alone cannot guarantee a finite price level, despite the fact that society as a whole is better off when money has value.

8.3.5.5   A Hybrid Fiat Currency System: Guaranteeing Monetary Equilibrium with Fractional Backing

Returning to the model at hand with a constant money supply, suppose the government guarantees that it will redeem money for goods at rate $1/P^{\mathrm{MIN}} < 1/\bar{P}$ per dollar. That is, the government offers real backing to the currency, but at a value below what currency would be worth in the monetary steady state. Assuming the government has adequate resources (for example, tax revenues) to buy back the currency at the price it guarantees, it is easy to see that such a policy will prevent hyperinflations. Since the real value of money is bounded from below by $1/P^{\mathrm{MIN}}$, any candidate equilibrium path along which the nominal price level is exploding must eventually come to a halt—and therefore the whole equilibrium unravels. Such a policy will work even if $1/P^{\mathrm{MIN}}$ is extremely small and, as Obstfeld and Rogoff (1983) show, even if the policy is not completely credible. Of course, as long as the economy avoids a hyperinflationary path, the government will never actually need to honor its guarantee. It would seem that in theory, governments desiring seignorage revenues have only to fulfill a very weak criterion to ensure that their money will be accepted, and that they have every incentive to do so. We take care not to overemphasize this result, since it is based on a very simplistic model of money. Ultimately, the answer to the question of whether

---

34. **Proof:** Because $v(\cdot)$ is monotonically increasing, $\lim_{M/P\to 0} v(M/P) = a_0$ exists, but may be $-\infty$. Suppose (contrary to the assertion of the theorem) that a_0 is finite. As $\lim_{M/P\to 0}(M/P)v'(M/P) > 0$, there exists a positive number c_0 and a level of real balances M_0/P_0 such that $(M/P)v'(M/P) > c_0$ for all $M/P < M_0/P_0$. The strict concavity of $v(\cdot)$ implies that for $M/P < M_0/P_0$, $v(M/P) - a_0 > (M/P)v'(M/P) > c_0$. But if a_0 is finite, M/P can be chosen small enough so that $M/P < M_0/P_0$ and $v(M/P) - a_0 < c_0$; and this contradicts the foregoing string of inequalities. Therefore, $a_0 = \lim_{M/P\to 0} v(M/P) = -\infty$.

hyperinflationary bubbles occur in practice must also be informed by the empirical evidence.

Application: Testing for Speculative Bubbles

Several empirical tests for the existence of speculative nominal price bubbles build on an imaginative method devised by West (1987).[35] To illustrate the basic idea, we return to the small-country monetary model of exchange rates from section 8.2.7. The money demand equation for that model is

$$m_t - p_t = -\eta i_{t+1} + \phi y_t + \epsilon_t$$

(where, in preparation for empirical estimation, we have added a statistical disturbance ϵ_t interpretable as a shift in money demand). PPP and uncovered interest parity turn this equation into

$$(m_t - \phi y_t + \eta i^*_{t+1} - p^*_t) - e_t = -\eta(E_t e_{t+1} - e_t) + \epsilon_t. \tag{55}$$

Equation (55) is the same as eq. (29) from section 8.2.7 except for the addition of the money demand shock ϵ_t. Equation (55) has the reduced-form solution

$$e_t = \frac{1}{1+\eta} \sum_{s=t}^{\infty} \left(\frac{\eta}{1+\eta}\right)^{s-t} E_t\{m_s - \phi y_s + \eta i^*_{s+1} - p^*_s - \epsilon_s\}, \tag{56}$$

which is analogous to eq. (30), and is similarly valid only when bubbles are excluded.

West's approach recognizes that direct estimation of the reduced form eq. (56) yields consistent estimates of the money demand parameter η only if speculative bubbles are indeed absent. Otherwise, there is an omitted bubble term which, if not included, biases estimation results. On the other hand, eq. (55) holds and can be estimated directly whether or not there are speculative bubbles. [Estimates of η based on eq. (55) are generally less efficient than ones based on eq. (56) because the latter impose more of the restrictions of the model.] West's test therefore involves estimating η using both approaches and statistically comparing the results. If the two estimates of η are not significantly different, the null hypothesis of no speculative bubbles is not rejected.[36]

---

35. The seminal paper on bubble tests in monetary models is Flood and Garber (1980). Their approach, however, applies only to a restricted class of bubbles, and the validity of their hypothesis tests requires strong assumptions. So we concentrate on West's (1987) later test, which is more versatile.

36. Because the expected rate of currency depreciation is an endogenous variable, estimation of eq. (55) requires instrumental variable techniques. Estimation of eq. (56) can be carried out by maximum likelihood. The estimation methodology involves positing a statistical model for the exogenous forcing variable $m_t - \phi y_t + \eta i^*_{t+1} - p^*_t - \epsilon_t$ and then calculating e_t based on the statistical model and the rational expectations assumption [as when we derived eq. (14) based on eq. (13)]. The final step is to

Applications of West's test to hyperinflation data generally fail to reject the no-bubbles null hypothesis.[37] When applied to less turbulent periods, the results are less uniform. Meese (1986), for example, finds mixed results for the post-1973 dollar–deutsche mark and dollar-pound exchange rates. He emphasizes that West's test must be interpreted as a joint test of the no-speculative-bubbles hypothesis, the monetary model itself, and assumptions about the statistical model market participants use for forecasting. If a component of the empirical model is misspecified, the two estimates of η may diverge even if there are no bubbles, in which case the test results can be misleading.

Since it is well known that monetary models of exchange rates perform poorly (Meese and Rogoff 1983a, 1983b), misspecification is likely to be a serious problem. Therefore, as a second approach, Meese tests for cointegration of exchange rates, money supplies, and the other fundamental variables in eq. (56). In principle, if there is no bubble in the exchange rate, it should be possible to find some stationary linear combination of the exchange rate and its supposed fundamentals. Meese finds that this second, less structural test also tends to reject the no-speculative-bubbles null. More recent research such as that of Chinn and Meese (1995) and Mark (1995), however, suggests that over long enough periods there is indeed a stationary relationship between exchange rates and standard fundamentals.

On the whole, the empirical literature suggests that one cannot reject the no-speculative-bubbles hypothesis for hyperinflation price data. The record is mixed for exchange rates in more normal times but offers no definitive evidence of rational bubbles of the type we have discussed. There certainly do not appear to be any historical examples of extreme inflations that were not accompanied by extreme rates of increase in the money supply.   ∎

8.3.6   Cash-in-Advance Models of Money Demand

Another popular way of modeling the demand for money is to assume a cash-in-advance constraint (a device introduced by Clower, 1967). There are several variations, but the central assumption is that money *must* be used to purchase goods, or at least some specified subset of goods. The cash-in-advance model is in essence a very extreme transactions-technology model in which money does not simply economize on transactions, it is essential for carrying any out. An appeal of cash-in-advance models is that they can deliver extremely tractable money demand

---

estimate jointly the parameters of the statistical process governing the exogenous variables and of the e_t equation. The parameters of these two equations will be interrelated.

37. For example, Casella (1989) fails to reject the no-speculative-bubbles hypothesis when monetary factors are assumed exogenous but finds that the results may be sensitive to that assumption.

equations while preserving the central advantages of an approach based on micro-foundations.[38]

In the most popular variant of the cash-in-advance model, agents must acquire currency in period $t - 1$ sufficient to cover all consumption purchases they make in period t. Following Lucas (1982), one can think of "agents" as households that consist of two specialized individuals, a "producer" and a "shopper." Each morning the shopper sets out with the money proceeds of the output the producer sold the day before, and the two household members have no further contact until the evening, when markets have closed for the day. Formally, the representative agent's problem is to maximize

$$U_t = \sum_{s=t}^{\infty} \beta^{s-t} u(C_s) \tag{57}$$

subject to period budget constraints of the form

$$B_{t+1} + \frac{M_t}{P_t} = (1 + r)B_t + \frac{M_{t-1}}{P_t} + Y_t - C_t - T_t$$

[which is the same as eq. (34) in the last model] and subject to the additional cash-in-advance constraints

$$M_{t-1} \geq P_t C_t. \tag{58}$$

Money doesn't enter the utility function, either directly or indirectly. Notice that if the nominal interest rate is positive, the cash-in-advance constraint will always *bind*: people never hold money in excess of next period's consumption requirements when they could instead earn a higher return by lending the money out. If we restrict our attention to equilibria with positive nominal interest rates, then

$$M_{t-1} = P_t C_t$$

always will hold, and we can use this equality to eliminate M_t and M_{t-1} from eq. (34), leaving the simplified constraint

$$B_{t+1} = (1 + r)B_t + Y_t - T_t - \frac{P_{t+1}}{P_t} C_{t+1}. \tag{59}$$

The final term on the right-hand side of eq. (59) comes from the substitution $M_t/P_t = (P_{t+1}/P_t)C_{t+1}$. Its influence will become apparent shortly.[39]

---

38. Our earlier discussion suggests that inflationary speculative bubbles cannot arise in any cash-in-advance model that makes money an absolute necessity. See also Woodford (1994).

39. Note that our formulation does not require agents to hold foreign currency between periods even if their country is running a current-account deficit and therefore making net consumption purchases from abroad. The implicit assumption here (similar to that of our earlier model) is that agents can convert previously acquired home currency into foreign currency that can be spent without delay. This

The intertemporal Euler condition is derived by maximizing

$$U_t = \sum_{s=t}^{\infty} \beta^{s-t} u \left\{ \frac{P_{s-1}}{P_s} \left[(1+r)B_{s-1} - B_s + Y_{s-1} - T_{s-1} \right] \right\}$$

with respect to B_s. Notice that because $C_t = M_{t-1}/P_t$, with M_{t-1} given on date t, C_t is predetermined—given by past history—in the individual's problem, and not subject to choice on date t.

The result of differentiating with respect to B_s (for $s > t$) is

$$\frac{P_{s-1}}{P_s} u'(C_s) = (1+r) \frac{P_s}{P_{s+1}} \beta u'(C_{s+1}).$$

Making use of the Fisher parity equation $1 + i_{s+1} = (1+r)(P_{s+1}/P_s)$, we divide both sides by $1 + r$ to derive

$$\frac{u'(C_s)}{1+i_s} = (1+r)\beta \frac{u'(C_{s+1})}{1+i_{s+1}} \tag{60}$$

for $s > t$. To understand the difference between eq. (60) and the usual consumption Euler equation, remember that consumption involves an additional cost here, since the agent must wait one full period between the date he converts bonds or output into cash and the date he can consume. That additional cost is i_s for money held between $s - 1$ and s, and it is i_{s+1} for money held between s and $s + 1$. The nominal interest rate thus acts as a consumption tax. Of course, in a stationary equilibrium with constant money growth, nominal interest rates and the implied consumption tax are constant, so eq. (60) boils down to the usual Euler equation.

Note that the "money demand" equation for this cash-in-advance model is simply the constant-velocity equation

$$\frac{M_{t-1}}{P_t} = C_t.$$

Again, it is consumption expenditure and not income that enters the money demand equation.

The fact that anticipated inflation does not affect money demand (given consumption) is an unappealing and empirically unrealistic feature of the cash-in-advance model, but one that can be amended in more general formulations. Lucas and Stokey (1987) allow for both cash and credit goods. Credit goods can be

---

assumption seems plausible, since both currencies are assumed to be highly liquid. An alternative structure requires that, one period in advance, agents must set aside enough domestic currency to cover domestic purchases and enough foreign currency to cover net foreign imports. Appendix 8A develops a two-country cash-in-advance model. See also the discussion in Helpman and Razin (1984).

purchased directly with currently earned income or bonds, so their cost does not include interest forgone while holding cash for a period. In this model, changes in the inflation rate affect the relative price of the two goods by raising the implicit tax on cash goods. Thus a higher nominal interest rate reduces money demand (given total consumption purchases) by shifting spending toward credit goods. Models like these can yield money demand functions analogous to those we obtain with the money-in-the-utility-function model, but they are somewhat more complicated.

A simple variant of the cash-in-advance model, proposed by Helpman (1981) and Lucas (1982), allows consumers to use cash acquired in period t for consumption later in period t. The producers who receive the cash must hold it between periods. The cash-in-advance constraint (58) is replaced by

$$M_t \geq P_t C_t.$$

In this case, inflation does not distort consumption decisions, and the usual consumption Euler condition holds. However, inflation does enter the budget constraints of *producers*, who hold cash between periods in proportion to current sales. Inflation is a production tax rather than a consumption tax in this model but producers supply their endowments inelastically and production therefore is not distorted.[40] Yet another version of the cash-in-advance model posits that enough money must be set aside in advance to cover later purchases of both bonds and goods; see, for example, Grilli and Roubini (1992).

Overall, the cash-in-advance framework yields results similar to those of the money-in-the-utility-function approach. Either approach represents a major advance over the Cagan model because it permits an integration of money-demand and consumption analysis. In the remainder of the book, we will favor the money-in-the-utility-function approach but deploy the cash-in-advance model when it offers analytical convenience or special insight.

8.3.7   Alternative Models of Money

A complete treatment of the various alternative models of money is beyond the scope of this book. A brief discussion of other variants, however, helps put in perspective those considered thus far. Overlapping generations models, building on Samuelson (1958), can generate an endogenous demand for money entirely out of its store-of-value function. No appeal to an ad hoc transactions technology is made. A drawback, however, is that the store-of-value role generates a demand for money only if agents have no more remunerative alternative such as capital, government bonds, or foreign lending (Wallace, 1980). As soon as any of these dominating

---

40. Aschauer and Greenwood (1983) build a labor-leisure choice into the model. Since goods produced currently can be consumed only after they are sold for money that is held for a period and meanwhile earns no interest, the nominal interest rate affects the relevant real wage, leading to a failure of the real-monetary dichotomy.

assets is introduced, one must introduce a transactions technology, cash-in-advance constraint, or legal restriction to obtain a monetary equilibrium. Thus overlapping generations models do not truly deliver an independent theory of money demand, a point emphasized by McCallum (1983).

More recently, Kiyotaki and Wright (1989) have developed a model that looks at the microfoundations of market trading structures. They show how money can arise as a social convention that improves on the barter equilibrium. The Kiyotaki-Wright model is based on a general equilibrium matching setup in which each agent produces one type of good but seeks to consume another. Agents are randomly matched in pairs each period and, if each has the good the other wants to consume, then they will always trade. Interestingly, even if only one of the agents has the good the other wants, they may still want to trade if the other agent carries a commodity that is highly "salable," that is, likely to be accepted by others in future trades. The model makes possible monetary equilibria in which agents use fiat money in trades even though no one actually wants to consume fiat money. Kiyotaki and Wright are forced to make a number of very strong and unrealistic assumptions, however, to characterize the equilibria of their dynamic general equilibrium matching model. (For example, credit could easily fill the role of money.) Nonetheless, the model effectively underscores the tenuousness of pure fiat money equilibria.

8.3.8   Dollarization

In the models we have looked at so far, tight legal restrictions prevent a country's residents from using foreign currency for domestic transactions. Real life is more complex. Many governments would have great difficulty persuading their citizens to use domestic currency without some kind of legal restrictions. Even in the presence of legal restrictions, however, agents often hold and use foreign currency anyway. Foreign currency may be held legally to buy imports or illegally for use in the underground economy. In this section, we consider an extension of the money-in-the-utility-function model in which the penalties for transacting domestically in foreign currency are not always sufficient to discourage its use entirely.

Consider a small open economy. The lifetime utility of the representative resident is a variation on eq. (33) from section 8.3.1:

$$U_t = \sum_{s=t}^{\infty} \beta^{s-t} \left\{ u(C_s) + v \left[\frac{M_s}{P_s} + g \left(\frac{\mathcal{E}_s M_{F,s}}{P_s} \right) \right] \right\}. \tag{61}$$

Here M_F denotes nominal holdings of foreign currency, which have real value $\mathcal{E} M_F / P$, and

$$g \left(\frac{\mathcal{E} M_F}{P} \right) = a_0 \left(\frac{\mathcal{E} M_F}{P} \right) - \frac{a_1}{2} \left(\frac{\mathcal{E} M_F}{P} \right)^2, \tag{62}$$

where $1 - \beta < a_0 \leq 1, a_1 > 0$. To rationalize the $g(\cdot)$ function in eq. (62), think of legal restrictions on local foreign currency use being easier to evade in some transactions than in others, resulting in a continuum of evasion costs. When anticipated home inflation is less than or equal to anticipated foreign inflation, it will turn out that there is no point to using foreign currency since $a_0 \leq 1$ (as we shall confirm). But when home inflation is higher than foreign inflation, the foreign currency share of total domestic transactions will turn out to be an increasing function of the inflation differential.[41] This model is especially plausible for developing countries in which high levels of "dollarization" typically arise when inflation rates are high.

Because domestic residents now accumulate foreign currency in addition to foreign bonds, the financing constraint (34) becomes

$$B_{t+1} + \frac{M_t}{P_t} + \frac{\mathcal{E}_t M_{F,t}}{P_t} = (1+r)B_t + \frac{M_{t-1}}{P_t} + \frac{\mathcal{E}_t M_{F,t-1}}{P_t} + Y_t - C_t - T_t. \quad (63)$$

Maximizing lifetime utility (61) subject to eq. (63), and assuming $(1+r)\beta = 1$ and PPP, $P_t = \mathcal{E}_t P_t^*$, we find the following first-order conditions with respect to bonds and the two monies:

$$u'(C_t) = u'(C_{t+1}), \quad (64)$$

$$\frac{1}{P_t}u'(C_t) = \frac{1}{P_t}v'\left[\frac{M_t}{P_t} + g\left(\frac{M_{F,t}}{P_t^*}\right)\right] + \frac{1}{P_{t+1}}\beta u'(C_{t+1}), \quad (65)$$

$$\frac{1}{P_t^*}u'(C_t) = \frac{1}{P_t^*}v'\left[\frac{M_t}{P_t} + g\left(\frac{M_{F,t}}{P_t^*}\right)\right]g'\left(\frac{M_{F,t}}{P_t^*}\right) + \frac{1}{P_{t+1}^*}\beta u'(C_{t+1}). \quad (66)$$

Equations (64) and (65) are the same as in our earlier money-in-the-utility-function model in section 8.3.2 and have the same interpretation. The new eq. (66) says that an optimizing agent must be indifferent at the margin between spending a unit of foreign currency on date t consumption or holding it for one period and then spending it on date $t+1$ consumption.

If we multiply both sides of eq. (66) by P_t^* and both sides of eq. (65) by P_t, and then use eq. (64) to eliminate $u'(C_{t+1})$, the resulting two equations combine to yield

$$g'\left(\frac{M_{F,t}}{P_t^*}\right) = \frac{1 - \beta \dfrac{P_t^*}{P_{t+1}^*}}{1 - \beta \dfrac{P_t}{P_{t+1}}}.$$

---

41. Clearly, the quadratic function $g(\cdot)$ assumed in eq. (62) is an approximation that applies only in the range where the marginal contribution of foreign balances to total liquidity, $a_0 - a_1(\mathcal{E}M_F/P)$, is positive. Notice that if foreigners have a similar utility-of-money function or are unrestricted as to their money holdings, they will never hold the small country's currency if its inflation exceeds the inflation they face at home. Thus we can safely assume foreigners hold none of the small country's money.

The quadratic functional form for $g(\cdot)$ assumed in eq. (62) yields the foreign currency demand equation

$$\frac{M_{F,t}}{P_t^*} = \frac{1}{a_1}\left(a_0 - \frac{1-\beta\dfrac{P_t^*}{P_{t+1}^*}}{1-\beta\dfrac{P_t}{P_{t+1}}}\right) \tag{67}$$

for interior equilibria where $M_{F,t} > 0$. [When the right-hand side of eq. (67) is less than or equal to zero, $M_{F,t} = 0$.] Equation (67) shows that agents will hold the foreign currency despite legal restrictions if the domestic inflation rate is sufficiently above the foreign one, but not if inflation rates are equal. The equation also shows that if a_1 is small (so that the penalties to foreign currency use are small), then very small changes in inflation differentials can induce huge swings in foreign currency use. Another observation concerns inflationary bubbles. Currency substitution renders the domestic currency decidedly nonessential, expanding the scope for self-validating domestic price spirals. In sum, if weak legal restrictions and an inflationary environment lead to currency substitution, considerable instability in prices and exchange rates can result.[42]

One can easily use the model to compare steady states with constant rates of foreign inflation and domestic money growth. An unanticipated permanent rise in home money growth leads to a portfolio shift from foreign bonds to foreign money. Agents therefore permanently cut consumption to finance the initial acquisition of more foreign currency. If the foreign country has a positive inflation rate, domestic residents will have to accumulate more foreign currency each period to hold their real foreign-currency balances steady. The resulting ongoing domestic trade balance surpluses reflect the seignorage revenues received by the foreign government from domestic citizens who wish to use its currency. We do not analyze the dynamics of the dollarization model in any detail as these are more complex than those of the earlier one-currency model, but major qualitative results are similar.

Matsuyama, Kiyotaki, and Matsui (1993) develop a model without legal restrictions in which the currencies chosen for various transactions are determined endogenously. As in the Kiyotaki-Wright (1989) model, people are randomly matched every period, each hoping to trade the good he holds but does not consume for one he would like to consume. A home resident is more likely to be paired with another home resident than with a foreign-country resident in any period, with the likelihood of meeting foreign agents providing a natural measure of the degree of economic integration. Matsuyama, Kiyotaki, and Matsui show that

---

42. Girton and Roper (1981) and Kareken and Wallace (1981) both emphasize that currency substitution can magnify small swings in expected money growth differentials into large changes in exchange rates. Weil (1991) studies bubbles under currency substitution. For surveys of the topic, see Giovannini and Turtelboom (1994) and Calvo and Végh (1996).

their model has an equilibrium in which only the local currency is used in purely local exchanges, and another in which one currency circulates as an international currency and may be used for trades even between residents of the same country.

8.4   Nominal Exchange Rate Regimes

Until now we have treated the money supply as exogenous. We have assumed that the government sets a path for the money supply, allowing the price level, exchange rate, and nominal interest rate to respond endogenously to clear the money market. This state of affairs seldom applies in practice. Monetary policy might be set to stabilize inflation, the exchange rate, nominal interest rates, output, employment, or some combination of all these variables and others. In this section, we will analyze one important class of endogenous monetary policy regimes that is of great practical importance, exchange rate targets.

The price-level flexibility assumed in this chapter makes the choice between fixed and floating exchange rates less interesting and important than it will be in the sticky-price environments of Chapters 9 and 10. If all nominal prices and interest rates are either instantly changeable or fully indexed to inflation, the role for stabilization policy is sharply reduced. Nonetheless, the flexible-price case still yields vital insights into the basic mechanics of alternative monetary regimes. In this section, we first review the basics and then look at models of speculative exchange-rate attacks.

8.4.1   Monetary and Fiscal Policies to Fix the Exchange Rate

The most straightforward case is that in which the government literally *fixes* the exchange at a constant level. This policy makes the money supply an endogenous variable that the government cannot directly set, as we shall show using Cagan's model. (Our discussion of exchange rate targeting will revert back to the basic Cagan model whenever it is sufficient for illustrating the central points.)

8.4.1.1   Monetary Policy to Fix the Exchange Rate

Consider a special case of the small-open-economy Cagan exchange-rate model,

$$m_t - e_t = -\eta(E_t e_{t+1} - e_t). \tag{68}$$

This equation is eq. (29) with y, i^*, and p^* all normalized to zero. Suppose now that the government wishes to fix the nominal exchange rate *permanently* at $\bar{e}$. What path of the money supply is consistent with having $e_t = \bar{e}$ permanently? Substitute $e_t = e_{t+1} = \bar{e}$ into eq. (68) to derive

$$m_t - \bar{e} = -\eta(\bar{e} - \bar{e})$$

or

Box 8.2
Growing Use of the Dollar Abroad

Exact estimates of currency holdings by foreigners do not exist, but it appears that the United States dollar is the currency most widely used outside national borders, followed by the Deutsche mark and the Japanese yen. Several pieces of indirect evidence support the view that a large share of the U.S. currency stock, which was roughly $350 billion at the end of 1994, is held abroad (although it is not easy to distinguish foreign holdings from holdings by the domestic underground economy). First, surveys show that household currency stocks now account for less than 7 percent of total currency outstanding and only 18 percent of total household transactions. Second, the number of $100 bills (the largest denomination) has been rising sharply, accounting for 80 percent of all new currency (in dollar terms) during the 1990s. By the end of 1994, $100 bills accounted for 60 percent of all currency. Third, measured currency shipments abroad have risen sharply. A cumulative total above $30 billion have been shipped to Argentina alone (Kamin and Ericsson, 1993), though some of this may have ultimately gone to other destinations. Some estimates of dollars circulating in the former Soviet Union exceed $60 billion. A past history of inflation, arbitrary currency restrictions, and confiscation make dollars particularly appealing in countries such as Russia.

Porter and Judson (1995), using a number of different approaches, conclude that between 50 and 70 percent of U.S. currency is held abroad. One of their approaches involves comparing changing seasonal currency demand patterns in America and Canada. In the 1960s the seasonal influence on currency demand was fairly similar in the two countries. But while Canada's seasonal demand has remained relatively stable, the seasonal component of U.S. money demand has been declining steadily. Porter and Judson attribute this decline to growing use of the American greenback in global underground transactions, which tend to be much less seasonal. A second approach Porter and Judson take is to compare changes in the ratio of currency to coins in the United States and Canada, and a third approach examines the percentage of bills issued in or after 1990 that have recirculated through U.S. Federal Reserve banks. All methods give broadly similar results.

If Porter and Judson's estimates are correct, a significant fraction of the roughly $20 billion in seignorage profits that the Federal Reserve turns over to the U.S. Treasury each year can be accounted for by foreign demand. Their conclusion also implies that shifts in the foreign demand for dollars could have a significant impact on the overall price level in the United States!

$m_t = \bar{m} = \bar{e}.$

Under our special assumptions, a fixed exchange rate implies a level of the money supply that also is permanently fixed. More generally, the money supply becomes an endogenous variable. Why? Under a permanently fixed exchange rate, currency appreciation and depreciation aren't possible, so uncovered interest parity forces the home nominal interest rate to equal the foreign rate, $i = i^*$. Since the price level is tied down by PPP (given the fixed exchange rate) and output is given at its full-employment level, *all* the determinants of money demand become exogenous to the small country. As a result, it is the money supply that must adjust to equilibrate markets.[43]

The real world, unlike the model, is complex and ever changing. Wouldn't a government need a vast amount of up-to-the-second information to know which level of money supply equates the exchange rate precisely to $\bar{e}$? The answer is no. The job requires *no* information and could be performed by an automaton. All the government has to do is "make a market" in foreign exchange at rate $\bar{e}$, that is, stand ready to meet any excess private demand or absorb any excess private supply of home currency at that relative currency price. The private sector is certain to initiate the trades with the government necessary to ensure continuous money-market equilibrium at the fixed rate. Indeed, it is in this way that fixed exchange rates and related regimes are implemented in practice. For theoretical purposes, however, it is essential to keep in clear view that exchange rate targets implicitly entail decisions about monetary policy.

A close relative of the fixed exchange rate is the *crawling peg*, under which the government announces a fixed *path* for the exchange rate but not necessarily a constant path. Suppose, for example, that the government sets today's exchange at $\bar{e}_t$, but thereafter allows the rate at which it is pegging to rise by μ percent per period, so that $\bar{e}_{s+1} - \bar{e}_s = \mu$ for $s \geq t$. Substituting this depreciation rate into eq. (68) implies

$$m_t - \bar{e}_t = -\eta\mu$$

and therefore that $m_{s+1} - m_s = \bar{e}_{s+1} - \bar{e}_s = \mu$ for $s \geq t$. In this case, the home interest rate must be μ percent above the foreign interest rate, $i = i^* + \mu$.[44] Abstracting from the credibility issues we take up in Chapter 9, the deceptively simple

---

43. This result generally also holds in sticky-price models with endogenous output.

44. It is sometimes argued that pegging the nominal interest rate is equivalent to a crawling peg for the exchange rate. While this statement is essentially correct when uncovered interest parity holds, there is an important qualification. A monetary policy that only specifies a path for nominal interest rates is incomplete unless it also specifies at least one point on the money-supply path. Otherwise, interest rate pegging ties down the expected rate of change of the exchange rate, but leaves the *level* of the exchange rate indeterminate. To see why, suppose that the government announces that it is going to use monetary policy to peg the nominal interest rate at $\bar{i}$. Then on date t, money-market equilibrium requires

$$m_t - e_t = -\eta\bar{i}.$$

It follows that any exchange rate e_t the private sector believes to be the equilibrium rate will be, since to fix interest rates the monetary authorities must validate the private sector's belief by setting $m_t = e_t - \eta\bar{i}$. The monetary authorities can avoid this problem if they specify a value for any m_s, $s \geq t$. (See Canzoneri, Henderson, and Rogoff, 1983, for a discussion of the same problem in the context of interest rates and prices.) This point arises in more subtle forms in a number of other contexts. See exercise 1 on future fixing of the exchange rate.

point is that if the government wishes to fix the exchange rate, it can do so by subordinating monetary policy to the exchange rate goal.[45]

8.4.1.2   Adjusting Government Spending to Fix the Exchange Rate

Is there any way for a small-country government to fix the exchange rate without completely abandoning monetary independence? In theory, one possible alternative is to use government spending. Consider the money demand equation for a small country that we derived from the money-in-the-utility-function model in section 8.3.2. In that model, the monetary equilibrium condition is eq. (37). Assuming the period utility function

$$u\left(C, \frac{M}{P}\right) = \log C + \log\left(\frac{M}{P}\right),$$

PPP, and a constant foreign price level $P^* = 1$, eq. (37) becomes

$$\frac{M_t}{\mathcal{E}_t} = \bar{C}\left[\frac{1+r}{1+r-(\mathcal{E}_t/\mathcal{E}_{t+1})}\right], \tag{69}$$

where $\mathcal{E}$ is the level (not the log) of the exchange rate. [Additive period utility ensures consumption is constant at $\bar{C}$ if $\beta(1+r) = 1$.] In Chapters 1 and 2 we saw that a rise in the permanent level of government spending $\bar{G}$ lowers $\bar{C}$ by the same amount. Thus a rise in government spending will cause the demand for real balances to fall. Holding the path of the money supply constant, this action implies that the exchange rate $\mathcal{E}_t$ must rise.[46] For example, if we assume that $\bar{Y}$ and $\bar{G}$ are constant, that $M_{t+1}/M_t = 1 + \mu$, and that there are no speculative bubbles, eq. (69) implies

$$\frac{M_t}{\mathcal{E}_t} = (\bar{Y} + rB_t - \bar{G})\left[\frac{(1+\mu)(1+r)}{(1+\mu)(1+r) - 1}\right].$$

While in principle government spending adjustments can relieve monetary policy of some of the burden of fixing the exchange, in practice fiscal policy is not really a useful tool for exchange rate management. Even leaving aside the politics of fiscal policy, fiscal changes simply take too long to implement to deal with

---

45. Note our implicit assumption that the public expects the monetary authority always to follow a monetary policy consistent with its announced path for the exchange rate. Suppose the public is not so trusting. For example, suppose that the government announces a fixed exchange rate, but the public expects future depreciation at the rate $\mu > 0$, perhaps because the government is sure to need seignorage revenues. Faced with such expectations, the monetary authorities can still support their target level for $\bar{e}$, but will have to set $m_t = \bar{e} - \eta\mu$ to do so.

46. Note that our result that a rise in government spending leads to a fall in money demand assumes an asymmetry between the government and private transactions technologies. If the government uses currency in the same proportion to transactions as the private sector, a rise in government spending would have no effect on the exchange rate.

fast-moving financial markets. In addition, adjusting government spending to fix the exchange rate would require unrealistically prompt and comprehensive information about the economy.

8.4.1.3   Financial Policies to Fix the Exchange Rate

We have seen that a government fixes an exchange rate by standing ready to trade domestic for foreign currency at the relative price $\bar{e}$. Generally (but not always), it is the central bank that carries out any required foreign exchange trades. The proximate effect of a central bank sale of domestic for foreign currency is a rise in the domestic money supply. That of the reverse transaction is a decline in the domestic money supply as currency goes out of circulation. It is these endogenous money supply changes that guarantee continuous money-market equilibrium. (Of course, we are now relaxing our earlier assumption that the government neither issues nor holds interest-bearing assets, because any foreign exchange acquired in intervention operations generally will be held as official *foreign reserves* in an interest-bearing form.)[47]

Often, governments try to influence the exchange rate without changing the money supply through a financial policy known as *sterilized intervention*. We describe the mechanics of intervention policies in detail in appendix 8B, but the basic idea of sterilized intervention is easy to grasp. In a nonsterilized intervention operation the government might buy foreign-currency-denominated bonds with domestic currency. To "sterilize" the first step of this intervention, the government reverses its expansive impact on the home money supply by selling home-currency-denominated bonds for domestic cash. The net effect is to change the relative supply of home-currency and foreign-currency bonds held by the public and, in a stochastic model, the risk composition of the public's marketable financial assets. We will discuss possible rationales for sterilized intervention policies after we analyze individual maximization under uncertainty in section 8.7.

8.4.2   Speculative Attacks on Fixed-Exchange-Rate Regimes

Since the final demise of the Bretton Woods system of fixed exchange rates in the early 1970s, numerous countries have sought to stabilize their currencies in foreign exchange markets for periods of up to several years. In virtually every case,

---

47. If Ricardian equivalence holds, an increase in the money supply accomplished through a foreign asset purchase (an official capital outflow) has the same impact on private budget constraints as the same increase effected through a higher level of transfer payments (as in Milton Friedman's famous parable of the money-spewing helicopter). Because money demand has risen, the government is financing its purchase of foreign assets from the private sector through seignorage. While the private sector's interest-bearing financial wealth declines, its human wealth rises *pro tanto* because the government's higher foreign interest income permits lower taxes. (We are assuming that the path of government spending does not change.) Domestic open-market operations, in which the government swaps money for its own interest-bearing debt, have parallel effects under Ricardian equivalence.

however, the rate has eventually collapsed, often after a convulsive speculative attack that embarrasses the government and depletes its foreign exchange reserves. Britain is rumored to have lost over $7 billion within a few hours trying to fend off the September 1992 attack that forced the pound off its peg against the mark. Mexico's 1994 intervention to support the peso-dollar rate exceeded $50 billion, yet it failed to prevent the currency's collapse at year's end. Speculative attacks are hardly a new phenomenon, though they have arguably become harder to resist and more widespread as international capital markets have deepened since the 1970s. The Bank of England, for example, was attacked by speculators in 1931, 1949, and 1967, to mention only some leading post–World War I episodes! In this section, we take a first look at models of the timing and causes of speculative attacks.

8.4.2.1   The Model

The model we highlight here shows that speculative attacks on a country's foreign exchange reserves, while sometimes appearing arbitrary and capricious to the naked eye, can occur even in a world where all speculators are completely rational. Indeed, under some conditions, speculative attacks are not only possible; they are *inevitable*.[48]

The basic idea is illustrated by a perfect-foresight model in which profligate fiscal policy makes a fixed exchange rate ultimately unsustainable. Consider a small open economy characterized by both purchasing power parity and uncovered interest parity, and in which monetary equilibrium is described by a continuous-time version of Cagan equation (68),

$$m_t - e_t = -\eta \dot{e}_t. \tag{70}$$

As long as the (log) exchange rate is fixed at $\bar{e}$, the (log) money supply must remain fixed at

$$\bar{m} = \bar{e}. \tag{71}$$

It is convenient to suppose that there are two branches of the domestic government. One is a fiscal branch of government that runs an exogenously determined deficit. The other is a central bank that issues currency by open-market operations in domestic and foreign bonds. The central bank is required to monetize part of the fiscal deficit by buying a steady stream of home government bonds. It also has the task of intervening as necessary to defend the exchange rate, though the requirement to monetize home government debt takes precedence. In the model,

---

48. The original model of speculative attacks on fixed exchange rates is due to Krugman (1979), who drew on the work of Salant and Henderson (1978) on the breakdown of gold-price-fixing schemes. The text model follows Flood and Garber (1984) except for using a log-linear rather than a linear approximation. For alternative discussions of the speculative attack literature, see Obstfeld (1994d) and Garber and Svensson (1995).

inconsistency between the two central bank objectives will imply that ultimately the fixed exchange rate must give way to a floating rate. The interesting question is when and how the exchange rate's collapse takes place.

At time t the asset side of the central bank's balance sheet (see appendix 8B) consists of domestic-government ($B_{H,t}^{cb}$) and foreign ($B_{F,t}^{cb}$) bonds, each denominated in the issuer's currency. The foreign-currency bonds are the central bank's foreign-exchange reserves, which we assume can never fall below zero. (We assume nominal bonds to capture the institutional reality, but all the results would go through if the bonds were real.) The balance sheet's liability side is made up of currency in circulation, M_t. If $\bar{\mathcal{E}}$ is the level at which the exchange rate is fixed, a simplified version of the central bank's balance sheet (in levels, not logs) is

$$M_t = B_{H,t} + \bar{\mathcal{E}} B_{F,t}. \tag{72}$$

To reduce notational clutter, we have omitted the cb superscripts that might be needed in other contexts to distinguish the central bank bond holdings in eq. (72) from private-sector holdings. The preceding balance-sheet equality says that any currency in private hands at time t must have been issued by the central bank at one time or another either to buy domestic or foreign currency debt.[49]

8.4.2.2   Domestic Credit Policy

Suppose that the central bank is required to expand its *nominal* holdings of domestic government debt at rate μ, regardless of events in the foreign exchange market. Thus

$$\frac{\dot{B}_H}{B_H} = \dot{b}_H = \mu, \tag{73}$$

where $b_H \equiv \log B_H$ in our usual notation. Assumption (73) is admittedly simplistic, but it serves (however crudely) to capture the central bank's subservient role as it passively monetizes the fiscal branch's steady stream of IOUs.

If the consolidated government is essentially printing money to finance expenditures, how can the exchange rate remain fixed? The answer is that the central bank must use its foreign currency reserves to soak up any currency the public does not want to hold at the fixed rate $\bar{\mathcal{E}}$. That way, the total currency supply in the hands of the public remains fixed at $\bar{\mathcal{E}}$, as equilibrium condition (71) requires.

As the central bank's holdings of domestic government debt expand, its foreign-currency assets must contract in order to keep the money supply, and therefore the exchange rate, fixed. By eq. (72), $\dot{M} = 0$ implies

49. We implicitly assume that the central bank must rebate to the fiscal branch any interest it receives on either type of bond. We also ignore the net worth item on the balance sheet, which absorbs any capital gains and losses on the central bank's asset holdings. These conventions simplify notation and are inconsequential in the present context.

$$\bar{\mathcal{E}} \dot{B}_\mathrm{F} = -\dot{B}_\mathrm{H}. \tag{74}$$

Therefore, the central bank's purchases of domestic government debt are precisely matched in value by foreign reserve losses.

Clearly this situation is unsustainable. Eventually, the central bank will run out of foreign reserves, at which point it will no longer be able both to finance government deficits and to keep the money stock and exchange rate fixed. Since we have assumed that printing money to help finance the deficit always takes precedence, it is the fixed rate that must ultimately give way. (In a more general model the central bank might extend the life of the exchange parity by borrowing more foreign reserves. But the fiscal branch of the government would have to provide the resources to repay creditors.)

8.4.2.3   The Necessity of a Speculative Attack

How will the inevitable transition from fixed to floating rates take place? The model's important and surprising prediction is that the exchange rate will have to be abandoned *before* the central bank has completely exhausted its reserves through debt monetization. Why? Otherwise, there would have to be a perfectly anticipated discrete rise in the exchange rate. Such a jump implies an instantaneously infinite rate of capital gain, and therefore presents an incipient arbitrage opportunity that motivates speculators to buy all the central bank's remaining reserves before they gradually reach zero on their own.

To see the problem, observe that once the central bank runs out of reserves B_F, the money supply M will begin to expand at rate μ. [Domestic assets B_H then are the only remaining asset on the central bank's balance sheet, and these are assumed to be expanding at rate μ; recall eq. (73).] Our earlier solutions to the Cagan model show that once the exchange rate begins to float, the expected rate of depreciation (and price inflation) will jump from 0 to μ, the rate of money growth. As a consequence, the demand for real balances will drop sharply by $\eta\mu$ percent on the day of the transition from a fixed to a floating rate.[50]

If the fixed-rate regime were to last without a speculative attack until the last penny of reserves leaked away, the only way the required drop in real balances could happen would be through a fully anticipated discrete $\eta\mu$ percent rise in the newly floating exchange rate from $\bar{\mathcal{E}}$. Such a path, as we have just argued, cannot be an equilibrium. In the instant prior to depreciation, each speculator would try to shift out of domestic money and into foreign reserves to avoid a capital loss.

But if the exchange rate cannot jump along a perfect-foresight path, then the required fall in real balances must take place entirely through a fall in *nominal* balances. The transition to a floating exchange rate therefore requires a speculative

---

50. Our asserted solution can be confirmed by inspection of the Cagan equation (70). We derived analogous solutions earlier for the price level; see eq. (18).

attack in which agents abruptly exchange currency for the remnants of the central bank's foreign reserves. To say more about the size and timing of the attack, we return to the formal model.

8.4.2.4   Timing the Attack

In Figure 8.4 we graph the log of the actual exchange-rate path together with the log of a *shadow* floating exchange rate, $\tilde{e}_t$. The shadow exchange rate is defined as the floating exchange rate that would prevail if the attack had already occurred (that is, if all the central bank's foreign assets had already passed into private hands).[51] The shadow exchange rate is

$$\tilde{e}_t = b_{H,t} + \eta\mu, \tag{75}$$

as implied by the (bubble-free) Cagan monetary model when $m_t = b_{H,t}$ and $\dot{m}_t = \dot{b}_{H,t} = \mu$.

The collapse of the exchange rate must take place on date T when the two schedules in the top panel of Figure 8.4 intersect to give $\tilde{e}_T = \bar{e}$. Only on this precise date can the transition from fixed to floating take place without a perfectly foreseen discontinuous change in the exchange rate. We have argued that the fixed rate cannot collapse after time T, but Figure 8.4 shows it cannot collapse before T either. Were speculators to buy all the central bank's reserves prematurely, the currency would immediately *appreciate* to reach the shadow rate. Anticipating a large negative return on speculation against the home currency, no individual would wish to attack the central bank, and therefore no attack would occur.

Figure 8.4 also shows the paths of the money supply and reserves; note the discrete fall in reserves on date T when the attack takes place. The log of reserves declines at an increasing rate over time because, as B_H rises and B_F falls, reserves constitute an ever-declining fraction of total central bank assets.

It is easy to solve for the exact time of the attack. Equation (73) implies that

$$b_{H,t} = b_{H,0} + \mu t,$$

where time 0 is an initial date.[52] Combining this equation with eq. (75) for the shadow floating rate, and noting that $\tilde{e}_T = \bar{e}$, we find

$$\bar{e} = b_{H,0} + \mu T + \eta\mu.$$

Solving for T yields

$$T = \frac{\bar{e} - b_{H,0} - \eta\mu}{\mu}. \tag{76}$$

---

51. The shadow exchange rate concept was introduced by Flood and Garber (1984).

52. Recall that if X grows at proportional rate μ, then $X_t = X_0 e^{\mu t}$ and $\log X_t = \log X_0 + \mu t$.

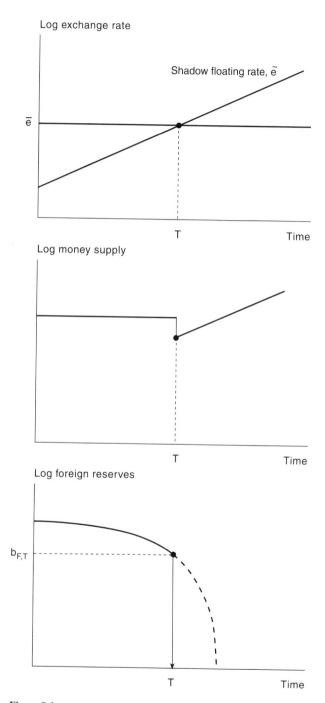

Figure 8.4
Anatomy of a speculative attack

Note that for all t prior to floating (that is, for $t < T$), $\bar{e} = \log(B_{H,t} + B_{F,t})$. Thus we can rewrite the preceding equation as

$$T = \frac{\log(B_{H,0} + B_{F,0}) - b_{H,0} - \eta\mu}{\mu}. \tag{77}$$

We see that the larger initial foreign reserve holdings $B_{F,0}$ are, the longer the fixed-rate regime will last. There is no guarantee that the right-hand side of eq. (77) is positive; it will definitely not be if $B_{F,0}$ is too small relative to μ. If the right-hand side of eq. (77) is negative, one should interpret the analysis as showing that a speculative attack must take place immediately on date 0.

It may seem obvious that a fixed-exchange-rate system suppresses speculative bubbles, but this is not always the case. Equation (75) for the shadow floating exchange rate assumes that speculative bubbles cannot arise. But if we do not impose this restriction, the general solution for the post-attack floating rate is given by

$$\tilde{e}_t = \log B_{H,t} + \eta\mu + b_T e^{(t-T)/\eta},$$

where b_T is an arbitrary constant. [See eq. (19) in our analysis of the continuous-time Cagan model.] Following the same steps to solve for the timing of an attack, we see that

$$T = \frac{\log(B_{H,0} + B_{F,0}) - b_{H,0} - \eta\mu - b_T}{\mu}.$$

If the arbitrary constant $b_T > 0$, then the attack occurs earlier than it would in the absence of post-attack speculative bubbles. Indeed, as Flood and Garber (1984) pointed out, if b_T is large enough, a speculative attack can cause the immediate collapse of a fixed-rate regime even when $\mu = 0$! That is, if speculative bubbles are a problem under a floating exchange rate, they can also bring down a viable fixed-rate regime. This analysis provides a first example of how expectations can lead to multiple equilibria under a fixed-rate regime, albeit one that relies somewhat mechanically on the possibility of speculative monetary price bubbles. Later on, in Chapter 9, we will consider more realistic models of how multiple equilibria can arise as a result of government attempts to fix exchange rates.

We formally introduce uncertainty into the analysis only after developing the mathematics of target-zone exchange rates. But it isn't hard to explain informally how uncertainty would work. Suppose that the process governing central-bank credit to the fiscal authorities is random with drift μ. Under plausible conditions, the probability of an attack rises over time as reserves fall and the exchange rate becomes vulnerable to smaller and smaller domestic-credit shocks. The regime collapses as soon as a shock pushes the shadow exchange rate above $\bar{e}$, and it is possible that the exchange rate will depreciate discretely but unexpectedly because of the unanticipated component of the shock (see Flood and Garber, 1984).

The main qualitative difference between the stochastic model and the certainty model is that the stochastic model implies a generally rising differential between home- and foreign-currency nominal interest rates in the run-up to a collapse. This differential is dictated by interest parity and compensates bond holders for the one-sided risk of a home-currency depreciation. In contrast, the deterministic version of the model leaves the home and foreign nominal interest rates equal until the moment of the attack, at which instant the home rate rises by μ.

8.4.2.5   Discussion

The preceding model combines elegant simplicity with a profound demonstration that speculative crises, far from being irrational panics, sometimes can be predicted from the most basic principles of efficient asset-price arbitrage. Nonetheless, the model has some serious shortcomings. From a theoretical perspective, it is asymmetric in its treatment of public and private behavior. The private sector is portrayed as completely rational and capable of fully anticipating events, whereas the monetary and fiscal authorities live by mechanical rules without any apparent regard for the long-term sustainability of the exchange rate. Certainly, the model does not provide any explanation why a rational government would not prefer to smooth its consumption of foreign exchange reserves over a long horizon, rather than spending them all during the finite life of the fixed exchange rate.

From an empirical perspective, the classical speculative attack model's emphasis on insolvency as the ultimate force underlying the collapse of fixed exchange rates is not very realistic. Virtually all of the countries forced off fixed rates by speculative attacks during the 1990s had the means to defend their exchange rates were their governments fully committed to doing so. For a range of countries, Table 8.1 compares the monetary base (corresponding to M in our model) and foreign exchange reserves in September 1994.

Table 8.1 shows that virtually all the major countries that suffered attacks on their exchange rates during the early 1990s had enough foreign exchange reserves and gold to buy back at least 80 to 90 percent of their monetary bases, had they been so inclined. For several countries, the ratio of total reserves to base was well in excess of 100 percent. Even the country with the lowest ratio, Italy, could have repurchased nearly half its base. And foreign reserves generally reflect only a small fraction of the resources that a country can bring to bear in defending its exchange rate. A government can always borrow to increase foreign exchange reserves, as long as markets regard it as solvent. Few of the countries listed in Table 8.1 would face insolvency if their debts were increased by even 10 percent of GNP. Such an

Table 8.1
Foreign Exchange Reserves and Monetary Base, September 1994

	Monetary Base (percent of GNP)	Reserves (percent of GNP)	Reserves/Base (percent)
Belgium	6.7	12.1	180
Denmark	8.6	8.1	94
Finland	11.2	10.4	93
France	4.6	4.6	100
Germany	9.9	6.2	63
Ireland	9.1	16.1	177
Italy	11.9	5.6	48
Mexico	3.9	4.7	120
Netherlands	10.0	13.6	136
Norway	6.3	18.7	297
Portugal	25.0	28.0	112
Spain	12.6	9.6	76
Sweden	13.0	12.1	93
United Kingdom	3.7	4.3	116

Source: Obstfeld and Rogoff (1995c).

amount, combined with their reserves, would be more than enough cushion to beat back even the most determined speculative attack.[53]

If these OECD governments had the financial resources to fight off speculative attacks, why didn't they successfully do so? To address this question adequately, we need a model with nominal rigidities in which the defense of a currency may have serious real effects. We also need a model in which the objectives and constraints of the government can be sensibly discussed. Chapter 9 will fill these gaps.

8.4.3 Multilateral Arrangements to Fix Exchange Rates

Since an exchange rate is the relative price of two currencies, the costs of resisting a speculative attack should be smaller if both countries' governments cooperate. To illustrate this point most clearly, we develop a two-country version of our log-linear exchange rate model. Assume that money-market equilibrium condition (24) applies to the home country and that an identical condition applies in the foreign country, with asterisks denoting foreign variables. Subtracting eq. (24) from the parallel foreign equation yields

---

53. We have argued that the OECD countries whose fixed exchange rates were broken by speculators in the early 1990s generally had ample resources to maintain their pegs. Then why didn't the massive interventions reported by the press over that period work? The short answer is that most of this intervention was sterilized. The Bank of England, for example, reportedly engaged in over $70 billion in intervention within a few hours during the September 1992 attack on the pound, largely using forward markets (see section 8.7.6 for a discussion of the equivalence between sterilized intervention and forward intervention). It suffered a substantial capital loss on these contracts after it ultimately decided to let the pound float.

$$p_t - p_t^* = m_t - m_t^* - \phi(y_t - y_t^*) + \eta(i_{t+1} - i_{t+1}^*).$$

Purchasing power parity, eq. (26), and uncovered interest parity, eq. (28), turn the preceding relationship into a stochastic difference equation for e_t,

$$e_t = m_t - m_t^* - \phi(y_t - y_t^*) + \eta(E_t e_{t+1} - e_t). \tag{78}$$

Given $y - y^*$, it is clear from this equation that fixing the exchange rate now means fixing the *relative* money supply, $m - m^*$. Indeed, this perspective makes it plain that if two governments wish to cooperate in fixing their mutual exchange rate, their combined monetary authorities can *never* run out foreign currency reserves.

8.4.4   Multilateral Currency Arrangements in Practice

The European Monetary System (EMS) set up in 1979 is the leading recent example of a cooperative multilateral system for targeting exchange rates. For the most part, however, Germany has historically set its own monetary policy independently and left its partners to bear the burden of fixing the exchange rate. True, Germany does intervene in foreign exchange markets and did so extensively during the 1992–93 EMS crises. Because it quickly sterilizes virtually all of its intervention, however, no shift in its monetary policy is necessarily implied.

Any multilateral peg must have some mechanism for determining overall monetary growth in the exchange rate union. An agreement to fix the exchange rate limits movements in relative money supplies but does nothing to tie down overall inflation. In the EMS, Germany has long set the system-wide inflation anchor unilaterally, though in principle this could be a coordinated decision. If and when some countries in Europe adopt a single currency as now planned—thereby irrevocably fixing their exchange rates—some mechanism for the joint design of monetary policy will be needed. Countries will also have to agree on the division of seignorage revenues from issuing the single currency.[54]

In practice the comprehensive postwar Bretton Woods system (1946-71) worked similarly to the EMS, but with the United States setting the system's monetary policy and other countries left to peg their exchange rates against the U.S. dollar. The eventual collapse of the Bretton Woods system at the beginning of the 1970s had many causes (see the essays in Bordo and Eichengreen, 1993), but two stand out. First, the United States began experiencing inflation during the late 1960s. (This inflation had its roots in fiscal problems associated with the rapid buildup of social programs and the funding of the Vietnam War.) Europe and Japan were reluctant to "import" U.S. inflation by continuing to buy as many dollars as needed to keep their dollar exchange rates fixed. Second, the continual evolution, growth, and

---

54. See Casella (1992) and Sibert (1994) for formal models of seignorage division.

deregulation of world capital markets increased pressure on the system by magnifying the potential for speculative attacks on currencies perceived to be weak. Eventually the dollar itself succumbed. After a period of convulsions from 1971 to 1973, the world entered the much less structured global exchange rate system with which it still, as of this writing, lives.

Both the EMS and Bretton Woods raise an important conceptual problem underlying any multilateral fixed exchange rate system. With N currencies there can be only $N-1$ independent exchange rates. Since only $N-1$ countries ever need to intervene to maintain parities, one country can direct its monetary policy toward some other goal.

A fruitful way to analyze multilateral currency systems is to ask how they resolve this "$N-1$ problem." In the EMS through the 1990s, Germany has played the role of Nth country, gearing its monetary policy toward low domestic inflation. Under Bretton Woods, the United States' intended monetary role was to peg the market price of gold at $35 per ounce. When this constraint on policy became binding, however, the United States quickly abandoned its gold commitment and, some would argue, turned its back on its systemic responsibilities. The EMS was designed to be perfectly symmetric in its operation, but it quickly evolved into a "hegemonic" system with Germany at its center.[55] Bretton Woods had an asymmetric design from the start, but it was primarily the willingness of countries outside the United States to hold their foreign reserves in the form of American dollars that gave the United States its freedom in monetary policy. Monetary scholars have perennially and inconclusively debated whether the emergence of a hegemon follows inevitably from the $N-1$ problem.[56]

The most important example of a fairly symmetric pegged exchange rate system is the classical gold standard that flourished in the late nineteenth century and ended with World War I. Under the gold standard, each currency's value in terms of gold was fixed by its issuer. In principle, gold could be freely used in domestic as well as international transactions, and international gold flows preserved equilibrium in national money markets. Except for some minor discrepancies relating to transport costs, exchange rates between currencies were determined simply by their relative gold values. Thus the system tied down exchange rates symmetrically, and the growth of world gold supplies determined global monetary growth.

This last feature of the system was a major drawback, as it allowed changes in gold's relative price to cause steep swings in overall price levels. Furthermore, gold parities were not immune to speculative attacks, which often accompanied domestic financial crises. The international gold standard's problems became especially acute after World War I when countries tried to reestablish it on a much slimmer

---

55. For interpretations of the EMS and its 1992-93 crisis, see Eichengreen and Wyplosz (1993) and Buiter, Corsetti, and Pesenti (in press).

56. For a discussion and references, see Eichengreen (1995).

base of monetary gold. As we shall see in the next chapter, there is now a scholarly consensus that the gold standard's flaws played a key role in deepening and propagating the global Great Depression of the 1930s.[57]

8.5   Target Zones for Exchange Rates

In a *target-zone* exchange-rate system, governments announce different rates at which they will sell and buy their currencies, with the gap between the selling and buying rate defining a zone of flexibility. In truth, the distinction between fixed rates and target zones is somewhat arbitrary, since most fixed rate regimes allow at a least a narrow band for fluctuation. Thus the Bretton Woods system of worldwide fixed exchange rates mandated a 2 percent gap between central banks' selling and buying rates against the U.S. dollar. Even under the pre–World War I gold standard, the cost of insuring and shipping gold implied a narrow band ("gold points") between which bilateral exchange rates could fluctuate. Contemporary advocates of target-zone systems generally have a somewhat wider band in mind, with the idea of trying to achieve a balance between exchange rate flexibility and predictability.

The most prominent example of a target zone is the European Monetary System. At various points since its inception in 1979, the multilateral exchange-rate grid of the EMS has included official bilateral zones of ±2.25 percent, ±6 percent, and ±15 percent. Developing countries such as Chile and Israel have used moving target zones that allow trend depreciation of the central exchange rate; see Leiderman and Bufman (1995).

In this section we study the operation of target zones, distilling the literature that builds on the seminal paper by Krugman (1991a). As with speculative attacks, the basic economics of target zones turn out to be easiest to grasp in a continuous-time model. The mathematics is considerably more difficult, however, since uncertainty is essential. Some readers may wish to skip this section entirely on a first reading of the chapter, though it isn't too hard to grasp the main points while skipping only the starred material.

8.5.1   Setting Up a Basic Model

As with speculative attacks, the ideas are most easily illustrated with the simple Cagan-type monetary model of section 8.2.7. However, since either partner in a target-zone system can intervene, it is convenient to use the two-country setup in which the exchange rate is given by eq. (78),

---

57. For further discussion of the gold standard, which is the subject of a vast literature, see Cooper (1982) and Eichengreen (1992). For theoretical discussions of the seignorage implications of various unilateral and bilateral exchange rate arrangements, see Helpman (1981), Fischer (1982), and Persson (1984).

$$e_t = m_t - m_t^* - \phi(y_t - y_t^*) + \eta(E_t e_{t+1} - e_t).$$

In preparation for our shift to a continuous-time formulation, let us assume that the time interval is very small, of length h, and denote the small change $e_{t+h} - e_t$ by de_{t+h}. Then, in analogy to the generalized discrete-time model of section 8.2.5, the difference equation representing the two-country equilibrium becomes

$$e_t = m_t - m_t^* - \phi(y_t - y_t^*) + \frac{\eta}{h} E_t de_{t+h}. \tag{79}$$

Let us define the composite variable $k_t \equiv m_t - m_t^* - \phi(y_t - y_t^*)$ as the *fundamentals* for the exchange rate (that is, the combination of exogenous forcing variables determining the exchange rate's path). If we rule out speculative bubbles, then difference equation (79) has an exchange-rate solution analogous to the small-country model's solution (30) (except that we have now endogenized the foreign interest rate and price level),

$$e_t = \frac{1}{h + \eta} \sum_{s=t}^{\infty} \left(1 + \frac{h}{\eta}\right)^{-(s-t)/h} E_t\{k_s\}h, \tag{80}$$

where the summation is over t, $t + h$, $t + 2h$, etc. This solution, valid for *any* fundamentals process, gives e_t as a discounted value of expected fundamentals. The reader will recognize this solution as analogous to the one derived from eq. (17) for the generalized discrete-time Cagan model.

The problem in working with eq. (80) is that in a target zone setting, the expected values on its right-hand side are hard to compute. (The barriers of the zone make monetary policy, and therefore the fundamentals, endogenous in a very complicated way.) Thus we will use economic reasoning to develop an alternative solution method useful in thinking about target zones.

8.5.2 Modeling a Target Zone

We assume that the "authorities"—meaning the Home or Foreign central bank, or a committee representing both—announce a target zone with an upper bound $\bar{e}$ (at which they *buy* Home currency with Foreign currency) and a lower bound $\underline{e} < \bar{e}$ (at which they *sell* Home currency for Foreign currency). Intervention sales and purchases affect the fundamentals by altering relative national money supplies, $m - m^*$, thereby keeping the exchange rate within its bounds. Note that with this intervention rule, the relative money supplies are endogenous. But they respond endogenously *only* when the exchange rate hits its ceiling or floor. (For the moment we won't worry about foreign reserve constraints, as the two countries clearly could coordinate their interventions so as to avoid large reserve changes for either.)

To close the model, we need to specify the stochastic process governing the fundamentals during periods where there is no intervention. We assume that as long as the exchange rate lies *strictly within* its band, the fundamentals follow a random-walk process,

$$dk_{t+h} = h^{1/2}vdz_{t+h},$$

(81)

where $dk_{t+h} \equiv k_{t+h} - k_t$ and $dz_{t+h} \equiv z_{t+h} - z_t$. The random variable dz_{t+h} has a mean-zero, i.i.d., normal distribution with unit variance [from which the change in fundamentals inherits an i.i.d. $\mathcal{N}(0, hv^2)$ distribution]. We assume that the variance of the change in fundamentals is proportional to the interval length h in eq. (81). This assumption implies that the variance is constant over any time span of *given* length as we vary the trading interval h. (Because we think of h as being infinitesimally small, we can assume there is no possibility that a large discrete shock drives the exchange rate from a point strictly within the band to the band's edge.)

Absent the exchange rate band, eqs. (80) and (81) together would give the very simple exchange rate solution $e_t = k_t$, which we refer to as the "free float" solution. That is, absent intervention, if the fundamentals follow a random walk, so does the exchange rate. But how does a solution look when the money supply is always altered at the boundaries of the zone to prevent the exchange rate drifting outside of it?

8.5.3   A General Solution for the Exchange Rate

The key to solving the model is to recognize that if the fundamentals follow a random walk within specified bounds, all information about the future probability distribution of fundamentals is summarized in their current level, k. Thus we may write a general or "candidate" solution for the exchange rate as

$$e = G(k),$$

where we assume the function $G(\cdot)$ is twice continuously differentiable.

If $e = G(k)$ is a solution, it must satisfy equilibrium condition eq. (79), meaning that

$$G(k_t) = k_t + \frac{\eta}{h}E_t dG(k_{t+h})$$

$$= k_t + \frac{\eta}{h}E_t\{G(k_{t+h}) - G(k_t)\}.$$

(82)

Let us consider a second-order Taylor approximation (at $k_{t+h} = k_t$) to the expected value on the right-hand side of the preceding equation:

$$E_t\{G(k_{t+h}) - G(k_t)\} \approx E_t\{G'(k_t)dk_{t+h} + \tfrac{1}{2}G''(k_t)(dk_{t+h})^2\}.$$

(83)

By eq. (81), $E_t\{G'(k_t)dk_{t+h}\} = G'(k_t)E_t\{dk_{t+h}\} = 0$. Furthermore,

$$E_t\{(dk_{t+h})^2\} = E_t\{hv^2(dz_{t+h})^2\} = hv^2.$$

Thus we have the approximation

$$E_t dG(k_{t+h}) \approx \frac{h v^2}{2} G''(k_t).$$

For h arbitrarily small, we can regard this approximation as an equality. [The higher-order terms in the infinite Taylor expansion corresponding to eq. (83) are multiplied by powers of h equal to or higher than $h^{3/2}$, and therefore they all go to zero more quickly than h does as the continuous-time limit is approached.] Plugging the implied equation into eq. (82) shows that any function $G(\cdot)$ that is a candidate to describe the equilibrium must satisfy

$$G(k) = k + \frac{\eta v^2}{2} G''(k) \tag{84}$$

as long as the fundamentals take a value for which the exchange rate $e = G(k)$ is *strictly* between $\bar{e}$ and $\underline{e}$.[58]

The time subscripts have been dropped from eq. (84) by design. We do so because the equation is most usefully thought of as a second-order stochastic differential equation describing the exchange rate's evolution as a function of fundamentals k rather than of time. As you can verify by differentiating it, a *general* solution to eq. (84) is

$$G(k) = k + b_1 \exp(\lambda k) + b_2 \exp(-\lambda k),$$

where b_1 and b_2 are arbitrary constants and

$$\lambda = \sqrt{\frac{2}{\eta v^2}}.$$

(Some readers may have already noticed the close analogy between target-zone analysis and option-pricing theory.)

This general solution is not enough to describe the exchange rate's behavior in the target zone. To do that, we have to tie down the arbitrary boundary conditions b_1 and b_2. We can find b_1 and b_2 by using our assumption that the authorities limit the exchange rate's range to the interval $[\underline{e}, \bar{e}]$.

8.5.4   The Target-Zone Solution

To simplify the algebra we assume that $\underline{e} = -\bar{e}$, making the zone symmetric about $e = 0$. Since we have assumed in eq. (81) that there is no deterministic drift in the fundamentals, the exchange rate solution must also be symmetric; that is, $b_1 = -b_2 = -b$, giving the relevant exchange-rate solution the general form

$$G(k) = k - b[\exp(\lambda k) - \exp(-\lambda k)]. \tag{85}$$

---

58. Recall that we used eq. (81) to derive eq. (84), and eq. (81) doesn't hold when $e = \bar{e}$ or $\underline{e}$.

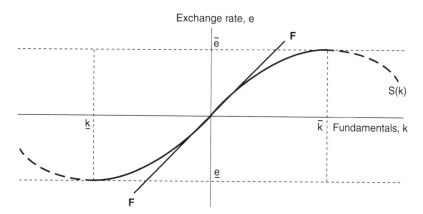

Figure 8.5
The exchange rate in a target zone

Let $S(\mathsf{k})$ be the *particular* solution to this equation that describes the exchange rate's actual behavior, that is, the solution with the correct value for the constant *b*. Figure 8.5 graphs $S(\mathsf{k})$ as an S-shaped curve. The 45° line is labeled **FF**, since this line would describe the relation between the exchange rate and fundamentals under a free float (given that the fundamentals would follow a random walk if there were no intervention at the boundaries). We will formally derive the path shown in a moment, but it is useful to refer to Figure 8.5 as we go through the proof. The key properties of the solution to notice are the following:

1. The exchange rate band determines upper and lower limits on the fundamentals, labeled $\overline{\mathsf{k}}$ and $\underline{\mathsf{k}}$, respectively, such that $S(\overline{\mathsf{k}}) = \overline{\mathsf{e}}$ and $S(\underline{\mathsf{k}}) = \underline{\mathsf{e}}$.

2. $S'(\mathsf{k}) \geq 0$ within the target zone; that is, the exchange rate is a nondecreasing function of the fundamentals over $[\underline{\mathsf{k}}, \overline{\mathsf{k}}]$.

3. $S'(\overline{\mathsf{k}}) = S'(\underline{\mathsf{k}}) = 0$, that is, $S(\mathsf{k})$ is tangent to the top and bottom of the band at the band's endpoints. (In the target-zone literature this is referred to as the *smooth pasting condition*, over the objections of finance theorists and stochastic control specialists who reserve the term for something else.)

The economic reasoning underlying the smooth pasting condition derives from a no-arbitrage argument, but it is somewhat subtle. Notice that before k actually hits a boundary (say $\overline{\mathsf{k}}$), its expected change is zero [because that is what eq. (81) assumes]. But once k reaches $\overline{\mathsf{k}}$, the exchange rate is at the top of its band, and the monetary authorities will only allow k to go down, not up. Thus, at the top of the band, $E_t\{dk_{t+h}\}$ must change discontinuously from zero to a negative value. If $S(\mathsf{k})$ were not tangent to the horizontal $\overline{\mathsf{e}}$ line as in Figure 8.5, this discontinuous jump in $E_t\{dk_{t+h}\}$ would imply a discontinuous jump in $E_t\{de_{t+h}\}$ and therefore in e itself. (This is the same logic as in the speculative attack model: a discontinuous change in expected depreciation changes money demand discontinuously and necessitates a discrete change in real balances.) No equilibrium path can approach such a point since speculators would anticipate arbitrage profits. The implication is that here, not only must the path of the exchange rate itself be continuous, the exchange rate's expected rate of change must be continuous as well. The final step in the logic is to note that the only way expected exchange rate depreciation can change continuously as the edge of the band is approached is for the $S(k)$ curve to be horizontal there.

The reader should note that we are considering only the most basic type of target zone here. The monetary authorities could, for example, commit to taking stronger action when $\bar{e}$ is reached, changing k by enough to throw the exchange rate back into the middle of the zone (this is an easy generalization). Alternatively, they could intervene before the zone's edge is actually reached, a policy called intramarginal intervention. We return to this point shortly in our discussion of target zones in practice. First, however, we provide a formal proof of the necessity of the smooth pasting condition.

*8.5.5   Proof of Smooth Pasting and Solution for b, $\bar{k}$, and $\underline{k}$

To derive smooth pasting rigorously and solve for the specific parameters of $S(k)$, we ask what happens when date t fundamentals are at $\bar{k}$, with $S(\bar{k}) = \bar{e}$. (The argument for the band's lower edge is symmetric.)

At $\bar{k}$, a small increase in fundamentals would push the exchange rate out of its band, so any incipient rise in k is automatically prevented by intervention. Using the same argument that led to eq. (83)—which, recall, is an equality for arbitrarily small h—we see that

$$E_t\{S(\bar{k} + dk) - S(\bar{k})\} = S'(\bar{k})E_t\{dk \mid dk \le 0\} + \tfrac{1}{2}S''(\bar{k})E_t\{(dk)^2 \mid dk \le 0\}, \quad (86)$$

where expectations are conditional on $dk \le 0$ because at $\bar{k}$, intervention is sure to keep fundamentals from rising.

According to eq. (81) the random variable dk is distributed symmetrically around zero, so $E_t\{(dk)^2 \mid dk \le 0\} = E_t\{(dk)^2\} = hv^2$. Plugging eq. (86) into eq. (79), we thus find

$$S(\bar{k}) = \bar{k} + \frac{\eta}{h}S'(\bar{k})E_t\{dk \mid dk \le 0\} + \frac{\eta v^2}{2}S''(\bar{k}). \quad (87)$$

Earlier we showed that $S(k)$ must satisfy eq. (84) when the exchange rate is within the target zone's interior, that is,

$$S(k) = k + \frac{\eta v^2}{2}S''(k).$$

We have also argued that the exchange rate must change continuously as the fundamentals change to rule out the arbitrage opportunity offered by an instantaneously infinite expected rate of capital gain. If the preceding equation holds within the band, then continuity implies that

$$S(\bar{k}) = \lim_{k \to \bar{k}} S(k) = \bar{k} + \frac{\eta v^2}{2} S''(\bar{k}).$$

At $k = \bar{k}$, however, $S(k)$ also satisfies eq. (87), as we have seen. Because the conditional expectation $E_t\{dk \mid dk \leq 0\}$ is strictly negative, our proof is complete, for $S(k)$ plainly cannot satisfy both the last equation and eq. (87) at $k = \bar{k}$ unless $S'(\bar{k}) = 0$.[59]

With the smooth pasting condition in hand it is straightforward to solve for b in eq. (85) and for the limiting fundamentals consistent with the target zone. Our symmetry assumptions imply that $\underline{k} = -\bar{k}$, so the solutions for b and $\bar{k}$ are all that remain to be found. They come from solving the pair of equations

$$S(\bar{k}) = \bar{k} - b\left[\exp\left(\lambda\bar{k}\right) - \exp\left(-\lambda\bar{k}\right)\right] = \bar{e},$$

$$S'(\bar{k}) = 1 - \lambda b\left[\exp\left(\lambda\bar{k}\right) + \exp\left(-\lambda\bar{k}\right)\right] = 0.$$

The second of these shows that $b > 0$, which assures us that, as Figure 8.5 suggests, $S''(k) = -\lambda^2 b[\exp(\lambda k) - \exp(-\lambda k)]$ is negative for $k > 0$ [making $S(k)$ strictly concave over the positive range of fundamentals] and positive for $k < 0$ [making $S(k)$ strictly convex over the negative range].

8.5.6   Target Zones in Practice

Figure 8.5 reveals one of the main reasons a country might adopt a target zone. The S-shaped exchange rate locus implies that the zone exerts a stabilizing effect, reducing the exchange rate's sensitivity to a given change in fundamentals. As a corollary, the threat of intervention at the margins keeps the exchange confined between $\bar{e}$ and $\underline{e}$ for a wider range of fundamentals than would a free float. Thus the target zone buys some exchange-rate flexibility with less variability than a free float would allow. If exchange rate variability per se is bad because of incomplete markets or other factors (some of which we discuss in Chapter 9), the stabilizing property of a zone will be viewed as an advantage. For this reason target zones have been advocated by Williamson (1985, 1993) and others.

A related property of target zones is that they can allow much more independence for domestic interest rates than a rigid peg. For short-term rates this is possible even when the zone is quite narrow, as pointed out by Keynes (1930, pp.

---

59. For alternative derivations see Flood and Garber (1991), Froot and Obstfeld (1991), and Bertola (1994).

319–331) and, much earlier, by Goschen (1861, pp. 129–131). Suppose the exchange rate of the home against the foreign currency can fluctuate within a ±1 percent band. Then the difference between the home and foreign per annum nominal interest rates on one-year, default-free securities can never exceed the maximal exchange rate change of 2 percent over a year.[60] But an exchange rate change of 2 percent over six months is a change of 4 percent on a per annum basis. Thus, quoted on an annual basis, home-foreign interest differentials on instruments maturing in six months could be as high as 4 percent per year. At a one-month maturity, the maximum interest differential would be 24 percent per year!

Given the elegance of the analysis, we are sad to report that empirical tests of this simple target-zone model have not confirmed its main predictions. One very fundamental inconsistency is that interest differentials often suggest considerable investor skepticism over the credibility of the bands (see the evidence cited by Garber and Svensson, 1995). The target zone model can be extended to allow for imperfect credibility, but the model becomes messier and its predictions less sharp. At a more subtle level, the empirical evidence does not support the basic Krugman (1991a) model's prediction that exchange rate observations should tend to be clustered near the boundaries of the band. The S-shaped exchange rate locus implies that the exchange rate should become less sensitive to fundamentals as the fundamentals approach their limits. Thus, once it is near the boundaries, the rate tends to sit there a long time.

One important reason for exchange rates to cluster near a zone's center is that in practice, monetary authorities typically do not wait to intervene until an exchange rate reaches its upper or lower limits. Intramarginal intervention is motivated in part by the authorities' fear that extreme values of the exchange rate may signal vulnerability to speculators.[61] Both factors, the lack of credibility of the bands and intramarginal intervention, can change the curvature of the S-curve in Figure 8.5. In practice, the elegant and simple nonlinearity emphasized by the basic target-zone model may not be very important.

*8.6   Speculative Attacks on a Target Zone

The finding that most target zones enjoy only partial credibility suggests that a realistic target-zone model must incorporate from the start the possibility of some kind of realignment. One possibility is to proceed in analogy to our earlier model

---

60. This statement is true even if investors are risk averse. Can you see why?

61. When two or more exchange rates are being targeted simultaneously by three or more countries, as in the European Monetary System's grid, intramarginal intervention may occur in one bilateral currency market as a result of intervention at the margin in another. For analyses of multilateral target zones, see Pill (1994), Flandreau (1995), Serrat (1995), and Jørgensen and Mikkelsen (1996).

of speculative attacks. Assume that only one country, the home country, pegs its currency's exchange rate and that the foreign reserves at its disposal are finite. As in our earlier attack model, we assume that the exhaustion of reserves initiates a freely floating currency.

Since the attack can occur only when the home central bank is selling foreign reserves to prevent the price of foreign currency from rising past $\bar{e}$, we can simplify the analysis, following Krugman and Rotemberg (1992), by assuming a "one-sided" zone in which there is a ceiling on the exchange rate but no floor. (As we shall see, this asymmetry effectively gives reserves a negative trend.) The equilibrium exchange rate locus $S(k)$ no longer is symmetric, but it still belongs to the family of general solutions $G(k) = k + b_1 \exp(\lambda k) + b_2 \exp(-\lambda k)$ derived earlier. It is, however, easy to tie b_2 down in this case. Because what happens at $e = \bar{e}$ must become increasingly irrelevant for the current exchange rate as k becomes smaller, $S(k)$ should approach the free-float locus, $e = k$, as k falls without bound. But $\lim_{k \to -\infty} G(k) = k$ if and only if $b_2 = 0$. Thus $S(k)$ must take the form $k + b_1 \exp(\lambda k)$ for an appropriate b_1.

To close the model, suppose that, because the money supply declines in an attack, fundamentals fall from an endogenously determined value $\bar{k}$ to $\bar{k} - \mathfrak{R}$ as speculators strip the central bank of reserves during its vain effort to defend the ceiling $\bar{e}$. Then two conditions jointly determine b_1 and $\bar{k}$. First, the exchange rate must equal $\bar{e}$ at the time of an attack,

$$S(\bar{k}) = \bar{k} + b_1 \exp(\lambda \bar{k}) = \bar{e}. \tag{88}$$

Second, as in our earlier attack model, and for the same reason, the exchange rate cannot jump in the transition to a free float,

$$S(\bar{k}) = \bar{k} + b_1 \exp(\lambda \bar{k}) = \bar{k} - \mathfrak{R}, \tag{89}$$

where $\bar{k} - \mathfrak{R}$ equals the postattack floating exchange rate. Since $\bar{k} - \mathfrak{R} < \bar{k}$, the second condition requires that $b_1 < 0$.

Figure 8.6 shows $S_1(k)$, which lacks the smooth pasting property, as the resulting exchange rate locus. Below $\bar{k}$, rising fundamentals push the exchange rate up along $S_1(k)$. As soon as $\bar{k}$ is reached, however, there is a sharp attack that reduces the fundamentals by $\mathfrak{R}$ but leaves the exchange rate momentarily at $\bar{e}$ on **FF**.

In contrast to the fixed-exchange-rate attack model of section 8.4.2, attacks can occur here even with no trend growth in the fundamentals (for example, continuing relative money supply growth), although it is easy to modify the model to allow for trends (see exercise 5). But if there is no unfavorable trend in the fundamentals, why doesn't the sharp fall in the money supply that an attack causes lead to a corresponding sharp appreciation of the home currency? The reason is that the preattack exchange rate already stands at an appreciated level relative to a free float,

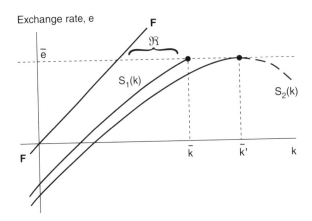

Figure 8.6
Speculative attack on a target zone

because of the expectation that the monetary authorities will defend the exchange rate ceiling.

In the case Figure 8.6 illustrates by $S_1(k)$, a small positive shock to fundamentals that pushes e to $\bar{e}$ sets off an attack. If it did not, the authorities would still have to use *some* reserves to maintain $\bar{e}$. Thus, on any future occasion that e reached $\bar{e}$, the no-arbitrage condition (89) would fail. Fundamentals that follow a random walk, however, must hit $\bar{k}$ frequently enough to exhaust any finite reserve stock in finite time; so collapse at some point is inevitable. Unless the attack occurs the first time it can succeed, the switch to a free float therefore will entail a discrete currency depreciation and excess anticipated profits. [A critical assumption making reserve exhaustion inevitable is that there is no floor to the band, so that the authorities never buy foreign reserves, but only sell them at $\bar{e}$. With a floor on the band, however, ultimate reserve exhaustion would still be inevitable if the fundamentals process in eq. (81) included a positive trend term μh.]

The type of locus shown as $S_1(k)$ in Figure 8.6 is not the only possibility. If reserves are high enough (implying a large $\Re$), the relevant exchange rate solution may be one like $S_2(k)$, which pastes smoothly to $\bar{e}$ at some $\bar{k}' > \bar{k}$. The critical value of $\Re$ at which smooth pasting first becomes possible, $\Re'$, is defined by eq. (88), eq. (89), *and* the derivative condition

$$S'(\bar{k}) = 1 + \lambda b_1 \exp(\lambda \bar{k}) = 0. \tag{90}$$

Combining eq. (90) with eq. (89) (for $\Re = \Re'$) shows that for smooth pasting to be possible, $\Re$ must be at least $\Re'$, where

$$\Re' = \frac{1}{\lambda}.$$

For reserve levels such that $\Re > \Re'$, $S(k)$ is determined entirely by eqs. (88) and (90), as in a fully credible target zone. The exchange rate locus therefore must be the same as $S_2(k)$ in Figure 8.6. Reserve levels are irrelevant to the solution in such cases because a speculative attack is impossible: $\Re'$ satisfies eq. (89), the condition that rules out a discrete exchange-rate jump, so the home currency would *appreciate* were an attack to reduce fundamentals by an amount $\Re$ greater than $\Re'$. Only for $\Re \leq \Re'$ is the target zone currently susceptible to attack.

Repeated interventions as e hits $\bar{e}$ must eventually lead to $\Re$ falling to $\Re'$, however. At this point the system will become vulnerable to attack. Indeed, as soon as $\Re'$ is reached and $k = \bar{k}'$, any further rise in the fundamentals will trigger an attack.

8.7   A Stochastic Global General Equilibrium Model with Nominal Assets

In this section we generalize our earlier maximizing models of money to encompass stochastic national outputs and money supplies. Though fundamentally a very straightforward extension of the models in Chapter 5, the stochastic monetary model permits analysis of a host of important issues, including the forward exchange premium, the hedging of nominal risks, and the effects of sterilized intervention.

8.7.1   Equilibrium Real Asset Pricing and Consumption Allocations

We begin with a money-in-the-utility-function model, which extends readily to the stochastic case.[62] Assume that the infinitely-lived representative resident of country n has a period utility function that is additive in consumption and real balances:

$$U_t^n = E_t \sum_{s=t}^{\infty} \beta^{s-t} \left[u(C_s^n) + v \left(\frac{M_s^n}{P_s^n} \right) \right], \qquad n = 1, \ldots, N. \tag{91}$$

The N country endowments of the lone consumption good fluctuate randomly, and may be correlated across time and across countries.[63] Money supplies are also random and, similarly, may be correlated across countries and time. Money and output shocks may be correlated with each other. As in our earlier money-in-the-utility-function formulations, we assume that home money is useful only to home residents. This assumption makes money services a nontraded good. Countries can, however, trade in a full spectrum of N country mutual equity funds. That is, assuming HARA preferences (see p. 293), they can trade a range sufficient

---

62. A related partial-equilibrium analysis is Kouri (1977). See also Branson and Henderson (1985). Alternative general-equilibrium approaches are followed by Stulz (1987) and Dufresne and Shi (1995). We will take up a cash-in-advance model later, as does Lucas (1982).

63. A few mild technical restrictions are needed to ensure the existence of equilibrium.

to achieve full sharing of idiosyncratic consumption risks, as in Chapter 5. In addition, countries may trade nominal bonds indexed to any currency (or to any basket of currencies). Finally, because purchasing power parity holds,

$$P^n = \mathcal{E}^{nm} P^m, \tag{92}$$

where $\mathcal{E}^{nm}$ is the price of country m's currency in terms of country n's. We spare you the budget constraint for a country n resident, since it involves real returns on all possible mutual funds and nominal bonds, as well as on currency n. We can skip the details because, with money services a nontraded good, the model's equilibrium conditions follow directly from the traded-nontraded goods setup developed in section 5.5. (Strictly speaking, the nontraded goods model of Chapter 5 had only two periods, but the extension of the additive preference case to an infinite horizon is immediate.) As in Chapter 5, the equilibrium naturally would be more complicated with nonadditive period utility.

The Euler condition governing the equilibrium return r^m on *any* asset is

$$u'(C_t) = \beta E_t\{(1 + r^m_{t+1})u'(C_{t+1})\}, \tag{93}$$

where we have suppressed country superscripts on consumption because eq. (93) must hold for *any* country's consumption.[64] With period utility additive in money and consumption, the presence of money has no effect whatsoever on allocation of the consumption good or on the real prices of country mutual funds. Because money may be thought of as a nontraded durable good here, it doesn't affect international risk sharing in tradables if its use doesn't affect marginal substitution rates for consumption on different dates and in different states. For the case of CRRA-isoelastic consumption preferences, we know that each country sells all claims to its own output in exchange for a share in a global country mutual fund. Ownership shares in this fund are time-invariant and determined just as in section 5.5.3. Therefore, the equilibrium has

$$C^n_t = x^n Y^W_t \tag{94}$$

for all n and t, where Y^W_t is per capita global output and $\sum_n x^n = 1$.

---

64. Recall our definition of r^m from section 5.4.1.2. For a country mutual fund, the multiperiod analog is given by

$$1 + r^m_{t+1} = \frac{V^m_{t+1} + Y^m_{t+1}}{V^m_t},$$

where Y^m_{t+1} is country m's output on date $t + 1$ and V^m_t is the date t market price of the claim to all of country m's future output (starting on date $t + 1$). Equation (93) can be derived from eq. (57) in Chapter 5. See also the discussion in Supplement A to Chapter 5.

8.7.2   Pricing Nominal Bonds and Money

Assets with payoffs specified in currencies can be priced in the same way as any other asset. Consider first a nominal bond denominated in a generic country's currency, which we refer to as "dollars." One dollar's worth of currency bonds returns a certain $1 + i_{t+1}$ dollars in period $t + 1$, where i is the nominal interest rate on dollars. The first-order Euler condition for a nominal bond thus is given by

$$\frac{1}{P_t}u'(C_t) = (1 + i_{t+1})\beta E_t \left\{ \frac{1}{P_{t+1}}u'(C_{t+1}) \right\}$$

or, in more familiar real terms [see eq. (93)], as

$$u'(C_t) = \beta E_t \left\{ (1 + i_{t+1})\frac{P_t}{P_{t+1}}u'(C_{t+1}) \right\}, \tag{95}$$

where $(1 + i_{t+1})P_t/P_{t+1}$ is the bond's ex post gross real return. Notice that in general, a naive expectations analog of Fisher parity equation (3) does *not* hold. That is, the return on a riskless real bond, $1 + r_{t+1}$, is not necessarily equal to the expected real return on a bond with a riskless nominal payout, $(1 + i_{t+1})E_t\{P_t/P_{t+1}\}$. The reason is that a bond that is riskless in nominal terms is not necessarily riskless in real terms. The pricing equation for a riskless real bond is the usual condition

$$u'(C_t) = (1 + r_{t+1})\beta E_t\{u'(C_{t+1})\}. \tag{96}$$

Equating the right-hand sides of eqs. (95) and (96) yields

$$(1 + r_{t+1})E_t \left\{ u'(C_{t+1}) \right\} = (1 + i_{t+1})E_t \left\{ \frac{P_t}{P_{t+1}}u'(C_{t+1}) \right\},$$

which reduces to a certainty-equivalence Fisher parity equation

$$1 + r_{t+1} = (1 + i_{t+1})E_t \left\{ \frac{P_t}{P_{t+1}} \right\} \tag{97}$$

only if

$$E_t \left\{ \frac{P_t}{P_{t+1}}u'(C_{t+1}) \right\} = E_t \left\{ \frac{P_t}{P_{t+1}} \right\} E_t\{u'(C_{t+1})\}.$$

The preceding factorization is valid, however, only if the covariance of inflation and the marginal utility of consumption is zero. As we shall see, this is not generally the case unless consumption (and therefore world income) is deterministic.

We next consider the stochastic Euler equation for money, which is

$$\frac{1}{P_t}u'(C_t) = \frac{1}{P_t}v'\left(\frac{M_t}{P_t}\right) + \beta E_t \left\{ \frac{1}{P_{t+1}}u'(C_{t+1}) \right\}. \tag{98}$$

Combining this equation with the bond Euler equation (95), we find

$$\frac{v'\left(\frac{M_t}{P_t}\right)}{u'(C_t)} = \frac{i_{t+1}}{1+i_{t+1}}.$$

Perhaps surprisingly, this is exactly the same as eq. (37) for the nonstochastic case even though currency holdings are subject to price-level risk here. Equation (37) still holds, however, because nominal bonds and currency have identical price-level risk, so that the opportunity cost of holding money rather than nominal bonds for a period is completely captured by the nominal interest rate, which is known when the money-demand decision is made.[65] The parallel with the nonstochastic case is a bit deceptive, since in general equilibrium uncertainty affects the nominal interest rate, the price level, and consumption.

Indeed, with period utility additive in consumption and money, nominal interest rates adjust in general equilibrium so that everyone is content with *no net trade* of nominal bonds. The logic is the same as in the nontraded goods model of section 5.5.3. Trade in contingent output claims brings countries' marginal rates of consumption substitution into equality across all dates and states of nature. Since all gains from trade are exhausted by trading real securities, trade of additional securities indexed to nontraded goods can yield no further benefit. Here, nominal bonds are claims indexed to the nontraded good—nominal money balances. Given trade in the global output equity funds, nominal bonds therefore do not expand opportunities for risk sharing. (The fact that the bonds are not traded does not, of course, prevent us from constructing their prices, as we shall see.)[66]

8.7.3 Determination of the Price Level and Exchange Rates

Given that real consumption is determined independently of nominal money supplies and prices, eq. (98) may be viewed as a nonlinear stochastic difference equation in P, with exogenous forcing variables C and M. In general there is no closed-form solution for the price level, though one can demonstrate existence and uniqueness (assuming no monetary bubbles) using standard methods.

It is helpful, therefore, to look at the special case

$$u(C_t) + v\left(\frac{M_t}{P_t}\right) = \frac{C^{1-\rho}}{1-\rho} + \log\left(\frac{M_t}{P_t}\right)$$

(in which country superscripts still are suppressed and ρ is the constant coefficient of relative risk aversion). Apply this period utility function to eq. (98) and recall eq. (94), which holds under the CRRA-isoelastic consumption preferences now assumed. The result is

---

65. The envelope theorem gurantees that, at an optimum, the individual would as soon shift a dollar of money holdings into dollar bonds as into any other nonmoney asset.

66. Under incomplete markets matters would be different. See Bacchetta and van Wincoop (1995).

$$1 = \frac{P_t (x Y_t^W)^\rho}{M_t} + \beta E_t \left\{ \frac{P_t}{P_{t+1}} \left(\frac{Y_t^W}{Y_{t+1}^W} \right)^\rho \right\}. \tag{99}$$

(Recall that x is the generic country's constant equilibrium share of world output.)
This difference equation has a closed-form solution for the special case

$$\frac{M_{t+1}}{M_t} = (1 + \mu)\epsilon_{t+1}, \tag{100}$$

with $1 + \mu > \beta$ and ϵ a nonnegative random variable with $E_t\{1/\epsilon_{t+1}\} = 1.$[67] To
confirm that claim, let us try the educated guess

$$\frac{M_t}{P_t} = \omega (x Y_t^W)^\rho, \tag{101}$$

where ω is a constant to be determined. After substituting eq. (101) into eq. (99),
and solving the resulting equation, we find that

$$\omega = \frac{1 + \mu}{1 + \mu - \beta} = \frac{1}{1 - \dfrac{\beta}{1 + \mu}} > 0.$$

Our conjecture is now verified. Just as in the Cagan model, high current income
raises the demand for real balances, while a high expected rate of money growth
lowers demand.

The last two equations imply that a country's price level is

$$P_t = M_t \left(1 - \frac{\beta}{1 + \mu} \right) (x Y_t^W)^{-\rho}$$

in equilibrium. Exchange rates are then determined by purchasing power parity
[eq. (92)]. It may seem puzzling that expected future output changes play no role
in determining the current price level. The reason is that higher expected future
output has two opposite effects on money demand. It depresses expected inflation,
if other things are equal. But it also must raise the real rate of interest to make
people content with a more steeply falling expected path for the marginal utility
of consumption. For the carefully chosen utility function in this example, the two
effects just cancel, leaving the nominal interest rate steady at $i = [(1 + \mu)/\beta] - 1$
independent of the distribution of future output.

If we relax the assumption that money supplies follow a random walk with drift,
it still may be possible to solve explicitly a log-linearized version of the model,
as we solved the stochastic growth model in Chapter 7. Suppose, for example, that
the log of the country's money supply and the log of world output follow stationary

---

67. In this case the log money supply follows a random walk with drift if ϵ is lognormal.

stochastic processes with independent, normally distributed, homoskedastic innovations. In addition, let $\log(1 + \mu)$ denote the deterministic drift in the mean of m
and $\log(1 + g)$ that in the mean of y^w. A logarithmic approximation to eq. (99)
around the nonstochastic steady-state equilibrium path is

$$m_t - p_t = \rho y_t^w - \left(1/\bar{i}\right) E_t \left\{p_{t+1} - p_t\right\} - \left(\rho/\bar{i}\right) E_t \left\{y_{t+1}^w - y_t^w\right\},$$

where $\bar{i} = [(1 + \mu)/\beta] - 1$ is the nominal interest rate in the nonstochastic steady-
state.[68] This equilibrium condition resembles the Cagan equation except for the
final term in expected output growth, which captures the money-demand effect of
the real interest rate. The solution of the preceding price-level difference equation
is

$$p_t = -\rho y_t^w + \left(\frac{\bar{i}}{1 + \bar{i}}\right) \sum_{s=t}^{\infty} \left(\frac{1}{1 + \bar{i}}\right)^{s-t} E_t \left\{m_s\right\},$$

which relates p_t to current world output and to the expected present value of the
money supply, discounted at the nominal interest rate.

8.7.4   A Stochastic Cash-in-Advance Model

The preceding analysis can easily be recast in a multicountry cash-in-advance
setup. The utility function of the representative agent in country n is given by

$$U_t^n = E_t \sum_{s=t}^{\infty} \beta^{s-t} u(C_s^n). \tag{102}$$

As in our earlier cash-in-advance model, we assume that all purchases of country
n output must be made in country n currency. Importantly, they must be made in
country n currency even when carried out by a resident of some other country.
However, we will slightly modify our timing assumptions to match the Helpman-
Lucas cash-in-advance model discussed in section 8.3.6. Before, we assumed that
consumers had to set money aside in $t - 1$ to make purchases in period t. Now we
will assume that consumers acquire the cash they need for period t consumption
purchases by first visiting asset markets that meet at the beginning of period t, *after*
period t shocks have been observed.

Shareholders receive money dividends—the proceeds from output sales—but
must hold these receipts in the currency they are paid until asset markets reopen
the following period. Outputs are inelastically supplied, so this delay imposes no

---

68. A constant term has been omitted. The omitted term is

$$\text{Var}_t \left\{\log \left[\frac{P_t}{P_{t+1}} \left(\frac{Y_t^w}{Y_{t+1}^w}\right)^\rho\right]\right\},$$

which is constant under the maintained assumptions about the exogenous variables M and Y^w.

distortion on the production side. Since each government makes stochastic money transfers to its own residents exclusively at the beginning of each period (before markets meet), shareholders face between-period currency risk, which they diversify by trading claims to their stochastic government transfer streams.[69]

Given these modifications, the model shares important similarities with our last model. In particular, there is again a dichotomy between the real and monetary economies, with the real allocation the same as in section 5.3. Given binding cash-in-advance constraints, price levels are trivially given by

$$P_t^n = \frac{M_t^n}{Y_t^n} \tag{103}$$

in every country n, and exchange rates are given by purchasing power parity, eq. (92). Nominal interest rates and other asset prices are determined just as in the preceding money-in-the-utility-function model. But the model differs, unrealistically so, in its prediction of a constant velocity of money. The assumption that expected inflation can never affect money demand makes the model unsuitable for many applications.

8.7.5   The Forward Foreign-Exchange Premium

Our stochastic monetary models can be used to understand *forward* exchange pricing. So far we have only discussed *spot* exchange rates, the rates applicable to immediate trades. A T-period dollar-yen forward contract written in period t is an agreement to purchase 1 yen on date $t + T$ with a number of dollars specified on date t. The terms of exchange for the date $t + T$ transaction define the T-period forward dollar-yen exchange rate.[70]

Forward foreign-exchange markets actually are superfluous if a full range of nominal bonds is traded. If $\mathcal{E}_t$ is the spot dollar-yen exchange rate, $\mathcal{F}_t$ the one-period forward dollar-yen rate, i_{t+1} the one-period dollar nominal interest rate, and i_{t+1}^* the one-period yen nominal interest rate, then *covered interest arbitrage* at one-period horizons ensures that

$$1 + i_{t+1} = (1 + i_{t+1}^*)\frac{\mathcal{F}_t}{\mathcal{E}_t}. \tag{104}$$

Corresponding relationships hold for longer instrument maturities. Equation (104) must hold since an agent can borrow one dollar, buy $1/\mathcal{E}_t$ worth of yen, invest in

---

69. The model would work quite differently if people had to acquire money for date t purchases *before* date t uncertainty was resolved. For models in this vein, see Stockman (1980) and Svensson (1985).

70. A related instrument is the *futures* contract. Futures contracts are typically written for a specific date and traded in organized markets; their value is backed by the exchange. Forward contracts, typically intermediated by banks, may involve counterparty default risk. These institutional nuances need not concern us here. For discussion, see Hodrick (1987).

yen-denominated bonds paying $1 + i^*_{t+1}$ per bond, and then lock in a future dollar payout by selling the return forward at rate $\mathcal{F}_t$. Because this entire operation can be conducted at time t, it involves no risk (abstracting from default risk) and thus its gross payout must equal the gross cost of the initial dollar borrowing, $1 + i_{t+1}$.[71] Notice that if we leave aside transaction costs (which are indeed very, very small for large players in the foreign exchange market), then forward contracts may be thought of as a pure bet, involving zero payment until the date when the bet is settled.

8.7.5.1 Siegel's Paradox

Because forward contracts are pure bets, one of the most natural and frequently asked questions in international finance is whether the forward rate is equal to the expected value of the future spot rate. That is, does the relationship

$$\mathcal{F}_t = E_t\{\mathcal{E}_{t+1}\} \tag{105}$$

hold? The motivation underlying eq. (105) is the rather naive but superficially appealing view that if it does not hold, agents will have the possibility of earning arbitrarily large expected profits by speculating in forward foreign exchange (since it is a pure bet). Having just studied the relationship between risk and return in general equilibrium, you probably realize that this argument must be missing something. Nevertheless, it is instructive to dissect it before we bring to bear the heavy artillery of the consumption capital asset pricing model.

Continue to think of the two currencies as being the dollar and the yen. One obvious problem with the arbitrage condition (105) is that it implies that expected *dollar* profits are zero, but not necessarily expected *yen* profits. This implication follows because, in general,

$$E_t\left\{\frac{1}{\mathcal{E}_{t+1}}\right\} > \frac{1}{E_t\{\mathcal{E}_{t+1}\}}$$

as a result of Jensen's inequality $[1/(\cdot)$ is a convex function]. Thus, if eq. (105) holds, we cannot simultaneously have

$$\frac{1}{\mathcal{F}_t} = E_t\left\{\frac{1}{\mathcal{E}_{t+1}}\right\},$$

which asserts that the yen-dollar forward rate equals the expected yen-dollar exchange rate. This phenomenon is often referred to as Siegel's (1972) paradox.

---

71. In practice, covered interest arbitrage holds exactly when one looks at quotes from the same trading room, and nearly exactly across the major money-trading centers. Obviously, it need not hold when a forward rate quote is taken from a country with an open, deregulated capital market but one of the interest rates used in the comparison is quoted in a country with significant capital controls.

Crudely put, the paradox is that there can be no equilibrium if risk-neutral Japanese investors care only about yen returns and if risk-neutral U.S. investors care only about dollar returns.[72] One way to think about the size of the Jensen's inequality term behind the paradox is to take $\mathcal{E}_{t+1}$ as lognormally distributed, in which case eq. (105) in logs is

$$f_t = E_t\{e_{t+1}\} + \tfrac{1}{2}\operatorname{Var}_t(e_{t+1}).\tag{106}$$

[From the Japanese perspective, the corresponding relationship is $f_t = E_t\{e_{t+1}\} - \tfrac{1}{2}\operatorname{Var}_t(e_{t+1})$.] Much empirical work on the forward premium simply tests whether $f_t = E_t\{e_{t+1}\}$, a log specification that is preferred because its results seemingly are independent of which country's currency is used as numeraire. Simple calculations suggest that while the Jensen's inequality term may be small relative to typical exchange rate movements, it can be of the same order of magnitude as typical forward premiums. For example, if the one-year standard deviation of the log exchange rate is 0.1, or 10 percent, then the variance will be 0.01, or 1 percent. Thus, in this case, the Jensen's inequality term would be 0.5 percent, smaller than typical forward premiums but not necessarily second order.[73]

One obvious objection to the preceding discussion is that even risk-neutral investors should care about real returns and not nominal returns.[74] The condition that expected *real* returns be zero is given by

$$E_t\left\{\frac{\mathcal{F}_t - \mathcal{E}_{t+1}}{P_{t+1}}\right\} = 0.\tag{107}$$

If purchasing power parity holds, then it is easily shown that it no longer matters which country's currency is the numeraire. Substituting $\mathcal{E}_{t+1}P^*_{t+1} = P_{t+1}$ into eq. (107) and multiplying numerator and denominator by $-1/\mathcal{F}_t\mathcal{E}_{t+1}$ yields

$$E_t\left\{\frac{\frac{1}{\mathcal{F}_t} - \frac{1}{\mathcal{E}_{t+1}}}{P^*_{t+1}}\right\} = 0\tag{108}$$

(remember, $\mathcal{F}_t$ is known at time t). Thus, if PPP holds (indeed, relative PPP is sufficient), the condition for expected real profits for a U.S. consumer implies

---

72. Actually, even taken at its own terms, the paradox is misleading. Suppose there is a single risk-neutral Japanese investor who cares only about expected yen returns and a single risk-neutral U.S. investor who cares only about expected dollar returns. Assume further that there are credit constraints limiting the maximum dollar trade they can make. Then the equilibrium would involve having the quantity bound be reached, with the forward dollar-yen exchange rate ending up as a negotiated rate between $E_t\{\mathcal{E}_{t+1}\}$ and $1/E_t\{1/\mathcal{E}_{t+1}\}$. Both agents see their utility rise, but this increase simply reflects normal gains from trade for agents with different objective functions. Introducing a new risky asset into an environment with incomplete markets can raise welfare because trade is not a zero-sum game.

73. Obviously, one can devise examples where the Jensen's inequality term is large.

74. See Frenkel and Razin (1980) and Engel (1984).

that expected real profits are also zero for a Japanese consumer. [The equivalence between eqs. (107) and (108) breaks down, however, when PPP fails, either due to a failure in the law of price or due to U.S. and Japanese consumers having different consumption baskets.]

Note that despite expected real profits' being zero for both U.S. and Japanese speculators, a wedge between the forward rate and the expected future exchange rate still appears when eq. (107) is expressed in logs. Assuming that prices and exchange rates are jointly lognormally distributed, eq. (107) in log form becomes

$$f_t = E_t\{e_{t+1}\} + \tfrac{1}{2}\,\text{Var}_t(e_{t+1}) - \text{Cov}_t(e_{t+1}, p_{t+1}). \tag{109}$$

It is common in the literature for the last two right-hand-side terms to be associated with Siegel's paradox, but we have just seen that there is no paradox in this special case. Rather the higher moments enter because the true equation characterizing equilibrium is not log-linear.[75]

8.7.5.2   Empirical Tests for Prediction Bias in the Forward Rate

Naive or not, the simple hypothesis that the forward exchange rate equals the expected value of the future spot rate has been subjected to an enormous amount of empirical testing, generally using a log specification. For example, if the empirical specification is written in terms of the forward premium $f_t - e_t$ as

$$e_{t+1} - e_t = a_0 + a_1(f_t - e_t) + \epsilon_t, \tag{110}$$

then the typical forward-market "efficiency" test asks whether one can reject the null hypothesis that $a_0 = 0$, $a_1 = 1$. If the forward rate indeed embodies all information available at time t, then it should also be true that ϵ_t is serially uncorrelated. The overwhelming majority of evidence, as surveyed by Hodrick (1987), Lewis (1995), Engel (in press), and others, suggests that the log forward rate is *not* equal

---

75. Because prices move very slowly relative to exchange rates, the term $\text{Cov}_t(e_{t+1}, p_{t+1})$ tends to be very small for most countries; see Chapter 9.

To derive the last equation, write eq. (107) as

$$E_t \exp(f_t - p_{t+1}) = E_t \exp(e_{t+1} - p_{t+1}).$$

Note that $\text{Var}_t(f_t - p_{t+1}) = \text{Var}_t\, p_{t+1}$ and $\text{Var}_t(e_{t+1} - p_{t+1}) = \text{Var}_t\, e_{t+1} + \text{Var}_t\, p_{t+1} - 2\text{Cov}_t(e_{t+1}, p_{t+1})$. The usual formula for the mean of a lognormal variate (see footnote 41 in Chapter 5) therefore implies

$$E_t\{\exp(f_t - p_{t+1})\} = \exp(f_t - E_t p_{t+1} + \tfrac{1}{2}\,\text{Var}_t\, p_{t+1})$$

and

$$E_t\{\exp(e_{t+1} - p_{t+1})\} = \exp[E_t e_{t+1} - E_t p_{t+1} + \tfrac{1}{2}\,\text{Var}_t\, e_{t+1} + \tfrac{1}{2}\,\text{Var}_t\, p_{t+1} - \text{Cov}_t(e_{t+1}, p_{t+1})].$$

From this eq. (109) follows after taking logs. [Equation (106) follows upon assuming P is non-stochastic.]

to the expected value of the future log spot rate, at least for cross-exchange rates between major countries' currencies.[76]

In itself, the finding that forward rates are biased predictors would not be at all surprising if there were a (possibly time-varying) risk premium on one country's currency relative to another's.[77] What is surprising is the widespread finding that realized exchange rate changes tend to be, if anything, in the *opposite* direction to that predicted by the forward premium. That is, not only does virtually every test of eq. (110) reject the null that $a_1 = 1$, but the point estimates are often negative. Froot and Thaler (1990) point out that for 75 published estimates of eq. (110) across various exchange rates and time periods, the average point estimate of a_1 is -0.88! Only a few studies find positive point estimates of a_1, and of those, none has $a_1 > 1$.[78] If taken literally, the finding that a_1 is negative, and often significantly so, is startling. It suggests that one can make predictable profits by betting against the forward rate.

What are the implications of these findings, and what restrictions do they put on theories of the forward premium bias? Fama (1984) offers an illuminating interpretation of the problem. He shows that finding a small positive or a negative slope coefficient in eq. (110) implies that the rational expectations risk premium on foreign exchange must be extremely variable. If a_1 is estimated to be below $\frac{1}{2}$ in a large sample, then the risk premium must in fact be more variable than the expected change in the exchange rate. In addition, if a_1 is estimated to be negative in a large sample, then the covariance between the risk premium and the expected rate of change in the spot rate must be negative. To understand Fama's results, observe that the asymptotic ordinary least squares (OLS) estimate of a_1 for eq. (110) is given by

$$\text{plim}(a_1^{\text{OLS}}) = \frac{\text{Cov}(f_t - e_t, e_{t+1} - e_t)}{\text{Var}(f_t - e_t)}. \tag{111}$$

Define the risk premium rp as the bias in the (log) forward premium,

---

76. The reader should not infer that all tests for forward rate bias take the simple form of (110). For an alternative see, e.g., Cumby (1988). However, the text's representation of one standard test facilitates a useful interpretation of the results.

77. We focus on the risk-premium explanation of the bias in forward exchange rates, but there are others. Rogoff (1980) argues that in small samples, exchange-rate distributions may have fat tails, so that convergence to normality is slow. (For example, many exchange-rate regimes are characterized by relatively fixed rates over long periods with infrequent devaluations.) If the econometrican does not look at a sufficiently long period, it may appear that the forward rate is a biased predictor when it is not. See Lewis (1995) for further discussion of the evidence. Infrequent events such as wars may imply that even a thirty-year sample is insufficient to eliminate this "peso problem."
   Froot and Frankel (1990) and Engel (in press) discuss the possibility of irrational investor expectations, which of course can also explain biased prediction by forward rates.

78. More recent research has generally obtained similar findings, with the exception of rates across EMS countries prior to the system's partial collapse in 1992–93 (Lewis, 1995).

$rp_t = f_t - E_t\{e_{t+1}\},$

with the implication that

$$f_t - e_t = E_t\{e_{t+1}\} - e_t + rp_t. \tag{112}$$

Then note that under rational expectations, the difference between the expected and the realized exchange rate,

$e_{t+1} - E_t\{e_{t+1}\},$

must be uncorrelated with all variables observable on date t, including that date's forward premium. (If not, forecasters would be ignoring information that should be useful in predicting.) Because, therefore,

$E_t\{(f_t - e_t)(e_{t+1} - E_t\{e_{t+1}\})\} = 0$

under rational expectations, we can write eq. (111) as

$$\text{plim}(a_1^{\text{OLS}}) = \frac{\text{Cov}\left[f_t - e_t, E_t\{e_{t+1}\} - e_t\right]}{\text{Var}(f_t - e_t)}. \tag{113}$$

We are now ready to demonstrate Fama's two results. His claim concerning $a_1^{\text{OLS}} < 0$ follows from substituting eq. (112) for $f_t - e_t$ to write the numerator of the preceding equation as

$\text{Cov}[f_t - e_t, E_t\{e_{t+1}\} - e_t] = \text{Var}(E_t\{e_{t+1}\} - e_t) + \text{Cov}[E_t\{e_{t+1}\} - e_t, rp_t].$

Since variances are nonnegative, the right-hand side of this expression, and therefore $\text{plim}(a_1^{\text{OLS}})$, can be negative only if

$\text{Cov}(E_t\{e_{t+1}\} - e_t, rp_t) < 0.$

To obtain Fama's result on the implications of $a_1^{\text{OLS}} < \frac{1}{2}$, multiply both sides of eq. (113) by $\text{Var}(f_t - e_t)$, and again use eq. (112) to substitute out for $f_t - e_t$:

$\text{plim}(a_1^{\text{OLS}})\{\text{Var}(E_t\{e_{t+1}\} - e_t) + 2\text{Cov}[E_t\{e_{t+1}\} - e_t, rp_t] + \text{Var}(rp_t)\}$

$$= \text{Var}(E_t\{e_{t+1}\} - e_t) + \text{Cov}[E_t\{e_{t+1}\} - e_t, rp_t]. \tag{114}$$

Using eq. (114), we see that $\text{plim}(a_1^{\text{OLS}}) < \frac{1}{2}$ implies that

$\frac{1}{2}[\text{Var}(E_t\{e_{t+1}\} - e_t) + \text{Var}(rp_t)] > \text{Var}(E_t\{e_{t+1}\} - e_t),$

so that

$$\text{Var}(rp_t) > \text{Var}(E_t\{e_{t+1}\} - e_t). \tag{115}$$

Fama's condition that the risk premium must be more variable than expected future exchange changes is generally viewed as a significant challenge to attempts to model exchange risk. One must be careful, however, not to overstate the puzzle posed by inequality (115). In Chapter 9, we will show that whatever our theoretical priors, expected changes in the exchange rate are typically very small empirically for most major currencies. Indeed, it is not easy to reject the hypothesis that log exchange rates follow a random walk, in which case $\mathrm{Var}(\mathrm{E}_t\{e_{t+1}\} - e_t) = 0$. Thus the surprising fact may be that expected exchange rate changes are typically so small, not that the variance of the risk premium is so large.

8.7.5.3   The Forward Rate in General Equilibrium

Can the global general-equilibrium model developed earlier in this section be reconciled with the empirical evidence? To evaluate the consumption CAPM's implications for the risk premium, deduce from eq. (93) that the ex post return differential $r^n_{t+1} - r^m_{t+1}$ between any two assets n and m must satisfy

$$0 = \mathrm{E}_t\left\{ (r^n_{t+1} - r^m_{t+1}) \frac{u'(C_{t+1})}{u'(C_t)} \right\}, \tag{116}$$

for any individual's consumption. (The left-hand side is zero because we are comparing rates of return on investments that both cost one consumption unit on date t.)

The difference between the ex post real return on a nominal home-currency bond and that on a nominal foreign-currency bond is

$$\frac{(1 + i_{t+1})P_t}{P_{t+1}} - \frac{(1 + i^*_{t+1})P^*_t}{P^*_{t+1}}.$$

Covered interest parity, eq. (104), and PPP, eq. (92), imply that this difference equals

$$\frac{(1 + i_{t+1})P_t}{\mathcal{F}_t}\left(\frac{\mathcal{F}_t - \mathcal{E}_{t+1}}{P_{t+1}} \right).$$

Substituting this expression for $r^n_{t+1} - r^m_{t+1}$ in eq. (116) and factoring out the term $(1 + i_{t+1})P_t/\mathcal{F}_t$ (which is date t information) yields

$$0 = \mathrm{E}_t\left\{ \left(\frac{\mathcal{F}_t - \mathcal{E}_{t+1}}{P_{t+1}} \right) \frac{u'(C_{t+1})}{u'(C_t)} \right\}. \tag{117}$$

A forward position, which requires no money down in period t, must yield zero expected utility in equilibrium.

For the case of CRRA preferences, the preceding equation becomes

$$0 = \mathrm{E}_t\left\{ \left(\frac{\mathcal{F}_t - \mathcal{E}_{t+1}}{P_{t+1}} \right) \left(\frac{C_t}{C_{t+1}} \right)^\rho \right\}. \tag{118}$$

Assuming that all variables in eq. (118) are jointly lognormally distributed, this equation can be written in logarithmic form as

$$f_t - E_t\{e_{t+1}\} = \tfrac{1}{2}\operatorname{Var}_t(e_{t+1}) - \operatorname{Cov}_t(e_{t+1}, p_{t+1}) - \rho\operatorname{Cov}_t(e_{t+1}, c_{t+1}).\qquad(119)$$

This relationship follows from the same type of derivation that produced eq. (109).[79] When $\rho = 0$, the preceding expression reduces to eq. (109) (which held for risk-neutral investors who care about real returns). The first two terms on the right-hand side of eq. (119) thus come from accounting for Jensen's inequality when expressing the risk premium in logs. The last term is a true risk premium. Just as in our analysis of the equity-risk-premium puzzle in section 5.4, it is difficult to rationalize a large absolute-value risk premium because consumption simply is not that variable. Either one has to assume that agents are extremely risk averse (ρ very high) or appeal to one of the various attempts to solve the equity premium puzzle, such as habit-formation preferences.[80] For major currencies, the absolute size of the risk premium, which appears to be roughly the same as that of the forward premium itself, is typically not quite as large as the equity premium (one-year forward discounts of 5 percent or more are the exception, not the rule). But since theory has a hard time explaining even half the equity premium, this fact is cold comfort.

A further problem in understanding the foreign-exchange risk premium is that it changes sign as expected depreciation does [an implication of the empirical finding $a_1 < 0$ in the forward discount regression eq. (110)]. Sometimes the risk premium runs against a country's currency and sometimes in favor of it. To think about this relationship, note that since each country's consumption growth is proportional to world income growth with CRRA utility, we could have written eq. (118) as

$$0 = E_t\left\{\left(\frac{\mathcal{F}_t - \mathcal{E}_{t+1}}{P_{t+1}}\right)\left(\frac{Y_t^W}{Y_{t+1}^W}\right)^{\rho}\right\}$$

and eq. (119) as

$$f_t = E_t\{e_{t+1}\} + \tfrac{1}{2}\operatorname{Var}_t(e_{t+1}) - \operatorname{Cov}_t(e_{t+1}, p_{t+1}) - \rho\operatorname{Cov}_t(e_{t+1}, y_{t+1}^W).$$

The covariance term $\operatorname{Cov}_t(e_{t+1}, y_{t+1}^W)$ may well change sign over the course of the world business cycle, but no study yet has succeeded in convincingly relating the stochastic properties of national outputs to forward-premium prediction bias. Indeed no study yet has explained the results of regressions such as eq. (110) in terms of *any* coherent model of the risk premium.

---

79. Hint: Factor C_t, known as of date t, out of the equation. Then observe that the covariance between log C_{t+1} and log P_{t+1}, as well as those variables' means and variances, drops out.

80. See, for example, Sibert (1996) and Bekaert (in press).

Whatever the explanation for the forward rate's highly biased predictions, it is not the thinness of the exchange markets. The Bank for International Settlements estimates that *daily* turnover in foreign exchange markets far exceeds $1 trillion.[81]

8.7.6   Sterilized Intervention, Forward Intervention, and Portfolio-Balance Effects

We have already mentioned the mechanics of sterilized intervention. Here we take a more detailed look at the possible effects of such operations.

8.7.6.1   Forward Intervention

The net effect of a sterilized intervention is to change the ratio of home- to foreign-currency denominated bonds held by the public. An equivalent way for a government to bring about the same change is through forward market intervention. (The transaction is fully equivalent in its economic effects, but as an accounting matter a forward contract is an "off balance sheet" item that need not affect the government's books until the contract's value date.)

To see the equivalence of forward and sterilized intervention, suppose the U.S. government signs a forward contract to buy $1 + i_{t+1}$ worth of dollars with $(1 + i_{t+1})/\mathcal{F}_t$ yen on date $t + 1$. Since the counterparty to the deal becomes committed to hand the U.S. government $\$(1 + i_{t+1})$ next period, the *net* stock of dollar-denominated one-period debt held by the market falls by the present value of the amount due to the U.S. government, $1. At the same time, the U.S. government's commitment to deliver yen *raises* the net stock of yen-denominated one-period debt the market is holding on date t by the present value of the future U.S. yen payment, or

$$\frac{1}{1 + i^*_{t+1}}(1 + i_{t+1})/\mathcal{F}_t = 1/\mathcal{E}_t$$

yen, also worth $1. (We have just used covered interest parity.) The net result of the forward deal therefore is to reduce the net supply of dollar debt to the public on date t by $1 while raising the net supply of yen debt by $1. The U.S. government could effect the same outcome by a $1 sterilized purchase of dollars with yen.

Equivalently, realize that dollar bonds are claims to future dollars and yen bonds are claims to future yen. By entering the forward market to buy future dollars with future yen, a government increases the net supply of future yen to the private sector and reduces the net supply of future dollars. This is precisely what the parallel sterilized intervention does. In practice most sterilized interventions are carried out through a forward deal, which is cheaper than two separate trades in the domestic and foreign bond markets would be.

---

81. For a theory of the high turnover rate in foreign exchange markets, see Lyons (1996).

8.7.6.2   Is There a Portfolio Effect?

The standard rationale for sterilized (or forward) intervention is the *portfolio-balance effect*. The public will willingly hold a higher ratio of nominal yen to dollar debt, so the reasoning goes, only if the yen depreciates in the foreign exchange market, reducing the *real* supply of yen debt relative to that of dollar debt.[82] Governments wishing to stabilize their currencies' exchange values without altering domestic monetary policies—that is, almost all governments at some time or other—find sterilized intervention very attractive.

Our discussion of Ricardian equivalence in Chapter 3 should leave you a bit uncomfortable with the portfolio-balance effect. In fact, the partial-equilibrium reasoning behind the portfolio effect becomes plain once we take a broader view of the private sector's assets and liabilities as encompassing not only financial assets but also future net tax payments to governments. A sterilized intervention changes the currency denomination of private financial portfolios through a mirror-image change in the government's. But the private sector's net taxes ultimately will reflect the performance of the government's financial portfolio, provided government spending doesn't adjust. So the reduction in private-sector dollar risk due to a sterilized official purchase of dollars is an illusion. It doesn't matter that your portfolio exposure to the risk of a dollar movement falls if your tax exposure rises by an equivalent amount.

In a model without Ricardian equivalence, such as the stochastic overlapping generations model of section 5.6, sterilized intervention can have a portfolio effect. All the other reasons for the apparent failure of Ricardian equivalence, documented in Chapter 3, also suggest that the portfolio effect could be theoretically relevant. Nonetheless, a large body of empirical research finds very little evidence of a portfolio-balance effect on foreign exchange risk premiums.[83] The problem with the portfolio model is in some ways reminiscent of that with the standard equity-premium model set out in Chapter 5. In the latter model the equity premium depends on consumption risk, which (for industrial countries) is relatively small at the aggregate national level. In the portfolio-balance model the risk premium depends on relative outside supplies of currency-denominated debt. Global government debt levels simply change too slowly and predictably, however, to explain the size and the volatility of the exchange-rate risk premium.

8.7.6.3   Intervention Signaling

It is still possible that sterilized intervention may affect exchange rates by signaling to markets official intentions about future macroeconomic policies (see,

---

82. See Branson and Henderson (1985) for a survey of early theoretical work on portfolio-balance models and the effects of sterilized intervention.

83. See, for example, Frankel (1982). For surveys of relevant literature, see Rogoff (1984), Hodrick (1987), and Edison (1993).

for example, Dominguez and Frankel, 1993). There certainly seem to have been episodes in which sterilized interventions, when concerted among large groups of countries, have clarified governments' views on exchange rates and shifted market opinion.

From a theoretical perspective, however, it is not clear at all why sterilized intervention should be a particularly powerful or credible tool for signaling the government's intentions. Governments put some money at risk when they intervene, but the sums involved are minuscule compared to annual tax revenues. Also unclear is the reason for preferring intervention over many other possible signaling devices. In any event, governments plainly believe that sterilized intervention has its uses, for they continue to practice it despite the lack of any hard evidence that it is consistently and predictably effective.

Appendix 8A   A Two-Country Cash-in-Advance Model

In this appendix we consider a general equilibrium version of the nonstochastic cash-in-advance model from section 8.3.6. Suppose there are two countries, Home and Foreign, each specialized in its endowment of a distinct good. Representative agents from both countries have preferences described by identical lifetime utility functions, with the Home agent's given by

$$U_t = \sum_{s=t}^{\infty} \beta^{s-t} u(C_s).$$

(120)

In this expression, C is a composite real consumption index defined by the CES aggregator

$$C = \left[\gamma^{\frac{1}{\theta}} C_H^{\frac{\theta-1}{\theta}} + (1-\gamma)^{\frac{1}{\theta}} C_F^{\frac{\theta-1}{\theta}} \right]^{\frac{\theta}{\theta-1}},$$

(121)

and C_H and C_F denote Home consumption of the Home good and the Foreign good, respectively. (Recall our discussion of such preferences in section 4.4.) Foreign preferences are the same with C_H^* and C_F^* replacing C_H and C_F. The Home-currency price of the Home (Foreign) good is p_H (p_F), and the Foreign-currency price of the Home (Foreign) good is p_H^* (p_F^*). We assume that the law of one price holds so that

$$p_H = \mathcal{E} p_H^*,$$

(122)

$$p_F = \mathcal{E} p_F^*.$$

(123)

To purchase the Home (Foreign) good in period t, agents must set aside Home (Foreign) currency in $t - 1$. The cash-in-advance constraints are therefore given by

$$M_{H,t-1} \geq p_{H,t} C_{H,t},$$

(124)

$$M_{F,t-1} \geq p_{F,t}^* C_{F,t},$$

(125)

where M_H and M_F denote Home holdings of the Home and Foreign currencies. The Foreign agent's cash-in-advance constraints are given by

$$M^*_{H,t-1} \geq p_{H,t} C^*_{H,t},$$

$$M^*_{F,t-1} \geq p^*_{F,t} C^*_{F,t},$$

where M^*_H and M^*_F denote Foreign holdings of the Home and Foreign currencies.[84]

The consumption-based Home-currency price index P corresponding to the CES consumption index (121) is

$$P = \left[\gamma p_H^{1-\theta} + (1-\gamma) p_F^{1-\theta} \right]^{\frac{1}{1-\theta}}, \tag{126}$$

where P solves the problem of minimizing $p_H C_H + p_F C_F$ subject to $C = 1$ [recall eq. (20) of Chapter 4]. The Foreign-currency consumption-based price index is

$$P^* = \left[\gamma (p_H^*)^{1-\theta} + (1-\gamma) \left(p_F^* \right)^{1-\theta} \right]^{\frac{1}{1-\theta}}. \tag{127}$$

Because people in the two countries have identical preferences, eqs. (126)–(127) and (122)–(123) imply that PPP holds:

$$P = \mathcal{E} P^*.$$

We continue to assume that bonds are real, but with two goods we need to be careful to specify exactly what that assumption means. Our assumption is that bonds are denominated in units of the index of total real consumption C, as in section 4.5. Thus giving up 1 unit of C to buy a bond entitles the buyer to a payment equivalent to $1 + r$ units of C a period later.

Next consider the period budget constraints of Home and Foreign residents. With so many individual prices and indexes to keep track of, it is easiest to specify budget constraints in nominal terms. The Home individual's constraint is

$$P_t B_{t+1} + M_{H,t} + \mathcal{E}_t M_{F,t}$$

$$= P_t (1 + r_t) B_t + M_{H,t-1} + \mathcal{E}_t M_{F,t-1} + p_{H,t} Y_t - p_{H,t} C_{H,t} - p_{F,t} C_{F,t} - P_t T_t, \tag{128}$$

where we have assumed that taxes T are also indexed to the consumption basket. Notice that r is generally endogenous and carries a time subscript. The corresponding constraint for the Foreign individual, written in foreign-currency terms, is

$$P_t^* B_{t+1}^* + M_{F,t}^* + \frac{M_{H,t}^*}{\mathcal{E}_t}$$

$$= P_t^* (1 + r_t) B_t^* + M_{F,t-1}^* + \frac{M_{H,t-1}^*}{\mathcal{E}_t} + p_{F,t}^* Y_t^* - p_{H,t}^* C_{H,t}^* - p_{F,t}^* C_{F,t}^* - P_t^* T_t^*.$$

Finally, if one abstracts from Home and Foreign government spending, asset holdings, and debt issue, the two government budget constraints are

---

84. As per our basic convention in this book, subscripts generally refer to a type of good (e.g., home or foreign, traded or nontraded). Superscripts refer to the agent who produces, holds, or consumes the good. Therefore M^*_H is Foreign holdings of Home money. In earlier models money was nontraded, and we used the natural convention of M^* to denote Foreign holdings of Foreign money.

$$T_t = \frac{M_{H,t} + M^*_{H,t} - M_{H,t-1} - M^*_{H,t-1}}{P_t},$$

$$T^*_t = \frac{M_{F,t} + M^*_{F,t} - M_{F,t-1} - M^*_{F,t-1}}{P^*_t}.$$

Note that Home's government earns seignorage from Foreign holdings of its currency, and Foreign's government benefits similarly.

The first-order conditions for this model are analogous to those of the first cash-in-advance model in section 8.3.6, and are derived similarly. As long as the nominal interest rate is positive, the cash-in-advance constraints hold with equality. Use the binding cash-in-advance constraints (124) and (125) to substitute for M_H and M_F in terms of C_H and C_F in the Home budget constraint (128). Then substitute PC for $p_H C_H + p_F C_F$ in constraint (128). The maximization problem becomes exactly the same as in the small county cash-in-advance model of section 8.3.6. For $s > t$, the resulting first-order conditions are

$$\frac{P_{s-1}}{P_s} u'(C_s) = (1+r)\frac{P_s}{P_{s+1}} \beta u'(C_{s+1}), \tag{129}$$

$$C_{H,s} = \frac{\gamma}{1-\gamma}\left(\frac{p_{F,s}}{p_{H,s}}\right)^\theta C_{F,s}. \tag{130}$$

It is straightforward to calculate the steady-state equilibrium of the model when output and expected money growth in both countries are constant. Aggregating eq. (130) together with its foreign counterpart, and assuming that goods markets clear in each period, we find

$$\frac{p_H}{p_F} = \left[\frac{\gamma Y_F}{(1-\gamma)Y_H}\right]^{1/\theta}. \tag{131}$$

Similarly, the real interest rate is given by

$$r = \frac{1-\beta}{\beta}.$$

Appendix 8B   The Mechanics of Foreign-Exchange Intervention

In this appendix we present additional institutional detail on foreign-exchange intervention, including the fundamental distinction between sterilized and nonsterilized intervention.

To understand how such foreign-exchange-market interventions work, it is helpful to separate the government into two arms, one a "fiscal authority" and one a "central bank." The central bank's balance sheet furnishes a useful accounting framework illustrating how monetary policy is conducted in practice.[85]

---

85. Keep in mind that in a sense, the distinction between the monetary and fiscal authority is completely artificial. In some countries, the fiscal authority simply prints money and uses it to make government purchases or transfers. In most countries, though, there is a veil between the fiscal and money authorities. The fiscal authority issues bonds and uses the proceeds to buy goods. If the central bank were then to print money and buy up the bonds, the net result would be the same as if the fiscal authorities had printed the money themselves. After all, the central bank pays all its profits to its owner, the state.

A typical central bank holds four types of assets. First, it holds claims on foreign entities; the bulk of these consists of foreign money M_F^{cb} and foreign-currency-denominated bonds B_F^{cb} (which may or may not be issued by a foreign government). The central bank generally also holds gold. Finally, it holds claims on domestic entities, usually consisting of home-currency-denominated bonds, B_H^{cb} (which, unless stated otherwise, we will assume are issued by the domestic government). These government bonds net out, of course, in a consolidated government balance sheet. But separating out the central bank's holdings will prove convenient for analyzing the mechanics of foreign-exchange-market intervention.

The *liabilities* of the central bank include the monetary base, equal to currency plus required reserves held at the central bank, $M_H + RR$. It also includes net worth (NW), an accounting item that makes the two sides of the balance sheet equal. The net worth item can vary because the market value of the central bank's assets is subject to fluctuations.

Central Bank Balance Sheet	
Assets	Liabilities
Net foreign-currency bonds	Monetary base
Net domestic-currency bonds	Net worth
Foreign money	
Gold	

In symbols, the central bank's balance sheet identity can be expressed in nominal domestic-currency terms as

$$P^g \text{Gold}^{cb} + \mathcal{E} B_F^{cb} + B_H^{cb} + \mathcal{E} M_F^{cb} = M_H + RR + NW,$$

with P^g the nominal price of gold. Arcane central bank accounting conventions sometimes require it to use a nonmarket price for gold *valuation* (buying and selling generally is done at market prices). The difference shows up in the net worth item.

When the central bank wishes to reduce the money supply, it sells one of its assets to the public. When it wants to increase the money supply, it buys assets from the public. *Nonsterilized* foreign-exchange-market intervention is simply the case in which the bank chooses to alter the monetary base through sales and purchases of foreign money or bonds.

Another form of intervention is *sterilized intervention*. Sterilized intervention is really a combination of two transactions. First, the central bank conducts a nonsterilized intervention by (say) buying foreign-currency bonds with home currency that it issues.

A Central Bank One-Dollar Purchase
of Foreign-Currency Bonds

Central Bank Balance Sheet	
Assets	Liabilities
Foreign-currency bonds (+1)	Monetary base (+1)

Then the central bank "sterilizes" the effects on the monetary base by selling a corresponding quantity of home-currency-denominated bonds to soak up the initial home currency increase.

A Central Bank One-Dollar Sale
of Home-Currency Bonds

Central Bank Balance Sheet	
Assets	Liabilities
Home-currency bonds (-1)	Monetary base (-1)

The net effect of the two operations is the same as a swap of home- for foreign-currency bonds with no change in the money supply.

Net Effect of a One-Dollar Sterilized
Foreign-Exchange Purchase

Central Bank Balance Sheet	
Assets	Liabilities
Home-currency bonds (-1)	Monetary base $(-\!\!-)$
Foreign-currency bonds $(+1)$	

Exercises

1. *Future fixing of the exchange rate.* During the beginning of the U.S. Reagan administration in 1981, some U.S. officials seriously discussed the possibility of making a transition to a fixed exchange rate for the dollar. However, they argued that it would be presumptuous for government officials to decide the best exchange rate $\bar{\mathcal{E}}$ and that they should instead let the market decide. The policy they proposed was to announce today that at some future date (say T) they would permanently fix the exchange rate (using monetary policy) at whatever level prevailed in the market at time $T - 1$. Is this a coherent policy? You may answer using the simplest Cagan exchange rate model if you so choose. [Hint: See footnote 44.]

2. *Variants of the money-in-the-utility-function model.* Assume a small open monetary economy as in section 8.3.1, but one in which utility depends directly only on consumption and not on leisure or real money balances. Thus, eq. (33) is replaced by

$$U_t = \sum_{s=t}^{\infty} \beta^{s-t} u(C_s).$$

We capture the transactions benefits of money instead by modifying the individual's budget constraint eq. (34) so that

$$B_{t+1} + \frac{M_t}{P_t} = (1+r)B_t + \frac{M_{t-1}}{P_t} + Yg\left(\frac{M_t}{P_t}\right) - C_t - T_t,$$

where Y is assumed constant and the transactions technology satisfies $g \geq 0$, $g' > 0$, $g'' < 0$, and $\lim_{M/P \to \infty} g(M/P) = 1$.

(a) Derive the individual's first-order conditions.

(b) Assuming a constant rate of money supply growth $M_t/M_{t-1} = 1 + \mu$, and assuming no speculative bubbles, characterize the equilibrium path of the money price level P.

(c) (Hard.) Now assume a slightly different form for the transactions technology so that

$$B_{t+1} + \frac{M_t}{P_t} = (1+r)B_t + \frac{M_{t-1}}{P_t} + Y_t - \frac{X_t}{P_t} - T_t$$

and

$$P_t C_t = X_t g \left(\frac{M_t}{P_t} \right),$$

where $g(M/P)$ has the same properties as before. Here X denotes total nominal expenditure on consumption, some of which is dissipated on costs of transacting. The higher the level of real balances an agent holds, the lower the costs of transacting. Again solve for the agent's first-order conditions. [Warning: Don't expect a neat solution.]

(d) (Very hard.) In the model of parts a and b, can one rule out speculative price-level bubbles? (Assume $\mu = 0$.)

3. *Equilibrium budget constraints and consumption with money in the utility function.* This exercise explores some implications of the nontradability of money in the money-in-the-utility-function model of section 8.3. (None of the consumption functions derived in this problem is a reduced-form description of equilibrium consumption until the *equilibrium* nominal price level is substituted in. See Supplement A to this chapter for a continuous-time analysis.)

(a) Combine the private intertemporal budget constraint (38) with the government intertemporal constraint in footnote 26 to derive the economy's aggregate constraint vis-à-vis the rest of the world,

$$\sum_{s=t}^{\infty} \left(\frac{1}{1+r} \right)^{s-t} (C_s + G_s) = (1+r)B_t + \sum_{s=t}^{\infty} \left(\frac{1}{1+r} \right)^{s-t} Y_s.$$

Explain this result.

(b) How would your answer change in the presence of government asset holdings or debt?

(c) In the setup of section 8.3.3, assume that θ, the intratemporal substitution elasticity between consumption and money, is 1. Show that an alternative way to represent equilibrium optimal consumption is as

$$C_t = \frac{(1+r)B_t + \sum_{s=t}^{\infty} \left(\frac{1}{1+r} \right)^{s-t} (Y_s - G_s)}{\sum_{s=t}^{\infty} \left[\prod_{v=t+1}^{s} (1 + r_v^C) \right]^{\sigma-1} \beta^{\sigma(s-t)}},$$

where $1 + r_{t+1}^c = (1 + r)(P_t^c/P_{t+1}^c)$. [Hint: A related problem is solved in section 4.4.2. It will help to derive the intertemporal Euler equation for C, which, for $\theta = 1$, takes the form

$$C_{t+1} = (P_t^c/P_{t+1}^c)^{\sigma-1}(1 + r)^\sigma \beta^\sigma C_t,$$

in analogy to eq. (34) of Chapter 4.] What happens when $\sigma = 1$?

(d) How does the answer change if $\theta \neq 1$?

4. *Generalizing eq. (60).* Prove that eq. (60) in section 8.3.6 holds even when the real interest rate varies over time.

5. *Trending fundamentals in the target zone model (Froot and Obstfeld, 1991).* Suppose that instead of eq. (81), fundamentals follow

$$dk_{t+h} = \mu h + h^{1/2} v dz_{t+h}$$

within the zone. Show that eq. (84) is replaced by

$$G(k) = k + \eta\mu G'(k) + \frac{\eta v^2}{2} G''(k),$$

which has a solution of general form $G(k) = \eta\mu + k + b_1 \exp(\lambda_1 k) + b_2 \exp(\lambda_2 k)$. How would you now find the target zone particular solution? (This is harder.)

6. *The foreign exchange risk premium with many commodities (Engel 1992).* Let the individual's period utility function over N commodities take the form $u(C) = u[\Omega(C_1, \ldots, C_N)]$ where $\Omega(C_1, \ldots, C_N)$ is homogeneous of degree 1 and $u(\cdot)$ is twice differentiable, with $u' > 0$ and $u'' \leq 0$. Let $(p_1, \ldots, p_N)$ be the vector of domestic money prices, and define the consumption-based *money* price level P as the minimal expenditure of domestic money allowing $\Omega(C_1, \ldots, C_N) = 1$.

(a) Prove that for every good j, $\partial C/\partial C_j = p_j/P$.

(b) Show that the relationship between the ex post profit from a forward position and consumption is

$$0 = E_t \left\{ \left(\frac{\mathcal{F}_t - \mathcal{E}_{t+1}}{P_{t+1}} \right) \frac{u'(C_{t+1})}{u'(C_t)} \right\},$$

which is analogous to eq. (117) of the chapter except that P is the consumption-based money price level for a multicommodity economy.

(c) Assuming foreigners have the same consumption preferences, derive the corresponding relationship involving real forward position profits in the foreign currency, $[(1/\mathcal{F}_t) - (1/\mathcal{E}_{t+1})]/P_{t+1}^*$. Assuming risk neutrality ($u'' = 0$), is there a Siegel's paradox here?

(d) Prove that for every good j,

$$0 = E_t \left\{ \left(\frac{\mathcal{F}_t - \mathcal{E}_{t+1}}{p_{j,t+1}} \right) \frac{u_j(C_{t+1})}{u_j(C_t)} \right\},$$

where $u_j(C) \equiv u'(C)(\partial C/\partial C_j)$.

(e) Now consider a two-country, two-good version of the stochastic cash-in-advance model considered in section 8.7.4, where each country is specialized in production of a *distinct* good X or Y, $C = \Omega(C_X, C_Y) = C_X^\gamma C_Y^{1-\gamma}$, and $u'' < 0$, so that consumers are risk averse. (On this model, see Lucas, 1982.) Also, assume a perfectly pooled risk-sharing equilibrium such that the two countries Home and Foreign have equal wealths that remain equal regardless of any shocks that occur. Let M (M^*) be the random level of the Home (Foreign) money supply. Show that the equilibrium spot rate $\mathcal{E}_t$ is

$$\mathcal{E}_t = \left(\frac{1-\gamma}{\gamma}\right) \frac{M_t}{M_t^*}.$$

If money and output shocks are independently distributed, prove that the equilibrium forward rate $\mathcal{F}_t$ is

$$\mathcal{F}_t = \left(\frac{1-\gamma}{\gamma}\right) \frac{E_t\left\{1/M_{t+1}^*\right\}}{E_t\left\{1/M_{t+1}\right\}}.$$

[Hint: Use the result in part d.]

(f) Infer from the result of part e that, despite risk-averse consumers, we get the "risk-neutral" forward rate equation (107),

$$\mathcal{F}_t = \frac{E_t\left\{\mathcal{E}_{t+1}/P_{t+1}\right\}}{E_t\left\{1/P_{t+1}\right\}}.$$

Can you give an intuitive explanation for this result? Show that the preceding equation still holds when P_{t+1} is replaced by $p_{X,t+1}$, and that

$$\frac{1}{\mathcal{F}_t} = \frac{E_t\left\{(1/\mathcal{E}_{t+1})/P_{t+1}^*\right\}}{E_t\left\{1/P_{t+1}^*\right\}}$$

also holds.

7. *Time series properties of time-averaged exchange rates.* In many settings, official statistics report exchange rates in time-averaged form, for example, as monthly averages of daily exchange rates. To understand the implications of this practice, consider the following example. Without worrying about the underlying macroeconomic model, assume that the exchange rate follows a random walk

$$\mathcal{E}_t = \mathcal{E}_{t-1} + \epsilon_t,$$

where ϵ_t is a serially uncorrelated white noise disturbance term, so that $E_{t-1}\{\epsilon_t\} = 0$. Think of the time periods as being weekly, and define the two-week average exchange rate as $\tilde{\mathcal{E}}_t = \frac{1}{2}(\mathcal{E}_t + \mathcal{E}_{t-1})$

(a) Suppose one takes every other observation of the two-week average series $\tilde{\mathcal{E}}$. That is, suppose one forms the series $\tilde{\mathcal{E}}_t$, $\tilde{\mathcal{E}}_{t+2}$, $\tilde{\mathcal{E}}_{t+4}$, ... Does this biweekly average series follow a random walk, i.e., is $E_t\{\tilde{\mathcal{E}}_{t+2}\} = \tilde{\mathcal{E}}_t$?

(b) Would the same problem arise if we simply took a biweekly series consisting of every other exchange rate observation, $\mathcal{E}_t$, $\mathcal{E}_{t+2}$, $\mathcal{E}_{t+4}$, without averaging?

8.   *Time series properties of overlapping forward exchange rate prediction errors.* This exercise shows a problem that can arise when one analyzes weekly data on one-month forward rates. Assume that forward rate data are available only at two-week horizons, so that a forward contract signed in period t governs a contract that comes due in period $t + 2$. Also suppose (for the sake of the example) that the log forward rate is an unbiased and efficient predictor of the two-week hence future spot rate, so that $f_{t,2} = E_t\{e_{t+2}\}$. That is, there is no risk premium, and we will not worry about any Jensen's inequality term.

(a) Form the *weekly* series of two-week forward rate prediction errors, $f_{t,2} - e_{t+2}$. Is this series serially uncorrelated? Explain.

(b) What if one formed a series consisting only of every other observation on $f_{t,2} - e_{t+2}$. Is this series serially uncorrelated?

(c) (Harder.) Briefly, show how, using a general method of moments estimator, an econometrician might get around the problem of having to throw out every other week of data. [Hint: See Hansen and Hodrick, 1980.]

9 Nominal Price Rigidities: Empirical Facts and Basic Open-Economy Models

One of the most difficult tasks in international macroeconomics is building a bridge between the real economy and its monetary side. Chapter 8 showed that even when money prices are completely flexible, monetary policy can have a real impact through its effects on seignorage, real money holdings, the consumption-based real interest rate, or risk premiums on currency-denominated assets. But most practical-minded economists would regard these channels as being of second-order importance compared with the short-run aggregate demand shifts that monetary shocks can produce when nominal prices or wages are even somewhat rigid. Indeed, many classic issues at the center of international macroeconomics, including optimum currency areas, choice of an exchange rate regime, the real effects of disinflation, and international monetary policy coordination, would be of relatively little consequence in a flexible-price world.

This chapter begins by illustrating the compelling empirical case for incorporating nominal price rigidities into open-economy macroeconomic analysis. We then review Rudiger Dornbusch's (1976) perfect-foresight extension of the essentially static Keynesian approach to modeling nominal exchange rates due to Fleming (1962) and Mundell (1963, 1964). The best-known facet of Dornbusch's famous model is its demonstration that sticky nominal output prices can induce *overshooting* behavior in exchange rates.

On a theoretical plane, the Dornbusch overshooting model has several methodological drawbacks. The most fundamental is the model's lack of explicit choice-theoretic foundations. In particular, there are no microfoundations of aggregate supply. Thus the model cannot predict how incipient gaps between aggregate demand and output are resolved when prices are set in advance and fail to clear markets. The Dornbusch model also is ill-equipped to capture current account dynamics or the effects of government spending, as it does not account for private or government intertemporal budget constraints. Perhaps most fundamentally, the model's lack of microfoundations deprives it of any natural welfare metric by which to evaluate alternative macroeconomic policies. In Chapter 10 we try to address the problem of reconciling the realistic implications of price stickiness with more satisfactory dynamic foundations.

In an economy where monetary policy surprises can systematically affect output and relative prices, the government could have an incentive to try creating unexpected inflation, either to reduce an inefficiently high unemployment level or simply for political advantage. Such incentives create a *credibility* problem for policymakers. Rational private-sector actors will build their inflationary expectations into price- and wage-setting decisions, thereby putting the government in the position of choosing between accommodative monetary policy and a slump. Since government promises to allow a slump often aren't credible, an upward wage-price-money supply spiral can result.

A number of actual episodes suggest that this type of inflation trap is more than a theoretical possibility. We will model the problem formally, explore its bearing on exchange-rate policy and on the theory of speculative currency crises, and ask whether institutional or other mechanisms can help governments maintain monetary policy credibility.

9.1   Sticky Domestic Goods Prices and Exchange Rates

Domestic macroeconomists have endlessly debated whether actual economies can usefully be characterized by flexible-price models. Much of the debate is over aesthetics: it is difficult to find a single compelling theoretical story that convincingly explains why nominal price adjustment appears sluggish in practice. Indeed, largely because of theoretical difficulties, the fashion for some time among some closed-economy macroeconomists has been to ignore price rigidities altogether. For anyone who looks even casually at international data, however, the idea that nominal price rigidities are irrelevant seems difficult to sustain. Figure 9.1 graphs the log Deutsche mark-dollar exchange rate against the log difference between German and U.S. consumer price indexes. A glance at the diagram, which is extremely typical for countries with floating currencies and open capital markets, shows that exchange rates are an order of magnitude more volatile than CPIs. (Figure 9.2, which graphs first differences in the two series, makes the point even more dramatically.) An immediate corollary of this result is that the short-run volatility of real exchange rates is very similar to that of nominal exchange rates. This striking empirical regularity is totally at odds with the monetary model of Chapter 8 except when most significant shocks buffeting the economy are real.

It is highly implausible, however, that most of the variability in real exchange rates is attributable to real shocks. Contradicting this view most strikingly is the fact that real exchange rates are always much less volatile when nominal exchange rates are fixed than when they are floating. This point has been forcefully documented by Mussa (1986), who compared real exchange-rate volatility under fixed and floating rates across a broad range of industrial-country pairings. Invariably, he found that volatility is dramatically higher under floating rates.[1] Skeptics might argue that the choice of exchange-rate regime is endogenous, and countries experiencing episodes of large real (that is, goods-market) shocks will switch to floating. It is true that the standard literature on choice of exchange-rate regimes prescribes floating rates when real shocks dominate and prescribes fixed rates when monetary and financial shocks dominate (see section 9.4.1). But Mussa found that the phenomenon is universal across numerous episodes of switches between fixed and

---

1. Mussa's finding has been confirmed in other studies, including Baxter and Stockman (1989) and Flood and Rose (1995).

Figure 9.1
Germany and the United States, exchange rate and prices

flexible rates, including some switches that seem clearly exogenous. It is also remarkable that a rise in real exchange-rate volatility tends to occur immediately upon a switch from fixed to floating rates, while a volatility decline occurs immediately upon the reverse switch.

Figure 9.3, which shows the nominal and real lira–French franc exchange rates, is illustrative. During the Bretton Woods period through December 1971 and the realignment-free EMS period from January 1987 until September 1992, the nominal exchange rate was relatively fixed. Over these periods, real exchange rate volatility was fairly low. During periods when the relative value of the two currencies was not effectively fixed (the early 1970s through 1987, and after September 1992), real exchange-rate movements were much more volatile and short-run real changes virtually mirrored short-run nominal exchange-rate changes. When the lira was forced to leave the EMS in September 1992, its real and nominal exchange rates moved sharply upward in tandem. The parallel movement of real and nominal exchange rates also characterizes the three Bretton Woods realignments (two at the end of the 1950s, the last a decade later) that preceded the general Smithsonian realignment at the end of 1971. Plainly the choice of exchange-rate regime can have important effects on at least one real variable.[2]

---

2. It is not as easy to document the effects of choice of exchange-rate regime on other real variables, such as output, the trade balances, and interest rates. Baxter and Stockman (1989) and Flood and Rose (1995) argue that in fact the choice of exchange-rate regime affects *only* the real exchange rate. Given the relatively small sample periods available, the considerable measurement error in data on variables such as GNP, and econometric problems (such as how to deal with unit roots and detrending), the

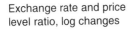

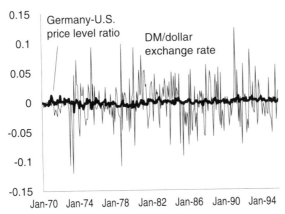

Figure 9.2
Germany and the United States, exchange rate and price changes

At the microeconomic level, an impact of exchange-rate volatility on the inter-country relative prices of similar commodities has been extensively documented. Many studies find that deviations from the law of one price are highly correlated with nominal exchange-rate changes.[3] Engel (1993) compares U.S. with Canadian consumer price data for a large variety of goods including fuel, men's clothing, and apples. In more than 2,000 pairwise comparisons, Engel finds that with only a few exceptions, the relative prices of *similar* goods across the United States and Canada are more volatile than the relative prices of *dissimilar* goods within either country. These findings are reinforced in Engel and Rogers (1995), who extend the comparisons to 23 American and Canadian cities. Even after controlling for dis-tance between two cities, they find an enormous "border effect" on volatility.[4] For example, the volatility of relative prices for very similar consumer goods appears to be much greater between closely neighboring American and Canadian city pairs such as Buffalo and Toronto or Seattle and Vancouver, than between cities such as New York and Los Angeles, which lie on opposite sides of the North American continent but within the same country.

This evidence motivates a look at a classic sticky-price extension of the flexible-price monetary model of Chapter 8.

---

issue remains controversial. We will argue in section 9.3.3 that the choice of exchange-rate regime had dramatic consequences for the international transmission of the Great Depression of the 1930s.

3. See, for example, Isard (1977) and Giovannini (1988).

4. For surveys of evidence on deviations from the law of one price, see Froot and Rogoff (1995) and Rogoff (1996).

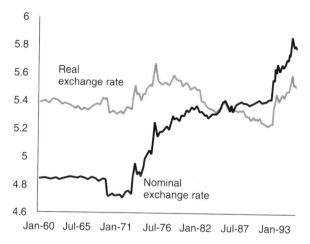

Log real and nominal
lira/franc exchange rates

Figure 9.3
France and Italy, exchange rate and prices (liras/franc, natural logarithms)

9.2   The Mundell-Fleming-Dornbusch Model

Since the early 1960s, the dominant policy paradigm for studying open-economy monetary and fiscal policy issues has been the Keynesian framework developed by Mundell (1963, 1964) and Fleming (1962). This section presents a variant of Dornbusch's (1976) famous perfect-foresight extension of the Mundell-Fleming model. As we have already noted, Dornbusch's model has important deficiencies, including its inability to deal adequately with current-account and fiscal-policy dynamics or, more fundamentally, with welfare issues. Nevertheless, the model remains so influential as to warrant discussion in any serious treatment of international monetary theory. Nothing here is essential for understanding the more complete models of Chapter 10. The Dornbusch setup will, however, help the reader frame many of the basic questions in international monetary economics and give perspective on some of the newer developments in the area.

9.2.1   A Small-Open-Economy Model with Sticky Prices and Endogenous Output

The Dornbusch model includes some of the same building blocks as the Cagan-type monetary models we discussed in Chapter 8. A small country faces an exogenous world (foreign-currency) interest rate i^*, which is assumed constant. With open capital markets and perfect foresight, uncovered interest parity must hold:

$$i_{t+1} = i^* + e_{t+1} - e_t. \tag{1}$$

[As in Chapter 8, $i_{t+1} = \log(1 + i_{t+1})$ is the logarithm of the gross domestic nominal interest rate between periods t and $t + 1$, $i^* = \log(1 + i^*)$, and e is the logarithm of the exchange rate, defined as the domestic price of foreign currency.][5] As in the basic monetary model of Chapter 8, only domestic residents hold the domestic money, and domestic monetary equilibrium is characterized by the Cagan-type aggregate relationship

$$m_t - p_t = -\eta i_{t+1} + \phi y_t, \tag{2}$$

where m is the log of the nominal money supply, p is the log of the domestic-currency price level, and y is the log of domestic output.

Let p^* be the (log of the) foreign price level measured in foreign currency. The model assumes that purchasing power parity (PPP) need not hold, so that the (log) real exchange rate, $e + p^* - p \equiv \log(\mathcal{E}P^*/P)$, can vary. Here we take the domestic consumption basket as numeraire and define the real exchange rate as the relative price of the foreign consumption basket. (See Chapter 4 for a discussion of real exchange rates. As in that chapter, we refer to a rise in $\mathcal{E}P^*$ relative to P as a home real depreciation or, alternatively, as a real depreciation of the home currency. A fall in $\mathcal{E}P^*$ relative to P is a real appreciation for the home country.)

The Dornbusch model effectively aggregates all domestic output as a single composite commodity and assumes that aggregate demand for home-country output, y^d, is an increasing function of the home real exchange rate $e + p^* - p$:

$$y_t^d = \bar{y} + \delta(e_t + p^* - p_t - \bar{q}), \qquad \delta > 0. \tag{3}$$

(We hold p^* constant throughout.) Interpret the constant $\bar{y}$ in eq. (3) as the "natural" rate of output. If we denote the real exchange rate by

$$q \equiv e + p^* - p, \tag{4}$$

then we can interpret $\bar{q}$ in eq. (3) as the *equilibrium* real exchange rate consistent with full employment. For simplicity, we usually assume both $\bar{y}$ and $\bar{q}$ to be constant.

The assumption in eq. (3) that a rise in the foreign price level relative to that in the home country (a rise in $e + p^*$ relative to p) shifts world demand toward home-produced goods could be justified through several mechanisms. Mundell, Fleming, and Dornbusch assume that the home country has monopoly power over the tradables it produces (despite its smallness in asset markets) and that home-produced tradables have a greater CPI weight at home than abroad. Real depreciation might

---

5. When Mundell and Fleming wrote, macroeconomists had not yet applied methods for handling rational expectations. In their principal models, Mundell and Fleming basically assumed static exchange rate expectations by requiring that $i_t = i^*$ under perfect capital mobility. Equation (1) plays a central role in Dornbusch's (1976) extension of the Mundell-Fleming model.

also increase demand for home goods by shifting domestic spending from foreign tradables to domestic nontradables.

Positing an aggregate demand function such as eq. (3) without deriving it from underlying microfoundations constitutes a sharp methodological departure from the approach we have generally adopted in most other parts of this book. However, like the Cagan and Solow models of earlier chapters, the Dornbusch model yields some important insights that survive more careful derivation. Chapter 10 will model the demand side in more detail.

Although asset markets clear at every moment as in the models of Chapter 8, output markets need not in the Dornbusch model. If goods prices were fully flexible, as in the models of Chapter 8, output would always equal its natural level, so that $y_t^d = y_t = \bar{y}$, and thus q would always equal $\bar{q}$. As we have already seen, the assumption of flexible prices is quite unrealistic. In practice, nominal goods prices adjust much more slowly than exchange rates. In the Dornbusch model, the empirical reality of sticky prices is captured by assuming that p is *predetermined*, and responds only slowly to shocks.

If the price level cannot move immediately to clear markets, however, then unanticipated shocks plainly can lead to excess demand or supply. In the absence of market clearing, one must make some kind of assumption about how the actual level of output is determined. Here we will follow Keynesian tradition and simply assume that output is demand determined, so that $y_t = y_t^d$. For the moment, we are not able to offer any justification for this assumption, and we will leave all details of aggregate supply in the background. Fortunately, it will be possible to give a much more satisfactory treatment once we have introduced microfoundations for aggregate supply in Chapter 10.[6]

Although p_t is predetermined and cannot respond instantly to date t shocks, it does adjust slowly over time in response to excess demand. Specifically, the price level adjusts according to the inflation-expectations-augmented Phillips curve

$$p_{t+1} - p_t = \psi(y_t^d - \bar{y}) + (\tilde{p}_{t+1} - \tilde{p}_t), \tag{5}$$

where

$$\tilde{p}_t \equiv e_t + p_t^* - \bar{q}_t$$

is the price level that would prevail if the output market cleared (*given* e_t, p_t^*, and $\bar{q}_t$). Intuitively, the first term on the right-hand side of eq. (5) embodies the price inflation caused by date t excess demand, while the second term provides for the price-level adjustment needed to keep up with *expected* inflation or productivity

---

6. A model with implications very similar to those of the Dornbusch model introduces a labor market and assumes that it is the nominal wage, rather than the price level, that is predetermined. (See, for example, Obstfeld, 1985, or Rogoff, 1985a.) Qualitatively similar results also follow from a variant of the model in which some prices are temporarily rigid while others are fully flexible.

growth. That is, the second term captures the movement in prices that would be needed to keep $y = \bar{y}$ if the output market were in equilibrium.[7] Differencing the definition of $\tilde{p}_t$ gives

$$\tilde{p}_{t+1} - \tilde{p}_t = (e_{t+1} + p^*_{t+1} - \bar{q}_{t+1}) - (e_t + p^*_t - \bar{q}_t).$$

Substituting this expression into eq. (5), and recalling that p^* and $\bar{q}$ are assumed constant, we find

$$p_{t+1} - p_t = \psi(y^d_t - \bar{y}) + e_{t+1} - e_t. \tag{6}$$

This completes our description of the Dornbusch model.

9.2.2 Graphical Solution of the Dornbusch Model

To solve the model, we begin by using eqs. (3) and (4) to express eq. (6) as

$$\Delta q_{t+1} = q_{t+1} - q_t = -\psi\delta(q_t - \bar{q}). \tag{7}$$

We will assume $1 > \psi\delta$, which ensures that shocks to the real exchange rate damp out monotonically over time. Next, we substitute eqs. (1), (3), and (4) into eq. (2). Together with the simplifying normalizations $p^* = \bar{y} = i^* = 0$, this step yields

$$m_t - e_t + q_t = -\eta(e_{t+1} - e_t) + \phi\delta(q_t - \bar{q}) \tag{8}$$

or

$$\Delta e_{t+1} = e_{t+1} - e_t = \frac{e_t}{\eta} - \frac{(1 - \phi\delta)q_t}{\eta} - \left(\frac{\phi\delta\bar{q} + m_t}{\eta}\right). \tag{9}$$

Equations (7) and (9) constitute a system of two first-order difference equations in q and e. It is not difficult to solve them analytically (see Supplement C to Chapter 2), but it is instructive to consider first the simple phase diagram in Figure 9.4, which is drawn under the assumption that m_t is constant at $\bar{m}$. Under eq. (7), the $\Delta q = 0$ schedule is vertical at $q = \bar{q}$. Thus the speed of anticipated real adjustment is independent of nominal factors. The $\Delta e = 0$ schedule has vertical-axis intercept $\phi\delta\bar{q} + \bar{m}$, and it is upward-sloping as drawn provided $1 > \phi\delta$, a condition we provisionally assume. (Note that the slope must be below 45 degrees.) The steady-state pair $(\bar{q}, \bar{e})$ lies at the intersection of the two curves. It follows from eq. (8) that

$$\bar{e} = \bar{m} + \bar{q}, \tag{10}$$

which, using the definition of q [eq. (4)], implies $\bar{p} = \bar{m}$ (recall that $p^* = 0$).[8]

---

7. There are several ways to allow for price-level adjustment in the Dornbusch model, and eq. (5) is based on Mussa (1982). The original Dornbusch (1976) model was designed only to analyze one-time shocks, and is not general enough to allow for anticipated disturbances; see Frankel (1979), Mussa (1982, 1984), Obstfeld and Rogoff (1984), and Obstfeld and Stockman (1985).

8. The solution for $\bar{e}$ follows because in the steady state, $q = \bar{q}$, $m = \bar{m}$, and $e_{t+1} = e_t$.

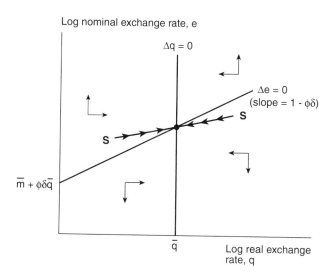

Figure 9.4
The Dornbusch model

Figure 9.4 also describes the system's dynamics away from the steady state. The dynamic arrows show that the Dornbusch model has the saddle-path property familiar from earlier chapters. That is, along all paths beginning anywhere but along the upward-sloping saddle path, **SS**, the exchange rate will eventually implode or explode. Since we did not derive the money demand function (2) from microfoundations, there is no way to argue rigorously that the economy is constrained to be on **SS**. One can, however, appeal to the close analogy between this model and the maximizing models of Chapter 8, and to the fact that the no-bubbles path is the only one that tightly links prices to fundamentals.

Now let's consider the time-honored thought experiment of an unanticipated permanent rise in the money supply from $\bar{m}$ to $\bar{m}'$. In the long run, of course, both the exchange rate e and the price level p must increase in proportion to the change in the money supply,

$$\bar{p}' - \bar{p} = \bar{e}' - \bar{e} = \bar{m}' - \bar{m},$$

as is easily shown using eqs. (7) and (9); the long-run interest rate remains i^*. In the short run, however, the price level p is predetermined and cannot respond to the unanticipated money change. Assuming that the economy initially occupies the steady-state equilibrium corresponding to $m_t = \bar{m}$ for all t, then, on initial date 0,

$$p_0 = \bar{m}, \tag{11}$$

which implies that

$$q_0 = e_0 - \bar{m}. \tag{12}$$

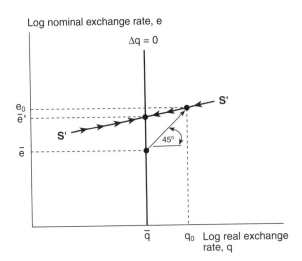

Figure 9.5
Exchange rate overshooting

The economy's immediate response to the unanticipated money shock and its transition to the new steady state are graphed in Figure 9.5. The new saddle path $S'S'$ passes through the new steady state $(\bar{q}, \bar{m}' + \bar{q})$. The 45° arrow in the figure is the initial condition described by eq. (12), which has a slope of unity. (Note that the slope of the saddle path $S'S'$ must be less than unity since it is shallower than the $\Delta e = 0$ schedule, which itself has slope less than one.) Thus, in response to the unanticipated money supply increase, the economy initially jumps to point (q_0, e_0) at the intersection of the new (post-shock) saddle path and the initial condition (12). Note the $e_0 > \bar{e}'$. That is, the exchange rate initially changes *more than proportionately* to the money shock.

This is Dornbusch's celebrated "overshooting" result. One reason it captured the imagination of many international economists and policymakers was its implication that the surprising volatility of floating exchange rates might be consistent with rational expectations. The 1970s were years of monetary instability throughout the industrialized world. If volatile money supplies had amplified effects on exchange rates, Dornbusch reasoned, they might be substantially responsible for the sharp exchange-rate fluctuations observed after the onset of floating in 1973.

The intuition underlying Dornbusch's overshooting result is easily seen by referring to the money demand equation (2), rewritten here:

$$m_t - p_t = -\eta i_{t+1} + \phi y_t.$$

The increase in m causes an increase in real money balances of $\bar{m}' - \bar{m}$, since p is initially fixed. Suppose the exchange rate jumped immediately to its new steady state. Then eq. (3) implies that output would rise (on impact) by $\delta(\bar{m}' - \bar{m})$;

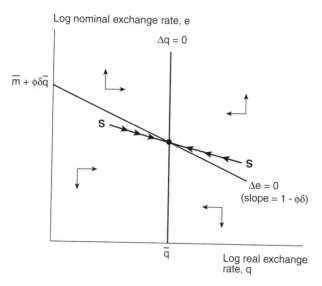

Figure 9.6
Exchange rate undershooting

money demand would thus rise by $\phi\delta(\bar{m}' - \bar{m})$. If, as we assumed in drawing Figures 9.4 and 9.5, $\phi\delta < 1$, then the rise in money demand is less than the rise in money supply. Thus, the home nominal interest rate i must fall below i^* to restore money-market equilibrium. This conclusion contradicts our initial supposition that e jumps immediately to its new steady state, for $i < i^*$ implies an expected *fall* in e, by interest parity equation (1). What does happen? By the preceding logic, the exchange rate cannot rise in the short run by *less* than $\bar{m}' - \bar{m}$. There would again have to be a fall in i, and therefore an expected appreciation—an impossibility, for then the exchange rate would be traveling away from rather than toward its steady state. The only possibility, when $\phi\delta < 1$, is for the currency initially to *overshoot* its long-run level. In the short-run equilibrium i still falls, but future appreciation is a rational expectation if the initial exchange rate e_0 is above its eventual steady state $\bar{e}'$.[9]

The preceding discussion suggests that overshooting will not necessarily occur if output responds sharply to exchange rate depreciation (δ is large) and if the income elasticity of money demand, ϕ, is large. Figure 9.6 graphs the case $\phi\delta > 1$, in which the $\Delta e = 0$ schedule is downward sloping. The saddle path SS now has a negative slope, as the arrows of motion show. An unanticipated permanent rise in the money supply therefore makes the exchange rate e rise less than proportionately to the money-supply increase. (The postshock exchange

---

9. Uncovered interest parity is an ex ante relationship that need not hold ex post if there are unanticipated shocks. Since we are allowing for an unanticipated shock at time 0, uncovered interest parity places no constraint on the initial movement in e_0.

rate e_0 lies below the new long-run rate $\bar{e}'$.) Notice that, regardless of whether the exchange rate undershoots or overshoots, the dynamics of the real exchange rate and output are qualitatively the same. The nominal depreciation of domestic currency implies a real depreciation (since prices are sticky). This real depreciation raises aggregate demand, so output rises temporarily above its steady-state value $\bar{y}$.

9.2.3   Analytical Solution of the Dornbusch Model

We have illustrated the main ideas of the Dornbusch model graphically. For completeness, however, we now show the model's analytical solution. Our approach to solving the model exploits its recursive structure.

Given any date t deviation of the real exchange rate from its long-run value, the solution to eq. (7) [rewritten as $q_{t+1} - \bar{q} = (1 - \psi\delta)(q_t - \bar{q})$] is

$$q_s - \bar{q} = (1 - \psi\delta)^{s-t}(q_t - \bar{q}), \qquad s \geq t. \tag{13}$$

(Recall that we have assumed $1 - \psi\delta > 0$.)[10] Having solved for the path of the real exchange rate (as a function of q_t), we can derive the path of the nominal exchange rate e with relative ease. For an exogenously given path of q, eq. (9) can be viewed as a first-order difference equation virtually identical to the Cagan model of Chapter 8, and it is solved similarly. Solving eq. (9) for e_t, and then subtracting $\bar{q}$ from both sides, yields

$$e_t - \bar{q} = \frac{\eta}{1 + \eta}(e_{t+1} - \bar{q}) + \frac{1 - \phi\delta}{1 + \eta}(q_t - \bar{q}) + \frac{m_t}{1 + \eta}.$$

By iterative forward substitution for $e_s - \bar{q}$, one obtains

$$e_t - \bar{q} = \frac{1}{1 + \eta}\sum_{s=t}^{\infty}\left(\frac{\eta}{1 + \eta}\right)^{s-t}m_s + \frac{1 - \phi\delta}{1 + \eta}\sum_{s=t}^{\infty}\left(\frac{\eta}{1 + \eta}\right)^{s-t}(q_s - \bar{q}) \tag{14}$$

after eliminating speculative bubbles by imposing the condition

$$\lim_{T \to \infty}\left(\frac{\eta}{1 + \eta}\right)^{T}e_{t+T} = 0.$$

If the money supply is constant at $\bar{m}$ as is assumed in the figures, eq. (14) reduces to

$$e_t - \bar{q} = \bar{m} + \frac{1 - \phi\delta}{1 + \eta}\sum_{s=t}^{\infty}\left(\frac{\eta}{1 + \eta}\right)^{s-t}(q_s - \bar{q}). \tag{15}$$

To evaluate eq. (15), we substitute for $q_s - \bar{q}$ using eq. (13) to get

---

10. See Supplement C to Chapter 2.

$$e_t - \bar{q} = \bar{m} + \frac{1 - \phi\delta}{1 + \eta}(q_t - \bar{q})\sum_{s=t}^{\infty}(1 - \psi\delta)^{s-t}\left(\frac{\eta}{1 + \eta}\right)^{s-t},$$

which simplifies to the equation for the saddle path **SS**,

$$e_t = \bar{m} + \bar{q} + \frac{1 - \phi\delta}{1 + \psi\delta\eta}(q_t - \bar{q}). \tag{16}$$

Notice that we constrained the economy to lie on the saddle path by imposing the no-speculative-bubbles condition following eq. (14). Also note that the slope of the saddle path depends on $1 - \phi\delta$, as demonstrated in the earlier diagrammatic analysis.

We can now solve analytically for the initial jumps in the real and nominal exchange rate that occur if the economy is at a steady state on initial date 0 when an unanticipated permanent increase in the money supply from $\bar{m}$ to $\bar{m}'$ occurs. The (postshock) date 0 real exchange rate, q_0, is found by combining the initial condition (12) (which embodies the assumption that $p_0 = \bar{m}$ is predetermined) together with saddle-path equation (16) (putting $\bar{m}'$ in place of $\bar{m}$, and setting $t = 0$). The second equilibrium condition embodies the assumption that the economy jumps immediately to the new, *postshock*, saddle path. The result is

$$q_0 = \bar{q} + \frac{1 + \psi\delta\eta}{\phi\delta + \psi\delta\eta}(\bar{m}' - \bar{m}).$$

Since, by eq. (12), $e_0 = q_0 + \bar{m}$,

$$e_0 = \bar{m} + \bar{q} + \frac{1 + \psi\delta\eta}{\phi\delta + \psi\delta\eta}(\bar{m}' - \bar{m}). \tag{17}$$

We see that the nominal exchange rate overshoots its new long-run equilibrium if $1 > \phi\delta$. Finally, to obtain the nominal exchange rate's transition path leading to the new long-run equilibrium, we combine the equation preceding eq. (17) with eqs. (13) and (16) to obtain

$$e_t = \bar{m}' + \bar{q} + (1 - \psi\delta)^t\left[\frac{1 - \phi\delta}{\phi\delta + \psi\delta\eta}(\bar{m}' - \bar{m})\right].$$

Can *real* shocks also lead to overshooting? Suppose that at time 0, there is an unanticipated fall in $\bar{q}$ to $\bar{q}'$. What is the adjustment process? The answer, as one can most easily deduce by comparing the steady-state relationship (10) and the initial condition (12), is that the domestic currency appreciates immediately to its new long-run level, $\bar{m} + \bar{q}'$, and the economy immediately goes to the new steady state.[11] The reason is that the required adjustment in the *real* exchange rate can be

---

11. That is, eqs. (7) and (9) will continue to hold with $\Delta q_{t+1} = \Delta e_{t+1} = 0$ if e_{t+1}, e_t, q_t, and $\bar{q}$ all change by the same amount $\bar{q}' - \bar{q}$.

accommodated in equilibrium entirely by a change in the *nominal* rate. It therefore does not necessitate any change in the long-run price level.

9.2.4   More General Money-Supply Processes

Our analysis has focused on one-time permanent increases in the money supply, but it is straightforward to extend the model to allow for temporary money-supply increases. Indeed, we have already done most of the work needed to solve the general case. Using eq. (13) once again to simplify the second summation term in eq. (14) yields

$$e_t - \bar{q} = \frac{1}{1+\eta} \sum_{s=t}^{\infty} \left(\frac{\eta}{1+\eta} \right)^{s-t} m_s + \frac{1-\phi\delta}{1+\psi\delta\eta}(q_t - \bar{q})$$

or

$$e_t - e_t^{flex} = \frac{1-\phi\delta}{1+\psi\delta\eta}(q_t - \bar{q}), \tag{18}$$

where

$$e_t^{flex} \equiv \bar{q} + \frac{1}{1+\eta} \sum_{s=t}^{\infty} \left(\frac{\eta}{1+\eta} \right)^{s-t} m_s = \bar{q} + p_t^{flex}. \tag{19}$$

One can interpret e_t^{flex} and p_t^{flex} as the exchange rate and price level that would obtain if output prices were perfectly flexible (in which case q_t would equal $\bar{q}$).[12] Instead of thinking of a one-time unanticipated change in the money supply, consider a date 0 change in the (perhaps very general) money supply process that (unexpectedly) changes e_t^{flex} and p_t^{flex} to $(e_t^{flex})'$ and $(p_t^{flex})'$ respectively, where $(e_t^{flex})' - e_t^{flex} = (p_t^{flex})' - p_t^{flex}$, since money shocks don't affect the real exchange rate when prices are flexible. We assume $p_0 = p_0^{flex}$. Then it is straightforward to use eq. (18) together with a generalized version of the initial condition (12),

$$q_0 = e_0 - p_0^{flex},$$

and eq. (19) to obtain

$$e_0 - e_0^{flex} = \frac{1+\psi\delta\eta}{\phi\delta+\psi\delta\eta}[(e_0^{flex})' - e_0^{flex}]. \tag{20}$$

[Compare eq. (20) with eq. (17) for the case of a permanent increase in the money supply, remembering that e_0^{flex} changes one-for-one with $\bar{q}$.] Finally, eqs. (13), (18), and (20) imply

---

12. Notice that $\tilde{p}_t$ defined just after eq. (5), differs from p_t^{flex} in being the hypothetical price level that would clear the output market at the *current* (possibly disequilibrium) nominal exchange rate, not, as in eq. (19), at the flexible-price nominal exchange rate e_t^{flex}. Indeed p_t^{flex} is precisely the equilibrium price level we derived in the flexible-price Cagan model [see eq. (9) in Chapter 8].

$$e_t - (e_t^{flex})' = (1 - \psi\delta)^t [e_0 - (e_0^{flex})']. \tag{21}$$

Assuming that $1 > \phi\delta$, eq. (20) implies that any date 0 disturbance that causes an unanticipated rise in e_0^{flex} will cause an even larger unanticipated rise in e_0. With very general money supply processes, it is no longer meaningful to talk about overshooting with respect to a fixed long-run equilibrium nominal exchange rate. But one can say that the *impact* exchange-rate effect of a monetary shock is greater when prices are sticky than when they are flexible. Thus price stickiness affects the conditional variance of the exchange rate. Equation (21) says the exchange rate converges to its (moving) flexible-price equilibrium value after a shock at a rate given by $\psi\delta$.

So far, our entire analysis has been for the perfect-foresight case, augmented by one-time unanticipated shocks. Because the model is (log) linear, however, it is straightforward to generalize it to the case where the money supply is explicitly stochastic, much along the lines of the log-linear models we considered in earlier chapters.[13] We leave this as an exercise.

9.2.5   Money Shocks, Nominal Interest Rates, and Real Interest Rates

Perhaps the most important insight gained by introducing more general money-supply processes concerns the different patterns of exchange-rate correlation with real and nominal interest rates.[14] In the simplest version of the Dornbusch model, in which there are only permanent unanticipated changes in the level of the money supply, lower nominal interest rates on a currency are associated with depreciation. In the flexible-price models of Chapter 8, however, we found that shocks to the *growth rate* of the money supply lead to the opposite correlation: increases in the nominal interest rate are associated with currency depreciation. When there is a money-supply growth-rate shock, which effect dominates?

Unlike money-supply-level shocks, growth-rate shocks lead to a positive correlation between nominal interest rates and exchange rates in the Dornbusch model. Suppose that the money supply is initially governed by the process

$$m_t = \bar{m} + \mu t$$

and that the economy is in a steady state (i.e., has converged to the long-run flexible-price equilibrium). The nominal interest rate in this steady state must be $i^* + \mu$. Then, at time 0, there is an unanticipated rise in the expected *future* money growth rate from μ to μ' so that

---

13. See, for example, Mussa (1982, 1984).

14. Frankel (1979), in a classic paper, stressed the importance of distinguishing between real and nominal interest rates in empirical exchange-rate modeling. Frankel's paper was the first serious effort to implement the Dornbusch model empirically.

$$m_t = \bar{m} + \mu' t, \quad \forall t \geq 0.$$

It is easy to confirm that the flex-price exchange rate depreciates immediately by

$$(e_0^{flex})' - e_0^{flex} = \eta(\mu' - \mu), \tag{22}$$

because the expected future rate of depreciation under flexible prices rises from μ to μ'. Assuming there is overshooting, the actual exchange rate e_0 rises even more than e_0^{flex}, as we saw in eq. (20).

Solving for the impact effect on the nominal interest rate is trickier. We calculate the new path of the nominal interest rate (for all $t \geq 0$) to be

$$i_{t+1} = i^* + e_{t+1} - e_t = i^* + (e_{t+1}^{flex})' - (e_t^{flex})' - \psi\delta(1 - \psi\delta)^t[e_0 - (e_0^{flex})']$$

using eqs. (1) and (21).[15] Since $(e_{t+1}^{flex})' - (e_t^{flex})' = \mu'$, the change in the nominal interest rate's path is

$$i_{t+1} - (i^* + \mu) = (\mu' - \mu) - \psi\delta(1 - \psi\delta)^t[e_0 - (e_0^{flex})']. \tag{23}$$

There are two countervailing effects in eq. (23). A permanent rise in the money growth rate from μ to μ' implies an equal rise in the trend rate of depreciation. But the remaining term on the right-hand side of eq. (23) is negative in the overshooting case. In the long run, the rise in trend depreciation clearly dominates, but is this necessarily the case in the short run? The answer is yes. Solve eq. (20) for $e_0 - (e_0^{flex})'$ and combine the result with eqs. (22) and (23) (for $t = 0$) to derive the impact change in the nominal interest rate, $i_1 - (i^* + \mu)$:

$$(\mu' - \mu) - \psi\delta\eta\left(\frac{1 - \phi\delta}{\phi\delta + \psi\delta\eta}\right)(\mu' - \mu) = \phi\delta\left(\frac{1 + \psi\delta\eta}{\phi\delta + \psi\delta\eta}\right)(\mu' - \mu).$$

Since $\mu' - \mu > 0$, the correlation between i and e induced by one-shot money-supply growth-rate shocks is unambiguously positive. This result stands in contrast to the correlation induced by one-shot changes in money-supply levels.

Although the correlation between nominal exchange rates and interest rates is ambiguous when money shocks are dominant, the Dornbusch model does offer a strong and clear prediction about the correlation between *real* exchange rates and *real* interest rates when the long-run real exchange rate, $\bar{q}$, is constant. Indeed, in our formulation that correlation is embodied in the price level adjustment mechanism, eq. (6). Defining the real interest rate as $i_{t+1} - (p_{t+1} - p_t)$, we normalize $i^* = 0$ and use eqs. (1), (3), and (6) to express it as

$$i_{t+1} - (p_{t+1} - p_t) = (e_{t+1} - e_t) - (p_{t+1} - p_t) = -\psi\delta(e_t + p^* - p_t - \bar{q}). \tag{24}$$

---

15. To derive the second equality, forward eq. (21) by one period and subtract eq. (21) itself from the resulting expression.

Higher real interest rates thus are associated with a currency that has appreciated in real terms.[16] In a more general setting where foreign interest rates and prices can vary, this relationship is easily generalized to

$$[i_{t+1} - (p_{t+1} - p_t)] - [i^*_{t+1} - (p^*_{t+1} - p^*_t)] = -\psi\delta(e_t - p_t + p^*_t - \bar{q}). \tag{25}$$

According to this generalized formulation, it is the *difference* between the home and foreign real interest rates that is inversely related to the degree of home-currency real depreciation.[17]

9.3   Empirical Evidence on Sticky-Price Exchange-Rate Models

The Mundell-Fleming-Dornbusch model is widely regarded as offering realistic predictions on the exchange rate, interest rate, and output effects of major changes in monetary policy. Countries that adopt dramatic monetary tightening almost invariably appear to experience real currency appreciation and higher real interest rates; examples include the Volcker deflation of the 1980s in the United States, Britain's monetary tightening under Prime Minister Margaret Thatcher starting in 1979 (see Buiter and Miller, 1983), and the attempts by European countries such as Italy and France to deflate by pegging to the Deutsche mark within the European Monetary System. In the 1990s, several Latin American countries drastically tightened monetary policy after the severe inflations of the 1980s, with similar effects on real interest rates and real exchange rates.

---

16. Our derivation of the real-interest-rate–real-exchange-rate relationship is much simpler than in Frankel (1979) because we adopted the Mussa (1982) price adjustment mechanism. But the intuition is the same. Expected trend movements in the equilibrium real exchange rate would add a trend adjustment term to the right-hand side of eq. (24).

17. To derive the last relationship, use interest parity, condition (1), to write

$$i_{t+1} - (p_{t+1} - p_t) = i^*_{t+1} + (e_{t+1} - e_t) - (p_{t+1} - p_t)$$

or, adding $p^*_{t+1} - p^*_t$ to both sides,

$$[i_{t+1} - (p_{t+1} - p_t)] - [i^*_{t+1} - (p^*_{t+1} - p^*_t)] = (e_{t+1} - e_t) + (p^*_{t+1} - p^*_t) - (p_{t+1} - p_t).$$

Notice next that eq. (6) becomes

$$p_{t+1} - p_t = \psi(y^d_t - \bar{y}) + e_{t+1} + p^*_{t+1} - e_t - p^*_t$$

with a variable foreign price level (but still assuming a constant long-run real exchange rate). Using eq. (3) to eliminate $y^d_t - \bar{y}$ as before, we therefore can write

$$(e_{t+1} - e_t) + (p^*_{t+1} - p^*_t) - (p_{t+1} - p_t) = -\psi(y^d_t - \bar{y})$$

$$= -\psi\delta(e_t + p^* - p_t - \bar{q}).$$

Combining this result with the preceding expression for the international real interest-rate differential, we reach eq. (25).

While conventional wisdom holds the Mundell-Fleming-Dornbusch model to be useful in predicting the effects of major shifts in policy, its ability to predict systematically interest-rate and exchange-rate movements is more debatable. In this section, we look at some of the evidence, beginning with the model's predictive power for interest rates and exchange rates, and then turning to output, where the model arguably is more successful. More detailed surveys can be found in Frankel and Rose (1995) and Isard (1995).

9.3.1   The Real-Interest-Differential–Real-Exchange-Rate Relationship

Many studies have attempted to detect the relationship (25) between the real interest rate and the real exchange rate predicted by the Dornbusch model, generally with little success. Meese and Rogoff (1988) could not reject the null hypothesis of no cointegration between the real exchange rate and the real interest rate differential for various cross rates among the dollar, yen, and Deutsche mark. Campbell and Clarida (1987) find that movements in expected interest differentials have not been large enough, or persistent enough, to account for variability in the real dollar exchange rate. Edison and Pauls (1993) have applied cointegration tests and error-correction mechanisms in equations that control for third variables (such as cumulated current accounts), but again with generally negative results.

A casual look at the evidence on the trade-weighted United States dollar may leave you surprised that researchers have had such difficulty detecting the negative real-exchange-rate–real-interest-rate correlation predicted by eq. (25). Figure 9.7 graphs quarterly data on the real value of the dollar against a trade-weighted average of other OECD countries' currencies. The real interest rate differential is measured by using interest rates on long-term bonds less one-year CPI changes. (Other standard expected inflation measures yield similar results.) For ease of visual interpretation, the real exchange rate in the figure is defined as $p - p^* - e$, making a real appreciation an upward movement in the exchange rate index. [Note well that under this convention, eq. (25) predicts a *positive* association between the two series.][18] As Figure 9.7 illustrates, the dollar's sharp upward appreciation during the mid-1980s occurred during a period when real interest rates in the United States were extremely high compared to those in its trading partners. Even apart from this episode, the figure seems loosely to suggest that long-term movements in the real-interest-rate differential do indeed have some correlation with long-term dollar exchange rate swings, even if the two variables do not move in lockstep.

---

18. The real exchange rate and interest rate data are taken from *International Financial Statistics* (the source for all the data in Figures 9.7–9.9). The countries included in multilateral averages are: Australia, Austria, Belgium-Luxembourg, Canada, Denmark, Finland, France, Germany, Greece, Ireland, Italy, Japan, the Netherlands, New Zealand, Norway, Portugal, Spain, Sweden, Switzerland, the United Kingdom, and the United States. One limitation of the real exchange rate measure used in Figure 9.7 is that it does not account for trade with developing countries.

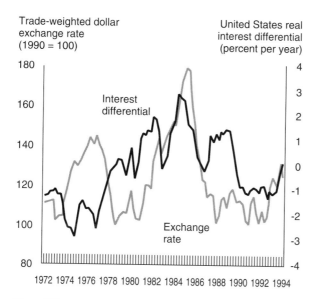

Figure 9.7
The dollar and relative U.S. real interest rates

Why doesn't the visual impression come through in regression analysis? Baxter (1994) suggests that most tests have focused too much on high-frequency (short-term) correlations and not enough on low-frequency movements. She uses methods better suited to detecting low-frequency movements and finds some correlation. She attributes its relatively small size to the preponderant role of high-frequency exchange-rate movements in explaining the total variance of exchange-rate movements.

Figures 9.8 and 9.9 show similar graphs for the trade-weighted yen and Deutsche mark. For these currencies, correlations between real interest differentials and real trade-weighted exchange rates seem, if anything, to go in the wrong direction (a relatively high real interest rate associated with a real currency depreciation). Overall, then, the empirical evidence on the real-interest-rate–real-exchange-rate correlation hardly provides overwhelming support for the Mundell-Fleming-Dornbusch model with a fixed long-run real exchange rate. Perhaps this outcome should not be surprising given the large literature on the speed of convergence to purchasing power parity. As Froot and Rogoff (1995) show, consensus estimates for the rate at which PPP shocks damp out are very slow. Consider a regression of the form

$$q_t = a_0 + \rho q_{t-1} + \epsilon_t,$$

where q is the real exchange rate and ϵ is a random disturbance. On annual panel data for industrialized countries, a typical estimate of ρ is 0.85. This implies an average half-life of deviations from PPP of roughly 4.2 years [where the half-life X

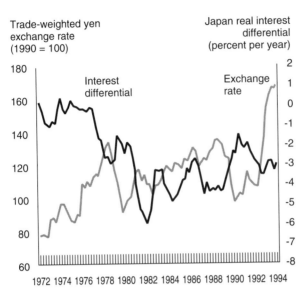

Figure 9.8
The yen and relative Japanese real interest rates

solves the equation $(0.85)^X = 1/2$]. Such slow convergence might make any systematic relationship between real exchange rates and the real interest rate difficult to detect except over fairly long horizons. The long half-life of PPP deviations remains something of a puzzle (see Rogoff, 1992, 1996).

9.3.2   Explaining the Nominal Exchange Rate

However badly the Mundell-Fleming-Dornbusch model fares in predicting the correlation between real exchange rates and real interest rates, its performance in predicting nominal exchange rates can only be described as worse (though it is not clear that a better model exists). Meese and Rogoff (1983a) analyzed the forecasting performance of a variety of monetary models of exchange rate determination, including the Dornbusch model and the flexible-price monetary model of Chapter 8. They showed that for major nominal exchange rates against the dollar, a random-walk model outperforms any of the structural models at one- to twelve-month forecast horizons. Remarkably, the random-walk model performs better *even if the structural-model forecasts are based on actual realized values of their explanatory variables.* In other words, the models fit very poorly out of sample, so that exchange rate movements are hard to rationalize on the basis of standard models even with the benefit of hindsight. As Frankel and Rose (1995) note, this awkwardly negative result has withstood numerous attempts to overturn it. The reasons behind the models' poor performances are not yet fully understood. Meese

Figure 9.9
The Deutsche mark and relative German real interest rates

and Rogoff (1983b) consider a variety of explanations, including the breakdown
of money demand functions and prolonged deviations from long-run purchasing
power parity, without reaching a decisive answer. They do, however, find that the
structural models may outperform the random walk at two- to three-year horizons. More conclusive evidence is presented by Chinn and Meese (1995) and Mark
(1995), who show that the superior performance of various monetary models at
very long horizons is statistically significant.[19]

The undeniable difficulties that international economists encounter in empirically explaining nominal exchange rate movements are an embarrassment, but
one shared with virtually any other field that attempts to explain asset price data.
Prescott (1986) has expressed the view that the difficulties of explaining asset price
fluctuations are such that macroeconomic models should be judged mainly on their

---

19. In an interesting paper, Eichenbaum and Evans (1995) try using some alternative measures of
money innovations for the United States, including statistical innovations in nonborrowed reserves and
the federal funds rate. Their reasoning is that such measures better capture the exogenous component
of monetary policy. (Foreign monetary policy is measured using the foreign interest rate.) Eichenbaum
and Evans also try Romer and Romer's (1989) dates marking deliberate monetary contractions; these
are based on minutes of the Federal Reserve's Open Market Committee. With all three measures, they
find that monetary contractions lead to dollar appreciations as in the Dornbusch model. Somewhat
surprisingly, however, they find roughly a two-year lag before the effect of the monetary contraction
peaks. To date the Eichenbaum-Evans analysis has not been subjected to out-of-sample testing. Clarida
and Gali (1994) find a similar delayed effect of money on exchange rates.

Table 9.1
Comparing Exchange-Rate and Stock-Price-Index Volatility, January 1981–August 1994
(standard deviation of month-to-month log changes)

Dollar/DM	Dollar/yen	S&P 500	Commerzbank	Nikkei
2.9	2.8	3.4	5.7	5.9

ability to explain fluctuations in output, consumption, investment, and other real quantity variables.

In trying to understand the difficulties in empirically modeling exchange rates, it is probably wrong to look for a special explanation of exchange-rate volatility. Instead, one should seek a unifying explanation for the volatility that all major asset prices display, including those of stocks and bonds as well as currencies. Indeed, nominal exchange rates typically are *less* volatile than, say, national stock-price indexes. Table 9.1 compares standard deviations of month-to-month changes in the log of the dollar/DM and dollar/yen exchange rates with those of the Standard and Poor's 500 stock index for the United States, the Commerzbank index for Germany, and the Nikkei 300 index for Japan.[20]

The standard deviation of month-to-month exchange rate changes is just under 3 percent, but the volatility of stock prices is even higher. One loose rationale for the higher volatility of stock prices is that currency values depend on GNP, which is more diversified than even a broad national stock market index.

9.3.3   Monetary Contraction and the International Transmission of the Great Depression

A central prediction of the Mundell-Fleming-Dornbusch model, and indeed of most Keynesian models, is that unanticipated monetary contractions lead to temporary declines in output. This assertion is perhaps the model's most controversial. For example, the real business cycle approach discussed in Chapter 7 argues that one can explain a substantial part of business cycle regularities by a model in which money has no real effects. In contrast, Friedman and Schwartz (1963) assign monetary shocks a dominant role. Resolving this debate empirically by estimating the effects of monetary shocks is not easy. First, it can be difficult to separate anticipated from unanticipated money shocks. (In theory unanticipated shocks should be much more important.) Second, if the monetary authorities follow any sort of money feedback rule (for example, a rule making money depend on exchange rates or interest rates), the money supply becomes endogenous. In this case, it can be difficult to distinguish the effects of money on output from the effects of third factors

---

20. Controlling for time trends does not qualitatively affect the results.

that simultaneously influence both.[21] Finally, the constant evolution of transactions technologies is making it increasingly difficult to find a measure of monetary policy that has a stable relationship with prices and output.

Partly as a result of these difficulties, economists recently have refocused their attention on the Great Depression of the 1930s. The Great Depression stands out for its severity and length. In the United States, unemployment rates exceeded 25 percent, the stock market dropped by 90 percent, and almost 50 percent of all banks failed. To varying degrees, countries in Europe, Latin America, and Asia experienced similarly precipitous declines. To paraphrase Bernanke (1983), a theory of business cycles that has nothing to say about the Great Depression is like a theory of earthquakes that explains only small tremors.

9.3.3.1   New International Evidence on the Great Depression

Until the 1980s most research on the Great Depression concentrated on the U.S. experience. In their classic book, Friedman and Schwartz (1963) placed the Depression at the doorstep of the U.S. Federal Reserve. According to Friedman and Schwartz, the young Fed (it was less than 20 years old at the outset of the Depression), whether by accident or design, initiated a sharp contraction in the U.S. money supply toward the end of the 1920s. This contraction was exacerbated by the banking crises of the early 1930s. A leader among skeptics of the monetary view was Temin (1976), who argued that money contractions were a response to the decline in output rather than vice versa, and that the main cause of the Depression in the United States was a large autonomous drop in consumption demand (a shift in the Keynesian *IS* curve, rather than the *LM* curve) that occurred in 1930.

More recently, economists have taken account of the worldwide scope of the Great Depression, drawing on evidence from twenty to thirty countries instead of just the United States. Leading examples of this research are Choudhri and Kochin (1980), Díaz-Alejandro (1983), Eichengreen and Sachs (1985), Hamilton (1988), Eichengreen (1992), and Bernanke and Carey (1995).

The new view is that the Depression was indeed caused by an exogenous worldwide monetary contraction, originating mainly in the United States and transmitted abroad by a combination of policy errors and technical flaws in the interwar gold standard. These problems forced any country pegging its currency to gold to contract its money supply sharply to maintain exchange parity. Countries outside the gold bloc—"floaters"—were free to devalue their currencies as necessary to avoid deflation. In an insightful paper, Choudhri and Kochin (1980) first noticed the clear divergence in economic performance between countries that abandoned the gold standard early in the Depression and others that stubbornly clung to gold.

---

21. As noted above, Romer and Romer (1989) try to overcome this endogeneity problem by using minutes of Federal Reserve Open Market Committee meetings to identify conscious monetary tightening. They find that their measure of monetary tightness helps predict downturns in GNP.

Comparing four countries outside the gold bloc (three Scandinavian countries and Spain) with four countries that stayed on gold (Belgium, Italy, the Netherlands, and Poland), Choudhri and Kochin found that the gold peggers suffered significantly sharper declines in output and employment. In a more comprehensive study, Eichengreen and Sachs (1985) showed that by 1935, countries that abandoned gold had substantially recovered from the Great Depression, while the gold bloc countries remained immersed in it.

Figure 9.10, based on data from Bernanke and Carey (1995), illustrates the finding. The vertical axis measures the ratio of real industrial production in 1935 to real industrial production in 1929, and the horizontal axis gives the corresponding ratio for the wholesale price level. The figure shows a striking positive correlation between cumulative inflation and the speed at which a country recovered from the Depression. A simple cross-section least squares regression of the cumulative industrial production change $\log(IP_{1935}/IP_{1929})$ on cumulative inflation $\log(WPI_{1935}/WPI_{1929})$ yields

$$\log(IP_{1935}/IP_{1929}) = 2.45 + 0.49 \log(WPI_{1935}/WPI_{1929}), \qquad R^2 = 0.17.$$
$$(0.21) \quad (0.23)$$

Thus a 1 percent increase in cumulative 1929–35 inflation is correlated with a 0.5 percent cumulative increase in industrial production. Countries that left the gold standard earliest in the period had the greatest latitude to inflate (though not all countries exercised this option with equal vigor), and monetary expansion seems systematically positively correlated with output growth.

9.3.3.2   Was the Global Monetary Contraction Simply an Endogenous Response to Output Decline? Flaws in the Interwar Gold Standard

If regressions such as the one in the preceding subsection were the only evidence linking adherence to the gold standard with the local severity of the Great Depression, one might still be able to argue that somehow output contraction induced countries to stay on the gold standard, rather than vice versa. This view—basically an international extension of Temin's (1976) hypothesis that monetary contraction was endogenous—is no longer sustainable in the face of a massive body of evidence assembled by Eichengreen (1992). Eichengreen considers in detail the political and technical underpinnings of the monetary contraction. He forcefully argues that the deflation experienced under the interwar gold standard was not the result of passive responses to declining output, but rather the unintended consequence of flawed central bank institutions, poor policy decisions, and difficult economic conditions that remained in the wake of World War I.

We touched on the history of the gold standard in our discussion of alternative monetary regimes in Chapter 8. Between 1870 and World War I the gold standard supported vigorous world trade and enjoyed a high degree of credibility. During that period, of course, central banks did not confront the political mandate to main-

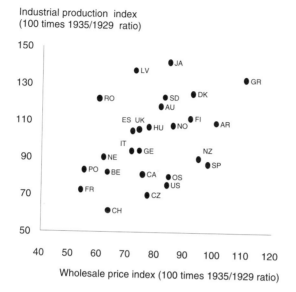

Figure 9.10
Industrial production and price levels in the Great Depression (1935; 1929 = 100)

tain full employment that emerged in the interwar years. In addition, the period was punctuated only by smallish, local wars.

The international gold standard was suspended when World War I broke out, but with a great deal of effort it was rebuilt after peace had been made. By 1929 virtually all market economies had returned to gold.

As Eichengreen (1992) and Bernanke (1995) argue, however, the reconstituted gold standard was built on much shakier ground than its prewar predecessor. First and perhaps foremost, having demonstrated their willingness to abandon the gold standard as a result of World War I (without necessarily returning to prewar exchange parities afterward), many countries were more vulnerable to speculators who might doubt the credibility of their commitment to gold. Second, in the interwar period, most countries maintained only fractional gold backing of their currencies, and most central banks held major currencies such as the dollar or pound in lieu of gold. This practice effectively increased the leverage of the world monetary gold stock, implying a heightened multiplier effect on the world money supply whenever hoarders pulled gold out of the system. Third, as with any fixed-exchange-rate regime, there was an asymmetry between deficit and surplus countries. Deficit countries were ultimately forced to deflate to maintain their currencies' exchange values while surplus countries faced no comparable pressure to inflate. Under the supposed gold standard "rules of the game," surplus countries were supposed to inflate as they gained gold through balance of payments surpluses, but instead the surplus countries, especially the United States and France, simply stockpiled the world's gold.

All these weaknesses in the interwar gold standard system helped propagate a deflationary monetary contraction that appears to have originated in the United States.

9.3.3.3   Summary

There is now overwhelming evidence suggesting that countries that abandoned gold early in the Great Depression and inflated did much better than countries that tried to stay linked to gold. A careful reading of the historical record also suggests that the monetary contraction initiating the Depression was exogenous, rather than a passive response to output, and that the international gold standard was a powerful transmission mechanism for the exogenous deflationary impulse. In sum, evidence from the interwar years provides some of the strongest support for a systematic effect of monetary policy on output.

From a welfare perspective, it is interesting to contrast the modern view of devaluation in the Great Depression with the older view of Nurkse (1944), who viewed devaluation as a "beggar-thy-neighbor" policy that raises the devaluer's income mainly at trading partners' expense. In Chapter 10, we will look at a model that suggests a different interpretation: countries that devalued their currencies (in order to inflate) may have actually helped their neighbors by expanding global aggregate demand. Under plausible assumptions, this positive effect can outweigh any trade-balance effects that occur because of shifts in competitiveness.

An important question that remains largely unresolved is why the Great Depression lasted so long, ending decisively only shortly before World War II. Bernanke (1983) argues that Depression had a devastating impact on financial intermediation, especially in the United States. It took many years for the country to rebuild its banking and financial industry. One piece of evidence he offers is that small firms without access to equity markets took more of a beating than large firms. (Looking at modern data, Gertler and Gilchrist, 1994, also find that monetary contractions tend to hit small firms harder than large firms.) Skeptics argue that a sector that accounts for only a very small fraction of GNP cannot account for such prolonged and severe dislocations. A different hypothesis is advanced by Eichengreen and Sachs (1985) and Bernanke and Carey (1995). These studies present cross-country evidence that nominal wage rigidities may have been sustained far beyond the one or two years most macroeconomists think of as an upper bound for delay in nominal wage adjustment. The studies do not, however, offer a detailed theory to explain their findings. Thus there still is no fully satisfactory explanation of the Great Depression's remarkable duration.

9.4   Choice of the Exchange-Rate Regime

Despite limited predictive and explanatory power, the Mundell-Fleming-Dornbusch model has deeply influenced thinking on a broad range of policy issues. One of the most important applications of the model is to the choice of exchange-rate regime.

9.4.1   Fixed versus Flexible Exchange Rates

A central result of the Mundell-Fleming-Dornbusch framework is that with sticky prices and flexible exchange rates, purely monetary shocks can spill over into the real economy, leading to large changes in prices and output and prolonged periods of adjustment. This prediction lies at the heart of a literature that argues that fixed exchange rates are superior to floating rates when money-demand shocks are the dominant source of disturbance buffeting the economy.[22] To understand the logic of the case for fixed rates, we need to extend our model to incorporate money-demand shocks. Suppose we modify the money-demand equation (2) to include a money-demand shock, so that now

$$m_t - p_t = -\eta i_{t+1} + \phi y_t + \epsilon_t,$$

where ϵ_t is an unpredictable shift in money demand. One might think of money-demand shocks as arising from changes in the transaction technology or the money multiplier, or from portfolio shifts. Clearly, it changes nothing essential to modify all formulas for a stochastic version of the log-linear Dornbusch model by replacing m_t with $m_t - \epsilon_t$. Money-demand shocks simply have effects equal but opposite to those of money-supply shocks.

A fixed exchange rate fully and automatically eliminates any real effects of money-demand shocks. Why? Because, as our analysis in section 8.4.1 showed, fixing the exchange rate implies setting the money supply so as to keep $m_t - \epsilon_t$ fixed, other things being equal. Thus fixing the exchange rate requires the monetary authority instantly to satisfy all money-demand shifts through (nonsterilized) foreign exchange intervention. Though there are some subtleties involving the timing of money-supply infusions, using the current money supply to peg the home nominal interest rate to the foreign nominal interest rate is an essentially equivalent policy. Again, if money-demand disturbances are the only shock buffeting the economy and the authorities fix i, they automatically fix $m_t - \epsilon_t$.

When shocks are real (that is, originate in the goods market), a policy of holding the money supply constant will often dominate a policy of trying to fix the

---

22. See, for example, the discussion in Garber and Svensson (1995). For a discussion of exchange-rate policy focusing on developing countries, see Edwards (1989).

exchange rate. We saw an example of this in our analysis of a fall in the long-run equilibrium exchange rate q̄ (a domestic real appreciation) in the Dornbusch model. (Recall the last paragraph of section 9.2.3.) In the example, adjustment to a new full-employment equilibrium was immediate under a floating exchange rate. Significantly, the shift to the new equilibrium required only an appreciation of the nominal exchange rate, which eliminated the need for a change in the nominal price level. Had the authorities been pursuing a fixed exchange-rate policy, however, domestic goods' money prices would have borne the entire burden of downward adjustment. Because these are sticky, the economy would have reached its new long-run equilibrium only gradually, after a period of unemployment.

Thus far, we have really discussed only pure fixed rates and pure floating rates (exogenous money). If Keynesian stabilization issues are the only problem, then, in general, the optimal exchange-rate policy does not call for fixing either the exchange rate or the money supply. Instead, the optimal policy takes the form of a feedback rule such as

$$m_t - \bar{m} = \Phi(e_t - \bar{e}),$$

where the optimal choice of Φ depends on the parameters of the model and the relative variance of the two types of economic shock. As the ratio of the variance of real shocks to the variance of monetary shocks goes to zero, the optimal regime will approach a fixed rate, implying $\Phi \to \infty$. (See Marston, 1985, and exercise 3. In a model where sterilized intervention is effective, the feedback rule can be generalized to incorporate shifts in portfolio preferences; see Branson and Henderson, 1985.)

We will not explore the literature on fixed versus flexible exchange rates in any great detail. One reason is that most of the literature is based on models that lack the microfoundations needed for meaningful welfare analysis. (Nevertheless, the key result that fixed exchange rates are optimal when financial disturbances dominate is likely to hold in more complete models.) Another reason for not dwelling too much on stabilization comparisons across exchange-rate regimes is that *credibly* fixed rates may not be a viable long-run option for most countries, given the pervasive possibility of speculative attacks on fixed exchange rates. Finally, many countries that adopt fixed exchange rates are more concerned with the effect on anti-inflation credibility than on short-term stabilization. We will discuss links among monetary-policy credibility, inflation, and exchange rates at the end of this chapter.

9.4.2 Optimum Currency Areas

A further step beyond fixed exchange rates is for two countries to share a common currency, as do, for example, the various states in the United States. Compared to a fixed exchange rate, a currency union is much harder to break, but it also requires a higher degree of policy coordination among members. The theory of optimal currency areas is one of the classic issues in international finance, dating back to the work of Mundell (1961), McKinnon (1963), and Kenen (1969). In recent years, with Europe's attempt to institute a common currency and the monetary problems facing the formerly communist bloc, the question of currency unions has again come to the forefront of international economic policy. Whereas a detailed analysis of optimum currency areas is well beyond the scope of this book, we will try in this section to give the reader at least a brief overview of the basic issues.

The main *benefits* two countries reap from having a common currency are generally thought to include the following:

1. Reduced transaction costs from currency conversion. Though the fees on large currency transactions are quite small, currency turnover is extremely high, so cumulative costs can be higher than one might imagine. Using bank data collected by the Bank for International Settlements, economists at the Commission of the European Communities (1990) estimated these costs to be between 0.25 and 0.4 percent of gross community product. (The bulk of the implied savings, about 70 percent, would come from eliminating margin and transaction fees paid to banks.)

2. Reduced accounting costs and greater predictability of relative prices for firms doing business in both countries.

3. Insulation from monetary disturbances and speculative bubbles that might otherwise lead to temporary unnecessary fluctuations in real exchange rates (given sticky domestic prices).

4. Less political pressure for trade protection because of sharp shifts in real exchange rates.

The main *costs* of having a common currency include these:

1. Individual regions in a currency union forgo the ability to use monetary policy to respond to region-specific macroeconomic disturbances. When labor mobility is high across regions, it is less necessary for each area to stabilize regional employment with its own independent monetary policy. Labor mobility is relatively high within the United States, but it is low within many European countries. Some authors, including Stockman (1988b), have argued that for Europe nation-specific productivity shocks play a substantial role in explaining aggregate national output fluctuations. This and similar findings suggest that asymmetric shocks should be an important consideration in deciding upon an exchange-rate regime.

2. Regions in a currency union give up the option to use inflation to reduce the real burden of public debt. (See Calvo and Leiderman, 1992, for a formal welfare analysis.) This budgetary inflexibility might be particularly important in extreme circumstances such as wars, for example. Also, as Sachs and Sala-i-Martin (1992) emphasize, currency unions such as the United States that share a national income

tax and transfer system have less need for region-specific monetary policy. Income taxes, for example, automatically transfer resources from boom regions to those in slump, thereby providing some measure of automatic stabilization.

3. Related to the last point, political and strategic problems arise in determining how member countries split seignorage revenues. (Regions that do not otherwise share a common fiscal policy must determine how to share seignorage revenues from printing the joint currency.) See, for example, Casella (1992) and Sibert (1994). Comparable problems arise in determining the currency union's joint monetary policy; see Alesina and Grilli (1992) and Canzoneri and Rogers (1990).

4. Avoiding speculative attacks in the transition from individual currencies to a common currency can be a major problem; witness the currency crises in Europe during the early 1990s. For a model of this problem, see Froot and Rogoff (1991), who argue that accelerating the speed of transition will not necessarily help temper speculative attacks and might simply hasten their occurrence.

An issue closely related to optimal currency areas is the choice of fixed or flexible exchange rates for two countries with different currencies. Of course, if exchange rates could be credibly fixed *forever*, then the differences between having a fixed exchange rate and a common currency would be fairly minor, and would mainly have to do with how leadership in monetary policy is determined. In practice, however, fixed exchange rate regimes never can be 100 percent credible. "Fixed" exchange rates are, in fact, more realistically thought of as "fixed but adjustable." As a practical matter, fixing the exchange rate for any length of time is not simple in a world of highly liquid and highly integrated world capital markets. Given the right conditions, speculative attacks can swiftly and ruthlessly undermine a country's commitment to a fixed exchange rate.[23]

Because it is difficult to separate stabilization from credibility issues in the choice of exchange-rate regime, we next turn to a formal exploration of credibility in monetary policy.

9.5 Models of Credibility in Monetary Policy

Our discussion of the choice of fixed versus flexible rates assumed that the monetary authorities can commit to a policy reaction function, and that this commitment will be perceived as fully credible by the public. In reality, credibility is a central problem in monetary design. If monetary expansions can raise output, won't monetary authorities be tempted to try routinely to raise employment above its natural

---

23. Garber and Svensson (1995) argue that the problem of speculative attacks is so severe that it dominates any practical analysis of the choice of exchange rate regime. See also the overviews of the international monetary system by Eichengreen (1994) and Goldstein (1995).

rate? Since the late 1970s, the recognition that strategic considerations are central to macroeconomic policy has led to a revolution in the theory of policy design, both at the domestic and at the international levels. We have alluded to credibility issues at several points in this book, but apart from our discussion of dynamic inconsistency in international borrowing in Chapter 6, we have not explored the subject systematically. This section provides a very basic introduction to the credibility problems that arise in making monetary policy. The macroeconomic model underlying our analysis is deliberately stylized, because we wish to highlight the gaming aspects of monetary policy rather than the technicalities of the transmission mechanism. Many of the results of the overly simple framework that follows can, however, be reinterpreted in terms of the more sophisticated models of Chapter 10.

9.5.1   The Kydland-Prescott, Barro-Gordon Model

In this section we present a simplified but very useful and influential model of monetary policy credibility. The basic ideas were first described by Kydland and Prescott (1977), though Barro and Gordon (1983b) showed the model's potential for explaining the stagflation that many industrialized countries experienced during the 1970s.[24] Barro and Gordon viewed their model as a positive account of inflation, but the subsequent literature, beginning with Rogoff (1985b) and more recently including Walsh (1995), Persson and Tabellini (1993), and Svensson (1995), has shown that the approach has important normative implications for the design of monetary institutions.

9.5.1.1   The Model

Consider a world in which private agents commit to nominal contracts one period before the contracts come into effect. For concreteness, let's think of nominal wage contracts, though the example here readily extends to other nominal rigidities. Of course, wage setters care about the real wage, not the nominal wage, so they must form forecasts of next period's inflation to know what nominal wage to commit to today. If these forecasts turn out to be wrong, real wages will deviate from their market-clearing level. Following standard Keynesian convention, we assume firms are always on their demand curves for labor, so that (all else equal) when inflation is higher than expected, employment rises, and when inflation is unexpectedly low, employment falls. Thus output is determined entirely by firms' demand for labor.

To capture these assumptions algebraically, we assume that the log of date t output, y_t, differs from its natural or flexible-price equilibrium level, $\bar{y}$, by an amount inversely proportional to the (log) real wage $w - p$. Thus,

---

24. Working roughly at the same time as Kydland and Prescott, Calvo (1978) developed a somewhat different model based on government seignorage needs. A broad survey is included in Persson and Tabellini (1990). See also Fischer (1990).

$$y_t = \bar{y} - (w_t - p_t) - z_t, \tag{26}$$

where we have assumed a proportionality constant of 1 to simplify the notation, and z_t is a conditional mean-zero, i.i.d. output supply shock. If workers always commit to a wage that sets expected output at its natural level, then the nominal wage for date t set in period $t - 1$ satisfies

$$w_t = E_{t-1}p_t. \tag{27}$$

The monetary authorities set period t policy *after* wage setters form inflation expectations on date $t - 1$ and after observing any date t shocks. For simplicity we will assume that they directly set inflation, defined by

$$\pi_t \equiv p_t - p_{t-1}. \tag{28}$$

The loss function that the monetary authorities *minimize* is a weighted sum of squared deviations from an output target of $\tilde{y}$ and an inflation target of 0:

$$\mathcal{L}_t = (y_t - \tilde{y})^2 + \chi \pi_t^2. \tag{29}$$

The quantity

$$\tilde{y} - \bar{y} = k > 0 \tag{30}$$

represents a positive wedge between the output level targeted by the authorities and the natural level of output. Such a wedge could arise even if the monetary authorities maximize social welfare. For example, if insider labor negotiators do not take into account the welfare of outsider workers, employment will be inefficiently low even if nominal wages are fully flexible. Alternatively, the socially optimal level of unemployment might be below the natural rate because income taxes separate the social and private returns to labor, or because of hard-to-repeal minimum-wage laws. (The model of Chapter 10 will yield another interpretation, that the market-determined output level is too low because of monopolistic producers or labor unions.) The constant χ in the authorities' loss function (29) weights the cost of inflation relative to that of suboptimal output. It may also reflect the private sector's preferences (though the choices of wage setters at a single atomistic firm have only an infinitesimal effect on economy-wide inflation). Inflation has several social costs. Higher *anticipated* inflation reduces the demand for money, which costs (virtually) nothing to produce but yields liquidity services at the margin (Bailey, 1956). Even *unanticipated* inflation is costly in the model, however. Higher unexpected inflation sharpens random income redistributions, degrades the allocation signals in relative prices, and raises the distortions a nonindexed tax system inflicts. In practice, the latter costs probably dwarf the liquidity cost of expected inflation. Driffill, Mizon, and Ulph (1990) survey the evidence.

Successively substituting eqs. (26), (27), and (30) into eq. (29), we obtain $\mathcal{L}_t = (p_t - E_{t-1}p_t - z_t - k)^2 + \chi \pi_t^2$ or, using the definition of inflation in eq. (28),

$$\mathcal{L}_t = (\pi_t - \pi_t^e - z_t - k)^2 + \chi \pi_t^2, \tag{31}$$

where $\pi_t^e \equiv E_{t-1}\pi_t = E_{t-1}p_t - p_{t-1}$.

Clearly, the model is ad hoc compared with the models considered in other chapters of this book. It nonetheless provides a useful (if rough) depiction of the typical tensions between monetary authorities and wage setters in many countries. The authorities would like output to be above its market-clearing level, whereas each individual wage setter, while perhaps agreeing with the general social goals of high aggregate employment and low inflation, wishes to avoid being among those who work at unexpectedly low real wages.[25]

We have assumed that the monetary authorities set actual inflation π_t *after* the private sector sets nominal contracts (which embody π_t^e), but does this fact mean that the authorities will always choose to set inflation high enough to force unemployment below the natural rate? Perhaps surprisingly, the answer is no. To see why, we need to consider how equilibrium is determined.

9.5.1.2   Equilibrium in the One-Shot Game

The presence of the wedge k between the target and natural output levels creates a *dynamic consistency* problem for the monetary authorities (in the sense we used that term in Chapter 6). The authorities would like to be able credibly to announce a zero-mean distribution of future inflation. But if such an announcement were believed by wage setters, the monetary authorities would be in a position to raise output above its natural level through an inflationary surprise at very little cost. Absent a mechanism for enforcing a promise of zero average inflation, a monetary authority whose promises are believed will never find $\pi = 0$ optimal ex post.

Though they move first, the atomistic wage setters understand the loss function (31) that the monetary authorities will minimize in the following period. They realize that for given values of π_t^e and z_t, the first-order condition for the authorities [found by differentiating eq. (31) with respect to π_t] will be

$$\frac{d\mathcal{L}_t}{d\pi_t} = \underbrace{2(\pi_t - \pi_t^e - z_t - k)}_{\substack{\text{(minus) marginal benefit of} \\ \text{higher inflation}}} + \underbrace{2\chi\pi_t}_{\substack{\text{marginal cost of} \\ \text{higher inflation}}} = 0, \tag{32}$$

which implies

$$\pi_t = \frac{k + \pi_t^e + z_t}{1 + \chi}. \tag{33}$$

---

25. Each worker will wish to avoid a cut in his own real wages even if the government redistributes the higher national output ex post to make everyone in the economy better off. The reason is that an atomistic worker regards the redistributive tax and transfer payments as exogenous to his own employment situation.

Thus the inflation level chosen by the monetary authorities is a function of inflationary expectations.

Because expectations are rational and wage setters understand that inflation will be set ex post according to eq. (33), the *equilibrium* inflation expectation π_t^e on date $t - 1$ satisfies

$$\pi_t^e = \mathrm{E}_{t-1}\pi_t = \mathrm{E}_{t-1}\left\{\frac{k + \pi_t^e + z_t}{1 + \chi}\right\},$$

or, since $\mathrm{E}_{t-1}z_t = 0$,

$$\pi_t^e = \frac{k}{\chi}. \tag{34}$$

Observe that expected inflation is higher, the greater is the wedge k between the authorities' target output level and the natural rate. Expected inflation is lower, the greater is χ, the relative weight the authorities place on inflation stabilization versus employment stabilization. Finally, substituting eq. (34) into eq. (33) yields ex post inflation,

$$\pi_t = \frac{k}{\chi} + \frac{z_t}{1 + \chi}. \tag{35}$$

Comparing the last two equations, we find that in equilibrium, the monetary authorities do *not* succeed in systematically surprising wage setters, for realized and expected inflation differ only by the unpredictable exogenous shock z_t. How is this possible if the monetary authorities move after wages are set and can always set inflation above the level anticipated in wage contracts? The intuition is seen most easily by referring to first-order condition eq. (32) and, temporarily, abstracting from the z shocks. Suppose that private agents were to set $\pi_t^e = 0$. Then, if the monetary authorities chose $\pi_t = 0$, they would perceive the marginal cost of higher inflation, $2\chi\pi_t$, as zero. But the marginal benefit from slightly higher inflation [that is, the reduction in the first (output) component of the monetary authorities' loss function], $-2(\pi_t - \pi_t^e - k)$, would be a positive number (a positive reduction in the loss function). Thus zero inflation cannot be an equilibrium. In the "time-consistent" equilibrium (Kydland and Prescott's perhaps unfortunate terminology), the marginal benefit to higher inflation exactly offsets the marginal cost at $\pi_t = \pi_t^e$. The monetary authorities *could* inflate above and beyond the private sectors' expectations, *but it is not in their interest to do so.* (We are ignoring second-order conditions, but it is easy to check that they are met here.) Reintroducing the supply shock z does not change the basic intuition of the equilibrium. The monetary authorities partially counteract the output effects of the z shocks, but private sector expectations are still correct on average.[26]

---

26. While it may appear that wage setters must explicitily coordinate in order to reach the equilibrium characterized by eq. (34), this is not the case. We have derived the equilibrium under the assumption that each wage-setting unit acts independently.

9.5.1.3   Equilibrium with a Commitment Technology

Clearly, the equilibrium is not optimal from anyone's perspective. It entails a costly inflationary bias to monetary policy with no mean gain in output. One possible solution would be for the country to adopt a constitutional amendment to have zero inflation so that $\pi_t = 0$, in which case $\pi_t^e = 0$ as well. But this situation is not optimal because it prevents the authorities from using monetary policy to stabilize the economy in response to the supply shocks z. (If you don't like that story, think of the monetary authorities as needing flexibility to deal with financial crises.) Ideally, the monetary authorities would like to convince wage setters that they will only use monetary policy to offset shocks. Rather than commit to zero inflation, they would like to commit ex ante to the optimal policy rule

$$\pi_t = \frac{z_t}{1 + \chi}, \tag{36}$$

which, as you can show, minimizes $E_{t-1}\mathcal{L}_t$ [derived from eq. (31)] subject to $\pi_t^e = E_{t-1}\pi_t$.[27]

The question is whether there is any practical way to make such a binding commitment, especially when one takes into account that in reality an optimal ex ante rule such as eq. (36) must be able to deal with a wide array of possible disturbances.

9.5.1.4   Reputational Equilibria

An optimistic view of the credibility problem in monetary policy is that it largely disappears in a more realistic long-horizon setting. Suppose, for example, that instead of minimizing the static loss function (31), the monetary authorities seek to minimize the present-value loss function

$$E_t \left\{ \sum_{s=t}^{\infty} \beta^{s-t} \mathcal{L}_s \right\}, \tag{37}$$

where $\mathcal{L}_s = (\pi_s - \pi_s^e - z_s - k)^2 + \chi\pi_s^2$. Then trigger-strategy equilibria in which expected inflation is lower than the "one-shot-game" level k/χ in eq. (34) may exist (in analogy to those we studied in Chapter 6).

Again, the idea is easiest to illustrate by assuming that the z shocks are absent. Suppose that private sector expectations are given by

$$\pi_t^e = \begin{cases} 0 & \text{if } \pi_{t-s} = \pi_{t-s}^e, \ \forall s > 0 \\ k/\chi & \text{otherwise.} \end{cases} \tag{38}$$

---

27. This is really only a second-best policy, of course, since it does not eliminate the underlying distortion causing the wedge k between the target and natural output levels. If that wedge could be eliminated, for example, through tax or labor-market reform, there would be no need for the monetary authorities to bind themselves in advance.

Thus expected inflation is zero in period t provided the monetary authorities set $\pi = \pi^e$ in all earlier periods. Otherwise, inflation expectations revert permanently to those of the one-shot game (there is an infinite period of "punishment"). To see whether these expectations are consistent with a zero-inflation equilibrium, we need to compare the cost and benefit to the monetary authorities of cheating by setting inflation greater than zero. Assuming that $\pi_t^e = 0$, the discounted cost of *not* setting $\pi_t = 0$ is simply $[\beta/(1 - \beta)]\chi(k/\chi)^2 = [\beta/(1 - \beta)]k^2/\chi$, the present value of the future costs from having equilibrium inflation at its one-shot-game level instead of zero from date $t + 1$ on.[28] The maximum date t benefit from cheating when $\pi_t^e = 0$ is found by minimizing

$$\mathcal{L}_t = (\pi_t - k)^2 + \chi\pi_t^2,$$

which yields $\pi_t = k/(1 + \chi)$. If the monetary authorities cheat, their minimized date t loss function therefore is

$$\left(\frac{k}{1 + \chi} - k\right)^2 + \chi\left(\frac{k}{1 + \chi}\right)^2 = \frac{\chi}{1 + \chi}k^2,$$

which is less than the date t loss k^2 that would obtain if instead π_t were set at $\pi_t^e = 0$. The short-term "gain" from cheating is thus $k^2(1 - \frac{\chi}{1+\chi}) = k^2/(1 + \chi)$. We see that if the government does not discount the future too much (β is near 1), then the cost of cheating, which we calculated as $[\beta/(1 - \beta)]k^2/\chi$, can easily outweigh the short-term benefit, $k^2/(1 + \chi)$. If $\beta < \chi/(1 + 2\chi)$, however, zero inflation isn't an equilibrium. Even if β is too low to support the zero-expected inflation equilibrium under the trigger-strategy expectations in eq. (38), it will still generally be possible for eq. (38) to support a positive equilibrium inflation rate below the one-shot-game level.[29]

It is straightforward to reintroduce the z shocks. The analysis is much the same except that trigger strategy expectations are given by

$$\pi_t^e = \begin{cases} 0 & \text{if } \pi_{t-s} = \pi_{t-s}^e + z_{t-s}/(1 + \chi), \ \forall s > 0 \\ k/\chi & \text{otherwise.} \end{cases} \tag{39}$$

Notice that in this case, the monetary authorities are allowed to stabilize in response to observable supply shocks without compromising their "reputation."

As in Chapter 6, the trigger-strategy equilibrium that we have discussed would unravel backward if the monetary authorities had a finite rather than an infinite horizon. (There would be no incentive to adopt anything but the one-shot-game

---

28. Note that, given the expectations in eq. (38), the monetary authorities will always set inflation at its one-shot-game level k/χ once they have already cheated and are suffering punishment anyway.

29. Even with a one-period (rather than infinite) punishment interval, it is always possible to support an expected inflation rate lower than that of the one-shot game (again in analogy with Chapter 6). For details and discussion of more complex punishment strategies, see Rogoff (1987). The trigger strategy type of equilibrium was proposed by Barro and Gordon (1983a).

inflation rate in the last period T, but then there can be no incentive to maintain a reputation in $T - 1$, etc.) One should not take this apparent fragility of the trigger-strategy equilibrium too literally though, since there are ways to resurrect "reputational" equilibria when policymakers' horizons are finite (e.g., if there is some degree of imperfect information about the policymakers' costs of breaking commitments; see Rogoff, 1987). The fairly robust point is that if monetary policy is a repeated game (and it certainly is), then the authorities' incentives to engage in surprise inflation in the current period may be tempered by concern for future reputation. It is sometimes even possible to support the optimal (with commitment) policy.

Unfortunately, there are good reasons for not relying too heavily on reputational considerations as a solution to the government's credibility problems in conducting monetary policy. First and foremost, reputational models generally admit a multiplicity of equilibria. In the preceding trigger-strategy model, even when zero expected inflation is sustainable as an equilibrium, the one-shot-game expected inflation rate $\pi^e = k/\chi$ remains an equilibrium, as does any inflation rate between 0 and k/χ. (Indeed, even negative expected inflation rates are sustainable.) As a result, there is a substantial coordination problem in achieving the most favorable reputational equilibrium. This coordination problem is likely to be quite severe in a macroeconomic setting with a very large number of agents. Even in setups where the equilibrium is unique, it typically turns out to be quite sensitive to the parameterization of the model.

9.5.2   Institutional Resolutions of the Dynamic Consistency Problem

If credibility is a problem in monetary policy, are there institutional reforms a country can adopt to lower inflationary expectations without sacrificing all flexibility in monetary policy?

9.5.2.1   The Conservative Central Banker

One possible way societies might confront the problem of monetary-policy credibility is to create an independent central bank that places a high weight on inflation stabilization. Suppose, for example, that the government delegates monetary policy to an independent "conservative" central banker with known preferences

$$\mathcal{L}_t^{CB} = (\pi_t - \pi_t^e - z_t - k)^2 + \chi^{CB}\pi_t^2,$$

where $\chi^{CB} > \chi$. That is, the central banker is conservative in the sense of placing a higher relative weight on inflation stabilization than does society as a whole. This scenario is not unrealistic: central bankers are often chosen from among conservative elements in the financial community. Following the same steps as in deriving eqs. (34) and (35), one can show that the (one-shot-game) equilibrium is now characterized by

$$\pi_t^e = \frac{k}{\chi^{CB}}, \tag{40}$$

$$\pi_t = \frac{k}{\chi^{CB}} + \frac{z_t}{1 + \chi^{CB}}. \tag{41}$$

Equations (40) and (41) reveal the pros and cons of having a conservative central banker. On the plus side, expected inflation in eq. (40) is lower than in eq. (34) since $\chi^{CB} > \chi$. However, comparing eqs. (41) and (35), we see that the conservative central banker reacts less to supply shocks than would a central banker who shared society's preferences. A conservative central banker is too concerned with stabilizing inflation relative to stabilizing employment. Clearly, if $k = 0$, so there are no distortions and no inflation bias, it makes no sense to have a conservative central banker. On the other hand, if $k > 0$ and there are no supply shocks, it is optimal to have a central banker who cares only about inflation ($\chi^{CB} = \infty$). Rogoff (1985b) shows that, in general, the optimal central banker has $\chi < \chi^{CB} < \infty$, and thus is conservative but not "too" conservative. The proof involves an envelope theorem argument. When χ^{CB} is very large, π^e is very small, and therefore the marginal cost of allowing slightly higher expected inflation is small. Thus the stabilization benefits of lowering χ^{CB} toward χ are first-order whereas the inflation cost is second-order. On the other hand, when $\chi^{CB} = \chi$, the monetary authorities are stabilizing optimally, and the inflation benefits to raising χ^{CB} are first-order while the stabilization costs are second-order.[30] There is thus a trade-off between flexibility and commitment. Lohmann (1992) shows that this trade-off may be mitigated by setting up the central bank so that the head may be fired at some large fixed cost. In this case, society will fire the conservative central banker in the face of very large supply shocks.[31]

9.5.2.2   Optimal Contracts for Central Bankers

One alternative to appointing a conservative central banker is to impose intermediate monetary targets on the central bank, perhaps through clauses in the central bank governor's employment contract.[32] Walsh (1995) has shown that the optimal contract in this class my eliminate the inflation bias of monetary policy without any sacrifice in stabilization efficacy.[33]

---

30. Effinger, Hoeberichts, and Schaling (1995) develop a closed-form solution to the model.

31. See also Flood and Isard's (1989) "escape clause" model of fixed exchange rates. Obstfeld (1991), however, shows that escape clauses such as Lohmann's and Flood and Isard's can lead to multiple equilibria and therefore be destabilizing. We will see such an example later on when we revisit models of speculative attacks on fixed exchange rates.

32. See Rogoff (1985b), who considers the credibility implications of a variety of intermediate targets, including inflation and nominal GNP. Using interest rate targets—nominal or real—to anchor inflation actually turns out to be counterproductive.

33. Persson and Tabellini (1993) expand Walsh's idea to look at various alternative monetary institutions. See also Persson and Tabellini (1995).

Suppose again that society creates an independent central bank, this time choosing a central banker who places the same relative preference weight on inflation stabilization as society [as reflected in eq. (31)]. In addition to society's welfare, however, the central banker also responds to monetary incentives. Suppose that these incentives are set so that the central banker's loss function is given by

$$\mathcal{L}_t^{CB} = (\pi_t - \pi_t^e - z_t - k)^2 + \chi \pi_t^2 + 2\omega \pi_t. \tag{42}$$

This objective function is the same as the social welfare function (31) except for the additional linear term in inflation tacked on the end. Imagine that the central banker receives a bonus that is reduced as inflation rises.

In place of first-order condition (32), the first-order condition for the central bank in setting inflation now becomes

$$\frac{d\mathcal{L}_t^{CB}}{d\pi_t} = 2(\pi_t - \pi_t^e - z_t - k + \chi \pi_t + \omega) = 0.$$

Taking $t-1$ expectations of the above equation and setting $\pi_t^e = E_{t-1}\pi_t$, we see that the equilibrium is now described by

$$\pi_t^e = \frac{k - \omega}{\chi}, \tag{43}$$

$$\pi_t = \frac{k - \omega}{\chi} + \frac{z_t}{1 + \chi}, \tag{44}$$

so that if $k - \omega$ is set equal to zero, the central bank will be induced to adopt the same monetary policy [eq. (36)] that it would in the presence of a commitment technology! The trick is that the added incentive term is linear, so that it mitigates the average inflation bias without affecting the central bank's marginal incentives for responding to z shocks. One of the most impressive features of the optimal linear incentive contract is that it turns out to be robust to incorporation of some types of private information (e.g., if the central bank has private information about its inflation forecasts, as in Canzoneri, 1985).[34]

What are some drawbacks to optimal incentive contracts? The most troubling question is whether a government that cannot itself be trusted to resist the temptation to inflate can be trusted to properly monitor the central bank's anti-inflationary incentives. Walsh (1995) and Persson and Tabellini (1993) argue that the contract may be encoded legally, but this justification is not sufficient. Even a government bound to make the payments specified in the contract may be hard to deter from offering a self-interested central banker extra-contract incentives that outweigh those specified in the original agreement. For example, the ex ante contract may give the central banker $1 million minus $100, 000 for every point of inflation. However, ex

---

34. Svensson (1995) shows that a system of intermediate inflation targets shares many of the desirable features of the optimal-contracting approach.

post, the government can offer the banker other incentives, explicitly or under the table, that more than offset his pecuniary loss from inflating. Any cost to bribing the central banker is likely to be small relative to the potential gains as perceived by the government. Government officials often find creative *sub-rosa* ways to pay themselves, so there is no reason to assume they could be prevented from tempting a central banker if the stakes were high enough.

Another problem with the optimal contract scheme is that there may be uncertainty about the relative weight the banker places on public welfare versus personal financial remuneration. If so, uncertainty about, say, the central banker's financial needs (e.g., private information about a costly impending divorce) may lead to uncertainty over inflation and introduce extraneous noise into inflation policy. Such uncertainty is above and beyond any uncertainty that might exist over the central banker's value of χ^{CB} (relative weight on inflation stabilization).[35] Finally, as Herrendorf and Lockwood (1996) point out, the efficiency of the contract approach may be reduced when the private sector resets its wage contracts at more frequent intervals than the government is able to reset the terms of the central banker's contract. (Given political constraints, this assumption seems highly plausible.) In this case, an appropriately structured contract can still reduce the mean inflation rate to zero but the response to supply shocks is no longer optimal. Herrendorf and Lockwood derive conditions under which the conservative central banker approach is more robust to this problem. While these criticisms are important, the optimal contract approach remains valuable in providing a concrete framework for designing optimal institutions.

9.5.3   Political Business Cycles

One interesting theoretical and empirical application of models of monetary policy credibility is to the study of political business cycles. During much of the postwar period, many Western democracies could be characterized as having had a conservative political party that placed a relatively high weight on keeping inflation in check and a liberal party more concerned about unemployment. Hibbs (1977) showed that these differences have led empirically to a type of political business cycle in which inflation and output growth tend to be high when liberals are in office, and low when conservative regimes are in power. His model, however, assumes a very crude static Phillips curve framework in which the monetary authorities can systematically raise output growth by raising inflation. Alesina (1987) presents a clever refinement of the Hibbs model that allows the private sector to form expectations in a more rational manner.

Suppose that the preferences of the monetary authority are determined by the party in power (we drop any consideration of whether these preferences coincide

---

35. See exercise 4 at the end of the chapter.

with society's preferences or a utilitarian social welfare function). When liberals are in power, the monetary authorities' objective function is

$$\mathcal{L}_t^L = -(\pi_t - \pi_t^e - k) + \frac{\chi^L}{2}\pi_t^2, \tag{45}$$

where L superscripts pertain to the "liberal" party. (We abstract from supply shocks z, which are not important here.) Notice also that we have chosen a functional form in which the term $\pi_t - \pi_t^e - k$ enters linearly. This change turns out to simplify the analysis and also corresponds to the notion that liberal parties always prefer more output to less. The conservative party places no weight on employment stabilization, so that its objective function is simply

$$\mathcal{L}_t^C = \pi_t^2. \tag{46}$$

Thus the conservative party always sets inflation at $\pi = 0$.

When the public knows in advance that the liberal party is going to be in power, equilibrium inflation is

$$\pi_t^e = \pi_t = \frac{1}{\chi^L}. \tag{47}$$

[Differentiate eq. (45) with respect to π_t holding π_t^e constant, then solve the resulting equation for π_t and observe that $\pi_t^e = \pi_t$ in equilibrium.] When the preferences of the policymaker in office are known in advance by wage setters, there is no difference in real wages and employment under the two regimes, since monetary policy is fully anticipated. The only difference is that equilibrium inflation is higher under the liberal party (it is zero under the conservatives).

Suppose, however, that there is an election in period t, and that when setting wages in $t - 1$, the public does not know which party is going to win. For simplicity, assume that the probability of either party winning is exogenous and equal to $\frac{1}{2}$. In this case, expected inflation is given by

$$\pi_t^e = \frac{1}{2} \cdot 0 + \frac{1}{2} \cdot \frac{1}{\chi^L} = \frac{1}{2\chi^L}. \tag{48}$$

[The problem is simplified by the fact that with the functional form (46), the liberal party's choice of inflation is independent of π_t^e.] If the conservative party actually wins the election, inflation will be lower than anticipated, real wages will be high and output growth low. If the liberal party wins, inflation will be higher than anticipated and output growth high.

Alesina's analysis suggests the following prediction. Throughout a liberal government's term inflation will be high, and throughout a conservative government's term inflation will be low. But output growth will be different for the two types of government only during the first part of a term in office, when contracts have not fully adjusted to the new government's preferences. During the second part of a government's term in office, output growth will be the same regardless of which party holds power. This is an interesting and strong refinement of the Hibbs model. Remarkably, Alesina (1987) finds that "rational partisan" political business cycles are evident across a broad range of Western democracies. Growth tends to be higher under liberal parties but only during the first year or two after an election, while inflation tends to be higher under liberal parties throughout their term in office.

One can criticize the Alesina model on a number of grounds. If elections are such a major source of inflation uncertainty, why aren't contracts timed to expire just before predictable elections so that new contracts can take into account the preferences of the winner? Won't the cycle be sharply mitigated in a lopsided election where there is little uncertainty about the ultimate victor? Nevertheless, the simple crisp empirical predictions of the model, together with its apparent empirical power, make this one of the most interesting pieces of evidence in favor of the general Kydland-Prescott and Barro-Gordon approach.

We note that this type of political business cycle is strikingly different from the classic Nordhaus (1975) cycle in which incumbents attempt to expand output prior to elections to try to convince voters to reelect them. For rational expectations refinements of the Nordhaus model based on cycles in budget policy, see Rogoff and Sibert (1988) and Rogoff (1990).

Application: Central Bank Independence and Inflation

The preceding discussion suggests that the inflation bias in monetary policy may be reduced by making the central bank independent of political pressures. In reality the degree of central bank independence is measured on a continuum. Variables such as the length of directors' terms, the process through which directors are appointed, and even the budgetary resources over which the bank has control may all have a bearing on its true independence in formulating monetary policy. Alesina and Summers (1993), Cukierman, Webb, and Neyapti (1992), and Grilli, Masciandaro, and Tabellini (1991), among many others, have noted a negative correlation between long-run industrial-country inflation rates and various indicators of central bank independence.

Figure 9.11 plots the Cukierman, Webb, and Neyapti (1992) measure of central bank independence (CBI) against average 1973–94 CPI inflation rates for 17 industrial countries. The least squares regression line for the cross section is

$$\pi_{1973-94} = 8.30 - 6.02CBI, \qquad R^2 = 0.30$$
$$\phantom{\pi_{1973-94} = }(1.57) \;\; (2.35)$$

(with standard errors in parentheses). The slope coefficient is of the hypothesized sign, and significant.

A number of authors have questioned whether results such as these really imply a strong causal link from CBI to low inflation. For one thing, this empirical cor-

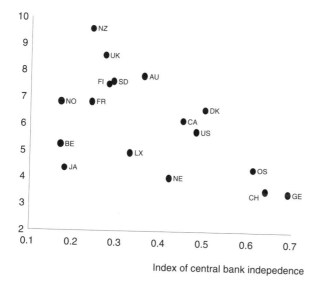

Average inflation, 1973-94

Index of central bank independece

Figure 9.11
Central bank independence versus inflation

relation does not extend easily beyond the set of industrialized countries. It may also be that CBI and low inflation arise from a common source. Posen (1995) argues that the political influence of a country's financial industry is instrumental in explaining both the independence of its central bank and its inflation record. In his framework, CBI in itself has no favorable inflation effect unless the central bank's directorate is more "hawkish" on inflation than the rest of government, and an influential financial community can best ensure this outcome. In addition, there are countries evident in Figure 9.11, notably Japan, with relatively dependent central banks yet low average inflation. (However, the main outside influence over the Bank of Japan is the Ministry of Finance, which is itself both conservative and very independent.) Milesi-Ferretti (1995) suggests that countries dominated by conservative politicians may avoid setting up institutions conducive to low inflation. The conservatives in power are themselves averse to inflation, but they wish to keep voters fearful of what the liberal opposition might do if elected. Campillo and Miron (in press) find little evidence that CBI affects long-run inflation even in high-income countries once other determinants of inflation, such as the size of the public debt, are included in cross-section regressions.

Because institutions are endogenous in the long run, the critics who view inflation and CBI as jointly determined have a point. At this stage, the evidence linking central bank independence to low inflation may be regarded as highly suggestive but not decisive.

■

9.5.4   Pegging the Exchange Rate to Gain Anti-Inflation Credibility

The basic lessons of the preceding closed-economy analyses readily extend to the open economy. The same institutional resolutions of the credibility problem available in the closed economy (an independent central bank, inflation targeting) are available in the open economy. In the open economy, however, another instrument for trying to commit to low inflation is available, the exchange rate. Indeed, pegging the exchange rate against the currency of a low-inflation country has been an extremely popular approach to developing or maintaining anti-inflation credibility. Giavazzi and Pagano (1988) argue that during the 1980s, many EMS countries effectively designated Germany's Bundesbank as their "conservative central banker" by pegging their nominal exchange rates to the Deutsche mark. Most developing countries have made exchange-rate stability the centerpiece of their inflation stabilization attempts.

In Chapter 8, however, we showed that fixed exchange rates can be susceptible to speculative crises. There we treated the government's behavior as mechanical. Here we show how speculative attacks can arise in a setting where the government's objectives are spelled out explicitly. An important implication of our discussion is that fixed exchange-rate commitments, like reliance on reputational mechanisms, may do little to buttress the credibility of governments with otherwise strong incentives to inflate. Indeed, they may give rise to multiple equilibria and the possibility of currency crises with a self-fulfilling element.[36]

9.5.4.1   The Model

Let's return to this section's basic model of monetary policy credibility. Reinterpret the model as applying to an open economy in which PPP holds, so that $P = \mathcal{E}P^*$, or, in log notation with P^* normalized to 1, $e = p$. Suppose the government minimizes the loss function

$$\mathcal{L}_t = (y_t - \tilde{y})^2 + \chi \pi_t^2 + C(\pi_t), \tag{49}$$

where, because of the PPP assumption, π_t corresponds to $e_t - e_{t-1}$, the realized rate of currency depreciation, as well as to the inflation rate. Under a fixed exchange rate, $\pi_t = 0$.

The loss function in eq. (49) is of the same general category as eq. (42), but with a different supplementary inflation-cost term $C(\pi_t)$. In an attempt to temper its credibility problems, the government here has adopted a "fixed but adjustable" exchange rate. It has placed itself in a position such that any upward change in e (a devaluation, implying $\pi_t > 0$) leads to an extra cost to the government of $C(\pi_t) = \bar{c}$, whereas any downward change in e (a revaluation, implying $\pi_t < 0$) leads to a

---

36. This section's analysis is based on Obstfeld (1996b).

cost of $C(\pi_t) = \underline{c}$. The fixed cost of a parity change could be viewed as the political cost of reneging on a promise to fix the exchange rate (for example, an EMS exchange-rate mechanism commitment).[37] If there is no change in parity, $C(0) = 0$. As we shall see, the fixed cost to breaking the exchange rate commitment may help reduce expected inflation but also may leave the economy open to speculative attacks.

Wages are again determined by eq. (27) and aggregate supply as in eq. (26). Output therefore is described by an expectations-augmented Phillips curve

$$y = \bar{y} + (\pi - \pi^e) - z;$$
(50)

that is, output net of the natural rate depends on unexpected currency depreciation (equals inflation) and a random supply shock, as before. Again, $\tilde{y} - \bar{y} = k > 0$. We have dropped time subscripts under the assumption that the equilibrium is time invariant, which will turn out to be consistent with our assumptions.

9.5.4.2   Equilibria

We will focus here only on equilibria of the one-shot game. We remind you that the private sector chooses depreciation expectations π^e before observing either z or π. In contrast, the government chooses π after observing both z and π^e.

Let us initially ignore the fixed cost term $C(\pi)$. If there were no fixed cost, the government would choose

$$\pi = \frac{k + \pi^e + z}{1 + \chi}$$
(51)

just as in eq. (33). Substituting this solution back into eqs. (50) and (49), we see that the resulting output level is

$$y = \bar{y} + \frac{k - \chi\pi^e - \chi z}{1 + \chi},$$
(52)

and that the government's ex post policy loss is

$$\mathcal{L}^{\text{FLEX}} = \frac{\chi}{1 + \chi}(k + \pi^e + z)^2.$$
(53)

Without *any* option of altering the exchange rate, the government's ex post loss would instead be

$$\mathcal{L}^{\text{FIX}} = (k + z + \pi^e)^2 > \mathcal{L}^{\text{FLEX}}.$$
(54)

Now take into account the fixed costs of currency realignment, $C(\pi)$. Given those costs, the authorities will change the exchange rate only when z is high

---

37. It is quite plausible that the public would not know $C(\pi)$ but would only have priors on it. For a characterization of the reputational equilibria that can arise in this case, see Rogoff (1987) and Froot and Rogoff (1991).

enough to make $\mathcal{L}^{\text{FIX}} - \mathcal{L}^{\text{FLEX}} > \bar{c}$ (in which case the currency is devalued), or low enough to make $\mathcal{L}^{\text{FIX}} - \mathcal{L}^{\text{FLEX}} > \underline{c}$ (in which case the currency is revalued). Devaluation thus occurs when $z > \bar{z}$, where

$$\bar{z} = \sqrt{\bar{c}(1 + \chi)} - k - \pi^{\text{e}}, \tag{55}$$

and devaluation when $z < \underline{z}$, where

$$\underline{z} = -\sqrt{\underline{c}(1 + \chi)} - k - \pi^{\text{e}}. \tag{56}$$

For shock realizations $z \in [\underline{z}, \bar{z}]$, the fixed exchange rate is maintained.

This policy response is akin to the escape-clause models of Flood and Isard (1989) and Lohmann (1992). The monetary authorities defend the fixed exchange rate against all but very large (in absolute value) shocks, in which case they pay the fixed costs of devaluation (revaluation) in order to use monetary policy for output stabilization. (Of course, once the fixed cost is paid, it will no longer serve as a check on the monetary authorities' aspirations to raise output systematically.)

The rational expectation of inflation (depreciation) π in the next period, given wage setters' expectations π^{e}, is

$$E\pi = E\{\pi \mid z < \underline{z}\}\Pr(z < \underline{z}) + E\{\pi \mid z > \bar{z}\}\Pr(z > \bar{z}), \tag{57}$$

where $\Pr(\cdot)$ denotes probability. (Recall that depreciation is zero when $\underline{z} \le z \le \bar{z}$.) Expected inflation π^{e} enters here both in determining the inflation rate the government chooses conditional on choosing to realign, and in determining the probability of a realignment. The fact that ex post inflation depends on π^{e} in a potentially very complicated way gives rise to the possibility that there are multiple equilibrium expected inflation rates under the "fixed but adjustable" exchange-rate scheme.

To see a parametric example of how multiple equilibria can arise, let us assume that z is uniformly distributed on $[-Z, Z]$.[38] Making use of eqs. (55)–(57) and (51), we calculate

$$E\pi = \frac{1}{1 + \chi}\left[\left(1 - \frac{\bar{z} - \underline{z}}{2Z}\right)(k + \pi^{\text{e}}) - \frac{\bar{z}^2 - \underline{z}^2}{4Z}\right] \tag{58}$$

---

38. In this case z is bounded and we must formally modify eq. (55) to read

$$\bar{z} = \max\left[\min\left\{\sqrt{\bar{c}(1 + \chi)} - k - \pi^{\text{e}}, Z\right\}, -Z\right],$$

whereas eq. (56) becomes

$$\underline{z} = \min\left[\max\left\{-\sqrt{\underline{c}(1 + \chi)} - k - \pi^{\text{e}}, -Z\right\}, Z\right].$$

For example, if $\sqrt{\bar{c}(1 + \chi)} - k - \pi^{\text{e}} > Z$ (implying that the cost of devaluing is prohibitively high given χ, k, and π^{e}), devaluations will never occur.

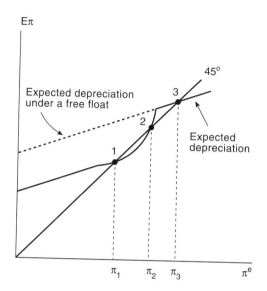

Figure 9.12
Multiple equilibria for expected depreciation

for a uniformly distributed shock z.

In equilibrium, wage setters' depreciation expectations must be rational,

$$\pi^e = E\pi,$$

where $E\pi$ is given by eq. (58), with $\bar{z}$ and $\underline{z}$ given by eqs. (55) and (56). In the basic one-shot-game credibility model of section 9.5.1, there was only one solution π^e to this last equation. But now there can be several such equilibria. To illustrate the fixed points of eq. (58), Figure 9.12 graphs it together with the 45° line. Let $-i^*$ denote the minimum possible level of π^e,[39] and assume that $\underline{c}$ and $\bar{c}$ are small enough so that at $\pi^e = -i^*$, $\underline{z} > -Z$ and $\bar{z} < Z$.

We calculate the slope of eq. (58) by differentiating it using formulas (55) and (56) to ascertain how $\bar{z}$ and $\underline{z}$ change as π^e rises. You can verify that $d\bar{z}/d\pi^e = d\underline{z}/d\pi^e = -1$ as long as $\underline{z} > -Z$. But as π^e rises, $\underline{z}$ falls. Output conditional on no realignment is falling, so progressively larger (in absolute value) negative shocks are needed to justify incurring the fixed cost of revaluation. Eventually as π^e rises, $\underline{z}$ hits its minimum value of $-Z$. Plainly, $d\underline{z}/d\pi^e = 0$ once this has happened.

Similarly, $\bar{z}$ too falls as π^e rises, because even relatively small positive shocks may warrant devaluation when output conditional on no devaluation is very low. Eventually as π^e rises, $\bar{z}$ reaches $-Z$, meaning that devaluation occurs for any

39. Assuming interest parity, this assumption gives the domestic nominal interest rate a lower bound of 0.

shock realization. At this point, obviously, $d\bar{z}/d\pi^e = 0$. Putting this information together, we find that the slope of eq. (58) is

$$\frac{dE\pi}{d\pi^e} = \begin{cases} \dfrac{1}{1+\chi} & \text{(for } \underline{z} > -Z) \\[2ex] \dfrac{1}{1+\chi}\left[\dfrac{1}{2} + \dfrac{1}{2Z}\left(k+\pi^e\right)\right] & \text{(for } \underline{z} = -Z, \ \bar{z} > -Z) \\[2ex] \dfrac{1}{1+\chi} & \text{(for } \bar{z} = -Z). \end{cases}$$

Once π^e has risen high enough that the devaluation threshold $\bar{z}$ is stuck at $-Z$, the government's reaction function reduces to eq. (51) and depreciation expectation (57) is the same as under a completely flexible exchange rate.

Figure 9.12 illustrates a situation with three possible equilibria, corresponding to different devaluation probabilities and different realignment magnitudes conditional on devaluation. In equilibrium 3, the expected rate of depreciation is given by $\pi^e = k/\chi$, which is exactly the mean expected rate of depreciation that would obtain under a free float; recall eq. (34). Equilibria 2 and 1 entail successively lower expected inflation.[40]

What are the implications of multiple equilibria? Having adopted a fixed but adjustable exchange rate, the government is powerless to enforce its favored low-inflation equilibrium at point 1. It may even end up being gamed into a free float, paying the fixed cost $\bar{c}$ with no benefit from having partially committed to a fixed rate. The root problem is that high expected depreciation in and of itself, by incipiently raising unemployment, creates an incentive for the government to validate expectations ex post by devaluing.

With multiple equilibria some seemingly unimportant event could trigger an abrupt change in expectations, shifting the equilibrium from one in which only a very bad realization of z forces the government off the fixed rate to one in which even a relatively small z does so. Such an event would look much like the sudden speculative attacks on exchange rates we analyzed using a very different setup in Chapter 8. But here the situation is analogous to a bank run in which withdrawals sparked by depositor fears can themselves cause an otherwise viable bank to fail.

It is important to note that a government with strong fundamentals (e.g., $\bar{c}$ and χ large, k low) is less vulnerable to speculative attacks taking the form of a shift in

---

40. For the free-float equilibrium to exist, we require the parameter restriction

$$\frac{1+\chi}{\chi}k - Z \geq \sqrt{\bar{c}(1+\chi)},$$

a condition that is more likely to be met if inflation aversion χ is low, $\bar{c}$ is low, and the "credibility distortion" k is high. One can see from the figure that there can only be multiple equilibria if this condition is met (though for more general probability distributions of z, there can be multiple equilibria even if there is no free-float equilibrium).

equilibria. (Conversely, a government with weak inflation fundamentals is more likely to find itself in a situation with multiple equilibria.) This point holds in a wide range of models (see Jeanne, 1995; Obstfeld, 1996b; or Velasco, 1996). Thus, even if speculative attacks are driven by "sunspots," countries with weak fundamentals are more likely to be vulnerable to them. For example, fears that a government will fail to service a big debt can themselves induce debt devaluation, possibly through an exchange rate change (see Calvo, 1988; Obstfeld, 1994d; and Cole and T. Kehoe, in press). Speculative attacks can contain a self-fulfilling element, being somewhat arbitrary in timing and weakening currency pegs that might have been sustainable for some time absent the attack. But it would be wrong to view the type of speculative attack analyzed here as being entirely divorced from fundamentals.

In stochastic versions of the classical balance-of-payments crisis model from Chapter 8, attacks typically are preceded by a period of rising domestic-foreign interest differentials, reflecting rising expectations of depreciation. But as Rose and Svensson (1994) show for the September 1992 attacks on the EMS, and Obstfeld and Rogoff (1995c) show for the December 1994 Mexican peso collapse, one-month to one-year interest differentials often remain fairly constant prior to an attack, rising sharply only when a crisis is imminent. Models with multiple equilibria, of the type considered in this section, may better be able to explain this phenomenon.

Application: Openness and Inflation

The preceding analysis treats the inflation problem in open economies in exact analogy to the closed-economy case. The dynamic consistency problem may be somewhat mitigated, however, in an open economy that takes world monetary policy as exogenous. The case of a flexible exchange rate is easiest to understand, though that assumption is not necessary. In the Dornbusch model discussed earlier in this chapter, we saw that unanticipated monetary expansion by a small open economy will, in general, lead to a real currency depreciation. Rogoff (1985a) has shown that this tendency for the exchange rate to depreciate following a monetary expansion may temper the incentives of a country's monetary authorities to inflate, unless the country's trade partners inflate at the same time. If the price index that the monetary authorities seek to stabilize includes foreign goods, real currency depreciation exacerbates the CPI inflation cost of unilateral monetary expansion. At the same time, if wages are partially indexed to the CPI or if foreign goods enter as intermediate goods into the production function, the employment (output) gain to monetary expansion is reduced when the real exchange rate depreciates. Overall, the output-inflation Phillips curve trade-off is worse in an open economy than in a closed economy. Therefore, if other things are equal, the monetary authorities have less temptation to inflate, and the time-consistent rate of inflation is lower.

D. Romer (1993) tests the proposition that more open economies have lower inflation rates. (He gauges openness by the ratio of imports plus exports to GDP.) Looking at average inflation rates and openness across a broad cross-section of countries, Romer finds that more open countries indeed appear to have lower inflation, and he generally finds this conclusion to be quite robust. The main qualification is that openness and inflation do not appear to be correlated for OECD countries. Romer argues that these countries may have already found institutional resolutions to the dynamic consistency problem (for example, an independent central bank), so that their degree of openness is not so important.[41]   ∎

9.5.5   International Monetary Policy Coordination

Two-country sticky-price models, even of the traditional ad hoc variety, can quickly become quite elaborate. For this reason, we have not given them much role in this chapter, preferring to defer our discussion until Chapter 10, where we develop a newer framework based on microfoundations for analyzing sticky-price economies. However, we cannot conclude our discussion of strategic considerations in monetary policy without at least some mention of the global dimensions of the problem. International policy cooperation is a fundamental topic in international economics, one that flows naturally from the fact that the world is populated by sovereign governments answerable mainly to domestic residents. Hamada (1974) was the pioneer in formally modeling the macroeconomic policy coordination problem.

For large actors such as the United States, the European Union, or Japan, monetary policies have spillover effects on the rest of the world. When a large country inflates, the shift in world demand toward its goods can have a big impact on other countries, and there can also be an important effect on world real interest rates. As in any setting with spillovers, there can be gains to cooperation. A simple example illustrates the basic problem. (For the example, we temporarily abstract from any wedge between the natural level of output and the output level targeted by the authorities.) Consider a crude Keynesian setting in which Home output is given by

$$y_t - \bar{y} = a_1[\Delta m_t - E_{t-1}\Delta m_t] + a_2[\Delta m_t^* - E_{t-1}\Delta m_t^*] + \epsilon_t,$$

where $\Delta m_t \equiv m_t - m_{t-1}$. Think of the above equation as a reduced form from a two-country Keyensian model in which nominal prices (wages) are set a period

---

41. Lane (1995) argues that country size should be an important determinant of inflation as well. He finds that, controlling for country size, openness and inflation are negatively correlated even for OECD countries. For additional evidence, see Campillo and Miron (in press) and Terra (1995).

in advance. Monetary policy induces deviations in Home output from its natural rate only to the extent it is unanticipated; the shock ϵ captures other exogenous shocks. Foreign money growth shocks enter the preceding equation for reasons we have just discussed. In the canonical two-country Mundell-Fleming-Dornbusch model, the sign of the spillover term (the sign of a_2) is ambiguous. Foreign monetary expansion leads to a short-run real appreciation of Home's currency, with an expenditure-switching effect that tends to lower global demand for Home output. But (unanticipated) Foreign inflation also lowers the world real interest rate, producing a general rise in world demand that tends to raise Home output. Which effect dominates typically depends on the empirical parameters of the model.

An equation similar to the preceding one holds for Foreign,

$$y_t^* - \bar{y} = a_1[\Delta m_t^* - E_{t-1}\Delta m_t^*] + a_2[\Delta m_t - E_{t-1}\Delta m_t] + \epsilon_t^*$$

where we have imposed structural symmetry (though ϵ_t need not be perfectly correlated with ϵ_t^*).

If the only goal of both countries were to stabilize output around its natural rate, then it would not matter whether or not they conducted their monetary policies in concert. Holding constant $E_{t-1}\Delta m_t$ and $E_{t-1}\Delta m_t^*$, which are predetermined as of time t, the monetary authorities have two instruments (Home and Foreign money growth) to hit two targets. Both countries can stabilize output exactly with or without cooperation. What if, however, countries have more targets than instruments? Suppose, for example, that authorities also care about the absolute levels of money growth, Δm_t for Home and Δm_t^* for Foreign. In particular, suppose they have loss functions given by

$$\mathcal{L}_t = (y_t - \bar{y})^2 + \chi(\Delta m_t)^2,$$
$$\mathcal{L}_t^* = (y_t^* - \bar{y})^2 + \chi(\Delta m_t^*)^2.$$

(Think of the money-growth terms on the right-hand sides as capturing trend inflation.) Now there are four targets in all but still only two instruments, and it therefore makes a difference whether the countries cooperate. In the absence of cooperation (and assuming a one-shot-game Nash equilibrium), the Home authority sets Δm_t (it actually chooses m_t, since m_{t-1} is predetermined) so that

$$\frac{\partial \mathcal{L}_t}{\partial m_t} = 2a_1(y_t - \bar{y}) + 2\chi\Delta m_t = 0.$$

This first-order condition plainly ignores the spillover effect of m_t on y_t^*. (Remember, $t - 1$ expectations have been determined by the time monetary authorities move on date t.) Foreign similarly sets

$$\frac{\partial \mathcal{L}_t^*}{\partial m_t^*} = 2a_1(y_t^* - \bar{y}) + 2\chi\Delta m_t^* = 0.$$

Suppose instead that Home and Foreign monetary policy were set by a central planner aiming to maximize

$$x\mathcal{L}_t + (1 - x)\mathcal{L}_t^*.$$

The first-order conditions for the planner are

$$x\frac{\partial \mathcal{L}_t}{\partial m_t} + (1 - x)\frac{\partial \mathcal{L}_t^*}{\partial m_t} = 0,$$

$$x\frac{\partial \mathcal{L}_t}{\partial m_t^*} + (1 - x)\frac{\partial \mathcal{L}_t^*}{\partial m_t^*} = 0,$$

which generally differ from those underlying the Nash equilibrium if there are international spillover effects (if $a_2 \neq 0$).[42] Depending on whether the spillover effects are positive or negative, the planning solution may involve higher or lower levels of monetary expansion than the noncooperative Nash solution. This is the fundamental insight of the literature on international monetary cooperation. Anyone schooled in the basics of game theory (or indeed who has read the preceding material in this chapter) will realize that one can introduce a host of strategic complexities into this setup, such as allowing for cooperation via repeated play, information problems, and so on.[43]

One very important nuance becomes evident if we restore the assumption that there may be a wedge between the rate of output targeted by the monetary authority and the rate targeted by wage setters. In this case, the strategic interactions across the two monetary authorities can become intertwined with the strategic interactions of each monetary authority with its own private sector. Rogoff (1985a) demonstrates that in this case, one can no longer automatically assume that the monetary authorities will enjoy systematically higher utility if they cooperate with each other. Because coordinated monetary expansion may yield greater output expansion for any given level of inflation, cooperation may actually raise the monetary authorities' incentives to inflate. This can in turn exacerbate their credibility problem vis-à-vis their own private sectors and lead to a higher time-consistent rate of inflation.

A serious treatment of international monetary policy cooperation is somewhat beyond the scope of this book. Our main justification for not treating the issue in more detail is that virtually all of the literature is based on obsolete Keynesian models, which lack the microfoundations needed for proper welfare analysis. While some may view microfoundations as being of second-order importance in this context, they are quite wrong as the model of Chapter 10 will illustrate. Because ad

---

42. Exercise: Solve for the levels of monetary growth in both the Nash and planner solutions.

43. For a discussion of some of the many gaming issues in monetary policy coordination, see Hamada (1985) and Canzoneri and Henderson (1991). See also Persson and Tabellini (1995), who emphasize the importance of institutional reform in promoting better outcomes.

hoc Keynesian analyses of cooperation can yield seriously misleading policy prescriptions, there is a compelling case for basing policy-coordination analysis on
choice-theoretic models such as the ones we consider in the next chapter.[44]

Exercises

1. *Disinflation with sticky prices.* Consider the small-country sticky-price exchange rate
    model presented in section 9.2. Suppose a small open economy is initially in a steady
    state with a high, constant inflation rate of $m_t - m_{t-1} = \mu$. In the initial steady
    state, prices and exchange rates are also rising at rate μ. Suppose that at time 0, the
    government unexpectedly initiates a draconian deflation plan, whereby money growth
    is immediately reduced to $m_t - m_{t-1} = 0$, $\forall t \geq 0$.

    (a) Analyze the effects on the path of output, real interest rates, and the real exchange
    rate.

    (b) Is there any way (in this model) for the monetary authorities to lower the inflation
    rate to 0 without putting the economy through a prolonged spell of low output? (This
    is tricky!) Briefly discuss why or why not, and how reasonable your answer is.

2. *Anticipated real depreciation.* Analyze the effects of an anticipated rise in the equi-
    librium real exchange rate from $\bar{q}$ to $\bar{q}'$ in the sticky-price exchange rate model of
    section 9.2. News of the change is learned at time 0, but the rise actually takes place
    at time T.

3. *The optimal exchange rate feedback rule.* Consider the following stochastic small-
    open economy model in which all exogenous variables are constant except for serially
    uncorrelated shocks, and p^*, i^*, $\bar{y}$, and $\bar{q}$ are all normalized to 0:

    $$i_{t+1} = E_t e_{t+1} - e_t,$$

    $$y_t^s = \theta(p_t - E_{t-1}p_t),$$

    $$y_t^d = \delta(e_t - p_t) + \epsilon_t,$$

    $$m_t - p_t = -\eta i_{t+1} + \phi y_t + \upsilon_t.$$

    Here, $\epsilon \sim N(0, \sigma_\epsilon^2)$ and $\upsilon \sim N(0, \sigma_\upsilon^2)$ are independent, serially uncorrelated, nor-
    mally distributed shocks. The second equation above is a simple rational-expectations
    supply curve, in which one-period price surprises can raise or lower output. (One
    rationalization for this would be if nominal wage contracts were set a period in ad-
    vance.) The shock ϵ may be thought of as a shock to the demand for the country's
    goods, and υ is a shock to the demand for real money balances. We assume that the
    objective function of the monetary authorities is to minimize the one-period condi-
    tional variance of output, $E_{t-1}\{y_t^2\}$. (In this example, one can think of the objective of
    the monetary authorities as trying to smooth prices to save the private sector the cost
    of indexing.)

---

44. Issues of international policy coordination naturally arise in spheres other than that of monetary
policy, and can be important even when prices are flexible. For discussions of fiscal policy coordination,
see, for example, Hamada (1986) and Kehoe (1987). Once again, Persson and Tabellini (1995) provide
a good overview.

(a) First consider a fixed money supply rule under which $m_t = \bar{m}$ in all periods, and calculate $E_{t-1}\{y_t^2\}$ as a function of σ_ϵ^2, σ_v^2, and the other parameters of the model. [Hint: You will find that under this policy, $E_t e_s = E_t p_s = \bar{m}$, $\forall s > t$.]

(b) Now suppose that the monetary authorities fix the exchange rate at $\bar{e} = \bar{m}$ by adjusting $m_t - \bar{m}$ in response to the shocks each period as necessary to hold the exchange rate constant. They do not, however, alter the announced future path of money, which is expected to remain at $\bar{m}$ in the absence of future shocks. (That is, $E_t m_{t+s} = \bar{m}$, $\forall s > t$.) Again calculate $E_{t-1}\{y_t^2\}$.

(c) Show that as $\sigma_\epsilon^2/\sigma_v^2 \to 0$, the policy in part b of a fixed exchange rate is always superior to the policy in part a of a fixed money supply (a pure float).

(d) (Very hard.) Suppose that instead of limiting themselves to a pure fixed rate or a pure float, the monetary authorities adopt an exchange rate feedback rule, $m_t - \bar{m} = \Phi(e_t - \bar{e})$. Find the optimal value of Φ, and show that, in general, it is intermediate between 0 (pure float) and ∞ (fixed rate). [Hint: This is not conceptually difficult, but there is a fair amount of algebra. For an intuitive solution approach to this class of problems, see Canzoneri, Henderson, and Rogoff (1983).]

4. *Optimal contracts for central bankers with uncertainty over the relative weight on public versus own welfare.* Suppose that eq. (42) in this chapter is replaced with

$$\mathcal{L}_t^{CB} = (\pi_t - \pi_t^e - z_t - k)^2 + \chi\pi_t^2 + 2\lambda_t \omega\pi_t,$$

where $\lambda > 0$ is a random variable that captures the relative weight a policymaker places on his own bonus versus public welfare; $E_{t-1}\lambda_t = 1$, $\mathrm{Var}_{t-1}\lambda_t = \sigma_\lambda^2$.

(a) Solve for π_t^e and π_t assuming a one-shot-game equilibrium.

(b) Assuming a social loss function of the form

$$\mathcal{L}_t = (\pi_t - \pi_t^e - z_t - k)^2 + \chi\pi_t^2,$$

solve for $E_{t-1}\mathcal{L}_t$.

(c) What choice of ω minimizes $E_{t-1}\mathcal{L}_t$?

5. *Central bank secrecy.* Suppose that in section 9.5.1's model of money and inflation, we replace the monetary authority's loss function (31) by one analogous to eq. (45),

$$\mathcal{L}_t = -\lambda_t(\pi_t - \pi_t^e - k) + \tfrac{1}{2}\pi_t^2,$$

in which there is no supply shock ($z = 0$), but where λ is a random variable such that $\lambda = 0$ with probability $\frac{1}{2}$, and $\lambda = 2$ with probability $\frac{1}{2}$. One may think of λ as capturing shocks that change the relative benefits of output versus inflation (e.g., a war).

(a) Solve for the one-shot-game equilibrium levels of π_t^e and π_t.

(b) Suppose the central bank can commit to a reaction function for $\pi_t(\lambda_t)$. Find the optimal reaction function such that $\pi_t^e = 0$. Is $E_{t-1}\mathcal{L}_t$ lower than in part a?

(c) Suppose now that the central bank knows λ_t in period $t - 1$. Calculate $E_{t-2}\mathcal{L}_t$ under two different regimes. In one, the central bank always reveals λ_t before π_t^e is set. In the other, it never reveals λ_t.

As Chapter 9 showed, many of the central issues in international monetary economics, including exchange-rate determination, the choice of exchange-rate regime, and the design of a central bank constitution, take on much greater significance when monetary policy can affect real output. Unfortunately, the Keynesian models we employed in Chapter 9 have many shortcomings. Given their lack of microfoundations for intertemporal choice, the models have very little to say about current accounts or budget deficits, and even less to say about welfare. But the older Keynesian models do have one very important feature that gives them an empirical edge over flexible-price monetary models: they allow for nominal rigidities. Fortunately, it is possible to introduce nominal rigidities without abandoning the insights of modern intertemporal economics, and in this chapter we illustrate how to do so.

A central element of our analysis involves introducing a monopolistic supply sector. Recent research in macroeconomics and trade theory has emphasized the possible importance of monopoly in explaining a range of phenomena, from business cycle regularities to growth. Monopoly plays a key role in our analysis because it permits one to justify rigorously the Keynesian assumption that output is demand-determined in the short run when prices are fixed. Monopoly also has important welfare implications for the international transmission of macroeconomic policy, and helps justify Chapter 9's assumption that a small country can temporarily affect its terms of trade through unanticipated monetary changes. Most of our analysis assumes sticky prices, but as we show toward the chapter's end, very similar results obtain in the presence of nominally rigid wages.

The reader should be warned that the models of this chapter may appear more challenging technically than most we have presented up until now. If broken down into their component parts, however, the models should seem familiar. For example, we make extensive use of consumption-based price indexes, which we first developed in Chapter 4. Our modeling of product differentiation exploits the constant-elasticity-of-substitution functional form used in Chapters 4, 5, 7, and 8. The money-in-the-utility-function formulation here will be familiar from Chapter 8. Finally, we make extensive use of log-linearizations to obtain closed-form solutions, a device used in Chapter 7's discussion of real business cycle models and in Chapter 4's Dornbusch-Fischer-Samuelson model. The only really new element is the introduction of nominal prices that are preset because of price-adjustment costs.

Our approach in this book generally has been to set out the small-country case before proceeding to more complex general-equilibrium models. Here, however, we plunge immediately into a full-blown two-country model, treating the small-country case as a limit in which one country's relative size goes to zero. Hopefully, the reader will find the greater intuition this strategy yields worth the extra effort. In the first model we develop, all goods are traded. Later in the chapter we consider a small-country model in which some goods are nontraded. This second model does not yield the interesting cross-country transmission effects of the global model, but it is a good deal simpler and, in some cases, yields the Dornbusch (1976) overshooting result of Chapter 9.

Most of this chapter's analysis focuses on monetary shocks. But the framework also yields some striking results concerning the effects of government spending and productivity shocks. An unanticipated permanent government spending increase, for example, both moves the world interest rate and causes a current-account surplus for the country where the shock originates. With sticky prices, output is demand-determined in the short run, so unexpected permanent changes in government spending tilt the path of world output. In contrast, the corresponding flexible-price model implies that permanent government consumption changes do not alter the time profile of output available for private consumption.

10.1   A Two-Country General Equilibrium Model of International Monetary Policy Transmission

In this section, we develop a perfect-foresight two-country general equilibrium monetary model with preset prices.[1] We consider only the perfect-foresight case because it suffices to illustrate the main new points of the chapter. To start, we specify tastes and technology and derive individual decision makers' first-order optimality conditions. The next step is to solve for a symmetric steady state where initial net foreign assets are zero. We linearize the model around its symmetric steady state and show how unanticipated permanent shocks affect the long-run equilibrium. (The economy would go immediately to this steady state if there were no nominal rigidities.) We then look at the economy's dynamics in the presence of preset nominal prices that can be adjusted only after a period.

10.1.1   Preferences, Technology, and Market Structure

The world is inhabited by a continuum of individual monopolistic producers, indexed by $z \in [0, 1]$, each of whom produces a single differentiated good, also indexed by z. All producers reside in two countries, Home and Foreign. Home consists of producers on the interval $[0, n]$, whereas Foreign producers are located on

---

1. The model is based on Obstfeld and Rogoff (1995a), who discuss related earlier analyses. The supply side of the model derives from the static closed-economy models of Blanchard and Kiyotaki (1987) and Ball and Romer (1989). The closest precursor to the model here is probably Svensson and van Wijnbergen (1989), who also embed monopolistic competition in a two-country sticky-price model. Their model, however, differs from the one we develop in many respects, perhaps the most important being its assumption of comprehensive international risk pooling. The assumption of comprehensive insurance in asset markets, aside from coexisting uneasily with their assumptions of nominal price rigidities and quantity rationing in goods markets, prevents monetary shocks from affecting the international distribution of wealth. This precludes current account effects and thus rules out some of the key issues we wish to study. In the model developed here, markets clear and there is no need for quantity rationing.

$(n, 1]$. It may seem strange to think of individuals as being the locus of monopoly power rather than firms, but this device is just a useful simplification. As usual, the results here can easily be extended to the case of decentralized factor markets. There is no capital or investment, but we stress that this is not an endowment economy because labor supply is elastic. Thus, it will turn out that period t output of good z, $y_t(z)$, is chosen in a manner that depends on the marginal revenue of higher production, the disutility of effort, and the marginal utility of consumption. Many important features of the model revolve around the endogeneity of output.

10.1.1.1 Preferences

All individuals throughout the world have identical preferences over a consumption index, real money balances, and effort expended in production. Since all agents within a country will have symmetric preferences and constraints, we analyze the maximization probems of representative national consumer-producers designated by the index value $j \in [0, 1]$. The intertemporal utility function of typical Home agent j is given by

$$
U_t^j = \sum_{s=t}^{\infty} \beta^{s-t} \left[\log C_s^j + \chi \log \frac{M_s^j}{P_s} - \frac{\kappa}{2} y_s(j)^2 \right].
$$

(1)

We discuss in turn each component of the period utility function.

The variable C is a real consumption index

$$
C^j = \left[\int_0^1 c^j(z)^{\frac{\theta-1}{\theta}} dz \right]^{\frac{\theta}{\theta-1}},
$$

(2)

where $c^j(z)$ is the jth Home individual's consumption of good z, and $\theta > 1$.[2] You will recognize eq. (2) as a natural generalization of the two-good constant-elasticity-of-substitution (CES) function that has appeared in several earlier chapters (beginning with Chapter 4).[3]

The price deflator for nominal money balances is the consumption-based money price index corresponding to (2). Let $p(z)$ be the Home-currency price of good z. Then the Home money price level is

$$
P = \left[\int_0^1 p(z)^{1-\theta} dz \right]^{\frac{1}{1-\theta}}.
$$

(3)

---

2. The parameter θ will turn out to be the price elasticity of demand faced by each monopolist. Since marginal revenue is negative when the elasticity of demand is less than 1, we require $\theta > 1$ to ensure an interior equilibrium with a positive level of output. This relationship will become apparent later when we solve for the steady state.

3. We also used a formulation analogous to eq. (2) for modeling how different types of capital affected aggregate output in the P. Romer (1990) model of Chapter 7.

This formula is a straightforward extension of the price index for the two-good CES case, and it can be derived similarly using the general approach developed in Chapter 4.[4]

The final term in the period utility functions in eq. (1), $-\frac{\kappa}{2} y_s(j)^2$, captures the disutility the individual experiences in having to produce more output. Suppose, for example, that the disutility from effort ℓ is given by $-\phi\ell$ and that the production function is $y = A\ell^\alpha$ ($\alpha < 1$). Inverting the production function yields

$$\ell = \left(\frac{y}{A}\right)^{1/\alpha}.$$

Then if $\alpha = 1/2$ and $\kappa = 2\phi/A^{1/\alpha}$, we have the output term that appears in eq. (1). It is very easy to relax the assumption $\alpha = 1/2$ in the following analysis, but doing so would only complicate some expressions without modifying any of our main qualitative conclusions. Note that a rise in productivity A may be captured in this model by a *fall* in κ.

A Foreign individual's utility function is completely analogous to that of a Home agent, except that Home money is held only by Home agents and Foreign money only by Foreign agents. The deflator for Foreign money balances M^* is

$$P^* = \left[\int_0^1 p^*(z)^{1-\theta}dz\right]^{\frac{1}{1-\theta}},$$

where $p^*(z)$ is the Foreign-currency price of good z.

10.1.1.2 Consumption-Based Purchasing Power Parity

To derive a relationship between P and P^*, we will assume that there are no impediments to trade, so that the law of one price holds for each individual good. That is, if we denote by $\mathcal{E}$ the nominal exchange rate (the Home-currency price of Foreign currency), then because $p(z)$ is the Home-currency price of good z and $p^*(z)$ is the Foreign-currency price of the same good,

$$p(z) = \mathcal{E}p^*(z). \tag{4}$$

---

4. Formally, the price index P solves the problem

$$\min_{c(z)} Z = \int_0^1 p(z)c(z)dz$$

subject to

$$\left[\int_0^1 c(z)^{\frac{\theta-1}{\theta}}dz\right]^{\frac{\theta}{\theta-1}} = 1.$$

We leave the derivation of expression (3) as an exercise for the reader.

Under the law of one price, we can rewrite the Home price index, eq. (3), as

$$
P = \left[\int_0^1 p(z)^{1-\theta} dz \right]^{\frac{1}{1-\theta}} = \left[\int_0^n p(z)^{1-\theta} dz + \int_n^1 [\mathcal{E} p^*(z)]^{1-\theta} dz \right]^{\frac{1}{1-\theta}}, \tag{5}
$$

since goods 0 to n are made at home, and the rest are produced abroad. Similarly, the Foreign price index P^* can be written as

$$
P^* = \left[\int_0^1 p^*(z)^{1-\theta} dz \right]^{\frac{1}{1-\theta}} = \left[\int_0^n [p(z)/\mathcal{E}]^{1-\theta} dz + \int_n^1 p^*(z)^{1-\theta} dz \right]^{\frac{1}{1-\theta}}. \tag{6}
$$

Comparing eqs. (5) and (6), we see that the Home and Foreign consumer price indexes are related by purchasing power parity:

$$
P = \mathcal{E} P^*. \tag{7}
$$

It is important to understand that PPP holds here because preferences are identical across countries and because there are no departures from the law of one price. Relative prices of various individual goods need not remain constant. Indeed, changes in the terms of trade—the relative price of Home and Foreign tradables—will play a large role here.

10.1.1.3   Individual Budget Constraints

To complete our specification of the individual's problem, we present the agent's budget constraint. We assume that the only internationally traded asset is a riskless real bond denominated in the composite consumption good. (We made the same assumption in the Dornbusch-Fisher-Samuelson model of section 4.5.) It would not be at all difficult to reformulate the model to incorporate greater asset diversity, but the assumption of complete asset markets would seem incongruous alongside the nominal rigidities we will introduce later on. The bonds-only formulation is also the more natural one if the object is to provide microfoundations for the Mundell-Fleming-Dornbusch setup. Under these assumptions, the period budget constraint for a representative Home individual j can be written in nominal terms as

$$
P_t B_{t+1}^j + M_t^j = P_t (1 + r_t) B_t^j + M_{t-1}^j + p_t(j) y_t(j) - P_t C_t^j - P_t \tau_t, \tag{8}
$$

where r_t denotes the real interest rate on bonds between $t - 1$ and t, $y_t(j)$ is output of good j (for which agent j is the sole producer), and $p_t(j)$ is its domestic-currency price. Because there is product differentiation, $p_t(j)$ need not be the same for all j. (Symmetric Home producers will, however, find it optimal to choose the same prices for their distinct products in equilibrium.) The variable M_{t-1}^j is agent j's holdings of nominal money balances entering period t, and τ_t denotes lump-sum taxes (payable in the composite consumption good C_t).

10.1.1.4 Government Budget Constraint

Since Ricardian equivalence holds in this setup, we can, without loss of generality, assume that the government runs a balanced budget each period.[5] For the moment, we will assume that there is no government spending so that all seignorage revenues are rebated to the public in the form of transfers:

$$0 = \tau_t + \frac{M_t - M_{t-1}}{P_t}. \tag{9}$$

10.1.1.5 Demand Curve Facing Each Monopolist

Given the constant-elasticity of substitution consumption index, eq. (2), it is easy to show that a Home individual's demand for z is given by[6]

$$c^j(z) = \left[\frac{p(z)}{P} \right]^{-\theta} C^j$$

and a Foreign agent's demand is

$$c^{*j}(z) = \left[\frac{p^*(z)}{P^*} \right]^{-\theta} C^{*j}.$$

Integrating demand for good z across all agents (that is, taking a population-weighted average of Home and Foreign demands), and making use of eqs. (4) and

---

5. As Woodford (1996) points out, Ricardian equivalence holds in monetary models with nominal rigidities only under somewhat more stringent assumptions than in real models.

6. Maximizing

$$C = \left[\int_0^1 c(z)^{\frac{\theta-1}{\theta}} dz \right]^{\frac{\theta}{\theta-1}}$$

subject to the nominal budget constraint

$$\int_0^1 p(z)c(z)dz = Z$$

(where Z is any fixed total nominal expenditure on goods), one can show that for any two goods z and z',

$$c(z') = c(z) \left[\frac{p(z)}{p(z')} \right]^{\theta}.$$

Plugging this expression into the preceding budget constraint and using eq. (3) shows that the representative agent's demand for good z is given by

$$c(z) = \left[\frac{p(z)}{P} \right]^{-\theta} \frac{Z}{P} = \left[\frac{p(z)}{P} \right]^{-\theta} C,$$

where the second equality uses the fact that P is the (minimum) money cost of one unit of composite consumption.

(7) [which imply that $p(z)/P = p^*(z)/P^*$ for any good z], we see that the total world demand for good z takes the constant-elasticity-of-substitution form

$$y^d(z) = \left[\frac{p(z)}{P}\right]^{-\theta} C^W, \tag{10}$$

where world consumption C^W is given by

$$C^W \equiv \int_0^n C^j \mathrm{d}j + \int_n^1 C^{*j} \mathrm{d}j = nC + (1-n)C^*. \tag{11}$$

In this equation, C (C^*) is consumption for a representative Home (Foreign) country agent. Equation (11) is the first of many times we drop the j superscript and impose symmetry on the identical agents within each country in order to simplify notation.

10.1.2   First-Order Conditions for the Representative Individual's Problem

To solve the model, use demand curve (10) [implying that $p_t(j)y_t(j) = P_t y_t(j)^{\frac{\theta-1}{\theta}}(C_t^W)^{\frac{1}{\theta}}$] to substitute for $p_t(j)$ in the period budget constraint (8). Then use the resulting expression to substitute for C_t^j in the intertemporal utility function (1). The result is the unconstrained maximization problem

$$\max_{y(j),M^j,B^j} U_t^j = \sum_{s=t}^{\infty} \beta^{s-t} \left\{ \log\left[(1+r_s)B_s^j + \frac{M_{s-1}^j}{P_s} + y_s(j)^{\frac{\theta-1}{\theta}}(C_s^W)^{\frac{1}{\theta}} \right.\right.$$

$$\left.\left. -\tau_s - B_{s+1}^j - \frac{M_s^j}{P_s} \right] + \chi \log\left(\frac{M_s^j}{P_s}\right) - \frac{\kappa}{2}y_s(j)^2 \right\}. \tag{12}$$

In performing this maximization, the individual takes C^W as given. The first-order conditions with respect to B_{t+1}^j, M_t^j, and $y_t(j)$, respectively, can then be written as

$$C_{t+1} = \beta(1+r_{t+1})C_t, \tag{13}$$

$$\frac{M_t}{P_t} = \chi C_t \left(\frac{1+i_{t+1}}{i_{t+1}}\right), \tag{14}$$

$$y_t^{\frac{\theta+1}{\theta}} = \frac{\theta-1}{\theta\kappa}(C_t^W)^{\frac{1}{\theta}}\frac{1}{C_t}, \tag{15}$$

where we have suppressed the indexes denoting agent j and i_{t+1} is the nominal interest rate for Home-currency loans between t and $t+1$, defined as usual by

$$1+i_{t+1} = \frac{P_{t+1}}{P_t}(1+r_{t+1}).$$

Equation (13) is, of course, the standard first-order consumption Euler equation for the case where the intertemporal elasticity of substitution is 1. Note that intertemporal consumption smoothing can be characterized entirely in terms of the composite index C and the consumption-based real interest rate r, just as in the multigood models of Chapter 4. Equation (14) is familiar from money-in-the-utility-function models of Chapter 8. It arises from the equilibrium condition that agents must be indifferent between (a) consuming a unit of the consumption good on date t or (b) using the same funds to raise cash balances, enjoying the derived transactions utility in period t, and then converting the extra cash balances back to consumption in period $t + 1$. The labor-leisure trade-off condition (15) is less familiar. It comes from the first-order condition that ensures that the marginal utility cost of producing an extra unit of output (implicitly due to forgone leisure) equals the marginal utility from consuming the added revenue that an extra unit of output brings. Analogous equations hold for the foreign country.

Note that, as usual, the first-order conditions (13)–(15) and the period budget constraint (8) do not fully characterize the equilibrium. Equilibrium also requires the transversality condition that[7]

$$\lim_{T \to \infty} R_{t,t+T} \left(B_{t+T+1} + \frac{M_{t+T}}{P_{t+T}} \right) = 0. \tag{16}$$

10.1.3 Global Equilibrium

In the aggregate, the domestic nominal money supply must equal domestic nominal money demand in each country, and global net foreign assets must be zero:

$$n B_{t+1} + (1 - n) B^*_{t+1} = 0. \tag{17}$$

Given these asset-market-clearing conditions, one can derive an aggregate global goods-market-clearing condition. Divide both sides of the Home period budget constraint (8) by P_t (and similarly divide both sides of the corresponding Foreign constraint by P^*_t), and then take a population-weighted average of the transformed budget constraints across Home agents and Foreign agents. Finally, impose condition (17) and the Home government budget constraint (9) (together with its Foreign analog) to obtain

$$C^W_t \equiv n C_t + (1 - n) C^*_t = n \frac{p_t(h)}{P_t} y_t(h) + (1 - n) \frac{p^*_t(f)}{P^*_t} y^*_t(f) \equiv Y^W_t, \tag{18}$$

where $y(h)$ and $p(h)$ are output and price of the representative Home good, and $y^*(f)$ and $p^*(f)$ are corresponding values for the representative Foreign good.[8] In

---

7. The transversality condition is derived by iterating the period budget constraint (8), as in Chapter 2.

8. The government budget constraint (9) implies that the τ terms must cancel the M terms in the aggregated period budget constraints (since money supply equals money demand), and condition (17) implies that at the world level the B terms must also cancel. The result is

$$\int_0^n C^j_t dj + \int_n^1 C^{*j}_t dj = \int_0^n \frac{p_t(j)}{P_t} y_t(j) dj + \int_n^1 \frac{p^*_t(j)}{P^*_t} y^*_t(j) dj$$

interpreting the preceding aggregate goods-market-clearing condition, remember that this is *not* a one-good model. We are able to aggregate here by using market prices to value all goods in terms of composite real consumption. Equation (18) thus states that world real consumption equals world real income.

10.1.4   A Symmetric Steady State

Because of monopoly pricing and endogenous output, the model here does not yield simple closed-form solutions for general paths of the exogenous variables. We could analyze the effects of exogenous shocks through numerical simulations. The intuition of the model, however, is much more easily seen by examining a linearized version. In order to linearize the system, we need to find a well-defined flexible-price steady state around which to approximate. The most convenient one corresponds to the case where all exogenous variables are constant, and this case is sufficient for illustrating our main points.

Because consumption and output are constant in the steady state, the real interest rate r is tied down by the consumption Euler equation (13) and is given by the now familiar condition

$$\bar{r} = \delta \equiv \frac{1 - \beta}{\beta},\tag{19}$$

where overbars indicate a steady state, and the parameter δ is the *rate* of time preference. (We first mentioned this notational convention in Chapter 1, footnote 1.)

Steady-state consumption must equal steady-state real income in both countries:

$$\bar{C} = \delta\bar{B} + \frac{\bar{p}(h)\bar{y}}{\bar{P}},\tag{20}$$

$$\bar{C}^* = -\left(\frac{n}{1 - n}\right)\delta\bar{B} + \frac{\bar{p}^*(f)\bar{y}^*}{\bar{P}^*}.\tag{21}$$

Equation (20) is just the usual condition one obtains for consumption when $\beta(1 + r) = 1$ (that is, when $\delta = r$) and income is constant. The only nuance is that here all variables are expressed in composite consumption units. Thus, as noted above, $\bar{p}(h)\bar{y}/\bar{P}$ is *real* income. As we shall see, $\bar{p}(h)/\bar{P}$ is not necessarily equal to 1 in the steady state if countries have different levels of wealth, since then their marginal utilities of leisure differ. Formally, one obtains eq. (20) by integrating the individual's period budget constraint (8) over time and then imposing the transversality condition (16) to obtain the present-value lifetime budget constraint. After imposing the government budget constraint (9) and domestic money-market equilibrium, one can show that the lifetime constraint reduces to eq. (20) in a steady

---

which reduces to eq. (18) because all individuals within a country are symmetric.

state with $\delta = r$. (For details, see Supplement A to Chapter 8.) The corresponding Foreign condition is derived similarly except that we have expressed $\bar{B}^*$ in terms of $\bar{B}$ using equilibrium condition (17).

In general, there is no simple closed-form solution for the steady state, but one does exist when initial foreign assets $\bar{B}_0 = 0$. In this special case, the equilibrium is completely symmetric across the two countries implying

$$\bar{p}_0(h)/\bar{P}_0 = \bar{p}_0^*(f)/\bar{P}_0^* = 1 \tag{22}$$

and

$$\bar{C}_0 = \bar{C}_0^* = \bar{y}_0 = \bar{y}_0^* = \bar{C}_0^{\mathrm{w}}, \tag{23}$$

where 0 subscripts on barred variables denote the initial preshock symmetric steady state where $\bar{B}_0 = 0$. [Equation (22) holds because in the globally symmetric equilibrium, any two goods produced anywhere in the world have the same price when prices are measured in the same currency.] The first-order condition governing each individual's optimal choice of output, eq. (15), then implies that in equilibrium,

$$\bar{y}_0 = \bar{y}_0^* = \left(\frac{\theta - 1}{\theta \kappa}\right)^{\frac{1}{2}}. \tag{24}$$

With flexible prices, output is determined independently of monetary factors.

Because each agent has monopoly power over the good he produces, global output is suboptimally low in the decentralized competitive equilibrium. To see this result, suppose that output is controlled by a planner interested in maximizing the utility of consumption net of the costs of forgone leisure

$$\max_y \left(\log y - \frac{\kappa}{2} y^2\right).$$

The solution is

$$y^{\mathrm{PLAN}} = \left(\frac{1}{\kappa}\right)^{\frac{1}{2}} > \left(\frac{\theta - 1}{\theta \kappa}\right)^{\frac{1}{2}} = \bar{y}_0. \tag{25}$$

In the decentralized equilibrium, in contrast, the marginal value of an additional unit of composite consumption exceeds the cost of forgone leisure. Monopolistic individual producers have no incentive to increase output of their own individual goods $y(j)$ unilaterally, since the benefits accrue mainly to other agents through a lower relative price. A planner, on the other hand, could coordinate jointly higher production. The inefficiency of the decentralized economy will play an important role in driving some of our later welfare results. Note that as the various goods become close substitutes (as θ becomes large), the distortions caused by monopoly abate.

Making use of money-demand equation (14) and the steady-state real interest rate condition (19), one can also solve for steady-state real balances,

$$\frac{\bar{M}_0}{\bar{P}_0} = \frac{\bar{M}_0^*}{\bar{P}_0^*} = \frac{\chi(1+\delta)}{\delta}\bar{y}_0, \tag{26}$$

where we have imposed the no-speculative-bubbles assumption.[9] In the next section, we linearize the model around the symmetric steady state we have just characterized.

10.1.5   Log Linearizing around the Symmetric Steady State

In this section, we develop linear versions of all of the model's equilibrium conditions. The general log-linearization approach is already quite familiar from Chapters 4 and 7, so we won't belabor the technique. Though the process is very straightforward, it is time-consuming. You should not feel obliged to check all of the linearizations on your first pass through the chapter, though you would probably find it helpful to check at least a couple of them. Again note that we are restricting our attention to a perfect-foresight setting (excepting initial shocks).

We begin with the price index equations (5) and (6). Assuming symmetry among each country's producers, these equations reduce to

$$P_t = \left\{ np_t(h)^{1-\theta} + (1-n)\left[\mathcal{E}_t p_t^*(f)\right]^{1-\theta} \right\}^{\frac{1}{1-\theta}},$$

$$P_t^* = \left\{ n\left[p_t(h)/\mathcal{E}_t\right]^{1-\theta} + (1-n)p_t^*(f)^{1-\theta} \right\}^{\frac{1}{1-\theta}}.$$

Linearizing around the symmetric steady state where $\bar{p}_0(h) = \mathcal{E}_0\bar{p}_0^*(f)$ yields

$$\mathsf{p}_t = n\mathsf{p}_t(h) + (1-n)\left[\mathsf{e}_t + \mathsf{p}_t^*(f)\right], \tag{27}$$

$$\mathsf{p}_t^* = n\left[\mathsf{p}_t(h) - \mathsf{e}_t\right] + (1-n)\left[\mathsf{p}_t^*(f)\right], \tag{28}$$

where we define $\mathsf{p}_t \equiv dP_t/\bar{P}_0$, $\mathsf{e}_t \equiv d\mathcal{E}_t/\bar{\mathcal{E}}_0$, $\mathsf{p}_t(h) \equiv dp_t(h)/\bar{p}_0(h)$, and $\mathsf{p}_t^*(f) \equiv dp_t^*(f)/\bar{p}_0^*(f)$.

NOTE: This notation for log approximations is the same one we used in Chapter 7, and it is more compact than the "hat" notation for log changes that we used in some earlier chapters. The more compact notation makes sense here because we will be extensively studying the approximate linear system, and it would be tedious to remind the reader constantly that the system we are looking at is only an approximation.[10]

---

9. The reader may be puzzled that nominal interest rates do not appear to affect steady-state money demand in eq. (26), but recall that with zero money and consumption growth and no bubbles, the steady-state nominal interest rate $\bar{\imath}$ equals the steady-state real interest rate $\bar{r}$, which in turn equals δ.

10. Superficially, the log differential notation here may seem inconsistent with our notation for the Mundell-Fleming-Dornbusch model in Chapter 9 (where e denoted log $\mathcal{E}$). But if one views the ad hoc linear model of Chapter 9 as a linearization of a more general system—which would seem to be the only natural interpretation—then the apparent inconsistency disappears.

The purchasing power parity equation (7) requires no approximation:

$$e_t = p_t - p_t^*. \tag{29}$$

The log-linearized versions of the world demand schedules for representative Home and Foreign products, eq. (10) and its Foreign counterpart, are

$$y_t = \theta \left[p_t - p_t(h) \right] + c_t^w, \tag{30}$$

$$y_t^* = \theta \left[p_t^* - p_t^*(f) \right] + c_t^w. \tag{31}$$

Note that if one takes a population-weighted average of eqs. (30) and (31) [that is, if one multiplies both sides of eq. (30) by n and both sides of eq. (31) by $1 - n$, and adds the results] all the price terms cancel [by eqs. (27) and (28)]. One then arrives at the world goods market equilibrium condition[11]

$$c_t^w = nc_t + (1 - n)c_t^* = ny_t + (1 - n)y_t^* \equiv y_t^w. \tag{32}$$

Log-linear versions of the labor-leisure trade-offs [eq. (15) and its Foreign counterpart] are

$$(\theta + 1)y_t = -\theta c_t + c_t^w, \tag{33}$$

$$(\theta + 1)y_t^* = -\theta c_t^* + c_t^w, \tag{34}$$

while the consumption Euler equations [(13) and its Foreign counterpart] take the log-linear form

$$c_{t+1} = c_t + \frac{\delta}{1 + \delta} r_{t+1}, \tag{35}$$

$$c_{t+1}^* = c_t^* + \frac{\delta}{1 + \delta} r_{t+1} \tag{36}$$

near the symmetric steady state, where $r_{t+1} \equiv dr_{t+1}/\bar{r}$ (recall that $\bar{r} = \delta$). Finally, log-linear versions of the money-demand equations [(14) and its Foreign counterpart] are

$$m_t - p_t = c_t - \frac{r_{t+1}}{1 + \delta} - \frac{p_{t+1} - p_t}{\delta}, \tag{37}$$

$$m_t^* - p_t^* = c_t^* - \frac{r_{t+1}}{1 + \delta} - \frac{p_{t+1}^* - p_t^*}{\delta}. \tag{38}$$

Note that if one subtracts eq. (38) from eq. (37) and applies the purchasing power parity equation (29), the result is

---

11. One can also derive eq. (32) directly by linearizing eq. (18) and applying eqs. (22), (23), (27), and (28).

$$m_t - m_t^* - e_t = c_t - c_t^* - \frac{1}{\delta}\left(e_{t+1} - e_t\right).\tag{39}$$

This equation is very similar to the exchange-rate equation that arises in the Cagan model (Chapter 8, p. 570) except that Home and Foreign consumption differentials appear in place of output differentials.

With the preceding linearizations in hand, we are now ready to solve the model, first for the steady state that is reached when prices are fully flexible, and then for short-run dynamics due to temporary price rigidities.

10.1.6   Solving for the Steady State

We now solve for the steady-state effect of a shift in the distribution of world wealth, indexed by $\bar{b}$. This solution will turn out to play a key role in tracing out the short- and long-run impacts of monetary shocks. If prices are perfectly flexible and all shocks are permanent, there are no dynamics and the world economy jumps instantly to the steady state governed by the existing distribution of wealth. With sticky nominal prices, which we will introduce shortly, the economy reaches the steady-state equilibrium characterized here only in the long run. Even though the price rigidities we introduce are merely temporary, it will turn out that unanticipated monetary factors still have a long-run impact through the world distribution of wealth. (Later in the chapter we will also analyze the impacts of productivity and government spending shocks which, if permanent, can have direct effects on the long-run equilibrium beyond their effects on wealth.)

To find closed-form solutions for the effects of wealth transfers (changes in $\bar{b}$) on the steady state, it is necessary to linearize one last pair of equations, (20) and (21), which equate steady-state income and expenditure in each country. The linearized versions are

$$\bar{c} = \delta\bar{b} + \bar{p}(h) + \bar{y} - \bar{p},\tag{40}$$

$$\bar{c}^* = -\left(\frac{n}{1-n}\right)\delta\bar{b} + \bar{p}^*(f) + \bar{y}^* - \bar{p}^*,\tag{41}$$

where a bar on a lowercase sans serif variable denotes the (approximate) log change in its steady-state value, for example, $\bar{c} = d\bar{C}/\bar{C}_0 = (\bar{C} - \bar{C}_0)/\bar{C}_0$. Since $\bar{B}_0 = 0$ in the initial symmetric steady state, we define $\bar{b} \equiv d\bar{B}/\bar{C}_0^W$. (Given that $\bar{C}_0 = \bar{C}_0^W = \bar{y}_0$, we could just as well have normalized changes in Home bond holdings by initial Home consumption or output.) Equations (40) and (41) are valid only for steady-state changes, so they are not time subscripted.

To solve for the long-run equilibrium as a function of net foreign assets $\bar{b}$, we observe that since eqs. (27)–(38) hold at all points, they must also hold once the economy has reached a steady state. The linear system characterizing the steady state is thus governed by eqs. (40) and (41) and barred versions of eqs. (27)–(38). This system of fourteen simultaneous equations may seem daunting, but the model's symmetry admits a simple solution approach. Specifically, it turns out to be quite easy to solve first for differences between per capita Home and Foreign variables, and then for population-weighted world aggregates (as in Aoki, 1981). This approach also makes the intuition underlying the results much clearer.

10.1.6.1   Solving for Differences between Home and Foreign Variables

Subtracting eq. (31) from eq. (30), eq. (34) from eq. (33), and eq. (41) from eq. (40), and making use of PPP equation (29), yields[12]

$$y_t - y_t^* = \theta[e_t + p_t^*(f) - p_t(h)], \tag{42}$$

$$y_t - y_t^* = -\frac{\theta}{1+\theta}(c_t - c_t^*), \tag{43}$$

$$\bar{c} - \bar{c}^* = \left(\frac{1}{1-n}\right)\delta\bar{b} + \bar{y} - \bar{y}^* - [\bar{e} + \bar{p}^*(f) - \bar{p}(h)]. \tag{44}$$

Substituting barred versions of eqs. (42) and (43) into eq. (44) yields

$$\bar{c} - \bar{c}^* = \left(\frac{1}{1-n}\right)\left(\frac{1+\theta}{2\theta}\right)\delta\bar{b}. \tag{45}$$

If output were exogenous (implying fixed labor input in the present model), a wealth transfer of $\bar{b}$ to Home would lead to a steady-state per capita international consumption differential of $[1/(1-n)]\delta\bar{b}$; Home residents would each raise consumption by the per capita interest $\delta\bar{b}$ on the transfer, and Foreign residents would each lower consumption by $n\delta\bar{b}/(1-n)$. But here output is *endogenous*, and the impact of wealth transfers on consumption differentials is less (recall $\theta > 1$). The reason is that with higher interest income, Home agents shift out of work into leisure, while poorer Foreign residents do the opposite. For the same reason, Home's steady-state terms of trade, given by

$$\bar{p}(h) - \bar{e} - \bar{p}^*(f) = \left(\frac{1}{1-n}\right)\left(\frac{1}{2\theta}\right)\delta\bar{b}, \tag{46}$$

improve when it receives a transfer. These transfer effects are all driven by the labor-leisure decision, but transfers can have a similar terms-of-trade effect in a model where output is exogenous but a country's residents have a preference for domestically manufactured goods.

---

12. Note that the relative price of typical Foreign and Home products, $e + p^*(f) - p(h)$, generally will change when the international wealth distribution becomes unequal. Home and Foreign producers then are no longer symmetric and may set different prices for their representative national products (with prices still compared in a common currency).

10.1.6.2   Solving for Population-Weighted Sums of Home and Foreign Variables

Multiply the home country labor-leisure equation (33) by n and the corresponding foreign equation (34) by $1 - n$, and then add to obtain an equation relating world income to world consumption:

$$(1 + \theta)y_t^W = (1 - \theta)c_t^W.$$

Combining a barred version of this equation with the steady-state version of eq. (32) implies that

$$\bar{y}^W = \bar{c}^W = 0. \tag{47}$$

Because of the symmetry of the model, small wealth transfers have no first-order effect on *global* consumption or income.

10.1.6.3   Solving for Levels of Individual Variables

Given the solutions for differences and world aggregates, it is easy to solve for the actual levels of all variables. For any variable x, these are related by the identities $x_t = x_t^W + (1 - n)\left(x_t - x_t^*\right)$ and $x_t^* = x_t^W - n\left(x_t - x_t^*\right)$. Thus, combining eq. (47) for aggregate consumption and eq. (45) for the difference between Home and Foreign consumption yields

$$\bar{c} = \left(\frac{1 + \theta}{2\theta}\right)\delta\bar{b}, \tag{48}$$

$$\bar{c}^* = -\left(\frac{n}{1 - n}\right)\left(\frac{1 + \theta}{2\theta}\right)\delta\bar{b}. \tag{49}$$

The solutions for other variables can be found similarly.

Note that we have been able to determine the long-run real equilibrium of the economy without reference to the money-demand equations because, of course, changes in the level of the money supply have no effect on real variables here when prices are flexible. Solutions for steady-state equilibrium price levels follow directly from the linearized money-demand equations (37) and (38):

$$\bar{p} = \bar{m} - \bar{c}, \tag{50}$$

$$\bar{p}^* = \bar{m}^* - \bar{c}^*. \tag{51}$$

Subtracting eq. (51) from eq. (50) and applying the purchasing power parity equation (29) gives the long-run exchange rate as

$$\bar{e} = \bar{m} - \bar{m}^* - (\bar{c} - \bar{c}^*). \tag{52}$$

10.1.7   Short-Run Equilibrium with Preset Prices

So far, but for a richer supply side, the model here is very much in the spirit of the flexible-price models of Chapter 8. We now introduce the assumption that the domestic-currency price of domestic goods, $p(h)$, and the foreign-currency price of foreign goods, $p^*(f)$, are set one period in advance, but adjust to flexible-price levels after a period, absent new shocks. Why might prices be set a period in advance? It is profoundly difficult to rationalize nominal price rigidities in a way that is both theoretically elegant and empirically sensible. There are basically two categories of explanations, those that rely on costs of price adjustment and those that portray inflexible price equilibria as a focal equilibrium in a world of multiple equilibria.[13] Multiple-equilibria explanations have the appeal of not having to posit a cost-of-adjustment technology for prices. On the other hand, they ultimately beg the question of why sticky prices are a relatively universal phenomenon. Specifically, multiple-equilibrium models do not explain why the sticky-price equilibrium would be consistently chosen across different eras and different countries if there are other, more efficient, equilibria.

10.1.7.1   Menu Costs and a Rationale for Demand-Determined Output

Probably the best extant rationalization for the approach we adopt here is the menu cost approach of Akerlof and Yellen (1985) and Mankiw (1985). In the present model, producers set prices to maximize real revenue net of the cost of forgone leisure. Because prices are set optimally by utility-maximizing monopolists, the envelope theorem implies that small changes in an individual's price will have only a second-order impact on his welfare. If there are finite menu costs to changing prices—even if these costs are fairly small—producers will not necessarily find it profitable to change prices in the face of sufficiently small demand shocks. Since in linearizing the model we are already restricting our attention to small shocks, the menu costs justification is quite appropriate.

   An important feature of the model is that it explains why output becomes demand determined in the short run if prices are rigid. When output markets are perfectly competitive and prices cannot adjust, there is no particularly strong argument for assuming that output adjusts to accommodate demand rather than being supply-determined. Here there is a strong argument, because under monopoly, prices are set above marginal cost. Thus if a small unanticipated shock raises demand, it will be profitable for a producer to raise output even if he cannot change his price. (A fall in demand will similarly lead to lower output if prices are fixed.)

---

13. Geanakoplos and Polemarchakis (1986) show that in principle one can rationalize sluggish price adjustment without appealing to non-Walrasian frictions. In their model, there are multiple equilibria, one of which exhibits sticky prices. See also Benhabib and Farmer (1994). For an application of this approach to exchange-rate models, see Beaudry and Devereux (1995).

Note that even with $p(h)$ and $p^*(f)$ set a period in advance, the Home-currency price of Foreign goods, $p(f)$, and the Foreign-currency price of Home goods, $p^*(h)$, must be able to fluctuate with the exchange rate in order for the law of one price to hold. Assuming that agents can freely buy and resell goods across borders, it is not possible for all goods to have fixed nominal prices in all countries. Later in the chapter we will consider a "pricing to market" version of the model in which there are impediments to trade and monopolists can price-discriminate across markets.

10.1.7.2   An Unanticipated Permanent Shock to the Money Supply

We are now ready to reconsider the classic Dornbusch exercise of an unanticipated permanent increase in the relative Home money supply occurring at time 1. That is, relative money supplies change according to

$$\bar{m} - \bar{m}^* = m - m^*, \tag{53}$$

where m is the percentage deviation of the time 1 money supply from the initial steady state: $m \equiv (M_1 - \bar{M}_0)/\bar{M}_0$. Note that we are able to drop time subscripts completely by taking advantage of the fact that the economy reaches its long-run equilibrium in just one period (because that is how long nominal prices take to adjust). Thus barred variables denote the long run (period 2 and beyond) and variables without time subscripts or bars denote period 1 variables.[14]

In the short run, at time 1, the Home-currency price of Home goods, $p_1(h)$, and the Foreign-currency price of Foreign goods, $p_1^*(f)$, are fixed at $\bar{p}_0(h)$ and $\bar{p}_0^*(f)$ (corresponding to the long-run symmetric equilibrium). For reasons we have already discussed, output becomes demand-determined when prices are sticky. *Therefore, the labor-leisure trade-off equations (33) and (34) do not bind.* The other equilibrium equations (27)–(32) and (35)–(38) still apply, even in the sticky-price short run.

One further difference between the short run and long run is that in the period when a shock hits, income need not equal expenditure, contrary to long-run eqs. (40) and (41). Instead, Home may run a current account surplus, given by

$$B_{t+1} - B_t = r_t B_t + \frac{p_t(h)y_t}{P_t} - C_t \tag{54}$$

(recall $G = I = 0$). Of course, the same must be true for Foreign. The linearized short-run (period 1) current account equations are therefore

$$\bar{b} = y - c - (1 - n)e, \tag{55}$$

---

14. As we have already noted, in a dynamic setting richer price adjustment mechanisms are possible. Restricting our attention to one-period menu costs, however, facilitates finding an analytical solution. Richer dynamic structures can, of course, be explored using numerical methods; see Aizenman (1989), Bergin (1995), or Sutherland (1995). Analytical models based on wage or price staggering are developed by Calvo (1983) and Calvo and Végh (1993).

Box 10.1
More Empirical Evidence on Sticky Prices

In Chapter 9 we discussed the substantial body of macroeconomic evidence showing that domestic price levels are considerably more sticky than exchange rates. Many international economists regard this as prima facie evidence that one must account for nominal price rigidities in any empirically plausible model of monetary policy. What is the microeconomic evidence on price rigidities? Using a data set on actual transactions prices, Carlton (1986) finds significant evidence of price rigidities for a wide range of intermediate goods. Carlton's results suggest that it is not unusual in some industries for prices to remain unchanged for several years. Blinder (1991) reaches similar conclusions using survey evidence on prices in manufacturing. Blinder finds that the modal period of price adjustment is one year. Based on his results, he estimates that fully 55 percent of GNP is repriced no more often than once per year. Both authors are careful, however, to emphasize that price is not the only mechanism that can be used to allocate goods, and that sellers can often change nonprice attributes (e.g., time of delivery) as a partial alternative to changing prices. There is, of course, a long empirical literature documenting the importance of nominal wage rigidities (see, for example, J. Taylor, 1983). (We will show in section 10.4 that our main results go through in a model making wages rather than prices the source of nominal rigidity.)

In an interesting study, Kashyap (1995) studies the price adjustment patterns for three large mail-order suppliers of consumer goods, L.L. Bean, Inc., the Orvis Company, Inc., and Recreation Equipment, Inc. For six items (two types of shoes, a chamois shirt, a wool blanket, a duffel bag, and a fishing fly), Kashyap's data set continuously spans the period 1953–87. Catalog pricing is interesting both because it encompasses a specific type of menu cost (it is expensive to reissue a catalog) and because the periodicity of the main company catalogs (generally six months) is fairly stable. Kashyap does indeed find that nominal rigidities are quite important and, like Blinder, finds that the average time between price changes for the various goods is twelve to eighteen months. (There is however, a considerable amount of variation.) Also consistent with the menu cost model is the finding that the (excess) kurtosis of price increases is 31.2 while the kurtosis of price cuts is 4.6; with general inflation and costly price adjustment, large price cuts will not be necessary as often as large price increases. One puzzling finding, though is that there is also a great dispersion across the size of price changes, with small price changes being very common. Kashyap argues that whereas the frequent small price changes are difficult to reconcile with fixed stationary menu-cost models, they may be consistent with newer dynamic menu-cost models where the cost of changing prices is itself a random variable (for example, the model of Caballero and Engel, 1994).

The microfoundations of nominal price rigidities remain a fundamental topic for macroeconomic research today. In our analysis, we assume an extremely simple model of price rigidities in order to develop a tractable analysis of other dynamic issues such as the current account. We do not deny the importance of introducing richer models of price rigidities, and this is one important area where the models of this chapter might be advanced in the future.

$$\left(\frac{-n}{1-n}\right)\bar{b} = \bar{b}^* = y^* - c^* + ne, \tag{56}$$

where we have made use of eqs. (27) and (28), and the fact that $p(h)$ and $p^*(f)$ are preset. Note that $\bar{b}$ appears in eqs. (55) and (56). Why? Given one-period price setting, whatever net foreign asset stocks arise at the end of the first period become the new steady-state levels from period 2 on. That is,

$$b_t = \bar{b}, \qquad \forall t \geq 2,$$

because all agents have equal discount rates and outputs are constant. This equality provides a crucial link between the equations of short-run and long-run equilibrium. Remember that in section 10.1.6, we gave solutions for steady-state variables as functions of $\bar{b}$, but $\bar{b}$ is affected by short-run current-account imbalances.

As with the steady-state system, it is much easier and more intuitive to approach the system by solving for country differences and world aggregates.

10.1.7.3   Solving the Short-Run System for Differences between Home and Foreign Variables

We first solve for differences between Home and Foreign variables, including the terms of trade and the exchange rate (which depend on price differences).

Subtracting the foreign Euler equation (36) from its domestic counterpart, eq. (35), yields

$$\bar{c} - \bar{c}^* = c - c^*, \tag{57}$$

where the left-hand side is the difference in long-run consumption changes and the right-hand side is the difference in short-run (period 1) changes. Equation (57) shows that changes in *relative* Home and Foreign consumption levels are permanent, even though short-run real interest rate changes can tilt individual-country consumption profiles. Loosely speaking, relative consumptions follow a random walk. The reason is that with integrated bond markets and identical consumption baskets, agents in both countries face the same real interest rate. Therefore, interest rate changes tilt their consumption profiles proportionately.[15]

We have already differenced the linearized money demand equations to arrive at eq. (39). Given that we are (for the moment) looking only at one-time permanent changes in the money supply, such that $e_t = \bar{e} \ \forall t > 2$, eq. (39) can be rewritten as

$$m - m^* - e = c - c^* - \frac{1}{\delta}(\bar{e} - e). \tag{58}$$

---

15. In general, with different consumption baskets, two countries will face different consumption-based real interest rates even when capital markets are perfectly integrated and uncovered interest parity obtains. Allowing for this effect complicates the model but would not reverse the main qualitative conclusions that follow.

To solve this dynamic equation, we begin by combining eq. (52) (the solution for $\bar{e}$) and eq. (57) to obtain

$$\bar{e} = (\bar{m} - \bar{m}^*) - (c - c^*). \tag{59}$$

Using eq. (59) to substitute for $\bar{e}$ in eq. (58), and eq. (53) to substitute $m - m^*$ for $\bar{m} - \bar{m}^*$, we obtain

$$e = (m - m^*) - (c - c^*). \tag{60}$$

Comparing eqs. (60) and (59), we see from eq. (53) that $e = \bar{e}$, implying that the exchange rate jumps immediately to its new long-run equilibrium following a permanent relative money shock. The intuition for the immediate adjustment is apparent from eq. (58). If money-supply and consumption differentials are both expected to be constant, then the exchange rate must be expected to be constant as well. A similar case can arise in the Mundell-Fleming-Dornbusch model of Chapter 9 when the $\Delta e = 0$ schedule has slope zero, which is the borderline case between overshooting and undershooting. The fact that the present version of the model does not yield overshooting is of no great concern. As we saw in Chapter 9, the evidence in support of overshooting is thin indeed. There is nothing intrinsic in the approach that precludes overshooting, however, and in section 10.2 we will look at a variant in which overshooting can occur.

One can easily extend the analysis here to allow for more general money-supply processes. The extension throws further light on the last paragraph's results. Solving eq. (39) forward in a manner exactly analogous to our mode of analyzing the flexible-price Cagan model in Chapter 8, one obtains

$$e_t = -(c_1 - c_1^*) + \frac{\delta}{1+\delta} \sum_{s=t}^{\infty} \left(\frac{1}{1+\delta} \right)^{s-t} (m_s - m_s^*), \tag{61}$$

which holds for all $t \geq 1$. (Recall that $c - c^*$ is constant after the initial date 1 shock.) The general result is that following an unanticipated perturbation to the path of the money supply, the exchange rate jumps to the flexible-price path corresponding to the new permanent consumption differential. One cannot press this analogy with the Cagan exchange rate model too far, however, since consumption differentials are not exogenous here and can be affected by unanticipated money shocks.

Figure 10.1 shows eq. (60) as the downward-sloping **MM** schedule; its slope is -1. The curve is downward sloping because an increase in relative Home consumption raises Home money demand. Therefore, Home's relative price level must fall, implying an appreciation of the exchange rate. The schedule intersects the vertical e axis at $m - m^*$, which would be the equilibrium exchange rate response if prices were fully flexible. Note that in deriving the **MM** schedule, we made use not only of the money demand equations but also of the consumption Euler equations.

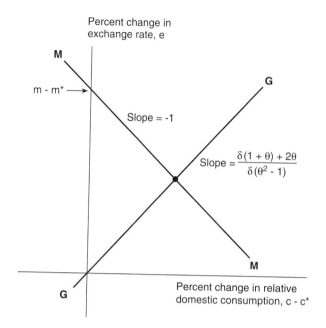

Figure 10.1
Short-run equilibrium

The **MM** schedule gives one relationship between e and $c - c^*$. A second schedule in e and $c - c^*$ may be derived using the short-run equilibrium conditions other than the money demand equations, together with eq. (45). The latter equation gives steady-state consumption differentials as a function of net foreign asset positions; this provides a crucial link between the short-run and long-run systems.

We first subtract eq. (56) from eq. (55) to obtain

$$\bar{b} = (1 - n)\left[(y - y^*) - (c - c^*) - e\right]. \tag{62}$$

We eliminate $y - y^*$ here by noting that eq. (42) implies

$$y - y^* = \theta e, \tag{63}$$

since $p(h)$ and $p^*(f)$ are fixed in the short run. To eliminate $\bar{b}$ we use eq. (45), which relates $\bar{b}$ to the *long-run* consumption differential, $\bar{c} - \bar{c}^*$. Finally, we note that by eq. (57), $\bar{c} - \bar{c}^* = c - c^*$. Effecting these substitutions in eq. (62) yields

$$e = \frac{\delta(1 + \theta) + 2\theta}{\delta(\theta^2 - 1)}(c - c^*), \tag{64}$$

which is the upward-sloping schedule **GG** in Figure 10.1. The **GG** locus has a positive slope because Home consumption can rise relative to Foreign's only if the exchange rate depreciates in the short run and permits Home output to rise relative to Foreign's.

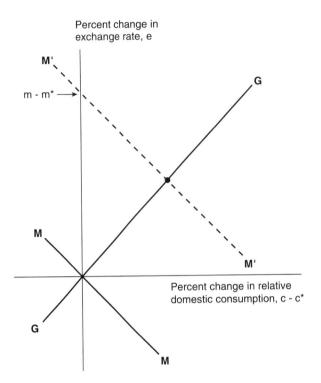

Figure 10.2
An unexpected relative rise in the domestic money supply

We are now ready to combine the two schedules to solve jointly for e and $c - c^*$. In Figure 10.2 the solid **MM** line corresponds to the preshock equilibrium where $m - m^* = 0$. The broken line is the postshock $\mathbf{M'M'}$ schedule.

The short-run (and long-run) equilibrium exchange rate and consumption differential lie at the intersection of the $\mathbf{M'M'}$ and **GG** curves. The exchange-rate effect of a money-supply increase is smaller, the larger is the price elasticity of aggregate demand θ. As $\theta \to \infty$, the **GG** schedule becomes horizontal. As Home and Foreign goods become very close substitutes, small exchange-rate changes lead to very large shifts in demand with preset prices.

Interestingly, the Home currency depreciates less than proportionately in response to a (surprise) relative Home money-supply increase *even in the long run.* (Recall that $e = \bar{e}$ for a permanent money shock.) The intuition is that the short-run depreciation temporarily raises Home real income relative to Foreign's so that the home country runs a current-account surplus, via the usual intertemporal consumption-smoothing channel. Home's higher long-run wealth leads to substitution into leisure (vice versa for foreigners), a fall in the supply of Home goods, and therefore an improvement in Home's terms of trade. Because the home country's real income and consumption rise in the long run, the nominal exchange rate does not need to depreciate as much as it would under fully flexible prices.[16]

The long-run *nonneutrality* of money is a significant difference between the present model and the model of Chapter 9, but one must be careful not to overstate it. First, in an overlapping generations version of the present model, the real effects of the money shock would eventually die out, albeit over a much longer horizon than the price frictions. (The time frame would be in life spans rather than one or two years.) Second, the long-run effect is likely to be much smaller empirically than the short-run effect. To see this difference, it is helpful to examine the closed-form solution of the model, which we now derive.

Together, eqs. (60) and (64) (the **MM** and the **GG** schedules) imply

$$e = \frac{\delta(1+\theta)+2\theta}{\theta\delta(1+\theta)+2\theta}(m-m^*) < m-m^*, \tag{65}$$

where the inequality holds because $\theta > 1$. Since domestic prices of domestic goods are preset, e also gives the short-run change in the terms of trade. Combining eqs. (60) and (65), we find that

$$c - c^* = \frac{\delta(\theta^2-1)}{\theta\delta(1+\theta)+2\theta}(m-m^*). \tag{66}$$

The output differential is found by combining eqs. (65) and (63). Finally, to find the short-run current account (which here equals the long-run change in net foreign assets $\bar{b}$) we substitute eqs. (63), (65), and (66) into eq. (62) to obtain

$$\bar{b} = \frac{2(1-n)(\theta-1)}{\delta(1+\theta)+2}(m-m^*). \tag{67}$$

Naturally, the larger is Home (the larger is n), the smaller the impact of a Home money shock on its current account.

Having solved for $\bar{b}$, one can now easily solve for all the long-run steady-state changes induced by the money shock. For example, combining eqs. (46) and (67) yields

$$\bar{p}(h) - \bar{e} - \bar{p}^*(f) = \frac{\delta(\theta-1)}{\theta\delta(1+\theta)+2\theta}(m-m^*). \tag{68}$$

---

16. The diagrammatic analysis is easily extended to the case of a temporary money shock. The **MM** schedule is replaced by eq. (61) while the **GG** schedule remains the same. Thus the slope of **MM** is the same as before, but the intercept is the discounted sum of present and future money changes given in eq. (61). The effects of a temporary money shock are, in general, smaller than that of a permanent one. It is no longer the case, however, that the diagram portrays both short-run and long-run equilibrium. The level of $c - c^*$ given by the diagram is permanent, but eq. (61) must be used to calculate the exchange rate after the initial sticky-price period.

Thus the long-run terms-of-trade impact of a money-supply shock is of the order of magnitude of the equilibrium interest rate $\bar{r}$ ($= \delta$), which makes sense given that it is the flow of interest income on net foreign assets that drives a wedge between the incentives to work in the two countries. Comparing eq. (65), which gives the short-run fall in Home's terms of trade, with the long-run rise in eq. (68), we see that the short-run effect is unambiguously larger in absolute value.

10.1.7.4   Solving for Short-Run World Aggregates

To solve for the effects of money expansion on short-term world consumption c^W and the short-term world real interest rate r (on loans between periods 1 and 2), we begin by multiplying the Home consumption Euler equation (35) by n and adding it to $(1 - n)$ times the Foreign consumption Euler equation (36) to obtain

$$\bar{c}^W = c^W + \frac{\delta}{1 + \delta} r. \tag{69}$$

Equation (47) shows, however, that $\bar{c}^W = 0$; the long-run effects of a money shock come entirely through wealth redistributions, so that global consumption remains fixed. Therefore,

$$c^W = -\frac{\delta}{1 + \delta} r. \tag{70}$$

A second equation in c^W and r may be obtained by multiplying the Home money-demand equation (37) by n and adding it to $(1 - n)$ times the Foreign money-demand equation (38). The result is

$$m^W = c^W - \frac{r}{1 + \delta} - \frac{m^W}{\delta}, \tag{71}$$

where $m^W \equiv nm + (1 - n)m^*$ is the weighted change in the world money supply. In deriving eq. (71), we have made use of eqs. (27) and (28) [noting that $p(h) = p^*(f) = 0$], eqs. (50) and (51) for long-run price levels, and $\bar{c}^W = 0$. Combining eqs. (70) and (71) yields

$$c^W = m^W = y^W, \tag{72}$$

$$r = -\left(\frac{1 + \delta}{\delta}\right) m^W, \tag{73}$$

where the second equality in eq. (72) follows from eq. (32). A monetary expansion at home or abroad temporarily lowers world real interest rates in proportion to the size of the expanding country; world consumption therefore expands. (Remember that in the long run, world interest rates and world consumption return to their preshock values.) Thus global monetary policy is not a zero-sum game, even if the effects may be asymmetric.

10.1.7.5   Solving for Short-Run Levels of Individual Variables

Given solutions for all the sums and differences, one readily solves for levels as before (a task left for the reader).[17] One item of particular interest is the short-run effect of a unilateral Foreign monetary expansion on Home output, often an item of great contention in international monetary policy discussions. Combining eqs. (63) and (72) yields

$$y = m^W + (1 - n)\theta e.$$

A unilateral Foreign monetary expansion raises world output by raising m^W. At the same time, however, it causes e to fall and shifts the composition of world demand toward Foreign goods. Substituting eq. (65) into the preceding expression and simplifying yields

$$y = \frac{\delta(1 + \theta) + 2[n(1 - \theta) + \theta]}{\delta(1 + \theta) + 2} m + \frac{(1 - n)2(1 - \theta)}{\delta(1 + \theta) + 2} m^*, \tag{74}$$

so that the net effects of Foreign monetary expansion on Home output are negative (recall that $\theta > 1$).[18]

10.1.8   Welfare Effects of Monetary Shocks

So far, our discussion has focused entirely on the positive analysis of monetary policy shocks, but one of the great advantages of this approach is that it also yields normative insights.

10.1.8.1   Equiproportionate Money-Supply Increases

An unanticipated equiproportionate increase in Home and Foreign money—one that raises m^W but keeps $m - m^* = 0$—must raise welfare in both countries. An equiproportionate money shock has no terms-of-trade or exchange-rate effects, nor does it affect the current account or any long-run variables. The only effect is to cause global output to rise in the short run; by eq. (72), $c^W = m^W = y^W$. This output increase raises world welfare because, as we have already shown, steady-state global output is inefficiently low when there is monopoly in final goods production. (With preset prices, an unanticipated money shock raises aggregate demand, which raises output and mitigates the distortion.) Clearly, real balances must rise in the short run in both countries as well. One should not interpret this result as saying that the monetary authorities can use activist policy to raise world output

---

17. Recall again that solving for levels simply requires noting that for any Home variable x, $x = x^W + (1 - n)(x - x^*)$.

18. In a more general version of the model, with non-unit consumption elasticities of money demand, the effects of Foreign money supply increases on short-run Home output would be ambiguous; see Obstfeld and Rogoff (1995a).

systematically. We have only looked at the case of an exogenous money-supply shock here. If monetary policy is determined endogenously as in the models in the second part of Chapter 9, price setters will take this fact into account in forming their price expectations. As we show in an end-of-chapter exercise, one can solve for the game-equilibrium level of money growth and inflation in a manner similar to that of the Kydland-Prescott, Barro-Gordon model of Chapter 9. In equilibrium, the monetary authorities do not succeed in systematically raising output, though they may help stabilize the economy in response to unanticipated shocks. Thus the present model can provide microfoundations for the more stylized models used to explore inflation credibility in Chapter 9.

10.1.8.2 Asymmetric Money Shocks

Determining the welfare effects of asymmetric money shocks would appear to be much more difficult. Not only do they engender exchange-rate effects, they also influence the current account and therefore affect the long-run equilibrium. For example, it might well seem from our preceding analysis that Foreign money-growth shocks have an adverse impact on Home welfare. In the short run, an unanticipated Foreign money increase causes Home's output to fall and its current account balance to go into deficit. In the long run, Home's terms of trade deteriorate, its consumption falls, and Home agents' work effort rises. On the plus side of the ledger, Home's consumption rises in the short run, and its short-run terms of trade also improve. To add up these effects formally and see how overall utility changes, we log-linearize the intertemporal utility function (1) and evaluate it. We will focus on the "real" component of a representative agent's utility

$$U_t^R \equiv \sum_{s=t}^{\infty} \beta^{s-t} \left(\log C_s - \frac{\kappa}{2} y_s^2 \right)$$

that depends only on output and consumption, and does not depend on real money balances. One can show that as long as the derived utility from real balances is not too large as a share of total utility—a very reasonable assumption that will hold as long as χ is not too large—changes in U^R dominate total changes in utility.

Taking advantage of the fact that the new steady state is reached after just one period, one finds after total differentiation of the preceding equation that

$$dU^R = c - \kappa \bar{y}_0^2 y + \frac{1}{\delta} \left(\bar{c} - \kappa \bar{y}_0^2 \bar{y} \right).$$

Equation (24) giving initial steady-state output $\bar{y}_0$ shows that this equation can be rewritten as

$$dU^R = c - \left(\frac{\theta - 1}{\theta} \right) y + \frac{1}{\delta} \left[\bar{c} - \left(\frac{\theta - 1}{\theta} \right) \bar{y} \right]. \tag{75}$$

One could evaluate this welfare effect directly by using the reduced-form solutions for c, $\bar{c}$, y, and $\bar{y}$, simply plugging them into eq. (75) to express dU^R in terms of money shocks. This is straightforward but requires a fair bit of algebra. A simpler approach is to find quasi-reduced-form solutions for the consumption and output variables in eq. (75) in terms of m^W and e. Such an approach has the advantage of separating global (associated with m^W) from country-specific (associated with e) effects.

The equation immediately preceding eq. (74) gives such an expression for y, $y = m^W + (1 - n)\theta e$. Using eqs. (32), (65), (66), and (72), we find

$$c = \frac{\delta(1 - n)(\theta^2 - 1)}{\delta(1 + \theta) + 2\theta} e + m^W.$$

Using eqs. (48), (65), and (67), we derive

$$\bar{c} = \frac{\delta(1 - n)(\theta^2 - 1)}{\delta(1 + \theta) + 2\theta} e.$$

Finally, eqs. (33), (47), and the last expression imply

$$\bar{y} = -\frac{\delta\theta(1 - n)(\theta - 1)}{\delta(1 + \theta) + 2\theta} e.$$

Substituting these four expressions into eq. (75), we find that all the terms in e (the country-specific terms) cancel, leaving the simple end result

$$dU^R = \frac{c^W}{\theta} = \frac{m^W}{\theta}. \tag{76}$$

Equation (76) thus states that the change in (the real component of) Home utility is proportional to the shock to world money, *regardless of its origin*.[19]

How is it possible that so many of the different factors that have an impact on Home welfare offset each other when there is a Foreign money-supply increase? And how is it possible that the impact on Home welfare is *identical* to that of a Home money shock, holding m^W constant? The answer comes from the fact that in the initial equilibrium, all producers are setting their relative prices at (individually) optimizing levels. Therefore, small changes in relative prices induced by exchange rate changes have no first-order effect on welfare. By the same token, agents are optimally smoothing consumption over time, so small current-account imbalances

---

19. Note that a Home monetary expansion unambiguously raises all components of Home welfare, since Home real balances rise in all periods. Foreign money growth raises Home real balances in the initial period (since Home money is constant and Home's currency appreciates). In future periods, however, Home real balances fall, since M is fixed and Home's long-run price level rises [see eq. (50)]. This one negative effect will not outweigh the various positive effects provided χ is not too large, as asserted in the text.

have only a second-order welfare effect. The sole *first-order* welfare effect is the one due to the initial monopoly distortion.

Strictly speaking, of course, our analysis applies only to *marginal* changes in the money supply. For large changes, the linearizations we have employed may break down, and numerical methods must be used to solve the model. Also, if one tries to rationalize the results here by small menu costs to changing prices, then of course one cannot rely on prices to remain constant when the shocks are large.[20] Nevertheless, the analysis here shows that many effects often emphasized in ad hoc policy analyses may be offsetting when taken together. The simplicity and clarity of the welfare results here provide a strong argument for having careful microfoundations.

10.1.9 Distorting Income Taxes and Welfare: An Important Caveat

The welfare results of the preceding section are striking indeed, and they illustrate the power of the approach. One must be careful, however, not to overstate their generality because in the model, monopolistic suppliers are the only source of distortion in the real economy. With additional sources of distortion, the welfare results will in general depend on the nature of the inefficiencies they create and their relative magnitudes.

Suppose, for example, that governments tax income. This creates a second distortion in the economy because income taxes distort the labor-leisure decision. Since the marginal domestic social revenue from higher production now exceeds marginal cost, a country can gain at foreigners' expense by depreciating its currency and thereby lowering the prices of its exports.

Let us assume that income from labor is taxed in both countries at the same constant rate τ^L. Assume further that both governments rebate all revenues from income taxation and money creation by varying lump-sum taxes τ_t (which will be negative in the case of transfer payments).[21] In this case, a representative agent's intertemporal budget constraint is given by

$$P_t B_{t+1} + M_t = P_t(1 + r_t)B_t + M_{t-1} + (1 - \tau^L)p_t y_t - P_t C_t - P_t \tau_t. \tag{77}$$

With revenues from both income taxes and money creation, the Home government's budget constraint (9) becomes

---

20. One subtle issue that arises if we justify preset prices by small menu costs is that there may be multiple equilibria. Holding own price $p(j)$ constant, there are two effects on the demand curve facing an individual firm j when all other firms raise their prices. Overall aggregate demand falls (holding M constant), but demand shifts toward firm j's good, since $p(j)/P$ falls. These two effects pull in opposite directions. For this reason, it may pay for a firm to absorb the menu cost of price adjustment if all other firms raise their prices, but not pay to change price if other firms keep their prices fixed. (In the terminology adopted by Cooper and John, 1988, the various firms' pricing decisions are strategic complements.) This multiplicity of equilibria is pointed out by Rotemberg and Saloner (1986).

21. Having the tax also apply to interest income does not alter the main qualitative results that follow.

$$0 = \tau_t + \frac{\tau^L}{nP_t} \int_0^n p_t(z) y_t(z) dz + \frac{M_t - M_{t-1}}{P_t},$$

where division by n is needed to put aggregate income taxes in the same per capita form as the other variables. Assuming a symmetric equilibrium within each country, this equation becomes

$$0 = \tau_t + \frac{\tau^L p_t(h) y_t(h)}{P_t} + \frac{M_t - M_{t-1}}{P_t}. \tag{78}$$

The foreign-country representative-agent and government-budget constraints are similar, with the same tax rate τ^L. With these modifications, all the first-order conditions of the model remain the same except for the labor-leisure trade-off, eq. (15), which becomes

$$y_t^{\frac{\theta+1}{\theta}} = \left(1 - \tau^L\right) \frac{\theta - 1}{\theta \kappa} \left(C_t^W\right)^{\frac{1}{\theta}} \frac{1}{C_t}. \tag{79}$$

In this case, in place of eq. (24), the steady-state output levels with zero net foreign assets become

$$\bar{y}_0 = \bar{y}_0^* = \left[\frac{(\theta - 1)\left(1 - \tau^L\right)}{\theta \kappa} \right]^{\frac{1}{2}}. \tag{80}$$

An income tax reduces individual incentives to work and lowers steady-state output.

Although allowing for an income tax changes the equation for steady-state output, the log-linearization of the model goes through exactly as before [except, of course, that the percent deviations are from the steady state of eq. (80) rather than from that of eq. (24)]. Therefore, the solutions for e, y, c, and so on are unchanged; an income tax shifts the steady state, but it does not here change the response of the variables (in percentage terms) to money shocks. However, although the presence of an income tax does not lead to different *positive* predictions concerning how the economy reacts to money shocks, it does lead to different *normative* predictions. In particular, it is no longer the case that Foreign money shocks benefit Home and Foreign residents equally.

The income tax distortion has different implications than the monopoly distortion because it leads to an asymmetry in the spillovers from increased work effort by Home agents. With monopoly the only distortion, an increase in output by a single Home agent equally benefits Foreign residents and other Home residents. But with an income tax, the marginal revenue from taxation is rebated entirely to domestic residents.

To compare the magnitudes of the various effects formally, we again evaluate the log-linearized utility function (75), this time using eq. (80) to substitute for $\bar{y}_0$. After a bit of algebra, one finds that the effect of an unanticipated permanent foreign monetary shock on domestic welfare is given by

$$dU^R = \left[\frac{(1-n)m^*}{\theta}\right]\left[1 - \frac{\tau^L(\theta-1)^2}{\delta(1+\theta)+2}\right]. \tag{81}$$

[Follow the same steps that led to eq. (76), but with m set to zero.] For θ near one, the effect of m^* on home welfare is unambiguously positive; with inelastic demand the distortions from monopoly dominate. As $\theta \to \infty$, however, the economy becomes more competitive and the tax distortion becomes the more important issue. For large enough θ, Foreign monetary expansion lowers Home welfare.

The cynical reader might conclude from this caveat that the welfare results lack robustness and are therefore unreliable. A more balanced—and more appropriate—conclusion would be that in understanding the welfare effects of international monetary policy, it is important to study the major sources of distortion empirically, and to weigh the impact of monetary policy on mitigating or exacerbating these distortions. It is certainly clear from our analysis that the standard approach adopted in Keynesian analyses, which treat output and the current account balance as measures of welfare, can be very misleading.

10.1.10 Country Size and Economic Welfare

The small-country case can be derived by taking the limit of the two-country model as $n \to 0$. Monetary expansion at Home then has no effect on the world interest rate r or on world consumption c^W. It does, of course, affect Foreign consumption of the Home good, $c^*(h)$, but Home goods comprise only an infinitesimal percentage of total consumption. However, although a small country's monetary policy has no effect on world aggregates, all the results we derived for the *difference* between per capita Home and Foreign variables still hold. Note that country size n did not enter into the results (short-run or long-run) for the exchange rate e, the terms of trade $p(h) - e - p^*(f)$, the current account, $c - c^*$, or $y - y^*$. Monetary expansion in the home country still lowers the relative price of its goods and raises its output. There is, however, no welfare benefit, even for the home country [see eq. (76)]. This result very much depends on the assumption that the small country consumes only an infinitesimal fraction of its own production. In the nontraded-goods version of the model given in section 10.2, there is a welfare benefit at home, even for a small country.

It is worth noting one difference between the closed- and open-economy analyses of monetary policy in the preceding monopolistic model. We have argued that (in either case) monopolists are willing to meet unanticipated demand at preset prices because they initially set their prices above marginal cost. Of course, they will be willing to meet unanticipated demand only up to the point where ex post marginal cost equals ex post marginal revenue. In the open economy, this point will be reached at a lower output level because the rise in import prices accompanying a

Box 10.2
The Role of Imperfect Competition in Business Cycles

Since the welfare results emphasized in section 10.1.8 depend on the presence of monopoly distortions in the economy, it is fair to ask how important these distortions are empirically. A number of recent studies have emphasized a central role for imperfect competition in explaining business-cycle fluctuations. Hall (1986) looks at microeconomic data for fifty industries covering all major sectors of the U.S. economy and argues that there is substantial evidence of imperfect competition. In particular, he finds that in most industries, price exceeds marginal cost. He argues that any business-cycle model must take into account how markups change over the cycle. Rotemberg and Woodford (1991) present a model in which markups are countercyclical, because firms' ability to collude is enhanced in a recession. They argue that a model such as theirs is needed to explain procyclical behavior of real wages and consumption because the only alternative explanation gives an implausibly large role to production function shifts. One fact they point to in support of their approach is that prices of raw materials are very procyclical over the business cycle, followed by intermediate goods and then final goods. Final goods prices, they argue, are the least procyclical because in booms they reflect not only lower direct markups, but lower markups on inputs as well.

Recent research has also emphasized the role of imperfect competition in explaining a host of issues in international trade and finance; see G. Grossman and Rogoff (1995) and Matsuyama (1993). Thus, while there plainly are many other important distortions in the economy, there is good reason to believe that imperfect competition is one of the more important ones.

domestic monetary expansion lowers each monopolist's real marginal revenue. (In the closed economy version, the only force working to limit output expansion is rising marginal disutility of work effort.) In general, the smaller the economy, the smaller the maximum output increase that an unexpected monetary expansion can achieve. Thus, in this class of models, there is again a sense in which the scope for monetary policy is more circumscribed in more open economies. Even for a very small economy, however, a monetary shock can raise output somewhat if there is an initial gap between price and marginal cost.

10.2   Imperfect Competition and Preset Prices for Nontradables: Overshooting Revisited

In the model of the preceding section, the presence of monopoly in the traded goods sector was a key feature in governing the international welfare spillovers in monetary policy. Here we consider a small-country model in which the nontraded goods sector is the locus of monopoly and sticky-price problems, and where the traded sector has a single homogeneous output that is priced in competitive world markets. As we shall see, the model has somewhat different welfare implications from the model of the last section, and it also yields a simple example of overshooting à la Dornbusch (1976).

10.2.1 The Model

Each representative home citizen is endowed with a constant quantity of the traded good each period, $\bar{y}_T$, and has a monopoly over production of one of the nontradables $z \in [0, 1]$.

The lifetime utility function of representative producer j is

$$U_t^j = \sum_{s=t}^{\infty} \beta^{s-t} \left[\gamma \log C_{T,s}^j + (1-\gamma) \log C_{N,s}^j + \frac{\chi}{1-\varepsilon} \left(\frac{M_s^j}{P_s} \right)^{1-\varepsilon} - \frac{\kappa}{2} y_{N,s}(j)^2 \right],$$

(82)

where C_T is consumption of the traded good and C_N is composite nontraded goods consumption, defined by

$$C_N = \left[\int_0^1 c_N(z)^{\frac{\theta-1}{\theta}} dz \right]^{\frac{\theta}{\theta-1}}.$$

Note that in eq. (82) we allow real balances to enter utility additively according to a general isoelastic function, instead of specializing to the log case in which $\varepsilon \to 1$. The parameter ε will turn out to be the critical determinant of whether overshooting can occur. The variable P in eq. (82) is again the consumption-based price index (defined as the minimum money cost of purchasing one unit of composite real consumption $C_T^{\gamma} C_N^{1-\gamma}$), here given by

$$P \equiv P_T^{\gamma} P_N^{1-\gamma} / \gamma^{\gamma} (1-\gamma)^{1-\gamma},$$

(83)

where P_T is the price of tradables. The law of one price holds in tradables, so that $P_T = \mathcal{E} P_T^*$ (P_T^* is exogenous and constant). The variable P_N is the nontraded goods price index

$$P_N = \left[\int_0^1 p_N(z)^{1-\theta} dz \right]^{\frac{1}{1-\theta}},$$

where $p_N(z)$ is the money price of nontraded good z. Bonds are denominated in tradables, with r denoting the constant world net interest rate in tradables and $\beta(1+r) = 1$. The typical individual j's period budget constraint in money terms is

$$P_{\mathrm{T},t}B_{t+1}^j + M_t^j = P_{\mathrm{T},t}(1+r)B_t^j + M_{t-1}^j + p_{\mathrm{N},t}(j)y_{\mathrm{N},t}(j) \tag{84}$$

$$+ P_{\mathrm{T},t}\bar{y}_{\mathrm{T}} - P_{\mathrm{N},t}C_{\mathrm{N},t}^j - P_{\mathrm{T},t}C_{\mathrm{T},t}^j - P_{\mathrm{T},t}\tau_t,$$

where per capita taxes τ are denominated in tradables.

As in the preceding section, we abstract from government spending and (since Ricardian equivalence holds) assume that the government balances its budget each period. The government budget constraint, in units of tradables, is therefore given by

$$0 = \tau_t + \frac{M_t - M_{t-1}}{P_{\mathrm{T},t}}. \tag{85}$$

Finally, in analogy with eq. (10), the preferences assumed here imply that non-traded goods producers face the downward-sloping demand curves

$$y_{\mathrm{N}}^d(j) = \left[\frac{p_{\mathrm{N}}(j)}{P_{\mathrm{N}}}\right]^{-\theta} C_{\mathrm{N}}^{\mathrm{A}}, \tag{86}$$

where $C_{\mathrm{N}}^{\mathrm{A}}$ is aggregate per capita nontraded goods consumption.

10.2.2   First-Order Conditions

The first-order conditions for individual maximization are found by maximizing eq. (82) subject to constraints (84) and (86). They are

$$C_{\mathrm{T},t+1} = C_{\mathrm{T},t}, \tag{87}$$

$$\frac{\gamma}{C_{\mathrm{T},t}} = \chi \frac{P_{\mathrm{T},t}}{P_t}\left(\frac{M_t}{P_t}\right)^{-\varepsilon} + \beta \frac{P_{\mathrm{T},t}}{P_{\mathrm{T},t+1}}\left(\frac{\gamma}{C_{\mathrm{T},t+1}}\right), \tag{88}$$

$$C_{\mathrm{N},t} = \frac{1-\gamma}{\gamma}\left(\frac{P_{\mathrm{T},t}}{P_{\mathrm{N},t}}\right)C_{\mathrm{T},t}, \tag{89}$$

$$y_{\mathrm{N},t}^{\frac{\theta+1}{\theta}} = \left[\frac{(\theta-1)(1-\gamma)}{\kappa\theta}\right](C_{\mathrm{N},t}^{\mathrm{A}})^{\frac{1}{\theta}}\frac{1}{C_{\mathrm{N},t}}, \tag{90}$$

where we have suppressed the individual j index. The first-order conditions are analogous to those in section 10.1.2, except for the additional equation (89) that governs allocation between traded and nontraded goods.[22] Note that eq. (87) implies that agents smooth consumption of traded goods independently of nontraded goods production or consumption. This result is due, of course, to the additive separability of period utility that eq. (82) imposes. We will assume the economy has

---

22. One approach to deriving the first-order conditions is to use eq. (86) to substitute for p_{N} in eq. (84), then use the resulting equation to substitute for C_{T} in eq. (82). The first-order conditions follow from differentiating with respect to B_{t+1}, M_t, $C_{\mathrm{N},t}$, and $y_{\mathrm{N},t}$, taking $C_{\mathrm{N},t}^{\mathrm{A}}$ as given.

zero initial net foreign assets. Given that production is constant at $\bar{y}_T$, this assumption implies that

$$C_{T,t} = \bar{y}_T, \qquad \forall t. \tag{91}$$

Thus in the absence of shocks to traded-goods productivity, the economy has a balanced current account regardless of shocks to money or nontraded-goods production. Substituting eq. (87) into eq. (88), we can express money demand as

$$\frac{M_t}{P_t} = \left\{ \frac{\chi}{\gamma} \left[\frac{C_{T,t} P_{T,t} / P_t}{1 - (\beta P_{T,t} / P_{T,t+1})} \right] \right\}^{1/\varepsilon}. \tag{92}$$

10.2.3 Steady-State Equilibrium

We are now prepared to solve for the steady state corresponding to the case where all prices are fully flexible and all exogenous variables, including the money supply, are constant. In the symmetric equilibrium, $C_{N,t} = y_{N,t}(z) = C_{N,t}^A$ for all z; thus eq. (90) implies that steady-state output of nontraded goods is given by

$$\bar{y}_N = \bar{C}_N = \left[\frac{(\theta - 1)(1 - \gamma)}{\kappa \theta} \right]^{\frac{1}{2}}. \tag{93}$$

In the steady state, prices of traded goods must be constant with a constant money supply, assuming no speculative bubbles. (Since monetary shocks will not turn out to affect $\bar{y}_N$ or $\bar{C}_N$, we do not use zero subscripts in the preceding equation.) The initial equilibrium price level, $\bar{P}_0$ (corresponding to the initial equilibrium money supply $\bar{M}_0$), may be found using eqs. (83), (89), and (91)–(93), together with $P_{T,t+1} = P_{T,t}$, which follows from the no-speculative-bubbles condition. Since money shocks have no effects on wealth, the long-run effects of a money shock are to raise both traded and nontraded goods prices proportionately.

10.2.4 Short-Run Equilibrium Response to an Unanticipated Money Shock

We now consider the effects of an unanticipated permanent money shock that occurs at time 1. Prices in the competitive traded goods sector are fully flexible, but prices in the monopolistic nontraded goods sector are set a period in advance; they adjust to the shock only by period 2. As in our earlier model, the economy reaches its long-run equilibrium in just one period (by period 2). Here, however, because there are no current-account effects, money is neutral in the long run, and only nominal variables change across steady states.

In the short run, prices of nontraded goods are fixed at $\bar{p}_{N,0}$, and therefore, by the same logic as before, nontraded output is demand determined. Given symmetry across the various domestic producers, it must be the case that

$$\frac{\bar{p}_{N,0}}{\bar{P}_{N,0}} = 1.$$

Short-run demand is given by

$$y_N^d = C_N. \tag{94}$$

As in the previous section, a variable without a time subscript is a short-run (period 1) variable. By combining eqs. (89), (91), and (94), recalling the assumption of zero net foreign assets, and noting that P_N is temporarily fixed, one derives

$$y_N = C_N = \frac{1-\gamma}{\gamma} \left(\frac{P_T}{\bar{P}_N} \right) \bar{y}_T, \tag{95}$$

which gives y_N and C_N as functions of P_T. To solve for P_T (traded goods prices are fully flexible), we log-linearize the money-demand equation (92),

$$\varepsilon(m - p) = p_T - p + \frac{\beta}{1-\beta}(p_T - \bar{p}_T), \tag{96}$$

where we denote short-run percentage deviations from the initial steady state by $x \equiv (X_1 - \bar{X}_0)/\bar{X}_0$, and long-run deviations from the initial steady state (which is reached in period 2) by $\bar{x} \equiv (\bar{X} - \bar{X}_0)/\bar{X}_0$.[23] Log differentiating the price-index equation (83) with P_N fixed yields the short-run change in the consumption-based price index

$$p = \gamma p_T. \tag{97}$$

Finally, the long-run neutrality of money in this model implies that

$$\bar{p}_T = \bar{m} = m, \tag{98}$$

where the second equality holds because the money supply increase is permanent. Substituting the two preceding relationships into eq. (96) yields

$$p_T = \frac{\beta + (1-\beta)\varepsilon}{\beta + (1-\beta)(1-\gamma+\gamma\varepsilon)} m. \tag{99}$$

Note that the price of traded goods changes in proportion to the exchange rate,

$$p_T = e,$$

since the law of one price holds here and the country does not have any market power in tradables. Therefore, from eq. (99), we can see that if $\varepsilon > 1$, the nominal exchange rate overshoots its long-run level (that is, $e > m = \bar{m}$).

One can understand the role of ε in overshooting by recognizing that in this model $1/\varepsilon$ is the consumption elasticity of money demand [see eq. (92)]. If p_T were to rise in proportion to m, the supply of real balances would rise by only $1 - \gamma$ that

---

23. In deriving eq. (96), remember that in the steady state $\bar{P}_T$ is constant, since the steady-state money supply is constant.

amount (since p_N is fixed). How much does the demand for real balances rise? A rise in p_T causes an equiproportionate rise in C_N in the short run. A percent rise in C_N leads in turn to a $1 - \gamma$ percent rise in *real* consumption. If $\varepsilon > 1$, the demand for real balances rises by less than the supply if $p_T = m$. Therefore, p_T must rise by more and, by the law of one price, the exchange rate must overshoot.

Note that an unanticipated rise in the money supply unambiguously improves welfare by coordinating an increase in output across agents in the monopolistic nontraded goods sector. It is easy to see that real balances rise temporarily as well. The analysis here was all for a small country facing an exogenous world interest rate, but in fact all the results would still go through if the country were large. The intuition is that in this particular setup, a money shock produces no current-account imbalance and therefore has no global spillover effect. If the period utility function were not additive in tradables and nontradables, nontraded goods consumption would affect the marginal utility of traded goods consumption, and money shocks would generally affect the current account and net foreign assets.

Application: Wealth Effects and the Real Exchange Rate

The models we have looked at suggest that even short-term macroeconomic disturbances can lead to wealth transfers with long-term implications for the real exchange rate. Theoretically, these long-term effects are of the order of the interest rate relative to short-term effects. But does this fact imply that they are empirically negligible? This question is closely related to the transfer problem we introduced in Chapter 4. In the models of this chapter, the effect of a transfer on the terms of trade comes from effects on labor supply. As we have observed, it can also arise through other channels, such as different consumption preferences at home and abroad.

Refer back to Figure 4.14, which plots the percent change in the trade-weighted WPI real exchange rate, denoted by p, against the change in the ratio of net foreign assets to output for a cross section of 15 OECD countries. (The former variable can be viewed as a terms-of-trade proxy.) A simple least squares cross-section regression using the data in the figure yields

$$\Delta \log p = 0.039 + 1.042 \Delta B / Y, \qquad R^2 = 0.31.$$
$$(0.027) \quad (0.433)$$

(Standard errors are in parentheses.) The regression indicates that an increase of 1 percent in the ratio of net foreign assets to output is associated with a 1 percent appreciation of the real exchange rate. Of course, one must be careful not to draw any strong conclusions from this simple nonstructural relationship. Estimating structural versions of sticky-price intertemporal models such as the one developed in this chapter is an important research issue.

Table 10.1
Dynamic Response of the U.S. Current Account
to a 20 Percent Real Dollar Depreciation
(percent of GDP)

Year	Change in Current Account
1	−0.24
2	0.61
3	1.22
4	1.36
5	1.46
6	1.54

Source: Bryant, Holtham, and Hooper (1988),
Table II-5, p. 113.
The table averages estimates from the DRI,
EPA, MCM, OECD, NIESR-GEM, and Taylor
models; simulations cover the years 1986–91.

A large empirical literature uses variants of the Mundell-Fleming-Dornbusch model to analyze how cumulated current-account deficits affect real exchange rates (see, for example, Williamson, 1985; Helkie and Hooper, 1988; and Krugman, 1991b). While we have identified a number of important theoretical failings with such models, it is still very useful to consider this substantial body of evidence. Generally speaking, the results of this literature, which has focused to a great extent on the case of the United States, is quite consistent with the nonstructural evidence in Figure 4.14. Very large real currency depreciations seem to be required to offset apparently quite small current-account deficits. Table 10.1, based on Bryant, Holtham, and Hooper (1988), is representative. The entries in the table are averaged estimates from six independent econometric models.

The initial negative response of the current account to a depreciation is generally termed the "J-curve" effect and is due to the fact that short-run elasticities of demand and supply are generally much smaller than long-run elasticities. In the short run, a real depreciation of the dollar implies that imports cost more and exports yield less, so that a higher current-account deficit results. Only over time do the quantity responses outweigh the price effects. As the table indicates, even a very substantial permanent depreciation has only a relatively modest impact on the current account. One implication typically drawn from these and similar calculations is that for the United States, fairly large real exchange-rate changes are required to change substantially the course of the current account. The United States, of course, is a relatively closed economy: 1994 gross exports and imports combined amounted to slightly less than 20 percent of GNP. While the ratio for Japan is similar, most other OECD countries (for example, Germany) have trade shares closer to 40 percent of GNP. For economies more open than the United

States, real exchange-rate changes have a considerably greater impact on the current account.   ∎

10.3   Government Spending and Productivity Shocks

Thus far in the chapter, we have focused almost exclusively on monetary shocks, but it is possible to use sticky-price intertemporal models to analyze a far wider range of issues. In this section, we return to the general equilibrium model of section 10.1 to illustrate how sticky-price dynamics change the economy's response to government spending and productivity shocks. As we shall see, the answers are sometimes surprisingly different from those offered by the standard flexible-price models considered in Chapters 1 and 2.

10.3.1   Productivity Shocks

We begin by considering the effects of temporary and permanent productivity shocks. Recall from our discussion on p. 662 that a positive productivity shock (a rise in A) may be captured in this model by a *fall* in κ, which multiplies output y in the period utility function

$$\log C + \chi \log \frac{M}{P} - \frac{\kappa}{2} y^2.$$

The higher productivity—the lower κ—the less labor is required to produce a given quantity of output. How does modifying the model of section 10.1 to allow for shocks to productivity change our analysis? The first-order conditions and the symmetric steady state of the two-country model stand unaltered. All the linearized equations of section 10.1.5 remain the same except for the linearized labor-leisure trade-off equations in the section, eqs. (33) and (34), which become

$$(\theta + 1)y_t = -\theta c_t + c_t^W + \theta a_t, \tag{100}$$

$$(\theta + 1)y_t^* = -\theta c_t^* + c_t^W + \theta a_t^*, \tag{101}$$

where

$$a_t \equiv -\frac{\kappa_t - \bar{\kappa}_0}{\bar{\kappa}_0}.$$

(Our use of a to denote proportional rises in productivity seems natural given the implicit inverse relationship between κ and A.) With this minor modification, we follow the same steps as in sections 10.1.6 and 10.1.7 to solve the model. The differenced labor-leisure equation (43) becomes

$$y_t - y_t^* = -\frac{\theta}{1+\theta}(c_t - c_t^*) + \frac{\theta}{1+\theta}(a_t - a_t^*),$$

and the solution for the difference between Home and Foreign steady-state consumption, eq. (45), is replaced by

$$\bar{c} - \bar{c}^* = \left(\frac{1}{1-n}\right)\left(\frac{1+\theta}{2\theta}\right)\delta\bar{b} + \left(\frac{\theta-1}{2\theta}\right)(\bar{a} - \bar{a}^*), \tag{102}$$

where

$$\bar{a} \equiv -\frac{\bar{\kappa} - \bar{\kappa}_0}{\bar{\kappa}_0}$$

is the steady-state percentage change in productivity. Holding net foreign assets constant, a relative rise in steady-state Home productivity leads to a rise in Home relative consumption. The rise, however, is less than proportional to the rise in $\bar{a} - \bar{a}^*$, in part because Home residents respond by working less, and in part because the relative price of Home goods falls as a result of the rise in relative (physical) output. The change in the steady-state terms of trade is given by

$$\bar{p}(h) - \bar{e} - \bar{p}^*(f) = \left(\frac{1}{1-n}\right)\left(\frac{1}{2\theta}\right)\delta\bar{b} - \frac{\bar{a} - \bar{a}^*}{2\theta}. \tag{103}$$

Of course, changes in world productivity also affect steady-state global output and consumption. Taking a population-weighted average of the labor-leisure trade-off equations (100) and (101)—which bind only in the steady state when prices become fully flexible—together with the relation $c_t^W = y_t^W$ [eq. (32)] yields[24]

$$\bar{c}^W = \bar{y}^W = \frac{\bar{a}^W}{2}. \tag{104}$$

A permanent rise in global productivity raises steady-state global output, but less than proportionately because agents substitute into leisure [look at the effect of a fall in κ in eq. (24)].

Now let us turn to the short run. Consider first an unanticipated *temporary* rise in Home productivity. What is the output effect? *Absolutely none*; the entire productivity rise is absorbed by a rise in Home leisure. Why? The labor-leisure equations (100) and (101) are not binding in the short run when prices are preset. Price exceeds marginal cost by a finite amount, and a small marginal productivity shock does not alter this fact. Output thus will still be demand determined. Therefore, if Home productivity rises, Home production stays constant, and Home agents simply supply the same quantity with less effort.

---

24. The fraction $\frac{1}{2}$ appearing in eq. (104) corresponds to the exponent on y in the period utility function. In the more general case where we allow the exponent to take on an arbitrary value $\mu > 1$ (that is, if the output term in the period utility function is given by $\frac{\kappa}{\mu}y^\mu$), eq. (104) is replaced by

$$\bar{c}^W = \bar{y}^W = \frac{\bar{a}^W}{\mu}.$$

We now turn to the more interesting case of a permanent positive productivity increase, so that $a = \bar{a}$ rises. (We will continue to allow for money shocks as well, which is not difficult because the two effects are additive in the linearized system.) The **MM** schedule is unaffected and remains as in eq. (60):

$$e = (m - m^*) - (c - c^*).$$

The **GG** schedule, however, which embodies the steady-state consumption equation (102), does change. Equation (64) is replaced by

$$e = \frac{\delta(1 + \theta) + 2\theta}{\delta(\theta^2 - 1)} (c - c^*) - \frac{\bar{a} - \bar{a}^*}{\delta(1 + \theta)}, \tag{105}$$

where we have used eqs. (57), (62), (63), and (102). The equilibrium is depicted in Figure 10.3, which illustrates the case of a permanent rise in relative Home productivity, holding relative money supplies constant. As one can see from the figure, the nominal exchange rate *appreciates*. The intuition for the appreciation is as follows. Although there is no short-run effect on output, Home output rises in the long run. Therefore, to smooth consumption, Home residents will dissave and raise current consumption, thereby raising the demand for Home money relative to Foreign money (per the **MM** schedule). This increase in turn leads to an appreciation of the Home currency. The current-account deficit will temper the long-term difference between Home and Foreign consumption, but will not reverse it. Solving eqs. (60) and (105) for the exchange rate yields

$$e = \frac{\delta(1 + \theta) + 2\theta}{\theta\delta(1 + \theta) + 2\theta} (m - m^*) - \frac{\theta - 1}{\theta\delta(1 + \theta) + 2\theta} (\bar{a} - \bar{a}^*), \tag{106}$$

confirming that a rise in $\bar{a} - \bar{a}^*$ indeed leads to an appreciation of the Home currency (a fall in e).

To solve for the impact of changes in productivity on the short-run real interest rate, we again combine eq. (69), the population-weighted average of the consumption Euler equations, with the population-weighted average of the money-demand equations. In contrast with the earlier case of a pure money shock, changes in world productivity generally affect steady-state consumption, as per eq. (104). Thus, the future world price level is expected to fall by $\bar{a}^w/2$, and the relevant population-weighted money demand equation average is not eq. (71) but

$$m^w = c^w - \frac{r}{1 + \delta} - \frac{m^w}{\delta} + \frac{\bar{a}^w}{2\delta}.$$

Substituting eq. (104) into eq. (69) and using the result to eliminate short-run world consumption in the preceding equation yields

$$r = \left(\frac{1 + \delta}{\delta} \right) \left(\frac{\bar{a}^w}{2} - m^w \right). \tag{107}$$

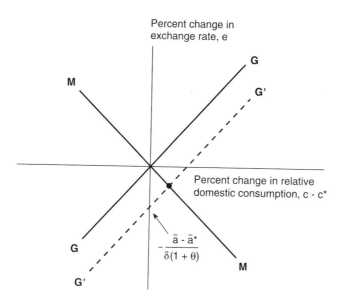

Figure 10.3
An unexpected relative rise in domestic productivity

Equation (107) shows that a permanent rise in world productivity $\bar{a}^w$ leads to a rise in short-term real interest rates. In the short run, agents do not wish to raise output. Therefore, short-run output is lower than long-run output, and the real interest rate rises as saving falls. Notice that in the short run the *nominal* interest rate doesn't change: expected deflation exactly offsets the rise in the real interest rate.

These results sharply contrast with the intuition we developed in the flexible-price models of Chapters 1 and 2. There, absent investment, a permanent productivity shock had no effect on the current account or interest rates, since it did not tilt the country or global income profiles. It would seem that the interest-rate result here should hold across a fairly general class of sticky-price models.[25]

Finally, note that we have interpreted κ as a productivity shock, but from our earlier discussion it is apparent that one could also interpret a rise in κ as a change in preferences favoring leisure over consumption. We will leave the welfare analysis of the international transmission of productivity disturbances as an exercise. One

---

25. Since a short-run change in κ (a) has no effect on any variables except leisure, it follows that an anticipated permanent change in κ that is learned in period 1 but does not take place until period 2 will have the same effect as a permanent shock that takes effect immediately (for all variables except leisure).

can show that a permanent rise in Home productivity unambiguously raises both Home and Foreign welfare.

10.3.2 Government Spending Shocks

We now turn to examining how preset prices can affect the response of the economy to temporary and permanent government spending shocks. Again, our analysis is a straightforward extension of the two-country model of section 10.1. In interpreting the results of this section, it is important to keep in mind that there are many ways to introduce government spending. Even in a basic flexible-price model, government investment spending has different effects from government consumption spending, and the effects of the latter are very sensitive to whether government consumption is a complement or a substitute for private consumption.[26] There is a similar range of possibilities for modeling G in a sticky-price setting. Here we will focus on the simplest case where government spending is purely dissipative and does not affect productivity or private utility. While this case is special in some respects, some of the basic insights it gives on how sticky-price models differ from flexible-price models turn out to be quite general. Furthermore, the *positive* results that follow would be the same if government spending entered separably into preferences.

10.3.2.1 Modifications to the Model to Allow for Government Consumption Spending

For simplicity, and to focus on the dynamic aspects of fiscal policy, we will assume that the government's real consumption index takes the same general form as the private sector's, given by eq. (2), and with the same elasticity of substitution θ:

$$G = \left[\int_0^1 g(z)^{\frac{\theta-1}{\theta}} dz \right]^{\frac{\theta}{\theta-1}}, \quad G^* = \left[\int_0^1 g^*(z)^{\frac{\theta-1}{\theta}} dz \right]^{\frac{\theta}{\theta-1}}.$$

Here G and G^* are per capita in each country. If governments act as price takers, then their demand functions for individual goods will also have the same form as the private sector's:[27]

$$g(z) = \left[\frac{p(z)}{P} \right]^{-\theta} G.$$

---

26. Older Keynesian models such as the ones in Chapter 9 do not make any of these distinctions, which is one of many reasons they are inadequate for studying the effects of fiscal policy.

27. In fact, governments may have an incentive to act as strategic monopsonists in this model, preferring to buy home goods to foreign to bid up their price. (For the same reason, governments may have an incentive to place tariffs on foreign goods.) We abstract from this possibility here, treating governments as behaving competitively in goods markets.

With government spending, the public budget constraint (9) is replaced by

$$G_t = \tau_t + \frac{M_t - M_{t-1}}{P_t},$$ (108)

and an analogous constraint holds abroad. Next, the demand function for the representative agent's output, eq. (10), is replaced by

$$y^d = \left(\frac{p}{P}\right)^{-\theta} (C^W + G^W),$$ (109)

where $G^W \equiv nG + (1-n)G^*$. Under eq. (109), the first-order condition (15) governing the Home representative agent's labor-leisure trade-off becomes

$$y^{\frac{\theta+1}{\theta}} = \frac{\theta-1}{\theta\kappa} (C^W + G^W)^{\frac{1}{\theta}} \frac{1}{C}.$$ (110)

Introducing the government also requires suitably modifying our current-account equations. Equations (20) and (21) governing steady-state current-account behavior are now

$$\bar{C} = \delta\bar{B} + \frac{\bar{p}(h)\bar{y}}{\bar{P}} - \bar{G},$$ (111)

$$\bar{C}^* = -\left(\frac{n}{1-n}\right)\delta\bar{B} + \frac{\bar{p}^*(f)\bar{y}^*}{\bar{P}^*} - \bar{G}^*.$$ (112)

Government spending, of course, subtracts from the total resources available for private spending.[28]

10.3.2.2   Modifications to Linearized Equations

We will linearize the model around a symmetric steady state in which $\bar{B}_0 = \bar{B}_0^* = \bar{G}_0 = \bar{G}_0^* = 0$, and again restrict our attention to perturbations in which all exogenous variables are constant in the long run. Since we are starting from an initial situation of zero government expenditure, the initial steady state is the same as before. The linearized model is also the same as that in section 10.1.5, except for the equations corresponding to eqs. (30)–(34) and (40)–(41),

$$y_t = \theta \left[p_t - p_t(h) \right] + c_t^W + g_t^W,$$ (113)

$$y_t^* = \theta \left[p_t^* - p_t^*(f) \right] + c_t^W + g_t^W,$$ (114)

$$y_t^W = c_t^W + g_t^W,$$ (115)

---

28. As in Chapter 8, we have assumed that the government does not have a transactions demand for currency. This approach, while the conventional one, may produce somewhat misleading results for price-level effects if the government has a need for transaction balances similar to the private sector's. It is not difficult to modify the model to allow for government money holdings.

$$(\theta + 1)y_t = -\theta c_t + c_t^W + g_t^W, \tag{116}$$

$$(\theta + 1)y_t^* = -\theta c_t^* + c_t^W + g_t^W, \tag{117}$$

$$\bar{c} = \delta \bar{b} + \bar{p}(h) + \bar{y} - \bar{p} - \bar{g}, \tag{118}$$

$$\bar{c}^* = -\left(\frac{n}{1-n}\right)\delta \bar{b} + \bar{p}^*(f) + \bar{y}^* - \bar{p}^* - \bar{g}^*, \tag{119}$$

where we define $g_t^W \equiv dG_t^W / \bar{C}_0^W$ and $\bar{g} \equiv d\bar{G}/\bar{C}_0^W$. (We normalize by initial world consumption because we have assumed that initial government spending is zero.) Changes in world government consumption affect world aggregate demand. Steady-state Home government consumption reduces income available for private Home consumption, and the same is true for Foreign.

One final set of equations that must be modified are the short-run current-account equations (governing the current account in the period of the shock). For Home, eq. (54) now becomes

$$B_{t+1} - B_t = r_t B_t + \frac{p_t(h)y_t}{P_t} - C_t - G_t. \tag{120}$$

Linearizing eq. (120) and using eqs. (27) and (28) [taking into account that $p(h)$ and $p^*(f)$ are preset in the short run] yields

$$\bar{b} = y - c - (1-n)e - g, \tag{121}$$

and the corresponding Foreign equation is

$$\left(\frac{-n}{1-n}\right)\bar{b} = \bar{b}^* = y^* - c^* + ne - g^*. \tag{122}$$

10.3.2.3 The Effects of Government Spending on the Steady State

We are now prepared to solve for the steady-state effects of permanent government spending shocks when prices are flexible and all exogenous variables other than government spending variables are constant. (Obviously, when government spending shocks are purely temporary, the steady-state equations are unchanged from those in section 10.1.6.)[29] As before, the simplest way to solve the system is to look at differences between Home and Foreign variables, and at population-weighted world aggregates. For example, multiplying eq. (116) by n and eq. (117) by $1-n$, then adding, yields

$$(\theta + 1)y_t^W = (1 - \theta)c_t^W + g_t^W.$$

---

29. Note, though, that with sticky prices, temporary government spending shocks can still affect the steady state indirectly by inducing short-run current-account deficits and thereby affecting $\bar{b}$.

Combining this expression with eq. (115) and substituting bars for t subscripts to denote the steady state yields

$$\bar{y}^w = \tfrac{1}{2}\bar{g}^w, \tag{123}$$

$$\bar{c}^w = -\tfrac{1}{2}\bar{g}^w. \tag{124}$$

A permanent rise in government spending raises steady-state world output, because people respond by substituting into work and out of leisure. For this reason, world consumption falls by less than the rise in government spending. Paralleling the derivation of eq. (45), one can use differenced versions of eqs. (113)–(119) to obtain

$$\bar{c} - \bar{c}^* = \left(\frac{1}{1-n}\right)\left(\frac{1+\theta}{2\theta}\right)\delta\bar{b} - \frac{1+\theta}{2\theta}\left(\bar{g} - \bar{g}^*\right). \tag{125}$$

Similarly, eq. (46) becomes

$$\bar{p}(h) - \bar{e} - \bar{p}^*(f) = \left(\frac{1}{1-n}\right)\left(\frac{1}{2\theta}\right)\delta\bar{b} - \frac{1}{2\theta}\left(\bar{g} - \bar{g}^*\right). \tag{126}$$

A relative rise in steady-state Home government spending induces a rise in relative Home output. It therefore leads to a deterioration in Home's steady-state terms of trade.

It is easy to check that in a flexible-price world, a rise in Home government spending would lower Home welfare (private consumption and leisure both fall), but raise welfare abroad. Higher Home government spending leads to an outward shift in the demand curve facing Foreign residents [from eq. (115) we see that global aggregate demand, $c^w + g^w$, rises], and therefore allows them to raise their prices at any given level of output.[30]

10.3.2.4   Short-Run Effects of Government Spending

We now examine the short-run effects of shocks to the path of government spending that are announced and implemented in period 1. We allow for both temporary and permanent shocks. As before, with $p(h)$ and $p^*(f)$ set one period in advance, the economy reaches its new steady state beginning in period 2.

Since government spending does not affect the money demand or the consumption Euler equations, the **MM** schedule [eq. (60)] remains as before:

$$e = (m - m^*) - (c - c^*). $$

---

30. We have ignored real balance effects in the welfare discussion of the text, but these reinforce the real effects for reasonable parameter values.

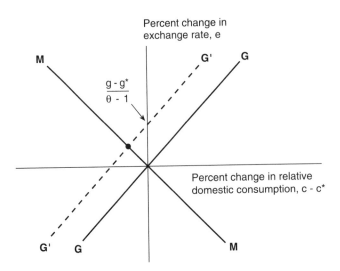

Figure 10.4
An unexpected temporary rise in Home government spending

As usual, variables without bars denote short-run (period 1) values, while variables with bars denote values for all periods beginning in period 2.

The **GG** schedule does change, since government spending shocks enter short-term aggregate demand, the current account, and, if they are permanent, steady-state consumption differentials. With government spending, the **GG** schedule, eq. (64), becomes

$$e = \frac{\delta(1 + \theta) + 2\theta}{\delta(\theta^2 - 1)} (c - c^*) + \frac{1}{\theta - 1}\left[g - g^* + \left(\frac{1}{\delta}\right)(\bar{g} - \bar{g}^*)\right]. \tag{127}$$

Notice that the steady-state component of the government spending differential is multiplied by $1/\delta$ $(= 1/\bar{r})$, reflecting that current consumption behavior depends on the present discounted value of government spending in all future periods.[31]

In Figure 10.4, we graph the **GG** schedule for the case of a purely temporary government spending shock, so that $\bar{g} - \bar{g}^* = 0$. Money is held constant, so the postshock **MM** schedule still passes through the origin. From the diagram, we can see that a rise in Home government spending leads to a depreciation of the Home currency. What causes the depreciation? A rise in Home government spending leads to an immediate fall in relative Home consumption; relative Home output goes up, but not by enough to offset the rise in taxes. Lower consumption implies lower money demand, requiring a rise in the price level and a depreciation of the currency. Analytically, one can solve the **MM** and the **GG** schedules (with

---

31. To derive eq. (127), use eqs. (57), (63), (121), (122), and (125).

$m - m^* = 0$) to obtain

$$e = \frac{\delta(1+\theta)}{\theta\delta(1+\theta) + 2\theta} \left[g - g^* + \left(\frac{1}{\delta}\right)(\bar{g} - \bar{g}^*) \right].$$

(128)

When $m - m^* = 0$, the **MM** equation (60) implies that $c - c^* = -e$, and the demand equations (113) and (114) imply that with preset prices, $y - y^* = \theta e$. Substituting these expressions into the difference between eqs. (121) and (122) and substituting for e using eq. (128) yields

$$\bar{b} = \frac{(1-n)\delta(1+\theta)}{\delta(1+\theta) + 2} \left[g - g^* + \left(\frac{1}{\delta}\right)(\bar{g} - \bar{g}^*) \right] - (1-n)(g - g^*).$$

(129)

It is easy to see that in the case of a transitory relative increase in Home government spending, Home runs a deficit as in a standard flexible-price intertemporal model. But as one can readily check, in the case of a permanent relative rise in Home government spending, $g - g^* = \bar{g} - \bar{g}^*$, Home actually runs a *surplus*. With preset prices, short-run Home income rises by more than long-run Home income, so Home residents adjust current consumption downward by more than the change in government spending. In analogy to the productivity example considered earlier, even though a permanent rise in government spending does not directly induce any tilting into the time profile of aggregate demand, it does introduce a tilt in the path of output net of government consumption.[32]

It should be apparent from the preceding discussion that a permanent rise in world government spending will lead to a fall in the short-run real interest rate. Solving for the world real interest rate as in our previous examples for monetary and productivity shocks [eqs. (73) and (107)], one obtains

$$r = -\left(\frac{1+\delta}{\delta}\right)\frac{\bar{g}^w}{2}.$$

(130)

A rise in steady-state government spending indeed lowers the contemporaneous real interest rate. Note, however, that only the steady-state (future) level of government spending enters into expression (130). Current government spending does not appear. Thus a temporary rise in world government spending has no effect at all on the real interest rate! The reason, of course, is that output is demand determined in the short run with preset prices. Thus an unanticipated temporary rise in world government spending induces an equal temporary rise in world output, with no effect on the net output available to the private sector. Hence there is no tilting of net output profiles and no interest-rate effect.

---

32. Mankiw (1987b) derives a short-run "multiplier" effect on output in a static closed-economy Keynesian-cross model.

How robust are the results here to changes in the particular way we have introduced government spending? Different approaches to modeling government spending can lead to different predictions about the impact on interest rates, even in the flexible-price case. One should interpret the results here as giving some indication of the direction of effects one would expect to see in a world with preset prices, *relative to a base case of flexible prices*.

Finally, there is the topic of welfare analysis, which again straightforwardly parallels our discussion of monetary disturbances. Regardless of the directions of the positive effects, overall Foreign benefits and Home loses when Home's government spends more. Home loses because it is forced to foot the bill for the entire expansion in world aggregate demand. Of course, these welfare results are also sensitive to the way in which government spending affects private agents' utility. If government spending directly enters the utility function, and if the initial share of government consumption in total consumption is suboptimally low, a rise in Home government spending can raise Home welfare. Again, the interesting question is how the results for a sticky-price model differ from those of a flexible-price model.

10.4 Nominal Wage Rigidities

There is a long tradition in macroeconomics, dating back to Keynes (1936), that emphasizes *wage* rigidity as the central monetary nonneutrality in the economy. Up to this point in the chapter our analysis has depended on price rigidities in the final goods sector, but that setup was assumed partly for ease of exposition. Here we show that all the main results that we have derived extend to the case of monopolistic supply in the labor market and preset nominal wages.

10.4.1   A Small Country Producing Nontraded Goods Using Differentiated Labor

10.4.1.1   The Model

The general point is perhaps easiest to demonstrate in the context of a slightly modified version of the small-country model with nontraded goods of section 10.2. Instead of assuming a continuum of monopolistically supplied nontradable goods, we assume that there is a single nontraded good that is supplied competitively. However, to produce the nontraded good, the representative firm must employ different types of labor $\ell(z)$, $z \in [0, 1]$ according to the linear-homogeneous CES production function

$$Y_{N,t} = \left[\int_0^1 \ell_t(z)^{\frac{\phi-1}{\phi}} \, dz \right]^{\frac{\phi}{\phi-1}}, \tag{131}$$

where $\phi > 1$. Each agent j in the economy is a monopoly supplier of $\ell(j)$ and considers his market power in deciding how much labor to supply. (One might think of each worker as the representative of a monopolistic union.) The utility function of the representative agent j is given by

$$
U_t^j = \sum_{s=t}^{\infty} \beta^{s-t} \left[\gamma \log C_{T,s}^j + (1-\gamma) \log C_{N,s}^j + \frac{\chi}{1-\varepsilon} \left(\frac{M_s^j}{P_s} \right)^{1-\varepsilon} - \frac{\kappa}{2} \ell_s(j)^2 \right],
$$

(132)

where the price index is the same as in section 10.2,

$$
P \equiv P_T^\gamma P_N^{1-\gamma} / \gamma^\gamma (1-\gamma)^{1-\gamma},
$$

except that P_N is now the money price of a single type of nontraded good rather than a price index. Note that otherwise the only difference between the utility function (132) and eq. (82) is that the disutility from work ℓ now enters directly instead of implicitly via y_N. As before, each agent receives a constant endowment of the traded good $\bar{y}_T$ each period, and can borrow and lend tradables at the fixed world interest rate r, where $\beta(1+r) = 1$. In addition, he earns $w_t(j)\ell_t(j)$ each period from labor income, where $w_t(j)$ is the nominal wage for differentiated labor of type j. The budget constraint of the representative agent therefore is

$$
P_{T,t} B_{t+1}^j + M_t^j = P_{T,t}(1+r)B_t^j + M_{t-1}^j + w_t(j)\ell_t(j)
$$

(133)

$$
+ P_{T,t}\bar{y}_T - P_{N,t}C_{N,t}^j - P_{T,t}C_{T,t}^j - P_{T,t}\tau_t,
$$

where $P_T = \mathcal{E} P_T^*$ is tied down by the law of one price, as usual.

The single representative competitive firm in the nontraded goods sector maximizes profits

$$
P_N Y_N - \int_0^1 w(z)\ell(z)\mathrm{d}z,
$$

(134)

subject to the production function (131). The firm's maximization problem yields the labor demands

$$
\ell_t^d(j) = \left[\frac{w_t(j)}{P_{N,t}} \right]^{-\phi} Y_{N,t}.
$$

(135)

A type-j worker takes this demand function into account when maximizing his utility.

10.4.1.2   The First-Order Conditions and the Steady-State Equilibrium

The implications of this setup, with monopolistically supplied labor instead of output, turn out to be remarkably similar to those of the previous model. Because the steps for deriving the steady-state equilibrium and for analyzing the effects of money shocks are virtually identical to the earlier sticky-price model, we will characterize them only briefly.

The first-order conditions for individual maximization subject to constraints (133) and (135) can still be characterized by eqs. (87)–(89), but the earlier "labor-leisure" equation (90) is now replaced by

$$\ell_t^{\frac{\phi+1}{\phi}} = \left[\frac{(\phi-1)(1-\gamma)}{\kappa\phi} \right] Y_{N,t}^{\frac{1}{\phi}} \left(\frac{1}{C_{N,t}} \right), \tag{136}$$

where the j indexes are now omitted since individuals are symmetric. To solve the model, it is helpful to note that in the symmetric equilibrium where all agents ask the same wage w_t, firms will hire equal quantities of each type of labor. With symmetric inputs, the representative firm's production function takes the simple linear form

$$Y_{N,t} = \ell_t, \tag{137}$$

where ℓ is the labor supply of the representative agent. Since the representative firm behaves competitively, workers must be paid their marginal products. Under symmetry, therefore

$$w_t = P_{N,t}. \tag{138}$$

Finally, clearing in the market for nontraded good implies

$$Y_{N,t} = C_{N,t}. \tag{139}$$

Substituting this condition together with eq. (137) into the first-order condition (136) and solving for the steady-state value of labor supply yields

$$\bar{\ell} = \left[\frac{(\phi-1)(1-\gamma)}{\kappa\phi} \right]^{\frac{1}{2}} = \bar{Y}_N. \tag{140}$$

Comparing eq. (140) with the similar expression (93) from the earlier setup, we see that monopolistic supply of labor pushes output below its efficient value in the same way as monopolistic supply of final goods. Steady-state prices and traded-goods consumption are determined as before.

10.4.1.3 Effects of an Unanticipated Permanent Money Shock with Preset Wages

Suppose now that wages w_t are set a period in advance (on date $t-1$), but that both $P_{N,t}$ and $P_{T,t}$ are fully flexible. (This assumption makes sense here because output markets are competitive.) Consider the effects of a one-time unanticipated increase in the money supply on date $t=1$. With nominal wages fixed, labor supply will be demand determined in the short run. The rationale for why labor and hence output is demand determined is exactly as in the earlier model with preset output prices.

The marginal utility of the initial real wage exceeds the marginal disutility from labor, so that if wages cannot be raised in response to an increase in labor demand, workers will fully accommodate the demand shift. Short-run demand is given by eq. (135) with $w_1 = \bar{w}_0$. Because firms producing output behave competitively, the zero-profit condition (138) implies $w/P_N = 1$ even when nominal wages cannot adjust, so that short-run aggregate demand is given by

$$\ell = Y_N = C_N.$$

From this point on, the model is solved exactly as in section 10.2, and in fact one arrives at the *identical* expression (99) for the impact effect on traded goods prices (and therefore the exchange rate) of a money shock. The condition for overshooting is the same, as are the essential welfare implications. Even the effect on nontraded-goods prices is the same despite the fact that P_N is flexible here. From a welfare perspective, the shock once again coordinates an efficient increase in labor supply and, therefore, in output.

One can easily extend the analysis to incorporate monopoly both in labor supply and in the final goods sector, in which case one can have sticky prices or wages or both.[33] We have focused on the sticky-wage interpretation of the model. The analysis can be adapted to incorporate rigidities in the prices for intermediate goods as in Basu (1995), who argues that small menu costs in intermediate-goods price setting can generate much larger business cycles than small menu costs in final-goods price setting alone.

10.4.2   A Two-Country Model with Preset Wages

One can similarly reformulate our earlier two-country model in terms of preset wages rather than preset prices, and obtain results closely analogous to those of section 10.1. We very briefly sketch the idea here in a formulation that can accommodate price discrimination across the two markets.[34]

Consider a slight extension of the two-country model of section 10.1 in which there are both a continuum of differentiated final goods and a continuum of differentiated labor inputs. The representative Home agent j is the monopoly supplier of labor of type j, and has lifetime utility function

$$U_t^j = \sum_{s=t}^{\infty} \beta^{s-t} \left[\log C_s^j + \chi \log \frac{M_s^j}{P_s} - \frac{\kappa}{2} \ell_s(j)^2 \right], \tag{141}$$

where C is again the consumption index given by eq. (2) and P is the consumption-based price index given by eq. (3). Home agents reside on the interval $z \in [0, \frac{1}{2}]$,

---

33. Blanchard and Kiyotaki (1987) allow for menu costs in both price setting and wage setting in their one-period model.

34. The model here is a simplified version of Hau (1996), who also allows for nontraded goods.

while Foreign agents reside on $(\frac{1}{2}, 1]$. Similarly, Home firms produce goods on the interval $z \in [0, \frac{1}{2}]$, and Foreign firms produce goods $(\frac{1}{2}, 1]$; all goods are traded. The production function for the representative Home good j is given by

$$y_t(j) = \frac{1}{2}\left[2\int_0^{\frac{1}{2}} \ell_t(z)^{\frac{\phi-1}{\phi}} dz\right]^{\frac{\phi}{\phi-1}}, \tag{142}$$

$\phi > 1$, where we normalize so that when all domestic labor inputs are used symmetrically at level ℓ, $y(z) = \frac{1}{2}\ell$. [It is not necessary to constrain the two countries to be the same size, but it simplifies the analysis. When the two countries are of different sizes, the larger country enjoys an advantage from having access to a larger variety of labor inputs. There are increasing returns as in the P. Romer (1990) model of Chapter 7.] Output of good z is monopolistically supplied by Home firm z. Home agents each hold equal shares of a portfolio of all Home firms (which now earn profits), and Foreign agents hold shares in Foreign firms. International asset trade is again constrained to riskless real bonds. The representative Home firm takes wages as given and chooses period t prices and labor inputs to maximize

$$p_t(j)y_t(j) - \int_0^{\frac{1}{2}} w_t(z)\ell_t(z)dz$$

subject to production function (142) and demand function (10). Each laborer faces a downward-sloping labor demand function analogous to eq. (135) of the preceding model but depending on an aggregate wage index. The first-order condition governing the individual's labor-leisure decision is analogous to eq. (136).

Solving the firm's problem and recognizing that wages and labor input will be symmetric in equilibrium yields the markup pricing rule

$$p_t(j) = \frac{\theta}{\theta - 1} w_t$$

where w_t is the symmetric wage rate. This type of formula is standard for profit-maximizing monopolists facing a constant price elasticity demand function, and we have already seen a version of it in Chapter 7.

With flexible prices and zero initial net foreign assets, the initial steady-state equilibrium level of production and consumption can be shown to be

$$\bar{y}_0 = \bar{y}_0^* = \left[\left(\frac{\phi - 1}{\phi}\right)\left(\frac{\theta - 1}{\theta}\right)\frac{1}{\kappa}\right]^{\frac{1}{2}}, \tag{143}$$

so that output is lower due to monopoly distortions in both the labor market and the output market. Otherwise the analysis is the same as in the earlier model. For example, if final-goods prices are flexible, wages are preset, and the law of one price holds, the effects of a surprise permanent money increase on both consumption differentials and the exchange rate are the same as in the section 10.1.

An interesting alternative version of the model relaxes the law-of-one-price assumption and allows for the possibility that monopolistic firms price-discriminate across countries (see the following application). In this case, because the production function is linear when all factors are used symmetrically, a firm's pricing decisions in the two markets are independent. (With a linear production function, a rise in production for the Home market does not affect the marginal cost of producing for the Foreign market.) The result is that the pricing rule for the representative Home good is given by

$$p_t(h) = \mathcal{E}_t p_t^*(h) = \frac{\theta}{\theta - 1} w_t. \tag{144}$$

Since the elasticity of demand is the same in both the Home and Foreign markets, the markup over nominal wages is the same. Even though deviations from the law of one price are possible (since we are implicitly precluding goods market arbitrage), they do not occur. More generally, if the constant elasticity of demand is different in the two markets, the levels of prices will differ. But domestic producers will still lower their foreign prices proportionately in response to a money shock that causes the domestic currency to depreciate. With constant elasticities of demand, there is complete *exchange-rate pass-through* to import prices. Complete pass-through can fail in theory and in practice, as the following application shows.

Application: Pricing to Market and Exchange-Rate Pass-Through

Throughout most of the analysis of this chapter, we have assumed that the law of one price obtains, so that, adjusted for exchange rates, the same good must sell for the same price throughout the world. An implicit assumption is that firms cannot price-discriminate across the countries; they are prevented from doing so by arbitrage through the resale market. But there are some classes of goods—automobiles are the leading example—for which firms sometimes can effectively charge different prices in different markets. With cars, standards may be slightly different across countries (a nontariff barrier), or firms may be able to withhold warranty service except in the country of origin. Also, for big-ticket items such as cars, it is easier for firms to enforce exclusive distribution agreements. (Similar agreements in small electronics goods are much more difficult to enforce because of an active "gray market" that arbitrages prices across regions.) The price discrimination explanation of departures from the law of one price is sometimes termed "pricing to market." In principle, pricing-to-market models can explain not only short-term but also longer-term departures from PPP.[35]

---

35. For a more complete discussion of pricing-to-market models, see Feenstra (1995).

One question that has received widespread attention is the degree of exchange rate pass-through in goods where producers can price-discriminate. During the early 1980s, when the dollar appreciated sharply against the Deutsche mark, the price of luxury German cars became much higher in the United States than in Europe. This is an example of incomplete exchange-rate pass-through, since German carmakers did not proportionately lower their U.S. prices when the dollar appreciated. The pricing-to-market model of the last section cannot explain this anomaly, since there, pass-through of monetary shocks is always one for one. (However, the empirical evidence could still be rationalized by recognizing that most "traded" goods contain substantial nontraded inputs, including local transportation, advertising costs, retail costs, and so on, as discussed in Chapter 4.) If pass-through is indeed less than one for one, what might be some explanations? One answer is that an appreciation of the dollar may reduce the elasticity of U.S. demand for imports; this would be the case if the demand curve facing foreign monopolists were linear rather than of constant elasticity. It is also possible to have incomplete pass-through because of supply-side factors such as irreversible investment costs in establishing a "beachhead" in the foreign market (Krugman, 1987; see also Dornbusch, 1987; Baldwin, 1988; Dixit, 1989; Betts and Devereux, 1996). Obviously, even with nonconstant demand elasticity or irreversible investment costs, monetary shocks will not affect the real markups charged by firms in different locations unless there is some type of nominal rigidity.

The empirical evidence on pricing to market as the explanation of incomplete pass-through is mixed. Knetter (1989) and others have found that incomplete exchange-rate pass-through is more pronounced for German and Japanese exporters than it is for American exporters. (Knetter studies pricing to market by looking at the prices charged by, say, German companies to Japanese and American importers.) Some of this difference appears to be due to the nature of the U.S. export industries, which tend to be more competitive (e.g., agricultural products). Knetter (1993) finds that U.S. pricing-to-market behavior becomes more similar to Germany's and Japan's if one controls for industry effects.

Froot and Klemperer (1989), Kasa (1992), and Ghosh and Wolf (1994) present empirical evidence showing that costs of price adjustment rather than oligopolistic price-setting behavior provide the most likely explanation of incomplete pass-through. Froot and Klemperer look at a model where consumers face costs of switching across products. They reason that if their costs-of-adjustment explanation is correct, then exchange-rate fluctuations that are expected to be permanent should have a much greater impact on markups than exchange-rate fluctuations that are expected to be temporary. United States data from the mid-1980s, Froot and Klemperer argue, provide evidence consistent with their model.

Of course even if pricing to market is genuinely important for some classes of goods, it is not obvious that they constitute a large fraction of total trade.   ∎

Exercises

1. *Shocks to the money growth rate.* Take the two-country model of section 10.1, but allow for steady-state money growth such that $\bar{M}_t/\bar{M}_{t-1} = 1 + \mu$ and $\bar{M}^*_t/\bar{M}^*_{t-1} = 1 + \mu^*$. Assume that in the initial steady state $\mu = \mu^*$.

   (a) How must eqs. (26), (37), (38), (39), (50), (51), and (52) be revised when $\mu > 0$?

   (b) Suppose there are short-run, one-period price rigidities as in the text and analyze the short-run impact on the exchange rate of an unanticipated permanent rise in the home rate of money growth from μ to μ', holding μ^* constant. You may use a diagram analogous to Figure 10.1; it is not strictly necessary to solve for the closed-form solution.

2. *The real exchange rate–real interest rate correlation revisited.* Consider the small-country model with nontradable goods of section 10.2.

   What is the short-run effect of an unanticipated permanent money shock on the real exchange rate and on the consumption-based real interest rate? Do unanticipated money shocks cause a temporary decrease in real interest rates and a real domestic currency depreciation as in the Dornbusch model of Chapter 9?

3. *The small-country case.* This exercise asks you to derive the small-country case directly without solving the full two-country model.

   Assume that the small country consumes only a single imported good and produces only a single export good over which it has some monopoly power. In particular, the demand curve faced by the small country is

   $$y^d = p^{-\theta} C^W,$$

   where p is the relative world price of the domestic good and C^W is the exogenous level of world demand. Finally, the small country faces an exogenous world own-rate of interest rate r on the imported good. (The small country, of course, has no effect on any world aggregate variables.) Derive the equilibrium by following steps parallel to those for deriving the results for differences between the home and foreign variables in the chapter's model.

4. *Credibility and monetary policy.* Consider a cash-in-advance variant of the model of section 10.2, in which representative agent j's utility function is given by

   $$U^j_t = \sum_{s=t}^{\infty} \beta^{s-t} \left[\gamma \log C^j_{T,s} + (1-\gamma) \log C^j_{N,s} - \frac{\kappa}{2} y_{N,s}(j)^2 \right].$$

   The model is otherwise the same except for the (contemporaneous) cash-in-advance constraint

   $$M^j_t \geq P_{T,t} C^j_{Tt} + \int_0^1 P_{N,t}(z) C^j_{N,t}(z) dz,$$

   which you may assume will always hold with equality in equilibrium. (One subtlety we abstract from here is that if consumers can obtain cash needed for transactions within the same period, it is producers that must hold cash between periods. In this formulation, therefore, inflation is a production tax instead of a consumption tax.

Implicitly we are assuming that the government pays interest on currency so that this issue—which is not important here—can be ignored.)

(a) Show that under flexible prices, the equilibrium level of nontraded goods output is given by

$$\bar{y}_N = \bar{C}_N = \left[\frac{(\theta - 1)(1 - \gamma)}{\kappa\theta} \right]^{\frac{1}{2}}.$$

(b) Show that if output were set by a planner, then the planner would choose

$$\bar{y}_N^{\text{PLAN}} = \left[\frac{(1 - \gamma)}{\kappa} \right]^{\frac{1}{2}}.$$

(c) Assume nontraded goods' prices are set one period in advance at a level consistent with M_t^e (the expected money supply), and denote the actual level of the money supply as M_t. Traded goods prices are fully flexible. Show that

$$y_{N,t} = \frac{M_t}{M_t^e} \bar{y}_N.$$

(d) Now suppose that the monetary authorities' objective function is given by

$$U_t - \frac{\chi}{2} (P_{T,t}/P_{T,t-1})^2,$$

so that they are interested in maximizing the utility function of the representative agent subject to an additional inflation term (this term depends only on traded-goods inflation but this is not important since nontraded goods prices are preset). This model is now analogous to the inflation credibility models we considered in Chapter 9, except that we have provided a motivation for the distortion between the natural rate of output targeted by the monetary authorities and the one targeted by wage setters. Show that once period t nontraded goods prices are set, assuming a one-shot-game equilibrium, the monetary authorities set M_t to maximize

$$(1 - \gamma) \log C_{N,t} - \frac{\kappa}{2} (y_{N,t})^2 - \frac{\chi}{2} (P_{T,t}/P_{T,t-1})^2.$$

(e) Show that the one-shot-game equilibrium level of money growth is given by

$$\frac{M_t}{M_{t-1}} = \frac{P_{T,t}}{P_{T,t-1}} = \left(\frac{1 - \gamma}{\chi\theta} \right)^{\frac{1}{2}},$$

where the right-hand side of this equation can also be written as

$$\{\kappa[(\bar{y}_N^{\text{PLAN}})^2 - (\bar{y}_N)^2]/\chi\}^{\frac{1}{2}}.$$

Supplements to Chapter 2

Supplement A   Methods of Intertemporal Optimization

In Chapter 2—as in much of this book—intertemporal optimization problems usually are solved by substituting constraints into the objective function so that necessary first-order conditions of optimality can be derived using simple differential calculus. Occasionally, however, alternative optimization methods are more convenient. You will encounter these alternative methods in this book and in reading the literature, so a brief description of how one goes about applying them is worthwhile. This supplement offers a nontechnical account of two leading approaches to solving dynamic maximization problems, the methods of *Lagrange multipliers* and *dynamic programming*. The supplement makes clear why the method of substitutions we used in the body of the chapter, when applicable, always yields the same results.

A.1   Optimization Using Lagrange Multipliers

To make our main points it is sufficient to work with the simplest multiperiod problem analyzed in the text: find a sequence C_t, $C_{t+1}, \ldots$ of consumption levels that maximizes

$$U_t = \sum_{s=t}^{t+T} \beta^{s-t} u(C_s)$$

subject to the two constraints

$$\sum_{s=t}^{t+T} \left(\frac{1}{1+r}\right)^{s-t} C_s + \left(\frac{1}{1+r}\right)^T B_{t+T+1} = (1+r)B_t + \sum_{s=t}^{t+T} \left(\frac{1}{1+r}\right)^{s-t} Y_s,$$

$$\left(\frac{1}{1+r}\right)^T B_{t+T+1} \geq 0,$$

where output levels are exogenous and there is no government.

The second of these constraints, the one that rules out Ponzi games of unbounded borrowing, is an *inequality* constraint. In Chapter 2, we finessed the technical problems it poses by arguing, from first principles, that an optimizing consumer always arranges matters so that $(1+r)^{-T} B_{t+T+1} = 0$. We can derive this conclusion more formally, however, by applying a classic mathematical result on optimization subject to inequality constraints, the *Kuhn-Tucker theorem*. (Actually, the original 1951 paper by Kuhn and Tucker contains a broader result than the one described here, but we will not need to invoke it in this book.) The theorem is as follows:

KUHN-TUCKER THEOREM   Let $f(\mathbf{z})$ and $g_j(\mathbf{z})$ $(j = 1, \ldots, N)$ be differentiable functions defined over $M \times 1$ vectors, with $f(\mathbf{z})$ concave and all of the $g_j(\mathbf{z})$ convex. A necessary and sufficient condition for $\mathbf{z}^0$ to be the global solution to the problem

$$\max_{\mathbf{z}} f(\mathbf{z}) \text{ subject to } g_1(\mathbf{z}) \leq 0, \ldots, g_N(\mathbf{z}) \leq 0$$

is that there exist nonnegative numbers λ_j $(j = 1, \ldots, N)$ such that

1. $g_j(\mathbf{z}^0) \leq 0$ for each constraint $j = 1, \ldots, N$;
2. $-\lambda_j g_j(\mathbf{z}^0) = 0$ for each constraint $j = 1, \ldots, N$;
3. $\partial f(\mathbf{z}^0)/\partial z_l = \sum_{j=1}^{N} \lambda_j \partial g_j(\mathbf{z}^0)/\partial z_l$ for each partial derivative with respect to $z_l, l = 1, \ldots, M$.

One implements the Kuhn-Tucker theorem mechanically by forming the Lagrangian

$$\mathcal{L} = f(\mathbf{z}) - \sum_{j=1}^{N} \lambda_j g_j(\mathbf{z})$$

and differentiating it partially with respect to each of the M components of $\mathbf{z}$ to get the first-order conditions listed in item 3. Each of the nonnegative Lagrange multipliers λ_j can be interpreted as the shadow value of the associated constraint j, that is, as the increase in maximized $f(\mathbf{z})$ that would result if the constraint were to be eased marginally. The conditions in item 2, which ensure that if a constraint is not strictly binding at the optimum—that is, if $g_j(\mathbf{z}^0) < 0$—its shadow value λ_j is zero, are called *complementary slackness* conditions. Finally, the conditions in item 1 simply ensure feasibility.[1]

Let's apply this abstract result to our initial maximization problem. We can rewrite the problem in Kuhn-Tucker form as maximization of $\sum_{s=t}^{t+T} \beta^{s-t} u(C_s)$ subject to the single inequality constraint

$$\sum_{s=t}^{t+T} \left(\frac{1}{1+r} \right)^{s-t} C_s - (1+r)B_t - \sum_{s=t}^{t+T} \left(\frac{1}{1+r} \right)^{s-t} Y_s \leq 0. \tag{1}$$

The associated Lagrangian is

$$\mathcal{L}_t = \sum_{s=t}^{t+T} \beta^{s-t} u(C_s) - \lambda \left[\sum_{s=t}^{t+T} \left(\frac{1}{1+r} \right)^{s-t} C_s - (1+r)B_t - \sum_{s=t}^{t+T} \left(\frac{1}{1+r} \right)^{s-t} Y_s \right].$$

Differentiation with respect to consumption levels yields the necessary conditions

---

1. For intuitive discussions of the Kuhn-Tucker theorem, including examples, see Dixit (1990), the first appendix of Kreps (1990), and Simon and Blume (1994, chs. 18–19).

$$\beta^{s-t}u'(C_s) = \lambda\left(\frac{1}{1+r}\right)^{s-t}.$$

By combining this condition with its date $s + 1$ counterpart, one obtains (because λ is the same in both expressions) the Euler equation, $u'(C_s) = (1 + r)\beta u'(C_{s+1})$ [eq. (5) of Chapter 2]. Notice, in particular, the implication that $\lambda = u'(C_t)$: the shadow value of the budget constraint is the initial marginal utility of consumption.

The complementary slackness condition can be expressed as

$$\lambda\left[\sum_{s=t}^{t+T}\left(\frac{1}{1+r}\right)^{s-t}Y_s + (1+r)B_t - \sum_{s=t}^{t+T}\left(\frac{1}{1+r}\right)^{s-t}C_s\right] = 0. \tag{2}$$

Unless $\lambda = u'(C_t) = 0$, something that is never true when there is meaningful economic scarcity, constraint (1) must hold as an equality at an optimum.

Thus, as argued in Chapter 2, the Euler equation plus the equality version of constraint (1) are necessary and sufficient to yield an optimal consumption program.

By iterating the Euler equation in the forward direction, one deduces that

$$u'(C_t) = (1+r)\beta u'(C_{t+1}) = (1+r)\beta[(1+r)\beta u'(C_{t+2})] = (1+r)^2\beta^2 u'(C_{t+2}).$$

Indeed, for any $T \geq 0$,

$$u'(C_t) = (1+r)^T\beta^T u'(C_{t+T}). \tag{3}$$

Go back to the original maximization problem set out at the start of this subsection; you will see that eqs. (2) and (3) can be combined to imply

$$\lambda\frac{B_{t+T+1}}{(1+r)^T} = u'(C_t)\frac{B_{t+T+1}}{(1+r)^T} = \beta^T u'(C_{t+T})B_{t+T+1} = 0.$$

This complementary slackness requirement is often referred to as the *transversality condition*, as is its infinite-horizon limit,

$$\lim_{T\to\infty}\beta^T u'(C_{t+T})B_{t+T+1} = 0. \tag{4}$$

The "transversality condition" we identified in the text for the infinite-horizon case, eq. (13) of Chapter 2, appears at first glance to be somewhat different, but it isn't really. To obtain it from the preceding equation, notice that, by eq. (3), $\beta^T u'(C_{t+T}) = u'(C_t)/(1+r)^T$. We have already observed that $u'(C_t)$ is strictly positive whenever we have a nontrivial economic allocation problem. Hence, for any economic application, eq. (4) is equivalent to eq. (13) of Chapter 2, $\lim_{T\to\infty}(1+r)^{-T}B_{t+T+1} = 0$.

Notice how the transversality condition follows from the constraint on running Ponzi games: if it is a binding constraint not to engage in a Ponzi game oneself, it cannot be optimal to allow others to do so by accumulating a stock of claims on them that grows in the limit at or above the rate of interest.

The preceding line of argument demonstrates that the transversality condition is necessary as well as sufficient for optimality in a finite-horizon setting. We have also presented an alternative argument (alongside that in section 2.1.2) that the transversality condition is necessary and sufficient in the present infinite-horizon setting with discounting.

In many applications a utility function is maximized subject to equality constraints, not inequalities. We saw such a case in Chapter 2 when we analyzed the q investment model. In this type of problem one can still derive necessary first-order conditions by equating the partial derivatives of the Lagrangian to zero. The only difference is that we know in advance that the equality constraints must bind.[2]

A.2   Dynamic Programming

The method of dynamic programming furnishes a second approach to intertemporal problems. You may be struck that its implementation sometimes appears to be more of an art than a science! Nonetheless, it is the method of choice in many contexts, notably, in stochastic finance theory, so it is important to be acquainted with the basic idea.

Consider the problem of maximizing $U_t = \sum_{s=t}^{\infty} \beta^{s-t} u(C_s)$ subject to the sequence of constraints

$$B_{s+1} = (1+r)B_s + Y_s - C_s, \quad s \geq t,$$

and a constraint ruling out Ponzi schemes, $\lim_{T \to \infty} (1+r)^{-T} B_{t+T+1} \geq 0$. (Dynamic programming is also applicable with a finite horizon, of course.) The latter constraint makes it reasonable to assume that there is a function, called the *value function*, that gives us the maximal constrained value of U_t as a function of overall initial wealth W_t. [Here, wealth would be given by eq. (19) of Chapter 2 with $I = G = 0$]. We write the value function as $J(W_t)$, and we assume it is differentiable.[3] For use in a moment, we note that W_t evolves according to a simple dynamic equation:

$$W_{t+1} = (1+r)B_{t+1} + \sum_{s=t+1}^{\infty} \left(\frac{1}{1+r} \right)^{s-(t+1)} Y_s$$

$$= (1+r)\left[(1+r)B_t + Y_t - C_t \right] + (1+r) \sum_{s=t+1}^{\infty} \left(\frac{1}{1+r} \right)^{s-t} Y_s$$

---

2. See Chapter 2 of Dixit (1990).

3. The attributes of the value function—existence, differentiability, and so on—are the subject of a vast technical literature. For main results and references, the interested reader should delve into Stokey and Lucas (1989).

$$= (1+r) \left[(1+r)B_t + \sum_{s=t}^{\infty} \left(\frac{1}{1+r} \right)^{s-t} Y_s - C_t \right]$$

$$= (1+r)(W_t - C_t). \tag{5}$$

Dynamic programming rests on a fundamental recursive equation involving the value function. That equation, called the *Bellman equation*, characterizes intertemporally maximizing plans through the following logic.[4] A consumption plan optimal from the standpoint of date t must maximize U_{t+1} subject to the future wealth level W_{t+1} produced by today's consumption decision C_t. (If not, the individual could raise utility by behaving differently after date t.) The foregoing property means, however, that a maximizing agent can behave as if $U_t = u(C_t) + \beta J(W_{t+1})$, where $J(W_{t+1})$ is the constrained maximal value of U_{t+1}. If this is so, then the choice of C_t maximizing lifetime utility is the one maximizing $U_t = u(C_t) + \beta J(W_{t+1})$ subject to $W_{t+1} = (1+r)(W_t - C_t)$. In symbols, the resulting Bellman equation is

$$J(W_t) = \max_{C_t} \left\{ u(C_t) + \beta J(W_{t+1}) \right\} \text{ subject to } W_{t+1} = (1+r)(W_t - C_t). \tag{6}$$

Translated into words, Bellman's principle states that an individual who plans to optimize starting tomorrow can do no better today than to optimize taking future optimal plans as given.

The maximization in eq. (6) can be expressed as

$$J(W_t) = \max_{C_t} \left\{ u(C_t) + \beta J \left[(1+r)(W_t - C_t) \right] \right\}. \tag{7}$$

The first-order necessary condition for maximization is

$$u'(C_t) - (1+r)\beta J'(W_{t+1}) = 0. \tag{8}$$

We transform this expression into something more familiar by appealing to the envelope theorem. For an optimizing individual, an increment to wealth on any date has the same effect on lifetime utility regardless of the use to which the wealth is put, consumption or saving. (An initial allocation in which, say, the marginal value of saving exceeds that of consumption cannot be optimal. The individual could raise lifetime utility by reducing consumption a bit and saving more.) The implication is that

$$J'(W) = u'(C) \tag{9}$$

on every date under a maximizing consumption plan.[5]

---

4. The original reference is Bellman (1957). For a lucid discussion, see the second appendix of Kreps (1990).

5. More formally, observe that first-order condition (8), which can be rewritten in the alternative form $u'(C) = (1+r)\beta J'[(1+r)(W-C)]$, gives optimal consumption as an implicit function of current

Combining eq. (9) with eq. (8) shows that the dynamic programming approach leads to the usual consumption Euler equation

$$u'(C_t) = (1+r)\beta u'(C_{t+1}).$$

Let's see how to use dynamic programming to solve explicitly for optimal consumption in the isoelastic case,

$$u(C) = \frac{C^{1-\frac{1}{\sigma}}}{1-\frac{1}{\sigma}}.$$

Our strategy is to *guess* the form of the value function—this is where the "art" of dynamic programming comes in—and then to use Bellman's equation to show the guess was right. Think of the argument as being analogous to a proof by mathematical induction.[6]

A natural guess is that the value function takes a form that is parallel to the isoelastic period utility function,

$$J(W) = \frac{\Theta}{1-\frac{1}{\sigma}} W^{1-\frac{1}{\sigma}}.$$

Substituting this conjectured solution into eq. (8), we see that the corresponding consumption function has to satisfy

$$C^{-\frac{1}{\sigma}} = (1+r)\beta\Theta\left[(1+r)(W-C)\right]^{-\frac{1}{\sigma}},$$

with the implication that

$$C = C(W) = \frac{1}{1 + \beta^\sigma (1+r)^{\sigma-1}\Theta^\sigma} W. \qquad (10)$$

It remains to solve for Θ with the aid of the Bellman equation. Use our conjecture about the isoelastic form of $J(W)$, together with the implied consumption function [eq. (10)] to write the Bellman equation

---

wealth, $C = C(W)$. Substitution of this function into the Bellman equation yields

$$J(W) = u\left[C(W)\right] + \beta J\{(1+r)[W - C(W)]\}.$$

Differentiation with respect to W results in

$$J'(W) = u'(C)C'(W) + (1+r)\beta J'\left[(1+r)(W-C)\right]\left[1 - C'(W)\right],$$

which, by eq. (8), reduces to

$$J'(W) = (1+r)\beta J'\left[(1+r)(W-C)\right].$$

A third application of eq. (8) now shows that $J'(W)$ must equal $u'(C)$.

6. In the example we look at here, the value function has a closed-form analytical representation. Usually no such solution can be found, and numerical methods must be used instead.

$$J(W) = u\left[C(W)\right] + \beta J\left[(1+r)(W-C)\right]$$

as

$$\frac{\Theta}{1-\frac{1}{\sigma}}W^{1-\frac{1}{\sigma}} = \left[\frac{1}{1+\beta^\sigma(1+r)^{\sigma-1}\Theta^\sigma}\right]^{1-\frac{1}{\sigma}}\frac{W^{1-\frac{1}{\sigma}}}{1-\frac{1}{\sigma}}$$

$$+ \beta\Theta\left[\frac{\beta^\sigma(1+r)^\sigma\Theta^\sigma}{1+\beta^\sigma(1+r)^{\sigma-1}\Theta^\sigma}\right]^{1-\frac{1}{\sigma}}\frac{W^{1-\frac{1}{\sigma}}}{1-\frac{1}{\sigma}}.$$

We can solve for Θ by equating the coefficients of wealth that appear on the two sides of this equation. Admittedly, this task appears impossible at first glance. But do not despair. All will become simple momentarily.

Since $1 - \frac{1}{\sigma} = \frac{\sigma-1}{\sigma}$, the result of equating coefficients can be written in the simplified form

$$\Theta = \frac{1}{\left[1+\beta^\sigma(1+r)^{\sigma-1}\Theta^\sigma\right]^{1-\frac{1}{\sigma}}} + \frac{\beta^\sigma(1+r)^{\sigma-1}\Theta^\sigma}{\left[1+\beta^\sigma(1+r)^{\sigma-1}\Theta^\sigma\right]^{1-\frac{1}{\sigma}}}$$

$$= \left[1+\beta^\sigma(1+r)^{\sigma-1}\Theta^\sigma\right]^{\frac{1}{\sigma}}.$$

After raising both sides to the power σ, this equation is easily solved for Θ:

$$\Theta = \left[\frac{1}{1-\beta^\sigma(1+r)^{\sigma-1}}\right]^{\frac{1}{\sigma}}.$$

We are done. Using this solution for Θ, we see that our guess about the value function's form is verified, with

$$J(W) = \left[\frac{1}{1-\beta^\sigma(1+r)^{\sigma-1}}\right]^{\frac{1}{\sigma}}\frac{W^{1-\frac{1}{\sigma}}}{1-\frac{1}{\sigma}}.$$

What is the optimal consumption function? Substitute Θ into eq. (10) to get

$$C = \left[1-\beta^\sigma(1+r)^{\sigma-1}\right]W.$$

You can check that this is exactly the same consumption function that we reached by a very different route in Chapter 2, eq. (16). That equation has the form $C = (r+\vartheta)W/(1+r)$, which reduces to the preceding consumption formula because $\vartheta \equiv 1 - \beta^\sigma(1+r)^\sigma$.

A.3   Stochastic Dynamic Programming

Dynamic programming provides a particularly convenient conceptual framework for handling stochastic maximization problems.

Consider the individual's problem of maximizing

$$U_t = E_t \left\{ \sum_{s=t}^{\infty} \beta^{s-t} u(C_s) \right\}$$

subject to

$$B_{s+1} = (1+r)B_s + Y_s - C_s,$$

where Y_s is a stochastic endowment. Let the value function $J_t\left[(1+r)B_t + Y_t\right]$ describe the maximized value of U_t. This value function depends on resources at the start of date t, and also (the reason for the t subscript) on the information available then. Such information affects maximized lifetime expected utility if it helps to forecast future levels of Y.

The stochastic Bellman equation corresponding to eq. (7) is

$$J_t\left[(1+r)B_t + Y_t\right]$$

$$= \max_{C_t} \left(u(C_t) + \beta E_t J_{t+1} \left\{ (1+r)\left[(1+r)B_t + Y_t - C_t\right] + Y_{t+1} \right\} \right).$$

The first-order condition for a maximum with respect to C_t is

$$u'(C_t) = (1+r)\beta E_t J'_{t+1}\left[(1+r)B_{t+1} + Y_{t+1}\right].$$

The same envelope-theorem reasoning leading to condition (9) implies

$$u'(C_{t+1}) = J'_{t+1}\left[(1+r)B_{t+1} + Y_{t+1}\right].$$

When combined with the first-order condition for C_t, the envelope condition gives

$$u'(C_t) = (1+r)\beta E_t \left\{ u'(C_{t+1}) \right\},$$

which corresponds to eq. (29) of Chapter 2.

As we mentioned earlier, closed-form consumption rules are difficult to derive in the present setting. The problem becomes easier if all unpredictable income comes from marketable financial wealth; see Supplement A to Chapter 5.

Supplement B   A Model with Intertemporally Nonadditive Preferences

We noted in Chapter 1 that without further restrictions, a completely general intertemporal utility function of the form $U_t = U(C_t, C_{t+1}, \ldots)$ would not lead to sharp, testable predictions about individual behavior. In an infinite-horizon context, moreover, it is not even clear how we would write down such a utility function and find its maximum!

Koopmans (1960) initiated the modern work on generalized utility functions by defining a class of intertemporal preferences that has since come to be known as the class of *recursive* preferences. Such preferences have the representation

$$U_t = A\left[u(C_t), U_{t+1}\right],$$

where $A(\cdot, \cdot)$ is called the *aggregator* function. One attraction of such preferences is that their implications can be explored through the method of dynamic programming described in Supplement A to Chapter 2.

The utility function we used throughout Chapter 2, given in eq. (11) on p. 63, is clearly recursive: its aggregator function is

$$U_t = A\left[u(C_t), U_{t+1}\right] = u(C_t) + \beta U_{t+1}.$$

But there are other, much richer, possibilities. We illustrate one through an example in which a small country's rate of time preference is endogenous, so that the country can have steady states for consumption and wealth at any world interest rate.

Let's assume that individuals still maximize discounted sums of period utilities, but that the subjective discount factor between any two periods s and $s+1$ is a function $\beta(C_s)$ of date s consumption. More formally, we take as the Koopmans aggregator function

$$U_t = A\left[u(C_t), U_{t+1}\right] = u(C_t) + \beta(C_t)U_{t+1},$$

which implies that

$$U_t = u(C_t) + \beta(C_t)u(C_{t+1}) + \beta(C_t)\beta(C_{t+1})u(C_{t+2}) + \cdots. \tag{1}$$

This intertemporal utility function was first proposed by Uzawa (1968).

Recall the simple intertemporal problem studied in Supplement A to Chapter 2. Here, the corresponding problem is to maximize eq. (1) subject to finance constraints of the form eq. (5) of Supplement A and a constraint barring Ponzi games. Dynamic programming is the most convenient tool for our purposes. The Bellman equation can be written

$$J(W_t) = \max_{C_t} \left\{u(C_t) + \beta(C_t)J\left[(1+r)(W_t - C_t)\right]\right\},$$

and the associated first-order condition for consumption is

$$u'(C_t) + \beta'(C_t)J(W_{t+1}) = \beta(C_t)(1+r)J'(W_{t+1}). \tag{2}$$

Intuitively, the right-hand side has the same interpretation as in the standard Euler equation: the discounted future value of an extra unit of saving on date t. The left-hand side is the date t cost of generating the extra saving: the forgone marginal utility of date t consumption plus a novel element, the change in the subjectively discounted value of future period utility flows.

The envelope condition [eq. (9) of Supplement A to Chapter 2] is replaced here by the more complicated relation

$$J'(W_t) = u'(C_t) + \beta'(C_t)J(W_{t+1}),$$

although the basic intuition is the same.[7] Combining this equation with the first-order condition (2) yields the equation

$$J'(W_t) = \beta(C_t)(1+r)J'(W_{t+1}), \tag{3}$$

which is essentially an intertemporal Euler equation.

To illustrate the dynamics the model implies, we assume that optimal consumption is an increasing function of wealth, that is, $C_t = C(W_t)$ with $C'(W_t) > 0$. Substituting this consumption function into eq. (3) leads to a difference equation in W,

$$J'(W_{t+1}) = \frac{J'(W_t)}{\beta\left[C(W_t)\right](1+r)}. \tag{4}$$

Equation (4) implies a steady-state wealth level $\bar{W}$ that equates $\beta\left[C(\bar{W})\right]$ to $1/(1+r)$: in the long run, and only in the long run, the subjective and market discount factors are the same. A steady state in wealth implies, of course, a steady-state consumption level of $C(\bar{W})$. The existence of a steady state stands in sharp contrast to the small-country case in Chapter 2, in which β is exogenously fixed and a steady state does not exist when $(1+r)\beta \neq 1$.

Equation (4) also implies different dynamics from the fixed time-preference case. Figure B.1 shows the behavior of that difference equation for the case $\beta'(C) < 0$, in which an increasing consumption level causes increasing impatience. If we make the standard concavity assumption on the value function, $J''(W) < 0$, the $J'(W)$ schedule in the figure is downward sloping as shown. On the assumption that $\beta'(C)$ isn't too large in absolute value, the schedule $J'(W)/\{\beta\left[C(W)\right](1+r)\}$ also has a negative slope. But when wealth is not much different from $\bar{W}$, this second schedule is flatter than $J'(W)$, as shown. Why? Rising wealth raises consumption, lowering $\beta(C)$ and making $J'(W)/[\beta(C)(1+r)]$ fall by less than $J'(W)$. Starting from any initial wealth level W_t, the figure shows the level of W_{t+1} implied by eq. (4). As you can see, the economy must always converge to the steady-state wealth level, which is uniquely determined. When β is a fixed constant, in contrast, the economy reaches a steady state only when $\beta(1+r) = 1$, and it does so immediately and at whatever level of wealth the economy happens to have at the moment. These results follow easily after one notices that eq. (4) applies to the case in which β is constant. It

---

7. The proof is exactly parallel to the one in footnote 5 of the preceding supplement.

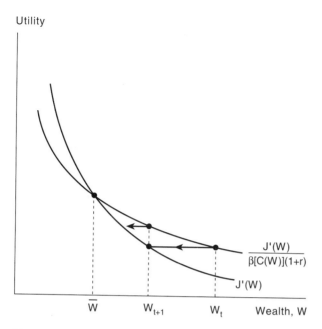

Figure B.1
Steady-state wealth under endogenous time preference

is a useful exercise for you to redraw Figure B.1 in the special case $\beta'(C) \equiv$ 0.[8]

If we imagine that output Y is fixed, then $W_t = (1+r)[B_t + (Y/r)]$. Therefore, constant steady-state wealth W implies constant steady-state net foreign assets. In general, if Y varies predictably over time, the model's current-account prediction for an economy in its steady state is exactly the same as that of the $(1+r)\beta = 1$ case in Chapter 2. But the response to unexpected shocks that move the economy out of the steady state will be different, as consumption will contain a mean-reverting component.

Our tentative assumption that $\beta'(C) < 0$ means that a person becomes more impatient to consume as he gets wealthier. This notion may strike you as counterintuitive. If $\beta'(C) > 0$, however, the analog of Figure B.1 implies *unstable* dynamics because the $J'(W)$ curve becomes the relatively flatter of the two schedules. This instability reflects the implication of $\beta'(C) > 0$, which you may also find counterintuitive, that a person's desire to accumulate wealth rises as he becomes richer!

---

8. The many details swept under the rug in the preceding paragraphs are worked out in full in the literature. For a review, the interested reader should consult Obstfeld (1990).

We leave it to you to decide whether the assumption $\beta'(C) < 0$ is too high a price to pay for a stable, well-behaved dynamic system.[9]

Supplement C   Solving Systems of Linear Difference Equations

At several points the chapter presented solutions for dynamic economic systems described by linear difference equations, that is, equations involving lagged as well as current values of relevant endogenous variables. To deepen understanding of the results in the text, this supplement exposits a unified methodology for solving linear difference-equation systems.[10]

C.1   First-Order Scalar Systems

The variable z_t follows a first-order linear difference equation if its dynamics can be described by the equation

$$z_t = az_{t-1} + m_t, \tag{1}$$

where m_t is an exogenous function of time (sometimes referred to as a forcing function). To *solve* such a difference equation is to express z_t as a function of the current, future, and lagged values of m_t as well as some initial value z_0 prevailing on the date the system begins its evolution.

C.1.1   The Stable Case: $|a| < 1$

The most sensible approach to solution may depend on whether $|a|$ is below 1 or above. We start with the case $|a| < 1$.

For any variable X_t define the *lag operator*, denoted L, by

$$LX_t = X_{t-1}.$$

The lag operator thus maps a variable to its value in the previous period. Equation (1) can now be rewritten as

$$(1 - aL)z_t = m_t. \tag{2}$$

Define the inverse of the operator $1 - aL$ in eq. (2), $(1 - aL)^{-1}$, as

$$(1 - aL)^{-1} = 1 + aL + a^2L^2 + a^3L^3 + \cdots, \tag{3}$$

an operator that "converges" in a formal sense because $|a| < 1$. The motivation for this definition is the observation that

---

9. One might imagine more complicated possibilities, involving a positive derivative $\beta'(C)$ for some consumption levels and a negative derivative for others. In this case there could be multiple steady states, some of them dynamically unstable.

10. Readers may also want to consult the recent treatise on dynamic models and methods by Turnovsky (1995).

$$(1 - aL)\left(1 + aL + a^2L^2 + a^3L^3 + \cdots\right) = \left(1 + aL + a^2L^2 + \cdots\right) - \left(aL + a^2L^2 + \cdots\right)$$

$$= 1.$$

Using definition (3), we find a solution to eq. (2) by observing that

$$z_t = (1 - aL)^{-1}(1 - aL)z_t = (1 - aL)^{-1}m_t$$

$$= m_t + am_{t-1} + a^2m_{t-2} + \cdots = \sum_{s=-\infty}^{t} a^{t-s}m_s. \qquad (4)$$

We can check that this solution satisfies eq. (1) by verifying the equality

$$az_{t-1} + m_t = a\left(\sum_{s=-\infty}^{t-1} a^{t-1-s}m_s\right) + m_t = \sum_{s=-\infty}^{t} a^{t-s}m_s = z_t.$$

However, it is important to notice that eq. (4) is not the *only* solution to eq. (1). If b_0 is any constant, then adding the term b_0a^t to eq. (4) yields another solution:

$$\sum_{s=-\infty}^{t} a^{t-s}m_{t-s} + b_0a^t = a\left(\sum_{s=-\infty}^{t-1} a^{t-1-s}m_s + b_0a^{t-1}\right) + m_t.$$

We therefore refer to

$$z_t = \sum_{s=-\infty}^{t} a^{t-s}m_s + b_0a^t \qquad (5)$$

as the *general solution* to eq. (1). The term b_0a^t is called the *homogeneous* component of the solution, whereas $\sum_{s=-\infty}^{t} a^{t-s}m_s$ is called the *nonhomogeneous* component. Thus the lag operator formalism is a way to find the solution's nonhomogeneous component; the homogeneous component is the equation's general solution when the m_t all are zero.[11]

The arbitrary constant b_0 is determined by an initial condition on the variable z_t. Suppose we know the date 0 value z_0, with all subsequent z_t determined by eq. (1). Then eq. (5) can correctly describe the evolution of z_t only if the initial condition

$$z_0 = \sum_{s=-\infty}^{0} a^{-s}m_s + b_0$$

holds, that is, if

$$b_0 = z_0 - \sum_{s=-\infty}^{0} a^{-s}m_s.$$

---

11. In this case we would have the *homogeneous* difference equation $z_t = az_{t-1}$.

Substituting the preceding equality into eq. (5) gives the *particular solution* (corresponding to the initial value z_0):

$$z_t = \sum_{s=1}^{t} a^{t-s} m_s + a^t z_0.$$ (6)

The particular solution in eq. (4) corresponds to a situation in which the system has been evolving for so long that the influence of the initial condition on dynamics is negligible. When $|a| \geq 1$, eq. (6) remains a correct particular solution as you can verify, but it cannot be derived through eq. (4).

EXAMPLE   Redefine K_t (for this example only) as the capital stock at the end of period t (rather than $t - 1$). Consider the resulting equation of motion for K_t,

$$K_t = (1 - \delta) K_{t-1} + I_t,$$

where $\delta \geq 0$ is a depreciation rate and I_t is gross investment during period t. The solution to this difference equation is

$$K_t = \sum_{s=1}^{t} (1 - \delta)^{t-s} I_s + (1 - \delta)^t K_0.$$ (7)

The date t capital stock equals the still-undepreciated portion of the initial, date 0, stock, $(1 - \delta)^t K_0$, plus the sum of still-undepreciated investments made between dates 1 and t. Observe that we would get the same answer via the method of iterative substitutions used in Chapter 2. Since $K_1 = (1 - \delta) K_0 + I_1$, $K_2 = (1 - \delta) [(1 - \delta) K_0 + I_1] + I_2 = I_2 + (1 - \delta) I_1 + (1 - \delta)^2 K_0$, and so on, so that, in general, eq. (7) follows.

C.1.2   The Unstable Case: $|a| > 1$

We have observed that even when $|a| > 1$, the particular solution (6) remains valid. But for the purpose of solving economic models, this solution is not always the most enlightening one. As we illustrate in a moment, unstable roots usually govern the behavior of forward-looking economic variables, such as equity prices, in which the influence of past forcing-variable levels is irrelevant (except insofar as they help in predicting the future). Yet solution (6) gives the misleading impression that the past matters directly for such variables.[12]

---

12. There *are* cases in which $|a| > 1$, but eq. (6) is exactly what we want to use to answer a specific question. As an example, suppose you put z_0 in the bank and deposit an additional m_s in every period $s > 0$. If the net interest rate on money is i per period, then at the end of t periods you will have a total of

$$z_t = \sum_{s=1}^{t} (1 + i)^{t-s} m_s + (1 + i)^t z_0$$

in the bank, which has the form of eq. (6) with $a = 1 + i > 1$.
   Moral: Always think about the economics of a problem before applying cookbook solution methods.

To handle cases of eq. (1) with $|a| > 1$, we now extend our lag operator formalism. Define the *lead operator*, L^{-1}, as the inverse lag operator, such that

$$L^{-1}X_t = X_{t+1}$$

for any variable X_t. With this notation, eq. (1) becomes, not eq. (2), but

$$(L^{-1} - a)z_{t-1} = L^{-1}m_{t-1},$$

or, after forwarding by one period and multiplying by $-a^{-1}$,

$$\left(1 - a^{-1}L^{-1}\right)z_t = -a^{-1}L^{-1}m_t. \tag{8}$$

If $|a| > 1$, then $\left|a^{-1}\right| < 1$, so, just as $1 - aL$ had a well-defined inverse operator when $|a| < 1$, $1 - a^{-1}L^{-1}$ has the inverse operator

$$(1 - a^{-1}L^{-1})^{-1} = 1 + a^{-1}L^{-1} + a^{-2}L^{-2} + a^{-3}L^{-3} + \cdots$$

now. Applying this inverse to eq. (8) gives the nonhomogeneous part of the general solution to eq. (1),

$$z_t = -a^{-1}(1 - a^{-1}L^{-1})^{-1}L^{-1}m_t$$

$$= -a^{-1}\left(1 + a^{-1}L^{-1} + a^{-2}L^{-2} + \cdots\right)L^{-1}m_t$$

$$= -\sum_{s=t+1}^{\infty} \left(\frac{1}{a}\right)^{s-t} m_s. \tag{9}$$

Notice that eq. (9) indeed satisfies eq. (1), because

$$az_{t-1} + m_t = a\left[-\sum_{s=t}^{\infty}\left(\frac{1}{a}\right)^{s-(t-1)}m_s\right] + m_t = -\sum_{s=t+1}^{\infty}\left(\frac{1}{a}\right)^{s-t}m_s = z_t.$$

However, the infinite forward sum in eq. (9) is convergent when (and only when) $|a| > 1$, just as the infinite backward sum in eq. (4) is convergent when (and only when) $|a| < 1$.[13] This is the mechanical rationale for solving stable systems backward and unstable systems forward.

---

13. Strictly speaking, the last statement is true only if the forcing variable m_t is "well-behaved," that is, does not change at too high or low an absolute rate. For example, in the case $|a| > 1$, if m_t were to follow $m_t = a'm_{t-1}$ with $|a'| > |a|$, the infinite sum

$$\sum_{s=t+1}^{\infty}\left(\frac{1}{a}\right)^{s-t}m_s = m_t\sum_{s=t+1}^{\infty}\left(\frac{a'}{a}\right)^{s-t}$$

in eq. (9) would be divergent, and hence ill defined, whereas the sum in eq. (4),

$$\sum_{s=-\infty}^{t} a^{t-s}m_s = m_t\sum_{s=-\infty}^{t}\left(\frac{a}{a'}\right)^{t-s} = \frac{m_t}{1 - (a/a')},$$

would be perfectly well defined. Throughout the book we rule out such pathological cases unless otherwise stated.

As before, we find a general solution by adding to the solution's nonhomogeneous component the homogeneous term $b_0 a^t$. The resulting general solution to eq. (1) for the case $|a| > 1$ is

$$z_t = -\sum_{s=t+1}^{\infty} \left(\frac{1}{a}\right)^{s-t} m_s + b_0 a^t. \tag{10}$$

But what initial condition determines b_0? Any choice for b_0 other than $b_0 = 0$ would lead to z_t exploding (for $b_0 > 0$) or imploding (for $b_0 < 0$) irrespective of the behavior of m_t. Thus, while it is mathematically correct to determine b_0 through an initial condition z_0, as in the case $|a| < 1$ discussed previously, in many models of economic interest we know in advance that z_t cannot explode or implode, and, therefore, that z_0 must have adjusted automatically to ensure that $b_0 = 0$.[14] An implication is that, for purposes of economic modeling, we can often take the particular solution in eq. (9) to be the case that is of economic interest. This property is intimately related to the condition that rules out self-fulfilling speculative asset-price bubbles, as the next example makes plain.

EXAMPLE   Consider arbitrage condition (53) of Chapter 2 equating the real interest rate to the rate of return on claims to a firm's future profits. This relation, lagged one period, can be written as a difference equation in the firm's ex dividend market value,

$$V_t = (1+r)V_{t-1} - d_t.$$

According to eq. (10), the general solution for V_t is

$$V_t = \sum_{s=t+1}^{\infty} \left(\frac{1}{1+r}\right)^{s-t} d_s + b_0(1+r)^t.$$

In appendix 2B, we saw the rationale for imposing a condition ruling out speculative bubbles in V_t,

$$\lim_{T \to \infty} \left(\frac{1}{1+r}\right)^T V_{t+T} = 0.$$

If $b_0 \neq 0$, however, this last condition won't hold. So $b_0 = 0$ is the appropriate initial condition for the model, implying that the firm's ex dividend value is simply the discounted value of future dividends, as in eq. (56) of Chapter 2, which we derived by iterative substitution coupled with a prohibition on bubbles. The implication is that efficient asset markets set the initial value V_0 to ensure that $b_0 = 0$. This initial

---

14. In our earlier example of money earning interest at rate i in the bank, the size of your account *would* explode (at rate i) if you never made net withdrawals. Thus there is no justification for assuming $b_0 = 0$.

value is the only one that removes the influence of the inherently unstable dynamics implied by $a = 1 + r > 1$.

C.1.3   Stochastic Linear Difference Equations

In stochastic models, forcing functions may include random variables, and variables may enter in expectational form. For example, instead of eq. (1) the equation to be solved may be

$$E_{t-1}z_t = az_{t-1} + E_{t-1}m_t. \tag{11}$$

Since expectations of the future typify forward-looking equations, we assume $|a| > 1$ and consider forward solutions.

To solve we forward eq. (11) by one period and take date t expectations, obtaining

$$E_t z_{t+1} = aE_t z_t + E_t m_{t+1}.$$

If we now think of the lead operator L^{-1} as mapping the date t expectation of a variable into the date t expectation of its next-period value,

$$L^{-1}E_t X_t = E_t L^{-1} X_t = E_t X_{t+1},$$

we may write the preceding expectational difference equation as

$$\left(1 - a^{-1}L^{-1}\right)E_t z_t = -a^{-1}L^{-1}E_t m_t$$

following the same steps that led to eq. (8). Multiplication by $\left(1 - a^{-1}L^{-1}\right)^{-1}$ and imposition of $b_0 = 0$ on the homogeneous part of the difference-equation solution, $b_0 a^t$, gives the answer

$$E_t z_t = -a^{-1}(1 - a^{-1}L^{-1})^{-1}L^{-1}E_t m_t$$

$$= -\sum_{s=t+1}^{\infty} \left(\frac{1}{a}\right)^{s-t} E_t m_s.$$

The only new wrinkle here is that we are interested in knowing z_t, not $E_t z_t$. But eq. (11) implies

$$E_t z_{t+1} = az_t + E_t m_{t+1},$$

so that z_t is a function only of information known on date t. Thus $E_t z_t = z_t$ and

$$z_t = -\sum_{s=t+1}^{\infty} \left(\frac{1}{a}\right)^{s-t} E_t m_s. \tag{12}$$

EXAMPLE   The stochastic analog of eq. (53) of Chapter 2 under risk neutrality is

$$1 + r = \frac{E_t \left(d_{t+1} + V_{t+1} \right)}{V_t}.$$

This condition can be expressed as the stochastic difference equation

$$E_t V_{t+1} = (1 + r) V_t - E_t d_{t+1},$$

which is simply an example of eq. (11) forwarded by one period. The solution for V_t implied by eq. (12) is

$$V_t = \sum_{s=t+1}^{\infty} \left(\frac{1}{1+r} \right)^{s-t} E_t d_s.$$

Under risk neutrality the firm's ex dividend value on date t is the present value of expected future dividends.

C.2   First-Order Vector Systems

If the quantities in eq. (1) are reinterpreted as vectors rather than scalars, and the parameter a as a conformable square matrix, we can still obtain solutions through methods analogous to those we have discussed. The main difference is in determining which variables in the system require forward solution (in terms of L^{-1}) and which require backward solution (in terms of L). A typical dynamic economic model involves inherently unstable dynamics (such as those associated with asset prices) as well as inherently stable dynamics (such as those associated with capital stocks). In general, therefore, both forward and backward elements enter into the model's solution.

C.2.1   The General Two-Variable Case

Consider the system

$$\begin{bmatrix} z_{1t} \\ z_{2t} \end{bmatrix} = A \begin{bmatrix} z_{1t-1} \\ z_{2t-1} \end{bmatrix} + \begin{bmatrix} m_{1t} \\ m_{2t} \end{bmatrix}, \tag{13}$$

where

$$A = \begin{bmatrix} a_{11} & a_{12} \\ a_{21} & a_{22} \end{bmatrix}$$

is nonsingular.

To solve this system, we need to recall some concepts from linear algebra. Let $\text{tr}A = a_{11} + a_{22}$ denote the trace of matrix A and let "det" denote the determinant operator. The system's characteristic roots ω_1 and ω_2 (also called eigenvalues) are the roots of the characteristic equation

$$\det \begin{bmatrix} a_{11} - \omega & a_{12} \\ a_{21} & a_{22} - \omega \end{bmatrix} = (a_{11} - \omega)(a_{22} - \omega) - a_{12}a_{21}$$

$$= \omega^2 - (a_{11} + a_{22})\omega + (a_{11}a_{22} - a_{12}a_{21})$$

$$= \omega^2 - (\text{tr}\mathbf{A})\omega + \det \mathbf{A}$$

$$= 0.$$

Two important results to remember are that

$$\text{tr}\mathbf{A} = \omega_1 + \omega_2,$$

$$\det \mathbf{A} = \omega_1\omega_2. \tag{14}$$

To derive these two equations, observe that ω_1 and ω_2 can be roots of the characteristic equation $\omega^2 - (\text{tr}\mathbf{A})\omega + \det \mathbf{A}$ only if that equation can be expressed as $(\omega - \omega_1)(\omega - \omega_2) = \omega^2 - (\omega_1 + \omega_2)\omega + \omega_1\omega_2 = 0$.

We assume that the characteristic roots ω_1 and ω_2 are real and distinct.[15] By the quadratic formula, this assumption requires

$$(\text{tr}\mathbf{A})^2 = (a_{11} + a_{22})^2 > 4(a_{11}a_{22} - a_{12}a_{21}) = 4 \det \mathbf{A}.$$

The system's two eigenvectors are defined as scalar multiples of vectors $[\, e_1 \quad 1\,]^{\mathcal{T}}$ and $[\, e_2 \quad 1\,]^{\mathcal{T}}$ (the superscript $\mathcal{T}$ denotes matrix transposition) such that

$$\mathbf{A} \begin{bmatrix} e_i \\ 1 \end{bmatrix} = \omega_i \begin{bmatrix} e_i \\ 1 \end{bmatrix}, \qquad i = 1, 2.$$

Since the last equation implies

$$e_i = (\omega_i - a_{22})/a_{21} = a_{12}/(\omega_i - a_{11}), \tag{15}$$

the two eigenvectors are distinct, and therefore the matrix

$$\mathbf{E} = \begin{bmatrix} e_1 & e_2 \\ 1 & 1 \end{bmatrix}$$

is invertible with inverse matrix

$$\mathbf{E}^{-1} = (e_1 - e_2)^{-1} \begin{bmatrix} 1 & -e_2 \\ -1 & e_1 \end{bmatrix}. \tag{16}$$

Next we apply these mathematical constructs. Let Ω be the diagonal matrix

$$\Omega = \begin{bmatrix} \omega_1 & 0 \\ 0 & \omega_2 \end{bmatrix}.$$

---

15. Distinct, real roots are always assumed in this book unless otherwise stated. On solving systems with complex roots, see Sargent (1987, ch. 9).

By the definition of the eigenvectors,

$$\mathbf{AE} = \mathbf{E}\Omega,$$

as you can check. Thus,

$$\mathbf{A} = \mathbf{E}\Omega\mathbf{E}^{-1}.$$

Now return to eq. (13), which the preceding equality allows us to express as

$$\begin{bmatrix} z_{1t} \\ z_{2t} \end{bmatrix} = \mathbf{E}\Omega\mathbf{E}^{-1} \begin{bmatrix} z_{1t-1} \\ z_{2t-1} \end{bmatrix} + \begin{bmatrix} m_{1t} \\ m_{2t} \end{bmatrix}.$$

Premultiplication by $\mathbf{E}^{-1}$ yields the equation

$$\mathbf{E}^{-1} \begin{bmatrix} z_{1t} \\ z_{2t} \end{bmatrix} = \Omega\mathbf{E}^{-1} \begin{bmatrix} z_{1t-1} \\ z_{2t-1} \end{bmatrix} + \mathbf{E}^{-1} \begin{bmatrix} m_{1t} \\ m_{2t} \end{bmatrix}.$$

Define the transformed vectors $\mathbf{z}'_t = \mathbf{E}^{-1}\mathbf{z}_t$ and $\mathbf{m}'_t = \mathbf{E}^{-1}\mathbf{m}_t$. The last matrix equation becomes

$$\begin{bmatrix} z'_{1t} \\ z'_{2t} \end{bmatrix} = \Omega \begin{bmatrix} z'_{1t-1} \\ z'_{2t-1} \end{bmatrix} + \begin{bmatrix} m'_{1t} \\ m'_{2t} \end{bmatrix}.$$

Because Ω is diagonal, the matrix transformation of eq. (13) has expressed the system in terms of two variables, z'_{1t} and z'_{2t}, with noninteracting dynamics. By eq. (16), the decoupled pair of scalar difference equations is

$$z'_{1t} = \omega_1 z'_{1t-1} + \frac{m_{1t} - e_2 m_{2t}}{e_1 - e_2},$$

$$(17)$$

$$z'_{2t} = \omega_2 z'_{2t-1} + \frac{e_1 m_{2t} - m_{1t}}{e_1 - e_2}.$$

Each of these can be solved separately using the scalar methods already described, and solutions for the original variables $\mathbf{z}_t$ can be retrieved by applying the reverse transformation $\mathbf{z}_t = \mathbf{E}\mathbf{z}'_t$.

C.2.2 Time-Invariant Forcing Variables

As a simple example, consider the case in which m_{1t} and m_{2t} are both constant at m_1 and m_2. In this case eq. (13) implies that the system has a stationary position or steady state defined by $z_{1t} = z_{1t-1} = \bar{z}_1$ and $z_{2t} = z_{2t-1} = \bar{z}_2$:

$$\bar{z}_1 = \frac{(1 - a_{22})m_1 + a_{12}m_2}{1 - \mathrm{tr}\mathbf{A} + \det\mathbf{A}},$$

$$(18)$$

$$\bar{z}_2 = \frac{a_{21}m_1 + (1 - a_{11})m_2}{1 - \mathrm{tr}\mathbf{A} + \det\mathbf{A}}.$$

By definition,

$$\bar{z}_1 = a_{11}\bar{z}_1 + a_{12}\bar{z}_2 + m_1,$$

$$\bar{z}_2 = a_{21}\bar{z}_1 + a_{22}\bar{z}_2 + m_2,$$

and subtraction of the foregoing from the original system expresses the latter as a homogeneous system in deviations from the steady state,

$$\begin{bmatrix} z_{1t} - \bar{z}_1 \\ z_{2t} - \bar{z}_2 \end{bmatrix} = \mathbf{A} \begin{bmatrix} z_{1t-1} - \bar{z}_1 \\ z_{2t-1} - \bar{z}_2 \end{bmatrix}.$$

Applying eq. (17) gives

$$(z_{1t} - \bar{z}_1)' = \omega_1 (z_{1t-1} - \bar{z}_1)',$$

$$(z_{2t} - \bar{z}_2)' = \omega_2 (z_{2t-1} - \bar{z}_2)',$$

with general solutions

$$(z_{1t} - \bar{z}_1)' = b_{10}\omega_1^t, \qquad (z_{2t} - \bar{z}_2)' = b_{20}\omega_2^t.$$

Premultiplication by $\mathbf{E}$ yields general solutions for the original variables:

$$z_{1t} - \bar{z}_1 = e_1 b_{10}\omega_1^t + e_2 b_{20}\omega_2^t,$$

$$z_{2t} - \bar{z}_2 = b_{10}\omega_1^t + b_{20}\omega_2^t.$$

Many dynamic economic models imply that $\omega_1 > 1$ and $0 < \omega_2 < 1$, so we analyze that case in detail. (Generally speaking, well-behaved economic models include an unstable root for each variable that depends on expectations about the future, and a stable root for each variable that is predetermined by the economy's history. The q investment model, to which we turn in a moment, illustrates this property.)

To prevent explosive bubbles, we impose the initial condition $b_{10} = 0$, which eliminates the unstable terms involving ω_1^t. Notice that once $b_{10} = 0$ is imposed, z_{1t} converges to $\bar{z}_1$ and z_{2t} converges to $\bar{z}_2$; the system's evolution is described by the unique stable *saddle path*

$$z_{1t} - \bar{z}_1 = e_2 (z_{2t} - \bar{z}_2),$$

the slope of which is the eigenvector associated with the stable root ω_2. Thus the steady state is saddle-point stable.

The coefficient b_{20} is determined by an initial value of z_{2t}, z_{20}. (Typically z_{20}, which is associated with the stable characteristic root ω_2, will be a predetermined variable like a capital stock, possessing a well-defined and historically determined initial value that determines the system's subsequent evolution.) The appropriate initial condition is $z_{20} - \bar{z}_2 = b_{20}$ which gives the particular solution

$$z_{1t} - \bar{z}_1 = e_2 \left(z_{20} - \bar{z}_2 \right) \omega_2^t,$$

$$\text{(19)}$$

$$z_{2t} - \bar{z}_2 = \left(z_{20} - \bar{z}_2 \right) \omega_2^t.$$

EXAMPLE   We can rewrite eqs. (69) and (68) of Chapter 2 (both lagged by one period) to show that the dynamics of Chapter 2's q investment model near the steady state take the form

$$\begin{bmatrix} q_t - \bar{q} \\ K_t - \bar{K} \end{bmatrix} = \begin{bmatrix} 1 + r - A\bar{K}\bar{F}_{KK}/\chi & -A\bar{F}_{KK} \\ \bar{K}/\chi & 1 \end{bmatrix} \begin{bmatrix} q_{t-1} - \bar{q} \\ K_{t-1} - \bar{K} \end{bmatrix}$$

(where derivatives are evaluated at the steady state and $\bar{q} = 1$). The system's characteristic equation is

$$\omega^2 - \left(2 + r - A\bar{K}\bar{F}_{KK}/\chi \right) \omega + (1 + r) = 0.$$

To be concrete, assume a Cobb-Douglas production function, $F(K, L) = K^\alpha L^{1-\alpha}$. Because $A F_K(\bar{K}, L) = \alpha A \left(L/\bar{K} \right)^{1-\alpha} = r$, the characteristic equation takes the form

$$\omega^2 - \left[2 + r + \frac{(1 - \alpha)r}{\chi} \right] \omega + (1 + r) = 0,$$

and the quadratic formula gives its roots as

$$\omega_1, \omega_2 = \frac{1}{2} \left\{ 2 + r + \frac{(1 - \alpha)r}{\chi} \pm \sqrt{ \left[2 + r + \frac{(1 - \alpha)r}{\chi} \right]^2 - 4(1 + r) } \right\}.$$

Since

$$\left[2 + r + \frac{(1 - \alpha)r}{\chi} \right]^2 > 4(1 + r),$$

ω_1 and ω_2 are real and distinct, and it is clear that the larger root, ω_1, exceeds 1. And, since $\omega_1 \omega_2 = 1 + r$ by eq. (14), $\omega_2 > 0$. To see that $\omega_2 < 1$, observe that this inequality is equivalent to

$$r + \frac{(1 - \alpha)r}{\chi} < \sqrt{ \left[2 + r + \frac{(1 - \alpha)r}{\chi} \right]^2 - 4(1 + r) }.$$

This is equivalent in turn (just square both sides) to

$$0 < \frac{4(1 - \alpha)r}{\chi},$$

which always holds because $\alpha < 1$. In summary, the model has an unstable root, ω_1, corresponding to the forward-looking price variable q, and a stable root, ω_2, corresponding to the predetermined capital stock K. The particular solution corresponding to the stable path **SS** in Figure 2.9 is [recall eq. (15)]

$$q_t - \bar{q} = \frac{\omega_2 - 1}{\bar{K}} \times \left(K_0 - \bar{K}\right) \omega_2^t,$$

$$K_t - \bar{K} = \left(K_0 - \bar{K}\right) \omega_2^t,$$

where the initial condition $z_{20} = K_0$ has been used. Because $\omega_2 < 1$, the solution provides algebraic confirmation of Figure 2.9's implication that q is above $\bar{q}$ when K starts below $\bar{K}$.

C.2.3   Time-Varying Forcing Functions When $\omega_1 > 1$ and $0 < \omega_2 < 1$

Turn now to the general system, eq. (17) with (possibly) nonconstant forcing variables. Since $|\omega_1| > 1$, the general solution for z'_{1t} is given by eq. (10),

$$z'_{1t} = -\sum_{s=t+1}^{\infty} \left(\frac{1}{\omega_1}\right)^{s-t} \left(\frac{m_{1s} - e_2 m_{2s}}{e_1 - e_2}\right) + b_{10}\omega_1^t.$$

Since $|\omega_2| < 1$, the general solution for z'_{2t} is, by eq. (5),

$$z'_{2t} = \sum_{s=-\infty}^{t} \omega_2^{t-s} \left(\frac{e_1 m_{2s} - m_{1s}}{e_1 - e_2}\right) + b_{20}\omega_2^t.$$

We will see the initial conditions determining b_{10} and b_{20} after expressing the system in terms of the original variables z_{1t} and z_{2t}. Premultiplying the foregoing solution for $[\, z'_{1t} \quad z'_{2t}\,]^{\mathsf{T}}$ by $\mathbf{E}$ gives

$$\begin{bmatrix} z_{1t} \\ z_{2t} \end{bmatrix} = \mathbf{E} \begin{bmatrix} z'_{1t} \\ z'_{2t} \end{bmatrix} = \begin{bmatrix} e_1 z'_{1t} + e_2 z'_{2t} \\ z'_{1t} + z'_{2t} \end{bmatrix},$$

or, using eq. (15),

$$z_{1t} = \frac{\omega_1 - a_{22}}{a_{21}} \left\{ -\sum_{s=t+1}^{\infty} \left(\frac{1}{\omega_1}\right)^{s-t} \left[\frac{a_{21} m_{1s} - (\omega_2 - a_{22}) m_{2s}}{\omega_1 - \omega_2}\right] + b_{10}\omega_1^t \right\}$$

$$+ \frac{\omega_2 - a_{22}}{a_{21}} \left\{ \sum_{s=-\infty}^{t} \omega_2^{t-s} \left[\frac{(\omega_1 - a_{22}) m_{2s} - a_{21} m_{1s}}{\omega_1 - \omega_2}\right] + b_{20}\omega_2^t \right\},$$

$$z_{2t} = -\sum_{s=t+1}^{\infty} \left(\frac{1}{\omega_1}\right)^{s-t} \left[\frac{a_{21} m_{1s} - (\omega_2 - a_{22}) m_{2s}}{\omega_1 - \omega_2}\right] + b_{10}\omega_1^t$$

$$+ \sum_{s=-\infty}^{t} \omega_2^{t-s} \left[\frac{(\omega_1 - a_{22}) m_{2s} - a_{21} m_{1s}}{\omega_1 - \omega_2}\right] + b_{20}\omega_2^t.$$

Setting $b_{10} = 0$ above removes speculative bubbles and places the economy on its saddle path. To determine b_{20}, we use the initial value z_{20} and find

$$b_{20} = z_{20} + \sum_{s=1}^{\infty} \left(\frac{1}{\omega_1} \right)^s \left[\frac{a_{21}m_{1s} - (\omega_2 - a_{22})m_{2s}}{\omega_1 - \omega_2} \right]$$

$$- \sum_{s=-\infty}^{0} \omega_2^{-s} \left[\frac{(\omega_1 - a_{22})m_{2s} - a_{21}m_{1s}}{\omega_1 - \omega_2} \right].$$

(20)

Substitution of this solution for b_{20} gives the particular solution of interest. To economize on notation, define the variables $\bar{z}_{1t}$ and $\bar{z}_{2t}$ (think of them as "moving steady-state" values) by

$$\bar{z}_{1t} = -\frac{\omega_1 - a_{22}}{a_{21}} \sum_{s=t+1}^{\infty} \left(\frac{1}{\omega_1} \right)^{s-t} \left[\frac{a_{21}m_{1s} - (\omega_2 - a_{22})m_{2s}}{\omega_1 - \omega_2} \right]$$

$$+ \frac{\omega_2 - a_{22}}{a_{21}} \sum_{s=-\infty}^{t} \omega_2^{t-s} \left[\frac{(\omega_1 - a_{22})m_{2s} - a_{21}m_{1s}}{\omega_1 - \omega_2} \right],$$

$$\bar{z}_{2t} = - \sum_{s=t+1}^{\infty} \left(\frac{1}{\omega_1} \right)^{s-t} \left[\frac{a_{21}m_{1s} - (\omega_2 - a_{22})m_{2s}}{\omega_1 - \omega_2} \right]$$

$$+ \sum_{s=-\infty}^{t} \omega_2^{t-s} \left[\frac{(\omega_1 - a_{22})m_{2s} - a_{21}m_{1s}}{\omega_1 - \omega_2} \right].$$

Then eq. (20) shows that $b_{20} = z_{20} - \bar{z}_{20}$. In analogy with eq. (19), the appropriate solution for the system therefore is

$$z_{1t} - \bar{z}_{1t} = e_2(z_{20} - \bar{z}_{20})\omega_2^t,$$

(21)

$$z_{2t} - \bar{z}_{2t} = (z_{20} - \bar{z}_{20})\omega_2^t,$$

where e_2 is given by eq. (15).[16]

C.2.4   A Shortcut Solution for the Case of $\omega_1 > 1$ and $0 < \omega_2 < 1$

A shortcut solution approach based on the lag operator can be used when $\omega_1 > 1$ and $0 < \omega_2 < 1$. Return to the original first-order vector autoregression in eq. (13), writing it as

$$\begin{bmatrix} 1 - a_{11}L & -a_{12}L \\ -a_{21}L & 1 - a_{22}L \end{bmatrix} \begin{bmatrix} z_{1t} \\ z_{2t} \end{bmatrix} = \begin{bmatrix} m_{1t} \\ m_{2t} \end{bmatrix}.$$

---

16. It is a good exercise to check, using eq. (14), that when m_{1t} and m_{2t} are constant, $\bar{z}_{1t} = \bar{z}_1$ and $\bar{z}_{2t} = \bar{z}_2$, as given in eq. (18).

Multiplying through by the inverse of the coefficient matrix, we get

$$\begin{bmatrix} z_{1t} \\ z_{2t} \end{bmatrix} = \begin{bmatrix} 1 - a_{11}L & -a_{12}L \\ -a_{21}L & 1 - a_{22}L \end{bmatrix}^{-1} \begin{bmatrix} m_{1t} \\ m_{2t} \end{bmatrix}$$

$$= \frac{1}{(1 - a_{11}L)(1 - a_{22}L) - a_{12}a_{21}L^2} \begin{bmatrix} 1 - a_{22}L & a_{12}L \\ a_{21}L & 1 - a_{11}L \end{bmatrix} \begin{bmatrix} m_{1t} \\ m_{2t} \end{bmatrix}$$

$$= \frac{1}{1 - \text{tr}(\mathbf{A})L + \det(\mathbf{A})L^2} \begin{bmatrix} 1 - a_{22}L & a_{12}L \\ a_{21}L & 1 - a_{11}L \end{bmatrix} \begin{bmatrix} m_{1t} \\ m_{2t} \end{bmatrix}$$

$$= \frac{L^{-2}}{(L^{-1} - \omega_1)(L^{-1} - \omega_2)} \begin{bmatrix} 1 - a_{22}L & a_{12}L \\ a_{21}L & 1 - a_{11}L \end{bmatrix} \begin{bmatrix} m_{1t} \\ m_{2t} \end{bmatrix}$$

$$= \frac{-(1/\omega_1)L^{-1}}{[1 - (1/\omega_1)L^{-1}](1 - \omega_2 L)} \begin{bmatrix} 1 - a_{22}L & a_{12}L \\ a_{21}L & 1 - a_{11}L \end{bmatrix} \begin{bmatrix} m_{1t} \\ m_{2t} \end{bmatrix},$$

where we have used eq. (14) to write the right-hand side in terms of the character-istic roots of $\mathbf{A}$. Multiply both sides by $1 - \omega_2 L$. The preceding equation can then be expressed as

$$\begin{bmatrix} z_{1t} \\ z_{2t} \end{bmatrix} = \omega_2 \begin{bmatrix} z_{1t-1} \\ z_{2t-1} \end{bmatrix} - \frac{1/\omega_1}{[1 - (1/\omega_1)L^{-1}]} \begin{bmatrix} (L^{-1} - a_{22}) m_{1t} + a_{12}m_{2t} \\ a_{21}m_{1t} + (L^{-1} - a_{11}) m_{2t} \end{bmatrix}$$

$$= \omega_2 \begin{bmatrix} z_{1t-1} \\ z_{2t-1} \end{bmatrix}$$

$$- \frac{1}{\omega_1} \sum_{s=t}^{\infty} \left(\frac{1}{\omega_1}\right)^{s-t} \begin{bmatrix} (L^{-1} - a_{22}) m_{1s} + a_{12}m_{2s} \\ a_{21}m_{1s} + (L^{-1} - a_{11}) m_{2s} \end{bmatrix}, \tag{22}$$

a solution form useful in many applications. [Because the preceding method is based on factoring the lag-operator polynomial $1 - \text{tr}(\mathbf{A})L + \det(\mathbf{A})L^2$, it is called the *polynomial factorization method*.]

To see why this solution and eq. (21) are the same, retrace the steps that led to eq. (21) to show that, in matrix notation, it can be written as

$$\begin{bmatrix} z_{1t} \\ z_{2t} \end{bmatrix} = \mathbf{E} \begin{bmatrix} -(1/\omega_1)L^{-1}[1 - (1/\omega_1)L^{-1}]^{-1} & 0 \\ 0 & (1 - \omega_2 L)^{-1} \end{bmatrix} \mathbf{E}^{-1} \begin{bmatrix} m_{1t} \\ m_{2t} \end{bmatrix}$$

$$+ \mathbf{E} \begin{bmatrix} 0 \\ (z_{20} - \bar{z}_{20})\,\omega_2^t \end{bmatrix}$$

$$= \mathbf{E}(\mathbf{I} - \mathbf{\Omega}L)^{-1}\mathbf{E}^{-1} \begin{bmatrix} m_{1t} \\ m_{2t} \end{bmatrix} + \mathbf{E} \begin{bmatrix} 0 \\ (z_{20} - \bar{z}_{20})\,\omega_2^t \end{bmatrix},$$

in which $\mathbf{I}$ is the 2×2 identity matrix.[17] Therefore,

$$(1 - \omega_2 L) \begin{bmatrix} z_{1t} \\ z_{2t} \end{bmatrix} = (1 - \omega_2 L)\mathbf{E}(\mathbf{I} - \mathbf{\Omega}L)^{-1}\mathbf{E}^{-1} \begin{bmatrix} m_{1t} \\ m_{2t} \end{bmatrix}$$

$$= (1 - \omega_2 L) \left(\mathbf{E}\mathbf{E}^{-1} - \mathbf{E}\mathbf{\Omega}\mathbf{E}^{-1}L \right)^{-1} \begin{bmatrix} m_{1t} \\ m_{2t} \end{bmatrix}$$

$$= (1 - \omega_2 L)(\mathbf{I} - \mathbf{A}L)^{-1} \begin{bmatrix} m_{1t} \\ m_{2t} \end{bmatrix},$$

where the final equality uses the equation $\mathbf{A} = \mathbf{E}\mathbf{\Omega}\mathbf{E}^{-1}$.[18] This last equation, however, is simply another way of writing eq. (22).

C.2.5   Stochastic Models

Consider the stochastic model

$$\begin{bmatrix} E_{t-1}z_{1t} \\ E_{t-1}z_{2t} \end{bmatrix} = \mathbf{A} \begin{bmatrix} z_{1t-1} \\ z_{2t-1} \end{bmatrix} + \begin{bmatrix} E_{t-1}m_{1t} \\ E_{t-1}m_{2t} \end{bmatrix},$$

which we will assume to be saddle-path stable as in our preceding example. Leading this equation a period (as in the univariate case of section C.1.3) and diagonalizing $\mathbf{A}$ (exactly as in the deterministic case), we proceed as before to obtain the stochastic analog of eq. (21),

$$z_{1t} - E_t\bar{z}_{1t} = e_2(z_{20} - E_0\bar{z}_{20})\omega_2^t,$$

$$z_{2t} - E_t\bar{z}_{2t} = (z_{20} - E_0\bar{z}_{20})\omega_2^t.$$

---

17. Since

$$\mathbf{I} - \mathbf{\Omega}L = \begin{bmatrix} 1 - \omega_1 L & 0 \\ 0 & 1 - \omega_2 L \end{bmatrix},$$

its inverse is

$$(\mathbf{I} - \mathbf{\Omega}L)^{-1} = \begin{bmatrix} \frac{1-\omega_2 L}{(1-\omega_1 L)(1-\omega_2 L)} & 0 \\ 0 & \frac{1-\omega_1 L}{(1-\omega_1 L)(1-\omega_2 L)} \end{bmatrix}$$

$$= \begin{bmatrix} -(1/\omega_1)L^{-1}\left[1 - (1/\omega_1)L^{-1}\right]^{-1} & 0 \\ 0 & (1 - \omega_2 L)^{-1} \end{bmatrix}.$$

18. To establish the first of the preceding equalities, note that

$$(1 - \omega_2 L)\mathbf{E} \begin{bmatrix} 0 \\ (z_{20} - \bar{z}_{20})\omega_2^t \end{bmatrix} = \mathbf{E} \begin{bmatrix} (1 - \omega_2 L) \cdot 0 \\ (z_{20} - \bar{z}_{20})\left(\omega_2^t - \omega_2 \cdot \omega_2^{t-1}\right) \end{bmatrix} = 0.$$

Division of the first of these by the second gives the stochastic saddle-path relationship

$$z_{1t} = E_t \bar{z}_{1t} + \frac{\omega_2 - a_{22}}{a_{21}} (z_{2t} - E_t \bar{z}_{2t}) . \tag{23}$$

C.3   Higher-Order Systems

Higher-order difference equations, for example,

$$z_t = a_1 z_{t-1} + a_2 z_{t-2} + m_t$$

(a second-order equation), can be written as first-order vector systems. Define $z'_t = z_{t-1}$. Then the preceding equation is equivalent to the equation pair

$$z_t = a_1 z_{t-1} + a_2 z'_{t-1} + m_t,$$

$$z'_t = z_{t-1},$$

which has the matrix representation

$$\begin{bmatrix} z_t \\ z'_t \end{bmatrix} = \begin{bmatrix} a_1 & a_2 \\ 1 & 0 \end{bmatrix} \begin{bmatrix} z_{t-1} \\ z'_{t-1} \end{bmatrix} + \begin{bmatrix} m_t \\ 0 \end{bmatrix} .$$

The solution methods just discussed therefore apply.

An alternative tack is to write the difference equation in terms of lag operators, for example,

$$(1 - a_1 L - a_2 L^2) z_t = m_t$$

in the second-order case. A solution can then be found by factoring the lag polynomial $1 - a_1 L - a_2 L^2$, as in section C.2.4 of this supplement.

Supplement A   Multiperiod Portfolio Selection

This supplement generalizes to an infinite-horizon setting the two-period problem of saving with portfolio selection that was central to section 5.3. Let Q_s denote an individual's *financial* wealth at the end of date $s - 1$ (the sum of all marketable assets accumulated through the end of $s - 1$). Assume the individual has no other income source. The general problem we start with is to maximize

$$U_t = E_t \left\{ \sum_{s=t}^{\infty} \beta^{s-t} u(C_s) \right\}$$

subject to the two constraints

$$Q_{s+1} = \sum_{n=1}^{N} x_{n,s}(1 + r_s^n) Q_s - C_s, \quad \sum_{n=1}^{N} x_{n,s} = 1,$$

for all $s \geq t$, with $W_t \equiv \sum_{n=1}^{N} x_{n,t}(1 + r_t^n) Q_t$, the value of total resources at the start of date t, given. Here, $x_{n,s}$ is the share of Q_s invested in asset n on date $s - 1$, and r_s^n is the (possibly uncertain) net rate of return on asset n between $s - 1$ and s.

Following Merton (1969) and Samuelson (1969), we characterize a solution via dynamic programming (see Supplement A to Chapter 2). Let $J_t(W_t)$ denote the value function for date t. As usual this function depends on total start-of-period-t resources, W_t. It also depends on date t information (hence the t subscript) if current and past asset returns contain information useful for predicting future returns. Notice that we can reformulate the wealth-accumulation constraint in terms of W:

$$W_{s+1} = \sum_{n=1}^{N} x_{n,s+1}(1 + r_{s+1}^n)(W_s - C_s).$$

After this constraint and the adding-up constraint $\sum_n x_{n,s} = 1$ are incorporated into the maximand, the Bellman equation for date t is

$$J_t(W_t)$$

$$= \max_{C_t, x_{n,t+1}} \left(u(C_t) + \beta E_t J_{t+1} \left\{ \left[1 + r_{t+1}^N + \sum_{n=1}^{N-1} x_{n,t+1}(r_{t+1}^n - r_{t+1}^N) \right](W_t - C_t) \right\} \right).$$

Differentiating and invoking the envelope theorem's implication that $J_{t+1}'(W_{t+1}) = u'(C_{t+1})$, we find the first-order conditions

$$u'(C_t) = \beta E_t \left\{ \left[1 + r_{t+1}^N + \sum_{n=1}^{N-1} x_{n,t+1}(r_{t+1}^n - r_{t+1}^N) \right] u'(C_{t+1}) \right\} \tag{1}$$

with respect to C_t and

$$E_t \left\{ (r_{t+1}^n - r_{t+1}^N) u'(C_{t+1}) \right\} = 0 \tag{2}$$

with respect to each of the $N - 1$ unconstrained portfolio shares $x_{n,t+1}$.[1]

Let us assume provisionally that $u(C) = \log C$ (we return to the CRRA case with $\rho \neq 1$ later). An educated guess is that the optimal consumption function has the proportional form

$$C_s = \mu W_s,$$

where μ is a constant. Given this guess, we can solve for portfolio shares by solving the $N - 1$ equations implied by eq. (2) and the reformulated wealth-accumulation identity,

$$E_t \left[(r_{t+1}^n - r_{t+1}^N) \left(\mu \left\{ \left[1 + r_{t+1}^N + \sum_{n=1}^{N-1} x_{n,t+1}(r_{t+1}^n - r_{t+1}^N) \right] (1-\mu) W_t \right\} \right)^{-1} \right]$$

$$= 0.$$

The optimal portfolio solution is messy in general.[2] We want to stress one important feature of the portfolio decision, however. Multiplication of both sides of the last equation by W_t shows that the optimal portfolio shares are independent of the level of wealth, a property that also holds for general CRRA-isoelastic preferences if uncertainty is i.i.d. Thus we have a separation between the saving and portfolio decisions, which would not occur if risk aversion varied with wealth.

Let r_{t+1}^o denote the return on the optimal (wealth-invariant) portfolio:

$$r_{t+1}^o \equiv r_{t+1}^N + \sum_{n=1}^{N-1} x_{n,t+1}(r_{t+1}^n - r_{t+1}^N).$$

Then eq. (1) simplifies to

$$\frac{1}{C_t} = \beta E_t \left\{ (1 + r_{t+1}^o) \frac{1}{C_{t+1}} \right\}.$$

We can use this equation to solve for μ. Since $C_s = \mu W_s$ for $s = t, t+1$, the wealth accumulation identity allows us to rewrite this Euler equation as

---

1. This last condition actually is

$$E_t \{ (r_{t+1}^n - r_{t+1}^N)(W_t - C_t) u'(C_{t+1}) \} = 0,$$

but since we will consider here only utility functions such that $u'(C) \to \infty$ as $C \to 0$, we can assume that $W_t > C_t > 0$ at an optimum so that division by $W_t - C_t$ always is permissible.

2. Merton (1969) discusses how the problem can simplify in continuous time.

$$\frac{1}{\mu W_t} = \beta E_t \left\{ \frac{1 + r^o_{t+1}}{\mu(1 - \mu)(1 + r^o_{t+1})W_t} \right\} = \frac{\beta}{\mu(1 - \mu)W_t}.$$

Solving for μ yields $\mu = 1 - \beta$, thus confirming the original guess.

For CRRA preferences with risk-aversion coefficient ρ, μ is a function of time (but not of individually chosen variables such as wealth) in general; that is, $C_t = \mu_t W_t$, where μ_t varies only because of variation in the conditional distribution of expected future returns. One can show that μ_t obeys the recursion

$$\mu_t = \left(1 + \left[\beta E_t \left\{ (1 + r^o_{t+1})^{1-\rho} \mu^{-\rho}_{t+1} \right\} \right]^{1/\rho} \right)^{-1}.$$

If returns are i.i.d., the return on the optimal portfolio is constant and μ therefore is constant (as it always is in the log case),

$$\mu = 1 - \left[\beta E \left\{ (1 + r^o)^{1-\rho} \right\} \right]^{1/\rho}.$$

Since ρ is the inverse of the intertemporal substitution elasticity, the ambiguous effect of the mean rate of return on consumption, given W, reflects the familiar tension between income and substitution effects.

Supplement A   Continuous-Time Maximization and the Maximum Principle

This supplement explores a continuous-time version of the money-in-the-utility function model of section 8.3. That version is a good vehicle for illustrating a continuous-time optimization technique that is used often in macroeconomic dynamics, the *maximum principle* or *method of optimal control* (see Arrow and Kurz 1970 or Dixit 1990).

A.1   The Continuous-Time Limit of the Monetary Model

As usual we start by rewriting the model for an arbitrary time interval h. Thus, the individual lifetime utility function becomes

$$U_t = \sum_{s=t}^{\infty} \left(\frac{1}{1+\delta h} \right)^{(s-t)/h} u\left(C_s, \frac{M_s}{P_s} \right) h \tag{1}$$

instead of eq. (33) of Chapter 8, where $\delta > 0$ is the *rate* of time preference, C_s is the (constant) rate of consumption over period s, and the summation is over $t, t + h, t + 2h$, etc. Rather than the analog of eq. (34), the individual's period budget for date s is

$$B_{s+h} + \frac{M_s}{P_s} = (1+rh)B_s + \frac{M_{s-h}}{P_s} + Y_s h - C_s h - T_s h, \tag{2}$$

because $C_s h$ is total consumption spending over the period.

To facilitate later comparison with the solution the maximum principle implies, we solve this problem by the method of Lagrangians, using a separate multiplier λ_s for each of the preceding period budget constraints. The resulting Lagrangian is

$$\mathcal{L} = \sum_{s=t}^{\infty} \left(\frac{1}{1+\delta h} \right)^{(s-t)/h} \left\{ u\left(C_s, \frac{M_s}{P_s} \right) h \right.$$

$$\left. - \lambda_s \left[B_{s+h} + \frac{M_s}{P_s} - (1+rh)B_s - \frac{M_{s-h}}{P_s} - Y_s h + C_s h + T_s h \right] \right\}.$$

First-order conditions with repect to C_s, M_s, and B_{s+h} are, for all $s \geq t$:

$$u_C\left(C_s, \frac{M_s}{P_s} \right) = \lambda_s, \tag{3}$$

$$\frac{1}{P_s} u_{M/P}\left(C_s, \frac{M_s}{P_s} \right) h = \frac{\lambda_s}{P_s} - \left(\frac{1}{1+\delta h} \right) \frac{\lambda_{s+h}}{P_{s+h}}, \tag{4}$$

$$\lambda_s = \left(\frac{1+rh}{1+\delta h} \right) \lambda_{s+h}. \tag{5}$$

By combining the first and third of these conditions, taking $h = 1$, and noting that $\beta = 1/(1 + \delta)$ in that case, we obtain the consumption Euler equation (35) of Chapter 8. By combining the first and second optimality condition, we likewise obtain the Euler equation for real money demand, eq. (36), when $h = 1$. Thus the Lagrangian method yields the same answers as in section 8.3.2.

Now let $h \to 0$. Because

$$\lim_{h \to 0} \left(\frac{1}{1 + \delta h} \right)^{(s-t)/h} = \exp\left[-\delta(s - t)\right],$$

the utility objective (1) becomes

$$U_t = \int_t^\infty \exp\left[-\delta(s - t)\right] u\left(C_s, \frac{M_s}{P_s}\right) ds \tag{6}$$

in the limit of continuous time. Dividing budget constraint (2) by h and going to the continuous-time limit gives

$$\dot{B}_s + \frac{\dot{M}_s}{P_s} = r B_s + Y_s - T_s - C_s. \tag{7}$$

Having derived the continuous-time versions of the individual's objective function and constraints, we next seek the continuous time limit of necessary first-order optimality conditions (3)–(5). Equation (3), of course, doesn't change. If we use eq. (5) to eliminate λ_{s+h} from eq. (4), however, the result is

$$\frac{1}{P_s} u_{M/P}\left(C_s, \frac{M_s}{P_s}\right) h = \frac{\lambda_s}{P_s} - \left(\frac{1}{1 + rh}\right) \frac{\lambda_s}{P_{s+h}},$$

which can be rearranged using eq. (3) as

$$\frac{u_{M/P}(C_s, M_s/P_s)}{u_C(C_s, M_s/P_s)} = \frac{1}{h}\left[1 - \left(\frac{1}{1 + rh}\right) \frac{P_s}{P_{s+h}}\right]$$

$$= \frac{r}{1 + rh} + \left(\frac{P_{s+h} - P_s}{h}\right) \left[\frac{1}{(1 + rh) P_{s+h}}\right].$$

Taking the limit as $h \to 0$ gives

$$\frac{u_{M/P}(C_s, M_s/P_s)}{u_C(C_s, M_s/P_s)} = r + \frac{\dot{P}_s}{P_s} = r + \pi_s = i_s, \tag{8}$$

where π_s is the inflation rate at time s and i_s is the nominal interest rate.[1] Thus, we obtain the continuous-time analog of money demand equation (37) on p. 533.

---

1. With a trading interval of length h, Fisher parity gives the nominal interest rate by $1 + i_{s+h} h = (1 + rh)(P_{s+h}/P_s)$, so that

Equation (5) is equivalent to

$$\frac{\lambda_{s+h} - \lambda_s}{h} = \lambda_s \left(\frac{\delta - r}{1 + rh} \right).$$

Once again taking the limit as $h \to 0$ gives

$$\dot{\lambda}_s = \lambda_s (\delta - r). \tag{9}$$

Together, eqs. (3), (8), and (9) therefore are the necessary first-order conditions for maximizing lifetime utility (6) subject to the financing constraint (7).

Before illustrating how to apply the maximum principle to the foregoing problem, it is convenient to reformulate it. Define

$$Q_s = B_s + \frac{M_s}{P_s} \tag{10}$$

as the individual's total financial wealth in this model. Differentiation of Q shows that

$$\dot{Q}_s = \dot{B}_s + \frac{\dot{M}_s}{P_s} - \pi_s \frac{M_s}{P_s},$$

which implies that eq. (7) has the equivalent form

$$\dot{Q}_s = r Q_s + Y_s - T_s - C_s - i_s \frac{M_s}{P_s}. \tag{11}$$

Equation (11) states that the change in financial wealth equals disposable income less total expenditure on consumption plus monetary services. In eq. (11), "income" includes the additional real interest payment one would receive were real balances held as nonmonetary wealth, while "expenditure" includes that forgone real interest payment. A maximization problem equivalent to the one we have been considering is to maximize utility (6) subject to constraints (10) and (11).

A.2   Dynamic Optimization Using the Maximum Principle

The maximum principle is designed to handle such problems. Here we describe how to apply it in general and show that for the problem of the last subsection, it leads to the same first-order condtions we have already derived.

Consider the generic problem of maximizing

$$i_{s+h} = (1 + rh) \left(\frac{P_{s+h}}{h P_s} \right) - \frac{1}{h} = r \left(\frac{P_{s+h}}{P_s} \right) + \left(\frac{P_{s+h} - P_s}{h P_s} \right).$$

Letting $h \to 0$ yields

$$i_s = r + \pi_s.$$

$$U_t = \int_t^\infty u[C_s(1), \dots, C_s(n)] \exp\left[-\delta(s-t)\right] ds \qquad (12)$$

with respect to the path $\{C_s(1), \dots, C_s(n)\}_{s=t}^\infty$, subject to the constraints

$$\dot{Q}_s = F[Q_s, C_s(1), \dots, C_s(n), s], \qquad Q_t \text{ given}, \qquad (13)$$

and

$$G[Q_s, C_s(1), \dots, C_s(n), s] = 0. \qquad (14)$$

This framework corresponds to the problem of maximizing lifetime utility (6) subject to eqs. (11) and (10), with $C(1)$ interpreted as consumption, $C(2)$ as nominal money holdings, $C(3)$ as bond holdings, and Q as financial wealth. In the preceding problem, Q is referred to as a *state variable* and the $C(j)$, $j = 1, \dots, n$, as *control variables*. (State variable levels are predetermined "stocks" but their rates of change are determined by the levels of the controls, which can be varied freely.) The technique we will describe is easily extended to cover arbitrary numbers of state variables, additional constraints, state variables that enter utility directly, and (through the Kuhn-Tucker theorem) inequality constraints.[2]

The following very useful result characterizes a solution:

MAXIMUM PRINCIPLE   Define the *Hamiltonian* for the problem of maximizing objective (12) subject to constraints (13) and (14) as

$$\mathcal{H}[C_s(1), \dots, C_s(n), Q_s, s] = u[C_s(1), \dots, C_s(n)] + \lambda_s F[Q_s, C_s(1), \dots, C_s(n), s]$$
$$- v_s G[Q_s, C_s(1), \dots, C_s(n), s],$$

where λ_s (which must be nonnegative) is called the *costate variable* and v_s is a Lagrange multiplier. The necessary conditions for an optimum include constraints (13), (14), and

1. $\partial\mathcal{H}/\partial C_s(j) = 0$ for each control variable, $j = 1, \dots, n$,
2. $\dot{\lambda}_s = \delta\lambda_s - \partial\mathcal{H}/\partial Q_s$ (the equation of motion for the costate variable).

Together with the preceding first-order conditions and concavity conditions that are spelled out in Arrow and Kurz (1970), for example, a sufficient condition for an optimum is the transversality condition

$$\lim_{T \to \infty} \exp(-\delta T)\,\lambda_{t+T} Q_{t+T} = 0. \qquad (15)$$

In standard economic applications with positive discounting, condition (15) is necessary also, as in discrete-time maximization problems (recall section 2.1.2 and Supplement A to Chapter 2).

---

2. Indeed, in the monetary problem there is an implicit inequality constraint that financial wealth can never fall below -1 times the present value of human wealth. As usual, this constraint will never bind if the marginal utility of goods becomes arbitrarily large near zero consumption.

To make this abstract proposition seem more concrete, let us apply it to the previous problem of maximizing the utility function (6) subject to eqs. (11) and (10). In that case the Hamiltonian is

$$\mathcal{H}\left(C_s, \frac{M_s}{P_s}, Q_s, B_s, s\right) = u\left(C_s, \frac{M_s}{P_s}\right) + \lambda_s\left(rQ_s + Y_s - T_s - C_s - i_s\frac{M_s}{P_s}\right)$$

$$- \nu_s\left(Q_s - B_s - \frac{M_s}{P_s}\right).$$

The first-order conditions for the controls C_s, M_s, and B_s are

$$\frac{\partial \mathcal{H}}{\partial C_s} = u_C\left(C_s, \frac{M_s}{P_s}\right) - \lambda_s = 0,$$

$$\frac{\partial \mathcal{H}}{\partial M_s} = \frac{1}{P_s}\left[u_{M/P}\left(C_s, \frac{M_s}{P_s}\right) - \lambda_s i_s + \nu_s\right] = 0,$$

$$\frac{\partial \mathcal{H}}{\partial B_s} = \nu_s = 0,$$

and the costate variable's equation of motion is

$$\dot{\lambda}_s = \delta\lambda_s - \frac{\partial \mathcal{H}}{\partial Q_s} = \delta\lambda_s - \lambda_s r + \nu_s = \lambda_s(\delta - r).$$

Plainly, however, the preceding four equations boil down to the first-order conditions (3), (8), and (9) that we derived earlier through a limiting argument.

A.3   Solving for the Equilibrium Consumption Level

As in the analogous discrete-time model analyzed in section 8.3.3, one can solve for consumption in terms of individual lifetime wealth and real consumption-based interest rates. For some special cases, however, one can go further in the continuous-time model and obtain a true reduced-form solution showing how consumption depends on monetary policy.

A.3.1   The Economy's Consolidated Budget Constraint

As a first step we consolidate the intertemporal budget constraints of the private and public sectors to derive the economy's aggregate resource constraint. We now distinguish private bond holdings, B^P, from national net claims on foreigners, B. You can verify that for any starting date t and terminal date $t + T$, differential equation (11) for financial wealth Q implies

$$Q_{t+T} = \exp(rT)Q_t + \int_t^{t+T}\left(Y_s - T_s - C_s - i_s\frac{M_s}{P_s}\right)\exp[r(t + T - s)]\,ds.$$

Division by $\exp(rT)$ yields

$$\int_t^{t+T} \left(C_s + i_s \frac{M_s}{P_s} \right) \exp\left[-r\,(s-t)\right] ds + \exp(-rT) Q_{t+T}$$

$$= Q_t + \int_t^{t+T} (Y_s - T_s) \exp\left[-r\,(s-t)\right] ds. \tag{16}$$

Now consider the infinite-horizon limit ($T \to \infty$). The transversality condition (15) requires that $\lim_{T\to\infty} \exp\left(-\delta T\right) \lambda_{t+T} Q_{t+T} = 0$ here. Equation (9), however, has the solution

$$\lambda_{t+T} = \lambda_t \exp\left[(\delta - r)\, T\right]$$

(again, differentiate with respect to T to verify). By eq. (3), the transversality condition can thus be written as

$$\lim_{T\to\infty} \exp\left(-rT\right) u_C(C_t, M_t/P_t) Q_{t+T} = 0.$$

Since $u_C(C_t, M_t/P_t) > 0$ when there is economic scarcity, the transversality condition effectively becomes $\lim_{T\to\infty} \exp\left(-rT\right) Q_{t+T} = 0$, which is the same as eq. (13) of Chapter 2. [See also the parallel discussion of eq. (4) in Supplement A to Chapter 2.]

Equation (16) therefore implies that the relevant individual intertemporal budget constraint for an infinite horizon is

$$\int_t^\infty \left(C_s + i_s \frac{M_s}{P_s} \right) \exp\left[-r\,(s-t)\right] ds$$

$$= B_t^P + \frac{M_t}{P_t} + \int_t^\infty (Y_s - T_s) \exp\left[-r\,(s-t)\right] ds, \tag{17}$$

where we have used eq. (10) to substitute private assets $B^P + (M/P)$ for Q. Constraint (17) equates the present value of expenditures (on consumption and money services) to the sum of financial and human wealth.

Let B^G denote the assets of the domestic government. The government budget constraint is written, analogously to the private constraint, as

$$\int_t^\infty G_s \exp\left[-r\,(s-t)\right] ds = B_t^G + \int_t^\infty \left(T_s + \frac{\dot{M}_s}{P_s} \right) \exp\left[-r\,(s-t)\right] ds, \tag{18}$$

so that the present value of government expenditures equals initial assets plus the present value of conventional tax revenue and seignorage. Recall that

$$\pi = \frac{\dot{P}}{P}$$

denotes the inflation rate and that

$$\frac{\dot{M}_s}{P_s} = \frac{d(M_s/P_s)}{ds} + \pi_s \frac{M_s}{P_s}.$$

Substituting this result into eq. (18) and integrating by parts leads to

$$\int_t^\infty G_s \exp\left[-r\,(s-t)\right]ds = B_t^G + \int_t^\infty \left(T_s + \pi_s \frac{M_s}{P_s}\right)\exp\left[-r\,(s-t)\right]ds$$

$$+ \lim_{T\to\infty} \exp(-rT)\left(\frac{M_{t+T}}{P_{t+T}}\right) - \frac{M_t}{P_t}$$

$$+ \int_t^\infty r\,\frac{M_s}{P_s}\exp\left[-r\,(s-t)\right]ds$$

$$= B_t^G - \frac{M_t}{P_t} + \int_t^\infty \left(T_s + i_s \frac{M_s}{P_s}\right)\exp\left[-r\,(s-t)\right]ds,$$

where we have imposed a condition ruling out self-fulfilling hyperdeflations, $\lim_{T\to\infty} \exp(-rT)\left(M_{t+T}/P_{t+T}\right) = 0$. [This limit condition follows from the reasoning that led to eq. (50) in Chapter 8.]

The last of the preceding equalities is the same one derived in footnote 26 of Chapter 8, although it generalizes the latter by allowing for initial public-sector interest-bearing assets. By combining it with the private sector's intertemporal constraint (17), we reach the economy's consolidated budget constraint vis-à-vis the rest of the world,

$$\int_t^\infty (C_s + G_s)\exp\left[-r\,(s-t)\right]ds = B_t + \int_t^\infty Y_s \exp\left[-r\,(s-t)\right]ds, \tag{19}$$

where $B = B^P + B^G$, as usual. This constraint reflects the nontradability of money services.

A.3.2 Consumption as a Function of Nominal Interest Rates

We next solve for equilibrium consumption, initially paralleling the discussion in section 8.3.3. For this purpose we assume CES-isoelastic preferences, so that the period utility function is

$$u\left(C, \frac{M}{P}\right) = \frac{\left\{\left[\gamma^{\frac{1}{\theta}} C^{\frac{\theta-1}{\theta}} + (1-\gamma)^{\frac{1}{\theta}} \left(\frac{M}{P}\right)^{\frac{\theta-1}{\theta}}\right]^{\frac{\theta}{\theta-1}}\right\}^{1-\frac{1}{\sigma}}}{1 - \frac{1}{\sigma}} \tag{20}$$

and the consumption-based price index is

$$P^C = \left[\gamma + (1-\gamma)i^{1-\theta}\right]^{\frac{1}{1-\theta}}. \tag{21}$$

For the preferences in eq. (20), eq. (8) implies that

$$M/P = \frac{(1-\gamma)}{\gamma} i^{-\theta} C. \tag{22}$$

Substituting the money-demand equation (22) into eq. (3) for the present case,

$$u_C\left(C, \frac{M}{P}\right) = \gamma^{\frac{1}{\theta}}\left[\gamma^{\frac{1}{\theta}} C^{\frac{\theta-1}{\theta}} + (1-\gamma)^{\frac{1}{\theta}}\left(\frac{M}{P}\right)^{\frac{\theta-1}{\theta}}\right]^{\left(\frac{\theta}{\theta-1}\right)\left(\frac{\sigma-1}{\sigma}\right)-1} C^{-\frac{1}{\theta}} = \lambda,$$

yields

$$C^{-\frac{1}{\sigma}}\left(P^c\right)^{\frac{\theta-\sigma}{\sigma}} = \lambda$$

(aside from an irrelevant multiplicative constant), where eq. (21) has been used. Taking logs of the preceding equation, differentiating, and using eq. (9) leads to the consumption Euler equation

$$-\frac{1}{\sigma}\left(\frac{\dot{C}}{C}\right) + \frac{\theta-\sigma}{\sigma}\left(\frac{\dot{P}^c}{P^c}\right) = \frac{\dot{\lambda}}{\lambda} = \delta - r,$$

or

$$\frac{\dot{C}}{C} = (\theta-\sigma)\frac{\dot{P}^c}{P^c} + \sigma(r-\delta).$$

From this equation the solution

$$\log C_s = \log C_t + \int_t^s\left[(\theta-\sigma)\frac{\dot{P}^c(v)}{P^c(v)} + \sigma(r-\delta)\right]dv$$

follows (as can be verified by differentiating with respect to s). Exponentiating gives the consumption-level equation

$$C_s = C_t \exp\left\{\int_t^s\left[(\theta-\sigma)\frac{\dot{P}^c(v)}{P^c(v)} + \sigma(r-\delta)\right]dv\right\}. \tag{23}$$

We can solve for equilibrium private consumption by using the integrated Euler equation (23) to substitute for C_s in the economy's intertemporal budget constraint, eq. (19). The result is

$$C_t = \frac{B_t + \int_t^\infty (Y_s - G_s)\exp[-r(s-t)]\,ds}{\int_t^\infty \exp\left\{\int_t^s\left[(\theta-\sigma)\frac{\dot{P}^c(v)}{P^c(v)} + (\sigma-1)r - \sigma\delta\right]dv\right\}ds}. \tag{24}$$

Notice that this expression differs from the consumption functions derived in section 8.3.3 by eliminating all endogenous variables other than the consumption-based price index, which depends on the nominal interest rate. Thus, the equation shows more transparently how anticipated variation in the nominal interest rate (unless $\theta = \sigma$) will affect consumption. Indeed, eq. (24) is quite analogous to eq. (35) in Chapter 4, which described optimal consumption in the presence of non-traded goods. The analogy will appear sharper if you use the fact that

$$\int_t^s \left[\frac{\dot{P}^C(v)}{P^C(v)} \right] dv = \int_t^s \frac{d \log P^C(v)}{dv} dv = \log \left[\frac{P^C(s)}{P^C(t)} \right]$$

to rewrite eq. (24) in the simplified form

$$C_t = \frac{B_t + \int_t^\infty (Y_s - G_s) \exp[-r(s-t)] \, ds}{\int_t^\infty \exp\left\{[(\sigma - 1)r - \sigma\delta](s-t)\right\} \left[\frac{P^C(t)}{P^C(s)} \right]^{\sigma - \theta} ds}. \tag{25}$$

Note that if the nominal interest rate is constant, equilibrium consumption behaves as it would in a model without money.

A.3.3   A True Reduced-Form Solution

Equation (25) is not a true reduced-form solution because it expresses consumption in terms of the endogenous variable P^C, which depends on the nominal interest rate. For the special case $\theta = 1$, however, one can express P^C explicitly in terms of underlying monetary policies. [Recall that in this special limiting case, period utility (20) is an isoelastic function of the real consumption index $C^\gamma (M/P)^{1-\gamma}$.] Assume that $\delta = r$ and define $\zeta \equiv \gamma + (1 - \gamma)\sigma$. One can then show that the nominal interest rate is given in equilibrium by

$$i_t = \left\{ \frac{1}{\zeta} \int_t^\infty \exp\left[-r(s-t)/\zeta\right] \left[\frac{M(s)}{M(t)} \right]^{-\frac{1}{\zeta}} ds \right\}^{-1}.$$

Combining this with eq. (25) and noting that $P^C = i^{1-\gamma}$ in the case $\theta = 1$ allows a complete characterization of the equilibrium paths of consumption, the current account, and the exchange rate. You can check that for constant money-supply growth at rate μ, $M(s)/M(t) = \exp[\mu(s-t)]$, the preceding equation for the equilibrium nominal interest rate implies $i = r + \mu$.

References

Abel, Andrew B. (1989). "Birth, death and taxes." *Journal of Public Economics* 39 (1989): 1–15.

Abel, Andrew B., Avinash K. Dixit, Janice C. Eberly, and Robert S. Pindyck (1995). "Options, the value of capital, and investment." Working paper 5227, National Bureau of Economic Research (August).

Abel, Andrew B., N. Gregory Mankiw, Lawrence H. Summers, and Richard J. Zeckhauser (1989). "Assessing dynamic efficiency: Theory and evidence." *Review of Economic Studies* 56 (January): 1–19.

Abraham, Katharine G., and John C. Haltiwanger (1995). "Real wages and the business cycle." *Journal of Economic Literature* 33 (September): 1215–64.

Aghion, Philippe, and Peter Howitt (1992). "A model of growth through creative destruction." *Econometrica* 60 (March): 323–51.

Aiyagari, S. Rao (1993). "Explaining financial market facts: The importance of incomplete markets and transaction costs." *Federal Reserve Bank of Minneapolis Quarterly Review* (Winter): 17–31.

Aiyagari, S. Rao, and Mark Gertler (1991). "Asset returns with transactions costs and uninsured individual risk." *Journal of Monetary Economics* 27 (June): 311–31.

Aizenman, Joshua (1989). "Monopolistic competition, relative prices and output adjustment in the open economy." *Journal of International Money and Finance* 8 (March): 5–28.

Akerlof, George A. (1970). "The market for 'lemons': Quality uncertainty and the market mechanism." *Quarterly Journal of Economics* 84 (August): 488–500.

Akerlof, George A., and Janet L. Yellen (1985). "Can small deviations from rationality make significant differences to economic equilibria?" *American Economic Review* 75 (September): 708–21.

Alesina, Alberto (1987). "Macroeconomic policy in a two-party system as a repeated game." *Quarterly Journal of Economics* 102 (August): 651–78.

Alesina, Alberto F., and Vittorio U. Grilli (1992). "The European central bank: Reshaping monetary policies in Europe." In Matthew B. Canzoneri, Vittorio U. Grilli, and Paul R. Masson, eds., *Establishing a central bank: Issues in Europe and lessons from the U.S.* Cambridge, UK: Cambridge University Press.

Alesina, Alberto, and Lawrence H. Summers (1993). "Central bank independence and macroeconomic performance: Some comparative evidence." *Journal of Money, Credit and Banking* 25 (February): 151–62.

Allais, Maurice (1947). *Economie et intérêt*. Paris: Imprimerie Nationale.

Altonji, Joseph G., Fumio Hayashi, and Laurence J. Kotlikoff (1992). "Is the extended family altruistically linked? Direct tests using micro data." *American Economic Review* 82 (December): 1177–98.

Aoki, Masanao (1981). *Dynamic analysis of open economies*. New York: Academic Press.

Arrow, Kenneth J. (1962). "The economic implications of learning by doing." *Review of Economic Studies* 29 (June): 155–73.

Arrow, Kenneth J. (1964). "The role of securities in the optimal allocation of risk bearing." *Review of Economic Studies* 31 (April): 91–96.

Arrow, Kenneth J., and Frank H. Hahn (1971). *General competitive analysis*. San Francisco: Holden-Day.

Arrow, Kenneth J., and Mordecai Kurz (1970). *Public investment, the rate of return, and optimal fiscal policy.* Baltimore and London: The Johns Hopkins Press.

Aschauer, David, and Jeremy Greenwood (1983). "A further exploration in the theory of exchange rate regimes." *Journal of Political Economy* 91 (October): 868–75.

Asea, Patrick K., and Enrique G. Mendoza (1994). "The Balassa-Samuelson model: A general-equilibrium appraisal." *Review of International Economics* 2 (October): 244–67.

Atkeson, Andrew (1991). "International lending with moral hazard and risk of repudiation." *Econometrica* 59 (July): 1069–89.

Atkeson, Andrew, and Tamim Bayoumi (1993). "Do private capital markets insure regional risk? Evidence from Europe and the United States." *Open Economies Review* 4 (3): 303–24.

Atkeson, Andrew, and Robert E. Lucas, Jr. (1992). "On efficient distribution with private information." *Review of Economic Studies* 59 (July): 427–53.

Attanasio, Orazio P., and Guglielmo P. Weber (1993). "Consumption growth, the interest rate and aggregation." *Review of Economic Studies* 60 (July): 631–49.

Attanasio, Orazio P., and Guglielmo P. Weber (1995). "Is consumption growth consistent with intertemporal optimization? Evidence from the Consumer Expenditure Survey." *Journal of Political Economy* 103 (December): 1121–57.

Auerbach, Alan J., Jagadeesh Gokhale, and Laurence J. Kotlikoff (1991). "Generational accounting: A meaningful alternative to deficit accounting." In David F. Bradford, ed., *Tax policy and the economy*, vol. 5. Cambridge, MA: MIT Press.

Auernheimer, Leonardo (1974). "The honest government's guide to the revenue from the creation of money." *Journal of Political Economy* 82 (May–June): 598–606.

Bacchetta, Philippe, and Eric van Wincoop (1995). "Trade in nominal assets." Mimeo, Studienzentrum Gerzensee and Boston University.

Backus, David K., Patrick J. Kehoe, and Finn E. Kydland (1992). "International real business cycles." *Journal of Political Economy* 100 (August): 745–75.

Bailey, Martin J. (1956). "The welfare cost of inflationary finance." *Journal of Political Economy* 64 (April): 93–110.

Balassa, Bela (1963). "An empirical demonstration of classical comparative cost theory." *Review of Economics and Statistics* 4 (August): 231–38.

Balassa, Bela (1964). "The purchasing power parity doctrine: A reappraisal." *Journal of Political Economy* 72 (December): 584–96.

Baldwin, Richard E. (1988). "Hysteresis in import prices: The beachhead effect." *American Economic Review* 78 (September): 773–85.

Ball, Laurence, and David Romer (1989). "Are prices too sticky?" *Quarterly Journal of Economics* 104 (August): 507–24.

Barro, Robert J. (1974). "Are government bonds net wealth?" *Journal of Political Economy* 82 (November/December): 1095–117.

Barro, Robert J. (1979). "On the determination of the public debt." *Journal of Political Economy* 87 (October): 940–71.

Barro, Robert J. (1989). "The Ricardian approach to budget deficits." *Journal of Economic Perspectives* 3 (Spring): 37–54.

Barro, Robert J. (1990). "Government spending in a simple model of endogenous growth." *Journal of Political Economy* 98 (October): S103–S125.

Barro, Robert J. (1991). "Economic growth in a cross-section of countries." *Quarterly Journal of Economics* 106 (May): 407–43.

Barro, Robert J., and David B. Gordon (1983a). "Rules, discretion and reputation in a model of monetary policy." *Journal of Monetary Economics* 12 (July): 101–21.

Barro, Robert J., and David B. Gordon (1983b). "A positive theory of monetary policy in a natural-rate model." *Journal of Political Economy* 91 (August): 589–610.

Barro, Robert J., N. Gregory Mankiw, and Xavier Sala-i-Martin (1995). "Capital mobility in neoclassical models of growth." *American Economic Review* 85 (March): 103–15.

Barro, Robert J., and Xavier Sala-i-Martin (1990). "World real interest rates." *NBER Macroeconomics Annual* 5: 15–61.

Barro, Robert J., and Xavier Sala-i-Martin (1991). "Convergence across states and regions." *Brookings Papers on Economic Activity* 1: 107–82.

Barro, Robert J., and Xavier Sala-i-Martin (1992a). "Convergence." *Journal of Political Economy* 100 (April): 223–51.

Barro, Robert J., and Xavier Sala-i-Martin (1992b). "Regional growth and migration: A Japan–United States comparison." *Journal of the Japanese and International Economies* 6 (December): 312–46.

Barro, Robert J., and Xavier Sala-i-Martin (1994). *Economic growth.* New York: McGraw-Hill.

Basu, Susanto (1995). "Intermediate goods and business cycles: Implications for productivity and welfare." *American Economic Review* 85 (June): 512–31.

Baumol, William J. (1986). "Productivity growth, convergence and welfare: What the long-run data really show." *American Economic Review* 76 (December): 1072–85.

Baumol, William J. (1993). "Social wants and dismal science: The curious case of the climbing costs of health and teaching." Paper presented at the American Philosophical Society Anniversary Meeting.

Baumol, William J., Sue Anne Batey Blackman, and Edward N. Wolf (1989). *Productivity and American leadership: The long view.* Cambridge, MA: MIT Press.

Baumol, William J., and William G. Bowen (1966). *Performing arts: The economic dilemma.* New York: Twentieth Century Fund.

Baxter, Marianne (1994). "Real exchange rates and real interest differentials: Have we missed the business-cycle relationship?" *Journal of Monetary Economics* 33 (February): 5–37.

Baxter, Marianne (1995). "International trade and business cycles." In Gene M. Grossman and Kenneth Rogoff, eds., *Handbook of international economics,* vol. 3. Amsterdam: North Holland.

Baxter, Marianne, and Mario J. Crucini (1995). "Business cycles and the asset structure of foreign trade." *International Economic Review* 36 (November): 821–54.

Baxter, Marianne, and Urban J. Jermann (1993). "The international diversification puzzle is worse than you think." Working paper 350, Rochester Center for Economic Research.

Baxter, Marianne, Urban J. Jermann, and Robert G. King (1995). "Nontraded goods, nontraded factors, and international nondiversification." Working paper 5175, National Bureau of Economic Research (July).

Baxter, Marianne, and Alan C. Stockman (1989). "Business cycles and the exchange rate regime: Some international evidence." *Journal of Monetary Economics* 23 (May): 377–400.

Bayoumi, Tamim, and Michael W. Klein (1995). "A provincial view of capital mobility." Working paper 5115, National Bureau of Economic Research (May).

Bayoumi, Tamim, and Ronald MacDonald (1995). "Consumption, income, and international capital market integration." *International Monetary Fund Staff Papers* 42 (September): 552–76.

Bayoumi, Tamim A., and Paul R. Masson (1994). "Fiscal flows in the United States and Canada: Lessons for monetary union in Europe." Discussion paper 1057, Centre for Economic Policy Research (November).

Bean, Charles R. (1986). "The terms of trade, labour supply and the current account." *Economic Journal* 96: 38–46.

Beaudry, Paul, and Michael B. Devereux (1995). "Money and the real exchange rate with sticky prices and increasing returns." *Carnegie-Rochester Conference Series on Public Policy* 43 (December): 55–101.

Bekaert, Geert (in press). "The time variation of risk and return in foreign exchange markets: A general equilibrium perspective." *Review of Financial Studies.*

Bellman, R. E. (1957). *Dynamic programming.* Princeton, NJ: Princeton University Press.

Ben-David, Dan (1993). "Equalizing exchange: Trade liberalization and income convergence." *Quarterly Journal of Economics* 108 (August): 653–79.

Benhabib, Jess, and Roger E. A. Farmer (1994). "Indeterminacy and increasing returns." *Journal of Economic Theory* 63 (June): 19–41.

Bergin, Paul (1995). "Mundell-Fleming revisited: Monetary and fiscal policies in a two-country dynamic equilibrium model with wage contracts." Mimeo, Yale University (June).

Bernanke, Ben S. (1983). "Nonmonetary effects of the financial crisis in the propagation of the Great Depression." *American Economic Review* 73 (June): 257–76.

Bernanke, Ben S. (1995). "The macroeconomics of the Great Depression: A comparative approach." *Journal of Money, Credit and Banking* 27 (February): 1–28.

Bernanke, Ben S., and Kevin Carey (1995). "Nominal wage stickiness and aggregate supply in the Great Depression." Mimeo, Princeton University.

Bernanke, Ben S., and Mark Gertler (1995). "Inside the black box: The credit channel of monetary policy transmission." *Journal of Economic Perspectives* 9 (Fall): 27–48.

Bernard, Andrew N., and Steven N. Durlauf (1994). "Interpreting tests of the convergence hypothesis." Technical working paper 159, National Bureau of Economic Research (June).

Bernheim, B. Douglas (1987). "Ricardian equivalence: An evaluation of theory and evidence." *NBER Macroeconomics Annual* 2: 263–304.

Bernheim, B. Douglas, and Kyle Bagwell (1988). "Is everything neutral?" *Journal of Political Economy* 96 (April): 308–38.

Bernheim, B. Douglas, Andrei Shleifer, and Lawrence H. Summers (1985). "The strategic bequest motive." *Journal of Political Economy* 93 (December): 1045–76.

Bertola, Giuseppe (1994). "Continuous-time models of exchange rates and intervention." In Frederick van der Ploeg, ed., *The handbook of international macroeconomics*. Oxford, UK: Basil Blackwell.

Betts, Caroline, and Michael B. Devereux (1996). "The exchange rate in a model of pricing-to-market." *European Economic Review* 40 (April): 1007–22.

Bhagwati, Jagdish N. (1958). "Immiserizing growth: A geometrical note." *Review of Economic Studies* 25 (June): 201–5.

Bhagwati, Jagdish N. (1984). "Why are services cheaper in the poor countries?" *Economic Journal* 94 (June): 279–86.

Bishop, William W., Jr. (1971). *International law: Cases and materials*. 3rd edition. Boston: Little, Brown.

Blanchard, Olivier J. (1983). "Debt and the current account deficit in Brazil." In Pedro Aspe Armella, Rudiger Dornbusch, and Maurice Obstfeld, eds., *Financial policy and the world capital market: The problem of Latin American countries*. Chicago: University of Chicago Press.

Blanchard, Olivier J. (1985). "Debt, deficits, and finite horizons." *Journal of Political Economy* 93 (April): 223–47.

Blanchard, Olivier J. (1993). "Movements in the equity premium." *Brookings Papers on Economic Activity* 2: 75–118.

Blanchard, Olivier J., and Nobuhiro Kiyotaki (1987). "Monopolistic competition and the effects of aggregate demand." *American Economic Review* 77 (September): 647–66.

Blanchard, Olivier J., and Lawrence H. Summers (1984). "Perspectives on high world real interest rates." *Brookings Papers on Economic Activity* 2: 273–324.

Blinder, Alan S. (1991). "Why are prices sticky? Preliminary results from an interview study." *American Economic Review* 81 (May): 89–96.

Bliss, Christopher J. (1975). *Capital theory and the distribution of income*. Amsterdam: North Holland.

Bohn, Henning (1992). "Budget deficits and government accounting." *Carnegie-Rochester Conference Series on Public Policy* 37: 1–84.

Bohn, Henning, and Linda L. Tesar (1995). "The U.S. investment portfolio and ICAPM." Mimeo, University of California, Santa Barbara.

Bordo, Michael D., and Barry Eichengreen, eds. (1993). *A retrospective on the Bretton Woods system: Lessons for international monetary reform*. Chicago: University of Chicago Press.

Bosworth, Barry, Gary Burtless, and John Sabelhaus (1991). "The decline in saving: Evidence from household surveys." *Brookings Papers on Economic Activity* 1: 183–256.

Bottazzi, Laura, Paolo Pesenti, and Eric van Wincoop (1996). "Wages, profits and the international portfolio puzzle." *European Economic Review* 40 (February): 219–54.

Brainard, William C., and James Tobin (1992). "On the internationalization of portfolios." *Oxford Economic Papers* 44 (April): 533–565.

Branson, William H., and Dale W. Henderson (1985). "The specification and influence of asset markets." In Ronald W. Jones and Peter B. Kenen, eds., *Handbook of international economics*, vol. 2. Amsterdam: North Holland.

Brock, Philip L. (1988). "Investment, the current account, and the relative price of non-traded goods in a small open economy." *Journal of International Economics* 24 (May): 235–53.

Brock, William A. (1974). "Money and growth: The case of long run perfect foresight." *International Economic Review* 15 (October): 750–77.

Brown, Stephen J., William N. Goetzman, and Stephen A. Ross (1995). "Survival." *Journal of Finance* 50 (July): 853–73.

Bryant, Ralph C., Gerald Holtham, and Peter Hooper, eds. (1988). *External deficits and the dollar: The pit and the pendulum*. Washington, DC: Brookings Institution.

Buiter, Willem H. (1981). "Time preference and international lending and borrowing in an overlapping-generations model." *Journal of Political Economy* 89 (August): 769–97.

Buiter, Willem H. (1988). "Death, birth, productivity growth and debt neutrality." *Economic Journal* 98: 279–93.

Buiter, Willem H. (1989). *Budgetary policy, international and intertemporal trade in the global economy*. Amsterdam: North Holland.

Buiter, Willem H., Giancarlo M. Corsetti, and Paolo A. Pesenti (in press). *Financial markets and international monetary policy cooperation: The lessons of the 92–93 ERM crisis*. Cambridge, UK: Cambridge University Press.

Buiter, Willem H., and Marcus Miller (1983). "Changing the rules: Economic consequences of the Thatcher regime." *Brookings Papers on Economic Activity* 2: 305–79.

Bulow, Jeremy I. (1982). "Durable goods monopolists." *Journal of Political Economy* 90 (April): 314–32.

Bulow, Jeremy I., and Kenneth Rogoff (1988a). "Multilateral negotiations for rescheduling developing country debt: A bargaining-theoretic framework." *International Monetary Fund Staff Papers* 35 (December): 644–57.

Bulow, Jeremy I., and Kenneth Rogoff (1988b). "The buyback boondoggle." *Brookings Papers on Economic Activity* 2: 675–98.

Bulow, Jeremy I., and Kenneth Rogoff (1989a). "A constant recontracting model of sovereign debt." *Journal of Political Economy* 97 (February): 155–78.

Bulow, Jeremy I., and Kenneth Rogoff (1989b). "Sovereign debt: Is to forgive to forget?" *American Economic Review* 79 (March): 43–50.

Bulow, Jeremy I., and Kenneth Rogoff (1990). "Cleaning up third world debt without getting taken to the cleaners." *Journal of Economic Perspectives* 4: 31–42.

Bulow, Jeremy I., and Kenneth Rogoff (1991). "Sovereign debt repurchases: No cure for overhang." *Quarterly Journal of Economics* 106 (November): 1219–35.

Bulow, Jeremy I., Kenneth Rogoff, and Afonso S. Bevilaqua (1992). "Official creditor seniority and burden-sharing in the former Soviet bloc." *Brookings Papers on Economic Activity* 1: 195–234.

Bulow, Jeremy I., Kenneth Rogoff, and Ning Zhu (1994). "Variability and the option value of default under moral hazard." Working paper, World Bank.

Burda, Michael C., and Stefan Gerlach (1992). "Intertemporal prices and the U.S. trade balance." *American Economic Review* 82 (December): 1234–53.

Caballero, Ricardo J. (1991). "Earnings uncertainty and aggregate wealth accumulation." *American Economic Review* 81 (September): 859–71.

Cabellero, Ricardo J., and Eduardo M. R. Engel (1994). "Explaining investment dynamics in U.S. manufacturing: A generalized (S, s) approach." Mimeo, Massachusetts Institute of Technology.

Cagan, Phillip (1956). "The monetary dynamics of hyperinflation." In Milton Friedman, ed., *Studies in the quantity theory of money*. Chicago: University of Chicago Press.

Calvo, Guillermo A. (1978). "On the time inconsistency of optimal policy in a monetary economy." *Econometrica* 46 (November): 1411–28.

Calvo, Guillermo A. (1983). "Staggered prices in a utility-maximizing framework." *Journal of Monetary Economics* 12: 983–98.

Calvo, Guillermo A. (1988). "Servicing the public debt: The role of expectations." *American Economic Review* 78 (September): 647–61.

Calvo, Guillermo A., and Leonardo Leiderman (1992). " Optimal inflation tax under precommitment: Theory and evidence." *American Economic Review* (March): 179–94.

Calvo, Guillermo A., and Maurice Obstfeld (1988). "Optimal time-consistent fiscal policy with finite lifetimes: Analysis and extensions." In Elhanan Helpman, Assaf Razin, and Efraim Sadka, eds., *Economic effects of the government budget*. Cambridge, MA: MIT Press.

Calvo, Guillermo A., and Carlos A. Végh (1993). "Exchange-rate based stabilisation under imperfect credibility." In Helmut Frisch and Andreas Wörgötter, eds., *Open-economy macroeconomics*. London: Macmillan.

Calvo, Guillermo A., and Carlos A. Végh (1996). "From currency substitution to dollarization and beyond: Analytical and policy issues." In Guillermo A. Calvo, ed., *Money, exchange rates, and output*. Cambridge, MA: MIT Press.

Campbell, John Y. (1987). "Does saving anticipate declining labor income? An alternative test of the permanent income hypothesis." *Econometrica* 55 (November): 1249–73.

Campbell, John Y. (1994). "Inspecting the mechanism: An analytical approach to the stochastic growth model." *Journal of Monetary Economics* 33 (June): 463–506.

Campbell, John Y., and Richard H. Clarida (1987). "The dollar and real interest rates: An empirical investigation." *Carnegie-Rochester Conference Series on Public Policy* 27 (Autumn): 103–40.

Campbell, John Y., and John H. Cochrane (1995). "By force of habit: A consumption-based explanation of aggregate stock market behavior." Working paper 4995, National Bureau of Economic Research (January).

Campbell, John Y., and Robert J. Shiller (1987). "Cointegration and tests of present value models." *Journal of Political Economy* 95 (October): 1062–88.

Campillo, Marta, and Jeffrey A. Miron (in press). "Why does inflation differ across countries?" In Christina D. Romer and David H. Romer, eds., *Reducing inflation: Motivation and strategy*. Chicago: University of Chicago Press.

Canova, Fabio, and Morten O. Ravn (1994). "International consumption risk sharing." Discussion paper 1074, Center for Economic Policy Research (December).

Cantor, Richard, and Nelson C. Mark (1988). "The international transmission of real business cycles." *International Economic Review* 29 (August): 493–507.

Canzoneri, Matthew B. (1985). "Monetary policy games and the role of private information." *American Economic Review* 75 (December): 1056–70.

Canzoneri, Matthew B., and Dale W. Henderson (1991). *Monetary policy in interdependent economies*. Cambridge, MA: MIT Press.

Canzoneri, Matthew B., Dale W. Henderson, and Kenneth Rogoff (1983). "The information content of the interest rate and optimal monetary policy." *Quarterly Journal of Economics* 98 (November): 545–66.

Canzoneri, Matthew B., and Carol Ann Rogers (1990). "Is Europe an optimal currency area?" *American Economic Review* 80 (June): 419–33.

Carlton, Dennis W. (1986). "The rigidity of prices." *American Economic Review* 76 (September): 637–58.

Carroll, Christopher D. (1992). "The buffer-stock theory of saving: Some macroeconomic evidence." *Brookings Papers on Economic Activity* 2: 61–156.

Carroll, Christopher D., and Lawrence H. Summers (1991). "Consumption growth parallels income growth: Some new evidence." In B. Douglas Bernheim and John B. Shoven, eds., *National saving and economic performance*. Chicago: University of Chicago Press.

Casella, Alessandra (1989). "Testing for rational bubbles with exogenous or endogenous fundamentals: The German hyperinflation once more." *Journal of Monetary Economics* 24 (July): 109–22.

Casella, Alessandra (1992). "Participation in a currency union." *American Economic Review* 82 (September): 847–63.

Cass, David (1965). "Optimum growth in an aggregative model of capital accumulation." *Review of Economic Studies* 32 (July): 233–40.

Cass, David (1972). "On capital overaccumulation in the aggregative, neoclassical model of economic growth: A complete characterization." *Journal of Economic Theory* 4 (April): 200–223.

Chinn, Menzie D., and Richard A. Meese (1995). "Banking on currency forecasts: How predictable is change in money?" *Journal of International Economics* 38 (February): 161–78.

Choudhri, Ehsan U., and Levis A. Kochin (1980). "The exchange rate and the international transmission of business cycles: Some evidence from the Great Depression." *Journal of Money, Credit and Banking* 12: 565–74.

Clarida, Richard H. (1990). "International lending and borrowing in a stochastic stationary equilibrium." *International Economic Review* 31 (August): 543–58.

Clarida, Richard H. (1993). "International capital mobility and growth." Working paper 4506, National Bureau of Economic Research (October).

Clarida, Richard, and Jordi Gali (1994). "Sources of real exchange rate fluctuations: How important are nominal shocks?" *Carnegie-Rochester Conference Series on Public Policy* 41 (December): 1–56.

Clower, Robert W. (1967). "A reconsideration of the microfoundations of monetary theory." *Western Economic Journal* 6 (December): 1–8.

Cochrane, John H. (1991). "A simple test of consumption insurance." *Journal of Political Economy* 99 (October): 957–76.

Cogley, Timothy, and James M. Nason (1995). "Output dynamics in real-business-cycle models." *American Economic Review* 85 (June): 492–511.

Cohen, Daniel M. (1985). "How to evaluate the solvency of an indebted nation." *Economic Policy* 1 (November): 140–67.

Cohen, Daniel M. (1990). "Debt relief: Implications of secondary market discounts and debt overhang." *World Bank Economic Review* 4 (January): 45–53.

Cohen, Daniel M. (1993). "Low investment and large LDC debt in the 1980's." *American Economic Review* 83 (June): 437–49.

Cohen, Daniel M., and Jeffrey D. Sachs (1986). "Growth and external debt under risk of debt repudiation." *European Economic Review* 30 (June): 529–60.

Cole, Harold L. (1988). "Financial structure and international trade." *International Economic Review* 29 (May): 237–59.

Cole, Harold L., and Patrick J. Kehoe (1995). "The role of institutions in reputation models of sovereign debt." *Journal of Monetary Economics* 35 (February): 45–64.

Cole, Harold L., and Patrick J. Kehoe (1996). "Reputation spillover across relationships: Reviving reputation models of debt." Working paper 5486, National Bureau of Economic Research (March).

Cole, Harold L., and Timothy J. Kehoe (in press). "A self-fulfilling model of Mexico's 1994–95 debt crisis." *Journal of International Economics*.

Cole, Harold L., and Maurice Obstfeld (1991). "Commodity trade and international risk sharing: How much do financial markets matter?" *Journal of Monetary Economics* 28 (August): 3–24.

Commission of the European Communities (1990). *One market, one money.* In *European Economy*, special issue. European Commission: Brussels.

Constantinides, George (1990). "Habit formation: A resolution of the equity premium puzzle." *Journal of Political Economy* 98 (June): 519–43.

Cooper, Richard N. (1982). "The gold standard: Historical facts and future prospects." *Brookings Papers on Economic Activity* 1: 1–45.

Cooper, Russell, and Andrew John (1988). "Coordinating coordination failures in Keynesian models." *Quarterly Journal of Economics* 103 (August): 441–63.

Crucini, Mario (1992). "International risk sharing: A simple comparative test." Mimeo, Ohio State University.

Cukierman, Alex, Sebastian Edwards, and Guido Tabellini (1992). "Seignorage and political instability." *American Economic Review* 82 (June): 537–55.

Cukierman, Alex, Steven B. Webb, and Bilin Neyapti (1992). "Measuring the independence of central banks and its effect on policy outcomes." *World Bank Economic Review* 6 (September): 353–98.

Cumby, Robert E. (1988). "Is it risk? Explaining deviations from uncovered interest parity." *Journal of Monetary Economics* 22 (September): 279–300.

Dean, Edwin R., and Mark K. Sherwood (1994). "Manufacturing costs, productivity, and competitiveness, 1979–93." *Monthly Labor Review* (October): 3–16.

Deardorff, Alan V. (1980). "The general validity of the law of comparative advantage." *Journal of Political Economy* 88 (October): 941–57.

Deaton, Angus (1992). *Understanding consumption.* Oxford, UK: Clarendon Press.

Deaton, Angus, and John Muellbauer (1980). *Economics and consumer behavior.* Cambridge, UK: Cambridge University Press.

Deaton, Angus, and Christina Paxson (1994). "Intertemporal choice and inequality." *Journal of Political Economy* 102 (June): 437–67.

Debreu, Gerard (1959). *Theory of value.* New Haven, CT: Yale University Press.

De Gregorio, José, Alberto Giovannini, and Holger C. Wolf (1994). "International evidence on tradables and nontradables inflation." *European Economic Review* 38 (June): 1225–44.

De Long, J. Bradford (1988). "Productivity growth, convergence, and welfare: Comment." *American Economic Review* 78 (December): 1139–54.

Detragiache, Enrica (1994). "Sensible buybacks of sovereign debt." *Journal of Development Economics* 43 (April): 317–33.

Devereux, Michael, and Fabio Schiantarelli (1990). "Investment, financial factors, and cash flow: Evidence from U.K. panel data." In R. Glenn Hubbard, ed., *Asymmetric information, corporate finance, and investment.* Chicago: University of Chicago Press.

Devereux, Michael B., Allan Gregory, and Gregor W. Smith (1992). "Realistic cross-country consumption correlations in a two-country, equilibrium, business-cycle model." *Journal of International Money and Finance* 11 (February): 3–16.

Devereux, Michael B., and Gregor W. Smith (1994). "International risk sharing and economic growth." *International Economic Review* 35 (August): 535–50.

Diamond, Peter A. (1965). "National debt in a neoclassical growth model." *American Economic Review* 55 (December): 1126–50.

Díaz-Alejandro, Carlos F. (1983). "Stories of the 1930s for the 1980s." In Pedro Aspe Armella, Rudiger Dornbusch, and Maurice Obstfeld, eds., *Financial policies and the world capital market: The problem of Latin American countries.* Chicago: University of Chicago Press.

Díaz-Alejandro, Carlos F. (1985). "Good-bye financial repression, hello financial crash." *Journal of Development Economics* 19 (September/October): 1–24.

Diwan, Ishac, and Dani Rodrik (1992). *External debt, adjustment, and burden sharing: A unified framework.* Princeton Studies in International Finance 73 (November).

Dixit, Avinash K. (1989). "Hysteresis, import penetration, and exchange rate pass-through," *Quarterly Journal of Economics* 104 (May): 205–28.

Dixit, Avinash K. (1990). *Optimization in economic theory,* 2nd ed. Oxford, UK: Oxford University Press.

Dixit, Avinash K., and Victor Norman (1980). *Theory of international trade: A dual, general equilibrium approach.* Welwyn, UK: James Nisbet and Cambridge University Press.

Dominguez, Kathryn M., and Jeffrey A. Frankel (1993). "Does foreign exchange intervention matter? The portfolio effect" *American Economic Review* 83 (December): 1356–69.

Dooley, Michael P. (1995). "A retrospective on the debt crisis." In Peter B. Kenen, ed., *Understanding interdependence: The macroeconomics of the open economy.* Princeton, NJ: Princeton University Press.

Dornbusch, Rudiger (1976). "Expectations and exchange rate dynamics." *Journal of Political Economy* 84 (December): 1161–76.

Dornbusch, Rudiger (1983). "Real interest rates, home goods, and optimal external borrowing." *Journal of Political Economy* 91 (February): 141–53.

Dornbusch, Rudiger (1987). "Exchange rates and prices." *American Economic Review* 77 (March): 93–106.

Dornbusch, Rudiger, Stanley Fischer, and Paul A. Samuelson (1977). "Comparative advantage, trade, and payments in a Ricardian model with a continuum of goods." *American Economic Review* 67 (December): 823–39.

Dowrick, Steve, and Duc-Tho Nguyen (1989). "OECD comparative economic growth 1950–1985: Catch-up and convergence." *American Economic Review* 79 (December): 1010–30.

Drazen, Allan (1978). "Government debt, human capital, and bequests in a life-cycle model." *Journal of Political Economy* 86 (June): 505–16.

Driffill, John, Grayham E. Mizon, and Alastair Ulph (1990). "Costs of inflation." In Benjamin M. Friedman and Frank H. Hahn, eds., *Handbook of monetary economics*, vol. 2. Amsterdam: North-Holland.

Duffie, Darrell, and Chi-fu Huang (1985). "Implementing Arrow-Debreu equilibria by continuous trading of few long-lived securities." *Econometrica* 53 (November): 1337–56.

Dufresne, Pierre Collin, and Wei Shi (1995). "Asset prices, interest rates, and exchange rates in an international monetary economy: A general equilibrium model." Mimeo, HEC School of Management and Bank of America.

Dumas, Bernard (1994). "Partial equilibrium versus general equilibrium models of the international capital market." In Frederick van der Ploeg, ed., *The handbook of international macroeconomics*. Oxford, UK: Basil Blackwell.

Eaton, Jonathan (1988). "Foreign-owned land." *American Economic Review* 78 (March): 76–88.

Eaton, Jonathan, and Raquel Fernandez (1995). "Sovereign debt." In Gene M. Grossman and Kenneth Rogoff, eds., *Handbook of international economics*, vol. 3. Amsterdam: North Holland.

Eaton, Jonathan, and Mark Gersovitz (1981). "Debt with potential repudiation: Theory and estimation." *Review of Economic Studies* 48 (April): 289–309.

Edison, Hali J. (1993). *The effectiveness of central-bank intervention: A survey of the literature after 1982*. Princeton Special Papers in International Economics 18 (July).

Edison, Hali J., and B. Dianne Pauls (1993). "A re-assessment of the relationship between real exchange rates and real interest rates: 1974–1990." *Journal of Monetary Economics* 31 (April): 165–67.

Edwards, Sebastian (1989). *Real exchange rates, devaluation, and adjustment*. Cambridge, MA: MIT Press.

Effinger, Sylvester C. W., M. Hoeberichts, and E. Schaling (1995). "Optimal commitment in the Rogoff (1985) model: A graphical and closed form solution." Tilburg University, Center for Economic Research discussion paper.

Eichenbaum, Martin, and Charles Evans (1995). "Some empirical evidence on the effects of monetary policy shocks on real exchange rates." *Quarterly Journal of Economics* 110 (November): 975–1009.

Eichengreen, Barry (1991). "Historical research on international lending and debt." *Journal of Economic Perspectives* 5 (Spring): 149–69.

Eichengreen, Barry (1992). *Golden fetters*. London: Oxford University Press.

Eichengreen, Barry (1994). *International monetary arrangements for the 21st century*. Washington, DC: Brookings Institution.

Eichengreen, Barry (1995). "The endogeneity of exchange-rate regimes." In Peter B. Kenen, ed., *Understanding interdependence: The macroeconomics of the open economy*. Princeton, NJ: Princeton University Press.

Eichengreen, Barry, and Jeffrey D. Sachs (1985). "Exchange rates and economic recovery in the 1930s." *Journal of Economic History* 45 (December): 925–46.

Eichengreen, Barry, and Charles Wyplosz (1993). "The unstable EMS." *Brookings Papers on Economic Activity* 1: 51–143.

Ekern, Steinar, and Robert Wilson (1974). "On the theory of the firm in an economy with incomplete markets." *Bell Journal of Economics and Management Science* 5 (Spring): 171–84.

Eldor, Rafael, David Pines, and Abba Schwartz (1988). "Home asset preference and productivity shocks." *Journal of International Economics* 25 (August): 165–76.

Engel, Charles M. (1984). "Testing for the absence of expected real profits from forward market speculation." *Journal of International Economics* 17 (November): 299–308.

Engel, Charles M. (1992). "On the foreign exchange risk premium in a general equilibrium model." *Journal of International Economics* 32 (May): 305–19.

Engel, Charles M. (1993). "Is real exchange rate variability caused by relative price changes? An empirical investigation." *Journal of Monetary Economics* 32 (August): 35–50.

Engel, Charles M. (in press). "The forward discount anomaly and the risk premium: A survey of recent evidence." *Journal of Empirical Finance.*

Engel, Charles, and John H. Rogers (1995). "Regional patterns in the law of one price: The role of geography versus currencies." Working paper 5395, National Bureau of Economic Research (December).

Epstein, Larry G., and Stanley E. Zin (1989). "Substitution, risk aversion, and the temporal behavior of consumption and asset returns: A theoretical framework." *Econometrica* 57 (July): 937–69.

Ethier, Wilfred J. (1984). "Higher dimensional issues in trade theory." In Ronald W. Jones and Peter B. Kenen, eds., *Handbook of international economics*, vol. 1. Amsterdam: North Holland.

Fama, Eugene (1984). "Forward and spot exchange rates." *Journal of Monetary Economics* 14 (November): 319–38.

Fazzari, Steven M., R. Glenn Hubbard, and Bruce C. Peterson (1988). "Financing constraints and corporate investment." *Brookings Papers on Economic Activity* 1: 141–95.

Feeney, JoAnne, and Ronald W. Jones (1994). "Risk aversion and international markets: Does asset trade smooth real income?" *Review of International Economics* 2 (February): 13–26.

Feenstra, Robert C. (1986). "Functional equivalence between liquidity costs and the utility of money." *Journal of Monetary Economics* 17 (March): 271–91.

Feenstra, Robert C. (1995). "Estimating the effects of trade policy." In Gene M. Grossman and Kenneth Rogoff, eds., *Handbook of international economics*, vol. 3. Amsterdam: North Holland.

Feis, Herbert (1930). *Europe the world's banker, 1870–1914: An account of European foreign investment and the connection of world finance with diplomacy before the war.* New Haven, CT: Yale University Press.

Feldstein, Martin, and Charles Horioka (1980). "Domestic savings and international capital flows." *Economic Journal* 90 (June): 314–29.

Fischer, Stanley (1982). "Seigniorage and the case for a national money." *Journal of Political Economy* 90 (April): 295–313.

Fischer, Stanley (1990). "Rules versus discretion in monetary policy." In Benjamin M. Friedman and Frank H. Hahn, eds., *Handbook of monetary economics*, vol. 2. Amsterdam: North Holland.

Fisher, Irving (1930). *The theory of interest.* New York: Macmillan.

Fishlow, Albert (1985). "Lessons from the past: Capital markets during the 19th century and interwar period." *International Organization* 39 (Summer): 383–439.

Flandreau, Marc (1995). "The burden of intervention: Externalities in multilateral exchange rate arrangements." Mimeo, Centre Nationale de la Recherche Scientifique, Paris.

Fleming, J. Marcus (1962). "Domestic financial policies under fixed and under floating exchange rates." *International Monetary Fund Staff Papers* 9 (November): 369–79.

Flood, Robert P., and Peter M. Garber (1980). "Market fundamentals versus price level bubbles: The first tests." *Journal of Political Economy* 88 (August): 745–70.

Flood, Robert P., and Peter M. Garber (1984). "Collapsing exchange rate regimes: Some linear examples." *Journal of International Economics* 17 (August): 1–13.

Flood, Robert P., and Peter M. Garber (1991). "The linkage between speculative attack and target zone models of exchange rates." *Quarterly Journal of Economics* 106 (November): 1367–72.

Flood, Robert P., and Peter Isard (1989). "Monetary policy strategies." *International Monetary Fund Staff Papers* 36 (September): 612–32.

Flood, Robert P., and Andrew K. Rose (1995). "Fixing exchange rates: A virtual quest for fundamentals." *Journal of Monetary Economics* 36 (August): 3–37.

Foley, Duncan K., and Miguel Sidrauski (1970). "Portfolio choice, investment and growth." *American Economic Review* 60 (March): 44–63.

Folkerts-Landau, David, and Morris Goldstein (1994). *International capital markets: developments, prospects, and policy issues.* Washington, DC: International Monetary Fund.

Frankel, Jeffrey A. (1979). "On the mark: A theory of floating exchange rates based on real interest differentials." *American Economic Review* 69 (September): 610–22.

Frankel, Jeffrey A. (1982). "In search of the exchange risk premium: A six-currency test assuming mean-variance optimization." *Journal of International Money and Finance* 1 (April): 255–74.

Frankel, Jeffrey A., and Andrew K. Rose (1995). "Empirical research on nominal exchange rates." In Gene M. Grossman and Kenneth Rogoff, eds. *Handbook of international economics,* vol. 3. Amsterdam: North Holland.

French, Kenneth R., and James M. Poterba (1991). "Investor diversification and international equity markets." *American Economic Review* 81 (May): 222–26.

Frenkel, Jacob A. (1976). "A monetary approach to the exchange rate: Doctrinal aspects and empirical evidence." *Scandinavian Journal of Economics* 78 (May): 200–224.

Frenkel, Jacob A., and Assaf Razin (1980). "Stochastic prices and tests of efficiency of foreign exchange markets." *Economics Letters* 6: 165–70.

Frenkel, Jacob A., and Assaf Razin (1992). *Fiscal policies and the world economy,* 2nd ed. Cambridge, MA: MIT Press.

Fried, Joel (1980). "The intergenerational distribution of the gains from technical change and from international trade." *Canadian Journal of Economics* 13 (February): 65–81.

Fried, Joel, and Peter Howitt (1988). "Fiscal deficits, international trade and welfare." *Journal of International Economics* 24 (February): 1–22.

Friedman, Milton (1957). *A theory of the consumption function.* Princeton, NJ: Princeton University Press.

Friedman, Milton, and Anna J. Schwartz (1963). *A monetary history of the United States, 1867–1960.* Princeton, NJ: Princeton University Press.

Froot, Kenneth A., and Jeffrey A. Frankel (1990). "Forward discount bias: Is it an exchange risk premium?" *Quarterly Journal of Economics* 104 (February): 139–61.

Froot, Kenneth A., Michael Kim, and Kenneth Rogoff (1995). "The law of one price over seven hundred years." Working paper 5132, National Bureau of Research (May).

Froot, Kenneth A., and Paul Klemperer (1989). "Exchange rate pass-through when market share matters." *American Economic Review* 79 (September): 637–54.

Froot, Kenneth A., and Maurice Obstfeld (1991). "Exchange-rate dynamics under stochastic regime shifts: A unified approach." *Journal of International Economics* 31 (November): 203–29.

Froot, Kenneth A., and Kenneth Rogoff (1991). "The EMS, the EMU, and the transition to a common currency." *NBER Macroeconomics Annual* 6: 269–317.

Froot, Kenneth A., and Kenneth Rogoff (1995). "Perspectives on PPP and long-run real exchange rates." In Gene M. Grossman and Kenneth Rogoff, eds., *Handbook of international economics,* vol. 3. Amsterdam: North Holland.

Froot, Kenneth A., and Richard Thaler (1990). "Anomalies: Foreign exchange." *Journal of Economic Perspectives* 4 (Summer): 179–92.

Gale, Douglas (1983). *Money in disequilibrium.* New York: Cambridge University Press.

Gale, William G., and John Karl Scholz (1994). "Intergenerational transfers and the accumulation of wealth." *Journal of Economic Perspectives* 8 (Fall): 145–60.

Garber, Peter M. (1990). "Famous first bubbles." *Journal of Economic Perspectives* 4 (Spring): 35–54.

Garber, Peter M., and Lars E. O. Svensson (1995). "The operation and collapse of fixed exchange rate regimes." In Gene M. Grossman and Kenneth Rogoff, eds., *Handbook of international economics,* vol. 3. Amsterdam: North Holland.

Gavin, Michael (1990). "Structural adjustment to a terms of trade disturbance: The role of relative prices." *Journal of International Economics* 28 (May): 217–43.

Geanakoplos, John, and Heracles Polemarchakis (1986). "Walrasian indeterminacy and Keynesian macroeconomics." *Review of Economic Studies* 53 (October): 755–79.

Gertler, Mark (1988). "Financial structure and aggregate economic activity: An overview." *Journal of Money, Credit and Banking* 20 (August, Part 2): 559–88.

Gertler, Mark, and Kenneth Rogoff (1990). "North-South lending and endogenous capital-market inefficiencies." *Journal of Monetary Economics* 26 (October): 245–66.

Gertler, Mark, and Simon Gilchrist (1994). "Monetary policy, business cycles, and the behavior of small manufacturing firms." *Quarterly Journal of Economics* 109 (May): 309–40.

Ghosh, Atish R. (1995). "Capital mobility amongst the major industrialized countries: Too little or too much?" *Economic Journal* 105 (January): 107–28.

Ghosh, Atish R., and Jonathan D. Ostry (1995). "The current account in developing countries: A perspective from the consumption-smoothing approach." *World Bank Economic Review* 9 (May): 305–33.

Ghosh, Atish R., and Paolo Pesenti (1994). "International portfolio diversification, human wealth and consumption growth: Some puzzles and interpretations." Discussion paper TI94-107, Tinbergen Institute.

Ghosh, Atish R., and Holger Wolf (1994). "Pricing in international markets: Lessons from the *Economist*." Working paper 4806, National Bureau of Economic Research.

Giavazzi, Francesco, and Marco Pagano (1988). "The advantage of tying one's hands: EMS discipline and central bank credibility." *European Economic Review* 32 (June): 1055–82.

Gilbert, Milton, and Irving B. Kravis (1954). *An international comparison of national products and purchasing power of currencies: A study of the United States, the United Kingdom, France, Germany, and Italy*. Paris: Organization for European Economic Cooperation.

Gilchrist, Simon, and Charles Himmelberg (1995). "Evidence on the role of cash flow for investment." *Journal of Monetary Economics* 36 (December): 541–72.

Giovannini, Alberto (1988). "Exchange rates and traded goods prices." *Journal of International Economics* 24 (February): 45–68.

Giovannini, Alberto, and Bart Turtelboom (1994). "Currency substitution." In Frederick van der Ploeg, ed., *The handbook of international macroeconomics*. Oxford, UK: Basil Blackwell.

Girton, Lance, and Don Roper (1981). "Theory and implications of currency substitution." *Journal of Money, Credit and Banking* 13 (February): 12–30.

Glick, Reuven, and Kenneth Rogoff (1995). "Global versus country-specific productivity shocks and the current account." *Journal of Monetary Economics* 35 (February): 159–92.

Goldstein, Morris (1995). *The exchange rate system and the IMF: A modest agenda*. Washington, DC: Institute for International Economics.

Golub, Stephen S. (1994). "International diversification of social and private risk: The U.S. and Japan." *Japan and the World Economy* 6: 263–84.

Golub, Stephen S., and Chang-Tai Hsieh (1995). "The classical theory of comparative advantage revisited." Mimeo, Swarthmore College and University of California, Berkeley.

Goschen, George J. (1861). *The theory of the foreign exchanges*. London: Effingham Wilson.

Gourinchas, Pierre-Olivier, and Jonathan A. Parker (1995). "Consumption over the lifecycle." Mimeo, Massachusetts Institute of Technology.

Grauer, Robert R., and Nils H. Hakansson (1987). "Gains from international diversification: 1968–1985 returns on portfolios of stocks and bonds." *Journal of Finance* 42 (July): 721–39.

Green, Edward J. (1987). "Lending and the smoothing of uninsurable income." In Edward C. Prescott and Neil Wallace, eds., *Contractual arrangements for intertemporal trade*. Minneapolis: University of Minnesota Press.

Green, Edward J., and Soo-Nam Oh (1991). "Contracts, constraints and consumption." *Review of Economic Studies* 58 (October): 883–99.

Greenspan, Alan (1989). "The economic value of ideas: Looking to the next century." *Japan Society of New York Newsletter* 36 (July).

Greenwood, Jeremy, and Stephen D. Williamson (1989). "International financial intermediation and aggregate fluctuations under alternative exchange-rate regimes." *Journal of Monetary Economics* 23 (May): 401–31.

Grilli, Vittorio, Donato Masciandaro, and Guido Tabellini (1991). "Political and monetary institutions and public financial policies in the industrial countries." *Economic Policy* 13 (October): 341–92.

Grilli, Vittorio, and Nouriel Roubini (1992). "Liquidity and exchange rates." *Journal of International Economics* 32 (May): 339–52.

Grossman, Gene M., and Elhanan Helpman (1990). "Trade, innovation and growth." *American Economic Review* 80 (May): 86–91.

Grossman, Gene M., and Elhanan Helpman (1991). *Innovation and growth in the global economy.* Cambridge, MA: MIT Press.

Grossman, Gene M., and Elhanan Helpman (1994). "Endogenous innovation in the theory of growth." *Journal of Economic Perspectives* 8 (Winter): 23–44.

Grossman, Gene M., and Kenneth Rogoff (1995). "Introduction." In Gene M. Grossman and Kenneth Rogoff, eds., *Handbook of international economics*, vol. 3. Amsterdam: North Holland.

Grossman, Herschel I., and John B. Van Huyck (1986). "Seigniorage, inflation, and reputation." *Journal of Monetary Economics* 18 (July): 21–31.

Grossman, Herschel I., and John B. Van Huyck (1988). "Sovereign debt as a contingent claim: Excusable default, repudiation, and reputation." *American Economic Review* 78 (December): 1088–97.

Grossman, Sanford J., and Oliver D. Hart (1980). "Takeover bids, the free-rider problem, and the theory of the corporation." *Bell Journal of Economics* 11 (Spring): 42–64.

Guiso, Luigi, Tullio Japelli, and Daniele Terlizzese (1992). "Saving and capital market imperfections: The Italian experience." In Erkki Koskela and Jouko Paunio, eds., *Savings behavior: Theory, international evidence, and policy implications.* Oxford, UK: Blackwell.

Hall, Robert E. (1978). "Stochastic implications of the life cycle-permanent income hypothesis: Theory and evidence." *Journal of Political Economy* 86 (December): 971–87.

Hall, Robert E. (1986). "Market structure and macroeconomic fluctuations." *Brookings Papers on Economic Activity* 2: 285–338.

Hamada, Koichi (1974). "Alternative exchange rate systems and the interdependence of monetary policies." In Robert Z. Aliber, ed., *National monetary policies and the international financial system.* Chicago: University of Chicago Press.

Hamada, Koichi (1985). *The political economy of international monetary interdependence.* Cambridge, MA: MIT Press.

Hamada, Koichi (1986). "Strategic aspects of international fiscal interdependence." *Economic Studies Quarterly* 37 (June): 165–80.

Hamilton, James D. (1988). "The role of the gold standard in propagating the Great Depression." *Contemporary Policy Issues* 6: 67–89.

Hansen, Lars Peter, and James J. Heckman (1996). "The empirical foundations of calibration." *Journal of Economic Perspectives* 10 (Winter): 87–104.

Hansen, Lars Peter, and Robert J. Hodrick (1980). "Forward exchange rates as optimal predictors of future spot rates: An econometric analysis." *Journal of Political Economy* 88 (October): 829–53.

Hansen, Lars Peter, and Ravi Jagannathan (1991). "Implications of security market data for models of dynamic economies." *Journal of Political Economy* 99 (April): 225–62.

Harberger, Arnold C. (1980). "Vignettes on the world capital market." *American Economic Review* 70 (May): 331–37.

Harris, Milton, and Robert M. Townsend (1981). "Resource allocation under asymmetric information." *Econometrica* 49 (January): 33–64.

Harrod, Roy F. (1933). *International economics.* London: James Nisbet and Cambridge University Press.

Hau, Harald (1996). "Exchange rate determination: The role of factor price rigidities and market segmentation." Mimeo, Princeton University.

Hayashi, Fumio (1982). "Tobin's marginal q and average q: A neoclassical interpretation." *Econometrica* 50 (January): 213–24.

Hayashi, Fumio (1987). "Tests for liquidity constraints: A critical survey and some new observations." In Truman F. Bewley, ed., *Advances in econometrics: Fifth world congress*, vol. 2. Cambridge, UK: Cambridge University Press.

He, Hua, and David M. Modest (1995). "Market frictions and consumption-based asset pricing." *Journal of Political Economy* 103 (February): 94–117.

Heaton, John, and Deborah Lucas (1995). "The importance of investor heterogeneity and financial market imperfections for the behavior of asset prices." *Carnegie-Rochester Conference Series on Public Policy* 42 (June): 1–32.

Heckman, James J. (1993). "What has been learned about labor supply in the past twenty years?" *American Economic Review* 83 (May): 116–21.

Heichelheim, Fritz M. (1958). *An ancient economic history,* vol. 1. Leiden: A.W. Sijthoff's Uitgevers-maatschappij N.V.

Helkie, William L., and Peter Hooper (1988). "The U.S. external deficit in the 1980s." In Ralph C. Bryant, Dale Henderson, Gerald Holtham, Peter Hooper, and Steven Symansky, eds., *Macroeconomics for interdependent economies.*" Washington, DC: Brookings Institution.

Helpman, Elhanan (1981). "An exploration of the theory of exchange rate regimes." *Journal of Political Economy* 89 (October): 865–90.

Helpman, Elhanan (1989). "Voluntary debt reduction: Incentives and welfare." In Jacob A. Frenkel, Michael P. Dooley, and Peter Wickham, eds., *Analytical issues in debt*. Washington, DC: International Monetary Fund.

Helpman, Elhanan, and Assaf Razin (1984). "The role of saving and investment in exchange rate determination under alternative monetary mechanisms." *Journal of Monetary Economics* 13 (May): 307–26.

Herrendorf, Berthold, and Ben Lockwood (1996). "Rogoff's 'conservative' central banker restored." Discussion paper 1386, Centre for Economic Policy Research (April).

Hibbs, Douglas (1977). "Political parties and macroeconomic policy." *American Political Science Review* 71 (December): 1467–87.

Hicks, John R. (1937). "Mr. Keynes and the 'classics': A suggested interpretation." *Econometrica* 5 (April): 147–59.

Hodgson, Godfrey (1984). *Lloyd's of London*. New York: Viking.

Hodrick, Robert J. (1987). *The empirical evidence on the efficiency of forward and futures foreign exchange markets*. Chur, Switzerland: Harwood Academic.

Hoshi, Takeo, Anil Kashyap, and David Scharfstein (1991). "Corporate structure, liquidity, and investment: Evidence from Japanese industrial groups." *Quarterly Journal of Economics* 106 (February): 33–60.

Hubbard, R. Glenn, Jonathan Skinner, and Stephen P. Zeldes (1994). "The importance of precautionary motives in explaining individual and aggregate saving." *Carnegie-Rochester Conference Series on Public Policy* 40 (June): 59–125.

Ingersoll, Jonathan E., Jr. (1987). *Theory of financial decision making*. Totowa, NJ: Rowman & Littlefield.

Isard, Peter (1977). "How far can we push the law of one price?" *American Economic Review* 67 (December): 942–48.

Isard, Peter (1995). *Exchange rate economics*. Cambridge, UK: Cambridge University Press.

Jappelli, Tullio, and Marco Pagano (1989). "Consumption and capital market imperfections: An international comparison." *American Economic Review* 79 (December): 1088–1105.

Jeanne, Olivier (1995). "Models of currency crises: A tentative synthesis." Mimeo, ENPC-CERAS, Paris.

Johnson, Harry G. (1955). "Economic expansion and international trade." *Manchester School of Economic and Social Studies* 23 (May): 95–112.

Jones, Larry E., and Rodolfo E. Manuelli (1990). "A convex model of equilibrium growth: Theory and policy implications." *Journal of Political Economy* 98 (October): 1008–38.

Jones, Ronald W. (1961). "Stability conditions in international trade: A general equilibrium analysis." *International Economic Review* 2 (May): 199–209.

Jørgensen, Bjørn N., and Hans Ole Æ. Mikkelsen (1996). "An arbitrage free trilateral target zone model." *Journal of International Money and Finance* 15 (February): 117–34.

Judd, Kenneth L. (1985). "On the performance of patents." *Econometrica* 53 (May): 567–85.

Kamin, Steven B., and Neil R. Ericsson (1993). "Dollarization in Argentina." International Finance Discussion Papers 460. Washington, DC: Board of Governors of the Federal Reserve System.

Kandel, Shmuel, and Robert F. Stambaugh (1991). "Asset returns and intertemporal preferences." *Journal of Monetary Economics* 27 (February): 39–71.

Kang, Jun-Koo, and René M. Stulz (1995). "Why is there a home bias? An analysis of foreign portfolio equity ownership in Japan." Working paper 5166, National Bureau of Economic Research (July).

Kareken, John, and Neil Wallace (1981). "The indeterminacy of equilibrium exchange rates." *Quarterly Journal of Economics* 96 (May): 207–22.

Kasa, Kenneth (1992). "Adjustment costs and pricing to market: Theory and evidence." *Journal of International Economics* 32 (February): 1–30.

Kashyap, Anil K. (1995). "Sticky prices: New evidence from retail catalogs." *Quarterly Journal of Economics* 110 (February): 245–74.

Kehoe, Patrick J. (1987). "Coordination of fiscal policies in a world economy." *Journal of Monetary Economics* 19 (May): 349–76.

Kenen, Peter B. (1969). "The theory of optimum currency areas: An eclectic view." In Robert A. Mundell and Alexander K. Swoboda, eds., *Problems of the international economy*. Chicago: University of Chicago Press.

Kenen, Peter B. (1985). "Macroeconomic theory and policy: How the closed economy was opened." In Ronald W. Jones and Peter B. Kenen, eds., *Handbook of international economics,* vol. 2. Amsterdam: North Holland.

Keynes, John Maynard (1929). "The German transfer problem"; "The reparation problem: A discussion. II. A rejoinder"; "Views on the transfer problem. III. A reply." *Economic Journal* 39 (March): 1–7; (June): 172–8; (September): 404–8.

Keynes, John Maynard (1930). *A treatise on money*. Vol. 2: *The applied theory of money*. London: Macmillan.

Keynes, John Maynard (1936). *The general theory of employment interest and money*. London: Macmillan.

Khan, Mohsin S., and Abbas Mirakhor, eds. (1987). *Theoretical studies in Islamic banking and finance*. Houston: Institute for Research and Islamic Studies.

Kindleberger, Charles P. (1978). *Manias, panics and crashes*. New York: Basic Books.

King, Mervyn A., and Don Fullerton, eds. (1984). *The taxation of income from capital: A comparative study of the United States, the United Kingdom, Sweden, and West Germany*. Chicago: University of Chicago Press.

King, Robert G., Charles I. Plosser, and Sergio Rebelo (1988a). "Production, growth and business cycles: I. The basic neoclassical model." *Journal of Monetary Economics* (March/May): 195–232.

King, Robert G., Charles I. Plosser, and Sergio Rebelo (1988b). "Production, growth and business cycles: II. New directions." *Journal of Monetary Economics* (March/May): 309–41.

Kirman, Alan P. (1992). "Whom or what does the representative individual represent?" *Journal of Economic Perspectives* 6 (Spring): 117–36.

Kiyotaki, Nobuhiro, and John Moore (1995). "Credit cycles." Working paper 5083, National Bureau of Economic Research (April).

Kiyotaki, Nobuhiro, and Randall Wright (1989). "On money as a medium of exchange." *Journal of Political Economy* 97 (August): 927–54.

Kletzer, Kenneth M. (1989). "Sovereign debt renegotiation under asymmetric information." In Jacob A. Frankel, Michael P. Dooley, and Peter Wickham, eds. *Analytical issues in debt*. Washington, DC: International Monetary Fund.

Kletzer, Kenneth M. (1994). "Sovereign immunity and international lending." In Frederick van der Ploeg, ed., *The handbook of international macroeconomics*. Oxford, UK: Basil Blackwell.

Knetter, Michael M. (1989). "Price discrimination by U.S. and German exporters." *American Economic Review* 79 (March): 198–210.

Knetter, Michael M. (1993). "International comparisons of pricing to market behavior." *American Economic Review* 83 (June): 473–86.

Kollmann, Robert (1995). "Consumption, real exchange rates, and the structure of international asset markets." *Journal of International Money and Finance* 14 (April): 191–211.

Koopmans, Tjalling C. (1960). "Stationary ordinal utility and impatience." *Econometrica* 28 (April): 287–309.

Koopmans, Tjalling C. (1965). "On the concept of optimal economic growth." In *The econometric approach to development planning*. Amsterdam: North Holland.

Kornai, Janos (1992). *The socialist system: The political economy of communism*. Princeton, NJ: Princeton University Press.

Kotlikoff, Laurence J. (1988). "Intergenerational transfers and savings." *Journal of Economic Perspectives* 2 (Spring): 41–58.

Kouri, Pentti J. K. (1977). "International investment and interest rate linkages under flexible exchange rates." In Robert Z. Aliber, ed., *The political economy of monetary reform*. London: Macmillan.

Kraay, Aart, and Jaume Ventura (1995). "Trade and fluctuations." Mimeo, Massachusetts Institute of Technology.

Kravis, Irving B., and Robert E. Lipsey (1983). *Toward an explanation of national price levels*. Princeton Studies in International Finance 52 (November).

Kremer, Michael (1993). "Population growth and technological change: One million B.C. to 1990." *Quarterly Journal of Economics* 108 (August): 681–716.

Kreps, David M. (1990). *A course in microeconomic theory*. Princeton: Princeton University Press.

Krugman, Paul R. (1979). "A model of balance of payments crises." *Journal of Money, Credit and Banking* 11 (August): 311–25.

Krugman, Paul R. (1987). "Pricing to market when the exchange rate changes." In Sven Arndt and J. David Richardson, eds., *Real-financial linkages among open economies*. Cambridge, MA: MIT Press.

Krugman, Paul R. (1989). "Market-based debt-reduction schemes." In Jacob A. Frenkel, Michael P. Dooley, and Peter Wickham, eds., *Analytical issues in debt*. Washington, DC: International Monetary Fund.

Krugman, Paul R. (1991a). "Target zones and exchange rate dynamics." *Quarterly Journal of Economics* 116 (August): 669–82.

Krugman, Paul R. (1991b). "Has the adjustment process worked?" In C. Fred Bersgten, ed., *International adjustment and financing*. Washington, DC: Institute for International Economics.

Krugman, Paul R., and Julio Rotemberg (1992). "Speculative attacks on target zones." In Paul Krugman and Marcus Miller, eds., *Exchange rate targets and currency bands*. Cambridge, UK: Cambridge University Press.

Kuhn, Harold W., and Albert W. Tucker (1951). "Nonlinear programming." In Jerzy Neyman, ed., *Proceedings of the second Berkeley symposium on mathematical statistics and probability*. Berkeley: University of California Press.

Kydland, Finn E., and Edward C. Prescott (1977). "Rules rather than discretion: The inconsistency of optimal plans." *Journal of Political Economy* 85 (June): 473–92.

Kydland, Finn E., and Edward C. Prescott (1982). "Time to build and aggregate fluctuations." *Econometrica* 50 (November): 1345–70.

Kydland, Finn E., and Edward C. Prescott (1996). "The computational experiment: An econometric tool." *Journal of Economic Perspectives* 10 (Winter): 69–86.

Laitner, John (1991). "Modeling marital connections among family lines." *Journal of Political Economy* 99 (December): 1123–41.

Lane, Philip R. (1995). "Inflation in open economies." Mimeo, Columbia University.

Leiderman, Leonardo, and Gil Bufman (1995). "Searching for nominal anchors in shock-prone economies in the 1990s: Inflation targets and exchange rate bands." Paper presented at the sixth annual meeting of the International Forum on Latin American Perspectives (November).

Leland, Hayne E. (1968). "Saving and uncertainty: The precautionary demand for saving." *Quarterly Journal of Economics* 82 (August): 465–73.

Leme, Paulo (1984). "Integration of international capital markets." Mimeo, University of Chicago.

Levine, Ross, and David Renelt (1992). "A sensitivity analysis of cross-country growth regressions." *American Economic Review* 82 (September): 942–63.

Lewis, Karen K. (1995). "Puzzles in international financial markets." In Gene Grossman and Kenneth Rogoff, eds., *Handbook of international economics*, vol. 3. Amsterdam: North Holland.

Lewis, Karen K. (1996). "What can explain the apparent lack of international consumption risk sharing?" *Journal of Political Economy* 104 (April): 267–97.

Lindert, Peter H., and Peter J. Morton (1989). "How sovereign debt has worked." In Jeffrey D. Sachs, ed., *Developing country debt and economic performance*, vol. 1. Chicago: University of Chicago Press.

Ljungqvist, Lars (1993). "Economic underdevelopment: The case of a missing market for human capital." *Journal of Development Economics* 40 (April): 219–39.

Lohmann, Susanne (1992). "Optimal commitment in monetary policy: Credibility versus flexibility." *American Economic Review* 82 (March): 273–86.

Long, John B., Jr., and Charles I. Plosser (1983). "Real business cycles." *Journal of Political Economy* 91 (February): 39–69.

Loury, Glenn C. (1981). "Intergenerational transfers and the distribution of earnings." *Econometrica* 49 (July): 843–67.

Lucas, Robert E., Jr. (1976). "Econometric policy evaluation: A critique." In Karl Brunner and Allan H. Meltzer, eds., *The Phillips curve and labor markets*. Amsterdam: North Holland.

Lucas, Robert E., Jr. (1982). "Interest rates and currency prices in a two-country world." *Journal of Monetary Economics* 10 (November): 335–60.

Lucas, Robert E., Jr. (1987). *Models of business cycles*. Oxford, UK: Basil Blackwell.

Lucas, Robert E., Jr. (1988). "On the mechanics of economic development." *Journal of Monetary Economics* 22 (July): 3–42.

Lucas, Robert E., Jr. (1992). "On efficiency and distribution." *Economic Journal* 102 (March): 233–47.

Lucas, Robert E., Jr., and Nancy L. Stokey (1987). "Money and interest in a cash-in-advance economy." *Econometrica* 55 (May): 491–513.

Ludvigson, Sydney (1995). "The macroeconomics effects of government debt in a stochastic growth model." Mimeo, Princeton University.

Lyons, Richard K. (1996). "Foreign exchange volume: Sound and fury signifying nothing?" In Jeffrey A. Frankel, Giampaolo Galli, and Alberto Giovannini, eds., *The microstructure of foreign exchange markets*. Chicago: University of Chicago Press.

MacDougall, G.D.A. (1951). "British and American exports: A study suggested by the theory of comparative costs: Part I." *Economic Journal* 61 (December): 697–724.

MacDougall, G.D.A. (1960). "The benefits and costs of private investment from abroad: A theoretical approach." *Economic Record* 36, Special Issue (March): 13–35.

Mace, Barbara (1991). "Full insurance in the presence of aggregate uncertainty." *Journal of Political Economy* 99 (October): 928–56.

Machina, Mark (1987). "Choice under uncertainty: Problems solved and unsolved." *Journal of Economic Perspectives* 1 (Summer): 121–54.

Machlup, Fritz (1943). *International trade and the national income multiplier*. Philadelphia: Blakiston.

Maddison, Angus (1982). *Phases of capitalist development*. Oxford, UK: Oxford University Press.

Maddison, Angus (1991). *Dynamic forces in capitalist development*. Oxford, UK: Oxford University Press.

Magill, Michael, and Martine Quinzii (1996). *Theory of incomplete markets*, vol. 1. Cambridge, MA: MIT Press.

Mankiw, N. Gregory (1985). "Small menu costs and large business cycles: A macroeconomic model of monopoly." *Quarterly Journal of Economics* 100 (May): 529–39.

Mankiw, N. Gregory (1987a). "Government purchases and real interest rates." *Journal of Political Economy* 95 (April): 407–19.

Mankiw, N. Gregory (1987b). "Imperfect competition and the Keynesian cross." *Economics Letters* 26: 7–14.

Mankiw, N. Gregory, David Romer, and David N. Weil (1992). "A contribution to the empirics of economic growth." *Quarterly Journal of Economics* 107 (May): 407–37.

Mankiw, N. Gregory, Julio J. Rotemberg, and Lawrence H. Summers (1985). "Intertemporal substitution in macroeconomics." *Quarterly Journal of Economics* 100 (February): 225–51.

Mankiw, N. Gregory, and Stephen P. Zeldes (1991). "The consumption of stockholders and nonstockholders." *Journal of Financial Economics* 29 (March): 97–112.

Mark, Nelson C. (1995). "Exchange rates and fundamentals: Evidence on long-horizon predictability." *American Economic Review* 85 (March): 201–18.

Marston, Richard (1985). "Stabilization policies in open economies." In Ronald W. Jones and Peter B. Kenen, eds., *Handbook of international economics,* vol. 2. Amsterdam: North Holland.

Mas-Colell, Andreu, Michael D. Whinston, and Jerry R. Green (1995). *Microeconomic theory.* New York: Oxford University Press.

Matsuyama, Kiminori (1987). "Current account dynamics in a finite horizon model." *Journal of International Economics* 23 (November): 299–313.

Matsuyama, Kiminori (1988). "Terms-of-trade, factor intensities and the current account in a life-cycle model." *Review of Economic Studies* 55 (April): 247–62.

Matsuyama, Kiminori (1993). "Modelling complementarity in monopolistic competition." *Bank of Japan Monetary and Economic Studies* 11 (July): 87–109.

Matsuyama, Kiminori, Nobuhiro Kiyotaki, and Akihiko Matsui (1993). "Toward a theory of international currency." *Review of Economic Studies* 60 (April): 283–307.

McCallum, Bennett T. (1983). "The role of overlapping generations models in monetary economics." *Carnegie-Rochester Conference Series on Public Policy* 18 (Spring): 9–44.

McKenzie, Ian M. (1982). *Essays on the real exchange rate, investment and the current account.* Unpublished doctoral dissertation, Massachusetts Institute of Technology.

McKinnon, Ronald I. (1963). "Optimum currency areas." *American Economic Review* 53 (September): 717–25.

McKinsey Global Institute (1993). *Manufacturing productivity.* Washington, DC: McKinsey & Co.

Meade, James E. (1951). *The balance of payments.* London: Oxford University Press.

Meese, Richard A. (1986). "Testing for bubbles in foreign exchange markets: A case of sparkling rates?" *Journal of Political Economy* 94 (April): 345–73.

Meese, Richard A., and Kenneth Rogoff (1983a). "Empirical exchange rate models of the seventies: Do they fit out of sample?" *Journal of International Economics* 14 (February): 3–24.

Meese, Richard A., and Kenneth Rogoff (1983b). "The out-of-sample failure of empirical exchange rate models: Sampling error or misspecification?" In Jacob A. Frenkel, ed., *Exchange rates and international macroeconomics.* Chicago: University of Chicago Press.

Meese, Richard A., and Kenneth Rogoff (1988). "Was it real? The exchange rate-interest differential relation over the modern floating-rate period." *Journal of Finance* 43: 933–48.

Mehra, Rajnish, and Edward C. Prescott (1985). "The equity premium: A puzzle." *Journal of Monetary Economics* 15 (March): 145–61.

Mendoza, Enrique G. (1995). "The terms of trade, the real exchange rate, and economic fluctuations." *International Economic Review* 36 (February): 101–37.

Merton, Robert C. (1969). "Lifetime portfolio selection under uncertainty: The continuous-time case." *Review of Economics and Statistics* 51 (August): 247–57.

Metzler, Lloyd A. (1942a). "Underemployment equilibrium in international trade." *Econometrica* 10 (April): 97-112.

Metzler, Lloyd A. (1942b). "The transfer problem reconsidered." *Journal of Political Economy* 50 (June): 397–414.

Metzler, Lloyd A. (1960). "The process of international adjustment under conditions of full employment: A Keynesian view." In Richard E. Caves and Harry G. Johnson, eds., *Readings in international economics.* Homewood, IL: Richard D. Irwin.

Milesi-Ferretti, Gian Maria (1995). "The disadvantage of tying their hands: On the political economy of policy commitments." *Economic Journal* 105 (November): 1381–1402.

Milne, Frank (1979). "Consumer preferences, linear demand functions and aggregation in competitive markets." *Review of Economic Studies* 46 (July): 407–17.

Mishkin, Frederic S. (1978). "The household balance sheet and the Great Depression." *Journal of Economic History* 38 (December): 918–37.

Mitra-Stiff, Pritha (1995). *Empirical studies in international equity markets.* Unpublished doctoral dissertation, Princeton University.

Modigliani, Franco (1970). "The life cycle hypothesis of saving and intercountry differences in the saving ratio." In W. A. Eltis, M. FG. Scott, and J. N. Wolfe, eds., *Induction, growth and trade: Essays in honour of Sir Roy Harrod.* Oxford, UK: Clarendon Press.

Modigliani, Franco (1988). "The role of intergenerational transfers and life cycle saving in the accumulation of wealth." *Journal of Economic Perspectives* 2 (Spring): 15–40.

Modigliani, Franco, and Richard Brumberg (1954). "Utility analysis and the consumption function: An interpretation of cross-section data." In Kenneth K. Kurihara, ed., *Post Keynesian economics.* New Brunswick, NJ: Rutgers University Press.

Modigliani, Franco, and Richard Brumberg (1980). "Utility analysis and aggregate consumption functions: An attempt at integration." In Andrew Abel, ed., *The collected papers of Franco Modigliani,* vol. 2. Cambridge, MA: MIT Press.

Mundell, Robert A. (1961). "A theory of optimum currency areas." *American Economic Review* 51 (September): 657–65.

Mundell, Robert A. (1963). "Capital mobility and stabilization policy under fixed and flexible exchange rates." *Canadian Journal of Economics and Political Science* 29 (November): 475–85.

Mundell, Robert A. (1964). "A reply: Capital mobility and size." *Canadian Journal of Economics and Political Science* 30 (August): 421–31.

Mussa, Michael (1976). "The exchange rate, the balance of payments, and monetary and fiscal policy under a regime of controlled floating." *Scandinavian Journal of Economics* 78 (May): 229–48.

Mussa, Michael (1982). "A model of exchange rate dynamics." *Journal of Political Economy* 90 (February): 74–104.

Mussa, Michael (1984). "The theory of exchange rate determination." In John F. O. Bilson and Richard C. Marston, eds., *Exchange rate theory and practice.* Chicago: University of Chicago Press.

Mussa, Michael (1986). "Nominal exchange rate regimes and the behavior of real exchange rates: Evidence and implications." *Carnegie-Rochester Series on Public Policy* 25 (Autumn): 117–214.

Muth, John F. (1961). "Rational expectations and the theory of price movements." *Econometrica* 29 (July): 315–35.

Myerson, Roger B. (1979). "Incentive compatibility and the bargaining problem." *Econometrica* 47 (January): 61–73.

Neal, Larry (1990). *The rise of financial capitalism.* Cambridge, UK: Cambridge University Press.

Nordhaus, William (1975). "The political business cycle." *Review of Economic Studies* 42 (April): 169–90.

Nurkse, Ragnar (1944). *International currency experience: Lessons of the interwar period.* Geneva: League of Nations.

Obstfeld, Maurice (1982). "Aggregate spending and the terms of trade: Is there a Laursen-Metzler effect?" *Quarterly Journal of Economics* 97 (May): 251–70.

Obstfeld, Maurice (1985). "Floating exchange rates: Experience and prospects." *Brookings Papers on Economic Activity* 2: 369–464.

Obstfeld, Maurice (1986). "Capital mobility in the world economy: Theory and measurement." *Carnegie-Rochester Conference Series on Public Policy* (Spring): 55–104.

Obstfeld, Maurice (1989). "How integrated are world capital markets? Some new tests." In Guillermo Calvo, Ronald Findlay, Pentti Kouri, and Jorge Braga de Macedo, eds., *Debt, stabilization and development: Essays in memory of Carlos Díaz-Alejandro.* Oxford, UK: Basil Blackwell.

Obstfeld, Maurice (1990). "Intertemporal dependence, impatience, and dynamics." *Journal of Monetary Economics* 26 (August): 45–75.

Obstfeld, Maurice (1991). "Destabilizing effects of exchange rate escape clauses." Working paper 3603, National Bureau of Economic Research (January).

Obstfeld, Maurice (1994a). "Are industrial-country consumption risks globally diversified?" In Leonardo Leiderman and Assaf Razin, eds., *Capital mobility: The impact on consumption, investment, and growth.* Cambridge, UK: Cambridge University Press.

Obstfeld, Maurice (1994b). "Evaluating risky consumption paths: The role of intertemporal substitutability." *European Economic Review* 38 (August): 1471–86.

Obstfeld, Maurice (1994c). "Risk-taking, global diversification and growth." *American Economic Review* 85 (December): 1310–29.

Obstfeld, Maurice (1994d). "The logic of currency crises." *Cahiers Économiques et Monétaires* 43: 189–213.

Obstfeld, Maurice (1995). "International capital mobility in the 1990s." In Peter B. Kenen, ed., *Understanding interdependence: The macroeconomics of the open economy.* Princeton, NJ: Princeton University Press.

Obstfeld, Maurice (1996a). "Intertemporal price speculation and the optimal current acccount deficit: Reply and clarification." *Journal of International Money and Finance* 15 (February): 141–47.

Obstfeld, Maurice (1996b). "Models of currency crises with self-fulfilling features." *European Economic Review* 40 (April): 1037–48.

Obstfeld, Maurice, and Kenneth Rogoff (1983). "Speculative hyperinflations in maximizing models: Can we rule them out?" *Journal of Political Economy* 91 (August): 675–87.

Obstfeld, Maurice, and Kenneth Rogoff (1984). "Exchange rate dynamics with sluggish prices under alternative price-adjustment rules." *International Economic Review* 25 (February): 159–74.

Obstfeld, Maurice, and Kenneth Rogoff (1986). "Ruling out divergent speculative bubbles." *Journal of Monetary Economics* 17 (May 1986): 346–62.

Obstfeld, Maurice, and Kenneth Rogoff (1995a). "Exchange rate dynamics redux." *Journal of Political Economy* 103 (June): 624–60.

Obstfeld, Maurice, and Kenneth Rogoff (1995b). "The intertemporal approach to the current account." In Gene M. Grossman and Kenneth Rogoff, eds., *Handbook of international economics*, vol. 3. Amsterdam: North Holland.

Obstfeld, Maurice, and Kenneth Rogoff (1995c). "The mirage of fixed exchange rates." *Journal of Economic Perspectives* 9 (Fall): 73–96.

Obstfeld, Maurice, and Alan C. Stockman (1985). "Exchange-rate dynamics." In Ronald W. Jones and Peter B. Kenen, eds., *Handbook of international economics*, vol. 2. Amsterdam: North Holland.

O'Connell, Stephen A., and Stephen P. Zeldes (1992). "Ponzi games." In Peter Newman, Murray Milgate, and John Eatwell, eds., *The new Palgrave dictionary of money and finance*, vol. 3. New York: Stockton Press.

Ohlin, Bertil (1929). "The reparation problem: A discussion. I. Transfer difficulties, real and imagined"; "Mr. Keynes' views on the transfer problem. II. A rejoinder." *Economic Journal* 39 (June): 172–82; (September): 400–404.

Ostry, Jonathan D., and Carmen M. Reinhart (1992). "Private saving and terms of trade shocks." *International Monetary Fund Staff Papers* 39 (September): 495–517.

Otto, Glenn (1992). "Testing a present-value model of the current account: Evidence from US and Canadian time series." *Journal of International Money and Finance* 11 (October): 414–30.

Özler, Sule (1993). "Have commercial banks ignored history?" *American Economic Review* 83 (June): 608–20.

Persson, Torsten (1984). "Real transfers in fixed exchange rate systems and the international adjustment mechanism." *Journal of Monetary Economics* 13 (May): 349–69.

Persson, Torsten (1985). "Deficits and intergenerational welfare in open economies." *Journal of International Economics* 19 (August): 67–84.

Persson, Torsten, and Guido Tabellini (1990). *Macroeconomic policy, credibility and politics.* Chur, Switzerland: Harwood Academic.

Persson, Torsten, and Guido Tabellini (1993). "Designing institutions for monetary stability." *Carnegie-Rochester Conference Series on Public Policy* 39 (Fall): 53–89.

Persson, Torsten, and Guido Tabellini (1995). "Double-edged incentives: Institutions and policy coordination." In Gene M. Grossman and Kenneth Rogoff, eds., *Handbook of international economics*, vol. 3. Amsterdam: North Holland.

Persson, Torsten, and Guido Tabellini (1996). "Federal fiscal constitutions: Risk sharing and moral hazard." *Econometrica* 64 (May): 623–46.

Pesenti, Paolo, and Eric van Wincoop (1994). "International portfolio diversification and nontraded goods." Mimeo, Princeton University.

Phelps, Edmund (1961). "The golden rule of capital accumulation: A fable for growthmen." *American Economic Review* 51 (September): 638–43.

Pill, Huw (1994). "The behaviour of exchange rates in multilateral target zones." Mimeo, Department of Economics, Stanford University.

Porter, Richard D., and Ruth A. Judson (1995). "The location of U.S. currency: How much is abroad?" Mimeo, Board of Governors of the Federal Reserve System.

Posen, Adam S. (1995). "Declarations are not enough: Financial sector sources of central bank independence." *NBER Macroeonomics Annual* 10: 253–74.

Prescott, Edward C. (1986). "Theory ahead of business-cycle measurement." *Carnegie-Rochester Conference Series on Public Policy* 25 (Autumn): 11–44.

Ramsey, Frank P. (1928). "A mathematical theory of saving." *Economic Journal* 38 (December): 543–59.

Ray, Debraj (1987). "Nonpaternalistic intergenerational altruism." *Journal of Economic Theory* 41 (February): 112–32.

Razin, Assaf, and Efraim Sadka (1995). *Population economics.* Cambridge, MA: MIT Press.

Rebelo, Sergio (1991). "Long-run policy analysis and long-run growth." *Journal of Political Economy* 99 (June): 500–21.

Ricardo, David (1951). *On the principles of political economy and taxation*, ed. Piero Sraffa. Cambridge, UK: Cambridge University Press.

Rivera-Batiz, Luis A., and Paul M. Romer (1991). "Economic integration and endogenous growth." *Quarterly Journal of Economics* 106 (May): 513–55.

Rogoff, Kenneth (1980). "Tests of the martingale model for foreign exchange futures markets." In *Essays on expectations and exchange rate volatility*. Ph.D. dissertation, Massachustts Institute of Technology.

Rogoff, Kenneth (1984). "On the effects of sterlized intervention: An analysis of weekly data." *Journal of Monetary Economics* 14 (September): 133–50.

Rogoff, Kenneth (1985a). "Can international monetary policy be counterproductive?" *Journal of International Economics* 18 (May): 199–217.

Rogoff, Kenneth (1985b). "The optimal degree of commitment to an intermediate monetary target." *Quarterly Journal of Economics* 100 (November): 1169–89.

Rogoff, Kenneth (1987). "Reputational constraints on monetary policy." *Carnegie-Rochester Conference Series on Public Policy* 26 (Spring): 141–81.

Rogoff, Kenneth (1990). "Equilibrium political budget cycles." *American Economic Review* 80 (March): 21–36.

Rogoff, Kenneth (1992). "Traded goods consumption smoothing and the random walk behavior of the real exchange rate." *Bank of Japan Monetary and Economic Studies* 10 (November): 1–29.

Rogoff, Kenneth (1996). "The purchasing power parity puzzle." *Journal of Economic Literature* 34 (June): 647–88..

Rogoff, Kenneth, and Anne Sibert (1988). "Elections and macroeconomic policy cycles." *Review of Economic Studies* 55 (January): 1–16.

Rolnick, Arthur J., François Velde, and Warren Weber (1994). "The debasement puzzle: An essay on medieval monetary policy." Working paper 536, Federal Reserve Bank of Minneapolis (October).

Romer, Christina D. (1989). "The prewar business cycle reconsidered: New estimates of gross national product, 1869–1908." *Journal of Political Economy* 97 (February): 1–37.

Romer, David (1993). "Openness and inflation: Theory and evidence." *Quarterly Journal of Economics* 108 (November): 870–903.

Romer, David H., and Christina D. Romer (1989). "Does monetary policy matter? A new test in the spirit of Friedman and Schwartz." *NBER Macroeconomics Annual* 4: 121–70.

Romer, Paul M. (1986). "Increasing returns and long-run growth." *Journal of Political Economy* 94 (October): 1002–37.

Romer, Paul M. (1987). "Crazy explanations of the productivity slowdown." *NBER Macroeconomics Annual* 2: 163–202.

Romer, Paul M. (1990). "Endogenous technological change." *Journal of Political Economy* 98 (October): S71–S102.

Rose, Andrew K., and Lars E. O. Svensson (1994). "European exchange rate credibility before the fall." *European Economic Review* 38 (May): 1185–1216.

Rotemberg, Julio, and Garth Saloner (1986). "A supergame theoretic model of price wars." *American Economic Review* 76 (June 1986): 390–407.

Rotemberg, Julio, and Michael Woodford (1991). "Markups and the business cycle." *NBER Macroeconomics Annual* 6: 43–129.

Rubinstein, Ariel (1982). "Perfect equilibrium in a bargaining model." *Econometrica* 50 (January): 97–109.

Rubinstein, Mark (1974). "An aggregation theorem for securities markets." *Journal of Financial Economics* 1 (September): 225–44.

Ruffin, Roy J., and Young Deak Yoon (1993). "International capital movements in the Solow and overlapping generations growth models." *Review of International Economics* 1 (June): 123–35.

Sachs, Jeffrey D. (1981). "The current account and macroeconomic adjustment in the 1970s." *Brookings Papers on Economic Activity* 1: 201–82.

Sachs, Jeffrey D. (1982). "The current account in the macroeconomic adjustment process." *Scandinavian Journal of Economics* 84: 147–59.

Sachs, Jeffrey D. (1984). *Theoretical issues in international borrowing*. Princeton Studies in International Finance 54 (July).

Sachs, Jeffrey D. (1989). "The debt overhang of developing countries." In Guillermo Calvo, Ronald Findlay, Pentti Kouri, and Jorge Braga de Macedo, eds., *Debt, stabilization and development: Essays in memory of Carlos Díaz-Alejandro*. Oxford, UK: Basil Blackwell.

Sachs, Jeffrey D., and Xavier Sala-i-Martin (1992). "Fiscal federalism and optimum currency areas." In Matthew B. Canzoneri, Vittorio U. Grilli, and Paul R. Masson, eds., *Establishing a central bank: Issues in Europe and lessons from the U.S.* Cambridge, UK: Cambridge University Press.

Sachs, Jeffrey D., and Andrew Warner (1995). "Economic reform and the process of global integration." *Brooking Papers on Economic Activity* 1: 1–118.

Salant, Stephen W., and Dale W. Henderson (1978). "Market anticipations of government policies and the price of gold." *Journal of Political Economy* 86 (August): 627–48.

Samuelson, Paul A. (1958). "An exact consumption-loan model of interest with or without the social contrivance of money." *Journal of Political Economy* 66 (December): 467–82.

Samuelson, Paul A. (1964). "Theoretical notes on trade problems." *Review of Economics and Statistics* 46 (May): 145–54.

Samuelson, Paul A. (1969). "Lifetime portfolio selection by dynamic stochastic programming." *Review of Economics and Statistics* 51 (August): 239–46.

Sargent, Thomas J. (1987). *Macroeconomic theory*, 2nd ed. Orlando, FL: Academic Press.

Savage, Leonard J. (1954). *The foundations of statistics*. New York: John Wiley.

Scheinkman, José A. (1984). "General equilibrium models of economic fluctuations: A survey of theory." Mimeo, University of Chicago.

Sen, Partha (1994). "Savings, investment, and the current account." In Frederick van der Ploeg, ed., *The handbook of international macroeconomics*. Oxford, UK: Basil Blackwell.

Serrat, Angel (1995). "Exchange rate dynamics in a multilateral target zone." Mimeo, Sloan School of Management, Massachusetts Institute of Technology.

Shafer, Jeffrey R., Jorgen Elmeskov, and Warren Tease (1992). "Saving trends and measurement issues." In Erkki Koskela and Jouko Paunio, eds., *Savings behavior: Theory, international evidence, and policy implications*. Oxford, UK: Blackwell.

Sharpe, William F. (1964). "Capital asset prices: A theory of market equilibrium under conditions of risk." *Journal of Finance* 19 (September): 425–42.

Sheffrin, Steven M., and Wing Thye Woo (1990). "Present value tests of an intertemporal model of the current account." *Journal of International Economics* 29 (November): 237–53.

Shiller, Robert J. (1993). *Macro markets: Creating institutions to manage society's largest economic risks*. Oxford, UK: Clarendon Press.

Sibert, Anne C. (1994). "The allocation of seigniorage in a common currency area." *Journal of International Economics* 37 (August): 111–22.

Sibert, Anne C. (1996). "Unconventional preferences: Do they explain foreign exchange risk premia?" *Journal of International Money and Finance* 15 (February): 149–65.

Sidrauski, Miguel (1967). "Rational choice and patterns of growth in a monetary economy." *American Economic Review* 57 (May): 534–44.

Siegel, Jeremy J. (1972). "Risk, interest rates and the forward exchange." *Quarterly Journal of Economics* 86 (May): 303–309.

Siegel, Jeremy J. (1995). *Stocks for the long run*. New York: Irwin Professional Publishing.

Simon, Carl P., and Lawrence Blume (1994). *Mathematics for economists*. New York: Norton.

Sims, Christopher A. (1996). "Macroeconomics and methodology." *Journal of Economic Perspectives* 10 (Winter): 105–20.

Solow, Robert M. (1956). "A contribution to the theory of economic growth." *Quarterly Journal of Economics* 70 (February): 65–94.

Stockman, Alan C. (1980). "A theory of exchange rate determination." *Journal of Political Economy* 88 (August): 673–98.

Stockman, Alan C. (1988a). "Fiscal policies and international financial markets." In Jacob A. Frenkel, ed., *International aspects of fiscal policies*. Chicago: University of Chicago Press.

Stockman, Alan C. (1988b). Sectoral and national aggregate disturbances to industrial output in seven European countries." *Journal of Monetary Economics* 21 (March/May): 387–409.

Stockman, Alan C., and Harris Dellas (1989). "International portfolio nondiversification and exchange rate variability." *Journal of International Economics* 26 (May): 271–89.

Stockman, Alan C., and Lars E. O. Svensson (1987). "Capital flows, investment, and exchange rates." *Journal of Monetary Economics* 19 (March): 171–201.

Stockman, Alan C., and Linda L. Tesar (1995). "Tastes and technology in a two-country model of the business cycle: Explaining international comovements." *American Economic Review* 85 (March): 168–85.

Stokey, Nancy L., and Robert E. Lucas, Jr. (1989). *Recursive methods in economic dynamics*. Cambridge, MA: Harvard University Press.

Stolper, Wolfgang F., and Paul A. Samuelson (1941). "Protection and real wages." *Review of Economic Studies* 9 (November): 58–73.

Strotz, Robert H. (1956). "Myopia and inconsistency in dynamic utility maximization." *Review of Economic Studies* 23 (June): 165–80.

Stulz, René M. (1981). "A model of international asset pricing." *Journal of Financial Economics* 9 (December): 383–406.

Stulz, René M. (1987). "An equilibrium model of exchange rate determination and asset pricing with nontraded goods and imperfect information." *Journal of Political Economy* 95 (October): 1024–40.

Summers, Robert, and Alan Heston (1991). "The Penn World Table (Mark 5): An expanded set of international comparisons, 1950–1988." *Quarterly Journal of Economics* 106 (May): 327–68.

Sutherland, Alan (1995). "Exchange rate dynamics and financial market integration." Mimeo, University of York (October).

Svensson, Lars E. O. (1985). "Currency prices, terms of trade, and interest rates: A general equilibrium asset pricing cash-in-advance approach." *Journal of International Economics* 18 (February): 17–41.

Svensson, Lars E. O. (1988). "Trade in risky assets." *American Economic Review* 78 (June): 375–94.

Svensson, Lars E. O. (1995). "Optimal inflation targets, 'conservative' central banks, and linear inflation contracts." Discussion paper 1249, Centre for Economic Policy Research (October).

Svensson, Lars E. O., and Assaf Razin (1983). "The terms of trade and the current account: The Harberger-Laursen-Metzler effect." *Journal of Political Economy* 91 (February): 97–125.

Svensson, Lars E. O., and Sweder van Wijnbergen (1989). "Excess capacity, monopolistic competition, and international transmission of monetary disturbances." *Economic Journal* 99 (September): 785–805.

Swan, Trevor W. (1956). "Economic growth and capital accumulation." *Economic Record* 32 (November): 334–361.

Taub, Bart (1990). "The equivalence of lending equilibria and signalling-based insurance under asymmetric information." *RAND Journal of Economics* 21 (Autumn): 388–408.

Taylor, Alan M. (1994). "Domestic savings and international capital flows reconsidered." Working paper 4892, National Bureau of Economic Research (October).

Taylor, John B. (1983). "Union wage settlements during a disinflation." *American Economic Review* 73 (December): 981–93.

Temin, Peter (1976). *Did monetary forces cause the Great Depression?* New York: Norton.

Terra, Maria Cristina Trinadae (1995). "Openness and inflation: A new assessment." Mimeo, Pontifical Catholic University, Rio de Janeiro.

Tesar, Linda L. (1993). "International risk-sharing and nontraded goods." *Journal of International Economics* 35 (August): 69–89.

Tesar, Linda L. (1995). "Evaluating the gains from international risk sharing." *Carnegie-Rochester Conference Series on Public Policy* 42 (June): 95–143.

Tesar, Linda L., and Ingrid Werner (1995). "Home bias and high turnover." *Journal of International Money and Finance* 14 (August): 467–92.

Thomas, Jonathan, and Tim Worrall (1990). "Income fluctuation and asymmetric information: An example of a repeated principal-agent problem." *Journal of Economic Theory* 51 (August): 367–90.

Thomas, Jonathan, and Tim Worrall (1994). "Foreign direct investment and the risk of expropriation." *Review of Economic Studies* 61 (January): 81–108.

Tirole, Jean (1982). "On the possibility of speculation under rational expectations." *Econometrica* 50 (September): 1163–81.

Tirole, Jean (1985). "Asset bubbles and overlapping generations." *Econometrica* 53 (November): 1499–1528.

Tobin, James (1967). "Life-cycle saving and balanced growth." In William Fellner et al., eds., *Ten economic studies in the tradition of Irving Fisher*. New York: John Wiley & Sons.

Tobin, James (1969). "A general equilibrium approach to monetary theory." *Journal of Money, Credit and Banking* 1 (February): 15–29.

Turnovsky, Stephen J. (1995). *Methods of macroeconomic dynamics.* Cambridge, MA: MIT Press.

Uzawa, Hirofumi (1968). "Time preference, the consumption function, and optimum asset holdings." In J. N. Wolfe, ed., *Value, capital and growth: Papers in honour of Sir John Hicks*. Chicago: Aldine.

van Wijnbergen, Sweder (1991). "Mexico and the Brady plan." *Economic Policy* 12 (April): 13–56.

van Wincoop, Eric (1994). "Welfare gains from international risk sharing." *Journal of Monetary Economics* 34 (October): 175–200.

Velasco, Andrés (1996). "Fixed exchange rates: Credibility, flexibility and multiplicity." *European Economic Review* 40 (April): 1023–36.

Ventura, Jaume (1994). "Growth and interdependence." Mimeo, Harvard University.

Wallace, Neil (1980). "The overlapping generations model of fiat money." In John H. Kareken and Neil Wallace, eds., *Models of monetary economies*. Minneapolis: Federal Reserve Bank of Minneapolis.

Walsh, Carl (1995). "Optimal contracts for central bankers." *American Economic Review* 85 (March): 150–67.

Wan, Henry Y., Jr. (1971). *Economic growth*. New York: Harcourt Brace Jovanovich.

Warner, Andrew M. (1992). "Did the debt crisis cause the investment crisis?" *Quarterly Journal of Economics* 107 (November): 1161–86.

Weil, Philippe (1989a). "Overlapping families of infinitely lived agents." *Journal of Public Economics* 38 (March): 183–98.

Weil, Philippe (1989b). "The equity premium puzzle and the risk-free rate puzzle." *Journal of Monetary Economics* 24 (November): 401–21.

Weil, Philippe (1990). "Nonexpected utility in macroeconomics." *Quarterly Journal of Economics* 105 (February): 29–42.

Weil, Philippe (1991). "Currency substitution and the evolution of multicurrency regions." In Alberto Giovannini and Colin Mayer, eds., *European financial integration*. Cambridge, UK: Cambridge University Press.

Weil, Philippe (1992). "Equilibrium asset prices with undiversifiable labor income risk." *Journal of Economic Dynamics and Control* 16 (July/October): 769–90.

West, Kenneth D. (1987). "A specification test for speculative bubbles." *Quarterly Journal of Economics* 102 (August): 553–80.

Wilcox, David W. (1989). "Social security benefits, consumption expenditure, and the life cycle hypothesis." *Journal of Political Economy* 97 (April): 288–304.

Williamson, John (1985). *The exchange rate system,* 2nd ed. Washington, DC: Institute for International Economics.

Williamson, John (1993). "Exchange rate management." *Economic Journal* 103 (January): 188–97.

Woodford, Michael (1994). "Monetary policy and price level determinacy in a cash-in-advance economy." *Economic Theory* 4: 345–80.

Woodford, Michael (1996). "Control of the public debt: A requirement for price stability?" Mimeo, Princeton University.

Worrall, Tim (1990). "Debt with potential repudiation." *European Economic Review* 34 (July): 1099–109.

Yaari, Menahem E. (1965). "Uncertain lifetime, life insurance, and the theory of the consumer," *Review of Economic Studies* 32 (April): 137–50.

Yotsuzuka, Toshiki (1987). "Ricardian equivalence in the presence of capital market imperfections." *Journal of Monetary Economics* 20 (September): 411–36.

Young, Alwyn (1992). "A tale of two cities: Factor accumulation and technological change in Hong Kong and Singapore." *NBER Macroeconomics Annual* 7: 13–54.

Young, Alwyn (1994). "Lessons from the East Asian NICs: A contrarian view." *European Economic Review* 38 (April): 964–73.

Young, Alwyn (1995). "The tyranny of numbers: Confronting the statistical realities of the East Asian growth experience." *Quarterly Journal of Economics* 110 (August): 641–80.

Zeldes, Stephen P. (1989a). "Consumption and liquidity constraints: An empirical investigation." *Journal of Political Economy* 97 (April): 305–46.

Zeldes, Stephen P. (1989b). "Optimal consumption with stochastic income: Deviations from certainty equivalence." *Quarterly Journal of Economics* 104 (May): 275–98.

Notation Guide and Symbol Glossary

Introduction

This notation guide and symbol glossary provides a brief summary of the book's basic notational conventions. Symbol usage is generally covered by the self-contained discussion within each chapter, but for convenience we also include here a listing of major symbol conventions that recur throughout the book.

Label Conventions

A number of basic conventions for labeling variables can best be explained using consumption as an example.

One-Good, Representative-Agent Models

c^i: Consumption of agent i.

c: Average per capita consumption.

C: Total aggregate consumption.

However, in representative-agent models, we typically normalize the population size to 1 and use C to denote both aggregate as well as individual consumption. (Nuance: In Chapters 4 and 10, C is a representative agent's consumption of a utility-weighted basket of different goods.)

c: The lowercase sans serif font refers to $\log C$ (or, in Chapters 7 and 10, an approximate log deviation of C from an initial baseline path).

Subscripts

C_t: Date t consumption (or C_s, for date s consumption)

Subscripts alongside t or s denote a type of good. For example:

$C_{N,t}$: Consumption of nontradables on date t.

(T is used for traded goods, H for home goods, F for foreign goods.)

Superscripts

Superscripts other than i or j refer to a type of agent, for example:

$c^{o,i}$: Consumption of agent i, a member of the old generation.

c^v: Per capita consumption of agents in generation v.

C^*: Foreign consumption in a two-country model (where C is home consumption).

C^n: Aggregate consumption of country n.

Other examples include P for private agent, Y for member of young generation. Superscripts may also be given special meanings in different chapters:

r^A: Autarky interest rate.

r^C: Consumption-based real interest rate.

r^τ: World interest rate in the presence of a tax on capital inflows.

Other examples include w for world, D for domestic.

Parentheses

It is sometimes more convenient to avoid subscript and superscript clutter by using an alternative convention:

$c_t^i(z)$ is agent i's consumption of good z on date t.

In Chapter 5, s denotes one of several possible randomly occurring states of nature:

$c_t^i(s)$ is the date t consumption of agent i in state s.

An Example

$c_{N,t}^i(s)$: Home agent i's date-t consumption of nontraded good N in state of nature s.

Bars, Primes, and Hats

Bars over a variable generally denote its steady-state or long-run constant value, for example:

$\bar{C}$: Steady-state aggregate consumption.

Exception: Overbars and underbars are used in combination to denote range of a variable; for example, $\bar{z}$ and $\underline{z}$ are upper and lower bounds for z.

Primes denote first derivative when attached to a function of a single variable:

$C'(x) = dC/dx$.

However, a prime attached to a variable as opposed to a function denotes a specific value of that variable. Thus:

$\bar{M}'$ is a specific value of the steady-state money supply, $\bar{M}$.

Logarithmic changes and logarithmic approximations near steady-state values may be denoted by "hats," for example:

$\hat{C} = \frac{C - \bar{C}}{\bar{C}}$ is the percent deviation of variable C from steady state.

$\widehat{C} = \frac{\bar{C}' - \bar{C}}{\bar{C}}$ is the percent deviation of variable C's new steady state from its initial steady state.

Exception: In Chapter 10 and in the stochastic growth model of Chapter 7, we use logarithmic changes so extensively that the hat notation (especially hatted barred variables) would be tedious. There we use c in place of $\widehat{C}$, and $\bar{c}$ in place of $\widehat{\bar{C}}$.

Operators

Most operators are written as Roman letters.

$E\{X\}$ = expectation of X.

$E_t\{X_{t+1}\}$ = conditional (on date t information) expectation of X_{t+1}.

$Var\{X\}$ = variance of X.

$Var_t\{X_{t+1}\}$ = conditional (on date t information) variance of X_{t+1}.

$Std\{X\}$ = standard deviation of X.

$Std_t\{X_{t+1}\}$ = conditional (on date t information) standard deviation of X_{t+1}.

$Cov\{X, Y\}$ = covariance of X and Y.

$Cov_t\{X_{t+1}, Y_{t+1}\}$ = conditional (on date t information) covariance of X_{t+1} and Y_{t+1}.

$Corr\{X, Y\}$ = correlation coefficient of X and Y.

$Corr_t\{X_{t+1}, Y_{t+1}\}$ = conditional (on date t information) correlation of X_{t+1} and Y_{t+1}.

d = differential operator, $df(X)/dX = f'(X)$.

Other operators include:

Lag operator, L: $LX_t = X_{t-1}$.

Lead (or forward) operator, L^{-1}: $L^{-1}X_t = X_{t+1}$. (In linear stochastic models, $L^{-1}E_t X_s = E_t X_{s+1}$).

First difference operator: $\Delta X_t = X_t - X_{t-1} = (1 - L)X_t$.

Matrix transposition operator: $\mathcal{T}$, defined so that for any matrix $[a_{ij}]$, $[a_{ij}]^{\mathcal{T}} = [a_{ji}]$.

Timing of Asset Stocks and Interest Rates

The capital stock accumulated by the end of period t, and available for production in period $t + 1$, is denoted K_{t+1}. Our timing convention for riskless bonds (private bonds and government debt) is the same. Correspondingly, r_{t+1} is the net real return on a riskless bond between periods t and $t + 1$. These timing conventions are standard for discrete-time growth models; they are the main ones we employ.

However, in Chapter 5, we follow standard finance notation and denote by V_t the end-of-period t market value of an asset that next yields dividends in period $t + 1$. This timing convention for prices of claims to assets is also used on occasion elsewhere.

In the special case of money, we denote by M_t the stock of nominal balances accumulated during period t. This notation, which we also use for other durable goods in section 2.4, is logical because we assume that durable goods begin to yield a service flow immediately upon purchase.

Sundry Conventions

Partial derivatives are generally written as, say, $F_L(K, L)$ rather $\partial F(K, L)/\partial L$, though we use the latter notation when it is clearer.

Major Variable and Parameter Definitions

Generally, the discussion of parameter usage within each chapter or set of related chapters is self-contained. Below, we list some of the recurring usages. Departures from these conventions are clearly discussed in context.

Uppercase English Alphabet

A: Productivity shift variable. $A(z)$ is relative productivity function in Chapter 4. Superscript A denotes autarky.

B: Net foreign assets. B^G denotes net government assets, B^P net private assets.

C: Aggregate consumption (equals per capita consumption when population is normalized to equal 1). In Chapters 4 and 10, index of real consumption.

D: Government debt ($= -B^G$). Foreign debt ($= -B$) in Chapter 6. Stock of consumer durables in Chapter 2. Superscript D denotes "defaulting state" in Chapter 6 and indicates domestic interest rate in Chapter 7.

E: Level of Harrod-neutral technological change. $E\{\cdot\}$ is the expectations operator. $\mathbf{E}$ is eigenvector matrix in Supplement C to Chapter 2.

F: Production function $F(\cdot, \cdot)$. When it appears as super- or subscript, F indicates "foreign."

G: Government spending. $G(\cdot, \cdot)$ is a production function.

H: Human capital. When it appears as super- or subscript, H indicates "home."

I: Investment.

J: The function $J(\cdot)$ is the value function in dynamic programming.

K: Capital stock.

L: Labor supply. $\bar{L}$ denotes total time endowment. Gross lending in Chapter 6.

M: Money supply.

N: Total population, or total size of a generation. Superscript N denotes "non-traded."

O: Superscript o denotes "old" generation.

P: Price level.

Q: Financial wealth (total of securitized assets).

R: Market discount factor. ($R_{t,s}$ is the market discount factor between periods t and $s \geq t$.)

S: National saving. S^G is government saving, S^P private saving.

T: Aggregate taxes paid to government. Terminal time period. Superscript T denotes "traded."

U: Lifetime utility.

V: Market value of asset.

W: Beginning-of-period wealth, including the present value of wage income.

X: Generic variable.

Y: Gross domestic product. Endowment income. Superscript Y denotes "young."

Z: Net output $Y - G - I$ in Chapter 2. Nominal expenditure.

Lowercase English Alphabet

a: Generic constant.

b: Per capita net foreign assets. b_0 is a speculative bubble term in Chapter 8.

c: Per capita consumption.

d: Per capita government debt. d is the differential operator.

e: Harrod-neutral productivity growth-rate parameter. Eigenvector component.

f: $f(\cdot)$ is intensive form of a linear-homogeneous production function, $f(k) \equiv F(K/L, 1)$.

g: Output growth rate. Per capita government spending

h: Per capita human capital. Length of time interval.

i : Investment per capita. Individual index variable. Nominal interest rate.

j: Individual index variable.

k: Per *worker* capital stock. In Chapter 8, k is (log) exchange-rate fundamentals.

l: Index variable.

m: Per capita nominal money holdings.

n: Population growth rate.

p: Relative price of nontraded goods. $p(s)$ is price of state s Arrow-Debreu security. Relative price of durable goods in Chapter 2.

q: Tobin's q. In Chapter 9, q denotes (log) real exchange rate.

r: Real interest rate. Rental price of capital. Rate of return on an asset.

s: Index variable for time, states of nature. Per capita saving.

t: Index variable for time.

u: Period utility function of the individual is $u(\cdot, \ldots, \cdot)$.

v: Period derived utility from real balances, $v(\cdot)$.

w: Wage.

x: Generic weight variable.

y: Per capita GDP or endowment.

z: Index variable for commodities. Shock to output in Chapter 9.

Uppercase Greek Alphabet

Δ: First-difference operator.

Π: Profits. Product operator.

Σ: Summation operator.

Ω: Linear-homogeneous real consumption indexes are denoted by $\Omega(\cdot, \ldots, \cdot)$.

Ψ: Matrix of vector autoregression parameters in Chapter 2.

Lowercase Greek Alphabet

α: Capital's share in Cobb-Douglas production function.

β: Discount factor in individual intertemporal maximization problems.

γ: Generic weight parameter in utility function.

δ: Rate of subjective discount. Depreciation rate of capital. In Chapter 9, elasticity of aggregate demand with respect to the real exchange rate.

ϵ: Random shock.

ε: Inverse of consumption elasticity of demand for real balances.

ζ: In Chapter 1, import demand elasticity with respect to interest rate.

η: In Chapter 6, share of income creditors can destroy in event of default. In Chapter 8, semi-elasticity of money demand with respect to nominal interest rate (or inflation rate in the Cagan model).

θ: Elasticity of intratemporal substitution across different consumer goods. In Chapter 7, productivity parameter in production function for new capital-good varieties.

ϑ: Composite parameter equal to $1 - (1 + r)^{\sigma} \beta^{\sigma}$ in Chapter 2.

ι: Implicit rental cost (user cost) of consumer durable.

κ: Proportional transport cost in Chapter 4. Parameter for labor disutility in Chapter 10.

λ: Lagrange multiplier. Costate variable in Hamiltonian.

μ: Generic share parameter. Money-supply growth rate. Alternative Lagrange multiplier in Chapter 6.

ν: Alternative Lagrange multiplier.

ξ: Generic variable.

π: Inflation rate. As $\pi(s)$ in Chapter 5, denotes probability of state of nature s. In Chapter 6, $\pi(A)$ denotes probability density function of future investment productivity.

ρ: Coefficient of relative risk aversion. Autoregressive parameter.

σ: Elasticity of intertemporal substitution.

ς: Share of government spending in output in Chapter 2.

τ: Lump-sum per capita taxes or tax rate.

υ: Standard deviation of fundamentals in Chapter 8.

ϕ: Income elasticity of money demand. Production function parameter.

φ: Generic parameter.

χ: Installation cost parameter in q model, Chapter 2. Utility-of-money weight in Chapter 10.

ψ: Vector autoregression parameters in Chapter 2. ψ_L is labor's share of GNP in Chapter 4. Alternative Lagrange multiplier in Chapter 6. Sensitivity of inflation to excess demand in Dornbusch model of Chapter 9.

ω: Global output shock in Chapter 6. Undetermined coefficient in Chapters 7 and 8. Eigenvalue.

Other

$\mathcal{A}$: $\mathcal{A}[u(c_t), U_{t+1}]$ denotes Koopmans's (1960) aggregator function.

$\mathcal{E}$: Nominal exchange rate (home price of foreign currency).

$\mathcal{F}$: Forward exchange rate (home price of foreign currency).

$\mathcal{L}$: Lagrangian.

$\mathfrak{L}$: Loss function of monetary authorities in Chapter 9.

ℓ: Labor supply per worker in Chapter 10.

$\mathfrak{R}$: Repayment on debt in Chapter 6.

$\mathfrak{R}$: Reserve loss in speculative attack on a target zone, Chapter 8.

$\mathcal{S}$: Set of states of nature.

$\int$: Integral operator.

Author Index

Subject Index

Bold page numbers indicate primary definitions and concepts.